The Encyclopedia of Contemporary American Fiction 1980–2020

The Encyclopedia of Contemporary American Fiction 1980–2020

Volume I
A–K

Edited by
Patrick O'Donnell, Stephen J. Burn,
and Lesley Larkin

WILEY Blackwell

This edition first published 2022
© 2022 John Wiley & Sons Ltd

All rights reserved. No part of this publication may be reproduced, stored in a retrieval system, or transmitted, in any form or by any means, electronic, mechanical, photocopying, recording or otherwise, except as permitted by law. Advice on how to obtain permission to reuse material from this title is available at http://www.wiley.com/go/permissions.

The right of Patrick O'Donnell, Stephen J. Burn, and Lesley Larkin to be identified as the authors of the editorial material in this work has been asserted in accordance with law.

Registered Offices
John Wiley & Sons, Inc., 111 River Street, Hoboken, NJ 07030, USA
John Wiley & Sons Ltd, The Atrium, Southern Gate, Chichester, West Sussex, PO19 8SQ, UK

Editorial Office
The Atrium, Southern Gate, Chichester, West Sussex, PO19 8SQ, UK

For details of our global editorial offices, customer services, and more information about Wiley products visit us at www.wiley.com.

Wiley also publishes its books in a variety of electronic formats and by print-on-demand. Some content that appears in standard print versions of this book may not be available in other formats.

Limit of Liability/Disclaimer of Warranty
While the publisher and authors have used their best efforts in preparing this work, they make no representations or warranties with respect to the accuracy or completeness of the contents of this work and specifically disclaim all warranties, including without limitation any implied warranties of merchantability or fitness for a particular purpose. No warranty may be created or extended by sales representatives, written sales materials or promotional statements for this work. The fact that an organization, website, or product is referred to in this work as a citation and/or potential source of further information does not mean that the publisher and authors endorse the information or services the organization, website, or product may provide or recommendations it may make. This work is sold with the understanding that the publisher is not engaged in rendering professional services. The advice and strategies contained herein may not be suitable for your situation. You should consult with a specialist where appropriate. Further, readers should be aware that websites listed in this work may have changed or disappeared between when this work was written and when it is read. Neither the publisher nor authors shall be liable for any loss of profit or any other commercial damages, including but not limited to special, incidental, consequential, or other damages.

Library of Congress Cataloging-in-Publication Data

Names: O'Donnell, Patrick, 1948– editor. | Burn, Stephen, editor. | Larkin,
    Lesley, editor.
Title: The encyclopedia of contemporary American fiction 1980-2020 / edited
    by Patrick O'Donnell, Stephen J. Burn, and Lesley Larkin.
Description: First edition. | Hoboken, NJ : Wiley-Blackwell, 2022. |
    Includes bibliographical references and index.
Identifiers: LCCN 2021054298 | ISBN 9781119431718 (cloth)
Subjects: LCSH: American fiction–20th century–Encyclopedias. | American
    fiction–21st century–Encyclopedias.
Classification: LCC PS379 .E53 2022 | DDC 813/.540903–dc23/eng/20220207
LC record available at https://lccn.loc.gov/2021054298

Cover Design: Wiley
Cover Image: © AerialPerspective Works/Getty Images sebastian-julian/Getty Images

Set in 10/12.5pt MinionPro by Straive, Pondicherry, India
Printed and bound by CPI Group (UK) Ltd, Croydon, CR0 4YY

Contents

Volume I

Alphabetical List of Entries — vii
About the Editors — xi
Contributors — xiii
Introduction — liii

Contemporary American Fiction 1980–2020 A–K — 1

Volume II

Contemporary American Fiction 1980–2020 L–Z — 787

Index — 1479

Alphabetical List of Entries

Abu-Jaber, Diana	1	*The Bolaño Effect*	166
Acker, Kathy	6	*Book Clubs*	175
Adichie, Chimamanda Ngozi	11	*Border Fictions*	184
Afrofuturism	17	Boyle, T.C.	194
After Postmodernism	26	*The Brain and American Fiction*	199
Alameddine, Rabih	35	Braschi, Giannina	208
Alarcón, Daniel	40	Brooks, Geraldine	214
Alexie, Sherman	45	Burroughs, William S.	219
Allende, Isabel	50	Butler, Octavia	225
Allison, Dorothy	56		
Álvarez, Julia	60	Carver, Raymond	231
Anaya, Rudolfo	65	Castillo, Ana	235
Anders, Charlie Jane	70	Chabon, Michael	240
Antrim, Donald	76	Chiang, Ted	246
Apostol, Gina	82	*Chick Lit and the New Domesticity*	251
Auster, Paul	87	Cisneros, Sandra	260
		Cleage, Pearl	265
Baker, Nicholson	93	Cliff, Michelle	270
Ball, Jesse	98	Cole, Teju	275
Bambara, Toni Cade	102	*Contemporary Fictions of War*	280
Banks, Russell	107	*Contemporary Regionalisms*	289
Barth, John	112	Cooper, Dennis	298
Beattie, Ann	117	Coover, Robert	303
Beatty, Paul	122	*The Culture Wars*	308
Bennett, Brit	128	Cunningham, Michael	316
Berger, Thomas Louis	133	*Cyberpunk*	321
Big Data	138		
Biological Fictions	147	Danielewski, Mark Z.	333
Black Atlantic	156	Danticat, Edwidge	338

Dara, Evan	342	Gray, Amelia	581
Davis, Lydia	347	Groff, Lauren	586
Debut Novels	352		
Delany, Samuel R.	357	Hagedorn, Jessica	593
DeLillo, Don	362	Hannah, Barry	598
Díaz, Junot	367	Harrison, Jim	603
Doctorow, E.L.	373	Hawkes, John	609
Ducornet, Rikki	377	Heller, Joseph	613
		Hemon, Aleksandar	618
Ecocriticism and Environmental Fiction	383	Hempel, Amy	623
		Hijuelos, Oscar	628
Egan, Jennifer	393	Hinojosa, Rolando	633
Eggers, Dave	398	Hogan, Linda	638
Elkin, Stanley	404	Homes, A.M.	643
Ellis, Bret Easton	410	Hosseini, Khaled	647
Ellroy, James	416	Hustvedt, Siri	653
Englander, Nathan	420	*Hypertext Fiction and Network Narratives*	658
Erdrich, Louise	425		
Erickson, Steve	430		
Eugenides, Jeffrey	434	*Illness and Disability Narratives*	667
Everett, Percival	440	*Indigenous Narratives*	675
		Intermedial Fiction	684
Federman, Raymond	447	Irving, John	694
Feinberg, Leslie	452		
Ferré, Rosario	457	James, Marlon	701
Ferris, Joshua	462	Jarrar, Randa	706
Fiction and Affect	467	Jen, Gish	711
Fiction and Terrorism	476	Johnson, Charles	716
Fictions of Work and Labor	486	Johnson, Denis	721
Foer, Jonathan Safran	495	Johnson, Mat	726
Ford, Richard	501	Jones, Edward P.	732
Franzen, Jonathan	506	Jones, Gayl	738
Frazier, Charles	511	Jones, Stephen Graham	744
Gaddis, William	517	Kennedy, William	751
Gaines, Ernest J.	522	Kincaid, Jamaica	756
García, Cristina	527	King, Stephen	760
Gass, William H.	532	Kingsolver, Barbara	765
Gay, Roxane	538	Kingston, Maxine Hong	770
Gibson, William	542	Krauss, Nicole	775
Glancy, Diane	547	Kushner, Rachel	780
Globalization	552		
Golden, Marita	562	Lahiri, Jhumpa	787
Gomez, Jewelle	567	LaValle, Victor	792
The Graphic Novel	572	Leavitt, David	797

Lee, Chang-rae	802	Palahniuk, Chuck	1043
Lee, Don	806	Patchett, Ann	1048
Le Guin, Ursula K.	812	*Periodization*	1053
Lerner, Ben	818	Perkins-Valdez, Dolen	1063
Lethem, Jonathan	823	Phillips, Jayne Anne	1068
Literary Magazines	828	Piercy, Marge	1074
Literature of the Americas	835	*Post-9/11 Narratives*	1079
		Posthumanism	1088
Mailer, Norman	845	*Post-Soul and/or Post-Black Fiction*	1097
Major, Clarence	850		
Marcus, Ben	854	Power, Susan	1107
Marshall, Paule	860	Powers, Richard	1112
Maso, Carole	865	*Program Culture*	1118
Mason, Bobbie Ann	870	Proulx, Annie	1125
Maupin, Armistead	876	Pynchon, Thomas	1130
McBride, James	881		
McCarthy, Cormac	884	*Queer and LGBT Fiction*	1137
McElroy, Joseph	890		
McKnight, Reginald	895		
McMillan, Terry	900	*Realism after Poststructuralism*	1147
Mengestu, Dinaw	907	Reed, Ishmael	1156
Millennial Fiction	912	*Religion and Contemporary Fiction*	1162
Millhauser, Steven	920		
Minimalism and Maximalism	925	Revoyr, Nina	1172
Mixed-Genre Fiction	934	Robinson, Marilynne	1177
Momaday, N. Scott	943	Roth, Philip	1182
Moody, Rick	948	Russell, Karen	1187
Moore, Lorrie	953		
Morrison, Toni	958	Saunders, George	1193
Mosley, Walter	963	Schwartz, Lynne Sharon	1198
Mukherjee, Bharati	969	Scott, Joanna	1204
Multiculturalism	973	Senna, Danzy	1210
		Serros, Michele	1215
Nava, Michael	983	Shteyngart, Gary	1220
Naylor, Gloria	987	Siegel, Lee	1225
The New Experimentalism/The Contemporary Avant-Garde	993	Silko, Leslie Marmon	1230
		Simpson, Mona	1235
Ng, Celeste	1001	Smiley, Jane	1240
Ng, Fae Myenne	1006	Sontag, Susan	1245
Nguyen, Viet Thanh	1011	Sorrentino, Gilbert	1251
		Spiotta, Dana	1256
Oates, Joyce Carol	1017	Stephenson, Neal	1261
O'Brien, Tim	1022	Stone, Robert	1267
Ortiz Cofer, Judith	1027	*Story Cycles*	1271
Ozeki, Ruth	1033	Strout, Elizabeth	1280
Ozick, Cynthia	1037	*Suburban Narratives*	1285

Tan, Amy	1295	Walker, Alice	1383
Tartt, Donna	1300	Wallace, David Foster	1388
Third-Wave Feminism	1306	Ward, Jesmyn	1393
Tomasula, Steve	1315	Washburn, Frances	1398
Trauma and Fiction	1319	Welch, James	1404
Truong, Monique	1328	White, Edmund	1410
		Whitehead, Colson	1415
Updike, John	1335	Wideman, John Edgar	1421
Urban Fiction	1340	Williams, Sherley Anne	1426
Urrea, Luis Alberto	1348	Wolfe, Tom	1432
		Wolitzer, Meg	1437
		Writers' Collectives	1442
Vidal, Gore	1355		
Viramontes, Helena María	1360	Yamanaka, Lois-Ann	1453
Vizenor, Gerald	1366	Yamashita, Karen Tei	1458
Vollmann, William T.	1371	*Young Adult Boom*	1463
Vonnegut, Kurt	1376	Yu, Charles	1472

About the Editors

Patrick O'Donnell is Professor Emeritus of English and American Literature at Michigan State University, where he served as department chair for twelve years. He is the author of many essays and books on modern and contemporary British and American fiction, including most recently *The American Novel Now: Reading American Fiction Since 1980*, *A Temporary Future: The Fiction of David Mitchell*, and *Knowing It When You See It: Henry James/Cinema*. He is a co-editor of the Wiley Blackwell *Encyclopedia of Twentieth Century American Fiction*, and has taught at several universities in the United States, France, Germany, and The Netherlands.

Stephen J. Burn is Professor of Contemporary American Literature at the University of Glasgow. He is the author or editor of seven books, most recently *American Literature in Transition: 1990–2000* (2018) and (with Mary K. Holland) *Approaches to Teaching the Works of David Foster Wallace* (2019).

Lesley Larkin is a Professor of English at Northern Michigan University and the author of *Race and the Literary Encounter: Black Literature from James Weldon Johnson to Percival Everett* (2015). She is currently working on a monograph about contemporary American literature, genomics, race, and the humanities tentatively titled *Reading in the Postgenomic Age*.

Contributors

Verena Adamik currently works as a teaching and research assistant for American studies at the University of Potsdam. Her first book, *In Search of the Utopian States of America: Intentional Communities in Novels of the Long Nineteenth Century*, came out in 2020. Her work on more contemporary literature has been published in *Utopian Studies* and with *Current Objectives of Postgraduate American Studies*. Other research interests include African American literature, horror, and science fiction. In addition, she is the host and creator of the podcast Talking American Studies.

Jon Adams grew up in Britain and Saudi Arabia, and studied at the universities of Keele and Durham. His first book, *Interference Patterns* (2007), examined the possibility of making a science of literary criticism. As a researcher at the London School of Economics he worked on the dissemination of science, and the overlaps between popular science and popular fiction. In 2011, he was selected as a "New Generation Thinker" by the BBC. Until 2020, he worked as a filmmaker, interviewing academics and producing short films.

Crystal Alberts is a tenured Associate Professor of English and Director of the UND Writers' Conference. Alberts specializes in post-1945 literatures and cultures, including Indigenous literatures. Her book *Art & Science in the Works of Don DeLillo* is under contract. She is the co-editor of *William Gaddis, "The Last of Something": Critical Essays* (2009). Her scholarship has also appeared or is forthcoming in *The Salt Companion to Diane Glancy* (2010), *Transatlantic Literature and Culture After 9/11* (2014), *Transmotion*, and *Don DeLillo in Context*. Alberts is also a digital humanist, who is building the UND Writers Conference Digital Collection (funded in part by the National Endowment for the Arts). She serves as the principal investigator (PI) for the NEH-funded "Strengthening North Dakota's Humanities Infrastructure" project.

Jameel Alghaberi is a member of the English Department at Thamar University (Yemen) and is currently a research fellow at Saurashtra University in India. His research interests include diaspora literature, postcolonial studies, and cultural identity.

Laura Alonso-Gallo, Professor of English at Barry University, has authored articles and contributions to books in the field of US contemporary fiction, including Latino/a literature, such as "Deconstructing Mexican Masculinity in Denise Chávez's *Loving Pedro Infante*" in *Teaching Late-Twentieth-Century Mexicana and Chicana Writers* (ed. Elizabeth Coonrod Martínez, 2020) and "Cuerpos perdidos: Violencia y hambre en la narrativa femenina cubanoamericana" in *Reading Cuba: Discurso literario y geografía transcultural* (ed. Alberto Sosa Cabanas, 2018). She is editor and co-editor of critical essays collections, among them *Guayaba Sweet: Literatura Cubana en Estados Unidos* (2003), *American Voices: Interviews with American Writers* (2004), and *Identidad y postnacionalismo en la cultura cubana* (2019).

Marissa L. Ambio is Assistant Professor of Hispanic Studies at Hamilton College. She specializes in nineteenth-century and contemporary US Latinx literature. Forthcoming publications include "Nuyorican *mestizaje* or *la gran familia neorriqueña* in Piri Thomas's *Down These Mean Streets*" in *Centro Journal*, "*Drown*-ed Out: Silence in Junot Díaz's Short Stories" in *Revista Canadiense de Estudios Hispánicos*, and "Diaspora," a chapter on New York's Cuban émigré newspapers to appear in the Cambridge Latin American Transitions series.

Eric Karl Anderson is a writer, book blogger, and YouTuber also known as LonesomeReader (www.LonesomeReader.com). His novel *ENOUGH* won the Pearl Street Publishing First Book Award. He has judged numerous book awards including the Lambda Literary Awards (2010), Green Carnation Prize (2015), the British Book Awards (2017), and the Costa Book Awards (2020). His MA dissertation at the University of East Anglia, "Acting Out: Performance and the Self in the Fiction of Oates and Sontag," made a comparison between Oates's *Blonde* and Susan Sontag's *In America*, examining the way the novels represented acting as profession and performativity.

Pascale Antolin is Professor of American Literature at Bordeaux Montaigne University in France, and head of the research group CLIMAS. A specialist of American modernism and naturalism, she has published books and articles on F. Scott Fitzgerald, Nathanael West, Frank Norris, and Stephen Crane, including *L'Objet et ses doubles. Une relecture de Fitzgerald* (2000) and *Nathanael West. Poétique de l'ecchymose* (2002). She has focused her research on illness in literature (autobiography and fiction) for several years and published articles on the subject in French, European, and American journals. More recently, she has developed a special interest in brain literature.

Stephen Carl Arch is Professor of English at Michigan State University. He is the associate lead editor of The Writings of James Fenimore Cooper, and the volume editor of Cooper's 1838 novel *Home as Found* (2021). His article on Doctorow and the Gothic was published in *E.L. Doctorow: A Reconsideration* (2019).

Paul Ardoin teaches courses on filmic and literary narrative as an Associate Professor at the University of Texas at San Antonio. His monograph, *Not a Big Deal: Narrating to Unsettle* (2021), is part of the Frontiers of Narrative series published by the University of Nebraska Press.

María Guadalupe Arenillas is an Associate Professor in the Department of Languages, Literatures, and International Studies at the University of Northern Michigan. She has published in national and international journals, including *A Contracorriente: Revista de Estudios Latinoamericanos*, *Alba de América*, *Vanderbilt e-journal of Luso-Hispanic Studies*, and *Revista Cine Documental*. She co-edited, with Michael J. Lazzara, *Latin American Documentary Film in the New Millennium* (2016). During 2012–2018, Dr. Arenillas was the co-editor of the series Memory Politics and Transitional Justice. Her current research focuses on Southern Patagonia in documentary film. She analyzes the relationship between images of Indigenous people, law, the State, and science and technology.

Jason Arthur is Associate Professor and Chair of English at Rockhurst University in Kansas City, Missouri, where he teaches and writes about twentieth- and twenty-first-century American literature and culture. His first book, *Violet America: Regional Cosmopolitanism in U.S. Fiction Since the Great Depression* (2013) is a literary history of resistance to red/blue polarization. Beginning with the Federal Writers' Project and extending to Oprah Winfrey's Book Club, *Violet America* examines interactions between literature and social welfare and finds that a civically engaged spirit of "regional cosmopolitan" persists in US fiction.

Ted Atkinson is Associate Professor of English at Mississippi State University and editor of *Mississippi Quarterly: The Journal of Southern Cultures*. His areas of research interest include modernism, US literature and culture of the 1930s, and literature and culture of the US South. He is currently working on a book project about modernism, infrastructure, and cultural representations of the Tennessee Valley Authority (TVA). Atkinson's most recent publication is a chapter titled "Working toward a Southern Erostocracy: The Wages of Homosocial Labor in the *Magic Mike* Films" published in *Queering the South on Screen* (2020).

Jacqueline Bach is the Elena and Albert LeBlanc Professor of English Education and Curriculum Theory at Louisiana State University. Her scholarship on how young adult literature engages educators and students in conversations about social issues has appeared in the *English Journal*, *Discourse: Studies in the Cultural Politics of Education*, and *Theory into Practice*. She is the author of *Reel Education: Documentaries, Biopics, and Reality Television* (2016) and was a co-editor of *The ALAN Review* (2009–2014), a journal dedicated to the study and teaching of young adult literature. She is a former high school English teacher and an avid fan of young adult fiction.

David Banash is the author of *Collage Culture: Readymades, Meaning, and the Age of Consumption* (2013) and editor of *Steve Tomasula: The Art and Science of New Media Fiction* (2015). He teaches at Western Illinois University.

Corinne Bancroft is an Assistant Professor at the University of Victoria. Her research focuses on narrative strategies, such as the braided narrative and child narrators, that contemporary authors use to help readers address issues of racial and sexual violence. She recently published "The Braided Narrative" in *Narrative*. Her other publications appear in *Style* and *Cognitive Semiotics*.

Antonio Barrenechea holds a PhD in comparative literature from Yale University. He has been a Professor of Literature of the Americas at the University of Mary Washington since 2005. His monograph, *America Unbound: Encyclopedic Literature and Hemispheric Studies* (2016), examines New World colonial archives in contemporary maximalist fiction from the United States, Latin America, and Canada. He is currently working on a new book project titled *One Hemisphere, Many Nations: The Americas in Literary History*.

Laura Barrett is Professor of English and Dean of the College of Liberal Arts and Sciences at SUNY New Paltz. Her research, focusing on representations of media and the uncanny in American literature since the nineteenth century, can be found in *Studies in the Novel, PLL: Papers on Language and Literature, Literature & History, South Atlantic Review*, and other journals and collections. Her essays on Don DeLillo have appeared in *Modern Fiction Studies, Journal of Modern Literature, The Cambridge Companion to American Fiction after 1945* (ed. John N. Duvall, 2012), and *Don DeLillo: Mao II, Underworld, and Falling Man* (ed. Stacey Olster, 2011).

Michael Basseler is Academic Manager at the International Graduate Centre for the Study of Culture, Justus Liebig University Giessen, Germany. He has published widely on twentieth- and twenty-first-century American literature and culture, with a focus on narrative, literary, and cultural theory, African American literature, the short story, and the contemporary US novel. His most recent publications include the monograph *An Organon of Life Knowledge: Genres and Functions of the Short Story in North America* (2019) and an edited volume on *The American Novel in the 21st Century: Cultural Contexts – Literary Developments – Critical Analyses* (2019, with Ansgar Nünning).

Diana Benea is an Assistant Professor in the English Department at the University of Bucharest and a former Fulbright Senior Scholar at the City University of New York – The Graduate Center (2017–2018). Her publications include a monograph entitled *The Political Imagination of Thomas Pynchon's Later Novels* (2017). Her current research focuses on the relationship between politics and performance, particularly documentary and community-based theater. She has recent and forthcoming chapters in *The Palgrave Handbook of Theatre and Race* (2021), and *American Dramaturgies for the 21st Century* (2021).

Lucy Biederman is Assistant Professor of English at Heidelberg University in Tiffin, Ohio. Her essays have appeared in the *The Emily Dickinson Journal, Henry James Review, Women's Studies*, and *Studies in the Literary Imagination*. Her hybrid scholarly/creative work has appeared in *Early American Literature, Poetry, Ploughshares*, and *North American Review*. She is the author of *The Walmart Book of the Dead* (2017).

Nicholas Birns is the author most recently of *The Hyperlocal in Eighteenth- and Nineteenth-Century Literary Space* (2019). His other books include *Theory After Theory: An Intellectual History of Literary Theory from the 1950s to the early 21st Century* (2010) and *Contemporary Australian Literature: A World Not Yet Dead* (2015). He has co-edited *Roberto Bolaño as World Literature* (2017, with Juan E. De Castro), *The Contemporary Spanish American Novel* (2013, with Will H. Corral and Juan E. De Castro), and *Vargas Llosa and Latin American Politics* (2010, with Juan E. De Castro). He is currently co-editing *The Cambridge Companion to the Australian Novel*. He teaches at New York University.

Kyle Bladow is Assistant Professor of Native American Studies at Northland College. His research interests include contemporary Indigenous literature, material ecocriticism, and environmental justice. He is co-editor of the collection *Affective Ecocriticism: Emotion, Embodiment, Environment* and has been published in *Feminist Studies*, *The Journal of Popular Culture*, and *Studies in American Indian Literature*.

Kasia Boddy is Reader in American Literature at the University of Cambridge. She is the author of *Boxing: A Cultural History* (2008), *The American Short Story Since 1950* (2010), *Geranium* (2013), and *Blooming Flowers* (2020), and editor of several anthologies, including *The New Penguin Book of American Short Stories* (2011). She has also published numerous essays on modern and contemporary American fiction and culture.

Kyung-Sook Boo is Professor of English and American Culture at Sogang University in Korea. She teaches American studies courses focusing on emergent literatures and film, critical race studies, and popular culture, with a concentration on Asian American studies and Native American studies. Her main research interests lie in the intersection of race, ethnicity, class, and gender in the sociocultural construction of identities. She has published in both Korea and the United States and has been the recipient of numerous teaching and service awards at New York University, Hongik University, and Sogang University, as well as of the L.G. Yonam Foundation International Research Award.

Marshall Boswell is the author of *John Updike's Rabbit Tetralogy: Mastered Irony in Motion*, *Understanding David Foster Wallace* (2001), and *The Wallace Effect: David Foster Wallace and the Contemporary Literary Imagination* (2019), as well as two works of fiction, *Trouble with Girls* (2003) and *Alternative Atlanta* (2005). With Stephen Burn, he is the co-editor of *A Companion to David Foster Wallace Studies* (2013) and he is the editor of *David Foster Wallace and "The Long Thing": New Essays on the Novels* (2014). He is a Professor of English literature at Rhodes College in Memphis, Tennessee, where he teaches twentieth- and twentieth-century American literature.

Jana Evans Braziel is Western College Endowed Professor in the Department of Global and Intercultural Studies at Miami University (Ohio). Braziel is author of five monographs: *"Riding with Death": Vodou Art and Urban Ecology in the Streets of Port-au-Prince* (2017), *Duvalier's Ghosts: Race, Diaspora, and U.S. Imperialism in Haitian Literatures* (2010), *Caribbean Genesis: Jamaica Kincaid and the Writing of New Worlds* (2009), *Artists, Performers, and Black Masculinity in the Haitian Diaspora* (2008), and *Diaspora: An Introduction* (2008).

Manuel Broncano is a Regents Professor of English at Texas A&M International University. From 2015 to 2019 he served as the president of the International American Studies Association (IASA). Before moving to Texas, he taught for two decades at the University of León (Spain).

Broncano has published scholarly works on Flannery O'Connor, Willa Cather, Faulkner, Melville, Poe, and others. His latest book is *Religion in Cormac McCarthy's Fiction: Apocryphal Borderlands* (2014). Broncano has also kept an active agenda as a translator. His latest translation is Giannina Braschi's *United States of Banana* (2016).

Joseph Brooker is Professor of Modern Literature at Birkbeck, University of London. The author of *Joyce's Critics* (2004), *Flann O'Brien* (2005), *Literature of the 1980s* (2010), and *Jonathan Lethem and the Galaxy of Writing* (2020), he has edited and co-edited special issues of the *Journal of Law and Society*, *New Formations*, *Textual Practice*, and *Critical Quarterly*.

Lillie Anne Brown is an Associate Professor of English at Florida A&M University and teaches African American literature and composition studies. She has published and lectured extensively on the works of Ernest J. Gaines and served as the 6th Annual Ernest J. Gaines Lecturer at the University of Louisiana at Lafayette. Her work has appeared in national and international publications, including *Revista Lingua & Literatura*, *Pakistaniaat*, *Southern Quarterly*, and *Black and White Masculinities in the American South (1800–2000)* (2009). She served as contributing editor of *New Criticisms on the Works of Ernest J. Gaines: Man of Letters* (2016). Her most recent work on Gaines is included in *Ernest J. Gaines: Conversations* (2019). She holds a PhD in nineteenth-century American literature from Florida State University.

Cedric Gael Bryant holds the Lee Family Chair in English and American Literature at Colby College in Waterville, Maine. His specializations include African American literature and Southern literature. His scholarship been published in *The Southern Review*, *MELUS*, *Modern Fiction Studies*, *The African American Review*, MLA's *Approaches to Teaching Faulkner's Absalom, Absalom!*, and *The Oxford Companion to African American Literature*. His current research includes a book-length project on violence as an aesthetic in contemporary literature of the American South.

Martyna Bryla holds an MA in English philology from the Jagiellonian University in Cracow, Poland, and a PhD in English studies from the University of Málaga in Spain, where she works as a researcher and lecturer. Her research interests include literary imagology, particularly in relation to East-Central Europe, and the construction of selfhood and otherness in multinational contexts. She has published articles and book chapters on hybridity and migrant experience in Gary Shteyngart's fiction.

David Buehrer is a retired Professor of English from Valdosta State University, where he taught courses in world literature, critical theory, and modern and contemporary American literature. He currently serves as a part-time Professor of English at Kennesaw State University, Georgia, where he teaches survey courses in modern world literature. He has published on a variety of twentieth- and early twenty-first century novelists, with articles on García Márquez, Bellow, Heller, Gaddis, Russell Banks, and Denis Johnson in journals such as *Critique: Studies in Contemporary Fiction*, *Philological Papers*, and *The Saul Bellow Journal*. His most recent book-length publication is the monograph *The Psychology of Social Class in the Fiction of Russell*

Banks, Denis Johnson and Harry Crews: Neo-Realism, Naturalism, and Humanism in Contemporary Fiction* (2014).

Imola Bülgözdi is an Assistant Professor teaching American literature and popular culture at the Institute of English and American Studies, University of Debrecen, Hungary. Her academic interests range from Southern studies to novel-to-film adaptation and fantasy and science fiction. Her recent publications include "Space and Translocality: Revisiting Bradbury's Mars" (in *Critical Insights: Ray Bradbury*, 2017) and "Spatiality in the Cyber-World of William Gibson" (in *Cityscapes of the Future: Urban Spaces in Science Fiction*, 2018). She co-edited, with Ágnes Györke, the volume *Geographies of Affect in Contemporary Literature and Visual Culture: Central Europe and the West* (2021).

Brianna R. Burke is an Associate Professor of Environmental Humanities and American Indian Studies in the English Department at Iowa State University. Currently she is working on a book titled *Becoming Beast: The Humanimal in Climate Justice Literatures*, which explores the morphing ideology of what it means to be (considered) Animal in a world of decreasing resources, and she publishes on environmental and social justice, as well as on the pedagogy of both.

J.J. Butts teaches American literature and film at Simpson College in Iowa. His essays have appeared in *African American Review, American Studies, Digital Humanities Quarterly*, and *The Space Between: Literature and Culture, 1914–1945*. He is the author of *Dark Mirror: African Americans and the Federal Writers' Project* (2021).

Keith Byerman is Professor of English, African American Studies, and Gender Studies at Indiana State University. He is the author of eight books (including one on the life and art of Clarence Major) on African American literature, as well as numerous articles on Southern and African American writing.

Thomas B. Byers is Professor Emeritus of English at the University of Louisville, where for more than a decade he directed the Commonwealth Center for Humanities and Society and the US Department of State Study of the US Institute on Contemporary American Literature. He has been a visiting Professor in Denmark, Ukraine, Brazil, and Italy, and at the University of Paris IV (the Sorbonne). He has published widely on contemporary US literature and film.

Marta Caminero-Santangelo is the Director of the Center for Latin American and Caribbean Studies (CLACS) at the University of Kansas. Her research focuses on twentieth- and twenty-first century US Latinx literary studies; she teaches classes in migration studies, US Latinx literatures, and literature of social justice. Her books include: *Documenting the Undocumented: Latina/o Narrative and Social Justice in the Era of Operation Gatekeeper* (2016), *On Latinidad: US Latino Literature and the Construction of Ethnicity* (2007), and *The Madwoman Can't Speak: Or Why Insanity Is Not Subversive* (1998). She earned a PhD from the University of California, Irvine, and a BA from Yale University.

Beth Widmaier Capo is Professor of English at Illinois College, where she teaches courses in American literature and gender and women's studies. She is the author of *Textual Contraception: Birth Control and Modern American Fiction* (2007) and co-editor of *Reproductive Issues in Popular Media: International Perspectives* (2017). She has published articles on an array of twentieth- and twenty-first-century American writers.

Eric Casero is a full-time lecturer in English at the University of Massachusetts-Dartmouth whose interests include modernism, contemporary literature, and cognitive literary theory. His work has appeared in the *Southern Literary Journal* and *Critique*.

Youngsuk Chae is a Professor of English at the University of North Carolina, Pembroke. She is the author of *Politicizing Asian American Literature: Towards a Critical Multiculturalism* (2008) and a co-editor of *Asian American Literature and the Environment* (2015). Her research focuses on Asian American literature, critical race studies, ecocriticism, and postcolonial studies.

David Chase is a Professor of English at Raritan Valley Community College in Branchburg, New Jersey. He earned his doctorate in English from UCLA. His current areas of research include mid- to late twentieth-century gay American novelists and the queer reconstruction of the family and home. Currently, he is revising sections of his dissertation ("Homing Desires/Desiring Home: The Construction of Queer Domestic Space in Contemporary American Literature") for future publication. His essay "Feels Like Home" was included in *My Gay New Orleans: 28 Personal Reminiscences on LGBT+ Life in New Orleans* (2016).

Biling Chen is an Associate Professor of English at the University of Central Arkansas, where she teaches a range of courses, including Asian American literature and Postcolonial literature. She is co-editor of *Conversation with Gish Jen* (2018).

Flore Chevaillier is Coordinator of Graduate Programs in the Department of English at Texas State University. Her first book, *The Body of Writing: An Erotics of Contemporary American Fiction* (2013), examines readers' experience of sensuality in their engagement with the language of fiction. Her second book, *Divergent Trajectories: Interviews with Innovative Fiction Writers* (2017), explores textual materiality and embodied reading practices through a series of interviews with some of today's most cutting-edge fiction writers. Her essays have appeared in *Journal of Modern Literature*, *Critique*, *College Literature*, and *European Journal of American Studies*.

Monica Chiu, Professor of English at the University of New Hampshire, teaches courses in Asian American studies, American studies, comics and graphic narrative, and race and ethnic studies. Her most recent edited collection, *Drawing New Color Lines: Transnational Asian American Graphic Narratives* (2015), is the first to address this transnational medium. She currently is working on a monograph on graphic pathographies, or graphic narratives by and about subjects who are ill. Her publications appear in journals such as *MELUS*, *Mosaic*, *Journal of American Literature*, and *LIT: Literature, Interpretation, Theory*, among others.

Birte Christ teaches American literature and culture at Justus-Liebig-University Giessen, Germany. One of her fields of expertise is American middlebrow literature and culture. She has published a monograph on *Modern Domestic Fiction* (2012), which traces the middlebrow variants of the nineteenth-century domestic novel into the twentieth century, and is currently working on a project on the shaping of West German postwar middlebrow reading culture through American novels in translation. Her second area of expertise is law and literature. A book on representations of the death penalty in American literature, film, and television is forthcoming.

Ralph Clare is Associate Professor of English at Boise State University, specializing in post-45 American literature. He is the author of *Fictions Inc.: The Corporation in Postmodern Fiction, Film, and Popular Culture* (2014) and the editor of *The Cambridge Companion to David Foster Wallace* (2018). His latest book project, *Metaffective Fiction: Structuring Feeling in Contemporary American Literature*, explores the role of emotion and affect in post-postmodern fiction and the neoliberal era in works by David Foster Wallace, Salvador Plascencia, Sheila Heti, Dave Eggers, and Ben Lerner, among others.

Miriam Marty Clark is Associate Professor of English at Auburn University, where she teaches and writes about modern and contemporary American literature. Her current project focuses on late poetry, the twenty-first-century work of American poets born in the 1920s and 1930s.

Christopher K. Coffman is a Senior Lecturer in Humanities at Boston University. His most recent book is *Rewriting Early America: The Prenational Past in Postmodern Literature* (2019). Among his other scholarly publications are three co-edited volumes and dozens of articles, essays, and reviews.

Lance Conley is PhD candidate in the English Department at Michigan State University. His research focuses on manifestations of pessimism in post-millennial American fiction and their political implications. He has published writing on films, philosophy, and popular culture.

Joseph M. Conte is Professor of English at the University at Buffalo, where he teaches twentieth- and twenty-first-century literature with an emphasis on post-9/11 literature, the global novel, and the literature of migration. He is the author of *Transnational Politics in the Post-9/11 Novel* (2019), which argues for a post-9/11 novel that pursues transversal approaches to global conflicts. Book chapters and essays on a wide range of contemporary literature appear in *Shifting Twenty-First-Century Discourses, Borders, and Identities* (2020), *Trump Fiction: Essays on Donald Trump in Literature, Film, and Television* (2019), and *American Literature in Transition: 1990–2000* (2017), among others.

David Cowart, Distinguished Professor Emeritus at the University of South Carolina (Columbia), is the author of a number of books on contemporary fiction, including *Don DeLillo: The Physics of Language* (2002), *Trailing Clouds: Immigrant Writing in Contemporary America* (2006), *Thomas Pynchon and the Dark Passages of History* (2011), and *Tribe of Pyn: Literary*

Generations in the Postmodern Period (2015). He has been a National Endowment for the Humanities (NEH) Fellow, toured Japan as a Fulbright Distinguished Lecturer, and held Fulbright chairs at the University of Helsinki and at the Syddansk Universitet in Odense, Denmark. He is working on a study of Cormac McCarthy's work.

Rebecca Cross is a program manager at the ANU College, the pathway college for the Australian National University, operated by Study Group Australia. Her research interests center on the contemporary short story cycle and the way the form encourages the reader to interact with and become engaged in the meaning-making process between the stories.

Jurrit Daalder is a Marie Curie COFUND Fellow at the Georg-August-Universität Göttingen, Germany, and Columbia University, where he is working on a monograph on the personal essay in postwar America. Before joining Göttingen, he completed his doctorate at Oxford and held a Government of Ireland Postdoctoral Fellowship in the School of English at Trinity College Dublin. Recent essays of his have appeared in *The Cambridge Companion to David Foster Wallace* (2018) and *George Saunders: Critical Essays* (2017).

Rita B. Dandridge is a Professor at Virginia State University, where she teaches African American literature. Her most recent book is *The Collected Essays of Josephine J. Turpin Washington: A Black Reformer in the Post-Reconstruction South* (2019). Her essays have appeared in *African American Review, Black American Literature Forum, CLA Journal*, and *Journal of Popular Romance Studies*. In 2004, she was the recipient of the TIAA-CREF Virginia Outstanding Faculty Award from the State Council of Higher Education for Virginia.

Kimberly Chabot Davis is Professor of English and Director of the Graduate English Program at Bridgewater State University in Massachusetts, where she teaches twentieth- and twenty-first-century American literature and film studies. She is the author of two books in the field of reception studies – *Beyond the White Negro: Empathy and Anti-Racist Reading* (2014) and *Postmodern Texts and Emotional Audiences* (2007). *Beyond the White Negro* won the Lois P. Rudnick book prize from the New England American Studies Association. Her current research focuses on satire, African American literature, and critical race studies.

Leanne Day is an Assistant Professor in English at the University of Hawai'i at Hilo. She was the inaugural Daniel K. Inouye Post-Doctoral Fellow at the University of Hawai'i at Mānoa, where she was co-hosted by Ethnic Studies and the Public Policy Institute. She also was the Florence Kay Fellow in Asian American Pacific Islander Studies and Women's, Gender, and Sexuality Studies at Brandeis University, where she started programming to develop a minor in Asian American and Pacific Islander studies. She received her PhD from the University of Washington and her research interests include Indigeneity, Asian American studies, settler colonialism, and Oceania.

Pauline Amy de la Breteque is a teacher at the Sorbonne Nouvelle University in Paris. She defended her PhD dissertation about poetics of creolization in the works of Jean Rhys, Paule Marshall, Olive Senior, Jamaica Kincaid, and Michelle Cliff in 2020 at the Sorbonne University. She is the author of several articles and book chapters such as "Textes rhizomes et créolisation chez Jean Rhys et Michelle Cliff" (2020) and "Memorial Excursion and Errancy in Paule Marshall's *Praisesong for the Widow*" (2019).

Melissa Dennihy is Associate Professor of English at Queensborough Community College of the City University of New York. Her scholarship focuses on contemporary multiethnic US literatures and reading and writing pedagogies. Dr. Dennihy's work has been published in journals including *MELUS*, *Pedagogy*, *Teaching English in the Two-Year College*, and *Teaching American Literature*, as well as numerous essay collections.

Vanessa Holford Diana is Professor of English and Director of the Honors Program at Westfield State University, in Westfield, MA, where her courses include Native American literature and public writing. Her essay "'I Am Not a Fairytale': Contextualizing Sioux Spirituality and Storytelling Traditions in Susan Power's *The Grass Dancer*" appeared in *Studies in American Indian Literatures* in 2009.

Thaomi Michelle Dinh teaches American ethnic studies at the University of Washington. Her writing has appeared in *Amerasia*, *Journal of Asian American Studies*, *International Examiner*, and The Asian American Writers' Workshop, *The Margins*. She specializes in postwar Vietnamese American cultural production.

Tamas Dobozy is a Professor in the Department of English and Film Studies at Wilfrid Laurier University. He lives in Kitchener, Ontario, Canada. He has published three books of short fiction, *When X Equals Marylou* (2002), *Last Notes and Other Stories* (2005), and, most recently, *Siege 13: Stories* (2013), which won the 2012 Rogers Writers Trust of Canada Fiction Prize and was shortlisted for both the Governor General's Award: Fiction, and the 2013 Frank O'Connor International Short Story Award. He has published over seventy short stories in journals such as *One Story*, *Fiction*, *Agni*, and *Granta*, and won an O. Henry Prize in 2011 and the Gold Medal for Fiction at the National Magazine Awards in 2014. His scholarly work – on music, Utopianism, American literature, the short story, and post-structuralism – has appeared in journals such as *Canadian Literature*, *Genre*, *The Canadian Review of American Studies*, *Mosaic*, and *Modern Fiction Studies*, among others. He has also published numerous chapters in peer-reviewed anthologies published by Routledge, University of Nebraska Press, University of South Carolina Press, and Wilfrid Laurier University Press, among others.

Lynn Domina is the author of several books, including most recently an annotated edition of Nella Larsen's *Passing* (2018). She has written on Leslie Marmon Silko, Zora Neale Hurston, Gerard Manley Hopkins, the Harlem Renaissance, and other topics. She is currently editing a volume on Harriet Jacobs' *Incidents in the Life of a Slave Girl* for the Modern Language Association's Options for Teaching series, and she serves as Head of the English Department at Northern Michigan University.

David Dougherty is Professor Emeritus of English and Liberal Studies at Loyola University Maryland. Lately he's been writing about detective fiction, especially Ross Macdonald and Laura Lippman. His most recent book is *Compelling Evidence: New Detective Stories*, a collection he edited in 2016.

Corinne Duboin is Professor of English at the University of Reunion Island (France) in the South-West Indian Ocean. Her essays on African American and postcolonial literatures have appeared in such journals as *CLA Journal, Mississippi Quarterly, Obsidian, Southern Literary Journal, Commonwealth, Etudes Littéraires Africaines,* and *Transatlantica.* Her publications also include a range of book chapters and co-edited collections such as *Diasporas, Cultures of Mobilities, 'Race' 3: African Americans and the Black Diaspora* (2016). Her current research focuses on contemporary transnational African writers who explore the immigrant experience in a globalizing world as well as the complexities of race relations in twenty-first-century America.

Allard den Dulk is Senior Lecturer in Philosophy, Literature, and Film at Amsterdam University College and Research Fellow at the Faculty of Humanities of the VU University Amsterdam (The Netherlands). He is the author of *Existentialist Engagement in Wallace, Eggers and Foer: A Philosophical Analysis of Contemporary American Literature* (2015). Currently, he is working on a book tentatively titled *Wallace's Existentialist Intertexts: Comparative Readings with the Fiction of Kafka, Dostoevsky, Camus and Sartre.* For more information and publications, see: www.allarddendulk.nl.

David F. Eisler is a postdoctoral research associate at the Heidelberg Center for American Studies in Heidelberg, Germany. His first book is titled *Unburdened: Civil–Military Relations and American War Fiction.* Prior to earning his PhD, David was a research analyst at the Institute for Defense Analyses near Washington, DC. He also served five years on active duty in the United States army, earning the rank of captain and completing overseas tours in Germany, Iraq, and Afghanistan. David received a BA in astrophysics from Cornell University in 2007 and an MA in international affairs from Columbia University's School of International and Public Affairs in 2014.

Hagar Eltarabishy is currently an Assistant Professor in the Faculty of Languages (Al-Alsun) at the Ain Shams University, Cairo, Egypt. She earned her BA in English in 2007, her MA in contemporary American drama in 2013, and her PhD in 2018 which focuses on a comparative study on hyphenated ethnic writers. She earned a Fulbright Fellowship at the College of William and Mary, Williamsburg, Virginia, in 2011, and then was awarded a teaching fellowship at Northern Michigan University, Marquette, Michigan, in 2014. Her interests are ethnic and gender studies, theater, and both Arabic and American literature.

Jonathan Evans is Senior Lecturer in Translation Studies at the University of Glasgow, Scotland, UK. His research interests include film remakes, the circulation of queer cinema, and the role of translation in English-language literatures. He is the author of *The Many Voices of Lydia Davis* (2016) and co-editor of *The Routledge Handbook of Translation and Politics* (2018).

Brian Evenson is the author of over a dozen books of fiction, most recently the story collection *Song for the Unraveling of the World* (2019). He is the recipient of three O. Henry Prizes as well as an NEA Fellowship and a Guggenheim Fellowship. His critical work includes *Understanding Robert Coover* (2003), *Ed vs. Yummy Fur, or What Happens When a Serial Comic Becomes a Graphic Novel* (2015), and *Raymond Carver's* What We Talk About When We Talk About Love (2018). He lives in Los Angeles and teaches at CalArts.

Cecilia Konchar Farr is Dean of the College of Liberal and Creative Arts and Professor of English at West Liberty University in West Virginia. She teaches, studies, and writes about popular literature, modernism, feminist and reception theory, and the history of the novel. Her books include a study of literary merit, *The Ulysses Delusion* (2016), and a forthcoming companion to reading Gertrude Stein's *The Making of Americans*, as well as several examinations of the *Harry Potter* novels and Oprah's Book Club. She is also a member of several book clubs and an avid novel reader.

Sarah Farrell is a full-time lecturer at the University of Texas at Arlington with a concentration on the Scientific Revolution and cross-comparisons to 1970s female utopian science fiction. Her main focus is Margaret Cavendish and her utopian work *The Blazing World*. She has also been an editor for several publications and a review contributor for fifteen years. Dr. Farrell has also served as a subject matter expert for online institutions.

Tikenya Foster-Singletary is an educator and scholar whose research interests include African American and American literature and television. She frequently presents at conferences by the College Language Association and the Popular Culture Association of the South. Her work has been published in *Obsidian: Literature of the African Diaspora* and *Southern Quarterly*; her essay "Dirty South: *The Help* and the Problem of Black Bodies" is also included in the edited volume *Like One of the Family* (2016). She is co-editor of an essay collection titled *Pearl Cleage and Free Womanhood* (2012). She is a faculty member in the English Department of Clark Atlanta University.

Hikaru Fujii is an Associate Professor of Contemporary Literary Studies at the University of Tokyo, Japan. His research in contemporary American fiction includes *Outside, America: The Temporary Turn in Contemporary American Fiction* (2013) as well as essays on American immigrant writers for whom English is their second language. He has also translated a number of works by contemporary authors such as Denis Johnson's *Tree of Smoke* (2007), Anthony Doerr's *All the Light We Cannot See* (2014), and Colson Whitehead's *The Nickel Boys* (2019).

Alison Gibbons is Reader of Contemporary Stylistics at Sheffield Hallam University, UK. She is the author of *Multimodality, Cognition, and Experimental Literature* (2012) and co-editor of *Mark Z. Danielewski* (2011), *Routledge Companion to Experimental Literature* (2012), *Metamodernism: Historicity, Affect, and Depth after Postmodernism* (2017), *Pronouns in Literature: Positions and Perspectives in Language* (2018), and *Style and Reader Response: Minds, Media, Methods* (2021). She uses stylistics, including empirical responses, to explore contemporary fiction, particularly autofiction, Anthropocene fiction, and metamodernist fiction.

Loren Glass is Professor of English at the University of Iowa, specializing in twentieth- and twenty-first-century American literature and culture. His first book, *Authors Inc.: Literary Celebrity in the Modern United States*, was published in 2004. His history of Grove Press, *Counterculture Colophon: Grove Press, the Evergreen Review, and the Incorporation of the Avant-Garde*, originally published in 2013, has recently been republished under the title *Rebel Publisher: Grove Press and the Revolution of the Word* (2018). He is a member of the Post45 collective and co-edits their book series.

Liliana C. González is Assistant Professor of Gender and Women's Studies at California State University, Northridge. She earned her PhD from the University of Arizona in Latin American literature and culture. Her work is at the crossroads of Chicanx, Latinx, and Latin American cultural and literary studies with an emphasis on narco studies, border studies, and queer theory. She is currently working on a book project titled *Narcosphere: The Intimate Politics of Narco Culture*.

Christopher González is a Professor of English and the founding director of the Latinx Cultural Center at Utah State University. He is the author and editor of many books, including the International Latino Book Award-winning *Reel Latinxs: Representation in U.S. Film & TV* (2019). His research and teaching areas include twentieth-century American literature; multi-ethnic literatures of the United States; Latinx literary and cultural production; film; comics and graphic novels; narrative theory; and American studies.

James Gourley is a Senior Lecturer in Literary Studies at Western Sydney University, where he is a member of its Writing and Society Research Centre. His research addresses twentieth- and twenty-first-century literature. His recent work has been published in *ISLE: Interdisciplinary Studies in Literature and Environment*, *Sydney Review of Books*, *English Studies*, *College Literature*, and *Thomas Pynchon in Context*.

Mark S. Graybill is a Professor of English and director of the Honors Program at Widener University. His scholarly work focuses on modern and contemporary American writers, and Southern authors in particular. He has published articles and/or chapters on Don DeLillo, James Dickey, Faulkner, Hannah, Josephine Humphreys, Bobbie Ann Mason, and Flannery O'Connor, among others. His essay "Nostalgia, Race, and Authoritarianism in Flannery O'Connor's Fiction" is forthcoming during summer 2021 in the scholarly journal *Americastudien/American Studies*.

Geoffrey Green is Professor of English at San Francisco State University. He is Executive Editor of the journal *Critique: Studies in Contemporary Fiction*. Current areas of research include contemporary fiction, pulp fiction and film noir, literature and psychology, and history and culture in contemporary fiction. His works include *Literary Criticism and the Structures of History: Erich Auerbach and Leo Spitzer* (1982), *Freud and Nabokov* (1988), *The Vineland Papers: Critical Takes on Pynchon's Novel* (1994), and *Novel vs. Fiction: The Contemporary Reformation* (1981). Most recently, he is the author of a short story cycle, *Voices in a Mask* (1988).

Sharony Green is an Associate Professor of History at the University of Alabama. A native of Miami, Florida, with ancestral roots in the Bahamas and the US South, she explores the across-time complexities of race and gender in US history. Green's awards include the 2020 PEN American Jean Stein Grant for Literary Oral History to complete an upcoming book addressing the experiences of people of African descent in a greater Miami neighborhood. As a 2021 Newberry Fellow, Green is also writing a book delving into the significance of Zora Neale Hurston's postwar visit to Honduras.

Brenda M. Greene, Professor of English, is Founder and Executive Director of the Center for Black Literature and Director of the National Black Writers Conference at Medgar Evers College, CUNY. Professor Greene's research and scholarly work include composition and African American literature. She is editor of *The African Presence and Influence on the Cultures of the Americas* (2010) and co-editor of *Meditations and Ascensions: Black Writers on Writing* (2008) and *Rethinking American Literature* (1997). She has written reviews and essays on Toni Morrison, Sonia Sanchez, Amiri Baraka, Haki Madhubuti, and Louise Meriwether.

Christine Grogan is an Assistant Professor of English at the University of Delaware, Dover campus. She has published articles on works including Ralph Ellison's *Invisible Man*, Azar Nafisi's *Reading Lolita in Tehran*, and Dorothy Allison's *Bastard Out of Carolina*. She came across the fiction of Robert Stone ("Bear and His Daughter") while writing her book, *Father-Daughter Incest in Twentieth-Century American Literature: The Complex Trauma of the Wound and the Voiceless*, which was published in 2016.

Ambreen Hai is Professor and current Chair of the Department of English Language and Literature at Smith College. She teaches literature of British imperialism and anglophone postcolonial literature with a focus on South Asia, Africa, and the Caribbean. She is the author of *Making Words Matter: The Agency of Colonial and Postcolonial Literature* (2009), and of many scholarly articles on a range of postcolonial and diasporic subjects. Her research interests include women's and gender studies, critical humor studies, transnationalism and migration, film, and ethics in literature. Her current project is on domestic servitude in global South Asian English fiction.

Amy T. Hamilton is a Professor of English at Northern Michigan University, where she teaches classes on Indigenous American literature, ecocriticism and environmental justice, early American literature, and Western American literature. She is the author of *Peregrinations: Walking in American Literature* (2018) and a co-editor (with Tom J. Hillard) of *Before the West Was West: Critical Essays on Pre-1800 Literature of the American Frontiers* (2014).

Donal Harris is an Associate Professor of English and Director of the Marcus W. Orr Center for the Humanities at the University of Memphis. He is the author of *On Company Time: American Modernism in the Big Magazines* (2016).

Sheri-Marie Harrison is an Associate Professor of English at the University of Missouri, where she researches and teaches contemporary global anglophone literature and mass culture of the African diaspora. She is the author of the book *Negotiating Sovereignty in Postcolonial Jamaican Literature* (2014) as well as essays in *Modern Fiction Studies*, *Small Axe*, *The Journal of West Indian Literature*, *The Oxford Research Encyclopedia*, and the *Los Angeles Review of Books*.

Michael Patrick Hart is an Assistant Professor of English at Lane College, where he researches experimental literary studies as well as fictional representations of academia. He is working on his first book, *The Glass Canon: A History of Experimental English*.

Juanita Heredia is Professor of Spanish at Northern Arizona University specializing in US Latinx and Latin American literature and cultural studies. She is the author of *Transnational Latina Narratives in the Twenty-first Century: The Politics of Gender, Race, and Migrations* (2009), editor of *Mapping South American Latina/o Literature in the United States: Interviews with Contemporary Writers* (2018), and co-editor of *Latina Self-Portraits: Interviews with Contemporary Women Writers* (2000). She earned a postdoctoral fellowship at the Institute of American Cultures at UCLA to work on her monograph, *Transnational Latinas/os and the City: Negotiating Urban Experiences in Twenty-first Century Literature and Culture*.

Achim Hescher is Senior Lecturer in English at the University of Koblenz-Landau, Landau Campus, Germany. He has published on graphic novels, postmodern literary theory, and TEFL methodology.

Diarmuid Hester teaches contemporary literature at the University of Cambridge, where he is a research associate of Emmanuel College. He has held research fellowships at the Rothermere American Institute at Oxford University, the John W. Kluge Center for the Humanities at the Library of Congress, and the Fales Library and Special Collections at New York University. His writing has appeared in *American Literature*, *GLQ: A Journal of Lesbian and Gay Studies*, *Journal of American Studies*, *Critical Quarterly*, the *Los Angeles Review of Books*, and other venues.

Andy J. Hicks completed his undergraduate degree at Royal Holloway University of London, his MA at the University of Exeter, and his PhD at the University of Bristol, UK. His work focuses on American and postmodern literature and posthumanist critical theory. He currently resides in Exeter, UK.

Susanna Hoeness-Krupsaw is Associate Professor of English at the University of Southern Indiana. She has over thirty years of teaching experience at the undergraduate and graduate level. Her research interests include modern American and Canadian fiction as well as graphic narratives. She has recently published on Maxine Hong Kingston's *Warrior Woman*, Marguerite Abouet's *Aya*, and John Lewis's *March*. She co-edited a collection of essays titled *Performativity, Cultural Construction, and the Graphic Narrative* (2019). She earned her PhD in English at Southern Illinois University.

Yonina Hoffman is postdoctoral faculty at United States Military Academy at West Point. Yonina's research interests include twentieth- and twenty-first-century literature, narrative theory, systems theory, and phenomenology, and Yonina's dissertation was entitled "The Voices of David Foster Wallace: Comic, Encyclopedic, and Sincere." Yonina has articles forthcoming at *Twentieth-Century Literature* (on David Foster Wallace and John Updike) and in *The Handbook of Diachronic Narratology* (on the first person).

Mary K. Holland is Professor of English at SUNY New Paltz, where she teaches contemporary literature and theory. She is the author of *Succeeding Postmodernism: Language and Humanism in Contemporary American Literature* (2013) and *The Moral Worlds of Contemporary Realism*

(2020), and of numerous essays on contemporary literature and film. She is the co-editor of *Approaches to Teaching the Work of David Foster Wallace* (2019) and of *#MeToo and Literary Studies: Reading, Writing, and Teaching about Sexual Violence and Rape Culture* (2021).

Cheryl R. Hopson is an Assistant Professor of English and African American Studies at Western Kentucky University in Bowling Green. Her research interests are in twentieth-century African American literature and 1970s/1990s Black women's fiction, memoir, and feminist writings. Notable publications include *Zora Neale Hurston as Womanist* (2013), *Alice Walker's Womanist Maternal* (2017), *Tell Nobody but God: Reading Mothers, Sisters, and "The Father" in Alice Walker's* The Color Purple (2018), and more recently, *Not Tragically Fat! On Shame* (2019). She is currently writing a literary biography of twentieth-century novelist and anthropologist Zora Neale Hurston.

Ray Horton is Assistant Professor of English at Murray State University in Murray, Kentucky. He recently served a term as President of the American Religion and Literature Society, an affiliate of the American Literature Association. He is currently working on a book project, tentatively titled *American Fiction's Secular Faith*, which examines how American novelists from the late nineteenth century to the present refigure the secularization thesis by crafting their aesthetics of quotidian experiences and ephemeral images out of sustained engagement with religious beliefs and practices. His articles have appeared in *PMLA*, *Christianity & Literature*, and *LIT: Literature, Interpretation, Theory*.

Kaisa Ilmonen is a university lecturer at the Department of Comparative Literature, University of Turku, Finland. Her doctoral dissertation (2012) considered Michelle Cliff's rebellious textuality. Ilmonen has published widely on the topics of Caribbean women's writing and intersectionality, queer, and postcolonial studies. Her articles have been published in journals such as *Signs: Journal of Women in Culture and Society*, *Journal of West Indian Literatures*, and *European Journal of Women's Studies*.

Fiorenzo Iuliano is Associate Professor of American literature at the University of Cagliari, Italy. His interests include modernism and twentieth-century American fiction, cultural studies and critical theory, graphic novels, and music and literature. He has published on Henry James, Sherwood Anderson, Sherman Alexie, and Alison Bechdel. He is currently completing a book on the cultural and subcultural scene of Seattle in the 1990s.

Alla Ivanchikova is an Associate Professor of English and comparative literature at Hobart and William Smith Colleges and the author of *Imagining Afghanistan: Global Fiction and Film of the 9/11 Wars* (2019).

Kristin J. Jacobson is a Professor of American Literature, American Studies, and Women's, Gender, and Sexuality Studies at Stockton University. She earned her PhD from Penn State, her MA from the University of Colorado-Boulder, and her BA from Carthage College. Her book *Neodomestic American Fiction* (2010) examines post-1980 domestic novels. Her current book,

The American Adrenaline Narrative (2020), defines the generic characteristics of extreme adventure narratives and analyzes them from an ecofeminist perspective. She was also the lead editor for *Liminality, Hybridity, and American Women's Literature: Thresholds in Women's Writing* (2018).

Brian Jarvis is a Senior Lecturer at Loughborough University in the United Kingdom. His research is mainly focused on contemporary US fiction and film and he is currently working on a book entitled *Don DeLillo and the Visual*.

Christina Jarvis is Professor of English at the State University of New York at Fredonia, where she teaches courses in twentieth-century American literature and culture, including several major author seminars on Kurt Vonnegut. She is the author of *The Male Body at War: American Masculinity during World War II (2004)*, and has published articles on war and gender in journals such as *Women's Studies*, *The Southern Quarterly*, *The Journal of Men's Studies*, and *War, Literature & the Arts*. She is currently completing a book about Kurt Vonnegut's planetary citizenship.

Jerry Rafiki Jenkins is a Professor of English at Palomar College in San Marcos, California. Rafiki's research focuses on African American speculative fiction and film, and his articles have been published in *Screening Noir*, *African American Review*, *Journal of Children's Literature*, and *Pacific Coast Philology*. Rafiki is also the author of *The Paradox of Blackness in African American Vampire Fiction* (2019), and he co-edited (with Martin Japtok) *Authentic Blackness/Real Blackness: Essays on the Meaning of Blackness in Literature and Culture* (2011) and *Human Contradictions in Octavia E. Butler's Work* (2020).

Christopher "CW" Johnson is an Associate Professor of Literacy Education at the University of Minnesota Duluth. He is a veteran classroom educator with a thirty-five-year-long career in language arts education. He has published and presented research in educational foundations, literacy education, teacher preparation, and literary criticism. He is chair for the Jim Harrison Association of ALA, and he is currently working on a book which considers Jim Harrison and the natural world.

Alex Jones is a PhD candidate in the Department of English at Vanderbilt University. He works in the field of post-45 and contemporary literature, with interests in the literary field, late modernism, and transnationalism.

Scott J. Juengel is an Associate Professor of English at Vanderbilt University. His research and teaching interests lie in the history and theory of the novel, the literature of the long eighteenth century, and critical theory. His work has appeared in *Modernism/modernity*, *ELH*, *Novel*, *Cultural Critique*, *Studies in Romanticism*, and a wide range of additional journals. He is currently completing a book-length manuscript entitled *The Right to the Novel*.

Nathan Jung is a lecturer at the University of Wisconsin–Milwaukee. His research interests include diaspora studies, media studies, and public sphere theory, and his work has been published in journals including *ARIEL*, *The Journal of Commonwealth Literature*, and *Philosophy and Literature*.

Ubaraj Katawal is Associate Professor of English at Valdosta State University, where he teaches courses in multicultural literature, world literature, and contemporary British and American literature. His works have appeared in numerous literary journals, including *boundary 2*, *South Central Review*, *Postcolonial Text*, *South Asian Review*, and *Symploké*.

Izabella Kimak is an Assistant Professor at the Department of British and American Studies at Maria Curie-Skłodowska University in Lublin, Poland. Her research interests encompass American ethnic literature, race, postcolonial and gender studies, and the intersection of literary and nonliterary arts. She has published extensively on South Asian American women's literature, with a special focus on literary representations of female sexuality and the female body. She is a member of the Steering Committee of the European Association for American Studies Women's Network and of the editorial board of the *Polish Journal for American Studies*.

Sara Kippur is Associate Professor and Chair of the Department of Language and Culture Studies at Trinity College, Connecticut. Her research focuses on modern French literature and translation studies. She is the author of *Writing It Twice: Self-Translation and the Making of a World Literature in French* (2015) and co-editor of *Being Contemporary: French Literature, Culture, and Politics Today* (2016). Her articles have appeared in venues such as *PMLA*, *Yale French Studies*, and the *Los Angeles Review of Books*, and she is currently at work on a new book, *Transatlantic Pacts: America and the Production of Postwar French Literature*. For more, see www.sarakippur.com.

Anson Koch-Rein is Assistant Professor of Liberal Arts at the University of North Carolina School of the Arts. His work as a teacher–scholar is situated in trans and queer studies, American studies, rhetorics and theories of metaphor, and disability studies. His recent publications have appeared in *European Journal of English Studies*, *LIT: Literature Interpretation Theory*, *Transgender Studies Quarterly*, and in edited volumes including *Becoming TransGerman* (2019) and *TransGothic in Literature and Culture* (2018).

Joe Kraus is Chair of the Department of English and Theatre at the University of Scranton, where he teaches contemporary American literature and creative writing. He is also president of MELUS (the Society for the Study of Multi-Ethnic Literature of the United States) and the author of *The Kosher Capones* (2019).

Ryan Ku is a Visiting Assistant Professor in the Department of English Literature at Swarthmore College and was previously the inaugural Postdoctoral Associate in Asian American and Diaspora Studies at Duke University. A theorist of Asian diaspora, Southeast Asian, and multiethnic American literatures after World War II, he intersects ethnic, sexuality, and postcolonial studies by tracing the contradictions of the United States as a nation to its traumatic history of imperialism in the Philippines, which has rendered the Filipino structurally queer. *Insurrecto*, Gina Apostol's latest novel, is one of the texts he is writing about in one of his book projects, *Alternate War Histories of Asia/America*.

Lejla Kucukalic teaches at Khalifa University, Abu Dhabi. She is the author of *Philip K. Dick, Canonical Writer of the Digital Age* (2008) and *Biofictions: Literary and Visual Imagination in the Age of Biotechnology* (2021) as well as articles about biotechnology in American literature and about Arabic science fiction.

Lauren Kuryloski is an Assistant Professor of Teaching at the University at Buffalo. Her work analyzes depictions of "madness and badness" in twentieth- and twenty-first-century American literature and visual culture, interrogating the ways in which gender, race, and sexuality influence societal constructions of deviance. She has previously published on the transgressive nature of race and gender passing in Fannie Hurst's *Imitation of Life* and its film adaptation (*Journal of Narrative Theory*, 2019), and is currently at work on a project that traces literary and visual depictions of female criminality across the twentieth century.

Michael Lackey is a Distinguished McKnight University Professor, a scholar of twentieth- and twenty-first-century intellectual, political, and literary history. He has published and edited nine books, including *The Modernist God State: A Literary Study of the Nazis' Christian Reich* (2012), *Truthful Fictions: Conversations with American Biographical Novelists* (2014), *The American Biographical Novel* (2016), and *Conversations with Biographical Novelists: Truthful Fictions across the Globe* (2016). He has guest-edited numerous special issues for journals like *a/b: Auto/Biography Studies*, *The American Book Review*, *Éire-Ireland: An Interdisciplinary Journal of Irish Studies*, and *The Mississippi Quarterly*. His most recent work includes two books, *Conversations with Joanna Scott* (2020), which is a collection of Scott's interviews, and a monograph titled *Ireland, the Irish, and the Rise of Biofiction* (2021).

Jo Langdon has a PhD from Deakin University, Australia, where she teaches in writing and literature. Her scholarship, published in journals such as *Critique*, *Current Narratives*, and *Life Writing*, has focused on magical realism, trauma, and elegy. She has served as an editor at the Australian-based literary journal *Mascara Literary Review*, and her own stories and poems have been widely published. She is the author of a chapbook of poetry, *Snowline* (2012), which was co-winner of the 2011 Whitmore Press Manuscript Prize. Her second poetry collection, *Glass Life*, was published by Five Islands Press in 2018.

Linda Gould Levine is Professor Emerita of Spanish at Montclair State University, where, as Full Professor, she chaired the Department of Spanish and Italian and was Director of the Women's Studies Program. She also taught at Rutgers University and Dartmouth College. She received a BA from New York University and an MA and a PhD from Harvard University. She is the author, co-author, and co-editor of seven books on feminism in Spain, and contemporary Spanish and Latin American writers, among them Isabel Allende (2002). She currently directs the theater group "Cruzando Caminos," which has performed plays by Spanish and Latina writers in various venues in New Jersey.

Sara Tanderup Linkis, PhD in comparative literature, is a postdoc at Lund University, Sweden. Her research project "Serialization in Contemporary Literary Culture" (2018–2020) was funded by Independent Research Fund Denmark. She has published various articles on intermediality, book objects, transmedial storytelling, and serialization in acclaimed journals such as *Narrative*, *Orbis Litterarum*, *Children's Literature Association Quarterly*, *Image & Narrative*, and *Paradoxa*, and she is the author of the monographs *Memory, Intermediality, and Literature* (2019) and *Serialization in Literature between Media and Markets* (2021).

Marta J. Lysik is Assistant Professor in the Institute of Journalism and Social Communication at the University of Wroclaw, Poland. She holds degrees in English, American studies, and journalism. In *Dialogism or Interconnectedness in the Work of Louise Erdrich* (2017) she applied the Bakhtinian notion of dialogism to Erdrich's writing practice. She researches literary, nonfiction, and media genres. Her research interest is American literature in general, and the contemporary American novel in particular. She is also interested in life-writing narratives and forms of self-referential writing: academic novels (she maintains a website about campus fiction: schoolsville.wordpress.com), literary memoirs, and bibliomemoirs. In 2019–2020 she held the Fulbright Fellowship at Carnegie Mellon University, and she is currently at work on her second book on representations of writers in American academic novels.

John Macintosh is a Lecturer in English at the University of Maryland, College Park. He is currently at work on a manuscript on contemporary fiction and service work. His recent publications have appeared in *Post45*, *Studies in the Novel*, and the *Los Angeles Review of Books*.

David W. Madden is Professor Emeritus of Modern American and Irish Literatures at California State University, Sacramento. He is editor of *Critical Essays on Thomas Berger* (1995) and author of "Thomas Berger's Comic-Absurd Vision in *Who is Teddy Villanova*" (*Armchair Detective* 14: 37–43 [1981]) and "The Renegade Mood in Thomas Berger's Fiction" (*Studies in American Humor* 2 (2): 130–141 [1983]), as well as numerous reference entries and reviews of Berger's works.

Deborah Madsen is Professor of American Literature and Culture at the University of Geneva, Switzerland. She is the editor of *The Routledge Companion to Native American Literature* (2015) and the author of a number of books and articles in the field of Indigenous cultural studies.

Hanna Mäkelä received her PhD in comparative literature at the University of Helsinki in 2014. She has been an Academic Visitor at the University of Cambridge on a Kone Foundation scholarship (2015–2016) and a university lecturer at the University of Helsinki (2016–2018). She is currently conducting postdoctoral research at the University of Tartu. Mäkelä's articles include "Player in the Dark: Mourning the Loss of the Moral Foundation of Art in Woody Allen's *Match Point*" (2012) and "Horizontal Rivalry, Vertical Transcendence: Identity and Idolatry in Muriel Spark's *The Prime of Miss Jean Brodie* and Donna Tartt's *The Secret History*" (2015).

Jim Mancall is Assistant Provost at Wheaton College in Norton, Massachusetts. He is the author of *James Ellroy: A Companion to the Mystery Fiction* (2014). His current book project is on Elmore Leonard.

Benjamin Mangrum is an Assistant Professor in the English Department at the University of the South. He is the author of *Land of Tomorrow: Postwar Fiction and the Crisis of American Liberalism* (2019). His research has also appeared in *PMLA*, *New Literary History*, *American Literary History*, *Contemporary Literature*, and elsewhere.

Joelle Mann is currently a Senior Lecturer in the Writing Initiative at Binghamton University, where she teaches courses on composition, literature, and media. Her research explores the intersections among cultural polemics, aesthetic forms, and changing media in the twenty-first century. Particularly, she investigates changing medial tropes manifest in novel forms. She has published articles on teaching composition and literature. She has most recently been published in *Critique: Contemporary Studies in Fiction* and is forthcoming in *Callaloo, A Journal of African Diaspora Arts and Letters*.

Melanie A. Marotta is a Lecturer in the Department of English and Language Arts at Morgan State University. Marotta's research focuses on American literature (in particular African American), young adult literature, the American West, science fiction, and ecocriticism. She is working on a monograph about young adult literature featuring female characters of African descent. She co-edited *Critical Pedagogy: Diversity, Inclusion, and the Visual in Higher Education* (2021, with Susan Flynn) included in Routledge's series Race and Ethnicity in Education. Her collection, *Women's Space: Essays on Female Characters in the 21st Century Science Fiction Western*, was published in 2019 as part of the Critical Explorations in Science Fiction and Fantasy series.

Kyoko Matsunaga is an Associate Professor at Hiroshima University, Japan, and a former Fulbright Fellow at the University of Nebraska–Lincoln. She specializes in Indigenous American literature, nuclear/atomic literature, and environmental literature. Her critical articles have appeared in such books and journals as *Reading Aridity in Western American Literature* (ed. Jada Ach and Gary Reger, 2020), *Ecocriticism in Japan* (ed. Hisaaki Wake, Keijiro Suga, and Yuki Masami, 2017), *Critical Insights: American Multicultural Identity* (ed. Linda Trinh Moser and Kathryn West, 2014), *Journal of Transnational American Studies*, and *Southwestern American Literature*. Her book, *American Indigenous Writers and Nuclear Literature: From Apocalypse to Survivance*, was published in Japan in 2019.

Derek C. Maus is Professor of English and Communication at the State University of New York at Potsdam, where he teaches courses on contemporary literature. He is the author of *Jesting in Earnest: Percival Everett and Menippean Satire* (2019) and *Understanding Colson Whitehead* (2014, 2nd. rev. ed. 2021), as well as the co-editor (with James J. Donahue) of *Post-Soul Satire: Black Identity* (2014). He is currently working on a comparative study of contemporary fiction by African American and Black Canadian authors.

E.L. McCallum, Professor of English and Film Studies at Michigan State University, wrote *Object Lessons: How to Do Things with Fetishism* (1999) and *Unmaking The Making of Americans: Toward an Aesthetic Ontology* (2018). She co-edited *After Queer Studies: Literature, Theory, and*

Sexuality in the 21st Century (2019). Recent essays appeared in *Quarterly Review of Film and Video*, *Postmodern Culture*, and *camera obscura*. Her current writing draws on queer quantum theory and biosemiotics to analyze how art cinema represents the animacy of the nonhuman world.

Scott McClintock is the author of *Topologies of Fear in Contemporary Fiction: The Anxieties of Post-Nationalism and Counter Terrorism* (2015), co-author of a chapter in *Thomas Pynchon in Context* (2019), a contributing co-editor of *Pynchon's California* (2015), and has contributed chapters to *The Pharmakon: Concept Figure, Image of Transgression, Poetic Practice* (2018), *Cruzar las Américas: Perspectivas Hemisféricas en Lenguajes, Literaturas y Culturas Visuales* (2016), and *Hemingway, Cuba and the Cuban Works* (2014), as well as numerous journal articles. He lives in Big Bear, California.

Anna McFarlane is a British Academy Postdoctoral Fellow at Glasgow University with a project entitled "Products of Conception: Science Fiction and Pregnancy, 1968–2015." She has worked on the Wellcome Trust-funded Science Fiction and the Medical Humanities project and holds a PhD from the University of St. Andrews on William Gibson's science fiction novels. She is the editor of *Adam Roberts: Critical Essays* (2016), co-editor of *The Routledge Companion to Cyberpunk Culture* (2020), and the author of *Cyberpunk Culture and Psychology: Seeing Through the Mirrorshades* (2021).

Laura B. McGrath is Assistant Professor of English at Temple University. Her research interests include contemporary US fiction, literary sociology, and digital humanities. She is at work on her first book, a study of the literary agent in the United States, 1960–present. Her writing has appeared in *American Literary History*, *Post45*, *CA: The Journal of Cultural Analytics*, the *Los Angeles Review of Books*, and *Public Books*.

Brian McHale is Arts and Humanities Distinguished Professor of English at the Ohio State University. He is the author of four books about postmodern literature and culture, including *Postmodernist Fiction* (1987), *Constructing Postmodernism* (1992), and *The Cambridge Introduction to Postmodernism* (2015), and co-editor of five other books. Co-founder of Ohio State's Project Narrative, which he directed in 2012–2014, he also served as president of the Association for the Study of the Arts of the Present (2010–2011) and the International Society for the Study of Narrative (2016). From 2015 through 2019 he edited the Duke University Press journal, *Poetics Today*.

Michele Meek is Assistant Professor of Communication Studies at Bridgewater State University, Massachusetts. Her research focuses on contemporary American female filmmakers and writers, with a particular emphasis on representations of sexual consent. She edited the book *Independent Female Filmmakers: A Chronicle through Interviews, Profiles, and Manifestos* (2019), and she presented a TEDx talk "Why We're Confused about Consent – Rewriting Our Stories of Seduction." Her scholarly publications include "'It Ain't For Children': 'Shame-Interest' in the Adaptations *Precious* and *Bastard Out of Carolina*" in *Literature/Film Quarterly* and "Exposing

Flaws of Affirmative Consent through Contemporary American Teen Films" in *Girlhood Studies*. For more, see www.michelemeek.com.

Bénédicte Meillon is an Associate Professor at the University of Perpignan Via Domitia, where she runs the ecopoetics workshop. She specializes in contemporary literature, focusing on ecopoetics of re-enchantment, ecofeminism, and magical realism. She has published papers on fiction by Barbara Kingsolver, Linda Hogan, Annie Proulx, Ann Pancake, and Ron Rash, as well as by Russell Banks, Roald Dahl, and Paul Auster. She is on the EASCLE advisory board. She has co-edited *Lieux d'enchantement: approches écocritiques et écopoét(h)iques des liens entre humains et non-humains* (*Crossways Journal*, 2018) and edited an international volume, *Dwellings of Enchantment: Writing and Reenchanting the Earth* (2020). She is finishing a monograph titled *An Ecopoetics of Reenchantment: Liminal Realism and Poetic Echoes of the Earth*. She has also co-edited two transdisciplinary issues of *Textes & Contextes* dealing with the reenchantment of urban wildness, the first, with Rachel Bouvet and Marie-Pierre Ramouche, dealing with eco- and geo-poetic approaches (June 2021), and the second, co-directed with Sylvain Rode and Hélène Schmutz, including takes on the subject from the environmental humanities (November 2021).

Jaime Armin Mejía, originally from the lower Rio Grande Valley of South Texas, teaches at Texas State University, San Marcos. His research focus has long been to bring together Mexican American literary studies with rhetoric and composition studies.

Erin Mercer is Programme Coordinator and Senior Lecturer in English at Massey University, New Zealand. She is the author of *Telling the Real Story: Genre and New Zealand Literature* (2017) and *Repression and Realism in Post-War American Literature* (2011). Her research interests include Gothic, and her work on Stephen King has been published as articles in *The Journal of Popular Culture* and *The Journal of American Culture*. She is currently at work on a book project called *Returns, Repeats, Repressions: Stephen King's Uncanny Imaginary*.

Gretchen Michlitsch is Professor of English and Director of the Ethnic Studies Program at Winona State University in Winona, Minnesota. She has taught graduate and undergraduate classes on slave narratives, African American literature, and American narrative traditions. She earned her PhD in English from the University of Wisconsin–Madison in 2005 and her published work includes essays on the books of Sherley Anne Williams, Nalo Hopkinson, Laura Esquivel, Louise Erdrich, and Toni Morrison. Michlitsch's current research focuses on narrative structures and on concepts of liberty and independence in American literature.

D. Quentin Miller is Professor of English at Suffolk University in Boston, where he teaches courses on contemporary American literature, African American literature, and fiction writing. He is the author, editor, or co-editor of a dozen books. His most recent books are *James Baldwin in Context* (2019), *Understanding John Edgar Wideman* (2018), *American Literature in Transition 1980–1990* (2018), and *The Routledge Introduction to African American Literature* (2016). He is the co-editor of the recently published 12th edition of *The Compact Bedford Introduction to Literature* (2020) and its briefer companion, *Literature to Go* (2020).

Leah Milne is an Assistant Professor of English at the University of Indianapolis, where she teaches multicultural American literature, postcolonial literature and theory, and young adult literature. Her articles have appeared in journals such as *MELUS*, *African American Review*, and *College Literature*. Her book, published in 2021 by University of Iowa Press, is entitled *Novel Subjects: Authorship as Radical Self-Care in Multiethnic American Narratives*.

Keith B. Mitchell is an Associate Professor of English at the University of Massachusetts Lowell. He has co-edited two collections of essays on Percival Everett's work: *Perspectives on Percival Everett* (2013) and *Percival Everett Writing Other/Wise* (2014), and he has published numerous articles on contemporary African American fiction.

Heike Mißler is a senior lecturer at the English Department of Saarland University, Germany. Her research interests include feminist theory, gender and queer studies, and contemporary literature. She is the author of *The Cultural Politics of Chick Lit: Popular Fiction, Postfeminism, and Representation* (2017).

Steven Moore is an independent scholar and the author/editor of several books and essays on William Gaddis. He is also the author of a two-volume survey entitled *The Novel: An Alternative History* (2010, 2013). His most recent books are *My Back Pages: Reviews and Essays* (2017) and *Alexander Theroux: A Fan's Notes* (2020).

Alexander Moran is the Faculty Chair for Writing at Stanbridge University. He is the author of *Understanding Jennifer Egan* (2021) and has published in *Orbit: A Journal of American Literature* and in *Textual Practice*. He currently serves on the editorial board of the *Journal of David Foster Wallace Studies*, and is the editor of *Conversations with Jennifer Egan* (2022).

Christian Moraru is Class of 1949 Distinguished Professor in the Humanities and Professor of English at University of North Carolina, Greensboro. He specializes in contemporary American fiction, critical theory, and world literature. His publications include monographs such as *Cosmodernism: American Narrative, Late Globalization, and the New Cultural Imaginary* (2011) and *Reading for the Planet: Toward a Geomethodology* (2015), and he is co-editor of the essay collections *The Planetary Turn: Relationality and Geoaesthetics in the Twenty-First Century* (2015) and *The Bloomsbury Handbook of World Theory* (2021).

Paula M.L. Moya is the Danily C. and Laura Louise Bell Professor of Humanities and Burton J. and Deedee McMurtry University Fellow in Undergraduate Education at Stanford University. She is the author of *The Social Imperative: Race, Close Reading, and Contemporary Literary Criticism* (2016) and *Learning from Experience: Minority Identities, Multicultural Struggles* (2002). She has also co-edited three collections of original essays, *Doing Race: 21 Essays for the 21st Century* (2010), *Identity Politics Reconsidered* (2006), and *Reclaiming Identity: Realist Theory and the Predicament of Postmodernism* (2000).

Damjana Mraović-O'Hare specializes in contemporary American literature, particularly contemporary American fiction by US-based/foreign-born American authors. She has published about American and world literature in *Criticism*, *Modern Language Studies*, *MELUS*, and *World*

Literature Today and has participated in many conferences both in the United States and in Europe. She is currently an Assistant Professor of English at Carson-Newman University, where she is also the Writing Center director.

Gerald David Naughton is Associate Professor of American Literature at Qatar University. He received his PhD from University College Dublin, where he specialized in nineteenth- and twentieth-century African American literature and culture. His other research interests include comparative American literature, postwar American fiction, and transnational literatures. His essays have appeared in such journals as *African American Review, Symplokē, Ariel: A Review of International English Literature*, and *Critique: Studies in Contemporary Fiction*.

Heather Neilson is a Senior Lecturer in the School of Humanities and Social Sciences at the Canberra campus of the University of New South Wales, Australia. She is a past president of the Australian and New Zealand American Studies Association and a former editor of the *Australasian Journal of American Studies*. Her monograph entitled *Political Animal: Gore Vidal on Power* was published in 2014. She is currently researching the work of Jay Parini.

Marguerite Nguyen is Associate Professor of English at Wesleyan, where she specializes in twentieth- to twenty-first-century American and Asian American literature, refugee cultures, and literary history. She is author of *America's Vietnam: The* Longue Durée *of U.S. Literature and Empire* (2018) and co-editor of *Refugee Cultures: Forty Years after the Vietnam War* (*MELUS* 41 (3) [2016]). Her next book project, tentatively titled *Refugee Ecologies*, argues for ecocritical readings of refugee cultures.

Justus Nieland is Professor and Chairperson of the Department of English at Michigan State University. His research and teaching interests lie in modernism and film and media studies. He is the author of four books, including *Happiness by Design: Modernism and Media in the Eames Era* (2020), *David Lynch* (2012), *Film Noir: Hard-Boiled Modernity and the Cultures of Globalization* (2010, with Jennifer Fay), and *Feeling Modern: The Eccentricities of Public Life* (2008). He is co-editor of the Contemporary Film Directors book series at the University of Illinois Press.

Keenan Norris teaches American literature and creative writing at San José State University. His novel *Brother and the Dancer* won the 2012 James D. Houston Award. He served as editor for the anthology *Street Lit: Representing the Urban Landscape* (2014). His novel *The Confession of Copeland Cane* was published in June 2021. He serves as guest editor for the Oxford African American Studies Center. Norris was a 2020 Public Voices Fellow and a 2017 Marin Headlands Artist-in-Residence Fellow. His editorials have been published in *The Los Angeles Times* and the *Los Angeles Review of Books*.

Milo W. Obourn is a Professor of English and Women & Gender Studies and Chair of Women & Gender Studies at SUNY Brockport. They teach courses in critical race theory, gender and sexuality studies, disability studies, and US literature and culture. Milo is the author of *Reconstituting Americans: Liberal Multiculturalism and Identity Difference in Post-1960s US Literature* (2011) and *Disabled Futures: A Framework for Radical Inclusion* (2020).

Elizabeth Lloyd Oliphant is faculty in English at Northland Pioneer College, where she teaches courses about American literature, Native American literature, genre fiction, and writing. Her work has appeared in *American Literature, ESQ*, and *Great Plains Quarterly*. In 2017 she received a PhD in literature and cultural studies from the University of Pittsburgh. She was born in Mississippi and now lives in New Mexico and Arizona.

Andrea Opitz is an Assistant Professor in the Department of English and the Director of the American Studies Program at Stonehill College. Her scholarship and courses emphasize race and gender in contemporary American literature and culture. Her articles on James Welch have appeared in *American Indian Quarterly, Studies in American Indian Literature,* and *All Our Stories Are Here* (2009), a critical anthology on Montana literature.

Sharada Balachandran Orihuela is Associate Professor of English and Comparative Literature at the University of Maryland, College Park. Her first book, *Fugitives, Smugglers, and Thieves: Piracy and Personhood in Hemispheric American Literature* (2018), examines depictions of illegal trade and makes them prominent in the analysis of American literature and in the construction of minoritarian racial, national, and gendered identities in the United States. Her articles and reviews have appeared in *Early American Literature, American Literary History, Arizona Quarterly, J19: The Journal of Nineteenth-Century Americanists, Environmental Communication, MELUS,* and *e-misférica*.

Hugh Charles O'Connell is an Assistant Professor of English at the University of Massachusetts Boston. His current research examines the relationship between speculative fiction and speculative finance. He is the co-editor (with David M. Higgins) of *Speculative Finance/Speculative Fiction* a special issue of *CR: The New Centennial Review* (19 (1) [2019]). Recent essays on contemporary and postcolonial science fiction have appeared in *Utopian Studies, The Cambridge History of Science Fiction, Postcolonial Literary Inquiry, Modern Fiction Studies, Paradoxa, Science Fiction Film & Television, The Routledge Companion to Cyberpunk Culture,* and the *Los Angeles Review of Books*.

Cyrus R.K. Patell is Global Network Professor of Literature at NYU Abu Dhabi and Professor of English at NYU in New York. The author of *Lucasfilm: Filmmaking, Philosophy, and The Star Wars Universe* (2021), as well as *Emergent U.S. Literatures: From Multiculturalism to Cosmopolitanism in the Late Twentieth Century* (2014) and *Cosmopolitanism and the Literary Imagination* (2015), he also is the co-editor (with Deborah Lindsay Williams) of *The Oxford History of the Novel in English, Volume 8: American Fiction since 1940* (2022).

Leila Moayeri Pazargadi is Associate Professor of English at Nevada State College, currently teaching composition, postcolonial literature, life writing, ethnic American literature, and Middle Eastern literature courses. She received her doctorate of philosophy in comparative literature with a certification in gender studies from the University of California, Los Angeles, in 2012. Her research focuses on Middle Eastern women writers producing autobiographical material in fiction and nonfiction after 9/11, but it also extends to include scholarship on the visual forms of comics, in addition to Persian photography of the Qajar era.

James Peacock is Senior Lecturer in English and American Literatures at Keele University in the UK. He specializes in contemporary American fiction, with particular interests in New York fictions and gentrification stories. His monographs include *Understanding Paul Auster* (2010), *Jonathan Lethem* (2012), and *Brooklyn Fictions: The Contemporary Urban Community in a Global Age* (2015). He has also published on detective fiction, the music of The Clash, and Quakerism and American literature.

Wendy Gay Pearson is an Assistant Professor in Gender, Sexuality, and Women's Studies at the University of Western Ontario. She specializes in work on (mainly queer) sexuality and its intersections with gender, race, Indigeneity, and class in science fiction, Canadian literature and film, and worldwide Indigenous film cultures. She is co-editor of *Reverse Shots: Indigenous Film and Media in an International Context* (2015), co-editor of *Queer Universes: Sexualities in Science Fiction* (2008), and co-author of *Zero Patience* (2011). She won the 2000 Pioneer Award for best published article in the field of science fiction and is also a 3M National Teaching Fellow.

Rubén Peinado Abarrio teaches at the School of Arts, Languages and Cultures at the University of Manchester in the UK. He earned his PhD in English studies at the University of Oviedo, Spain, in 2013. His doctoral work led to the publication of his first monograph, *Learning To Be American: Richard Ford's Frank Bascombe Trilogy and the Construction of a National Identity*, in 2014. His current research interests include the interconnections between the literatures of the United States and the Spanish-speaking world, and the intersections between space and trauma theory.

Dana Phillips is Professor of English at Towson University in Maryland. He is the author of *The Truth of Ecology: Nature, Culture, and Literature in America* (2003, 2007), and of numerous articles, chapters, and review essays on topics in American literature, ecocriticism, and the environmental humanities. In his recent work, he focuses on narratives of environmental decline, catastrophe, collapse, apocalypse, and the end of nature; on climate change; and on ideas of the human and the posthuman.

Beatrice Pire is Associate Professor of American Literature at the University of Sorbonne Nouvelle, Paris. She is the author of *Hart Crane: l'Âme extravagante* (2003) and *Figures de la décomposition familiale dans le roman américain contemporain* (2018), and editor of *David Foster Wallace: Presences of the Other* (2017). She has published numerous academic articles and book reviews on contemporary American fiction.

Jason S. Polley is Associate Professor of English at Hong Kong Baptist University. His research interests include Indian English fiction, experimental criticism, literary journalism, critical pedagogy, comics, SF, Stephen King, and Hong Kong studies. He has written articles on John Banville, *District 9*, Jane Smiley, *Watchmen*, Wong Kar-wai, *House of Leaves*, Joel Thomas Hynes, and R. Crumb. His co-written article on *A Suitable Boy* is forthcoming. He's co-editor of the volumes *Poetry in Pedagogy* (2021) and *Cultural Conflict in Hong Kong* (2018). His monograph is *Jane Smiley, Jonathan Franzen, Don DeLillo: Narratives of Everyday Justice* (2011). He has two creative nonfiction books: *Cemetery Miss You* (2011) and *Refrain* (2010).

Daniel Punday is Professor and Head of the Department of English at Mississippi State University, as well as a past president of the International Society for the Study of the Narrative. He is the author of six books, the most recent of which is *Playing at Narratology: Digital Media as Narrative Theory* (2019).

Daniel Enrique Pérez is an Associate Professor of Chicanx and Latinx studies at the University of Nevada, Reno, and a Jotería studies scholar. He is the author of *Rethinking Chicana/o and Latina/o Popular Culture* (2009) and a collection of poetry entitled *Things You See in the Dark* (2018). He also edited *Latina/o Heritage on Stage: Dramatizing Heroes and Legends* (2015) and has published several articles centering on the intersections of gender, race, ethnicity, sexuality, and class. He obtained his PhD from Arizona State University.

Vincent Pérez is an Associate Professor of English at the University of Nevada at Las Vegas. His scholarly interests include Hemispheric American studies, Chicanx and Latinx literature, critical theory, and popular culture. Pérez has published in American (US), Mexican American, and African American literary studies in a range of scholarly journals. His most recent essay, "Spanish and Mexican Literature of California," was published in *A History of California Literature* (ed. Blake Allmendinger, 2015). His next book is an interdisciplinary study of immigration narratives titled *Fictions of the Americas: Latino/a Migrants and Transnational Memory*. His book *Remembering the Hacienda: History and Memory in the Mexican American Southwest* (2006), examines nineteenth-century US Hispanic fiction and autobiography. Anthologies in which his articles appear include: *Look Away! The U.S. South in New World Studies* (ed. John Smith and Deborah Cohn, 2004), *María Amparo Ruiz de Burton: Critical and Pedagogical Perspectives* (ed. Amelia María de la Luz Montes and Anne Elizabeth Goldman, 2004), *Autobiography Without Apology: The Personal Essay in Chicanx and Latinx Studies* (ed. Chon A. Noriega, Wendy Laura Belcher, and Charlene Villaseñor Black, 2020), *Recovering the U.S. Hispanic Literary Heritage*, and *I Am Aztlán: The Personal Essay in Chicano Studies* (ed. Chon A. Noriega and Wendy Laura Belcher, 2011).

Verónica Quezada completed her undergraduate and graduate studies at the University of California, Irvine. She received her doctorate in Spanish, with emphasis on Latin American and Chicano literatures. She wrote her dissertation on the performance of the Chicana and Latina identity in contemporary literature. She is Assistant Professor in the Language and Culture Program at Soka University of America, Aliso Viejo, California, where she teaches all levels of Spanish language courses. In addition, she analyzes and teaches Latin American literatures, Chicanx studies, border studies, and mass culture.

Nicholas F. Radel is Professor of English at Furman University, South Carolina. Author of *Understanding Edmund White* (2013) and co-editor of *The Puritan Origins of American Sex* (2000), he has written numerous articles on modern literature and sexuality, including early scholarly and biographical studies of Edmund White.

Art Redding is Professor of English at York University in Toronto, Canada. He is the author of *Radical Legacies: Public Intellectuals in the United States* (2016), *Haints: American Ghosts,*

Millennial Passions, and Contemporary Gothic Fictions (2011), *Turncoats, Traitors, and Fellow Travelers: Culture and Politics of the Early Cold War* (2008), and *Raids on Human Consciousness: Writing, Anarchism, and Violence* (1998).

Amy Reddinger holds a PhD in English from the University of Washington. Her literary scholarship includes work on James Baldwin and other twentieth-century African American LGBTQIA+ writers. Other areas of scholarship include food studies, gender studies, and the study of teaching and learning. She was a tenured English faculty member at the University of Wisconsin Colleges prior to becoming the Dean of Arts and Sciences at Bay de Noc Community College in Escanaba, Michigan.

Jamie Redgate lives in Scotland. His PhD in English literature was funded by the Arts and Humanities Research Council and completed at the University of Glasgow in 2017, resulting in the book *Wallace and I: Cognition, Consciousness, and Dualism in David Foster Wallace's Fiction* (2019). Jamie's essays and fiction have been published in *David Foster Wallace in Context* (2021), *Electric Literature*, *Gutter*, *Unwinnable*, and elsewhere, and can be found at www.jamieredgate.co.uk.

Christopher Rieger is Professor of English and Director of the Center for Faulkner Studies at Southeast Missouri State University. He is the author of *Clear-Cutting Eden: Ecology and the Pastoral in Southern Literature* (2009) and the co-editor of six essay collections, including *Faulkner and Hemingway* (2018) and *Faulkner and García Márquez* (2020). He has published essays on a range of authors, including Ernest Gaines, Larry Brown, Karen Russell, Marjorie Kinnan Rawlings, Zora Neale Hurston, Mo Yan, and Yukio Mishima.

Carmen Haydée Rivera is Professor of English at the University of Puerto Rico. Her teaching and research interests include diasporic Puerto Rican writers in the US, US Latino/a literature, literature of Caribbean migration, and women's studies. Her publications include a co-edited collection of essays titled *Writing Off the Hyphen: New Perspectives on the Literature of the Puerto Rican Diaspora* (2008) and a critical biography titled *Border Crossings and Beyond: The Life and Works of Sandra Cisneros* (2009). She also co-edited a collection of critical essays titled *Two Wings of the Same Bird: Transdisciplinary Approaches to Puerto Rican and Cuban American History, Literature, and Culture* (forthcoming). Additional critical articles appear in *The Ethnic Studies Review, CENTRO Journal, Camino Real, Op-Cit, Revista Umbral, New West Indian Guide, Latino/a Research Review, Caribbean Studies*, and *Sargasso*.

Carmen S. Rivera, PhD, is a Professor of Spanish, Latino Studies, and Women's and Gender Studies at SUNY Fredonia. She is the author of *Kissing the Mango Tree: Puerto Rican Women Rewriting American Literature* (2002). Currently, she is working on a book, *Las casitas de Rosario Ferré: Foundations, Structures, Spaces*, that examines Ferré's complete works.

James Emmett Ryan teaches at Auburn University, where he serves as Jean Wickstrom Liles Endowed Professor of English. His books include *Imaginary Friends: Representing Quakers in*

American Culture, 1650–1950 (2009) and *Faithful Passages: American Catholicism in Literary Culture, 1844–1931* (2013). His research on American literature and culture has appeared in journals including *American Literary History, Religion & American Culture, Leviathan, Studies in American Fiction, American Quarterly, Journal of American Culture, Book History, Quaker History, Studies in Travel Writing,* and *Journal of Modern Literature*.

Michelle Ryan-Sautour is *Maître de Conférences* (Associate Professor) at the Université d'Angers, France, where she co-directs the "Short Fiction and Short Forms" section of the CIRPaLL research group and oversees the European Network for Short Fiction Research. Her research focus is the speculative fiction and short stories of Angela Carter, Rikki Ducornet, Ali Smith, Sarah Hall, and other contemporary writers, with a special emphasis on authorship, reading pragmatics, game theory, and gender. Ms. Ryan-Sautour's research has been published in various collections and journals such as *Marvels & Tales, Journal of the Short Story in English, Etudes Britanniques Contemporaines,* and *Short Fiction in Theory and Practice*.

Yomna Saber is Associate Professor of English Literature at Qatar University. Her areas of research include African American literature, women's literature, and gender studies. Among her recent publications are: "Blurring the Contours of Memory in June Jordan's *Soldier: A Poet's Childhood*" in *a/b: Auto/Biography Studies* (2019), "Toni Cade Bambara's *The Salt Eaters*: Hearing the Silent Voice of Pain," in *Voices of Illness: Negotiating Meaning and Identity* (2019), "The Conjure Woman's Poetics of Poisoning in Gloria Naylor's *Mama Day*" in *Folklore* (2018), and *Gendered Masks of Liminality and Race: Black Female Trickster's Subversion of Hegemonic Discourse in African American Literature* (2017).

Jeffrey A. Sartain teaches courses in literature, composition, and professional writing at the University of Houston-Victoria. His studies focus on the culture of the digital age, posthumanism, contemporary authors, and literary minimalism. He is the editor of two books, *Sacred and Immoral: On the Writings of Chuck Palahniuk* (2009) and *The Many Lives of the Evil Dead: Essays on the Cult Film Franchise* (co-edited with Ron Riekki, 2019). He currently serves as the managing editor for *American Book Review*.

Theophilus Savvas is Senior Lecturer in English Literature at the University of Bristol in the UK. He is the author of *American Postmodernist Fiction and the Past* (2011) and several articles on American literature of the twentieth and twenty-first centuries. He is the co-editor (with Christopher K. Coffman) of a 2019 special issue of *Textual Practice* titled "American Fiction after Postmodernism." He is working on a literary history of vegetarianism.

Melissa E. Schindler is Assistant Professor of English at the University of North Georgia. She earned her PhD from SUNY University at Buffalo. She has been a Fulbright Research Fellow in Brazil and a Peace Corps volunteer in Mozambique. Her interdisciplinary research interests include: Luso-Afro-Brazilian studies; Indian Ocean studies; sexuality studies; second language acquisition; and first-year composition. Her work can be found in journals such as *Research in African Literatures, Caesura,* and *Obsidian*. She has also contributed essays to *Porn Archives* (ed.

Tim Dean, Steven Ruszczycky, and David Squires, 2014) and *Libre Acesso: Latin American Literature and Film through Disability Studies* (ed. Susan Antebi and Beth Ellen Jörgensen, 2016).

Vince Schleitwiler is a lecturer in the Department of American Ethnic Studies at the University of Washington. A comparative ethnic studies scholar specializing in Asian American and African American literatures and cultures, he is the author of *Strange Fruit of the Black Pacific: Imperialism's Racial Justice and Its Fugitives* (2017), as well as scholarly essays in *Comparative Literature*, *Global Performance Studies*, *African American Review*, and elsewhere.

Stefanie Schäfer (PhD Heidelberg) has worked as Professor of North American Studies at the universities of Jena, Erlangen, and Augsburg, Germany, and is currently a research fellow at the University of Vienna, Austria. Her research interests include narrative, visual and popular culture, and gender studies in the United States and in Canada. Her second book, *Yankee Yarns: Storytelling and the Invention of the National Body in Nineteenth-Century American Culture* (2021), examines the transatlantic origins of the United States' national allegory.

Florian Sedlmeier is Assistant Professor of North American Literature at the John F. Kennedy Institute, Freie Universität Berlin, Germany. He is a former recipient of grants by the German Research Foundation and has taught at the Universities of Hamburg and Salzburg, Austria. Recent publications include *The Postethnic Literary: Reading Paratexts and Transpositions around 2000* (2014) and *Anecdotal Modernity: Making and Unmaking History* (ed. with James Dorson, MaryAnn Snyder-Körber, and Birte Wege, 2020). He is currently working on a book about William Dean Howells and the literary field imagination in the late nineteenth century.

Barbara Kitt Seidman holds a BA, MA, and PhD in literature. She taught at Linfield College, a liberal arts college in western Oregon, for thirty-five years, retiring as Professor Emerita of English in 2018. Her scholarly writing has focused on US and Canadian literature, particularly by women writers, writers of color, and writers of literary autobiography. In forty years of teaching, she offered courses in all these areas, as well as in film studies and composition. While at Linfield she also served in administrative roles, including as the college's first female vice president of academic affairs/dean of faculty. She currently lives in Chandler, Arizona, with her husband.

Kascha Semonovitch holds a PhD in philosophy from Boston College and an MFA in poetry from Warren Wilson College. Her poems and essays have appeared in *The Bellingham Review*, *Zyzzyva*, *The Crab Creek Review*, *The Colorado Review*, and *The Kenyon Review*, among others, and in the chapbook *Genesis* (2012) by Dancing Girl Press. She has taught philosophy at Seattle University and Boston College, edited two collections of philosophical essays, and published numerous essays on early twentieth-century thought, recently in *Simone Weil and Continental Philosophy* (2017) and *The Bloomsbury Companion to Arendt* (2021). She now teaches at The Hugo House, a center for writers in Seattle.

Jeffrey Severs is Associate Professor of English at the University of British Columbia, where he specializes in US fiction since 1945. He is the author of *David Foster Wallace's Balancing Books: Fictions of Value* (2017) and co-editor of *Pynchon's Against the Day: A Corrupted Pilgrim's Guide* (2011). He has published articles on Wallace, Pynchon, Wideman, Roth, and others in *Critique, Modern Fiction Studies, Twentieth-Century Literature, Textual Practice, MELUS, Studies in American Fiction*, and other journals.

W. Andrew Shephard is an Assistant Professor of African American Literature in the University of Utah's English Department. His research focuses on modes of genre fiction such as science fiction, fantasy, and horror, as they intersect with questions of race, gender, and sexuality, and the ways in which marginalized peoples utilize the conventions of genre to address concerns specific to their communities. He is the author of the chapter "Afrofuturism of the Nineteenth and Twentieth Centuries" published in *The Cambridge History of Science Fiction* (2019), as well as the article "'All is Always Now': Slavery, Retrocausality, and Recidivistic Progress in Samuel R. Delany's *Empire Star* (1966)" published in *New Centennial Review*.

Matthew Shipe is a Senior Lecturer and the Director of Advanced Writing in the English Department at Washington University in St. Louis. He is co-editor (with Scott Dill) of *Updike and Politics: New Considerations* (2019), and his work has appeared in *The John Updike Review, Philip Roth Studies, A Political Companion to Philip Roth* (2017), *Roth and Celebrity* (2012), and *Perspectives on Barry Hannah* (2006). He currently serves as President of the Philip Roth Society and is on the executive board of the John Updike Society.

Debra Shostak is Mildred Foss Thompson Professor Emerita of English Language and Literature at the College of Wooster. The author of *Fictive Fathers in the Contemporary American Novel* (2020) and *Philip Roth: Countertexts, Counterlives* (2004), and the editor of *Philip Roth: American Pastoral, The Human Stain, The Plot Against America* (2011), she has published on numerous contemporary American novelists and on film. She recently served as executive co-editor of *Philip Roth Studies*.

Jason Shrontz is an English Professor at Klamath Community College in Klamath Falls, Oregon. He earned his PhD from the University of Rhode Island. His research examines American literature and the practices of human connection in the digital world. In the classroom, he is an avid digital literacy advocate.

David Siglos, Jr. is a PhD candidate in English at the University of California, Riverside. He received his BA in English from the University of Nevada, Las Vegas, and his MA in English from the University of California, Riverside. His research interests include Asian American literature, Filipino American literature, Philippine anglophone literature, theater and performance, and postcolonial theory, among others. He was born and raised in Negros Oriental, Philippines, and moved to the United States when he was aged 16.

Robin Silbergleid is a writer who works in the areas of poetry, creative nonfiction, and innovative literary criticism. She is the author of several books, including the poems *The Baby Book* (2015) and the memoir *Texas Girl* (2014), and is co-editor (with Kristina Quynn) of *Reading and Writing Experimental Texts: Critical Innovations* (2017). Her current projects include an autotheoretical analysis of contemporary queer mother memoir and a hybrid critical-creative monograph on the work of Carole Maso. She is Associate Professor of English and Director of Creative Writing at Michigan State University.

Bryn Skibo is a postdoctoral researcher at the University of Geneva, Switzerland. She has published extensively on the use of Anishinaabe philosophies as narrative theory and is the senior book reviews editor of *Transmotion*, a peer-reviewed journal inspired by the work of Gerald Vizenor.

Jennifer J. Smith is an Associate Professor and Chair of the English Department at North Central College. Her book, *The American Short Story Cycle* (2018), spans two centuries to tell the history of a genre that includes both major and marginal authors. Her work on story cycles has been published in *Pedagogy*, *Journal of the Short Story in English*, *Short Fiction in Theory and Practice*, and a number of essay collections.

Maritza Stanchich, PhD, is Professor of English at University of Puerto Rico-Río Piedras, where she teaches Puerto Rican diaspora, Latinx, Caribbean, and US American literatures, has directed MA and doctoral programs in English, and served in the Academic Senate. Her scholarship on William Faulkner, Puerto Rican diaspora literature, and the crisis in Puerto Rico has been published in peer-reviewed journals and books. Her columns starting in 2010 for the *Huffington Post*, *The New York Times*, and the *Guardian* helped bring international attention to Puerto Rico's crisis. She has also collaborated as an activist in various social movements, including academic unionization, most recently with the Asociación Puertorriqueña de Profesores Universitarios (APPU).

Cristina Stanciu is an Associate Professor of English and Director of the Humanities Research Center at Virginia Commonwealth University, where she teaches US multiethnic and Indigenous literatures. She has published and has essays forthcoming in *American Indian Quarterly*, *MELUS*, *Studies in American Indian Literatures*, *College English*, *NAIS*, *JGAPE: Journal of the Gilded Age and Progressive Era*, *Italian American Review*, and others. She is the co-editor of *Our Democracy and the American Indian and Other Writings by Laura Cornelius Kellogg* (2015) and the co-editor of the *MELUS* special issue "Pedagogy in Anxious Times" (Winter 2017). Her research has been supported by research grants at the Newberry Library and the Beinecke Rare Book and Manuscript Library, a postdoctoral fellowship from the American Association of University Women (AAUW), an NEH summer stipend award, and others. She is a recent recipient of an Obama Fellowship at Johannes Gutenberg University of Mainz, Germany, and a Fulbright Scholar Award. Her first monograph is forthcoming from Yale University Press.

Alexander Starre is Assistant Professor of North American Culture at the John F. Kennedy Institute at Freie Universität Berlin, Germany. He is a former Humboldt Foundation Fellow and has previously taught at the University of Göttingen and at Brown University. Recent publications include *Metamedia: American Book Fictions and Literary Print Culture after Digitization* (2015), *Projecting American Studies: Essays on Theory, Method, and Practice* (ed. with Frank Kelleter, 2018), and *The Printed Book in Contemporary American Culture: Medium, Object, Metaphor* (ed. with Heike Schaefer, 2019). He is currently working on a book about knowledge institutions in the United States around 1900.

Emmett Stinson is a lecturer in writing and literature at Deakin University. He is the author of *Satirizing Modernism* (2017) and *Known Unknows* (2010), which was shortlisted for the Steele Rudd Award. He is a co-author of *Banning Islamic Books in Australia* (2011).

Billy J. Stratton is an Associate Professor in the Department of English at the University of Denver. His research focuses on contemporary Native/American literatures, postcolonial theory, and captivity narratives, with secondary interests in Southern Gothic literature, postmodernism, dystopian literature, posthumanism, and film studies. His scholarship primarily addresses contemporary Native American/American writers and poets, while he has also written on Native American history and society, especially as it relates to Indigenous knowledge. He has produced two books: *Buried in Shades of Night: Contested Voices, Indian Captivity, and the Legacy of King Philip's War* (2013) and *The Fictions of Stephen Graham Jones* (2016), with a fiction project set in Appalachian coal country currently underway. Finally, Stratton has been a frequent contributor to news and popular media outlets including the *Los Angeles Review of Books, Time, Salon, The Independent,* and *The Hill*.

Seth Studer is an instructor in the English Department at South Dakota State University in Brookings. He earned his doctorate from Tufts University. His dissertation ("Backlash Realism: The American Novel during the Long 1980s") dealt with the intersection of literary realism and conservative political rhetoric in US fiction. He has published articles on the popular reception of Jonathan Franzen's novels and literary representations of Richard Nixon.

Rachel Sykes is Senior Lecturer in Contemporary American Literature at the University of Birmingham, UK. They are the author of *The Quiet Contemporary American Novel* (2018) and have published work in *Critique, Signs: Journal of Women in Society and Culture, C21: Twenty-First Century Writing,* and the *Journal of American Studies*. They are currently working on a project about the politics of disclosure in contemporary American and online cultures.

Tereza M. Szeghi is Professor of Comparative Literature and Social Justice at the University of Dayton in Ohio. Her research focuses on ways American Indian and Latinx writers use literature to achieve social and political change pertaining to their human rights. Her publications have appeared in such journals as *Aztlán, Studies in American Indian Literature, Comparative Literature, MELUS,* and *Western American Literature*.

Stuart J. Taylor is a lecturer at Edinburgh Napier University and educator at the University of Glasgow, where he recently completed his doctoral project, "Encyclopedic Architectures: Mathematical Structures in the Works of DeLillo, Pynchon, and Wallace." Researching interrelations of mathematics and literature, he is working on a debut monograph provisionally entitled *Mathematics in Postmodern U.S. Fiction*. Recent publications include "Mathematics of the Infinite" in *David Foster Wallace in Context* (ed. Clare Hayes-Brady, 2021) and "Mathematical Clinamen in the Encyclopedic Novel: Pynchon, DeLillo, Wallace," in *The Palgrave Handbook of Literature and Mathematics* (ed. Robert Tubbs, Alice Jenkins, and Nina Engelhardt, 2021).

Peter Templeton is Associate Lecturer in the Faculty of Arts and Social Sciences for the Open University, UK, and Fellow of the School of the Arts, English and Drama at Loughborough University. His first book, *The Politics of Southern Pastoral Literature, 1785–1885: Jeffersonian Afterlives*, was published in 2019. He is also one of the editors of the collection *Violence from Slavery to #Black Lives Matter: African American History and Representation* (2020), and the author of the 2021 volume *Clerks: "Over the Counter" Culture and Youth Cinema*. As well as these longer projects, he has contributed scholarly articles on a significant number of American authors.

Lucas Thompson is a Lecturer in English at the University of Sydney. He is the author of *Global Wallace: David Foster Wallace and World Literature* (2017), and has published widely on contemporary US literature. His articles have appeared in *New Literary History*, *Comparative Literature Studies*, *Texas Studies in Literature and Language*, and *The New Review of Film and Television Studies*, among other venues.

Jason Tougaw is the author of the memoir *The One You Get: Portrait of a Family Organism* (2017), winner of the Dzanc Nonfiction Prize, *The Elusive Brain: Literary Experiments in the Age of Neuroscience* (2018), and *Strange Cases: The Medical Case History and The British Novel* (2006). His essays have appeared in *Literary Hub*, *OUT* magazine, *Electric Literature*, *Modern Fiction Studies*, and *Literature and Medicine*.

Daria Tunca works in the Department of Modern Languages at the University of Liège, Belgium, where she is a member of the Center for Postcolonial Studies CEREP (www.cerep.uliege.be). Her research focuses on stylistics and African literatures, with a particular emphasis on contemporary Nigerian fiction. She is the author of *Stylistic Approaches to Nigerian Fiction* (2014) and the editor of *Conversations with Chimamanda Ngozi Adichie* (2020).

Agnieszka Tuszynska is an Associate Professor of English at Queensborough Community College-City University of New York, where she teaches courses in African American literature and writing. She also volunteers as an educator in a prison with College Justice Program, teaching college-prep workshops and facilitating book discussion groups. Her research focuses on African American literature of the Jim Crow era and the Harlem Renaissance and prison literature. Her work has previously appeared in *MELUS*, *English Language Notes*, *The CLA Journal*, *Dialogues in Social Justice: An Adult Educational Journal*, and other publications.

Eleanor Ty is Professor of English and Film Studies at Wilfrid Laurier University in Ontario, Canada. She was a Fulbright Visiting Research Chair at the University of California, Santa Barbara, in 2019. She has published books on cultural memory, Asian North American, and eighteenth-century literature. *Asianfail: Narratives of Disenchantment and the Model Minority* (2017) won the Asian/Pacific American Librarians Association Award for Literature in the adult nonfiction category for 2017. Other monographs include *Unfastened: Globality and Asian North American Narratives* (2010) and *The Politics of the Visible in Asian North American Narratives* (2004).

Ji-Young Um received her PhD in English from the University of Washington in Seattle and currently teaches in the English and Cultural Studies Department at Seattle Pacific University. Dr. Um's areas of teaching and research include American culture and US wars in Asia/Pacific, US multiethnic literature, race in media and popular culture, and Asian American literature, among other topics.

Jerry Varsava is Professor of Comparative Literature and English at the University of Alberta in Edmonton, Canada. He has published widely on the fiction of the twentieth and twenty-first centuries. His current work focuses on the depiction of economic life in the contemporary global novel across a spectrum of areas including the environment, economic precarity, economic inequality, and globalization, among others.

Martha L. Viehmann is a retired instructor of American studies, English, and composition. Viehmann writes about Indigenous literatures of North American literature and their intersections with European American culture. She is currently working on an article analyzing Tim Tingle's middle grades novels about the Choctaw Trail of Tears. She has published articles on Pauline Johnson and Mary Austin and book chapters on Mourning Dove and on literature of the US West.

Kirin Wachter-Grene is Assistant Professor of Liberal Arts at the School of the Art Institute of Chicago. She holds a PhD in English and focuses on African American literature and gender and sexuality studies. Dr. Wachter-Grene's work is published in *African American Review*, *The Black Scholar*, *Callaloo*, *Feminist Formations*, *Legacy: A Journal of American Women Writers*, and more. She is guest editor of *At the Limits of Desire: Black Radical Pleasure*, a special issue of *The Black Scholar* (50 (2) [2020]), and is currently working on her manuscript titled *Into the Scorpion Garden: Samuel R. Delany and Transgressive African American Literature*.

Belinda Waller-Peterson is an Assistant Professor of English at Moravian University and President of the African American Literature and Cultural Society. She is also a licensed registered nurse. She teaches courses in African American literature and culture and the health humanities. Her most recent publications include: "*The Art of Death* by Edwidge Dandicat, Book Review," (*Journal of Medical Humanities*, 2021), "'nobody came/cuz nobody knew': Shame and Isolation in Ntozake Shange's 'Abortion Cycle #1'," (*CLA Journal*, 2019), and "'Are You Sure, Sweetheart, That You Want to be Well?' The Politics of Mental Health and Long-Suffering in Toni Cade Bambara's *The Salt Eaters*," (*Religions*, 2019).

Alys Eve Weinbaum is Professor of English at the University of Washington, Seattle. She is the author, most recently, of *The Afterlife of Reproductive Slavery: Biocapitalism and Black Feminism's Philosophy of History* (2019).

CONTRIBUTORS

Alex Wermer-Colan, PhD, is the Digital Scholarship Coordinator at Temple University Libraries' Loretta C. Duckworth Scholars Studio, where he directs research and pedagogical projects integrating emerging technologies across the disciplines. His editorial scholarship and literary criticism explore the politics of decadent literature from the modernist period to the era of new media. He has edited two collections of archival materials and criticism on William S. Burroughs, *The Travel Agency is on Fire* (2015) and *William S. Burroughs Cutting Up the Century* (2019). His writing has also appeared in *PAJ: A Journal of Performance and Art, The Journal of Interactive Technology and Pedagogy, Twentieth Century Literature, The Yearbook of Comparative Literature, American Book Review, The D.H. Lawrence Review,* and the *L.A. Review of Books.*

Mark West researches contemporary American historical and eco-fiction, with a focus on representations of the 1960s. He recently published "'Observacion of these Articles': Surveillance and the 1970s in David Foster Wallace's *The Pale King*" in *Critique: Studies in Contemporary Fiction* and "Apocalypse Without Revelation?: Shakespeare, Salvagepunk and *Station Eleven*" in the *Open Library of Humanities.*

Brian Willems is Associate Professor of Literature at the University of Split, Croatia, Faculty of Humanities and Social Sciences. His most recent publications include *Sham Ruins: A User's Guide* (2021), *Speculative Realism and Science Fiction* (2017), *Shooting the Moon* (2015), and the novella *Henry, Henry* (2017).

Jeffrey J. Williams is the author or editor of seven books, including *PC Wars: Politics and Theory in the Academy* (1995) and *How to Be an Intellectual: Criticism, Culture, and the University* (2014). He serves as one of the editors of *The Norton Anthology of Theory and Criticism* (2001; 3rd ed. 2017) and was editor of *The Minnesota Review* from 1992 to 2010. In 2019 he was Distinguished Visiting Fellow at the Advanced Research Collaborative at CUNY Graduate Center, and he is Professor of English and of Literary and Cultural Studies at Carnegie Mellon University.

Roberta Wolfson is a Lecturer in the Program in Writing and Rhetoric at Stanford University. Her research focuses on contemporary Asian American, African American, and Latinx American literatures, comparative race studies, critical mixed-race studies, and risk and security studies. Her scholarly work has been published in *MELUS, American Literature,* and *African American Review,* and she is currently working on a book manuscript that considers how writers of color engage anti-racist narratives to trouble the operations of the contemporary US security state.

Isabel Quintana Wulf is an Assistant Professor of English at Salisbury University, Maryland, where she teaches multiethnic US literatures, Native American literature, and critical theory. Focusing on contemporary fiction, her research examines the representation of borders and border spaces in Native American and Chicana/o/x literature, as both geopolitical and metaphorical formations. Paying attention to narratives of nation building, racialization, and settler colonialism, her research teases out the forces of inclusion and exclusion embedded in border logics, focusing on the ways racialization and discrimination processes transform into commonsense principles of social organization.

Justyna Włodarczyk holds a PhD in American literature and works at the Institute of English Studies at the University of Warsaw, Poland. Her research interests combine animal studies and gender studies, with a particular interest in how human–animal relationships are entangled in broader ideological projects. She has published in *Genders, Society and Animals*, and *Medical Humanities*. She is the author of *Ungrateful Daughters: Third Wave Feminist Writings* (2010). Her most recent book is *Genealogy of Obedience: Reading North American Dog Training Literature* (2018). She is currently working on a project on depictions of interspecies harmony in American literature and culture.

James P. Zappen is a Professor in the Department of Communication and Media, Rensselaer Polytechnic Institute, Troy, New York. His recent publications include "Affective Identification in Jennifer Egan's *A Visit from the Goon Squad*" in *Literature Interpretation Theory*; "New York City as Dwelling Place: Reinventing the American Dream in Steven Millhauser's *Martin Dressler*, Joseph O'Neill's *Netherland*, and Atticus Lish's *Preparation for the Next Life*" in *The Journal of American Culture*; and "Affective Rhetoric in China's Internet Culture" in *Present Tense: A Journal of Rhetoric in Society*.

Introduction

PATRICK O'DONNELL, STEPHEN J. BURN, AND LESLEY LARKIN

The introduction of the honored speaker at the stereotypical awards ceremony all too often begins with a gag-line: "and now, someone who needs no introduction." Not necessarily needing an introduction could be said of many of the authors and topics included in this survey of contemporary American fiction of the last forty years, but just as many are – in the view of the editors – genuinely in need and deserving of a good introduction. In truth, so proliferate and diverse is the American fiction of the last four decades that no encyclopedia could contain all of it, and no introduction could fully chart its energies and trajectories. Our effort in this compendium is to provide a large-scale mapping of contemporary American fiction since 1980 – one that is symptomatic rather than comprehensive, and one whose many details await completion by readers who will add their own experience reading the authors included here and countless others, contemplating the range of questions the subjects pose and raising more than can be accommodated in an encyclopedia ten times, fifty times longer.

The first horizon of this encyclopedia is its chronological time-frame: four decades, forty years extending, in terms of US presidential history, from the beginning of the Reagan era to the end of the Trump presidency. In between, a succession of presidents and events no one could have foreseen in 1980 and which we are still digesting and assimilating at the end of, and well beyond, 2020. We have chosen 1980 as a starting point because it ushers in a decade of deep change in American life and culture in the turn toward a new millennium: in Britain and America, Thatcher and Reagan were in power; in American writing, the "high postmodernism" that blossomed in the 1960s and 1970s was just beginning to wane, even as poststructuralist theory, largely imported from Europe, was in ascendency. Of equal significance, the 1980s in America saw the institutionalization of multiculturalism in the academy via the development of ethnic and gender studies curricula and the canonization of writing by people of color as the impact of changes brought about by the "canon wars" were felt both in universities and publishing houses, and reflected both in course syllabi and bestseller lists. At the same time, the United States retreated from the movement for greater race and gender equity as a new conservatism ascended in US politics, along with mass incarceration and the so-called War on Drugs. This was also the decade that saw the advent of the Internet and digital culture: ARPANET, the predecessor to what we now call the Internet, produced the first series of internet protocols in the early 1980s, and the "World Wide Web" was invented and made publicly available toward the end of the decade. The forty years that extend from 1980 to 2020 have seen the emergence of a system of communication and information exchange unprecedented in human history, and new forms of writing, from hypertext to Twitter fiction, with attendant changes to traditional conceptions of the author following in their wake. Concepts such as "posthumanism" and "the Anthropocene" have established themselves as key terms for the first part of the twenty-first century; climate change has become *the* primary planetary concern of the last decades – one that seems to defy both political and imaginative capacities. Creative writing as a social institution has been charted by such works as Mark McGurl's *The Program Era* (2009), and the continuance of the novel, increasingly taking place amidst putatively competing online forms, first blogs, and now tweets and Instagram posts, has been formulated in widely-publicized critiques such as David Shields' *Reality Hunger* (2010). In short, the last forty years have brought "enormous changes at the last minute," to borrow the title of a story by an extraordinary writer, Grace Paley, who is not included in the author's list of this work for reasons described below.

The first and one of the primary challenges facing the editors of *The Encyclopedia of Contemporary American Fiction, 1980–2020* is who and what to include, and who and what not to include. Given the limitations of, even, a capacious format (up to 1,000,000 words in two volumes) and the more complicated limitations of how many scholars could be recruited within a reasonable time-frame to contribute their considerable energies to this project, the editors began with a rudimentary plan: about 200 authors to be covered in entries of approximately 3000 words each; approximately fifty topics to be covered in entries of 5000 words. (This is not to mention the third, and unexpected constraint imposed by COVID-19, which inevitably impacted the scheduling, deadlines, and the final contents of the *Encyclopedia*). Given the proliferation and quality of contemporary American writing over the last forty years, the lists could easily have been twice as long and still seemed too short, inevitably leaving gaps we would otherwise wish to fill. In drawing up and discussing our initial lists, the editors arrived at one conclusion that might be regarded as both a limitation and an opening early on: the *Encyclopedia* could only be indicative, not exhaustive; many would have to be left out for the relatively fewer to be included in what intentionally would be a compendium that is representative of four decades of American fiction, but only in the sense that a fractal graph of a shoreline is representative of the actual coast of a national seashore. As editors, we suffer under no delusion that our final choices and the entries we have been successful in recruiting will be satisfactory to all, or even to any. While we have attempted to be professionally objective in our choices and to follow certain self-imposed rules (mentioned below), it would be dishonest for us to claim there is not a subjective element in our choices, though we would also wish to have it noted that both the objective and subjective perspectives brought to bear upon this project are based upon a collective experience of over seventy-five years teaching and writing about contemporary American fiction. Any volume of this sort is both enriched and limited by the specific perspectives and experiences of its editors. Rather than lamenting the exclusions that any given reader will find here, we hope that the result of noting these will be a source of discussion and inspiration, as much as the inclusions may be a source of information and adventure in reading authors and works newly discovered.

The objectives we pursued in determining the lists of authors and topics to be included in the *Encyclopedia* are straightforward in theory but turned out to be complicated to parse in practice.

First, any author, both those born decades before the entry point of 1980 as well as those born after, must have published at least two highly visible works (novels or short story collections) during the forty-year period: for more established writers, visibility was indicated in available critical commentary; for newer, less-established writers, visibility was more often indicated by the presence of book reviews and/or online commentary that suggested the writer had achieved a consensus among readers of their evolving importance. For the older, most well-established writers, especially those who had already garnered a wealth of information and critique available elsewhere, we additionally agreed to include them only if they had published work of considerable significance after 1980 in terms of the overall trajectories of their careers. Thus, we have included Norman Mailer, who published his first and, still, among two or three of his most important novels, *The Naked and the Dead*, in 1948, but who also published post-1980 five weighty novels indicative of a career continuing to evolve. We did not, however, include Donald Barthelme, who had achieved recognition as a leading proponent of postmodern and experimental fiction and who was still alive and writing in 1980, but whose most important work, in our view, had already been published in the preceding two decades. The decision is certainly not uncontroversial, and can only additionally be understood in the context of a desire to generate a compendium that included as many newer energies and voices as possible while still maintaining a balance between older and younger generations of writers. Thus, once more, we decided to include an entry on Ursula K. LeGuin, who published her first novel in 1966, but who continued in a steadily prolific writing career up until her death in 2018; but we decided not to include Grace Paley, one of the most remarkable story writers of the twentieth century who continued to write well into the first decade of the twenty-first century, but whose most accomplished work in prose narrative occurred before the 1980s, when she began to focus more on poetry. In striving to balance established with emergent writers, our inclusion of younger generations of writers was based not only upon their visibility as defined above, but also on our capacity to attract contributors from the scholarly community. Writers such as Viet Thanh Nguyen and Brit Bennett – each, with two novels to their credit, the first coming in 2015 and 2016 respectively – have been included, but, following our "at least two works of fiction" rule, other acclaimed young writers such as Ta-Nehisi Coates and Tommy Orange, both with a single, highly-regarded work of fiction to date, have not. In inviting contributors for this project, we have encouraged entry authors not to provide, simply, overviews of the work at hand, but to offer specific critical perspectives; not incidentally, many of these contributors teach and write abroad, giving this project focused on a single national literature, by intention, a broad, international perspective.

Several other elements factored into our decisions. Especially since so much contemporary fiction is intermedial and cross-genre, we wanted to include authors who worked in multiple genres (science fiction, crime fiction, romance) but not strictly or primarily in a single genre, especially as existing encyclopedias are already focused on writers in these genres. Highly popular fiction writers like Stephen King or LeGuin or Joyce Carol Oates are included both because of the impact of their work well into the twenty-first century as well as the fact that they work across several genres, sometimes within a single novel. The growing visibility, importance, and impact of fiction by writers of color and LBGTQ writers in the period of the *Encyclopedia*, as well as important critiques of institutional racism, homophobia, and transphobia within the publishing industry and the academy, have guided our attempt to create a diverse authors list in which relative newcomers, such as Charlie Jane Anders and Roxane Gay, rub virtual shoulders with literary giants like Toni Morrison and Louise Erdrich. The *Encyclopedia* is well-focused on a national literature, but our selection, the contributions, and the authors and topics included consistently raise the questions: What is a national literature? What is an American national literature within the context of a hemispheric conception of "American" literature? What do these terms actually mean in a moment when, on the global scale, recondite nationalisms contend with planetary sensibilities and increasingly complex communication networks generate new notions of singularity and collectivity? While operating within fairly conventional parameters – work written in English by those who have lived much or all of their lives within the United States – we hope that the international perspective provided by our many contributors who work outside the United States also extends to many of the writers whose presence, visibility, and impact extends well beyond that of the boundaries of the United States. With all of this comes the editors' understanding that any writer occupies multiple categories of nation, genre, and identity at any given time, including, of course, the many immigrant and cosmopolitan writers represented herein as well as those Native American writers who belong to sovereign nations that exist within US borders.

We had two primary aspirations when it came to the selection of topics for the *Encyclopedia*: first, that the topic reflect the energies and tendencies of contemporary American fiction as it has evolved in the last forty years; and second, ideally, that many of the topics entries would touch upon authors and works that we were not able to include in the author's list. As with the list of authors, the included topics came about as the result of extensive conversation between the editors and much longer lists that needed to be trimmed, some topics collapsed into each other if possible, others retained or discarded based upon a consensus about what seemed most important and who we might recruit to write a substantial entry on complex matters within the limitation of 5000 words. As with the author entries, we encouraged contributors of the topic entries to develop the entry according to their own lights, providing needed information but, at the same time, developing a critical "edge" or angle that would bring the contributor's unique perspective to the work at hand. In several cases, we discussed the horizons and perspective of the entries with an individual contributor whom we were attempting to recruit, such that we feel it is fair to say that there is a strong element of collectivity in the *Encyclopedia*. That, at least, has been one of our primary goals both in selection and outcome. The result is a diverse collection of entries that runs from subjects salient early in our period and now subject to critical rethinking (e.g. "Multiculturalism"), to subjects (e.g. "Posthumanism") currently ascendant in discussions of American fiction.

The editors would like to express our gratitude to the editing and production teams at Wiley, who guided us throughout the staging and assembly of the *Encyclopedia*; we especially wish to thank our editorial assistants, first, Yashoda Balasubramanian, and then, Aruna Pragrasam, for their prodigious efforts in managing all of the contributions, corresponding with all of the contributors, and keeping the project on track from beginning to end – all with grace, patience, and the highest level of professionalism. We also wish to thank Dan Finch at Wiley, who got things rolling with the Scholar One system and made sure we had a solid foundation for the project, and Nicole Allen, who was involved in the project at the outset and who was always there along the way to help us sort out things out. Our thanks as well to Giles Flitney, who has done an admirable job as project manager. Patrick O'Donnell thanks Diane O'Donnell for her love and steadfast support, and colleagues and friends Justus Nieland, Scott Juengel, Stephen Arch, David Madden, and Cedric Bryant for their encouragement throughout the project, as well as their fine contributions to it. Lesley Larkin thanks Northern Michigan University for partially funding her participation in this project as well as the many colleagues who offered ideas and contributions, particularly Amy Reddinger and Amy Hamilton; she also thanks Mark Romanski for love and laughter, Killian Larkin and Alexander Larkin for patience and good humor, and Tom Frank for the kind of personal and intellectual support that is simply impossible to ever repay. Stephen Burn thanks Marshall Boswell and Mary Holland for wisdom and recommendations throughout this project, and, at Glasgow, is grateful for support and advice from Chris Gair, Alice Jenkins, and Helen Stoddart.

Literary criticism, like literature itself, is never a solo endeavor, nor is it practiced in a vacuum. Recent social and political events have necessarily shaped and shadowed the analyses collected herein, and perhaps chief among these is the racial reckoning that followed the murder of George Floyd by a police officer in Minneapolis in 2020. The protests against police brutality, and other forms of violent and systemic racism, that arose – in the midst of a pandemic which disproportionately affected Black and brown people (more on this below) – were unprecedented in breadth and notably shifted public discourse on race. The long-term effects of this shift remain to be seen (and we are currently in the midst of a powerful backlash). But these events – like the uptick in anti-Asian hate crimes, the separation of migrant families at the US/Mexico border, the epidemics of violence against Indigenous women and girls and transwomen of color – are powerful reminders of the real stakes involved in reading and writing about contemporary American lives. In this volume, we have attempted, however imperfectly, to make space for a wide range of voices, acknowledging that institutionalized racism continues to constrain who is published, taught, and written about – and by whom. As white scholars, we recognize our own privilege within this system and acknowledge those scholars who, subject to racism themselves, wrote under the challenging conditions of discrimination and protest. Their work is a reminder of the promise that literature can and does matter in ways that affect us all.

Much of this project has been conducted during the long months and (now) years of the onslaught of a global pandemic, and as editors we could not let the occasion of an introduction pass without commenting briefly on COVID-19. We are pleased, and honored, to reflect that the vast majority of our contributors remained committed to this project and finalized their work during an exceedingly difficult time in their professional and personal lives. We are immensely grateful for their perseverance and their writing. While we regrettably lost a very few entries along the way due to circumstances beyond anyone's control (those on Joshua Cohen, John Rechy, Lynne Tillman, and Literary Prizes, for example), we have been cheered by the number of entries we have *not* lost, and once more by the commitment of everyone involved to this project. Nevertheless, we (only, inadequately) recognize the enormous losses so many have suffered during this unprecedented time – a recognition and mourning in the midst of which this project and its celebration of imaginative life and work takes place.

A

Abu-Jaber, Diana

HAGAR ELTARABISHY
Ain Shams University, Egypt

Diana Abu-Jaber is a contemporary American Jordanian writer, a professor at Portland State University, and a novelist. She was born in Syracuse, New York, in 1959, to an American mother and a Jordanian father, Patricia and Ghassan Abu-Jaber. As a child, she lived in Jordan with her family, before returning to the United States. Later on, and on a Fulbright Fellowship (1996), she returned to Jordan to explore her roots and her writing tools, doing research for her books. Hence, she moved between Jordan and America within her lifetime creating a sense of in-betweenness that is also evident in her writing. In 1980, she studied at SUNY Oswego, majoring in English, and earned her BA. Then, she attained her MA from the University of Windsor in 1982, and in 1986, she earned her PhD from SUNY Binghamton. Throughout her teaching career, she taught literature, film studies, and writing at numerous American universities which include: Iowa State University, University of Oregon, University of Nebraska, University of Michigan, UCLA, and University of Miami. Besides teaching, she has also published articles in *The Washington Post* and *The New Yorker*, along with her many literary reviews issued in established publications. In addition, Abu-Jaber has published seven books, highlighting her various literary narrative techniques and themes, exploring her hyphenated identity along the way.

Abu-Jaber started her literary career in the 1990s showcasing her writing talent that developed from one book to the next. She has published four novels and two memoirs which include: *Arabian Jazz* (1993), *Crescent* (2003), *The Language of Baklava: A Memoir* (2005), *Origin* (2008), *Birds of Paradise* (2011), and *Life without a Recipe: A Memoir* (2016). Moreover, in 2020, a new novel was published, entitled *Silverworld*.

Throughout her literary career, Abu-Jaber has received recognition and awards for her distinguished writing, and many of her books have been bestsellers. For instance, she was awarded the Oregon Book Award in 1994 for her first novel, *Arabian Jazz*; she also won the PEN Center USA Award for Literary Fiction as well as the American Book award for *Crescent* in 2004. In 2012, she won the Arab American Book Award for her latest novel, *Birds of Paradise*.

In most of her work, Abu-Jaber addresses the question of identity, and her characters are often on a journey of identity formation.

For instance, in *Arabian Jazz*, considered the first mainstream Arab American novel, the quest for identity is evident through a hybrid family and first generation children (reminiscent of Diana Abu-Jaber's own life). In this novel, the liminal state the first generation children find themselves in is formed because of their hybridity; moreover, the creation of what postcolonial theorist Homi Bhabha called a "Third Space" is in progress in a vibrant, humorous, detailed description of a family with an Arab father, a deceased American mother, and their daughters living in the United States. Here, Bhabha's concept is highlighted in the girls, who are living at borderlines of cultural difference; they find it hard to belong to either the Arab or the American side, and they learn to create a new horizon for their hyphenated identities. The extended Arab family members, the American jazz music that plays throughout, the talk of marriage, the search for "home" for both the father and the daughter create a mood of confusion, but also represent reality for those who question their identities and try to find home. All of this is written with a passion for food, especially Arabic food as a tribute to Abu-Jaber's Jordanian roots. The collision of cultures cannot be evaded and is exemplified in the Ramound family: Mutassem, the father, is pulled apart between his nostalgia for his home country and his life in America; Jemorah, his daughter, is in search of who she is, still struggling with her hyphenated identity; and his other daughter, Melvina, seems to have it all figured out and leads her American life. Consequently, with a symbolic title to testify to such cultural collision, *Arabian Jazz* is prolific with cultural allusions, yet it opens a way for identifying with immigrants, and speaks of first-generation identity loss. It is loaded with many humorous tales and character details, as the reader is swallowed in a different world where no chronological order is present but, rather, time is distorted by spiraling backwards at times with abrupt shifts to present moments; the blurred distinction between the past and the present needs an attentive reader to follow. In addition, the novel touches upon politics in a subtle manner, with some embedded criticism conveyed through typical family discussions over dinner. On another level, *Arabian Jazz* defies the American media that broadcasts ugly stereotypes of Arabs and whatever is Arabian. The novel is about music, food, family, love, and death, thus humanizing Arabs, making them less precarious, all through reading about the Jordanian Ramound family. Abu-Jaber makes the novel relatable to any hyphenated character who is trying to find his/her way and acquire Homi Bhabha's Third Space, where negotiating a unique hybrid identity is possible.

In *Crescent*, written before 9/11 but published after, in 2003, Abu-Jaber moves away from Jordan to include more Middle Eastern identities, such as Lebanese, Iraqi, and Persian. She continues to address hybridity, but this time with her Iraqi American chef, Sirine. Though set in Los Angeles, the novel does not leave out Middle Eastern food; an Arabic Thanksgiving banquet, aromatic tea, and mouthwatering crisp baklava are all fully described, among other delicious Arabic food in Um-Nadia's café. Though the novel may seem to be simply about love, it is not so simple. Abu-Jaber revisits Arabic oral tradition and plays with technicalities of narration in *Crescent*. She introduces a magic realist story with jinns and mermaids that is interwoven in her novel with the love story of Sirine and Hanif, till both stories unfold themselves by the end and become one. Portions of a mythical adventure story about Abdelrahman Salahadin precede her main events in each chapter, which might seem unrelated at times, but eventually, Salahadin, Sirine, and Han's stories connect. It is a symbolic, witty maneuver that invites the reader to become attentive and decipher the codes in Abu-Jaber's main plot.

On another note, politics and media manipulation, as well as the precarity of Arab life, are clear themes in this novel, with direct criticism of both dictatorship in Iraq (in a previous period) and the silence of Western media. Arabic literature and arts are explored, too, and Abu-Jaber takes the reader to wander in the streets of Egypt, Lebanon, and Iraq. She introduces her characters as Arab intellectuals who recite poetry, visit art galleries, and teach in American universities. They are well educated and cultured; they represent the opposite of the stereotype of the ignorant, barbaric Arab. *Crescent* thus addresses a different Iraq to the one known to the Western community and media. It is not the Iraq that is full of terrors as a result of the Gulf war and the dictatorship of Saddam Hussein; rather, it is Iraq the minaret and lighthouse of arts and knowledge where all those interesting tales, adventures, food, and literature come from. All of these cultural gifts are juxtaposed to the theme of exile and the sense of Diaspora most of the novel's immigrant and hybrid characters feel. "What is home?" is an important question that keeps popping up in their quest for identity, and especially through Abu-Jaber's hybrid main heroine in *Crescent*. A love story it is, but talk of political and cultural exile, finding home, and hunger for memories are all embedded in the novel. It is worth mentioning that the timing of the novel's publication, though not intentional, helped make the novel part of Arab/American dialogue after 9/11 and during the Iraq War. *Crescent* represented a different version of Iraqis than the one proposed in the media.

In 2008, Abu-Jaber developed her writing tools and introduced her favorite themes of identity, home, and family with fresh devices in her third novel. *Origin* does step away from direct references to Arab identity, but it is still a novel about questioning identity, this time in the form of a thriller. The main character, Lena, is a fingerprint examiner in search of her origins and roots. The Tarzan-like childhood that Lena remembers of her past and her search for her origins and biological parents, with an ambiguous reference to her ethnic identity that will never be resolved, are all interwoven with a mysterious case she is investigating. *Origin* investigates the theme of home, with Lena's various memories of childhood and talk of forests and apes, an orphanage, and foster homes. Lena's quest for identity is a long journey, as she tries to make connections between vague memories, small details, and a weird token she is left with. Satisfaction with what one has, and the bitterness of dissatisfaction because of what has been buried forever, revolve around Lena and her foster family. Thus, dysfunctional families, love, mysterious ethnicity, and unknown roots are all topics addressed in *Origin*, through a thrilling, breath-stopping fiction with surprises that unveil themselves with the progression of narration typically found in a crime novel.

Finally, in her fourth novel *Birds of Paradise*, Abu-Jaber steps even farther from her Arab roots to a full multicultural setting in Miami. This gives her space to demonstrate more narrative techniques in writing of family issues, relationships, isolation, visibility/invisibility, and freedom. This time, each chapter is colonized by one of the Muir family members (father, mother, son, and daughter) to tell their part of the story. This narrative device recalls Egyptian novelist and Nobel Laureate Naguib Mahfouz's technique of narrating each chapter through the perspective of a different character, as in his novel, *Morning and Evening Talks* (1987). However, Abu-Jaber maintains her unique style; while Mahfouz divides his chapters in *Morning and Evening Talks* alphabetically, for his sixty-seven characters of different generations to narrate their side of the story (and along the way their lives intersect), Abu-Jaber's four characters jump in to show their side of the story where needed and in no specific pattern. The readers have, therefore, to weave the loose threads, fill in the gaps between the different chapters as if looking into a big puzzle they have to complete by the end of the novel. Moreover, readers must wait for each character to reappear and take over the chapter to know what happened in subsequent chapters to follow what they previously recounted. Abu-Jaber again infuses this novel with food metaphors; kneading and baking are intrinsic here to sweeten the bitterness of life experienced by the shattered Muir family. In *Birds of Paradise*, Abu-Jaber proves that she is not essentially talking about Arabs alone; she is, rather, universal in her imagination and not limited to her ethnic identity. In fact, both *Origin* and *Birds of Paradise* give way to her universality as a writer.

Diana Abu-Jaber gets personal too in her writing and makes the personal universal. This is clear in her two published memoirs, where Abu-Jaber opens her heart and pours it out on paper, unfolding her full life, talking of her past and future. In her famous culinary memoir *The Language of Baklava*, Abu-Jaber focuses on the past; she introduces her family, her relationship with her father "Bud," but most importantly she adds recipes to each of her chapters to involve the readers. Recipes are present to celebrate at times, or soothe the pain – and counteract what has just been brutally revealed –with comfort food. Abu-Jaber interweaves recipes in such a witty manner that it is clear they are not simply recipes but also potent metaphors. She makes cooking an act of love rooted in memories and people. But *The Language of Baklava* serves another purpose, for it is a memoir of how Abu-Jaber's hybrid identity was formed. The in-betweenness evoked in her novels is obvious with her Arab family and the American context she lives in; her cultural and even linguistic alienation are expressed and confessed, as she tackles stereotypes through witty narration, till she reconciles with her identity and comes to terms with it throughout adulthood. Consequently, this is a book on the journey of identity formation of this established writer. As in her early novels, the memoir carries themes of confusion, identity formation, hybridity, liminality, cultural alienation and isolation, family, race and ethnicity, but also power. The distinction of her technique lies in how the narration is not interrupted but rather strengthened by the ingredients, steps, and number of servings she puts into her personal accounts.

A decade later, Abu-Jaber published her second memoir, *Life without a Recipe*, a book about adulthood and surprises that life throws at you, where no direct recipes are to be found. It is a very relatable book, as it explores failed marriages, finding true love (when Abu-Jaber talks of her husband Scott), loss of a parent (when readers cry over the death of "Bud" whom they loved in *The Language of Baklava*), but most importantly motherhood and adoption (when she talks of her experience with her daughter, Grace). It is a memoir about dealing with loss, grief, and disappointments; hence, there are no steps to follow to make life better. Rather, it is about learning to appreciate the little details. As a result, it is a very human memoir. It is no longer about racial and ethnic identity, as this was already resolved with her first memoir. Rather, this is a book dedicated to every struggling human being. It bluntly speaks of divorce, love, death, and career, but most importantly of the beauty of parenthood and of overcoming the losses and challenges of life – conquering them with love, food, and family. It is thus a memoir that speaks to every human being despite their color and culture, a memoir of life.

Looking at both memoirs, in Diana Abu-Jaber's world, food is a prominent trademark.

Naturally, then, food is a recurring motif in her books. Food is memory, identity, culture, cure, ritual, legacy, nostalgia, love, and security. It also always appeals to her readers' gastronomy and makes her books mouthwatering with her detailed description of every dish to ease the pain and wipe away tears.

Overall, common themes can be traced across Abu-Jaber's six books: hybridity, questioning identity, exile, finding home, liminality, family relationships, cultural alienation, isolation, ethnicity, precarity, feminism, and empowerment are all present themes. Moreover, Abu-Jaber often addresses politics in her books, especially the politics of the Middle East, and directs criticism at political leaders and institutions, at times. On the other hand, she also attacks Western stereotypes, racism, and blindfolded media.

However, Abu-Jaber does not try to beautify the Arab world to make it appealing to the American reader; she does not hide Arab ailments, stubbornness, politics, nor faults, but she presents their gray-like life as no different from anyone else's in the world. They are not the abhorrent terrorist of the Western media, but neither are they the saints of folk tales. Arabs are mere human beings with secrets, fears, disturbed families who cause trouble; they love and are nostalgic, and believe their countries are the best in the world but still flee them for a better life or bigger dreams. Hence her originality as a writer is recognized, as well as her ability to create multilayered characters who are universal, relatable despite cultural differences. In fact, Abu-Jaber's readers will now grasp more of the cultural background and understand it, rather than blindly reject it. The Arab and the Arab American are no longer precarious, but fully dimensional characters with a roller coaster of emotions. They are not to be shunned but accepted and understood; they are not merely stereotypically exotic and mysteriously dark – thus evil – but part of the melting pot, preserving their origins and roots to maintain the uniqueness of their identities, but remaining essentially human after all.

As for her writing devices and techniques, Abu-Jaber gives credit to the Arab oral tradition she learned from her father and his stories. She admits (Field 2006, p. 221) that she was influenced by his tales, and it affected her style of writing and narration. Therefore, her narrative devices often take different forms and shapes. Moreover, her language is also distinguished by how detailed and vibrant it is. Her characters are vivacious and relatable despite their different ethnic backgrounds; as a result, empathy is a common feature that readers experience while stepping into the world of Abu-Jaber's characters.

All in all, Diana Abu-Jaber is a prominent contemporary Arab American novelist who does not run away from what has shaped her as a writer whether her father's love for food and storytelling, or her mother's keenness on reading and holding the family together. Pride in her roots both as an Arab and as an American is perceived in her works. Hence, Abu-Jaber uses parts of her own life and personality and develops them into something grander in her writing. She is not pigeonholed in ethnic writing alone, but rather proves her universality as a writer.

SEE ALSO: Alameddine, Rabih; Jarrar, Randa; Multiculturalism; Post-9/11 Narratives

REFERENCE

Field, Robin E. (2006). A prophet in her own town: an interview with Diana Abu-Jaber. *MELUS* 3 (4): 207–225.

FURTHER READING

Al-Joulan, Nayef A. (2010). Diana Abu-Jaber's *Arabian Jazz*: an orphic vision of hybrid cultural identity. *Neophilologus* 94: 637–652.

Bhabha, Homi. (1994). *The Location of Culture*. Routledge: London.

Limpár, Ildikó. (2009). Narratives of misplacement in Diana Abu-Jaber's *Arabian Jazz, Crescent*, and *Origin. Hungarian Journal of English and American Studies (HJEAS)* 15 (2): 249–268.

Masood, Khalid. (2017). Negotiating borders: cultural communication in Abu-Jaber's literary works. *International Journal of English Language, Literature in Humanities (IJLLH)* 5 (9): 997–1015.

Michael, Magali C. (2011). Arabian nights in America: hybrid form and identity in Diana Abu-Jaber's *Crescent. Critique: Studies in Contemporary Fiction* 52 (3): 313–331.

Stevens, Jay. (2005). An interview with Diana Abu-Jaber. *CutBank* 1 (63): 20–33.

Zbidi, Nawel. (2015). Postmodernist generic transgressions, fragmentation and heteroglossia in Diana Abu Jaber's *Crescent. International Journal of Humanities and Cultural Studies* 2 (1): 661–671.

Acker, Kathy

PATRICK O'DONNELL
Michigan State University, USA

Kathy Acker (1947–1997) is one of the best-known and prolific avant-garde/experimental writers of the post-1980 era in contemporary American fiction. Often viewed as an "underground" writer in the same company as William S. Burroughs (who served as an informal mentor), Henry Miller, and the Beats, she is intentionally scandalous and transgressive in work that challenges limits of all kinds – aesthetic, social, moral, corporeal. Her work and visibility reached their apogee when French poststructuralist theory and third-wave feminism combined to consequentially transform notions of gender identity and sexuality in ways that continue to confront the repressions wrought by late capitalism operating within a patriarchal social order. Acker's oeuvre is voluminous, and includes over thirty novels, novellas, and stories, as well as dozens of other works in multiple genres: poetry, essays, spoken-word and musical recordings, plays and filmscripts. Acker's life was equally adventurous: writer, performance artist, university lecturer, stripper, alternative musician – in all of these roles, she relentlessly attacked the ideologies of normalcy as they apply to the accepted constructions of family, state, sexuality, and identity. She has often been linked with figures such as performance artist Laurie Anderson and photographer Cindy Sherman in her critiques of bodily images of women imposed by the social order, and her exposure of the damage done to the bodies of women in the Western world. Her reputation has declined somewhat from its heights in the 1980s and 1990s (though a 2019 article about an Acker exhibition at the Institute of Contemporary Arts in London is entitled "Why post-punk pioneer Kathy Acker is making a comeback"), but through her writing, teaching, and example, Acker has influenced over two generations of contemporary writers.

Acker was born in New York City and matriculated at Brandeis University majoring in Classics before transferring to the University of California-San Diego where she studied with avant-garde writers such as David Antin and Jerome Rothenberg; she graduated with a BA in 1968. She continued postgraduate education in Classics at the City University of New York, though she did not graduate, becoming immersed in the 1970s New York punk scene and commencing a serious writing career. Her first notable work (initially self-published and circulated in xeroxed copies) came in 1973 with the distinctively-titled *The Childlike Dream of the Black Tarantula: Some Lives of Murderesses*; this was followed quickly by a second novel, *I Dreamt I was a Nymphomaniac: Imagining* (1974), both published under her working pseudonym at the time, the Black Tarantula. A third novel, *The Adult Life of Toulouse Lautrec* (1975), completed what is considered to be an early trilogy of novels sharing features that will become the signatures of Acker's work throughout her career: a collage-like mixture of genres, styles, and narrative identities (the notorious "cut-up method" of Burroughs re-invented); autobiographical elements freely mixed with fictional elements; a heavy infusion of surrealistic dreams, visions, and memories; and use of materials from multiple discursive regimes, including direct "appropriation" of passages from other works. This last feature later led in her career to charges of plagiarism – an accusation that can only be countered with the recognition that Acker believed we inhabit a textual universe accessible to all, like the atmosphere we breathe; authors do not "own" this universe any more than we own the air we inhale, they merely channel and mediate it. Obviously there is irony in this position taken by an author who became famous for her own signature style, made available in books primarily published by Grove, the independent (but, nevertheless, corporate) press known for its publication of Acker's predecessors – Burroughs, Miller, and the major figures of the Beat movement – and thus a proper (and copyrighted) home for her own work.

Acker's next novel seems like the title of a first novel or a memoir: *Kathy Goes to Haiti* (1978), and like the initial trilogy, it contains mixes heavy doses of autobiography with fiction as the titular "Kathy" takes a road trip and undergoes a multitude of sexual experiences in what one critic has termed "a twisted Nancy Drew porn novel" that is representative of critique of language and her exposure of "the ways that language worked on her body" (Rice 2011, p. 427). The novel sets the tone for much of the work Acker will accomplish in the years leading to strong international recognition in the late 1980s with the publication of *Empire of the Senseless* (1988). Flagrant, scandalous, pornographic, psychotic, plagiaristic, excessive, violent – these are all terms that can be applied to this work that insists on contesting the norm, wherever that term lands. For example, in *Great Expectations* (1983), titled in the face of Dickens's classic novel, Acker's narrative pastiche intersperses passages blatantly lifted and, occasionally, slightly modified from a number of nineteenth-century writers, including Dickens himself, whose *Bildungsroman* initially provides the form and occasion for Acker's story of a young man's adventures on the streets of life. But the novel quickly switches gender, narrator, and story into that of a young woman who experiences sexual violence as she navigates a world predominated by war in search of her heritage. In a similar fashion, *Blood and Guts in High School* (copyrighted in 1978, but not published by Grove until 1984) is a female *Bildungsroman* that depicts its protagonist engaging with multiple sexual partners, living in poverty, and being forced into prostitution before she escapes "the life" and travels to Morocco where she befriends the novelist and political activist Jean Genet with whom she travels extensively, eventually dying of cancer. Nathaniel Hawthorne's *The Scarlet Letter* (1850) serves as one of the plagiarized sources for this story of survival in a degraded world.

Interspersed with a prodigious amount of material in the mid- to late 1980s including poetry, plays, essays, and revised and repackaged earlier work, two novels appeared: *My Life My Death by Pier Paolo Pasolini* (1984) is an imagined autobiographical account of the surrealist Italian filmmaker; and in *Don Quixote, Which Was a Dream* (1989), the female protagonist impersonates the famous male fictional character inhabiting the persona of a knight who sets about reforming contemporary America. In 1988, she published what many consider to be her most important work, *Empire of the Senseless*, which this correspondent has characterized as "a comedy of exteriority in which everything is outed... the tabooed hyperbolically externalized and acted out under millennial conditions in which the unthinkable, strangely normalized, operates beneath and contests against 'the concrete of repression'" (O'Donnell 2000, p. 98; interpolated citation from Acker 1988, p. 119). Borrowing from the form and content of Mark Twain's *The Adventures of Huckleberry Finn* (1884), *Empire of the Senseless* is the story of two terrorists, Abhor and Thivai, roaming the streets of a post-apocalyptic Paris where they encounter various gangs and cults as they attempt to subvert the combined efforts of official and parental authorities to thwart their efforts at revolution. In the novel, narratives and identities shift so rapidly that the entire work has the quality of a dimly-remembered dream where dissociation and displacement rule the day. The novel's title clearly echoes that of Nagisa Ōshima's 1976 film *In the Realm of the Senses*, which considered in pornographic detail the intense sexual relationship between a hotel owner and a maid; the "empire" of the novel's title is accordingly an anti-rational construct where taboo, criminality, and anarchy are pitted against law and order, but as the narrative develops, it becomes clear that empire and anti-empire mirror each other in the quest for power. Acker ponders in this novel whether or not there is any escape from a system in which all binary formations (male/female; father/daughter; conformity/revolution; conscious/unconscious) appear to constantly be at war over what, or who, controls and administers reality. This may be said to characterize Acker's writing as a whole, which seems obligated to use recognized, "official" languages (even if these are syntactically skewed) and all-too-familiar stories in order to imagine the possibility of a language, story, and reality that is thoroughly "other" in its contours and horizons. The story of the father violating the daughter, for example, which occurs in many of Acker's novels, including *Empire*, seems to be one Acker cannot get away from, or transform into a different story about patriarchy and paternal repression. Yet this is not a cause for despair in Acker's novels; rather, the "old story" serves as a source of inspiration and motivation in her work, where the experimentation with language and narrative form – even with forms of repetition – intimates, if it cannot fully express, something new.

In this context, it seems appropriate that Acker's next novel, *In Memoriam to Identity* (1990), is a collage of stories about self-destruction and self-preservation in a social order that either imposes a normative sense of self or annihilates the "aberrant." A passage from the chapter entitled "Rimbaud," named after the French symbolist poet known for his transgressive verse (and one of Acker's influences) provides a sense of the extreme conditions within which her characters struggle to survive:

> R's mother hated him . . . this draconian woman who could tolerate no slight to authority decided to become the Mother of Maternal Crimes (MMC): she was going to murder pitiful R, not exactly by killing him, but by destroying and annihilating every shred of his will and soul while he still lived on . . . R grew up to be a wild animal, unsocialized. He was filthy. His mother taught him nothing, wanted nothing to do with him. He was disinherited. He lived on bare sunlight and played with forms of natural violence as if they were knives and chains. Tied to his mother the more miserable she made him, the more he did whatever he wanted.
>
> (Acker 1990, pp. 3–4)

Much of this may or may not have relevance to the real life of Arthur Rimbaud, but in the novel, the character "R" is the embodiment of self-hatred. He flees into the world of art and imagination in order to temporarily rescue himself from dire straits, but art is just as dangerous as life because it necessitates the exposure of his fragmented identity and a reopening of all of the wounds he has suffered; art, in much Acker's work, is the exacerbation of suffering, not its cure. Apparently the practice of his art was so caustic for the historical author Rimbaud that he stopped writing poetry at the age of 20, even though he had seventeen years remaining in his short life. In *In Memoriam*, the effort involved to construct an identity is prodigious, and for the novel's characters, existing in various tortured circumstances and time schemes, always temporary.

A fair amount of Acker's work after 1990 involves the republication and reshaping of earlier work. *Hannibal Lecter, My Father* (1991), for example, includes her first work, a prose-poem entitled *Politics* (1972); a short story, *New York City in 1979*, first published in that year (and an early sign of future success, as it won the prestigious Pushcart Prize for short fiction following its publication); *The Birth of the Poet* (1987), a performance piece; and *Algeria: A Series of Invocations Because Nothing Else Works* (1984), which charts an alternative fictional landscape both within and outside the American empire. Similarly, *Portrait of an Eye: Three Novels* (1992), is a republication of the originally self-published *The Childlike Life of the Black Tarantula, I Dreamt I Was a Nymphomaniac*, and *The Adult Life of Toulouse Lautrec*; the collection was published by Grove and serves as sign of Acker's rapidly rising star in the late 1980s and early 1990s. In 1997, Acker published *Bodies of Work*, a diverse collection of essays covering topics from body building and science fiction to the conceptual films of Peter Greenaway and the work of Hannah Arendt.

In 1994 and 1996, Acker published her final two novels, respectively, *My Mother: A Demonology*, and *Pussy, King of the Pirates*. *My Mother* is structured as a female *Bildungsroman*, related in the voice of Laurie, a young woman who experiences childhood abuse both at home and in the boarding school she attends, and who survives these to become a free spirit perennially on the road. In some ways, this fictional memoir reads, in parts, more traditionally and lyrically than previous work by Acker, yet it is still replete scenes of violence and graphic sexuality, and serves as an echo chamber for the voices of other writers, politicians, and philosophers acting as a "plagiarized" chorus to the protagonist's interior monologues. Purportedly based on the relationship between the French philosopher, Georges Bataille, and Colette Peignot, an avant-garde author and poet whose work was published posthumously under the pseudonym "Laure," *My Mother* takes us into familiar Acker territory, where a woman's identity is constantly destroyed and rebuilt in the face of authoritarian repression and abuse. As in other Acker novels, "mother" is of no help; in fact she, as an embodiment of the reproducibility of the male system, is complicit with it.

Pussy, King of the Pirates, is very loosely modeled on Robert Louis Stevenson's *Treasure Island* (1883) and Pauline Reage's erotic novel *The Story of O* (1954). Following an oracular beginning in the voice of the French surrealist poet, dramatist, and filmmaker Antonin Artaud, it traces the adventures of two former prostitutes, O and Ange, as they form a band of female pirates and go in search of buried treasure, a quest interspersed with dreamlike passages and masochistic fantasies. The novel is at once absurdist, comic, and alienating in its scenes of violence and its exploration of tabooed subjects. It is intensely centrifugal in its references, engaging in what Steven Shaviro, critic and friend of Acker's, terms "splicing":

> on page 16 of *Pussy, King of the Pirates*, Acker splices an account of how her biological father abandoned her mother when she was pregnant, with an account of the suicide of the French Romantic poet Gerard de Nerval. Both of these are then juxtaposed with a reading of the Hanged Man card from the Tarot deck, together with a passage lifted

from James Miller's biography of the French philosopher Michel Foucault, explaining why Foucault retained an interest in the German philosopher Martin Heidegger, despite the latter's having been a Nazi.

(Shaviro 2019)

Like many of Acker's works, *Pussy* is a picaresque novel, one of the oldest traditional forms of narrative that recounts in episodic fashion the adventures of a male rogue. Daniel Defoe's *Moll Flanders* (1722) is one of the first novels to portray a female protagonist in this genre. The protagonist, a prostitute turned con artist who deceives numerous men in order to steal their fortunes, suddenly reforms at the end and lives out her final years repenting for her deeds; Acker's female picaros, deformed from the beginning and reshaped throughout their lives, characteristically remain unreformed and scandalous in their piratical pursuits.

Acker's continuing influence can be observed in a number of contemporary writers, both those of her own time and those of the current generation, including Jeanette Winterson, Dennis Cooper, Chuck Palahniuk, Alissa Nutting, and Chris Kraus (who is also Acker's biographer). Yet it remains an open question as to how Acker's fiction might be regarded in the current moment, when sexual mores and gender identity are being refashioned, and when social behavior and acceptability is generating new boundaries and policies – ones that might seem inimical to, or at least quite different from the transgressive sensibilities inherent in the heady mix of Acker's influences in the late 1960s and 1970 when she began writing: the fiction of William Burroughs, punk rock, high postmodernism, the drug culture, the sexual liberation movement. Literary critic Ralph Clare provides one view of how Acker can be regarded today (and, perhaps, tomorrow) in his 2018 essay, "Why Kathy Acker Now?" On the question of identity and current identity politics, Clare suggest that Acker would resist the neoliberalism extant even in more progressive notions of diversity and gender identity:

> The left's version of neoliberalism has marketed its commitment to diversity quite well over the last couple of decades without adequately addressing underlying issues such as income inequality, sexism, or racism. Acker, in contrast, is not interested in celebrating diversity if it means adding to a drop-down menu of identity choices. She wants to preserve the notion of diversity before it is tamed by an acceptable category. Thus, her works question and defy categorization itself. Nor, however, does Acker end up blindly equating "freedom" with the "free market," which comprises the right's justification of neoliberalism.

(Clare 2018)

Clare views Acker's work in the same manner that she might view it herself: as something that lies outside of rules and categories of all kinds, be they those of the law, politics, language or identity. It is because Acker's work strives for this "before" and "beyond" in its essential transgressions that it will continue to be relevant – precisely in its trespass – to changing times and values.

SEE ALSO: Cooper, Dennis; Fiction and Affect; Maso, Carole; Millennial Fiction; Palahniuk, Chuck; Queer and LGBT Fiction; Third-Wave Feminism

REFERENCES

Acker, Kathy. (1988). *Empire of the Senseless*. New York: Grove.
Acker, Kathy. (1990). *In Memoriam to Identity*. New York: Grove.
Clare, Ralph. (2018). Why Acker now? *Los Angeles Review of Books* (May 2, 2018). https://www.lareviewofbooks.org/article/why-kathy-acker-now (accessed August 5, 2021).
Little, Harriet Finch. (2019). Why post-punk pioneer Kathy Acker is making a comeback.

Financial Times (April 26, 2018). https://www.ft.com/content/d5d7574c-65c7-11e9-b809-6f0d2f5705f6 (accessed August 3, 2021).

O'Donnell, Patrick. (2000). *Latent Destinies: Cultural Paranoia in Contemporary U.S. Fiction.* Durham, NC: Duke University Press.

Rice, Doug. (2011). Kathy Acker. *Encyclopedia of Twentieth Century American Fiction* (ed. Patrick O'Donnell, David W. Madden, and Justus Nieland), 427–428. New York: Wiley-Blackwell.

Shaviro, Steven. (2019). Remembering Kathy Acker. *The Pinocchio Theory* blog (September 13, 2019). http://www.shaviro.com/Blog/?p=1586 (accessed August 8, 2021).

FURTHER READING

Borowska, Emilia. (2019). *The Politics of Kathy Acker: Revolution and the Avant-Garde.* Edinburgh: Edinburgh University Press.

Colby, Georgina. (2016). *Kathy Acker: Writing the Impossible.* Edinburgh: Edinburgh University Press.

Henderson, Margaret A. (2020). *Kathy Acker: Punk Writer.* New York: Routledge.

Kraus, Chris. (2017). *After Kathy Acker: A Biography.* Cambridge, MA: MIT Press.

Scholder, Amy, Harryman, Carla, and Ronnell, Avital. (eds.) (2006). *Lust for Life: On the Writings of Kathy Acker.* New York: Verso.

Adichie, Chimamanda Ngozi

DARIA TUNCA
University of Liège, Belgium

Chimamanda Ngozi Adichie divides her time between Nigeria, where she was born in 1977, and the United States, where she came to study on a scholarship at Drexel University in Philadelphia in 1997. More than two decades after her arrival in the United States, Adichie still does not hold an American passport. As the writer has recently stated in interviews, this is a choice that she may soon modify, but her current citizenship status usefully symbolizes the authorial stance that she has adopted throughout her career as an "American" writer: even though Adichie is now an important figure on the contemporary American literary scene, she has deliberately retained her position as an outsider of sorts. This has manifested in her creative works in different ways, with the writer often featuring Nigerian characters who emigrate to the United States and are baffled by American habits, disoriented by unspoken cultural expectations, or oppressed by racial hierarchies in the country.

Over the years, Adichie has recounted various stories in interviews that are useful in delineating her evolving sense of Americanness. One such anecdote, which she has repeated in different forms since the mid-2000s, features the writer, freshly arrived in the United States, encountering an African American man in Brooklyn. The man addresses her as "sister," an affiliative term that the young Adichie vehemently rejects at the time because of the negative stereotypes associated with African Americans. In narrating the story, however, the author consistently reports how her views have evolved since then, helped by the knowledge that she has acquired about African American history. While this anecdote positions Adichie as a now discerning participant in American society who has learned to navigate the country's cultural and racial codes, on other occasions the writer has cultivated more ambiguous familial affiliations with the United States, stating that "America is like my distant uncle who doesn't remember my name but occasionally gives me pocket money" (quoted in Cohen 2008).

When Adichie arrived in the United States at the age of 19, she had already published a collection of poems covering themes such as politics, religion, and love (*Decisions* [1997]), and a play on the 1967–1970 Nigeria–Biafra War (*For Love of Biafra* [1998]). She soon left poetry and drama aside to focus on writing both long and short fiction. Her breakthrough on the international scene came with the publication of her first novel, *Purple Hibiscus* (2003), which received prestigious prizes such as the Hurston/Wright Legacy Award for Debut Fiction (2004) and the Commonwealth Writers' Prize for Best First Book (2005). The novel is a first-person narrative told through the eyes of Kambili, a teenager living in military-ruled Nigeria in the late twentieth century. Against this background of national terror, the narrator grows up in the shadow of her devoutly Catholic father, Eugene, a pro-democracy champion, who is also a domestic tyrant who regularly beats his family in the name of religious righteousness. When *Purple Hibiscus* was released, critics were quick to point out the similarities between Eugene and Okonkwo, the stubborn traditionalist of Chinua Achebe's *Things Fall Apart* (1958). The comparison was aided by the first sentence of Adichie's novel, which announced its literary genealogy: "Things started to fall apart at home when . . ." (2003, p. 3). Although the author claims that the allusion to her compatriot Achebe's seminal novel was "unintentional," she recognizes that it was probably an "unconscious tribute" to the man whom she has consistently identified as "the writer whose work has been most important to me" (Lalami 2004). In her 2009 TED talk, "The Danger of a Single Story," in which Adichie speaks of the power of literature to either reinforce or disrupt stereotypes, the writer also credits Achebe (as well as Guinean Camara Laye) for her realization, as a young reader, that fiction could include other characters than the white people featured in the British and American books that she had so far been reading as a child.

During her early years in the United States, Adichie combined her writing activities with her university education. After attending Drexel, she transferred to Eastern Connecticut University to be able to move in with her sister, who had set up a medical practice in Connecticut. She graduated with a major in communication and a minor in political science from that institution in 2001, and then completed an MA in creative writing at Johns Hopkins University in 2003 before obtaining an MA in African studies at Yale University in 2008. In the period leading up to the publication of *Purple Hibiscus*, Adichie also established herself as a successful short story writer. Several of these early stories feature Nigerian immigrants in the United States whose diverse experiences are explored using a range of different styles and through various thematic lenses, which together testify to Adichie's career-long interest in issues of cultural, racial, and gender-based power dynamics. One of her earliest stories, "You in America" (2001, later published in revised version as "The Thing around Your Neck" [2009]), is a narrative written in the second person that follows a young woman, Akunna, who, after winning the American visa lottery, moves to Maine to stay with a male relative, who then attempts to sexually abuse her. The protagonist leaves Maine for Connecticut, where she starts working in a restaurant and begins dating a white man – a relationship that, despite the man's apparent kindness, is fraught with obstacles linked to differences in race, culture, social status, and nationality between the two lovers, problems that coalesce into a seemingly unbridgeable chasm. Such divergences are reminiscent of the difficulties in maintaining interracial relationships that Adichie would later explore in her novel *Americanah* (2013), where the white and privileged American Curt is unable to understand the racism and administrative restrictions that affect the life of his Nigerian girlfriend Ifemelu.

In a manner similar to "You in America," several of Adichie's early stories present the United States as a place of cultural or emotional disconnection for its Nigerian characters. In "Imitation" (2003), the protagonist, Nkem, leads an isolated life with her children in Philadelphia, while her husband, Obiora, infrequently visits from Nigeria, where he spends most of his time on alleged business but actually has a younger lover. At the end of the story, Nkem tells Obiora about her decision to move back to Nigeria, but the narrative does not mention whether this expression of agency eventually allows her to reclaim her dignity. In "New Husband" (later revised as "The Arrangers of Marriage" [2009]), Chika Agatha Okafor (named Chinaza Agatha Okafor in later versions) moves from Nigeria to the United States to marry Ofodile Udenwa, an obnoxious resident doctor. Ofodile is a caricature: he is obsessed with blending into American society and renames himself Dave Bell (and wants his wife to go by Agatha Bell); he admonishes Chika/Chinaza for speaking Igbo, corrects her use of British rather than American words, and forbids her to cook Nigerian food. Throughout Chika/Chinaza's marital ordeal, the only consistent moral support that she receives is from her African American neighbor Nia. This friendship is emblematic of the many connections between African and African American characters that Adichie establishes throughout her work, including in the story "Women Here Drive Buses" (2003), in which a Nigerian immigrant in Philadelphia, Ken, meets and eventually asks out a Black female bus driver, Carol, whose positive response to his request augurs the possibility of romance.

Adichie's short stories earned her her first literary accolades. "You in America" was nominated for the Caine Prize for African Writing in 2002, but it is mostly the author's Nigeria-based short fiction that won prestigious prizes: "The American Embassy" received the O. Henry Prize in 2003; "That Harmattan Morning" was the joint winner of the BBC Short Story Competition in 2002; and "Half of a Yellow Sun" was awarded the David T. Wong International Short Story Prize in 2002–2003. The latter two stories, along with another piece entitled "Ghosts" (2004), explore the Nigeria–Biafra war, and may be considered early fictional sketches of the conflict that Adichie would extensively write about in her second novel, *Half of a Yellow Sun* (2006). This book is often considered the author's most important and most personal work to date. Its importance lies in the combined exploration of characters' emotional lives and of the political events that fueled the Nigeria–Biafra war, a conflict precipitated by the secession of Biafra (located in Southeast Nigeria) following a series of ethnically motivated massacres of Igbo people, the majority ethnic group in that region. In *Half of a Yellow Sun*, the third-person narration alternates between chapters set in the early and in the late 1960s, and the story is told from the perspective of three main characters: a teenage houseboy, Ugwu; his female employer, Olanna, a sociologist who comes from a rich Igbo family; and Richard Churchill, a white Englishman who is also a keen admirer of ancient Igbo art. Adichie, who was born seven years after the end of the conflict, has often commented on how the war had shaped her family history – both her grandfathers died in refugee camps – and how the novel had been a way for her to come to terms with this legacy, even as the process of researching and writing it was emotionally draining. The book won numerous awards, including the Orange Broadband Prize for Fiction in 2007, an award later renamed Women's Prize for Fiction, of which Adichie's novel was declared "Winner of Winners" in 2020. *Half of a Yellow Sun* was also made into a film of the same title (2013, directed by Biyi

Bandele). In the years following the publication of the novel, the writer received many additional prestigious distinctions, including a so-called Genius Grant from the MacArthur Foundation in 2008.

At this point in Adichie's career, it is with some self-avowed cynicism that she published a collection of short stories, *The Thing around Your Neck* (2009), as she and her editor felt that "it was time for [Adichie] to gesture to the American audience" (Tunca 2020, p. 190) by publishing a volume containing stories set in the United States. The collection features one previously unpublished piece, "The Shivering," about two US-based Nigerians' different approaches to religion, along with previously published material, some of which was mentioned above – "The Thing around Your Neck," "The Arrangers of Marriage," "The American Embassy," and "Ghosts." Other oft-discussed stories in the volume include "Jumping Monkey Hill," a fictional exploration of the racism and sexism that Adichie experienced during a Caine Prize writing workshop that she attended in South Africa in 2003; "On Monday of Last Week," which subtly narrates a Nigerian woman's attraction to the African American mother of the child that she is babysitting in Philadelphia; and "The Headstrong Historian," which has often been read as a feminist rewriting of Achebe's fiction and was inspired by Adichie's assertive great-grandmother Omeni.

The Thing around Your Neck did not enjoy the anticipated success on the American market. By contrast, Adichie's third novel, *Americanah*, was not only published to wide critical acclaim – for example, it won the National Book Critics Circle Award in 2013 – but it also became a bestseller in the United States, despite the writer's expectations to the contrary. Indeed, the author had anticipated that American readers might not like the book because of its irreverence: *Americanah* is what Adichie refers to as her "fuck you" novel, that is, the book that she wrote because she wanted to, without feeling any sense of responsibility (Smith 2014). The result was a narrative that, according to Adichie's editor, lacked nuance (Tunca 2020, p. 190), but which most critics have positively assessed as a candid exploration of the absurdities of race in the United States. The book is also a love story between its protagonist, Ifemelu, and her high school boyfriend, Obinze, as well as a commentary about the social and political situation in Nigeria, in which large portions of the narrative are set. However, it is the novel's depiction of the United States that has drawn the most extensive critical attention. The narrative opens as Ifemelu is about to return to Nigeria after thirteen years spent on the East Coast of the United States. During her time in the country, she has discovered the workings of a society divided along racial lines, rather than along ethnic lines as in Nigeria, where her awareness of race was minimal: as Ifemelu states, "I only became black when I came to America" (Adichie 2013, p. 290). This statement reflects Adichie's own sentiment, captured in strikingly similar terms: "I wasn't black until I came to America. I became black in America" (Reese 2018).

The novel's blunt exposure of the workings of race in the United States relies on a pivotal narrative device: the blog written by the novel's protagonist. Indeed, in *Americanah*, Ifemelu becomes the author of a successful blog about race, several excerpts of which are featured throughout the book. In these entries, the protagonist sometimes takes on the stance of an amused anthropologist, sometimes that of a more serious social commentator but, in all cases, she uses a forthright tone to discuss issues such as American "tribalisms" (of which "[t]here are four kinds – class, ideology, region, and race" [2013, p. 184]), illogical race- and ethnicity- based hierarchies and systems of categorization, and the problematic politicization of Black women's hairstyles. While

Americanah's explorations of race highlight the discrimination suffered by both Africans and African Americans in the United States, the novel also evokes far more visibly than the early short stories the tensions between these two groups – for example, *Americanah* features a scene in which an African American student accuses an African classmate of having sold African Americans into slavery, and the book also stages a decisive rift between Ifemelu and her African American partner Blaine, which occurs as a result of the protagonist's choice to attend a professional lunch rather than participate in a racial protest organized by her boyfriend.

If *Americanah* contributed to making Adichie a recognizable figure in US literary circles and even popular culture (her views on Black women's hair, for example, received extensive coverage in the press and were widely discussed on blogs and websites), her feminist nonfiction is another element that has helped her to achieve this status. In 2012, Adichie delivered a talk at TEDxEuston in London, "We Should All Be Feminists," some of whose passages were sampled by Beyoncé in her song "Flawless" (2013), and whose title was later used on a T-shirt designed by Maria Grazia Chiuri of the fashion house Christian Dior. The TED talk was published under its original title in book format (2014) and was followed some years later by another feminist pamphlet, *Dear Ijeawele, or a Feminist Manifesto in Fifteen Suggestions* (2017), which grew out of a Facebook post in which Adichie advised a Nigerian friend on how to raise her daughter to be a feminist.

Adichie's two short but impactful texts present feminism in simple and uncompromising terms. They adopt a standard definition of the word "feminist" ("*a person who believes in the social, political and economic equality of the sexes*" [2014, p. 47]) and insist that women's full equality with men is not subject to nuanced negotiation: "Being a feminist is like being pregnant. You either are or you are not" (2017, p. 21). Adichie's views on feminism are expressed in largely jargon-free language, a choice that has met with some resistance in academia, where the author is sometimes perceived to overly simplify complex gender issues. However, the writer's accessible idiom partakes of a deliberate communicative strategy that draws on the rhetorical power of vivid anecdotes, and that gives pride of place not to feminist scholars but to remarkable women from Adichie's immediate environment or from her family – such as, once again, her great-grandmother, who already provided inspiration for "The Headstrong Historian."

As a corollary to this "bottom-up" approach to feminism, Adichie's two texts focus on women's everyday experiences. Some of the issues that she discusses, such as the disproportionate amount of domestic work usually performed by women, reverberate across the world's patriarchal societies, while other topics, including the importance assigned to marriage in girls' education, have stronger resonance in Nigeria than they do in the Global North. Accordingly, the reception of Adichie's feminism has also followed different trajectories across geographies. Illustrative of this is the response to Adichie's suggestion to Hillary Clinton, during a 2018 interview, that the latter should change the first descriptor of her Twitter profile (which was "wife") to a word emphasizing her professional achievements. In the mainstream US media, Adichie's idea was largely hailed as a marker of progressive feminism; in Nigeria, the incident sparked considerable outrage, as the writer was accused of disrespecting the institution of marriage (Tunca 2020, p. 185).

Adichie, however, is not deterred by such reactions, and she keeps holding out hope for greater equality between the sexes in the future. This hope is grounded in her firm belief that culture can change. As she writes in *We Should All Be Feminists*, "Culture does not make people. People make culture" (2014,

p. 46). In a 2021 interview with Ebuka Obi-Uchendu, she illustrated this principle by sharing the revelation that her name, "Chimamanda," which is now widely popular in Igboland following the writer's literary success, is in fact one that she invented shortly before the publication of her first novel. "Chimamanda," which means "My God will never fall" in Igbo, is based on Adichie's Catholic confirmation name, "Amanda," which the author decided to abandon after arriving in the United States and finding out that it was particularly common in the country, where it was additionally pronounced in a way that she felt did not reflect her identity. (The middle component of Adichie's pen name, Ngozi, is actually her given name – she was born Ngozi Grace Adichie – but she felt that this was also too common to use as a first name.) On one level, Adichie's Igboization of the name "Amanda" after coming to the United States aptly symbolizes her attachment to her native Igbo culture and her resistance to American cultural assimilation, a stance reflected both in her short stories and in *Americanah*. On another level, Adichie's personal redefinition may be said to reflect one of her most distinctive qualities as a writer, namely her propensity to constantly reinvent, reshape, and reimagine – be it herself, her Igbo culture, or her part-time American home.

SEE ALSO: Globalization; Multiculturalism

REFERENCES

Adichie, Chimamanda Ngozi. (2003). *Purple Hibiscus*. Chapel Hill: Algonquin Books of Chapel Hill.
Adichie, Chimamanda Ngozi. (2009). The danger of a single story. TED (July 2009). https://www.ted.com/talks/chimamanda_ngozi_adichie_the_danger_of_a_single_story?language=en (accessed September 20, 2021).
Adichie, Chimamanda Ngozi. (2013). *Americanah*. London: Fourth Estate.
Adichie, Chimamanda Ngozi. (2014). *We Should All Be Feminists*. New York: Anchor.
Adichie, Chimamanda Ngozi. (2017). *Dear Ijeawele, or a Feminist Manifesto in Fifteen Suggestions*. London: Fourth Estate.
Cohen, Patricia. (2008). 25 receive $500,000 "genius" fellowships. *New York Times* (September 23, 2008). http://www.nytimes.com/2008/09/23/arts/23fell.html (accessed July 21, 2021).
Lalami, Laila. (2004). A conversation with Adichie. *Laila Lalami* (April 16, 2004). http://lailalalami.com/2004/a-conversation-with-adichie/ (accessed July 21, 2021).
Obi-Uchendu, Ebuka. (2021). BLACKBOX INTERVIEW Feat Chimamanda Ngozi Adichie, Part 1. (January 1, 2021). http://www.youtube.com/watch?v=z_Ec4dtjn1Y (accessed July 21, 2021).
Reese, Hope. (2018). Chimamanda Ngozi Adichie: I became Black in America. *JSTOR Daily* (August 29, 2018). http://daily.jstor.org/chimamanda-ngozi-adichie-i-became-black-in-america/ (accessed July 21, 2021).
Smith, Zadie. (2014). Between the lines: Chimamanda Ngozi Adichie with Zadie Smith. *Livestream* (March 20, 2014). http://livestream.com/schomburgcenter/events/2831224 (accessed July 21, 2021).
Tunca, Daria. (2020). The novelist as therapist: a conversation with Chimamanda Ngozi Adichie. In: *Conversations with Chimamanda Ngozi Adichie* (ed. Daria Tunca), 182–200. Jackson: University Press of Mississippi.

FURTHER READING

Emenyonu, Ernest. (ed.) (2017). *A Companion to Chimamanda Ngozi Adichie*. Martlesham: Boydell & Brewer.
Feldner, Maximilian. (2019). Biafra and Nigerian identity formation in Chimamanda Ngozi Adichie's *Half of a Yellow Sun* (2006). In: *Narrating the New African Diaspora: 21st Century Nigerian Literature in Context*, 37–60. Cham: Palgrave Macmillan.
Hallemeier, Katherine. (2015). To be from the country of people who gave: national allegory and the United States of Adichie's *Americanah*. *Studies in the Novel* 47 (2): 231–245.
Hewett, Heather. (2005). Coming of age: Chimamanda Ngozi Adichie and the voice of the third generation. *English in Africa* 32 (1): 73–97.

Tunca, Daria. (ed.) (2020). *Conversations with Chimamanda Ngozi Adichie*. Jackson: University Press of Mississippi.

Afrofuturism

LESLEY LARKIN
Northern Michigan University, USA

In her introduction to the anthology *Octavia's Brood: Science Fiction Stories from Social Justice Movements* (2015), Walidah Imarisha writes, "Whenever we try to envision a world without war, without violence, without prisons, without capitalism, we are engaging in speculative fiction. All organizing is science fiction" (2015, p. 3). By arguing that movements for social change depend upon a speculative imaginary, Imarisha broadens the definition of speculative fiction to include narratives and practices that are not overtly science fictional (or even literary) but nevertheless engage in the work of imagining alternative presents and futures. Imarisha's revolutionary work, which includes writing workshops for community organizers, is a culmination of longstanding efforts to wrest science fiction, fantasy, and horror from a dominant white male point of view and to deploy speculative techniques toward a multifarious fight for justice.

These efforts have been pioneered by Afrofuturism, a movement that places Black people at the center of future-tense imaginings. Black visions of the future, and speculative assessments of the past and present, are everywhere in the twenty-first century, including Jordan Peele's horror films *Get Out* (2017) and *Us* (2019), science fiction and horror television series by Misha Green (*Lovecraft Country* [2020]) and Little Marvin (*Them* [2021]), the futuristic music and videos of Janelle Monáe and Erykah Badu, and the reemergence of the Black Panther superhero in comic books (written by Ta-Nehisi Coates, Nnedi Okorafor, and Roxane Gay) and films (written and directed by Ryan Coogler) – not to mention numerous works of fiction. Meanwhile, science fiction studies has seen an increase in critical attention paid to Black writers as well as an expansion of critical vocabulary to address Black perspectives. Furthermore, "futurism" and "speculation" have surfaced as key concepts in the study of Black literature, regardless of genre, as well as in movements for racial justice, which focus on the imaginative work remaking the world requires.

HISTORY AND DEFINITIONS

"Afrofuturism" can describe a range of techniques that center Black people and their relation to past, present, and future. Black voices in speculative genres were relatively few when Mark Dery coined the term "Afrofuturism" in 1994. However, there was an identifiable Afrofuturist trend across the arts. Dery cites painter Jean-Michel Basquiat; filmmaker John Sayles; musicians Jimi Hendrix, George Clinton, Herbie Hancock, Sun Ra, and Parliament-Funkadelic; and writers Samuel Delany, Octavia Butler, Steve Barnes, and Charles Saunders as key figures. In fact, as Sheree Thomas and others have shown, Black science fiction can be identified as early as the nineteenth and early twentieth centuries, in works by Martin Delany, W.E.B. Du Bois, Charles Chesnutt, Pauline Hopkins, and George Schuyler. Furthermore, the Black literary tradition has long evinced strains of the surreal, supernatural, and otherworldly – after all, the experience of being Black in America has, from the beginning, involved estrangement and alienation. As critic Greg Tate puts it, "being Black in America is a science fiction experience" (Dery 1994, p. 208). Several contemporary scholars, such as Isiah

Lavender III and Lisa Yaszek, have read classic works of African American literature, from *Incidents in the Life of a Slave Girl* (1861) to *Invisible Man* (1952), through an Afrofuturist lens. In recent years, Black speculative and Afrofuturist traditions have blossomed into a recognized movement that includes novels and stories by Ta-Nehisi Coates, Tananarive Due, Jewelle Gomez, Andrea Hairston, Nalo Hopkinson, N.K. Jemisin, Victor LaValle, Walter Mosley, Nnedi Okorafor, Nisi Shawl, Rivers Solomon, Cadwell Turnbull, and Colson Whitehead, among others.

In his initial definition of the term, Dery describes Afrofuturism as "Speculative fiction that treats African American themes and addresses African American concerns in the context of twentieth-century technoculture – and, more generally, African American signification that appropriates images of technology and a prosthetically enhanced future" (1994, p. 180). Following Tate, Dery also asserts that Afrofuturism is an apt vehicle for Black writers inasmuch as "African Americans, in a very real sense, are the descendants of alien abductees; they inhabit a sci-fi nightmare in which unseen but no less impassable force fields of intolerance frustrate their movements; official histories undo what has been done; and technology is too often brought to bear on Black bodies" (p. 180). There are three levels to Dery's definition: (i) Afrofuturism can describe any Black cultural production that engages technological themes and employs futuristic or speculative techniques; (ii) Afrofuturism might especially describe narratives that use speculative techniques to engage Black social, political, or historical concerns; and (iii) speculative tropes and techniques are especially relevant to Black history and experience. From this perspective, the story of European colonialism, the transatlantic slave trade, racialized chattel slavery, jim crow segregation, and racial terrorism – and their ongoing aftermath – is a story of first contact, alien abduction, and apocalypse. In the wake of the police killings of George Floyd, Breonna Taylor, and Daunte Wright – only the latest victims of an ongoing assault on Black life – and in the midst of a global pandemic that disproportionately affects Black people, Dery's insights remain apt.

Another important definition comes from social scientist Alondra Nelson, who launched an online community devoted to Afrofuturism in 1998 and became one of its clearest exponents. (Nelson is currently Deputy Director of the Office of Science and Technology Policy; as scholar Leah Milne (2021) has remarked, "There's an Afrofuturist in the White House"). In her introduction to a 2002 special issue of *Social Text*, Nelson highlights counternarrative as a key feature of Afrofuturism, which consists of "African American voices with other stories to tell about culture, technology, and things to come" (2002, p. 9). Nelson emphasizes the challenges African American writers pose to narratives that erase the technological contributions of Black people, present Black people as technologically retrograde, and imply that technological advances will eliminate racism. Also important, in Nelson's view, is Afrofuturism's complex treatment of time. Nelson offers Ishmael Reed's *Mumbo Jumbo* (1972) as a signal example of how Afrofuturist texts draw from a "usable past" and "synchronize" asynchronous histories in order to supersede facile representations of Black pasts and futures (2002, pp. 7, 8).

More recently, Ytasha Womack, author *Afrofuturism: The World of Black Sci-Fi and Fantasy Culture* (2013), has also emphasized Afrofuturism as a discourse of resistance. Womack sees in Afrofuturism not just the novel combination of "elements of science fiction, historical fiction, speculative fiction, fantasy, Afrocentricity, and magical realism with non-Western beliefs" but also the critical and artistic "intersection of imagination, technology, the future, and liberation" (2013,

p. 9). For Womack, the Afrofuturist imagination is aimed at changing the world.

Taking these definitions together, we might define Afrofuturism in this way: an artistic and intellectual movement of the African diaspora that draws from a range of speculative techniques in order to articulate complex counter-narratives of past, present, and future and to enable the creation of a more just world.

COMPLEX TEMPORALITIES

As this definition suggests, and as Paula M.L. Moya and I have written in relation to "ethno-speculative fiction," (forthcoming) a central feature of Afrofuturism is a complex approach to time. Afrofuturist authors challenge ideas about historical progress, interrupt the deferral of Black dreams, and reveal the presence of the past. In so doing they also challenge science fictional tropes and expectations.

For example, Afrofuturist fiction upends expectations about the temporality of apocalypse. Mainstream apocalyptic narratives often focus on forestalling catastrophe, showing readers where we will end up if we don't change course. In contrast, Afrofuturist narratives often reveal that the apocalypse has already happened or is happening now. Such narratives oppose naïve claims that racism is a "thing of the past" or that technology will allow us to transcend it. As author Junot Díaz writes, taking a presentist approach, "[I]t seems that the future has already arrived. And that future is dystopian" (2017, p. 5). The refiguration of apocalyptic temporality is regularly intertwined with the representation of intergenerational trauma: the collective and inherited injury – emotional, psychological, physical – resulting from genocide, slavery, and other mass ordeals.

Octavia Butler's *Kindred* (1979) and Toni Morrison's *Beloved* (1987) are classic works that reveal the present as postapocalyptic. *Kindred* tells the story of Dana, a contemporary Black woman repeatedly pulled back to the antebellum South to save a white slaveowning ancestor, a paradoxical situation in which refusing to help her Black ancestors' tormentor might eliminate her own existence. *Beloved*, a ghost story set in the 1870s but responding to a retreat from racial justice in the 1980s, dramatizes Morrison's concept of rememory, whereby the past rears its head in the present. Both novels offer literal, violent, depictions of the presence of the past: Dana loses a limb in her final return to the present, and her white husband is aged and scarred by his own journeys to the past; Morrison's title character is the incarnation not only of a child killed by her mother in a desperate attempt to protect her from bondage but also of a whole host of lives destroyed by the Middle Passage and slavery. Butler and Morrison illustrate what Alys Weinbaum calls the "afterlife of slavery," the "residue" that remains in "our biocapitalist present" (2013, p. 65).

Many Afrofuturists also pursue the "usable past": history reclaimed or reimagined for the purposes of surviving the present and pursuing a liberated future. Nigerian American novelist Nnedi Okorafor (2019) elucidates this idea in her definition of "Africanfuturism," the term she prefers for work, like her own, that is "directly rooted in African culture, history, mythology, and point-of-view," that "does not center the West," and that explores not "what could have been" but "what has been" and "what is and can/will be." For Okorafor, "grappling" with the past is always a forward-looking endeavor. This perspective is also evident in Nisi Shawl's *Everfair* (2016), a steampunk novel set in an alternate-history Belgian Congo, where a free state for refugees from King Leopold's reign of terror has been founded. Rather than a utopian vision of what could have been if only African societies had industrialized sooner,

Everfair explores the advantages and conflicts that attend efforts to create a just future.

The excavation of a usable past necessarily expands our understanding of what counts as "science" in "science fiction," as writers draw upon traditional ecological, medicinal, and celestial knowledge. In Okorafor's novella *Binti* (2015), a young Himba woman deploys ancient technologies and materials to protect herself, heal others, and pursue peace amidst an intergalactic, interspecies conflict. Jamaican-Canadian author Nalo Hopkinson's postapocalyptic *Brown Girl in the Ring* (1998) draws upon Afro-Caribbean cultural traditions to create a fictional spiritual practice that "functions as the basis for a unique pan-Caribbean identity" (Coleman 2009, p. 1). Shawl also challenges the opposition of "science/technology" and "belief/tradition," writing that "There are solid connections between [the West African religion] Ifa and the realm of science," and drawing upon those connections in her work (2016, p. 221).

In several texts, Black music is presented as a technology – specifically, as a time machine. This is the central conceit of Amiri Baraka's story "Rhythm Travel" (1995), in which a man has created a machine that, running on music, sends him to an antebellum plantation (via the work song "Take This Hammer") and to an imaginary destination "inside gravity" (via the music of Sun Ra) (2000, p. 115). Baraka's inventor has mastered a temporal superpower that Ralph Ellison suggests is possessed by all Black people (i.e. "the invisible"): "Instead of the swift and imperceptible flowing of time, you are aware of its nodes, those points where time stands still or from which it leaps ahead. And you slip into the breaks and look around" (1952, p. 8). In *Invisible Man*, the music of Louis Armstrong unlocks this ability for the narrator, prompting a vision of enslaved ancestors that is also a journey through time. Nabeel Zuberi explains that the features of Black music "express a yearning for an African origin that is impossible to satisfy" and articulate a "diasporic response to time and space" (2007, p. 286). One might view Black music as necessarily expressing – even enabling – alternative temporalities. Langston Hughes's *Montage of a Dream Deferred* (1951), for example, uses the rhythmic shifts of bebop to interrupt audience expectations about the temporality of racial progress ("You think it's a happy beat?") (1994, p. 221). And in *Jazz* (1992), Toni Morrison's jazz technique culminates in the apparent transformation of the book into a knowing, speaking being; here, jazz is the technology by which the West African tradition of the "Talking Book" manifests in the present.

In its complex temporalities, Afrofuturism rejects both the primitive stereotypes assigned to Black people and the violence that cuts Black lives short; it reimagines past, present, and future in the service of Black liberation. Consider how the recent *Black Panther* (2018) film draws upon alternate history in its presentation of a hypertechnological African state unhampered by the legacies of colonialism. Importantly, the film's representation of Wakanda is not pure idealism. The film turns on a significant ethical questions. What responsibilities do powerful and wealthy nations have to the rest of the world? What responsibilities do Black people have to one another? Exploiting the historical coincidence of the Black Panther superhero and the Black Panther Party (both created in 1966), the film juxtaposes drastically different political projects – T'Challa's nationalist protectionism and Killmonger's pan-Africanism – that are both visions of a Black community independent of white or Western control.

The society in Octavia Butler's postapocalyptic *Parable* series (1993, 1998), characterized by environmental catastrophe, wealth inequity, mass illiteracy, violence, and the erosion of democratic institutions, could not be more different from Wakanda. However, within this bleak setting Butler imagines a young, "hyper-empathetic" Black woman who becomes the emancipatory leader of a futuristic, interstellar religion. As in *Black Panther*, the utopian vision raises ethical dilemmas about how to construct sustainable and just communities – "the very hard choices and the unexpected new social forms that interstellar colonization might make possible" (Canavan 2019, p. 62). In Butler's "Bloodchild" (1984), the *Xenogenesis* series (1987, 1988, 1989), and *Fledgling* (2005), these dilemmas are explored in communities in which one species has significant intellectual, physical, and/or technological advantages over another.

As *Black Panther* and Butler's works suggest, Afrofuturist texts also articulate complex spatialities, as writers extend their vision beyond the nation and even the earth itself – or reveal physical spaces to be repositories of conflicting realities and histories. Some works, like W.E.B. Du Bois's 1920 short story "The Comet," in which a white woman and a Black man believe themselves to be the only survivors of an apocalyptic event, reveal the multiple worlds that exist in a shared space governed by the "color-line." Others, like N.K. Jemisin's *Broken Earth* series (2015, 2016, 2017), focus on the environmental degradation linked to systems of oppression.

Two recent novels play with the time-space continuum while reimagining the path from slavery to freedom. In Colson Whitehead's *The Underground Railroad* (Bianculli 2016), adapted as a television series by Barry Jenkins in 2021, the title is literal: escapees travel on an underground train to different states, each "located" at a distinct point in a (fictional) timeline of American racial progress – what Whitehead refers to as "different state[s] of American possibility" ("Colson"). South Carolina, for example, is characterized by racial progress (emancipation and economic opportunity) and racial terror (eugenics). This uncanny mix belies narratives of racial progress as they are expressed temporally (racism is a thing of the past) and spatially (racism belongs to the South, freedom to the North). In Ta-Nehisi Coates's *The Water Dancer* (2019), slaves are carried to freedom by the historical Underground Railroad and through the supernatural power of "conduction." To access this power, Hiram, the protagonist, must recount a memory in as much detail as possible; through narration, he folds time and space, helped by a chain of ancestors. Coates, like Whitehead, upends conventional timelines and geographies of escape; although Hiram conducts people to freedom in the North, his story ends at the plantation of his youth, now an underground station from which he can pursue his radical emancipatory vision. "We sought not merely to improve the world," Hiram writes, "but to remake it" (2019, p. 252).

VISIONARY FICTION AND NONFICTION

This emphasis on remaking the world explains why Afrofuturism and other forms of "visionary fiction" have transcended media and genres and gained traction among activists. In defining "visionary fiction," Imarisha and her collaborators "distinguish science fiction that has relevance toward building new, freer worlds from the mainstream strain of science fiction, which most often reinforces dominant narratives of power." Visionary fiction works toward the "decolonization of the imagination," from which "all other forms of decolonization are born" (2015, p. 4). In *Octavia's Brood*, Imarisha and co-editor adrienne maree brown feature science fiction and fantasy written by activists, many of whom have no prior literary experience; their works assert the powerful role speculation can play in "sculpting reality from our dreams." Imarisha also offers a novel spin on the science fictionality of Black experience: "[F]or those of us from communities with historic collective trauma, we must understand that each of us is already science fiction walking around on two legs. Our ancestors dreamed us up and then bent reality to create us." The ancestral imagination was science fictional, Imarisha insists, and writers and activists have a responsibility to advance their ancestors' "visionary legacy" (p. 5).

The use of speculative techniques to critique the status quo and imagine/create a freer world is not limited to works of fiction. Indeed, there is an emerging trend of contemporary antiracist texts that are not categorized as fiction but can be categorized as Afrofuturist. Such works offer complex treatments of time, call upon ancestral imagination, expose the fictionality of white supremacy, and limn the science fictional contours of Black experience. Authors of these texts turn to speculative techniques perhaps because, as Seo-Young Chu (2010) explains, the deeply estranging traumas of racism resist realist representation. Their works are evidence of the broad influence of Afrofuturist fiction on contemporary Black letters.

Like *Octavia's Brood*, Kimberly Drew and Jenna Wortham's innovative archive *Black Futures* (2020) blurs the line between art and activism. A compendium of essays, visual art, dialogues, poetry, recipes, songs, and social media posts, *Black Futures* is an encyclopedia of the Afrofuturist imagination – a Borgesian volume that shatters ossified ways of thinking about the world and the place of Black people in it. Making inspired connections across time and space, *Black Futures* invites nonlinear reading and prompts readers to engage online sources, undertake creative and physical activities, donate time and money, or otherwise act. Like Middleton A. Harris's "scrapbook" of Black history *The Black Book* (1974), which Drew and Wortham cite as an influence, *Black Futures* is a multimodal catalogue of Black experience and achievement, but while *The Black Book* brings suppressed history into view, *Black Futures* asserts the future that Black people are literally and imaginatively denied. Contributor Alisha Wormsley's statement, "THERE ARE BLACK PEOPLE IN THE FUTURE," initially a response to the underrepresentation of Black people in science fiction media, is the central thesis of the book: Black people must imagine and shape a future in which they thrive (2020, p. 44). Given the ongoing destruction of Black life, the erasure of Black people from mainstream science fiction is nothing less than a genocidal aesthetic – and Afrofuturism significantly more than demographic correction.

In her memoir *When They Call You a Terrorist* (2018), co-written with asha bandele, Black Lives Matter co-founder Patrisse Khan Cullors responds to the assault on Black life by articulating an interstellar and intergenerational vision of Black humanity. In the opening passage, Cullors recalls a video in which astrophysicist Neil deGrasse Tyson explains "that we . . . are literally made out of stardust" (2020, pp. 3–4). This account of humanity's relation to the universe squares with Cullors's understanding of her family history and Black survival. Of the thirteen generations who endured slavery and its aftermath, she asks, "What could they be but stardust, these people who refused to die . . .?" She then, like Imarisha, turns to ancestral imagination: "Our foreparents imagined our families out of whole cloth . . . They had to. It is the only way I am here, today, . . . learning to find hope while navigating the shadows of hell even as I know it might have been otherwise" (p. 5). In making this claim, Cullors draws together past, present, and future – along with unrealized timelines (what "might have been") – to express the complex temporality of Black survival.

Ta-Nehisi Coates, who entered the realm of speculative fiction with *The Water Dancer* and Black Panther comics, also employs speculative figures in his nonfiction, though he arrives at a different temporal intervention than Cullors. Throughout *Between the World and Me* (2015), Coates uses phrases like "a world apart," "beyond the firmament," and "past the asteroid belt" to articulate the alienating experience of living in a body under threat. He describes the West Baltimore of his childhood as a "portion of the American galaxy ... where bodies were enslaved by a tenacious gravity" and Howard University as a spiritual "Mecca" where the Black diaspora, in its geographical and temporal multiplicity, materializes – and in which Black exceptionalism is a technology of escape from white supremacy's orbit (2015, pp. 20, 39). Even Coates's discussion of the "robbery of time," whereby Black people lose years to "readying the mask, or readying ourselves to accept half as much," resembles a kind of time dilation (p. 91).

Coates's explorations of Black space-time coalesce in a specific critique: The "moral arc of the universe" does not automatically "bend toward justice"; all too often it bends, for Black people, "toward chaos then conclude[s] in a box" (2015, p. 28). Coates rejects utopian temporalities and demands that we do not reduce Black ancestors to plot points in stories of triumph:

> Slavery is not an indefinable mass of flesh. It is a particular, specific enslaved woman, whose mind is as active as your own, whose range of feeling is as vast as your own; who prefers the way the light falls in one particular spot in the woods, who enjoys fishing where the water eddies in a nearby stream, who loves her mother in her own complicated way, thinks her sister talks too loud, has a favorite cousin, a favorite season, who excels at dressmaking and knows, inside herself, that she is as intelligent and capable as anyone.
>
> (2015, p. 69)

Coates turns to fictional characterization here, a move that recalls the story of a "wagonload of slaves" that a group of children invents at the end of Toni Morrison's 1993 Nobel Lecture. This miniature story-within-an-essay seems to leave behind the "realism" of the essay in favor of the "unrealism" of fiction – but the story is realer than a history that would reduce a complex human being to a "mass of flesh."

Claudia Rankine's 2014 work of poetry and essay, *Citizen: An American Lyric*, also uses speculative techniques to account for the estranging traumas of racism. In one of many chilling encounters, a white therapist erupts in rage and fear at the Black patient who arrives for a forgotten appointment. Rankine writes, "It's as if a wounded Doberman pinscher or a German shepherd has gained the power of speech" (2014, p. 25). On the opposite page, readers encounter another human-animal hybrid: a photograph of artist Kate Clark's "Little Girl," a taxidermied infant caribou with the face of a human child. This second figure is clearly prey, underscoring Rankine's point that predation is a component of whiteness, not Blackness. Rankine's work abounds with speculative figures, from the materialization of a white woman's fear as an empty space that follows around the Black man she won't sit next to on the train, to the floodwaters of Hurricane Katrina and the Atlantic Ocean, which appear as the deadly manifestations of anti-Black racism. These figures estrange readers from an upside-down world in which the fiction of white supremacy is treated as real. They work to "decolonize" the imagination, making space for new, liberatory possibilities.

AFROFUTURISM'S "FICTIVE KIN"

Afrofuturism, whether fictional or nonfictional, is not alone in undertaking this decolonizing work. Parallel movements – Indigenous futurism, Chicanafuturism, Asian American futurisms, and others – are the "fictive kin" of Afrofuturism, to use Catherine Ramírez's phrase. Drawing upon longstanding and distinct speculative traditions, as well as specific histories of oppression and exclusion, they articulate unique concerns and sensibilities while also sharing the goal of building more just worlds.

Chicanafuturism, for example, "explores the ways that ... technologies ... transform Mexican American life and culture. It questions the promises of science, technology, and humanism for Chicanas, Chicanos, and other people of color. And [it] articulates colonial and postcolonial histories of *indigenismo*, *mestizaje*, hegemony, and survival" (Ramírez 2008, p. 187). Speculative themes and techniques are apt tools for exploring Chicanx experience and culture because, as novelist Ernest Hogan puts it (in terms familiar to Afrofuturists): "Chicano is a science fiction state of being" (quoted in Merla-Watson and Olguín 2017, p. 4). Speculative elements have "always been a mainstay of Chican@ and Latin@ literary, visual and performing arts" and are connected to a politics of liberation: "The exposés, critiques, and utopian alternatives modeled within the Latin@ speculative arts promise to combat ... old monsters with newer ones that might help set us all free" (pp. 1, 32). Contemporary Chicanx and Latinx writers of speculative fiction include Kathleen Alcalá, Giannina Braschi, Ana Castillo, Junot Díaz, Ernest Hogan, Carmen Maria Machado, and Daniel José Older, among others. Inspired by Ramírez's question – "What happens to Chicana/o texts when we read them as science fiction?" – critics have also taken speculative approaches to a wide variety of works, from folk stories about the Chupacabras (Calvo-Quirós) to Gloria Anzaldúa's theoretical writings (Ramírez 2008).

At the heart of Indigenous futurism is the insight, shared with Afrofuturism and Chicanx and Latinx futurisms, that the apocalypse has already happened in the form of settler colonialism, genocide, and environmental destruction, afflicting its survivors with "post-apocalypse stress syndrome" (Gross 2003, p. 128). Indigenous futurism integrates science fictional techniques and "Indigenous scientific literacies" to imagine decolonization, renewal, and balance among human and more-than-human beings (Dillon 2012, p. 7). Indigenous writers insist not only that there are Native people in the future but also that there are Native people in the present (challenging the myth of the "Vanishing Indian") – and that Native people are vital to the creation of a livable future for all. Like Afrofuturism, Indigenous futurism can be identified in works that precede the coining of the term; as Otoe-Missouria and Choctaw writer Johnnie Jae says, "Indigenous Futurism comes as naturally as breathing ... we all imagine how differently the world would be without ... colonization." Grace Dillon (Anishinaabe) argues that the Indigenous imagination has transformed science fiction, expanding what is meant by "science" and shaping the development of "slipstream" fiction, which blurs the boundary between science fiction and realism. Native authors who work under the speculative umbrella include Sherman Alexie (Spokane), Celu Amberstone (Cherokee), Louise Erdrich (Turtle Mountain Chippewa), Stephen Graham Jones (Blackfeet), Darcie Little Badger (Lipan Apache), Gerald Vizenor (White Earth Chippewa), and Gerry William (Splatsin).

Asian American futurisms have a somewhat unique valence, inasmuch as Asian people have largely been associated, in the United States, not with primitivity but with a hypertechnological future and perpetual alienness – whether represented as the "model minority" or the "yellow peril" (Lavender 2017, pp. 5, 8). As writer and critic Dawn Chan explains, "[T]he myth of an

Asian-inflected future has infiltrated imaginations worldwide ... Think of the vertical neon signs, the sleep-deprived gamers, the flesh-meets-machine of conveyor-belt sushi" (Chan 2016) Many contemporary Asian American writers challenge these "techno-orientalist" tropes (Roh *et al.* 2015), often revealing that the systems of economic exploitation with which Asian people are identified also oppress Asian (and Asian American) people. The use of speculative techniques to account for Asian diasporic experiences, and to articulate a "transpacific imagination" (Lavender 2017, p. 6), is neither new nor limited to writers working in overtly speculative genres, such as Ted Chiang, Wesley Chu, Larissa Lai, Ken Liu, and Alyssa Wong. Classic works from the Asian American canon, such as Maxine Hong Kingston's *The Woman Warrior* (1976) and Karen Tei Yamashita's *Through the Arc of the Rainforest* (1990), use magical realist and slipstream techniques, and many Asian American (and Canadian) writers, such as Chang-rae Lee, Ruth Ozeki, and Charles Yu, move freely across generic boundaries.

It seems that these authors recognize what Afrofuturist authors also insist upon: Reimagining the past, present, and future is crucial to world-building, both fictional and literal.

SEE ALSO: Butler, Octavia; Delany, Samuel; Díaz, Junot; Gay, Roxane; Gomez, Jewelle; Jones, Stephen Graham; LaValle, Victor; Morrison, Toni; Whitehead, Colson; Yu, Charles

REFERENCES

Baraka, Amiri. (2000). Rhythm travel. In *Dark Matter: A Century of Speculative Fiction from the African Diaspora* (ed. Sheree R. Thomas), 113–115. New York: Warner Books; 1st ed. 1996.

Bianculli, David. (2016). "Underground Railroad" is a literal train to freedom. *Fresh Air* (November 18, 2016). https://www.npr.org/2016/11/18/502558001/colson-whiteheads-underground-railroad-is-a-literal-train-to-freedom (accessed July 24, 2021).

Canavan, Gerry. (2019). Eden, just not ours yet: on *Parable of the Trickster* and Utopia. *Women's Studies* 48 (1): 59–75.

Chan, Dawn. (2016). Asia-Futurism. *Artforum* (Summer). https://www.artforum.com/print/201606/asia-futurism-60088 (accessed July 24, 2021).

Chu, Seo-Young. (2010). *Do Metaphors Dream of Literal Sleep? A Science-Fictional Theory of Representation*. Cambridge, MA: Harvard University Press.

Coates, Ta-Nehisi. (2015). *Between the World and Me*. London: One World.

Coates, Ta-Nehisi. (2019). *The Water Dancer*. London: One World.

Coleman, Monica. (2009). Serving the spirits: the Pan-Caribbean African-derived religion in Nalo Hopkinson's *Brown Girl in the Ring*. *Journal of Caribbean Literatures* 6 (1): 1–13.

Cullors, Patrisse Khan and bandele, asha. (2020). *When They Call You a Terrorist: A Black Lives Matter Memoir*. New York: St. Martin's Griffin; 1st edition 2018.

Dery, Mark. (1994). Black to the future: interviews with Samuel R. Delany, Greg Tate, and Tricia Rose. In: *Flame Wars: The Discourse of Cyberculture* (ed. Mark Dery), 179–222. Durham, NC: Duke University Press.

Díaz, Junot. (ed.) (2017). Editor's note. *Global Dystopias*. Special issue of *Boston Review* (July): 5–6.

Dillon, Grace. (ed.) (2012). *Walking the Clouds: An Anthology of Indigenous Science Fiction*. Chicago: University of Arizona Press.

Drew, Kimberly and Wortham, Jenna. (2020). *Black Futures*. London: One World.

Ellison, Ralph. (1952). *Invisible Man*. New York: Random House.

Gross, Lawrence W. (2003). Cultural sovereignty and native American hermeneutics in the interpretation of the sacred stories of the Anishinaabe. *Wičazo Ša Review* 18 (2): 127–134.

Hughes, Langston. (1994). Montage of a Dream Deferred. In: *The Collected Poems of Langston Hughes* (ed. Arnold Rampersad), 218–272. New York: Vintage, 1994.

Imarisha, Walidah and brown, adrienne maree. (eds.) (2015). *Octavia's Brood: Science Fiction Stories from Social Justice Movements*. Oakland, CA: AK Press.

Lavender, Isiah, III. (2017). *Dis-Orienting Planets: Racial Representations of Asia in Science Fiction.* Jackson: University Press of Mississippi.

Merla-Watson, Cathryn Josefina and Olguín, B.V. (eds.) (2017). *Altermundos: Latin@ Speculative Literature, Film, and Popular Culture.* Los Angeles: UCLA Chicano Studies Research Center Press.

Milne, Leah. (2021). Introduction to Afrofuturism. Lecture to Northern Michigan University (February 2, 2021), Marquette.

Moya, Paula M.L. and Larkin, Lesley. (forthcoming). The decolonial virtues of ethnospeculative fiction. In *Cultivating Virtue in the University* (ed. Michael Lamb and Jonathan Brant). Oxford: Oxford University Press.

Nelson, Alondra. (2002). Introduction. Future Texts. Special issue of *Social Text* 20 (2): 1–15.

Okorafor, Nnedi. (2019). Africanfuturism defined. *Nnedi's Wahala Zone Blog* (October 19, 2019).

Ramírez, Catherine. (2008). Afrofuturism/Chicanafuturism: fictive kin. *Aztlán: A Journal of Chicano Studies* 33 (1): 185–194.

Rankine, Claudia. (2014). *Citizen: An American Lyric.* Minneapolis: Graywolf Press.

Roh, David S. et al. (eds.) (2015). *Techno-Orientalism: Imagining Asia in Speculative Fiction, History, and Media.* New Brunswick, NJ: Rutgers University Press.

Shawl, Nisi. (2016). Ifa: reverence, science, and social technology. *Extrapolation* 57 (1–2): 221–228.

Weinbaum, Alys Eve. (2013). The afterlife of slavery and the problem of reproductive freedom. *Social Text* 31 (2): 49–68.

Womack, Ytasha. (2013). *Afrofuturism: The World of Black Sci-Fi and Fantasy Culture.* Chicago: Lawrence Hill.

Zuberi, Nabeel. (2007). Is this the future? Black music and technology discourse. *Science Fiction Studies* 34 (2): 283–300.

FURTHER READING

Eshun, Kodwo. (2003). Further considerations of Afrofuturism. *CR: The New Centennial Review* 3 (2): 287–302.

Kilgore, DeWitt Douglas. (2003). *Astrofuturism: Science, Race, and Visions of Utopia in Space.* Philadelphia: University of Pennsylvania Press.

Lavender, Isiah, III. (2014). *Black and Brown Planets: The Politics of Race in Science Fiction.* Jackson: University Press of Mississippi.

Lavender, Isiah, III and Yaszek, Lisa. (eds.) (2020). *Literary Afrofuturism in the Twenty-First Century.* Columbus: Ohio State University Press.

Shawl, Nisi. (ed.) (2019). *New Suns: Original Speculative Fiction by People of Color.* Oxford: Solaris.

After Postmodernism

JAMIE REDGATE
Independent scholar, Glasgow, Scotland

It should be quite simple to summarize everything that happened to America and its literature after the end of postmodernism, given that the era ended with the end of history itself. According to Francis Fukuyama, writing in the summer of 1989 before the Berlin Wall fell, "we may be witnessing not just the end of the Cold War ... but the end of history as such: that is, the endpoint of mankind's ideological evolution and the universalization of Western liberal democracy" (1989, p. 4). When the Soviet Union was finally dissolved in December 1991, Fukuyama's prediction seemed assured. The Cold War was over. The Western Enlightenment "idea," upon which the United States had been founded, had, despite a century of apparent setbacks, won out in the end. After a century of endings – a century of "posts" of all sorts: postmodernism, posthumanism, postcolonialism, and now posthistory – it looked like we were in for a sort of posthumous age, a conflictless, post-victory era of unstoried "boredom."

The American novel in the 1990s was certainly marked by a sense that things had come to an end. David Foster Wallace described the "despair and stasis" (1993, p. 49) that seemed to infect the culture after the radicalism of postmodernism was institutionalized, its tools taken up by television and marketing to serve the very system they'd been developed to critique. Because the postmodernists' primarily ironic mode "serves an almost exclusively negative function," wrote Wallace, it is "singularly unuseful when it comes to constructing anything to replace the hypocrisies it debunks" (p. 67). The same was true in the academy, where poststructuralist theory – which, like the postmodern novel which evolved in tandem with it, emphasized the groundlessness of not-so-stable value systems – came to dominate. Hence the stasis: though American cultural life had been hollowed of the very values on which its political victory was supposed to be based, postmodernism (in both its ironic and deconstructionist modes) cleverly preempted any criticism of *itself* by celebrating that lack.

The trap Wallace describes was apparent in works from the time, such as Daniel Clowes's *Ghost World* (1993–1997). Aptly named, Clowes's comic portrays two young women who are prisoners of irony, as one-note as the monotone palette in which they are colored: "Oh man, that's so pathetic. It's not even a joke." / "I know … isn't he great!" (2000, p. 9). Other writers, such as Bret Easton Ellis and Chuck Palahniuk, described the empty amorality of a posthistorical generation in more violent terms. *American Psycho* (1991), an obscene Dantean portrait of "uh, how life presents itself … in New York, maybe *anywhere*, at the end of the century" (p. 399), suggested that the grotesque material comforts certain Americans were set to enjoy in the new millennium would render them utterly nihilistic. Palahniuk's bluer-collar characters in *Fight Club* (1996) were slaves to the same future. For a "generation of men raised by women" (1997, p. 50), with neither a "great war" to fight nor "a great depression" to endure (p. 149), it was apparently only anarchy that could give their lives direction.

As it turned out, 1989 was not the beginning of the end so much as the start of a period of profound transition. This seems obvious in hindsight, and this entry will attempt to untangle some of the different threads that make up this story, but throughout the 1990s artists, writers, and critics in every corner of the culture were already calling for an end to the endings, a post- to the post-ness of the preceding century. Wallace's own essay, published in 1993, was diagnostic but also a call to arms for a new generation of "*anti*-rebels" who would make literature new by having "the childish gall actually to endorse and instantiate single-entendre principles" (1993, p. 81). Wendy Steiner suggests that the end of the century was an "aesthetic turning point" (2001, p. 191) for fine art as well, and for the artists who, after a century of visual deprivation (in the form of the avant-garde celebration of abstraction, obscenity, and obscurantism), were rediscovering the humanizing effect of beauty and perspective. William T. Vollmann argued that it was about time writers escaped "the structuralist smog that has hovered so long over our universities" and put their faith back in the idea "that truth exists" (Vollmann 1990). In order to have a future beyond postmodernism, there was a sense that one had to look back to what had been there before its ascendency, a sense that "maybe," as Witold Rybczynski (1997) put it, "we should be picking up the pieces."

The problem for the "post-postmodernists" was that, as Robert L. McLaughlin puts it, "neither America nor the fiction that seeks to represent it can return to a state of pre-postmodern innocence" (2004, p. 66). How does one critique postmodernism when postmodernism crippled the means of critique? How can you speak with authority after the death of authorities, with language when language cannot describe the concrete? The Enlightenment was "excellent for debunking quite a lot of beliefs, powers, and illusions," writes Bruno Latour, but "it found itself totally disarmed" when it was "eaten up by the same debunking impetus" (2004, p. 232).

Those of a more scientific bent had an easy answer to the damage done. Aghast on behalf of the humanities, scientists such as Alan D. Sokal lamented the anti-Enlightenment sentiment of much postmodern theory, and in the follow-up to the infamous hoax article he had published in the postmodern cultural studies journal *Social Text* (which pretended to challenge the "dogma" that "there exists an external world"), he called for a revival of the so-called "*naïve*" belief that there are in fact facts, and that scientific "objectivity" is attainable (1996, p. 339). In the best-selling *The Blank Slate: The Modern Denial of Human Nature* (2002), Steven Pinker argued that by treating human nature as a text to be rewritten, the postmodernists in the academy had engendered moral relativism, induced campus hysteria about biological determinism, and facilitated the production of art that was "ugly, baffling, insulting, pretentious, [and] unintelligible" (p. 416). Echoing Sokal, Pinker suggested that the answer to this crisis was for the humanities to re-embrace Enlightenment values and draw from fields such as cognitive science, which offered a material foundation for human study and a bridge back to reality.

The construction of this bridge between the two cultures was welcomed by many on the humanities' side. In his 1991 book *Reading Minds: The Study of English in the Age of Cognitive Science*, Mark Turner decried "theory" for being "scattered and elitist" (p. vii) and blamed it for literary studies' failure to "spea[k] to the world" (p. 11). In a series of manifestos published in the following decade, Alan Richardson, Mary Thomas Crane, and Francis F. Steen formalized the routine calls for a "revolution" by proposing a new kind of cognitive literary studies. Linguistic meaning, they wrote, "is not arbitrary, but is instead motivated by experiences of perception and embodiment" (Crane and Richardson 1999), just as theory's central concerns about the "fragmented self" and the "problematic" concept of "individual agency" might be helpfully regrounded in a scientifically literate account of the realities of our brains (Richardson 1999, p. 159). If postmodern theory was, as Michael Drolet puts it, the "manifestation of ... the breakdown of rationality and of the Western philosophical tradition" (2004, p. 3), the newly sophisticated science of brain and body offered a coherent foundation on which to rebuild.

The major elements of postmodern theory – the dominance of Text, the suspicion of causality, the metaphysics of absence – were all evident in postmodern fiction, and we can see the same transition toward a newly material aesthetic taking place in the novels of the period. Robert Coover's *The Adventures of Lucky Pierre: Directors' Cut* (2002), part elegy to postmodernism and part greatest hits, perhaps best exemplifies what post-postmodern writers were pushing against. The novel, which plays *Rosencrantz and Guildenstern are Dead* (1966) with a 1961 pornographic cartoon, follows the titular character as he lives out his confusing – at times ontologically harrowing – life in "Cinecity" (2002, p. 32), a filmreel-flat backdrop to his escapades that obeys whatever wacky metaphysics Coover's next gag requires. Like Stoppard's metafiction, in which *Hamlet*'s bit characters only exist when the text summons them – "Words, words. They're all we have to go on" (Stoppard 1967, p. 31) – Coover's characters are image only. In one scene, for instance, where Pierre is "sandwiched [between] mirrors," he is described as "heav[ing] frenziedly in an infinite series" (Coover 2002, p. 47), an endless sequence of perfect reproductions that renders the original man completely diffuse. Is Pierre the Pierre having sex? Or is he the one "on the other soft screen ... watching her through the keyhole ... surrounded by mirrors and cameras" (p. 51)? Because no one image has any more weight than another, it is impossible for us – and, more alarmingly, for him – to tell. At the very moment Pierre should be most connected to his own bodily experience, he is, rather, the consummate postmodern subject: less a character than "a sequence of dead stills in rapid succession" (p. 333).

In 1989 – the same year that the fall of the Berlin Wall put an end to another old order – the publication of Katherine Dunn's *Geek Love* marked the beginning of the material turn in the American novel. Though *Geek Love* shares much with the work of Coover and Thomas Pynchon – it is vaudevillian, freakish, literally carnivalesque – it regrounds their postmodern play in what Peter Boxall calls the "stubborn materiality of the body" (2013, p. 16). This is most evident in the scene in which Oly, the narrator, watches a tape of another woman's voluntary disfigurement. The narrative setup is a clever example of postmodern recursion – we watch as the characters watch the screen – but unlike Coover's novel, *Geek Love* treats the camera as a device that emphasizes the subject's presence, not their absence. Where the women in Coover's novel are vaguely woman-shaped configurations of sex organs, Dunn's scene of disassembly is freighted with the weight of the body of the woman at it's center. The footage on *Geek Love*'s camera is certainly unsettled – the image "skids" and "staggers and blurs past in a fizz of colour" (1989, p. 179) – but Dunn implies a direct causal connection between screen and subject: the "fizz" (p. 181) in the film-edit necessarily means that flesh is "bubbling" in the surgical "edit" of the woman being filmed.[1]

Dunn anticipated a sequence of novels in the 1990s that enacted the same material critique of postmodernism. Richard Powers's *The Gold Bug Variations* (1991) is an account of the molecular biologist Stuart Ressler, who wrestles with the enigma of the human genetic code: that "4 letter tune" (p. 15) from which we "all derive" (p. 25). From the premise up, Powers's novel is a revision of one of the central tenets of postmodernism. As Patricia Waugh puts it, the lesson of poststructuralism was that "our knowledge" of the world is "mediated through language"; the postmodern novel's self-conscious status as text, therefore, was a way to ask questions about the "construction of 'reality' itself" (1984, p. 41). Powers makes reference himself to these ideas ("Words are a treacherous sextant, a poor stand-in for the thing they lay out" [1991, p. 352]), and the genetic code in some ways proves them right: his characters, too, are literally a combination of four letters. The point of the genetic code, however, is that it is a representational system that maps directly (reliably, dependably, testably) onto a biological reality. Though *Gold Bug* is arguably a rewrite of Pynchon's *The Crying of Lot 49* (1965) – a sort of detective story, triggered by a bequest from a dead man – their opposing conclusions are revealing. Where Pynchon makes an amusing mockery of Oedipa's search for answers, Jan, on the other hand, grows from amateur to expert as she climbs the shoulders of science's giants: "this surge of strange confidence: I have turned up a solution" (1991, p. 165). Like Dunn, Powers doesn't reject the postmodern project outright. His characters begin, rather, where Oedipa ended. They are unmoored and uncertain, but – like their author – they find stable ground by re-excavating their own foundations: by "dig[ging] all the way down, to the *bottom*" (p. 604).

It is telling, given Roland Barthes's declaration that there is no such thing as "The Great Family of Man" (1957, p. 100), that so many of the big novels of the 1990s told the stories of families, and told them in evolutionary terms. As Stephen Burn has argued, the post-postmodern novel was characterized by a "more fundamental belief in the shaping influence of temporal process – that the things that happen to you in the past make a difference to who you are in the present" (2008b, p. 25). Unlike Pierre, who doesn't recognize his own children (Coover 2002, p. 181), or Joseph Heller's Bob Slocum, who can't recall his own father (1974, p. 77), the post-postmodern hero cannot escape their genealogy. Jeffrey Eugenides's *Middlesex* (2002), for example, digs down through several generations in order to explain the genetic map which so "dictates" the main character's "destiny" (p. 37). That character is a "hermaphrodite" (p. 413) who, because of the "blank slate" (p. 478) theory of human development, was raised as a gender at odds with his innate sense of self. Explicitly critical of that theory, which was "popular in the early seventies" (p. 478), Eugenides realigns his predecessors' concerns about identity, nurture, and the self around a different center of gravity: "Biology gives you a brain. Life turns it into a mind" (p. 479). In *The Corrections* (2001), Jonathan Franzen unpacks the fraught effects one set of parents has on their children: "The universe was mechanistic: the father spoke, the son reacted" (p. 174). Wallace's *Infinite Jest* (1996) tells the etiology of Don Gately's addiction in reverse, starting with his recovered state in the present and going back in time with him as he re-remembers his mother's own addiction, and the causes and effects that got him into trouble with drugs in the first place. Hal Incandenza, meanwhile, goes in the other direction, and over the course of his slow fall toward addiction the reader pieces together the chain of unhappinesses he is fleeing from, beginning in the novel as far back as his father's father.

Unlike the heroes of the postmodern fictions that came out of the Cold War, the characters in these novels are not dissolute victims of chaos and conspiracy but logically constrained by their upbringings and their biologies. This is not to say that the post-postmodern novel is naively optimistic. Fiction in the 1990s has its fair share of ontological crises, but it is important to note how they manifest. Where Slothrop and Lucky Pierre disintegrate on the page, Jimmy's loss of language in *Gold Bug* is due to a "hemorrhage" that affects the "switches" and "wir[ing]" of his brain (Powers 1991, p. 545), while in *Middlesex* it is "blood pool[ing] in [the] brain" that "wash[es] even the last fragments of [a] self away" (Eugenides 2002, p. 269). In Jonathan Lethem's *Motherless Brooklyn* (1999), reality disintegrates and needs "knitting" back together, but this is because the narrator has Tourette's, an atypical cognitive experience which highlights how much language really does matter (p. 43). Percival Everett's *Erasure* (2001) plays up the "death of the author" when the character Thelonious Ellison writes a parody of the kind of "racial self-expression" (p. 238) he is expected to write, and it becomes a bestseller. Thelonious is never replaced by his pseudonym, however, but lingers on to suffer the insult. The real death happens when his mother, who suffers from dementia, forgets him, and he becomes a tragically "blank space" in her "universe" (p. 229). If "cause-and-effect ... ha[d] been taken as far as it [would] go" in the paranoid, indeterministic universe of *Gravity's Rainbow* (Pynchon 1973, p. 105), now it was the be-all.

The world outside the novel certainly continued to operate according to the rigid laws of causality, and our transitionary period had another beginning in 1989, when, on February 14, the Ayatollah Khomeini sentenced Salman Rushdie to death for the crime of writing *The Satanic Verses* (1988). In the fallout of the fatwa, the political left's limp defense of the right to freedom of thought and expression was blamed on decades of postmodernist moral relativism. "The flame of the Enlightenment is waning," Rushdie writes in his memoir, quoting Gunter Grass: "But ... there is no other source of light" (Rushdie 2012, p. 161). If that flame was guttering in the 1990s, it seemed to go out altogether on September 11, 2001. The terrorist attacks on the Twin Towers threw all the issues haunting the prior decade – cultural relativism, Western disaffection, the clash of ideologies – into sudden sharp focus. The "New Atheist" movement that emerged in the aftermath saw postmodernism and religious fundamentalism as two sides of the same anti-Enlightenment coin (Dawkins 1998, p. 141; Dennett 2006, p. 262; Harris 2005, pp. 138–139; Hitchens 2005, p. 18). The movement was a direct response to 9/11, but also to the ongoing revival of Christian fundamentalism in America, which was making a concerted (some would say *postmodern*) effort to rewrite evolutionary fact as "just a theory," equal in value to the theory of "Intelligent Design." At the same time, a version of the New Atheists' defense of the Enlightenment would be embraced by the political (and, confusingly, Christian) right to both frame the attacks on 9/11 as a "hat[red] of our freedoms" and legitimize the "war on terror" (Bush 2001). The debate about Western and American values that had been so much a part of the postmodern project was being played out in the political realm.

Fiction after 9/11 was neither so jingoistic nor so atheistic. But what did fiction writers believe in? One of the recurring motifs in the postmodern novel was the tarot deck, which appears variously in *Gravity's Rainbow* (Pynchon 1973, p. 180), *The Tunnel* (Gass 1999, p. 154), *Naked Lunch* (Burroughs 2014, p. 65), *The Magus* (Fowles 1966, p. 477), and *Underworld* (DeLillo 1997, p. 495), to take examples from some of the major works. (Of the post-postmodern novels discussed in this entry, tarot cards appear only in *Infinite Jest*, though they are associated in that novel with an older, bygone generation: Hal's father, James Incandenza, makes a film in which "God and Satan play poker with Tarot cards for the soul of an alcoholic" [Wallace 1996, p. 988n. 24]). The tarot pack is a fitting motif for that generation, since the stories and meanings one makes out of its random arrangements can be reshuffled and reinterpreted indefinitely. As Samuel Chase Coale puts it, "the postmodern celebration of radical scepticism clashes with a deeper yearning for unity and wholeness ... everything becomes a sign, a clue, a piece of a larger puzzle" (2005, p. 4). In the post-postmodern novel the yearning was still there, but writers were looking for more coherent answers. As we've seen, there was grandeur to be found in the evolutionary view of life. Postmodernism had challenged the "assumption that literature embodied *universal* value" (Eagleton 1996, p. 191), but if, as George Saunders puts it, "our minds are built on common architecture," then that meant we could speak, across boundaries, to one another (Saunders 2017).

Yet the turn away from postmodernism was shaped as much by the increasingly overt religiosity of writers such as Saunders and Wallace as it was by their scientific literacy. Saunders's "Escape from Spiderhead" (2010), in which a team of sinister neuroscientists chemically induce moods in human subjects, is a proof-of-concept of materialism, yet it ends with the narrator committing suicide, breaking his body until his soul escapes the confines of its material prison: "right out through the roof" (Saunders 2013, p. 79). Wallace's *Infinite Jest* depicts a community of addicts who, after giving away their souls to narcotics, have become, in the process, "empty shell[s]" (1996, p. 508). The soul, for these writers, is neither simplistically religious, nor overtly Christian, nor indeed entirely faithful, but it is a humanistic metaphor, a lingering ghost of the idea that a part of us survives the dying animal we are all fastened to. The post-postmodern novel is borne forward not just by a material turn, but a dualistic one. Though the post-postmodern hero is a slave to determinism and their own materiality, it is precisely those constraints that create a space for coherent identity, albeit one that perhaps requires a little faith.

The question of faith had a parallel development in the metafictional novel, which began, in this period, to play a slightly different game. Where John Barth, in his autobiographical novel *Once Upon a Time* (1994), continually points to his own narrative inventions and the status of the book as text – "I understand that the people and objects in these scenes are ... mere images, projections insubstantial as light – although something tells me it's *words* they're made of" (pp. 143–144) – Wallace insists that his novel *The Pale King* (2011) is "really true" (pp. 68–69), though the autobiographical sections are based in far less fact. Where John Fowles, in the historical fiction *The French Lieutenant's Woman* (1969), never lets the reader settle into his constructed history ("had news reached [the characters] out of the future of the aeroplane ..." [1969, p. 17]), Michel Faber's neo-Victorian novel *The Crimson Petal and the White* (2002) invites the reader instead to be a part of the illusion: "still holding on to me ... your feet are wet ... I've brought you here to make: connections" (pp. 3–4). The difference is subtle, but where the former poke holes through the text and claim to speak to the reader directly – Wallace would come to call this "a highly rhetorical sham-honesty" (1999, p. 125) – a new generation is embracing the lie.

The best-selling novel *Life of Pi* (Martel 2001) put this lie front and center. In the novel's final part, after the narrator has recounted a magical story of a boy stranded on a lifeboat in the ocean with an enormous tiger, he offers his interrogators a more realistic version of events, changing the animals on the boat into members of the crashed ship's crew. Where Fowles famously offered two different conclusions to *The French Lieutenant's Woman*, each as valid as the other (1969, p. 390), Martel gives two interpretations of the same story: the question is not about which ending is right, or about resisting narrative closure, but about "Which is the better *story*" (2002, p. 317, my emphasis). In other words, where the postmodern novel encourages skepticism, the post-postmodern novel assumes the reader is already skeptical. Instead of beating a dead author, it insists on the fact of fiction, and invites the reader to suspend their disbelief. "It's an offer," writes Jennifer Egan, in her metafictional, neo-gothic novel *The Keep* (2006), "to believe in his nonsense ... it's like all the pretending *made* me believe" (p. 100).

The end of postmodernism had many beginnings, but one of them – again in 1989 – will have a greater lasting impact than any of the others. In March of that year, Tim Berners Lee wrote a modest document titled "Information Management: A Proposal." By October of 1990, Lee "had written the three fundamental technologies that remain the foundation of today's web ... HTML ... URI ... HTTP" (Web Foundation n.d.). By 2008, the crowdsourced Wikipedia had more articles than "all the world's paper encyclopaedias combined" (Gleick 2012, p. 379). In some ways the Internet has been a boon for American literature: a democratizing force that has diversified the work that garners acclaim and legitimized neglected forms and genres. But the explosion of new voices has also drowned most of them out. Mark McGurl concluded *The Program Era* (2009) on a hopeful note, arguing that the end of the era of great individual writers spoke not to a lack of talent but to "an embarrassment of riches" (p. 410). Milan Kundera was less hopeful when, in 1979, he predicted social media: "Once the writer in every individual comes to life (and that time is not far off), we are in for an age of universal deafness and lack of understanding" (1996, p. 147).

Though the post-postmodern movement may have marked the end of the postmodern novel, the arguments at the heart of postmodernism have, in the megaphone of the Internet, been entirely amplified. The Sokal affair was not resolved at all but "Squared" when James Lindsay, Helen Pluckrose, and Peter Boghossian published seven hoax papers to discredit what they called a thriving "postmodern discourse" (Mounk 2018). But the debate is not just academic. Having spread online, it is now being "co-opt[ed]" by right-wing authoritarians in Westminster and Washington who want to discredit the "woke" political left (Trilling 2020). In an ever-worsening culture war, critical theory – like the other offshoots of the postmodern era: identity politics and grievance studies, sex differences and biological determinism, climate denial and cancel culture, fake news and free speech – is now, in the manner one speaks of it, a signifier of allegiance.

What shape the novel will take in the twenty-first century is impossible to predict. The least we can hope for is that it makes some sense of the noise.

SEE ALSO: Barth, John; The Brain and American Fiction; The Culture Wars; DeLillo, Don; Egan, Jennifer; Everett, Percival; Franzen, Jonathan; Palahniuk, Chuck; Post-9/11 Narratives; Powers, Richard; Pynchon, Thomas; Realism after Poststructuralism; Saunders, George; Wallace, David Foster

NOTE

1 *Geek Love* is not a literal reimagining of Coover's novel, of course, since *Lucky Pierre* was published thirteen years later. The latter's collection of postmodern tropes makes it an exemplary postmodern text, however, and a helpful comparison. As Stephen Burn points out, Coover's novel is an "obituar[y]" that "paradoxically testif[ies]" to postmodernism's "continued vitality" (2008a, p. 223).

REFERENCES

Barth, John. (1994). *Once Upon a Time: A Floating Opera*. London: Sceptre.

Barthes, Roland. (1957). *Mythologies* (trans. Annette Lavers). New York: The Noonday Press.

Boxall, Peter. (2013). *Twenty-First-Century Fiction: A Critical Introduction*. Cambridge: Cambridge University Press.

Burn, Stephen J. (2008a). The end of postmodernism: American fiction at the millennium. In: *American Fiction of the 1990s: Reflections of History and Culture* (ed. Jay Prosser), 220–234. London: Routledge.

Burn, Stephen J. (2008b). *Jonathan Franzen at the End of Postmodernism*. London: Continuum.

Burroughs, William S. (2014). *Naked Lunch: The Restored Text*. London: Penguin Books.

Bush, George. (2001). President Bush addresses the nation. *The Washington Post* (September 20, 2001). https://www.washingtonpost.com/wp-srv/nation/specials/attacked/transcripts/bushaddress_092001.html (accessed July 15, 2021).

Clowes, Daniel. (2000). *Ghost World*: London: Jonathan Cape.

Coale, Samuel Chase. (2005). *Paradigms of Paranoia: The Culture of Conspiracy in Contemporary American Fiction*. Tuscaloosa: Alabama University Press.

Coover, Robert. (2002). *The Adventures of Lucky Pierre: Directors' Cut*. New York: Grove.

Crane, Mary Thomas and Richardson, Alan. (1999). Literary studies and cognitive science: toward a new interdisciplinarity. *Mosaic* 32 (2): 123–140.

Dawkins, Richard. (1998). Postmodernism disrobed: review of *Intellectual Impostures* by Alan Sokal and Jean Bricmont. *Nature* 394: 141–143. https://physics.nyu.edu/sokal/dawkins.html (accessed July 15, 2021).

DeLillo, Don. (1997). *Underworld*. London: Picador.

Dennett, Daniel C. (2006). *Breaking the Spell: Religion as Natural Phenomenon*. London: Penguin Books.

Drolet, Michael. (2004). *The Postmodernism Reader: Foundational Texts*. London: Routledge.

Dunn, Katherine. (1989). *Geek Love*. London: Abacus.

Eagleton, Terry. (1996). *Literary Theory: An Introduction*, 2nd ed. Oxford: Blackwell.

Egan, Jennifer. (2006). *The Keep*. London: Abacus.

Ellis, Bret Easton. (1991). *American Psycho*. London: Picador.

Eugenides, Jeffrey. (2002). *Middlesex*. London: Bloomsbury.

Everett, Percival. (2001). *Erasure*. London: Faber.

Faber, Michel. (2002). *The Crimson Petal and the White*. Edinburgh: Canongate.

Fowles, John. (1966). *The Magus*. London: Vintage.

Fowles, John. (1969). *The French Lieutenant's Woman*. London: Vintage Books.

Franzen, Jonathan. (2001). *The Corrections*. London: Fourth Estate.

Fukuyama, Francis. (1989). The end of history? *The National Interest* 16: 3–18.

Gass, William H. (1999). *The Tunnel*. Normal, IL: Dalkey Archive Press.

Gleick, James. (2012). *The Information: A History, a Theory, a Flood*. London: Fourth Estate.

Harris, Sam. (2005). *The End of Faith: Religion, Terror, and the Future of Reason*. London: Free Press.

Heller, Joseph. (1974). *Something Happened*. London: Vintage Books.

Hitchens, Christopher. (2005). Transgressing the boundaries: review of *The Johns Hopkins Guide to Literary Theory and Criticism*. *The New York Times* (May 22, 2005). https://www.nytimes.com/2005/05/22/books/review/transgressing-the-boundaries.html (accessed July 15, 2021).

Kundera, Milan. (1996). *The Book of Laughter and Forgetting*. London: Faber; 1st ed. 1979.

Latour, Bruno. (2004). Why has critique run out of steam? From matters of fact to matters of concern. *Critical Inquiry* 30: 225–248.

Lethem, Jonathan. (1999). *Motherless Brooklyn*. London: Faber.

Martel, Yann. (2002). *Life of Pi*. Edinburgh: Canongate; 1st ed. 2001.

McGurl, Mark. (2009). *The Program Era: Postwar Fiction and the Rise of Creative Writing*. Cambridge, MA: Harvard University Press.

McLaughlin, Robert L. (2004). Post-postmodern discontent: contemporary fiction and the social world. *Symplokē* 12 (1/2): 53–68.

Mounk, Yascha. (2018). What an audacious hoax reveals about academia. *The Atlantic* (October 5, 2018). https://www.theatlantic.com/ideas/archive/2018/10/new-sokal-hoax/572212/ (accessed July 15, 2021).

Palahniuk, Chuck. (1997). *Fight Club*. London: Vintage Books; 1st ed. 1996.

Pinker, Steven. (2002). *The Blank Slate: The Modern Denial of Human Nature*. London: Penguin Books.

Powers, Richard. (1991). *The Gold Bug Variations*. New York: Harper Perennial.

Pynchon, Thomas. (1973). *Gravity's Rainbow*. London: Vintage Books.

Richardson, Alan. (1999). Cognitive science and the future of literary studies. *Philosophy and Literature* 23 (1): 157–173.

Rushdie, Salman. (2012). *Joseph Anton: A Memoir*. New York: Random House.

Rybczynski, Witold. (1997). Think tank: lofty ideas that may be losing altitude. *The New York Times* (November 1, 1997). http://www.nytimes.com/1997/11/01/arts/think-tank-lofty-ideas-that-may-be-losing-altitude.html (accessed July 15, 2021).

Saunders, George. (2013). *Tenth of December*. London: Bloomsbury.

Saunders, George. (2017). What writers really do when they write. *The Guardian* (March 4, 2017). https://www.theguardian.com/books/2017/mar/04/what-writers-really-do-when-they-write (accessed July 15, 2021).

Sokal, Alan D. (1996). Transgressing the boundaries: an afterword. *Philosophy and Literature* 20 (2): 338–346.

Steiner, Wendy. (2001). *Venus in Exile: The Rejection of Beauty in 20th-Century Art*. New York: Free Press.

Stoppard, Tom. (1967). *Rosencrantz and Guildenstern are Dead*. London: Faber.

Trilling, Daniel. (2020). Why is the UK government suddenly targeting "critical race theory"? *The Guardian* (October 23, 2020). https://www.theguardian.com/commentisfree/2020/oct/23/uk-critical-race-theory-trump-conservatives-structural-inequality (accessed July 15, 2021).

Turner, Mark. (1991). *Reading Minds: The Study of English in the Age of Cognitive Science*. Princeton: Princeton University Press.

Vollmann, William T. (1990). American writing today: a diagnosis of the disease. *Conjunctions* 15. https://www.conjunctions.com/print/article/william-t-vollmann-c15 (accessed July 15, 2021).

Wallace, David Foster. (1993). E unibus pluram. Repr. in: *A Supposedly Fun Thing I'll Never Do Again*, 21–82. London: Abacus.

Wallace, David Foster. (1996). *Infinite Jest*. London: Abacus.
Wallace, David Foster. (1999). *Brief Interviews with Hideous Men*. London: Abacus.
Wallace, David Foster. (2011). *The Pale King: An Unfinished Novel* (ed. Michael Pietsch). London: Penguin Books.
Waugh, Patricia. (1984). *Metafiction: The Theory and Practice of Self-Conscious Fiction*. London: Routledge.
Web Foundation. (n.d.). History of the Web. *World Wide Web Foundation*. https://webfoundation.org/ (accessed July 15, 2021).

FURTHER READING

Burn, Stephen J. (ed.) (2018). *American Literature in Transition: 1990–2000*. Cambridge: Cambridge University Press.
Green, Jeremy. (2005). *Late Postmodernism: American Fiction at the Millennium*. New York: Palgrave Macmillan.
Prosser, Jay. (ed.) (2008). *American Fiction of the 1990s: Reflections of History and Culture*. London: Routledge.
Vermeulen, Timotheus and van den Akker, Robin. (2010). Notes on metamodernism. *Journal of Aesthetics and Culture* 2: 1–10.

Alameddine, Rabih

LEILA MOAYERI PAZARGADI
Nevada State College, USA

Rabih Alameddine is a Lebanese American writer and painter of Druze descent. Born in 1959 in Amman, Jordan, to Lebanese Druze parents, Alameddine is sometimes described as atheist or nonreligious. Growing up between Kuwait, Lebanon, and England, he proceeded to earn an engineering degree at UCLA, followed by an MBA at the University of San Francisco in 1982 (Freeman 2016). However, his literary contributions are more widely known as he has become a prolific novelist, who often explores states of displacement and liminality between Lebanon and the United States, in addition to themes concerning exile, fragmentation, homelessness, and sexuality. About his early life, he recalls in an interview with *Literary Hub*, "I was born into a wonderful family. Again, my father, my mother, my sisters … My greatest gift, in many ways, is that I was loved. With all my craziness. And I cursed them, and I lived in San Francisco, and they are in Beirut, and there is a reason for that. But I … I love them dearly" (Freeman 2016). Although themes concerning sexuality and family are running currents throughout his texts, about his own gay identity, he notes that he has not struggled with the knowledge, and that his family accepts that he is gay (Curiel 2008).

As an accomplished painter, Alameddine was formerly active in the art world with high-selling abstract pieces and commissions, two of which later served as covers for *Koolaids* (1998) and *The Angel of History* (2016). Although he was competitive and active in the art market, Alameddine eventually came to declare in a 2008 interview with *SF Gate*, "I didn't like it - I didn't like what was happening to me as a painter … I was successful, but I always felt like I was a fraud, whether it was true or not" (Curiel 2008). Refocusing his energy on writing novels instead, Alameddine's works have contributed to the growing body of Arab American literature that explores themes of identity and in-betweenness as they relate to the nation.

Alameddine's literary works include the following: *Koolaids: The Art of War*, *The Perv: Stories* (1999), *I, the Divine: A Novel in First Chapters* (2001), *The Hakawati* (2008), *An Unnecessary Woman* (2013), and *The Angel of History: A Novel*. All of his novels take up the perspective of marginalized or oft-ignored protagonists who are working through personal and emotional moments stemming from transnational movement and border crossings. Exile is a running current throughout his narratives, not just displacement caused by the Lebanese Civil War (1975–1990), but escape from family dynamics, particularly when the protagonists confront their own sexuality and agency. Confronting marginalization, Alameddine frequently takes on sexism, heterosexism, racism, and ableism throughout his oeuvre.

In terms of his literary contribution to the field, scholars, such as Layla al Maleh, Nouri Gana, Waïl Hassan, Syrine Houte, Therí Pickens, and Steven Salaita, have all noted the way in which his corpus transcends national boundaries; in so doing, his works are exemplary of exilic cultural production that investigates layered transnational identities. Andreas Pflitsch also observes that Lebanese writers in exile, like Alameddine, exist in a "double state of outside-ness," (2006, p. 281), which simultaneously prevents writers from idealizing their origins or conversely eschewing their culture for a standardized "Western mode of living" (Hout 2012, p. 9).

In reference to Alameddine's body of work, Steven Salaita notes its literary quality in *Modern Arab American Fiction: A Reader's Guide*, stating "one function (or result) of good literature is to usher readers beyond two-dimensional views of the world and its inhabitants" (2011, p. 8). Often transcending binary relationships, particularly as they concern cultural identity, Alameddine creates fictional texts that are as much works of world literature as they are models within Arab American literature. One of the primary reasons for this dual register is that he is often consumed with questions of belonging and identity inherent in transnational crossings. About his own identity and the paradox of belonging, he disclosed in a radio interview with Ramzi Salti and Nadia Barhoum, on Stanford University's *Arabology* in 2016, "But somewhere along the line, the two integrated – and I don't mean that I did not become an American, or I did not become Lebanese. The dichotomy left, because I became sort of my own person. I no longer cared to listen to this or to listen to that. I still think it's really important when there is a part that collates and at that time specifically, when I wrote in Lebanon, I belonged. In America, I fit but do not belong. But in Lebanon I belong, but I do not fit" (Salti and Barhoum 2016).

In Alameddine's groundbreaking novel, *Koolaids: The Art of War*, the author masterfully interweaves vignettes from characters either suffering from HIV/AIDS or losing friends to the epidemic during the 1980s. Taking place between San Francisco and Beirut, the novel begins with the story of Mohammad, a gay Lebanese man watching his friends and community battle two wars: the AIDS virus and the Lebanese Civil War. What is notable about this work is not only the attention to war-torn Lebanon, but the exploration of gay, Middle Eastern identity. About writing and his identity, Alameddine states, "How I started writing was being frustrated with reading books that did not reflect my experience particularly being an Arab and a gay man during the AIDS crisis" (Salti and Barhoum 2016). His treatment of and sensitivity toward his characters offers a refreshing and compelling discussion of AIDS and illness that refuses to victimize his protagonists. Therí Pickens notes in "Feeling Embodied and Being Displaced: A Phenomenological Exploration of Hospital Scenes in Rabih Alameddine's Fiction," that his novels, particularly *Koolaids*, often present the "hospital space and lines as a means of working through displacement. Characters reject the idea that normalcy or belonging is a state to which they should aspire, regardless of whether that norm or belonging is constituted in sexual, bodily, or mental terms" (2013, p. 67). Through the lens of disability studies, the text yields much about doctor/patient dynamics, themes of death, illness, and reevaluation of victimhood as it depicts illness as more than just disease.

Often breaking from expectations about Lebanese men and women as straight, docile, or monolithic, Alameddine presents complicated characters who grapple with sexuality, alienation, trauma, violence, and relocation as they confront life in-between Lebanon and the US. In *The Perv*, Alameddine further explores identities of those infected with the AIDS virus, often showing the alienation and sense of displacement of his characters beyond physical exile. (Pickens 2014, p. 71). His collection of short stories explores not only gay identity, but also the sexual agency of straight Lebanese men and women impacted by the Lebanese Civil War. Ultimately, throughout the collection, he metaphorizes illness for the condition of exile. Like *Koolaids*, this collection is injected with a somber cynicism flecked with humor, creating a sobering exploration of identities torn apart by war.

In Alameddine's third work, *I, the Divine: A Novel in First Chapters*, the author presents a fictional autobiography written in a series of first chapters by the Lebanese American protagonist, Sarah Nour El-Din. The first female protagonist to have a primary storytelling role in Alammedine's oeuvre, Sarah explores her life in-between Lebanon and the US, her relationship to her family, and her negotiation of two cultures and geographies. Every chapter begins as "Chapter One," as Sarah, a writer and artist, attempts to craft her memoir more than twenty years after she leaves Lebanon in 1989. Moving between genres, perspectives, and languages, Alameddine structures a complex narrative that is unfinished, just as the protagonist's life is unfinished. Prophetically published on September 11, 2001, the fictional autobiography anticipates the Middle Eastern women's memoir boom that would ensue following the catastrophic events of that day. In using fragmented aesthetics to show the complexity of retelling a life in transit, Alameddine also denies the "knowability" of the fictional autobiographical protagonist. The narrative becomes more about process than product, particularly as it discusses Alameddine's favorite themes: exile, displacement, and alienation with respect to the search for belonging. Caught between Lebanon and the United States, the search for Sarah's identity, as it relates to home, also depicts themes of fragmentation that are aesthetically mirrored in the production of the first-chapters memoir. The aesthetic effect produces a "'literary cubism' that distances the reader from fully understanding Sarah's life experiences and feeling as they if they can know what it means to be a Lebanese American woman caught in conflict. Furthermore, the complexity of the shifting autobiographical voices undermines monolithic portrayals and fabrication appearing in post-9/11" memoirs (Pazargadi 2018, p. 55). In terms of autobiographical studies, the text is particularly useful for discussing how Sarah uses varying first-, second-, and third-person voices to defy autobiographical convention and assert her agency as a female storyteller through her polyphonous narrative.

While many view writing and autobiographical life storytelling as cathartic, Alameddine notes that he finds it the opposite, disclosing in an interview appendixed in *I, the Divine*, "I do not believe in writing as a form of therapy. At times, writing can be therapeutic, but most of the time, writing is *un*therapy, something akin to torture. A writer goes to therapy to work out problems that are exacerbated by writing . . . My writing makes no sense and does not help me; therefore I pursue it" (2003, p. 314). He adds in 2016, "Usually what I write about are things that I'm obsessed with, and usually things that I'm obsessed with are things that I am angry about. So what usually comes out is uncomfortable for people. But my existence is uncomfortable for people" (Freeman 2016).

The complexity of storytelling is evident throughout his work, wherein he often explores it as an art related to psychological trauma. In his fourth work, *The Hakawati*, the author invokes the Sheherazadian storytelling tradition to explore themes of isolation, exile, and belonging. Employing the frame narrative structure of *A Thousand and One Nights* within *The Hakawati*, the author creates an epic tale about a Lebanese grandfather and grand storyteller ("hakawati" in Arabic), whose grandson, Osama al-Kharrat, visits his sick father in Beirut in 2003. Having spent many years in America, the narrative explores generational storytelling that jumps in time and space. The narrative focuses as much on the art of storytelling as the story itself, opening with the memorable line, "Listen. Allow me to be your god. Let me take you on a journey beyond imagining. Let me tell you a story" (Alameddine 2008, p. 5). These prophetic lines herald a sweeping narrative, which like Alameddine's other texts, moves between cultures, political conflicts, and family memories set against the backdrop of the 1967 Israeli-Arab war and the Lebanese Civil War. The author draws attention to the power of Middle Eastern storytellers in stylistic ode to *A Thousand and One Nights* and the work of Egyptian Nobel Laureate Naguib Mahfouz with fantastical mergers of drama and folklore. About this tradition, Alameddine enthuses in a 2008 interview: "It's *how* we tell the stories that are different. I think the way the Arabs tell the story, which is how I try to do it (in *The Hakawati*) is to invite the reader to sit and listen - as much as it's storytelling, it's *involvement* with the listener" (Curiel 2008). Not unlike *I, the Divine*, the text becomes more about process than product in its meditations on storytelling as a vehicle exploring diasporic themes.

Further reflections on the Lebanese Civil War are explored in *An Unnecessary Woman* from the vantage point of a 72-year-old "unnecessary" woman, Aaliya. Employing a pronounced feminist approach reminiscent of *I, the Divine*, the author provides feminist critiques of patriarchal modes found throughout Aaliya's life. As Dina Al-Khatib and Yousef Awad note, Aaliya's assertive voice allows for a gender-based critique of issues facing Arab women every day, including "biased social conventions that govern matters of marriage, education, and financial independence, in addition to other issues of violence, sexual harassment and most importantly, marginalization" (2019, p. 9). Ultimately, Aaliya's rejection of her own alienation defies those seeking to cast her aside because of perceived difference or abnormality.

Perhaps this is a text wherein Alameddine metadiegetically infuses his love for literature via his book-loving protagonist. Literary references abound, ranging from Leo Tolstoy to Franz Kafka to Marguerite Duras to J.M. Coetzee. What chiefly occupies her time is reading; once a year, Aaliyah chooses one manuscript to translate just for herself. However, the focus of *An Unnecessary Woman* is not literary analysis, but the isolation and strength of an aging woman confronting her own mortality. The narrator is thoughtful and meditative, drawing the reader's attention to the profundity of the quotidian and the triumphs of the everyday, as opposed to the impact of extraordinary events. Asserting her agency, she combats perceived invisibility through defiant visibility. When asked how he convincingly writes from the perspective of a woman, Alameddine replies,

> It was not written by a man. It was written by me. I mean the trouble is that we think of the separation – of, "this is a man and this is a woman." That kind of dichotomy for me

never really existed. I did not write a book about a woman. I wrote a book about Aaliya. So this book is Rabih writing about Aaliya ... I sit down to think, "How can I make Aaliya real, come to life? So, that's how it's done. I don't know how a man would do such a thing. I know how I would do such a thing, and that's a big difference.

(Salti and Barhoum 2016)

Aaliya's agency is achieved by refusing otherness, as Alameddine moves her from the periphery of the story to the center, especially in resistance to her marginalization by others (Al-Khatib and Awad 2019, p. 6).

Alameddine's latest novel to date, *The Angel of History: A Novel*, departs from the usual Lebanese protagonist to focus on a Yemeni-born poet, Jacob, who is living in San Francisco and checking into a mental health facility. The frame narrative takes place during one single night spent in the waiting room. Aesthetically, the novel experiments with form as it switches between interviews with Satan and Death, Jacob's journals, and his autobiographical descriptions at the clinic. While Jacob is at the clinic, Satan and Death battle in allegorical struggle for his soul. The text features the haunting familiarity of loss at the hands of AIDS, which is compared to the US drone onslaught during the ongoing Yemeni Civil War. Deviating from the familiar Lebanese backdrop of his novels, Alameddine instead compares past loss to current political conflicts ravaging the Middle East, particularly Yemen. Alameddine cynically draws parallels between those bombed into adopting American values in Yemen with gay men bullied by heteronormativity in San Francisco, and beyond. As Aminatta Forna proclaims in *The Guardian*, "This is a story of one life and many themes: death and sex; religion; war; love and loss and the need to remember" (Forna 2016).

As a talented and accomplished writer, it is not surprising that Rabih Alameddine has earned many awards and recognitions for his masterful storytelling. To date, he has won the following: Guggenheim Fellowship in 2002, National Book Critics Circle Award finalist (2014), California Book Award's Gold Medal Fiction for *An Unnecessary Woman* (2014), and both the Arab American Book Award (2017) and the Lambda Literary Award for Gay Fiction (2017) for *The Angel of History*. Humble about his accolades while also inspiring others to write, he retorts to those praising his work: "Don't read my work, go out there and make your own narratives." (Salti and Barhoum 2016).

SEE ALSO: Literature of the Americas; Mixed-Genre Fiction; Multiculturalism; Queer and LGBT Fiction; Trauma and Fiction

REFERENCES

Alameddine, Rabih. (1998). *Koolaids: The Art of War*. London: Picador.
Alameddine, Rabih. (2003). *I, the Divine: A Novel in First Chapters*. London: Phoenix; 1st ed. 2001.
Alameddine, Rabih. (2008). *The Hakawati: A Story*. New York: Anchor.
Al-Khatib, Dina and Awad, Yousef. (2019). Unfolding the female journey in Pynchon's *The Crying of Lot 49* and Alameddine's *An Unnecessary Woman*. *International Journal of Comparative Literature and Translation Studies* 7 (2): 6–14.
Curiel, Jonathan. (2008). Alameddine. *SF Gate* (April 29, 2008). http://www.sfgate.com/entertainment/article/Alameddine-3217366.php (accessed July 5, 2021).
Forna, Aminatta. (2016). *The Angel of History* by Rabih Alameddine review – a gloriously political tale of survival. *The Guardian* (October 13, 2006). https://www.theguardian.com/books/2016/oct/13/the-angel-of-history-by-rabih-alameddine-review (accessed July 5, 2021).
Freeman, John. (2016). Rabih Alameddine: "My existence is uncomfortable for people." *Literary Hub* (October 26, 2016). https://lithub.com/rabih-alameddine-my-existence-is-uncomfortable-for-people/ (accessed July 5, 2021).
Hout, Syrine. (2012). *Post-War Anglophone Lebanese Fiction: Home Matters in the Diaspora*. Edinburgh: Edinburgh University Press.

Pazargadi, Leila M. (2018). Unfixing the autobiographical subject: fragmentation as aesthetics in Rabih Alameddine's *I, the Divine*. In: *Arab American Aesthetics: Literature, Material Culture, Film, and Theatre* (ed. Therí A. Pickens), 42–59. New York: Routledge.

Pflitsch, Andreas. (2006). To fit or not to fit: Rabih Alameddine's novels *Koolaids* and *I, the Divine*. In: *Arab Americas: Literary Entanglements of the American Hemisphere and the Arab World* (ed. Ottmar Ette and Friederike Pannewick), 275–283. Frankfurt: Vervuert.

Pickens, Therí A. (2013). Feeling embodied and being displaced: a phenomenological exploration of hospital scenes in Rabih Alameddine's fiction. *MELUS* 38 (3): 67–85.

Pickens, Therí A. (2014). *New Body Politics: Narrating Arab and Black Identity in the Contemporary United States*. New York: Routledge.

Salaita, Steven. (2011). *Modern Arab American Fiction: A Reader's Guide*. Syracuse: Syracuse University Press.

Salti, Ramzi and Barhoum, Nadia. (2016). Arabology interviews Rabih Alameddine. *Arabology* (January 23, 2016). www.arabology.org/2016/01/arabology-interviews-rabih-alameddine.html (accessed July 5, 2021).

FURTHER READING

Al Maleh, Layla. (ed.) (2009). *Arab Voices in Diaspora: Critical Perspectives on Anglophone Arab Literature*. Amsterdam: Rodopi.

Awad, Yousef. (2012). *The Arab Atlantic: Resistance, Diaspora, and Trans-cultural Dialogue in the Works of Arab British and Arab American Women Writers*. Saarbrücken: LAP LambertAcademic.

Hassan, Waïl S. (2011). *Immigrant Narratives: Orientalism and Cultural Translation in Arab American and Arab British Literature*. New York: Oxford University Press.

Hartman, Michelle. (2013). Rabih Alameddine's *I, the Divine*: a Druze novel as world literature. In: *The Edinburgh Companion to the Arab Novel in English: The Politics of Anglo Arab and Arab American Literature and Culture* (ed. Nouri Gana), 339–359. Edinburgh: Edinburgh University Press.

Hout, Syrine. (2008). The tears of trauma: memories of home, war, and exile in Rabih Alameddine's *I, the Divine*. *World Literature Today* 82 (5): 58–62.

Salaita, Steven. (2007). *Arab American Literary Fictions, Cultures, and Politics*. New York: Palgrave Macmillan.

Shanahan, Dervla. (2011). Reading queer a/theology into Rabih Alameddine's Koolaids. *Feminist Theology* 19 (2): 129–142.

Alarcón, Daniel

JUANITA HEREDIA
Northern Arizona University, USA

In the twenty-first century, American literature has taken a new turn as more authors of international and culturally mixed backgrounds in the United States have shifted their literary geographies beyond the borders of the United States, according to Heredia in *Transnational Latina Narratives* (2009). Daniel Alarcón, who emerged on the literary stage with the publication of his collection of short fiction *War by Candlelight: Stories* (2005), belongs to this generation of transnational authors. In his first story collection, he not only includes stories of migration that take place in New York City, but he also captures the emotional trauma of civilians living during a civil war in Peru that began in the 1980s. Alarcón had already published selected stories from this anthology in venues such as *The New Yorker*, *Harper's*, and *Granta* to much national critical acclaim, some comparing him to a young Mario Vargas Llosa or Flannery O'Connor. When he published his first novel, *Lost City Radio* (2007), Alarcón garnered an international reputation as he further expanded on the consequences of a civil war in an unmentioned South American country. He earned an International Literature Award from the Haus der Kulturen der Welt for the German translation of this novel. This honor attests to the fact that Alarcón not only writes for a US readership but, like many authors concerned with transnational matters, the translations of his works have made them accessible to a global audience. Alarcón hopes his fiction can reach readers from various corners of the world, from countries in Latin America to Ghana, India, and Palestine.

In the 1980s and early 1990s, Peru underwent a turbulent civil war initiated by Maoist-leaning terrorists called the Shining Path. They used violence to recruit thousands of Andean migrants, many of whom died in the process or were displaced to the capital of Lima. In 1980, Daniel Alarcón migrated at the age of three with his parents and two siblings from his birthplace in Lima, Peru, to the United States. Although not formally trained in literature, Alarcón credits his family, his father in particular, for his masterful storytelling ability. While Alarcón obtained a traditional formal education until high school in Birmingham, Alabama, graduated with a bachelor's degree in anthropology at Columbia University, and then obtained a master of fine arts at the Iowa Writers Workshop in English, he grew up in a bilingual and bicultural household always attentive to his family's stories in Spanish. In fact, he recalls that his family sent cassette recordings of stories in Spanish from the United States to relatives in Peru to maintain strong family ties. Despite the geographic distance and technological limitations between the United States and South America in the 1980s, the emotional bond between Alarcón and his relatives in Peru has always been solid. This exposure to two languages and two cultures simultaneously contributes to Alarcón's cosmopolitan sensibility in his literary formation in fiction, journalism, and eventually, in his award-winning international podcast *Radio Ambulante* in Spanish.

Alarcón has earned prestigious awards such as a Whiting Award, a Fulbright, a Guggenheim Fellowship, a Lannan Fellowship, and has been nominated for honors such as "One of 21 Young American Novelists under 35" by *Granta* magazine as well as "One of 39 under 39 Latino American Novelists" at the international Hay Festival in Colombia that have made him a recognized writer beyond the United States. He has received positive reviews for his fiction by *The Washington Post*, *The Los Angeles Times*, *The Chicago Tribune*, and *The Financial Times* (London) to name a few. After discovering his publication in *The New Yorker*, the editors at the award-winning Peruvian literary magazine *Etiqueta Negra* invited Alarcón to join their team as an associate editor. In turn, he served as a liaison between *Etiqueta* and the *Virginia Quarterly Review* for which he co-edited with Ted Genoways a special issue called *South America in the 21st Century* (2007), which included fiction, journalism, and photography from an array of contemporary writers, artists, and translators from South America and the United States. In 2010, Alarcón edited *The Secret Miracle*, a collection of conversations and reflections from a myriad of critically acclaimed writers, such as Edwidge Danticat, Haruki Murakami, and Mario Vargas Llosa, who discuss the craft of writing. As an author, editor, and translator, Alarcón is in a unique position to navigate diverse literary worlds and bridge them in his creative and editorial outputs.

An important theme for Alarcón in his fiction and journalism is the city. Much happens in cities, both ugly and dangerous, but also beautiful and inspiring. Since Alarcón has traveled extensively, he is able to compare and contrast cities globally, finding common ground as well as differences. Other than living in Lima and various cities in the United States, he has studied abroad in Ghana as an undergraduate, taught photography in Ramallah, and covered stories in different metropolises in Latin America. On the representation of urban themes, experiences, and cities, Alarcón has stated in an interview:

> Like a lot of people, I find cities to be fascinating places to live because there is so much going on simultaneously. You have people living side by side, in what amounts to different centuries. These places, for all their disconnects, tell us a great deal about what it means to be human and what it means to be alive right now. I do find a great deal of inspiration from seeing in these very cold, chaotic, difficult places, how people find ways to survive and thrive.
>
> (Heredia 2012, p. 401)

Evidently, Alarcón embraces a modern perspective of what it means to live in cities and have multifaceted experiences in contemporary times. He does not view the city as a utopic place but rather acknowledges and accepts living in a city with realistic eyes. Cities are not perfect, but they do offer opportunities for work, resources for leisure, and a sense of home.

In fact, two important experiences that would affect Daniel Alarcón's life and professional writing are connected to urban contexts. After completing his undergraduate studies at Columbia University, Alarcón decided to work as a counselor and teacher for two years in a high school in central Harlem, New York City. He then won a Fulbright Fellowship to travel, research, and teach in Lima, Peru, in 2001. It was the first time in his life that he had returned to the country of his birth to live for an extended period. He decided to live in a neighborhood called San Juan de Lurigancho, inhabited by Andean migrants on the edges of Lima. He felt that he needed to be situated close to his place of work, teaching photography to youngsters from this area. The students he encountered had families whose lives had been affected by the Shining Path civil war in the 1980s. Both of these experiences in major metropolises, New York and Lima, would prove pivotal and influential in the making of his first major fiction publication, *War by Candlelight*, and subsequent fiction. Alarcón later expanded one of the stories, "City of Clowns," from *War by Candlelight* into a graphic novel, *Ciudad de Payasos* (2010), in Spanish in collaboration with Peruvian graphic artist, Sheila Alvarado.

In *War by Candlelight*, Alarcón delivers heart-wrenching stories on a local, national, and international scale as he dives into themes of migration, urbanization, and corruption. He incorporates urban experiences from Lima to New York City, exemplifying that he can move swiftly in a transnational context. The most well-known story of this collection, "City of Clowns," (first published in *The New Yorker* in 2003) chronicles the migratory experiences of Andean people settling in Lima, Peru, in search of a better life by escaping the devastating circumstances and lack of economic opportunities in their hometown, Cerro de Pasco, during the Shining Path years. Likewise, "Lima, Peru, July 28, 1979" and the title story, "War by Candlelight," provide an insightful look at migrants escaping the civil war by moving from Andean towns to the capital of Lima, always on the verge of leading precarious lives as violence and death are constant threats. One character observes, "Dying is the local sport" (2005, p. 19). It is worthwhile to note that Alarcón also maps narratives in the United States to show how Peruvian immigrants and their children experience cultural dis/encounters with other cultural groups in the examples of "Third Avenue Suicide," "Absence," and "A Science for Being Alone." While he creates culturally specific characters from the Andes, Peru, Ecuador, and the United States, he is attentive to the modern conditions of loneliness and solitude in a metropolis and the search for a viable community in urban contexts for new groups of immigrants in the United States, thereby changing the patterns of past Latin American immigrant groups such as Mexicans and Cubans.

In *Lost City Radio*, Alarcón focuses on the plight of migrants who move from the

Amazonian and Andean provinces to a metropolitan capital during an unstable postwar period in an unnamed South American country in which the government is characterized as authoritarian. By using the media instrument of the radio, Alarcón situates his novel in a radio station in a capital city alluding to Lima to show the significance of remembering the victims, dead or disappeared, of a civil war. Rather than represent the two opposing forces of the civil war, Alarcón captures the emotional trauma of the consequences of this political moment of violence for the victims and their loved ones. He explores how this political turmoil can separate families, parents from their children, and disrupt communities in the Andean and Amazonian provinces, all of which leads to migrations and the expansion of the capital city. But Alarcón does more. He evokes sympathy and compassion for characters with flaws, dreams, and yearnings who search for social justice in a rapidly changing and chaotic world.

In *Lost City Radio*, Alarcón narrates a romance between a young revolutionary migrant student, Rey, living in a capital city, who falls in love with a future journalist of a radio talk show, Norma. Through flashbacks, Alarcón shifts between the past and present, showing how the characters' lives are intertwined. Alarcón plays with fiction within fiction as the character of Rey has a tendency to invent stories and tests the boundaries of the truth with his love interest, Norma. Because Rey becomes involved as an activist in political matters in the city, he is arrested and then must go into hiding away from the city, leaving behind Norma. Since Rey must lead a clandestine life, he separates from Norma and does so in an Amazonian region of his country where he becomes involved with another woman and fathers a child he wishes to take to the city. As time passes, Norma does not know if Rey is alive or not. As a radio broadcaster, she relays news and reports on the disappearance of people affected by the civil war. As destiny would have it, one day a boy named Victor, who lost his mother to a natural disaster, appears at the radio station where Norma works looking for his father. After putting the pieces of the puzzle together, Norma learns that Victor is Rey's lost son whom, as a consequence of the civil war, he will never raise.

Lost City Radio has been translated into at least thirteen languages. In order to promote this important work, Alarcón spent two years traveling to different corners of the globe. He has commented that what most affected him from this experience was the way people of diverse backgrounds talked to him after a reading and thanked him for writing this fiction because they or their families had undergone similar traumatic experiences during times of war. This response speaks to the power of Alarcón's storytelling and his ability to convey empathy in his fiction beyond national and cultural borders.

In his second novel, *At Night They Walk in Circles* (2013), Alarcón reaches another literary milestone as he explores the lives of three actors in a guerrilla theatre troupe often testing the boundaries between reality and fiction in a nameless South American country. He unravels a narrative of mystery, intrigue, and suspense, showing the human side of relationships in a contemporary post-civil war period. In readings, Alarcón has stated that this novel took about seven years to complete, his most challenging work yet. He constructs characters of different generations and regions in an unspecified Andean country to show how historical events can be erased unless someone keeps the memory of these alive. Nelson is the city youngster playwright who has never left the metropolis and expects his brother in the United States to help him with a visa. Henry is an older revolutionary playwright, also a migrant from the provinces, who lived during the civil war and was arrested for his political ideas. He is a mentor to Nelson. Finally, Patalarga, is an actor from the provinces who mediates the worlds between the two characters. Alarcón not only represents different perspectives on art and politics in this novel but he also shows how characters with irreconcilable differences can reach common ground on a human level in a new era of political stability.

In his second short fiction collection, *The King Is Always Above the People* (2017), Alarcón expands his literary canvass of characters temporally and spatially, but he is still preoccupied with migration, urban experience, violence, and relationships on a quotidian basis.

Alarcón constructs a variety of stories with characters ranging from a fallen gang member to an imaginary Abraham Lincoln. He writes a range of short fiction – from a concise but profound three-page story, "The Thousands," to an elaborate fifty-page novella, "The Auroras" – with the same intensity. Geographically, Alarcón sets his stories in California, Illinois, Andean provinces, and a capital city in an unspecified South American country, to name a few locations. Historically, he moves between contemporary times and the age of Abraham Lincoln in the nineteenth century, twisting familiar plots to evoke a human side of a historical figure. In spite of the versatility of the stories in this collection, the theme of migration, be it internally within a country or from one country to another, unites the experiences of most of the characters. Alarcón astutely moves from the realist portrayals of his earlier fiction to hypothetical situations, as in "The Ballad of Rocky Rontal," which offers the possibility of different endings. While he is not focused solely on the context of the civil war in a South American country, Alarcón continues to be preoccupied with the injustices of corruption, violence, and the search for intimacy and fulfillment in personal relationships affecting both men and women. He balances the social and the personal in these stories with a careful look at the characters' abilities to transcend their flaws and reach a better understanding of humankind in a fragmented society, be it in the United States or abroad. This work was one of three finalists for the Story Book Prize. He had published a version of this collection by the same title, *El rey está por encima del pueblo* (2009), in Spanish translation in Mexico City.

Since his time as a graduate student at the Iowa Writers Workshop, Alarcón has met South American authors and collaborated with translations of their work into English. He has also embarked on other projects of fiction and journalism, such as *Zoetrope All Story: The Latin America Issue* (2009), co-edited with Diego Trelles Paz, and the abovementioned collaboration on the special issue *South America in the 21st Century* for the *Virginia Quarterly Review*. These professional endeavors make Alarcón not only a necessary voice but also a transnational ambassador in disseminating work by new literary voices from the Spanish-speaking world to an English-reading audience. Similar to his role as author and editor, Alarcón's role as translator is another credit to his achievements, especially when it comes to revealing further artistic talent from Latin America. In his English translation of the memoir *The Book of Emma Reyes* (2017), not only is he responsible for undertaking this linguistic enterprise, but he recovers a gem of an artist admired by the likes of Nobel-winning Colombian Gabriel García Márquez. In this major translation endeavor, Alarcón introduces the world to a forgotten Colombian artist, Emma Reyes, who lived in poverty and misery before leading the life of a Bohemian and who was discovered posthumously for her creative talents.

One of Alarcón's greatest contributions to social media narrative is the creation of his

Spanish podcast, *Radio Ambulante*, in 2012 (distributed by the National Public Radio starting in 2016). Reminiscent of the radio production *This American Life*, Alarcón and his team of journalists, including his Colombian wife Carolina Guerrero, interview people from all walks of life in the Spanish-speaking world in Latin America and the United States to share their stories about everything from immigration and politics to World Cup soccer and transgender identity. In 2014, Alarcón and his collaborators earned the Gabriel García Márquez Award for Innovation in Journalism for *Radio Ambulante*.

Although Daniel Alarcón has published a variety of literary works – and a podcast – in a relatively short period (2003–2017), he has contributed substantially to the different fields of literature, journalism, and media as much for a Spanish-listening public and readership as an English one. Very few authors in the United States have achieved this kind of literary and media range in such a relatively brief amount of time. Furthermore, Alarcón is influencing a younger generation of writers like Peruvian Jack Martínez Arias, demonstrating that his fiction crosses linguistic and cultural borders. Scholars and critics should note Alarcón's contributions as versatile, urgent, and important to American literature and letters of the Americas in a transnational fashion.

SEE ALSO: After Postmodernism; The Culture Wars; Fictions of Work and Labor; Globalization; The Graphic Novel; Indigenous Narratives; Literature of the Americas; Millennial Fiction; Trauma and Fiction; Urban Fiction

REFERENCES

Heredia, Juanita. (2005). *War by Candlelight: Stories*. New York: HarperCollins.
Heredia, Juanita. (2009). *Transnational Latina Narratives in the Twenty-first Century: The Politics of Gender, Race, and Migrations*. New York: Palgrave Macmillan.
Heredia, Juanita. (2012). The task of the translator: an interview with Daniel Alarcón. *Latino Studies* 10 (3): 395–409.

FURTHER READING

Aguirre, Carlos and Walker, Charles. (eds.) (2017). *The Lima Reader: History, Culture, Politics*. Durham, NC, and London: Duke University Press.
Bost, Suzanne and Aparicio, Frances. (eds.) (2012). *The Routledge Companion to Latino/a Literature*. New York and London: Routledge.
Falconi, José Luis and Mazzotti, José Antonio. (ed.) (2008). *The Other Latinos: Central and South Americans in the United States*. Cambridge, MA: Harvard University Press.
González, John Morán and Lomas, Laura. (eds.) (2018). *The Cambridge History of Latina/o American Literature*. Cambridge and New York: Cambridge University Press.
Heredia, Juanita. (ed.) (2018). *Mapping South American Latina/o Literature in the United States: Interviews with Contemporary Writers* (Literatures of the Americas Series). Cham, Switzerland: Palgrave Macmillan.

Alexie, Sherman

BRIANNA R. BURKE
Iowa State University, USA

Sherman Alexie is one of the most notorious writers of the late twentieth and early twenty-first centuries. He is known for his prodigious literary production, his scathing wit and charm, his controversial views on cultural traditions and reservation life, the wide dissemination of his works, and recent revelations of his sexual misconduct by the #MeToo Movement. Sherman Alexie has written four novels, five short story collections, seven volumes of poetry, two screenplays, a children's book, and a memoir. He has been an active member of the literati, serving on the Board of Directors for the National Indian College Fund and the Presidential Panel for the National Dialog on Race, and he promotes his work almost endlessly. Many of his pieces have earned awards, including the PEN/Faulkner Award for Fiction, The PEN/Malamud Award for Short Fiction, the PEN/Hemingway Citation for Best First Fiction, and the National Book Award for Young People's Literature. The film *Smoke Signals*, his first screenplay, won the Audience Award and the Filmmaker's Trophy at Sundance when it premiered in 1998; in 2019 it was added to the National Film Registry in the Library of Congress. His work is known for being brutally honest, funny, and insightful, and consistently challenges the idea that there has ever been a singular, iconic Indian, or a singular way to be American Indian.

Alexie was born on October 7, 1966, both Coeur d'Alene and Spokane, and grew up on the Spokane reservation in Wellpinit, Washington, one of six siblings. As he references many times in his work, he was born with hydrocephalus (or "water on the brain") and was not expected to live. Tenacious, he was reading by the age of two, tackling *The Grapes of Wrath* (1939) by kindergarten. His mother made quilts and worked in the Wellpinit trading post; his most recent book, a memoir titled *You Don't Have to Say You Love Me* (2017) is about her, who he describes as "brilliant, funny, beautiful, generous, vindictive, deceitful, tender, manipulative, abusive, loving, and intimidating" (Alexie n.d.). His mother rarely appears in his early work, but fathers are a frequent topic throughout his oeuvre, notably in *Smoke Signals* as well as the heartbreaking and hilarious titular short story "War Dances" that details his father's struggle with alcoholism, diabetes, and eventual death. As a young adult, Alexie decided to attend school in Reardon, a predominately white high school about thirty miles away from the reservation, the subject of his graphic novel *The Absolutely True Diary of a Part-Time Indian* (2007). Getting him to Reardon was a struggle for his family, and there he experienced frequent racism, but he also flourished, becoming the captain of the basketball team – ironically called the "Reardon Indians" – class president, and a member of the championship debate team. After high school, he attended Gonzaga University, where he floundered, started to drink, and then enrolled at Washington University, a critical turning point in his life. There, he took his first poetry class with Alex Kuo and stopped drinking when his first collection of poems, *I Would Steal Horses* (1992), was accepted for publication. Since, Alexie has seemingly never stopped writing.

I Would Steal Horses was quickly followed by *The Business of Fancydancing* (1992), a collection of poems, prose poems, and short pieces of fiction that establishes Alexie's style, and in which he tackles many of the themes that become recurrent tropes throughout his work: alcoholism, poverty, and the racism beating at the heart of the American empire well into the twenty-first century, but also love, popular culture, American history, family relationships, basketball, and what it means to be Indigenous when "authenticity" and belonging are measured by blood quantum and ceremony attendance. All of Alexie's poetry collections – seven in total – experiment with genre, style, and form. Many include short pieces that are proto versions of later stories, like "Pawn Shop," a precursor to "What You Pawn, I Will Redeem," a story that Alexie often says is the best he's ever written. In "Pawn Shop," the narrator walks into a bar to find "all the Indians are gone"; he wanders, entering a pawn shop where he finds "a single heart beating under glass, and I know who it used to belong to, I know all of them" (1992, p. 79). Many of Alexie's stories reappear years later, fully fleshed and with bite, creating a running cast of characters that return repeatedly.

The Lone Ranger and Tonto Fistfight in Heaven, released in 1993, vaulted Alexie into literary fame. Winning the PEN/Hemingway Citation for Best First Fiction, the collection is comprised in a style that will become typical of Alexie's work: a mix of brutal and destabilizing honesty and startling and often dark humor, written with a wild, lyrical beauty. The topics that Alexie broaches in this first short story collection also repeat through his work, as if through writing he sharpens his ideas through time and experimentation; some of the pieces, like "Because My Father Always Said" and "This is What it Means to Say Phoenix, Arizona," appear rewritten in *Smoke Signals*. *Lone Ranger* is devastating in its portrayal of alcoholism and the cyclical nature of poverty, but such hardship is mitigated by tender moments where characters confront the difficulties of reality together, and in doing so create survival. In "Traffic Signal," Alexie writes, "Indians have a way of surviving. But it's almost like Indians can easily survive the big stuff. Mass murder, the loss of language and land rights. It's the small things that hurt the most. The white waitress who wouldn't take an order, Tonto, the Washington Redskins" (1993, p. 49). In the most heartrending piece in the collection, "Jesus Christ's Half-Brother is Alive and Well on the Spokane Indian Reservation," James, a baby, is thrown from the window of a burning home, and the narrator *breaks* his fall, but doesn't catch him. This metaphor of not-quite-catching James, but trying to save him repeatedly, becomes a story about building family and salvation despite loss through love.

One of the consistent themes in Alexie's work is cultural hybridity. In poems and through characters, in his early writing years Alexie wrestled with what it meant to be American Indian in the late-twentieth and early twenty-first century, sometimes criticizing the cultural values espoused by the work of his contemporaries. His writing often plays with historical and political representations of Indigenous people in the media, and initially, whether or not his work ultimately reinforced these stereotypes or disrupted them was a subject of vigorous critical debate. In early interviews, Alexie claimed that he wanted to be different from what he derisively called the "corn pollen and eagle feather school" of writing (Bellante and Bellante 1994, p. 15) and he asserted that many of his fellow American Indian artists wrote not about who they are as Indigenous peoples, but about "the kind of Indian they wish they were" (Purdy 1997, p. 10). This ambivalence, marked by a tension between the individual and the community, between tradition and modernization, inflects *Reservation Blues* (1995), many of his short stories, *Smoke Signals*, and the film version of *The Business of Fancydancing* (2002).

Playing with popular culture and American history, *Reservation Blues* begins when Thomas Builds-the-Fire offers a ride to the blues iconoclast Robert Johnson, who leaves behind his legendary guitar endowed with sinister power by the "gentleman at the crossroads." The guitar leads Thomas to begin a rock band that becomes Coyote Springs. In typical style, Alexie explodes stereotypes and expectations, since New Age hippies attending Coyote Springs concerts hope to "hear some ancient Indian wisdom" but get "a good dose of Sex Pistols covers instead" (1995, p. 41). As Coyote Springs tours and gets into trouble, plagued by liquor and white female roadies, Calvary Records sends them an invitation to audition for a recording contract. The entire novel takes place on a parody of a reservation – with a "man who was probably Lakota" because every reservation needs at least one Sioux – which in the end is abandoned for city life.

Alexie's next novel, *Indian Killer* (1996), once again plays with tropes of Indianness, and takes on the serious issue of how Indigenous identities are drowned in the ideology and media of the empire, what James Cox labels "white noise" (Cox 2006). In the novel, a brutal serial killer stalks the streets of Seattle, scalping and murdering white men. The prime suspect for the murders is John Smith, an American Indian man adopted and raised by white parents who begins to fall into madness, in part because his identity is unstable. The novel is disturbing, dark, gothic, unresolved. In a compelling twist on authenticity, one of the characters in *Indian Killer* is a faux-Indigenous white mystery author who is outed by an American Indian activist. A few years later, Alexie identified a faux-native writer, the self-named "Nasdijj" (aka Tim Barrus), who had published a highly-praised "memoir" claiming to be Diné. In 2006, Alexie published "When the Story Stolen is Your Own" in *Time Magazine* after an investigation unveiled the masquerade.

When Alexie publishes his next short story collection – *The Toughest Indian in the World* in 2000 – he seemingly no longer needs to prove cultural authenticity. In this collection, his characters have left the reservation; they are urban, professionals – journalists, lawyers, writers. Their struggles with identity are not internal but are caused by having to confront stereotypes. In "Assimilation," the main character wishes that tribal identification, Coeur d'Alene, was merely a "description" not an "excuse, reason, prescription, placebo, prediction, or diminutive" (2000, p. 2). In "Dear John Wayne," an old lady hijacks a conversation with an anthropologist who wants to learn about her tribe; instead, she tells him about a love affair she had with John Wayne on the set of *The Searchers* (1956). *Toughest Indian in the World* is most known for its titular story where a journalist picks up a hitchhiker and spends the night with him in a consensual sexual encounter between two men. The piece sparked conversation, but it is not the first story Alexie has written with queer characters. In his earliest short story collection *Lone Ranger*, Alexie writes in "Somebody Kept Saying Powwow" that "Years ago, homosexuals were given special status within the tribe [. . .] even though our tribe has assimilated into homophobia" (1993, p. 203). In typical Alexie style, the stories in *Toughest Indian* are touching, scathing, and funny, but "The Sin Eaters," a story about boarding schools and forced breeding programs, is a horror story, skewering a cannibalistic capitalism that has consumed Indigenous bodies in various ways since the age of Empire. In the story, although the exploitation of Indigenous bodies is met with large-scale protests that transcend race and class divisions, the entire process happens anyway, like a racist perpetual motion machine.

Released just three short years after *The Toughest Indian in the World*, *Ten Little Indians* (2003) continues Alexie's exploration of urban American Indian people as they struggle to create lives in a world that refuses to see them as anything other than icons of the past. The most famous story in the collection, "What You Pawn, I Will Redeem," first appeared in *The New Yorker*; in the story, Jackson, a homeless man, happens upon a pawn shop where he discovers the dance regalia of his grandmother, stolen years before. He proves it was his grandmothers' and the pawn shop owner gives him twenty-four hours to earn the money to purchase it back. The story follows him hour by hour as he tries desperately to earn the money. Having failed, he returns to the shop without the money, but the shop owner gives it to him anyway, and he puts it on. "I wrapped myself in my grandmother's regalia and breathed her in" (2003, p. 194). In "The Search Engine," Corliss begs, borrows, and steals an education, sometimes trading on the romantic stereotypes of her people to get ahead, when she discovers a book of poems written by a member of her tribe. As if responding to the American Indian writing community's early concerns about Alexie's work, the tracked-down writer admits, "no matter what I wrote, a bunch of other Indians will hate it because it isn't Indian enough, and a bunch of white people will like it because it is Indian" (p. 41).

After these two short story collections – and a poetry collection released in between, *One Stick Song* in 2000 – Alexie returns to novels. *Flight* (2007) and *Absolutely True Diary of a Part-Time Indian* are both Young Adult Literature. Narrated by a 15-year-old, time-traveling, often homeless boy called Zits, *Flight* is about reckoning with the past in order to find oneself – a challenge for anyone, let alone a teenage boy without a family. Zits travels through multiple time periods and inhabits multiple bodies, literally "walking in other people's shoes," until he arrives back in the present, decides to make different choices, and ultimately lives with the brother of a police officer who has repeatedly detained him in the past. The narrators in both *Flight* and *Absolutely True Diary* must make difficult decisions that will shape them as adults. These texts meditate on how to navigate a system built on racism and inequality, and how destructive anger can become. *Absolutely True Diary* won the National Book Award for Young People's Literature (later rescinded) and has been widely taught in classrooms throughout the United States.

Mixed-genre and experimental, *War Dances* (2009) is mature and masterful and won the PEN/Faulkner Award for Fiction. In the powerfully biographical titular stories, Alexie writes about being diagnosed with meningioma, worrying that his childhood health problems have come back to claim him, and explores his family history as it leads to his own two sons. Broken into segments, the most touching piece in "War Dances" is "Blankets," an exemplar of Alexie's particular iconic style: as his father recovers from the loss of his foot due to diabetes, Alexie roams the hospital looking for blankets to keep his father warm and happens upon another Indigenous family in the hospital celebrating a birth. Knowing that blankets are often given within Indigenous communities as gifts, Alexie approaches the family, writing jokingly about the family's "new Indian tradition" to bless the baby. "The Indian world is filled with charlatans, men and women who pretended – hell, who might have come to believe – that they were holy," Alexie writes (2009, p. 36). The family gives him a blanket and sings a healing song, despite his protests, and when he returns to his father and places the blanket around him, "he pulled the thick wool up to chin. And then he began to sing" (p. 40). Alexie, the dutiful son, joins him. *War Dances* as a collection also explores the capriciousness of power and those who wield it, like in "The Senator's Son," and in "Breaking and Entering." It is his most recent, completely new collection of short stories, followed by *Blasphemy* in 2013, which combines previous stories with 16 new, short pieces.

In 2017, Alexie released a memoir about his mother, *You Don't Have to Say You Love Me*, which quickly became a bestseller. Promoting the book, Alexie commented that the memoir was difficult to write, part "eulogy" and part "self-portrait," and the strain of reading it to audiences on a regular basis began to take a toll; in the midst of a book tour, Alexie cancelled the rest of his appearances, writing, "I have been rebreaking my heart night after night" (Alexie n.d.).

Shortly after, in 2018 during the rise of the #MeToo movement, Alexie was accused by several women of sexually predatory acts; ten women went on record with National Public Radio (NPR) about his behavior, not without considerable risk to their personal lives and their careers. The majority of these women – many Indigenous – were young at the time and seeking professional mentorship from Alexie, who, they say, promised to read their work and help their careers. In response to the accusations, Alexie released a statement admitting that he "has harmed" others and that he "is sorry," though he has "no recollection of physically or verbally threatening anybody or their careers" (Alexie n.d.). Afterward, he declined the 2018 Carnegie Medal from the American Library Association for his memoir and the American Indian Literary Association rescinded their award for best Young Adult novel. As a result, many scholars, teachers, and critics are debating whether or not to teach his work in college and high school classrooms. What are the ethics of teaching brilliant work by writers who have done terrible things? Alexie's ultimate legacy as a writer is, at this time, in question.

SEE ALSO: Díaz, Junot; Erdrich, Louise; Everett, Percival; Hogan, Linda; Jones, Stephen Graham; Momaday, N. Scott; Vizenor, Gerald; Welch, James

REFERENCES

Alexie, Sherman. (n.d.). fallsapart.com (accessed July 23, 2021).
Bellante, John and Bellante, Carl. (1994). Sherman Alexie, literary rebel. *Bloomsbury Review* 14 (1994): 14–15, 26.
Cox, James H. (2006). *Muting White Noise: Native American and European American Novel Traditions*. Norman: University of Oklahoma Press.
Purdy, John. (1997). Crossroads: a conversation with Sherman Alexie. *SAIL* 9 (4): 2–19.

FURTHER READING

Bird, Gloria. (1995). The exaggeration of despair in Sherman Alexie's *Reservation Blues*. *Wičazo Ša Review* 11 (2): 47–52.
Lincoln, Kenneth. (1993). *Indi'n Humor: Bicultural Play in Native America*. New York: Oxford University Press.
Lincoln, Kenneth. (2007). *Speak Like Singing: Classics of Native American Literature*. Albuquerque: University of New Mexico Press.
Moore, David L. (2005). Sherman Alexie: irony, intimacy, and agency. *The Cambridge Companion to Native American Literature* (ed. Joy Porter and Kenneth M. Roemer), 297–310. New York: Cambridge University Press.

Owens, Louis. (1998). *Mixedblood Messages: Literature, Film, Family, Place*. Norman: University of Oklahoma Press.

Allende, Isabel

LINDA GOULD LEVINE
Montclair State University, USA

In 2018, Isabel Allende was the first Spanish-language author to receive the National Book Foundation Lifetime Achievement Award for Distinguished Contribution to American Letters. This award, which cited Allende's "expertly crafted and propulsive narratives" that "elevate the stories and lives of women," represents an important expansion of the category of American fiction. Allende's twenty-four works, including novels, memoirs, short stories, essays, and young adult fiction, have been translated into forty-two languages and have sold 70 million copies, a testimony to her success as a storyteller who crosses cultural divides. Her books invite readers on journeys to different parts of the world and are marked by feminist sensitivity, commitment to social justice, blurring of boundaries, memory, loss, sensuality, creativity, and love.

Allende's narrative style is agile, humorous, and lyrical. It fuses penetrating psychological portrayals with journalistic and sociological accounts. Historical characters coexist with fictional ones, erasing the line between fact and invention. Examples of magical realism appear throughout her fiction, inspired by Nobel Prize Laureate Gabriel García Márquez and her own belief in the power of the spirit and the transcendence of rational thought. While her novels reveal that history follows an unbridled cycle of violence, Allende is a fervent believer in love as an antidote against hate and in breaking down divides among nations and individuals. Above all, she demonstrates a masterful ability to create works that are politically relevant and emotionally satisfying, while providing much needed hope in a world spiraling out of control. Her extensive body of fiction invites comparisons with Amy Tan, Maxine Hong Kingston, Toni Morrison, and Lisa See.

Allende's works mirror the multiple paths their author has taken. Born in Peru in 1942, she has lived in several countries and since 1988 has made the United States her home. Her father, a Chilean diplomat who disappeared from her life when she was three years old, was first cousin to Salvador Allende, whom Isabel considered an uncle. She spent her childhood in her grandparents' home in Santiago, Chile.

During her adolescence, Allende lived in Bolivia and Lebanon with her mother and stepfather, a Chilean diplomat. Her return to Chile in 1958 and early adulthood – including her graduation from high school, career in journalism and television, marriage to engineer Miguel Frías, and the birth of her first child – are told with great humor in her first memoir, *Paula* (1994). As a magazine and television celebrity in the early 1970s, Allende satirically railed against machismo in her first published work of nonfiction, *Civilize Your Troglodyte* (1974).

The election of socialist Salvador Allende as president of Chile in 1970, followed by the United States-backed military coup on September 11, 1973 – which led to the rise of dictator Augusto Pinochet – marked a dramatic change in the lives of thousands of Chileans. Isabel Allende joined the underground opposition, eventually putting herself and her family in substantial danger. After receiving death threats, Allende left Chile in 1975 and settled in Venezuela with her husband and children, Nicolás and Paula. On January 8, 1981, a date which would form part of the Allende lore, she began a farewell letter to her 99-year-old grandfather who lay dying in Chile. Fueled by nostalgia, this letter became her debut novel, *The House of the Spirits*, published in Spain in 1982.

The House of the Spirits is a gripping saga of the Trueba-del Valle family, from the 1920s to 1974, in an unidentified country that is clearly the author's homeland. Allende structures her novel around four female characters and their relationship to Esteban Trueba, the family patriarch and conservative landowner whose rape of his servant Pancha García marks his family history. Nívea, Clara, Blanca, and Alba, Trueba's respective mother-in-law, wife, daughter, and granddaughter, are strong women whose names suggest luminosity and whose actions represent different forms of resistance to patriarchal and military power. A fusion of opposites characterizes the novel in its blending of the magical and the real, fiction and history, past and present. As the magical occurrences which characterize the early chapters of the work give way to harsh realism associated with a military coup, Allende recreates the terror of the Pinochet dictatorship. Alba's activism in the underground opposition leads to her rape and torture by Colonel García, Trueba's vengeful illegitimate grandson. Upon her release from jail, achieved through her grandfather's connections, Alba uses her grandmother Clara's journals and other documents, as well as her own experiences, as a means of understanding her family's history and her country's plight. While pregnant with a child that may be her lover's or her torturer's, Alba gestates both powerful words and new life, fusing conventional male and female spheres. By explicitly rejecting a prolongation of hatred, she expresses Allende's belief in the need to dismantle her country's cycle of violence.

Critical response to *The House of the Spirits* was as diverse and complex as its narrative world. Among Allende's novels, it remains the most commented on by academics and writers. While some critics labeled it an imitation of García Márquez's *One Hundred Years of Solitude* (1967), others were quick to point out differences: García Márquez's concept of magical realism – the expansion of reality to include the magical and unforeseen – together with the novel's pessimistic ending and implied narrator in a room of "his own," are replaced in Allende's novel by a feminist spirit and sense of hope. Critics on the right denied the political reality Allende presented; those on the left questioned her attempt to break the cycle of vengeance through Alba's ultimate act of forgiveness. Smuggled into Chile in diaper bags during the Pinochet regime, the novel is a singular achievement in the recording of Chilean history. It also marks the beginning of Allende's international success and provides a roadmap of the themes, techniques, and vision that define her writing. Allende's second novel, *Of Love and Shadows* (1984), is similarly located in Chile and concentrates on the discovery of a mine in Lonquén, where the military dictatorship buried the bodies of assassinated *campesinos*.

The sustained focus on Chilean history present in many of Allende's novels is notably absent from her third, *Eva Luna* (1987). Written in the mode of a female *Bildungsroman* tinged with picaresque, metafictional, and postmodern aspects, it features, as in *The House of the Spirits*, a strong woman as both narrator and historical participant. It is also a celebration of storytelling and the power of the word, and highlights the theme of *mestizaje*. The concept of a *mestizo* heritage, which will reappear in Allende's recreation of the Indian and European roots of the legendary hero Zorro in her 2005 novel of the same name, is an apt metaphor for the blending of lives which shapes this novel and Allende's fiction in general.

Eva Luna, who lives in a country that resembles one of Allende's adopted homelands, Venezuela, is the offspring of a European mother and a father of the Luna tribe. Orphaned at six, she becomes, like Allende herself, a Latin American Scheherazade, in this case the writer of an autobiographical *telenovela* called *Bolero*. The novel is narrated by both Eva and Rolf Carlé, an Austrian immigrant and photographer fleeing the horror of World War II and his father's ignominious role in it. It follows Eva and Rolf from the 1940s through the late 1960s, their passionate romance, and their relationship to the guerrilla movement that shakes Venezuela. A colorful cast of characters assists Eva in her evolution from servant to writer, among them the Turkish merchant Riad Halabí, who gives Eva gifts essential to Allende's female characters: literacy, a love of words, and sensuality.

Following the publication of *Eva Luna*, and her divorce from Miguel Frías, the experience of moving to a new country marked another stage in Allende's writing career. While on a book tour in the United States in 1987, Allende fell in love with San Francisco attorney William Gordon. A long-distance courtship evolved, and Allende, with characteristic resolve and adventure, uprooted her life and moved to California. While adjusting to a new domestic reality, she wrote *The Stories of Eva Luna* (1989), a companion text to her previous novel.

Allende's move to the United States and her marriage to Gordon provided her with fertile material for a major shift in her narrative focus, which subsequently includes North and South America. Her fourth novel, *The Infinite Plan* (1991), is situated primarily in California. Divided in four parts, this ambitious *Bildungsroman* is set against the backdrop of critical moments of social unrest, including the cultural revolution in Berkeley in the 1960s and the Vietnam War. It recreates in great measure the life of Gordon himself, told through first- and third-person narration. This novel represents Allende's foray into a terrain occupied by the greats of American fiction: the American dream. It also captures, in the spirit of Chicana feminist Gloria Anzaldúa, the borderland of an east Los Angeles barrio. The novel's protagonist, Gregory Reeves, spends his childhood there and experiences the cultural clashes, gang warfare, and so-called reverse racism that mark his life as a gringo.

Allende develops Reeves's inner transformation as he studies in Berkeley, discovers a sense of peace in a remote Vietnam village, abandons his quest for wealth and obsession with conventional manhood, and finds meaning in his small law firm devoted to the disenfranchised. She also critiques patriarchal norms through Reeves's childhood friend, Carmen Morales, whose odyssey similarly evokes Anzaldúa as she traverses multiple borders to fashion her identity.

In 1991, Allende's promotional tour in Madrid for *The Infinite Plan* coincided with the hospitalization of her daughter, Paula. Previously diagnosed with the hereditary disease porphyria, she fell ill and went into a coma from which she never emerged. Allende's attempt to save her daughter's life, as well as give her a testimony of her 28-year-old existence, is recorded in her moving memoir, *Paula*. If Allende's previous works are characterized by the blending of different spheres, nowhere are the boundaries more tenuous than in this work, which unites life and death, the personal and the political, humor and grief, the author's desire to save her daughter and her acceptance of the need to let go. Ensconced in the tradition of Latin American autobiography, which blends personal and collective memory, the narrative sweep of *Paula* includes the life of its protagonist, her family, and Chilean history.

In *Paula*, as in *The House of the Spirits*, Allende describes the military coup of 1973 and situates her family in the midst of the reign of terror that led to their exile in Venezuela. She creates, with strands of words and memory, a portrait of her country, of the grace and intelligence of her first-born child, and of her own life. Closing with the words "Farewell Paula woman, welcome Paula spirit," Allende offers her readers a glimpse of the power of the spirit that survives beyond death. An international bestseller, *Paula* initiates a dialogue with her daughter that Allende continues in her later memoir, *The Sum of Our Days* (2007).

Three years passed after Paula's death before Allende published *Aphrodite: A Memoir of the Senses* (1997), which celebrates the pleasures of living, eating, and sensuality. The process of writing it fueled Allende's return to fiction and led to her fifth novel, *Daughter of Fortune* (1999), an Oprah Book Club selection and *New York Times* bestseller. In this work, she turns again to Chile and California, together with a new geographical space: China. Situated primarily in 1843–1853 during the turbulent time of the California gold rush, when discrimination against Chinese and Mexicans abounds and women are scarce, *Daughter of Fortune* features two protagonists from different worlds who meet under inauspicious circumstances. Eliza Sommers is an orphan brought up in an upper-class British household in Chile; Tao Chi'en is Fourth Son to an impoverished family in China. They come together as they journey to California, Eliza, a pregnant stowaway who miscarries during the voyage, and Tao Chi'en, the ship's cook who uses his Eastern healing skills to save her.

Each character discards firmly engrained prejudices about gender identity and tradition. Eliza dresses like a man while searching for her Chilean lover, and Tao Chi'en learns English and dons a suit and short hair while studying Western medicine. Allende thus offers a new version of gender and cultural hybridity in the American West. As in previous novels, she places her protagonists in the midst of compelling historical events, including their efforts to rescue the "Singsong Girls" from San Francisco's Chinatown brothels.

While the search for freedom fuels *Daughter of Fortune*, memory, a constant in Allende's writings, inspires her sixth novel, *Portrait in Sepia* (2000). A complex work that unites *Daughter of Fortune* and *The House of the Spirits*, its action unfolds in California and Chile. Its three-part structure completes the story of Eliza and Tao Chi'en, who marry in a Buddhist ceremony and raise their children in San Francisco's Chinatown, each negotiating the contours and strictures of American reality. It also captures the beginning of the Nívea and Severo del Valle lineage and introduces, as protagonist, Aurora del Valle, Eliza and Tao Chi'en's granddaughter.

Allende unites characters from her previous novels in an intriguing story that occupies the first part of the novel. Aurora's mother, Lynn Sommers, dies in childbirth, after having been abandoned by the child's father, Matías del Valle, and saved from dishonor through her marriage to Matías's cousin, Severo. Upon the outbreak of the Pacific War, Severo returns to Chile, leaving Aurora with her maternal grandparents, Eliza and Tao Chi'en, who call her by her Chinese name, Lai Ming. Following Tao Chi'en's death, when Lai Ming is five years old, Eliza takes her husband's body to China and asks Lai Ming's paternal grandmother, Paulina del Valle, to raise her. Paulina takes Lai Ming to Chile and erases all traces of her previous existence, including her Chinese name. Aurora traverses multiple cultural, linguistic, and geographical spaces as she searches for images of her past. A gifted photographer, she uses her camera to immortalize tumultuous moments of Chilean history, including the massacre of Chilean workers in 1907. The personal and the communal, fiction and history, reflection and writing – all constants in Allende fiction – are artfully woven together in Aurora's life. *Portrait in Sepia* testifies to Allende's celebration of hybrid identities as Aurora embraces her Chilean, Chinese, and British heritage.

The presence of Chile in Allende's fiction reappears in a different form in Allende's 2004 memoir, *My Invented Country*, a work which resounds with her debt to Chilean Nobel Prizewinning poet Pablo Neruda. This textured memoir not only offers additional insights into the author's life but is also an important link to her eighth novel, *Inés of My Soul* (2006). In this book, Allende gives life to an historical figure frequently erased from accounts of the founding of Chile. Inés Suárez, from Plasencia, Spain, occupies center stage and defines herself – together with her lover and companion Pedro de Valdivia – as conqueror and founder of the kingdom of Chile in 1537. Crisscrossing continents and gender norms as she searches for her Spanish husband in the New World, Inés assimilates male codes of violence. She dresses in full armor, fights like a conqueror, saves fellow Spaniards, and decapitates members of the formidable Mapuche enemy. She writes herself out of anonymity through such deeds while also inscribing in her chronicle the traditionally female talents which contribute to her legacy. Allende gives her character ample space to describe her admiration for Indigenous healers and for the Mapuche, whose language and culture she assimilates. Through this nuanced portrayal built on extensive research, Allende interrogates the relationship between the female conqueror and the male vanquished and writes a compelling addition to the life of Inés Suárez.

Allende's interest in crucial moments of national history leads to her recreation of the founding of Haiti in her ninth novel, *Island Beneath the Sea* (2010). A sweeping historical narrative, it traverses the multiple boundaries that separate Haiti, Cuba, and the United States, as well as those that separate races, the enslaved, and the free. The first-person narration of the colonizer Inés Suárez gives way to the first-person account of the colonized subject, the mixed-race slave Zarité. Zarité's rape by her French master, Toulouse Valmorain, cannot help but evoke the rape of Pancha García by Esteban Trueba in *The House of the Spirits*. Ideology, romance, and the union of different spheres, basic components of Allende's fiction, reappear here. As in *The House of the Spirits*, Allende explores the consequences of rape through the story of the tragic love affair of Valmorain's offspring: the "quadroon" Rosette, born from his rape of Zarité, and Maurice, his legal heir born of a Spanish wife. Allende's third-person narration captures the struggle for freedom by people of color in Louisiana and Saint-Domingue and the founding of the Black Republic of Haiti in 1803. Parallels between African voodoo rites and Christianity, and between African healing rituals and Western medicine, provide another variation of Allende's vision of an inclusive cultural space where hierarchies of dominance disappear.

Allende again pays tribute to those who seek freedom in her thirteenth novel, *In the Midst of Winter* (2017). She unites three characters from different worlds who meet by accident. Lucía Moraz is a resourceful visiting professor of Latin American Studies in New York who, like Allende, was exiled from Chile to Venezuela following the 1973 coup. Richard Bowmaster is the scholarly and neurotic chairperson of the Latin American Studies Department, who is scarred from the suicide of his Brazilian wife and tragic death of his two children. Evelyn Ortega is an undocumented immigrant traumatized by violence in Guatemala and rape by the criminal gang MS-13. Allende brings these characters together during the New York snowstorm of 2015 in what is perhaps the most improbable narrative scenario in her writings – the need to dispose of a dead body in Evelyn's borrowed car. In the process of finding a burial place, they reveal complex psychological and political demons and unite in solidarity and love. Allende's sensitive rendition of the experience of an undocumented immigrant is given broader meaning in the novel's final chapter. A US citizen since 2003, she critiques the xenophobia unleashed against Latinx by Donald Trump's 2016 presidential campaign.

Allende's fourteenth novel, *A Long Petal in the Sea* (2019), revisits the theme of exile and the Chilean military coup. An historical novel that spans fifty-five years (1936–1991), it pays homage to Chilean poet Pablo Neruda, whose verses appear throughout and who contracted the boat that transported refugees of the Spanish Civil War from southern France to Chile – a "long petal in the sea" – in 1939. Set against the backdrop of two major events of the twentieth century, this compelling novel traverses continents and political upheavals.

Allende's desire to create literature that addresses her concern for the environment and regard for non-Western cultures extends to young adults in her trilogy *City of the Beasts* (2002), *Kingdom of the Golden Dragon* (2003), and *Forest of the Pygmies* (2004). Allende has also created The Isabel Allende Foundation to honor the life of her daughter Paula. Its mission is to provide help for women and girls, especially in Chile and California.

Allende has received over thirty international awards, many marking her inclusion in the canon of American writers. Most notable are the Presidential Medal of Freedom (2014) and the Chilean National Prize for Literature (2010). Allende's acceptance speech at the National Book Awards ceremony in 2018 characterized the current era as "a time of nationalism and racism, of cruelty and fanaticism," but added a very Allendian note of hope: "I believe in the power of stories. If we listen to another person's story, if we tell our own story, we start to heal from division and hatred. Because we realize that the similarities that bring us together are many more than the differences that separate us."

SEE ALSO: Border Fictions; Debut Novels; Indigenous Narratives; Kingston, Maxine Hong; Literature of the Americas; Mixed-Genre Fiction; Morrison, Toni; Tan, Amy; Young Adult Boom

FURTHER READING

Cox, Karen Castellucci. (2003). *Isabel Allende: A Critical Companion*. Westport, CT: Greenwood Press.
Craig, Bonnie M. (2013). *Rewriting American Identity in the Fiction and Memoirs of Isabel Allende*. New York: Palgrave Macmillan.
Levine, Linda Gould. (2002). *Isabel Allende*. New York: Twayne.
Rodden, John. (ed.) (2011). *Critical Insights: Isabel Allende*. Pasadena, CA, and Hackensack, NJ: Salem Press.
Snodgrass, Mary Ellen. (2013). *Isabel Allende: A Literary Companion*. Jefferson, NC: MacFarland & Co.

Allison, Dorothy

MICHELE MEEK
Bridgewater State University, USA

Dorothy Allison's poetic yet brutally frank writing depicts Southern poverty, childhood sexual abuse, and lesbian desire. Perhaps best known for her National Book Award nominated and best-selling semi-autobiographical novel *Bastard Out of Carolina* (1992), Allison's writing has spanned poetry in *The Women Who Hate Me* (1983), nonfiction essays in *Skin: Talking About Sex, Class and Literature* (1994), memoir in *Two or Three Things I Know For Sure* (1995), and, of course, fiction through her short stories in *Trash* (1988) and novels – *Bastard Out of Carolina* and *Cavedweller* (1998) – both of which have been adapted into films, directed by Anjelica Huston and Lisa Cholodenko, respectively.

Born in 1949 in Greenville, South Carolina, Allison describes the defining aspect of her life as the shame of being born into poverty by an unwed teenage mother who had quit the seventh grade to be a waitress. She often details the indignity that her family faced by not fitting the definition of the "good" poor and being judged as the undeserving and irredeemable "white trash" who steal, do drugs, get into fights, drop out of school, and wind up in jail – or dead.

Allison's stepfather raped her from the time she was five years old – a secret that compounded her shame and rage growing up. At age 11, Allison confided in her cousin about the abuse. Allison's mother, the only one who believed her, vowed that the sexual abuse would stop, although both his sexual and physical abuse continued for years afterwards, until her teen years when she found ways to avoid him. At age 16, Allison attempted suicide and her mother promised to help her make her way out of their surroundings, although she had little actual means to do so. It was when her mother, stepfather, sisters, and she moved to Florida that Allison began to reimagine herself beyond the confines of her upbringing. She obtained a National Merit Scholarship to Florida Presbyterian College (now called Eckerd College) in 1967, left home, and earned her BA in 1971. She was not only the first member of her family to graduate college; she was the first to graduate high school.

Allison's early career combined odd jobs and non-profit work. Not long after college, she took a job at the Social Security Administration in Tallahassee. On her second day in the city, she wandered into the Women's Center to attend what she thought was a meeting for their magazine. Instead, she found herself part of a consciousness-raising group. Allison describes her epiphany when a well-dressed heterosexual woman opened up about being sexually assaulted by her father and wanting to murder him – Allison was shocked that the experiences of a middle- to upper-class heterosexual woman could resonate so strongly with her, and she had never witnessed someone express so openly such feelings. She took to feminism with what she calls a religious fervor; as she puts it, the women's movement saved her. The exposures, discoveries, and connections it unveiled helped her find a way to talk about – and ultimately write about – the traumas that she had experienced growing up. In her twenties, Allison learned that she had contracted gonorrhoea from her stepfather, which, untreated, left her unable to have children – a fact that later inspired her short story "Don't Tell Me You Don't Know." Before long, she was running the Women's Center and working as editor of its publication *Amazing Grace, A Feminist Magazine* (1973–1974), where she published her first poems, although her writing at that time mostly took the form of articles.

After a brief stint in Washington, DC, working as editor of the political theory magazine, *Quest: A Feminist Quarterly*, Allison moved to New York to attend the New School for Social Research for a master's in anthropology. She initially pursued more academic and journalistic forms of publications, keeping her persistent desire to write poems and stories mostly private. Her career as a storyteller had actually started long before as a young girl who invented violent and partially true tales for the audience of her sisters and cousins. But even when she began writing down her stories, she ritually burned them every year until the age of 24 when a woman in her collective interrupted her ritual and persuaded her to wait. Her obstacle, as she describes it, was feeling discouraged by the typical middle-class white male writer who seemed to be getting published – and with whom she felt she had little in common. She simply could not imagine how her terrifyingly dark stories would find a place in their world.

Through the process of writing and rewriting, Allison reshaped her experiences and those she witnessed into her first short stories and essays, which were published in the early to mid-1980s in feminist and lesbian journals, such as *New York Native* and *Conditions Magazine*, where she also worked as an editor. Many of these early writings have since been compiled into her book *Skin: Talking About Sex, Class and Literature*. She often details how the initial blunt meanness of her stories in drafts became more nuanced with compassion through revision. Allison's stories capture the complex undercurrents of love and resentment beneath the surface of family relationships, and a defining characteristic of her writing remains her portrayal of the choices people make out of desperation, disillusionment, hope, and love.

Because of her matter-of-factness about the way sexual desire emerges despite and amidst sexual abuse and her explicitness about butch/femme lesbian sexuality, Allison has had a fraught history with certain factions of the feminist movement. In 1982, Allison was invited to speak on a panel "Politically Correct, Politically Incorrect Sexuality" at the Barnard Conference on Sexuality. Conference organizers, including Jane Gould, Carole Vance, Gayle Rubin, and others, positioned the event to investigate the complexities of sexual pleasure and danger. However, the conference evoked a significant backlash – not from a conservative standpoint, but a feminist one. Radical feminists from the Women Against Pornography group, including Susan Brownmiller and Andrea Dworkin, contended that they had been omitted from the conference, which they had been since conference organizers sought to move beyond an anti-pornography stance. The detractors lambasted and picketed the conference; called the president of the college to complain; and denounced participants, including Allison, as "antifeminist terrorists." They accused panelists of justifying female sexual exploitation and child molestation – an ironic claim, considering Allison has always been a strong advocate against both. Nevertheless, Allison's acknowledgement that children too experience sexual awareness, desire, and pleasure made her a target. The college shrunk from its support, confiscating over a thousand copies of the conference publication "Diary of a Conference on Sexuality." The considerable controversy around the conference ultimately marked the clear division between "pro-sex" and "anti-porn" feminists. Allison's response took the form of a series of poems later published in her book *The Women Who Hate Me* in 1983 by Long Haul Press, and adapted to the chapbook, *The Women Who Hate Me: Poetry 1980–1990* published by Firebrand Books.

Throughout the 1980s, Allison published numerous essays and short stories, which became adapted and compiled in her book *Trash: Short Stories* in 1988 by Firebrand Books. Allison's writing has been compared with writers like William Faulkner, Flannery O'Connor, and Harper Lee, but Allison also found much inspiration in the writing of Toni Morrison, Audre Lorde, and James Baldwin. Characterized by a strong voice and raw depictions of sex, violence, and classism, Allison's stories dare to go where few writers have the courage to go. Her story "River of Names," for example, tells the story of a woman who invents stories from her childhood to share with her lover while experiencing nightmares from the actual violence that shaped her youth. The stories that the narrator holds inside her – much like Allison's – seem too cruel to share with her naïve lover raised by a university professor father and a mother who made her daughter's dresses. The protagonist's stories turn into demented jokes – "What's a South Carolina virgin?" "'At's a ten-year-old can run fast." But they're no jokes – the speaker tells us that her cousins and she were raped. Several of Allison's stories have been anthologized – such as "A Lesbian Appetite" in the *Penguin Book of Lesbian Short Stories* (1993) and *Women on Women: An Anthology of American Lesbian Fiction* (1990); "Her Thighs" in *The Persistent Desire: A Femme-Butch Reader* (1992); "Deciding to Live" in *Writing Women's Lives: An Anthology of Autobiographical Narratives by Twentieth-Century Women Writers* (1994); among others. *Trash* won two Lambda Literary Awards in 1989 for Best Lesbian Fiction and Best Small Press Book, as well as the American Library Association's Prize for Lesbian and Gay Writing. In 2002, she republished the collection with Plume with a new introduction and the addition of "Compassion," a story about three adult daughters who come together as their mother dies from cancer. "Compassion" was selected for the *Best American Short Stories 2003* and *Best New Stories from the South 2003*.

Two of Allison's stories – one for the anthology *High Risk: An Anthology of Forbidden Writings* (1991) and "A Bastard Out of Carolina" (1986) in the fiction section of the *Village Voice Literary Supplement* – became the inspiration and beginnings of her novel *Bastard Out of Carolina*. Afraid of having her work censored, Allison presented the most sexually explicit sections of the book to publishers when seeking a contract so there was no misunderstanding her work. After having worked on the story already for many years, she signed on with Dutton for a $37,000 advance, providing her the motivation to complete her novel in three more years. Her resulting tour de force, *Bastard Out of Carolina*, became a bestseller and garnered overwhelmingly positive reviews, propelling Allison far beyond the queer and feminist communities that had long admired her writing and speaking. The book became a finalist for the 1992 National Book Award, a *New York Times* Notable Book of the Year, a finalist for the Lillian Smith prize, a Ferro Grumley prize winner, and an American Library Association prize winner, and it has been published internationally in over a dozen languages.

Through the point of view of the young girl Bone, the novel depicts a girl who, like Allison, is born to an unwed woman in South Carolina and then physically and sexually abused by her stepfather. Highly autobiographical but nonetheless fiction, the book remakes Allison's childhood into a story in which the girl comes of age amidst abuse, finding both her strength and her sexuality within that abuse. Certainly, the novel speaks not only to lesbian women who have experienced abuse – in fact, Allison has found men and women of all ages and backgrounds who approach her at readings or write her to thank her for telling their story. Allison's storytelling pushes beyond the boundaries of other novels depicting incest. Here, we see how Bone's rage and sexual desire grow uncomfortably together as her masturbatory fantasies begin to shape how she imagines herself within and beyond her abuse. Her novel too addresses the particularly challenging relationship between mother and daughter – as much as Bone's mother seeks to protect her children, she finds herself unable to turn her back on their abuser. Through writing, Allison says that she enacts a kind of justice – which is perhaps one of the reasons her work has resonated with so many. As she puts it, "I wrote to release indignation and refuse humiliation, to admit fault and to glorify the people I loved who were never celebrated" (2002, p. xii). And yet, her work never offers pat happy endings – rather her stories and novels, including *Bastard Out of Carolina*, present the shreds of hope that linger after trauma.

Director Anjelica Huston adapted *Bastard Out of Carolina* into a film produced by TNT. Again, however, Allison's themes attracted controversy. In its adaptation, the film had already omitted some of the most sexually transgressive aspects of the novel – in particular how Bone's masturbatory fantasies incorporate her abuse. However, it did contain two scenes of sexual abuse – a scene when Bone's stepfather sexually molests her in their car and a violent rape scene. After seeing the film before its release, network executives insisted that Huston cut both scenes. Supported by Allison, Huston stood firm against censorship, which left the film in limbo for months while Ted Turner himself publicly expressed his disgust at the sexual violence of the film. Ultimately, the film was invited to screen at Cannes Film Festival and was acquired by Showtime, where it aired in 1996. Although many reviewers commented on the violence of the film, most recognized the bravery and brilliance of a film that so compelling told the disturbing story of Bone's coming-of-age.

Bastard Out of Carolina boosted Allison into more fame, if not fortune – in fact, Allison often talks openly about how difficult it is to make a living as a writer, even a renowned one. She followed up her novel with a memoir book of essays, *Two or Three Things I Know For Sure*, also published by Dutton in 1995. Although more squarely in the nonfiction genre, Allison still plays with the way memory and storytelling blur the line between the real and the imagined, and her essays read like free verse, poetically shaping the characters and moments throughout her life.

Allison published her second novel, *Cavedweller*, with Dutton in 1998. The book tells the story of Delia Byrd and her daughter Cissy who embark on a journey from Los Angeles to Georgia when Cissy's rock star father, Randall Pritchard, dies suddenly. Years earlier, Delia had abandoned her two daughters, Amanda and Dede, in Georgia to run off with Randall's band Mud Dog after her husband threated to kill her. Now, she urgently wants the girls back in her and Cissy's lives. The novel brims with bad choices and the redemption that follows, along with the children who come of age in the midst of it all. Still mourning the loss of her father, Cissy must contend with her new life in a new town with her two half-sisters, Amanda and Dede, and their own father who is dying from terminal cancer. A bestseller and a *New York Times* Notable Book, *Cavedweller* won the Lesbian General Fiction Lambda Award, an American Library Association Prize, and was a finalist for the Lillian Smith Prize. The novel was adapted to a 2003 stage play written by Kate Moira Ryan, directed by Michael Greif, and featuring music by composer Stephen Trask. Simultaneously, it was adapted into a film produced by Showtime Independent Films and directed by Lisa Cholodenko. Starring Kyra Sedgwick, Aidan Quinn, Kevin Bacon, and Regan Arnold, the film was praised by many critics for its subtle beauty and excellent performances. It premiered at Tribeca Film Festival, won the New American Cinema award at the Seattle International Film Festival, and brought Independent Spirit Award acting nominations for Sedgwick and Quinn.

Allison now lectures and performs at events across the world and is working on her third novel, *1972*. She served for over a decade as a member of the board of the Fellowship of Southern Writers and won the 2007 Robert Penn Warren Award for Fiction and the 2008 Emory University Center for Humanistic Inquiry's Distinguished Visiting Professor. Duke University houses drafts of her manuscripts, as well as personal journals, correspondence and other materials dated from 1965–2010 in a collection for research access. Allison currently resides in Northern California with her partner, Alix Layman, and their son.

SEE ALSO: Fiction and Affect; Morrison, Toni; Queer and LGBT Fiction; Trauma and Fiction; Walker, Alice

REFERENCE

Allison, Dorothy. (2002). Introduction: stubborn girls and mean stories. *Trash*, vii–xvi. New York: Plume.

FURTHER READING

Blouch, Christine and Laurie Vickroy. (eds.) (2004). *Critical Essays on the Works of American Author Dorothy Allison*. New York: Edwin Mellen Press.

Claxton, Mae Miller. (ed.) (2012). *Conversations with Dorothy Allison*. Jackson: University of Mississippi Press.

Dorothy Allison. (n.d.). https://www.dorothyallison.com

Dorothy Allison Papers, 1965–2010. (n.d.). David M. Rubenstein Rare Book & Manuscript Library, Duke University. https://library.duke.edu/rubenstein/findingaids/allisondorothy/

Álvarez, Julia

MARÍA GUADALUPE ARENILLAS
Northern Michigan University, USA

Dominican American writer Julia Álvarez (b. 1950) is the author of more than two dozen works of fiction, poetry, non-fiction, and children's and young adult fiction and is one of the best-known Latino/a voices of the twentieth and twenty-first centuries. She was born in New York City, moved with her parents to their native land, the Dominican Republic, soon after, and returned with her family to the United States in 1960. This geopolitical duality, and the fact that she writes in English, has infused Álvarez's work with a hybrid consciousness. In the earlier stages of her work, Álvarez's characters try to find their home and voices, while inhabiting two different places, but as her work evolves, she departs from this search for cultural and national identity, and the preoccupation with identity gives way to questions of how to live better with others and have fair intercultural encounters. In this sense, her long trajectory moves from the identity politics that characterized the 1990s to concerns about environmental issues, sustainability, neoliberalism, borders, privilege, and immigration laws.

Álvarez's first novel, *How the García Girls Lost Their Accents* (1991), is the tale of the García Torres family that, like her own, fled the Dominican Republic in the 1960s, after the father's involvement in a plot against the dictator General Rafael Leónidas Trujillo (1930–1961). Like many of her novels, the work is a blend of memoir, autobiography, and fiction. Divided in three parts that range from the present (adulthood in the United States) to the past (childhood in the Dominican Republic), *How the García Girls Lost Their Accents* has fifteen chapters that do not follow a lineal temporality and, at first sight, seem to have no more connection to each other besides recurring topics and characters. Despite the experimental format of the novel and the inclusion of different points of views, the main characters, Mami, Papi and the four García girls, to a certain extent, do conform to established expectations about immigrants' eccentricity, displacement, struggles with identity and family unity. Critics have seen the novel as a traditional "moving tale of a family that prevails throughout considerable traumas, remaining loyal and loving to one another [and doing] so in spite of being suddenly uprooted from everything that has been familiar and placed in a country where the language and culture are alien" (Sirias 2001, p. 19).

This more canonical position of an "ethnic literature" in part is due to the assimilationist politics of the 1960s. As Álvarez explains in "Rapunzel's Ladder, Social Justice Education: A Way Down from the Ivory Tower," "[t]hose were the early days of the Civil Rights Movement, pre-bilingual education, pre-everything but the old assimilationist model of immigration. From the start, my American education was not about adding to and, therefore, expanding my heritage or preserving my native language, but replacing it with something *better*" (2010, p. xvi). Thus, Álvarez's earlier work focuses on the tensions of assimilation in the heart of a traditional Catholic and patriarchal Dominican family and on the lessons, grief, and joy that trying to blend in, in a foreign culture, brings. At the center of the losses is Álvarez's insecurity with her mother tongue, a quite common tragic experience that results from the assimilationist model. The success of the novel with the US audience is in part due to its universal appeal as a coming-of-age story and its portrait of an immigrant family with conventional values. As Arlene Dávila points out, there is "a contemporary United States discourse that too often over-ethnicizes or de-ethnicizes Latinos/as 'whether by presenting them as a threat or as contributors to the national community'; by highlighting their growing purchasing power and intrinsic 'values'; or because of their coming of age or eagerness to assimilate" (quoted in Myers 2016, p. 177).

However, as Marion Rohrleitner states, Álvarez's later work, particularly the novel *¡Yo!* (1997), complicates expectations of "ethnic literature." In doing so, Álvarez "refuses to idealize the family" (2013, p. 45) and shows gender, class and racial conflicts as central to the immigrant families themselves as well as their own communities. At the same time, the constructed character of the "ethnic writer" as someone who speaks for a group is opposed to individuality, the "inherent difference often overlooked in a culture" and "the artifice of the literary work" (p. 51).

The expectations for the "ethnic writer" and Álvarez's interest in her own individuality are illustrated very clearly in a chapter of her autobiography entitled "Doña Aída, with Your Permission." Álvarez tells an anecdote that took place at the Caribbean Studies Association conference in Santo Domingo. There, Dominican writer Aída Cartagena Portalatín, a keynote speaker alongside Álvarez, after hugging her in front of the audience, announced "This is unbelievable, a Dominican writing in English. Come back to your country, come back to your language. You are Dominican" (2000, p. 821, my translation). Álvarez's ironic answer, "You are right, Doña Aída, I'm also not *una norteamericana*" (p. 822) demonstrates a transcendence of a definite national literary and cultural identity and emphasizes the different experiences amongst Latinos/as. At the same time, Álvarez discusses in her novels her peripheral position as a woman who doesn't have children, and as a creative writer who works in US academia.

Álvarez uses a contradictory polyphony in many of her works. She relies on collective storytelling as a path to justice necessarily linked to activism. *In the Time of the Butterflies* (1994) tells the story of the Mirabal sisters' fight against Trujillo and the ultimate assassination of three of them by a government death squad. The successful novel was selected as the National Endowment of the Arts Big Read, and was later adapted into a film mainly because it brings to light one of the darkest moments of Dominican history through the eyes of four beautiful young women that belonged to a well-to-do, tight-knight family. It is not a coincidence that Álvarez considers Scheherezade of the *Arabian Nights* a storyteller and activist ("The Scheherezade Project"). Scheherezade confronts a man, who exploits and kills young women, through narration in a similar way to how the Mirabal sisters, *las Mariposas* (the butterflies), confront Trujillo's infamous predatory ways, while journaling their experiences. Storytelling can also prove deadly during dictatorship; consequently the tensions between silence and the need to speak are also central in Álvarez's work as the title of her book of poems, *The Woman I Kept to Myself* (2004) suggests.

Struggles for justice and activism in the face of gender, racial, and class oppression are never without their own contradictions and idealism both in and outside texts. For Rosa Linda Fregoso, *In the Time of the Butterflies* "raises profound political questions about the position of the women in the family and the nation. At the micro-level, Álvarez uses images of an authoritarian father and Catholicism to question the twin pillars of women's oppression in provincial Dominican society" (2003, p. 10). As Lisa Blackmore explains, critics have suggested that *In the Time of the Butterflies* is a metafictional text that challenges monumental and patriarchal history by mixing intimate stories, oral tales, and national narratives (2015, p. 106). However, Blackmore affirms that in Álvarez's attempt to narrate Trujillo's era through a story that can "touch hearts," lies a simplistic dichotomy of "sacrifice-redemption" and "oppression-liberation," in which the "good Catholic girls" react against the figure of the tyrannical oppressor (p. 106). Blackmore asks about a literature that idealizes the sisters and turns their history into a monument of freedom. The metonymic association of the sisters with freedom risks erasing the nuances of postdictatorship in the Dominican Republic, where the decline of *trujillato* brought, in the next five years, a series of different governments, a *coup d'état* and a US military intervention (p. 104). The idealization of the Mirabal sisters and the consideration that they were the last straw that ended dictatorship erases, then, the continuity of oppression and of the historical racial struggles of a divided island.

In the essay "A White Woman of Color" (1998), Álvarez speaks of her experiences with racism and illustrates many of the conflicts that her fictional characters experience with racialization and the intersection of class and race. Álvarez explains how growing up in the Dominican Republic there was a "hierarchy of beauty in the family dictated by [their] coloring," hair, and physical features (1998, p. 57). The lighter the skin and the straighter the hair, the better. Her mother's side of the family was well-off and considered "whiter" than her paternal line, but in New York City, Álvarez and her sisters are the "spics" of the playground. Álvarez mentions Trujillo's obsession with whitening the Dominican Republic:

> The denial of the Afro-Dominican part of our culture reached its climax during the dictatorship of Trujillo, whose own maternal grandmother was Haitian. To protect Dominican race purity, Trujillo ordered the overnight slaughter of thousands [. . .]. He also had the Dominican Republic declared a white nation despite the evidence of the mulatto senators who were forced to pass this ridiculous measure.
>
> (1998, p. 56)

Here, Álvarez is referring to the event, known as *El Corte* or the Parsley Massacre, that took place in October 1937, when the border between Haiti and the Dominican Republic was the center of a genocide against the Haitian people. Trujillo, who, as Álvarez states, had always imagined a white nation related to Spain, ordered the massacre of an estimated 9000–20,000 Haitian people. Notwithstanding, even if she denounces racist practices in her family and the horrific killings of *El Corte*, Álvarez fails to examine the lasting extent of racial oppression and attributes it mostly to a matter of aesthetic:

> So, black was not so good, kinky hair was not so good, thick lips were not so good. But even if you were *indio oscuro con pelo malo y una bemba de aquá a Baní*, you could still sit in the front of the bus and order at the lunch counter – or the equivalent thereof. There was no segregation of races in the halls of power. But in the aesthetic arena – the ones to which we girls were relegated as females – lighter was better. Lank hair and pale skin and small fine features were better. All I had to do was stay out of the sun and behave myself, and I could pass as a pretty white girl.
>
> (1998, p. 56)

Álvarez explains that she and her family were not considered "real Dominicans" because their privilege, "background, education, and most especially [their] pale skin had made mobility easier" and so they did not have to "undergo the same kind of race struggles as other Dominicans" (1998, p. 58). The economic privilege of her family, which separates them from the rest, proves in the end what was denied before: the fundamental "segregation of races in the halls of power."

Additionally, in "A White Woman of Color," Álvarez comments on the influence of her maids in her understanding of race. They are "dark-skinned" women, "some of Haitian background" (1998, pp. 57–58). Álvarez remembers one of the maids, Misiá, who escaped the 1937 massacre and was taken and hidden by the writer's family. She took care of the children and told stories that "spread the wings of our imaginations and connected us deeply to the land we came from" (p. 58). Relegated to the role of caretakers and storytellers, the portrait of these Haitian maids is a bit unidimensional. Álvarez does not include a critique of the system that relegated them to these roles, but, rather, offers a formulaic fascination with their folkloric tales. The same happens with many of the Haitian characters of her novels. In *How the García Girls Lost Their Accents*, for instance, Chucha, the Haitian maid, has served the García family for more than thirty years, since she escaped the massacre. She is described as "super wrinkled" and "Haitian blue black" (1994, p. 218). "Chucha always had a voodoo job going, some spells she was casting or spirit she was courting or enemy she was punishing" (p. 219). The family that takes the maids in and provides work, even if well intended and loving, perpetuates racial and economic divisions.

In her most recent work, Álvarez has become more conscious of institutionalized racism and the continuation of not only Trujillo's racial policies but also the long history of racial struggles in the Caribbean. The racial tensions in Hispaniola and the status of Haitians in the Dominican Republic are at the center of her travelogue *A Wedding in Haiti, the Story of a Friendship* (2012). Here Álvarez recounts the story of her relationship with a young immigrant worker from Haiti, Piti, and her trips to Haiti, first to attend Piti's wedding and then to take his wife back for a visit in the aftermath of the 2010 earthquake. Piti and the writer met on one of her trips to the Dominican Republic. He was working on a farm there and later on was hired to work at Álvarez's coffee farm.

A Wedding in Haiti relates to the children's book *A Cafecito Story* (2002), a fable about the encounter between Joe, a Nebraskan teacher, and the Dominican Republic farmers he befriends while on the island and ends up growing coffee with. Fighting against foreign corporations and the devastating effects of their methods on the soil, the Nebraskan teacher and the Dominican farmers unite to start a cooperative. At the same time, Joe teaches them how to read and write. A love song to the land, sustainability, and education, *A Cafecito Story* is a hopeful tale of productive intercultural encounters. In the afterword, Bill Eichner, Álvarez's husband, states the similarities of the parable and the couple's own story. What started with them buying a plot of land in the Dominican Republic transformed into Alta Gracia Coffee Cooperative, a space with a broader concept of sustainability that includes education, a public library, and the promotion of workers' rights. As a children's book, however, *A Cafecito Story* does not address some of the complexities of intercultural encounters, for instance, the power inequality of the situation, as it is someone from the United States who can afford and own the land, or the challenges that many farmers still face to support their families on "fair trade" wages.

It is worth mentioning that *A Wedding in Haiti* came out a year before the Dominican Republic rulings of 2013 and that many of Álvarez's concerns in *A Wedding in Haiti* are present in her critiques of the court rulings. In 2013, the Dominican Tribunal Court revoked the citizenship of Dominicans born to undocumented Haitian parents after 1929. This expression of institutionalized racism affected around 200,000 Dominicans of Haitian descent, many of whom, having spent their lives in the Dominican Republic, did not have any ties to Haiti. With a group of Dominican intellectuals, among them Junot Díaz and the Haitian-American Edwidge Danticat, Álvarez denounced publicly the ruling as a continuation of "constant abuse, including the infamous Dominican massacre" (Kurlansky et al. 2013). Additionally, in *A Wedding in Haiti*, Álvarez notes the silence that prevails on the issues between Haiti and the Dominican Republic, "[a]lthough it doesn't get the attention of say, the Middle East, there is a troubled history between the two small countries occupying this island. [. . .] [C]onflicts persist, as undocumented Haitians cross over into their comparatively richer neighbor country, willing to do work Dominicans won't do, often underpaid and poorly treated, a situation not unlike Mexicans who come to El Norte in search of a better life" (2012, p. 2).

The travelogue provides interesting insights as Álvarez, her husband, and an eclectic group, make the first road trip to the wedding and then, later, take Eseline, Piti's homesick wife, and their daughter for a much-needed stay in Haiti. The border crossing, with its unstable and changing permits, visas, or lack thereof, speaks to economic disparities, corruption, and oppression. The trip to the wedding brings Álvarez closer to her Haitian friends by showing their lives on the other side of the island. Houses, families and the wedding itself are described in detail and with interest. In the second trip, which takes place in the aftermath of 2010 earthquake, Álvarez reflects on the ethics of witnessing, as a foreign traveler, the reverberation of a natural disaster. These reflections are linked to her encounters with Haitians living amidst the rubble and barely surviving, and with those who came to the island, sometimes to help, and at other times to take advantage of its ruinous state and to profit from disaster. Once again, Álvarez finds herself in an uncomfortable in-between place and starts to confront her own position and privilege. When somebody asks her why she is in Haiti, she is a bit ashamed to answer that she "came to see," but in the end, admits that to witness allows her to tell, and we could add, ultimately, to try to understand.

SEE ALSO: Danticat, Edwidge; Debut Novels; Díaz, Junot; Fiction and Affect; Fictions of Work and Labor; Literature of the Americas; Mixed-Genre Fiction; Multiculturalism; Young Adult Boom

REFERENCES

Álvarez, Julia. (1994). *How the García Girls Lost Their Accents*. Chapel Hill, NC: Algonquin Books; 1st ed. 1991.
Álvarez, Julia. (1998). A white woman of color. *Hungry Mind Review* (Spring): 56–60.
Álvarez, Julia. (2000). Doña Aída, with your permission. *Callaloo* 23 (3): 821–823.
Álvarez, Julia. (2010). Foreword: Rapunzel's ladder, social justice education: a way down from the ivory tower. In: *Social Justice Education: Inviting Faculty to Transform Their Institutions* (ed. Kathleen Subikowski, Catharine Wright, and Roman Graft), xiii–xxiv. Sterling, VA: Stylus.
Álvarez, Julia. (2012). *A Wedding in Haiti, the Story of a Friendship*. Chapel Hill, NC: Algonquin Books.
Blackmore, Lisa. (2015). Violence in the Jardín de (la) Patria: the monumentalisation of the Mirabal sisters and the trauma site in the Dominican postdictatorship. *Mitologías Hoy* 12: 101–117.
Fregoso, Rosa Linda. (2003). Julia Álvarez, In the Times of the Butterflies. In: *Reading U.S. Latina Writers: Remapping American Literature* (ed. Alvina E. Quintana), 7–14. New York: Palgrave Macmillan.
Kurlansky, Mark, Díaz, Junot, Danticat, Edwidge, and Álvarez, Julia. (2013). Two versions of a Dominican tale. *The New York Times* (October 31, 2013). https://www.nytimes.com/2013/11/01/opinion/two-versions-of-a-dominican-tale.html (accessed October 4, 2021).
Myers, Megan Jeanette. (2016). Dos rayanos-americanos rewrite Hispaniola: Julia Álvarez y Junot Díaz. *Confluencia: Revista Hispana de Cultura y Literatura* 32 (1): 168–181.
Rohrleitner, M. (2013). ¡Yo! On the margins: dividing the family and the ethnic writer as traitor. In: *Inhabiting La Patria: Identity, Agency, and Antojo in the Work of Julia Álvarez* (ed. Rebecca L. Harrison, and Emily Hipchen), 43–61. Albany, NY: SUNY Press.
Sirias, Silvio. (2001). *Julia Álvarez: A Critical Companion*. Westport, CT: Greenwood Press.

FURTHER READING

Rodríguez, Néstor E. (2010). *Divergent Dictions: Contemporary Dominican Literature* (trans. Kerstin Oloff). Coconut Creek, FL: Caribbean Studies Press.

Anaya, Rudolfo

MANUEL BRONCANO
Texas A&M International University, USA

Novelist, essayist, poet, playwright, educator, social activist, even wine critic on occasion, but always a storyteller, Rudolfo Anaya avowedly was a born writer. As evidence, he would humorously cite the day when, a mere toddler, his parents sat him on a sheepskin and displayed around him several objects, among them a saddle, a notebook, and a pencil, and the child crawled unhesitatingly toward the writing utensils, ignoring everything else, thus choosing his path in life. When Anaya died on June 28, 2020, in Albuquerque, New Mexico, obituaries published across the nation signaled him as the "father," the "godfather," the "dean," a "founder," a "pioneer," and a "giant" of Chicano literature. The most widely read Mexican American author of all times and an unquestionable American classic, Rudolfo Anaya's literary legacy is a sustained celebration of hybridity and convergence, as well as a deconstruction of racial and cultural essentialisms. A regionalist with a keen eye for local color and a mythmaker who has recovered and endowed with new meaning the myths and legends of Indigenous America, Anaya occupies a privileged position at the crossroads of modernism, social realism and naturalism, magic realism, and postmodernism. Criticism has generally pigeonholed Anaya as an ethnic writer, and a critical reevaluation is necessary in order to gain a more nuanced understanding of his works in the broader context of Pan-American and world literature.

Born on October 30, 1937, in La Pastura, a railroad hamlet in Guadalupe County, New Mexico, and brought up in Santa Rosa, the county seat a few miles to the north, Rudolfo Anaya would find in the locale of his childhood an inexhaustible source of spiritual and poetic inspiration throughout his life. His father, Martín Anaya, descended from an old lineage of vaqueros who had been herding cattle and sheep for generations in the area of Llano Estacado, the extensive plateau that occupies parts of eastern New Mexico and northwestern Texas. His mother, Rafaelita Márez, descended from an equally old family of farmers from Puerto de Luna, also in Guadalupe County. Both families had been living in the region long before the annexation of the territory to the United States resulting from the Treaty of Guadalupe Hidalgo (1848). Growing up in a Spanish-speaking household in which storytelling provided a sense of self and community, the myriad tales and legends told by his elders in those early years left an indelible mark on Anaya's imagination. *Bless Me, Última* (1972), his first and most popular novel, became his lasting testimony of a vanishing world where the marvelous and the real coexisted harmoniously in a timeless equilibrium. In *Bless Me, Última*, young Antonio is the inheritor and repository of two opposing forces, the llano and the farm, and by means of his writing, the young boy is capable of reconciling those antagonistic forces, becoming the spokesman for the two, for one cannot truly exist without the other. Antonio is thus the catalyst for convergence, not only of the llano and the farm, but also of good and evil, day and night, Christianity and Indian religion, the past and the present, Última and Tenorio, God and the golden carp, the pagan deity that inhabits the river. And that convergence takes place on the written page, for Antonio is a writer-to-be who has found in synthesis his own completion as human being.

Anaya's family moved to Albuquerque in 1952 and settled in the barrio of Barelas, a working-class neighborhood near the downtown and a de facto ghetto for Mexican American peasants flocking to the city in large numbers, attracted by the prospect of well-paid jobs. While life in Santa Rosa had been almost paradisiacal, as Anaya would often reminisce in his writings, life in the city confronted him with the harsh realities of racial prejudice and discrimination, especially conspicuous at school. In his essay "On the Education of Hispanic Children," the writer evokes the feelings of shame and alienation that besieged him, as a Spanish-speaking mestizo trying to carve his niche in Anglo-America: "I was told too many times that I didn't belong . . . that my language and my parents didn't belong . . . [that] I was not like the other students . . . with an Anglo-American background" (Anaya 1995, p. 403). Anaya's elder brother Larry, already a resident of Barelas, introduced him to the neighborhood, thus facilitating his transition to city life. He found new friends and led the typical life of a teenager, playing baseball and basketball and listening to Elvis, driving customized cars and flirting with girls. However, he was always a diligent student and avoided the street gangs that proliferated in the barrio and kept mostly away from drugs, a real plague among the Mexican American youth. Barelas became the subject of *Heart of Aztlán* (1976), Anaya's second, semi-autobiographical novel, which narrates the migration to Albuquerque of the Chávez family, forced to sell their farm in the village of Guadalupe to cover multiple debts. An exercise in social realism, *Heart of Aztlán* combines ancient mythology and civic action, in what probably is Anaya's most political book.

At 16, Anaya suffered a tragic accident that changed the course of his life forever. Since there were no swimming pools in the neighborhood, he and his playmates frequented a spot not far from the barrio where an irrigation ditch created a deep pond that served the purpose. As he dove confidently into the water one summer afternoon, he fractured two vertebrae in his neck, resulting in instant paralysis of his whole body. Unable to swim, he floated face down for several minutes while his friends continued with their games, unaware of the situation. Drowning, Anaya had a near-death experience in which he saw himself detach from his body and soar above the whole scene, until one of his friends finally turned him over and he started breathing again. Despite the gloomy initial prognosis, and the long and torturous process of healing, Anaya would recover, against all odds, full mobility of his legs and arms. Years later, this experience became the basis for *Tortuga* (1979), the novel that completed the trilogy, loosely autobiographical, that traces the development of a Mexican American boy destined to become a writer. While Anaya considered *Tortuga* to be one of his best works, the novel has passed largely unnoticed by criticism, perhaps overshadowed by the popularity of *Bless Me, Última*. A profound meditation on trauma and healing, *Tortuga* weaves a dense web of intertextual allusions, from Dante's *Divine Comedy* (1472) to Thomas Mann's *Magic Mountain* (1927), Kafka's *Metamorphosis* (1915) or Pirandello's *Six Characters in Search of an Author* (1921), alongside classic and Native American myths and legends.

By the time of his high school graduation, Rudolfo Anaya's recovery was complete, although aftereffects from the accident would reappear periodically throughout his life. He attended business school for two years, but he realized business was not his vocation and decided to drop out and enroll instead in the English program at the University of New Mexico (UNM). Without money, Anaya pressed his way through college by working at any odd job available, until he completed his BA in 1963 and accepted a teaching position in a small town in New Mexico, and later in Albuquerque. In the following years, he completed two Master of Arts degrees, in English and in guidance and counseling, at UNM, and in 1974 he accepted a position at the English department to teach creative writing and Chicano literature, which he held until his retirement in 1993. During his college years, Anaya grew increasingly aware of the systemic racism against Mexican Americans and joined the crusade initiated by César Chávez and others in California in the early 1960s demanding equal rights for Latinos, part of the broader Civil Rights movement of the era. He was among the approximately 1500 Mexican American youths attending the National Youth and Liberation Conference in Denver, Colorado (March 23, 1969), which resulted in the adoption of the term "Chicanismo," as defined in the manifesto "El Plan espiritual de Aztlán," a true declaration of independence of the Mexican American community as a colonized people within the United States. The Chicano movement expanded rapidly across the country and soon internal dissension arose along ideological lines, especially in the early years, as a Marxist-Leninist faction attempted to impose an ultra-nationalist agenda in both Chicano politics and aesthetics.

In his 1989 essay "Aztlán: A Homeland without Boundaries," Anaya would contest such a narrow and intolerant stance, instead envisioning Aztlán, the imagined homeland of Mexican Americans, as a borderless and fluid space, a communal territory open to all races and all peoples deprived of a homeland, a place of healing and rebirth for the human spirit. A mestizo himself, Anaya celebrates mestizaje as the expression of convergence and reconciliation among races and nations. He keeps alive the memory of the tragic destiny of the American Indian after the fateful arrival of the European, especially the Pueblos of the American Southwest. However, Anaya looks into history, not to blame, but to understand the past and learn how to live together in mutual tolerance and respect. The mestizo is the offspring of such traumatic encounter, simultaneously being and not being, like the Americas themselves. Indian and white, European and Native, the mestizo speaks the American idiom, the coalescence of Spanish and English. The stories he tells derive from both the Indigenous oral traditions and the Spanish folktales, which in turn originated "in the subcontinent of India and centuries ago made their way into Persia, then to Europe," as Anaya observes in the epilogue to *Serafina's Stories* (2004, p. 188). Serafina is the Pueblo Indian reincarnation of Scheherazade, the narrator of the Persian *One Thousand and One Nights*, at the time of the 1680 Pueblo Revolt against the Spanish in Santa Fe. Like Scheherazade, Serafina possesses a rare beauty that matches her wisdom in Indian and white cultures alike, and is an accomplished storyteller who placates the governor's ire by means of her tales. Serafina stands for reconciliation, and mediates effectively between the Spanish conqueror and the vanquished Indian. She is the honorary "spiritual great-grandmother from our New Mexican past," Anaya writes, and "perhaps we are all Serafina's children" (2004, p. 189).

By the beginning of the 1980s, Anaya was widely recognized as one of the leading figures of Chicano letters, and he was the recipient of various distinctions and awards: the National Endowment for the Arts Fellowship (1979, 1980); the National Chicano Council for Higher Education Fellowship (1980); the Kellogg Foundation Fellowship (1983–1986); and the Mexican Medal of Friendship, Mexican Consulate of Albuquerque (1986), among others. He was invited for a public reading at the White House during the Carter administration, and received an honorary Doctor of Humane Letters from the University of Albuquerque (1981), the first of seven honorary doctorates awarded to him: Marycrest College, Iowa (1984); College of Santa Fe (1991); University of New England (1992); California Lutheran University (1994); University of New Mexico (1996); and University of New Hampshire (1997). Later in life, he was the recipient of the National Endowment for the Arts National Medal of Arts Lifetime Honor (2001); the Outstanding Latino/a Cultural Award in Literary Arts or Publications, from the American Association of Hispanics in Higher Education (2003); and the Robert Kirsch Award (2011). Despite his frail health and his need of a wheelchair, in September 2016 Anaya decided to attend the award ceremony at the White House, as one of the recipients of the 2015 National Endowment for the Humanities National Humanities Medal. In his speech, President Barack Obama commended the author for works "that celebrate the Chicano experience and reveal universal truths about the human condition." An unconditional admirer of the President, while a military escort wheeled him off the dais after his medal presentation, Rudolfo Anaya shouted at the top of his voice, "Viva Obama," which led those in attendance to break protocol and erupt in cheers and laughter. When asked by a journalist about the shout, he replied, "He is my hero, man" (Coleman 2016). In March 2018, Anaya attended a ceremony celebrating the newly named Rudolfo Anaya North Valley Library, in what would be his last public appearance. In 2019, the Governor of New Mexico and the State Legislature proclaimed October 30 a state holiday, "Rudolfo Anaya I Love to Read Day."

During the 1980s, Anaya traveled extensively, both within the United States and abroad, including a one-month visit to China that allowed him to seek commonalities between the Chinese and Chicano cultures, which he recorded in the journal *A Chicano in China* (1984). He visited Mexico City on several occasions, where he gathered the materials for his novella *The Legend of La Llorona* (1984), which revisits the legend of Aztec pre-Columbian origin that was a household tale both in Old and New Mexico. Anaya engaged in editorial work, collecting several short story anthologies by Chicano writers, as well as traditional tales from the Southwest. In the 1990s, Anaya's audience expanded considerably, due in part to Warner Books, the major publishing and distribution company that contracted him for six books, starting with *Alburquerque* (1992). *Alburquerque*, whose title restores the original name of the city, sets a new course in his fiction, exploring the intersection of politics and the environment, against the background of New Mexico's colonial heritage. It is the first installment in Anaya's highly successful Sonny Baca series, action-packed thrillers about the Chicano private eye who engages in twisted and dangerous investigations that will uncover the many environmental threats looming over the fragile ecosystem of New Mexico. *Alburquerque* dwells on the commodification of water and the corrupted practices to gain its control. His next title, *Zia Summer* (1995), exposes the dangers associated with nuclear waste. *Rio Grande Fall* (1996) expands into the underworld of cartels and corrupted public servants involved in the drug-dealing business. *Shaman Winter* (1999) and *Jemez Spring* (2005) complete the series, once more revisiting the nuclear menace and the connivance of wealthy entrepreneurs and unscrupulous politicians exposed in the previous novels.

Rudolfo Anaya was a teacher as much as a writer, and was involved in cultural and educational endeavors throughout his life. He fought the erasure of Mexican Americans in school curricula and contributed actively to the implementation of Chicano studies programs in colleges and the inclusion of literary works in the school reading lists. *Bless Me, Última* soon became a household title at middle and high schools across the country, although in several instances the novel was banished for its negative portrayal of Catholicism and the conspicuous presence of pagan elements, as well as its pervasive use of Spanish. In 1981, the Bloomfield School Board in New Mexico ordered all copies of *Bless Me, Última* to be burned. In 2010, Arizona passed legislation that led to the elimination of Mexican American studies from the Tucson Unified School District and the removal of books by Chicano writers from the curriculum, including Anaya's novel, which the writer publicly condemned. Concerned with the educational barriers affecting Mexican American children, Anaya and his wife Patricia sponsored numerous literacy programs across the state. Likewise, they opened a writer's retreat in Jemez Springs in support of aspiring authors. A champion of the Mexican American heritage, Anaya wrote several children's books in which he introduces legends and traditions of both Old and New Mexico, as well as historical figures of the Chicano movement, like the long poem *Elegy on the Death of César Chávez* (2000).

The loss in 2010 of Patricia, his wife of forty-four years, and his own declining health, tinged Anaya's final years with sorrow and nostalgia, while episodes of excruciating pain caused by arthritis in his back confined him to bed for extended periods. He wrote extensively about death and memory, love and bereavement, and his style became more lyrical. Both *Randy López Goes Home* (2011) and *The Old Man's Love Story* (2013) are highly poetic allegories that translate his personal experience of loss into a universal meditation on the human condition. Along the way, Anaya revisits his life and his works and brings both to a closure, as if in preparation for his own death. The circle completed, he is now ready, like Randy López, to go home in peace. Over fifty novels, short stories, plays, children's books, poetry, essays, and collections of traditional and contemporary tales secure his place in literary history. His legacy as an educator and philanthropist secures his place in the history of the Mexican American community and its struggle for equality and recognition.

SEE ALSO: Border Fictions; Contemporary Regionalisms; Ecocriticism and Environmental Fiction; Illness and Disability Narratives; Indigenous Narratives; Literature of the Americas; Trauma and Fiction

REFERENCES

Anaya, Rudolfo. (1989). Aztlán: a homeland without boundaries. In: *Aztlán: Essays on the Chicano Homeland* (ed. Rudolfo Anaya, Francisco A. Lomelí, and Enrique R. Lamadrid), 230–241. Albuquerque: El Norte Publications/Academia.
Anaya, Rudolfo. (1995). On the education of Hispanic children. In: *The Anaya Reader*, 399–403. New York: Warner Books.
Anaya, Rudolfo. (2004). *Serafina's Stories*. Albuquerque: University of New Mexico Press.
Coleman, Michael. (2016). Rudolfo Anaya honored for "pioneering stories." *Albuquerque Journal* (September 22, 2016). https://www.abqjournal.com/851424/rudolfo-anaya-honored-for-pioneering-stories.html (accessed July 7, 2021).

FURTHER READING

Anaya, Rudolfo. (1986). Rudolfo A. Anaya: an autobiography. In: *Contemporary Authors: Autobiography Series, Volume 4* (ed. Adele Sarkissan), 15–28. Detroit: Gale Research Company.
Baeza, Abelardo. (2001). *Man of Aztlan: A Biography of Rudolfo Anaya*. Austin: Eakin Press.
Cantú, Roberto. (ed.) (2016). *The Forked Juniper: Critical Perspectives on Rudolfo Anaya*. Norman: University of Oklahoma Press.
Dick, Bruce and Sirias, Silvio. (eds.) (1998). *Conversations with Rudolfo Anaya*. Jackson: University of Mississippi Press.
Fernández-Olmos, Margarite. (1999). *Rudolfo A. Anaya: A Critical Companion*. Westport, CT: Greenwood.

Anders, Charlie Jane

WENDY GAY PEARSON
University of Western Ontario, Canada

Charlie Jane Anders is the author of three novels, *Choir Boy* (2005, writing as Charlie Anders), *All the Birds in the Sky* (2016), and *The City in the Middle of the Night* (2019), the novella *Rock Manning Goes For Broke* (2018), and a short story collection called *Six Months, Three Days, Five Others* (2017). She has published short fiction in *Boston Review*, *Tin House*, *Conjunctions*, the *Magazine of Fantasy and Science Fiction*, *Wired* magazine, *ZYZZYVA*, *Catamaran Literary Review*, and *Asimov's Science Fiction*, as well as online at Tor.com, Lightspeed, McSweeney's Internet Tendency, and a number of anthologies. Anders won a Hugo Award for her story "Six Months, Three Days" (2011) and a Theodore Sturgeon Award for "Don't Press Charges And I Won't Sue" (2017). *The City in the Middle of the Night* won the 2020 Locus Award for best science fiction novel, while "The Bookstore at the End of America" (2019) won the Locus for best short story in the same year. *Choir*

Boy won a 2006 Lambda Literary Award and was a finalist for the Edmund White Award for Debut Fiction. Anders has also won the Emperor Norton Award, for "extraordinary invention and creativity unhindered by the constraints of paltry reason" (Anders 2020). Anders currently has a three-book contract with Tor Teen; the first book, *Victories Greater Than Death*, was published in 2021.

Anders is also the co-founder and editor, with her partner Annalee Newitz, of *other magazine*, which was published from 2002 to 2007. The couple also co-founded the website io9, which focuses on science, science fiction, and cultural criticism. In 2007, Anders and Newitz published a book of first-person stories by female geeks called *She's Such a Geek*. Anders also organizes the monthly bi-coastal Writers With Drinks reading series, and co-hosts the Hugo Award-winning podcast *Our Opinions Are Correct*, also with Annalee Newitz. In 1999, Anders founded the satirical website God Hates Figs, a very funny response to the Westboro Baptist Church's homophobic God Hates Fags website. Anders identifies as a trans woman and uses she/her pronouns. Anders has written specifically about trans issues in *Choir Boy* and in some of her short stories, notably "Love Might Be Too Strong a Word" (2008). In her online bio, Anders writes that, "I'm probably the only person to have become a fictional character in a *Star Trek* novel and in one of Armistead Maupin's *Tales of the City* books" (Anders 2020).

With the exception of *Choir Boy*, the majority of Anders's work is science fiction and fantasy. Anders's interests in science, technology, and futurism are showcased in all her work, particularly her fiction of the last decade and her work with io9 and Tor.com. Anders describes the founding of io9 in a 2016 article called "io9 Was Founded on the Idea that Science Fiction Belongs to Everyone" (Anders 2016). Anders talks about brainstorming the website with Newitz and Nick Denton of Gawker Media. They came up with four basic principles: (1) because of advances in science and technology, we already live in a science fiction world; (2) "science fiction is uniquely qualified to comment on the era we're living in, and is the only pop culture that accurately reflects the world around us"; (3) basic cultural literacy today takes for granted the mainstreaming of science fiction; and (4) science fiction belongs to everyone, not any particular group of fans, writers, or filmmakers. Science fiction, Anders writes, "should be about the future, and about newness" (Anders 2016).

Choir Boy, while not science fictional, is still about the future and about newness. The protagonist is a 13-year-old boy named Berry for whom singing in the church choir is the only worthwhile thing in a typically troubled teenage life. Berry's parents do not like each other, or Berry. They put him in the church choir because his mother wants him to learn music, and the choir not only does not charge for lessons, it actually pays a small stipend. Berry, who is small for his age, is mercilessly bullied in school. At 13 the thing he wants more than anything is to keep singing with the trebles, not to be bounced out of the choir or put into an "adult" singing role when his voice, inevitably, breaks. In his pursuit of this goal, Berry seeks out options for chemical castration, effectively becoming what the dust jacket refers to as "accidentally trans." The process of maturation closes possible futures for Berry, even as he struggles to find ways to keep them open. In this respect, even though this is a novel about a trans kid, its reflections on transness are as much allegorical as literal. At a time when attacks on transgender people are proliferating, particularly in the media, various US states have passed so-called "bathroom bills" designed to make public life inaccessible to trans people, and the UK courts have just banned the use of puberty blockers for anyone under 18 (rendering them largely pointless), Anders's first novel remains remarkably on point. What rights does our culture allow children to define their own identity and to grow up to be who they want to be? How can trans and nonbinary children imagine a future they can survive, particularly in the age of anthropogenic climate change and the looming threat of ecological disaster?

This potential for planetary catastrophe brought about by human activity lies at the heart of Anders's first science fiction and fantasy (SFF) novel, *All the Birds in the Sky*, another coming-of-age novel which features two protagonists, Patricia Delfine, a teenage girl who discovers that she's a witch, and Laurence Armstead, a techno-geek who has managed to construct a two-second time machine and is attempting to build an artificial intelligence (AI) in his bedroom closet. Both are ostracized at their private school for their inability to fit in, which is how we discover that Laurence's time machine has its uses, as Laurence can jump two seconds into the future, just enough to avoid a punch thrown at him. It also turns out to be the common denominator of juvenile techno-geeks. Laurence's parents are alarmed by his interests and embarrassed by his failure to be a "normal" teenager and send him to a military-style school intended to cure him of any tendency toward originality or rebellion. Patricia's parents are not much better; they live in an old spice house and allow their sadistic older daughter, Roberta, to bully her younger sister. Both young people escape parental constraints by joining with others like them: witches and geeks.

The protagonists meet again as young adults, Patricia having been educated at the Eltisley Maze magic school, where she learns to be a witch and to avoid the sin of Aggrandizement. Laurence's two-second time machine buys him the attention of older, more organized techno-geeks who are attempting to build a rocket. They're part of the Ten Percent Project, which believes the human race can only survive if 10% leave the planet for space. Both Patricia's magical training and Laurence's scientific education come to focus on saving the planet from climate change and the destruction wreaked by capitalism. This is one aspect in which the novel's playful take on genre becomes clear, as it moves from what looks like standard young adult (YA) fantasy to "cli-fi" (climate-focused science fiction), with multiple stops in between. There are echoes of all the magic schools of YA literature, from Ged's training in Le Guin's first Earthsea novel to Harry Potter's Hogwarts Academy. As adults, Patricia and Laurence become lovers, despite multiple forces interfering with their relationship (including Theodolphus Rose, the assassin sent to kill Patricia by the Nameless Order of Assassins in order to prevent her from interfering with the great Unraveling, the spell which will unmake the world).

Climate change and the probability of planetary destruction are forces to be reckoned with in this novel, and part of its tension lies in the very different approaches Patricia's magic and Laurence's engineering take. *Birds* rewrites the supposed historic conflict between arts and sciences with magic on one side and technology on the other. Both provide hope, but both also allow for the possibility of terrible mistakes and mass destruction. As Anders wrote on Tor.com, "we need to imagine the future in order to survive it" (2019b). *Birds* imagines a future in which magic and technology offer alternative visions of both saving and destroying the world. Is the Ten Percent Project really a good alternative? What happens to those left behind? Which will not be just 90% of humanity, but close to 100% of every other living thing on the planet. *Birds* taps into some of the posthumanist impulses of contemporary science fiction, even if it cannot really be defined as cyberpunk (despite the role of the AI, CH@NG3M3, that Laurence and Patricia create between them). The talking birds (and other animals) who permeate the novel are a reminder that climate change is not only a human disaster, but a planetary one that crosses species boundaries.

Birds begins and ends with Patricia making her way to the Tree – led there as a six-year-old by an injured sparrow and again as an adult, but this time with Laurence and Peregrine (CH@NG3M3's chosen name) in tow. The Parliament of Birds asks the child Patricia a question: "Is a tree red?" The Tree tells child Patricia that the role of witches is to serve nature. At the end, the narrative circles back to both these points, as Patricia finds herself still unable to answer whether or not a tree is red. "I don't know," is her only answer, but it's also the correct answer, as both question and answer trigger something for Peregrine. Laurence inserts the Caddy (tablet-like device) on which Peregrine is loaded into the Tree, resulting in a systemwide update that merges tree and artificial intelligence, who equally interpret their new relationship as love. Peregrine and the Tree between them create a complete history of magic in the world and undo the final spell, the Unraveling, because it has not yet been cast. Peregrine concludes that "Carmen and the other witches were right, people need to change ... now I can see the nonhuman interactions as well. I think we can empower people. Every human can be a wizard" (Anders 2017, loc. 4998). When Laurence intervenes to say "or a cyborg," Peregrine – the AI who has renamed itself after a raptor – says, "A cyborg ... will be the same thing as a wizard." The new future of humanity is decidedly posthuman, cyborgian, informed by a tearing down of the boundaries between humans and nature and between magic and technology. It is not much of a stretch to suggest that this is a novel deeply informed by postmodern, feminist, queer, and critical animal studies and particularly by the work of Donna Haraway, from "A Cyborg Manifesto" (1985) to *Staying with the Trouble: Making Kin in the Chthulucene* (2016).

Birds is also a novel about giving voice and silencing. Who has a voice? Who is silenced? And why? Patricia's first inkling of her magical abilities comes when she is able to understand Dirrp the sparrow, talk to the Parliament of Fowls and the Yggdrasil-like Tree that hosts it, and argue with her cat. All of these are voices that are not normally comprehensible – and possibly not even audible – to humans. Humans without magical powers, such as Laurence, can hear noises but are not able to recognize them as language. However, humans also have varying degrees of access to being heard, which one might theorize in Butlerian terms as differential access to cultural intelligibility. While dominant culture tells us animals other than humans are not capable of communication or intelligence, it also determines the degree of access humans themselves have to meaningful and recognizable speech. Patricia tells Laurence, "this planet is not just some 'rock.' It's not just some kind of chrysalis we can shed, either.. . . It's us. And this isn't just our story. As someone who's spoken to lots of other kinds of creatures, I kinda think they might want a vote" (Anders 2017, loc. 1991). In this respect, *Birds* critiques the humancentrism of Arthur C. Clarke's *Childhood's End* (1953), in which humans are transformed into a higher species and leave Earth to its destruction. *Birds*, by contrast, centers around the simple but largely unregarded fact that nonhuman beings also have a stake in the survival of the planet. However, outside of *Birds*, they have few ways of communicating that so that humans can hear. Silence/voice matters. And, in perhaps the most dramatic moment in the novel, Laurence defies the curse that he will never speak again if he talks about magic and saves Patricia's life precisely by giving up his voice. If that sounds like the silencing of technology by magic, it is not, because the ending of the novel brings the two together to create something entirely new. But it is a core sacrifice which negates Laurence's previous commitment to purely technological solutions to saving (some of) humanity while letting the planet die, while at the same time reminding savvy science fiction readers of Arthur C. Clarke's famous claim that all advanced technology looks like magic. Anders plays fascinating riffs that interrogate and complicate that claim.

Anders's most recent novel, *The City in the Middle of the Night*, is set on a planet called January, settled by humans but still largely inhospitable, due to both climate and alien life-forms. Adam Roberts has called this novel "classic SF in the mode of Ursula K. Le Guin or Octavia Butler" (2019). Even the name of the planet is a nod to Le Guin's planet Winter in *The Left Hand of Darkness* (1967). In this respect, *City* is quite different generically from the madcap mixture of genres in *Birds*, although it too falls partially within the genre of cli-fi. It's also very different from the zany near-apocalypse meets *Jackass* qualities of the intervening novella, *Rock Manning Goes For Broke*. Indeed, Rebecca Evans correctly identifies *City* as a climate justice narrative and notes that "Climate justice narratives . . . require an attention both to the likelihood of climate injustice in the future *and* to the way that such injustice is rooted . . . in the present moment. Second, representations of climate futures matter in terms of resisting heteronormative systems, or the vexed relationship that queer scholarship has identified between futurity and reproductive politics" (2017, p. 95).

Human settlers on January have had to adapt to the fact that the planet does not rotate relative to its sun. Both frozen and scorching sides are full of alien life-forms that seem monstrous to the settlers. There are two human cities in the temperate zone, each having opposing notions of governance. The oppressive Xiosphant is obsessed with efficiency and time management and also divided along class lines, while Argelo is chaotic, anarchic, fun, but short on resources. Both cities have to cope with the inevitable failures of the ancient technologies they've inherited from the first settlers, thus exacerbating the struggle to survive in an inhospitable environment. One of the protagonists, Sophie, is a working-class girl in homophobic Xiosphant who has won a scholarship to the Gymnasium to save herself from being forced into marriage. There she falls in love with her dorm-mate, Bianca, and sacrifices herself to stop Bianca from being punished for breaking the rules. Exiled to the ice outside the city, a de facto death sentence, Sophie is saved by a "crocodile." Much to Sophie's surprise, the Gelet are an intelligent species who communicate with her by sharing memories and thoughts. Sophie finds herself exiled from Xiosphant and unable to see her beloved Bianca. The other protagonist, Mouth, lives with the memory of the deaths of her nomadic group, the Citizens, who are violently and inexplicably killed on the road. Mouth is co-opted to Bianca's attempts at political revolution to overthrow the Xiosphanti government.

Alongside the political argument about how one deals with governments that are either chillingly oppressive or utterly disorganized while facing potential environmental disaster, *City* highlights alternative possibilities through Sophie's various experiences with the Gelet, who turn out to have been very gently shaping their planet's ecosystem for centuries. Mouth's Citizens were itinerant traders who discovered a type of moss in the vents of volcanoes and harvested everything they could. For the Gelet, who have spent centuries cultivating these blooms, this is a major ecological disaster, as the plants "laced throughout the world, collecting heat energy on the day side and redirecting it to the night, exhaling gases that calmed the skies" (2019a, p. 303). The resultant climatological imbalance creates a flood of caustic liquid that drowns a nest of thousands of Gelet infants. When the Citizens return to harvest more and unwittingly increase climate destabilization, the Gelet muster a blue swarm that overwhelms and kills the Citizens. The child Mouth is the sole survivor and has, until the Gelet show her, no idea what the Citizens have done.

While the novel focuses on anthropogenic climate change affecting January and harming its indigenous species, the narrative also dwells on human relationships, beginning with Sophie's forbidden love for Bianca. Bianca comes to understand and reciprocate that love only after Sophie is sent outside to die. Mouth also has a female love, Alyssa, but, not being from Xiosphant, she doesn't struggle with the relationship. Argelo has no interest in regulating people's intimate relations; the Argelan language has "a million different terms for relationships: lovers, parent/child, teacher/student, friend" (2019a, p. 171). However, the queerness of *City* does not lie only in the fact that both of its protagonists are women interested in same-sex relationships. Queer temporalities abound in *City*'s description of its characters' relationship to time and history. Humans on January have largely forgotten their past, but the Gelet remember and give Sophie back her people's history, particularly the ways in which their survival on January has been and still is dependent on the Gelet's ability to manage their planet. Without human binary gender or any sense of heteropatriarchal relations, the Gelet provide a queer alternative not only to understanding how to live on and with a harsh environment, but also multiple queer alternatives to how humans think about relationships and kin.

As a relatively new fiction author, Anders has yet to receive much critical attention for her work. That is a situation that is not likely to last, as her work has already made an impact, particularly within the worlds of science/speculative fiction.

SEE ALSO: Butler, Octavia; Cyberpunk; Ecocriticism and Environmental Fiction; Le Guin, Ursula; Queer and LGBT Fiction

REFERENCES

Anders, Charlie Jane. (2016). io9 was founded on the idea that science fiction belongs to everyone. Gizmodo (April 29, 2016). https://gizmodo.com/io9-was-founded-on-the-idea-that-science-fiction-belong-1773233193 (accessed July 7, 2021).

Anders, Charlie Jane. (2017). *All the Birds in the Sky*. London: Titan. Kindle e-book.

Anders, Charlie Jane. (2019a). *The City in the Middle of the Night*. New York: Tor Books. Kindle e-book.

Anders, Charlie Jane. (2019b). Why science fiction authors need to be writing about climate change right now. Tor.com (January 22, 2019). https://www.tor.com/2019/01/22/why-science-fiction-authors-need-to-be-writing-about-climate-change-right-now/ (accessed July 7, 2021).

Anders, Charlie Jane. (2020). Long bio, first person. In: *The City in the Middle of the Night*. https://www.cityinthemiddleofthenight.com/ (accessed November 12, 2020). The long bio can now be found at https://www.charliejaneanders.com/about (accessed July 23, 2021).

Evans, Rebecca. (2017). Fantastic futures? Cli-fi, climate justice, and queer futurity. *Resilience: A Journal of the Environmental Humanities* 4 (2/3): 94–110.

Roberts, Adam. (2019). *The City in the Middle of the Night* by Charlie Jane Anders review: another world. *The Guardian* (February 22, 2019). https://www.theguardian.com/books/2019/feb/22/city-middle-night-charlie-jane-anders-review (accessed July 7, 2021).

FURTHER READING

Andersen, Gregers. (2019). *Climate Fiction and Cultural Analysis: A New Perspective on Life in the Anthropocene*. New York: Routledge.

Antrim, Donald

JAMES GOURLEY
Western Sydney University, Australia

Donald Antrim, author of a loosely-defined trilogy of novels, a memoir, a collection of stories, and a significant number of stand-alone stories in high-profile literary magazines (especially the *New Yorker*, where he has a more than twenty-year publishing history) is, counterfactually perhaps, a shadowy character of the American literary world. His biographical note is performatively sparse: his works, his most prominent awards, and where he lives: either New York City or Brooklyn, New York. But, this sparseness is not the entire picture: Antrim, carefully reluctant in the literary spotlight, is also the author of the stridently personal *The Afterlife* (2006), which tells the story of his mother's life and death, and is determinedly upfront in its disclosure of the author's presence and role in that book: "The story of my life is bound up in this story, the story of [Antrim's mother's] deterioration" (Antrim 2008, p. 5).

Antrim appears to the reader both present and absent, simultaneously. This doubled procedure, of concealment and disclosure, of principled gravitas and exuberant imagination, is a regularly identifiable method within Antrim's works and his literary endeavor. This entry considers this dialectic in Antrim's texts, and in the common themes that link them. It does so, to a surprising extent, without any true critical interlocutors to engage with: despite considerable acclaim, Antrim's work has only attracted minimal scholarly response, and while there are a number of interviews conducted with him, even these are characterized by caution on the writer's part (aside from the moments in which Antrim's caution tips over into willing disclosure). As such, this entry seeks to present the importance of Antrim's *oeuvre*, and to map out a series of critical questions which it raises.

Born in 1958, Antrim was educated at the elite Woodberry Forest School in Virginia, and then at the Ivy League Brown University, where he graduated with a BA in 1981. As should already be obvious, absolutely trustworthy information beyond this is difficult to find. Indeed, in *The Afterlife*, where Antrim reflects upon his experience as a child and adolescent, the reader's trust in what is relayed is consistently undermined: "testimony from my parents' old crowd about [Antrim's mother's] later years [. . .] as a wife and mother [. . .] is hard to come by, as are memories of my own, memories of the sort that add up to form a coherent . . . what? Picture? Impression? Narrative?" (2008, p. 12). In lieu of a picture, impression, or narrative, Antrim does drip-feed details of his life: he relates living in Fort Knox, Kentucky (when a baby) and Fort Bragg, North Carolina (where Antrim's sister was born) (p. 168); Gainesville, Florida (as a six year old) (p. 148); Tallahassee, Florida – "my sister and I conspire to remember these as good years" (1966–1968) (p. 23); "thirty minutes west of" Charlottesville, Virginia (when twelve) (p. 169); and Miami, Florida (when Antrim was 14, so, say, 1972) (p. 40). Antrim then reports that: "When I was sixteen, I left Miami for boarding school in the foothills of the Blue Ridge Mountains. Two years after that, I went north to college, and four years later I moved to New York, where I still live" (p. 60). And thus, one imagines, to the present.

Beyond a sophomore short story, "Rocket Man" (1986), in *Columbia: A Journal of Literature and Art*, Antrim's literary debut was the first novel in his "trilogy," *Elect Mr. Robinson for a Better World* (1993). The trilogy develops a set of common themes and features: the naïve male narrator; the atmosphere of domestic American realism interrupted by the strangeness of a character's relation to that world; the sense of anxiety (especially environmental anxiety) that looms within the text. Despite this continuity, the label of "trilogy" is a strange one. Antrim speaks of the trilogy despite the fact that the three novels "do not form a continuous narrative; [and] characters do not appear in book after book" (Bolt 1997, p. 27). Indeed, in another example of the doubled nature of Antrim's method, he asserts their trilogy-status while acknowledging "[i]t may turn out this is not a trilogy at all" (p. 27).

Elect Mr. Robinson for a Better World is narrated by Pete Robinson, schoolteacher, sometime mayoral hopeful, and Inquisition-era torture enthusiast. Antrim evokes and subverts a suburban American idyll with the novel's opening lines: "See a town stucco-pink, fishbelly-white, done up in wisteria and swaying palms and smelling of rotted fruits broken beneath trees: mango, papaya, delicious tangerine; imagine this town rising from coral shoals bleached and cutting upward through bathwater seas [...]" (Antrim 1994, p. 1). The town, bewitching and troubled, is located in the Florida Antrim would remember from his childhood. *Elect Mr. Robinson* does not, however depict Antrim's childhood Florida. For this town is at war, fractured, crumbling, and increasingly militarized: family homes are fortified with moats, weapons, surveillance. Pete's charm leads him through the novel: meeting the town's collected citizens, attempting to bury pieces of the ex-mayor's body (drawn and quartered – at Pete's suggestion – during the novel's opening), and establishing a new school in the community. The novel's conclusion, in which schoolroom discipline meets Inquisition-era torture, reveals Pete's depravity, and places in a stark light the sympathy his narration generates. The reader is thus cast back to the beginning of the novel, where Pete narrates his confinement in an attic room, the house – and Florida – flooding as he waits and watches.

The second book in the trilogy, and Antrim's next novel, is *The Hundred Brothers* (1997). One-hundred brothers – or perhaps ninety-nine. . . – gather to eat in the library of their family home, and to come to a collective decision on how to dispose of their father's ashes. As the night veers toward its intoxicated conclusion, both of these two events prove impossible to satisfactorily complete. The novel's narrator is Doug, unstable and alcoholic. The brothers carouse through the library as it steadily decays, occasionally aware of their privilege in comparison to the huddled masses outside the great house:

> What must it be like, in this bitter season, to inhabit the shabby tent city that covers the meadow beyond the wall [of the house]? From time to time I will happen to peak out a rattling window and glimpse the trash-can fires here and there illuminating bleak lean-tos and crouched, windblown figures. Invariably I contemplate the happy fortune we in the room share; and I will offer, almost always, a silent prayer of thanks. . .
>
> (2013, pp. 60–61)

This perspective is, however, fleeting. The brothers change their allegiances constantly, as the dinner-party gives over to a hedonistic, no-holds barred search for pleasure, filial affirmation, or reassurance. Doug performs a ritual masked dance as the Corn King, provoking a response from his brothers that is ambiguous: either violent attack or caring restraint in the face of mania. The novel concludes with Doug immobilized, uncertain, the library increasingly decrepit.

The third novel in the trilogy is *The Verificationist* (2000). In it, a group of psychotherapist colleagues, all from the so-called Krakower Institute, meet for supper in a pancake restaurant. The narrator, Tom, is an outsider within the group: a practitioner of "Self/Other Friction Theory" and an individual constantly casting himself out of a group because of his desire to see – and to analyze – the whole (Antrim 2001, p. 3). Tom has a breakdown of sorts at supper: he attempts to start a food fight, something he has apparently done before, and is restrained in a massive bear hug by his peer, Richard Bernhardt. At this point, Tom becomes uncertain and floats up toward the ceiling, apparently dissociating. As he floats above his colleagues, he gains an alternate perspective: on his colleagues, his profession, and on his relationship with his wife, Jane. Later, he attempts a romance with a waitress from the Pancake House, flying across town to a Civil War battlefield. The novel concludes with Tom floating through the roof of the Pancake House and away from his body. He moves toward the hospital, to the ICU, where he hopes Jane will meet him.

It is clear that the publication of *The Verificationist* and the completion of the "trilogy" of novels marks, for Antrim, a conclusion of sorts. During this same period, Antrim's mother died, an event which had significant emotional and literary consequences. In a 2014 *New Yorker* interview, Antrim states: "my three novels exist pretty much as alternate worlds. But in my memoir [. . .] and in my stories, I've shifted a little away from more pronounced fantastic conceits [. . .] It seems to me that maybe I want to work toward [. . .] a more quietly embedded and less immediately apparent, perhaps more emotionally driven, fantastic" (Treisman 2014). *The Afterlife* is certainly "more emotionally driven." It tells the story of the life and death of Louanne Antrim; seamstress, mother, alcoholic, survivor. Additionally, and inevitably, it tells the story of Donald Antrim's life and family. Its various chapters intersperse the story of Louanne Antrim's life and loves (Antrim's father – they married and divorced *twice* – and the bottle) with Antrim's own story. Indeed, *The Afterlife*'s memoir-form facilitates the author's engagement with emotion, embedded here within the fantastic normality of everyday American family life. As of this article's publication, readers still await Antrim's reputed next novel, again focused through family: "a novel about [Antrim's] father" (Sullivan 2014).

Late 2014 saw, rather, the publication of *The Emerald Light in the Air*, a collection of stories, all previously published in the *New Yorker* (between 1999 and 2014). The collection is a testament to the long-standing relationship between Antrim and that arbiter of highbrow literary style: the collection is dedicated to the *New Yorker*'s fiction editor, Deborah Treisman. According to John Jeremiah Sullivan (2014), Antrim "refers to her as a 'teacher,' and says that in a funny way he considered himself to be working for her during all that time." The volume collects a series of primarily New York stories: of Manhattan relationships, enduring and falling apart; Manhattan moments, in their dual American-ness and cosmopolitanism. The collection culminates with "The Emerald Light in the Air," which moves away from New York and back to the Virginia where Antrim lived as a child and adolescent. The story's main character, Billy French, is troubled: his recent past contains "the locked ward and his sick brain and the torn-up suicide notes," all of which Antrim himself had experienced (Antrim 2015a, p. 145). Driving along, Billy finds himself enclosed: in the world and in his life. He takes the reasonable (at the time) option of guiding his car along a creek bed. But rather than a story of compounded woe, "The Emerald Light in the Air" presents this as a transformative moment. Billy drives up the creek, eventually encountering a young man looking for help from a doctor; his mother is sick. Billy dispenses what help he can provide, and then departs, suddenly beatified. The story signals a likely new direction for Antrim's writing, away from the anxiety of his new work and toward a new alternative.

Brian Evenson, himself a widely-published novelist, has written the only previous piece of academic criticism on Antrim. "Constructed Space in Donald Antrim's Trilogy" traces the increasing claustrophobia developed in the trilogy: in Elect Mr. Robinson, the novel's space is the town; in The Hundred Brothers, the library; and in The Verificationist, the Pancake House (but really in Richard Bernhardt's close embrace) (see Antrim 2001, pp. 10–15). While the scholarly response to Antrim's work has been limited, it has produced a significant body of high-profile literary journalism. Antrim has submitted to long-form interviews (in BOMB, 1997 and the New Yorker, 2013 and 2014), as well as prompting features (such as in bookforum, 2012 and The New York Times Magazine, 2014). Each novel of the trilogy has also been reissued with a "celebrity" introduction: Jeffery Eugenides introduces Elect Mr. Robinson, Jonathan Franzen The Hundred Brothers, and George Saunders The Verificationist.

Antrim's texts, and the trilogy especially, are masterpieces of absurdist comedy, where humor and anxiety intermingle. At the level of the sentence this comedy is developed in the juxtaposition of precisely matter-of-fact language and narration with strange or inconceivable narrative events. Antrim's grammatical precision is consistent, but most notable in The Hundred Brothers' opening sentence, which extends for almost two pages, listing each of the hundred brothers' names, most of their occupations, and much else besides. Narratorial matter-of-factness, combined with strange narrative events, produces wonderful comic effects, such as the moment Tom begins to float in The Verificationist:

> It was then, while Bernhardt squeezed and I held him – it was then that I began my ascent toward the ceiling. Up I went. I have to confess that I felt, ascending, a bit scared. I am not as a rule happy or comfortable on rocking boats or on airplanes thrown by turbulence, or on the average amusement-park ride [. . .] Bernhardt squeezed and up I went, up toward the Pancake House ceiling, drifting higher to float over the heads of clinicians and waitresses gathered around tables piled with waffles, uneaten bacon, biscuits. How I wished I had been sensible and ordered eggs over easy.
>
> (2001, p. 32)

The ostensibly obvious strangeness of this event – the subject floating up toward the ceiling as a consequence of being pulled into an involuntary hug – is presented as entirely unremarkable; in its place is a more commonplace concern about motion sickness. In fact, one of the distinctive comedic experiences of reading Antrim's work is reconciling the disjunction between the sober and precise prose employed with the unconventional narrative events it documents. The logic of Antrim's sentences and their grammatical precision are, of course, emblematic of the New Yorker's style (see Yagoda 2000 and Leitch 1997). This style can be characterized by intellectual complexity; Antrim's writing challenges expectations, however, by pushing its narrative into consistently strange territory, probing the reader's credulity. The particular type of humor Antrim's texts most consistently develop is, in a sense, a response to the overwhelming atmosphere of anxiety – and indeed its particularly real manifestation – his characters experience. While each novel in the trilogy presents this tension between humor and anxiety and its irresolution, it is most pervasively developed in "Another Manhattan," originally published in the New Yorker in 2008 and collected in The Emerald Light in the Air.

"Another Manhattan" draws together multiple narratives. These focus on two married Manhattan couples (Kate and Jim, Susan and Elliot), both failing marriages, who are sexually involved with the other couple (Kate with Elliot, Susan with Jim). The story focuses primarily on Jim, who strategizes how to recommence a relationship with Susan while keeping face with Kate. His immediate desire is to buy Kate a large bouquet of flowers. Flirting with the attractive florist, Jim ends up agreeing to a massive bouquet resplendent with roses which he cannot pay for himself. Instead, he has to call Kate and ask for her to pay for his gift herself. This neat comedic reversal – a gift designed to secure Kate's affection and trust instead resulting in her greater concern and distrust – is moderated by the increasingly urgent hints of anxiety and mental ill-health that emerge during these events. Jim enters the florist having walked from "the outpatient clinic" (2015a, p. 71); later he reflects upon the mental consequences of his "lithium [and] [. . .] antidepressant cocktail" (p. 78) before admitting that he has just been released from hospital. The reader discovers that the recent hospitalization is one of many, as a consequence of "anxiety and suicidality" (p. 83): "in the past six month, there had been three emergency-room visits and two locked-ward admissions" (p. 86). By the story's denouement, its humor has fallen to the wayside; it is still present but has limited operation.

As he finally departs the florist, Jim walks to the restaurant where the four intend to eat dinner, increasingly paranoid as he seeks to avoid being apprehended and hospitalized again: "[w]henever a siren sounded in the distance – and, once, beating helicopter blades in the night sky caused him to sprint up a side street – he dropped into a furtive, crouching gait" (2015a, p. 91). He arrives at the restaurant harried and bleeding (he is hiding within the bouquet and has been pricked by the rose's thorns), and suddenly the outside world intrudes. The story concludes with Jim re-hospitalized, Kate "on her knees on the emergency-room floor [. . .] extract[ing] the laces from his shoes" her total anguish an impediment to the story's previous humor (p. 95). Indeed, a story like "Another Manhattan" clearly illustrates the gravity of Antrim's humor; it provides no solace, but is instead an acknowledgment of the brutal anxiety of existence – it asks the reader to contemplate this fact directly.

Despite Antrim's capacity to entertain and confound the reader, both at the level of the sentence and the plot, there are elements of his texts which are less edifying. This is particularly the case in the fact that Antrim's writing is almost exclusively about men, and employs a masculine frame of reference.

The apparent exception here is *The Afterlife*, focused on Antrim's mother, in life and death. And yet in an interview with Deborah Treisman (2014), Antrim speaks of *The Afterlife* as "my memoir." Indeed, so much of *The Afterlife* is concerned with *Antrim's* experience of his mother's life and death. The opening chapter, initially published as "I Bought a Bed" in the *New Yorker* in 2002, is precise in its intent to perceive Louanne Antrim's life within Donald Antrim's own experience:

> The story of my mother's lifelong deterioration is, in some respects, the story of her life. The story of my life is bound up in this story, the story of her deterioration. It is the story that is always central to the ways in which I perceive myself and others in the world. It is the story, or at any rate it is my role in the story, that allows me never to lose my mother. With this in mind – the story of my mother and me, my mother *in* me – I will try to tell another story, the story of my attempt, during the weeks and months following her death, to buy a bed.
>
> (2014, p. 5, emphasis original)

There are two important elements here. The first is the continuation of the strategy which relates comedy and anxiety in Antrim's trilogy: that is, that one emotion-generating experience is effaced (or complicated) by its engagement with another event which is clearly comedic. Thus in *The Afterlife*, the emotional challenges of Antrim's mother's death are placed in an alternate perspective by their forced relation to the author's apparently mundane (but this is inevitably not the case) experience of bed-buying.

The second element, is the one originally highlighted. That while the object of *The Afterlife* is Louanne Antrim and her life and death, the true subject of the memoir in Antrim himself. The fact that the trilogy's three protagonist-narrators are all thirty-or forty-something men, all erudite and of an intellectual bent, suggest again the significant element of the personal that exists within Antrim's texts. (In a commencement address Antrim delivered at his former school – and subsequently published in the *New Yorker* – Antrim (2015b) wrote: "my characters are both me and not me." We might also consider here Antrim's increasing forthrightness in discussing his own mental health challenges [see Sullivan 2014].) Maturity itself is a significant feature of all three texts in the trilogy, most often focused on the question of fatherhood. Pete, Doug, and Tom are not fathers, and their desire for fatherhood is variously indirectly rebuffed or rejected outright. All three are both childless and often child*like*, men in name only.

While Antrim's writing is considered self-referential, the changes he forecast post-trilogy assist in thinking against the grain. While hermetic, Antrim's texts are not self-obsessed. Rather, they pay careful attention to the world in small but important ways. Thus in *Elect Mr. Robinson* Pete lauds a science fair project on "Annual Coastal Erosion Due to Global Temperature Shifts and Resultant Polar Ice Cap Meltdown Contributing to Rising Sea Levels," while the novel concludes with Pete locked in his attic, Florida slowly flooding (Antrim 1994, p. 42). Antrim's texts are consistently intuitive, and while his reputation remains less significant than his peers, his is work is powerful and important.

SEE ALSO: After Postmodernism; Barth, John; DeLillo, Don; Foer, Jonathan Safran; Franzen, Jonathan; Literary Magazines; Pynchon, Thomas; Roth, Philip; Saunders, George; Wallace, David Foster

REFERENCES

Antrim, Donald. (1994). *Elect Mr. Robinson for a Better World*. London: Minerva; 1st ed. 1993.

Antrim, Donald. (2001). *The Verificationist*. London: Bloomsbury; 1st ed. 2000.

Antrim, Donald. (2008). *The Afterlife*. London: Abacus; 1st ed. 2006.

Antrim, Donald. (2013). *The Hundred Brothers*. London: Granta; 1st ed. 1997.

Antrim, Donald. (2015a). *The Emerald Light in the Air*. London: Granta.

Antrim, Donald. (2015b). The unprotected life. *The New Yorker* (July 16, 2015). https://www.newyorker.com/books/page-turner/the-unprotected-life (accessed August 2, 2021).

Antrim, Donald. (2019). Everywhere and nowhere: a journey through suicide. *The New Yorker* (February 11, 2019). https://www.newyorker.com/magazine/2019/02/18/everywhere-and-nowhere-a-journey-through-suicide (accessed August 2, 2021).

Bolt, Thomas. (1997). Donald Antrim. *Bomb* 58: 26–29.

Evenson, Brian. (2002). Constructed space in Donald Antrim's trilogy. *Revue Française d'Études Américaines* 94: 10–15.

Leitch, Thomas. (1997). The *New Yorker* school. In: *Critical and Creative Approaches to the Short Story* (ed. Noel Harold Kaylor, Jr.), 123–149. Lewiston, NY: Edwin Mellen Press.

Sullivan, John. (2014). Donald Antrim and the art of anxiety. *The New York Times Magazine* (September 17, 2014). https://www.nytimes.com/2014/09/21/magazine/donald-antrim-and-the-art-of-anxiety.html (accessed August 2, 2021).

Treisman, Deborah. (2014). This week in fiction: Donald Antrim. *The New Yorker* (January 26, 2014). https://www.newyorker.com/books/page-turner/this-week-in-fiction-donald-antrim (accessed August 2, 2021).

Yagoda, Ben. (2000). *About Town: The New Yorker and the World It Made*. New York: Da Capo.

FURTHER READING

Eugenides, Jeffrey. (2012). Introduction. In: *Elect Mr. Robinson for a Better World* (by Donald Antrim). London: Picador.

Franzen, Jonathan. (2011). Introduction. In: *The Hundred Brothers* (by Donald Antrim). London: Picador.

Saunders, George. (2011). Introduction. In: *The Verificationist* (by Donald Antrim). London: Picador.

Apostol, Gina

RYAN KU
Swarthmore College, USA

Can the subaltern write a novel? This question underlies Gina Apostol's work, which straddles the Philippines and United States. Given the misremembered (if remembered at all) history of the US colonization of the Philippines (1898–1946), the inclusion of Apostol – following Bienvenido N. Santos, Carlos Bulosan, and Jessica Hagedorn – as a figure of American literature is a remarkable irony of history. Filipino novelists, it would seem, occasionally emerge in the US literary scene as a counterpoint to US disavowal of its past in the Philippines. Equally noteworthy is the chosen medium, which is hardly a simple means for the colonized to tell their story amid the colonizer's writing of history. Historically, the novel departed from the epic's unmediated representation of a coherent world in depicting life rendered irreducibly complicated, problematic, and contradictory by modernity. Accordingly, it is partial and, aware of its partiality, ironic. The complexity of its content and its cognizance of its formal limits has made the novel the most protean of literary genres (Puckett 2018). Its language is decentered and its subject – both writer and reader – is the solitary bourgeois individual because its stories arise out of a particular history. In fact, as the literary form of modernity, the novel does not only domesticate selves into subjects of its Western regimes of origin; it has also sought the other in the places that the West has tried to incorporate in its realization of modernity. That is, the anchoring of the novel to capitalism, the economic basis of modernity, also made the novel a part of modernity's colonial underside, indeed a commodity in the world system (Cooppan 2018).

If the novel provides narratives of history grounded in modernity, telling stories based on the structural conditions of the modern world, to what extent can the subaltern speak through the novel? For subjects subordinated in modernity – rendered *subaltern*, in Antonio Gramsci's terms; voiceless, according to postcolonial studies, in the context of colonizing Western representation – can the novel serve as a vehicle for the telling of one's own history, for the showing of other sides of the world? After independence in the postwar era, also known as late modernity, former colonies claimed the status of the nation-state, the political form that their colonizers adopted in the advent of modernity. Consistently, the metropolitan and postcolonial novel both have the nation as a frame of reference. Indeed, the novel from both ends of the colonial relation builds the nation, if in a primarily imaginative sense, by constituting individual *and* collective identity, mediating the subject's relation to a community – the nation – through a shared identity (Anderson 1983). In the Philippines, the gap that the novel is supposed to bridge is compounded by the genre's origins in the West, from which the Philippines had to wrest itself to become a nation like its Western colonizers. Like the nation itself, the novel is thus a double-edged sword for the Filipino, a harbinger of colonial and revolutionary modernity. No one embodies this more than José Rizal, the mestizo product of "the integration of [Spanish] colonial Philippines into the world market in the nineteenth century" (Hau 2008, p. 318), whose novels in Spanish inspired the Philippine Revolution (1896–1898). Beginning in the following period of US colonization, Rizal would become a national hero and a formative influence on Filipino writers – including Apostol, whose novels, by her own account, "all [. . .] speak to Rizal" (Nadal 2020).

In light of the ways that the subaltern cannot speak with their own voice, indeed alienate themselves, in the emblematic discursive form of Western modernity, Apostol "write[s] that novel anyhow" (2019b). To do so, she practices serial reading, following fellow postcolonial writer Jorge Luis Borges. Because even the colonized know themselves only through the colonizer's texts, she "pursue[s . . .] a rereading of the double in the [hegemonic] text, the elusive Filipino, who must be read awry through others' words: inverse, anew" (Apostol 2013). Unearthing the subaltern from texts that represent them as subjects of colonization entails a "mediated sense of self," a "sense of reality as mediation" (2019a) – that is, consciousness of the self as existing in relation to an other, of reality as mediated by irreducible factors like technology (e.g. texts) and politics (e.g. of colonization). This deconstruction of identity as double (constructed in part by an other) and unstable (deployed and redeployed for contradictory purposes) rests on a "global sense of self – [on the confrontation of one's] own scars and trauma [i.e. history, that enables one to be] steadfast in [one's . . .] multiple identities" (Fantauzzo 2018). Apostol thus points to the multiplicity of Filipino identity, to the different ways that Filipinos perform their identity along with other identities, to suggest that Filipino writers can find the truth of Filipino identity in Western, including American, discourse. In effect, writing novels, or rewriting the novel, is her means of letting the subaltern speak through the dominant. In this regard, her work is in keeping with the Filipino novel, which, in her reading, "was always an innovation," the transposition of a Western genre into another milieu, thereby its transformation (2019b). "Using Western [. . .] tricks [. . .] which are also [her] own" (2019b), she draws on both postmodernism, including the metafiction of her teacher John Barth, and realism, historically the dominant literary aesthetic in the Philippines, to posit postmodernism as a form of realism that, against its definition by the New Critics, matches the overdetermined construction of Filipino history in "mak[ing] the problem of this translated [or mediated] self both its subject and its form" (2017). In the same way that Filipino novels tend to "play on the perceived division between history and literature" (Nadal 2020), Apostol's "political art novel[s]" (2019b) are political precisely in their "narrative play" (Fantauzzo 2018), in employing Western forms to invert them, thereby unraveling the Filipino from its subordination.

Apostol has been narrating subaltern realities by postmodern means as early as in her first novel, *Bibliolepsy* (published in the Philippines in 1997). The novel begins by defining its title as a condition – sentimentality manifest physically, sexually, improperly – that describes the narrator Primi's life, of which the book is an account. Part one recollects her childhood in Tacloban and part two follows her as a young woman in Manila. In coining the term to name her condition, Primi uses the colonizer's language to convey her own meaning, akin to how her affliction is also her raison d'être. She must have gotten this love for books from her father, an animator and writer of *komiks* – that Filipino adaptation of the comic book, with its images that allegedly embody the obscenity of the book itself – or else from the books, including the *Kama Sutra*, that her *abuelita* gifted her as a kid. These are conflicting sources as the grandmother refuses to recognize the father, who is working class and part Chinese. Her improper relation to texts could have also come from the family attorney, who *may* have touched her at the library after the funeral for her parents, who disappeared when Primi was eight, on the day in 1972 when martial law was declared. In any case, bibliolepsy would bring Primi to Manila in the 1980s, to the writers whose words and bodies she would seek. One of these men would cause her to miss EDSA, the People Power Revolution that toppled the dictator in 1986, for a book. In depicting familial conflicts that reflect the nation's postcolonial hierarchies and ultimately place the protagonist at the margins of the revolution, *Bibliolepsy* looks like a classic realist Filipino novel. The social concerns of the book, however, function mainly as the backdrop for Primi's reflections on reading itself, for her elaboration and reclamation of her condition. This is not to say that the social context is unimportant; in fact, its specificities make the novel a veritable portrait of the reader as Filipina. Departing from realist conventions while lending the postmodern novel Filipino reality, *Bibliolepsy* finally posits the writer as a reader rather than a revolutionary. In failing to take part in the revolution, what work does the writer do? What work does the text do in the context of its failure to be revolutionary *and* of the things that the revolution fails to do?

Apostol's second novel, *The Revolution According to Raymundo Mata* (published in the Philippines in 2009, in the USA in 2021), is even more historical *and* experimental. If *Bibliolepsy* is a reader's journal, *Raymundo Mata* is an edition of its eponymous hero's notebooks – his papers, creative writings, and/or diary – in four parts, from his childhood in Cavite (the most rebellious of Spain's Philippine provinces) to his college years in Manila to his employment in a printing press to his generalship in the Philippine Revolution. With its jokes, puns, ironies, and other witticisms, the first part in particular reads like the narratives from the time in which Mata was being schooled (e.g. Voltaire), lending credence to the book as a historical novel that charts its night-blind hero's coming of age at the margins of history amid the Filipino Enlightenment (notably, as the friend of Emilio Aguinaldo, who would go on to become the first President of the Philippines). Like modernist texts, the writing is thick with allusions, except that while for someone like T.S. Eliot this amounts to comprehensive referentiality that both counters and conveys the otherwise baffling complexity of metropolitan modernity, for Apostol allusion reverses the hierarchy of knowledge as her references would be familiar to the colonized and not the colonizer. Apostol avoids being obscure, however, through annotations – especially footnotes that explain the allusions – thereby literally juxtaposing the high and the low while pointing to the narrative as a text. This postmodern hermeneutic embedded in the storytelling consists in multiple voices: those of the two editors, nationalist historian Estrella Espejo and quasi-Lacanian psychotherapist Diwata Drake – the postcolonial and the psychoanalytic critic, so to speak – and the translator, PhD student Mimi C. Magsalin (a pseudonym). Magsalin gets caught in between not only the conflicting editors but the multiple languages of the supposedly original text: Mata's Tagalog influenced by colonial Spanish along with a sprinkling of several other Philippine, not to mention European and Asian, languages, as well as the English of the Americans, with which the story ends without an account of the climactic events of the revolution. Instead, the narrative's highlight is an encounter with Rizal in which, from the periphery, Mata steals some of the First Filipino's burning drafts of a third novel – his attempt to write in Tagalog – of which *Raymundo Mata* may be a copy. Or maybe Magsalin, as Drake suggests, made the whole thing up, even as Espejo comes to discern its verity after "recovering" from the breakdown its reading had induced.

Apostol made her American debut with her third novel, *Gun Dealers' Daughter* (published in the Philippines in 2010, in the USA in 2012), which returns to the Philippines under martial law, perhaps the most well-known era in Philippine history, and zooms in on the Filipino oligarchy to ironically dramatize Filipino postcoloniality beyond official history. The narrator is Sol (Soledad Soliman), whose parents' wealth, as the title suggests, is rooted in the US arms trade, in which the conduit is Sol's American "uncle" Gianni. In college, Sol becomes politicized: she crosses class and sexual borders – in particular, with the couple Jed, another child of *caciques* (the natives who took over the position of the colonizers after decolonization), and Soli (Solidaridad Soledad), her name twin – and takes part in the plot to assassinate a US colonel, a former prisoner of war in Vietnam turned counterinsurgency expert in Marcos's Philippines. Vignettes of Sol's world evoke Hagedorn's *Dogeaters* (1990), the novel that, in depicting US neocolonialism in the Philippines, inaugurated the emergence of Filipino culture in America. Apostol traces this world to Leyte – the province where Tacloban, her hometown, is located; from where the First Lady and Sol's mother hail; and where Gianni's father fought in World War II and General MacArthur returned to liberate the then US colony from the Japanese. Sol's foray into adolescent radicalism despite her family's social status also harks back to F. Sionil José's socialist realist classic *My Brother, My Executioner* (1973) – except Sol actually does something, which leads her to the state in which she narrates her story: diagnosed with anterograde amnesia, her ability to form new memories stalled by a fixation on the events that led to the assassination. Sol can only remember what happened before, not after, trauma, which she attempts to account for in writing that is subject to fragmentation and repetition, not to mention her unreliability and dysgraphia. The novel's realism thus extends to, indeed relies on, its subject's mind, as in modernism, and is conveyed through postmodern techniques. Sol's trauma consists in guilt, but less about the assassination than about its collateral damage. To protect her, her family ends up framing Soli, whom she had already betrayed by sleeping with Jed, who persuaded her to take part in the plot. It was too late for her to stop the cover-up just as it was too late for her to stop the plot and it may be too late for her to come to terms with the past. Beyond personal trauma, the novel raises the question of whether complicity in power perverts the revolution, which implies revolution's impossibility to the extent that it entails power. Indeed, Sol's trauma rests on her complicity in the violence of the revolution, which is thereby unraveled as itself contradictory, like the power that enables Sol to be party to it. Ultimately, is not this double bind the Filipino position itself – between not only East and West, as the Philippines has historically been portrayed, but also post- and neocoloniality, given that the nation, including in its "one hundred years of solitude," has always been marked by the other?

Apostol tackles US imperialism and the Filipino subaltern most directly in a fourth novel, *Insurrecto* (published in the USA in 2018), an offshoot of another novel she had been at work on, *William McKinley's World*. Following an American filmmaker, Chiara Brasi, who hires a Filipina translator, Magsalin (a professional name that means *to translate*; the student in *Raymundo Mata* a decade later?), to accompany her to a forgotten site of the Philippine–American War, *Insurrecto* interweaves the frame narrative, set in 2018 amid an extrajudicial "drug war," with the women's "duel scripts." Chiara's script recounts the lead-up to the 1901 Balangiga incident – in which, in response to forty-eight deaths at the hands of Filipino villagers, US soldiers savaged the town – from the viewpoints of Cassandra Chase, the American socialite who captured images of the scene, and Casiana Nacionales, the townswoman who plotted the attack on the soldiers. Magsalin's script recreates the making of *The Unintended* – the Vietnam War film that Chiara's father shot in the Philippines in the martial law years (an allusion to *Apocalypse Now* [1979]) – from the perspectives of Virginie, the director's wife and investor who would leave him, taking the four-year-old Chiara with her, and Caz, the local teacher with whom he had an affair behind the scenes. Doubleness is a motif in the novel, from the diplopia of at least two characters to the development of stereography during the war to the dual perspectives of each narrative frame, indeed the narratives' doubling of each other. In relating the characters of the narratives in a "duel," Apostol alludes to the Philippine–American War as a primal scene, the origin of trauma that is repeated – from an episode in the war to the filming of another war like it to the storytellers' belated quest for truth – in the form of the contrapuntal relations between the women that trace the war's history. The intertwined national histories are only a part of the story, however, which may be why Magsalin writes about Chiara's family: to question Chiara's reasons for embarking on the journey, ironically enough because she herself cannot tackle her own inability to come home. Once again entangling the political and the personal, Apostol implies that the colonizer and the colonized need each other to work through their shared traumatic history. This is not to say that their positions are interchangeable. To date Apostol's most metafictional novel, *Insurrecto* calls attention to the narratives as film scripts, including the frame narrative – a reminder that they *are* all, including the novel, narratives. By the end of the novel, Magsalin and Chiara have exchanged scripts, as if in reading each other's stories they have become the author of the other's writing. In fact, it is never explicitly stated, or clear, who has been telling which story. While authorship can to some extent be traced, there are contrary evidences and unsolvable puzzles. It is key in this regard to keep in mind the early hint that Apostol drops: that Chiara is Magsalin's protagonist. If the "duel scripts" named in part two are stories within the story, the frame narrative (part one's "mystery"), Apostol reminds her readers, *is* a story. Who is the writer of this story, the frame narrative? Who else can this be but Magsalin, who is thus revealed to be the writer not only of her story but also of Chiara's story? In other words, the frame narrative is the subaltern's attempt to tell not only her story but also the story of the dominant, indeed to insert the dominant into the subaltern so as to narrate the other side – the inverse – of history.

These novels have been well received: the first two both won the Philippine National Book Award; the third, shortlisted for the William Saroyan International Prize for Writing, won the PEN Open Book Award; and the fourth was shortlisted for the Dayton Literary Peace Prize and was one of *Publishers Weekly*'s 10 Best Books. In addition, Apostol has published shorter work – e.g. "Cunanan's Wake," a story that traces the queerness of Filipino kinship amid US illegibility, in the anthology *Charlie Chan is Dead 2* (2004), edited by Hagedorn – not to mention critical essays and regular op-eds in both Philippine and US outlets (collected along with other materials on her website, www.ginaapostol.com). Traversing the boundaries of aesthetic traditions while bridging literary and civic life, Apostol has made writing in English her own, especially through her novels. Through writing, the subaltern emerges at the heart of empire.

SEE ALSO: After Postmodernism; Barth, John; Hagedorn, Jessica; Multiculturalism; Realism after Poststructuralism; Trauma and Fiction

REFERENCES

Anderson, Benedict. (1983). *Imagined Communities: Reflections on the Origin and Spread of Nationalism*. London and New York: Verso.

Apostol, Gina. (2013). Borges, politics, and the postcolonial. Borges Center at the University of Pittsburgh. https://www.borges.pitt.edu/news-events/bruce-rosenstein-borges-gina-apostol-borges-politics-and-postcolonial (accessed July 7, 2021).

Apostol, Gina. (2017). Narration and history. Gina Apostol: a novelist's blog. https://ginaapostol.wordpress.com/2017/03/23/narration-and-history/ (accessed July 7, 2021).

Apostol, Gina. (2019a). "My choices kept moving me toward the consciousness of women": an interview with Gina Apostol, by Thom Cuell. *Minor Literature[s]* (October 2, 2019). https://minorliteratures.com/2019/10/02/my-choices-kept-moving-me-towards-the-consciousness-of-women-an-interview-with-gina-apostol-by-thom-cuell/ (accessed July 7, 2021).

Apostol, Gina. (2019b). A doubling, troubling gaze. *Singapore Unbound* (April 15, 2019). https://singaporeunbound.org/blog/2019/4/6/tqt7q7lext6y9ex38mypq4fvcnroue (accessed July 7, 2021).

Cooppan, Vilashini. (2018). The novel as genre. In: *The Cambridge Companion to the Novel* (ed. Eric Bulson), 23–42. Cambridge: Cambridge University Press.

Fantauzzo, Laurel F. (2018). In multiplicity is truth: an interview with Gina Apostol. *Los Angeles Review of Books* (December 31, 2018). https://lareviewofbooks.org/article/in-multiplicity-is-truth-an-interview-with-gina-apostol/ (accessed July 7, 2021).

Hau, Caroline S. (2008). The Filipino novel in English. In: *Philippine English: Linguistic and Literary Perspectives* (ed. Maria Lourdes S. Bautista and Kingsley Bolton), 317–336. Hong Kong: Hong Kong University Press.

Nadal, Paul. (2020). The novel and technologies of empire: a conversation with Gina Apostol. Asian American Writers Workshop (February 28, 2020). https://aaww.org/technologies-of-empire-gina-apostol/ (accessed July 7, 2021).

Puckett, Kent. (2018). Epic/novel. In: *The Cambridge Companion to the Novel* (ed. Eric Bulson), 57–73. Cambridge: Cambridge University Press.

FURTHER READING

Balce, Nerissa S. (2016). Laughter against the state: on humor, postcolonial satire, and Asian American short fiction. *Journal of Asian American Studies* 19 (1): 47–73.

Myers, Cecilia N. (2016). Confession, hybridity, and language in Gina Apostol's *Gun Dealer's Daughter*. *Asian American Literature: Discourse & Pedagogies* 7: 102–114.

Pison, Ruth J.L. (2010). The narrativized body and history: Gina Apostol's *Bibliolepsy*. In: *Dangerous Liaisons: Sexing the Nation in Novels by Philippine Women Writers (1993–2006)*, 223–249. Quezon City, Philippines: University of the Philippines Press.

Ponce, Martin J. (2013). Revolution from above. *American Book Review* 34 (5): 10–11.

Quicho, Alex. (2019). Chaos will set you free. *The New Inquiry* (November 18, 2019). https://thenewinquiry.com/chaos-will-set-you-free

Tan, Jillian J.O. (2012). Discursive formations and the ambivalent nation in Gina Apostol's *The Revolution According to Raymundo Mata*. *Kritika Kultura* 19: 342–360.

Auster, Paul

LANCE CONLEY
Michigan State University, USA

Paul Auster's fictional oeuvre remains grounded by an apophatic impulse, a particular enigmatic negativity that permeates much of his fiction. In other words, starting with *The New York Trilogy* (1987) and continuing through to his most recent epic, *4321* (2017), Auster's novels depict a wide variety of characters that attempt to make meaning out of events and occurrences, often tragic and violent, that appear guided by the mystical powers of language, chance, and identity. His fiction can be divided into the decades in which each of his novels was published: the 1980s (five), the 1990s (four), the 2000s (six), and the 2010s (two). Subsequent to a brief recounting of relevant biographical details about Auster, the rest of this entry is structured around a decade-based organizational schema. When analyzed from such a perspective, Auster's fiction reveals a through-line of depictions of older male characters attempting to make meaning out of difficult situations wrought by the volatile interaction between the concepts mentioned above, language, chance, and identity. Following short summaries and discussions of each of his works, a bibliography appears composed of a series of secondary sources for further reading on Auster and his impact on American fiction published over the past forty years.

Auster was born on February 3 in Newark, New Jersey in 1947. After earning a BA and MA at Columbia University, Auster moved to Paris and worked on translating the writing of French writers such as Maurice Blanchot, André du Bouchet, Pierre Clastres, and Stéphane Mallarmé. He returned to the United States in 1974 and, after a marriage to acclaimed short story writer Lydia Davis, with whom he has one son, Daniel, Auster met his current partner, novelist and essayist Siri Hustvedt, whom he married in 1981. Auster later became involved in filmmaking, writing and co-directing with Wayne Wang acclaimed films such as *Smoke* (1995) and *Blue in the Face* (1995), the former garnering Auster the Independent Spirit Award for Best First Screenplay.

Auster published five novels in the 1980s: *City of Glass* (1985), *Ghosts* (1986), *The Locked Room* (1986) – the three of which comprise *The New York Trilogy* – *In the Country of Last Things* (1987), and *Moon Palace* (1989). Given conversations on Auster's writing remain oversaturated with analyses of *The New York Trilogy*, this entry will not say as much about that text in order to focus on the impact of some of his lesser-studied works. Nevertheless, the trilogy must be taken into account. The novels of *The New York Trilogy* constitute the first appearance of Auster's characters confronting a form of existential dread generated by (among other things) language's inability to capture the Real, the paradoxical nature of identity and its relationship to authorship, and the ways in which chance, randomness as such, hangs over all encounters and exchanges in the complex diegeses the author creates. From the fictional version of himself in *City of Glass* who recounts events as told to himself by the "author" of the "story" – a writer named Paul Auster – to the colorful characters that make up the cast of *Ghosts* – the narrative's major players are named Blue, Black, Brown, and White – to the mysterious Fanshawe of *The Locked Room*, a character that quite literally has his identity stolen from him by the novel's narrator, the characters that appear in *The New York Trilogy* represent a narrativized reckoning with the aporias at the heart of language, identity, and chance funneled through some of the fundamental elements of detective fiction.

Auster's second novel, *In the Country of Last Things*, depicts a post-apocalyptic diegesis in which the narrator, Anna Blume, bears witness to the perpetual decay of an unnamed city in what appears to be the United States. Auster's second novel is epistolary, meaning that it is constructed as a letter from Anna to an unknown individual as she documents the destruction of the city in which she lives, despite communal efforts made by both herself and the narrative's other characters to stabilize society. The narrative ends ambiguously, with the fate of Anna and her surviving accomplices left unknown, and readers never learn if her letter reached its intended reader(s). The conflict that drives *In the Country of Last Things* hinges on the unknown identity of Anna's possible audience because it brings a certain ethical element to the text. In the novel's apocalyptic diegesis of decay and ruin, where not only matter appears to have reached a point of unsurpassable finitude but also human identities and memories, the fact that Anna chooses to write, even if the world around her reaches its end, reveals the profound power of *In the Country of Last Things* and its epistolary form.

Moon Palace rounds out Auster's fictional production in the 1980s, and in the context of both his 1980s writing and his oeuvre, the novel stands out for its, by comparison, upbeat nature and somewhat hopeful conclusion. Telling the story of Marco Fogg, *Moon Palace* is the narrative of Fogg's attempt to construct a stable identity. Born an orphan and raised by his uncle, Victor – whose death early in the narrative throws the protagonist into a deep depression – Fogg struggles to possess a sense of self whose genesis he can pinpoint, making and breaking a series of personal relationships over the course of the text's three hundred-plus pages. He chooses to hit the proverbial road, and the latter parts of *Moon Palace* thus have the feeling of a road novel. *Moon Palace*'s powerful final scene, in which Fogg stops his car on an empty California beach in the wee hours of the morning and claims the beginning of a new life, closes the novel with an open-ended optimism with regards to the character's attempt to construct a stable identity, which makes *Moon Palace* feel somewhat different than the texts that both precede and follow it.

Auster's 1990s fictional output begins with *The Music of Chance* (1990). The novel takes elements of the road novel seen in *Moon Palace* and deploys them in the narrative of Jim Nashe, an existentially distraught firefighter who inherits a large sum of money after the death of his estranged father and decides, like Marco Fogg, to hit the road with no final destination. On his travels he comes across Jack Pozzi, a professional poker player, who proposes a get-rich-quick scheme that involves Nashe's investment in Pozzi defeating a couple of wealthy amateur players, Flower and Stone – who, over the course of the narrative, become more sinister and mysterious until they disappear altogether – in a series of high-stakes poker games. Perhaps more than any of Auster's other novels, *The Music of Chance*, as one might expect, is fundamentally invested in interrogating the ways in which chance rules the universe and how one's sense of identity can be destroyed by it in an instant.

Leviathan (1992) is perhaps Auster's most overtly political novel written to date. Though not explicitly stated in the text, the title can be read as a reference to Thomas Hobbes's famous treatise of the same name, and the novel includes an epigraph from Ralph Waldo Emerson: "Every actual State is corrupt." With arguably one of the most chilling opening passages in the history of American literature, *Leviathan* is composed as a novel within a novel, one that tells the story of Peter Aaron, an author who tasks himself with recounting the narrative of Benjamin Sachs, his old friend and a recently deceased domestic terrorist, because Aaron feels it is necessary to try to give a true account of what led to Sachs's suicide by bomb on the side of the road in Wisconsin. The text can be read as a fascinating attempt by Aaron to recreate the identity and thus the story of a deceased individual, Sachs, who will never get the chance to defend or explain his actions in person. However, acknowledging the intrinsic fallibility of his project, Aaron notes that there is a chance that "the words I am about to write might mean nothing" because they, unlike Sachs's acts of domestic terrorism, remain tethered by the limits of language (1992, p. 2).

Mr. Vertigo (1994) and *Timbuktu* (1999) are Auster's last works of the 1990s, and each text remains anomalous and yet similar to the rest of the author's corpus. This claim is based on the fact that the former represents Auster's most blatant attempt at addressing racism, a topic that does not appear in much of his writing. The latter is told from the perspective of a dog, Mr. Bones, who, over the course of *Timbuktu*, must deal with the looming death of his master, Willy G. Christmas, a homeless poet, and his own fear that he will not get into the afterlife, the fantastical locale of the novel's title. While *Timbuktu*, though tinged with similar existential questions to Auster's earlier novels, remains relatively light in terms of scale and scope, *Mr. Vertigo* confronts the racism that plagued the twentieth century in the United States head-on by depicting the socially ingrained racism of its protagonist, Walter "Walt" Rawley, and his quite literal attempts to rise above the ignorance and hatred of the environment in which he was raised. Much of the first half of the novel depicts Walt's rescue from abuse at the hands of his aunt and uncle by Master Yehudi, a Hungarian magician of sorts who teaches Walt how to levitate and also becomes a surrogate father for him. In each text, though of different species, the principal characters, Walt and Mr. Bones, confront the meaning of their individual identities by dealing with the tragic loss and violent chaos inherent in their separate worlds.

Auster's fictional output in the 2000s remains characterized by relatively short, cryptic narratives that return to the same themes and style seen in his earlier writings. Though *The Book of Illusions* (2002), *The Brooklyn Follies* (2005), and *Invisible* (2009) are longer than *Oracle Night* (2003), *Travels in the Scriptorium* (2006), and *Man in the Dark* (2008), each of these works employs varying experimental techniques to talk about the same recurrent themes: the mystical nature(s) of language, identity, and chance, as well as the relative nature of truth and the complicated relationship between author and reader. With *Invisible* serving as an outlier, all of the novels feature depictions of despondent male characters, often authors of some sort – another frequent motif in Auster's fiction – that use the act of writing as a means of communicating an acknowledgment of existential dread and yet, in some cases, a sense of communal responsibility, an ethical commitment to Others, despite declining circumstances dictated by the randomness of an uncaring universe.

For example, *The Book of Illusions* tells the story of David Zimmer, a college professor in Vermont devastated by the loss of his wife and daughter in a plane crash. Finding solace in the silent comedies of Hector Mann, an entirely fictional actor about whom Auster provides fascinating biographical details, Zimmer becomes obsessed with learning as much as he can about Mann's life for the purposes of writing a book about him. Zimmer's project thus functions as a means of working through his grief via the acquisition of knowledge of the minute details that comprise the identity of another person, Mann. Once he learns the details of the tragedy and chance that ruled Hector's life, Zimmer is able to begin to come to terms with the loss of his own family.

Oracle Night focuses on another writer, Sidney Orr, who, like the protagonist of *Man in the Dark* and *Travels in the Scriptorium*, faces the implications of his own looming finitude. In *Oracle Night*, this confrontation comes in the form of a devastating illness, but Sidney recovers, an anomaly in probability that represents the importance of chance in the narrative. Upon recovering, Orr purchases a blue notebook from a local stationery store and begins to compose a semi-autobiographical novel about the way in which life is dictated by chance. In terms of its existential themes, the metafictional narrative that follows, like *Man in the Dark* and *Travels in the Scriptorium*, possesses a more sinister tone than much of Auster's novels published in both the 2000s and 2010s.

Man in the Dark and *Travels in the Scriptorium* have been mentioned together because they share a number of characteristics. Each focuses on elderly male characters in perplexing situations in which their individual thoughts dictate much of their respective narratives. In *Man in the Dark*, journalist August Brill is recovering at his daughter's house in Vermont from a car accident. Plagued by a bout of insomnia stemming from the recent passing of his wife and other personal tragedies, Brill imagines an alternate reality in which America has been destroyed by a civil war, and, per usual, the novel becomes increasingly metatextual and existential over the course of its short narrative. *Travels in the Scriptorium* depicts the mysterious story of an elderly man called simply "Mr. Blank" who, at the novel's beginning, finds himself locked in a room with no recollection of who he is or how he got to his current location and only a handful of objects, a mysterious manuscript, and a stack of puzzling photos on a desk to help him learn the "truth" of his situation. The narrative reads as a tense examination of an individual deprived of his identity and the ways in which written material and fetishized objects can function as markers of and therefore breadcrumbs to a unique sense of self. While the details of the two novels differ, *Travels in the Scriptorium* and *Man in the Dark*, written in succession, represent a concentrated return to short and mysterious narratives that comprised *The New York Trilogy* but with older characters and different political and historical contexts reflective of Auster's age and response to, among other things, 9/11, the Iraq War, and his own looming mortality.

The Brooklyn Follies and *Invisible* are the last two novels published by Auster in the 2000s. As mentioned above, *Invisible* stands out from the others published in this time period because its content is unique and its form is used again (to an extent) in *4321*. Divided into four parts narrated by different characters within separate time periods, *Invisible* is the story of James/Jim, a famous author writing in the novel's present, 2007, who receives a manuscript for a memoir from a dying man named Adam Walker, but he never gets to meet Walker in person. In the first part of the novel, readers encounter Walker as a college student at Columbia University who becomes entangled in a love triangle with his political science professor, Rudolf Born, and Born's girlfriend, Margot, in the spring of 1967. After learning that much of Walker's memoir is fabricated, the narrative devolves into Jim's quest for some form of truth about the identity of Walker and his complicated relationship with Born and Margot, which was plagued by a violent incident in their younger years.

Along with *Moon Palace* and parts of *4321*, *The Brooklyn Follies* represents one of Auster's more cheerful approaches to the existential dread that tinges much of his works. The novel focuses on the redemptive relationship of Nathan Glass, another widowed, older male character plagued by pessimistic views of his own mortality, and his nephew Tom, who shares the same bleak views as Nathan, caring little about his life and future. In short, the negative feelings they share allow each character, over the course of the novel, to connect with another person in ways they thought not possible and make *The Brooklyn Follies* a significant work in the writer's bibliography.

To date, Auster has published only two novels in the 2010s: *Sunset Park* (2013) and *4321*. The former returns to the narrative structure and major themes of *The Brooklyn Follies* and focuses on Miles Teller, a college dropout with no hope or plan for his life in the wake of the 2008 global financial crisis, and his reconnection with an old friend, Bing, who lives in an abandoned home in Brooklyn. Through this rekindled friendship, Teller, like Nathan and Tom in *The Brooklyn Follies*, gains the necessary support and strength to reassemble his identity. Auster's most recent novel, *4321*, is also his longest by a great deal. Published in 2017 after three years of writing and coming in at a staggering 866 pages, *4321* feels like the author's magnum opus. The novel is divided into four large parts composed of seven chapters apiece, and each focuses on a different version of the life of Archie Ferguson, a Jewish boy born in Newark, New Jersey in 1947. All four of the narratives feature the same set of characters – for example, his parents and the love of his four lives, Amy Schneiderman – but the historical context and situational circumstances in which Archie finds himself remain unique in each instance. Perhaps the principal point of *4321* is the way in which chance reigns over the four distinct narratives of Archie Ferguson such that they feel separate yet strangely connected based on the shifting circumstances. Reader expectations are manipulated with the death and birth of the different Archies, and the effect is nothing short of staggering. In sum, *4321* is Auster's arguable masterpiece to date, and the text serves as an appropriate bookend to the author's incredible contribution to American letters over the past forty years.

SEE ALSO: Chabon, Michael; Contemporary Fictions of War; DeLillo, Don; Fiction and Terrorism; Hustvedt, Siri; Post-9/11 Narratives; Pynchon, Thomas; Realism after Poststructuralism

REFERENCE

Auster, Paul. (1992). *Leviathan*. New York: Viking Press.

FURTHER READING

Arce, María Laura. (2016). *Paul Auster and the Influence of Maurice Blanchot*. Jefferson, NC: McFarland.

Auster, Paul. (2017). *A Life in Words: Conversations with J.B. Siegumfeldt*. New York: Seven Stories Press.

Herzogenrath, Bernd. (1999). *An Art of Desire: Reading Paul Auster*. Atlanta: Amsterdam Press.

Krämer, Kathrin. (2008). *Walking in Deserts, Writing out of Wounds: Jewishness and Deconstruction in Paul Auster's Literary Work*. Heidelberg: Universitätsverlag Winter.

Peacock, James. (2010). *Understanding Paul Auster*. Columbia: University of South Carolina Press.

B

Baker, Nicholson

ERIC CASERO
University of Massachusetts, Dartmouth, USA

Nicholson Baker is an American novelist, essayist, and historical preservationist who has been active from the 1980s up to the present day. While his work spans several genres, he is best known for his novels, which display a signature style involving first-person narrators relaying intensely detailed observations within a constrained time frame. Baker's novels usually contain little in the way of traditional plot, involving few major conflicts or antagonists. Instead, the intrigue of his writing comes from the ways in which he follows the twists and turns of his protagonists' thoughts as they reflect on and describe everyday objects in unsparing detail. For example, *The Mezzanine* (1988), Baker's debut novel, consists entirely of the thoughts of Howie, a young office worker, as he takes a midday lunch break. The novel takes place within a single hour and features no major characters other than Howie. Like most of Baker's novels, it contains, in lieu of traditional plot, pages-long descriptions of everyday minutiae, all relayed from a narrator's delightfully obsessive point of view. Objects of sustained description in *The Mezzanine* include shoelaces, escalators, and shampoo bottles, and Howie freely associates such objects with a plethora of trivial factoids and personal memories. This unique narrative style reflects Baker's desire, as stated in the essay "Changes of Mind" (1982), to follow "each sequential change of mind in its true, knotted, clotted, vinyl multifariousness, with all of the colorful streamers of intelligence still taped on and flapping in the wind" (1996, p. 9). In both his fictional and his nonfictional work, Baker captures these subtle, "sequential change[s] of mind" with a unique sense of care, attention, and intellectual curiosity.

Nicholson Baker was born in 1957 in Rochester, New York. As a young man he demonstrated an interest in music, and even enrolled in music school. This interest informs early stories such as "K.590" (1981) and "Playing Trombone" (1982) as well as the later novel *Traveling Sprinkler* (2013), each of which highlights music as a major theme. Baker eventually transitioned to a full-time literary career and published *The Mezzanine* in 1988. *The Mezzanine* establishes many of the stylistic elements that would come to define Baker's fiction over the course of his career, using a series of far-flung extended metaphors and a wide-ranging, almost whimsical vocabulary to describe its 1980s-era office setting in a level of detail that, while potentially excruciating in the hands of a lesser writer, becomes imaginative, engaging, and refreshing when rendered in Baker's giddy, ultra-curious prose. The novel features several memorable phrasings, including Howie's descriptions of a sandwich's cream cheese as a "unitary scrum" and his office's ambient noise as a "universal lobby-sound" (2010, pp. 39, 98). Howie employs various odd, yet endearing, hyphenated constructions, referring to his use of a personalized stamp as a "life-ordering act" and unfamiliar co-workers as "the not-introduced-to-yet, the not-joked-about-the-weather-with" (pp. 22, 60). The keen-eyed descriptions and unusual vocabulary that mark Baker's writing draw our attention to the little things that make up our everyday experiences while simultaneously defamiliarizing these experiences through their author's striking vocabulary. By reading *The Mezzanine*, we are able to view things like shoelaces and shampoo bottles with fresh eyes, seeing them not simply as parts of the background noise of our existence, but as vital components of life as it is actually experienced.

In addition to its heavy emphasis on descriptions of minutiae, *The Mezzanine* is notable for its digressiveness, another hallmark of Baker's style. Among his impassioned descriptions of everyday objects, Howie will frequently shift from subject to subject, suddenly moving to new topics according to his whims. As Ross Chambers has pointed out (1994), these digressions are examples of what Baker refers to, in the nonfiction book *U and I* (1991), as narrative "clogs" – places where a novel's primary narrative is blocked or obstructed when the writer shifts focus to some seemingly unnecessary subject. Baker says in *U and I*, "I wanted my first novel to be a veritable infarct of narrative cloggers" (1991, p. 73), and Baker's writing, whether fictional or nonfictional, often consists almost entirely of these "clogs." Baker, much like his narrators, appears to delight in ruminating about whatever subjects cross his mind, with little regard for narrative momentum. Consequently, his writing often takes on a contemplative, almost meditative quality: thoughtful, unhurried, yet deeply immersive.

This digressiveness is enhanced by Baker's use of footnotes in *The Mezzanine*. Howie's thoughts often spill over into long footnotes that allow him to stray from the already threadbare narrative. Howie himself reflects on the role that footnotes can serve in a text, as he thinks (appropriately enough, in a long footnote) that writers such as Boswell "loved footnotes," because "they knew that the outer surface of truth is not smooth, welling and gathering from paragraph to shapely paragraph, but is encrusted with a rough protective bark of citations, quotation marks, italics, and foreign languages, a whole variorum crust of 'ibid.'s' and 'compare's' and 'see's' that are the shield for the pure flow of argument as it lives for a moment in one's mind" (2010, p. 122). Footnotes are just one device that allows Baker, in novels like *The Mezzanine*, to follow the rough, imperfect "outer surface of truth," tracking the thoughts of his characters (and, in his nonfiction work, himself) as they twist and turn in all kinds of unpredictable directions. Baker, interestingly enough, largely abandoned the use of footnotes in his later work (although they do appear sporadically). His writing, however, maintains an interest in digressions and narrative "clogs."

While Baker is best known for his detailed descriptions of everyday objects, this reputation perhaps underemphasizes his status as one of contemporary literature's foremost depicters of consciousness. The objects that Baker describes in his work are fascinating not simply for their own sake, but for the ways that they reveal the idiosyncrasies of characters' thought processes. Howie's thoughts about shampoo and milk delivery in *The Mezzanine* reveal a deep sense of nostalgia, while in *Room Temperature* (1990), a homemade mobile catalyzes the relationship between the narrator and his wife. For Baker, the things that people think about are vessels that connect them to the world, and even to other human beings.

However, while objects of thought often serve, for Baker, as points of connection between human consciousness and the wider world, they can also highlight some of the limitations and strangeness of thought. While Baker shows how everyday objects can provide a window into the inner workings of the world, that window is only partial, limited by gaps and inconsistencies. The book *U and I* is ostensibly a study of John Updike, but it is even more fascinating as a revealing portrait of Baker's own feelings and insecurities as a writer. Baker explicitly states in *U and I* that he avoided rereading any of Updike's work before writing the book, as doing so would "irreparably harm the topography of my understanding of him" (1991, p. 32). Rather than develop an objective, comprehensive study of Updike, Baker wants to "know how we think about a writer without the artifice of preparation, how we think about Updike in particular only when we *discover ourselves* thinking about him, when some feature of the world or of our own thoughts spontaneously recalls a tone or tick or glimpse of his work, or even merely brings up the image of his face in a particular jacket photo . . . or the memory of some fifth-hand story one has heard or read about him" (pp. 34–35, emphasis original). The object of study is, for Baker, interesting primarily because of what it reveals about human thought processes. He thus prefers a "fifth-hand" story about Updike to a more factual account, because although such a story may be inconsistent or spotty, it is more faithful to the way that Updike actually influences the author's life on a day-to-day basis. Baker's approach to writing *U and I* also highlights his dedication to capturing the spontaneousness of thought. He is less interested in staging narrative conflicts than he is in relaying the subtle, sudden changes of mind that attend consciousness on a moment-to-moment basis.

Another stylistic quirk that contributes to Baker's unique ability to capture the fine-grained aspects of human thought is his tendency to refer to thoughts in the manner of physical objects: as if they contain form, weight, and depth. This tendency is clearly present in the early essay "The Size of Thoughts" (1983), which begins, "Each thought has a size, and most are about three feet tall" (1996b, p. 10). Baker spins this whimsical metaphor into a meditation on the relationship between big, momentous, or "large" thoughts and more subtle, minor, or "small" thoughts. He eventually concludes, "Large thoughts depend more heavily on small thoughts than you might think." By objectifying thought in this essay, Baker creates another statement that sums up much of his approach to writing. He is a writer often concerned with "small" thoughts, and his books demonstrate the ways in which small thoughts are crucial in shaping human experience. His treatment of thoughts as objects helps to valorize the subtle movements of mind that characterize consciousness, providing these seemingly minor mental phenomena with dignity and significance. In *The Mezzanine*, for example, Howie refers to instances when he remembered his experiences with milk and cheese as "units of dairy thinking" (2010, p. 46). Similarly, in *Room Temperature*, narrator Mike wonders how well he is able to discern his wife's thoughts, thinking at one point that "this would be one of those times when if I did get a peek into her thoughts I would be rewarded by a specific clump of happiness that I would be permanently grateful to have learned" (p. 17). In Baker's vision of consciousness, a person can measure thoughts in "units" or experience "clumps" of happiness, and the author's style helps to emphasize the importance of these clumps and units.

Most of Baker's fiction can, broadly speaking, be divided into two primary strands. The first of these strands begins with *The Mezzanine* and its time-constrained, hyper-detailed style. It also contains Baker's second novel, *Room Temperature*, published in 1990, which is a sort of "spiritual sequel" to *The Mezzanine*. *Room Temperature* is narrated by Mike, a new father, as he rocks his infant daughter to sleep. Like Baker's first novel, *Room Temperature* consists almost entirely of its narrator's detailed descriptions of his observations and personal memories. The major difference is the domestic setting, which contrasts with the office environment of *The Mezzanine*. Later in his career, Baker published *A Box of Matches* (2003), another domestically themed "spiritual sequel." Two recent novels, *The Anthologist* (2009) and *Traveling Sprinkler* (2013), take a bit of a detour from the earlier fictions, but maintain much of the spirit and digressive, constrained style of the earlier novels. Both of these later novels are narrated by the poet Paul Chowder as he reflects on the subjects of poetry (in *The Anthologist*) and music (in *Traveling Sprinkler*).

The second major strand in Baker's fiction is his writing on sex and includes the erotic novels *Vox* (1992), *The Fermata* (1994), and *House of Holes* (2011). While these books clearly represent a separate class of novel for Baker, as they focus almost entirely on the subject of sex, they actually reveal many of the same concerns as his other books. Just as everyday phenomena reveal thoughts and emotions in *The Mezzanine* and *Room Temperature*, connecting characters with the world around them, similarly quotidian objects channel sexual desire in the erotic novels. Within the first few pages of *Vox*, for instance, main characters Jim and Abby flirt by discussing items such as bedspreads, packing slips, and meatball subs. Their conversation, which forms the entirety of the novel, even takes place over the telephone, further emphasizing the ways in which their relationship is conducted through nonhuman entities. While the novel is not as directly focused on consciousness as books like *The Mezzanine* and *U and I*, it shares a similar fascination with the way that everyday objects mediate our relationships to the world at large and to other people.

While Baker is known primarily as a novelist, he is almost equally prolific as a nonfiction writer. Like his fiction, Baker's nonfiction can be broadly divided into two separate strands. The first of these consists mainly of Baker's essays. In addition to *U and I* (a long essay in book form), Baker has published two essay collections: *The Size of Thoughts* (1996) and *The Way the World Works* (2012). His essays, much like his novels, often consist of minutely detailed descriptions, applying sustained thought and attention to objects in order to track the mind's movements as it considers the world around it. They also continue Baker's digressive style, as in the epic, seven-part essay "Lumber" (1995) in which Baker freely associates recollections of his research into the history of the word "lumber" with reflections on the lives of various poets and writers who have employed "lumber" as a metaphor in their writing. Like the best of his fiction, "Lumber" provides intensely detailed descriptions of its primary subject, while simultaneously self-reflexively tracking the thoughts of its speaker wherever they may wander. Other subjects of Baker's essays include everyday objects and technological advances such as movie projectors, nail clippers, and model airplanes. Such essays suggest that Baker shares with his fictional characters a restless sense of curiosity about the world that surrounds him.

The second major strand of Baker's nonfiction is his polemical writing. While his more essayistic writings tend to freely and pleasantly meander through discussions of their subjects, Baker has also published several books that make more pointed arguments, with more specific aims. *Double Fold* (2001) and *Human Smoke* (2008) both reflect Baker's interest in historical preservation. *Double Fold* argues that libraries ought to preserve, rather than throw away, many of their old books and newspapers. *Human Smoke* uses primary-source historical documents to argue against the popular conception that the Allied forces were drawn into World War II by Hitler's aggression. *Human Smoke* notably reflects Baker's advocacy of political pacifism, a theme also addressed in the short novel *Checkpoint* (2004), in which two men argue whether or not to assassinate then-president George W. Bush. Baker's most recent book, *Substitute* (2016), shows the author continuing his passionate advocacy for reform using a different approach. Instead of his usual historical research, Baker engages in a kind of immersive journalism in *Substitute*, working as a substitute teacher for twenty-eight days in order to formulate a critique of the current state of American schools.

Baker's interest in historical preservation, as evidenced in *Double Fold* and *Human Smoke*, is another crucial component to his career. While not directly related to his novels, his preservationist instinct informs his characters' interests in cataloguing and committing to memory the minutiae of daily life. Baker himself has helped found the American Newspaper Repository, an organization that maintains a collection of historical newspapers in order to protect them from destruction. Just like his fictional characters, Baker has an insatiable drive toward detailed descriptions, and preserving historical documents is a way for us, as a culture, to maintain as detailed a picture of the past as we can. It is also worth noting that while Baker's historicist tendencies and interest in the past may make him appear to be a luddite, stubbornly clinging to old ways, he actually celebrates technological advances. Many of his essays show an appreciation for engineering and design, and Howie's reflections on technology in *The Mezzanine* express joy in the little tweaks and improvements that go into office products like hand dryers and escalators. Most notably, Baker has written articles expressing his interest in Wikipedia, for which he has worked as an editor. Whether discussing new or old things, what holds Baker's interest is the quest to preserve the seemingly small, yet crucial twists and turns that constitute both historical progression and human consciousness.

While Baker does not easily fit into any recent literary movements, he does share certain key qualities with major authors of postmodernism. Notably, the digressive style of his narrations suggests a rejection of overarching historical metanarratives. Baker also tends to blend references to high and low culture, slotting discussions of Marcus Aurelius next to reveries on shampoo brands in *The Mezzanine*. His novels are indeed deeply embedded within the US consumer culture of the past forty years. However, where many postmodern writers, notably Don DeLillo and David Foster Wallace, treat consumer culture as an object of satire, Baker treats it as an object of fascination. His work is rarely, if ever, satirical, engaging closely with the fine-grained textures of reality rather than standing at a distance from it. When Howie makes "emotional analogies . . . between the history of civilization on the one hand and the history within the CVS pharmacy on the other," he is not speaking in a tongue-in-cheek manner (2010, p. 114). Rather, he sincerely believes that the various brands that line the shelves of a massive drugstore chain express crucial facets of human desire and culture.

Baker is thus a difficult writer to pin down, and yet it is his idiosyncrasy that continues to make his work vital. Whether through his essays, his preservation work, his erotic novels, or his (only slightly) more conventional literary fiction, Baker is one of the great cataloguers of the contemporary world, as well as one of the great depicters of consciousness. His work not only draws our attention to the minute details of our environment; it shows us how conscious thought is shaped and mediated by these details. He remains one of American literature's strangest, yet most important, authors.

SEE ALSO: After Postmodernism; The Brain and American Fiction; Debut Novels; Fictions of Work and Labor

REFERENCES

Baker, Nicholson. (1991). *U and I: A True Story*. New York: Vintage.

Baker, Nicholson. (1996a). Changes of mind (1982). In: *The Size of Thoughts: Essays and Other Lumber*, 3–9. New York: Vintage.

Baker, Nicholson. (1996b). The size of thoughts (1983). In: *The Size of Thoughts: Essays and Other Lumber*, 10–17. New York: Vintage.

Baker, Nicholson. (2010). *The Mezzanine*. New York: Grove Press; 1st ed. 1988.

Chambers, Ross. (1994). Meditation and the escalator principle: on Nicholson Baker's *The Mezzanine*. *Modern Fiction Studies* 40 (4): 765–806.

FURTHER READING

Marshall, Colin. (2010). Consciousness on the page: a primer on the novels of Nicholson Baker. *The Millions* (November 19, 2010). https://themillions.com/2010/11/consciousness-on-the-page-a-primer-on-the-novels-of-nicholson-baker.html

O'Mahony, John. (2003). Particular obsessions. *The Guardian* (January 11, 2003). https://www.theguardian.com/books/2003/jan/11/features reviews.guardianreview20

Pettersson, Bo. (2012). What happens when nothing happens: interpreting narrative technique in the plotless novels of Nicholson Baker. In: *Narrative, Interrupted: The Plotless, the Disturbing and the Trivial in Literature* (ed. Markku Lehtimäki, Laura Karttunen, and Maria Mäkelä), 42–56. Berlin: De Gruyter.

Saltzman, Arthur. (1999). *Understanding Nicholson Baker*. Columbia: University of South Carolina Press.

Thompson, Graham. (2011). Periodizing the 80s: "the differential of history" in Nicholson Baker's *The Mezzanine*. *Modern Fiction Studies* 57 (2): 300–317.

Ball, Jesse

KASCHA SEMONOVITCH
Hugo House, Seattle, USA

In Jesse Ball's books, it's not that bad things happen to good people. Bad things happen to people. In his minimalist prose, Ball depicts characters suffering under strange tyrannical regimes – oppressed family, illness, poverty, unjust political systems. The systems persecuting the characters are extreme and often almost allegorical, yet Ball gently shows us how we share the basic structure of these characters' lives. He prompts us to identify with not only the victims but the oppressors. These timeless issues provide again and again fodder for new novels as Ball continues to produce at the remarkable rate of nearly a book a year (at the time of writing). For this prolific writing, Ball has earned well-deserved attention as a productive and significant contributor to contemporary American fiction in the early twentieth-first century. His work has gathered attention as experimental fiction as well as popular fiction. In 2008, he won the *Paris Review*'s coveted The Plimpton Prize and has been long listed for the National Book award. He received fellowships from the National Education Association, Guggenheim Foundation, and Creative Capital. His work has been collected in *The Best Nonrequired Reading* (2018) and other anthologies.

In addition to his novels, Ball has collected drawings, poems, and what he calls "bestiaries." According to Ball, he generally writes entire books in a period of 4–14 days (Mitchell 2014); he wrote *How to Set Fire and Why* (2016) in just one week and a *Cure For Suicide* (2015) during a six-day period (Meno 2016). Such amazing productivity has driven Ball's career quickly from a few well-received novels to a long bibliography that will likely continue.

Medicine, spirituality, and literature shaped Ball's family life. Over the course of his career, Ball iterates on these themes which structure both the human condition generally and his own early life. His mother was a librarian, his father a seminarian turned Medicaid administrator. His brother had Down syndrome and required frequent medical care, bringing Ball in contact with the hospitals and medical imagery that appear in his work (Meno 2016).

These early personal experiences appear more or less overtly in different novels. Illness and mortality are persistent themes in his work. In *The Way Through Doors* (2009), doctors and medical terminology pursue the characters. In *Census* (2018), the narrator's son, like Ball's own brother, has Down syndrome. The novel's preface explicitly connects the novel to his brother's life and concludes with a set of photos of the author's brother. The narrator puzzles over what kind of self-understanding his son has; he concludes that it isn't much less clear than the self-understanding that any of us have whether or not we have some diagnosed condition. The narrator himself is a doctor and suffers a long illness. Others try to cure him, but his disease is incurable; in any case, the doctor resists the cure. He knows that there is no cure for what we truly suffer: He will ultimately die – we all will – and there is no cure for that.

Mortality itself recurs thematically. Ball once said that he "spent a long time in cemeteries" as a child because there was one near his house (Mitchell 2014). He claimed to have written *Samedi the Deafness* (2007) while staying near a cemetery. In nearly every book, Ball's characters explicitly face death in some form. In that sense, the title *A Cure for Suicide* serves as a synecdoche for his oeuvre overall. In this fractured narrative, a series of caretakers and patients attempt to heal one another and restore a desire to live. But given the world in which they live, there seems to be no healing possible. In *How to Set a Fire and Why* (2016), a young girl is so persecuted by family and institutions that she wants to become an arsonist – another type of death wish. At the end of the book, she manages to survive, but she leaves the reader with little evidence that she should want to live. The reader can do nothing for her nor for so many despairing young people.

How to Set a Fire and Why also shows an educational institution that is only another oppressive regime. In his own text on pedagogy, *Notes on My Dunce Cap* (2016), Ball writes that a teacher "should at all times resist authority" and say as little as possible, reframing education as a collaborative and open project. Education, if properly expressed, has great potential, according to Ball.

Ball recalls struggling in school as a child and even a psychological test that diagnosed him as possibly brain damaged. Nonetheless, after this difficult childhood experience with school, Ball manages to gain creative writing education at prestigious schools. After obtaining a BA at Vassar College, he pursued his writing practice with an MFA at Columbia University. Only a few years later, he found a post at the School of the Art Institute of Chicago where he still teaches.

This literary education was followed by an industrious career. He quickly published several books of poems and drawings through an Icelandic Press: *March Book* (2004), *Og svo kom nóttin* (2006), *Vera & Linus* (2006).

His first novel, *Samedi the Deafness*, appeared only a few years after graduate school; he received positive but cautious reviews and literary critical attention primarily as a writers' writer. The *New York Times* review of this first novel called it a success but nonetheless warned that it does not offer readers clarity. He followed this novel with several more increasingly well-received books: *Parables & Lies (2007)*, *Pieter Emily* (2009), *The Way Through Doors*, and *The Curfew* (2011). His poetry was collected in *The Village on Horseback: Prose and Verse* (2011) and later, his stories in *Deaths of Henry King* (2017).

With a review of *Silence Once Begun* (2014) by James Wood in *The New Yorker*, Ball gained more public attention outside the inner circles of the literary community. His subsequent novels, *A Cure for Suicide*, *How to Set a Fire and Why*, *Census*, and *The Divers' Game* (2019), have been critiqued carefully and prompted numerous interviews and profiles. After these novels, Ball also published nonfiction pieces *Sleep, Death's Brother* (2017) – a manual on lucid dreaming – and a book on teaching – *Notes on My Dunce Cap* (2016).

Ball's editor at Vintage Books, Jennifer Jackson, described a shift in his writing to become "more character driven, more emotionally resonant" (Meno 2016), and it may be this shift toward the intimate and emotional that has drawn in a wider audience. It may also be that the issues that shape Ball's work – death, family, and injustice – are profoundly human and inevitably endearing.

Ball has mentioned two early literary influences that are eerie, poetic, and fantastical. He remembers his father reciting Lewis Carrol's *Jabberwocky* and describes how this poem, which emphasizes sound and emotional effect of language, serves as an epitome of literature for him. In an in-depth profile in *Chicago Magazine*, Ball identified a childhood encounter with *Grendel*, by John Gardner as influential. In the first person, Grendel tells the story of a monster and its unjust persecution by humans who nonetheless fascinate the monster. Grendel asks philosophical questions about human existence and struggles merely to survive. Grendel is unjustly persecuted for his very being, and the book ends dramatically with Grendel's death. Ball's novels also contain monsters – but they are of the human sort. The human monster is both persecutor and persecuted. In *A Cure for Suicide*, for example, the reader follows a character along a plot line that finally reveals itself as a hopeless circle – patient becoming caretaker becoming patient.

Gardener's work verges on the fantastical as does the work of many authors to whom Ball is compared. Ball's stories have been frequently described as in the tradition of Borges, Kafka, and Jackson. A self-described "fabulist" according to his website, Ball's books have been called thought experiments and fables. He shares much with his contemporary Valeria Luiselli, and his work has been compared to the polemical Japanese Nobel-winner Kenzaburo Oe. Ball's work also shares much with speculative fiction, in the tradition of Margaret Atwood, given the way many of his books' worlds resemble yet diverge from our own. These authors share with Ball stylistic daring into the fantastical, and like Ball, they do not shy away from direct and directive metaphors aimed at social institutions.

In the novels *The Way through Doors*, *A Cure for Suicide*, *Census*, and *The Divers' Game*, hyperbolically oppressive governments and institutions rule character's daily lives. And yet these strange regimes are just close enough to our own that we can imagine how they might represent a future as dystopic as the worlds of Atwood. In *The Divers' Game* and *A Cure for Suicide*, society has become malicious and blatantly violent, with thinly veiled allusions to German concentration camps of the 1940s and American immigrant detention centers of the 2018s and on. In the end, the allusions and details effectively blur the two together.

In interviews, Ball affirms that his books are political acts, but amends that their focus is justice itself, not any particular political system. Nonetheless, with an op-ed in the *Los Angeles Times* in 2017, Ball gained attention by arguing that all Americans should serve a prison sentence once every ten years to ensure a fair system. This hyperbolic claim was seemingly put forward as a practical agenda. And, after reading the article, it seems a real proposal, if not solution, to address some of the injustice in the penitentiary system.

As in Kafka, Atwood, and Jackson, Ball's settings oscillate between the symbolic and recognizable – one has the sense that the world is *almost* one we inhabit. At the same time, Ball's settings are unmoored from any particular, recognizable place. Characters often live only in "the city" or in towns identified by letters or types of regimes. In an interview with *The Paris Review* about *Silence Once Begun*, Ball said, "I don't really think *Silence Once Begun* takes place in Japan so much as it takes place in this imaginary Japan" (Bates 2014). This statement may be applied to the settings of many of Ball's novels. The story unfolds in an idea of a country, a political or social context.

Like their settings, Ball's characters often feel like lightly sketched allegorical figures. A despairing Giacometti, he outlines pinched and disintegrating individuals. At first glance, Ball's characters, like Giacometti's figures, barely exist – he marks out a few minimal, well textured lines to indicate a form and an intention. Nonetheless, he imbues them with personality. Like Kafka's Gregor Samsa, the characters have quirks of speech, habits, and particular desires – and yet retain the status of figures in an allegory. Ball zooms in and shows details of particular and fully realized character lives. For example, in *A Cure for Suicide* and *The Divers' Game*, Ball gives realism and voice to tween and teenage girls. The colloquial dialogue brings the reader into intimate contact with the young adult experience. And then, the narrative perspective recedes and again takes on a global, metaphorical distance. This zooming out and zooming in reinforces the way individual differences recede when we consider the human experience of mortality, and justice as a whole. And, as James Woods noted, Ball's characters can be witty – in subtle, dry sentences, they remark slyly on events. Woods described Ball's style as "chastely lyrical" (Woods 2014). His narrators restrain themselves from adverbs, preferring sentences with a direct syntax and few dependent clauses. One often has the sense of listening to a transcript of a procedure or a recitation of a ritual.

In an interview, Ball remarked that a novelist creates "a world that is sort of half of the world" and the reader's mind fills in the rest (Bates 2014). Indeed, Ball's characters, settings, and worlds always circle around an open space that readers fill in with details of their own lives and political context. The participation of the reader in completing the novel's world makes the work feel more relevant, more real, more applicable to their own situation.

Like these other authors engaged in thought experiments, Ball's novels weave philosophical issues into his fiction more or less explicitly. Ball explains that he does not directly aim at philosophical questions: "I try to just think in terms of books," he said, and yet he also says that there doesn't need to be "a choice to move towards philosophy or towards fiction" (Bates 2014).

The narrator of *Census* remarks that "we as people make a kind of mistake" when we identify ourselves with images in photographs. "Is that really you in the photograph? Or is it someone you have a connection with?" the narrator asks. We cannot be sure of ourselves, he suggests. Once unseated from self-certainty, we may pose other questions, such as "What are you but your habits?" as Ball asked in an interview (Meno 2016).

Like Sartre, Ball questions our tendency to identify with stable, external labels. "I could determine myself to be 'born a worker' or to 'be born bourgeois,'" writes Sartre (1984, p. 132), but in doing so, I excuse myself from truly examining human being. The very structure of human existence means that we are not tied to particular details of physical identity; instead, we are radically independent from this world.

Ball offers no palliatives, no unjustified hope. His books can be difficult to finish as one learns that the end state may be very much like the opening state. Although his later works perhaps offer less frustration to the reader than his first novels, the books do not gift us with easy revelations. We cannot identify only with victims but must also undergo identification with those who uphold unjust systems. And, for at least the length of a novel, we cannot look away from our own mortality.

SEE ALSO: After Postmodernism; Illness and Disability Narratives; Mixed-Genre Fiction; The New Experimentalism/The Contemporary Avant-Garde

REFERENCES

Bates, Jennifer. (2014) Different ways of lying: an interview with Jesse Ball. *The Paris Review* (April 1, 2014). https://www.theparisreview.org/blog/2014/04/03/different-ways-of-lying-an-interview-with-jesse-ball/ (accessed August 23, 2021).

Meno, Joe. (2016). Inside the bizarre, brilliant world of Jesse Ball. *Chicago Magazine* (June 27, 2016). https://www.chicagomag.com/Chicago-Magazine/July-2016/Jesse-Ball/ (accessed August 23, 2021).

Mitchell, Shawn A. (2014). A good work is a moment of clear thought. *Fiction Writers Review* (March 6, 2014). https://fictionwritersreview.com/interview/a-good-work-is-a-moment-of-clear-thought-an-interview-with-jesse-ball-2/ (accessed August 23, 2021).

Sartre, Jean Paul. (1984). *Being and Nothingness* (trans. Hazel E. Barnes). New York: Washington Square Press.

Woods, James. (2014). But he confessed: Jesse Ball's *Silence Once Begun*. *The New Yorker* (February 10, 2014). https://www.newyorker.com/magazine/2014/02/10/but-he-confessed (accessed July 5, 2021).

FURTHER READING

Ball, Jesse. (2017). "The Edge of Sense." In: *Light in the Dark: Writers on Creativity* (ed. Joe Fassler), 173–177. New York: Penguin Books.

Ball, Jesse. (2017). Everyone should go to jail, say, once every ten years. *Los Angeles Times* (June 20, 2017).

Waldman, Katy. (2019). "The Divers' Game": Jesse Ball's unnerving parable of a country that feigns innocence. *The New Yorker* (September 23, 2019).

Bambara, Toni Cade

BELINDA WALLER-PETERSON
Moravian University, USA

Toni Cade Bambara, born Miltona Mirkin Cade, was an activist, writer, editor, documentary filmmaker, and teacher. Bambara's life and work were informed by the movements of the 1960s and 1970s. Both the Civil Rights movement (1960s) and the Black Power movement (1970s) inspired and were informed by corollary artistic movements cultivated across the broad spectrum of Black aesthetic production. Bambara's writing reflects the interstitial connections between both movements, as well as the burgeoning Pan-African movement. Throughout her life she operated as both an artisan and an activist committed to the advancement of Black life, Black culture, and political progress. This entry engages Bambara's major literary works and their development of health activism as a liberatory tool for Black people. Consistent with Bambara's coalition-building amongst women and marginalized communities, her literature raises generative questions about and offers innovative pathways toward healing and wholeness for Black people.

Raised in Harlem, New York during the 1940s, Bambara and her brother were immersed by their parents in creative and political experiences that shaped Bambara's definition of the Black community and Black success. Bambara's mother encouraged her artistic aspirations at an early age and empowered Bambara to literally name herself. As a young child, Bambara renamed herself Toni Cade. In 1970 she added the surname Bambara after discovering the name amongst her grandmother's belongings. Bambara also called herself a cultural worker, a name that reflects her commitment to elevating diverse communities of everyday people.

Bambara earned a Bachelor of Arts in theater arts and English from Queens College in 1959. While pursuing a Master of Arts degree in American literature from the City College of New York, Bambara worked as a social worker at the New York Department of Welfare and as the Director of Recreation at Metropolitan Psychiatric Hospital (Holmes and Wall 2008, p. 12). She earned her MA in 1965. Over the course of her career Bambara taught at City College of New York, Rutgers University, and Spelman College. She traveled to Cuba and Vietnam, amongst many other countries, to collaborate with and support women's collectives.

Bambara published a few short stories prior to editing *The Black Woman: An Anthology* in 1970 and *Tales and Stories for Black Folks* in 1971. She published her first collection of short stories, *Gorilla, My Love*, in 1972. Her second collection, *The Seabirds Are Still Alive*, followed in 1977. She published her most well-known work, *The Salt Eaters*, in 1980. In 1981, *The Salt Eaters* won the American Book Award. Shortly after, Bambara began working on *Those Bones Are Not My Child*, a novel that was edited and published in 1999 by her friend and editor Toni Morrison after Bambara's death in 1995. Morrison also edited and published *Deep Sightings and Rescue Missions: Fiction, Essays, and Conversations* in 1996.

In 1985 Bambara moved from Atlanta to Philadelphia where she transitioned into filmmaking. At Scribe Video Center in Philadelphia, Pennsylvania, Bambara co-produced (with Louis Massiah) several documentary film projects, including *The Bombing of Osage Avenue* (1986) and *W.E.B. Du Bois: A Biography in Four Voices* (1996). Bambara saw filmmaking as a natural progression of her art and activism.

Bambara's body of work reflects her penchant for activism; she develops a distinct political aesthetic across her corpus. According to Linda Holmes, she defined herself as "a Pan-Africanist-socialist-feminist in the United States" and "urged black women to begin deconstructing the myths that lead to their own self-destruction" (Holmes and Wall 2008, p. 14). Pan-Africanism is a global cultural and political movement that centers and embraces the common heritage, experiences, artistic production, and political challenges of Black people throughout the African diaspora. Wrestling with and struggling against those political challenges, including the history of slavery, colonialism, apartheid, racial capitalism, and white supremacy, is the vital substance of the Pan-African mission. For Bambara, Pan-Africanism was an essential pillar of her intersectional definition of herself. As a socialist, a feminist, *and* a Pan-Africanist artist, Bambara's worldview centered women, rejected capitalism, and probed the lived experiences of Black people throughout the diaspora.

Bambara clarified her perspective on this intersectional identity in an essay titled "On the Issues of Roles" in 1970: "We're so turned around about Western models, we don't even know how to raise the correct question. But raise them we must if we are to fashion a natural sense of self, if we are to develop harmonious relationships with each other. What are we talking about when we speak of revolution if not a free society made up of whole individuals?" (1970, pp. 128–129). For Bambara, Pan-Africanism, socialism, and feminism reflect a nexus of ideologies and identities through which she was able to establish models (in her fiction and in her activism) that would, in turn, cultivate the "harmonious" alliances required to sustain the societal revolution that would result in true liberation for Black people all over the world.

Toni Cade Bambara believed in the complexity of Black identity and reflected that complexity in and through her work. According to Nobel laureate Toni Morrison, "[h]er writing is woven, aware of its music, its overlapping waves of scenic action, so clearly on its way – like a magnet collecting details in its wake, each of which is essential to the final effect" (1996, p. viii). Morrison's poetic description of the form(s) of Bambara's writing also powerfully reflects the social, political, and cultural content of Bambara's novels and collections of short stories.

Bambara's body of work emphasizes activism in ways that center Black people, people of color, and women. Activism, as understood and articulated by Bambara, includes health activism. Health, wellness, and what constitutes wholeness emerge as primary concerns in the collected essays in *The Black Woman*, the short stories in *Gorilla, My Love* and *The Seabirds Are Still Alive*, the community health center setting of *The Salt Eaters*, and in the pages of *Those Bones Are Not My Child*. For Bambara health is our right. Note well here that health – not health care – is what Bambara claims as a human right, and in so doing she cultivates characters and fictional experiences in literature that ruminate on the critical issues at stake in terms of health and wellness for Black people and Black women especially.

The community health center wall in Bambara's first novel, *The Salt Eaters*, reads: *Health is our right*. This sign is at once a declarative statement, an assertion of agency and self – an affirmation of what *is*, not what is due or being asked. The *health is our right* sign is a reminder that Black people in the community have a right to access all of the resources that constitute health. This moves beyond medicine, doctors, and treatment into the more proactive provenance of nutrition, exercise, and the ongoing struggle to dismantle the systems of racism and economic exploitation that over-determine health and life expectancy for Black people. *Health is our right* underscores what is already a given or what should already be a given. *Health is our right* states that broader definitions of health, the resources that constitute health, the living conditions that support health, and so on, are always already understood as *our rights*. For Bambara, these are inalienable rights embedded in what it means to be human.

Much like the healthcare disparities and the cultural incompetency in medical diagnoses, Bambara finds that we regularly and systemically ask the wrong questions. Bambara challenges her readers to ask the right questions – generative questions that highlight the health concerns of Black women, children, men, and Black communities. Asking the right questions allows individuals and their communities to advocate for themselves and others in meaningful and impactful ways.

Bambara signals the declaration that health is our right throughout her body of literature. She defines health as including the physical sense of the body, the spirit of Black communities, the collective political action of women, and the financial wellbeing of individuals and their communities. Through her work and writing Bambara suggests that health is inextricably woven into how Black people create, embrace, and/or reject definitions of what it means to exist in the world as a Black person.

Bambara's first short story collection, *Gorilla, My Love*, is comprised of fifteen stories that meditate on childhood, betrayal, love, and womanhood. The collection considers the constitution of community by focusing on the interior desires of Black girls and women. While these stories wrestle with trauma and the challenges faced by oppressed people at various intersections of subjectivity and identity, several young Black girls emerge in bold defiance of gendered norms and societal expectations. Their examples demonstrate what is possible for Black communities when the health and wellness of Black girls and women are centered. In "Raymond's Run," young Hazel Parker articulates a confident sense of self that is strengthened in her dominance as a runner and commitment to her disabled older brother. Hazel embodies the caring ethic that Bambara suggested could "push against the synthetic conflicts that white society orchestrates in its interests, not ours" (Lewis 2012, p. 16). The young women in "The Johnson Girls" also affirm a caring ethic that speaks to some of the ways in which women offer themselves to one another as resources. Gathered in Inez's bedroom, the other young women act as her co-conspirators, advisers, and confidants as they assess the status of her relationship and discuss the nature of being women. Whether familial or sisters by choice, *Gorilla* reveals, collectives of women can create and normalize self-affirming spaces where they are centered, healthy, and whole even as they take on the pressures of living in a world of systemic racial and gender oppression.

Bambara's second collection of short stories, *The Seabirds Are Still Alive*, highlights political action, police brutality, tensions in relationships, exile and return, beginnings and endings. Girls, young women, and maternal figures continue to populate the intimate spaces of the stories. They embody contradictory ideas of girlhood, exercise bold declarations of girlhood, embrace blossoming womanhood, and settle into a seasoned, experienced womanhood. They do this alongside tumultuous and violent events that happen in their homes, communities, and the world. Similar to *Gorilla*, this collection takes up questions of agency and wholeness; however, *Seabirds* situates those questions within communities that are actively under siege, trapped in the memories of being set upon by agents of the government, and at times determined to organize and educate themselves in the face of racial oppression. In many instances, the health of the community hinges on smaller collectives (cultural and community centers, mentoring programs, women's groups, etc.) established to advocate and provide support and resources for the larger communal whole.

What emerges throughout *Seabirds* is a depiction of communities in crisis as a result of deteriorating health conditions caused by greedy, predatory organizations and racist, sexist institutions. These conditions include lack of healthy food options because they no longer own the land, and unsafe living conditions as a result of targeted police violence and disinvestment in community infrastructure. Individual acts of selfishness or carelessness invite in the opportunists that take advantage of the inexperienced and unrepresented members of the community. And at other times, it is the crushing relentlessness of capitalism, government bureaucracy, and white supremacy that Bambara exposes in *Those Bones Are Not My Child*. But always, it negatively impacts the community's ability to be healthy, to thrive, and to live.

Bambara foregrounds the question of what constitutes health and wholeness in *The Salt Eaters* and maps out a world in which the state of one person's health resonates beyond her own community. The novel opens with a question that becomes a refrain, adapted throughout the text: *"are you sure, sweetheart, that you want to be well?"* The primary story unfolds over the course of a single day and situates two Black women, one a healer, the other an activist, at its center. Velma, having suffered a mental crisis and attempted suicide, ends up in the community infirmary where she finds herself sitting on a stool opposite Minnie, who poses the question. For Velma, health hinges in part on acknowledging and accepting her spiritual inheritance while also managing her activist work. Velma is the primary example of the danger of sacrificing one's health at the altar of productivity, advocacy, or the demands that a community makes on its activists.

The pressing issue of the novel is to heal Velma. Her healing is enmeshed in the health and healing of the other characters in the narrative. The definition of "heal" is explored and expanded by the medical practitioners and "nontraditional" healers. Bambara sets aside modern medical knowledge and practice as the primary course of treatment. The treatment required for Velma to "be well" is beyond the expertise of modern medicine. The doctors can attend to the physical body, stitching the cuts on her wrists, but they cannot address the root cause of her illness. Through the reiteration of Minnie's question, the cost of wellness and wholeness becomes clear; Velma must identify past traumas and decide that she wants to be healed and whole. This process requires the support of her community, which constitutes an additional level of healing that is communal and distinct from allopathic medicine. In the novel, this type of communal support manifests as elders and spiritually rooted community members sitting in a circle around Velma and Minnie. They assist in the healing ceremony by praying, meditating, humming, and directing positive energy toward the women.

Velma's location at the novel's center serves as an anchor for the other characters who are also facing physical and psychic challenges. They also require the intervention of neighbors and friends. The stories of other characters oscillate between the past and the present, at times creating a sense of confusion and chaos that mirrors Velma's own inability to grasp her present condition or care for herself. The novel imagines healing in a way that requires community members, medical practitioners, and healers to work in community with each other. *Health is our right*, but this assertion works against the longstanding attitudes of perseverance and long-suffering that Bambara and other Black writers acknowledge. The kinds of questions *The Salt Eaters* forwards pose constructive opportunities for activists, artists, and thinkers to consider relevant ideas for the pathway forward in health and wellness for Black communities.

Those Bones Are Not My Child immerses the reader in the Atlanta kidnappings and grisly murders of children that occurred from 1979 to 1981. Bambara, who lived in Atlanta with her daughter during this horrific time, collected newspaper articles related to the cases and filled notebooks with information she gathered from task forces and other community-led groups. Bambara's journals and investigative work became the foundation for *Bones*, whose working title was *If Blessing Comes*. *Bones* follows a young Black mother, Marzala (Zala) Spencer, whose son disappears at the beginning of the novel. Zala, who has two younger children, is overwhelmed by the lack of access to accurate information and by the law enforcement and investigative bureaucracies that force her to spend time tracking down leads and relying on press conferences for updates on the cases.

According to Bambara, when writing *Bones*, she was asking, "do we understand what it means when you buy into the official version of things?" (Lewis 2012, p. 101). The question challenges readers to consider how official language, as Morrison refers to it in her 1993 Nobel prize acceptance lecture, inflicts violence on marginalized communities that have been victimized (Morrison 1993). In *Bones*, the violence of the official version of the Atlanta child murders comes in the form of omissions, denials, obfuscation, and character assassination, as the victims of crime are blamed for their own victimization. This blaming extends to the community that struggles to protect itself from the exact violence perpetuated and sustained by inaccurate reporting, the outcome of which erodes the mental, physical, and spiritual health of individuals within the community.

The thematics of Toni Cade Bambara's literary work pose challenging questions and cultivate compelling characters designed to probe the complexities of health and wellness as civil and human rights, particularly in the Black and African American community. Bambara grasps the individual experience through her characters and the community experiences in her characters' worlds. She reflects on the health of her community through her powerful prose and compelling subject matter to assert that individual wellness, health, and what constitutes wholeness are inclusive of, and in many ways dependent on, the health of the overall community.

SEE ALSO: Kincaid, Jamaica; Marshall, Paule; Morrison, Toni; Silko, Leslie Marmon; Trauma and Fiction; Walker, Alice; Writers' Collectives

REFERENCES

Bambara, Toni Cade. (ed.) (1970). *The Black Woman: An Anthology*. New York: Washington Square Press.

Holmes, Linda Janet and Wall, Cheryl A. (eds.) (2008). *Savoring the Salt: The Legacy of Toni Cade Bambara*. Philadelphia: Temple University Press.

Lewis, Thabiti. (ed.) (2012). *Conversations with Toni Cade Bambara*. Jackson: University Press of Mississippi.

Morrison, Toni. (1993). Nobel Lecture (December 7, 1993). https://www.nobelprize.org/prizes/literature/1993/morrison/lecture/ (accessed July 7, 2021).

Morrison, Toni. (ed.) (1996). *Deep Sightings and Rescue Missions: Fiction, Essays, and Conversations*. New York: Vintage Books.

FURTHER READING

Georgia Writers Hall of Fame. (n.d.). Toni Cade Bambara. https://www.georgiawritershalloffame.org/honorees/toni-cade-bambara

Holmes, Linda Janet. (2014). *A Joyous Revolt: Toni Cade Bambara, Writer and Activist*. Santa Barbara: Praeger.

Lewis, Thabiti. (2020). *"Black People Are My Business": Toni Cade Bambara's Practices of Liberation*. Detroit: Wayne State University Press.

Banks, Russell

JASON ARTHUR
Rockhurst University, USA

His earliest dust-jacket biographies concluded with the assertion that Russell Banks "grew up in a working-class environment, which has played a major role in his writing." As his career progressed and he acquired literary accolades, including the John Dos Passos Prize (1985) and the status of New York State Author (2004–2006), and academic appointments, including Howard G.B. Clark University Professor at Princeton, Banks's dust-jacket bio evolved into such upmarket understatements as, "His work has been translated into twenty languages and has received numerous international prizes and awards." This shift in promotional language, from foregrounding class to foregrounding international affiliations, can be seen as analogous of Banks's career in general. His earliest novels are rooted in legacies of New England regionalism. His more recent novels, though built from the very vernacular voices that Banks develops in his early career grappling with his working-class identity, express a cosmopolitan scope and sensibility.

Banks's career has spanned half a century. Beginning in 1969, with the publication of *Waiting to Freeze*, one of his two collections of poetry, the other being the 1974 collection, *Snow*, Banks has published thirteen novels, six collections of short stories, two collections of poetry, and three works of nonfiction. His novels are *Family Life* (1975), *Hamilton Stark* (1978), *The Book of Jamaica* (1980), *The Relation of My Imprisonment* (1983), *Continental Drift* (1985), *Affliction* (1989), *The Sweet Hereafter* (1991), *Rule of the Bone* (1995), *Cloudsplitter* (1998), *The Darling* (2004), *The Reserve* (2008), *Lost Memory of Skin* (2011), and *Foregone* (2021). His short story collections are *Searching for Survivors* (1975), *The New World* (1978), *Trailerpark* (1981), *Success Stories* (1986), *The Angel on the Roof* (2000), and *A Permanent Member of the Family* (2013). His nonfiction works are *Invisible Stranger* (1998), a photo–text collaboration with photographer Arturo Patten, *Dreaming Up America* (2008), a study of early American literature, and his most recent publication, *Voyager* (2016), a collection of his travel writings.

Two pre-career events helped to set the tone and themes of this very full, very eventful career. The first event occurred in 1958, when Banks, who had been awarded an academic scholarship to Colgate University and had thereby become the first member of his family to attend college, dropped out of Colgate midway through his first semester to head south with the intention, never realized, of joining the Cuban Revolution. The second strange, theme-setting event occurred in 1967, when Jack Kerouac crashed at Banks's house for four days. At that time, Banks was an undergraduate student at the University of North Carolina at Chapel Hill.

Banks's experience at Colgate, specifically the experience of being a working-class teenager trying, and failing, to fit in among some of America's most privileged coeds, was formative. *The Book of Jamaica*, *Continental Drift*, *Affliction*, *The Rule of the Bone*, and *Lost Memory of Skin* all explore the anxieties and pathologies that develop when rural, working-class men try to rise above their stations. By acquiring either academic credentials, as does the narrator of both *The Book of Jamaica* and *Affliction*, or forging cosmopolitan connections, as does the narrator of the coming-of-age novel *The Rule of the Bone* when he befriends a Jamaican migrant worker and as does the antihero of *Continental Drift* when he moves his family from rural New Hampshire to Miami, Banks's characters often face identity crises directly related to the shame and humiliation that accompanies finding oneself a provincial rube amid sophisticates. These same novels (*Affliction* excepted) explore the question of how stories of poverty and divestment in Caribbean countries can resonate with the lives of the very disparaged working-class men and boys who sit at the center of so many of his novels.

An even more prominent theme of Banks's fiction is self-destruction. That theme became entwined with Banks's own career ambitions the night that he met a literary hero at the sad end of his life. Kerouac, who was en route to Florida on what would be his last road trip, met a friend of Banks's, who phoned Banks from a bar in Chapel Hill and said that he'd just met Jack Kerouac and that Kerouac wanted a place to have a party. The "party" lasted four days, the main attraction of which was Kerouac's descent into alcohol-fueled madness. He oscillated between lucid recitations of Blake and the Upanishads and what Banks, in his *Paris Review* recounting of the experience, recalls as the disturbing antics of an "anti-Semitic, angry, fucked-up, tormented old drunk," a "real know-nothing" whom alcohol had wrecked (Banks 1998, p. 54). This experience of being at the start of a literary career and seeing one of his "literary heroes seem fragile and vulnerable" moved Banks, who went on to produce fiction that features male characters who are similar to Kerouac in their alarming, affecting self-destruction.

Witnessing the wreckage of late-life Kerouac also amounted to a career-defining cautionary tale for Banks. It was still on his mind when, in 2000, Banks wrote a screenplay adapting Kerouac's classic novel, *On the Road* (1957), for Francis Ford Coppola. That screenplay, over which Coppola ultimately passed in order to enlist the writing/directing duo of Walter Salles and José Rivera, is framed by a fourth-wall-breaking, autobiographical account of the strange weekend Banks spent with Kerouac. This metafictional component of Banks's screenplay is reminiscent of the metafictional exercises that characterize much of Banks's early work.

Metafiction, and other styles of literary experimentation typically associated with fiction that gets labeled "postmodern," was Banks's way of working through his connection to the unsavory side of working-class masculinity. Literary experimentation became for Banks a labor-intensive exercise through which he could sever his connection to working-class identity while also retaining some of its work ethic. More broadly speaking, to write metafiction in the 1970s was to approximate the formal preoccupations of a serious writer. Banks's stylistic difficulty applies explicitly to matters of representing class identity, suggesting that Banks understood experimental fiction as a kind of highbrow transcendence of class. When, in the early 1980s, specifically in the collection of interrelated stories titled *Trailerpark*, he abandons metafiction for the more straightforwardly realist narrators of his 11 most recent novels, Banks brings into these voices the paradoxical sensibility of the detached inhabitant.

Three of Banks's experimental novels, *Family Life*, *Hamilton Stark*, and *The Relation of My Imprisonment*, were later collected and reprinted by HarperPerennial under the title *Outer Banks* (2008). Each of these novels represents the complex, at times turgid, nature of Banks's early fiction. *Family Life* uses the generic shell of the fairytale to tell a story about the appetites and domestic dramas of a mock-royal family. Likewise, *The Relation of My Imprisonment* assumes an overtly antiquated narrative style reminiscent of seventeenth-century Puritanism. These works may be written off as the sophomoric anomalies of a career otherwise marked by allegiance to the narrative conventions of literary realism. However, especially in terms of *Hamilton Stark*, Banks's metafictional pretensions juxtapose literary sophistication and the distressingly perennial subject of toxic masculinity.

This juxtaposition of careful narrative introspection and thoughtless violence and self-destruction sets a tension that drives the narratives in such acclaimed works as *Affliction*, *Continental Drift*, *The Sweet Hereafter*, *Cloudsplitter*, and *Lost Memory of Skin*. In these works, the juxtaposition takes the form either (i) of oscillating between a sophisticated outsider narrator and characters who are shortsighted rural denizens (*Affliction*, *The Sweet Hereafter*), (ii) of shifting from a detached perspective to one borrowing heavily from the sensibility of a provincial antihero (*Continental Drift*), or (iii) of including characters whose interest in disparaged characters is ultimately academic (*Cloudsplitter*, *Lost Memory of Skin*).

This complexity begins to take shape with *Hamilton Stark*. That novel's "meta" component dramatizes the perplexing, sometimes absurd, incongruence that arises when a novel writer chooses to write about what Banks, in multiple novels (*The Book of Jamaica*, *Affliction*, *Cloudsplitter*), calls "remnant people." Banks uses this phrase to describe small, explicitly separatist groups that have survived into the present day virtually unchanged by national standardization. These groups include Jamaican Maroons and Francophone

Algonquins, enslaved and Indigenous peoples who narrowly escape extinction on a colonized continent indifferent, if not downright hostile, to their survival. In *Hamilton Stark* and *Affliction*, though, Banks uses the term to discuss people in a small town in New England. As opposed to being the results of heroic resistance, these "remnant people," whose roots in American literature stretch back into nineteenth-century literary regionalism, are deeply foolish. They stubbornly insist on making lives in places that have outlived their economic reasons for being. There is an underlying inevitability to the violence that occurs among these people, an inevitability arguably first represented in American fiction through Edith Wharton's *Ethan Frome* (1911). Unlike Wharton's titular character, Banks's Hamilton Stark is an antihero who relishes violent self-destruction.

Hamilton Stark is arguably Banks's attempt not to merely represent, or even to transcend, but to repurpose as a literary enterprise the most unsightly aspects of working-class masculinity. Stark is an unabashed misogynist. He evicts his mother from her home, destroys the furniture and possessions that his ex-wives, all five of them, leave behind. His wily, elaborate mode of destruction suggests that to smash to pieces one's world is a guaranteed way for rural working-class men to claim agency. Banks's treatment of the wreckage Stark creates may be a dramatization of his own working-class inheritance. His choosing to treat this wreckage in the language of high postmodernism represents Banks's flight into writing, into the kind of self-conscious language acts that are both a welcome contrast to physical labor and a way of aestheticizing the inelegant details of a laborer's life.

Though there is little detectable metafiction in them, the remainder of Banks's twentieth-century novels (*Continental Drift*, *Affliction*, *The Sweet Hereafter*, *Rule of the Bone*, and *Cloudsplitter*) can be characterized as spiteful, successful attempts to transcend their status as "New England novels." They are novels that want to leave their regional distinctions behind. For instance, *Continental Drift* begins with an alarmingly violent outburst of Bob DuBois, a "nice guy" oil-burner repairman at the start of an early-onset midlife crisis. After the outburst, and a failed attempt to articulate to his wife the nature of his crisis, DuBois and his wife decide to move the family to Florida, in search of that something "more" that drives so much fiction of domestic doom in America. In *Affliction*, a prodigal son has to return to his hated childhood hometown to tell the story of his brother's strange criminal behavior. In *The Sweet Hereafter*, a novel that revolves around a school bus accident that kills all of a small town's children, various characters give testimonials. One such testimonial, that of widower and father to two drowned children, Bill Ansel, describes his obdurate disposition as "not bitterness [but] what happens when you have eaten your bitterness" (Banks 1991, p. 47). This is the recalcitrance of one who must both own up to and rage against the limitations of being a "New Englander" nearly a century after New England has ceased being a literary or cultural capital. The narrative voices of these novels are thus dark, weathered sensibilities of men whom inertia has defeated. This quality of voice is a result of Banks's straining against regional limitations. Banks's narrators know a lot about their landscapes, and this knowledge is not something that they cherish. It's the despised, encyclopedic comprehension of a hated hometown.

Such hatred is most acutely rendered through Rolfe Whitehouse, narrator of *Affliction*. For Rolfe, local knowledge is a way out of the local, a way of gaining the evaluative means through which to explain why violence is so central to writing about the overlooked sites of America's once most beloved, now most backward, region. In *Affliction*, Banks clarifies that the object of critique is not the region per se but the type of provinciality whose myopia denies the existence of destructive impulses native to the region. Such myopia engenders a nostalgia that both stokes reactionary male violence and partitions it from the wider world. That Rolfe, who abandoned his hometown for the Boston suburbs and a life as a history teacher, is tasked to tell the story of his brother and father, both abusive drunks, is an acknowledgement of the extent to which one's past cannot be escaped. Rolfe is a native who wants to be an outsider. Through him, specifically through his desire to have a detached, objective perspective on his family and hometown, Banks begins to historicize self-destructive masculinity. Initially, the historicization is demystifying; things are bad in Lawford simply because Lawford is located too far north. No amount of reform can overcome the problems of Rolfe's hometown. At least that's what Rolfe wants to believe. Rolfe's description of northern New Hampshire is thus an object lesson in how to mobilize local knowledge as information in order to escape complicity.

But *Affliction* ultimately becomes a parable of paternal violence, something that Paul Schrader honed in on with his film adaptation. The novel projects itself as a vehicle for a universal theme and thus a novel that has finally abandoned the particularity of themes in regional fiction. Even Banks's decision about the title highlights the book's nonregional aspirations. The manuscript was originally titled "The Dead of Winter," a title that asserted the prominence of Rolfe's hometown's doomed northness. By becoming "*Affliction*," and by gaining a Simone Weil epigraph, the novel becomes supra-regional, and the New England writer's ability to abandon his region becomes a matter of philosophic seriousness.

Abandonment is the theme of *Rule of the Bone*, a novel about a homeless teenager who takes up with a Rastafarian drifter and eventually migrates to Jamaica. With *Rule of the Bone* comes a resurgence of Banks's teenage interest in the Caribbean, an interest that he explores initially in *The Book of Jamaica*, a dense exploration of political and cultural systems on the island. *Rule of the Bone* is a conventional *Bildungsroman*. It's been likened to such classics of the genre as Mark Twain's *Adventures of Huckleberry Finn* (1884) and J.D. Salinger's *The Catcher in the Rye* (1951).

In much the same way that *Rule of the Bone* is Banks's one coming-of-age novel, *Cloudsplitter* is singular among Banks's oeuvre in that it is his one comprehensive foray into historical fiction. A novel about the life of abolitionist John Brown as told to an academic by Brown's son, Owen, the last surviving member of the Brown family. In addition to being a novel that, faithful to its genre, expresses fidelity to its setting, historical period, and the domestic life and events of John Brown, *Cloudsplitter* is also Owen's confession of deeply held beliefs about race and deeply buried racist secrets. It's an admission of guilt that is at once hyper-particular to the conditions of the Brown family story and an allegory of transhistorical racial tension.

From his research into that novel, Banks discovered the subject of his next novel, *The Darling*, which is set primarily in Liberia, an African nation first settled by a group of antislavery white Americans, during its long, bloody civil war (1989–1996). The novel's narrator, Hannah Musgrave, is the daughter of a famous child psychologist (reminiscent of Benjamin Spock). When she was young, as rebellion against her father's more patrician, pacifist paradigm of civil rights advocacy, Hannah joined the Weather Underground. After a bombing gone awry, she escapes to Africa, where she meets and marries a Liberian politician and friend of Charles Taylor. As a reluctant member of the Liberian elite, Hannah experiences an identity crisis that develops into her starting a chimpanzee sanctuary. From this outrageously haphazard set of narrative conditions, which blend historical and invented events and figures, Banks builds a surprising, poignant critique of white management of the enduring legacies of slavery in America and beyond. That such an international, transhistorical story begins one morning on a farm in upstate New York suggests the degree to which Banks has achieved detachment through commitment to the local.

Banks's answer to the question of what it means to be a "New England writer" has thus been to assert that that badge is exchangeable for cosmopolitan affiliation. His commitment to representing regions and people that modern capital has abandoned has truly gone global, and his representations of such regions and peoples refract back to the reader some of the more poignant economic injustices brought about by globalization.

SEE ALSO: After Postmodernism; Fictions of Work and Labor; Minimalism and Maximalism; Realism after Poststructuralism

REFERENCES

Banks, Russell. (1991). *The Sweet Hereafter*. New York: HarperCollins.
Banks, Russell. (1998). Interview by Robert Faggen: The art of fiction no. 152. *The Paris Review* 147: 50–88.

FURTHER READING

Arthur, Jason. (2013). *Violet America: Regional Cosmopolitanism in U.S. Fiction Since the Great Depression*. Iowa City: Iowa University Press.
Banks, Russell. (2021). *Foregone*. New York: HarperCollins.
McEneaney, Kevin T. (2010). *Russell Banks: In Search of Freedom*. Santa Barbara: Praeger.
Niemi, Robert. (1997). *Russell Banks*. New York: Twayne.
Roche, David. (ed.) (2010). *Conversations with Russell Banks*. Jackson: University of Mississippi Press.

Barth, John

CHRISTOPHER K. COFFMAN
Boston University, USA

In January 1980, *The Atlantic* published John Barth's "The Literature of Replenishment," which piece serves as something of a corrective to common misunderstandings of his intentions and achievements as an author. Barth's first two novels, *The Floating Opera* (1956) and *The End of the Road* (1958), had earned him a place among the Black Humorists in the late 1950s, and his works of the 1960s and early 1970s, *The Sot-Weed Factor* (1960), *Giles Goat-Boy* (1966), *Lost in the Funhouse* (1968), and *Chimera* (1972), ensured him a spot among the Olympian figures of postmodernist metafiction. Furthermore, his nonfictional writing, especially the 1967 essay "The Literature of Exhaustion," defined the terms of the formally unconventional, anti-realist, and reflexively self-aware fiction with which he is most associated. Yet, as the 1980s opened, his reputation was in question: while fans saw his most recent novel, *LETTERS* (1979), as the culmination of his career thus far, many reviews echoed the sentiments of critics such as Gore Vidal and John Gardner, who saw Barth's prose as overly academic and lacking in moral and political edge. In "The Literature of Replenishment," Barth contends that he neither regards literature as a whole as having become irrelevant nor thinks a fictional project that accommodates moral concerns falls outside of American literature's purview. In addition to rebutting such negative assessments of his attitude and works, he also articulates a concern that the sort of literary projects for which his critics call are in fact themselves deficient due to an overextended commitment to outdated aesthetic assumptions, including those underpinning both the traditions of realism and the innovations of modernism. Furthermore, Barth argues, the future relevance of literary fiction depends upon a synthesis or other overcoming of the conventions of those earlier movements. Perhaps the best way to consider his works since 1980, then, is not to carry on with the unreasonably constrained interpretive framework with which his critics of the late 1970s and early 1980s operated, but instead with an eye to the question of whether or not he has realized, or at least pursued, effective and engaging narrative innovations.

Barth's first novel of the 1980s, *Sabbatical* (1982), follows the lead of its title and the arguments of "The Literature of Replenishment," proffering a stock-taking and readjustment of the course of his fictional project. Shorter and less formally and stylistically radical than *LETTERS*, *Sabbatical* also reads as a concession to those who had found his texts too daunting. The plot is a conventional one, although it is garbed in trappings typical of Barth's fictions: a middle-class married couple sort out their professional and personal lives while sailing Barth's beloved home waters of the Chesapeake Bay. In addition to much talk about sailing, there are reflections on fictions, the productivity of heterosexual sexuality, celebrations of the major figures of literary history, allusions to Barth's own earlier works, comments on the state of the Maryland estuarine, many doubles and twins, and a sense that the sea is of most interest to a writer as a symbol of the ocean of story, just as the divide in a road signals narrative opportunity. This is not to say the novel offers no forward movement, in terms of Barth's career. Against those who would claim he is disengaged, his development of a CIA plot explores the difference between those duplicitous schemers, who would use narrative to obscure reality, and the literary writer, who uses it to explore that which reality cannot offer (in this case, such wonders as a sea monster). Too, Barth here begins to make more space for the feminine in his work, primarily by sharing the narratorial voice between male and female figures to a greater degree than he ever had before. At the same time, the CIA plot verges on the territory of the narrative cliché, replicating in its own register the typical shape of a common murder mystery. *Sabbatical* is one of Barth's minor works, but it offers readers both reflections on his work to 1980 and signposts for much of his post-1980 career.

The Tidewater Tales (1987) is more ambitious and significantly more expansive than *Sabbatical*, although the two books call for a paired reading in several ways, not least because the earlier book finds many of its incidents and characters reprised in the later one. One of the central characters is Katherine Sherritt, a pregnant librarian who spends most of the novel sailing the Chesapeake Bay with the other central character, her writer husband, Peter Sagamore, who suffers from a case of writer's block. The upcoming birth of the couple's twin children and Peter's capacity to compose operate in tandem, with certain narrative structures needing to work their way to resolution before production can ensue in either case. Perhaps of more interest in *The Tidewater Tales* than the situation of its central couple is Barth's return to earlier narrative topics and strategies, which are fleshed out and approached from new perspectives. Hence, his interest in narrative theme and variation (Barth was at one point a performing musician) emerge clearly. Such developments are especially evident in the creation of a richer familial world than that presented in most of Barth's earlier works: parents, nephews, siblings, family friends, school chums, and the family doctor all take center-stage at various points. Likewise, their stories, both biographical and invented within the novel, are given extended attention, working in counterpoint to the primary narrative. Balanced against that local, if narratively rich, social world is the broader society of storytellers, manifest most strikingly in the novel in the Sagamore-Sherritt's encounters with what seem to be real-world (primary-narrative) versions of major literary figures, who embody the text's tendency to allow storytelling to cross the boundaries between real and fictional: Huck Finn, Don Quixote, Ulysses, and Scheherazade. Some passages seem a concession to Barth's critics, although they resist apologetics, as when Katherine and Peter are described as "just your average, sappy, middle-class, high-minded liberals," "mildly patriotic but nowise chauvinistic, opposed to imperialist aggression all around . . . Equal opportunity, justice for all, save the environment, no nuclear . . . beware the military-industrial complex, make our government obey the law" (Barth 1987, p. 238). The catalogue of attitudes may slide into self-mockery, but it also neatly encapsulates the controlling ideological attitude of Barth's fictions, even as the levity with which it is presented reminds readers that his concern is the story, rather than the narrowly political. To the extent he has an allegiance, it is to the muse, and his enemies are those who commit political crimes and then try to obscure those crimes with language, who "widen the gap between what things represent themselves to be and what they are" (p. 261). Against such disorienting forces are those of the storyteller, who recognizes that life operates in a fashion akin to narrative; as Loes Nas strongly expresses the point, "life equals story and story equals life" (Nas 2000, p. 187).

As Barth takes a negative view of those who widen the divide between narrative and life, the structure and events presented in his first novel of the 1990s, *The Last Voyage of Somebody the Sailor* (1991), counteract that tendency, identifying commonality of story and reality in such an elaborate way that the distinction between them becomes difficult to maintain. From the first, we are immersed in a multilayered frame tale, as a hospitalized narrator tells a visitor "The Last Story of Scheherazade," which story itself relates the sequence of tales Scheherazade told to Death when he visited her. The convolutions of plot and character multiply: Scheherazade's story tells of a twentieth-century journalist and sailor who falls overboard, and seemingly drowns, only to be reborn in the world of *The Thousand and One Nights*. The sailor (William Behler) then trades stories with Sindbad across a series of several evenings while insinuating himself into the merchant's household and the romantic life of Sindbad's daughter. The two narrative threads are eventually brought together, at which point the stage is set for Behler's return to America. The seemingly fantastic nature of the tale is brought into relief by one medieval Arab's claim that Behler's tale is nothing but fantasy, while the Arabian audience would prefer the "high ground of traditional realism . . . rocs and rhinoceri, ifrits and genies" (1991, p. 136). Too, against claims that Sindbad's or Behler's tales are too fantastic to countenance, one weighs remarks by Angela Carter, who asserts the text "is filled with white nights and golden days, a busy, bustling, wholly invented and self-sufficient world posing as a novel, with something in it for everybody" (Carter 1991). Additionally, there is Nicholas Birns's observation that *Somebody the Sailor* "partakes of . . . the porous, flexibly hybrid, and ecumenical spirit carried over from *The Tidewater Tales*" (1993, p. 133).

Barth's home territory of tidewater Maryland is central to his work, and the inclination to seek biographical elements in his texts is reinforced by the various author surrogates he introduces. These features are brought to the foreground most strongly in the fictional autobiography *Once Upon a Time: A Floating Opera* (1994). The book may be read as a *Künstlerroman*, but also as a testament to Barth's faith in the power of narrative to distinguish different versions of the self, which mingle together like the elements of Maryland's Bay: "Neither dry land nor sea, as the Chesapeake is neither salt nor fresh; emblematic equally of stagnation and regeneration, of death and new life – these inbetweenlands are my imagination's mise-en-scène.. . . I doubt the authority of any story of mine in which they do not figure" (1994, p. 35). Perhaps more than any of his earlier works, this text highlights Barth's increased interest in interrogating not only narrative potential but also authorial identity, which itself is treated as fluid, constructed, and multiple.

To the catalogue of developments in Barth's fictions of the 1990s must be added a preoccupation with endings of stories, an element that is obviously foreboding in terms of the narrative of one's life. Just as *The Last Voyage of Somebody the Sailor* begins with and returns to scenes of illness, confusion, and death, so Barth's later works maintain a preoccupation with terminality. Stephen J. Burn argues as much in an essay on Barth's late style, but additionally observes that Barth treats endings as opportunities for meditations on conclusion rather than movements to narrative silence. Indeed, a framing tale of his 1996 short story collection, *On with the Story*, is that an elderly couple, approaching death, keeps alive by telling stories. While one might also approach the sequence as a circling back to earlier themes and narrative structures in the author's career, or as paired with *Once Upon a Time*, Barth's second collection of shorter texts is finally a celebration of the power of narrative to confront the ultimate. As Burn accurately asserts, "Barth's late works absolutely refuse to concede art's right to organic wholeness in the face of natural decay and disintegration" (2016, p. 186).

The implications of another kind of end, that of an author's artistic relevance, is one preoccupation informing Barth's first work of the twenty-first century, 2001's *Coming Soon!!!*. In this novel, a young writing program student squares off against his aging mentor, a situation Barth uses as a means to express appreciation of ambition and as an excuse to reassess features of his earlier works. This aspect of the plot was enough to prompt a revival of critical assessments of Barth's texts that judge his efforts irrelevant to the cutting edge of narrative fiction, as does a review by Brian Evenson in *Bookforum* that is especially scathing because generally so insightful in its assessments of Barth in relation to such literary stars of the era as David Foster Wallace, whose own work is deeply indebted to and a partial rejection of Barth's own. At the same time, complaints that Barth continues circling back on his early narrative innovations rather than gaining new ground could equally be leveled against such reviews, which are not so different in many respects from those penned by figures like Gardner more than two decades earlier. Perhaps of more interest than the complaints regarding *Coming Soon!!!*'s place in the arc of Barth's career or the avant-garde of American fiction are Barth's engagements in the novel with digital media: his work is obviously a print one, but the opening conceit is a narrator's discovery, in the Chesapeake wetlands, of a waterproof package containing a floppy disc from which much of the rest of the book unfolds. Along the way, Barth frames portions of the text in such a manner that it resembles the buttons, dialog boxes, and menus of computer screens. So, one way to read *Coming Soon!!!* is as a recognition that technology has finally come close to catching up with at least one aspect of Barth's exploration of narrative possibility. While anxieties about the death of print fiction are certainly an element of the novel's digital media meditations, the book finally affirms Barth's ongoing assertions that narrative is adaptable and powerful enough to overcome that challenge.

The terrorist events of September 11, 2001, and their global aftershocks, registered as another sort of end in Barth's next book of fiction, *The Book of Ten Nights and a Night: Eleven Stories* (2004). A gathering of uncollected short fictions from across Barth's career, the whole coheres by virtue of a newly composed frame narrative preoccupied with a seemingly even more dangerous threat to narrative than the death of an author or a shift away from print as dominant medium: "TEOTWAWKI," or, "The End Of The World As We (Americans) Knew It" (2004, p. 3). As the title of the volume suggests, however, Barth's response is to return to the sources of his art, which include not only Scheherazade and *The Thousand and One Nights*, but also the tidal settings with which most narratives of his early life begin. In other words, Barth doubles down, again, on the trappings that have long decorated his affirmations of the relevance and power of storytelling in the face of seeming doom.

Barth's three most recent books of fiction, *Where Three Roads Meet: Novellas* (2005), *The Development* (2008), and *Every Third Thought* (2011) offer the various genres of narrative fiction with which he has grappled across his career, providing readers with, respectively, a trio of novellas (like *Chimera*), a collection of short stories, and a novel. All are much preoccupied with retrospective glances and the power of narrative to make sense of lives and the world in which they unfold. The latter two volumes particularly lend themselves to a reading as a pair: *The Development* describes life (and storytelling) among the aging residents of a gated community, Heron Bay Estates. Among the recurring characters is Tim Manning, whose sense of self is challenged by a narrative incoherence that particularly afflicts the aged: the loss of memory due to degenerative brain disease. In other words, one matter Barth explores with particular focus in the collection is a tension between written narrative as chronicle and life writing as an act of subjective meaning-making. Heron Bay Estates is eventually destroyed by a tornado-spawning hurricane, but, in typically Barthian fashion, that disaster is only the penultimate event, one that spurs the title and material of the final piece, "Rebeginning." A similar sense of narrative's endless power to start over shapes *Every Third Thought*, which follows one couple from *The Development* into their partially reassembled post-Estate lives. The couple are writers and academics, and their retreat from the recent past sees them traveling to the home of Shakespeare. During the excursion, the husband falls and injures his head, an event that initiates a series of five fugue-like flashbacks to his early life. Those flashbacks function in a suitably contrapuntal manner in relation to a present-time narrative sequenced to five seasons (from Fall to Fall) coordinated around the theme of the fall: Adamic, physical, seasonal, and so forth. As the Shakespearean title of the volume suggests, the author stands, Prospero-like, somewhat above the fray, while also deeply invested in it. The narrative closes with one of Barth's most tender moments: the protagonist-author reaches out in the dark to confirm the presence of his wife beside him. It is the image of any author, an image both affecting and powerful: hand stretching into the unknown, seeking contact.

SEE ALSO: After Postmodernism; Post-9/11 Narratives; Realism after Poststructuralism; Vidal, Gore; Wallace, David Foster

REFERENCES

Barth, John. (1987). *The Tidewater Tales: A Novel*. New York: Fawcett.
Barth, John. (1991). *The Last Voyage of Somebody the Sailor*. New York: Anchor.
Barth, John. (1994). *Once Upon a Time: A Floating Opera*. Boston: Little, Brown.

Barth, John. (2004). *The Book of Ten Nights and a Night: Eleven Stories*. Boston: Houghton Mifflin.

Birns, Nicholas. (1993). Beyond metafiction: placing John Barth. *Arizona Quarterly: A Journal of American Literature, Culture, and Theory* 49 (2): 113–136.

Burn, Stephen J. (2016). The end: an introduction to Barth's late style. In: *John Barth: A Body of Words* (ed. Gabrielle Dean and Charles B. Harris), 177–200. Victoria, TX: Dalkey Archive Press.

Carter, Angela. (1991). White nights and golden days. *The Washington Post* (February 3, 1991). https://www.washingtonpost.com/archive/entertainment/books/1991/02/03/white-nights-and-golden-days/2df5aa31-2475-4e6f-86eb-88246c5bddb0/ (accessed September 6, 2021).

Nas, Loes. (2000). "On with the story": the storage of cultural memory in John Barth's later fiction. In: *Genres as Repositories of Cultural Memory* (ed. Hendrik van Gorp and Ulla Musarra-Schroeder), 177–188. Amsterdam: Rodopi.

FURTHER READING

Barth, John. (1984). *The Friday Book: Essays and Other Nonfiction*. New York: Putnam.

Barth, John. (1995). *Further Fridays: Essays, Lectures, and Other Nonfiction, 1984–1994*. Boston: Little, Brown.

Barth, John. (2012). *Final Fridays: Essays, Lectures, Tributes and Other Nonfiction, 1995–*. Berkeley: Counterpoint.

Dean, Gabrielle and Harris, Charles B. (eds.) (2016). *John Barth: A Body of Words*. Victoria, TX: Dalkey Archive Press.

McLaughlin, Robert L. (2004). Post-postmodern discontent: contemporary fiction and the social world. *Symplokē* 12 (1/2): 53–68.

Beattie, Ann

MIRIAM MARTY CLARK
Auburn University, USA

The story of Ann Beattie's writerly beginnings is by now well known. Born in 1947, at the beginning of the extended baby boom that followed World War II, Beattie grew up in suburban Washington, DC. In 1968, as an undergraduate at American University, she won a coveted summer guest editorship at *Mademoiselle*, as Sylvia Plath had done fifteen years earlier. Her first *New Yorker* story, "A Platonic Relationship," appeared in April of 1974, when she was 27; by the end of 1979 she had published seventeen stories in the magazine, claiming a place alongside some of the best-known short story writers of the twentieth century, including Eudora Welty, J.D. Salinger, John Cheever, Alice Munro, and John Updike and establishing her reputation as the voice of her generation in stories that chronicled with cool precision the experience of white, middle-class young people who came of age in the late 1960s and early 1970s. In the decades that followed, Beattie's fiction was widely read and reviewed. Critics focused on her continuing interest in the attitudes and experiences of her generation; her attunement to popular culture and everyday life in middle-class America; and her "minimalism," a term that was as often used to place her – "in a clutch of collectively labeled artists," as John Barth puts it (1986, p. 1) – as to analyze her style. Literary scholarship on her work is scant, however. Among the aspects of Beattie's fiction that have not yet been addressed is its intellectual context, in particular its relationship to late-twentieth century American philosophy. The last section of this entry traces a connection between Beattie's fiction and philosopher Richard Rorty's arguments about the contingency of knowledge and truth.

Over the decades of Beattie's long career, the importance of literary fiction dwindled steadily in American culture. Mass circulation magazines like the *New Yorker*, *Harpers*, *Esquire*, and *Mademoiselle* reduced the number of stories they published or stopped publishing fiction altogether; newspaper book review pages shrank and disappeared;

book sales faltered, bookstores closed, and the subscription book clubs that flourished through the middle of the twentieth century folded. Despite this, Beattie continued to publish stories in the *New Yorker* and other prominent literary journals. Her books appeared with brisk regularity, a new novel or volume of stories every couple of years. Her new fiction was widely reviewed; *The New York Times* typically reviewed her books twice, once in the daily paper and a second time in the Sunday Book Review section. She became a key figure in "the Vintage Contemporary generation," writers who published under Gary Fisketjon's imprint at Random House in the 1980s and influenced a generation of aspiring fiction writers (Dames 2019). Long after she aged out as a famous young writer, she remained a literary celebrity; she has been, among other things, the subject of articles in *Time* (1980, 1990, 2019), *People* (1990), and *Vogue* (2015); and interviews and reviews on National Public Radio, most recently in April of 2019. In May of 2019, following the publication of her novel *A Wonderful Stroke of Luck* she did a guest spot on *Late Night with Seth Meyers*.

Despite this sustained attention, Beattie's body of work is difficult to characterize. From the beginning her stories were recognizable in the tradition of Chekhov, Hemingway, Welty, and Updike. But they also did something new; "You figured out how to write an entirely different kind of story," John Updike told her (Deresiewicz 2011). Stylistically, the difference could be described: Her sentences were shorter and more spare than readers were accustomed to seeing in literary fiction; her diction was plainer; her syntax was "atomized," reflecting the atomized consciousness of her characters and her generation (Deresiewicz 2011). From the beginning, her generational focus polarized literary critics. In his *New York Times* review of *Chilly Scenes of Winter* (1976) and *Distortions* (1976), J.D. O'Hara, noted with pleasure that Beattie "understands and dramatizes our formlessness" (1976, pp. 189–190). In her review of *Secrets and Surprises,* Beattie's second volume of stories, Ann Hulbert admired the deft depiction of "nondescript days," "marginal lives," and "lethargically offbeat characters" who came of age in the 1960s (1979, p. 34). For other critics, however, Beattie's style and subject were a source of irritation. Anatole Broyard wrote in *The New York Times* that Beattie's first two books made him feel "like a psychiatrist at the end of a long day" (1976, p. 27). Pico Iyer, writing in *Partisan Review* a few years later, described Beattie's fiction as "parched," "exhausted," and "numb"; her sentences "wan"; her cadences "neutral" and "chill," (1983, p. 550) and her characters "doomed to a life in the long, ambiguous shadow of the sixties" (p. 548).

Like her predecessor John Updike, Beattie writes within a realist tradition about the lives of white, upper-middle class Americans, people who do not need to worry about meeting basic needs or having enough money to get by. Like Updike, she is interested in her characters' experience of the social changes that transformed middle-class American life over the second half of the twentieth century, most notably the sexual revolution and the near-simultaneous idealization and destabilization of the nuclear family, but also evolving middle-class ideas about things like child-rearing, education, work, friendship, aging, and the increasingly mediated and commodified nature of everyday life. Like his fiction, hers sometimes focuses on middle-class experience of social upheavals and political events – the Vietnam War and the unrest it created, the Civil Rights Movement, the AIDS epidemic, and the 9/11 attacks.

In Updike's fiction, this middle-class experience becomes legible in psychologically coherent characters. Though many of his characters, including Richard Maples, Rabbit

Engstrom, and Henry Bech, develop over multiple texts and sometimes across decades and life-phases, even his stand-alone narratives imply a connection between the brief glimpse a story offers and a coherent self, an unfolding life story. This is also true in Alice Munro's fiction, which appeared regularly in the *New Yorker* over many of the same years Beattie was publishing there. But from the beginning Beattie resists this kind of psychological coherence. She has often remarked that she does not begin writing with characters or situations in mind; "I never have ideas. I don't plan or plot," she told an interviewer in 2015 (Dueben). Throughout her career she has used the same names for characters in unrelated stories, blurring distinctions among her fictional texts and pushing back against the notion that narrated experiences signify or might over time add up to coherent and memorable characters, as they do in Updike's Richard or Rabbit and Munro's Del, or Rose or Prue.

Nor do her characters imagine that they have the capacity to know themselves deeply or understand the experience and motives of others; what they think about themselves and the world around them is typically modest and circumstantial – a situation grasped, a feeling named, a fact reckoned with, though often only in the most provisional ways. The narrator of her story "The Burning House," which appeared in the *New Yorker* in 1979, lies in bed at night thinking about the housemates she has known for years and yet seems to know less and less as time goes by; "All those moments," she says, "and all they meant was that I was fooled into thinking I knew these people because I knew the small things, the personal things" (1982, p. 254).

Moreover, Beattie's narratives are "ensemble pieces" (O'Rourke 2011), focused on clusters of characters rather than on an individual protagonist. The stories are tightly framed in place and time – a weekend in Vermont, a crucial few days on the road to Florida, a winter in Cambridge, a summer in Maine – and in their cultural moment, represented in references to music, television, consumer products, and political and social events. In the novels, what happens within these frames is connected, though only in retrospect, to the motives and desires of her characters. In *Picturing Will* (1991), for example, Jody's artistic ambitions emerge as a driving force in the novel; Mel's desire to nurture and protect children – realized only late in the novel – is another. In the short stories, what happens just happens, a cascade of events or series of contingencies. After a freak accident at a wedding, the narrator of a late story called "The Little Hutchinsons," offers her own memorable image of the ineluctability of life. "In the great flip-book of heaven, where our movement is created and the story reveals itself," she wonders,

> what's to be made of some tragedy in miniature: not two people embracing to waltz with perfect steps and swirling tux tails and a voluminous skirt; not an agile fox chasing a rabbit that outwits him at the last second by burrowing into the hole of a tree . . . instead, one tiny figure approaching another, clasping that person's hand, both turning to face the viewer and to take a modest bow, then suddenly we see only the legs of one figure who levitates, the toes of tiny shoes dangling atop the page. Then nothing. Only the bride. White space.
>
> Our flipping thumb runs out of space and time. . .
>
> (2015, p. 153)

The word "minimalism," widely used in discussions of American literature in the 1980s and early 1990s, offered critics one way to think about the absence of psychological coherence and agency in Beattie's fiction. The term links her to Ernest Hemingway, whose theory and practice of "omission" and whose image of fiction as the tip of an iceberg, served as a model for many writers who came after him. It also links her to a very diverse group of late-twentieth century writers, including Raymond Carver, Donald Barthelme, Frederick Barthelme, Jayne Anne Phillips, Amy Hempel, Tobias Wolfe, and Richard Ford, whose work had also been characterized as "minimalist" by literary critics and scholars. Addressing the suppleness or slipperiness of the term, novelist John Barth wrote in a 1986 essay for *The New York Times* that fiction could be "minimalist in any or all of several ways." There are, he writes,

> minimalisms of unit, form, and scale ... There are minimalisms of style: a stripped-down vocabulary; a stripped-down syntax that avoids periodic sentences, serial predications and complex subordinating constructions; a stripped-down rhetoric that may eschew figurative language altogether; a stripped-down, non-emotive tone. And there are minimalisms of material: minimal characters, minimal exposition.
>
> (1986, p. 1)

Beattie's minimalism befits her minimally-emotive characters, their limited power to act purposefully in the world. "No one had written this way before," William Deresiewicz writes, "The sense was of an absent maker, characters abandoned to themselves... These were people who were going through their lives a moment at a time, trying to get to the next sentence" (2011).

Over time Beattie's fiction evolved. She explored new perspectives – Millennials, in *A Wonderful Stroke of Luck*; public figures in *Mrs. Nixon: A Novelist Imagines A Life* (2011); people who lived to tell the story of their own lives and the last decades of the century. As the twenty-first century advanced, she experimented with literary form, mixing fiction and biography, for example. Her short stories "took on flesh," and became "warmer" (O'Rourke 2011). Her more recent collections, *The Accomplished Guest* (2017) and *The State We're In* (2015), are more like those of Updike and Munro. *The State We're In*, for example, features linked stories about Jocelyn, a high school girl spending the summer in Maine with her uncle and his mentally ill wife while her mother recovers from surgery. Sometimes the later stories involve what David Means describes as "calm, revelatory moments" (2005) the kind of modest epiphany readers know to look for in modern short stories.

Beattie was among the most productive, longest-writing of the fiction writers widely characterized as minimalist in the 1980s and early 1990s, but what happens "after minimalism" as her work changes and the term falls out of vogue among critics, is a question that has not yet been adequately addressed. The late work invites retrospective consideration of Beattie's career and a return to the question of what it is her fiction omits, submerges, or detaches from and why. Though it is obscured by her droll descriptions of herself and her craft, Beattie's fiction shares with late-twentieth century philosophy an interest in epistemological questions – questions that have to do with how our minds work to produce thoughts and representations, how we legitimate these representations as "knowledge" and "truth," and how we understand the relationship between our ideas and the external world of "empirical facts."

It is no accident that in Beattie's story "A Windy Day at the Reservoir," first published in 1991, her character Chap discovers on the drafting table in the study of the house where he and his wife are staying, a copy of Richard Rorty's new book *Contingency, Irony, and Solidarity* (1989). The question that runs through Beattie's writing, intensifying as her characters grow older and the work of meaning making becomes more urgent, is like the one Rorty poses in his book: *can* we make meaning, tell coherent stories about our lives, be in meaningful relationships with others, and create a just society, if what we know is not moored to fundamental principles or empirical facts? What looks like detachment or omission in Beattie's work might be taken instead as fictional exploration of the same question. What would it mean to think of ourselves, our stories, as contingent? In the novels and stories of her early career, Beattie's interest is in the *experience* of contingency, of being unmoored from the foundations that once seemed to order both private and public life. In the later fiction she sometimes imagines, as Rorty does, a world in which we might, by understanding our values and beliefs – our "final vocabulary" (Rorty 1989, p. 73) – as *ours* and by regarding the final vocabularies of others with respect and generosity, discover shared vocabularies and build enduring connections to others.

Beattie's late stories sometimes imagine moments in which one person's deeply, but gently, held values and beliefs encounter another's. The narrator of "Yancey," published in 2015, is an aging, widowed poet. An Internal Revenue Service agent has come to her house to confirm that the room she has claimed as an office for writing poetry is really being used as an office. They chat about her dog, her work as a poet, his alcoholic wife, her difficult daughter. He helps her with a balky window. Out of politeness or mild curiosity, he asks her to recommend a poet he might like. She asks what kind of poetry he likes. He remembers reading Robert Frost in school but confesses that he skips over the poetry in the magazines that come to his house. "I'm an equal opportunity idiot, I guess you'd say," he says (2015, p. 49). The poet reflects on this, then chooses James Wright's "Lying in a Hammock at William Duffy's Farm in Pine Island, Minnesota" (1961), which she reads aloud to him.

He listens as the speaker of the poem describes what he can see from the hammock on a beautiful summer day – a bronze butterfly, wildflowers scattered down a ravine, a field of sunlight, old horse droppings that "blaze up into golden stones," a bird circling overhead (2015, p. 50). The agent observes that the last line of the poem – "I have wasted my life" – "seems to come out of nowhere" (p. 50). No, the poet says, Wright "gave us the scene so that we'd be seduced" and then he "changed the game on us" (p. 51). The agent responds ironically: "That's the kind of guy who'd stick a pin in a balloon. I mean, thank you very much for reciting that. I'll get a book of his poetry and write to let you know my reaction." "That's good," the poet replies, with a little irony of her own. "Any day's good when you get someone to buy a book of poetry who wouldn't ordinarily do it." The agent, turning serious says, "You thought I'd identify with the guy in the hammock. And I guess I do, to be honest." She responds with kindness: "Most people who are being honest feel that way at least some of the time, in my experience" (p. 51).

It is a moment of human connection arising from or within a set of contingencies – his work and hers, her perspective and his, and the random circumstances that brought them together. But their conversation is, in fact, framed by two other visions of life in a contingent world. One on side is the poem itself. What happens in sight of the hammock on William Duffy's farm happens without any intention or effort on the speaker's part; his purposelessness – his "wasted life" – is the very thing that allows him to see the beautiful contingencies of a summer afternoon. On the other side is the last scene of Beattie's story. After the agent leaves, the poet walks her dog, Yancey, to the edge of the field behind the house and unclips the leash to let her "sniff out the day's still dazzling possibilities" (2015, p. 51). "No day failed to contain the unexpected," she thinks with satisfaction as she watches a flock of starlings rise from the tall grass, "Which I suspect Yancey thought too" (p. 51).

The poet's pleasure in the chance encounter and then in the dazzle and drift of the world seems a long way from the aimlessness and anomie of Beattie's earliest characters. But the early fiction and the later are connected by her interest in the contingency of her characters' lives. In broad philosophical terms, she is interested in questions of how we live in a world without foundations. Sometimes her fiction focuses on the raw experience of living in such a world, sometimes on the varieties of what Rorty calls self-protective "knowingness" (1998, pp. 25–27) that her characters use to shield themselves against it. But sometimes, especially in late stories like "Yancey," contingency is liberating; to be unmoored is to be vitally connected to others and to the surprising world around us. As if it were not about what our lives rest on – the principles and foundations – but about what we bring, and what we are open to.

SEE ALSO: Book Clubs; Carver, Raymond; Literary Magazines; Minimalism and Maximalism; Story Cycles; Updike, John

REFERENCES

Barth, John. (1986). A few words about minimalism. *The New York Times Book Review* (December 28, 1986): 1.
Beattie, Ann. (1982). *The Burning House*. New York: Random House; 1st ed. 1979.
Beattie, Ann. (2015). *The State We're In*. New York: Scribner.
Broyard, Anatole. (1976). Books of the times. *The New York Times* (August 24, 1976): 27. https://www.nytimes.com/1976/08/24/archives/books-of-the-times-the-shock-of-unrecognition.html?searchResultPosition=2 (accessed July 31, 2020).
Dames, Nicholas. (2019). Millennials in Beattieland. *Public Books* (April 1, 2019). https://www.publicbooks.org/millennials-in-beattieland/ (accessed June 16, 2020).
Deresiewicz, William. (2011). Beattitudes: on Ann Beattie. *Nation* (November 22, 2011). https://www.thenation.com/article/archive/beattitudes-ann-beattie/ (accessed June 16, 2020).
Dueben, Alex. (2015). *The Millions* (October 7, 2015). https://themillions.com/2015/10/a-riddle-to-be-solved-the-millions-interviews-ann-beattie.html (accessed July 29, 2020).
Hulbert, Ann. (1979). Secrets and surprises by Ann Beattie. *New Republic* (January 20, 1979): 34–36. https://eds-b-ebscohost-com.spot.lib.auburn.edu/eds/pdfviewer/pdfviewer?vid=2&sid=aef71326-3e59-4c78-9148-f78e6954c256%40sessionmgr101 (accessed July 31, 2020).
Iyer, Pico. (1983). The world according to Beattie. *Partisan Review* 50 (4): 548–553. http://www.bu.edu/partisanreview/books/PR1983V50N4/HTML/files/assets/basic-html/index.html#553 (accessed July 31, 2020).
Means, David. (2005). "Follies," the goddess of small things. *The New York Times* (May 5, 2005). https://www.nytimes.com/2005/05/22/books/review/follies-the-goddess-of-small-things.html (accessed June 16, 2020).
O'Hara, J.D. (1976). Reviews. *The New York Times* (August 16, 1976): 189–190. https://archive.nytimes.com/www.nytimes.com/books/97/05/11/reviews/beattie-chilly.html (accessed June 16, 2020).
O'Rourke, Meghan. (2011). The visions of Ann Beattie. *New York Review of Books* (July 14, 2011). https://www.nybooks.com/articles/2011/07/14/visions-ann-beattie/ (accessed June 16, 2020).
Rorty, Richard. (1989). *Contingency, Irony, and Solidarity*. Cambridge: Cambridge University Press.
Rorty, Richard. (1998). *Achieving Our Country*. Cambridge, MA: Harvard University Press.

FURTHER READING

Trouard, Dawn. (ed.) (2006). *Conversations with Ann Beattie*. Oxford, MS: University of Mississippi Press.

Beatty, Paul

PAUL ARDOIN
University of Texas at San Antonio, USA

Though also an accomplished poet and editor, Paul Beatty is best known for his novels – first his widely taught debut, *The*

White Boy Shuffle (1996), and more recently *The Sellout* (2015), which made Beatty the first US winner of the Man Booker Prize. His career began with awards for his poetry, published in two collections, *Big Bank Take Little Bank* (1991) and *Joker, Joker, Deuce* (1994), but – though his novels often feature poets and poetry, and though he edited the near-500-page *Hokum: An Anthology of African-American Humor* (2006) – the twenty-five-plus years since have seen Beatty turn almost exclusively to fiction. Hailed for his biting wit but resistant to descriptions that reduce his work to the merely comic or satirical, Beatty makes resistance to all brands of pigeonholing, prejudging, universalizing, defining, and setting expectations for the individual, the group, or the work – *particularly on the basis of race* – central among the recurrent themes of his oeuvre. One could identify resistance as central to the *forms* of his narratives, as well: utilizing characteristics of what narratologist Kathryn Hume has called a "narrative speed" that results in a disorienting "feeling of excessive rapidity" (2005, p. 105), Beatty combines wide-ranging intertextual allusions, often large casts of supporting characters, and a barrage of barbed critiques aimed in seemingly every direction, with the result of resisting easy sense-making for readers.

Beatty's early *Big Bank Take Little Bank* – a collection of poems filled with clever portmanteaux and neologisms, irregular spacing and capitalization – serves as a sort of training ground for later, more successful experiments (with writing through personas, for example) and oeuvre-wide concerns (e.g. "the lure of" so-called "colorblind" viewpoints [1991, p. 28] and "meltin pot pie wishes" [p. 43]). Like the protagonist of the later *Tuff* (2000), the speakers in this collection praise (Spike Lee, Akira Kurosawa) and critique (*Field of Dreams*) film; and, like the protagonist of *The White Boy Shuffle*, a speaker here even has a childhood friend named Nick Scoby (1991, p. 70). But the collection is largely remarkable for its key differences from Beatty's later work, including an intensity and directness that those who imagine Beatty as primarily a satirist might find surprising.

His second collection of poetry, *Joker, Joker, Deuce*, finds Beatty's various personas grappling – as so many of his fictional characters do – with the expectations others hold for them. The first-person poet-speaker of "Verbal Mugging," for example, explicitly satirizes the expectations of readers and the poets who would cater to them, particularly when those readers are white. Related hallmarks of Beatty's later work show up throughout: critiques of white liberals and white readers who say things like "dont get upset but / why dont you [blacks and other oppressed etc.] / write more universally" (1994, p. 6), for example, and of those intellectuals who claim commitment to progressive politics but "Dont go into the projects" (p. 8).

Poetry continued to play a central role after Beatty's turn to fiction. Beatty's first novel, *The White Boy Shuffle*, tells the story of Gunner Kaufman, a poetic and athletic phenom who, "being a poet, and thus expert in the ways of soulful coercion," is "eminently qualified" to lead a nationwide suicide movement (1996, p. 1) in response to American racism:

> In the quest for equality, black folks have tried everything. We've begged, revolted, entertained, intermarried, and are still treated like shit. Nothing works, so why suffer the slow deaths of toxic addiction and the American work ethic when the immediate gratification of suicide awaits?
>
> (1996, p. 2)

Gunner, who descends from "a long cowardly queue of coons, Uncle Toms, and faithful boogedy-boogedy retainers" (1996, p. 5), spends his early years as the "cool black guy" in the "predominantly white sanctuar[y]" of Santa Monica (p. 27), until his mother becomes alarmed by her children's estrangement from Blackness and moves them to Hillside, a West Los Angeles "hood" (p. 41). Later, in the wake of Gunner's participation in the unrest and looting following the Rodney King verdict (during which his "pacifist Negro chrysalis peeled away, and a glistening anger began to test its wings" [p. 131]), his mother transfers him to a school in the Valley (p. 138). As a result, Gunner is in a familiar position for Beatty characters – an outsider in every environment – which eventually leads to his "unofficial ascension to poète maudit for" a local gang "and by extension the neighborhood" (p. 105), then basketball star, then college dropout, and, eventually, "messiah" of a "mass suicide" that serves as "the ultimate sit-in" (p. 2). Regardless of how much of an outsider Gunner feels (and is), he still finds himself lumped into the easy, socially constructed categories of race by a nation of people who – as Gunner writes in a poem-within-the-novel – all "claim to know my problem / when they don't even know my name" (pp. 172–173). Pointing his critiques in all directions, Gunner reserves his own right to recognize almost everyone – regardless of category or affiliation – as "selfish apathetic humans like everybody else" (p. 199).

Beatty's next novel, *Tuff*, opens with a vaudevillian pairing in the 320-pound Tuffy (Winston Foshay) and the crutch-propelled Fariq Cole, with whom Winston has been partner in crime since the fifth grade. The two have just survived a drug den "shoot-'em-up" (2000, p. 10) by fainting and hiding, respectively. Like *The White Boy Shuffle* and the later *The Sellout*, the novel's plot circulates (loosely) around the political career of its protagonist, but while Winston's near-accidental run for city council falls just short in the vote tally, it plays a more successful role in his coming of age. At the same time as *Tuff* often feels a happier and more optimistic novel than is typical for Beatty, the satire remains omnipresent and is, perhaps ironically for a *Bildungsroman*, situated largely around popular fixations *on* a successful coming of age for racial minorities (particularly Black and Latino boys) in the United States. (The satire here is familiar: *The White Boy Shuffle* sees Gunner attend – and mock – his high school's "monthly 'Young Black and Latino Men: Endangered Species' assembly" [1996, p. 112].) In fact, the novel's supporting cast has intentionally orchestrated an effort to inspire Winston's coming of age. If *Tuff* is a *Bildungsroman*, though, it is not the one they aimed to write for Winston (who specifically rejects, for example, the "bummy *Raisin in the Sun*" route [2000, p. 44]), and it emerges as much from his refusals and resistances of the paths they aim to chart for him as it does from their own plans and models. Winston sees his own model in philosophies of the universe, both from "one million light years" away (p. 71) and within the intimate circle drawn around the individual in a samurai story (p. 77). And his epiphanies arrive in art house movie theaters and sumo rings as much or more than they arrive in courtrooms or schoolrooms staged for intentional interventions (and not at all in some "condescending novel [. . .] orchestrated for political correctness" [p. 104]). At the same time, the novel warns against epiphanies – from the religious to the literary – when, for example, Winston encounters local fisherman "crazy old Siddhartha Jenkins [. . .] wildly wrestling with his pole as if he'd hooked Hemingway's giant marlin" (p. 136).

Just as Beatty's poetry can shed light on the forms and concerns of his fiction, so can his editorial project – *Hokum: An Anthology of African-American Humor* – help highlight a potential lineage not just behind his sense of humor but behind his larger philosophy surrounding humor, satire, absurdity, and the role and place of the humorist. In a general introduction and a few short section intros, Beatty describes his purpose in relationship not just to a climate of humor – "I compiled this book because I'm afraid that American humor is fading into Bolivian and that Will Smith, the driest man alive, will be historicized as the Oscar Wilde of Negro wit and whimsy" (2006, p. 3) – but to a climate of horror and "the absurdity of life," particularly the absurdity of life in a racist culture (p. 299): "My resentment has become so overbearing that these days I'm unable to take anything seriously, much less humorously. Everything is satirical. Not *Mad* magazine satirical but Orwellian dystopic" (p. 2). The volume recovers a strain of texts from a variety of authors – poets, novelists and short story writers, political leaders, musicians, comics writers, and so on – who reveal and revel in the dystopic. At the same time, the volume also works to belie the image of African American literature as fundamentally humorless, dour, sentimental. Almost always, argues Beatty, we have imagined "the defining characteristic of the African-American writer [as] sobriety – moral, corporeal, and prosaic" (p. 11). Beatty laments how much such strains of African American literature have dominated the cultural imaginary as *the only* strains of African American literature, leading, for example, to the near erasure of works like Fran Ross's hilarious (and intimidatingly hyper-referential, hypertextual, and polymathic) *Oreo*. *Hokum* does not simply rebut the view of African American literature as singular or singularly humorless. It also places Beatty's preoccupations – from insisting on the right to point critiques in any direction, to refusing to be easily pigeonholed – in a clear textual tradition.

Slumberland (2008) finds Beatty changing his primary intertextual focus to music and his geographical/cultural focus to Germany. Of course, setting the novel's story abroad allows Beatty new ways to talk about the US, and making the novel's protagonist a DJ on a quest to complete his perfectly crafted beat (rather than making him, say, a poet) allows Beatty new ways to talk about literary art.

This novel about free jazz and the Berlin Wall turns out to have plenty to say about Richard Wright's humorlessness (2008, p. 103), about Beckett's minimalism (p. 164), and about how "Faulkner's world literary existentialism never extends to blacks" (p. 172). Typical of Beatty, the book is thick with intertextual allusions, features a large cast of characters, and finds endless targets for critique. Perhaps in *Slumberland* even more than elsewhere in Beatty's oeuvre, these techniques I have classified under Hume's term – "narrative speed" – come into the service of Beatty's ongoing resistance to pigeonholing, classifying, and siloing, and they do so by way of the novel's fixation on art-making. The protagonist's art here, as a DJ, is about gathering, reassembling, curating extant sounds from everywhere (a view not all that far from Beatty's description of *Hokum* as "a mix-tape narrative dubbed by a trusted, though slightly smarmy, friend" [2006, p. 11]). Protagonist Ferguson W. Sowell, known professionally as DJ Darky, has a "phonographic" memory (2008, p. 22) that allows him to remember every sound – from every note in every song he has ever heard to less explicitly musical fare like the exact sound of "Brando's creaking leather jacket in *The Wild One*" (p. 34), "the sizzle of an Al's Sandwich Shop cheesesteak at the exact moment Ms. Tseng adds the onions" (p. 35), and "a McDonald's straw being inserted into a vanilla shake" (p. 235). He uses this mastery of sound and brilliant assembling ability, along with his impressive record collection, to curate a perfect jukebox in the Slumberland bar and to write a "near perfect" (p. 33) beat. His quest in the novel becomes perfecting that beat and having it "ratified" by his musical hero, The Schwa, "a little-known avant-garde jazz musician" (p. 36) who, in true Beatty style, is valued for being "indeterminate" and "indefinable" (p. 36) and for having "no sympathies of any kind, political or otherwise" (p. 38). Related questions of whether the artist has political or moral responsibilities recur throughout *Slumberland*. When the protagonist DJs a skinhead rally, for example, he reports, "I felt like a Class D war criminal, but being a DJ is like being an ACLU lawyer arguing for the Klansmen's right to march" (p. 174). Through much of the text, DJ Darky's quest suggests that taking from everywhere and being accountable to (definable by, categorizable by) no audience is a supreme aesthetic value. (Lest we take even that suggestion as an "answer" to or uncomplicated descriptor of Beatty's own view, though, the narrator also draws a straight line between Keats's epigram that "Beauty is truth, truth beauty" and Rudolf Hess's declaration that "Hitler ist Deutschland! Deutschland ist Hitler!" [p. 219].) Challenges to category and accountability in the novel accompany conversations about what Trey Ellis (1989) calls "The New Black Aesthetic" and about so-called post-racialism – the latter invoked in the question of whether The Schwa and DJ Darky have created "a beat so perfect as to render musical labels null and void. A melody so transcendental that blackness has officially been declared passé" (2016, p. 16), thereby liberating the protagonist: "You can do what you want. No demands. No expectations. The only person I have to please is myself" (p. 230).

Booker Prize-winning *The Sellout* asks – among other things – what Blackness *is*, particularly in a nation that so aggressively insists it is post-racial and post-racism. The novel's protagonist, Me, responds to confident claims to define Blackness with questions like, "what exactly is *our thing*?" (2016, p. 288). Utilizing both Beatty's own training in psychology and the protagonist's strange education in social science (and what his father called "Liberation Psychology" [p. 27]), the novel puts forth fictional theories of the stages of "black identity" and finally hypothesizes an ultimate stage (Stage IV) that includes Richard Pryor and Chester Himes (also anthologized in *Hokum*) along with the "Unmitigated Blackness" of figures like Jean-Luc Godard, Frida Kahlo, Louis-Ferdinand Céline, and Björk (p. 277). At the same time as the text offers omnipresent critiques of anti-Black racism in America, as well as repeated critiques of figures it imagines as in some ways complicit with or capitulating to white supremacy (like Bill Cosby, Condoleezza Rice, and Colin Powell), it also – like so much of Beatty's work – refuses to settle on a straightforward form of resistance or a singular way of (especially racial) being, and it refuses to reduce US ills to the country's long and ongoing anti-Black terror and racism: "what about the Native Americans? What about the Chinese, the Japanese, the Mexicans, the poor, the forests, the water, the air, the fucking California condor? When do they collect?" (p. 289). The protagonist asking these questions – accused "race pervert" (p. 130) Me – reveals his story in analepsis, from the US Supreme Court, which is hearing the case for his arrest on charges of reinstituting slavery and segregation in the unmapped city outside of Los Angeles formerly known as Dickens. In a large-scale, comical social science experiment, Me has accepted his neighbor Hominy (a former Little Rascal, whose childhood career centered around "Unabashedly Racist" depictions [p. 238]) as his volunteer slave and has officially segregated a bus and an already-all-Black school, all to unexpectedly positive results: higher test scores, less conflict, Hominy's great comfort, and so on. "[I]t's like the specter of segregation has brought Dickens together" (p. 163). Me's country – so intent on its view of itself as "post-racial" – is forced to grapple with what his experiment reveals and whether the apparently improved situation is tolerable in the face of its violation of the country's stated values: "this country," it turns out, "isn't quite as comfortable as it looks"

(p. 3). Me's plan, in such a country, is read as a "conspiracy to upset the apple cart just when things were going so well" (p. 15) – or at least just as we had convinced ourselves that things were going so well. He has "whispered 'Racism' in a post-racial world" (p. 262).

Unusually straightforward (for a Beatty novel) in its presentation of at least some of its theses and outcomes, *The Sellout* even has a judge "rub his tired eyes" and explain the contradiction Me's plan has exposed:

> In attempting to restore his community through reintroducing precepts, namely segregation and slavery, that, given his cultural history, have come to define his community despite the supposed unconstitutionality and nonexistence of these concepts, he's pointed out a fundamental flaw in how we Americans claim we see equality.
> (2016, pp. 265–266)

Perhaps it is the straightforwardness of such speeches that makes this novel feel so (relatively) accessible and has made it so attractive to award committees. Even the novel itself seems to tip its own hand at one moment when it adds to the lauded list of "Unmitigated Blackness" the case of "essays passing for fiction" (2016, p. 277) – that is, something very much like this thesis-declaring novel itself.

It is tempting – in light of that reference to genre – to imagine a larger trajectory of Beatty's work, growing increasingly prosaic – moving, roughly, from the early poetry, to fiction, to the bursts of essay and theory in the introduction, headnotes, and promotional periodical pieces in and around *Hokum*, to, finally, an essay masquerading as the novel *The Sellout*. At the same time, we can also recognize a more coherent Beatty than such genre-jumping would suggest, given that some of the images of the earliest poetry continue to show up even as late as *The Sellout*, and given that so many of the figures (and one rather lengthy joke) anthologized in *Hokum* are cited in the later novel. Arguably, from this perspective, an individual Beatty novel cannot even be entirely read unless read in both the context of his larger body of texts – prosaic and poetic – and the larger centuries-, continents-, and media-spanning contexts of its many intertexts.

SEE ALSO: Post-Soul and/or Post-Black Fiction

REFERENCES

Beatty, Paul. (1991). *Big Bank Take Little Bank*. New York: The Nuyorican Poets Café.
Beatty, Paul. (1994). *Joker, Joker, Deuce*. New York: Penguin.
Beatty, Paul. (1996). *The White Boy Shuffle*. London: Picador.
Beatty, Paul. (2000). *Tuff*. New York: Anchor.
Beatty, Paul. (ed.) (2006). *Hokum: An Anthology of African-American Humor*. London: Bloomsbury.
Beatty, Paul. (2008). *Slumberland*. London: Bloomsbury.
Beatty, Paul. (2016). *The Sellout*. London: Picador; 1st ed. 2015.
Ellis, Trey. (1989). The new Black aesthetic. *Callaloo* 38 (Winter): 233–243.
Hume, Kathryn. (2005). Narrative speed in contemporary fiction. *Narrative* 13 (2): 105–124.

FURTHER READING

Beatty, Paul. (2006). Black humor. *The New York Times* (January 22, 2006). https://www.nytimes.com/2006/01/22/books/review/black-humor.html
Donnelly, Elisabeth. (2015). Paul Beatty on writing, humor and race: "There are very few books that are funny." *The Guardian* (March 10, 2015). https://www.theguardian.com/books/2015/mar/10/paul-beatty-interview-the-sellout#
Jackson, Chris. (2015). Our thing: an interview with Paul Beatty. *The Paris Review* (May 7, 2015). https://www.theparisreview.org/blog/2015/05/07/our-thing-an-interview-with-paul-beatty/
Martin, Michelle. (2006). Finding the lighter side of African American lit. Talk of the Nation. *NPR* (February 6, 2006). https://www.npr.org/transcripts/5192289

Sandhu, Sukhdev. (2016). Paul Beatty: "Slam poetry, TED talks: they're for short attention spans." *The Guardian* (June 24, 2016). https://www.theguardian.com/books/2016/jun/24/paul-beatty-interview-the-sellout

Bennett, Brit

LESLEY LARKIN
Northern Michigan University, USA

Brit Bennett's fiction career, comprising two novels to date – *The Mothers* (2016) and *The Vanishing Half* (2020) – has coincided with a period of intense political polarization in the United States. The rise of openly antidemocratic and racist politicians, ongoing police brutality against Black people, and unprecedented support for the Black Lives Matter movement have shifted – and heightened – public discourse on race and racism. Concepts and slogans previously considered academically or politically fringe (e.g. "intersectionality," "defund the police") are now setting the terms of civic debate. And analyses of America's long history of structural racism, from the formerly esoteric field of "critical race theory" to the *New York Times*'s *1619 Project* (2019), have become the targets of rhetorical and legislative attack.

Within this bubbling stew, and despite resisting the role of "spokeswoman for young black people," Bennett has emerged as one of the most incisive voices on race and racism of her generation (Alter 2016). She first came to attention for her essays – published in venues such as *The New Yorker*, *New York Times Magazine*, and *Paris Review* – on topics such as racist violence and the racialization of childhood. Bennett's keen critiques of whiteness and subtle explications of the intersections of gender and race, in both fiction and nonfiction, have gained her an important place on the contemporary antiracist bookshelf. However, it is vital to recognize that the key motivation for her work – one shared with her clearest literary influence, Toni Morrison – is not the remediation of white racism but the desire to write about Black people *for* Black people. In her fiction, Bennett draws deeply from the African American literary well, signifying on traditional themes (e.g. mother-daughter relationships, racial passing, migration), while contributing a fresh voice and perspective. Her work is likely only to grow in stature in the coming years.

Bennett was born in 1990 and raised in Oceanside, California, an economically and ethnically mixed beach community fictionalized in *The Mothers*. Her father, Oceanside's first Black city attorney, grew up in South Central Los Angeles; her mother, a fingerprint analyst, grew up sharecropping in Louisiana and came to California in the last wave of the Great Migration. Her mother's experience has given Bennett a sense of the proximity of Jim Crow segregation, its lingering presence: "The idea that this is ancient history – it never felt ancient to me," she has explained. "I'm one generation away" (Brockes 2021).

Bennett grew up writing, beginning a draft of *The Mothers* while still a teenager. She earned a bachelor's degree in English from Stanford (including a stint at Oxford), followed by a master of fine arts degree in creative writing from the Helen Zell Writers' Program at the University of Michigan. In 2016, Bennett was selected by the National Book Foundation as a "5 under 35" honoree, alongside Yaa Gyasi, Greg Jackson, S. Li, and Thomas Pierce. *The Vanishing Half* was longlisted for the Aspen Words Literary Prize, the National Book Award, and the Women's Prize; there are also plans to adapt it for television.

Bennett entered the public eye with "I Don't Know What to Do with Good White People" (2014), an online essay that garnered more than a million views in three days (Alter 2016). Written after a grand jury failed to indict police officer Darren Wilson in the killing of Mike Brown in Ferguson, Missouri, the piece calls to task "good white people" whose responses to the "non-indictment" are, in Bennett's assessment, empty virtue signaling: "What a privilege, to concern yourself with seeming good while the rest of us want to seem worthy of life," she writes. The misapprehension of racism as a question of personal belief, rather than of systems and structures, causes real harm: "[W]hat good are your good intentions," Bennett asks, "if they kill us?" She extends this point in "White Terrorism is as Old as America" (2015), in response to the murder of Black churchgoers by a white gunman in Charleston, South Carolina. Here, Bennett eviscerates media coverage that perpetuates a mythology of "lone wolves" and "bad apples" instead of offering an analysis of white identity as central to racial violence – and vice versa. Bennett's critique of whiteness, particularly of white liberals, appears in her novels as well. In *The Mothers*, the narrator explains that "subtle racism was worse because it made you feel crazy. You were always left wondering, was that actually racist?" (2016, p. 113). And in *The Vanishing Half*, Bennett writes of the "fine people, good people" who admired Martin Luther King but "wouldn't have allowed the man to move into their neighborhood" (2020, p. 159).

In several essays, Bennett explores another theme central to her fiction: the intersectional experiences of Black women. In "Ta-Nehisi Coates and a Generation Waking Up" (2015), Bennett praises Coates's influential nonfiction work *Between the World and Me* (2015), while also noting its gendered limitations. By presenting grief for Black men as Black women's primary response to anti-Black violence, she argues, Coates and others imply that violence against Black women is natural. Bennett dramatizes this problem in a brief dialogue in *The Mothers*: "Black boys are target practice. At least black girls got a chance," says a young man (2016, p, 240). "I don't think that's true," counters his female companion. "I never feel safe." In "Body and Blood" (2018), Bennett elaborates on the challenge of living in a Black female body. She argues that the sexual self-discipline demanded of girls by the church, a major theme in *The Mothers*, is counterpart to the physical discipline taught to Black boys as a strategy for evading white violence; both exacerbate the alienation of young people from their bodies without actually protecting them. Paradoxically, Bennett describes writing as both a temporary escape from a vulnerable body and a means of reconnecting body and spirit; she cites writers James Baldwin, Alice Walker, and Toni Morrison as models for this reconnection.

Morrison's influence, in particular, looms large in Bennett's fiction. *The Mothers* is a worthy companion to Morrison's first novel, *The Bluest Eye* (1970); both focus on the experiences of Black girls as they strain against powerful, collective forces. While Morrison uses snippets from a reading primer to express normative views on the nuclear family that crush the young girl at the center of her book, Bennett offers "the Mothers," a chorus of gossiping church women who contextualize, analyze, and judge the behavior of her novel's main character. Gossip is, in fact, central to both books, each of which begins by inviting readers to share in a secret. Bennett and Morrison alike lend significance to a verbal form coded as feminine and dismissed as trivial; as Bennett has said, "[G]ossip has social power" (Jerkins 2016).

The "secret" that everyone is talking about in *The Mothers*, as in *The Bluest Eye*, is a pregnancy. Seventeen-year-old Nadia, involved in a hidden relationship with Luke, her pastor's son, has become pregnant and undergone an abortion. This scandal falls on the heels of another: Nadia's mother's suicide. Lonely and grieving after both events, Nadia begins an intense friendship reminiscent of the opposites-attract bond at the heart of another Morrison novel, *Sula* (1973). Although Nadia is adventurous and outspoken, and Aubrey is quiet and devout, their relationship is cemented by the shared experience of maternal abandonment. (Aubrey's mother has chosen her abusive boyfriend over her own daughter.) Aubrey's home briefly becomes a second home to Nadia, and her sister Mo – whose name suggests she is a partial maternal stand-in – and Mo's partner, Kasey, become Nadia's second family. Nadia then leaves Oceanside and stays away for years, attempting to avoid the palpable absence of both her mother and the "Baby" she chose not to carry. When she eventually returns, she embarks on an affair with Luke, now married to Aubrey. Bennett underscores the inverse trajectories of Aubrey and Nadia's lives when Luke abandons Aubrey at a fertility appointment just as, years before, he abandoned Nadia at an abortion clinic.

As several relationships threaten to implode, one is reminded that Oceanside lies in the shadow of a nuclear power plant whose "two white domes" are called "the boobs" by local schoolchildren. How easily the maternal ideal can "go boom," as it were: "All it takes is a storm," says an acquaintance, in reference to the nuclear plant, "and we all blow up" (2016, p. 34). Nadia responds by revealing her own fantasy of destruction/self-destruction, modeled, perhaps, on her mother's violent end: "That's how I wanna go someday ... Boom." The volatility of motherhood is the beating heart of Bennett's novel. What makes someone a mother – whether "by heart" or "by womb" (p. 22)? And can a mother forfeit her access to that title?

Bennett honors the significance of mothers while also making clear that no individual can live up to the cultural ideal of motherhood. The chorus of "Mothers" who criticize, cajole, and offer warnings about everything from "littlebit love" to "ain't shit men" are themselves complex, imperfect, vulnerable – a fact Nadia becomes aware of when she takes on a mothering role toward them (2016, pp. 22, 88). Only then do readers encounter actual dialogue among the Mothers, in place of a collective voice. Motherhood, toppled from its pedestal, becomes, in Bennett's hands, a signifier for the many selves we carry within us, the many lives we might give birth to – others' and our own. In a novel intensely focused on secrets and the tension between external and internal selves, pregnancy is a potent metaphor indeed.

If *The Mothers* is engaged in a rich dialogue with Toni Morrison's oeuvre, *The Vanishing Half* is a book "sashed in influences" (Sehgal 2020). Of special note are Bennett's many references to the longstanding genre of the passing narrative. Like Mark Twain's *Pudd'nhead Wilson* (1893), the novel centers on "twins" (Twain's are half-brothers) who exist on opposite sides of a strict but arbitrary color line; not incidentally, fingerprinting, a technology that has served both eugenics and racially unequal policing, plays a role in both novels. By naming one of her central characters Desiree, Bennett also evokes Kate Chopin's "Désirée's Baby" (1893), which, like *The Vanishing Half*, engages the complex racial dynamics of Louisiana and the precarious status of light-skinned Black women. But perhaps the text to which Bennett most directly alludes is Nella Larsen's *Passing* (1929). Both novels focus on a pair of light-skinned Black women who make diametrically opposed choices with regard to racial identity, and both trace the psychological and social reverberations of these choices – though Bennett is able to go further than her predecessor in this exploration.

The Vanishing Half makes good on the promise of the passing narrative not only to expose the contradictions of the American racial economy but also to follow identity development along multiple and intersecting vectors – and across time and space. The story begins in 1968, when Desiree Vignes returns to Mallard, Louisiana, daughter Jude in tow, several years after having fled her hometown as a teenager with her identical twin sister, Stella. Evoking, in inverted form, the dark-skinned town at the center of Morrison's *Paradise* (1997), Mallard is founded as a haven for light-skinned Black people, though Desiree and Stella learn, when their father is lynched in front of them, that proximity to whiteness is no guarantee of safety. Not long after their flight to New Orleans, the girls' paths diverge: Stella (like Larsen's Clare) marries a wealthy white man and passes permanently into white society, while Desiree (like Larsen's Irene) marries "the darkest man she could find" (2020, p. 4). Both women have a single daughter, and the novel follows their stories, too: Jude, as she grapples with growing up "blueblack" in her mother's "colorstruck" hometown and then launches a new life in California, and Kennedy, as she flounders, despite economic and racial privilege, and longs for a deeper connection to her mother (pp. 84, 20). When the cousins eventually meet, neither rupture nor reconnection follows; rather, Bennett imagines a tenuous thread among the Vignes women – or, rather, a "vine," whose course and offshoots are unpredictable.

Importantly, *The Vanishing Half* ends neither in tragedy for Stella, nor in a racial "homecoming" (Wald 2000, p. 34). Instead, Bennett makes clear that both Stella and Desiree have made choices within a racial binary that offers very few. Desiree lives with the consequences of raising her daughter in a community that largely rejects her, though she also creates a loving family there. Meanwhile, Stella lives in comfort and privilege, but with the constant fear of being exposed and with the regular invasion of racial trauma in her intimate relationships, as when her daughter's face morphs into the face of "everyone that she had ever hated" and her husband's body turns into the body of a member of the lynch mob that killed her father (Bennett 2020, pp. 199, 161). As Bennett alternates among various time periods (from the 1950s to the 1980s), she underscores the proximity and continuing relevance of "earlier" forms of racism, illustrating that passing, and the forces that provoke it, are not phenomena that "belong" to a bygone era.

Importantly, Bennett suggests that expressing – even experimenting with – various identities is not anathema to the authentic self but part and parcel of the human experience. We see every character engaging in race, gender, and class performances, whether in their personal lives or, as in the case of Kennedy, an actor, or Barry, a drag performer, on stage. Bennett's sensitive treatment of Reese, who is transgender, illustrates the point that gender, specifically, is both "performative" and "deep-seated" (Butler 1993, pp. 94, 107). Rather than suggesting that gender is merely a costume (like the cowboy hat and boots Reese is wearing when he first meets Jude) or a straightforward matter of genitals or DNA, Bennett presents gender as both a complex citation of social norms and an intimate matter of the heart. "A body could be labeled," muses Jude while studying anatomy and stroking Reese's arms, "but a person couldn't, and the difference between the two depended on that muscle in your chest" (Bennett 2020, p. 131). Bennett's inclusion of Reese's storyline is daring in the context of a contentious political debate that often involves the invalidation of transgender identities through spurious comparison to racial passing. But Bennett makes clear that race and gender are distinct aspects of identity in intricate relation; Reese and Stella's storylines are neither parallel nor perpendicular. Notably, just as Bennett rejects typical passing narrative tropes, she also avoids the trope of "forcible exposure" found in many in transgender narratives; neither Stella nor Reese is outed in *The Vanishing Half* (Carroll 2018, p. 5).

At the heart of Bennett's novel is her perception, also explored in *The Mothers*, that a person can be two people or more at once – and over a lifetime. Although this capacity can underwrite duplicity and betrayal, there is an inherent hopefulness to Bennett's recognition of the plural self, a faith in people's capacity to grow and change; after all, both Stella and Desiree make major life changes in middle age, including Stella's decision to tell Kennedy the truth about her life. A figure from the opening passage of the novel, when the narrator recounts Stella and Desiree's disappearance from Mallard, neatly captures Bennett's commitment to indeterminacy: "One morning, the twins crowded in front of their bathroom mirror, four identical girls fussing with their hair. The next, the bed was empty, the covers pulled back like any other day, taut when Stella made it, crumpled when Desiree did" (2020, p. 4). Here, the girls are reflections of themselves and of each other; they multiply from one to two to four and back again, anticipating the later, paradoxical, claim that they are "like one body split in two" and like "two bodies poured into one" (p. 36). They also disappear, the figure of the empty bed suggesting a present absence/absent presence. Although the bed is made "like any other day," the ambiguity of Bennett's sentence structure implies that it is somehow both "taut" and "rumpled" – a Schrodinger's bed that symbolizes the undecidability of identity, its fragile dependency on external interpretation or, put another way, on reading.

The role readers play in making narrative decisions, their intimate relation to the stories they read, is an important concept for understanding Bennett's work. Early on in *The Mothers*, the women who comprise the title chorus offer a commentary on prayer that we might take as a commentary on reading itself. They explain that "intercessory prayer" requires a feat of imagination understood in physical terms: "You close your eyes and listen to a request. Then you have to slip inside their body. . . . If you don't become them, even for a second, a prayer is nothing but words" (2016, p. 38). Here, language becomes a means of crossing the boundary between self and other, of connecting bodies and spirits. In the final passage of the book (which also recalls Morrison's metafictional move at the end of *Jazz* [1992]), the Mothers suggest that narrative is itself intercessory, entering the very bodies of readers: "We see the span of [Nadia's] life unspooling in colorful threads and we chase it," say the Mothers, "wrapping it around our hands as more tumbles out. She's her mother's age now. Double her age. Our age. You're our mother. We're climbing inside of you" (2016, p. 275). Blurring the lines between reading and interceding – and between authors and readers – Bennett offers her wide-ranging, unpredictable stories about the richness of Black lives as a prayer *to* and *for* her readers. Now we hold these stories inside ourselves, and the questions she leaves us with are: Will you carry this story? Which version will you give birth to? And how will you nurture it?

SEE ALSO: Allison, Dorothy; Gay, Roxane; Morrison, Toni; Third-Wave Feminism; Ward, Jesmyn

REFERENCES

Alter, Alexandra. (2016). *The Mothers*, a debut novel, is already creating a stir. *The New York Times* (October 9, 2016). www.nytimes.com/2016/10/10/books/the-mothers-brit-bennett.html?smid=url-share (accessed July 6, 2021).

Bennett, Brit. (2015). White terrorism is as old as America. *New York Times Magazine* (June 19, 2015). https://www.nytimes.com/2015/06/19/magazine/white-terrorism-is-as-old-as-america.html (accessed July 6, 2021).

Bennett, Brit. (2016). *The Mothers*. New York: Riverhead Books.

Bennett, Brit. (2020). *The Vanishing Half*. New York: Riverhead Books.

Brockes, Emma. (2021). Brit Bennett: Trump colonised our brains for years. Suddenly he's just gone? It feels surreal. Interview with Brit Bennett. *The Guardian* (May 15, 2021). https://www.theguardian.com/books/2021/may/15/brit-bennett-trump-colonised-our-brains-for-years-suddenly-hes-just-gone-it-feels-surreal (accessed July 6, 2021).

Butler, Judith. (1993). *Bodies That Matter: On the Discursive Limits of "Sex."* London: Routledge.

Carroll, Rachel. (2018). *Transgender and the Literary Imagination*. Edinburgh: Edinburgh University Press.

Jerkins, Morgan. (2016). Doubt and shame in "The Mothers": an interview with Brit Bennett. *Los Angeles Review of Books* (October 11, 2016). https://lareviewofbooks.org/article/doubt-shame-mothers-interview-brit-bennett/ (accessed July 6, 2021).

Sehgal, Parul. (2020). Brit Bennett's new novel explores the power and performance of race. Review of *The Vanishing Half*, by Brit Bennett. *The New York Times* (May 26, 2020). https://www.nytimes.com/2020/05/26/books/review-vanishing-half-brit-bennett.html (accessed July 6, 2021).

Wald, Gayle. (2000) *Crossing the Line: Racial Passing in Twentieth-Century U.S. Literature and Culture*. Durham, NC: Duke University Press.

FURTHER READING

Bennett, Brit. (2015). Addy Walker, American girl. *The Paris Review* (May 28, 2015). https://www.theparisreview.org/blog/2015/05/28/addy-walker-american-girl/

Eaton, Kalenda. (2018). Review of *The Mothers*. *Western American Literature* 53 (1): 139–141.

Hobbs, Allyson. (2016). *A Chosen Exile: A History of Racial Passing in American Life*. Cambridge, MA: Harvard University Press.

Wilkerson, Isabel. (2011). *The Warmth of Other Suns: The Epic Story of America's Great Migration*. New York: Vintage.

Berger, Thomas Louis

DAVID W. MADDEN
California State University, Sacramento, USA

Thomas Berger was a prolific writer who worked across genres but is known primarily for his efforts as a novelist. He published twenty-three novels, fourteen of which appeared after 1980, and two collections of shorts stories (*Granted Wishes: Three Stories* [1984] and *Abnormal Occurrences: Short Stories* [2013]). Of the five plays he wrote (*Other People* [1970], *Rex, Rita, and Roger* [1970], *The Siamese Twins* [1971], *At the Dentist's* [1981], and *The Burglars* [1988]), only *Other People* and *The Burglars* have been published. Other works include fifteen interviews and various uncollected articles and essays. Berger's novels range over a variety of genres, but the work which overshadows them all is *Little Big Man* (1964), which received the Richard and Hinda Rosenthal Award, the National Institute of Arts and Letters Award, and a Western Heritage Award and was adapted into a major motion picture in 1970.

Berger was completely devoted to the craft of writing, rarely taking teaching assignments and resistant to popular and avant-garde trends in the literary world, such as documentary realism, surrealism, and metafiction, to name only a few. Nevertheless, elements from each do occasionally appear in his works. Berger was a thoroughgoing independent, some might even argue an iconoclast, who gave very few full-length interviews, avoided the gatherings of other writers, and refused opportunities for self-promotion. Late in his career, after moving to a new publisher, he was encouraged to travel into Manhattan to have lunch with his new editor. Berger declined because he was uncomfortable with this type of socializing and because, as he told his agent, the editor would be replaced in a few months and Berger would be compelled to have lunch with yet another new face. Not surprisingly, then, he was never as celebrated as some of his contemporaries – Philip Roth, Saul Bellow, E.L. Doctorow, John Updike, Kurt Vonnegut, Don DeLillo, or Thomas Pynchon.

Perhaps the most important aspect of his writing is his dedication to language itself. He is a stylist par excellence, seeking in every novel to expand the range of his prodigious talents. As Brooks Landon, Berger's most adroit critic, points out, "One way of summarizing this overriding concern is simply to say that for Berger, the novel's most profound subject must always be the power of language" (1991, p. 14). In his relentless celebration of language and style, Berger explores a range of fictional genres: the Western (*Little Big Man* and *The Return of Little Big Man* [1999]), detective fiction (*Who is Teddy Villlanova?* [1977]), utopian/dystopia fiction (*Nowhere* [1985]), domestic narrative (*Sneaky People* [1975], *The Feud* [1983]), police procedural (*Killing Time* [1967], *Suspects* [1996]), knight errantry (*Arthur Rex* [1978]), futurism (*Regiment of Women* [1973]), fantasy (*Being Invisible* [1987], *Changing the Past* [1989], *Adventures of the Artificial Woman* [2004]), social commentary (*Crazy in Berlin* [1958], *Reinhart in Love* [1962], *Vital Parts* [1970], *Reinhart's Women* [1981]), moral dilemmas (*The Houseguest* [1988], *Meeting Evil* [1992], *Best Friends* [2003]), and specific reinventions of the Oresteia (*Orrie's Story* [1990]) and Robinson Crusoe (*Robert Crews* [1994]). The two significant exceptions are *The Houseguest* and *Neighbors* (1980), which along with *Little Big Man* is his favorite novel and which he described as being "like automatic writing: I never consciously thought about it at all, but would rush to typewriter each morning, eager to see what would happen next" (Madden 1995, p. 166).

Such a diverse canon would suggest there is little commonality among Berger's works, and while each is unique and independent of the others, there are some mainstays. A consistent feature is the status of his protagonists, who are always outsiders to one degree or another. The pattern is established early with *Crazy in Berlin* in the figure of Carlo Reinhart, a young soldier dispatched to Berlin in the American occupation forces during World War II. An eager, naive young man, Reinhart comes under the influence of a series of characters who hold divergent values and challenge his innocent view of the world. Berger returns to the character in *Reinhart in Love* to present his postwar experiences – marriage, children, friends, job – but through it all Reinhart remains alienated and naive, a fumbler in a society of ambitious contemporaries. *Vital Parts* continues the series as a 44-year-old Reinhart chafes against the culture of the late 1960s and wages a continuous battle with his defiant son, Blaine. By this time a confirmed loser, Reinhart seeks to escape an inhospitable life and world through cryogenic freezing.

Berger would not return to Reinhart for eleven years, when he appears as a 54-year-old recluse living with his daughter in her apartment, jobless and largely directionless. His joy in cooking suddenly catapults him into local celebrity when he appears on a morning news program as the resident chef. Unlike most of Berger's other outsiders, Reinhart finally finds a place of respect and equanimity, and Berger intended to continue with Reinhart into old age, but that novel never came to pass.

The ultimate Berger outsider is, of course, Jack Crabb, the hero of *Little Big Man* and *The Return of Little Big Man*. Jack is orphaned during his family's crossing of the plains, adopted by a tribe of Cheyenne, and raised as one of their own. His life is a quintessential picaresque journey, and like all picaros Jack is forever left to his own devices in a largely inhospitable, threatening world. He spends the first thirty-three years of his life shuttling between the tribe and the white world, seeking some purchase on stability and purpose as he reinvents himself again and again. Although he repeatedly refers to the white world as civilized and Native Americans as savages, Jack never abandons either nor establishes a hierarchy of values. For Jack, each culture has elements of nobility and disgrace, and ultimately Jack's is less a search for a profession, spouse, or singular achievement than a desperate quest for the self, a sense of identity dictated by the searcher and not the world at large. He is clearly most at home with the Cheyenne, but he agrees with his friend Lavender that inevitably he yearns to return to the white world to satisfy his curiosity yet regrets that one cannot simply become a Native American – that identity is a matter of birthright. When his adoptive grandfather, Old Lodge Skins, dies at the novel's close, Jack is left more profoundly alone than ever before.

The Return of Little Big Man continues the episodic journeys of Jack Crabb from 1876 into the dawn of the twentieth century. Crabb wanders endlessly, encounters more legendary figures of frontier history, and apart from a mangy dog he rescues, his life continues to be that of an isolate. For Berger the alienated are not the exceptions or the minority, these figures are the modern norm, and theirs is the true existential condition of American life.

In each of his novels, Berger presents figures who are victims of humiliations large and small, and their lives are typically devoid of great distinction or achievement. To protect themselves, they construct a personal armor of pride to shield them from threats they find everywhere. Earl Keese in *Neighbors* lives a quiet, uneventful life in a house at the end of a dead-end street. His encounter with a pair of exuberant, unpredictable new neighbors triggers his latent competitiveness. The wife of the new couple, Ramona, poses a central question about the essence of Keese's character, "How far would you go to avoid humiliation? That's what I always think when I look at somebody like you" (1980, p. 42), and the answer is nearly anything, including ruining the neighbors' car and firing a shotgun at their house.

The Feud, a finalist for a Pulitzer Prize which was overruled by the competition's administrators, is a sustained study in pride and its many calamities. The novel centers on two adjacent Midwestern towns whose inhabitants delude themselves that they are somehow superior to their neighbors. Through a comedy of errors, their insecurities and competitiveness explode into hilarious consequences. A simple misunderstanding in a hardware store devolves into the darkest of suspicions, and as the most paranoid of the townspeople, Reverton, says in exasperation, "We got our pride at stake here. They get away with that, and the next thing you know they'll be riding us down like dogs and violating our women and all" (1983, p. 27). More than income or opportunity, suffocating pride holds these people in their place, and their children, with their aspirations for something better or larger, are consumed by the stultifying values of their parents.

The Houseguest is based on the outlandish premise that a stranger has insinuated himself into the home and lives of a family for entirely obscure reasons. Chuck Burgoyne, the houseguest, learns the secrets of each member of the Graves family, who are supercilious, privileged creatures living in disdain of their neighbors. When they finally decide they have had enough of Chuck, the bankruptcy of their lives is fully revealed. A frequent theme in Berger's novels is the interplay between morality and manners, and the battle between Chuck and the Graves is a litmus test for this contrast. Each of the Graves is morally weak or deficient with their lassitude and ethical lapses. They replace moral distinction with possessions, property rights, and accepted behavior. The patriarch, a serial adulterer, puts the matter best when exclaiming, "Look this man has *abused our hospitality*! Can there be a greater crime? Think of what that means to the whole matter of civilization" (1988, p. 192). As he opines later, "This is beyond right and wrong: it is simple reality" (p. 211), and, of course, when seen in these terms, any action, even assassination of the houseguest, becomes acceptable.

Best Friends is an extended exercise in the distinctions between manners and morals, as the novel examines a life-long friendship between two middle-aged men, Roy Courtright and Sam Grandy. The two pledge loyalty to one another and operate on the standards of bourgeois acceptability, with Roy repeatedly providing increasing drafts of money for Sam's irresponsible lifestyle. Beneath the seeming bonhomie, there is tension: Roy is impatient with Sam's irresponsibility, and Grandy is a manipulator who plays on Courtright's weaknesses and inability to challenge Sam's exploitation. The novel teems with phrases such as "moral responsibility," "moral position," "moral essence," and "moral courage," and when Courtright betrays the friendship by falling in love and sleeping with Grandy's wife, Kristin, he rationalizes his behavior, "Love not only superseded morality; it transformed everything done in its interests, else he would have felt foolish after a roll in the backseat of a car. As it was, he felt like a hero" (2003, p. 164). As much as the two profess love, they despise each other as well, and in the end, when Grandy dies of a stroke and Courtright pledges to stand by Kristin through her ordeal, the narrator concludes, "So while escaping Roy's revenge, Sam had gotten his own at last. But in so doing, he had also given Roy a use. That's what best friends are for" (p. 209).

Perhaps the apogee of Berger's investigation of moral themes appears in *Meeting Evil*, his most relentlessly dark fiction, "I've been trying in recent years to be grimmer and grimmer and grimmer . . . I wanted to write a book no one could call comic" (Landon 1991, p. 29). As in *Best Friends*, Berger pits two antithetical people against one another in the figures of John Felton and Richie Maranville and sends them on a moral journey to the pit of hell. Felton is a quiet, responsible, but thoroughly unprepossessing man who consistently strives to do right by others and himself. His moral code is hardly rigorous but is serviceable for living at peace with family, neighbors, and colleagues. Richie, however, is vile and depraved, yet he sees in John a perverse reflection of himself, "It was their destiny to be brothers. Intuition was the faculty that most influenced what Richie did, though it might well seem to others that he acted altogether on sudden impulse" (1992, p. 129). Richie takes John on a crime spree of outlandish proportions, involving theft, battery, mayhem, and murder. Indeed, Berger has examined criminal types in other novels – Joe Detweiler in *Killing Time*, Lloyd Howland in *Suspects*, Buddy Sandifer in *Sneaky People*, and Esther Mencken and E.G. in *Orrie's Story* – but unlike Richie, these figures are largely ineffective bunglers. Richie is despicable, self-serving, self-aggrandizing, and powerfully lethal.

As their wild journey progresses, John must confront his own demons and acknowledge a grim fascination with Richie and his schemes. When Richie suggests they get rid of a witness, John finds what is "especially disturbing about this statement was that it did not appall him – as, in all decency, it should have" (1992, p. 52). Ultimately John must either continue with decency and propriety and be destroyed or wander into a moral hinterland and save himself. As the narrator describes at the novel's end, "Killing Richie in what was really cold blood had not yet horrified or sickened him, but he assumed that both reactions, and worse, might come when his sense of self returned. Perhaps he would not survive" (p. 220). As Berger commented in an interview, "I am happy to be called a moralist, which by the way does not conflict at all with my stated intention of writing only to amuse myself. What amuses me are tales of moral significance: my own are always personal inventions, even when I use history or established legend, but hardly ever self-regarding" (Madden 1995, p. 170).

John, along with so many other Berger protagonists, must contend with worlds that seem to defy comprehension, and they suggest another major Berger concern – the nature of reality itself. Reality, for Berger's characters, is hardly fixed, reliable, clearly definable. In fact, as John Felton discovers, it is often chaotic and fluid. Early in *Neighbors*, Earl Keese admits to bizarre visions that regularly confound:

> Were Keese to accept the literal witness of his eyes, his life would have been of quite another character, perhaps catastrophic, for outlandish illusions were, if not habitual with him, then at least none too rare for that sort of thing. Perhaps a half-dozen times a year he thought he saw such phenomena as George Washington urinating against the wheel of a parked car (actually an old lady bent over a cane), a nun run amok in the middle of an intersection (policeman directing traffic), a rat of record proportions (an abandoned football), or a brazen pervert blowing him a kiss from the rear window of a bus (side of sleeping workingman's face, propped on hand).
> (1980, pp. 1–2)

Russell Wren, the putative playwright and detective, in *Nowhere* is hustled off to the kingdom of San Sebastian to investigate a local terrorist group, the Sebastiani Liberation Front, and during his stay he discovers that police act as judges, blondes are reviled as social inferiors, scholars work to rewrite anything they disagree with, librarians are illiterate, and so on. At every turn logic and predictability are overturned, and when Wren returns home, he concludes, "... one result (perhaps the only) of my visit to San Sebastian was a diminishment of my capacity for wonder... Did things make any more sense elsewhere? Or, to be fair, any less?" (1985, p. 182). Before he can answer this question, he awakens from sleep to realize all of San Sebastian has been a dream.

A trio of later novels – *Being Invisible*, *Changing the Past*, and *Adventures of the Artificial Woman* – challenge accepted notions of reality. Each is founded on seeming impossibilities, yet those impossibilities offer looking glasses through which the seemingly normal or predictable is analyzed. In *Changing the Past* Walter Hunsicker, a stable, largely satisfied man, is offered the chance to alter his past, redo his life, and consequently alter the future. When he learns that his son is dying from AIDS, he jumps at the opportunity to become three different versions of himself in an attempt to alter the inevitable. Hunsicker becomes dissatisfied with each of his new incarnations and ultimately opts to resume life as himself. Ultimately, he realizes that he cannot escape reality, or in his case the life he has chosen, "Life is taking your medicine. That's [the condition of escape] not reality" (1989, p. 278).

Being Invisible offers another improbable alteration for Fred Wagner, a writer of mail-order copy who yearns to be a novelist. A dissatisfied nobody, Wagner suddenly discovers he can will his own invisibility, a power which he immediately puts to craven purposes: to avoid colleagues, to rob a bank, and to spy on his ex-wife. Gradually, through this series of misadventures and indignities, Wagner must confront some uncomfortable truths – he, like the rest of the world, is at the mercy of random events, invisibility cannot alter the "realistic morality for which [he] had hitherto frankly lacked the stomach" (1987, p. 241), and his old world is at an end. When he rescues a woman from an attacker, he not only develops a presumably meaningful relationship but discovers "that being invisible was not, underneath it all, only a self-serving delusion" (p. 262).

Certainly, the most extreme version of reality disrupted can be found in *Adventures of the Artificial Woman*. Ellery Pierce, a technician at an animatronics firm and a failure with women, creates his own female robot which, though a perfect imitation of a human being, lacks all the flaws and emotions of an actual woman. In rapid course she follows the other women in Pierce's life; she leaves for new opportunities, which include prostitute, stripper, porn star, and eventually actor. As her celebrity increases, Pierce's world crumbles into homelessness. Through accident, a prevailing force in nearly any Berger fiction, they are reunited; he becomes her manager and closest advisor in a political campaign that culminates as President of the United States. Ultimately, that other serious Berger concern, morality, or lack thereof in Phyllis's case, leads Pierce to dismantle his creation when she assumes frightening power.

In spite of extremes like those mentioned above, Berger's characters always inhabit a generally recognizable world, but one that often resembles a hall of mirrors in some of its particulars. In reviewing *Neighbors,* Michael Malone offered a helpful guide to many of Berger's fictions, "[they] must be read literally, but cannot be read realistically. Berger reminds us that the truth has very little to do with reality anyhow" (Malone 1980, p. 537).

SEE ALSO: Contemporary Fictions of War; Contemporary Regionalisms; DeLillo, Don; Doctorow, E.L.; Pynchon; Thomas; Realism after Poststructuralism; Suburban Narratives; Updike, John; Vonnegut, Kurt

REFERENCES

Berger, Thomas. (1980). *Neighbors*. New York: Delacorte Press/Seymour Lawrence.
Berger, Thomas. (1983). *The Feud*. New York: Delacorte Press/Seymour Lawrence.
Berger, Thomas. (1985). *Nowhere*. New York: Delacorte Press.
Berger, Thomas. (1987). *Being Invisible*. New York: Little, Brown.
Berger, Thomas. (1988). *The Houseguest*. New York: Little Brown.
Berger, Thomas. (1989). *Changing the Past*. New York: Little, Brown.
Berger, Thomas. (1992). *Meeting Evil*. New York: Little Brown.
Berger, Thomas. (2003). *Best Friends*. New York: Simon & Schuster.
Landon, Brooks. (1991). *Understanding Thomas Berger*. Columbia: University of South Carolina University Press.
Madden, David W. (1995). *Critical Essays on Thomas Berger*. Boston: G.K. Hall & Co.
Malone, Michael. (1980). American literature's Little Big Man. *Nation* (March 5, 1980): 537.

FURTHER READING

Hughes, Douglas. (1976). Thomas Berger's elan: an interview. *Confrontation* 12: 23–39.
Landon, Brooks. (1989). *Thomas Berger*. Woodbridge, CT: Twayne.
Lethem, Jonathan. (2003). Introduction: Berger's ambivalent usurpations. In: *Meeting Evil* (by Thomas Berger), ix–xviii. New York: Simon & Schuster.
Rowe, John Carlos. (1983). Alien Encounter: Thomas Berger's *Neighbors* as a critique of existential humanism. *Studies in American Humor* 2 (1): 45–60.
Weales, Gerald. (1983). Reinhart as hero and clown. *Hollins Critic* 20 (5): 1–12.

Big Data

BENJAMIN MANGRUM
University of the South, USA

A massive database of information is not, in itself, "big data." There is no self-evident scale or statistically significant line that must be crossed before *data* moves from its ordinary state to something novel and, well, *big*. Instead, the idea of big data refers to a way of imagining totality through computational tools. It is a structure of contemporary experience, not a discrete method or volume of empirical information.

The idea of big data does not emerge *ex nihilo* during the late-twentieth and twenty-first centuries. The philosopher Ian Hacking explains that scientists and citizens alike began to encounter an "avalanche of numbers" in the nineteenth century (1990, p. 5). There are important continuities between the scale and techniques of contemporary data science and the earlier developments charted by scholars like Hacking. Nonetheless, what's distinctive about big data is that it is rooted in the exponential growth of information-technology systems, digital media, and the rise of personal computing technologies. These material and technological developments have made an older numerical way of thinking newly imaginable and actionable.

This entry examines how contemporary literary fiction explores this way of thinking about vast scales of data via information technology. While most contemporary writers are critical of the societal and personal costs of this phenomenon, some present data systems and analysis are important components of utopian politics. I describe literary texts written by both skeptics and proponents as "data fictions," by which I mean works that take up big data as a structuring feature of contemporary experience. I begin by analyzing data fictions from the 1980s and 1990s before the idea of big data gained currency in tech circles, and then I examine a range of ways in which big data informs literary writing since the idea's formal articulation and the closely related advent of Google and related information-technology companies.

DATA FICTIONS BEFORE "BIG DATA"

The first usage of the term "big data" appears to be a 1997 article published in the proceedings of the 8th Institute of Electrical and Electronics Engineers Visualization Conference (Cox and Ellsworth 1997). Yet this appearance in a printed journal is not the only, or even primary, source of the idea. The nineteenth-century development of information infrastructure was a necessary precondition for big data (see Cortada 2016). Post-1945 ideas about a "global village" and the popularization of cybernetics were also influential (see Tierney 2018). The first personal computers of the late 1970s and 1980s later made it possible for American consumers to perceive data computation as relevant for their everyday lives. Perhaps most important, though, is that personal computing was a prerequisite for private corporations to gather large swaths of user data (Zuboff 2009, pp. 233–254).

Each of these developments made big data a key part of the structures of contemporary experience. However, these trends were highly uneven across the American public. The popularization of data culture has been marked by a persistent "digital divide," a term that designates the inequalities of access to computers and the Internet (see Chakraborty and Bosman 2005).

Marge Piercy's novel *He, She and It* (1991) takes up many of these political and social issues within contemporary data culture. The novel imagines a future world run by multinational technology companies, or "multis." These corporations are in control of affluent urban centers, but they bring in laborers from poorer areas of exurban sprawl. One such area is known as the Glop. Access to computer technology in the Glop is irregular, although residents are able to "plug in" to the Net, a kind of public utility akin to the Internet. Apart from the multi's urban centers and impoverished exurbs, there are also rare towns and enclaves that have developed their own information systems and technological defenses. Piercy's novel focuses on the town of Tikvah, which teeters on the edge of maintaining its independence from the multis.

The management of data is a major front in this struggle for independence. One of the novel's main characters, a woman named Malkah, maintains Tikvah's digital defenses. Malkah's daughter, Riva, "began to move from pure data piracy toward something more political and even more dangerous." Riva, we learn, is on a "crusade of liberating information from the multis" (1991, p. 29). Yet Riva does not view her activism as stealing information; rather, as she explains, "I liberate it. Information shouldn't be a commodity. That's obscene" (p. 194). Riva's activities make her a target of several multis. She eventually persuades Malkah and her own daughter to fight against a particularly powerful multi, and this resistance leads them to "project" themselves into data systems to steal information about the multi's strategy to conquer the town of Tikvah (p. 267).

Projecting oneself into data systems becomes a tool of political resistance and an opportunity for artistic self-creation. Data projections also call attention to the fluidity of identity, particularly in terms of gender and sexuality. *He, She and It* thus invokes the corporate politics and political promises of data, and it inflects those themes through feminist ideas about identity. These themes have resurfaced in more recent fiction on artificial intelligence, such as Annalee Newitz's *Autonomous* (2017). These novels differ from many other works on the cultural and social significance of information systems and data aggregation by exploring the forms of gendered and ethnic inequality that mark technology usage.

There are also important continuities between *He, She and It* and other early data fictions. William Gibson's short story "Burning Chrome" (1982), for instance, takes up the idea of information-technology monopolies, which exploit a vast area known as the Sprawl. These themes appear again in Gibson's novel *Neuromancer* (1984). This influential novel tells the story of a data thief named Henry Dorsett Case. Case is hired to steal information from a conglomerate called Sense/Net. Thus, like Piercy's *He, She and It*, Gibson's *Neuromancer* presents data as a commercial product and political tool of multinational corporations. Both novels imagine individual technology users – hackers and computer engineers – as morally compromised but nonetheless admirable heroes who resist data commodification. However, Case later learns that his job was coordinated by a powerful artificial intelligence system, so the nature of his agency or ability to resist data-coordinated schemes comes into question.

The largest scale and aggregation of data in *Neuromancer* is located in the novel's now-famous term *cyberspace*, which is a "graphic representation of data abstracted from the banks of every computer in the human system. Unthinkable complexity. Lines of light ranged in the nonspace of the mind, clusters and constellations of data" (Gibson 2016, p. 52). The novel presents data as an abstraction made visible through computational technology, but it also locates data as the object on the outer borders of the mind's capacity for thought. Data is *real* in the novel, but paradoxically it is also "unthinkable." It exists, but only in the mind's "nonspace," as though these "constellations of data" are situated in a vastness beyond any human capacity for comprehension. This gloss on the reality of cyberspace anticipates connections between big data and posthumanism, explored further below.

Data fictions from the 1980s and 1990s suggest how closely the advent of big data would be tied to the "electronic elsewheres" created by the Internet (see Berry, Soyoung, and Spigel 2010, p. vii). Other data fictions from this period include Samuel R. Delany's *Stars in My Pocket Like Grains of Sand* (1984), some stories in *Byte Beautiful* (1985) by James

Tiptree, Jr. (aka, Alice Bradley Sheldon), Pat Cadigan's *Synners* (1992), and Richard Powers's *Galatea 2.2* (1995).

BIG DATA AND THE KNOWLEDGE ECONOMY

Following the early period of data fictions, big data would figure into a diverse range of fiction writing, expanding beyond science fiction to works of literary realism. This breadth of influence is not surprising, because the term *data* is an interdisciplinary and genre-defying object (see Gregg and Nafus 2017). Indeed, many works of contemporary literary realism feature vast aggregations of data less as the text's governing thematic code than as a necessary element of contemporary plot and everyday experience. In such works, it's as if big data runs in the background, becoming visible only intermittently when characters engage with information technologies and digital media that express wider transformations in the knowledge economy of the twenty-first century.

In Jhumpa Lahiri's *The Lowland* (2013), a Bengali-American professor named Gauri worries that the rise of digital technologies has deleterious effects on her intellectual life: "Too much is within her grasp now. . . . Glowing screens, increasingly foldable, portable, companionable, anticipating any possible question the human brain might generate. Containing more information than anyone has need for" (2013, p. 334). Gauri contrasts the largely digitized forms of research in the contemporary university with her pre-digital educational experience. While digital media make it possible to find out about Indian history or her family members through a search engine, Gauri does not experience this availability as the democratization of knowledge. Instead, vast troves of data and the internet browsers that make them legible are merely "information" dislodged from comprehensible human "need." Big data is knowledge without the context of human finitude.

Similarly, in *A Person of Interest* (2008) by Susan Choi, a professor named Hendley is killed by a bomb mailed to him in a package bearing the logo of a large information-technology firm. Hendley is "only recently somewhat renowned, and only specifically for the computer-science branch of the math department" (2008, p. 6). This work, scorned by the pure mathematicians in the department, is shrouded in language of tech "evangelism," for his work is heralded as "midwifing an unprecedented information-technology age that would transform the world as completely as had the industrial revolution" (p. 6). Mathematics becomes an important component of the novel's suspense, but data functions as something like math's popular foil. In fact, the titular "person of interest" is Professor Lee, an aging Asian-born mathematician in the same department. Lee's work stands in contrast to Hendley's, because his status in the prestige hierarchy of US higher education is "laughable" (p. 6). The custodian of big-data information systems stands in for the trendy vanguard of the knowledge economy, while pure mathematics seems outmoded and irrelevant.

Lahiri's and Choi's novels suggest how big data appears in contemporary fiction as a symptom of the possible eclipse of traditional institutions of knowledge production. As Choi's novel suggests, this anxiety often leads to comparisons between the advent of digital information systems and the "industrial revolution." Yet the revolution in the Canadian-American writer Ruth Ozeki's *A Tale for the Time Being* (2013) extends beyond higher education and economic structures to how knowledge itself is being reformulated in the image of data. Ozeki's novel follows the parallel lives of a writer named Ruth and a teenager named Nao, who writes a diary that

Ruth later finds not long after the 2011 tsunami that devastated Japan. The diary leads Ruth to search the Internet for information about Nao, her family, the victims of the tsunami, the subsequent meltdown of a nuclear reactor, and a score of interrelated – or only tangentially related – queries. These searches lead Ruth to reflect on the effects of digital information on her intellectual life. Whereas she once was able to focus and think deeply, now the "spring [of thought] had dried up, the pool was clogged and stagnant. She blamed the Internet" (2013, p. 92).

Using online search engines, Ruth scans troves of information about such topics as ADHD, Japanese genres of writing, and remote Buddhist monasteries. Much like Gauri's concerns in *The Lowland*, Ruth's inquiries lead her to doubt the rightness or benefit of searching through so much information. "Is the Internet a kind of temporal gyre," she wonders, "sucking up stories, like geodrift, into its orbit?" (2013, p. 114). The answer to this question is both yes and no, for Ruth's searches do yield helpful information about the distressing events recorded in Nao's diary. Yet the truth also seems to escape the data compilers, and this possibility points to the fact that the big data running in the background of the novel has its limits. "Information," she finds, "is a lot like water; it's hard to hold on to, and hard to keep from leaking away" (p. 197). Like Emerson's claim that things tend to "slip through our fingers then when we clutch hardest," information in Ozeki's novel escapes us regardless of the far-reaching grasp of our media technologies and information systems (Emerson 1971–2013, vol. 2, p. 29).

This slipperiness becomes particularly complicated when Ruth connects information technology and knowledge production to modern theories of quantum physics. Such theories attend to "the smallest scales and atomic increments" that make up reality. The idea of quantum entanglement, in particular, eerily implies that "attention might have the power to alter reality" (2013, p. 409). The connections between quantum physics and information science are complicated, and their convergence in the novel underwrites certain mysterious turns of plot. The upshot, though, is that Ruth comes to believe that technology users' entanglement with information systems affect both the observer and the observed. The data running behind the novel is therefore not discrete; technology users – and novel readers – are entangled with the most minute and expansive scales of information.

These novels present big data as a signal phenomenon of wider changes in the structures of contemporary knowledge production. The ability to access information globally, and to find real-time results about the world, change how contemporary technology users come to know what they know and feel what they feel. Anxiety and discontent seem to be the prevailing sensibilities about automated assessments of data and massive aggregations of information, particularly as those technologies are often only felt as humming abstractly in the background.

BIG DATA AND THE POSTHUMAN

The idea of big data is often associated with the technological supersession of the human and humanistic scales of value. This technological version of posthumanism appears tacitly in the three Vs most often used to define big data: volume, variety, and velocity. Each of these characteristics ostensibly mark limits of prior modes of analysis and human reasoning. Thus, the journalist Chris Anderson announces a new age of big data in an influential 2008 article in *Wired* magazine: "Sixty years ago, digital computers made information readable. Twenty years ago, the Internet made it reachable. Ten years ago, the first search engine crawlers made it a single database. Now Google and like-minded companies are sifting through the most measured age in history, treating this massive corpus as a laboratory of the human condition" (Anderson 2008).

Such announcements exemplify how big data is often linked with a vexed kind of post-human discourse. The promises of big data are here focused on better understanding humanity, yet the very idea of big data also indicates how the human capacity for analytical thinking and value judgments are inadequate to the forms of knowledge made newly accessible by data science. Humanity is the limit that big data transcends but also the golden fleece that big data tries to capture through measurement.

This tension appears late in Richard Powers's novel *The Overstory* (2018). One of the novel's main characters, a programmer named Neelay, creates a powerful computer program to "learn what life wants from humans" (2018, p. 489). The machine-learning program crawls the Internet, gathering information from databases, social media, and a countless number of personal devices. It analyzes all living things, both human and nonhuman, at an incomprehensible speed and scale. In the time it takes a human being to "form one self-judging thought," the narrator explains, "a billion packets of program pass over. They course under the sea in great cables – buzzing between Tokyo, Chengdu, Shenzhen, Bangalore, Chicago, Dublin, Dallas, and Berlin. And the learners begin to turn all this data into sense" (p. 489). The "billion packets of program" is itself a vast network of algorithms, and that program runs across an even larger scale of information. This information lacks "sense" or meaningfulness apart from the analytical powers of the algorithms. It's not the data alone that matters, but it's what Neelay's program does with data that counts.

Powers's novel follows the branching narratives of several characters as they interact with one another and, more importantly, with forests and trees. Yet the later appearance of a big-data program is notable, for this form of machine learning comes to take the shape of the living organisms that have been the focus of so much of the novel. In effect, the data "learners" come to supplant the human thinkers. The novel depicts these "learners" in evolutionary language: "They split and replicate, these master algorithms that Neelay lofts into the air. They're just starting out, like simplest cells back in the Earth's morning. But already they've learned, in a few short decades, what it took molecules a billion years to learn to do" (2018, p. 489). In the attempt to understand life, the learning program becomes a living thing. The narrator even calls it "the next new species," a living and thinking entity that comes into existence "simply by placing billions of pages of data side by side" (p. 496).

Powers explores similar connections between the natural and the digital in his earlier work, including *Orfeo* (2014), which culminates in an attempt by a man named Peter Els to use DNA as a kind of musical score, as though genetics and data science were natural bedfellows with musical composition. Related aspects of the relation between data analysis and posthumanism also appear in Greg Bear's *Darwin's Radio* (1999) and *Darwin's Children* (2003), novels that imagine the gene-editing technologies made possible through data analysis.

Whereas these novels have a sense of admiration for technological experiments with the natural world, several stories in George Saunders's *In Persuasion Nation* (2006) criticize what one critic describes as the "the techno-scientific promises of consumer capitalism" (Lake 2013, p. 66). For example, the story "My Flamboyant Grandson" follows a man named Leonard Petrillo and his grandson Teddy. Records of consumer behavior enable real-time advertisements that Leonard cannot escape, as ads are beamed directly to technological implants worn by seemingly every person in the narrative world. In keeping with Saunders's characteristic satire, this technological fantasy devolves into the absurd: "in the doorway of PLC Electronics," Leonard recounts, "a life-size Gene Kelly hologram suddenly appeared, tap-dancing, saying, 'Leonard, my data indicates you're a bit of an old-timer like myself! [. . .] Why not come in and let Frankie Z. explain the latest gizmos!'" (2006, p. 16). Teddy does not see a holograph of Gene Kelly but instead "his hero Babar, swinging a small monkey on his trunk while saying that his data indicated that Teddy did not yet own a Nintendo" (p. 16).

The absurdity of these data projections becomes a source of absurd alienation for Leonard and his grandson. Indeed, Saunders's stories suggest how the world imagined by data transforms the human into an object of data-generated capital. Consumer behavior becomes a form of input, which in turn is processed by algorithms that underwrite a capitalist economy. Accordingly, "human" makes sense not as a product of humanist ideals or as a biological-metaphysical construct but as a resource for algorithmic computation.

BIG DATA AND EXTRACTIVE ECONOMIES

These technological transformations of what it means to be human highlight some of the important continuities between the politics of big data and earlier forms of quantitative techniques. The ledgers and accounting practices of the plantation economy is another source for the uses of big data, for these earlier practices created the need for another kind of numerical information. Novels such as Edward P. Jones's *The Known World* (1994), for example, explore this earlier form of information culture associated with a slave economy. Jones tells the story of a former slave named Henry Townsend, who soon builds his own plantation. Townsend purchases slaves "from a man down from Fredericksburg who had a lot of five slaves to sell and had the most informative leaflet full of the history of those slaves" (2003, p. 50). Such passages are indicative of the novel's engagement with a longer history of information culture, in which deeds, maps, ledgers, and other forms of numerical data underwrote the institutions of chattel slavery.

Even as Jones's novel shows how plantation accounting transformed human beings into numerical objects, other works of contemporary American fiction explore how big-data technologies reimagine individuals as objects of numerical value within a capitalist economy. Such works depict digital information-gathering as a new kind of extractive economy. For example, in Thomas Pynchon's *Bleeding Edge* (2013), a woman named Maxine Tarnow follows the implausible wealth associated with hashslingrz, a firm that offers computer security services. Tarnow eventually learns about a computer chip that "sits quietly in a customer's machine absorbing data, from time to time transmitting what it's gathered out to interested parties" (2013, p. 248). The chip extracts data and commodifies it for sale on an illicit market.

Pynchon's work takes digital technology as an opportunity for corporate extraction, but other works of contemporary fiction associate big data aggregations with governmental programs. In David Foster Wallace's unfinished novel *The Pale King* (2011), the "Author's Foreword" includes a long footnote about 1987, "the year that computers and a high-powered statistical formula known as the ANADA (for 'Audit-No Audit Discriminant Algorithm') were first used in the examination of nearly all individual US tax returns" (2011, p. 70). The footnote establishes vague connections between this program and the life and work of one of the novel's main characters, who works for the Internal Revenue Service. Through such connections *Pale King* overlays the idea of literary character onto governmental techniques for exploiting big data.

The maps made visible by big data also appear in Jonathan Franzen's *Purity* (2015), which follows a character named Andreas who twice receives "dumps of internal email and algorithmic software that plainly revealed how [Google] stockpiled personal user data and actively filtered the information it claimed passively to reflect" (2015, p. 478). Yet Andreas balks at going public with this information: "In both cases, fearing what Google could do to him, Andreas had declined to upload the documents. To salvage his self-regard, he'd been honest with the leakers: 'Can't do it. I need Google on my side'" (p. 478). The episode suggests that big data only cursorily leads to transparency and greater social order. In reality, the megacorporations that compile and deploy big data stifle dissent passively, in this case by simply offering other useful and more benign-seeming services.

Whereas earlier forms of extractive capitalism quantified the relation between human chattel and material resources, data-driven methods focus on transforming the details of users' habits and lives into commodities. Blake Crouch's *Recursion* (2019) offers an interesting reformulation of this view, imagining a world in which a neuroscientist named Helena Smith creates a technology that maps the human memory structure. She learns about a quantum processor that might allow for "the sort of enormous data-set mapping problem" characteristic of the human brain (2019, p. 33). Initially Helena imagines the project as a way to re-experience notable moments from one's past, but the prospect of extracting and reproducing memories leads her to stumble upon a larger conspiracy being investigated by a cop named Barry Sutton.

These contemporary data fictions represent big data as an extractive technique within what Shoshana Zuboff (2019) calls "surveillance capitalism," or the monitoring of users by private corporations, which intend to profit from user data.

BIG DATA AND SOCIALITY

If user data has become a commodity for exchange, big data has also altered how contemporary technology users understand collectivity. The advent of aggregative technologies has created a new form of what the philosopher Charles Taylor (2004) calls modern social imaginaries. Big data has presented itself as an image for social totality (see Wagner-Pacifici, Mohr, and Breiger 2015; Mangrum 2018).

The idea that big-data technologies somehow disclose the real shape of the social – but also become generative of new forms of collectivity – is a prominent theme of Barry Lyga and Morgan Baden's young-adult novel *The Hive* (2019). This dynamic also animates Dave Eggers's acclaimed *The Circle* (2013), which questions the kinds of utopianism underwriting seemingly benevolent companies like Twitter, Snapchat, and Facebook. The title of Eggers's novel refers to a global corporation, which purchases and absorbs the world's major tech firms (2013, p. 23). The result is the Unified Operating System, the first universal information system, which puts "all of every user's needs and tools" into "one account, one identity, one password, one payment system, per person" (p. 21).

This consolidation of online data allows the Circle to know seemingly everything about everyone, but more importantly it allows the company to make predictions on the basis of that information. This, of course, is the promise of big data: it can disclose patterns that are evident at scales simply too vast for the human mind, but it also purports to reveal future realities and aspects of our lives unknown even to ourselves. Eggers's novel interrogates this relationship between truth, sociality, and big-data technologies. The novel is particularly suspicious of the consolidation of digital technology under powerful corporate entities. However, *The Circle* also shows why such techno-idealism nonetheless seems plausible to many workers in this sector. As the novel's protagonist Mae Holland says, "Who else but utopians could make utopia?" (2013, p. 30).

A version of Mae's question echoes throughout Malka Older's *Infomocracy* (2016), which imagines a future political system of "centenals," or groups of 100,000 voters, who make both electoral and everyday decisions in response to real-time, fact-checked information. Wearable technology enables individuals to access verified data about seemingly anything. Unlike skeptical treatments of big data, though, *Infomocracy* imagines this future order as based on a wholly transparent system of global technology. This system is run by a trans-national corporation called Information, which strives to be politically neutral. This arrangement would be a recipe for disaster in the other novels discussed in this entry, but *Infomocracy* takes the thought experiment as a serious and laudable kind of utopian experimentation. After all, centenals have access to verified information, even if it is technologically mediated, and thus have greater democratic control. As one technologist says, "Information is a public good. [...] We cannot give ourselves the power to see and leave everyone else blind" (2016, p. 260).

Data – as an idea, but also as the product of institutional design and technological infrastructure – does come under scrutiny in *Infomocracy*. For example, an agent of Information named Mishima acknowledges "that neither elections nor Information are neutral, that subtle changes in where centenal boundaries are drawn would lead to completely different outcomes, and that as much as they try to balance it, Information workers end up transmitting their most minute preferences and prejudices through the subjective choices of their work" (2016, p. 291). Biases are baked into the algorithms and the institutions of big-data democracy. Nonetheless, recognizing these shortcomings does not lead Mishima to reject the system: "she casts her lot with [Information] anyway, because she can't think of anything better" (p. 291).

CONCLUSION

The novels and short stories discussed in this entry show how big data is a variable marker of contemporary sensibilities about information technology and corporatized media. These sensibilities most often gravitate around anxieties and deep-seated skepticism. The close proximity of corporate power to big data is the primary source of anxiety in contemporary fiction. However, some contemporary writers also deploy data science and computational analysis as resources for imagining utopian experimentation.

SEE ALSO: Cyberpunk; Eggers, Dave: Gibson, William; Lahiri, Jhumpa; Piercy, Marge; Pynchon, Thomas; Ozeki, Ruth; Powers, Richard; Saunders, George; Wallace, David Foster

REFERENCES

Anderson, Chris. (2008). The end of theory: the data deluge makes the scientific method obsolete. *Wired Magazine* (June 23, 2008). http://www.wired.com/2008/06/pb-theory/ (accessed July 18, 2021).

Berry, Chris, Soyoung, Kim, and Spigel Lynn (eds.) (2010). Introduction: here, there, and elsewhere. In: *Electronic Elsewheres: Media, Technology, and the Experience of Social Space*, vii–xxviii. Minneapolis: University of Minnesota Press.

Chakraborty, Jayajit and Bosman, M. Martin. (2005). Measuring the digital divide in the United States: race, income, and personal computer ownership. *The Professional Geographer* 57 (3): 395–410.

Choi, Susan. (2008). *A Person of Interest*. New York: Penguin.

Cortada, James W. (2016). *All the Facts: A History of Information in the United States since 1870*. New York: Oxford University Press.

Cox, Michael and Ellsworth, David. (1997). Application-controlled demand paging for out-of-core visualization. *Proceedings of the 8th IEEE Visualization Conference*: 235–244.

Crouch, Blake. (2019). *Recursion*. New York: Crown.

Eggers, Dave. (2013). *The Circle*. New York: Knopf.

Emerson, Ralph Waldo. (1971–2013). *Collected Works of Ralph Waldo Emerson*, 10 vols (ed. Robert Spiller et al.). Cambridge, MA: Harvard University Press.

Franzen, Jonathan. (2015). *Purity*. New York: Farrar, Straus and Giroux.

Gibson, William. (2016). *Neuromancer*. New York: Penguin; 1st ed. 1984.

Gregg, Melissa and Nafus, Dawn. (2017). Data. In: *Keywords for Media Studies* (ed. Laurie Ouellette and Jonathan Gray), 55–58. New York: New York University Press.

Hacking, Ian. (1990). *The Taming of Chance*. New York: Cambridge University Press.

Jones, Edward P. (2003). *The Known World*. New York: Amistad; 1st ed. 1994.

Lahiri, Jhumpa. (2013). *The Lowland*. New York: Vintage.

Lake, Christina Bieber. (2013). *Prophets of the Posthuman: American Fiction, Biotechnology, and the Ethics of Personhood*. Notre Dame, IN: University of Notre Dame Press.

Mangrum, Benjamin. (2018). Aggregation, public criticism, and the history of reading big data. *PMLA* 133 (5): 1207–1224.

Older, Malka. (2016). *Infomocracy*. New York: Tom Doherty Associates.

Ozeki, Ruth. (2013). *A Tale for the Time Being*. New York: Viking.

Piercy, Marge. (1991). *He, She and It*. New York: Fawcett Books.

Powers, Richard. (2018). *The Overstory*. New York: Norton.

Pynchon, Thomas. (2013). *Bleeding Edge*. New York: Penguin.

Saunders, George. (2006). *In Persuasion Nation*. New York: Riverhead.

Taylor, Charles. (2004). *Modern Social Imaginaries*. Durham, NC: Duke University Press.

Tierney, Matt. (2018). Cyberculture in the large world house. *Configurations* 26: 179–206.

Wagner-Pacifici, Robin, Mohr, John W., and Breiger, Ronald L. (2015). Ontologies, methodologies, and new uses of Big Data in the social and cultural sciences. *Big Data & Society* 2 (2): 1–11.

Wallace, David Foster. (2011). *The Pale King: An Unfinished Novel*. New York: Little, Brown.

Zuboff, Shoshana. (2019). *The Age of Surveillance Capitalism: The Fight for a Human Future at the New Frontier of Power*. New York: PublicAffairs.

FURTHER READING

Hayles, N. Katherine. (2020). *Postprint: Books and Becoming Computational*. New York: Columbia University Press.

Houser, Heather. (2020). *Infowhelm: Environmental Art and Literature in an Age of Data*. New York: Columbia University Press.

Hu, Tung-Hui. (2015). *A Prehistory of the Cloud*. Cambridge, MA: MIT Press.

Rhee, Jennifer. (2018). *The Robotic Imaginary: The Human and the Price of Dehumanized Labor*. Minneapolis: University of Minnesota Press.

Biological Fictions

LEJLA KUCUKALIC
Khalifa University, United Arab Emirates

Biological fictions include a corpus of novels, stories, and manifestos that reflect a growing engagement of American writers with genetic science. In the 1980s and 1990s, American writers (and their critics) focused on the cybernetic aesthetic, portraying life in virtual, digital, and networked worlds. Since the 1990s and especially in the twenty-first century, a paradigm shift occurred in language and themes to accurately represent life in the Age of Biology (1953–present). Writers of biofictions encapsulate the age in which human beings have discovered not only the rules and processes of genetic language but also how to manipulate biomolecules within that language. The resulting "biofictions" (not to be confused with biographical fictions) are formally hybrid literary fictions that exemplify a growing dialogue between biology, technology, and society. The literary works that portray processes and changes ushered in by genetics and present new genetic organisms and their lives include Charles Stross's "Rogue Farm" (2003), Michael Crichton's *Next* (2006), Ted Kosmatka's "N-Words" (2008), Paolo Bacigalupi's *The Windup Girl* (2009), Richard Powers's *Orfeo* (2014), Margaret Atwood's *MaddAddam* trilogy (2014), Edward Ashton's *Three Days in April* (2015) and *The End of Ordinary* (2017), and biopunk anthologies such as *Growing Dread: Biopunk Visions* (2011), edited by Caroline Dombrowski, and *Bio-Punk: Stories from the Far Side of Research* (2013), edited by Ra Page. In their fictions, these writers portray posthuman societies where biohacking is a lifestyle, where postapocalyptic ecosystems are depleted by various genetic interventions, and where transgenic animals and patented cell-lines, disillusioned postdocs and greedy Big Pharma CEOs enact everyday life. Biofictions (bi-fi) are also the new genetic "narratives," as beings that arise from bio-imagination and from manipulation of genetic language; this co-evolution unfolds as an artistic and scientific practice.

The dialogue between biology, technology, and society unfolds both on the level of language and on the level of fictional imagination. Works by Ashton, Crichton, Kosmatka, Atwood, and others feature worlds set in the alternative present or speculated future times, with characters and plots that highlight the complexity of the Biological Age, and a host of political, social, and cultural issues beyond genetics. These contemporary biofictions are often critical of the incursion of molecular biology into the body and society. One recurrent theme, for example, is the spread of contagions through viruses and pandemics, mostly resulting from human activity. They are often introduced as a background condition, as in, for example, *The Windup Girl*, where environmental neglect, food viruses, and unwanted infections and mutations lead to a depleted, altered world in the Age of Contraction. Bacigalupi's novel illustrates the world in which (post)humans have become more integrated into the natural environment around them, even though that environment has been altered into a less balanced and more hostile ecosystem. At other times, the contagions are at the center of the plot, as in Edward Ashton's *Three Days in April*, where hundreds of thousands of people die almost simultaneously from what appears to be a deadly virus. Ashton builds a world where sentient AIs who insist on being considered "Silico Americans" and "Engineered and Augmented" human beings with an array of biological or nanotech enhancements in their cells and bodies are sometimes attacked by the UnAltered. In this world, a group of hackers, a molecular biologist, and even an AI, work together to successfully solve the mystery of the virus. This world is further developed in Ashton's subsequent novel, *The End of Ordinary* (2017), where "the Stupid War" between the Engineered and the UnAltered has recently finished and "non-therapeutic genetic modification has only been legal in most of the United States for about thirty years" (2017, p. 32). Characters tend to pick a package known as "the Pretty set," the athletic package, or custom-engineered enhancements from one of the two competing companies, GeneCraft and Bioteka. Despite the reign of commercial and totalitarian outfits in this narrative world, it is ordinary people versed in (bio)technology, not politicians or business leaders, who stop the hazardous projects from unfolding.

A deadly virus that destroys people's digestive tract features also in Atwood's *Oryx and Crake* (2003), but with more ominous and much less hopeful vision. Like Ashton, Atwood makes clear that the role of individual scientists and individuals in general is extremely important in both creating and solving the conditions of epidemics and outbreaks. Her Crake is a difficult yet brilliant man, appreciated for his skills and talent as he is being educated and then employed in the field of transgenics. Crake's solution for the environmental damage inflicted by human beings is a coordinated distribution of a highly effective "rogue hemorrhagic" whose symptoms include "high fever, bleeding from the eyes and skin, convulsions, then breakdown of the inner organs, followed by death" (Atwood 2013, p. 380). Crake makes sure that he, too, is dead as the virus spreads, in order not to divulge the contents of an antidote.

The stories and metaphors with which we describe biotechnology play an important role in the negotiation of scientific meaning, public understanding of science, and policy decisions. They are often composite metaphors, produced by both literature and science. The term genetic engineering, for example, was coined by Jack Williamson in his novel about genetic science, *Dragon's Island* (1951) (Sargent 2009, p. 224). Now widely accepted, the term genetic engineering implies both a perceived level of control over genetic processes and the intimation of the constructed and calculated approach to the human body.

FROM SCIENTIFIC LANGUAGE
OF BIOFICTIONS TO BIOPUNK

While most of the novels that comprise literary biofiction belong to the genre of science fiction, some, like Powers's *Orfeo* and Michael Crichton's *Next*, are "mainstream" representations of the biotech world. Biofiction combines elements of realistic, postmodern, and science fiction to address processes such as genetic experimentation, biopolitical control, and posthuman transitions. These hybrid fictions might be understood to represent new realism, a literary expression that captures the complexities of the current techno-scientific life, with human and posthuman actors at their center. The subject matter of biofictions includes contagions and epidemics, transgenic organisms and their destinies, genetic cures and failures, media treatment of genetic science, commercial and political systems that developed around the use of biotechnology, environmental crises caused and solved by genetic interventions, and human behavior within the infrastructures of biotechnological enterprise. In addition to commercial and political institutions, corrupt, overambitious, irresponsible, weak individuals often make up scientific and legal systems in biofictional stories. These stories are also about ordinary people who encounter products and possibilities of genetics; the responses range from ingenious to naive and ignorant (both Atwood's *MaddAddam* trilogy and Crichton's *Next*, for example, lean toward the latter). Their stories show the vulnerability, corruptibility, and the agency of those performing the science and those either benefiting from or being impaired by it. Sometimes, the (dis)advantages affect the same person, such as the shadowy biotech CEO who dies from experimental genetic therapy in *Next* or the biohacking composer in *Orfeo* who achieves his artistic dreams by composing with pathogens, but is treated as a wanted terrorist.

Models proposed in biofiction range from dystopian and (post)apocalyptic to that of diversification and new possibilities (these models will be discussed below). Biofiction provides diverse points of view, including those of created organisms, and also examines the distinct points of view of various actors in the networks of biotechnology. The exploration of themes such as the relationship between creative and Faustian impulses in art and science that both seek to describe and alter life moves beyond the simplistic metaphors about biotechnology and its workings, often occurring in the media, and beyond the exact determinants of genre categories.

In order to portray the Age of Biology, biofictions notably incorporate precise scientific language into their narratives, with details pertaining to genes, viruses, and modified molecules and organisms. Michael Crichton's *Next*, a novel that exhaustively describes biotech industry's inventions and mistakes, is replete with the language of genetics. Wealth management advisers in the novel's world shrewdly discuss investments in lymphokines and cytokines while playing golf and politicians disinterestedly listen to scientists who try to explain how genes function. In a scene where a geneticist tells the congressional meeting that "a single ATGC sequence can code for multiple proteins. Some sections of code are basically switches ... [and others] lie silent unless activated by specific environmental stimuli," an "aide who received substantial contributions from drug companies" asserts that "yours is a minority opinion" to the speaker. He also asserts that "most scientists wouldn't agree with your view of the gene," to which the geneticist replies: "actually, most scientists do agree. And with good reason" (2006, p. 257). Crichton here illustrates, in his use of scientific language and the dramatic moment, a general unwillingness to grapple with the complexities and effects of molecular biology. The narrative voice adds further explanation to this scene, detailing how environmental stimuli and other conditions trigger gene activation and expression. "Some genes contained multiple coding sequences separated by regions of meaningless code. That gene could use any of its multiple sequences to make a protein. Some genes were activated only if several other genes were activated first" (p. 257). The narrator accurately describes the behavior of molecular mechanisms and dispels the false belief in direct correlation between a single gene and any human trait or behavior (p. 255). Such inclusions of scientific language into biofictions do not fictionalize genetics, but rather incorporate genetic science into the fictional worlds produced by writers.

By consciously using a high level of scientific content, biofictional novels function as active co-creators of current opinions about genetic science: they provide a space in which both our ignorance and unwillingness to grapple with science as well as the difficult bioethical questions become clearer. Bi-fi does not aim to be didactic, but with the high stakes of genetic material being literally bought, sold, and manipulated, biofictions do demand the active engagement of their readers in both the scientific and the literary aspects of the story. Biofictions operate both as dissenting and interpreting narratives: they mediate between society and science, giving us a way to participate in the increasingly complicated narratives of molecular genetics. Scientific details of genetics are interwoven into the narrative, as one stream of language is joined with another in hybrid, syncretic fictions that reflect our current reality and legitimize biotech knowledge.

Narrative interrogations of biotechnology play an important role in the attempts of both scientists and humanists to raise the levels of participation and understanding of trends in molecular biology. Literary critics Lennard Davis and David Morris, for example, in their "Biocultures Manifesto," suggest that, in order to deepen our knowledge, sciences and humanities must work together: "the biological without the cultural, or the cultural without the biological, is doomed to be reductionist at best and inaccurate at worst" (2007, p. 411). Celebrated geneticist James Watson notes that "we still have a long way to go on our journey toward understanding of how DNA does its work," and he recognizes an impulse in both "artists and scientists to explore the ramifications of our newfound genetic knowledge" (2010, p. 420). This joint endeavor to improve the way molecular biology is conceptualized and performed is particularly evident in the artistic-scientific movement of biopunk, which promotes renegade uses of molecular biology, but also produces manifestos and stories about rebellious science. Scientific "biopunks" insist on widely shared resources and easily accessible knowledge of genetics that would be performed as a citizen science; literary biopunk is a sub-category of biofictions that represents this world of biohackers, their experiments, and their critical role in the new society.

The renegade uses of biotechnology in scientific circles, known as biopunk, became popularized in Marcus Wohlsen's book *Biopunk: Solving Biotech's Biggest Problems in Kitchens and Garages* (2011), drawing attention to groups of trained and amateur scientists and biohackers who advocated community-based "elegant, creative, self-reliant solutions to doing biology" (2011, p. 5). The earliest substantial references to biopunk, however, appear in the popular science and general newspaper articles already in the late 1980s and early 1990s, when molecular scientists acknowledged the emergence of the homemade genetic rights movement with potential for further development. Since then, biopunk initiatives grew into larger networks of scientific collectives, labs, and institutes, such as the National Center for Biotechnology Information (NCBI) and International Open Facility Advancing Biotechnology (BIOFAB) with code libraries, collaborative project opportunities, research data, and webinars, tutorials, and manuals available to professional and amateur scientists worldwide. Biopunk experiments include sequencing genomes of organisms ranging from strawberries, which is a relatively simple task, to that of H1N1 and other viruses, testing oneself for the presence of certain genetic mutations that would indicate heritable diseases, or injecting oneself with home-made treatments (p. 15).

The earliest references to literary biopunk are recorded in studies such as Brian McHale's *Constructing Postmodernism* (1992), where biopunk is understood as a literary successor of the cyberpunk genre, presenting stories about the combined mechanical, digital, and biological alterations of human beings and their ensuing new identities (1992, p. 258). The genre's name comes from adding the suffix -punk to the thematic focus of bioengineering; the tradition started with the "cyberpunk" movement and the short story by Bruce Bethke with the same title (Bethke 1997). The author sought to describe a new subculture "that juxtaposed punk attitude with high technology" and the idea spread to other forms of rebellious sf writing including biopunk. The naming of cyberpunk and biopunk is a good example of the role that literary imagination plays in the shaping and mirroring of the practical and scientific side of these movements. Cyberpunk and biopunk have in common the DIY ethos toward science and social activism and their familiar use of informatics; they both also include scientific-artistic exchanges between practice and art, and art and practice of cyber- and biopunk.

Examples of biopunk fictions include, as a precursor, Thomas Disch's *Camp Concentration* (1967), Paul J. McAuley's "Gene Wars" (1991), Paul Di Filippo's *Ribofunk* (1996), Paolo Bacigalupi's *The Windup Girl*, Richard Powers's *Orfeo*, and Edward Ashton's *Three Days in April*, together with biopunk anthologies such as *Growing Dread: Biopunk Visions* (ed. Dombrowski) and *Bio-Punk: Stories from the Far Side of Research* (ed. Page). Biopunk literature presents stories about quirky scientists and novel organisms, genetically modified worlds, and lives of characters who often, DIY-style, find their way out of serious trouble through the use of genetic science. Their language is often the exacting scientific language usually reserved for the subgenre known as "hard sf." Such details – patented genetically modified organisms, potential accompanying diseases, and biohacking – serve to remind the reader that we are in the process of building a new world, based on a myriad of biological alterations and experiments. Giving attention to details of genetic science aids in understanding of its complexity and the impact of its potential benefits and risks through biofictional means. These attempts to involve us as complicit readers reflect biopunk science's goal of creating a "critical mass" of thinkers and science-doers outside of institutions and commercial outfits.

Biopunk science and biopunk literature revolve around shared goals and ideas; together they advocate for better uses of biotechnology that would support broad communities and give people access to both the knowledge and products of genetics. In science and in literature, the poetics of biopunk focuses not only on experimentation and hybridity, but also on resistance against the abuses of biopower. One such work is Richard Powers's *Orfeo*, a novel about an aging composer turned biotech hobbyist who is accused of bioterrorism and persecuted by the FBI for conducting experiments in his home lab.

RICHARD POWERS'S *ORFEO*

Orfeo addresses a problem of governmental power to control operations related to biotechnology, applying the US Patriot Act (referenced throughout the novel) in order to mark individuals as domestic terrorists with relative ease and stop them from conducting genetic research. In the novel, the protagonist, Peter Els, is quickly marked as a bioterrorist for trying to compose music in bacterial DNA. Even though the evidence against him is missing, he is hounded, possibly to his death, by the media, the public, and Homeland Security. Powers's novel is based on real-life events. The clash depicted in the novel between an amateur chemist-composer Els and the US authorities appears to be modeled on Dr. Steve Kurtz, at the time an associate professor of art at the University of Buffalo, who was arrested in 2004 on bioterrorism charges. Kurtz worked with "three harmless bacteria cultures" to produce artwork that was highly critical of germ warfare and the accompanying governmental discourse of panic and fear (Critical Art Ensemble 2004). Luckily, Dr. Kurtz did not suffer the same fate as Peter Els in the novel, but his case raised a number of questions about the level of control that the government can impose on artists and scientists who work with biomaterials.

By pitting individual acts of biotech science against the goals of the government, Powers draws attention to the governing mechanisms of control and their purveyors in the age of biohorror and bioterrorism. Els turns to molecular biology motivated by his lifelong desire to produce transcendent music and perhaps win against death. Els wants to "scribble down the tune that would raise everyone he ever knew from the dead and make them laugh with remembering" (Powers 2014, p. 221). In his youth, Els admits to his new wife that he "wants to write music that will change its listeners" by bringing them "to something outside themselves" (p. 130). His old ambition, combined with his DIY bioskills, becomes a driving force; however, what compels the aging composer to finally start his experiments is a chance at redemption, not of the past, but of "his youthful sense of future" (p. 334). And because both music and life happen "on scales a million times smaller than ours" (p. 207), for Els, the attempt to break these boundaries signifies an attempt to reach "the sublime" (p. 10). "Els had staked his life on finding that larger thing," we are told (p. 10). Biotechnology and art become the elements of the same aspiration to transcend our human limitations; music and chemistry are "long-lost twins" (p. 57). A biotech Orfeo, Els, realizes that "With a little time, patience, a web connection, the ability to follow instructions, and a credit card, he might send a tune abroad again . . . music for the end of time" (p. 334). The micro-organism that Els works on, however, is *Serratia marcescens*, a common bacterium found in a wide range of environments, but also a human pathogen. Used as a biological marker in lab studies until the 1950s, *S. marcescens* was eventually connected to hospital infections, which in the novel do breakout in an unrelated location simultaneously with Els's experiments. Els's meddling with *S. marcescens* does represent a transgression of biosafety; a "few casual experiments that now seemed criminal, even to him" (p. 102). Through his efforts, Els grows from an entirely marginalized, lost figure, an elderly divorced man estranged from his daughter, to an alleged criminal in a system that punishes individual transgressions in science much more harshly than institutional ones.

LEGITIMACY OF KNOWLEDGE AND CONTROL OF INFORMATION IN THE "BACTERIAL AGE"

Orfeo is a biopunk novel not just because it portrays an individual rebel confronted by a larger system of control, but also because it portrays a biotech-altered twenty-first-century America, continuously fabricating a fake sense of security and enjoying a pervasive collective oblivion. Echoing the conditions in David Foster Wallace's 1996 novel, *Infinite Jest* (which could be reread as a biofiction), Els lives in the country whose people suffer from a "chronic focal difficulty" problem, characterized by the inability to complete tasks and ignore distractions, "the country's collective concentration simply shot" (2014, p. 84). The media govern the country's attention economy, and the production of fear is an important element in the attempts to control and misrepresent Els's activities. After Els's equipment, documents, and music records are confiscated, the media and public go into a frenzy of harassment, dubbing the 70-year-old "Biohacker Bach" (p. 264). From hiding, Els eventually addresses the public in a series of tweets under the @*Terrorchord* handle. "I did what they say I tried to do. Guilty as charged" (p. 350). Despite the potential danger of Els's experiments, the real harm is never established, which does not prevent the authorities from persecuting him. This, however, is also America at the forefront of genetic editing, in what Peter Els refers to as the "American Bacterial Age," as well as the age of "Ameritrax saga" and the Sarin gas attacks (p. 332). Despite his sense of the "progress's forced march," Els is seeking to find solutions to his lifelong creative and personal questions with the newest means, combining art with technology and, in the end, with living matter (p. 53). He gets his inspiration to start modifying cells by reading "an article about the DIY biology movement" and educates himself about the process through an online course, video clips, and textbooks. "No one seems to realize how easy [it is]," Els explains to his former therapist. "Easier than learning Arabic" (p. 143). As does the real-life incident that inspired it, Powers's novel raises a host of questions about the possibilities of open science, the role of art when connected to science, and the extensive powers of the Patriot Act – that cover bioterrorism and biological agents – held over US citizens and residents since 2001. At the same time, the novel reminds us of the real dangers associated with the handling of biomaterials and bioengineered components, raising ethical and moral questions about the Faustian tendencies in science and art.

In *Orfeo*, Powers challenges the binaries between artistic courage and folly, biological experiment and hazard, biofreedom and bioterrorism, composed and emergent music. The world, consisting of "millions of species of bacteria, fungi, protozoa, micro-algae, actinomycetes, nematodes, and microscopic arthropods," sings in "a torrent of chemical signaling" (2014, p. 332). These "encoded songs" of the Earth's multitudes and the "durable medium" in which he can now work consume Els's thoughts and energies. As he endeavors to create an immortal musical work in cells, where he "found an instrument free of all [piano] bars," Els judges his behavior as both criminal and vain (p. 49). However, together with glimpses of the possible risks of Els's experiments, throughout the novel we also see glimpses of the universal human legacy, artistic and genetic, that Els considers as reasons that transcend his selfish artistic striving. Amateur bioengineers should be allowed to work and exchange information because, before death, "we're entitled to nothing, and soon to inherit. We're free to be lost, free to shine, free to cut loose, free to drown" (p. 346). Acting with this knowledge is Els's personal manifesto for his avant-garde, but also potentially dangerous, biopunk art.

By describing the chaos that Els creates with his experiments, evident in the frenzied response of the public and the authorities and the chaos that his trials create in Els's own life, Powers illustrates the underlining turmoil of biopunk that critics such as Paul Taylor present as an inherent characteristic of the movement. In "Fleshing Out the Maelstrom: Biopunk and the Violence of Information," Taylor discusses biopunk as a practice of uncertainty, anxiety, and instability, qualities inherited from the cyberpunk model (2000, p. 3). In Taylor's view, biopunk describes the world in which growth, hybridity, and fecundity cannot be escaped or fully controlled. This metaphor is also addressed by Peter Els: "Life is nothing but mutual infection. And every infecting message changes the message it infects" (Powers 2014, p. 95).

BIOLOGICAL IMAGINATION AND MOLECULAR LANGUAGE

The vision of humankind's future in the midst of rapid discoveries seems difficult to achieve without the construction of the poetics of molecular science, captured in biofictional imagination and language. By making the biological elements both specific and sublime, Powers's language effectively expresses the language of biofictional imagination, a language that intercrosses with the language of biomolecules: DNA, RNA, and proteins. This overlap between biological and artistic language is not purely metaphorical. On the one hand, the combinations of four nucleic acids (ATCG) and twenty amino acids (represented by one- and three-letter code) are considered as words by geneticists and the process of inserting DNA is now widely referred to as genetic editing, since biomolecules are cut and pasted, and genetic information stored in dictionaries, and so on. On the other hand, geneticists have been using properties of language such as Chomsky's syntactical rules and linguistic structures of dependency and nesting of words in order to accurately describe structures of biomolecules and to create grammars that enabled reading of the genome (Searls 2002, p. 212; Bralley 1996, p. 150). Scientists also realized that certain configurations of nucleic acids were not context free, but rather context sensitive, highly complex, and in possession of emergent properties (Searls 2002, p. 212; Bralley 1996, p. 152). In other words, natural language and the language of genetic structures both produce meaning. This unique parallel allows for a broad definition of biofictions as representational and cultural formations that unfold on the level of language, where textuality is understood both as letters and combinations of genetic code and as natural language. The overlap of human and genetic language, and the existence of meaning in biological processes, allows for understanding of both molecular and artistic processes of creation as forms of the bioimagination that generate biofictions.

In this wider context, the imagination of biofictions produces forms that are biological, semiotic, and textual. Newly created genetic organisms are texts of biofictions: this approach interprets genetically edited organisms – such as those with transgenic (multiple species), synthetic, and recombinant (lab-created) DNA – as new genetic "narratives." Examples include transgenic animals such as Alba, the GFP (green fluorescent protein) albino rabbit, designed by genetic researcher Louis-Marie Houdebine and artist Eduardo Katz, and genetically modified cells and genes that interact with malignant cells (Nogrady 2020). Alba's existence is mirrored in fiction by the characters of Dave and Gerard, a transgenic chimp and transgenic parrot with considerable agency and lived experience in Crichton's *Next*.

Other organisms dreamed up by fictional authors include miniature pet unicorns in Minerva Zimmerman's "Muffin Everlasting" (2011) or Charles Stross's multi-organism collective, the "rogue farm," in the story of the same title (Stross 2010). Stross's "farm" is potentially an emergent organism: it consists of "half a dozen human components subsumed into it ... cytocellular macroassemblies flexing and glooping in disturbing motions" (2010, p. 68) as well as hybrid "stage trees" with "nitrate cellulose in their walls," combined with the "custom-hacked fungal hyphae with a depolarizing membrane nicked from human axons" (p. 69). Such organisms, imagined by Stross and others, are art forms that integrate scientific information and are potentially achievable, latent in the fictional and genetic language as an imaginable possibility.

In addition to reader reception, the success of biofictions depends on the creation of a new critical vocabulary that will explore these narratives further. The hybrid, syncretic forms that encompass interactions between science, culture, and literary imagination on the molecular level can be effectively parsed and understood through the concept of biofictions. Connected to the concept of "bioimagination" and biological meaning, biofictional novels and stories not only vitally address the world of biotechnology, but they co-create new forms that are biological, semiotic, and textual, where textuality is understood both as letters and combinations of genetic code and as sequences of natural language.

Biofictions, as a critical concept and as a corpus of literature, examine the "human" and imagine the posthuman in the molecular-cybernetic futures. Texts that are biofictions operate both on the inside of the biodiscourse, where they often confirm the bias (promises of immortality, post-eugenics beliefs in genetic determinism), and outside of it, where they can create new approaches and ideas for the Biological Age (more equal use of biotechnology, human rights extended to other organisms). Biofictions represent the ideology of the Biological Age. They display hybridity and syncretism on the margins of American literature and science and cover a wide range of topics related to molecular biology, from cloning (e.g. Steven Polansky's *The Bradbury Report* [2010]) to viral biological disasters (Atwood, Ashton, and Powers, as mentioned above), resulting in science-oriented novels, created in literary modes that range from science fictional to realistic. Regardless of their form, the literature of American biofictions plays a role in the legitimization of biotech knowledge and it may help scientists and the public examine and further understand the professional and personal ethical issues at stake in the biotech enterprise.

SEE ALSO: After Postmodernism; The Brain and American Fiction; Cyberpunk; Ecocriticism and Environmental Fiction; Gibson, William; Illness and Disability Narratives; Millennial Fiction; Mixed-Genre Fiction; The New Experimentalism/The Contemporary Avant-Garde; Powers, Richard; Realism after Poststructuralism; Wallace, David Foster

REFERENCES

Ashton, Edward. (2017). *The End of Ordinary*. New York: Harper Voyager Impulse.

Atwood, Margaret. (2013). *Oryx and Crake*. London: Virago; 1st ed. 2003.

Bethke, Bruce. (1997). Cyberpunk. http://www.infinityplus.co.uk/stories/cpunk.htm (accessed July 11, 2021). First published in *Amazing Science Fiction Stories* 57 (November 4, 1983).

Bralley, Patricia. (1996). An introduction to molecular linguistics. *BioScience* 46 (2): 146–153.

Crichton, Michael. (2006). *Next*. New York: HarperCollins.

Critical Art Ensemble. (2004). Critical art is under attack (poster). http://critical-art.net/defense/posters/CAEflyerCombo.pdf (accessed July 12, 2021).

Davis, Lennard and Morris, David. (2007). Biocultures manifesto. *New Literary History* 38 (3): 411–418.

Dombrowski, Caroline. (ed.) (2011). *Growing Dread: Biopunk Visions*. Seattle: Timid Pirate.

McHale, Brian. (1992). *Constructing Postmodernism*. New York: Routledge.

Nogrady, Bianca. (2020). Natural killer cell therapies catch up to CAR T. *The Scientist* (April 1, 2020). https://www.the-scientist.com/bio-business/natural-killer-cell-therapies-catch-up-to-car-t-67332 (accessed July 11, 2021).

Powers, Richard. (2014). *Orfeo*. New York: Norton.

Sargent, Pamela. (2009). Science fiction and biology. In: *Reading Science Fiction* (ed. James Gunn, Marleen S. Barr, and Matthew Candelaria), 219–226. New York: Palgrave Macmillan.

Searls, David B. (2002). The language of genes. *Nature* 420 (November): 211–217.

Stross, Charles. (2010). Rogue farm. In: *Wireless*, 67–84. New York: Ace Books.

Taylor, Paul. (2000). Fleshing out the maelstrom: biopunk and the violence of information. *M/C: A Journal of Media and Culture* 3 (3).

Watson, James. (2010). *DNA: The Secret of Life*. London: Arrow Books.

Wohlsen, Marcus. (2011). *Biopunk: Solving Biotech's Biggest Problems in Kitchens and Garages*. New York: Penguin Books.

Zimmerman, Minerva Lise. (2011). Muffin everlasting. In: *Growing Dread: Biopunk Visions* (ed. Caroline Dombrowski), 5–12. Seattle: Timid Pirate.

FURTHER READING

Carpi, Daniela. (ed.) (2011). *Law and Literature: Bioethics and Biolaw through Literature*. Berlin: Walter de Gruyter.

DaCosta, Beatriz and Philip, Kavita. (eds.) (2008). *Tactical Biopolitics*. Cambridge, MA: MIT Press.

Disch, Thomas M. (1999). *Camp Concentration*. New York: Vintage Books.

Hamilton, Sheryl N. (2003). Traces of the future: biotechnology, science fiction, and the media. *Science Fiction Studies* 30 (2): 267–282.

Page, Ra. (ed.) (2011). *Litmus: Short Stories from Modern Science*. Manchester: Comma Press.

Schmeink, Lars. (2016). *Biopunk Dystopias*. Liverpool: Liverpool University Press.

Black Atlantic

MELISSA E. SCHINDLER
University of North Georgia, USA

ORIGINS OF THE BLACK ATLANTIC

In its strictest sense, the phrase "the Black Atlantic" originated in the monograph of the same name by cultural studies scholar Paul

Gilroy. As Gilroy himself notes, however, Black intellectual communities on both sides of the Atlantic were already developing this concept long before his 1993 publication gave it a name. Moreover, following the publication of *The Black Atlantic: Modernity and Double Consciousness* (1993), the book's central conceit has been revised, challenged, and expanded. Whether in criticism or praise, the phrase continues to be invoked both inside and outside academe – a testament to its ongoing salience.

Developed through readings of the work of twentieth-century intellectuals of African descent as well as Afro-diasporic music, Gilroy's notion of the Black Atlantic offers four central tenets. First, it argues that communities of African descent in Africa, the Americas, the Caribbean, and Europe identify more strongly with transnational ties than they do with national ones. The most prominent symbol of this international "crosscurrent" of identity, Gilroy suggests, is the slave ship, where people of African descent created community across linguistic, cultural, and regional borders. The forging of such connections continued wherever people of African descent landed in the Atlantic world, fomenting a transnational sensibility founded on a shared experience of forced migration and enslavement. The second tenet of Gilroy's book builds on W.E.B. Du Bois's notion of double-consciousness to highlight how experiences of alienation for descendants of enslaved Africans strengthened their transnational affiliations. Treated as second-class citizens in their countries of birth, people of African descent in the Atlantic world found solidarity across national borders. Third, Gilroy famously contends that centuries of transnational identification resulted in hybrid communities, cultures, and sensibilities. Whereas nationalisms claim unity in sameness, hybridity and creolization locate unity at the meeting of cultures of African descent in diaspora. He is careful to note that his is neither an essentialist claim nor an anti-essentialist one. Rather, it is "anti-anti-essentialist" (1993, p. 102). Gilroy's final claim is that the transnationalism of the African diaspora was not peripheral or even just resistant to Western modernity. Instead, the Black Atlantic acted as a dialectic "counterculture of modernity," making the civilizing mission of European and North American modernisms possible through an international resistance to the nation-state.

The concept of the Black Atlantic had immediate implications for literary studies. In many ways, it opened up discussions around common tropes in African American writing. Fiction set in the United States suddenly took on additional geocultural significances. Classic African American literature, such as Jean Toomer's *Cane* (1923), Nella Larsen's *Quicksand* (1928), and Toni Morrison's *Beloved* (1987), were seen as taking up transnational Atlantic concerns. Through a Black Atlantic lens, Langston Hughes's declaration "I, too, sing America" testified to the role of Africans and African descendants in New World modernity. What's more, the Black Atlantic also allowed scholars to trace the reverberations of African American authors across the Americas, so that poets such as Hughes spoke not only for Afro-descendants in the United States but also those spread throughout Latin America (Prescott 2012).

HISTORICAL CONTEXT

The concept of the Black Atlantic, like Gilroy's monograph, did not lack historical precedent. Indeed, several academic publications paved the way for the text and worked collectively to provide entrenched scholars a path around stalemated discussions. In 1993, Joseph Harris published the second edition of a then 10-year-old book-length collection of essays about the African diaspora. It contained contributions from twenty-five scholars, including Colin Palmer, George Shepperson, and Thomas Skidmore. This was followed in 1995 by a book-length history of five decades of the African diaspora as well as a collected essays edited by Carole Boyce Davies and Molara Ogundipe-Leslie about the "international dimensions of black women's writing." Then, in 1996, Colin Palmer's *The African Diaspora*, just one of several book-length works by Palmer on the experiences of Africans outside of the continent, was published. Indeed, since the mid-century pan-Africanist movements and the rise of the Black studies discipline in the United States in the late 1960s and early 1970s, scholars had been deeply invested in studying the dispersion of Afro-descendant people around the world (Kelley 1999).

At first, that work involved rewriting histories of the modern world to account for African migrations. Then it turned to deciphering the impact of said migration, particularly in the Americas. Indeed, by the early 1990s, an academic conflict had been established between the "retentionists" – those who argued that Africans transported cultural practices wholesale to the Americas and preserved them for generations – and the "creolists" – those who saw evidence that transatlantic slavery and European immigration had combined with Indigenous people in the West to create blended traditions. Fiction by authors of African descent across the Americas was typically read as exemplifying one of these approaches and disproving the other. For instance, Paule Marshall's *Praisesong for the Widow* (1983) provides evidence for the notion of African survivals, or retentions, because it incorporates Gullah cultural practices brought to the United States from Africa and preserved. (The Gullah–Geechee Corridor refers to the coastal areas of the lower Atlantic where communities of African descent settled. Gullah is both an identity and a language.) On the other hand, the work of authors such as Ernest J. Gaines is often interpreted as proof of creole American cultures. Novels like *Catherine Carmier* (1964) depict Louisiana as a multicultural space shaped by successes and challenges of cultural mixing.

Gilroy, however, came from a different academic discussion: British cultural studies. Influenced by a diverse array of scholars, including C.L.R. James and Stuart Hall, Gilroy's ideas were controversial in part because they deviated from the established definition of hybridity, one that was divorced from land and nation altogether. In conjunction with authors such as Homi Bhabha and James Clifford, Gilroy's notion of the Black Atlantic argued that "routes" rather than "roots" served as the foundation for the modern human. Gilroy sought to challenge the limited scope of British and American cultural studies, pushing it to become more international, even as the text encouraged scholars working in African and Black studies to become less essentialist.

BLACK ATLANTIC LITERATURES

Although the concept of the Black Atlantic has implications for every field, literary critics were some of the first to explore its significance. After all, several of Gilroy's chapter-length studies focused on African American authors, including W.E.B. Du Bois, Richard Wright, and Toni Morrison. Moreover, in the absence of complete and accurate histories as well as the relative paucity of primary documents authored by people of African descent, fiction writers often used literature to render the experiences of enslaved Africans and their descendants in the Atlantic world. The Black Atlantic enabled readers to identify specific gestures and themes in work that would have otherwise fallen under the larger umbrella of the African diaspora.

Many examples of Black Atlantic literature, for example, foreground the experiences of enslaved people, particularly those in the Americas. A focus on the lives of the enslaved and the inherited traumas of slavery was, in some respects, radical. After all, following Toni Morrison, Atlantic slavery was the unacknowledged foundation of the United States. It was a history so erased that it could no longer simply be remembered but was nevertheless still present as a repeated trauma, lived again and again as "rememory." Indeed, Gilroy invokes Morrison's theories about the shared cultural inheritance of North American slavery to structure his notion of the Black Atlantic. As a result, readers were quick to interpret novels such as Morrison's *Beloved* from within the Black Atlantic paradigm. Soon, a number of other African American literary genres came to share the identification. Nonfiction slave narratives, including the autobiographies of Harriet Jacobs, Frederick Douglass, and Olaudah Equiano, became emblematic of Black Atlantic literature, not because they depicted African American life but because they strategically positioned slavery at the heart of the (North) American experience.

Another common theme in Black Atlantic literature is transnational or transcultural relationships. For instance, David Chioni Moore used the theory of the Black Atlantic to reread the work of Langston Hughes and, in turn, interprets Hughes's work – specifically his travel writing – to define some of the limits of Gilroy's expansive concept (Moore 1996). Many others have examined Hughes's reflections on travels to Cuba as notable contributions to Black Atlantic literature, not just because Hughes sees Afro-Cuban life to parallel his own but also because his visits impacted the work of Afro-Cuban authors, such as Nicolás Guillén. Whether authors directly espoused international connections, as did Hughes in Cuba, or explored them more subtly between characters, fiction bearing the Black Atlantic label took on new meaning through transnational perspectives. Similarly, critics brought to the foreground previously marginalized elements of African American and diasporic literature that featured cross-cultural, hemispheric American relationships. The Black Atlantic perspective illuminates how often authors depict collaboration and conflict between African Americans, Native Americans, Latinos, and Latin Americans, among many others. From Octavia Butler's multilingual, multicultural Los Angeles to Afro-Native American folktales, exchanges across cultural groups are common to literatures of the Black Atlantic (Brennan 2003).

A third common theme is the use of the ocean as a symbol for diasporic, and specifically a Black Atlantic, consciousness. Gilroy's emphasis on the slave ship as modernity's stage and the Middle Passage as the figurative vessel of transnational counterculture set into motion a profound reflection on the psychical role of waterways in the process of slavery's "rememory." Maritime voyages can draw epistemological conflict to the surface of a character's mind. Avey Johnson, protagonist of Marshall's *Praisesong for the Widow*, serves as a clear example of the trope. During a Caribbean cruise, Avey is thrust into her ancestral past – not to Africa, but to her Black Atlantic transnational ancestors. Her personal journey begins even before she steps on the boat, as she waits with other passengers to board: "It didn't seem that they were just going on a day's outing up a river to a state park a few miles away, but on a voyage – a full-scale voyage – to someplace far more impressive. No one there could have said where this place was. No one could have called its name" (Marshall 1983, p. 109). Her impending sea travel recalls a journey that she made up the Hudson River in her youth, and both trips link her, along with fellow travelers, to African ancestors crossing the ocean through the Middle Passage. Such imagery pervades Black Atlantic literature. It is evident in Edwidge Danticat's harrowing descriptions of Haitian refugees taking to the sea in rafts and in Nicolás Guillén's poetry about the relationship between Black Caribbeans and the ocean in "El Negro Mar" ("The Black Ocean"). It can also take the form of rivers, lakes, and streams. For instance, in Wanda Coleman's tribute to Emmett Till, who was brutally murdered and left in the Tallahatchie River, the poet's reference to a "blood river" invokes the slave trade's cost in lives thrown overboard. Like many other examples of Black Atlantic literature, however, it also speaks of a shared awareness born of tragedy, since an awareness of "the deep dank murk of consciousness" of the river produces "a birth" (Coleman 1983). Thus, the lens of the Black Atlantic allowed readers to make new meaning out of Afro-diasporic, African American, and African texts.

THE BLACK ATLANTIC EXPANDS

Critical Response

By all accounts, *The Black Atlantic* enjoyed tremendous success. Nevertheless, it also faced immediate critique, most of which, according to Africanist studies scholar Simon Gikandi, centers on what readers assume to be Gilroy's "sins of omission" (2014, p. 241). For a study about the Atlantic world, the monograph focuses almost entirely on Black intellectuals from North America (Barnes 1996). Meanwhile, for a study of people of African descent, Africa is also largely absent, except, perhaps, as a signifier of a lost ancestral past (Dayan 1996). Others point to the book's erasure of the experiences of Black women and of enslaved people in the Americas. Scholars have repeatedly expressed concern about the limited scope of the monograph, which posits a theory of anti-essentialist Black internationalism based almost entirely on a mostly homogeneous group of North American, Afro-descendant men of similar experience and background. Critics also faulted the book for privileging culture over politics, for failing to live up to its own proposed scope. Yet, as Gikandi surmised in 1996 and again in 2014, perhaps the greatest contribution that Gilroy's book made was not to answer questions about the field but to open it to new ones. Without a doubt, the concept of the Black Atlantic quickly left behind Gilroy's initial rendering and was revised – sometimes stretched – to accommodate the wide spectrum of experiences that constitute the African diaspora.

The Black Atlantic Beyond the Atlantic

Interestingly, one of the first components of the Black Atlantic to expand outside of Gilroy's monograph was its geography. On the one hand, the estimated 12 million Africans forcibly moved from Africa to Europe and the Americas during nearly four centuries of the transatlantic slave trade testifies to the tremendous impact of Atlantic slavery on Western history. It also justifies Gilroy's focus on the Atlantic region. On the other hand, Africans traveled outside of Africa centuries before the Atlantic slave trade began, and slave trade routes to other parts of the globe existed long before the peculiar institution was established in the Atlantic. The African American intellectuals whose work Gilroy analyzed were keenly aware of the wide geography of the diaspora. The concept of a Black Atlantic, therefore, emerged relatively late. Paul T. Zeleza, whose work explores African diasporic routes around the world, emphasizes the importance for African and Africanist scholars of "decentralizing the Atlantic and putting it in its proper perspective" (2005, p. 63). He and others were quick to point to how research on African communities in Asia, the Middle East, and the South Pacific offers alternatives to theories of diaspora based on a Black Atlantic model. Not only do perspectives outside of the Atlantic more effectively contextualize diverse experiences of diaspora, but they also offer additional tools for interpreting Black Atlantic renderings of the wider diaspora. Through the lens of a decentered Atlantic, for instance, W.E.B. Du Bois's *The Dark Princess* (1928), a novel about an African American man falling in love with a princess in India, makes a weaker case for Black internationalism than the Atlantic model allows.

Nevertheless, owing to the momentum of Black Atlantic scholarship, researchers pushed the field further to define an Afro-Indian Ocean, an Afro-Mediterranean and Middle East, an Afro-Asia, and an Afro-Pacific. The Black Atlantic set the stage for regional analyses of transnational communities forged across waterways and national boundaries. In the 1990s and early 2000s, a cohort of scholars, including Omar Ali, Ed Alpers, Gwen Campbell, Joseph Harris, Isabel Hofmeyr, Pier Larson, H. Adlai Murdoch, Richard Pankhurst, Shihan de Silva Jayasuriya, and Pascale De Souza, consolidated a set of assumptions about the diaspora in the East. Like the Atlantic, they contended, diasporas in the Indian Ocean created transnational connections as a result of migration across borders. They also argued that these transnational connections and travels fueled the development of societies throughout the Indian Ocean littoral and across various island nations. At the same time, they noted several differences. For one, the symbol of the ship – and of the slave trade more generally – was not seen to be as instrumental in solidifying a Black political consciousness in the East. Because migration in the region, forced or chosen, started much earlier and happened at a much slower rate, not all communities maintained a strong diasporic consciousness. Other differences include the linguistic and cultural influences of hostlands as well as their ethnic diversity. Places such as South Asia, the Arabian Peninsula, and Indonesia already had a historically diverse populace, one whose diversity was mapped onto visible markers of presumed race. From critics' perspectives, this complicates one's ability to trace African migrations in ways that are purportedly simpler in the Atlantic. For instance, would communities of African descent in India trace their roots to recent ancestors, brought by the European slave trade, or to much older migrations, such as Arab trade routes on the east coast of Africa? Similarly, how is one's spoken language a reflection of diasporic ancestry? Of transnational identification? This scholarship challenged the centrality of the Black Atlantic model, suggesting that transnational connections, if they existed, resulted from very different, and often very local, contexts. The subsequent generation of scholars, however, challenged the claim that African diasporas in the East did not form a counterculture of modernity through shared consciousness (Jayawardene 2020).

The Non-Anglophone Black Atlantic

To some degree, the claims made about African migrations outside of the Atlantic apply to those areas of the Atlantic left out of Gilroy's initial rendering, including the Caribbean, Canada, Latin America, the coastal regions of Africa (even on the Indian Ocean side, from which a significant portion of nineteenth-century enslaved Africans were taken), and Europe. Indeed, much of the work by scholars of these fields is invested in expanding Gilroy's Black Atlantic paradigm to its own, underrepresented constituents while also weighing the value of his framework.

In the case of Latin America and the Spanish-speaking Caribbean, a number of important contributions have helped to broaden the field. First, as made evident in Emory University's *Slave Voyages Database*, some 40% of all enslaved Africans in the Americas ended up in Brazil (Emory Center for Digital Scholarship 2021). Another 45% landed in the Caribbean. Finally, around 12% went to the United States. These numbers have important implications for defining the Black Atlantic which, after all, was initially based on an Anglophone and largely African American perspective. If around 12% of enslaved Africans went to the United States and the Black Atlantic is US-centric, then how accurately does it reflect the realities of Afro-descendant communities in the rest of the Americas? For a number of scholars, the diasporic experience nonetheless remains parallel. Extensive research by Miriam DeCosta-Willis, Richard Jackson, and Antonio Tillis, among others, points to shared experiences akin to double-consciousness among Afro-Latin American communities, especially in Colombia, Brazil, Cuba, Puerto Rico, and the Dominican Republic. As they demonstrate, a number of Afro-Latin American writers speak to a hemispheric understanding of Black identity based on a common history. These scholars are responsible for bringing attention to authors such as Manuel Zapata Olivella, Candelario Obeso, Adalberto Ortiz, and Pilar Barrios, to name a few.

At the same time, other scholars have pointed out differences between the inheritances of New World slavery in the Anglophone United States and colonial slavery in Hispanophone and Lusophone countries, a difference which is at least borne out by the numbers themselves. Whereas the English-speaking world had ceased to participate in the slave trade – where abolition was fueled, in part, by a desire to limit economic growth of other countries – Spain, Portugal, and then an independent Brazil continued to participate illegally in the trade. In many respects, Spain and Portugal are thought to have colonized differently from the English. Due to its proximity to North Africa and history of cultural mixing, scholars have identified the Iberian Peninsula as "between" Europe and countries of the global South (Santos 2002). The position of Spain and Portugal relative to other parts of Europe, argue Santos and others, impacted their colonial practices. Many have used this sociocultural hierarchy to explain the seeming penchant among Portuguese and Spanish colonists for mixed-race relationships, as depicted in Gayl Jones's *Corregidora* (1975), and social mobility of some people of color in Latin America, evident in the popularity of Brazilian cultural icon Xica da Silva. They also draw attention to complex matrices of racial identifications (*casta*) that such relationships invariably produced, particularly in Spanish America. Finally, Spanish and Portuguese colonists attempted to spread the Catholic religion. For some, it is no accident that former colonies of the Iberian Peninsula have the greatest concentrations of syncretic Afro-Latin American religions, which blend Catholic or Christian practices with Indigenous African or Native American ones. Examples of syncretic Afro-Christian spiritual practices abound in the literatures of the Americas, ranging from Zapata Olivella's engagement with Afro-Colombian deities in *Chango, the Biggest Badass* (1980) to Ishmael Reed's invocation of Louisiana voodoo in *Mumbo Jumbo* (1972) to Zora Neale Hurston's research trips to Jamaica to study obeah.

More than simply a critique of what is missing from the theory of the Black Atlantic, scholarship that focuses on its underrepresented geographies raises the question of how its central tenets change when all regions are accounted for. If the Black Atlantic highlights a counterculture of modernity – a dialogic pair – then the perspectives of Latin American and even non-Atlantic African descendants may redefine modernity itself. Indeed, much of the Atlantic world, if not many human communities, are multilingual. To what extent are Africans and their descendants responsible for facilitating communication between populations that spoke different languages? Shihan de Silva Jayasuriya describes transnational Africans as "cultural brokers," raising the possibility that migration, forced or chosen, fosters transnational connections (Jayasuriya 2009).

One of the most pressing areas in Black Atlantic scholarship is the place of Africa itself. Some readers disregard the theory's applicability to African countries and communities precisely because the continent functions as a signifier of a lost homeland, necessarily vacated and static to preserve a diasporic nostalgia. Lucy Evans characterizes this critique as a division between those who wish to return diaspora theory to "roots" because the reality for many Africans is not based on "routes" (2009, p. 262). Evans highlights the work of Thomas Olver and Stephen Meyer, who curated a special issue of *Current Writing* on this issue. The collection of articles locates Africa in the Black Atlantic by highlighting the reverberations of transatlantic slavery. Saidiya Hartman's *Lose Your Mother: A Journey Along the Atlantic Slave Route* (2007) echoes this claim by traveling to Ghana to understand slavery's hidden legacies in West Africa. At the same time, a focus on contemporary African literatures suggests that migration shapes the lives of many who live on the continent. Some fiction emphasizes the experiences of people born in African countries who move abroad and then return to their homelands – experiences depicted in the work of Helen Oyeyemi's *The Icarus Girl* (2005) and Noo Saro-Wiwa's *Looking for Transwonderland* (2012). Contemporary migration literature also highlights journeys within Africa, raising the question of whether the concept of the Black Atlantic must include the Americas or Europe to be considered as such.

Gender and Sexuality in the Black Atlantic

Just as critics pointed out the geographic omissions of the initial Black Atlantic paradigm, they were quick to take its focus on men to task. Black women, however, have historically had less access to travel and fewer opportunities to author their own texts. As a result, scholars have employed a number of approaches to contextualize cultural practices as Black Atlantic creative acts – demonstrations of agency, and evidence of migration. As Katherine McKittrick shows in *Demonic Grounds* (2006), Black women negotiate geographic spaces of slavery as part of an embodied "practice of diaspora" (Hayes Edwards 2003). Their lived experiences and embodied practices redefine the meaning of the Black Atlantic, underscoring what Hershini Bhana Young identifies as the ghosts haunting a collective Black body (Young 2006). Meanwhile, according to Samantha Pinto, Black women authors revise the concept of the Black Atlantic by enacting "difficult diasporas" in experimental forms of writing (Pinto 2013). Where African American men travel physically in Gilroy's initial rendering of the concept, Pinto argues that Black women employ "experimental economies of form and a set of aesthetic practices that flow unevenly across national and geographic borders in the Anglophone diaspora" (2013, p. 3). The controversial, albeit now-treasured, African American author Zora Neale Hurston exemplifies Pinto's concept of "difficult diasporas" in her emphasis on the lived experiences of Black women in the diaspora, most famously in *Their Eyes Were Watching God* (1937), but also in her autobiographical work *Mules and Men* (1935).

The queer of color critique and, following Jafari S. Allen, "Black/Queer/Diaspora" studies (Allen 2012) provide yet another lens through which the Black Atlantic might be stretched and even distorted. If Pinto finds Black Atlantic practices in the formal experimentation of Black women writers, scholars claim countercultures of modernity and, arguably, postmodernity in Black queer diasporic practices – how texts "work" and "move" (Allen 2012, p. 215). From rereadings of classic LGBTQ+ African American authors, like James Baldwin, to contemporary Black queer authors, such as Nalo Hopkinson, Black queer studies encompasses several other critiques of the concept of the Black Atlantic. For Omise'eke Natasha Tinsley, neither Black Atlantic studies nor queer theory has accurately captured the Black queer experience, thus attesting to the need for a line of intellectual query that investigates the space between (Tinsley 2008). More significantly, Tinsley contends, Black Atlantic and queer theory are incomplete without a Black queer perspective. This is not because gender and sexuality can be "tacked on" to race and vice versa. Instead, Tinsley contends, the Black Atlantic is inherently queer because of its oceanic fluidities. At the same time, the queer Atlantic is inherently Black because of its oceanic materialities. Citing the affective relationships that most certainly developed in the hold of slave ships, Tinsley's work exemplifies the value of a Black/queer/diaspora approach in moving scholarship past ossified discussions of what Gilroy's Black Atlantic omits.

Black Atlantic, Afrofuturist Atlantic

On its surface, Afrofuturism appears to have little to do with Black Atlantic theory. Its geography is often otherworldly or runs contrary to the presumed truths of human maps. Yet from its roots to its most current iterations, Afrofuturism seeks to answer many of the same questions as Black Atlantic studies. Alondra Nelson defines Afrofuturism as "a critical perspective that opens up inquiry into the many overlaps between technoculture and black diasporic histories. [It] looks across popular culture . . . to find models of expression that transform spaces of alienation into novel forms of creative potential" (2000, p. 35). In the literary world, Afrofuturism frequently locates its origins in the fiction of twentieth-century Black writers of science fiction and fantasy, especially Octavia E. Butler and Samuel Delany. Both authors are invested in thinking through how social and systemic oppression will manifest in future worlds and alternate presents. Butler's *Dawn* (1987), for instance, imagines a near future where humans must mate with aliens in order for the species to survive at all. By positioning humans as a marginalized species, Butler exposes social division in the contemporary world and recalls the injustices of (human) colonialism. When Butler and Delany began publishing, they were some of the only writers of color in the world of science fiction, but many authors have since embraced the genre, including N.L. Jemisin, Nnedi Okorafor, and Nalo Hopkinson. Many readers understand the concept of the Black Atlantic to make a similar movement to Afrofuturism, insomuch as the transnational cultural space of the Atlantic Ocean was at once a "space of alienation" and a counterculture actively challenging human exploitation. In its simultaneous turn toward the past and the future, however, Afrofuturism allows readers to redefine history by imagining alternative or, perhaps, counterfutures. Afrofuturism also highlights the ingenuity of diasporic connections and Black technologies born out of the conditions of alienation that characterize the Black Atlantic.

Black Lives Matter in the Wake

Perhaps no movement has inherited the Black Atlantic's emphasis on transnational connections more evidently than Black

Lives Matter. Through its use of social media, the BLM movement draws parallels between the experiences of people of African descent and people of color around the world. By consistently centering the "interminable event" of the trauma of white supremacy, BLM embodies Christina Sharpe's notion of "wake work," a critical expansion of Gilroy's concept of the Black Atlantic. Sharpe describes "wake work" as a "theory and practice of the wake – a theory and praxis of being Black in diaspora" (2016, p. 19). Sharpe develops the metaphor of the wake, which she reads as referring to the space created behind a (slave) ship, to the state of being "woke" and to the part of some funeral practices. She asks, "In the midst of so much death and the fact of Black life as proximate to death, how do we attend to physical, social, and figurative death and also to the largeness that is Black life, Black life insisted from death?" (p. 17). The answer, she contends, "look[s] something like wake work." Literary texts that centralize Black experiences are one manifestation of wake work. Examples include Angie Thomas's *The Hate You Give* (2017), which speaks directly to Black death through policing – a central issue of BLM. They also include texts such as Dionne Brand's poem *thirsty* (2002), an exploration of the city of Toronto through the perspective of a Black man whose final words before death are "thirsty." Black Lives Matter, in its emphasis on the continued threat to Black life through racialized policing, housing and employment practices, gatekeeping mechanisms in education, gerrymandering, and other political interference, exemplifies Sharpe's concept of wake work. It operates in the wake of the Atlantic slave ship, insists on raising consciousness to wake people up, and forces the world to hold wakes for Black people whose lives have been taken. It embodies the creative principle of the wake – the "theory and praxis of being Black in diaspora."

SEE ALSO: Butler, Octavia; Danticat, Edwidge; Delany, Samuel; Jones, Gayl; Literature of the Americas; Marshall, Paule; Morrison, Toni; Queer and LGBT Fiction; Reed, Ishmael; Trauma and Fiction

REFERENCES

Allen, Jafari S. (2012). Black/queer/diaspora at the current conjuncture. *GLQ* 18 (2–3): 211–248.

Barnes, Natasha. (1996). Black Atlantic – Black America. *Research in African Literatures* 27 (4): 106–107.

Boyce Davies, Carole and Ogundipe-Leslie, Molara. (1995). *Moving Beyond Boundaries: International Dimensions of Black Women's Writing*. New York: NYU Press.

Brennan, Jonathan. (2003). *When Brer Rabbit Meets Coyote: African-Native American Literature*. Urbana: University of Illinois Press.

Coleman, Wanda. (1983). *African Sleeping Sickness: Stories and Poems*. Santa Rosa, CA: Black Sparrow Press.

Dayan, Joan. (1996). Paul Gilroy's slaves, ships, and routes: the Middle Passage as metaphor. *Research in African Literatures* 27 (4): 7–14.

DeCosta-Willis, Miriam. (1977). *Blacks in Hispanic Literature*. Port Washington, NY: Kennikat Press.

Emory Center for Digital Scholarship. (2021). *Slave Voyages Database*. https://www.slavevoyages.org/ (accessed July 12, 2021).

Evans, Lucy. (2009). The Black Atlantic: exploring Gilroy's legacy. *Atlantic Studies* 6 (2): 255–268.

Gikandi, Simon. (1996). Introduction: Africa, diaspora, and the discourse of modernity. *Research in African Literatures* 27 (4): 1–6.

Gikandi, Simon. (2014). Afterword: outside the Black Atlantic. *Research in African Literatures* 45 (3): 241–244.

Gilroy, Paul. (1993). *The Black Atlantic: Modernity and Double Consciousness*. Cambridge, MA: Harvard University Press.

Hartman, Saidiya. (2007). *Lose Your Mother: A Journey Along the Atlantic Slave Route*. New York: Farrar, Straus and Giroux.

Hayes Edwards, Brent. (2003). *The Practice of Diaspora: Literature, Translation, and the Rise of Black Internationalism*. Cambridge, MA: Harvard University Press.

Jackson, Richard. (2008). *Black Humanism and Literature in Latin America*. Athens: University of Georgia Press.

Jayasuriya, Shihan de Silva. (2009). *African Identity in Asia: Cultural Effects of Forced Migration*. Princeton: Marcus Wiener.

Jayawardene, Sureshi. (2020). Ceylon African Mānja performance: enactments of Black ways of being and knowing in Sri Lanka. *African and Black Diaspora* 13 (3): 256–268.

Kelley, Robin. (1999). "But a local phase of a world problem": Black history's global vision, 1883–1950. *Journal of American History* (December): 1045–1077.

Marshall, Paule. (1983). *Praisesong for the Widow*. New York: Plume.

McKittrick, Katherine. (2006). *Demonic Grounds: Black Women and the Cartographies of Struggle*. Minneapolis: University of Minnesota Press.

Moore, David Chioni. (1996). Local color, global "color": Langston Hughes, the Black Atlantic, and Soviet Central Asia, 1932. *Research in African Literatures* 27 (4): 49–72.

Nelson, Alondra. (2000). AfroFuturism: past-future visions. *Colorlines* (April 30, 2000): 34–37.

Pinto, Samantha. (2013). *Difficult Diasporas: The Transnational Feminist Aesthetic of the Black Atlantic*. New York: NYU Press.

Prescott, Laurence E. (2012). "Yo también soy América": Latin American receptions of Langston Hughes's American Dream. *Critical Insights: Langston Hughes* (ed. R. Baxter Miller), 255–274. Ipswich, MA: Salem Press.

Santos, Boaventura de Sousa. (2002). Between Prospero and Caliban: colonialism, postcolonialism, and inter-identity. *Luso-Brazilian Review*, 39 (2): 9–43.

Sharpe, Christina. (2016). *In the Wake: On Blackness and Being*. Durham, NC: Duke University Press.

Tillis, Antonio. (2012). *Critical Perspectives on Latin American Literature*. New York: Routledge.

Tinsley, Omise'eke Natasha. (2008). Black Atlantic, queer Atlantic: queer imaginings of the Middle Passage. *GLQ: A Journal of Lesbian and Gay Studies* 14 (2): 191–215.

Young, Hershini Bhana. (2006). *Haunting Capital: Memory, Text, and the Black Diasporic Body*. Hanover, NH: Dartmouth College Press.

Zeleza, Paul T. (2005). Rewriting the African diaspora: beyond the Black Atlantic. *African Affairs* 104 (414): 35.

FURTHER READING

Goebel, Walter and Schabio, Saskia. (2006). *Beyond the Black Atlantic: Relocating Modernization and Technology*. London: Routledge.

Harris, Joseph E. (1993). *Global Dimensions of the African Diaspora*, 2nd ed. Washington, DC: Howard University Press.

Segal, Ronald. (1995). *The Black Diaspora: Five Centuries of the Black Experience Outside Africa*. New York: The Noonday Press.

The Bolaño Effect

NICHOLAS BIRNS
New York University, USA

BOLAÑO AND HIS AFTERMATH

Roberto Bolaño was the first Latin American writer after the Boom generation of Gabriel García Márquez, Mario Vargas Llosa, and Carlos Fuentes to be widely influential in the United States. The work of the Chilean-born, Mexican-bred, Spanish resident marked a break with the magical realism and lyrical left-wing politics that characterized the Boom writers, and instead combined a fecund encyclopedism with a bitter sense of disillusionment as he bore witness to violence, misogyny, and terror. Bolaño's fiction gave younger American writers a new way to reflect on their own culture and recent past, fostering complexity while jettisoning outworn metaphysical assumptions.

Bolaño's first book translated into English and published in the United States was *By Night in Chile*, a short novel about the aftermath of the Pinochet coup in Chile in 1973 and featuring a Catholic priest and conservative intellectual, Sebastián Urrutia Lacroix, brought in to, incongruously, explain the works of Karl Marx to the newly installed right-wing military dictator. This novel was translated just before his death in 2003 at the age of 50. Bolaño's breakthrough, though, came with *The Savage Detectives,* translated in 2006. A feigned oral history of a group of young poets in Mexico, it is at once a buddy-novel, a travelogue of Mexico City a journey to Northern Mexico, and a reflection of the splendors and miseries of literary life and how youthful ideals turn and wither in maturity. The seal on Bolaño's reputation was set when his masterwork, *2666,* was translated in late 2008. This massive book contains several narratives including that of a search for Benno von Archimboldi, a reclusive German writer living in Northern Mexico and a harrowing testimonial to the victims of the "femicide" murders of female workers on the US-Mexican border.

After *2666,* the Bolaño estate released a mass of unpublished manuscripts. Some of these books, such as his poetry and the wargame-based novel *The Third Reich,* received considerable attention; others passed somewhat beneath notice as a kind of Bolaño fatigue set in. Nonetheless, the canonicity and resonance of the major works was unquestioned, which had a convulsive influence on the emerging generations of American novelists. Bolaño, importantly, was both a realist and experimentalist. He gleefully partook in the traditions of highbrow fiction while also, as his translator Chris Andrews pointed out, appealing to disaffected males who usually did not read the latest well-reviewed novels. He was first published by a prestigious experimental publisher (New Directions) who continued to publish some of his "smaller" books even while "big" books such as *The Savage Detectives* and *2666* were published by the United States' leading literary imprint, Farrar, Straus and Giroux. He had three different translators, the Australian Chris Andrews for his New Directions novels, the American Natasha Wimmer for his Farrar, Straus, and Giroux, novels and the American Laura Healy for his poetry, which suggested that there were almost three different literary personas emerging in English: the elegiac ironist of the shorter books, the apocalyptic prophet of the two long books, and the lyrical anti-poet of the verses. Bolaño also possessed multiple temporalities. He became popular in a US literary world still reeling from the attacks of 9/11 and wanting an orientation to a suddenly hostile and predictable world, even if his Chilean, Mexican, and Spanish subjects had little pertinence to the Arab world or to Islam. Most of his major work took place in the late 1960s and 1970s, in a world now a generation back, and which younger American writers knew only through childhood memories or as hearsay and history. And Bolaño's deep subject is the palpable lingering legacy of World War II and the Holocaust. This is manifest in the faux-biographical *Nazi Literatures in the Americas* and in *The Third Reich.* It is just beneath the surface in the character of the reclusive novelist Archimboldi in *2666,* And it is tacit in many of his other works. Bolaño found a way to connect the war and the genocide in the concentration camps not just to the atrocities of Latin American authoritarian regime but to the systemic violence of neoliberalism and of the militaristic rhetoric of twenty-first-century globalization and governance. García Márquez was perceived by his North American readership as coming from one place, the tropical jungles of Colombia, and one time – a near-present rendered qualitatively more past by the author's own sense of the separate development of Latin America from the rest of the Western world. Bolaño, on the other hand, was a writer who possessed multiple affiliations and evoked multiple temporalities.

It would be easy to say what the Boom writers were for their contemporaries in the United States and the Baby Boomer generation that followed them, Bolaño was for their Generation X or Millennial successors. This attitude, though, is complicated by a few notable factors. First, there were movements within Latin America that were tantamount to a Generation X "pure play." The McOndo movement, based in Chile and combining the name of the Macondo of García Márquez with the arch-capitalist conformism of McDonald's, and the Crack movement, based in Mexico and espousing a more experimental poetics, both arose in 1996. Their spearheads were both young male writers: Jorge Volpi in Mexico and Alberto Fuguet in Chile. Though very different writers – Fuguet wrote of the disillusioned world of his own generation, one that had grown up under the Pinochet dictatorship, and Volpi wrote of history, apocalypse, and secrets – both Fuguet and Volpi (who shared the same US translator, Kristina Cordero) assayed material that would later be canvassed by Bolaño. Like Fuguet, Bolaño wrote of post-Pinochet Chile in a way fiercely critical of the dictator but lacking the leftist sentimentality and moralism of older Chilean writers. Like Volpi, Bolaño wrote of a Latin America affected by Europe and permitted the contemporaneity of the rest of the world, foregrounding the way their culture was fundamentally a post-1945 one. Though older than either Volpi or Fuguet, Bolaño also came to prominence circa 1996.

Yet Fuguet, who was translated in the United States in 1997, before Bolaño was published, and Volpi, who was not translated until 2003, both failed to make a significant dent in America, whereas Bolaño – their generational elder by a decade, Baby Boomer rather than Generation X – achieved a convulsive success. Part of this was the post-9/11 timing, and, as with any successful writer, was a chain of tastemakers, publishers, and reviews whose discernments and preferences happen to align in a favorable way for Bolaño. But, as Will Corral has suggested, another part of Bolaño's greater success is that he continued all the new emphases in Latin American fiction that the generational rhetoric of Volpi and Fuguet tried to accentuate, but without the limits imposed by generational identity (2013, p. 12). Not only could Bolaño's novels speak to readers of any age, but they did not seem animated by a purely internal discussion among Latin American literati. This is particularly true since even though by the late 1990s magical realism and the far more central Boom preoccupation of the total novel was exhausted within Latin American fiction, in US fiction it still manifested a persistent appeal that could not simply be ascribed to one motivating factor. In seeking to overthrow magical realism, Fuguet and Volpi risked themselves – paradoxically given their internationalist and anti-local color bent – as being of only provincial importance. Bolaño, on the other hand, combined his clearly antithetical definition of himself vis-à-vis his predecessors with a larger ethical and aesthetic agenda. When Bolaño pronounced, for instance, in his 1999 speech in Caracas upon acceptance the Rómulo Gallegos Award, that Latin American intellectuals would have been ill-treated if a lot of the leftist revolutionary groups they supported would have ever in fact come to power, it did not seem a bratty rejoinder to entrenched literary elders. Bolaño had similar critiques of Latin American literary establishment to those of the Crack and McOndo writers. But his agenda and purport were not just generational, but literary and of world stature.

AUTOETHNOGRAPHY

Though Bolaño's name was widely known in the United States literary world by 2003, with an almost universal currency by the time of the translation *2666* in 2008, the full force of the Bolaño effect was not felt in the United States until the global financial crisis of 2007–2009. Part of this was just the normal lag the literary field needs to absorb new influences. Additionally, in the 2000s, magical realism, though past its prime, still sustained its usefulness, even as the signifier "Bolaño" in the United States suggested a highbrow Latin American literature after the Boom. Writers such as Isabel Allende, Laura Esquível, and Sara Gruen used the techniques in ways that offered images of the stranger and outsider to a relatively mass audience. Other writers such as David Foster Wallace, though comparatively uninfluenced by magic realism per se, did emulate the Latin American Boom idea of the total novel, in which the novel became a meta-genre synthesizing many genres and forms of information and expression. A third, and perhaps the most viable version is "autoethnographic" magic realism, following the term "autoethnography," coined by the scholar of Victorian literature James Buzard to describe England's turning the anthropological techniques applied to other cultures on itself. The first wave of this transpired in the 1980s when writers such as John Barth, in *The Tidewater Tales* (1987), and Joyce Carol Oates, in *Bellefleur* (1980), wrote of their "own" Macondo-like rural spaces; but what really fed into the Bolaño effect was the urban autoethnography represented most significantly by Jonathan Lethem in his novels *Motherless Brooklyn* (1999) and *the Fortress of Solitude* (2003). Lethem, writing of Brooklyn neighborhoods both traumatized and put on the conceptual map by demographic gentrification, strategically provincialized Latin American influences to make them part of a story not just of a particular urban area but of a Generation X that, like that of Fuguet and Volpi, wished to continue in a progressive political vein without the seemingly metaphysical certitudes of its immediate predecessors. If the result was sometimes what Elizabeth Gumport (2009) classified as "magic real-estate-ism," the achievement of Lethem, who has admiringly reviewed Bolaño, was to define an American literary generation that was suspectable to Bolaño's influence.

Junot Díaz's *Brief Wondrous Life of Oscar Wao*, published in 2007, is the first US novel to show any trace of the Bolaño effect. Indeed, it can be seen as a transition-point from the influence of the Latin American magic realists to that of Bolaño and the generation after him. Like Lethem and like the Latin American novelists of Generation X, Díaz alludes generously to pop culture – movies, fantasy novels, comic books – to both complement a magical-realist aesthetic and proffer a looser, more irreverent, and more contemporaneous version of that aesthetic. Like Bolaño – all of whose works have at their backbone a sense of *testimonio* to the traumatic aftereffects of violence – Díaz's novel produces a sense of the aftermath of catastrophe, in his case the Trujillo dictatorship in the Dominican Republic from which the parents of the narrator and protagonist have fled. The use of Yunior, the novelist's narrator, as a surrogate for the author is reminiscent of Bolaño's technique with Arturo Belano in *The Savage Detectives*, and the combination in Díaz's novel of pop-cultural brio and literary swagger yet coexisting with a more observational and sociopolitical witness-narrative is in a round sense similar to what Bolaño achieves.

The global financial crisis and the election of Barack Obama augured a new era in American culture, one in which the United States and its history were even less exempt from the suffering most of the rest of the world experienced as routine. Writers began to look back on the previous few decades, including the wars in the Middle East, the rise of inequality, and the hegemony of a right-leaning philosophy of neoliberalism – to see where things had gone wrong. Bolaño's oeuvre, from a Latin American vantage-point, was constellated around just that issue, and American writers looked to the 1970s and 1980s to find equivalents of what the 1973 Chilean coup was for Bolaño. Rachel Kushner, in *The Flamethrowers*, depicts a young women artist named Reno, who travels to New York from the American West in the 1970s and then goes to Europe and becomes involved with a wide spectrum of Italian political life ranging from an industrial family who had coexisted with the Fascist regime to radical left-wing terrorists. Kushner was familiar with Latin American culture, as evidenced by her pervious novel, 2008's *Telex Form Cuba*, and her novel shared a title with the 1931 novel by Roberto Arlt (*Los Lanzallamas*) which also involves terrorists as a site of social turbulence. She spoke of the role that Bolaño played in helping her conceive her canvas: "I had been really charged by a re-read of Roberto Bolaño's *The Savage Detectives*. Things happen, characters walk in and out, take over, tell stories. . . . and part of it, I believe, is the blank voice of the narrator, who can let the world he encounters speak through him, without having to offer wisdom on it every few sentences" (Cotton 2014). That Bolaño's narrator was absent, for Kushner, enables the author to let many voices speak and also to illuminate a politically agitated time without being too polemical or too neutral, and to criticize the right and the left but not in an equivalent way. Bolaño's deadpan tone, emulated by Kushner, conveys the importance of the content without insisting on any authorial interpretation. In positing the near past of the 1970s as the antechamber to the troubles of the time in which Kushner was writing, the American novelist learns from Bolaño's sense of writing in the aftermath of catastrophe and writes as it were an autoethnography of the unfinished agendas of the American political left and artistic avant-garde.

Garth Risk Hallberg, in *City On Fire* (2015) wrote a similar near-past autoethnography, a panoramic novel of the 1970s, this time in New York City leading up to the July 1977 blackout. His sense of an implicated distance from the events of forty years before echoed Bolaño, though the book's evident ambition drew it back into the total novel, a genre which even *2666*, with its emphasis on "parts" in its section titles traced only in a fractional way. The most adept American emulators of Bolaño position their works formally between the total novel-limning *Savage Detectives* and *2666* with *récits* like *By Night in Chile* and *Distant Star* (1996), with a touch of the faux-documentary of *Nazi Literature in the Americas* (2008) thrown in. Rebecca Makkai's *The Great Believers* (2018) parallels its main thread of a young, romantic art dealer dying in Chicago at the time of the AIDS crisis of the 1980s with crushed hopes and dreams of a would-be modernist painter working in Paris in the 1920s, parallelling the two time frames in *The Savage Detectives* between the crushed hopes and dreams of a new art movement in the 1920s and a similar sense of utter defeat and catastrophe in the 1970s incarnation of the visceral realists. Makkai's interrogation of how experiments in art, politics, and sexuality resists bourgeois conformism and the ravages of time is both elegiac and clear-eyed, possessing the essential substrate of witness on which all of Bolanos literary pyrotechnics stand.

Molly Prentiss's *Tuesday Nights in 1980* (2016), like *The Flamethrower, is* set in the avant-garde art world and in the time just before the rise of the political Right and of neoliberalism in the United States. But it begins in Buenos Aires, where a woman named Franca is documenting the atrocities and disappearances staged by the then-ruling military junta. Franca's story is tied into the main narrative of the artistic provocateur James Bennett by the presence of her brother Raúl and her son Julián in New York, but in a larger sense Prentiss is following in Bolaño's footsteps in suggesting that the transformation of the late-twentieth century world has a genesis or at least a foreboding in the Latin American authoritarianisms of the 1970s. Bolaño's precedent provides a model for a literary autoethnography in that the autoethnographies stemming from Bolaño are trying to explore the etiology of our own time and witness the victims of inimical forces in our own day.

AUTOFICTION

Bolaño is the rare writer with any kind of outsider, beatnik following, and a rare contemporary writer male or female, with a significant male following (see Chris Andrews, above). The broad audience Andrews describes Bolaño as achieving is somewhat striking, as Bolaño is hardly a crowd-pleaser. Adam Kirsch, who has written sympathetically about Bolaño's work, nonetheless describes Bolaño's novels as "actively burdensome to read" (2017). Kirsch, though, goes on to delineate what might be the element in Bolaño's prose that most explains his appeal to American writers and how it dovetails with that of previous Latin American authors. "Every moment of a novel, Bolaño suggests by precept as well as his own practice, must work the fantastic into the very texture of the prose, if it is to do justice to the ominous strangeness of our world."

Despite what Kushner says about his novels' lack of authorial intrusiveness, this linkage of the imaginative to the real justifies classifying Bolaño as a writer of what has been called autofiction. Although not all of even most of Bolaño's oeuvre can be termed autofiction – fiction that muddies the water between life and art, fiction and nonfiction even more than traditional autobiographical fiction did. In *Distant Star*, Bolaño's narrator talked about having hepatic issues (Bolaño also did so, and died of liver failure) and reminisces about Santiago in the early 1970s in tones that mirror Bolaño's own biographical experience, For instance, in *The Savage Detectives*, the co-protagonist Arturo Belano is a clear reflection of Bolaño himself as a youth, in his identity as a "visceral realist" (in real life, infrarealist poet) of Chilean background, and in the obviously similar last name, garnished by the more romantic "Arturo" which refers not only to King Arthur but to Arthur Rimbaud. Furthermore, Bolaño stated that the narrator of *2666* is Arturo Belano, thus bringing in a voice recognizably close to his own even in a novel where there is no active first-person narrator.

It is in *The Savage Detectives,* though, that Bolaño deals with memory in a wistful and yet unsentimental way, as he portrays his literary youth in ways both mocking and nostalgic, as something to at once repudiate and reclaim. Like more exclusively autofictional novelists who had a similarly convulsive effect on the American scene such as Elena Ferrante and Karl Ove Knausgaard, Bolaño's oeuvre registers the social and political changes that have made the twenty-first century different from, and in some ways a disappointing sequel to, the twentieth. There is a sense, of experience funneled through a deeply personal prism. This prism is one in which the author does not bother to disguise through fancy literary legerdemain. But there is an utter lack of commitment to a polemical *parti pris*, even as the authors make clear they are acquainted with and have a critical line on the political changes of the past seventy-five years, including the way our present is very different from what the twentieth century thought, hoped, or feared would be its future. Autofiction is thus never simply navel-gazing, as minute as it might be in its registering of the details of lived experience. There is a fundamental tie to society and to a life conceived in relation to a community which offsets the inevitable egoism of an autofiction venture.

Indeed, if there is one genre actively discouraged by autofiction, it is fantasy. That there is, as Kirsch observes, some latent fantasy in Bolaño only shows us how remarkable it is that he had thoroughly worked that element into the grain of reality. Indeed, one might say that the fantastic element in Bolaño, when it is not projected into apocalypse as in *2666*, is involuted into the grain of connecting self and society. American novelists who have written autofiction, such as Ben Lerner in *Leaving the Atocha Station* (2011) and its prequel, *The Topeka School* (2019) have benefited from Bolaño's ability to reach the political through the personal. This is particularly true in *The Topeka School*, which seeks to evoke the genesis of the political trends that led to the Trump administration in the ordinary life of middle America in the 1990s.

AUTOPOIESIS

Even as Bolaño's work honors the self, however, it also registers the presence of systems. Autopoiesis, or self-making, is a term coined in 1972 by two Chilean biologists, Humberto Maturana and Francisco Varela, one year before the Pinochet coup. They sought to adapt the processes of bodily self-regulation they observed in biology to the social sphere. Rather than focusing on society as the product of human actions, they saw society at the intersection of self-sustaining systems. Autopoiesis is not totally parallel with neoliberalism. Neoliberalism tended to believe, as Margaret Thatcher memorably stated, that there was in such thing as society. Autopoiesis, on the other hand, necessarily posits a society that can regulate itself. But autopoiesis in the way it refuses to affirm an attendant social solidarity as a challenge to neoliberalism, while nonetheless challenging it in terms of its establishment of a collective world, has been hearkened to as a philosophy that can in conceptual terms both accept and counter neoliberalism.

That autopoiesis, neoliberalism (in the form of the Pinochet regime's self-conscious embrace of free market economics), and Bolaño himself as a thinker all had their origins in the Chile of the early 1970s makes for a neat comparison. More compelling, though, is the way Bolaño's core aesthetic identity, as a poet, links up to autopoiesis. Bolaño made clear that he would have always preferred to be a poet and he turned first to entering fiction writing contests in coastal Catalonia, and then eventually to the large-scale book publication, in order to support his family financially. But he continued to write and publish poetry until he passed away. Furthermore, *The Savage Detectives* demonstrably elevated the poet even as it made fun of the heedless avant-garde hijinks of the visceral realists. But Bolaño aligned his poetry with the anti-poetry of Nicanor Parra rather than the politically committed, lyrical, and humanistic poetry of Pablo Neruda or César Vallejo. His poetry is pure, but also hard, Not hard in the sense of being difficult, but hard as opposed to soft, sentimental, subjective; hard in the sense of not privileging one's own subjectivity as a diametrical counter-force to malignant ideologies or governments.

This is another connection between Bolaño and Lerner as novelists, as Lerner has defended poetry as a mode in *The Hatred of Poetry* (2016) even as he sees it as always a record of "failure" (p. 8) and "impossible" (p. 9). Both writers share a dedication to poetry without romanticizing it. And this informs the practice of their fiction, in which the poetic is always a leavening substrate that enriches reality, without redeeming it. Lerner, like Bolaño, has continued to write and publish poetry even as he has attained great success as a novelist. Like Bolaño's, Lerner's is personal, but avoids personality; attentive to the world, but without the intrusion of a desiring or willful subjectivity.

> Ari, pick up. I'm a different person
> In a perfect world, this would be
> April, or an associated concept
> Green to the touch
> several feet away
>
> (2010, p. 29)

It is not a perfect world, and such a green April is inaccessible and even unreal. But its impossibility is something poetry can still undertake. Poetry can make the conditions of its own meaning, even as theories of autopoiesis assume that the systems, not individuals, are responsible for outcomes. While not denying individuality and the possibility for change, autopoiesis sidelines subjectivity and affective cognition. The self-inventing aspects of autopoiesis, especially as unfolded by the Swedish sociologist Niklas Luhmann, were thought for a time to be close to deconstruction. Yet autopoiesis is closer, in its skepticism about the efficacy of the subjective will, to speculative realism. Speculative realism, which gained intellectual popularity in the 2010s the wake of the perceived failure of deconstruction and of various more Marxist or action-oriented alternatives to deconstruction, is a totalizing but non-humanistic philosophy. Though it shares previous Continental philosophies' resistance to imitation by empirical constraints, it lacks both the emphasis on volition and the disappointment in the way knowledge is always experienced as falling short of what can be called "the totality of being" – a common trait of thinkers from Kant to Heidegger to Derrida.

This sense of the autopoietic is very different, far more (to use an adjective Lerner deploys to describe poetic logic) "astringent" than ideas of the metafictional deployed far earlier in literary circles (2016, p. 10). This is evidenced in several distinct aspects of Lerner's *The Topeka School*. The narratives in this novel move beyond the autobiographical or autofiction – there are three other points of view in the novel: that of Adam's father and mother, and the outlier of Darren, a mentally disadvantaged boy who is taunted by the same school bullies who Adam narrowly evades through his academic excellence. Adam ends up, like Lerner himself, a graduate of Brown University and a successful writer in New York, while Darren is last seen as a participant at a Donald Trump rally. Adam has married a Latinx woman and is a participant in Occupy Wall Street and the anti-Trump resistance. What saves this outcome from simply being autobiographical virtue-signaling is that Adam is a poet. The discipline of poetry is contrasted in Lerner's novel to the debate technique of "the spread," which seeks to overwhelm the audience with random words and facts in order to weaponize words as a kind of privileged violence. Not that poetry itself is something salvific or inherently elevating – it is not, either in Bolaño or Lerner – but that it assists on another way of thought that is distinct in a formal sense from the main stream of life as we know it. The plural narration of Lerner's novel and this sense of poetry is a distinct formal arena work in tandem.

Plural narration has become more and more a standard feature in the highbrow US novels since 2010. Even such popular works as Ann Patchett's *Commonwealth* (2016) and Bill Clegg's *Did You Ever Have A Family?* (2015) used plural narration to give a multitude of perspectives on a shared set of experiences, indicating that the narrative cannot be summed up by one privileged spectator. Whereas twentieth-century writers might have used this technique to foreground the manifold and irreducible nature of reality, the Bolaño effect comes in the way it dissipates uniform authorial agency while still centering a very clear narrative purpose.

Valeria Luiselli's *Lost Children Archive* (2019) was the first novel in English by a writer who, though still under 40, had already become a canonical Mexican and Latin American writer for her writing in Spanish. *Lost Children Archive* is a novel about an academic couple whose marriage falls apart during a cross-country trip from the East Coast of the US to the border with Mexico. The adult woman's narrative is studded with the effect of her research, and is full of represented to European philosophy and to modernist art and aesthetics, and is the major voice in the first half of the novel, but as the family reaches the border, the children themselves become lost, and encounter migrant children more permanently lost. It is in this section that the adult female voice hands off the narrative to the voice of the young boy in the family, making the book at once an elegy for the dead and what Maturana and Varela would call a realization of the living.

Luiselli's positioning the work at the border recalls the femicides of Ciudad Juárez so relentlessly depicted in *2666*, and her focus on children rather than adult women as victims of neoliberal state violence both revises and continues Bolaño's dark vision. Indeed, how the cognitively powerful narrative voice is an adult woman with agency in Luiselli's book speaks to the assigned passivity of the femicide victims in Bolaño's novel. Luiselli's writing in English can also be seen as a byproduct of Bolaño's oeuvre bridging the two tongues. Though Bolaño never visited the United States and did not know English well, he was somewhat of an Anglophile, read widely in classic and contemporary US literature. Although Luiselli writes about migrants and narrative blurs the border between English and Spanish, Mexican and American, her viewpoint is reminiscent less of the feminist mysticism of a Gloria Anzaldúa than of Bolaño's sage ferocity.

Beneath the dramatic images of Bolaño's meteoric career and his early death, his remarkable oeuvre has changed US fiction, not the least because it spoke to changes that were already occurring in the fabric of the American cultural system. The Bolaño effect on twenty-first-century American literature has been savage and apocalyptic, but also generative of thoughtful reflection on cultures, subjectivities, and systems.

SEE ALSO: After Postmodernism; Alarcon, Daniel; Allende, Isabel; Border Fictions; Fiction and Terrorism; Globalization; Lerner, Ben; Minimalism and Maximalism; Post-9/11 Narratives; Urban Fiction

REFERENCES

Andrews, Chris. (2015). *Roberto Bolaño's Fiction: An Expanded Universe*. New York: Columbia University Press.

Corral, Will. (2013). General introduction. *The Contemporary Spanish-American Novel: Bolaño and After* (ed. Will H. Corral, Juan E. De Castro, and Nicholas Birns), 12. London: Bloomsbury.

Cotton, Jess. (2014). Voiceless voices: an interview with Rachel Kushner. *The Quietus* (February 3, 2014). https://thequietus.com/articles/14407-rachel-kushner-the-flamethrowers-interview (accessed September 24, 2021).

Gumport, Elizabeth. (2009). Gentrified fiction. *N + 1* (November 2, 2009). https://nplusonemag.com/online-only/book-review/gentrified-fiction/ (accessed August 9, 2021).

Kirsch, Adam. (2017). Murakami vs. Bolaño: competing visions of the global novel. *Literary Hub* (April 24, 2017). https://lithub.com/murakami-vs-bolano-competing-visions-of-the-global-novel/ (accessed August 9, 2021).

Lerner, Ben. (2010). *Mean Free Path*. Port Townsend, WA: Copper Canyon Press.

Lerner, Ben. (2016). *The Hatred of Poetry*. New York: Farrar, Straus and Giroux.

Maturana, Humberto and Varela, Francisco. (1980). *Autopoiesis and Cognition: The Realization of the Living*. Dordrecht: Springer.

FURTHER READING

Castellanos Moya, Horacio. (2019). Bolaño Inc. *Guernica* (November 1, 2019). https://www.guernicamag.com/bolano_inc/

De Castro, Juan E. and Birns, Nicholas. (eds.) (2017). *Roberto Bolaño as World Literature*. New York: Bloomsbury.

Hallberg, Garth Risk. (2009). The Bolaño myth and the backlash cycle. *The Millions* (November 16, 2009). https://themillions.com/2009/11/the-bolano-myth-and-the-backlash-cycle.html

Hoyos, Héctor. (2016). *Beyond Bolaño: The Global Latin American Novel*. New York: Columbia University Press.

Lopez-Calvo, Ignacio. (ed.) (2015). *Roberto Bolaño: A Less Distant Star*. New York: Palgrave Macmillan.

Pollack, Sarah. (2013). After Bolaño: rethinking the politics of Latin American literature in translation. *PMLA* 128 (3): 660–667.

Book Clubs

CECILIA KONCHAR FARR
St. Catherine University, USA

As Toni Morrison pointed out to Oprah's Book Club in a discussion of *Paradise* in 1998, "Novels are for talking about and quarrelling about and engaging in some powerful way. However that happens, at a reading group, a study group, a classroom or just some friends getting together, it's a delightful, desirable thing to do . . . Reading is solitary, but that's not its only life. It should have a talking life, a discourse that follows" (Morrison 1998). It is impossible to fully explore contemporary fiction from 1980 to 2020 without paying attention to this "talking life," to the explosion of a book club culture that powered the publishing industry into the twenty-first century.

While Oprah Winfrey was at the epicenter of the book club phenomenon from the start of her Book Club in 1996, the reverberations of her influence spread outward in the early part of the new century. Consider this: When protests erupted all over the world in 2020 after the death of George Floyd in Minnesota, *The New York Times* Best Seller list immediately reflected a now-entrenched American reading habit – the impulse to join a group and talk about it. A month after Floyd, an unarmed Black man, was recorded being killed by a white police officer, thirteen of the fifteen nonfiction bestsellers the first week in July were about race – from Ibram X. Kendi's newly released *How to be an Antiracist* (2019) at number 1 to several former bestsellers, including Ta-Nehisi Coates's *Between the World and Me* (2015) and Michelle Alexander's *The New Jim Crow* (2010), returning to the list, and the persistent *Becoming* (2018), Michelle Obama's memoir, at number 15. And the trend continued through the summer, as booksellers in my community tweeted about being backordered on every title about race in the United States, novels and nonfiction alike. Across platforms, social media feeds were filled with invitations to read a book and join the conversation. Both of my longstanding book clubs, as well as my university community, chose titles that addressed race and white privilege to read together over the summer.

In *How to Read and Why* (2000), Yale Professor Harold Bloom (one of the most popular and influential literary scholars of the late twentieth century) articulates the traditional view of reading as "a solitary praxis," arguing that its "pleasures . . . are selfish rather than social. You cannot directly improve anyone else's life by reading better or more deeply" (2000, p. 22). Similarly, writer and cultural critic Judith Shulevitz asserts that "Despite what your teacher may have told you, literature does not make society better," and that talking about books in book clubs "has nothing to do with coming together and everything to do with breaking apart, with figuring out how to live as an independent intellect and a soul loyal to its own needs" (2002, p. 51).

Yet the social life of literature has increasingly gained the attention of critics and shifted the way we think about reading in the twenty-first century. As literary scholars Patrocinio

P. Schweickart and Elizabeth A. Flynn argue in their introduction to *Reading Sites: Social Difference and Reader Response* (2004), a broad consensus has developed among critics on principles that influence how reading is defined, including the tenets that "the text is not a container of stable objective meaning"; that "the reader is a producer of meaning"; and that, as a result, "readings are necessarily various" (2004, pp. 1–2).

Given these assumptions, the best readings aim to gather diverse insights rather than to adhere to a definitive, expert unveiling of a text. For intersectional feminist critics like Schweickart and Flynn, "The concern to develop reading strategies that attend to the otherness of the text is of a piece with the concern to attend to other people with different experiences and perspectives, to resist totalizing interpretive frameworks, and to recognize multiple systems of social and cultural domination" (2004, p. 18). With this in mind, that July 2020 Best Seller list becomes not an anomaly but evidence of the growing recognition that reading at its best is not "a solitary praxis" but a lively social one.

In its early days, Oprah's Book Club was criticized for using books to start conversations with readers – not just about literature but about issues such as domestic violence, immigration, poverty, and mental illness. Yet today's most successful online book clubs have followed her lead. Well-Read Black Girl, for example, an Instagram book forum started by Gloria Edim in 2015, tallied nearly half a million followers in its first five years and claims to "address inequalities and improve communities through reading and reflecting on the works of Black women" (Well-Read Black Girl n.d.). Celebrities Reese Witherspoon, Emma Watson, Jenna Bush Hager, and Sarah Jessica Parker all have book clubs with an explicit social purpose. Reese's Book Club, for instance, has presented itself on its website as "A community propelled by meaningful connections with stories, authors and fellow members." Its aim is to "spark thought, joy, and conversation – online and in real life," with a focus on books by and about women (Reece's Book Club n.d.).

Book clubs with ambitions like these owe their existence in the United States to a long line of talking readers – from the women's improvement societies formed by new immigrants, freed Black women, polygamous Mormon wives, factory girls, privileged society ladies and others in the nineteenth century to the bohemian expatriate circles that nurtured experimental modernism and the consciousness-raising groups that advanced the women's movement in the twentieth century. In fact, Black women's literary societies and feminist consciousness-raising groups were direct antecedents of Oprah's Book Club. And all of these groups established a firm foundation for today's lively landscape of book clubs and social reading practices.

SOCIAL AND HISTORICAL CONTEXTS

From our earliest days as a nation, literary societies and other women's clubs claimed a key place as instigators of cultural and religious reform in the United States. They were also initiators of political action on issues such as abolition, prohibition, and women's suffrage. For the most part, club women lacked mainstream access to power; they were years away from getting the vote; some were not yet defined as fully human; and nearly all of them were excluded from formal education. So, they built their own unique systems, inspired in part by European intellectual salons and religious forums, but made distinctive by the rigorous separation of spheres enforced by the United States' individualistic, white, patriarchal social mores. In *Intimate Practices: Literacy and Cultural Work in U.S. Women's Clubs, 1880–1920* (1997), Anne Ruggles Gere describes how these women's groups pursued intellectual goals while distinguishing themselves from what they perceived as more masculine academic practices:

> Gathering in one another's homes, libraries, or club rooms that carried a domestic imprint, clubwomen assumed a less formal posture than that enacted in the classroom. Academic discipline of the body was supplanted by comfortable chairs, handwork such as sewing or knitting, and the consumption of food and drink. These accommodations to the body never appeared in the classroom, where students occupied hard seats in lined rows, with the figure of the instructor often towering over them on a dais, and where handwork and refreshments of all sorts were explicitly forbidden.
>
> (1997, p. 35)

Gere uses the minutes from women's club meetings to demonstrate how their readers encountered books both intellectually and emotionally, using domestic and community-building practices associated with femininity. A Michigan woman reporting on a meeting in 1889 affirms this unique approach: "It seemed to me that we as a club have benefited from our association, in the matter of conversations – of being able to think aloud with less timidity and with more directness" (1997, p. 17). But the outcomes of these meetings were political as well as personal and social. One scholar notes that these women's clubs established almost 75% of public libraries, created kindergartens, set up college scholarships, and campaigned for universal education (Seaholm 1988, p. 272).

Similarly, Elizabeth McHenry explores how Black women's literary societies served club women across the South. She writes in *Forgotten Readers: Recovering the Lost History of African American Literary Societies* (2002) of "the tremendous thirst for education" among formerly enslaved people in the years after the Civil War (2002, p. 2). She points out that educating African Americans was illegal in every Southern state but Tennessee before the war, so the literary societies these women formed became "not only places of refuge for the self-improvement of their members, but acts of resistance to the hostile racial climate" of the United States, particularly in the backlash years post-Reconstruction when many of these groups were formed (p. 17). In these circles of trusted friends, women often read aloud, mentoring one another into literacy and rhetorical eloquence as a hopeful pathway to "respect, political voice, and citizenship" (p. 83).

Aspirations toward empowerment and increased respect also motivated recruitment for the largest, most successful "book club" of the early twentieth century, the Book of the Month Club (BOMC). Neither aligned with domesticity, connected to a small community, nor aimed at women readers, BOMC was a predecessor to today's vast online forums in its direct mail structure. As Joan Shelley Rubin explains in *The Making of Middlebrow Culture* (1992), while the publishing industry that established the BOMC intended to engage educated men in book buying, the growth of the club came from its appeal to millions of less educated, immigrant, and working-class Americans who aspired to do better, to be better. The hugely successful BOMC persisted, from its founding in 1926, throughout the twentieth century until today, capitalizing (literally) on a broad desire among the rising middle class to be well read and informed – and to read what "everyone else" was reading.

Janice A. Radway makes a similar point in *A Feeling for Books: The Book of the Month Club, Literary Taste, and Middle-Class Desire* (1997), exploring the preferences of "general readers" for whom the BOMC was a path to literacy as "the quintessential mark of privilege, as that which had to be both acquired and mastered in order to demonstrate assimilation to and participation within the public sphere" (1997, p. 243). Many working-class homes I encountered (and lived in) as a child had shelves lined with BOMC books and, likewise, with Reader's Digest Condensed Books, which had a similar purpose and direct mail structure (1950–1997).

Popular as BOMC was, it was not the only evidence of the enduring influence of the nineteenth-century ladies' literary societies, those communities of earnest women committed to "improvement," education, and the arts. Even the most avant-garde and bohemian circles of US expatriate Paris in the mid-twentieth century – Gertrude Stein's famous salon in rue de Fleurus, Natalie Clifford Barney's "L'Académie des Femmes" with its backyard recreations of "the golden age of Lesbos," and Sylvia Beach's Shakespeare and Company Bookstore – purposefully linked the social and the literary, creating communities and conversations around books, ideas, and art. The 1996 documentary film *Paris Was a Woman* captures archival footage and interviews with some of these expats, mostly lesbians who imagined together a world more welcoming than the one they left behind across the Atlantic (Schiller 1996). Beach's memoir, *Shakespeare and Company* (1956), is an enchanting account of how one unpretentious woman created the hospitable space and encouraged the crucial exchanges that became the modernist literary movement's social center.

With this history, it should come as no surprise that when communities of women began to form around the goal of liberation in the second-wave feminist movement in the 1970s, the established habits of women's literary societies were instrumental to unleashing the political uses of literature. Jaime Harker and I write about this connection in *This Book is An Action* (2016): "For many feminist writers of the Women's Liberation Movement, fiction became a means for transforming readers' politics. Reading was essential in early conceptions of second-wave feminism, as books became a provocation to conversation about readers' own lives and experiences" (Harker and Konchar Farr 2016, p. 4). And further, "that this moment of significant feminist social change was catalyzed in print, and its activists were united by a firm belief that books could be revolutionary, that language could remake the world, and that writing mattered in a profound way" (p. 4). The feminist writer Susan Faludi amplifies this insight in a passage about how a consciousness-raising (CR) novel affected her second-wave mother:

> I well recall returning home from college my freshman year to the flushed and fuming presence of my mother, who had just finished [Marilyn French's] *The Women's Room*. She felt, she said at the time, as if French had taken up residence in our living room and transcribed every detail into a novel. Then she realized that the similarities were no coincidence, because what had happened to her had happened to the wife across the street and the one next door to her. They had all been had, or let themselves be had, and she was filled with the sort of anger that is peculiarly bracing, the kind of fury that fuels small and big changes.
>
> (1988, p. 469)

As Lisa Maria Hogeland writes in *Feminism and its Fictions: The Consciousness-Raising Novel and the Women's Liberation Movement* (1998): "The CR novel was important and influential in introducing feminist ideas to a broader reading public" (1998, p. ix). And the organized conversations about these novels, in living rooms and at kitchen tables, circulated new and radical ideas, and again, as in the late nineteenth century, spurred political action and social change.

THE BOOK CLUB PHENOMENON

It wasn't until early in the twenty-first century that historians and critics, particularly feminist scholars, began to research this literary "women's work." Notably, Rita Felski, in her influential *Uses of Literature* (2008), called on literary critics to be more attentive to readers and what literature does for them, to them, and with them, and to "engage seriously with ordinary motives for reading – such as the desire for knowledge or the longing for escape – that are either overlooked or undervalued in literary scholarship" with its traditional focus on textual interpretation (2008, p. 14). Anticipating a shift in direction for criticism, she concluded, "There is no reason why our readings cannot blend analysis and attachment, criticism and love" (p. 22).

At about the same time, Elizabeth Long, a pioneer in the study of book groups, was marking "an almost explosive growth in the number of women participating in informal reading groups" in the last decades of the twentieth century (2003, p. 19). She wanted to explore the reasons for it, but quickly felt that many of her colleagues "could not understand why an intelligent person might consider women's reading groups a serious topic for investigation" (p. x). In her 2003 study, *Book Clubs: Women and the Uses of Reading in Everyday Life*, Long concludes, however, that "by looking at women's reading groups . . . one can see people in the process of creating new connections, new meanings, and new relationships – to the characters in the books or their authors, to themselves, to the other members of the group, to the society and culture in which they live." This activity, she writes, "is quite literally productive" (2003, p. 22).

Long's book, it turned out, joined several others in responding to book club culture and reading's various purposes in the United States at that moment. Observing the vitality of reading groups around her, Ellen Slezak gathered first-person accounts from book club members across the country in her 2002 collection, *The Book Group Book*. These narratives highlight the informality and personal connection that was typical of most groups at the time. Hedy N.R. Hustedde observes of her Iowa book group: "In the beginning, I think we joined a discussion group because we cared about literature. We kept coming back because we care about each other" (Slezak 2002, p. 143). Janet Tripp, a book club member in Minnesota, asserts that her experience of reading changed as she engaged with a group. "Books have more to say to me," she writes. "Previously, the conversations I held with my books were a quiet dialogue. There were just two voices, mine and the book's. It was nothing like the communion that goes on now – full of exclamations, impassioned pleas, confession and campaigning, enlightenment, and exchange" (p. 159).

By 2009, journalists were following the rise of book clubs in the United States. *MinnPost* reported that year of estimates that placed the number of book club members in the United States at five million. "Most clubs have ten or more members," the author added, and "70 to 80 percent of clubs are all-female" (Otto 2009). Katie Wu, writing for *McSweeney's* in 2011, summed up the state of book clubs: "In the past fifteen years, book clubs in the U.S. have become commonplace, if not ubiquitous. They are cultivated by celebrities, bookstores, libraries, community centers, municipalities, and of course the occasional beauty shop." One study posited that the number of book clubs in the United States doubled between 1990 and 2000, with "low estimates count[ing] at least 100,000 book clubs" that year. Wu also reports on hits for a Google search of the phrase "book clubs" in 2003 at 424,000, which she compares with her 2011 result of 40 million. (A Google search in 2020 yielded 424 million results for the search term "book clubs.")

BookBrowse, an organization that has surveyed readers regularly since 2004, offers a statistical window into this growing book club culture. In 2014 the editors interviewed 2,723 US women aged 25 and over who read at least one book a month. Of these readers,

56% were in a book club, 19% in more than one. The annual surveys reveal a fairly steep rise in book club engagement to get to that 56% with only 33% of those interviewed in 2004 reporting book club membership. In *The Inner Lives of Book Clubs: A Report on Who Joins Them and Why, What Makes Them Succeed, and How They Resolve Problems* (2019), the BookBrowse editors tally about a 75% book club membership rate among the 3705 regular readers who completed the organization's survey in 2017 and 2018 (BookBrowse 2019). The clubs they reported on were mainly private (74%), met monthly (85%), and were, for the most part, all-women groups (88% of private book clubs and 52% of public ones). But perhaps the most interesting aspect of the BookBrowse report is its insight into the dynamics of book clubs. The responses of club members to questions about group benefits echo the theory of literary scholars Schweickart and Flynn that links the effort to "develop reading strategies that attend to the otherness of the text" to "the concern to attend to other people with different experiences and perspectives." As one reader notes about her book group discussions, "The discourse enhances my opinion and understanding of the books, often due to learning from the members' lives and their experiences" (BookBrowse 2019, p. 19). Another reader sounds like a modern version of Gere's nineteenth-century women's club member cited earlier: "When I walk into the book club each month I get this sense that I belong and that over the next two hours I'll be engaging my brain and growing as a person" (p. 18).

Moreover, as Wu reminds us, today's book clubs aren't only a social or literary phenomenon worth noting, but also an economic one. "The sales power of these clubs [is] hard to measure, but the most conservative estimates point to some incredible numbers. If one assumes each club has ten members, and picks six books a year, that's 60 books sold per club." Multiply that by 100,000 clubs in and you get six million books. "And that's not even counting Oprah," she adds (Wu 2011).

Thus, while many observers credit Oprah Winfrey with the widespread expansion of women's book clubs in the late twentieth century, as Long, Slezak, and others observe, the movement was already in progress when Oprah burst on the scene with her book club late in 1996. And then it went viral, before we were even using that word for sharp upward trends in popular culture and media.

OPRAH'S BOOK CLUB

By tracing the evolution of Oprah's Book Club, we can also track more broadly the forms and purposes of US book clubs on the cusp of the twenty-first century. Like the women's literary societies before it, Oprah's Book Club (OBC) occupied a decidedly feminine space, distinguished by its difference from masculine models of textual exchange, which, again, were mainly academic, solitary, and "serious," rather than social and popular. The studio for the OBC television show, especially in its early years, looked like a living room rather than a talk show set or classroom; readers, writer, and host all sat in a circle of cushy couches and chairs, sometimes with the remains of a shared meal behind them. Because *Oprah!* was both daytime TV *and* a talk show, advertising targeted it as pretty much a women-only space. Also like its nineteenth-century predecessors, OBC's appeal was communal and conversational, extending reading beyond its solitary life into its talking life. Following the pattern of women's literary societies, particularly those comprised of Black women, Oprah's TV talk show consistently drew its members' attention to both self-improvement and justice issues. "Literature is powerful," Winfrey asserted as she encouraged participation in OBC. "It has the ability to change people, to change people's thoughts . . . Books expand your vision of yourself and your world" (Winfrey 2000). She also showed her cards for cultural change, aspiring from the very first OBC show to "get America reading again."

In its first iteration, 1996–2002, OBC expanded on these successful social reading practices as it drew millions of viewers and book buyers: It openly appealed to women and, pointedly, the less educated (it regularly featured women who confessed that they "hadn't read a book in years" – or ever); it was democratic in that it highlighted everyday readers and their perceptions; it aimed to build connections and conversations, modeling appropriate book club exchanges among a few selected guests for each show; it was aspirational, carrying forward the theme of the *Oprah!* show, "Live Your Best Life"; it was, again, staged as a warm and welcoming domestic space; it was both entertaining and educational, both light and socially aware.

And it worked, most markedly for the publishing industry. I observed in *Reading Oprah: How Oprah's Book Club Changed the Way America Reads* (2004) that every one of Winfrey's selections from the first six years of OBC became a bestseller, even debut novels by previously unknown authors (Konchar Farr 2004, p. 2). They averaged sixteen weeks on *The New York Times* Best Seller list. Sometimes up to six Oprah novels appeared on the fifteen-book fiction list at once. During that first stage, for six years "a week never went by without at least one Oprah book on national bestseller lists" (p. 2). The escalating popularity of OBC also influenced end-of-year *Publishers Weekly* tallies, where Oprah's fiction choices became the most successful annual sellers, rather than the nonfiction titles (what a publishing industry expert called "that familiar balance of spiritual solace, health, comics, and computer instruction") that had dominated book sales

for years (p. 21). OBC choices included a lively mix of popular authors – Wally Lamb, Maeve Binchy, and Sue Miller, for example – and literary works by Toni Morrison, Joyce Carol Oates, Barbara Kingsolver, Alice Hoffman, and Maya Angelou. These selections echo the range of many book clubs, as they move from light entertainment to more thought-provoking books, addressing the various tastes and desires of their members. Oprah's diverse recommendations and her online suggestions and support at Oprah.com and, later, *O* magazine evidently inspired the formation of many new reading groups, as membership in book clubs saw the steep rise that Long and others noted above.

Yet despite the rather astounding successes for publishers, novelists, book clubs, and television ratings, OBC had been besieged from the start by characterizations of its book choices as lightweight, lowbrow, even "schmaltzy and one-dimensional," in the words of Jonathan Franzen (quoted in Konchar Farr 2004, p. 75), whose ungrateful response to his novel's selection by Oprah became a topic of celebrity gossip in 2001. Apparently fed up with such (generally sexist and inaccurate) criticism, Winfrey cancelled the OBC altogether in 2002. When she returned a year later, she had revealingly shifted her focus to "classics," leading a more aspirational literary enterprise that echoed the early promises of BOMC and other academic-leaning clubs for democratic access to education and high culture.

Gone were the big yellow easy chairs, the wine glasses, and the ordinary women readers who had surrounded Oprah to talk about books. Much of the Classics OBC took place online, where readers could print out a bookmark with reading deadlines for *Anna Karenina* (1877), read a guide to *One Hundred Years of Solitude* (1967), or listen to a college professor lecture on William Faulkner. Gone, too, were many of OBC's fans – and book buyers. In the years when Oprah was not selecting contemporary novels, the OBC's ratings slid, and there were consistently fewer novels on the publisher's annual list of top sellers. In 2002, the year of Oprah's hiatus, only one book sold more than a million copies, a cookbook (Konchar Farr 2016, p. 73). In the previous active years of the OBC, novels had dominated that list, with 10 or more million-sellers every year.

Oprah's earlier preference for a conversational book club seemed to upend her newfound focus frequently as the Classics OBC moved through the first decade of the twenty-first century with far fewer selections and much more occasional announcements – there was an extended engagement with Eckhart Tolle and a year when the only book club choice was Elie Wiesel's 100-page *Night* (1956). Big, absorbing contemporary novels reappeared a few times (*Middlesex* [2002], *The Story of Edgar Sawtelle* [2008], *The Pillars of the Earth* [1989]) along with several memoirs and some lighter literary fiction, until Winfrey announced two Dickens novels for the final meeting of the Classics OBC in 2011. As she ended her 25-year run on network TV and moved to the Oprah Winfrey cable network (OWN), no new book announcements came for nearly two years.

I have noted elsewhere another crucial shift in OBC during its second iteration as a classics book club. The tone of increased seriousness, the emphasis on education and self-examination rather than political or social engagement, and the tendency to talk *at* rather than *with* readers led OBC to markedly different authors:

> It is revealing, considering the [women-dominated] demographics of Oprah's Book Club ... that from 2004 until the announcement of "Book Club 2.0," Oprah had not chosen a single book by a woman writer – *eight years and not a one* – and only a handful by men of color; whereas, all but nine of the 48 selections of the earlier book club were by women, eleven by women of color.
>
> (Konchar Farr 2016, p. 70)

This shift is easily explained by OBC's series of moves away from its foundation in the tradition of women's literary societies, with their commitment to connection and conversation, their history of social and political engagement, and their unabashed appeal to women. Without that footing, Oprah's house of books trembled as she led readers off into less inhabited hallways and wings. Meanwhile, morning TV shows and local libraries, Internet influencers and celebrities rushed to Oprah's neighborhood to build their own book clubs. Even at their best, their efforts have never met hers in size or influence – even at her worst.

Since those final Dickens novels, three notable things have happened at OBC in its third iteration, identified early on as "Book Club 2.0." One has been the return of the woman writer (and, we can assume, a return to courting women readers), with 11 of the 16 choices in the past eight years by women. The second is the refocus on contemporary literature, specifically fiction. All but three of those sixteen choices have been new novels. The final, most significant trend has been Winfrey's selection of Black writers – ten of sixteen, including Isabel Wilkerson's *Caste*, the August 2020 OBC book that fit with the race-related studies that dominated the Best Seller list in the midst of the political unrest that summer.

At the time of writing, the OBC on AppleTV and Instagram has been more active than it was on OWN, more active than it has been since the late 1990s, with seven new titles announced between September 2019 and August 2020. By all appearances, other book clubs arrived just a step behind OBC, coming into conversations about gender and race and, now, setting down their wine glasses and light reading to focus with Oprah on Black lives. A fascinating August 2020 *New York Times* article features several new book groups created by young Black women, highlighting the rapper

Noname and the vlogger Jouelzy. Citing both McHenry's work on nineteenth-century literary societies and Oprah Winfrey's sustained literacy efforts, Iman Stevenson describes how these new clubs grew from those roots to create a space "free of the white gaze" to learn, to build community, and to inspire activism (Stevenson 2020). A few groups invite only women of color to participate, and most feature the works of Black writers exclusively. As I read their aims, I recalled vividly a moment in 2000 when Winfrey proclaimed that "the world would be different" if everyone read Toni Morrison's *The Bluest Eye* (1970), which she called "a national treasure." Not only was she affirming Black women's substantial influence on literate culture in the United States, she was inviting her massive "ladies' improvement society" to take this novel's message about race and talk about it, then change because of it. Fast forward to 2020 where we find Oprah continuing the work she began more than twenty years ago, even more focused on elevating writers of color, and now with these young Black women following in her footsteps.

Because, simply stated, Oprah Winfrey has done more for books and readership in the past quarter century than any other force in American society. One word from her, still, and a novel becomes a bestseller, an author becomes a popular phenomenon. To this day, literally millions of regular readers trust her and follow her recommendations. No one else in the publishing industry, journalism, or the Academy has this kind of clout. A devoted reader, empathic listener, and avid talker, Winfrey's skills served her well as she fostered an expansive book club movement. Grounded in a uniquely American tradition, she continues to deploy the power of reading for personal growth, social engagement, and political change as she engages readers in the talking life of books.

It is no small coincidence, then, that in the United States in summer 2020, despite an unchecked pandemic and divisive political climate, surrounded by massive justice uprisings and shifting attitudes about race, many of us found ourselves occupied in the not-so-solitary praxis of reading in book clubs and Internet forums, coming together on Zoom in community, activist, college, and library book groups – and in Winfrey's reinvigorated online OBC. Urged to isolate, Americans responded by heading for havens of social reading and book clubs.

SEE ALSO: Chick Lit and the New Domesticity; Debut Novels; Fiction and Affect; Franzen, Jonathan; Kingsolver, Barbara; Literary Magazines; Morrison, Toni; Oates, Joyce Carol

REFERENCES

Bloom, Harold. (2000). *How to Read and Why*. New York: Scribner's.

BookBrowse. (2019). *The Inner Lives of Book Clubs: A Report on Who Joins Them and Why, What Makes Them Succeed, and How They Resolve Problems*. https://www.bookbrowse.com/wp/innerlives/ (accessed July 12, 2021).

Faludi, Susan. (1988). Afterword. In: *The Women's Room* (by Marilyn French). New York: Ballantine.

Felski, Rita. (2008). *The Uses of Literature*. Oxford: Blackwell.

Gere, Anne Ruggles. (1997). *Intimate Practices: Literacy and Cultural Work in U.S. Women's Clubs, 1880–1920*. Urbana: University of Illinois Press.

Harker, Jaime and Konchar Farr, Cecilia. (eds.) (2016). *This Book Is an Action: Feminist Print Culture and Activist Aesthetics*. Urbana: University of Illinois Press.

Hogeland, Lisa Marie. (1998). *Feminism and Its Fictions: The Consciousness-Raising Novel and the Women's Liberation Movement*. Philadelphia: University of Pennsylvania Press.

Konchar Farr, Cecilia. (2004). *Reading Oprah: How Oprah's Book Club Changed the Way America Reads*. Albany: SUNY Press.

Konchar Farr, Cecilia. (2016). *The Ulysses Delusion*. New York: Palgrave Macmillan.

Long, Elizabeth. (2003). *Book Clubs: Women and the Uses of Reading in Everyday Life*. Chicago: University of Chicago Press.

McHenry, Elizabeth. (2002). *Forgotten Readers: Recovering the Lost History of African American Literary Societies*. Durham, NC: Duke University Press.

Morrison, Toni. (1998). Book Club: Toni Morrison. *The Oprah Winfrey Show* (transcript, March 6, 1998). Florham Park, NJ: Burrelle's Information Services.

Otto, Audra. (2009). The evolution of American book clubs: a timeline. *MinnPost* (September 9, 2009). https://www.minnpost.com/books/2009/09/evolution-american-book-clubs-timeline/ (accessed July 12, 2021).

Radway, Janice A. (1997). *A Feeling for Books: The Book of the Month Club, Literary Taste, and Middle-Class Desire*. Chapel Hill: University of North Carolina Press.

Reece's Book Club. (n.d.). https://hello-sunshine.com/ (accessed July 12, 2021).

Rubin, Joan Shelley. (1992). *The Making of Middlebrow Culture*. Chapel Hill: University of North Carolina Press.

Schiller, Greta. (dir.) (1996). *Paris Was A Woman* (writer Andrea Weiss). Jezebel Productions, Cicada Films.

Schweickart, Patrocinio P. and Flynn, Elizabeth A. (2004). *Reading Sites: Social Difference and Reader Response*. New York: Modern Language Association of America.

Seaholm, Megan. (1988). "Earnest Women: The White Women's Movement in Progressive Era Texas." PhD dissertation, Rice University.

Shulevitz, Judith. (2002). You read your book and I'll read mine. *The New York Times Book Review* (May 19, 2002): 51.

Slezak, Ellen. (2002). *The Book Group Book: A Thoughtful Guide to Forming and Enjoying a Stimulating Book Discussion Group*. Chicago: Chicago Review Press.

Stevenson, Iman. (2020). The Black Book Club rises to the next level. *The New York Times* (August 2, 2020): 2.

Well-Read Black Girl. (n.d.). https://www.wellreadblackgirl.com/ (accessed September 11, 2021).

Winfrey, Oprah. (2000). *Drowning Ruth*. *The Oprah Winfrey Show* (transcript, November 16, 2000). Florham Park, NJ: Burrelle's Information Services. Book Club citations on *Bluest Eye* from personal recording (May 26, 2000).

Wu, Katie. (2011). The Book Club phenomena. *McSweeney's* (February 8, 2011). https://www.mcsweeneys.net/articles/the-book-club-phenomena (accessed July 12, 2021).

FURTHER READING

Aubry, Timothy. (2011). *Reading as Therapy: What Contemporary Fiction Does for Middle-class Americans*. Iowa City: University of Iowa Press.

Bhalla, Tamara. (2016). *Reading Together, Reading Apart: Identity, Belonging, and South Asian American Community*. Champaign: University of Illinois.

Cotten, Trystan. (2010). *Stories of Oprah: The Ophrahfication of American Culture*. Jackson: University Press of Mississippi.

Driscoll, Beth. (2014). *The New Literary Middlebrow: Tastemakers and Reading in the Twenty-first Century*. Basingstoke, UK: Palgrave Macmillan.

Harris, Jennifer, et al. (2007). *The Oprah Phenomenon*. Lexington: University Press of Kentucky.

Watson, Jay and Harker, Jaime. (eds.) (2013). Oprah's summer of Faulkner. Special issue of *Mississippi Quarterly* 66 (3).

Border Fictions

LILIANA C. GONZÁLEZ
California State University, Northridge, USA

Despite the US–Canada border being the longest international border in the world, the most politically, culturally, and historically prominent US national boundary is undoubtedly the US–Mexico border. The US annexation of Mexican territory in 1848 and the establishment of a new southern boundary led to the emergence of a unique US–Mexican border culture. Accordingly, border fictions suggest the very invention of the border and a history that tells of geographic intimacy, imperialism, and economic domination. Contemporary accounts of border experience are thus inevitably linked to a history of US aggression and the dispossession, lynching, and criminalization of Mexican and Indigenous peoples across the present US Southwest and Northern Mexico (Guidotti-Hernández 2011, p. 6). The creation of the notorious Mexican bandido narrative, for example, was an effort to legitimize the displacement and dispossession of Mexicans after 1848, resulting in a dominant, long-lasting image of Mexicans and Mexican Americans within the US collective imaginary (Berg 2002, p. 39). Since then, many border fictions have grappled with racist and limiting representations, at times engaging directly in countering stereotypes and at other times choosing more nuanced approaches to resisting such narratives. Border fictions are thus disputed zones in material and metaphoric terms. Like the US–Mexico border itself, border fictions have become more pronounced and contentious in the last forty years due to neoliberal economic policies like the Border Industrialization Program and the North American Free Trade Agreement (NAFTA), as well as the increased militarization of the border, including the push for the construction of a wall (Camacho 2005, p. 256).

This entry offers a brief and select account of contemporary border fictions within the historical context of the US–Mexico border. Just as the border straddles more than one national landscape, border fictions straddle more than a single medium, including historical narratives, self-narratives and popular stories, visual media, and music, especially *corridos* (the border ballad). In terms of literary genres, border fictions span semi-autobiographical and personal essays that fall somewhere between fiction and nonfiction as well as consisting of prose (novels and short stories) and poetry. Rather than emphasizing boundaries, contemporary understandings of borders call into question the traditional expectations of identity, language, culture, and literary genre. As such, border fiction, in its more expansive capacity, better articulates the lived experiences and narratives that are crucial to understanding border life and culture. Characteristic themes include language, biculturalism, and border crossings as well as thematic subgenres like drug (*narco*) narratives, which reiterate the violence of the US–Mexico border's contested terrain. While attached to geographic connotations, border fictions signal to the symbolical experience of border identities and marginality. Border fictions continue to be written from different perspectives, including not only border writers from Mexico and the United States, but also US white authors, Mexican writers, Chicanx, and Latinx authors.

WRITING AGAINST COLONIAL HISTORIES

Stories from within border life reject racist dominant narratives that differentiate border dwellers from US white populations and thus aim to rewrite the border, what José Pablo Villalobos calls "writing against the (other's) border" (2007, p. 35). Since the mid-1800s, an overabundance of fictionalized narratives and images have painted the US–Mexico border, border towns, and their people as wretched and deviant. For instance, Orson Welles's film noir classic from 1958, *Touch of Evil*, which depicts the main character Charlton Heston playing Mexican police detective Ramón Miguel Vargas in brownface, represents a dominant US outlook on the border that differentiates and distances itself from its proximity to Mexico. *Touch of Evil*, which is based on the Whit Masterson novel *Badge of Evil* (1956), in this respect, enables a US mainstream gaze that simultaneously rejects and needs the border's existence as a stand-in symbol of Mexico's supposed inferiority. As Villalobos argues, *Touch of Evil* "reminds us that the border is where the abject abounds" (2007, p. 35). Abjection is therefore understood within the film and many other US mainstream representations as being synonymous with the border as the material and symbolic buffer that protects the United States from Mexico. But the production of difference also aims to retroactively justify US imperialism and its continued economic dominance while simultaneously fabricating the necessity to curb migration from Mexico and beyond.

With the publication of Américo Paredes's *"With His Pistol in His Hand": A Border Ballad and Its Hero*, 1958 would prove to be a key year in the representation of the border – albeit with a counter-perspective. As Héctor Calderón describes it, the iconic border fiction is "a hybrid form, blurring the boundaries between disciplines: it is parts anthropology, folklore, history, and fiction," and it presents both a history and counter-story within the Rio Grande Valley which, since annexation, has perpetually been a zone of conflict and resistance (Calderón 1991, p. 16). As Calderón points out, some sections of the text serve as the basis for the 1983 film *The Ballad of Gregorio Cortez*, which signals to its continued relevance. *"With His Pistol in His Hand"* describes the "historical and social world of the Texas vaquero Gregorio Cortez" who was accused of killing a Texas sheriff in 1901 (Calderón 1991, p. 16). Paredes recreates the patriarchal ranch culture of the Rio Grande Valley and more importantly "rescued the border ballad from abandonment for study within both the Anglo and Hispanic academic worlds" (p. 15). Border ballads or *corridos*, both fictional and historically based folktales, centered rural patriarchal border heroes, including Gregorio Cortez and others such as Catarino Garza and Juan Cortina, who resisted and rebelled against the Texas Rangers and local sheriffs (p. 17). While these narratives of resistance toward US white and Anglo dominance represent a cultural tradition of struggle on the border, they often omitted or limited the role of women (Herrera-Sobek 1990, p. 54). On this note, a lesser known but notable narrative similar to Paredes's is *Caballero: A Historical Novel* (1996), by Jovita González and Eve Raleigh. Also set in South Texas during the mid-1800s, the novel portrays the struggle of Mexican Americans against the encroaching US white settlers. Although written during the 1930s, the novel suffered various failed attempts at publishing, most likely due to the prominent racist and sexist attitudes of the publishing industry at the time. The novel was finally published in 1996 by Texas A&M Press and co-edited by José E. Limón and María Cotera.

NEW BORDER CONSCIOUSNESS

The groundbreaking semi-autobiographical work of Gloria Anzaldúa, *Borderlands/La Frontera: The New Mestiza* (1987) represented a shift – a threshold for voicing a different kind of border experience – and gestured away from the patriarchal masculinist border heroes. While similar to Paredes's classic, as a hybrid text that replicates the border by merging different genres and styles, *Borderlands* pushes the bounds of identity, literature, and genre even further as a feminist and queer text that centers the Mexicana, Chicana, and Tejana border experience where language, sexuality, and gender are key to the development of a new border consciousness. Though Anzaldúa writes *Borderlands* from a contemporary perspective, she excavates the collective memory of Mexicans and their existence and resistance in the Rio Grande Valley. Anzaldúa weaves together a creative personal narrative of border experience that closely resembles the Latin American narrative genre *testimonio* (testimonial) (Calderón 1991, p. 25). Anzaldúa emphasizes that the borderlands not only are the physical manifestations of geopolitical boundaries but also indicate the psychological, sexual, and spiritual borders that expand well beyond the US Southwest.

Anzaldúa exquisitely represents the residual and emergent topics of border literature focusing on queer Chicana subjectivity on the margins of two worlds – one colonized by the other. Anzaldúa delivers a vivid image of US domination through a personal account of dispossession contextualized within a collective loss. As Sonia Saldívar-Hull contends, "But history in this New Mestiza narrative is not a univocal discursive exercise – in this new genre, a moving personal narrative about her Grandmother's dispossession occupies the same discursive space as a dry recitation of historical fact, while lyrics from a *corrido* about 'the lost land' butt up against a poetic rendition of an ethnocentric anglo historian's vision of U.S. domination over Mexico" (1999, p. 3). For Anzaldúa the border is "una herida abierta" (an open wound) "where the Third World grates against the first and bleeds. And before a scab forms it hemorrhages again, the lifeblood of two worlds merging to form a third country" (1987, p. 25). The wound as metaphor functions precisely because of the immense burden and pain the borderlands must contain, where the border as wound simultaneously embodies and represents "the third world" but also acts as a barrier to Latin America. Anzaldúa continues, "Borders are set up to define the places that are safe and unsafe, to distinguish *us* from *them*," echoing and critiquing the same narrative that we see in *Touch of Evil* (p. 25). But *Borderlands* does not remain at the level of critique; its poetic narrative does not shy away from boldly presenting a daring counternarrative within the context of US ethnocentric nationalism. In this regard, one of most symbolic and consequential sections in *Borderlands*, "How to tame a wild tongue," is a distinctive contribution to conceptualizing language and resistance in the borderlands. Anzaldúa argues that language is one of the ways in which US imperialism has ensured its domination over Chicano/as and Mexicana/os. Anzaldúa begins this section by citing artist Ray Gwyn Smith, "Who is to say that robbing a people of its language is less violent than war?" (p. 75), and incisively critiques how border and Chicanx language practices are chastised by both US Anglo and Mexican monolingual speakers of English and Spanish, something she calls "linguistic terrorism" (p. 80). "How to tame a wild tongue" has been a blueprint for understanding language practices and critically analyzing language politics, whether it be in relation to psychological, cultural, literary, or material borderlands. Indeed, Anzaldúa's impact is vast across the thematic and theoretical domains helping to complicate expectations within academic disciplines and literary genres. The importance of Anzaldúa's legacy in advancing Chicana feminism as praxis and border studies as a field cannot be understated. Anzaldúa's work has had particular significance for border literature, carving out a space for border fiction like Lucrecia Guerrero's short story collection *Chasing Shadows* (2000) and Ito Romo's novel *El Puente/The Bridge* (2000), among others.

Anzaldúa was a prolific editor of several influential volumes including *This Bridge Called My Back: Writings by Radical Women of Color* (1981), co-edited with Cherríe Moraga, and border fictions for children, such as *Prietita Has a Friend* (1991), *Friends from the Other Side – Amigos del otro lado* (1993), and *Prietita y la llorona* (1996). These books were not only bilingual, but also reflected border and bicultural stories that spoke to the experiences of brown children in the United States. Literary critic Tey Diana Rebolledo, for instance, observes that as an elementary school teacher at the time, Anzaldúa "understood that the bilingual and migrant children she taught needed to see their voices reflected in the stories they heard and read" (2006, p. 280). Anzaldúa's commitment to writing children's border fiction encapsulates and emphasizes both her influence and impact in the forging of a new consciousness around border reality and experience across the different yet connected fields of theory, literature, and education.

BORDER FICTIONS AS *RECONQUISTA* (RECONQUEST) NARRATIVE

Despite the influential work of authors like Anzaldúa, contemporary representations of the border have, nevertheless, continued to be written from an outsider's perspective. For example, Cormac McCarthy's writing has been influential in the shaping of border narratives and embodies the "outsider" writer subjectivity as a US white American not from the border. McCarthy's works include the so-called border trilogy which consists of *All the Pretty Horses* (1992), *The Crossing* (1994), and *Cities of the Plain* (1998), novels which prominently feature themes related to the US–Mexico border. *No Country for Old Men* (2005), published several years later, is not part of the border trilogy but also takes place on the border. The novel, which is set during the 1980s and was made into a film by the Coen brothers in 2007, presents some of the quintessential border themes of violence, drug cartels, and "disputed" territories. The opening scenes of the film show an arid and desolate terrain which serves as the setting to the bloody aftermath of a Mexican drug deal gone wrong, signaling to the violent context of the plot and the southwest Texas desert. This emphasis on violence is confirmed by several events in the novel and film's plot, including the ruthless actions of the hired killer Anton Chigurh, echoed by Sheriff Bell's uncle telling Bell that the region has always been violent. The region's violence is of course not coincidental but rather a product of sustained conflict and territory disputes from the violent confrontations between the Indigenous peoples and New Spain to the forceful displacement of both Mexican and Indigenous populations by white settlers. The novel and film are exemplary portrayals that remind the US-identified reader and spectator that the borderlands are still very much contested terrains that must be reconquered over and over again. The film, like the novel, fits perfectly into the modern Western genre where Mexicans are equated with drug traffickers and replace Native Americans as the archetypal enemy in the Wild West narrative. It is not difficult to see how *No Country for Old Men* (2007) replicates the Mexican bandit stereotypes and is further aggravated by the portrayal and embodied violence of the racially ambiguous hitman Anton Chigurh, played by Spanish actor Javier Bardem. Border representations like McCarthy's enact the "reconquering" and "securing" of the border through the continuous adaptation and restaging of US expansionism and the Mexican American War. While McCarthy's *No Country for Old Men* is illustrative of modern reconquest narratives of the frontier, there are other examples of US fiction that reproduce this narrative in its various iterations. For instance, *Streets of Laredo* (1993) and *Comanche Moon* (1997), by Larry McMurtry, as well as *Strong Justice* (2010), by Jon Land, and *El Paso*, by Winston Groom, posit Mexicans as the imminent threat of the US–Mexico border, a danger which must be subdued by an apparent US predisposition for law and order.

THE VIOLENCE OF THE BORDER: NARRATIVES ON CROSSING, FEMINICIDE, AND THE DRUG TRADE

The fervent claim "[w]e didn't cross the border, the border crossed us" holds true for those whom Anzaldúa would refer to as "los atravesados" (the crossed ones), Mexican nationals who found themselves living on US territory after the Treaty of Guadalupe Hidalgo. It is especially significant for Indigenous communities like the Yaqui of Arizona and Sonora that were divided once the international border was drawn (Anzaldúa 1987, p. 25). Yet the phrase also stands in relation to the imposition of geopolitical borders across continents intended to slow the free movement of people, which has happened for hundreds of years. Border fictions in the contemporary era continue to incorporate border crossing accounts; however, the conditions of border experience have drastically transformed. The effects of neoliberal policies since the 1960s are reflected in depictions from and about the border with narratives about narcotrafficking, "the war on drugs," poverty, mass migration, and feminicide shaping the core of border fictions.

Border Crossing and Migrant Narratives

In recent years, authors like Reyna Grande, with *The Distance Between Us: A Memoir* (2012), Marcelo Hernández Castillo, with *Children of the Land* (2020), and Karla Cornejo Villavicencio, with *The Undocumented Americans* (2020), have forged a space not only for attesting to the difficulties involved with border crossings but also for the telling of the day-to-day experiences of living as an undocumented immigrant in the United States as a direct result of geopolitical borders. Similarly, narratives like Oscar Martínez's *The Beast: Riding the Rails and Dodging Narcos on the Migrant Trail* (2013) detail the journey that many Central American migrants take along "La Bestia" (The Beast), a freight train route that begins in the Mexican Southern State of Chiapas, which borders Guatemala. Martínez's account details the hardships that many migrants face as they ride the train, often dealing with the dangers of injury or even death. Though Central American migration has been prominent since the late 1970s due to civil wars and civilian suppression, especially in Guatemala, Honduras, and El Salvador, recent border migrant fictions signal the intensification of border securitization, xenophobic sentiments, and harsher immigration laws that deny political asylum and detain Central American migrant families and children.

One of the most influential border crossing narratives is Luis Alberto Urrea's *The Devil's Highway* (2005), a border crossing account of the Wellton 26 – a group of twenty-six migrants who in 2001 attempted to cross the Arizona–Sonora border within the Sonoran Desert, one of the hottest and driest landscapes in North America. Urrea, who grew up on the US–Mexico border between Tijuana, Baja California, and San Diego, California, has written extensively about the hardships and complexities of border experience. Urrea's narration, a blend of fact and fiction, gives us a glimpse into the men's lives, their hometowns and families, and their distressing journey through the desert, a trek that only twelve survived. Urrea's chronicle emphasizes the dire conditions of border crossing as a result of US immigration and border policies, including "Operation Gatekeeper" (1994). Implemented during the Clinton era to "deter" migrants from crossing into the United States, Operation Gatekeeper instead forced migrants to cross along the harshest desert sections of the US–Mexico border, resulting in thousands of deaths from dehydration and heat exhaustion. Through harrowing details, Urrea reminds the readers that migrants must not only face the environmental hardship of the desert but must also deal with the US Border Patrol, possible desertion by coyotes (hired professional crossers), and criminal organizations.

In his reading of Urrea's *The Devil's Highway*, Abraham Acosta argues that Urrea's narrative reveals the Arizona–Sonora border region, rather than the more policed regions of the border, as constituting a real zone of indistinction that renders life as bare, life that can be lost without consequence (2014, p. 225). He writes, "Thus conceived, the events named after the Wellton 26 reveal a critical demonstration of the U.S.–Mexico border's juridical form; their errant itinerary serves to trace this border's innermost workings and processes. Urrea's narrative thus doubles as an attempt to critically grapple with the state of exception that exists along the southern Arizona border, where abandonment and not the application of law is sovereign, ultimately resulting in the deaths of the Wellton 26" (p. 225). For Acosta, abandonment in the desert heat to die indicates that the group of migrants were never considered as a sacrificial loss by either the United States or Mexico. Consequently, the adversity of border crossing expressed by works such as *The Devil's Highway*, in the context of NAFTA and Operation Gatekeeper, have emphasized the material and symbolic linkage between the US–Mexico border, the desert, violence, and death. Unfortunately, as the US–Mexico border's troubled history has dictated, the connection extends, in more than one way.

Border Writing on Feminicide

Although gender violence is endemic to patriarchal society, it undoubtedly becomes aggravated in zones of heightened neoliberal trade and transnational crossings. Since the early 1990s, hundreds of young women have been reported as missing in Ciudad Juárez, Chihuahua, Mexico, a city that borders El Paso, Texas (Monárrez Fragoso *et al*. 2015, p. 13). Though there are various journalistic accounts of feminicide and gender violence on the US–Mexico border, such as Sergio González Rodríguez's *Huesos en el desierto* [Bones in the Desert] (2002), there are also fictional narratives such as Roberto Bolaño's *2666* (2004) and Alicia Gaspar de Alba's *Desert Blood: The Juárez Murders* (2005). As the titles suggest, the Chihuahuan desert is center stage and witness to the corruption that reproduces such brutal violence. Border fictions that represent feminicide in Ciudad Juárez critique the conditions that have allowed such violence to occur and endure by exploring some of the theories and narratives that seek to explain the murders and lack of justice. The use of the term "feminicide" by scholars and activists, rather than "femicide," attempts to address the systemic prevalence of violence against women as foregrounded by the policing of sexuality and gender expression (Bueno-Hansen 2010, p. 304). Deficient forensic technology, the drug trade, machismo, transnational economic interests, as well as the complicity of police are cited as some of the reasons behind the unresponsiveness of investigative practices which have permitted the murders to continue. *Desert Blood: The Juárez Murders*, for instance, describes a sex-trafficking conspiracy between US Border Patrol and Mexican police that indicates the complicity of both the Mexican and US governments. Because many of the victims have been migrant, dark-skinned, working-class women employed in the maquiladoras (border factories), theories have specified maquiladora bus drivers and the employers themselves as the ones responsible for the killings. Yet precisely because of its location on the US–Mexico border, theories have also signaled drug cartels and US citizens crossing into Ciudad Juárez as the culprits behind the horrific violence. Border fictions that portray the murders of young women in Ciudad Juárez, in effect, not only become a way to bring awareness but also manifest a direct challenge to the inaction of Mexican authorities and complicity of US and other international economic interests.

Narco Fictions

González Rodríguez's journalistic account *Huesos en el desierto* emphasizes the magnitude of gender violence on the US–Mexico border not only as a product of misogyny and patriarchy but also as directly related to the surge of drug trafficking. As maquiladoras became more abundant with NAFTA, so did the illicit drug trade (Malkin 2001, p. 120). With increased pressure from the United States, Mexico, in 2006, declared a war on the drug trade. The subsequent "war on drugs" was, however, a contemporary iteration or phase of the larger "war on drugs" that began during the Nixon era with the creation of the Drug Enforcement Administration (DEA) in 1973. While drug trafficking narratives (narco narratives) have been popularized in the US mainstream media (TV series, films, music, and literature) within the last fifteen years, narco narratives, like the drug trade, have been historically associated with the US–Mexico border since the early to mid-twentieth century. Some of the earliest border fictions about the US–Mexico drug trade were *narco corridos* (drug trade ballads) that narrated bloody confrontations between Mexican drug dealers and police forces on both sides of the border. Since the 1980s, *narco corridos* have grown to the extent of including varied subgenres; for instance, one subgenre depicts more violent scenarios while another portrays the lifestyle associated with drug trafficking. Similarly, narco narratives have followed the *corrido* tradition and are wide ranging in depicting the drug trade, the violence of the war on drugs, narco lifestyle, as well as the social and political context associated with the drug trade. Narco narratives told from the Mexican perspective either explicitly or implicitly feature the US–Mexico border and borderlands. For example, Víctor Hugo Rascón Banda's *Contrabando* [Contraband] (1993) tells the story of three women from the Mexican border state of Chihuahua who are involved in narcotrafficking. *El Amante de Janis Joplin* [Janis Joplin's Lover] (2003), by acclaimed narco narrative author Elmer Mendoza, follows the protagonist David Valenzuela and his escape from the grasp of Sinaloa drug dealers. The novel eventually sees him travel to the United States and land a pitching tryout for the Los Angeles Dodgers. At the same time, Chicana/o/x, fronteriza/o/x (Mexican border dwellers), and US white authors have also written about drug culture in relation to the US–Mexico border from within the United States. Chicano border author Alberto Ríos's story "The Child" narrates the journey of two women traveling a bus route north in the Mexican border state of Sonora from Guaymas to Hermosillo and then to Nogales, which borders Nogales, Arizona (Ríos 1984). The two women are concerned with a child that appears to be sick, only to find out at the end that the child was deceased and had been filled with drugs to cross into the United States. The story reflects a common route taken by border dwellers and, as Mary Pat Brady argues, "[I]n portraying the bus ride's typicality, 'The Child' sets up the horror of its closing revelation, which makes the trip anything but typical" (Brady 2002, p. 185). Published in 1984, the story carries an implied resistance toward making narco narratives typical by emphasizing the horrific image of the lifeless child. Yet the proliferation of narco narratives since then has complicated any sort of rejection toward the normalization of common themes and stereotypes. Narco narratives in many ways have been an avenue for American exceptionalism and righteousness to flourish, leading more US white authors to write narco fiction. Don Winslow's *Power of the Dog* (2005), for example, tells the story of Art Keller, a half-white half-Mexican detective, a larger-than-life San Diego, California native attempting to single-handedly bring down a Mexican cartel. *Power of the Dog* later became the first part of Winslow's "Power of the Dog: Cartel Series," which also includes *The Cartel* (2015) and *The Border* (2019). Other examples of US white authors writing fiction related to drug trafficking and the drug war are Christopher Irvin's *Federales* (2014) and the controversial *American Dirt* (2019) by Jeanine Cummins.

CONTEMPORARY CHICANX BORDER FICTIONS

Several contemporary writers have taken a feminist and queer stance to counter the official sexist and racist historical records of the US Southwest. Chicana and Tejana Emma Pérez, in particular, has written queer counternarratives, including novels, such as *Gulf Dreams* (1996), as well as nonfiction works, such as *The Decolonial Imaginary: Writing Chicanas into History* (1999). Her novel *Forgetting the Alamo, or, Blood Memory* (2010) is the story of Micaela Campos, a lesbian *vaquera* (cowgirl) from Texas during the nineteenth century. By remembering the racially and ethnically diverse groups that inhabited Texas during this period and the violence they endured, Pérez not only counters the dominant US narrative about the Alamo but also challenges the erasure of queer Tejanas from history. In this way, Pérez extends the debate of the US–Mexico borderlands as contested terrain by intensifying the confrontation of history that vilifies queers and people of color. Other renowned Chicana authors who have written border fictions include Ana Castillo and Graciela Limón. Ana Castillo's *The Guardians* (2008) is set in a New Mexican border town that portrays the reality and effects of border life and Graciela Limón's novel *The River Flows North* (2009) renders the border crossing journey of a group of immigrants.

LIFE ON THE BORDER

Despite the abundance of representations of the border as violent, border literature also encompasses works which wittingly avoid depictions of violence and instead showcase the quotidian experiences of life on the border. Memoirs have been one way in which writers have chosen to portray border culture. While memoirs are typically considered nonfiction, border memoirs are hybrid works that blur genre lines and dialogue with historical "fictions" about the border. For example, authors like Norma Elia Cantú and Alberto Ríos have centered their most celebrated writings on portraying their own experiences within the rich cultural setting of the US–Mexico border. Cantú's memoir *Canícula: Snapshots of a Girlhood en la Frontera* (1995) is a narrative album of Cantú's upbringing in the Laredo/Nuevo Laredo border. *Canícula*, which Cantú herself defines as a "fictional auto-ethnobiography," expresses dynamic storytelling through photographs and fictionalized memories (Durán 2007, p. 70). Cantú's memoir represents a unique look at a girl's coming of age during the mid-twentieth century on the border, a rarity in comparison to the abundance of coming-of-age boyhood stories.

In *Capirotada: A Nogales Memoir* (1999), Alberto Ríos also uses photographs. *Capirotada* is in reference to a traditional Mexican dish popular in Sonora which is made from a varied mix of ingredients that in many ways resembles the diverse experience of living on the US–Mexico border. Border scholar Javier Durán notes that self-narratives have become an important genre for writing about border reality. Durán argues that "Contemporary border writing shows that life narratives and autobiographical texts are functional vehicles that allow readers to explore the complex negotiations involved in border identity positioning" (2007, p. 70). For Durán, Ríos's allusion to food on the border "re-creates an autotopography that links the materiality of food to an extended commemorative experience" (p. 69). Despite the lack of direct textual reference to the photographs, Ríos implicitly connects the different parts of *Capirotada* through the photographs in which he details the everyday joys of border living (p. 70). In this way, the border stories of Cantú and Ríos, as opposed to the border narratives of Paredes, Anzaldúa, or Pérez, take a more subtle approach to a representation of the border that implicitly counters the dominant historical narrative.

SEE ALSO: Castillo, Ana; Literature of the Americas; McCarthy, Cormac; Mixed-Genre Fiction; Queer and LGBT Fiction; Urrea, Luis Alberto

REFERENCES

Acosta, Abraham. (2014). *Thresholds of Illiteracy: Theory, Latin America, and the Crisis of Resistance*. New York: Fordham University Press.

Anzaldúa, Gloria E. (1987). *Borderlands/La Frontera: The New Mestiza*. San Francisco: Aunt Lute Books.

Berg, Charles Ramírez. (2002). *Latino Images in Film: Stereotypes, Subversion, and Resistance*. Austin: University of Texas Press.

Brady, Mary Pat. (2002). *Extinct Lands, Temporal Geographies: Chicana Literature and the Urgency of Space*. Durham, NC: Duke University Press.

Bueno-Hansen, Pascha. (2010). *Feminicidio*: Making the most of an "empowered term." In: *Terrorizing Women: Feminicide in the Americas* (ed. Rosa-Linda Fregoso and Cynthia Bejarano), 290–311. Durham, NC: Duke University Press.

Calderón, Héctor. (1991). Texas border literature: cultural transformation and historical reflection in the works of Américo Paredes, Rolando Hinojosa and Gloria Anzaldúa. *Dispositio* 16 (41): 13–27.

Camacho, Alicia Schmidt. (2005). Ciudadana X: gender violence and the denationalization of women's rights in Ciudad Juarez, Mexico. *CR: The New Centennial Review* 5 (1): 255–292.

Coen, Joel and Coen, Ethan. (dirs.) (2007). *No Country for Old Men*. Miramax Films.

Durán, Javier. (2007). Border voices: life writings and self-representation of the U.S.–Mexico *frontera*. In: *Border Transits: Literature and Culture Across the Line* (ed. Ana María Manzanas), 61–78. Amsterdam: Rodopi.

Guidotti-Hernández, Nicole M. (2011). *Unspeakable Violence: Remapping U.S. and Mexican National Imaginaries*. Durham, NC: Duke University Press.

Herrera-Sobek, María. (1990). *The Mexican Corrido: A Feminist Analysis*. Bloomington: Indiana University Press.

Malkin, Victoria. (2001). Narcotrafficking, migration, and modernity in rural Mexico. *Latin American Perspectives* 28 (4): 101.

Monárrez Fragoso, Julia Estela et al. (2015). *Vidas y territorios en busca de justicia*. Tijuana: El Colegio de la Frontera Norte.

Rebolledo, Tey Diana. (2006). Prietita y el otro lado: Gloria Anzaldúa's literature for children. *PMLA* 121 (1): 279–284.

Ríos, Alberto. (1984). The child. In: *The Iguana Killer: Twelve Stories of the Heart*, 12–21. Lewiston, ID: Blue Moon and Confluence Press.

Saldívar-Hull, Sonia. (1999). Introduction to the second edition. In: *Borderlands/La Frontera: The New Mestiza* (by Gloria E. Anzaldúa), 2nd ed., 1–15. San Francisco: Aunt Lute Books.

Villalobos, José Pablo. (2007). Up against the border: a literary response. *Critical Approaches to Ethnic American Literature* 2: 35–300.

Welles, Orson. (dir.) (1958). *Touch of Evil*. Universal-International.

FURTHER READING

Castillo, Debra A. and Córdoba, María Socorro Tabuenca. (2002). *Border Women: Writing from la Frontera*. Minneapolis: University of Minnesota Press.

Gaspar de Alba, Alicia and Guzmán, Georgina. (2010). *Making a Killing: Femicide, Free Trade, and la Frontera*. Austin: University of Texas Press.

Luiselli, Valeria. (2020). *Lost Children Archive*. London: Vintage Books.

Sadowski-Smith, Claudia. (2008). *Border Fictions: Globalization, Empire, and Writing at the Boundaries of the United States*. Charlottesville: University of Virginia Press.

Saldívar-Hull, Sonia. (2000). *Feminism on the Border: Chicana Gender Politics and Literature*. Berkeley: University of California Press.

Boyle, T.C.

VERENA ADAMIK
University of Potsdam, Germany

T.C. Boyle, or Thomas Coraghessan Boyle, is probably best known for his 1995 novel *Tortilla Curtain*, which quickly became a staple of high school and college syllabi. *Tortilla Curtain* deftly illustrates what Boyle does best: acerbically tracing the irrationality that governs human thought and the resulting contradictory and often unethical behavior (mostly in relation to xenophobia, environmentalism, and gender). Despite often casting a critical eye over US society, Boyle's works are accessible reads with fast-paced and eventful plots. This combination has produced a number of international bestsellers. In fact, Boyle is so popular in Germany that translations of his works have been published before the original versions came out in English (Clement 2018). However, his talent for depicting the impotence of reason in the face of base desires, selfishness, group dynamics, and indoctrinated ideologies is also a weakness: at times, Boyle's satire reproduces what it means to criticize, coming close to naturalizing the hedonistic, prejudiced, and emotionally charged behavior of his characters.

The self-styled "wise guy" and "punk" (Boyle 1999) was born 1948 as Thomas John Boyle in Peekskill, New York, where he grew up in a working-class household. Autobiographical elements can often be found in his fiction: young people with bleak prospects, drug use, and addiction are recurring themes that draw on Boyle's own experiences (both of his parents were alcoholics and Boyle himself is no stranger to a variety of substances). Like some of his literary influences, such as William Faulkner and Gabriel García Márquez, he frequently refers to a fictional town that is a thinly veiled version of his hometown: Peterskill (e.g. *World's End* [1987]; *Drop City* [2003]). He became interested in literature and writing when in college. After receiving his BA in English and History, Boyle continued his education at the Iowa Writers' Workshop at the University of Iowa, where he earned an MFA and PhD. During his studies, Boyle met numerous authors who came to affect his writing style, including Vance Bourjaily, Raymond Carver, and John Irving.

In particular, John Cheever – who advised Boyle against "fads" – had a significant impact on his writing. Indeed, Boyle often stresses that literature should be, above all else, entertaining. As a public persona, Boyle is something of an entertainer. He does not shy away from interviews and photographs, he dons eccentric outfits, discusses openly his writing process, gives animated readings, and posts regularly on social media.

Much of Boyle's works can be classified as "historiographical metafiction" (Freese 2017). This term, coined by Linda Hutcheon, describes postmodern novels that include real-world historic events, fictional elements, intertextual references, and metafictional statements. Historiographical metafiction thus contests "both any naive realist concept of representation and any equally naive textualist or formalist assertions of the total separation of art from the world" (Hutcheon 1989). Some of the authors that Hutcheon gives as examples, such as John Barth, Márquez, and Thomas Pynchon, are amongst those that Boyle himself has listed as his literary influences (Boyle 1999). However, Boyle's plots are not as convoluted and his style is not as experimental as commonly found in postmodern historiographical metafiction, his writing being more straightforward. He understands himself to write in the tradition of Cheever, as well as Flannery O'Connor, and popular Victorian authors, especially Charles Dickens. Nonetheless, the opaque relationship between fact and fiction in his works betrays the strong impact postmodern writers had on him.

Throughout his oeuvre, Boyle consciously plays with the idea that history is always also a narrative ("History on Wheels" [2001]). He does this by invoking generic conventions corresponding to the period and/or topic he engages with. In his debut novel, *Water Music* (1981), set in the late eighteenth and early nineteenth century, he draws on various conventions of eighteenth- and nineteenth-century novels, and travel writing. In *Budding Prospects* (1984), tellingly subtitled *A Pastoral*, he mimics the "pastoral" mode of idealizing agrarian life (Gleason 2009, p. 49), an idea that accompanied westward expansion, capitalist endeavors of land speculation, and various back-to-the-land discourses; this entanglement resurfaces in the novel. The frontier romance á la James Fenimore Cooper and more-or-less factual frontier stories underlie *World's End* (1987) and *The Harder They Come* (2015) (D'Haen 1994; Freese 2017), both of which are concerned at least in part with the national mythology of the United States. *Tortilla Curtain* invokes John Steinbeck's novels and, in this way, challenges the historical amnesia that underlies nativism. *A Friend of The Earth* (2000), an ecocritical work of speculative fiction revolving around an environmentalist who engages in acts of sabotage (so-called monkey wrenching), refers to Edward Abbey's *The Monkey Wrench Gang* (1975) as well as US nature writing from Henry David Thoreau and John Muir. When portraying the hippie counterculture in *Drop City*, he mixes traditions of nature writing with the style of the beat poets and Aldous Huxley. Two novels featuring controversial scientists – *The Inner Circle* (2004) about Alfred Kinsey's research into sexual practices and *Outside Looking In* (2019) about Timothy Leary's experiments with LSD – both mimic the language of scientific logs, which stands in stark contrast to the nonconventional self-experimentation conducted by the main characters. *The Terranauts* (2016) ponders the interrelations between ecological consciousness, science, and media spectacle by giving scandalous insights into the thoughts of the wannabe science-stars. In many of these novels, national US myths come under scrutiny. Boyle combines form and content in a way that draws attention to how the conventions of fiction, nonfiction, and historiography are strongly entangled with ideology.

Scholarly publications on Boyle's work generally include insights into Boyle's sources and the extent of his historical (un)faithfulness. The resulting effects of these changes merit further consideration. For example, the fictional caprices of the characters in *Water Music* suggest that the allegedly enlightened English society of the late Gregorian era acts upon irrational impulses such as greed, sexual desires, and romantic infatuation. Their capacity for self-reflection is minimal and what is left is a distorted worldview; they ignore the importance of chance and the existence of the preternatural even when the evidence is right in front of them. In *The Road to Wellville* (1993), events at Battle Creek Sanitarium are dramatically arranged to highlight their absurdity, showcasing that allegedly scientific health fads are part fantastical concoctions of fanatics, part sexual fetish, part capitalist calculation. The eponymous commune in *Drop City* is modeled after a real-life utopian community – Morning Star. While critics have accused Boyle of emphasizing the negative aspects of such communities, the book ends with happy couples recreating a modernized frontier romance, a plot twist that promotes the very fantasy of living off-the-grid that it initially satirizes. *The Harder They Come* features a fictionalized version of Aaron Bassler, a man who enjoyed short infamy in 2011 when he, in the throes of psychosis, shot two people, prompting a police manhunt that ended over a month later when he was killed by a SWAT team. As Peter Freese (2017) notes, Boyle here arranges more-or-less historic events so that they spell a "dire warning" of the violence underlying the US narrative. For example, the paranoid and hallucinating protagonist conjures the nineteenth-century pioneer John Colter as a role model in order to justify his increasingly antisocial behavior. This connection of national myth and violence is further emphasized by his romantic partner, who identifies as a sovereign citizen, and a father who is celebrated after he uses his military training to kill a man with his bare hands. *The Terranauts* revolves around a fictionalized version of Biosphere 2 – a research facility in Arizona which attempted to determine the viability of humans living within a closed ecological system. While basing the novel on the biosphere's two missions, it exaggerates the personal drama, managerial authoritarianism, and media spectacle, thus questioning the seemingly noble motivations behind scientific endeavors.

Here emerges one of Boyle's main interests: idealism and the complexities of effecting change; or rather, the problems that arise in the realization of idealistic visions. Scientists and reformers are not (exclusively) driven by the thirst for knowledge and improving the world but (also) by a desire for money, fame, and/or sex. Conversely, grand schemes are thwarted by mundane and chance occurrences, regardless of high expectations, noble intentions, and brilliant visions. Boyle also frequently reiterates this in short stories (e.g. "The Descent of Man" [1979], "The Siskiyou, July 1989" [2011]). One obstacle that many of his protagonists face is their own subject position. In Boyle's novels, consumerist and national ideologies, gender roles, class, racial identity, and genealogies continue to inform, or even determine, the thoughts and actions of supposed outsiders and revolutionaries. Thus, characters often change their names or dissociate completely. In this, one may detect a level of self-deprecating humor, as the author changed his name from Thomas John Boyle to Thomas Coraghessan Boyle in his late teens and then shortened it to T.C. Boyle when he was around 50.

The counterculture of the 1960s and 1970s looms large in much of Boyle's work. Even when hippies are not part of the narrative, his work is full of their associations: drugs, sexual liberation, and environmental activism. Many of his characters are disillusioned or delusional, or prone to be manipulated by a charismatic but ultimately authoritarian leader – a hallmark of Boyle's writing. Seemingly inevitable, doubts and disappointments then come to undermine supposedly firmly held convictions. As the revolutionary momentum of the 1960s subsided, it is tempting to read these motifs as Boyle's judgment of his generation. Yet Boyle does not insist on the binary between a counterculture and a "co-opting" mainstream, between "authentic" and "phony." Rather, his work consistently portrays people as products of their cultural environments, even when they withdraw into their own microcosms and disavow "the old" in favor of "the new" – be that off-the-grid hippies, survivalists, nineteenth-century reformers, adventurous explorers, scientists, or environmentalists.

Another recurring theme is the cognitive dissonance of privileged White men who seek to justify their prejudice and aggression. Here, a complex entanglement of environmentalism, class, gender, and race emerges. In these satirical portrayals of subject position and of human irrationality, Boyle rarely offers an alternative, resulting in an unsettling quality, which many contemporary reviewers have praised. Nevertheless, Boyle's cynicism flirts with defeatism in a way that risks effectively normalizing the status quo. For example, his portrayal of gender roles both satirizes power imbalances and stereotypes, and it normalizes them – as in the case of multiple rape scenes (for example, "Greasy Lake" [1985], "Rara Avis" [1998]). Similarly, men tend to fall into one of the two categories: either they ruthlessly pursue fame and sexual pleasures, or they are reliable partners and typical "good guys." When Boyle writes about sex it is often weirdly comic, especially if practices diverge even the slightest from heteronormative ideals. Boyle's characters often engage in more or less tabooed fetishes and practices: group sex, sex in public, voyeurism, bondage, anal play, enemas, and even bestiality. Despite this, his characters are mostly heterosexual and subscribe to heteronormativity in their daily life. In the end, most protagonists gravitate towards traditional relationships and family structures. Typically, the more reliable men are providing for their families, while women have a caring side to them and relish the thought of becoming mothers. In his more hopeful novels, these nuclear contingents act as a protective space in which the progressive ideals can survive in a moderate way (Gleason 2009, p. 67). In other novels and short stories, ideological realignments or turnabouts are the subject of mockery.

Race is another aspect in which Boyle's work is ambiguous: on the one hand, the inner monologue of privileged White characters often reveals their irrational, thus all the more emotionally charged, racism. On the other, minorities are largely depicted through the eyes of White people and rendered as "Other" – stereotyped as threatening, superstitious, old-fashioned, poor, criminal, and impulsive. In addition, Boyle selectively evokes traits of minority literature (bilingualism and engaging with territorial discourses; D'Haen 1994) but then gives such a bleak outlook on racial relations that his work tends to disempower his minority characters.

Boyle rarely delivers poetic justice, despite all the verbal acrobatics, whimsical characterizations, and improbable plotlines. Many of Boyle's works leave a powerfully acerbic aftertaste. The absence of a clear critical voice and firm moral statement at times calls into question whether the works are to deliver criticism at all. For example, in his first novel, *Water Music*, Boyle mimics the imperial discourse so effectively that the narrative reproduces orientalist and colonial stereotypes. Africans in the novel are not fully developed characters. The only exception is Johnson: a native African, who was enslaved in America before becoming an English gentleman, to be then imprisoned in a penal colony, before returning home to his tribe. Yet, he seems accessible largely because he received, and truly relished, his education, which was defined by the ethos of the European Enlightenment. The female characters also cannot fight their historic predetermination: one gives up science for her domestic role, another eventually kills herself, like the heroine of many a British eighteenth- and nineteenth century novel (even though the narrator initially assures the reader that she is cut from a different cloth, her tragic demise is a literary cliché). *Drop City* makes clear that racial prejudice persists in the progressive counterculture, despite the ideals of its hippy characters. Yet, the novel itself replicates a White gaze on African Americans and Native Americans, and it features a scene in which a Black man rapes an underage White girl. The only man who tries to intervene is Pan: White, somewhat racist, and generally morally dubious. Ironically, his community condemns him because he is suspected of having been an accomplice in this sexual assault, but he is never confronted about the sexual transgressions of which he is actually guilty; he manipulates his girlfriend to perform sexual acts. *The Harder They Come*, just as the iconic Jamaican movie of the same name, begins with a bus-driving scene featuring reggae music and criminal youths. But the novel then takes on a White, US perspective on the Caribbean and moves on to the USA and the toxic grand narrative of macho frontier individualism. In a metafictional comment typical for Boyle, one of the characters even notes that the story of the dead Caribbean youth is completely left out of the rest of the work. Instead, it is the White, schizophrenic protagonist who takes the place of the main character of this book named after a Jamaican movie. Questions abound: why this translation? Why cite the movie in the title and in the opening scenes and then focus solely on White US Americans? And why the crude, stereotypical portrayals of Latinos?

Tortilla Curtain, probably Boyle's most successful novel to date, is an exception in that it does take a clear moral stand. By narrating the perspective of a White, well-to-do couple, Boyle explores the social dynamics of their community rife with hypocrisy, moral myopia, and xenophobia. These US Americans are afraid to lose their amenities to the very people whose exploitation enables their lifestyle. The object of their anxiety is represented by a Mexican couple trying to make a living in the USA. This couple does not present a threat at all, and their story is heart-wrenching. Undocumented and homeless, they are horribly abused by every person who has more power than they do – which is everyone. Yet, even at their most desperate, they do not resort to anything more than petty crime. Nonetheless, the narrative focus remains on the White, male perspective and the Mexicans are never developed beyond the confines of stereotypes, so that a certain ambiguity remains (Paul 2001).

Boyle excels at illustrating the complexity of decision-making, especially when race, class, sexual orientation, and gender are involved. Yet, critical work on Boyle still needs to unpack more thoroughly how the self-styled "punk," for all his fascination with quirky outsiders, reproduces a rather conservative normativity, and how his cynical character portrayals run the risk of suggesting that idealism, activism, and progressive change are futile.

SEE ALSO: Barth, John; Carver, Raymond; Ecocriticism and Environmental Fiction; Irving, John; Pynchon, Thomas

REFERENCES

Boyle, T.C. (1999). This monkey, my back. https://www.tcboyle.com/author/essay.html (accessed July 5, 2021).

Clement, Kai. (2018). Schriftsteller T.C. Boyle wird 70: "Zeile für Zeile – diesem Fluss folge ich." *Studio 9.* https://www.deutschlandfunkkultur.de/schriftsteller-t-c-boyle-wird-70-zeile-fuer-zeile-diesem.2165.de.html?dram:article_id=434809 (accessed August 25, 2021).

D'Haen, Theo. (1994). The return of history and the minorization of New York: T. Coraghessan Boyle and Richard Russo. *Revue française d'études américaines* 62: 393–403.

Freese, Peter. (2017). T.C. Boyle's *The Harder they Come*: violence in America. *Anglia* 135: 511–542.

Gleason, Paul William. (2009). *Understanding T.C. Boyle.* Columbia: South Carolina University Press.

Hutcheon, Linda. (1989). Historiographic metafiction parody and the intertextuality of history. In: *Intertextuality and Contemporary American Fiction* (ed. Patrick O'Donnell and Robert C. Davis), 3–32. Baltimore: Johns Hopkins University Press.

Paul, Heike. (2001). Old, new and "neo" immigrant fictions in American literature: the immigrant presence in David Guterson's *Snow Falling on Cedars* and T.C. Boyle's *The Tortilla Curtain. Amerikastudien / American Studies* 46 (2): 249–265.

FURTHER READING

Kollin, Susan. (2012). North Alaska and other bad trips in T.C. Boyle's *Drop City. Genre: Forms of Discourse and Culture* 45: 329–350.

Madinabeitia, Monika. (2013). The myth of the frontier in T.C. Boyle's *The Tortilla Curtain.* In:

A Contested West. New Readings of Place in Western American Literature (ed. Martin Simonson, David Río, and Amaia Ibarraran), 189–205. Vitoria-Gastiez, Spain: Portal Editions.

Palmerino, Gregory. (2017). "This was nature": growing death and the necrophilous character in T.C. Boyle's "Greasy Lake". *The Explicator* 75: 239–241.

Ramuglia, River. (2018). Tearing down the greenhouse: visual ecology, savvy critics, and climate change in T.C. Boyle's *The Terranauts*. *Studies in the Novel* 50: 68–85.

Wright, Jill G. (2016). Tortillas from grapes: T. Coraghessan Boyle reimagines Steinbeck's social-protest novel. *Steinbeck Review* 13: 151–168.

The Brain and American Fiction

PASCALE ANTOLIN
Université Bordeaux Montaigne, France

To yoke the brain with fiction seems to suggest that the gap between "the two cultures" of science and the humanities that C.P. Snow noted in his famous 1959 lecture is now closed. For Andrew Gaedtke, "a discursive exchange has begun to develop across the notorious 'two cultures' divide" (Gaedtke 2015, p. 274), even though, so far, it has been more akin to "information transfer than true collaboration" (Birge 2012, p. 89). In the past fifty years, however, American fiction *has* incorporated material from neuroscience – broadly understood as brain sciences – hence the emergence of "brain fiction."

For centuries, the skull was the boundary between the observable and unobservable dimension of the human being – despite exploratory investigation procedures such as trepanation. Advances in neuroscience and neurotechnology in the twentieth century progressively unlocked the mystery of the brain, and provided insights into brain processes as well as their connections to mental states and observable behavior (Wickens 2015). In the 1990s, declared the "the Decade of the Brain" by President George H.W. Bush, a wide and rapidly expanding spectrum of neuroimaging technologies became available, resulting in a neuro-technological revolution. Popular books using the findings of neuroscience were published, and soon became bestsellers: the most famous included *Consciousness Explained* (1991) by philosopher Daniel Dennett and *How the Mind Works* (1997) by psychologist Steven Pinker. They propounded neural theories of mind and explained mental phenomena in terms of brain processes. From then on, not only has neuroscience developed but the application of neuroscience to fields beyond medicine has been widespread – to such an extent that Melissa M. Littlefield and Jenell M. Johnson have coined the phrase "neuroscientific turn" to refer to the new trend (Littlefield and Johnson 2012). Others speak more critically of "neuromania" to describe what they call "the mindless [use of] neuroscience" in all fields, from neuro-education to neuro-marketing and neuro-economics (Satel and Lilienfield 2013). According to Littlefield and Johnson, neuroscience is a "translational discipline" (2012, p. 3), in other words, it can be transferred to other fields, including literature.

One new genre of fiction that has emerged from this development is the "neuronovel," a word coined in 2009 by Marco Roth in a highly influential – though somewhat sketchy (Burn 2018, pp. 167–169) – essay in *n+1*. In contemporary Anglo-American fiction, Roth writes, "the novel of consciousness or the psychological or confessional novel – the novel, at any rate, about the workings of a mind – has transformed itself into the neurological novel, wherein the mind becomes the brain," and neurology replaces psychoanalysis. Roth decries the development of the neuronovel by way of comparison with the genre's predecessors, particularly the stream-of-consciousness writers of the Modernist period like James Joyce and Virginia Woolf. According to Roth, this shift – which, some contend, "he may have been overstating" (Ortega and Vidal 2013, p. 333) – began in 1997 with the publication of British writer Ian McEwan's *Enduring Love*. Among other instances of the same genre, Roth mentions American novels such as Jonathan Lethem's *Motherless Brooklyn* (1999), Richard Powers's *The Echo Maker* (2006), Rivka Galchen's *Atmospheric Disturbances* (2008), and John Wray's *Lowboy* (2009).

Actually, Roth was not the first to write about this new development. In 2008, Gary Johnson made a somewhat similar, albeit less negative, statement about what he called "neuronarratives": "a growing list of narrative works […] foreground[s] the emerging fields of neuroscience and neurobiology. These works, I propose, constitute an emerging subgenre of literature that can provide us with a glimpse of how authors are responding to scientific advances concerning the nature of human consciousness" (2008, pp. 170–171). Whether they are called "neuronovels" (Roth 2009), "neuronarratives" (Johnson 2008), "cognitive fiction" (Tabbi 2002), or "neurological realism" (Harris 2008), the defining feature of these works is that they reopen the "black box" of consciousness in neuroscientific terms.

Materialists, physicalists, or reductionists like Dennett and Pinker demystify consciousness and provide a materialist explanation of mind. They believe that the mind does not exist as a separate entity; it is merely a state of the brain, caused entirely by neurons and neurochemistry. "You are your brain" has become a widespread tenet among contemporary philosophers (Daniel Dennett and Patricia Churchland, for instance) and neuroscientists (Francis Crick and Dick Swaab, among others). This approach generates a "cerebral subject" and "reduc[es] the self to an organ of the body," while personhood is replaced by "brainhood" (Vidal 2009, p. 11). According to Jason Tougaw in *The Elusive Brain* (2018), however, theoretical neuroscientists – like Antonio Damasio, Stanislas Dehaene, Michael Gazzaniga, Joseph LeDoux, Jaak Panksepp, and Sebastian Seung – describe consciousness as emerging from but not fully explained by brain physiology alone. They consider that neuroscience will account for subjective experience one day, but it cannot do so yet. "While they often use language and rhetoric that suggest a physicalist stance implying that brains determine fate, end of story, the details of these writers' theories reveal much more interesting attempts to grapple with questions about how matter and mind, or physiology and consciousness, shape each other" (Tougaw 2018, p. 10). All are faced with what Joseph Levine in a 1983 essay, "Materialism and Qualia: The Explanatory Gap," calls "the explanatory gap" between objective, neural networks and subjective experience. The concept of qualia – the subjective first person of phenomenal experience – has been a cornerstone of debates about consciousness ever since. Descriptions of neurophysiology are all third person, yet consciousness is experienced in the first person. How then is the third-person matter in our brains related to our actual first-person experience? That is the most challenging question. In *The Character of Consciousness* (2010), philosopher David Chalmers distinguishes between the "easy problems of consciousness" that relate to objective phenomena – neurotransmitters and action potentials – and the "hard problem of consciousness" that is qualitatively different: the problem of subjectivity. He explains that the hard problem "persist[s] even when the performance of all the relevant functions [e.g. neurochemistry] is explained" (2010, p. 6). Neuroscience, then, has been unable so far to account for the complex relations among body, mind, self, and world.

The neuronovel is a direct response to advances in neuroscience, the neuroscientific turn, and especially contemporary neuromania. This does not mean that writers engage in the debate, let alone, as Roth contends, that they defend a reductionist approach. Instead, as "cultural producers," they "are addressing a paradigm shift in our understanding of the world and of ourselves" (Lustig and Peacock 2013, p. 5). Victorian phrenology finds its way into Charlotte Brontë's *Jane Eyre* (1847), Freud's ideas into Virginia Woolf's novels, and these authors similarly find themselves compelled to engage with contemporary theories of being. Fiction allows them to ask, even dramatize, questions about consciousness and selfhood that have remained unanswered so far. Emphasizing the brain allows them to question interiority and identity. They "experiment with narrative forms that may frame new views about the relationship between brain matter and the immaterial experiences that compose a self" (Tougaw 2018, p. 3).

However, the neuronovel is only "the newest way of fictionally elaborating brain-related issues" (Ortega and Vidal 2013, p. 333). In the 1970s, science fiction novels such as Philip K. Dick's *A Scanner Darkly* (1977) incorporated research on split-brain and hemispheric lateralization, and quoted articles by the neuroscientists Joseph E. Bogen (1969) and Michael S. Gazzaniga (1967). Medical thrillers also developed and often introduced brain-related theories and practices (Ortega and Vidal 2013, pp. 335–336). The prehistory of the genre, therefore, includes Joseph McElroy's *Lookout Cartridge* (1974), Tom Robbins's *Jitterbug Perfume* (1984), and John Barth's *Once Upon a Time* (1994).

Largely absent from brain-based literary studies, Don DeLillo's fiction has also been related to the neurological turn. Stephen Burn contends that characters in *Ratner's Star* (1976), DeLillo's fourth novel, "are often solidly anchored in the scientific discourse of the early seventies" and the novel should be classified as "a kind of neurofiction, a work that absorbs and carries on a dialogue with the contemporary sciences of mind" (2015, p. 210). Burn even mentions "neural architecture" in *Great Jones Street* (1973) and *Ratner's Star* (2013, p. 40). In a later essay, Burn distinguishes two periods in DeLillo's fiction. The premillennial novels use the brain to clarify fear responses: "the fictional geography of each book is typically organized according to a vertical axis, where a descent to lower levels normally indexes a corresponding cognitive descent to the realms of either primitive fear […] or violent action." The postmillennial work, by contrast, "shifts away from fear responses toward a more prominent engagement with the neurology of vision" (2018, pp. 170–171). The transition is perceptible in *White Noise* (1985), and confirmed in *The Body Artist* (2001) and *Point Omega* (2010). DeLillo's growing interest in the neurology of vision, Burn writes, is representative of a larger trend among writers like Lynne Tillman (*American Genius*, 2006), David Foster Wallace (*The Pale King*, 2011), and Robert Coover (*The Adventures of Lucky Pierre*, 2002). This approach is all the more significant since it affects not just the "figuration of external reality" but also the "shape of the same works" (Burn 2018, p. 174). The persistence of vision being a mere illusion which escapes conscious awareness, the fragmented narrative sequence is often privileged in these novels, and it belongs to the reader – as it belongs to the brain of the viewer – to bring together the static images in order to create a coherent whole.

The neuronovel, therefore, is not an orphan that suddenly came to life in the early years of the twenty-first century – "the century of the brain," according to the International Brain Research Association (Vidal 2009, p. 7). It belongs in a long history and carries a significant inheritance of fiction engaging with neuroscience. This history leads to questions about names and definitions. Most scholars tend to use the word "neuronovel," probably for the sake of simplicity, considering the popularity of Roth's label. They have also adopted the thematic definition suggested by Johnson: "a work of fiction that has cognitive science as a, or the, main theme" (2008, p. 170). Burn suggests a broader definition: "Some of the most revealing syndrome novels, in fact, are those that do not foreground cognitive models at the level of plot, but instead offer suggestive hints of their neural narratives through an author's formal and rhetorical choices or through carefully placed allusions that lie at the ragged edges of the central character's lives" (2013, p. 36). In this entry, "brain fiction" stands for the broader label referring to all fiction engaging with neuroscience formally or topically from the 1970s onward. "Neuronovel," "neurofiction," or "neuronarrative" – even neuro-literature – are used for fiction centering on the brain in a manner and to an extent not previously witnessed, as it has emerged in the contemporary "neurocultural" context, that is, the last thirty years – the prefix neuro- providing an easy means of differentiating them from earlier fictions.

Neuronovels come in very different forms. For instance, Roth mentions two categories, "soft" and "hard," Tougaw identifies five (2018, pp. 6–7), and Burn adopts a chronological approach, before and after the millennial (2013, p. 43). For the sake of simplicity, let us distinguish narratives featuring characters with neurological conditions from narratives with protagonists engaged or merely interested in brain research. Though significantly less numerous, the novels in this second category include *Galatea 2.2* by Richard Powers (1995), *The Blazing World* by Siri Hustvedt (2014), and *Andrew's Brain* by E.L. Doctorow (2014).

Published in the middle of the "Decade of the Brain," *Galatea 2.2* is one of the most popular and typical of its class, together with British writer David Lodge's 2001 *Thinks...* – many scholars have analyzed the two novels jointly. Set on a college campus, *Galatea 2.2* fictionalizes the two-culture debate described by Snow since it stages a humanist and a cognitive scientist as they "attempt collaboration and argue about the nature of consciousness, its biological connections, its phenomenological qualities, and its aesthetic implications" (Tougaw 2018, p. 55). In addition to telling a story, the novel "display[s], through some of [its] characters' inner conflicts and interpersonal relations, the challenges of writing a neuronovel" (Ortega and Vidal 2013, p. 337) – the humanist being a novelist. The originality of the plot lies in the purpose of the collaborative work between the writer and the scientist: they intend to develop a computer named Helen, capable of passing the final exam for a master's degree in English literature. The humanist spends months teaching Helen the literary classics until he is convinced that it can mimic self-consciousness and possesses the neural systems of a living brain. But Helen also wants full human embodiment – an allusion to the embodied mind thesis (Barrat 2013). "Being a brain or its functional equivalent is not enough for it. Thus, like other forms of fictional exploration of the relation between brain and personhood [...], neuronovels problematize rather than merely assert the neurological belief that humans are essentially their brains" (Ortega and Vidal 2013, p. 338).

Dennett praised Powers's novel for finding "brilliant ways of conveying hard-to-comprehend details of the field" and even concluded that "the novel is an excellent genre for pushing the scientific imagination into new places" (2008, pp. 152, 160). *Galatea 2.2* does borrow the language and theories of neuroscience, and has certainly contributed to their understanding among the reading public. However, it eventually spurns materialist philosophy in favor of humanism, showing the limits of artificial intelligence, and bringing the reader back to the explanatory gap. The concluding lines of the narrative – "I might have another fiction in me after all. I started to trot, searching for a keyboard before memory degraded" (Powers 1995, p. 328) – suggest that the humanist has overcome his writer's block and emerges from the encounter ready to write a novel that, in all likelihood, will be close to *Galatea 2.2*. The neuroscientific knowledge he has acquired has the potential to turn into a new source of inspiration. In a 2013 interview, Powers claimed the label "hybrid fiction" that his work was given by Daniel Grassian (2003), "in the sense of taking two species and combining them into a new form of life" (Sun 2013, p. 336). For other writers, the introduction of neuroscientific language and concepts is merely a strategy "to revitalize their field" (Ortega and Vidal 2013, p. 330).

American fiction has certainly been revitalized in the last thirty years by the emergence of the second category of neuronovel, or "syndrome novel" (Lustig and Peacock 2013), characterized by leading protagonists suffering from rare neurological conditions: Capgras syndrome (*The Echo Maker* and *Atmospheric Disturbances*), Tourette's (*Motherless Brooklyn*), paranoid schizophrenia (*Lowboy*), and amnesia (*Man Walks into a Room* [2002] by Nicole Krauss). These neuronovels, however, belong in a tradition of fiction narrated by or through characters with "atypical cognitive dispositions" (Tougaw 2018, p. 131): from Cervantes, Sterne, and Poe to Gilman, Woolf, Faulkner, or Morrison, among others. The key difference is that neuronovels participate in contemporary debates about neurocognitive difference and raise ethical questions about the representation of neurological difference. To shed light on this new trend, Jonathan Lethem evokes "new vocabularies for human perceptual life" (2000, p. xiv) provided in particular by the medicalization of contemporary existence. For Burn, the "syndrome often stands as a synecdoche for the larger sense of disorientation that haunts millennial life." These novels, like their postmodernist predecessors, make "the familiar strange" and "probe [...] the root conditions of modernity [...] or even the meaning of modern existence" (2013, p. 43).

However, the neuroscientific vocabulary so prominent in the first category of neuronovels is often far less obtrusive in the second: it is hardly present at all in *Motherless Brooklyn* and *Lowboy*. In *Atmospheric Disturbances*, it is not the vocabulary of neurology that prevails – while the hero-narrator, a psychiatrist, thinks his wife has been replaced by an impostor, he never mentions Capgras syndrome – but the jargon of a pseudo-meteorological science. In *Still Alice* (2007) by Lisa Genova – both a neuroscientist and a writer – which features a leading character suffering from early Alzheimer's, and *The Echo Maker* by Richard Powers, the language of neurology is set against the poetic language of recurrent lyric descriptions. In *Man Walks into a Room*, Krauss takes advantage of her character's amnesia to create entire paragraphs luxuriating in the small details of everyday life. "Such passages play to Krauss' traditional novelistic strengths – sensitive rendering of detail, heightened attention to ordinary moments – but the return to a largely conventional narrative form is connected to a wider argument the novel makes about literature's reaction against neuroscience's growing cultural authority" (Burn 2013, p. 44). In this sense, neurofiction often enacts a defense of literature, as a counternarrative to the dehumanized language of neuroscience.

This may be the reason why neuronovels are often more conventional than the more experimental fiction characteristic of postmodernism. While they return to character, they "do not limit themselves to incorporating neuroscientific concepts and vocabulary from a third-person perspective, as if it were a medical diagnosis [...]. [They] sometimes do so, thereby, both describing mental processes and 'defamiliarizing' them by means of scientific vocabulary [Lodge 2002, p. 88]. Yet they also bring a neuroscientific perspective and language into first-person narratives, thus recovering the patient's voice that is generally absent from scientific, including neuroscientific, writing" (Ortega and Vidal 2013, p. 332). Sarah Birge underlines the special contribution of this type of fiction: "Popular science writing, such as that of Oliver Sacks or V.S. Ramachandran, often depicts cognitive disorders (by exploring the doctor's experience with brain-damaged patients), but fiction is able to go one step further by representing the subjective viewpoint of people who might have a difficult time describing their own perspective narratively" (2012, p. 92). *Motherless Brooklyn* and *Atmospheric Disturbances* are good examples. *Lowboy* and *The Echo Maker* are third-person narratives but the omniscient narrator alternately adopts the viewpoints of the major characters – neurodivergent or not – which tends to bridge the gap between them, and contributes to a questioning of cognitive norms. For Burn, the dominance of the first-person perspective in contemporary neuronovels illustrates "literature's primal connection to subjective experience" (2013, p. 45), which neuroscience has failed to grasp. Gaedtke underlines in neuronovels "rich descriptions of the often bizarre, phenomenological circumstances" that compensate for the "lack of a global, explanatory framework" (2015, p. 273). In other words, neuronovelists devise strategies emphasizing both the power of literature and the limits of neuroscience.

As it returns to more conventional narrative forms, the neuronovel also returns to traditional genres – detective fiction (*Motherless Brooklyn*, *Lowboy*, *The Echo Maker*, *Atmospheric Disturbances*) and, occasionally, the coming-of-age narrative (*Motherless Brooklyn*, *Lowboy*). While it borrows from their conventions, it revises them as well. For Tougaw, "neuronovels build on detective fiction's speculative tendencies, weaving hypothetical questions about the physiological self into the mysteries of their plots." Nonetheless, Tougaw also points out that "neuronovels are almost always revisionist mysteries" (2018, p. 132) since "plot resolution depends only partly on the solving of crimes" (p. 157). In *Lowboy* – the eponymous story of a 16-year-old paranoid schizophrenic who has just escaped from a psychiatric hospital and is pursued by a Black detective and the boy's mother – the sense of mystery mostly relies on the breathless pace of the novel, a traditional feature of the genre. But "Lowboy's role is ambivalent and this is where Wray revises the conventions of the genre to serve his own purposes. The adolescent is both a victim of the American system of institutionalization and medication for disabled people, and potentially the victimizer – he could hurt people especially since he has stopped taking his medication" (Antolin 2019a). As for the detective, instead of playing the leading role, he has been given a bit part. Especially, the traditional ending of detective fiction is disturbed: after the young protagonist's death, the concluding metalepsis – that is, the narrator's intrusion into the diegetic universe – suggests that the narrator has turned as delusional as the young hero. The ending does not restore order, therefore, but creates further disorder.

Also a detective novel, *Motherless Brooklyn* stands apart since the Tourettic hero is also the first-person narrator, playing the role of a sleuth so as to find out who killed his mentor. While at first sight, with his verbal outbursts and motor tics, he seems to be wholly unfitted for the job, his neurological condition turns out to be an asset, and he identifies both the murderer and the reason for the crime. Tougaw explains that "[Lethem] creates a kind of dialectic between the symptoms of Tourette's and the conventions of detective fiction. They're both about interpretation" (2018, p. 147). But the novel continues after the murder has been solved, with the narrator falling back on his symptoms and syndrome. Relying on laughter and grotesque degradation, Lethem's novel turns into parody, in the Bakhtinian sense of the word that involves regenerating ambivalence; in other words, the book is both "a homage to and a rewriting of the conventional genre" (Antolin 2019b).

However, Tougaw warns, staging neurodivergent characters or narrators "risks dealing in caricature of neurological difference, reinforcing stereotypes, or making readers feel they are gaining genuine knowledge from fictional portraits" (2018, p. 133). It is true that neuro-literature has contributed to the public awareness so that even relatively rare neurological disorders and their names, like Tourette's or Capgras syndrome, are more familiar today than ever before. Yet, neither *Motherless Brooklyn* nor *Lowboy* falls into the trap of turning neurodivergent experience into stereotype. In *Lowboy*, the third-person narrative alternates Lowboy's viewpoint with the detective's or his mother's. This alternation juxtaposes the first-person experience of schizophrenia and the perspectives of observers, which prevents the stigmatization of schizophrenic subjectivity. In *Motherless Brooklyn*, "the Tourettic first-person narrator [...] presents himself as a freak and dramatically displays his recurrent tics through lexical and typographic variations in the narrative. Thus, he plays a double part: as a character, he is the freak on the freakshow platform, or the page, and as the narrator, he is the freakshow talker [...] constructing the freak from his condition. Thereby, the narrative turns into a freakshow, not in the sense of the sordid spectacle of the past, but as a construction questioning both the social and the literary order" (Antolin 2019b). *Motherless Brooklyn*, therefore, enacts a paradigm shift with the narrator's disability turning into a special ability.

Roth is mistaken, therefore, when he writes that "by turning so aggressively inward, to an almost cellular level, this kind of novel bypasses the self, let alone society, or history, to arrive at neurology" (2009). *Motherless Brooklyn* sends a powerful political message as it implicitly takes up sociologist Erving Goffman's 1963 theory of stigma. As for *Lowboy*, it "challenges confinement to institutions and the medication that goes with it, that is, mostly tranquilizers," which are repeatedly mentioned in the book (Antolin 2019a). But *The Echo Maker* may be the most significant example since it is not just a neuronovel but an ecological novel as well – Heather Houser (2014) calls it "ecosickness fiction." While the main plot features a character suffering from Capgras syndrome as a result of brain injury suffered in a car accident, the novel is also concerned with a breed of cranes whose nesting habitat is threatened by real estate development. The cranes appear at the beginning of each of the novel's five sections, when the narrative turns grandly lyric. However, the birds are ambivalent, both familiar and foreign to humans: "Cranes are souls that once were humans and might be again, many lives from now. Or humans are souls that once were cranes and will be again, when the flock is rejoined" (Powers 2006, p. 231). In fact, the cranes have not experienced the same evolution as humans, they have remained "feathered dinosaurs bugling, a last reminder of life before the self" (p. 351). The self, a human specificity, is at the root of ecological destruction as if humans were suffering from a collective Capgras syndrome toward the natural world. The self, and its definition, is also at the root of the characters' problems. All equally struggle to identify as subjects. The only solution for them is to be "intersubjectively connected to other selves" (Harris 2008, p. 237), that is, capable of adopting narratives coming from others. The equation of selfhood with narrative runs throughout the novel, particularly in a passage where the doctor is reading from a book he has just published: "Consciousness works by telling a story, one that is whole, continuous, and stable. When that story breaks, consciousness rewrites it. Each revised draft claims to be the original" (Powers 2006, p. 234). In the novel, not only does Powers defend the privileged role of human consciousness but he also propounds an Emersonian drive to connect (Dewey 2002), and achieves some transcendent spiritual meaning.

In a 2002 essay, Jonathan Franzen writes that "where I ought to recognize that, yes, the brain is meat, I seem instead to maintain a blind spot across which I tend to interpolate stories that emphasize the more soul-like aspects of the self" (p. 19). For Burn, "much post-postmodern fiction seems to yearn for at least a partial return to religion and spirituality presumed to be absent from the postmodern world." Despite the pronouncements of neuroscience, neuronovels, in Burn's view, are often characterized by "the stubborn persistence of the idea of a soul [which] acts as a placeholder for science to merge with a persistent mysticism" (Burn 2013, pp. 45–47). In *The Unnamed* (2010) by Joshua Ferris, while the main character suffers from an unspecified compulsion to keep walking, the novel explores "the deep metaphysical ache that lies at the core of post-postmodern fiction" (Burn 2013, p. 45). However, the narrative also displays the novel's dialogic abilitiy to combine the authoritative language of neuroscience with the more mystical "work of the divine" (Ferris 2010, p. 305).

While they focus on the brain, neuronovels express the writers' concern about "the biologization of the self and the medicalization of the mind." Neurofiction is "part of a project to rescue the singularity of human experience from phantom objectivity, to understand the intersubjective processes that constitute our sense of self-presence or loss of it" (Waugh 2013, pp. 25, 24). However, the novelists engaging in neurofiction also betray a certain fascination with neuroscientific discoveries and the hopes they seem to raise for insights into human nature. They are attracted to the authoritative, empirical language of neuroscience as well. Introducing this language into their narratives may be a means of appropriating, even controlling it. From this viewpoint, neuronovelists are reminiscent of Modernist writers' celebration and condemnation of the technology of their time. As Ortega and Vidal write, "unlike a scientific or philosophical argument, an artwork is allowed to be a locus of contradictions where opposites may coincide" (2011, p. 23).

Tougaw sheds light on these contradictions: "If writers of [...] neuronovels can tell us anything, it's that mystery defines the epistemology of relations between brain and self; and where you find mystery, you'll find contradictions too" (2018, p. 11). He even contends that "neuronovelists are contemporary heirs to Modernist experiments with interiority" (2017, p. 174). Taking up the metaphor used by Heather Houser (2014, p. 19), Tougaw suggests calling this new genre a "literary laboratory," that is, "a place for investigation" and experiments. It gives "narrative form to questions central to science" and tells "stories about brain-related experiences" (2018, p. 5). Powers expresses a more personal position in a 2013 interview: "the future of storytelling in our society is going to be more and more impacted by scientific narratives and technological narratives, and [...] we are assimilating and normalizing those stories in ourselves, sometimes without knowing it. So what I want to do is to expose the way in which those processes are already starting to change the way we tell the stories about ourselves" (Sun 2013, p. 340). Whatever their reasons, neuronovelists have certainly "refreshed" the field of literature (Johnson 2008, p. 184) and responded to neuromania – more than neuroscience. They have also proved that fiction can exhibit the same plasticity and adaptability as the brain. However, fiction does not need conclusive answers, it is merely trying to convey "the feeling of what happens" (Damasio 1999).

SEE ALSO: Barth, John; Coover, Robert; DeLillo, Don; Doctorow, E.L.; Ecocriticism and Environmental Fiction; Ferris, Joshua; Franzen, Jonathan; Hustvedt, Siri; Illness and Disability Narratives; Krauss, Nicole; Lethem, Jonathan; McElroy, Joseph; Millennial Fiction; Powers, Richard; Wallace, David Foster

REFERENCES

Antolin, Pascale. (2019a). "His cramped and claustrophobic brain": confinement and freedom in John Wray's *Lowboy*. *European Journal of American Studies* 14 (2). https://journals.openedition.org/ejas/14639?lang=en (accessed September 21, 2021).

Antolin, Pascale. (2019b). "I am a freak of nature": Tourette's and the grotesque in Jonathan Lethem's *Motherless Brooklyn*. *Transatlantica* 1. https://journals.openedition.org/transatlantica/13941 (accessed September 21, 2021).

Barrat, James. (2013). *Our Final Invention: Artificial Intelligence and the End of the Human Era*. New York: Thomas Dunne Books.

Birge, Sarah. (2012). Brainhood, selfhood, or "meat with a point of view." In: *The Neuroscientific Turn: Transdisciplinarity in the Age of the Brain* (ed. Melissa Littlefield and Jenell M. Johnson), 89–104. Ann Arbor: University of Michigan Press.

Burn, Stephen J. (2013). Mapping the syndrome novel. In: *Diseases and Disorders in Contemporary Fiction: The Syndrome Syndrome* (ed. Tim J. Lustig and James Peacock), 35–52. Abingdon, UK: Routledge.

Burn, Stephen J. (2015). Neuroscience and modern fiction. *MSF: Modern Fiction Studies* 61 (2): 209–225.

Burn, Stephen J. (2018). The neuronovel. In: *American Literature in Transition* (ed. Rachel Greenwald Smith), 165–177. Cambridge: Cambridge University Press.

Chalmers, David J. (2010). *The Character of Consciousness*. New York: Oxford University Press.

Damasio, Antonio. (1999). *The Feeling of What Happens: Body and Emotion in the Making of Consciousness*. New York: Houghton Mifflin Harcourt.

Dennett, Daniel C. (2008). Astride the two cultures: a letter to Richard Powers, updated. In: *Intersections: Essays on Richard Powers* (ed. Stephen J. Burn and Peter Dempsey), 151–161. Champaign, IL: Dalkey Archive Press.

Dewey, Joseph. (2002). *Understanding Richard Powers*. Columbia: University of South Carolina Press.

Ferris, Joshua. (2010). *The Unnamed*. New York: Reagan Arthur Books/Little, Brown.

Franzen, Jonathan. (2002). *How to Be Alone*. New York: Picador.

Gaedtke, Andrew. (2015). Neuromodernism: diagnosis and disability in Will Self's *Umbrella*. *MSF: Modern Fiction Studies* 61 (2): 271–294.

Grassian, Daniel. (2003). *Hybrid Fictions: American Fiction and Generation X*. Jefferson, NC: McFarland.

Harris, Charles B. (2008). The story of the self: *The Echo Maker* and neurological realism. In: *Intersections: Essays on Richard Powers* (ed. Stephen J. Burn and Peter Dempsey), 230–263. Champaign, IL: Dalkey Archive Press.

Houser, Heather. (2014). *Ecosickness in Contemporary U.S. Fiction: Environment and Affect*. New York: Columbia University Press.

Johnson, Gary. (2008). Consciousness as content: neuronarratives and the redemption of fiction. *Mosaic* 41: 169–184.

Lethem, Jonathan. (2000). Introduction. In: *The Vintage Book of Amnesia* (ed. Jonathan Lethem), xiii–xvii. New York: Vintage Books.

Levine, Joseph. (1983). Materialism and qualia: the explanatory gap. *Pacific Philosophical Quarterly* 64: 354–361.

Littlefield, Melissa M. and Johnson, Jenell M. (eds.) (2012). *The Neuroscientific Turn: Transdisciplinarity in the Age of the Brain*. Ann Arbor: University of Michigan Press.

Lodge, David. (2002). *Consciousness and the Novel*. London: Penguin Books.

Lustig, Tim J. and Peacock, James. (eds.) (2013). *Diseases and Disorders in Contemporary Fiction: The Syndrome Syndrome*. Abingdon, UK: Routledge.

Ortega, Francisco and Vidal, Fernando. (2011). Approaching the neurocultural spectrum: an introduction. In: *Neurocultures: Glimpses into an*

Expanding Universe (ed. Francisco Ortega and Fernando Vidal), 7–28. New York: Peter Lang.

Ortega, Francisco and Vidal, Fernando. (2013). Brains in literature/literature in the brain. *Poetics Today* 34 (3): 327–359.

Powers, Richard. (1995). *Galatea 2.2*. New York: Farrar, Straus and Giroux.

Powers, Richard. (2006). *The Echo Maker*. London: Vintage Books.

Roth, Marco. (2009). The rise of the neuronovel. *n+1* 8. https://nplusonemag.com/issue-8/essays/the-rise-of-the-neuronovel/ (accessed July 22, 2021).

Satel, Sally and Lilienfeld, Scott O. (2013). *Brainwashed: The Seductive Appeal of Mindless Neuroscience*. New York: Basic Books.

Snow, C.P. (1959). *The Two Cultures and the Scientific Revolution*. Cambridge: Cambridge University Press.

Sun, Jian. (2013). Fictional collisions: Richard Powers on hybrid narrative and the art of stereoscopic narrative. *Critique: Studies in Contemporary Fiction* 54 (4): 335–345.

Tabbi, Joseph. (2002). *Cognitive Fictions: Electronic Mediations* 8. Minneapolis: University of Minnesota Press.

Tougaw, Jason. (2017). The blood beating in his brain: where is consciousness in the modern novel? *The Scofield* 2 (2): 172–180.

Tougaw, Jason. (2018). *The Elusive Brain: Literary Experiments in the Age of Neuroscience*. New Haven: Yale University Press.

Vidal, Fernando. (2009). Brainhood, anthropological figure of modernity. *History of the Human Sciences* 22 (1): 5–36.

Waugh, Patricia. (2013). The naturalistic turn, the syndrome, and the rise of the neo-phenomenological novel. In: *Diseases and Disorders in Contemporary Fiction: The Syndrome Syndrome* (ed. Tim J. Lustig and James Peacock), 17–34. Abingdon, UK: Routledge.

Wickens, Andrew P. (2015). *A History of the Brain: From Stone Age Surgery to Modern Neuroscience*. New York: Psychology Press.

FURTHER READING

Antolin, Pascale. (2022). Introduction. The neuronovel (2009–2021). Special issue of *European Journal of American Studies*.

Gaedtke, Andrew. (2012). Cognitive investigations: the problems of qualia and style in the contemporary neuronovel. *Novel* 45 (2): 184–201.

Braschi, Giannina

MARITZA STANCHICH
University of Puerto Rico-Río Piedras

Giannina Braschi's *The United States of Banana* (2011) takes off from her groundbreaking quasi-novel *Yo-Yo Boing!* (1998) and culminates an unofficial trilogy that began with *El imperio de los sueños* (1994) to mark a paradigmatic shift in the dizzying millennial poetics of witness of José Martí's and Walt Whitman's New York. Live from New York for the new millennium, *The United States of Banana* bears witness to the end of the American century via a trans-canonical and trans-American postmodern performance that envisions Puerto Rico's liberation from US colonialism. The timing of its publication aftermath feels propitious, as the relationships between the US "colossus of the north" and Latin America play out in the Caribbean with an aborted rapprochement to Cuba and the economic collapse of Braschi's homeland of Puerto Rico. *Banana* enacts simultaneously postmodern and protest poetics in dizzying global/local contexts, as US global hegemony declines post-9/11, as the United States becomes the second largest Spanish-speaking country in the world, and as Puerto Rico drowns in debt crisis – worsened by hurricane and earthquake disasters, as well as the COVID-19 pandemic. Braschi's avant-garde Spanish–English bilingualism wrestles staggering legacies of both these colonial languages of the Americas to forge parity between them, exposing officializing discourses of national literary canons and imperial powers on a global stage. From the perspective of immigrant New York,

Braschi witnesses the "death of the salesman" in the apocalyptic ash of 9/11, with a rhetorically supercharged romp through genres, registers, canons, popular cultures, and dramatis personae, to imagine a carnivalesque end to US colonialism, forging what critic Madelena Gonzalez calls a "rogue aesthetic" that seeks to "rewrite radical politics as high art" (2014, sec. 10).

The three works as a creative oeuvre also work through the considerably charged linguistic tensions and terrains of bilingualism in Puerto Rican, US Latinx, and trans-American terms with *El imperio de los sueños*, *Yo-Yo Boing!*, and *The United States of Banana* in Spanish, avant-garde Spanglish, and English, respectively, and with all three translated to English or Spanish. Braschi's invocation of "high art" and cosmopolitan celebration of New York sets her apart from the protest poetics and working-class ethos of Nuyorican poets, as does her coming from a "high-bourgeois" Puerto Rican family (Ostriker 1994, p. vii), becoming a tennis champion and professional model in Puerto Rico, later studying in Madrid, living in Paris, Rome, and London before settling in New York. Yet because she has lived in New York since 1977, it would be remiss not to describe her as a diasporic, New York-based Puerto Rican author. In New York she worked as an academic and critic but increasingly dedicated herself to her art. Her readings/performances with panache and fashion flair seek a transformative audience experience linguistically and aesthetically that is dizzying in scope, abandoning North/South binaries, exalting in-betweenity as twenty-first-century praxis, and positioning a simultaneously colonized and cosmopolitan subjectivity. As Alicia Ostriker notes in the introduction to the translation of *Empire of Dreams* (1994), Braschi is "not a protest poet, though deeply aware of politics and power" (p. vii). At once mixing cultural references such as Fellini and Cher, modes such as philosophy and queer erotica, acts such as contemplating *Hamlet* and taking a shit, standup and soliloquy, Braschi's oeuvre mixes highbrow literary discourse with popular culture in ways that are unmistakably modern, urban, and sophisticated.

Of the three works, the most recent in English seems to be receiving more critical attention, in global/hemispheric/local contexts, being staged in New York (adapted and directed by Colombian director Juan Pablo Felix in 2015) and transformed into a graphic novel in Sweden (by Joakim Lindengren in 2017). One of the only other critics relating all three works together is Arnaldo Cruz Malavé (1996, 2014), on the arresting gender and sexuality implications of Braschi's poetic vision of New York City. Taking all three works together as an unofficial trilogy also serves to chart how Braschi's vanguard bilingualism in its multitude of registers breaks with previous theorizations of the functions of interlingualism in diasporic Puerto Rican and Chicano theory (Juan Bruce-Novoa 1990; Juan Flores and George Yúdice 1990; Frances Aparicio 1997, 1998), as well as with Puerto Rico's insular cultural nationalist linguistic discourses (Jorge Duany 2002; Juan Flores 1979; Zilkia Janier 2005). Indeed, Braschi's linguistic experimentation and generic hybridity challenge a trans-imperial history of global power relations between English and Spanish (as theorized by Walter Mignolo 2000) and exceed canonical traditions to put into relief their entanglements with hegemonic nation-state formations. Alexandra Vega-Merino describes the language of *Yo-Yo Boing!* as "shoring up creative energy for the challenge to develop a nuanced, original, playful and productive bilingualism." Evelyn Nien-Ming Ch'ien's suggestive readings of world literature in what she calls *Weird English* (2004) posit an English pollinated by other languages at the level of syntax in the oeuvres of writers such as Junot Diaz and Salman Rushdie, which also applies to Braschi. And critic Lourdes Torres's reading of Braschi's "radical bilingualism" goes further to deepen this critical term (Torres 2007, p. 86).

Braschi's language experiments also bring to the fore a vein of avant-garde literature of the Puerto Rican diaspora, as did the poet Pedro Pietri, along with the distinct recent projects of Urayoán Noel, Edwin Torres, Lawrence La Fountain-Stokes, and the late Edgardo Vega Yunqué, as well as what I and others elsewhere call "post-Nuyorican literature," including poets who uniquely venture into broadly comparative and international terrains. Among these are Victor Hernández Cruz, whose recent work explores Arabic and African linguistic influences in Spain, and Martín Espada, whose oeuvre straddles pan-Latino, trans-American literary traditions, engaging Latin American history as well as a global poetics of dissent. *United States of Banana*'s fantastic mode in particular brings to mind Stateside Puerto Rican authors who also use light sci-fi, fantasy, and magical realism to challenge and innovate gender, sexual, cultural, and aesthetic dictates, such as Lyn Di Iorio, Charlie Vazquez, and playwright Quiara Alegría Hudes.

Indeed, Braschi's so-called trilogy culminates with a fantastic send-up of Western literary canonicity, running the gamut of poetry, prose, drama, film, and philosophy, in modes by turns classical and absurd. A French afterword to *Banana* forthcoming by Madelena Gonzalez uses Julia Kristeva's observation of "exaggerated sophistication" of the outsider's words relying on "naked rhetorical force" to produce extravagant Baroque tendencies, characterizing Braschi's style for its "overloaded artifice, exaggerated effects and a certain grandiloquence" (para. 11). This lends a sense of the fantastic to all three of Braschi's books, though increasing considerably in scale with each. Critic Christina Garrigos (2012) reads *United States of Banana* as "The Waste Land" of the twenty-first century, though there is a big difference between Eliot's lament and Braschi's humor, and Braschi's multiple allusions point to the many linguistic and cultural fissures in such foundational civilizational thinking, rather than conservatively shoring them up. That Eliot aimed to be as much or more a British poet than an American poet, and is recognized as both, fits the tensions inherent in Braschi's many allusions, in terms of their linguistic, cultural, and national cross-currents, lending a frisson that feeds a particular sense of the fantastic. *Yo-Yo Boing!*'s English/Spanish bilingual performance defamiliarizes "Spanglish" to an extent that makes it almost impenetrably startling in an obnoxiously Gertrude Stein vein, while simultaneously invoking a cosmopolitanism reminiscent of Stein's extended Paris circles.

To further unpack *Yo-Yo Boing!*, by turns poetry, fiction, manifesto, treatise, memoir, drama, and song, and often referencing popular culture, consider how it unfolds in three sections labeled for filmic and theatrical techniques, as critics Laura Loustau and Ljudmila Mila Popovich (2012) (2002) note, titled "Close-Up," "Blow-Up," and "Black-Out." The first two section titles also refer to films that share affinities with Braschi's treatment of canonical literary tensions, linguistic patrimonies, and cross-cultural productions. *Close-Up* is the 1990 Iranian film masterpiece, in the docu-fiction genre, by director Abbas Kiarostami, who was also a poet, painter, graphic artist, and part of the Iranian New Wave cinema known for its poetic dialogues and allegorical, philosophical, and political subjects. The film is also a favorite at New York City art film houses, such as Film Forum. While blow-ups enlarge photographs, the second section also famously alludes to Michelangelo Antonioni's tour de force film *Blow-Up* (1966), considered a "mod masterpiece," the Italian director's first English-language film inspired by Julio Cortázar's short story "Las babas del diablo" (1959, "The Devil's Drool"), as noted by Debra A. Castillo (2005, p. 174) and María M. Carrión (1996, p. 185). "Black-Out" as a lighting technique in theater conveys to audiences that a play has ended (and drama is the key literary genre sustained in a more pronounced way later in *Banana*). No less concerned with local allusions, the book's title *Yo-Yo Boing!* refers to the stage name of the Puerto Rican comedian and radio personality Luis Antonio Rivera, probably known better by those on the island close to or of Braschi's generation.

The Socratic dialogues of *Yo-Yo Boing!* between a voice named Giannina Braschi, Zarathustra, and Hamlet at first strike a serious philosophical pose, yet as Plato's Socrates was not the real Socrates, Nietzsche's Zarathustra and Shakespeare's Hamlet are here simultaneously characters and non-characters, as "Giannina Braschi" is and is not the voice of the author, who all go on to take the stage again in *Banana*, which of the three creative works gives way more fully to drama as a literary genre. As *Yo-Yo Boing!* levels the playing field of power dynamics between English and Spanish, bookended front and back in its erudite Spanish, *The United States of Banana*, reversing and subverting assumptions about which country gets deemed a banana republic, while completely in English, brings in lead characters from the Spanish Golden Age, with Segismundo as a prisoner trapped by his father for 100 years under the skirt of the Statue of Liberty, as if to stave off a terrible prophecy à la Sophocles. This invokes Pedro Calderón de la Barca's *La vida es sueño* (1635), in which the imprisoned prince's father is king of Poland, on an equal footing with if not more central than Shakespeare's *Hamlet* (1603), of course the prince of Denmark, highlighting the trans-national subtexts of these enshrined texts in the English and Spanish literary canons. And as the following exchange in *Banana* shows, the New World setting exalts the internationalism and multilingualism of New York, while interrogating themes of belonging, displacement, language, tradition, and national literatures:

SPAIN: Where is Segismundo?
GIANNINA: He is the prince of Poland.
SPAIN: Return him to Spain where he belongs.
ENGLAND: No I won't return the Elgin Marbles to Greece, so you can keep Hamlet.
GIANNINA: In Denmark?
ENGLAND: In New York.

(2011, p. 254)

The Spanish Golden Age poetry Braschi invokes is also in part produced by that era's cross-cultural translation and influence, with Italianate poetry indebted to Petrarch. Braschi's experimentalism puts in relief these linguistic tensions inherent in canonicity, which also serves to highlight and undermine trans-American New Worldings. The relocation debate to "return the Elgin Marbles to Greece," sculptures acquired by the British government in 1816 and then passed on to the British Museum, also suggests the cultural appropriation of the so-called ideals of classical Western civilization.

A passage Braschi has read publicly from *Yo-Yo Boing!* highlights the artist's stance at the helm of such often-contested linguistic border crossings:

– If I respected languages like you do, I wouldn't write at all. El muro de Berlín fue derribado. Why can't I do same. Desde la torre de Babel, las lenguas han sido siempre una forma de divorciarnos del resto de la humanidad. Poetry must find ways of breaking distance. I'm not reducing my audience. On the contrary, I'm going to have a bigger audience with the common markets – in Europe – in America. And besides, all languages are dialects that are made to break new grounds. I feel like Dante, Petrarca, and Boccaccio, and I even feel like Garcilaso forging a new language. Saludo al nuevo siglo, el siglo del nuevo lenguaje de América, y le digo adiós a la retórica separatista y a los atavismos.

(1998, p. 142)

By invoking Dante, Petrarch, and Boccaccio, Braschi alludes to the official legitimizing processes of nation-states, turning to other European languages not included in Mignolo's aforementioned formulation, in recalling the way architects of Italy marshaled language excluding other regional dialects. And as critic Carrión notes, *El imperio de los sueños* also makes explicit this theme: "The idea of an only tongue ruling over a considerable number of different nations and peoples is fundamentally questioned in one of the most exaggerated instances of textual buffoonery" (1996, p. 172).

The seamless code-switch at the Berlin Wall introduces a poetic declaration, in which Braschi exalts the bi- or multilingual as the twenty-first-century subject par excellence by invoking the postmodern present, the Spanish Golden Age, which coincided with the rise of the Spanish empire, along with the globalization of free trade agreements and a unified post-Cold War Germany. While "Garcilaso" recalls the Spanish Golden Age poet Garcilaso de la Vega, a simultaneous Garcilaso reference for the Americas, El Inca Garcilaso de la Vega, the sixteenth-century mestizo Peruvian soldier, historian, and translator of Quechua and Spanish, was also forging new language terrains, arguing for the integrity of both languages as Spanish powerfully interpolated into the capitalist world system.

Of the three works, *Banana* is the only one written almost entirely in English and, perhaps ironically, more than the others takes a clear anticolonial stance on Puerto Rico's status as a US territory, with *Yo-Yo Boing!* being read by some critics as more status-quo oriented when it comes to local politics in her homeland (Torres-Padilla 2007). While performing philosophical intrigue as experimental art, *Banana* is rife with hilarious inside jokes and local vernacular references from Puerto Rico, which also enact canonical, linguistic, and nation-state interrogations, such as the repeated chorus on Puerto Rico's three main political parties: "wishy" (independence), "wishy-washy" (the free associated state), or "washy" (statehood), stand-ins for "Spanish, Spanglish or English," "nation, colony or state" (2011, p. 114), as seen in this dialogue between the three:

WISHY: You are only Fú
WASHY: You are only Fá
WISHY: You only wash
WISHY: You only wish. And I am sick at heart.
WISHY-WASHY: You say I'm neither Fú nor Fá. But I say I am Fú and Fá. You are only Fú. How can Fú be more Fú than Fá?

(2011, p. 107)

This playful local reference, the colloquial phrase "Ni fú, ni fá" (loosely translated as "neither here nor there" or "it makes no difference"), makes a pointed political commentary, as does the later burial of the sardine still performed in the carnival of Puerto Rico's southern city of Ponce (as it is in regions of Spain). In *Antillano* fashion, this word play echoes in theme and tone Junot Diaz's *fukú* from *The Brief Wondrous Life of Oscar Wao* (2007). Though parodying, these are serious matters to *Banana*'s chief storyline, the attempted prison break for Segismundo, for his freedom, tied up with Puerto Rico's, is also inextricably linked to Puerto Rico's party politics as a sham of colonial democracy:

If they vote for Wishy – Segismundo will be liberated from the dungeon. If they vote for Wishy-Washy, the status quo will prevail. If they vote for Washy, he will be sentenced to death, and nobody will have the honor of hearing his songs rise from the gutters of the dungeon of liberty. Every four years the citizens of Liberty Island vote for Wishy-Washy. They can choose between mashed potato, french fries or baked potato. But any way you serve it, it's all the same potato.

(2011, p. 7)

The play on Calderón de la Barca's Golden Age Spanish play as a dream doubles as the dream for Puerto Rico's more radical independence, at a time when the so-called American dream dies in Puerto Rico. And the obsession with dreaming also arches back to the trilogy's first *Imperio de los sueños*. The grand finale local burial of the sardine echoes the commuters packed like sardines in the subway at the first section of *Banana*, which bears witness to the World Trade Center Twin Towers collapsing, something Braschi actually did witness. The advertising jingle for Oliver Exterminator remains a motif – again, many on the island may well recall the pest control company Oliver Exterminator, though probably that particular advertisement will resonate only or mainly with those similarly born in the 1950s. References to crabs going backwards are not the "ragged claws" of Eliot's "Prufrock" (1915) but what both Ramon Grosfoguel (Grosfoguel et al. 1997) and Arcadio Díaz Quiñones (2000) have theorized as *jaiba* or *jaibería*, as a Puerto Rican ethos of avoiding confrontation.

The effect of these global/local references is as playful, serious, and vanguard as the Jean Tinguely sculpture "Narva" (1961) at the Met, satirizing mindless manufacturing in the Dada style, or his more massive sculpture "Homage to New York," which accidentally burst into flames when unveiled at the Museum of Modern Art in 1960. Braschi's closure to the American Century is fire and brimstone, just as the sardine gets burned at the end of its carnival procession and burial.

In the ultimate trans-American gesture, US passports are awarded to all Latin Americans, as if prophesizing a conceptual alternative to the United States completing a wall at its border with Mexico. Rather than reconcile the power relations and attendant tensions of all these multiple historical, political, linguistic, and canonical resonances, Braschi's oeuvre transcends and transforms them in poetic language that imagines ways to "make it new" and level the playing field between English and Spanish as perhaps only daring conceptual art can start to do.

SEE ALSO: Border Fictions; The Culture Wars; Fiction and Terrorism; Globalization; Literature of the Americas; Mixed-Genre Fiction; The New Experimentalism/The Contemporary Avant-Garde; Post-9/11 Narratives; Trauma and Fiction; Urban Fiction

REFERENCES

Aparicio, Frances. (1988). Tato Laviera y Alurista: hacia una poetica bilingüe. *Boletín del Centro de Estudios Puertorriqueños* 7 (13): 86–96

Aparicio, Frances. (1997). On subversive signifiers: tropicalizing language in the United States. In: *Tropicalizations: Transcultural Representations of Latinidad* (ed. Frances Aparicio and Susana Chávez-Silverman), 194–212. Hanover: University Press of New England.

Braschi, Giannina. (1994). *Empire of Dreams* (trans. Tess O'Dwyer). New Haven: Yale University Press.

Braschi, Giannina. (1998). *Yo-Yo Boing!* Minneapolis: Latin American Review Press.

Braschi, Giannina. (1999). *El imperio de los sueños*. San Juan: Editorial de la Universidad de Puerto Rico; 1st ed. 1988.

Braschi, Giannina. (2011). *United States of Banana*. Las Vegas: Amazon Crossing.

Braschi, Giannina. (2016). *Estados Unidos de Banana* (trans. Manuel Broncano). Luxembourg: Amazon Crossing.

Bruce-Novoa, Juan. (1990). *RetroSpace: Collected Essays on Chicano Literature*. Houston: Arte Público Press.

Carrión, María M. (1996). Geographies, (m)other tongues and the rôle of translation in Giannina Braschi's *El imperio de los sueños*. *Studies in Twentieth Century Literature* 20 (1): 167–191.

Castillo, Debra A. (2005). *Redreaming America: Toward a Bilingual American Culture*. Albany: State University of New York.

Cruz Malavé, Arnaldo. (2014). "Under the skirt of liberty": Giannina Braschi rewrites empire. *American Quarterly* 66 (3): 801–818.

Díaz Quiñones, Arcadio. (2000). *El Arte de Bregar: Ensayos*. San Juan: Ediciones Callejón.

Duany, Jorge. (2002). *The Puerto Rican Nation on the Move: Identities on the Island and in the United States*. Chapel Hill: University of North Carolina Press.

Flores, Juan. (1979). *Insularismo e ideología burguesa en Antonio Pedreira*. La Habana: Casa de las Américas.

Flores, Juan and Yúdice, George. (1990). Living borders/buscando America: languages of Latino self-formation. *Social Text* 24: 57–84.

Garrigos, Christina. (2012). Review. *Evergreen* 128 (June). https://evergreenreview.com/read/two-reviews-united-states-of-banana-giannina-braschi/ (accessed September 23, 2021).

Gonzalez, Madelena. (2014). *United States of Banana* (2011), *Elizabeth Costello* (2003) and *Fury* (2001): portrait of the writer as "bad subject" of globalisation. *Études Britanniques Contemporaines* 46: n.p.

Grosfoguel, Ramón, Negrón-Muntaner, Frances, and Georas, Chloé S. (1997). Introduction: beyond nationalist and colonialism discourses: the *jaiba* politics of the Puerto Rican ethno-nation. In: *Puerto Rican Jam: Rethinking Colonialism and Nationalism* (ed. Frances Negrón-Muntaner and Ramón Grosfoguel), 1–36. Minneapolis: University of Minnesota Press.

Janer, Zilkia. (2005). *Puerto Rican Nation-Building Literature: Impossible Romance*. Gainsville: University of Florida Press.

Lindengren, Joakim. (2017). *United States of Banana* (graphic novel in Swedish). Stockholm: Cobolt Förlag.

Loustau, Laura R. (2002). Conciencia nómada y traslados geo-literarios en *El imperio de los sueños* de Giannina Braschi. In: *Cuerpos Errantes: Literatura Latina y Latinoamericana en Estados Unidos*, 117–156. Rosario, Argentina: Beatriz Viterbo Editora.

Mignolo, Walter. (2000). *Local Histories/Global Designs: Coloniality, Subaltern Knowledges, and Border Thinking*. Princeton: Princeton University Press.

Nien-Ming Ch'ien, Evelyn. (2004). *Weird English*. Cambridge, MA: Harvard University Press.

Ostriker, Alicia. (1994). Introduction. In: *Empire of Dreams* by Giannina Braschi (trans. Tess O'Dwyer), viii–xvi. New Haven: Yale University Press.

Popovich, Ljudmila Mila. (2012). Metafictions, migrations, metalives: narrative innovations and migrant women's aesthetics in Giannina Braschi and Etel Adnan. *The International Journal of the Humanities* 9 (10): 117–127.

Torres, Lourdes. (2007). In the contact zone: code-switching strategies by Latino/a writers. *MELUS* 32 (1): 75–96.

Torres-Padilla, Jose L. (2007). When hybridity doesn't resist: Giannina Braschi's *Yo-Yo Boing!*. In: *Complicating Constructions: Race, Ethnicity and Hybridity in American Texts* (ed. David S. Goldstein), 290–307. Seattle: University of Washington Press.

FURTHER READING

Aldama, Frederick Luis and O'Dwyer, Tess. (eds.) (2020). *Poets, Philosophers, Lovers: On the Writings of Giannina Braschi*. Pittsburgh: University of Pittsburgh Press.

Stanchich, Maritza. (2005/6). Towards a post-Nuyorican literature. *Sargasso II: The Floating Homeland/La Patria Flotante*: 113–124.

Vega-Merino, Alexandra and Sommer, Doris. (1998). Either/and. Introduction to *Yo-Yo Boing!* (by Giannina Braschi), 11–18. Minneapolis: Latin American Review Press.

Brooks, Geraldine

STEFANIE SCHÄFER
University of Vienna, Austria

Geraldine Brooks's writing brings to life cultural history and the history of the book with a feminist spin. Her historical novels oscillate between feminist rewriting and reimagining events as they might have been, making creative use of gaps, oversights, and absences, and thus articulating historiographic criticism in a postmodernist vein. The protagonists are white eyewitness experiencers of historic events such as the Plague in England, the Venice Carnival, the early days of Harvard University, or, in the Pulitzer Prize-awarded novel *March* (2005), the American Civil War. Thematically, Brooks's oeuvre focuses on book culture and knowledge production, discussing literacy, the reception and afterlives of literary works, or the absences created by lost books. Her characters speak in period diction, often rendered in intimate and self-reflective genres, such as inner monologue, epistolary, or journal writing. To create these voices, Brooks turns to historical sources from the seventeenth, eighteenth, or nineteenth centuries. By virtue of her characters, Brooks thus foregrounds storytelling. In the sense of Hayden White's (1984) claim that history is always rendered in imaginary ways, Brooks's fiction interrogates authoritative historiographies and offers a gendered version or "gender history" (Canning 2006) of popular historic episodes and periods.

Next to five bestselling novels, Brooks's oeuvre spans a memoir (*Foreign Correspondence* [1997]) about her Australian upbringing and her writing to pen pals around the world, a travel report from the Middle East (*Nine Parts of Desire: The Hidden World of Islamic Women* [1995]), and the Australian Broadcasting Company's 2011 Boyer Lectures. Brooks's training and work as foreign correspondent for the *Wall Street Journal* provide the backdrop for the questions her novels raise. Her work combines archival research with confabulation and romance, and may be read, with Mitchum Huehls, as "postmodernized historical fiction" (2017, p. 143). Historical fiction of the 2000s, Huehls finds, reflects Francis Fukuyama's (now famously revoked) dictum of the "end of history" (p. 139), and, with Linda Hutcheon, captures "a deeper political truth about history's permanent mediation and ultimate indeterminacy" (p. 143).

Geraldine Brooks's writing can best be read through Hutcheon's look at the political potential of historical fiction, spelled out in a feminist take. With white female narrators glancing at the scene from overlooked niches, Brooks's novels critique the misrepresentation of white women in historiography, aiming to restore "women's self-representation" (Hutcheon 2002, p. 137) while acknowledging the fictionality of this endeavor. The protagonists affirm their subject position and stabilize a humanist notion of selfhood. They are self-reflexive, ironic, and tormented, but ultimately gratified narrators, whereas other historical fiction by writers such as E.L. Doctorow, Thomas Pynchon, or James McBride critiques "selfhood" as the very currency of Eurocentric discursive regimes.

Brooks's feminist stance also celebrates book culture. While she insists on "restor[ing] history and memory in the face of distortions of the 'history of forgetting'" (Hutcheon 1989, p. 10), Brooks avoids the metanarrative play of parody and pastiche. Her novels cover a distinct life span and often display women's experiences (mostly in tending to important, history-making men) in period diction. This reveals the vulnerability of the written word. Letters, confessionals, even printed books fail to tell the whole truth and are often compromised by the narrators' human failures. In some novels, the chapter headings are set in historical handwriting, creating an authenticity and reinforcing authorship. In *Caleb's Crossing*, the narrator's handwriting of the section titles shows lack of training when she is 15, swift elegance at 17, and a shaky hand at age 70 (2011, pp. 1, 109, 345); Bethia confesses: "My hand is unlovely, since father did not school me in writing" (p. 8). *March* also has handwritten chapter headings and graphically contrasts the husband's letters to his wife with his confession that he cannot impart to her the horrors of war he experiences. Brooks's political and epistemological commentary on book culture and historiography will be extrapolated in three exemplary readings.

Compared to her other novels, *People of the Book* (2008) is the most experimental narrative, with a book, the Sarajevo Haggadah, as protagonist. The novel follows the Haggadah across Europe and through the centuries, offering the book's hi/story quite literally through its people: The novel's title points to the imprint that owners, readers, and carriers leave on its material body, but also quotes the Islamic term "people of the book," which designates the book-based religions, Judaism, Christianity, and Islam. The Sarajevo Haggadah, an illuminated Hebrew codex originating in Barcelona in 1350 and rediscovered in 1894, is owned today by the National Museum of Bosnia and Herzegovina in Sarajevo. Brooks imagines its travels through various perspectives. In 1996, in the midst of the Yugoslavian War, Australian book restorer Hannah Heath uncovers the book's history through fragments found in its pages, including an insect wing, wine stains, and a single white hair. Her restoration is enlivened by flashbacks to figures both imagined and historical in the Haggadah's past; as Hanna speculates over her findings, the reader gets the actual story, from a Jewish partisan girl in 1940 Sarajevo, an Austrian book binder in 1890s Vienna, an Inquisition censor in 1609 Venice, and a Jewish book binder in 1492 Tarragona.

The Hagaddah's value as text, cultural artefact, and material archive offers a multifaceted view of book culture: its illuminations interrogate book history; it functions as ritual object at the Passover table; and its survival claims the victory of book lovers over anti-Semitic efforts seeking to destroy and disappear Jewish culture. Throughout the centuries, the Haggadah is salvaged by a coalition of "book people" from Jewish, Christian, and Muslim backgrounds. *People of the Book* thus asserts the value of books as archives, objects of material culture, and agents of interreligious coexistence. Its writing, according to Brooks (2008, p. 369), was urged by her experience of the burned libraries in war-torn Sarajevo and the risks taken by librarians and custodians to save the city's diverse cultural legacy.

In *Caleb's Crossing* (2011), writing represents a subversive act in the newly founded Puritan settlement on North America's Atlantic coast. In anticipation of the "national imperative" (Nelson 1998, p. 28) of white manhood in the USA, literacy, even in the 1660s, is a privilege granted to a few Native men selected by the settler Puritan authorities at Harvard University's Indian College, while it remains taboo to white women, such as the narrator Bethia Mayfield. In *Caleb's Crossing*, Bethia relates the settlement history of Martha's Vineyard and the story of two Indigenous boys educated at Harvard University's Indian College in a historically certified effort to kill two birds with one stone: first, to ease Harvard College's financial problems, and second, to educate "the English &Indian youth of this Country in knowledge: and godliness" (Peabody Museum 2011). Through Bethia's eyes, the contact between the Puritan settlers and the Indigenous peoples is rendered as a crossing, back and forth, between cultures, epistemologies, and life and death: as a girl, Bethia secretly befriends Cheeshahteaumauk of the Noepe, whom she calls Caleb, on Martha's Vineyard. The story ends in 1675 with King Philip's War, which violently terminates the relations between the settlers and the Indigenous tribes. Through Bethia's eyes, the novel triangulates different Puritanisms, settler colonialism, and regionalist historiographies. In the Afterword, Brooks attributes the story to the "remarkable environmental and cultural stewardship of the Wampanoag Tribe of Gay Head/Aquinnah," where she "first learned" of Cheeshahteaumauk and his graduation from Newtowne College (later Harvard University) in 1661. Cheeshahteaumauk's omission from historiography, she holds, might be due to either invisibility and assimilation, or to social isolation "by racial prejudice" (2011, p. 414). Fictional Caleb's survival struggle to syncretize his beliefs with rigid Protestant discipline spells out the US settler colonial myth of the vanishing Indian. His efforts are thwarted by many factors, including the turn of settler–native relations, his infection from tuberculosis (caused by what Bethia finds to be an unhealthy lifestyle of indoor study), and his recluse shaman uncle, who has foreseen the demise of his people at the hands of the settlers. With Orpheus's crossing into the underworld as epigraph, *Caleb's Crossing* reads as the eulogy for a utopian New World of Indigenous and settler exchange that might have been, but Brooks is careful to lay the blame at anyone's feet.

While Caleb perishes, Bethia's testimony persists. *Caleb's Crossing* embodies Bethia's diary, in three parts, as a teenager on the island, as an indentured servant at a Cambridge grammar school, and on her deathbed back on the island. Bethia calls her account a "spiritual diary," doubting that she will ever have the courage to accuse herself of her sins publicly in Puritan custom (2011, p. 8). The narrator transgresses social, gendered, and cultural boundaries in a battle without and within her community; drawn to the spiritual practices of the island tribes, she realizes she is not among those saved by the Puritan God (p. 92). Yet she also contrasts the teachings of her family, the Mayfields, with the hypocritical congregation of the Living Saints on the mainland, whom she describes as "whited sepulchres" and "base" (p. 286). And finally, she secretly battles with her inferior status as a woman, eavesdropping and learning both the teachings of her missionary father and the forbidden language of the Wampanoag ("Listening, not speaking, has been my way," p. 4). Against the rigid Puritan teachings, she holds up a pragmatic irony, for example, by observing that "they say the Lord's day is a day of rest, but those who preach this generally are not women" (p. 114).

Sticking with the intimacy and obsession of self-inspection, *March* fills a gap in an American literary classic, Louisa May Alcott's *Little Women* (1868/9). Where Alcott's novel shows the deprivations of the four March sisters whose father has gone to fight in the Civil War, Brooks provides the father's battlefield experience and remembrance of his youth. March's war travels are also a journey into his past. As a blueprint for the protagonist, Brooks takes Louisa May Alcott's father, Amos Bronson Alcott (1799–1888), a member of the Concord Transcendentalists, radical reformer, and pedagogue, whose failed experiments and bankruptcy prompted his daughter's career as bestselling author. Brooks thus imagines the life young Bronson might have had traveling the South as a peddler, the marriage of the Alcotts, and the war trauma afflicted on the March family and on the nation, when its capital Washington is turned into a war sickbay. March's telling voice is conjured from Bronson Alcott's writings (2005, p. 276), and his famous contemporaries Ralph Waldo Emerson and Henry David Thoreau also make appearances. *March* reiterates episodes readers might know from Alcott's *Little Women* and thus throws into relief its narrative perspective of Alcott's alter ego, Jo. Where *Little Women* anticipates the arrival of the New Woman at the end of the nineteenth century, *March* shows how the idealist father sees his world view, mind, and body shattered, and remains scarred for life. Brooks articulates a feminist enhancement of *Little Women* in various ways: on the story level, she interrogates the Marches' partnership; on the historiographic plane, she revises Bronson Alcott's role as reformer and Concord Light; and in pertaining to national memory and symbolism, she administers the demise of patriarchy lived through by March. *March* is not only a fictional retelling, but also an allegorical story of the USA. In Alcott's travels as peddler and his participation in the Transcendentalist movement, the reader may identify the narrative of the nation's "coming of age," fought out in the conflict over slavery in the carnage of the Civil War (see Haase and Schäfer 2019; Schäfer 2021).

In *March*, Brooks engages the US cultural craze of remembering the Civil War which "has never receded into the remote past in American life" (Fahs and Waugh 2004, p. 2). The suggested union between the northerner Alcott and the formerly enslaved Grace, the lover of his young life, and his preference for Grace over his wife, Marmee, spell out the romance of reconciliation (Thomas 2017) and pinpoint the blinding whiteness of the American classic *Little Women*. Grace is Brooks's only Black character of import, a sidelined helper figure who is at the same time the object of a supressed desire looming in the attic of the Marches' marriage. At March's Civil War sickbed, she is given the agency to care for him, then gracefully walk away from the oldish white man toward her own freedom. In turn, his wife, Marmee, describes Washington in "ruins," a capital under construction but already reeking of "lost grandeur" (2005, p. 215). The perspectives of these two women reiterate the paradoxical function of the Civil War in US cultural memory, both as cataclysm of internal conflict and as everlasting point of return and national self-reassurance.

Brooks's writing foregrounds the pragmatism its many female protagonists employ to make the world go round and exposes male vanity and weakness. As Bethia states "I am not a hero [...] But neither will I go to my grave a coward, silent about what I did, and what it cost" (2011, p. 410). The female characters are often empowered by romance, "true" love, and heterosexual fulfilment, which recalls nineteenth-century sentimental fiction. If read historically, the question remains whether the women who Brooks portrays had a chance at this very contemporary notion of female self-realization. Her choice of topic and historic personnel are easy points of entry for Western general educated readers, but specifically for Americans who are exposed to Puritanism and Civil War histories in school curricula and in everyday cultural practice. The rewritings Brooks offers, spiced up with romance and female self-empowerment, are easily accessible and question "master" narratives. Her bestselling novels are equipped with reader's guides, interviews with the author, and recommendations for book club discussions that address and engaged general readership with a pedagogic thrust, which might also explain why they have been overlooked in scholarly debates. She acknowledges taking liberties with her historic findings, such as creating Bethia's narrative voice from the writings of Puritan icons Anne Bradstreet, Anne Hutchinson, or Mary Rowlandson (all of which were edited and censored, of course, by well-meaning white men), or inventing the enigma of the Sarajevo Haggadah's lost silver clasps, courtesy of a syphilis-ridden Austrian. These inventions lend vivacity to a type of historical fiction seeking to revise historiographies too often read as authoritative. From a contemporary vantage point, Brooks's novels may be seen to cater to a white feminist desire for historic revisionism that overlooks intersectional subject positions. While she supports a pacifist stance in religious conflict, her novels also embrace US exceptionalism. The Puritan/national origin story in *Caleb's Crossing* or the Civil War mending administered by the Black woman in *March* affirm the greatness attributed to the US national project. So do Brooks's characters, who remind us that the Great Men of History were made, loved, and cared for by strong and no-nonsense white women.

SEE ALSO: Book Clubs; Chick Lit and the New Domesticity; Doctorow, E.L.; Fictions of Work and Labor; Hustvedt, Siri; Pynchon, Thomas; Realism after Poststructuralism; Third-Wave Feminism

REFERENCES

Alcott, Louisa May. (1989). *Little Women*. New York: Penguin; 1st ed. 1868/9.
Brooks, Geraldine. (2005). *March. A Novel*. London: Harper Perennial.
Brooks, Geraldine. (2008). *People of the Book*. London: Harper Perennial.
Brooks, Geraldine. (2011). *Caleb's Crossing*. London: Fourth Estate.
Canning, Kathleen. (2006). *Gender History in Practice: Historical Perspectives on Bodies, Class, and Citizenship*. Ithaca and London: Cornell University Press.
Fahs, Alice and Waugh, Joan. (eds.) (2004). *The Memory of the Civil War in American Culture*. Chapel Hill and London: University of North Carolina Press.
Haase, Felix and Schäfer, Stefanie. (2019). Revisioning and rewriting American history in Geraldine Brooks' *March* (2005), James McBride's *The Good Lord Bird* (2013), and E.L. Doctorow's *The March: A Novel* (2006). In: *The American Novel in the 21st Century* (ed. Michael Basseler and Ansgar Nünning), 87–100. Trier: WVT.
Huehls, Mitchum. (2017). Historical fiction and the end of history. In: *American Literature in Transition: 2000–2010* (ed. Rachel Greenwald Smith), 138–151. Cambridge: Cambridge University Press.
Hutcheon, Linda. (1989). *Historiographic Metafiction, Parody and the Intertextuality of History*. Baltimore: Johns Hopkins University Press.
Hutcheon, Linda. (2002). *The Politics of Postmodernism*. London: Routledge.
Peabody Museum. (2011). The Indian College. https://www.peabody.harvard.edu/node/2011 (accessed June 29, 2021).
Nelson, Dana. (1998). *National Manhood. Capitalist Citizenship and the Imagined Fraternity of White Men*. Durham, NC, and London: Duke University Press.
Schäfer, Stefanie. (2021). *Yankee Yarns. Storytelling and the Invention of the National Body in Nineteenth-Century American Culture*. Edinburgh: Edinburgh University Press.
Thomas, Brook. (2017). *The Literature of Reconstruction: Not in Plain Black and White*. Baltimore: Johns Hopkins University Press.
White, Hayden. (1984). The question of narrative in contemporary historical theory. In: *Metafiction* (ed. Mark Currie, 1995), 104–114. London: Longman.

FURTHER READING

Blight, David. (2001). *Race and Reunion: The Civil War in American Memory*. Cambridge: Harvard University Press.
Browne, Victoria. (2014). *Feminism, Time, and Nonlinear History*. London: Palgrave Macmillan.
Maynes, Mary Jo, Laslett, Barbara, Joeres, Ruth-Ellen Boetcher, et al. (eds.) (1997). *History and Theory: Feminist Research, Debates, Contestations*. Chicago: University of Chicago Press.
Rifkin, Julie and Ryan, Michael. (2004). Feminist paradigms. In: *Literary Theory. An Anthology* (ed. Julie Rifkin and Michael Ryan), 765–769. Oxford: Blackwell.
Smith, Bonnie. (2010). Women's history: a retrospective from the United States. *Signs: Journal of Women in Culture and Society* 35 (3): 723–747.

Burroughs, William S.

ALEX WERMER-COLAN
Temple University, USA

William Seward Burroughs (b. February 5, 1914, in St. Louis, Missouri – d. August 2, 1997, in Lawrence, Kansas) remains a paradoxical figure, standing as one of the most controversial, avant-garde, and popular writers of the twentieth century. In the post-World War II period, Burroughs's experimental works in fiction and autobiography bent the boundaries of American prose genres through surreal satire and obscene fantasy. Born into a family whose wealth derived from his grandfather's invention of the adding machine, Burroughs's thinking and writing broke further ground speculating on technology's imbrication with power, biology, and language. Graduating with a degree in English literature from Harvard University in 1936, Burroughs pursued postgraduate studies in anthropology and ethnology, and, briefly, medical school in Vienna. In the aftermath of World War II, Burroughs became addicted to heroin while living in New York City, where he acted as a mentor to young acolytes of the Beat generation like Jack Kerouac and Allen Ginsberg. After publishing such classic works of Cold War American fiction as *Naked Lunch* (1959) and the 1960s cut-up novels popularly known as the "Nova Trilogy," Burroughs was heralded as a spokesperson for the counterculture and a godfather of the punk movement. Bridging modernist and postmodernist literary traditions in American fiction, Burroughs's influence left its mark on such authors and artists as Kathy Acker and Thomas Pynchon, Iggy Pop and David Cronenberg. Burroughs's contradictory status as a cultural renegade, a notorious novelist, and a prophetic thinker has remained at the crux of his enduring appeal ever since. While Burroughs's most groundbreaking works of literature and art appeared at the helm of the 1960s countercultural revolution, even after his rise to prominence in the 1970s, Burroughs continued to create variegated and innovative works of American fiction and autofiction until the end of his long life. Since his death at the age of 83, archivists and scholars have recovered tens of thousands of Burroughs's unpublished materials, producing restored editions and releasing previously unknown writings and multimedia works that have brought Burroughs's transformative visions to life in the early decades of the new millennium.

Burroughs began writing in the 1930s, but he only completed a novel and found marginal success with his earliest, confessional work, *Junkie: Confessions of an Unredeemed Drug Addict* published under the pseudonym William Lee in 1953. His second novel, *Queer*, was written shortly thereafter, but remained unpublished until 1985, when Burroughs appended a preface where he reflected for the first time in print on his accidental killing of his wife, Joan Vollmer, during a drunken rendition of the William Tell act in Mexico City in 1951. That heinous act would haunt Burroughs for the rest of his life, driving him into twenty-five years of exile as he traveled and resided in Latin America, North Africa, and Europe, while pursuing through his writing a life-long quest to escape from what he called the "ugly spirit." Burroughs's two early novels, along with his epistolary novella co-authored with Allen Ginsberg, *The Yage Letters* (1963), exemplified an unusual willingness to speak explicitly about "deviant" behaviors in a style and tone far ahead of his time. These early confessional works presaged Burroughs's exorcistic experiments in literary form and content in the coming decades. Burroughs would soon become an infamous literary figure with the publication of his shocking collage-novel, *Naked Lunch*, notorious not least due to the series of legal cases challenging its distribution on the grounds of obscenity. Shortly after the books' publication, thanks to the artist Brion Gysin, Burroughs's discovery of the cut-up method commenced a decade-long effort to take the collage form further than any modernist predecessor. Burroughs produced not only short pieces, but eventually novel-length works, by cutting up tens of thousands of pages from the literary canon, contemporary newspapers and magazines, and any ephemera he could find. His cut-up novels of the 1960s caused a literary sensation, offending traditional standards of taste, conventions of authorship, and formal expectations of genre and narrative: *The Soft Machine* (1961, 1966, 1968), *The Ticket That Exploded* (1962, 1967), and *Nova Express* (1964) appeared in multiple permutations over the 1960s. His science-fictional world-building formulated a psychedelic, space-age mythology, prophesizing a ruling class whose manipulation of technology and viral forms of language would put contemporary society, and the planet's survival, at unprecedented risk.

Burroughs's paranoid vision of a dystopian present and future became increasingly mainstream at the turn of the 1970s with the publication of opinion pieces and interviews in such collections as *The Job* (1968) and his manifesto of technological pessimism and guerrilla warfare, *The Electronic Revolution* (1970, 1973). In this period, Burroughs transformed from an exile of the United States to a spokesperson for the youth counterculture, a role model whose writings and persona would become enshrined in the highest echelons of academic and popular culture in the coming decades. After being elected to the American Academy and Institute of Arts and Letters in 1983, Burroughs was awarded the Ordre des Arts et des Lettres by France a year later. Despite earning early in life the moniker of "the Invisible Man," Burroughs would go on to seem just as much at home performing a reading for *Saturday Night Live* in 1981, making cameos in films like Gus Van Sant's *Drugstore Cowboy* (1989), or starring in a Nike commercial in 1994 that blatantly commodified his outlaw iconicity. His novel *Naked Lunch* was adapted to film by David Cronenberg in 1991, and throughout the 1980s and 1990s, Burroughs released recordings from his reading tours and collaborated on albums with rock stars like Kurt Cobain for the piece "The 'Priest' They Called Him" (1993). He even wrote a libretto with Tom Waits for Robert Wilson's Faustian *The Black Rider* (1992).

The turn in American culture and literature marked by the year 1980, then, holds a pivotal place in the transformation of Burroughs's reputation. At the 1978 Nova Convention in New York City, Burroughs was given a seat of honor by such luminaries as Michel Foucault and Gilles Deleuze, John Cage and Patti Smith. In his keynote address, Burroughs articulated the pressing political stakes of his oeuvre for the present and the future: "If we see the earth as a spaceship and go further to invoke the comparison of a lifeboat, it is of course of vital concern to everybody on the boat if the crew and the passengers start polluting the supplies of food and water, distributing supplies on a grossly inequitable basis, knocking holes in the bottom of the boat, or worst of all plotting to blow the boat out from under us" (Burroughs 1979).

If Burroughs was unexpectedly canonized by the early 1980s, his personal life also went through seismic shifts during the last decade of the Cold War. After his twenty-five years of self-imposed exile from the United States, in 1974, Burroughs had finally returned to the United States to live in New York City at the center of the vibrant downtown art and music scene, meeting famous artists like Andy Warhol and a steady stream of fans and disciples. Burroughs's regular visitors to his apartment, known as the Bunker, exposed the recovering addict to unnumbered temptations. After spending the 1970s residing in New York City and making money touring as a literary celebrity around the globe, in 1981 Burroughs moved to Lawrence, Kansas, thanks to the urging and assistance of his literary agent and editor, his soon-to-be adopted son, and the eventual head of his literary estate, James Grauerholz. Burroughs wasn't only escaping the New York scene; a few years later downtown New York would find itself at the nexus of the HIV/AIDs epidemic. Burroughs's move was potentially lifesaving, but accompanied by an ominous premonition. By the late 1970s, Burroughs was putting the finishing touches to his first novel since *The Wild Boys:*

A Book of the Dead (1971), *The Cities of Red Night* (1981), a work oft credited with prophesizing a sexually transmitted virus akin to HIV/AIDS. This first work in his last prose trilogy was followed by *The Place of Dead Roads* (1983) and *The Western Lands* (1987). Just as his earliest prose trilogy arose out of collaborations and correspondence with Allen Ginsberg, and his second trilogy, the cut-up sci-fi novels of the 1960s, came into being through collaborations with Brion Gysin, Burroughs's last trilogy was the product of collaborations with James Grauerholz. It was also produced from a new vantage point in Burroughs's life, as he settled into relative seclusion in Kansas and took stock of his life.

Shortly after his move to the American Midwest, however, his son, William S. Burroughs III (also known as William S. Burroughs Jr. and Billy Burroughs), died at the young age of 33 from cirrhosis of the liver, leaving Burroughs rueful of the divide that had persisted between father and son throughout much of their lives. Not least because of this tragic event, in his late period, Burroughs would write his most significant works of autobiography, including his Preface to the belatedly published *Queer*, his short, but moving elegy, *The Cat Inside* (1986), his dream diary, *My Education: A Book of Dreams* (1995), and his posthumously published journals, *Last Words: The Final Journals of William S. Burroughs* (2000). During the 1980s, Ted Morgan also interviewed Burroughs for his first official biography, *Literary Outlaw: Life and Times of William S. Burroughs* (1988). Morgan's interviews with Burroughs offered an opportunity for Burroughs to recollect over his long life; the tape recordings remain a treasure trove of archival materials housed at Arizona State University's Rare Books and Manuscripts Library. Indeed, by the 1990s, Burroughs's work was becoming coveted by libraries and archives interested in acquiring the possessions of major literary estates.

Burroughs's ongoing collaborations with James Grauerholz not only led to new collections of his essays in *The Adding Machine* (1986) and of his fiction in *Interzone* (1990), but also ensured the preservation of his papers in special collections around the country, archival holdings that have enabled, posthumously, a rebirth in Burroughs scholarship through the recovery, analysis, and publication of misprinted, unpublished, and unknown works.

If by the 1980s the cut-up method was less central to his craft, in his late writing Burroughs nevertheless continued to experiment with avant-garde practices of writing and artmaking, including new narrative techniques in his novels and visual techniques in his shotgun paintings. For Burroughs, the creative process was always aimed at the transcendence of the written word by means of aural or visual arts that could serve as portals beyond the limitations of the rational mind and the physical body. Throughout his life, Burroughs's project to "rub out the word" manifested in wide-ranging media and forms: from artistic collages to newspaper mock-ups, from comics in Jeff Nuttall's 1960s mimeo magazine, *My Own Mag*, to the graphic novel *Ah Pook is Here* (1979) with Malcolm McNeill, from early recordings *Call Me Burroughs* (1965) to the tape remixes later collected in *Break Through In Grey Room* (1986) and his spoken word collaboration "Spare Ass Annie and other Tales" (1993). In 1994, Burroughs's art was exhibited at the Los Angeles County Museum of Art; along with the accompanying catalogue book *Ports of Entry: William S. Burroughs and the Arts* (1996), the show established Burroughs on the map of art historians, auction houses, galleries, and museums. Since that time, a series of books have collected and documented Burroughs's multimedia works, including *The Art of William S. Burroughs: Cut-ups, Cut-ins, Cut-outs* (2012), Axel Heil's and Ian

McFadyen's *William S. Burroughs: Cut (The Future of the Past)* (2013), Patricia Allmer's and John Sears's *Taking Shots: The Photography of William S. Burroughs* (2014), and Joan Hawkins's and Alex Wermer-Colan's edited collection *William S. Burroughs Cutting Up the Century* (2019).

Burroughs's death in 1997 hardly marked the end of his publishing career; in fact, in its aftermath, Burroughs's work experienced an unexpected renaissance, with restored editions of his published works, and publications of previously unseen materials from the archives and small press periodicals, revealing what had remained hidden under the iceberg of Burroughs's wide-ranging cut-up practices. While Burroughs's manuscripts are spread throughout special collections and private collectors' holdings in the United States and Europe, the vast majority are housed at Arizona State University's Rare Books and Manuscripts Library, Ohio State University's Rare Books and Manuscripts Library, and the New York Public Library's Henry W. and Albert A. Berg Collection of English and American Literature. Of all of Burroughs's archival holdings, the Berg Collection testifies to Burroughs's assertion in his title for Folio 58: "What Is Rejected For The Final Typescript Submitted To Publisher Is Often As Good Or Better Than What Goes In . . ." The Berg Collection contains over 11,000 pages of materials that even Burroughs never saw after archiving his work with Barry Miles's assistance in the early 1970 (after being sold into private hands, the so-called Vaduz archive remained hidden from the public until 2008, when it was acquired by the New York Public Library). Over the past two decades, James Grauerholz and Oliver Harris, most notably, have pursued unprecedented editorial projects to restore editions of Burroughs's first trilogy (*Junky: The Definitive Text of Junk* [2012], *Queer: 25th Anniversary Edition* [2010], and *The Yage Letters Redux* [2006], as well as *Naked Lunch: The Restored Text* [2013]), and the misnamed "Nova Trilogy" (*The Soft Machine: The Restored Text* [2014], *The Ticket That Exploded: The Restored Text* [2014], and *Nova Express: The Restored Text* [2014]). These restored editions represent a significant archival project in postmodern American literary studies, giving new life to these avant-garde works whose printings were riddled with errors, and whose conditions of publication and censorship kept confined to the archive much of the works' most compelling material. These speculative works are not only valuable critical editions of Burroughs's oeuvre, exhibiting archival perspectives and supplements to the original editions; these restored editions also testify to the way Burroughs's wide-ranging writings were always meant to be read as one large book, mutating in a constant state of metamorphosis, alive and adaptive to the present.

As in the case of such publications as Geoffrey D. Smith's and John M. Bennett's edited collections of *Everything Lost: The Latin American Notebook of William S. Burroughs* (2008) and *William S. Burroughs' "The Revised Boy Scout Manual": An Electronic Revolution* (2018), the trend in publishing Burroughs's works has increasingly shifted towards publishing new works of previously unseen archival materials. Burroughs's correspondence has appeared across two volumes, Oliver Harris's *The Letters of William S. Burroughs, Vol. 1: 1945–1959* (1994) and Bill Morgan's *Rub Out the Word: The Letters of William S. Burroughs, 1959–1974* (2012). His interviews have been collected in *Burroughs Live: The Collected Interviews of William S. Burroughs (1960–1997)* (2001). More recently published archival materials have shed light on such diverse subjects as Burroughs's cut-up method, his personal life, and the disparate influences on his work from such twentieth-century thinkers as the Freudian disciple Wilhelm Reich, the theorist of General Semantics, Alfred Korzybski, and the founder of Scientology, L. Ron Hubbard. Alex Wermer-Colan's edited collection, *The Travel Agency is on Fire* (2015), featured Burroughs's cut-up experiments with writers from William Shakespeare to T.S. Elliot. Joan Hawkins's and Wermer-Colan's anthology of criticism and archival materials, *William S. Burroughs Cutting Up the Century*, was born out of festivals and conferences in 2014 marking the centennial of Burroughs's birth, and showcased a new wave of Burroughs scholarship on the politics of the cut-up method and the archive in the age of new media. Over the past decade, thanks to the indefatigable work of Keith Seward and book collector Jed Birmingham, the website *RealityStudio.org* has also become an unprecedented repository of bootleg editions of Burroughs's publications throughout the mimeograph and small press revolution. Michael Stevens's *The Road to Interzone: Reading William S. Burroughs Reading* (2009) represents another milestone in Burroughs's scholarship, offering the most comprehensive view of Burroughs's reading practices throughout his life. These wide-ranging developments in Burroughs scholarship, while building upon previous generations of scholars' critical exegeses, has proven critical to rejuvenating and adapting Burroughs's idiosyncratic oeuvre to the contemporary period of digital new media and neoliberal dystopia, historical developments that the proto-cyberpunk author had arguably anticipated as early as the 1950s.

Burroughs's late period in the 1980s and 1990s is often discussed as the time when his outlaw status became commodified, and when the author retreated from militant politics, seeking instead through silent representations of inner space an escape from a planet rotting at the hands of virulent powers from outer/cyber space. The posthumous resurrection of Burroughs's unpublished works, however, has given a second life to his subversive influence on contemporary culture and art in the twenty-first century. Throughout his entire oeuvre, Burroughs wrote for the present and the future, trying to intervene into contemporary power dynamics, while altering how the people of his time looked at the past and imagined possible futures. In his late work, his writing became all the more speculative, as his pessimism deepened about the narrowing potential for new forms of human existence. As he reimagined how to challenge what his readers thought inevitable and natural, Burroughs increasingly turned in his late work to the deep past, reflecting on what life could have been like without European colonialism, and exploring how a sexually transmitted virus could irrevocably change the world. During this late period, as he witnessed the death of many of his closest friends and peers, including Allan Ginsberg's passing only months before his own, Burroughs's creative work became increasingly preoccupied with the possibility of an afterlife, and turned in his late writing to ancient practices for navigating the land of the dead. Nevertheless, Burroughs's late work remains the least studied period of his oeuvre, perhaps not least because these novels, especially *The Western Lands*, demonstrate such an intense meditation on the significance of and potential for immortality, or life beyond the limitations of the body and the mind. While Burroughs's post-1980 late works have yet to receive the critical attention given to his earlier works, his last prose trilogy, autobiographical writings, and artistic experiments, as well as his previously unpublished writing now being published posthumously, amount to an unprecedented afterlife for his oeuvre, offering readers of today prescient perspectives on the new millennium's crisis-ridden political, technological, and ecological landscape.

SEE ALSO: Cyberpunk; Delany, Samuel; DeLillo, Don; Gibson, William; Mixed-Genre Fiction;

The New Experimentalism/The Contemporary Avant-Garde; Pynchon, Thomas; Queer and LGBT Fiction; Reed, Ishmael; Sontag, Susan

REFERENCE

Burroughs, William S. (1979). *The Nova Convention*. New York: Giorno Poetry Systems. https://soundcloud.com/pir8m1k3y/nova-conspiracy-william-s (accessed August 27, 2021).

FURTHER READING

Burroughs, William S. (2005). *William S. Burroughs Papers (1951–1972)*. New York: The New York Public Library's Henry W. and Alban A. Berg Collection, Berg Coll MSS Burroughs Archive.
Harris, Oliver. (2003). *William Burroughs and the Secret of Fascination*. Carbondale: Southern Illinois University Press.
Hawkins, Joan and Wermer-Colan, Alex. (eds.) (2019). *William S. Burroughs Cutting Up the Century*. Bloomingdale: Indiana University Press.
Miles, Barry. (2014). *Call Me Burroughs: A Life*. New York: Twelve.
Walsh, Philip and Schneiderman, Davis. (eds.) (2004). *Retaking the Universe: William S. Burroughs in the Age of Globalization*. London: Pluto.
Wermer-Colan, Alex and Hawkins, Joan. (eds.) (2019). *William S. Burroughs Cutting Up the Century*. Bloomingdale: Indiana University Press.

Butler, Octavia

ALYS EVE WEINBAUM
University of Washington, USA

Octavia Estelle Butler was a reclusive and prolific writer of speculative fiction (SF) who maintained notoriously careful boundaries around her intimate life. Consequently, the same short list of personal details is repeatedly gleaned by Butler scholars from the interviews that she gave over the course of a writing career tragically cut short by a lethal fall on winter ice in front of her Lake Forest Park home, outside Seattle, on February 24, 2006, several months prior to her 58th birthday. Perhaps because of her reclusivity, public appearances made an especially forceful impression – indeed, Butler's writing and persona feed an ever-widening audience that she frequently described as composed of three cohorts: science fiction fans, feminists, and African American readers. As obituaries attest, at the time of Butler's untimely death she was acclaimed not only for transforming the SF genre from within but also as a major contributor to both feminist theory and contemporary African American literature. Butler had cult-like status among a range of cultural workers including Afrofuturists, posthumanists, Black feminists, and "cyborg theorists" (those inspired by the reading of Butler first offered by Donna Haraway). She was the first writer of SF to be awarded a McArthur "Genius Award," the first Black woman to garner the two most prestigious science fiction prizes, the Hugo and the Nebula, and, in retrospect, she is widely regarded as *the* trailblazer who pried opened the tightly locked doors of a resolutely white male genre to people of color, and especially to Black women.

Butler was born on June 22, 1947, in Pasadena California, to Octavia M. Butler. Her mother worked as a live-in maid, and it was in the homes of white employers that Butler recalls first witnessing the at once harsh and quotidian racism that characterized America in the early years of the Civil Rights era. Butler's father was a shoeshine man who died when she was an infant. Butler notes her appreciation for her mother's support in interviews, but this acknowledgment is often coupled with her expression of an abiding sense of isolation growing up. Butler felt herself to be an outsider among outsiders – "an out kid" who never fully belonged (Rowell 1997, p. 65). Butler sometimes attributes her isolation to her commanding physical stature (she was 6 foot 2 inches) and to her undiagnosed dyslexia. Butler scholars also attribute it to her experience of racism, sexism, and poverty. Her oft-cited self-description captures her understanding of her positionality, as well as her intersectional take on her life experience: "I'm comfortably asocial, a hermit in the middle of Seattle – a pessimist if I'm not careful, a feminist, a black, a former Baptist, an oil-and-water combination of ambition, laziness, insecurity, certainty and drive" (Francis 2010, p. xi).

Butler's "drive," imaginative and otherwise, propelled her forward from an early age. She was a young library-goer who quickly moved from reading stories to writing her own. The circumstances of her first foray into her chosen genre at age 12 are instructive. As Butler notes, she wrote in response to *Devil Girls from Mars*, a TV show she was certain she could best. After graduating from John Muir High School in 1965, Butler worked day jobs that enabled her to attend college at night. She completed a two-year degree at Pasadena City College in 1968, and then went on to enroll in the Screen Writers Guild Open Door Program at Cal State, Los Angeles. It was in a Guild course that Butler met Harlan Ellison, the science fiction writer who she claims was the first to offer honest critical feedback and to encourage her professional writing career. Ellison helped arrange for Butler's participation in the Clarion Science Fiction and Fantasy Writing Workshop, so-called because it was first convened in Clarion, Pennsylvania. The six-week program produced an anthology that included Butler's first publication. While holding down a series of day jobs that she notes were often boring and/or degrading, Butler wrote daily, building her craft, submission by submission. In 1976, she published her first novel, *Patternmaster*.

Collectors of early editions of Butler's novels know that the cover art, which occasionally depicts Black female protagonists as white, indexes the hesitance if not the outright unwillingness of the SF publishing industry to conceive of a Black woman as the heroine of a science fiction narrative that would appeal to fans. The cover art also indexes the early disavowal of Butler's persistent thematization of raced and gendered power dynamics throughout her corpus. Whether the story or novel in question is populated by slaves, aliens, telepaths, or shapeshifters, each represents a complex meditation on social power, on the intersections of race and gender, and on how complexly articulated social hierarchies subtend the interactions among all living beings. If there is an overarching question that can be said to animate the entirety of Butler's corpus, it is a question about the construction of concept of "human being" – about who is included within the ambit of the "human," and about how contests over the meaning of the concept are delimited by racial and gender distinctions as well as by racialized and gendered distinctions drawn among species.

Patternmaster turned out to be the first installment in a nonsequential series broadly concerned with the plight of those who possess heightened telepathic and psionic abilities (the so-called Patternists who are connected into a telepathic pattern), with the social and political consequences of feelings of superiority. In addition to *Patternmaster* the series includes *Mind of my Mind* (1977), *Survivor* (1977), *Wild Seed* (1980), and *Clay's Ark* (1984). Of these, *Wild Seed*, a novel about Doro, an Egyptian man-spirit or *ubange* who is immortal and has already been alive for 4000 years, and Anyanwu, a shape-shifting African woman who possesses the power to regenerate and thus reproduce her own immortality, has garnered the lion's share of critical attention. The novel robustly centers race and gender power dynamics, and vividly stages the contests between Doro and Anyanwu not only as epic in scope but also as allegorical.

After all, Doro and Anyanwu are embroiled in a battle over how to reproduce life itself. For his part, Doro hopes to breed a race of beings with heightened abilities that confer immortality and can therefore companion Doro into eternity. By turns, Anyanwu works to resist Doro's orchestrated breeding program and its eugenic agenda. Instead of killing and breeding to survive, Anyanwu nurtures the lives of the wayward beings whom she has healed and drawn into her powerful orbit through expression of empathy and solidarity. Though neither Doro nor Anyanwu are strictly speaking "human," the question of human futurity looms over the text, and the struggle for reproductive hegemony emerges as the stake in the conflict depicted. Indeed, as in all the other power struggles Butler depicts, one form of power over life itself (what the French theorist Michel Foucault has called "biopower") is pitted against another. Though Butler notes in interviews that she generally avoided literary criticism and cultural theory in the hope of sheltering her work from its influence, some critics regard Butler as a feminist theorist of biopower, and thus as a feminist theorist of the biological body. As Gregory Hampton explains, Butler's writings hold up a mirror that demystifies the ways that readers attribute meaning to bodies and to the gendered and racialized populations that these bodies collectively comprise.

Wild Seed, set during the first two centuries of the Atlantic slave trade, is thematically linked to Butler's best-known work, *Kindred* (1979). Whereas *Wild Seed* treats the Atlantic slave trade as a backdrop, *Kindred*, which is sometimes generically classified as a neo-slave narrative alongside works such as Toni Morrison's *Beloved* (1987), centers racial slavery in America by imagining enslavement from the vantage point of the enslaved. By employing the conceit of time travel, it rockets a Black woman living in Los Angeles in 1976 back and forth between her present moment and her life on an antebellum Maryland slave plantation inhabited by her ancestors. As Dana shuttles between supposed freedom and the deprivations and dangers of life as a slave, the indistinction between "freedom" and "enslavement" becomes increasingly palpable. In this way, Butler shows readers how slavery lives on in the minds and bodies of the enslaved and their descendants even in those instances in which the slave past is not consciously recognized as impressing itself on the present. At the novel's close, Dana returns to Los Angeles for what she hopes will be the last time. Tellingly, she does so with an arm that is so maimed by the powerful grip of her white progenitor as she travels through time that her limb must be violently amputated. Symbolically, slavery lives on in Dana's broken body as in her mind.

In Butler's second series, *Xenogenesis* or *Lilith's Brood* (the latter is the title of the single volume, first published in 2000, containing the novels that make up the trilogy: *Dawn* [1987], *Adulthood Rites* [1988], and *Imago* [1989]), Butler again homes in on racialized and gendered power dynamics, social hierarchy, and the question of human being. In this instance, these concerns play out through an evolving interspecies relationship between humans and extraterrestrials that is marked by racism, sexism, and a sense of superiority that is manifest by the aliens through their conquest of the humans, and by the humans through what can only be characterized as their "humanism" (in a torque on the familiar term). In *Dawn*, the most critically acclaimed novel in this series, Butler introduces the Oankali, a species differentiated into three genders (rather than two) whose bodies are clad in sensory tentacles variously used for communication, sexual pleasure, and reproduction. The Oankali inhabit a living spaceship that is traveling the universe "trading" genetic materials with those with whom the Oankali must breed to survive. Because the Oankali are biologically compelled to continuously transform themselves at the genetic level, for reasons simultaneously altruistic and self-interested they rescue as many survivors as possible from planet Earth after its inhabitants have rendered it uninhabitable through environmental assault and nuclear warfare. The Oankali keep their human captives in suspended animation for decades as they study their DNA and work to acclimate them to the idea that they must eventually breed with Oankali and blend the two species into an entirely new species neither entirely purely human nor Oankali. The nuclear holocaust that serves as *Dawn*'s backstory has led some critics to read the novel as a meditation on Cold War anxieties that animated the US–Soviet conflict during the historical moment in which the novel was written. Others read the gene trading as an uncannily prescient meditation on the Human Genome Project, which only succeeded in mapping the human genome two decades *after* the book's publication. This second reading has continued to amass resonance as gene patenting and the biocapitalist economy that depends on a global trade in genetic materials and bioinformatics accelerates.

As in her other novels, in *Dawn* Butler's protagonist is a Black woman. The near impossible task foisted on Lilith Iyapo is training a small group of fellow humans to survive after they and their Oankali "families" are transported back to Earth to repopulate it. While Lilith struggles with the psychological transformations that accompany the genetic transformations that she endures as she is adapted by the Oankali, she brings the reader into a world in which it is necessary to imagine trading pure humanness for hybridized survival. While Lilith is judged a traitor by some humans for acquiescence to the Oankali's reproductive agenda, her response to her impossible situation is so delicately and generously portrayed by Butler that it clears space for expanded meditation on her central question: What does it mean to be human when clinging to genetic purity amounts to suicide at the level of the species? When does the quest for human purity become a form of racism, or more aptly an expression humanism? And, at what tipping point does power over the reproduction of species morph into power over life itself?

The use of representations of interspecies relationships to recast familiar racial dynamics is a mainstay of SF. The signature of Butler's SF is that she intertwines her meditations on fictive interspecies conflicts with meditations on actual interracial conflicts as these have emerged over the course of American history. While Butler has occasionally issued disclaimers about specific texts, expressly stating that they are not about slavery, the history of dehumanization that is an adjunct of 400 years of racial slavery in the Atlantic world invariably inflects her corpus through her insistent return to the question of what it means to be human. Butler's repeated creation of Black female protagonists who must confront hierarchical behavior among fellow humans in the form of racism and sexism, and/or address power dynamics imposed by other species through control over reproduction, necessarily allegorizes the processes of dehumanization that characterize the long history of slavery in the Americas and the Caribbean and the specific culture of reproductive extraction on which racial slavery was uniquely predicated.

In Butler's third series, which tells the story of a dystopic United States rapidly collapsing under the pressure of the economic crisis, resource scarcity, violence, and environmental destruction, a young Black visionary, Lauren Olamina, establishes a new religion intended to help fellow humans survive beyond the crumbling of Earth by finding a home on another planet. Echoes of the Oankali's species-saving commitment to change and colonization can be readily located in Lauren's Earthseed faith whose central mantra is "All that you touch, you change. All that you change, changes you. The only lasting truth is change. God is change," and whose goal is human settlement of the far corners of the universe (Butler 1993, p. 3). It is also notable that Lauren believes that she possesses the capacity to be devastated by the physical pain that she senses in others – a capacity that recalls the empathic powers possessed by both the Oankali and the Patternists.

When, in *Parable of the Sower* (1993), Lauren's family is killed and their Los Angeles refuge destroyed, Lauren is forced to venture out into a post-apocalyptic landscape populated by dispossessed, desperate, and drug addicted people who behave more like animals than human beings. As Lauren moves north on a carless Interstate in search of a better climate and the possibility of fresh water, she gathers a group of followers whom she succeeds in moving to a safe, if temporary, haven. In the subsequent *Parable of the Talents* (1999), Lauren and her Earthseed settlement come under siege. An authoritarian Christian fundamentalist government has taken control of the United States and the new president (whose motto, "Make America Great Again," uncannily portends President Trump's) sends in armed forces to squelch Lauren's subversive non-Christian faith. After a period of enslavement, however, Lauren and her followers prevail in transporting Earthseed followers to a spaceship headed for Alpha Centauri. Butler's imagination of resilient Black life that both survives slavery and audaciously imagines a future on other planets has made the *Parable* novels favorites among the Afrofuturists – writers, musicians, and visual artists collectively invested in celebration of a Black futuristic aesthetic. Notably, the *Parable* novels are referenced in several hip-hop songs, SF television shows, and films, and they form the basis for a modern opera whose libretto was written by Toshi Reagon and her mother, legendary Black feminist musician Bernice Johnson Reagon. In interviews, Butler explores her plan for a third *Parable* novel set on Alpha Centauri. Though this novel was never completed, partial drafts of *Parable of the Trickster* are housed at the Huntington Library amongst the rest of Butler's carefully self-curated papers.

In the year before she died, Butler published a final novel, the vampire saga *Fledgling* (2005), which she claimed to have written to divert herself from the grim world of the *Patternist* series and the writer's block that working on the series produced. As in previous novels, in *Fledgling* Butler's protagonist is a Black woman, in this instance, a young vampire whose extra melanin – an intentional genetic modification – enables her to be active during daylight hours. And yet, because Shori is genetically modified she is regarded as "impure" and as a threat to an influential segment of the vampire world, one not only ancient but best described as white supremacist in its allegiance to preservation of vampiric "purity" (read whiteness). Like Lauren, who seeks to offer her people a new understanding of the world and the means to create a better one, Shori seeks to gather and lead people who condone genetic modification, affirm Blackness, and value the heightened abilities afforded by both. In this sense, the vampire world mirrors our own. It functions according to historically embedded racial dynamics that denigrate "impurity" and Blackness – qualities that in Shori's case perform a conceptual inversion in so far as they confer superiority. Though *Fledgling* is a vampire novel, it is closely linked to Butler's SF writings by its attention to racialized and gendered power dynamics, and through its critique of quests for biological "purity" that transform crusaders for purity into their own worst enemies – into racists, sexists, speciesists, and, as in the *Patternist* and *Xenogenesis* novels, into humanists. Ultimately in *Fledgling*, as in her previous novels, Butler suggests that rigid identity-based self-understanding leads to rejection of necessary changes to the self, and thus to foreclosure not only of the chance to become one's best self, but also to the chance to survive into a future that demands transcendence of rigidly organized ideas of self/other.

Over the course of a relatively short career as a writer, Butler not only gifted readers a body of work that allows us to apprehend the operations of gender and racial power in our world with new eyes, she lays the groundwork for Black feminist speculative fiction's emergence as a life force unto itself. This legacy is evident in the dismantling of SF's whiteness and maleness to the point that today it would no longer be possible for Butler to quip of the genre, as she once did in a 1980 interview, that as a Black woman writer she was its "smallest minority," a minority of one. Today Butler's concerns are echoed in the work of a fast-growing cohort of Black feminist SF writers including Tananarive Due, Nalo Hopkinson, N.K. Jemisin, Nisi Shawl, and Rivers Solomon, among many others.

SEE ALSO: Afrofuturism; Black Atlantic; Delany, Samuel; Gibson, William; Gomez, Jewelle; Mixed-Genre Fiction; Queer and LGBT Fiction

REFERENCES

Butler, Octavia. (1993). *Parable of the Sower*. New York and Boston: Grand Central.
Cobb, Jelani. (2010). Interview with Octavia Butler (1994). Reprinted in: *Conversations with Octavia Butler* (ed. Conseula Francis), 49–64. Jackson: University of Mississippi.
Francis, Conseula. (ed.) (2010). *Conversations with Octavia Butler*. Jackson: University Press of Mississippi.
Rowell, Charles H. (1997). An interview with Octavia E. Butler. *Callaloo* 20 (1): 47–66.

FURTHER READING

Canavan, Gerry. (2016). *Octavia E. Butler*. Urbana: University of Illinois Press.
Hampton, Gregory Jerome. (2010). *Changing Bodies in the Fiction of Octavia Butler: Slaves, Aliens, and Vampires*. Lanham, MD: Lexington Books.
Holden, Rebecca J. and Shawl, Nisi. (eds.) (2013). *Strange Matings: Science Fiction, Feminism, African American Voices, and Octavia E. Butler*. Seattle: Aqueduct Press.
Jamieson, Ayana and Bailey, Moya. (eds.) (2019). Octavia Butler, Part One, special issue of *Women's Studies* 47 (7) (2018): 695–764; and Part Two, *Women's Studies* 48 (1): 1–80.

Carver, Raymond

TAMAS DOBOZY
Wilfrid Laurier University, Canada

Although Raymond Carver was publishing in the late 1960s, and throughout the 1970s, it was during the 1980s that he became widely acknowledged as one of America's most prominent writers. Carver's literary output includes nonfiction, poetry, plays, and a screenplay, but it is his work in the short story that is considered his foremost contribution to American literature. Arguably, he is the emblematic writer of a new strain of American realism emerging from the 1960s, and which matured in the late 1970s and early 1980s. It is characterized by a concern with the society of late capitalism, particularly the experiences of the lower and working class, and its milieu of strip malls, anonymous consumerism, the erosion of regional identity and folkways under the pressures of globalization and pop culture, the loss of meaningful labor, and the breakdown of the family as a result of economic pressure, addiction, and domestic violence. Similarly, Carver's fictions, frequently rooted in his working-class background, depict family dysfunction, alcoholism, violence, joblessness, disenfranchisement, and poverty.

As Tess Gallagher commented in *Carver Country*, there is a political dimension to many of Carver's stories insofar as they comment on the advent of Reaganism, a time marked by attacks on working-class institutions, particularly unions, but also social programs, and a widening of the gap between rich and poor in America (Carver, Gallagher, and Adelman 1990). Bill Buford (1983), writing about Carver's realism in *Granta*, noted in the writing a politics rooted not in social protest per se, but in the conditions that give rise to it. While the writers engaged with this strain of realism were grouped under various critical terms – minimalism, K-mart realism, dirty realism, among others – Carver resisted such labels, regarding himself as working within a larger tradition that included Flaubert, Chekhov, and Hemingway, among others. It is equally true that while Carver's work is everywhere marked by an awareness of and compassion for the limitations imposed by precarious labor, some of his later work, particularly stories such as "Cathedral," "Blackbird Pie," and "Errand," are written with a metafictional flourish, directly interrogating the act of narrative. Carver's preferred term for his writing was "precisionism," which encapsulates his abiding interest in verbal economy not for its own sake but for its capacity to

The Encyclopedia of Contemporary American Fiction 1980–2020, First Edition. Edited by Patrick O'Donnell, Stephen J. Burn, and Lesley Larkin.
© 2022 John Wiley & Sons Ltd. Published 2022 by John Wiley & Sons Ltd.

render social truth aesthetically – to convey "how things out there really are, and how [the writer] sees those things" (Carver 1984, p. 18). Thus, Carver's fidelity to style – and he was noted throughout his career as much for his style and sensibility as for what he wrote about – was always rooted in the understanding that style conveyed more than simply itself. Throughout his work, Carver remained deeply devoted to "the right word," stripping down his writing to convey the essence of his subject. It is in this that his place in the lineage of writers such as Flaubert is most apparent.

Carver was born on May 25, 1938, in Clatskanie, Oregon, and his work was dominated by the region of the Pacific Northwest, though he spent considerable time living and writing in Iowa, California, and New York State. When Carver was young, his family relocated to Yakima, Washington, where his father worked in a lumber mill. It was here that Carver spent his childhood, and where he was exposed to the blue-collar values and worldview that occupy much of his work. As a young adult, Carver was employed as a fruit picker, millworker, clerk, and delivery man, while nurturing his talents as a writer of poems and short stories. In 1957, he married his first wife, Maryann Burk. They had two children.

In 1958 Carver attended Chico State College, where he took classes taught by one of one of his most lasting influences, the writer John Gardner. In his essay, "Fires," Carver acknowledges Gardner's influence on the verbal economy of his work, though the essay goes on at much greater length about the straitened circumstances of his early writing life, when the psychological pressures of raising two children, getting an education, and working in various jobs as unskilled labor all competed with his desire and time to write. Those years also saw Carver's growing allegiance to literary realism, and his outspoken aversion to what he calls in another essay, "On Writing," the "tricks" of "experimentation" and "formal innovation" (Carver 1984, pp. 14–15) characteristic of the metafictional writing of John Barth and others. As well, Carver's primary modes of literary production – the short story and the lyric poem – were, as the essays articulate, grounded in precarious living circumstances, which did not allow him the financial and existential security, not to mention the time, necessary for longer works such as the novel. Carver completed his Bachelor's degree in general studies in 1963 after transferring to Humboldt State College. From there, he attended the prestigious Writers' Workshop at the State University of Iowa, where the faculty included poets Donald Justice and Mark Strand, and fiction writer R.V. Cassill. His fellow students included Joy Williams, Clark Blaise, and Bharati Mukherjee. He left without completing the degree.

In 1976, Carver's first major collection of short fiction, *Will You Please Be Quiet, Please?* was published by McGraw-Hill. The book was a national success, and it earned Carver accolades in publications such as *The New York Times Book Review* and *Newsweek*, as well as a nomination for the National Book Award. The title story had already earned Carver a place in *Best American Short Stories 1967*. Told in the third person, it features a protagonist, Jackson, who attends college, is drawn to literature and teaching, marries a woman called Marian, with whom he has two children, and takes place in Arcata, a town in which Carver lived. The drama revolves around Marian confessing to a one-night stand she had years ago with a mutual friend, but the majority of the story follows Jackson after Marian's revelation, as he wanders a town that seems everywhere inflected, in a naturalistic vein, with his inner torment, the "catastrophe" that he feels marks an absolute transformation in his life (Carver 1976, p. 243). However, Jackson's problems seem to stem equally from his failure to articulate, or to find the words for conveying the issues he faces. The story thus revolves around a conflict Carver would return to again and again in his stories – simultaneously aesthetic and social – namely, the agency embodied in language. The story, like many written by Carver, turns on the contrast between the literary writing in which the story is delivered and the protagonist's attempts to embody his own experiences in a precise language. The narrative ends with Jackson's children begging for a story, but instead of delivering one Jackson goes to bed, his resentment of his wife's adultery giving way under her erotic touch. The work thus gives voice to a figure on the margins who is denied voice. At the same time, it charges his life, and by extension all such lives, with significance.

Many of the stories in *Will You Please Be Quiet, Please?* draw upon Carver's travels and experiences – though he insisted the autobiographical authenticity witnessed by critics resulted from writing about the world he knew rather than the life he'd lived – and depict lives where the betrayals and desperation resulting from material want exclude or undermine a moral or spiritual view. This collection was also noted for its style, colloquial and spare to the point of being self-consciously minimalist.

The book also marked Carver's association with Gordon Lish, who first published him in *Esquire* in the early 1970s, and who continued to promote his work as editor at McGraw-Hill, and, later, Knopf. A 1998 article by D.T. Max in *The New York Times Magazine*, "The Carver Chronicles," reveals the extent to which Lish's editing intervened in the final form of many of Carver's early stories, initiating a controversy over authorship that continues to surround Carver's work. Lish's editorial influence is most pronounced in Carver's second major collection, *What We Talk About When We Talk About Love* (1981). Carver strenuously objected to Lish's editorial interventions – excising pages, rewriting sentences, changing endings, rearranging paragraphs – as the editor distilled Carver's precisionism to a skeletal minimalism. Readers were confronted with stories as notable for what they don't contain as for what they do. Gone were much of the descriptions, moments of epiphany, and even the inner worlds of characters that marked the previous collection. The stories offered a bewildering world of surfaces, in which characters act out in enigmatic ways, such as the protagonist of "Why Don't You Dance?" who arranges his furniture on the front lawn of his home. Similarly, the story "Viewfinder" ends with the protagonist hurling rocks from the roof of his house, to which he's been urged to ascend by an armless man going door to door offering to take and then sell Polaroid photographs. In the title story, four characters sit outside, in oncoming darkness, trying and failing to define love. *What We Talk About When We Talk About Love* is everywhere marked by an unidentified woundedness, an inability to create a coherent narrative around personal trauma.

Many of the reviews of *What We Talk About When We Talk About Love* drew attention to the stripped-down style, particularly in comparison with *Will You Please Be Quiet, Please?* Reviewers were mixed on Carver's performance in this collection, alternately praising or condemning him for the sparseness of his prose. In fact, reading *What We Talk About When We Talk About Love* in the context of Carver's work as a whole is disjunctive for its emphasis on style. The highly wrought minimalism of Lish's editorial interventions is at odds with the more explicit social, political, and spiritual concerns that mark the rest of his oeuvre. Nonetheless, the book catapulted Carver to literary celebrity. As well, despite the dark subject matter, Carver's life had changed dramatically in the years between the two collections. In 1977, he managed to begin a period of sobriety that would last to the end of his life, and in 1978 he separated from his wife Mariann, though they would not be formally divorced until 1982. Shortly thereafter he began a relationship with the writer Tess Gallagher, which would continue until his death.

Perhaps as a result of his critical validation, and changes in his personal life, Carver resisted similar editorial interventions in his next collection, *Cathedral* (1983). Stylistically, the book marked a return to the more generous vision, and less foregrounded style, of his first collection. Appropriately, the titular story dwells on recovery, while also continuing Carver's longstanding interest in the power of art to aestheticize and thus redeem experience. However, unlike in the story "Will You Please Be Quiet, Please?" the first person narration serves to bridge the distance between the author's awareness and expertise and the protagonist's experience. "Cathedral" takes place over the course of an evening, and it involves the visit of a blind man to the home of the narrator and his wife, who has been involved in a longstanding correspondence with their visitor. The story turns on ocularcentrism – the idea that sight is the dominant organ of knowing – and the narrator's inability to "see" what his wife regards in the blind man, much less the blind man's own beneficent vision of the world. At the end, the blind man places his hand over the protagonist's and asks him to draw a cathedral, though it is the protagonist who, as a result, escapes the solipsism that confines his understanding. Many of the stories, such as "Chef's House," "Careful," and "Where I'm Calling From," deal with the effects of alcoholism and recovery. Others, "Preservation," "The Compartment," and "Fever," continue Carver's explorations of joblessness, low-income work, divorce, and family dysfunction. The story "A Small, Good Thing" restored the "The Bath," from *What We Talk About When We Talk About Love*, to its earlier, original version. The difference is marked. The Lish-edited version ends *in medias res*, on an ominous phone call that propels the narrative into a dark uncertainty; the expanded version ends on a moment of communal grace. The story confirmed the extent of Lish's editing process in *What We Talk About When We Talk About Love*, as well as Carver's desire for, and confidence in, redressing it.

The last major collection published in Carver's lifetime was *Where I'm Calling From: New and Collected Stories* (1988). This collection was both a culmination of Carver's writing and an intriguing indication of future directions, particularly in late stories such as "Blackbird Pie" and "Errand," which openly play with metafictional conceits, meditating on the construction of narrative as part of the action of the story itself. They are notably different from anything Carver had written to that point, while at the same time continuing his longstanding interest in the ways in which experience can be aesthetically configured in the interests of survival and redemption. Along with this new direction, the collection as a whole, developed by Carver and his new editor, Gary Fisketjon, restored many of the alternate versions of stories edited by Lish. In every case, the alternate versions are more elaborate on the level of description, character, and plot, and serve to some extent as correctives to Carver as a minimalist writer, clearly less concerned with the self-conscious stylistics on display in *What We Talk About When We Talk About Love*, and more with the mimesis and precisionism that suggest a fealty to the tradition of literary realism. A story such as "Distance" in *Where I'm Calling From* (entitled "Everything Stuck to Him" in the Lish version) restores details on setting and the characters' histories and psychological motivation, and thus dwells as much on what the writing conveys as how it conveys it. More significantly, these versions present a more prominent spiritual depth and social engagement.

The book was a success, garnering Carver rave reviews, and appearances in popular magazines, such as *People* and *Vanity Fair*. In 1987, he was inducted into the American Academy of Arts and Letters. However, by the time of its publication, Carver was suffering from the lung cancer that would ultimately end his life. A number of posthumous collections followed his death on August 2, 1988. *No Heroics, Please: Uncollected Writings* (1992) and *Call If You Need Me: The Uncollected Fiction and Other Prose* (2001) round out his fiction. In 2009, Carver was honored with the Library of America edition of his work, *Raymond Carver: Collected Stories*.

Carver's stature as the representative American short story writer of his generation has, if anything, grown since his death, with new editions, critical works, and even film treatments of his writing. While Carver's canonical place as a writer of realism is generally acknowledged, this does not accurately reflect the wide treatment given his work by scholars, many of whom regard a sophistication in the work equal to that of Carver's more demonstrably "postmodern" peers. The richness of Carver's allusions, his careful work with temporality, his evident concern for and sympathy with the underclass, his dark humor, his attention to the particulars of his historical moment, all of these suggest the rich critical legacy afforded by his work. Carver's fiction responded to much of the same social pressure as that of dissimilar writers – Pynchon, Bartheleme, Barthes – the rise of late capitalism and globalization, Cold War anxiety, a growing gap between rich and poor, the impoverishment of public discourse in politics and the media, although it did so by invoking a different strain in American literature. Carver's response was to attempt to reclaim language and narrative, and in the course of doing so illuminate lives on the margins of late twentieth-century America. In his work, literary art became not only a refuge from the pressures of social forces, but a form of resistance to them.

SEE ALSO: Contemporary Regionalisms; Fictions of Work and Labor; Ford, Richard; Globalization; Illness and Disability Narratives; Minimalism and Maximalism; Realism after Poststructuralism; Religion and Contemporary Fiction; Suburban Narratives; Trauma and Fiction

REFERENCES

Buford, Bill. (1983). Editorial. *Granta* 8: 4–5.
Carver, Raymond. (1976). *Will You Please Be Quiet, Please?* New York: McGraw-Hill.
Carver, Raymond. (1984). *Fires*. New York: Vintage; 1st ed. 1983.
Carver, Raymond, Gallagher, Tess, and Adelman, Bob. (1990). *Carver Country: The World of Raymond Carver*. New York: Arcade.
Max, D.T. (1998). The Carver chronicles. *The New York Times Magazine* (August 9, 1998): 34–40, 51, 56, 57.

FURTHER READING

Hallett, Cynthia Whitney. (1999). *Minimalism and the Short Story: Raymond Carver, Amy Hempel, and Mary Robison*. Lewiston: Mellen.
Kleppe, Sandra Lee, and Robert Miltner. (2008). *New Paths to Raymond Carver: Critical Essays on His Life, Fiction, and Poetry*. Columbia: University of South Carolina Press.
Runyon, Randolph. (1992). *Reading Raymond Carver*. Syracuse: Syracuse University Press.
Saltzman, Arthur. (1988). *Understanding Raymond Carver*. Columbia: University of South Carolina Press.
Sklenicka, Carol. (2009). *Raymond Carver: A Writer's Life*. New York: Scribner.

Castillo, Ana

TEREZA M. SZEGHI
University of Dayton, USA

Ana Castillo's (b. 1953) considerable critical and literary output has always been marked by her overt commitment to activism – specifically what, in her 1994 essay collection, *Massacre of the Dreamers*, she terms Xicanisma (or Chicana feminism). In her words, "Xicanisma is formed: in the acknowledgement of the historical crossroad where the creative power of woman became deliberately appropriated by male society. And woman in the flesh, therefore, was subordinated. It is our task as Xicanistas, to not only reclaim our indigenismo – but also to reinsert the forsaken feminine into our consciousness" (1994, p. 12). Castillo's conception of and commitment to Xicanisma variously manifest in her generically diverse body of work, which ranges from poetry to experimental novels, critical essay collections, drama, and translation. Both the content and the form of her writing prioritizes Chicanas – whom she has stated are her target audience – by not only privileging and valuing their experiences, but also writing in a manner that makes her work familiar and meaningful to them. With her second poetry chapbook, *The Invitation* (1979), for instance, Castillo overtly calls out the machismo of Chicanos active in the Chicano Movement and asks them to acknowledge the work and sexual identities of their Chicana colleagues (Spurgeon 2004, p. 11). Castillo joined other Chicana writers, such as Sandra Cisneros, Denise Chávez, Gloria Anzaldúa, and Cherie Moraga, in forging a body of literature and criticism that articulates Chicana perspectives, histories, experiences, identities, and activism.

Castillo's Xicanisma and the other activist elements of her writing are rooted, in many ways, in her upbringing. Born to a Mexican American father and a Mexican mother in Chicago (her mother was born in the United States but moved to her parents' native Mexico as a child and was raised there), Castillo grew up with a strong sense of her cultural identity, along with a resistance to the patriarchal elements of Chicano culture she saw reflected in her parents' relationship and an acute awareness of the racism and financial hardships that disproportionately affected members of her community. Since her youth, Castillo has been active in a range of social movements that bear particularly on the lives of Chicanxs, as well as Latinx peoples more generally. Castillo earned a bachelor's degree in art with a minor in secondary education – in spite of her parents' view that clerical work was the highest attainment a Chicana could hope for, and in opposition to the combined racism and sexism of the white male faculty who repeatedly questioned her talents and undermined her confidence. She went on to earn a master's degree from the University of Chicago and a PhD in American studies from the University of Bremen, Germany.

Key themes that define Castillo's oeuvre include: Chicana sexualities, Chicanas' negotiation of restrictive gender roles within Chicano and Euroamerican societies, religious syncretism (Indigenous spirituality and Catholic belief in tension with the Church's hierarchy and what she sees as its reductive, passive conceptions of women), mestizaje (the mixed cultural identities of Chicanxs, as they are constructed and experienced) and associated feelings of countrylessness, migration, and the human rights of the Indigenous peoples of the Americas.

Castillo's first novel, *The Mixquiahuala Letters* (1986), winner of the American Book Award from the Before Columbus Foundation, powerfully illustrates how her Xicanisma shapes the content and form of her writing. This epistolary novel is comprised of a series of letters written by Teresa to her friend and frequent travel companion, Alicia, as she moves repeatedly between the United States (where she is born and raised) and Mexico (where she feels culturally linked) – and this quest for identity as it is shaped by multiple cultures and nations for many Chicanas is a persistent theme of Castillo's oeuvre. Frustrated by her family's expectation that her marriage and husband be the primary factors in shaping her identity, Teresa travels to Mexico only to be frustrated by the sexual objectification she encounters there and the difficulty of meaningfully connecting to her Indigenous roots. In this way Teresa reflects Castillo's own experiences of resisting her family's normative conceptions of gender identity (her 1995 poetry collection *My Father Was a Toltec* provides extended meditations on this subject) and feeling alienated by both the United States and Mexico to the point of feeling countryless as a mestiza. Teresa's and Alicia's relationship with one another is strengthened and routinely shattered by their encounters with men on both sides of the border, as the women relish their freedom to travel without male companionship (despite being censured for it), but also are drawn to relationships with men, only to be objectified, misunderstood, and even threatened with violence when they refuse traditional gender norms. At the same time, perhaps most overtly through its unconventional form, the novel refuses any neat resolution to these complex issues of gender, identity, and sexuality.

As the author makes clear in the novel's front matter, *The Mixquiahuala Letters* can be read in almost any order desired, except from front to back, or taken individually. Through this structure Castillo suggests that there is no stable ending and no set sequence of events. Moreover, because the letters are written solely from Teresa's perspective, readers understand that their truth is subjective, and thus limited. Even as Castillo suggests three potential paths through the letters (for the "conformist," "cynic," and "quixotic"), these prescriptions do more to destabilize and multiply the potential meaning of a set of experiences, as the alternative possibilities are ever present. As Lesley Larkin argues, although Castillo highlights her readers' agency in deciding how to read the letters, she also plays a heavy hand in determining their paths through the letters (2012, pp. 142–143). In Tanya Long Bennett's view, "In giving such a flexible structure to the novel, Castillo creates a text that cannot be defined by any unified ideology. Similarly, her choice of 'i' as a pronoun for herself [Castillo uses the lower case 'i' in much of her writing, and has Teresa assign the 'i' to herself as well] undermines the notion of the authorial 'I' in that it refuses to indicate the authority representing dominant discourses. Yet in saying 'i,' Teresa, through her letters, can voice a self, a fragmented self that resists ideological definition" (Bennett 1996, p. 462). Ultimately, *The Mixquiahuala Letters'* form reinforces the novel's argument about the ways in which various social structures (the family, the nation, the Church) constrain Chicanas' ability to forge what they identify as an authentic and usable sense of self, while at the same time testifying to the importance of empowering Chicanas to do the complex work of self-identity formation.

With *So Far From God* (1993), Castillo's formal experimentations continue in new forms. As always, Castillo's experimentations are directed toward reaching her Chicana readership and exposing the structures of racism, sexism, capitalism, and colonialism that undermine their fundamental wellbeing. She adapts a broad range of source materials in her portrait of the lives and, in most cases, deaths of her central female characters (four daughters and their mother Sofia), such as: Mexican folklore, telenovelas, curanderismo (traditional healing practices of the Indigenous peoples of the Americas), Catholic legends, and the Bible. Castillo's adaptations of these materials all advance her Xicanisma. For instance, when one of the daughters, Caridad, is attacked by a mysterious evil force made of wool (a malogra), the language used to describe it is reminiscent of the European conquest of the Americas (García 1998; Alarcón 2004). Daniel Cooper Alarcón argues, "In linking La Malogra's attack on Caridad to the destructive conquest of the indigenous peoples of New Spain, Castillo situates this specific act of violence within a 'centuries old' pattern of violent oppression and genocide against indigenous peoples and suggests that the attack on Caridad is not an isolated event nor, regrettably, should it be viewed as a historical anomaly" (2004, p. 146). Indeed, contemporary manifestations of colonial violence thread throughout the novel and the lives and deaths of Sofia's daughters. For instance, *So Far From God* offers one of Castillo's earliest and most searing depictions of environmental racism – an issue that plays a prominent role in her more recent novel, *The Guardians* (2007), as well – when Fe, the daughter swept up by the promises of US capitalism and normative conceptions of marriage, is slowly and unknowingly poisoned by toxic chemicals in her workplace at the Acme Corporation. Ultimately, in Alarcón's words, "the death of each of Sofia's daughters can be viewed as some form of violence in which the safety of women or indigenous peoples is viewed as unimportant" (2004, p. 147).

As several critics have observed, after the death of each of her four daughters, Sofia emerges not as broken but as resolute, able to incorporate the lessons of her daughters' deaths, along with their best qualities, and become a leader in her economically floundering community, who draws upon and adapts the various cultures, religions, and social structures available to her. She founds "Los Ganados y Lana" (The Cattle and Wool Cooperative) and, with the support of her female friends, is declared mayor of the unincorporated town of Tome, New Mexico. The cooperative, among other things, provides the community space for cattle grazing in the face of widespread land loss to Euroamericans, facilitates the sale of meat and wool goods, at Sofia's butcher shop, and allows the community to access needed equipment through collective bartering. Sofi also instantiates a syncretic Xicana theology through her founding of Mothers of Martyrs and Saints, which serves to critique and parody the patriarchy and structural exclusions of the Catholic Church. Laura Gillman and Stacey M. Floyd-Thomas argue that each of the primary female characters in the novel exemplifies one of Chela Sandoval's modes of resistance, with Sofia embodying the differential mode, which moves flexibly between the others (represented by her daughters) as befitting the situation. They elaborate, "She is the incarnation of wisdom, as her name represents and she carries within her self faith (Fe), charity (Caridad), hope (Esperanza), and the wise folly of *la Loca* [the separatist] that results as a consequence of exercising these virtues in a tainted world" (Gillman and Floyd-Thomas 2001, p. 169).

So Far From God, along with several other of Castillo's publications, highlights the particular challenges related to parenting in the borderlands – whether the literal region where the United States and Mexico meet, or metaphorically, the margins of the dominant US culture where many Chicanxs are relegated. Only after the excruciating experience of having all four of her daughters die as a consequence of some manner of racism and/or sexism, is Sofia able to envision a way of helping to move her community into prosperity and community-based wellbeing. She is unable to save her daughters, but extends an ethic of care to the community at large. Likewise, as I detail elsewhere (Szeghi 2021), in *The Guardians* Regina engages in an activist, unconventional motherhood. Herself a virgin, out of necessity she becomes a mother figure to her undocumented nephew, Gabo, and advocates for his rights and education within the United States. In an even more striking turn, the novel concludes with her taking in the daughter of Tiny Tears, a gang member who murdered Gabo. Further, Regina's romantic interest, Miguel, works to expose environmental contamination in his community, which he holds culpable for his son's health problems. In her 2016 essay collection, *Black Dove: Mamá, Mi'jo, and Me*,

Castillo shares her own devastation when she learns her son has been arrested and imprisoned for robbery while under the influence of drugs. She reflects on the social pressures he faced growing up as a brown man in the United States and the limits of her ability to prepare him for or insulate him from these realities.

With *The Guardians* and *Black Dove* Castillo also returns to the desert landscapes of New Mexico (prominently featured in *So Far From God* and her 2001 poetry collection, *I Ask The Impossible*) and the thematizing of this space as deeply spiritual and menacing – particularly for its Indigenous (American Indian and Chicanx) inhabitants, who often have a strong connection to the land but also are marginalized by dominant forces of racism, sexism, and capitalism. In the years her son was incarcerated, the desert became a place of deep loneliness and contented solitude as she worked to understand what had happened to her son and what his future life would be. Her meditations on the desert landscape, captured in *Black Dove*, also generated the founding questions that motivate *The Guardians*: "What would it be like to be on this side waiting for that missing loved one? Who would I call? Better yet, could I call anyone for assistance in finding him or her?" (Castillo 2016, p. 222). In *The Guardians*, the spiritual aspects of the landscape emerge through the presence of the Franklin mountains as one of the novel's guardians and through Regina's earth-based spirituality, set against the backdrop of her brother Rafa's disappearance while crossing through this unforgiving landscape from one side to the other.

The Guardians powerfully illustrates that, as much as Castillo's primary focus has been on Chicana experiences and advocacy for their rights, her work has transnational elements as well, as I discuss more extensively elsewhere (Szeghi 2021). Castillo expresses here a broader commitment to the dignity of all persons and her view of international borders as undermining that goal. Through *The Guardians* Castillo variously documents the traumas related to undocumented migration as they are suffered by individuals with differential legal statuses in the United States, while testifying to the multiple legitimate reasons why people are compelled to cross and re-cross the border. The timeliness of and need for Castillo's critique is illustrated in part through the negative feedback she has received when giving public readings from this novel. She recalls, "It surprised me (and not in a good way) that for the first time in thirty years, since I read poetry as a labeled 'radical woman of color,' that there were people in the audiences who would get up and walk out. The stories of Mexicans crossing illegally, told from the enraged perspective of those waiting on this side, was (to some) not worthy of compassion" (Castillo 2016, p. 222). Castillo reflects that her work highlighting marginalized perspectives always has been hard-fought, as illustrated through this reception to *The Guardians* and through the challenges she faced when first attempting to publish *Massacre* (p. 223).

Ultimately, for all the weighty political content that defines Castillo's oeuvre, and the fierce commitment to social change that motivates Castillo's long and prolific career, it would be a mistake not to recognize the spirit of playful experimentation and the celebration of Chicana identities, experiences, and knowledge that infuse her writing as well. This playfulness and celebration can be seen in such aspects of Castillo's work as: the adaptation of literary forms to reflect Chicanas' experiences (as with the multiplicity of reading paths in *The Mixquiahuala Letters*, or the long chapter headings in *So Far From God*, reminiscent of eighteenth- and nineteenth-century novels and of telenovelas), the forging of characters who insist upon exploring their sexualities freely in the face of social disapproval (as with Palma in the Lambda Award-winning *Give It To Me* (2014)), and testaments to the power of Indigenous epistemologies (through such characters as Mamá Grande and Pastora in *Sapogonia* (1990), and *So Far From God*'s Felicia and Caridad). Of course, Castillo's social critiques are wed to these aspects of her craft, but as she makes clear, recognizing the complex identities and experiences of Chicanas means not only protesting the structures that deny their full humanity, but also celebrating what makes them unique and strong.

SEE ALSO: Álvarez, Julia; Border Fictions; García, Cristina; Indigenous Narratives; Literature of the Americas; Ortiz Cofer, Judith; Serros, Michele; Third-Wave Feminism; Urrea, Luis Alberto; Viramontes, Helena Maria

REFERENCES

Alarcón, Daniel Cooper. (2004). Literary syncretism in Ana Castillo's *So Far From God*. *Studies in Latin American Popular Culture* 23: 145–152.

Bennett, Tanya Long. (1996). No country to call home: a study of Castillo's *Mixquiahuala Letters*. *Style* 30: 462–478.

Castillo, Ana. (1994). *Massacre of the Dreamers: Essays on Xicanisma*. New York: Plume.

Castillo, Ana. (2016). *Black Dove: Mamá, Mi'jo, and Me*. New York: Feminist Press.

García, Alesia. (1998). "Aztec Nation: History, Inscription, and Indigenista Feminism in Contemporary Chicana Literature and Political Discourse." PhD dissertation, University of Arizona.

Gillman, Laura and Floyd Thomas, Stacey M. (2001). Con un pie a cada lado/with a foot in each place: Mestizaje as transnational feminisms in Ana Castillo's *So Far From God*. *Meridians: Feminism, Race, and Transnationalism* 2 (1): 158–175.

Larkin, Lesley. (2012). Reading as responsible dialogue in Ana Castillo's *The Mixquiahuala Letters*. *MELUS* 37 (3): 141–165.

Spurgeon, Sara L. (2004). *Ana Castillo*. Boise, ID: Boise State University Press.

Szeghi, Tereza M. (2021). Identity formation and dislocation: transnationalism in Ana Castillo's *The Mixquiahuala Letters* and *The Guardians*. In: *New Transnational Perspectives on Ana Castillo* (ed. Bernadine M. Hernández and Karen R. Roybal), 86–99. Pittsburgh: University of Pittsburgh Press.

FURTHER READING

Alberto, Lourdes. (2012). Topographies of Indigenism: Mexico, decolonial Indigenism, and the Chicana transnational subject in Ana Castillo's *Mixquiahuala Letters*. In: *Comparative Indigeneities of the Américas: Toward A Hemispheric Approach* (ed. M. Bianet Castellanos, Lourdes Gutiérrez Nájera, and Arturo J. Aldama), 38–52. Tucson: University of Arizona Press.

Cochran, James. (2016). Make the land shiver: Ana Castillo's ecopolitics in *The Guardians*. *Journal of South Texas English Studies* 6 (2): 67–77.

Fagan, Allison E. (2012). Damaged pieces: embracing border textuality in revisions of Ana Castillo's *Sapogonia*. *MELUS* 37 (3): 167–188.

Hernández, Bernadine M. and Roybal, Karen R. (eds.) (2021). *Transnational Chicanx Perspectives on Ana Castillo*. Pittsburgh: University of Pittsburgh Press.

Johnson, Kelli L. (2004). Violence in the borderlands: crossing to the home space in the novels of Ana Castillo. *Frontiers* 25 (1): 39–58.

Wehbe-Herrera, Aishih. (2013). A history teacher [who] calls himself Chicano: negotiating borders, masculinity, and ethnicity in Ana Castillo's *The Guardians*. *Interculturalism in North America: Canada, the United States, and Beyond* 8: 149–158.

Chabon, Michael

ALEXANDER MORAN
Stanbridge University, USA

Like Jennifer Egan, Jonathan Lethem, and Colson Whitehead, Michael Chabon has never settled into a singular style or form; indeed, this seems to be something of a generational trait, with all of these authors born within a decade of Chabon's 1963 birth in

Washington, DC. Each is an inheritor of the postmodern tradition, and as a result they are largely unencumbered by ideas of high and low, or of blending history and fiction. Nonetheless, Chabon stands out from his peers in two distinct ways: first, as Andrew Hoberek succinctly summarizes, Chabon's career serves as a "veritable allegory" for the turn against the style taught in university writing programs (2011, p. 484). Second, Chabon is perhaps the most vocal champion of genre fiction and popular forms. In tracing the arc of his career to date, though, it becomes clear that there are hints of his devotion to genre in his earlier fiction. Moreover, it becomes apparent that while Chabon dramatically changes style from book to book, he consistently explores issues of contemporary Jewish identity, masculinity, fatherhood (on which he has now published two essay collections), sexual fluidity, the legacies of World War II, and art's relationship to the market.

Chabon's early fiction focuses on creative writing students, professors, and campus life, and this period can be named, in a nod to Mark McGurl's seminal 2009 study, Chabon's "Program Era." His debut novel, *The Mysteries of Pittsburgh* (1988), was famously submitted to a publisher by his UC Irvine instructors and received a huge advance. It follows Art Bechstein, a recent graduate of the University of Pittsburgh, over a single summer. Art seeks to distance himself from his father (a money launderer for the mob), maintain a relationship with his mentally unstable girlfriend Phlox, and also navigate his growing feelings for his new friend, Arthur Lecomte. (In the forgettable 2008 film adaptation, Phlox's role is minimized, and Arthur Lecomte was bizarrely completely cut.) Due to the nuanced depiction of Art's bisexuality, Chabon's own sexuality was much discussed when *Pittsburgh* was published. However, what is particularly intriguing in the context of his later turn to genre is that Art constantly tries to resist his father's world of crime, despite his friend Cleveland's encouragement that Art use his connections. This allegorizes what Chabon was being taught in the university; that he would "not be taken seriously" if he presented genre works in his workshops (Costello 2015, p. 124). The allegory is made even stronger when Cleveland leads Art – whose pun of a name becomes relevant in this context – to make legal transgressions, as if Chabon is afraid to step over a boundary of some sort. Chabon's first novel, then, while it may reflect such writing workshop staples as "write what you know" and concludes with an epiphanic moment, also hints at the genre fiction he was soon to write.

Chabon struggled immensely with his second novel, and in the interim he published the collection *A Model World* (1991). Representative of what McGurl terms a "key genre of the Program Era" (2009, p. 50), these stories are largely set in California (where Chabon received his MFA), often on college campuses, and contain moments of revelation. The second half of this collection, "A Lost World," is a series of stories that follow Nathan Shapiro's teenage years as he comes to terms with the aftershocks of his parents' divorce, echoing Chabon's own adolescent experiences. As with *Pittsburgh*, genre fiction lurks in the background, as Nathan's father introduces him to science fiction classics such as A.E. Van Vogt's *Slan* (1940) and Alfred Bester's *The Demolished Man* (1952). So, in this partly autobiographical story, Chabon hints at his deep knowledge and long relationship with genre fiction.

Chabon's aborted second novel, *Fountain City*, only belatedly saw the light of day in 2010's *McSweeney's 36*, where Chabon published selected chapters with his acerbic edits and comments. After leaving this failed manuscript, *Wonder Boys* (1995), told in the voice of the adulterous Grady Tripp, a farcical middle-aged college writing instructor struggling to write his second novel, came quickly (a big screen adaptation was made in 2000, starring Michael Douglas and Tobey Maguire, which was a critical hit but a commercial failure). Sardonic and playful with his own failures, *Wonder Boys* signaled that Chabon was capable of radically changing styles. Moreover, with the creation of the character August Van Zorn, a pulp horror writer, he created a means to write genre fiction in his second collection, *Werewolves in Their Youth* (1999). Almost entirely set in the Pacific Northwest, *Werewolves* is by far his darkest work to date, replete with Freudian overtones (one story is called "Son of a Wolfman"), paedophilia, numerous forms of sexual violence, and many divorces, the last of which perhaps draws on Chabon's own marital breakdown. The final story in the collection, "In the Black Mill," is a Lovecraftian tale of horror credited to August Van Zorn, the fictional horror writer from *Wonder Boys*. This neatly signposted the next phase of his career: the Lovecraftian, comics-like, and Borgesian world-building that would define the second period of his career.

Chabon's third novel, *The Amazing Adventures of Kavalier and Clay* (2000), is a sweeping historical novel that seeks to situate comics as "a proud American cousin, in indigenous vitality and grace, of baseball and jazz" (2000, p. 75). Sam Clay and Josef Kavalier, a patchwork of the many underacknowledged Jewish pioneers from the Golden Age of comics, develop a comic book, *The Escapist* (which has spawned a real comics series). The title points to the key theme of the novel: Josef is an immigrant from Prague and longs for his family to escape to the United States, while Sam is secretly gay. These macho superheroes are therefore a way for them both to escape from the complex realities of their lives and identities. Moreover, Josef smuggles the Golem of Prague to America, and so the novel contains an element of magical realism that will pervade nearly all of Chabon's subsequent fiction. The theme of escape also serves as a metaphor for Chabon's writing, as in this text he removes the strictures he felt were imposed by what he learned in university.

Kavalier and Clay is the first of Chabon's novels to engage with what Daniel Punday calls "the ultimately metaphysical problem of personal identity in the marketplace" (2008, p. 298). Chabon's novel constantly explores this tension, which complicates what Rachel Greenwald Smith terms a "compromise aesthetic" – the process whereby artists make compromises with the market and therefore forgo any radical potential – as *Kavalier and Clay* shows the seemingly endless rounds of negotiation, as well as compromise, that mark any popular form (2014). Chabon has come to see even the quality of a writing program as defined by "the amount of financial support the program offers to students so that they can concentrate on their writing" (Costello 2015, p. 44). He has also acknowledged that he now rarely writes short stories because "children are expensive, and short stories just don't pay very well" (2018, p. 11). His turn to genre is the means by which he began to explore the relationship of art to commerce, one which he also discovered when writing in Hollywood for *Spiderman 2* (2004) and *John Carter* (2012), as well as numerous failed pilots for television (although he did serve as the showrunner for the first season of *Star Trek: Picard*, and will fulfill the same role for the upcoming series of *Kavalier and Clay*). In focusing on buried histories, Jewish identity, popular culture, and the economic needs of the artist, *Kavalier and Clay* signaled a clear shift in Chabon's literary priorities and marked the beginning of his most productive period of writing to date.

During *Kavalier and Clay*, Josef realizes that the violence of his superhero creations mirrors the fascists they fight. *Summerland* (2002), a young adult fantasy that, like

Werewolves, is set in the Pacific Northwest, is almost a direct rebuke to that glorification of violence. Inspired by the world-building of Ursula Le Guin's *A Wizard of Earthsea* (1967), Chabon follows her lead by eschewing violence; similar to the power of names in Le Guin's work, the world of *Summerland* is held together by magical "grammers," and generally celebrates the power of language and stories. A quest narrative where Ethan Feld and his friends must stop the trickster coyote's world-ending plans via a series of baseball games with mythical creatures, *Summerland* blends North American myths with the British fantasy fiction of J.R.R. Tolkien, C.S. Lewis, Terry Pratchett, and Michael Moorcock. It is also deeply indebted to Lewis Hyde's *Trickster Makes This World: Mischief, Myth, and Art* (1998), and Chabon provided a glowing foreword to the 2010 reissue of Hyde's book.

The Final Solution: A Story of Detection (2004) – whose subtitle points to its generic structure – is a mystery novel featuring an unnamed, aging, dementia-ridden Sherlock Holmes. The title echoes what was supposed to be Holmes's final story, "The Final Problem," as well as having obvious connotations of the Holocaust. Anna Richardson points out that *The Final Solution* questions the conventions of these two genres: "Like the popular crime narrative... the structure of a Holocaust testimony is indeed highly conventionalized, grounded in the 'before-during-after' of the narrator's Holocaust experience" (2010, p. 160). Chabon thematizes the patchwork nature of the novel within the text; as well as the "tatterdemalion" (2004, p. 50) clothing of the aging Holmes, Mr. Panicker's car "retain[s] few of its original constituent parts" (p. 87). Here, Chabon pastiches these two genres in order to query how many parts you can change before a generic object becomes something entirely new. Similarly, *Gentlemen of the Road* (2007) pastiches genre traditions: as well as its original serialization in the *New York Review of Books* (although Chabon had actually written it all before publication), it draws on the rollicking stories of Robert E. Howard and Fritz Leiber. The narrative follows Zelikman and Amram's travails in the largely forgotten, partly Jewish Khazar civilization, and so, as with *Summerland* and *Kavalier and Clay*, *Gentlemen* recovers a lost history. *Gentlemen* is perhaps most notable for Chabon's afterword. As well as revealing the working title was "Jews with Swords," he goes on to claim that *Pittsburgh* and *Wonder Boys* exemplify his previous use of "the genre of late-century naturalism" (2007, p. 200). In doing so, Chabon recasts his entire career as engaging with conventions and genres in some way, a trait he shares with his contemporaries: Egan has put forth that, "I see verisimilitude . . . as one of many possible approaches . . . I mean let's face it, this is *all* artificial" (Dinnen 2016).

Since the publication of *Kavalier and Clay*, Chabon has produced many essays, often about the value of genre fiction, most of which are collected in *Maps and Legends: Reading and Writing Along the Borderlands* (2008). He regularly argues that the genre fiction of such luminaries as Henry James and Joseph Conrad has been willfully etched out by literary critics. In his introduction to *The Best American Short Stories 2005*, he defines his embrace of genre as partially an attempt to shine a light on this literary legacy, but also "to reclaim entertainment as a job fit for artists and for audiences" (2005, p. xvi). Chabon argues that popular forms – such as comics or genre novels – are more than just copies of copies that can be mass-produced, and that there is far more to these works than simply eliciting pleasure.

The Yiddish Policemen's Union (2007) embodies how Chabon seeks to merge art and entertainment. It is a hard-boiled detective novel that, like Philip Roth's *The Plot Against America* (2004), explores a meticulously imagined alternate history. In Chabon's novel, a Yiddish-speaking Jewish protectorate was established during World War II in Sitka, Alaska. Partly a love letter to Raymond Chandler and Dashiell Hammett, the novel was also inspired, Chabon states, by his research into his 2002 essay, "Guidebook to a Land of Ghosts" (republished in *Maps and Legends* as "Imaginary Homelands"), regarding a Yiddish phrasebook. A detective, Meyer Landsman, is investigating the murder of the Rabbi's son, the mystical Mendel Shipman. Landsman discovers that Mendel is possibly also the "Tzaddik Ha-Dor," the potential messiah of his generation, echoing the Jewish mysticism of the Golem in *Kavalier and Clay*. In placing these myths in these settings, Chabon indicates that there are numerous similarities between these religious stories and genre fiction. Landsman uncovers a vast millenarian conspiracy that involves the US government and the more extreme parts of Sitka's society, who aim to blow up the Dome of the Rock in Jerusalem. While being another novel that pastiches genre – the clipped prose style reflects Hammett and Chandler in particular – *The Yiddish Policemen's Union* is also one of his clearest engagements with contemporary Jewish identity, particularly the relationship of the American Jewish community and Israel.

After *Yiddish*, Chabon states he was exhausted by the research these world-building novels require (Costello 2015, p. 102), so after returning to comic books and the clash of art and commerce in the 2012 short story "Citizen Conn," he returned to the near present, 2004, and to his adopted home, Oakland, California, for *Telegraph Avenue* (2012). Drawing on his early life experiences in the planned, integrated community of Columbia, Maryland, *Telegraph Avenue* follows two men, Archy and Nat, the former Black, the latter white and Jewish, and their slowly collapsing record store situated in the rapidly gentrifying area between Berkeley and Oakland. Like Dorothy in the short story "Son of a Wolfman" from *Werewolves*, Archy and Nat's wives, Gwen – who is heavily pregnant – and Aviva, are midwives, struggling for respect from the medical community. (Interestingly, *Telegraph Avenue* began as a pilot for TNT around the time *Werewolves* was published, so Chabon was clearly preoccupied with midwives around the end of the 1990s.) As well as exploring gentrification and the lasting effects of Blaxploitation on ideas of masculinity – Archy's largely absent father, Luther Stallings, is a fading Blaxploitation star – Chabon once again looks at the fluidity of sexual identity in the character of Julius, Aviva and Nat's son. Compared with the bleak millenarianism of *The Yiddish Policemen's Union*, *Telegraph Avenue* is a far more hopeful novel, a tonal shift that it appears can be credited to the election of Barack Obama. Set just after Obama's famous convention speech in 2004, Obama appears in the text and talks to Gwen about Archy's failings. *Telegraph Avenue* also ends on a hopeful note, where the young gay couple find online anonymity liberating. These scenes are oddly quaint; as Egan notes in her review, this depiction of the Internet "feels hopeful in a way that already seems nostalgic" (2012). While it does not involve any particular genre flourishes, that is not to say Chabon does not take risks; for instance, one section is a single twelve-page sentence told from the point of a view of a parrot as he swoops in and out of each of the characters' lives. Moreover, many interviewers queried whether it was okay for a white author to write in the voice of so many Black characters, a choice which has led this novel to be often compared to Quentin Tarantino, whose films form the basis of Julius and Titus's relationship. So, even when moving closer to his own experiences, Chabon continues to experiment, and inhabit different styles, forms, and voices.

His most recent novel, *Moonglow* (2016), is a fictionalized memoir, supposedly capturing the fragmented memories of his dying grandfather. However, as well as noting in the acknowledgments that *Moonglow* is a "pack of lies" (2016, p. 430), the protagonists are people he only refers to as "my grandfather" and "my grandmother." In the use of the possessive pronoun "my," Chabon constantly highlights that it is his version of these people. The plot of *Moonglow* involves V-2 rockets, space travel, and the wartime traumas that affected his grandmother's mental health. Literary allusions abound: the rocket is an obvious reference to Thomas Pynchon's *Gravity's Rainbow* (1973), J.D. Salinger is mentioned numerous times, and the television show he claims his grandmother hosted in the 1950s, *The Crypt of Nevermore*, is a nod to the character Madame Psychosis in David Foster Wallace's *Infinite Jest* (1996). It also fits within the contemporary genre of the fictional memoir, one that includes Paul Auster's *The Invention of Solitude* (1982), Dave Eggers's *A Heartbreaking Work of Staggering Genius* (2000), James Frey's *A Million Little Pieces* (2003), and Ron Currie's *Flimsy Little Plastic Miracles* (2013). *Moonglow* shows Chabon blending metafiction, memoir, history, and genre writing, and so it is another example of Chabon using a patchwork of genres to challenge these generic conventions.

Most recently Chabon and his partner, fellow writer Ayelet Waldman, co-edited the essay collection *Kingdom of Olives and Ash: Writers Confront the Occupation* (2017). While it is a fool's errand to guess where Chabon's fiction may turn next, this publication suggests he may perhaps return to the political overtones of *The Yiddish Policemen's Union* and *Telegraph Avenue* in response to the Trump administration. Chabon's fiction is representative of many of the shifts seen in fiction over the last thirty years: as well as the influence of creative writing programs, his work is particularly symptomatic of a contemporary turn to the lost or the forgotten, whether that be myths, histories, or genres. Embracing the lessons of postmodernism, Chabon concerns himself with entertaining himself and his audience as only he knows how.

SEE ALSO: After Postmodernism; Debut Novels; Egan, Jennifer; Lethem, Jonathan; Mixed-Genre Fiction; Periodization; Program Culture; Story Cycles; Whitehead, Colson; Young Adult Boom

REFERENCES

Chabon, Michael. (2000). *The Amazing Adventures of Kavalier and Clay*. New York: Picador.

Chabon, Michael. (2004). *The Final Solution: A Story of Detection*. New York: HarperCollins.

Chabon, Michael. (ed.) (2005). *The Best American Short Stories 2005*. Boston: Houghton Mifflin.

Chabon, Michael. (2007). *Gentlemen of the Road*. New York: Del Rey Books.

Chabon, Michael. (2016). *Moonglow*. New York: HarperCollins.

Chabon, Michael. (2018). *Pops: Fatherhood in Pieces*. New York: HarperCollins.

Costello, Brannon. (ed.) (2015). *Conversations with Michael Chabon*. Jackson: University of Mississippi Press.

Dinnen, Zara. (2016). "This is all artificial": an interview with Jennifer Egan. *Post45* (May 20, 2016). https://post45.org/2016/05/this-is-all-artificial-an-interview-with-jennifer-egan/ (accessed July 2, 2021).

Egan, Jennifer. (2012). Lost tracks. Review of *Telegraph Avenue*, by Michael Chabon. *The New York Times* (September 6, 2012). https://www.nytimes.com/2012/09/09/books/review/telegraph-avenue-by-michael-chabon.html (accessed July 2, 2021).

Greenwald Smith, Rachel. (2014). Six propositions on compromise aesthetics. *The Account: A Journal of Poetry, Prose, and Thought*. https://theaccountmagazine.com/article/six-propositions-on-compromise-aesthetics (accessed July 2, 2021).

Hoberek, Andrew. (2011). Cormac McCarthy and the aesthetics of exhaustion. *American Literary History* 23 (3): 483–499.

McGurl, Mark. (2009). *The Program Era*. Boston: Harvard University Press.

Punday, Daniel. (2008). *Kavalier & Clay*, the comic-book novel, and authorship in a corporate world. *Critique: Studies in Contemporary Fiction* 49 (3): 291–302.

Richardson, Anna. (2010). In search of the final solution: crime narrative as a paradigm for exploring responses to the Holocaust. *European Journal of English Studies* 14 (2): 159–171.

FURTHER READING

Chabon, Michael. (2019). *Bookends: Collected Intros and Outros*. New York: HarperCollins.

Dewey, Joseph. (2014). *Understanding Michael Chabon*. Columbia: University of South Carolina Press.

Kavadlo, Jesse and Batchelor, Bob. (eds.) (2014). *Michael Chabon's America: Magical Words, Secret Worlds, and Sacred Spaces*. Lanham, MD: Rowman & Littlefield.

Chiang, Ted

W. ANDREW SHEPHARD
University of Utah, USA

With just sixteen short stories and a novella to his name, Ted Chiang's body of work is relatively small. Yet he has become one of the leading voices in science fiction since his debut in 1990. Chiang has amassed four Nebula Awards, four Hugo Awards, four Locus Awards, and the John W. Campbell Award for Best New Writer. He has been nominated twice for the James Tiptree, Jr. Award for speculative works which enhance our understanding of gender and sexuality. Since the adaptation of his short story "Story of Your Life" (1998) into the film *Arrival* (2016), his work has garnered even more mainstream attention. Chiang's stories are often celebrated for their lucid prose, the diligent research process that informs them, and the deft manner in which they wed conceptual rigor with a deeply felt humanism.

Chiang was born in Port Jefferson, New York, in 1967, the son of Chinese nationals who fled to Taiwan during the Communist Revolution of China and later immigrated to the United States. His father is a professor of engineering at the City University of New York and his mother is a retired librarian. In 1989, Chiang graduated from Brown University with a degree in computer science and attended the Clarion Writing Workshop for authors of speculative fiction. Among his mentors at Clarion were Spider Robinson and Karen Joy Fowler; he credits the former with encouraging him to resubmit the story "Understand" (1991) for publication following several rejections. Shortly after attending Brown and Clarion, Chiang moved to Seattle, where he worked for Microsoft as a copy writer of technical manuals and met his partner, Marcia Glover, an interface designer turned photographer (Rothman 2017).

One of Chiang's major thematic concerns is free will versus determinism, a debate in which he takes a somewhat even-handed view. In an interview for *The New Yorker*, Chiang remarks: "I believe that the universe is deterministic, but that the most meaningful definition of free will is compatible with determinism" (Rothman 2017). This philosophy is reflected in several of his stories, including his most famous work, "Story of Your Life" (1998). The story concerns Dr. Louise Banks, a linguist who is recruited by the US government when sapient extraterrestrial life arrives on Earth. The aliens, called heptapods due to their biology, are possessed of cognition that works in a way drastically different than ours. They communicate through a language whose sense of causality presents unique difficulties in translation. In the process of learning to communicate with the heptapods, the protagonist discovers that thinking in their language radically reorients one's perception of time – a science fictional riff on the concept of linguistic relativism.

Instead of the linear model of time typically perceived by human beings, Louise begins to experience moments from her life as occurring simultaneously, in the process gaining a glimpse of her future – her love affair and marriage to a colleague, the daughter they have together, the eventual dissolution of their marriage, and the death of their child in early adulthood. Despite knowing the tragedies to come, Louise unreservedly chooses this path.

"The Merchant and the Alchemist's Gate" (2007), winner of the Nebula and the Hugo for Best Short Story, takes a similar approach to the subjects of grief and loss. The story is a thought experiment based on Kip Thorne's theorization of a mode of time travel that does not violate Einsteinian special relativity. The story concerns a merchant living in ancient Baghdad who, while at the town square market, encounters an alchemist selling access to a gate which allows one to travel through time. While traveling, one may interact with one's past or future self but is incapable of changing events. Heedless of this advice, the merchant travels into the past, desperate to prevent the death of his wife. He fails, but gains insights which allow him to make peace with his past and forgive himself. With its setting and nested narrative structure, Chiang's tale evokes the feeling of *The Thousand and One Nights*, while also delivering a predestination paradox as tightly constructed as any in science fiction.

A more pessimistic treatment of determinism occurs in "What's Expected of Us" (2005), which takes the form of a letter from one year in the future warning us about a piece of technology which has yet to be released. The device, called a Predictor, is ostensibly a toy but one which has devastating implications for humanity. It consists simply of a small remote control with a button and a green LED light; the light will inevitably flash a second before you push the button. Any attempts to trick or outsmart the device are doomed to failure. The implication that free will is an illusion leads large portions of the population to sink into catatonia and madness. The letter warns the reader that even if free will is an illusion, it is important for the sake of society to pretend that our choices matter. Of course, by implication, the letter is as futile a gesture as trying to outsmart the Predictor device itself.

One of Chiang's finest explorations of this theme is "Anxiety is the Dizziness of Freedom" (2019), set in a world in which the Many Worlds hypothesis of quantum theory has been proven true. In this story, a device called a PRISM allows you to send and receive messages to and from an alternate timeline. The story concerns Nat, a small-time con artist recruited into a scam involving the selling of PRISMs to people desperate to reconnect with loved ones who have died in their own timeline. Stories about alternate timelines traditionally focus on historical contingency, how a single decision can trigger a chain of events leading to a dramatically different outcome. However, in Chiang's story the multiverse also becomes a proving ground for one's character. The story implies that a person's character is not defined or determined by any one event but by the cumulative sum of his or her actions.

Other stories can be comfortably characterized as falling into the "gadget" model of science fiction story identified by Robert A. Heinlein. "Liking What You See: A Documentary" (2002) takes the form of a transcription of a fictional documentary concerning students, faculty, and administrators on a college campus and their opinions on a medical procedure which induces "calliagnosia" or "calli" for short – the inability to recognize physical beauty – as a means of eliminating lookism in their campus culture. In contrast to other stories with similar premises, notably Charles Beaumont's "Number 12 Looks Just Like You" (1952), and that presume that such a development would turn dystopian, Chiang takes a somewhat agnostic approach to the subject. The documentary form provides a variety of perspectives, from those in favor of implementing calli to those who vehemently oppose it. This ambivalence is perhaps best exemplified by Tamara, a college student who has recently gotten her implant removed and who goes through a spectrum of responses to her new circumstances.

Set in the near future, "The Truth of Fact, the Truth of Feeling" (2013) takes the form of a journalist's opinion piece on "Remem," a wearable technology which digitally records the life of the wearer. The narrator explores how the panopticon effect generated by the technology benefits society as a whole, by policing the behavior of law enforcement and reinforcing ethical business practices, while also acknowledging the damage that can be inflicted upon interpersonal relationships – the technology enables petty scorekeeping or games of oneupmanship and can stymie forgiveness. The narrator's skepticism toward the technology is shaken when he reviews the lifelog accounts of an argument with his daughter and its aftermath, discovering that he has misremembered the events in a way that flattered himself and contributed to their estrangement. While the story's premise bears a resemblance to the *Black Mirror* episode "The Entire History of You" (2011), Chiang eschews that narrative's pessimism in favor of meditating on the vagaries of human perception and the ways in which technology has mediated our fallible memories over the years. To drive home this point, the narrator contrasts his epiphany with another technological shift that changed humanity's relationship to memory – the transition from oral to print culture.

"Dacey's Patent Automatic Nanny" (2011) was originally written for the Jeff VanderMeer edited anthology *The Thackery T. Lambshead Cabinet of Curiosities* (2011) concerning a museum of imaginary technological artifacts. The story describes a device developed by Reginald Dacey, a Victorian-era mathematician and computer programmer, who, inspired by Charles Babbage's Analytical Engine, constructs an automated caretaker for his child following the death of his wife. The story takes a darkly humorous approach to the early growing pains of developmental psychology and the often bizarre practices proliferating in the field at this time, evoking the experiments of behaviorists like John B. Watson, as well as B.F. Skinner and his famous box.

Chiang's humanistic approach to ethics and technological innovation is perhaps best exemplified by the celebrated "The Lifecycle of Software Objects," which won the Locus and Hugo Awards for Best Novella in 2011. The story concerns Ana and Derek, employees of a software company which also manufactures "digiens" or digital entities, artificial intelligences analogous to sentient versions of the Tamagotchi digital pets from the 1990s. When the company goes under, Ana and Derek adopt digiens and effectively parent them to maturity. Chiang's AIs stand in striking contrast to many popular portrayals; they are not reflexively hostile, like the Terminator films' SkyNet, nor are they akin to the god-like AIs of William Gibson's Sprawl novels. Instead, Chiang's story convincingly points out that just as human consciousness requires years of maturation and careful guidance to make it suitable for labor and social relations, so might an intelligence comprised of computer code. The novella also considers how AI technology developed by private interests might entail different ethical and legal concerns than an AI technology developed by the military-industrial complex. In this respect, the story reflects the concerns expressed in Chiang's opinion piece "Silicon Valley is Turning Into Its Own Worst Fear" (2017).

Another popular theme within Chiang's oeuvre is cognition itself. The story

"Understand," written during his Brown days, concerns a man who is given an experimental neuro-regenerative treatment after suffering brain damage. The treatment not only repairs his damaged neural tissue, it dramatically increases his intelligence, causing him to notice patterns and find aesthetic significance in everyday phenomena. His enhanced cognitive capacity enables something beyond metacognition, a *para*-cognitive ability which allows him to develop a language to facilitate more efficient thinking and to optimize his consciousness for his own purposes. The narrator's activities eventually make him some enemies. He becomes of interest to the American intelligence community and later runs afoul of another cognitively enhanced metahuman, who has optimized himself for social intelligence and networking rather than aesthetics and considers the protagonist a threat to his plans to guide humanity to a better society.

"The Evolution of Human Science" (2000) considers the societal impact of cognitively enhancing human beings from an angle not often explored in science fiction: how it would affect academic life. The story takes the form of an editorial piece from a future where a prenatal gene therapy has created cognitively enhanced "metahumans" who have taken over scientific research, making new discoveries at a rate with which normal human beings cannot compete. While these beings are happy to share their findings for the common benefit, the metahumans' ability to transmit information to each other via a process called Digital Neural Transfer means that they are increasingly indifferent to the idea of publishing their research for humans to read – the majority of scientific articles at this point are secondhand accounts of metahumans' findings translated into human languages. Like Arthur C. Clarke's *Childhood's End* (1952), the story takes an elegiac approach to the notion of a posthuman singularity. But whereas the emergence of posthumans unambiguously means the end of humanity and any of its future accomplishments in Clarke's novel, Chiang points out that human beings may still have something to contribute to scientific study in the form of hermeneutics. In analyzing and extrapolating upon the gaps in metahuman science, the humans of Chiang's story call attention to concerns which would never occur to their cognitively enhanced brethren.

Chiang has explored the idea of consciousness from nonhuman perspectives as well. The story "Exhalation" (2008) concerns a scientist of a mechanical race of beings who inhabit a universe with physical laws drastically different from our own and whose cognition seems powered by a kind of pneumatic, rather than biochemical, process. Interested in understanding the nature of consciousness and memory, he undertakes a daring experiment to dissect his own brain and examine the processes of his own cognition and memory making. "The Great Silence" (2015) contemplates the Fermi paradox from the perspective of a tropical parrot, suggesting that humanity may have already encountered other intelligent life and simply not have noticed. The latter tale was later anthologized in *The Best American Short Stories of 2016*, a rarity for writers of science fiction and fantasy.

Faith and spirituality are also prominent themes in Chiang's work. Indeed, many of his stories explore theological concepts with the same degree of conceptual rigor that he applies to science fictional tropes. Often such tales coincide with the author's interest in what he calls "discredited worldviews" (Rothman 2017). Yet, rather than dismissing of spiritual belief, these tales highlight how abstract systems of knowledge, such as the sciences, often require leaps of faith. Take, for example, the story "Division by Zero" (1991), which concerns a mathematician who discovers an equation that allows one to divide by zero, thereby exposing an inconsistency in mathematics which threatens to undermine our most fundamental understanding of the way the world works; Chiang focuses on the psychological strain this revelation places upon the protagonist as she struggles to come to grips with its implications.

We also see this fascination play out in stories such as the Hugo Award-winning "Tower of Babylon" (1990), which retells the biblical tale of the Tower of Babel from the perspective of a stonecutter. Chiang's version is grounded in the logistical details of such an undertaking, including Bronze Age stonecutting techniques and the construction of makeshift communities on the tower. As the project reaches completion, the stonecutter and his compatriots tunnel through the firmament of sky – here conceptualized as a physical barrier to entering Heaven. The effect is that of a hard science fiction story written from the perspective of Bronze Age science. Though the protagonist never experiences a true encounter with the divine, the story evokes the mixture of fear and curiosity that would accompany such a feat.

The stories "Hell is the Absence of God" (1998) and "Omphalos" (2019) take similarly materialistic approaches to spiritual matters. The former takes place in a world where the existence of the Judeo-Christian God is an incontrovertible fact – miracles are commonplace, angels physically manifest on street corners, and people witness loved ones ascending to Heaven or languishing in Hell. The story concerns a man who struggles to love God because of too much proof rather than too little; his wife was killed in a natural disaster triggered by an angelic manifestation. In his endnotes, Chiang explains that the story was inspired by his dissatisfaction with moral inconsistencies within the Book of Job. "Omphalos" turns to the theory of "Young Earth creationism," exploring what it would be like to work in the sciences if the fossil record supported literalist interpretations of the Bible. Archaeologist Dorothea Morell is devout in her belief, having personally unearthed trees without growth rings and the mummified remains of primordial humans without navels. Yet, she is shaken to discover that though Earth was created by a divine being, there is proof of another world which is the true center of creation. Moreover, the lack of divine intervention on this world may be because we were really a trial run. The story's name "Omphalos," a Greek word meaning "center of the world," gestures toward the seismic impact such a revelation might have upon the faithful. The uniting theme of these three stories is how spiritual belief might be affected by the presence of material evidence.

Materialism and spirituality also collide in "Seventy-Two Letters" (2000). Set in an alternative Victorian London in which the golems of Jewish folklore and the outdated scientific theory of embryonic preformation are realities, the story focuses on a young kabbalist, or animator of golems, who is recruited into a conspiracy within the British Royal Society of Natural Philosophers who have discovered that, due to a hereditary defect in males, the human race will be incapable of reproducing within four generations. They propose to use the mystical techniques of kabbalism to construct new humans capable of self-replication in a manner similar to a Von Neumann machine. These men plot to keep this knowledge undisclosed to the public, ostensibly in the interest of preventing panic but also with more self-serving motives in mind: to control the rate at which the lower classes breed and to prevent women from discovering that they no longer need men for reproduction. The story contemplates how limiting access to knowledge can be used to preserve class hierarchies.

In an interview with the author, Joshua Rothman suggests that the overarching theme of Chiang's oeuvre is "the costs and the uses of knowledge" (2017). While Chiang himself demurs on this interpretation, the matter merits further consideration. After all, there are many ways of "knowing," each significant in its own way. Stories like "Division by Zero" contemplate the limits of empiricism as a way of knowing the world. Tales such as "Understand" and "Story of Your Life" consider how other modes of ontological perception might reveal seemingly unfathomable truths. "Anxiety is the Dizziness of Freedom" and "The Truth of Fact, the Truth of Feeling" explore the question of how well one can truly know oneself. "Liking What You See: A Documentary" proposes that certain types of sensory knowledge may blind us to other ways of knowing. And metaphysical tales such as "Omphalos" concern themselves with the age-old debate of faith and its relationship to concrete forms of knowledge. Moreover, in an era which has been declared "post-truth" and in which methods of inquiry are under increasing suspicion, perhaps such meditations are Chiang's greatest gift to the literary landscape – providing readers with a safe space in which to consider all that we don't know.

SEE ALSO: After Postmodernism; Mixed-Genre Fiction; Realism after Poststructuralism; Yu, Charles

REFERENCES

Chiang, Ted. (2002). *Stories of Your Life and Others*. New York: Vintage Books.
Chiang, Ted. (2017). Silicon Valley is turning into its own worst fear. Buzzfeed News (December 18, 2017). https://www.buzzfeednews.com/article/tedchiang/the-real-danger-to-civilization-isnt-ai-its-runaway (accessed July 3, 2021).
Chiang, Ted. (2019). *Exhalation: Stories*. New York: Knopf.
Rothman, Joshua. (2017). Ted Chiang's soulful science fiction. *The New Yorker* (January 5, 2017). https://www.newyorker.com/culture/persons-of-interest/ted-chiangs-soulful-science-fiction (accessed July 3, 2021).

FURTHER READING

Fan, Christopher T. (2014). Melancholy transcendence: Ted Chiang and Asian American postracial form. *Post45* (May 11, 2014). https://post45.org/2014/11/melancholy-transcendence-ted-chiang-and-asian-american-postracial-form/
Nicol, Bran. (2019). Humanities fiction: translation and "transplanetarity" in Ted Chiang's "Story of Your Life" and Denis Villeneuve's *Arrival*. *American, British, and Canadian Studies* 32 (1): 107–126.
Oates, Joyce Carol. (2019). Science fiction doesn't have to be dystopian. *The New Yorker* (May 6, 2019). https://www.newyorker.com/magazine/2019/05/13/science-fiction-doesnt-have-to-be-dystopian/amp

Chick Lit and the New Domesticity

HEIKE MIßLER
Saarland University, Germany

Chick lit started out as a marketing label for humorous, female-centered novels which soared to popularity in the 1990s and early 2000s. The term has come to designate a heterogeneous but well-established subgenre of popular fiction. Due to the fact that chick lit is related to the popular romance in that the heroine's search for happiness often culminates in a successful monogamous (and usually heterosexual) relationship and domestic bliss, the genre's critical reception has been mixed. At best, chick-lit novels are considered to represent an easily digestible, commercialized form of feminism, and at worst, they are considered an antifeminist backlash promoting regressive, neo-traditional ideals of femininity. As such, the novels are a prime example of the cultural phenomenon of post-feminism, which is most simply defined by its ambiguous representations of female empowerment.

THE EMERGENCE OF CHICK LIT

When the label chick lit ("chick" being a derogatory term for a young woman and "lit" the abbreviation of literature) began to circulate, it was mainly used as a dismissive designation. Cris Mazza and Jeffrey DeShell are credited with first using the term in print in the title of their edited collection of short stories *Chick-Lit: Postfeminist Fiction* (2000). As Mazza highlights, their use of the term was decidedly ironic and meant to draw attention to prevailing double standards about literary fiction by men and women (Ferriss and Young 2006, p. 3). The term gained popularity after the success of what are by now considered two of the foundational texts of the genre: Helen Fielding's *Bridget Jones's Diary* (1996) and Candace Bushnell's *Sex and the City* (1997), two novels dealing with a 30-something single woman in an urban setting and her search for happiness. In both *Bridget Jones's Diary* and *Sex and the City* finding happiness largely consists of finding Mr. Right, but also in building a career and maintaining friendships and family relationships, in other words, "having it all."

While the meaning of the term remains ambiguous, the publishing industries have since embraced it as a label for a genre of popular fiction, which took on shape with the wave of publications that followed in the footsteps of Bridget Jones and Carrie Bradshaw. In the United States, authors such as Meg Cabot, Emily Giffin, Kim Wong Keltner, Nicola Kraus and Emma McLaughlin, Terry Macmillan, Alisa Valdes, Jennifer Weiner, and Lauren Weisberger are by now part of a firmly established chick-lit canon, and in the United Kingdom and Ireland, novels by Cecilia Ahern, Jenny Colgan, Jane Green, Marian Keyes, and Sophie Kinsella feature dominantly on best-selling chick-lit lists. These authors' novels are recognizable as chick lit not just in terms of their content, but also because of their cover designs. These often feature items connoting a certain kind of pleasing and traditional femininity, ranging from luxury goods (stilettos and jewelry) to baked goods (cupcakes and cakes), pastel colors, and titles in cursive fonts. This extremely stereotypical marketing is still commonly applied. While it may be useful in terms of recognizability, it has been criticized by authors, readers, and scholars alike for its connotations of superficiality and consumerism.

DEFINING CHICK LIT

Initially, chick lit was defined as light-hearted, often humorous fiction largely written for, by, and about women. However, the single-girl(s)-in-the-city formula à la Bridget Jones and Carrie Bradshaw evolved relatively quickly and chick lit now features a broader range of protagonists, settings, and issues. It can have a female protagonist, or several protagonists, male or female, telling the story from different perspectives. It can also be written by men (examples include novels by Nick Alexander, Matt Dunn, David Nicholls, and Nicholas Sparks). This diversification has challenged the boundaries of the genre somewhat. However, it also shows that even within the formula, there is room for change.

This is necessarily so: like many other popular fiction genres, chick lit is caught up in marketing. A commercial genre such as chick lit must follow the demands of the market and adjust to what its target audience wants. Readers' tastes change over time, and the market is easily oversaturated. At the same time, authors cannot stray too far from the genre's core features, as the texts would then become unrecognizable as chick lit. In short, authors must be able to provide more-of-not-quite-the-same if they wish to keep their readership. Like many other popular fiction genres, chick lit also has a large and active fan community and a thriving online fan culture, which helps to shape and renegotiate the limits of the genre by reviewing and recommending novels. Chick-lit authors thus have a vested interest in interacting with fans and keeping a loyal following. Chick-lit fan websites such as Chicklit Club or Chick Lit Central offer guidance when it comes to what can or cannot be included in the chick-lit canon. Chicklit Club, for instance, offers its visitors the following definition of the genre, which emphasizes the female experience:

> Chick lit is a popular genre of contemporary fiction that focuses on the *transformational journey* of a woman or group of women. Storylines cover the many phases of life, from *starting a career, dating, moving to a new location, marriage, motherhood, mid-life transitions, divorce and death.* Romance is a common element but is not the sole focus of the book – *work, family or personal issues* play a big part. Often these novels are humorous, while its writers don't shy away from the *serious issues.*
>
> (Chicklit Club n.d., my italics)

As this definition shows, the quest motif lends a structure to the texts. The heroine is presented with a personal challenge which she must try to overcome to find happiness. Much like in coming-of-age plots, her character development is at the center of the action. Yet, as highlighted above, there is hardly a limit to potential plot elements.

A number of chick-lit subgenres focus on classic female life stages: teen lit, working-girl lit, bride lit, mommy lit, hen lit, and widow lit, showing no age limits to the genre. There are also subgenres dedicated to specific themes: "dieting lit," dealing with body image and weight issues; "sick lit," dealing with terminal illness and mental health issues; and there is even chick lit with a religious focus. "Ethnic chick lit" such as African American, Asian American, Latina, and Indigenous chick lit has also emerged, although many scholars point out that this moniker not only implies a problematic hierarchy within a genre that is predominantly associated with white, Western, middle-class, heterosexual authors and heroines, but also ignores the fact that some "ethnic chick lit" novels pre-date *Bridget Jones's Diary* and *Sex and the City* and were crucial in shaping the genre, such as African American author Terry MacMillan's *Waiting to Exhale* (1992). Thus, the term "ethnic chick lit" itself is questionable in its assumption of white being the default and chick lit being the unmarked term, with the implication that authors, readers, and characters are generally white.

Further broadening the chick-lit genre is what Suzanne Ferriss and Mallory Young call "chick culture," which they define as "mostly American and British popular culture media forms focused primarily on twenty- to thirty-something middle-class women" (Ferriss and Young 2007, p. 1). The concept of chick culture shows that the aesthetics and narrative tone of chick lit lend themselves well to transmedial adaptations not only for TV and film ("chick flicks"), but also for nonfiction genres such as magazines, blogs, and memoirs (Angela Clarke's *Confessions of a Fashionista* [2013]), travel writing (Jennifer Cox's *Around the World in 80 Dates* [2005]), and even cookbooks (Marian Keyes's *Saved by Cake* [2012]). Chick lit has also spawned a range of crossover subgenres, including 'vampire lit' (Stephanie Meyers's *Twilight* series [2005–2008]), "mystery lit" or "tart noir" (Janet Evanovich's *Stephanie Plum* series [1994–2017]), erotic fiction (E.L. James's *Fifty Shades* trilogy [2011–2012]), and young adult fiction (Meg Cabot's *Princess Diaries* series [2000–2015]). Note the belittling labels common to female-centered cultural products: chick lit, chick flicks, tart noir, and so on.

Because of the mutability of the formula and the heterogeneity of the content, a description of chick lit's formal and narrative features is helpful in order to pin down the quintessence of the genre. First, they are usually told in a confessional mode and use first-person narration, or a third-person narrator who privileges the heroine's perspective. Second, they are markedly humorous, ranging from gentle irony or self-deprecating humor to a downright satirical or even cynical narrative tone. Third, they are intertextual and hybrid, often mixing elements of high and low culture. A novel might thus contain literary references (see Harzewski's analysis of chick lit as a new novel of manners [2011]) and use the rhetorical style of women's magazines and self-help books (Smith 2008). Finally, the novels situate themselves firmly in late twentieth- and early twenty-first-century popular culture by making frequent references to contemporary culture and society, by name-dropping designer brands or names of celebrities.

The narrative is thus constructed in a way so as to make "offers of identification" (Jauss 1982, p. 93) to the readers. The conversational tone of the narrative sometimes even addresses readers directly, and gives them the impression of being involved in the heroine's life. In *Bridget Jones's Diary*, this impression is reinforced by the diary format, in which the heroine shares her secrets and thoughts with the readers. In Plum Sykes's *Bergdorf Blondes* (2004), for instance, the protagonist introduces herself to the readers directly: "Before I give you the rest of the goss from Mimi's [baby] shower, here are a few character traits you might want to know about me: [. . .]" (p. 4). The narrative is thus set out to engage its readers. However, the offers of identification do not have to be straightforward. Some novels might have more than one narrator-protagonist (e.g. Melissa Senate's *The Break-Up Club* [2006] and Alisa Valdes's *Dirty Girls Social Club* [2003]) and readers can choose who they identify with best; or they might feature a heroine who does not start out as a likeable character, but who comes of age in the course of the novel and makes amends. Heroines frequently endear themselves to their readers despite or perhaps even because of their flaws, since these are what makes them relatable. What is essential is that the chick-lit heroine is not perfect, but an ordinary character, an "everywoman," rather than a role model or a superwoman. Even if some readers might not be able to relate to the heroine at all, they will recognize the world that she lives in and the problems she encounters.

To sum up, there are only a few features in terms of content and form that can be ascribed to the multitude of texts labeled as chick lit. While the female experience and the quest motif remain constants of the genre, not only has the initial single-girl(s)-in-the-city formula expanded into numerous subgenres, it has also crossed over into other media, and its thematic scope is ever growing. The few formal features which mark a text recognizably as chick lit are the paratexts (notably the cover design) and the humorous confessional narrative.

GENEALOGIES AND DEVELOPMENTS

In an attempt to establish chick lit's literary history, scholars have traced the genre's origins back to a number of different authors, periods, and genres. *Bridget Jones's Diary* (1996) and *Sex and the City* (1997) are usually cited as urtexts, but the literary heritage of Jane Austen and other nineteenth- and early twentieth-century women writers such as Edith Wharton has also been noted. Jane Austen is often considered the godmother of chick lit due to the textual proximity of Helen Fielding's *Bridget Jones's Diary* and Austen's *Pride and Prejudice* (1813), and the enduring popularity and transmedial appeal of its main characters, Elizabeth Bennet and Fitzwilliam Darcy. In recent years, scholars have hinted that this genealogy contributes to a whitewashing of the genre and have suggested alternative genealogies, specifically for African American chick lit (Hurt 2019) and for Indian chick lit (Ponzanesi 2014). Hurt's and Ponzanesi's interventions are important in so far as chick lit is a global phenomenon with international reach and many variations of the genre in different national settings (Donadio 2006; Ponzanesi 2014; Folie 2020). Even so, Western chick-lit scholarship has dedicated most of its attention to white Anglo-American chick-lit titles, with some notable exceptions (Guerrero 2006; Butler and Desai 2008). This imbalance has been remedied by more recent studies, such as Sandra Ponzanesi's chapter on postcolonial chick lit in her monograph *The Postcolonial Cultural Industry* (2014), Tace Hedrick's study of chica lit entitled *Chica Lit: Popular Latina Fiction and Americanization in the Twenty-First Century* (2015), and Erin Hurt's edited collection *Theorizing Ethnicity and Nationality in the Chick Lit Genre* (2019).

The innovations brought to the genre by writers of color such as Kavita Daswani, Kim Wong Keltner, Terry Macmillan, Sofia Quintero, and Alisa Valdes have enriched the single-girl(s)-in-the-city formula by adding issues of race, assimilation, and belonging, and they have expanded the political dimensions of the genre. As Ponzanesi states, chick lit as part of popular culture "participates in forming and providing insights into national and global citizenship" (2014, p. 190), and ethnic chick lit makes this even clearer by featuring heroines who have to negotiate their status in society on a daily basis. Ponzanesi, Hurt, and Hedrick have argued that chick lit also fulfills important functions for writers and readers from ethnic minority backgrounds. Hedrick argues that the novels can take on an almost instructive function by laying out "in narrative form, prescriptions for attaining an American cultural citizenship for upwardly mobile Latinas, one that gestures toward a kind of 'value added' model of legal citizenship" (2015, p. 11). They can also serve as a corrective for prevailing cultural stereotypes and challenge the assumptions white readers may have about other cultures, by opening "a window into distant and exotic worlds," as Ponzanesi puts it (2014, p. 227). The minority ethnic protagonists of chick lit often reflect on their hyphenated identities and show how they negotiate questions of assimilation and cultural authenticity in their everyday lives: "These characters usually explain to readers that they do not fit the criteria often used to signify their ethnicity and often align themselves consciously with cultural practices that signify dominant culture" (Hurt 2019, p. 4). In challenging clichés about their culture and simultaneously addressing the expectations of their communities, these texts carve out a space for hybrid identities and cross-cultural experiences. Importantly, they promote the visibility and diversity of ethnic characters and give a voice to those who are often left out or silenced in mainstream Western popular culture. For (aspiring) authors of color, an additional incentive for writing chick lit might be the fact that the genre offers career opportunities in a book market that is interested in expanding its target audiences. Whereas (white) chick lit was declared dead by various news outlets and publishing houses at the end of the first decade of the twenty-first century due to falling sales figures, Ponzanesi and Butler and Desai claim that ethnic chick lit, particularly from India and China, for instance, has neither lost its appeal nor its readership and continues to grow strong (Ponzanesi 2014, pp. 179, 187; Butler and Desai 2008, p. 28).

It should be stressed that proclamations of chick lit's demise were greatly exaggerated in the West. What is noticeable, however, is that chick lit is a product of its time and aims to reflect issues that its readers will relate to. For instance, the genre generally reacted to the economic crisis of 2008. While early successful chick-lit titles were often set in middle and upper-class spheres, post-recession chick lit frequently features entrepreneurial heroines and heroines who worry more about their work than about their love life, although they do not always exactly suffer from economic hardship (cf. Scanlon 2013). Examples of post-recession chick lit include Erica Kennedy's *Feminista* (2009), Amy Silver's *Confessions of a Reluctant Recessionista* (2009), Sarah Strohmeyer's *The Penny-Pincher's Club* (2009), Melissa Senate's *The Love Goddess Cooking School* (2010), and Jenny Colgan's *Meet Me at the Cupcake Café* (2011) and *Welcome to Rosie Hopkins' Sweetshop of Dreams* (2012). As long as the chick-lit formula remains open to these alterations, its longevity is secured.

RECEPTION AND CRITICISM

Chick lit has been controversially received. Famous rebukes include Doris Lessing's accusation that the genre deals with "helpless girls, drunken, worrying about their weight" and Beryl Bainbridge's dismissal of the genre as a waste of time (both quoted in Ferriss and Young 2006, pp. 1–2). Another critic, Elizabeth Merrick, even went so far as to edit a collection entitled *This Is Not Chick Lit* (2006) to publicize her concerns over the genre's harmful effect on female readers, as it "numbs our senses [. . .]," as she claims (Merrick 2006, p. ix). This reaction may be partly due to the fact that chick lit is sometimes considered a subgenre of another popular fiction genre which has often been dismissed by the critics: the popular romance (Wherry 2014). Despite the fact that numerous studies have tried to vindicate the popular romance and to show its psychological complexity as well as its social function (see for example Tania Modleski [1982], Janice Radway [1984], and Jean Radford [1986]), discussions of chick lit's literary worth and feminist potential, or rather lack thereof, have repeated common prejudices (see for example Gill and Herdieckerhoff 2006). The criticism directed at chick lit is thus reminiscent of the kind of criticism that writing by women has always attracted, such as moral concerns about what women should read and what is considered "worthy" of their time and attention. Moreover, these concerns also often imply a misunderstanding about readers' responses to chick lit, since they suggest a strong influence of these books on the readers' lives, instead of acknowledging, as literary theory has done for years, that there are numerous ways of engaging with a text.

What is certainly true, however, is that the label chick lit is potentially harmful to some authors. Like the umbrella term "women's fiction," the label "chick lit" suggests that the issues addressed only concern women, although they are in fact very often universal. Moreover, the term is suggestive of low-brow writing and light entertainment, despite the fact that the texts often deal with serious issues such as dysfunctional relationships and families, illness, depression, anxiety, death, unemployment, and struggles in the workplace, for example. It is thus no surprise that many authors have contested the label and would not categorize their writing as chick lit (at least not exclusively), and many (e.g. Jenny Colgan, Jojo Moyes, and Jennifer Weiner) have spoken out against the negative connotations that the label implies, as well as the double standard inherent in it. Chick lit's male counterpart, "lad lit," has never had to face the same kind of stereotypical treatment by the publishing industries, nor has it received the trenchant criticism chick lit has, and it is generally enjoyed by readers of all genders. The same is true for many young adult novels with a female protagonist, such as John Green's best-selling *The Fault in Our Stars* (2012), which are similar in their narrative tone and thematic choice to many chick lit novels, but which have not been gendered to the same extent by the book industry nor by the critics.

As hinted at earlier, the main critical and popular debate about chick lit is whether it is a feminist or anti-feminist genre. Critics claim that the genre proliferates images of a shallow and consumerist femininity and of women who are largely interested in domestic bliss rather than female empowerment. This in itself is yet another example of the double standard applied to fiction written by women, since the same critical question ("is it feminist?") is not used to the same extent for fiction that is not distinctly gendered. However, in the case of chick lit, the first critical assessment always seems to be in how far the texts present progressive or regressive images of femininity. For a genre that offers a plethora of issues, this question cannot be answered conclusively. Chick lit's position in this debate is best understood in the context of post-feminism. Post-feminism is a somewhat elusive concept that has been variously defined as either a backlash against feminism or a continuation of it. One useful marker of orientation is temporal: post-feminism can be seen to describe the status of women in contemporary Western culture. Women are largely equal to men before the law and are, at least in theory, able to "have it all." The question is, however, how this sense of agency plays out in practice and whether the notion of "having it all" is a boon or a burden in disguise, as it comes with a whole new set of expectations and ideals. Rosalind Gill has provided a comprehensive and useful definition of post-feminism not as an "either/or" concept, a movement or a set of beliefs, but as a "both/and" "sensibility," which has marked Western contemporary popular culture in the aftermath of the second wave of feminism (Gill 2007). She lists the following elements of post-feminist media representations:

> [. . .] the notion that femininity is a bodily property; the shift from objectification to subjectification; the emphasis upon self-surveillance, monitoring and discipline; a focus upon individualism, choice and empowerment; the dominance of a makeover paradigm; the articulation or entanglement of feminist and anti-feminist ideas; a resurgence in ideas of natural sexual difference; a marked sexualization of our culture; and an emphasis upon consumerism and the commodification of difference.
>
> (2007, p. 255)

What qualifies these elements is that they all seem to negotiate, as Harzewski puts it, "the tensions between femininity and feminism" (2011, p. 150), and chick lit seems to be one of the foremost manifestations of this quandary.

The "both/and" quality of post-feminism is mirrored in chick-lit writing on two levels: form and content. On the level of form, the novels' humorous narrative voice frequently uses irony to produce ambiguities of meaning. On the level of content, the quest narrative of the chick-lit formula dictates that the heroine must pursue her desires and is usually rewarded with a happy ending. The possibility for subversion is inbuilt into this formula, because the heroine's desires are marked by two qualities: first, they are presented as "natural" and "normal" in a heteronormative sense (e.g. marriage, children, etc.), because they are never questioned, and second, they are shown to be difficult to achieve, despite the heroine's attempts at self-discipline in true Foucauldian fashion. The heroine will struggle so hard to achieve her aim that she will suffer and experience failure at least once during her quest. Cathy Yardley calls this the "life-implosion syndrome" – a common plot device in chick lit

(2007, p. 14). Thus, the most universal "normal" desires of a "good life," such as the happy heterosexual relationship, domestic bliss, the fulfilling career, motherhood, and/or the healthy and sexy body, are not only constructed as normative but as elusive and oppressive. Lauren Berlant calls this phenomenon of desiring something that will make you unhappy a relation of "cruel optimism" (2011, p. 1). The formula thus makes visible the norms which underlie the heroine's desires, and thereby opens them to criticism and weakens them. In the end, however, the heroine learns from her failure, grows as a character, and is rewarded with her happy ending and so the norm is reinstated as that which ultimately produces happiness. Readers can thus choose to privilege the heroine's long struggle to reach her aim and her "cruel optimism," or her moment of triumph at the end of the novel. Depending on one's focus, the texts can be interpreted as potentially subversive or as affirmative of dominant norms of femininity. The reduction of chick lit to a celebration of pre-feminist ideals and the promotion of a new domesticity thus misses one layer of interpretation, since the struggle to comply with normative ideals is a mainstay of chick lit. To give an example: in the novels which foreground the heroine's aspirations to reach a markedly consumerist feminine ideal, the heroine's consumer behavior is satirized through exaggeration, rather than embraced uncritically, such as in Sophie Kinsella's *Shopaholic* series (2000–2016), Candace Bushnell's *Sex and the City*, Helen Fielding's *Bridget Jones's Diary*, and Plum Sykes's *Bergdorf Blondes*. Although the heroines might appear to be mindless consumers pursuing the ideals of femininity proffered to them by women's magazines, advertisements, and popular media culture, their failed attempts to comply with the ideal dominate the plot. As Caroline Smith puts it in her study *Cosmopolitan Culture and Consumerism in Chick Lit*, it is in fact "the heroines' inability to navigate their own paths in the face of these ever-present consumer ideologies" that takes center stage (2008, p. 119). The heroine's failure to reproduce the ideal ultimately always exposes the ideologies that are the cause of her unhappiness in the first place, and thus it is these ideologies that are worthy of critical analysis.

The dominant ideology in chick lit is heteronormativity. Heteronormativity as defined by Michael Warner and Lauren Berlant designates "the institutions, structures of understanding, and practical orientations that make heterosexuality seem not only coherent – that is, organized as a sexuality – but also privileged" (1998, p. 548). Heteronormativity does not just relate to sexuality, but entails further regulations of the self and one's relationships, which becomes particularly clear in chick lit: the heroine's desires are almost always the same: self-optimization, finding a partner, getting married, having children. It seems that the chick-lit formula is not yet flexible enough to include desires which are not marked as "good" and "normal" by heteronormativity. Heroines who find their happy ending while being single, or promiscuous, or polyamorous, or who do not want to marry and have children are still relatively rare. Lesbian and queer heroines are slowly starting to become more visible in chick lit, in novels by Kiki Archer, Clare Lydon, Siera Maley, and Camille Peri for example, but they have not yet reached the mainstream success their heterosexual counterparts have. Non-normative desires thus have little space within the chick-lit formula so far, and hence the criticism that what the genre can offer must remain contained within a heteronormative framework.

Nevertheless, the debates about chick lit's cultural worth and its representation of womanhood, whiteness, and heteronormativity go to show that the genre not only marks an important moment in female cultural production, but continues to be relevant. Despite proclamations of chick lit's death as a genre, it remains a potentially subversive cultural narrative and a crucial reference point for new products of post-feminist media culture which have evolved from chick lit and will continue to do so.

SEE ALSO: McMillan, Terry; Multiculturalism; Third-Wave Feminism; Young Adult Boom

REFERENCES

Berlant, Lauren. (2011). *Cruel Optimism.* Durham, NC: Duke University Press.
Berlant, Lauren, and Warner, Michael. (1998). Sex in public. *Critical Inquiry* 24 (2): 547–566.
Butler, Pamela and Desai, Jigna. (2008). Manolos, marriage, and mantras: chick-lit criticism and transnational feminism. *Meridians* 8 (2): 1–31.
Chicklit Club. (n.d.). Chick Lit 101. https://www.chicklitclub.com/chicklitintro.html (accessed July 19, 2021).
Donadio, Rachel. (2006). The chick-lit pandemic. *The New York Times* (March 19, 2006). https://www.nytimes.com/2006/03/19/books/review/the-chicklit-pandemic.html (accessed July 19, 2021).
Ferriss, Suzanne and Young, Mallory. (eds.) (2006). *Chick Lit: The New Woman's Fiction.* New York and London: Routledge.
Ferriss, Suzanne and Young, Mallory. (eds.) (2007). *Chick Flicks: Contemporary Women at the Movies.* New York and London: Routledge.
Folie, Sandra. (2020). The ethnic labelling of a genre gone global: a distant comparison of African-American and African chick lit. In: *Translation, Reception, Transfer* (ed. Norbert Bachleitner), 313–325. Berlin and Boston: De Gruyter.
Gill, Rosalind. (2007). *Gender and the Media.* Cambridge: Polity Press.
Gill, Rosalind and Herdieckerhoff, Elena. (2006). Rewriting the romance: new femininities in chick lit? *Feminist Media Studies* 6 (4): 487–504.
Guerrero, Lisa. (2006). "Sistahs are doin' it for themselves": chick lit in Black and white. In: *Chick Lit: The New Woman's Fiction* (ed. Suzanne Ferriss and Mallory Young), 87–102. New York and London: Routledge.
Harzewski, Stephanie. (2011). *Chick Lit and Postfeminism.* Charlottesville: University of Virginia Press.
Hedrick, Tace. (2015). *Chica Lit: Popular Latina Fiction and Americanization in the Twenty-First Century.* Pittsburgh: University of Pittsburgh Press.
Hurt, Erin. (ed.) (2019). *Theorizing Ethnicity and Nationality in the Chick Lit Genre.* New York and London: Routledge.
Jauss, Hans Robert. (1982). *Aesthetic Experience and Literary Hermeneutics.* Minneapolis: University of Minnesota Press.
Mazza, Cris and DeShell, Jeffrey. (ed.) (2000). *Chick-Lit: Postfeminist Fiction.* Tuscaloosa: University of Alabama Press.
Merrick, Elizabeth. (ed.) (2006). *This Is Not Chick Lit.* New York: Random House.
Modleski, Tania. (1982). *Loving With A Vengeance: Mass-Produced Fantasies for Women.* Hamden, CT: Archon Books.
Ponzanesi, Sandra. (2014). *The Postcolonial Culture Industry: Icons, Markets, Mythologies.* Basingstoke: Palgrave Macmillan.
Radford, Jean. (ed.) (1986). *The Progress of Romance: The Politics of Popular Fiction.* London and New York: Routledge.
Radway, Janice. (1984). *Reading the Romance: Women, Patriarchy and Popular Literature.* Chapel Hill: University of Northern Carolina Press.
Scanlon, Jennifer. (2013). What's an acquisitive girl to do? Chick lit and the Great Recession. *Women's Studies* 42 (8): 904–922.
Smith, Caroline J. (2008). *Cosmopolitan Culture and Consumerism in Chick Lit.* New York: Routledge.
Sykes, Plum. (2004). *Bergdorf Blondes.* New York: Viking Press.
Yardley, Catherine. (2006). *Will Write for Shoes: How to Write a Chick Lit Novel.* New York: Thomas Dunne Books.
Wherry, Maryan. (2014). More than a love story: the complexities of the popular romance. In: *The Bloomsbury Introduction to Popular Fiction* (ed. Christine Berberich), 53–69. London: Bloomsbury.

FURTHER READING

Ferriss, Suzanne. (2014). Chick lit non fic: the comedic memoir. *Feminist Media Studies* 14 (2): 206–221.

Mißler, Heike. (2017). *The Cultural Politics of Chick Lit: Popular Fiction, Postfeminism, and Representation*. New York and London: Routledge.

Cisneros, Sandra

CHRISTOPHER GONZÁLEZ
Utah State University, USA

Sandra Cisneros is one of the most significant contributors to American letters, thanks to her intense focus on Chicana/o/x identity, specifically Chicana identity, and her outspoken advocacy for third-wave feminist issues. Her poetry, short stories, novellas, and novels serve as much-needed contributions to Chicana writing and to American letters writ large. Her collection of stories, *Woman Hollering Creek* (1991) and her novel *Caramelo* (2002) helped solidify the promise of her talent that was made manifest in her groundbreaking *The House on Mango Street* (1984), which, along with Rudolfo Anaya's *Bless Me Ultima* (1972), is arguably the most widely read and studied work by a Latinx author in the United States, especially in high school English classrooms. *The House on Mango Street* has never been out of print, and it is largely this book that cements Cisneros's legacy.

Born in Chicago, Illinois, on December 20, 1954, Sandra Cisneros has become one of the most indispensable writers for literature that focuses on Latinx women. She helps establish (along with Gloria Anzaldúa, Ana Castillo, and Helena Maria Viramontes) an articulated Chicana feminism that broke through the male-dominated Chicano movement for civil rights of the late 1960s and 1970s. Her father Alfredo Cisneros de Moral, Mexican by birth, and her mother Elvira Corsero Anguiano, a Mexican American from Chicago, came to have seven children, all of whom were male except Sandra, the third child. As the only girl among her six brothers, issues concerning the inequities and disparities often heaped on women in Chicano culture were ever at the forefront of her experiences, a fact that would later significantly impact the trajectory of her writings and her ideologies. The mobility of her family (they were consistently on the move, and lived in Chicago and Mexico City) seemed to cause a great degree of angst and disquiet in the young Cisneros, and it helped establish her notions of home and migration for Latinxs in the United States as expressed in her writings. The constant moving of her family was incredibly formative for the artist Cisneros would become; she reportedly had a difficult time establishing friendships, exacerbated by her brothers' paternalistic treatment of her: "Being an only daughter in a family of six sons forced me by circumstance to spend a lot of time by myself because my brothers felt it beneath them to play with a *girl* in public. But that aloneness, that loneliness, was good for a would-be writer – it allowed me time to think and think, to imagine, to read and prepare myself for my writer's profession" (Cisneros 2015, p. 92). Her Chicago neighborhood was predominately Puerto Rican, and it was that neighborhood that helped give shape to arguably what is her most impactful work, *The House on Mango Street*, which went on to win the American Book Award and became a staple in public schools and universities across the United States.

These challenges in her childhood compelled Cisneros to turn inwardly to books and writing. Her working-class roots also became an integral aspect of her writing, despite her education at Loyola University in Chicago and her MFA training at the prestigious Iowa Writers' Workshop. Cisneros realized that she wanted to be a writer around the time of her preteen years, even though she had kept such desires to herself for many years. One of the critical characteristics of Cisneros as a personality is her fierce and dogged determination to see something through despite what others may think.

Cisneros pursued an English degree while at Loyola. Her experiences in that program, and especially after a creative writing class she enrolled in, set her on a path to explore her world and experiences through writing. And though her talents were potent enough to gain her entry into the Iowa Writers' Workshop, she has since discussed how difficult her experience was in the program – a program that, at least at the time, did little to nurture her voice and honor her experiences as being as valid as those of her white peers. She has mentioned that she became a writer despite the Iowa Writers' Workshop rather than thanks to it, claiming it "failed her" (Cisneros 2015, p. 196). What this statement suggests is the nature of the structure of these educational institutions and spaces and how, even now, they are not designed with writers like Cisneros in mind – writers from historically marginalized and vulnerable communities in the United States.

As her career has unfolded, Cisneros has become a key figure in what would come to be known as the Chicana feminist movement of the 1980s. Latinx literature is a relatively nascent tradition in US literature, emerging fully in the 1970s, and it was initially dominated mainly by male writers, such as Rudolfo Anaya, Rudolfo "Corky" Gonzales, Cesar Chavez, and Oscar "Zeta" Acosta. Though notable women were writing during these times, it is not until the 1980s that more Latina/Chicana women began to be published, many by small and independent presses. Cisneros had several important early publications that helped to break up the logjam of men writing of their Hispanic heritage. For writers like Cisneros, the personal experiences born out of sociopolitical strife were necessary stories to tell, especially since they were stories that were not getting told at all. Like other Chicana feminist writers, Cisneros exposed the joys and sufferings of a community of women whose time to be heard had arrived, thanks mainly to the women themselves, who forged their opportunities as a result of having been denied for so long.

A fundamental theme of Cisneros's work is the struggle to feel like one truly belongs to a specific identity group. In her case, it is the difficulties reconciling her Mexican heritage with the aspect of her identity that is bound to the United States. Thanks in considerable measure to her moves from the United States to Mexico and back again, Cisneros experienced a very fluid sense of self, where at times she felt Mexican, at other times American, and nearly always never fully one or the other. She has explored this duality and hybridity throughout much of her work, and her conceptions of feminism and womanhood play crucial roles in not only shaping her understanding of herself but also her explorations of community and culture via these understandings of identity. In writing through her particular lens of identity, she has managed to capture something widespread and far-reaching not only in the Chicano community but across the world. Her books are prevalent worldwide, and her novels have been translated into a host of languages.

Beyond the significance of Cisneros as a writer, she has taken very prominent stances in political and sociological causes while also serving in various roles such as a teacher and writer in residence. Her activism has led her to create a variety of workshops and foundations with the intent of fostering talent from historically marginalized communities and vulnerable identity positions. Perhaps the most impactful of these has been the Macondo Foundation, a writing program based in San Antonio, Texas, to provide further mentorship and opportunity to develop for promising writers in the Southwest. She has recognized the power and influence that she has attained, and she has, in turn, used her influence and status to help others, and most especially women of color who share many of the struggles and hardships that Cisneros encountered in the early parts of her life.

Cisneros is the recipient of several key awards, including the National Endowment for the Arts Creative Writing Fellowship in Fiction and Poetry in 1981 and 1988. More recently, she was honored with the National Medal of Arts by President Barack Obama to recognize her many contributions to American letters and the arts. She has also managed to stay in the zeitgeist, which is both a function of her indispensability to Latinx culture and the volatile nature of her personality. In 2020 she was somewhat linked to a controversy surrounding the author Jeanine Cummins and her novel *American Dirt* (2018), which was accused of a kind of exploitation of migrant and refugee stories that embroiled its author, its publisher, and even Oprah Winfrey, who had selected the book for her highly influential book club. Cisneros had provided the book and its cover a radiant quote. Journalist Maria Hinojosa questioned Cisneros as to why she would lend her name and credibility to a book that arguably was built on many stereotypes of Mexican migrants (Hinojosa 2020). On a more positive note, Cisneros is referenced in Jon M. Chu and Lin-Manuel Miranda's film *In the Heights* (2021), where several influential Latinas are invoked in reverential roll call with the likes of Celia Cruz and Sonia Sotomayor. Cisneros is referenced simply as "Sandra," alongside a stylized image of her as a mural. Because the film is destined to be a kind of cultural touchstone, the mention of Cisneros is a reminder that she has achieved the status of an icon.

Her first published book was *Bad Boys*, a series of seven poems published in 1980. The poems take a penetrating view of childhood and a Chicano neighborhood in Chicago, a place she knew so well, wracked with poverty and struggle. This style of a poetry book, called a chapbook, is a small publication that belies its significance to the writing world because it introduces such an impactful author in such an unassuming way, and it reveals how Cisneros, who is mostly known now as a writer of prose, initiated her publishing career with a tiny book of poems published by a small independent press.

Nearly four years later, an independent publisher called Arte Público Press would publish *The House on Mango Street*, a book whose influence and staying power cannot be overemphasized. It is a book that deliberately works to upend a general reader's expectations for what a novel should be. Indeed, *The House on Mango Street* is not a novel at all, in the traditional sense. Instead, it is a compendium of forty-four connected vignettes – short stories that hover over a 12-year-old Chicana girl named Esperanza Cordero who lives in a Chicano area of Chicago. The book is a coming-of-age story that takes place over a year, and it arises from the experiences of Cisneros's childhood. As with *Bad Boys*, *The House on Mango Street* reveals Cisneros's ability to condense and compress such grand issues as social class and cultural understanding in only brief swatches of writing. The prose takes on the quality of Esperanza's worldview as a Chicana girl who comes of age with the knowledge that the world is often set against her, even within her own community. By giving her such authoritative perspective and voice, Cisneros ultimately empowers all women who make that transition from child to adolescent to young adult. It is at times funny, intelligent, daring, and poignant and would in many ways serve as a kind of prototype for everything else Cisneros would do from there on as a writer. It won the Before Columbus American Book Award, and today the book is considered a classic of Chicano and Chicana literature. As a measure of its standing, it has sold over six million copies and has been translated into many languages. It routinely appears in high school and college reading lists, despite its potentially controversial subjects, such as Esperanza's budding sexual awareness, that have landed it on several banned book lists.

My Wicked, Wicked Ways (1987), a book of poetry developed from her MFA project and enriched by experiences she had in Europe as she worked on her poems, casts its eyes on a variety of topics that would concern a Chicana: love, religion, guilt, friendships, and the evolution of an affair with a man named Rodrigo, who is the subject of so many of the poems they are included in a section titled "The Rodrigo Poems." The mélange of Mexican cultural heritage and its brand of Catholicism dominates the poems, as is indicated in its title. The poems take on the possibilities and permissions surrounding a woman's desires, her sexuality, and the dominion of religion over a woman's mind, body, and soul.

Cisneros would return once more to narrative form in her collection of short stories, *Woman Hollering Creek and Other Stories*. In twenty-two short stories (so short, she calls them *cuentitos*, though at least one, "The Eyes of Zapata," is nearly thirty pages long), Cisneros again makes excellent use of the vignette form she employed in *The House on Mango Street* and lays out many concerns for a life straddled by an arbitrary national border that cannot divide two national cultures. Here, rather than have the stories emanate from a specific character or narrator, the unifying aspect is the geographical environs of San Antonio, Texas. The many characters give a multi-faceted look at women negotiating an inhospitable culture dominated by sexist cultural traditions and systemic oppressions. The collection continues Cisneros's explorations of both sides of the United States and Mexico border, which were even more on her mind as she was living in San Antonio at the time. Perhaps the most potent aspect of *Woman Hollering Creek* is Cisneros's deliberate use of clichés and stereotypes to explore such issues as immigration, identity, and the humanity of her cast and thus her community.

Loose Woman (1994) is Cisneros's most extensive collection of poems to that point, with over sixty verses that emphasize the variety of emotions of love, ranging from the romantic to very nearly erotic. Unlike in *My Wicked, Wicked Ways*, Cisneros portrays a more sexually liberated woman in this book of powerful poetry. *Loose Woman* continued to solidify her as a significant poet to complement her status as an indispensable narrative storyteller.

Cisneros then turned her attention to storytelling for younger audiences by taking one of her vignettes from *The House on Mango Street* and recasting it as a children's picture book. *Hair / Pelitos* (1994). The book again demonstrates Cisneros's refusal to be cast as a creator of only one type of verbal art, moving from poetry to prose to children's books with absolute ease.

Caramelo signaled Cisneros's return to narrative, and it again underscored her interest in those experiences which shaped her into adulthood – specifically, her family that seemed strewn across the North American continent. Using short, vignette-styled chapters (by now a signature formal feature of Cisneros's style), *Caramelo* seeks to reclaim Cisneros's Mexican roots and cultural traditions. It also reaches into many of Cisneros's own experiences, and at times the author herself provides footnotes in her novel that serve as a commentary on various moments in the story. The novel is highly personal even by Cisneros's standards. It is an epic novel that spans the better part of a century and delves deeply into Mexican history. Narrated by Celaya Reyes, called Lala throughout, the novel is primarily a family history. Like

Cisneros's family, the Reyes frequently migrate between Mexico City and Chicago. *Caramelo* makes significant use of the rebozo, a specific type of shawl native to Mexico, as a metaphor of the ties that bind a family together.

More recently, Cisneros has continued her desire to reach into other forms of storytelling and literary expression. With her book *Bravo, Bruno!* (2011), Cisneros tells a story from the perspective of a poodle named Bruno, with illustrations placing the affable dog in various places in Italy. Notably, Cisneros wrote the book in Italian. *Have You Seen Marie?* (2012) is an illustrated tale that centers on a woman's search for her cat that becomes a search for meaning and self. Described as a fable for adults, the illustrations by Ester Hernández bring poignancy to a story about the loss of a loved one and the resiliency found in community. These works indicate Cisneros's growing comfort with visual storytelling as well as stories for children.

A House of My Own: Stories from My Life (2015) is a collection of Cisneros's writing that spans three decades and gives a powerful overarching perspective of the portrait of the artist as a Chicana. The book brings together uncollected and some previously unpublished writings, as well as a collection of personal photos, and is indispensable for those interested in the author as a person whose lived experiences have influenced her art. The collection serves as a kind of memoir, with recently written pieces by the older Cisneros providing context and perspective to the writings of her younger self.

Cisneros again returned to writing about animals with *Puro Amor* (2018), a bilingual chapbook illustrated by the author herself. In this short story, Cisneros reimagines Frida Kahlo and Diego Rivera in the sunset of their years (they are called Missus and Mister Rivera), as a couple in a house filled with a menagerie of animals. Missus Rivera cares for them all, as her own frail health prevents her from leaving the "caza azul," a house that is so blue it is almost cobalt. The story interrogates love and the strange forms it may take. This small book suggests that Cisneros is at a stage in her career where she is led more by her interests in exploring what art can do and what she can do with art, rather than be caught up in the expectations that she be a certain kind of writer. *Puro Amor* is the first publication for adults since *Caramelo*, and it is tantalizingly short.

Throughout her remarkable and influential career, Sandra Cisneros has given much-needed representation to Chicana women in US literature. Her steadfast explorations of Chicana identity, migration, stereotypes, religion, feminism, childhood, and sexuality are now regarded as classics of American literature. In this regard, her works bring diversity and a considerable understanding to the idea of womanhood across Anglo and Latinx cultures.

SEE ALSO: Álvarez, Julia; Anaya, Rudolfo; Castillo, Ana; Cofer, Judith Ortiz; García, Cristina; Hinojosa, Rolando; Multiculturalism; Third-Wave Feminism; Urrea, Luis Alberto; Viramontes, Helena Maria

REFERENCES

Cisneros, Sandra. (2015). *A House of My Own: Stories from My Life*. New York: Vintage.
Hinojosa, Maria. (2020). Digging into *American Dirt* (January 30, 2020). www.latinousa.org/2020/01/29/americandirt/ (accessed August 18, 2021).

FURTHER READING

Cisneros, Sandra. (2007). *Vintage Cisneros*. New York: Knopf.
Ganz, Robin. (2010). Sandra Cisneros: border crossings and beyond. In: *Critical Insights: The*

House on Mango Street, 190–204. Hackensack, NJ: Salem Press.

Madsen, Deborah L. (2000). *Understanding Contemporary Chicana Literature*. Columbia: University of South Carolina Press.

Rivera, Carmen Haydée. (2009). *Border Crossings and Beyond: The Life and Works of Sandra Cisneros*. Santa Barbara, CA: Praeger.

Cleage, Pearl

TIKENYA FOSTER-SINGLETARY
Clark Atlanta University, USA

Considerations of the work of Atlanta playwright, novelist, essayist, and poet Pearl Cleage should begin with the idea of free womanhood. The idea centers much of her work. The concept as she uses it is an attempt to unhinge women from the confines of social strictures. An early piece, "In the Time Before the Men Came" (1989), outlines the idea. The story crystallizes the key features of Free Womanhood: a group of supernatural Amazon-like women who live in isolation from men. They are self-contained and self-reliant until one of the women is lured away by neighboring men, interrupting the utopian space they have created and leaving the women vulnerable to subservience to men. It is a gesture towards a feminist worldview, which privileges women's productive (and reproductive) relationships with each other and warns that patriarchy lurks nearby to threaten that harmony.

In one of Cleage's best-known plays, *Flyin' West* (1992), the main characters also use the concept to convey the bonds of sisterhood they create. They chant lines very similar to ones in the earlier text, proclaiming their right to define themselves as Black women who are courageous, loving, and strong. Here, the idea of free womanhood is especially significant because it engages two generative themes in African American literature more broadly. The women have emerged from the end of enslavement and taken advantage of the mobility they had previously been denied. They avail themselves of the Homestead Act to claim and cultivate land in Kansas as part of American westward expansion. The narrative benefits from Cleage's research on the time period and cultural elements like the interactions between Native Americans and African Americans in the postbellum era. The context of American acquisition of land, post-Emancipation, and female-empowered space – along with confronting colorism and domestic violence – makes *Flyin' West* one of the most salient vehicles for embodying Cleage's worldview. This is, perhaps, why *Flyin' West* was the most produced play in the country in 1994.

Cleage's use of the free womanhood idea is directly iterative of the way she sees herself as a writer and of her upbringing. Born in Detroit, Michigan, Cleage was influenced by her father Albert Cleage (later known as Jaramogi Abebe Agyeman), who founded the Shrines of the Black Madonna of the Pan-African Orthodox Christian Church. His coupling of civil rights, religion, and Black nationalism provide a framework for Cleage's worldview, as did witnessing the Detroit riots of the 1960s. Her mother, Doris Graham Cleage, also provided a fertile environment for appreciating literature and the arts, ensuring that their home was filled with books and that Cleage and her sister appreciated the performing arts. These influences, in addition to her formal education at Howard University and, later, Spelman College, laid a landscape of critical inquiry and artistic value. Moreover, the political and social disruptions of her young adult years in the mid-twentieth century framed the focus on race, equality, and Black nationalism that is frequently reflected in her work. Free Womanhood echoes these foundational concepts rooted in race and gender equality.

Cleage's writing spans several genres. Early in her career she produced a column for the *Atlanta Tribune* and worked as press secretary in the mayor's office with Atlanta mayor Maynard Jackson. She also composed scripts for television, most notably when she worked as host of programs for WQXI-TV and WETV television stations in Atlanta in the early portions of her career. She is, however, best-known as a playwright and novelist. Some of her earliest produced work includes *The Bangs* and *The Sale* (written as a student at Howard University and Spelman College). Several plays, such as *Hospice* (1985), *Puppetplay* (1982), *Good News* (1994), *Essentials* (1983), *Bourbon at the Border* (1997), *Late Bus to Mecca* (1992), and *Chain* (1994), are anthologized in the collection *Flyin' West and Other Plays*. Also in that collection is *Blues for an Alabama Sky* (1995), an often-produced play set against the backdrop of the Harlem Renaissance that was part of the Cultural Olympiad for the 1996 International Olympic Games, held in Atlanta. In 2015, the Alliance produced the play again as part of its twentieth anniversary season. The Royal Academy of Dramatic Arts has also produced *Blues,* a testament to its wide-spread appeal (Billington 2017). Her most recent plays include *A Song for Coretta*, which premiered in 2007 and celebrates the life and legacy of Martin Luther King, Jr.'s widow Coretta Scott King, *The Nacirema Society Requests the Honor of Your Presence at a Celebration of Their First One Hundred Years*, which debuted at the Alabama Shakespeare Festival in 2010, and *What I Learned in Paris*, which debuted in 2012. In 2019 *Angry, Raucous, and Shamelessly Gorgeous* was performed at the Alliance Theater. In addition to composing drama, she has also worked as artistic director for Just Us theater in Atlanta, where a number of her plays have also been produced. During her tenure as playwright in residence there, she collaborated with her creative partner and husband, Zaron Burnett, Jr. to produce performance projects titled *Live at the Zebra Lounge*.

Cleage's work as an essayist has also been well-received. Her essay collection, *Mad at Miles: A Black Woman's Guide to Truth* (1990), became a lynchpin in her oeuvre. Across the essays included in the collection, she explores feminism, race, and violence against women, including her own experience of violence at the hands of a former lover. The title essay poses – and firmly answers – the question of whether lovers of jazz music can continue to purchase and enjoy Miles Davis's music, widely considered among the best of jazz artists. The ethics of separating art from heinous acts by the artist continues to loom large. Her conclusion is that Davis' behavior, in particular his extreme violence against then partner Cicely Tyson, is irredeemable because of his unrepentant bragging about his aggression; for Cleage, this warrants total rejection of his art. Her stance demonstrates the convergence of her own activism and art. Later, these essays became the basis of *Deals with the Devil and Other Reasons to Riot* (1993), which addresses political concerns, domestic violence, race, and popular culture. Of particular note is "The Other Facts of Life," which presents a blunt set of guidelines for women moving through American society. The essay warns against ignoring the frightening realities of violence against women, with sexual violence at the forefront. In addition, the collection includes a self-reflective essay, "Why I Write," that describes the development of Cleage's identity as activist and writer; it is a clarifying moment that expresses her desire to explore the crossroads of racism and sexism in hopes of exposing them as ills that manifest in individual human lives. Here she unpacks both for herself and for her audience the purpose of her work: to work towards healing and resist the violence and brutality of the oppression of Black women. Her writing is stark and pointed, using self-reflection and social commentary to impact an audience with whom she shares concern. In 2014 another work of nonfiction, *Things I Should Have Told My Daughter: Lies, Lessons, and Love Affairs*, revealed her self-examination through journal entries in the 1970s and 1980s. The book considers her earlier life as mother, wife, and emerging writer.

As a novelist, Cleage came to great prominence when her first novel, *What Looks Like Crazy on an Ordinary Day* (1997), was selected as a 1998 Oprah Book Club pick and was a *New York Times* bestseller for eight weeks. *Crazy* is almost as significant for its depiction and treatment of HIV, the diagnosis that the main character is faced with at the beginning of the text, as for its presentation of love, community, and family. The protagonist, Ava, enters into a romantic relationship after conceding that her diagnosis has made her undesirable to men and moving back to the small town where she was raised. Cleage shifted to the novel form when the story she wanted to tell was not served by writing for the stage. It is worth noting, however, that this was not Cleage's first work of prose fiction. *The Brass Bed and Other Stories* (1991) presents autobiographical short stories that are minimalist and genre mixing. In similar vein, *What Looks Like Crazy on an Ordinary Day* displays the frame at work in several of her other novels: the Black body personal demonstrates the sociopolitical workings of the Black body politic. Most often, the personal is represented in romantic partnerships. This first novel also includes a list of things every free woman should know, which includes growing flowers, guidelines for making sexual choices, and basic home and auto repair. An outgrowth of the earlier manifestations of free womanhood, this list makes tangible the abstract ideas suggested in *Flyin' West* and "In the Time Before the Men Came." The story demonstrates how free womanhood directs characters' focus on the self and invites authentic connection with other people. In line with feminist ideals, this is true for both female and male characters.

Though not situated as sequels, subsequent novels share characters and features with *What Looks Like Crazy on an Ordinary Day*. *I Wish I Had a Red Dress* followed Cleage's debut novel in 2001. It expands the story of the protagonist Ava's sister Joyce, who elevates her activist work and forges a romantic partnership of her own. The next novel, *Some Things I Never Thought I'd Do*, was published in 2003. It is the first novel set in Atlanta and the first in a series of books set in the city. Like much of her previous work, it tells the story of a woman in crisis and in search for truth. Here, the main character is contending with the aftermath of a struggle with substance abuse disorder. Additionally, *Some Things I Never Thought I'd Do* also explores romance and community. Cleage recasts West End Atlanta, which suffers from the ills of drugs, crime, and economic underdevelopment, as a lush, utopic landscape within a protective border. While in this novel and others, women are central figures who both work together and act against each other, the halo of protection in West End is created by men. This element may explain some critiques of these novels that note the focus on heterosexual relationships and respectability. Significantly, however, *Babylon Sisters* (2006) subverts the protective role of men by centering the female characters as heroines and protectors.

Continuing her interest in romance and sociopolitical commentary, Cleage followed these novels with four that both embrace and inquire into the social structure created by character Blue Hamilton, who provides protection for the imaginary West End community. *Baby Brother's Blues* (2006) explores the limits of that protection. Like Cleage's other works of fiction, it uses romantic and platonic relationships to explore social ills. *Till You Hear from Me* (2010) gestures toward the close relationship between the author and her father. It frames the story in the wake of Barack Obama's historic election as US President in 2008 and comments on the complicated intersection of media, religion, and generational divisions. In *Seen It All and Done the Rest*, published in 2009, and *Just Wanna Testify*, published in 2011, Cleage expands her vision to tackle American culture's preoccupation with vampires and addresses shifts in the urban environment. Putting Blue Hamilton at the center of these novels emphasizes the balance between the personal and the communal that holds together the reimagined West End Atlanta. *Seen It All and Done the Rest* follows *Baby Brother's Blues* in its focus on political vice and the less polished parts of the city. In fact, all of these novels include significant social and political concerns: the election of the first Black US President, the devastation of Hurricane Katrina, the effects of addiction on both individuals and community, the Iraq War, and Black America's often complicated relationship with citizenship.

Although her plays and novels have received a great deal of attention, Cleage's poetry, essays, and scripts are also significant parts of her work. In 2005 she co-wrote "We Speak Your Names" with Zaron Burnett, Jr. for Oprah Winfrey's Legends Ball. Like the ball itself, featuring both emerging and elder artists and activists, the work celebrates twenty-five selected African American women across fields such as film and television, music, literature, and activism. It acknowledges the women highlighted during the weekend by name. Cleage was designated one of the younger artists, and the poem expresses gratitude for the contributions of the more established women. Though the piece was read aloud during the Legends Ball weekend, it was later published as a book. Like much of her other work, "We Speak Your Names" underscores sisterhood and freedom, among other ideas. This work extends from the artistic foundation of her first book of poetry, *We Don't Need No Music* (1971), which she hoped would represent healing and positivity for Black people. That volume was followed by another book of poetry, *Dear Dark Forces*, in 1980. In addition, she is a founding editor of literary magazine *Catalyst*, which featured Cleage's own creative and editorial work as well the work of other artists. These publications further demonstrate Cleage's commitment to embracing work about the intersection of race and gender through a wide swath of platforms. As an outgrowth of her work as writer and the thrust of activism in her work, Cleage often lectures, teaches, and supports writers and artists through educational institutions and arts organizations. She has served as Endowed Chair in Fine Arts at Spelman College from 2005–2007, for instance. Moreover, she is a frequent participant in the National Black Arts Festival, an Atlanta area organization with a mission for promotion and education of the arts. Alliancetheater.org (n.d.) details her first work for young people, which debuted at the Alliance Theater in 2015, *Tell Me My Dream*. She has also composed a children's book with her husband titled *In My Granny's Garden* (2019), which reflects the novels' frequent interest in the value of homegrown food and flowers; *What Looks Like Crazy on an Ordinary Day*, for instance, includes growing food and flowers in its list of Ten Things Every Free Woman Should Know.

From her work on the campaign and administration of Atlanta's first Black mayor to her consistent presence in the city's cultural scenes, Cleage is, arguably, one of Atlanta's best-known writers. Atlanta functions as a character itself in novels like *Some Things I Never Thought I'd Do*, *Babylon Sisters*, and *Baby Brother's Blues*. In particular, the city's West End functions as an aspirational space; still, it is recognizable as a part of the city's actual landscape. The iconic Civil Rights

Movement-era restaurant Pascal's is featured often, as are the Victorian houses and the Krispy Kreme doughnut shop that help to define the area; in addition, other metro-Atlanta area landmarks, like Lenox Square Mall, situate the stories in Atlanta. Moreover, Cleage's longstanding relationship with the Alliance Theater further underscores the place of Cleage, her work, and associations with Atlanta. She has served as playwright in residence, and several of her plays have debuted there, including *What I Learned in Paris*. Atlanta also provides the backdrop for works like *Things I Should Have Told My Daughter*; the author's personal reflections illuminate the political and cultural setting of the city during the decades after the Civil Rights Movements. Cleage's varied experiences in the city allow for a layered and complex presentation of Atlanta both as it is and as it could be. Highbrow and more pedestrian lives are presented with dignity.

Cleage has received a number of awards in recognition of her work. The New Georgia Encyclopedia notes the Bronze Jubilee Award for Literature in 1983 and the Governor's Award for Arts and Humanities, along with the National Association for the Advancement of Colored People Image Award, an Honorary Doctorate from Spelman College, the outstanding columnist award from the Atlanta Association of Black Journalists, and the Bronze Jubilee Award for Literature (Seese 2019). She also been acknowledged by the Georgia Writers Association. Grants by the National Endowment for the Arts, the Georgia Council on the Arts, and the Coca-Cola Foundation have provided support for her work. In 2021, she was named the first poet laureate for the city of Atlanta.

As result of her long career as writer, Pearl Cleage has become a prominent voice in the arts and in the city of Atlanta more broadly. Moreover, her influence has extended to other writers as well, perhaps most notably Tayari Jones, who was a student in Cleage's creative writing course while she attended Spelman College and whose 2018 novel *An American Marriage* was a *New York Times* bestseller. Cleage's emphasis on racism and sexism, among other social concerns, is definitive of both her work and her personal values. These concerns, expressed clearly in her nonfiction work, also frame her plays and novels. Her novels, in particular, are intentional in their confrontation of domestic violence, politics, and so on. This focus in her novels and other work makes Cleage an especially conscious voice whose presence and influence continue into the twenty-first century.

SEE ALSO: Book Clubs; Debut Novels; Literary Magazines

REFERENCES

AllianceTheater.org. (n.d.). (accessed July 14, 2021).

Billington, Michael. (2017). *Blues for an Alabama Sky* review. *The Guardian* (February 12, 2017). https://www.theguardian.com/stage/2017/feb/12/blues-alabama-sky-review-1930s-harlem-pearl-cleage-royal-academy-dramatic-art-london (accessed August 2, 2021).

Seese, June Akers. (2019). Pearl Cleage. *The New Georgia Encyclopedia* (December 1, 2019). https://www.georgiaencyclopedia.org/articles/arts-culture/pearl-cleage-b-1948 (accessed July 30, 2021).

FURTHER READING

Critical Perspectives on Pearl Cleage. (2009). Special issue of Obsidian III: Literature in the African Diaspora 10 (1).

Foster-Singletary, Tikenya and Francis, Aisha. (eds.) (2012). *Pearl Cleage and Free Womanhood*. Jefferson, NC: McFarland.

Giles, Freda Scott. (1997). The motion of herstory: three plays by Pearl Cleage. African American Review 31 (4): 709–712.

Turner, Beth. (2007). The feminist/womanist vision of Pearl Cleage. In: *Contemporary African*

American Women Playwrights: A Casebook (ed. Philip C. Kolin), 99–114. New York: Routledge.

Weekley, Ayna. (2008). Why can't we flip the script: the politics of respectability in Pearl Cleage's *What Looks Like Crazy on an Ordinary Day*. Michigan Feminist Studies 21: 24–42.

Cliff, Michelle

KAISA ILMONEN
University of Turku, Finland

Born in Kingston, Jamaica, Michelle Cliff (1946–2016) belongs to the generation of diasporic, migrant writers who began their careers during the late 1970s and early 1980s, as well as US-based third-wave feminists of that time. Besides Cliff, writers such as Audre Lorde, Jamaica Kincaid, Sandra Cisneros, and Alice Walker explored the themes of intersecting identities, roots and place, female identity and sexuality, and marginalization. Cliff uses Caribbean and African American traditions and folklore in her novels to rewrite colonized cultural identity. In her much-cited essay "A Journey Into Speech" (1985), Cliff envisions storytelling "retracing the African past of ourselves, reclaiming as our own, and as our subject, a history sunk under the sea, or scattered as potash in the cane fields, or gone to bush" (1985, p. 14). Cliff's writing is often occupied with histories rewritten from oppressed points of view. Her histories of resistance, and rebellious textuality, highlight solidarities between marginalized groups. She addresses queer and intersectional identities, outsiderness and Creolization, displacement, memory, trauma, and traumatized sense of self in history.

Cliff's family moved to New York in the early 1960s. They were able to maintain their middle-class lifestyle and did not participate in the political movements of that time. Their economic status made it possible to travel between the United States and Jamaica. Her parents could and wanted to pass as white, even though they felt uncomfortable because of their experiences of racism. Cliff has called the racial passing of her light-skinned family a "schizophrenic experience" but also a mode of self-protection (Adisa 1994, p. 275). At university Cliff majored in European History and she later moved to London in order to complete her MA in Italian Renaissance art at the Wartburg Institute. After returning to the United States, Cliff began her career in publishing. In the late 1970s she published a lesbian feminist journal, *Sinister Wisdom*, together with the feminist scholar Adrienne Rich, who became her lifelong partner. In addition to her literary and publishing careers, Cliff also taught creative writing at several universities, and lived most of her life in California. Cliff died of liver disease in June 2016.

In all her writings Cliff highlighted Caribbean diasporic themes and claimed her Jamaican cultural identity, retaining her Jamaican citizenship (MacDonald-Smythe 2001; Adisa 1994; Schwartz 1993.) Cliff's first collection of poetry, *Claiming an Identity They Taught Me to Despise*, was published in 1980. The most recurrent themes of her works, the psychic displacement of a light-skinned Creole, her feelings of alienation, the prejudices of the surrounding society, and the problems of passing, are already present in this collection. One of her best-known novels, the semi-autobiographical *Abeng*, was published in 1984. It describes the life of a pre-teen light-skinned girl, Clare Savage, growing up in Jamaica and struggling with her contradictory sense of Jamaican history, ambivalent identity, and awakening sexuality. In 1985, Cliff published a collection of prose poems and essays called *Land of Look Behind*, which depicts the consequences of multiple simultaneous oppressions and feelings of alienation in more generalized terms: for example, the story of Anne Frank, which haunts the protagonist in *Abeng*, is included in the collection. In 1987,

Cliff published her second novel, *No Telephone to Heaven*, which today is probably her most acclaimed piece of writing. The novel continues the story of Clare Savage into her adult years, migrating between the United States, the United Kingdom, and Jamaica, but develops further the themes of queer and transnational identities, cultural traumas, and a sense of displacement.

In 1990, Cliff published a collection of short stories, *Bodies of Water*. The title refers to the legacy of the Black Atlantic; this collection also addresses loneliness and alienation due to racism, sexism, or homophobia. The Holocaust, the Vietnam War, domestic violence, slavery, and the violation of civil rights remain in the backgrounds of these traumatized characters. A shared experience of oppression is also the main focus of Cliff's next novel, *Free Enterprise* (1993). (The second edition, published in 2004, has the subtitle *A Novel of Mary Ellen Pleasant*.) *Free Enterprise* consists of an assemblage of historical storylines concerning abolitionist struggles in the United States during the nineteenth century, and focusing on the efforts of Mary Ellen Pleasant, a historical character who is said to have funded John Brown's famous raid on Harper's Ferry. The novel highlights the many different forms of resistance conducted by subordinate groups, whether Jews, Native Americans, African Americans, Creole Caribbeans, women, queers, or dis/abled people (sections of the novel are set at the Carville leper colony located in Louisiana, 1894–1999). *Free Enterprise* makes the reader particularly aware of multiple systems of oppression, intersectional solidarity beyond identity politics, and the marginalized histories of the Americas (Ilmonen 2017).

In 1998, Cliff published yet another collection of short stories, *Store of a Million Items*, which once again examines the experience of displacement shared by differently marginalized people. The United States, metaphorically represented as a store selling almost anything, cannot offer safety for the stories' characters. Ten years later, Cliff published a book-length collection of nonfictional essays called *If I Could Write This in Fire* (2008), reflecting her personal migrant experiences intertwined with the history of violence, colonialism, even genocide, and the plights of Jamaican history. The theme of history is continued in her most recent collection of short stories, published in 2009, *Everything is Now*. The title refers to the continued presence of the past in our lives on a psychological level. On a more collective level, the collection focuses on characters who need to gather their own history from oral stories and items not displayed in museums.

Cliff's last piece of writing, a novel called *Into the Interior*, was published in 2010. It is a collection of short story-like chapters depicting a young Caribbean woman's travel to the United Kingdom to study art history at the Warburg Institute. The chapters describe her peculiar encounters with people of several sexual obliquenesses, turning an examining "colonial gaze" towards the former colonizer and its perversions.

In Cliff's works, a complex and complicated sense of history, a multiplicity of memories, and transnational solidarities between differently oppressed people and their forgotten resistance are always highlighted. Collecting the pieces of memory becomes a leitmotif of her texts, and more often than not, the reader recognizes these collections as intersectional. *Abeng*'s omniscient narrator, for example, corrects Clare Savage's sense of history by conveying memories forgotten by the archives, by the history she learns in school. The narrator presents the reader with the foremothers of Cliff's mythical lineage of lesbian/feminist rebels. One of them is Mma Alli, a healer in a slave plantation Clare visits more than a hundred years later. Mma Alli is depicted as a "one breasted warrior woman" representing "a tradition which was older than the one which had enslaved them" (Cliff 1995, p. 34). Mma Alli "had never lain with a man" but "she was a true sister to the men – the Black men: her brothers" and "by being with her in bed, women learned all manner of the magic of passion [...]. *To keep their bodies their own*, even while they were made subject to whimsical violence." (p. 35.) Through such passages, Cliff unearths memories and histories that are not only postcolonial, but also feminist and queer.

Consequently, *Abeng* moves from male history to female archaeology. The narrator acts as a textual archaeologist who points out the crevices within historical discourse out of which another past can be detected, like the two sounds of the conch shell known as "abeng" (Edlmair 1999) The counter-history in *Abeng* is deeply attached to the Jamaican ground and to the sufferings of slaves. Cliff's textual archaeology becomes clear, for instance, when the narrator describes a drive to the Caymanas Racetrack, a place where Clare's father gambles: "The turn for Caymanas was on the Spanish Town Road, right by Tom Cringle's Cotton Tree, a huge silk cotton tree which was a Jamaican landmark, from whose branches human bodies had once swung" (1995, p. 144). Counter-memory is hidden in the bowels of the earth or scattered in fragments to be found in rocks, trees, old songs, ancient rites, or secrets remembered by women.

Cliff's literary voice undergoes some changes after the 1980s: her more recent works relocate the themes of reclaimed history, resistance, and remembering into a more transnational space (MacDonald-Smythe 2001, pp. 18–20, 181–184). Now, the sense of self is not connected to the idea of "origins," or homelands, but to diasporic solidarity. The search for Caribbean history in *Abeng* and *No Telephone to Heaven* is transformed into a project of retracing the genealogy of many kinds of resistances in *Free Enterprise*. The theme is echoed in the composition of the novel: like the history of resistance, *Free Enterprise* is itself a tapestry of pieces and voices. The most polyvocal part of *Free Enterprise* consists of stories told in the Carville leper colony. In Carville, the novel's protagonist, Annie, participates in storytelling sessions with the lepers as they remember the lives, names, and roots taken from them by the US Public Health Service. The lepers embody a variety of ethnic backgrounds, and during their storytelling they share not only their own individual tales but also those of their people. In Carville, all the lepers from different backgrounds are pathologized as "others," racialized and dis/abled in authoritarian discourse (Agosto 1999).

Carville becomes a metonym standing for the solitude of those considered unfit, other, alien, or different. The loneliness of those seen as inappropriate is the all-encompassing theme in Cliff's writings. It is often connected to white Caribbeanness, or Creoleness, but also to sexual otherness and queerness. Kim Robinson-Walcott writes about "the peculiar loneliness of the white Jamaican" and explains that "history has burdened the white West Indian with his own peculiar set of baggage: as past oppressor and present threatened minority, saddled with collective guilt but still holding the reins of power" (2003, pp. 98, 96). All the protagonists of Cliff's novels share what Robinson-Walcott calls "the trauma of a light-skinned person being trained to pass for white" (p. 99). In *No Telephone to Heaven*, Clare Savages's father counsels his daughter on invisibility, "Self-effacement. Blending in. The uses of camouflage" (Cliff 1996, p. 100), in order to make it in New York. This kind of self-effacement makes Clare's African-identified mother lose herself completely. Without the solidarity of her African American sisters, she decides to return to Jamaica, leaving her light-skinned daughter behind. The particular solitude of those almost white but not quite (cf. Bhabha 1995, p. 86) is not mitigated in Europe, where Clare and the art historian protagonist of *Into the Interior* feel an even denser loneliness.

Sexual otherness is a focal point in Cliff's depiction of otherness. Solitude and mutual longing for female love have sad results for cousins and lovers Alice and Clover Hooper in *Free Enterprise*. As Clover, an aspiring photographer, ponders her future role as a wife, she is terrified: "Accommodations would be made. She might even be kept at home. In a room where she would be forced to approximate a rounded, female figure. Maternal, feminine. Soft. She was not and it frightened her." (Cliff 1994, p. 158.) Alice also feels restricted by her status, but unlike Clover she cannot articulate what bothers her. Instead, she identifies herself and Clover with Emma Bovary in Flaubert's novel. Both Alice and Clover have tragic fates. Clover commits suicide by drinking the liquids she uses to develop her photographs, and Alice retires from the world into her bedroom in the attic, like Bertha Mason in *Jane Eyre* (1847) by Charlotte Brontë.

As demonstrated above, Cliff's texts are full of intertextual references, paratexts, hypotexts, citations, and moments of ekphrasis, when her narrators depict visual art. Her textual strategy is to present the reader with the recurrent theme of alienation and racism in the Western literary imagination. As her narrators keep referring to J.M.W. Turner's paintings, Dickens, Shakespeare, Columbus, Heathcliff, Madame Bovary, Conrad's Marlowe, or Bertha Mason, the reader realizes the way Western culture is preoccupied with the binary of "us versus them." Clare, for example, identifies herself with the English orphan Pip Pirring (Cliff 1995, p. 36), the Creole woman Bertha Mason (1996, p. 116), *Ivanhoe*'s dark Rebecca (1995, p. 72), and the Jewish Anne Frank (1995, p. 72). It becomes clear that Cliff's decolonizing literary strategy is based on mixing or co-opting several cultural myths which, as narrative acts, illustrate the multiple contrasts of postcolonial reality.

Furthermore, Cliff's textual network widens the postcolonial logic towards queer and feminist issues. The section in *No Telephone to Heaven* that describes Clare's lonely life in London is called "Et in Arcadia Ego" (Here I am in Arcadia), referring to Virgil's fifth eclogue where Death enters Arcadia. Some scholars interpret this title in terms of discovering the falseness of imperial myths (see e.g. Strachan 2002). However, from a queer point of view, yet another intertext may be acknowledged. In one of the most famous novels describing homosexual love, *Brideshead Revisited* (1945) by Evelyn Waugh, the first part is called "Et in Arcadia Ego." This section of Waugh's novel depicts the two male protagonists falling madly in love with one another. Like Clare, they study classics in an English university and feel distanced from their families. This intertext opens up the possibility of interpreting Clare's sense of outsiderness and depression also as yearning for a lesbian partnership (Ilmonen 2017). Thus, Cliff's novels "unfurl" differently depending on whether they are considered in the African American, Caribbean, queer, lesbian, Black feminist, postcolonial, US, or transnational migrant literary contexts.

As an author, Michelle Cliff never yielded to the commercial values of the publishing industry, and she described the difficulties of finding a publisher for *Into the Interior* (Stecher and Maxwell 2013). Cliff did not promote her works commercially, and there are only a few pictures published of her. In spite of her scarce publicity, Cliff's novels have been acclaimed by scholars and critics. Recently, her works have attracted new academic attention through the rise of trauma and memory studies. Several scholars have turned to Cliff's texts in order to theorize the ideas of cultural memories and trauma in more complex and multidirectional ways (Casteel 2014; Croisy 2007–2008; Ilmonen 2020). In his oft-quoted study *Multidirectional Memory: Remembering the Holocaust in the Age of Decolonization* (2009), Michael Rothberg emphasizes dialogue and interaction to "create new forms of solidarity and new visions of justice" (2009, p. 5) out of empathy, historical relatedness, and a shared sense of trauma. Rothberg describes Michelle Cliff as an "obviously multidirectional writer" who connects the Jewish experience to that of the Caribbean (p. 27).

Several scholars have suggested that Cliff's fiction potentially renews trauma studies in many ways, whether in terms of intersectionality, Creolization, or multidirectionality. (Ilmonen 2020; Croisy 2007–2008; Casteel 2014). For Sarah Phillips Casteel, Cliff's textuality reflects a sensibility that "privileges multiple and complex forms of identification over the dyads of black/white and victim/perpetrator" (2014, p. 797). In all of Cliff's fiction, her fundamental ethos is towards multilayered, ambivalent, and complex understanding of history and identity. Cultural identities emerge in her novels as palimpsests, revealing new stories and narrative layers, dissolving "either–or" definitions. Clare Savage, for instance, is able to recognize the different facets of her identity, as the narrator sums up in *No Telephone to Heaven*: "She is white. Black. Female. Lover. Beloved. Daughter. Traveler. Friend. Scholar. Terrorist. Farmer" (1996, p. 91). History, identity, and ethics emerge intertwined in Cliff's writing: the seeking of the rebellious, female self is always negotiated through several axes of experience.

SEE ALSO: Black Atlantic; Kincaid, Jamaica; Literature of the Americas; Multiculturalism; Queer and LGBT Fiction; Third-Wave Feminism; Trauma and Fiction; Walker, Alice

REFERENCES

Adisa, Opal. (1994). Journey into speech – a writer between two worlds: an interview with Michelle Cliff. *African American Review* 2, 273–281.

Agosto, Noraida. (1999). *Michelle Cliff's Novels. Piecing the Tapestry of Memory and History.* New York: Peter Lang.

Bhabha, Homi K. (1994). *Location of Culture.* London: Routledge.

Casteel, Sarah Phillips. (2014). Writing under the sign of Anne Frank: Creolized holocaust memory in Michelle Cliff and Caryl Phillips. *Modern Fiction Studies* 4: 796–820.

Cliff, Michelle. (1985). *Land of Look Behind.* New York: Firebrand Books.

Cliff, Michelle. (1990). *Bodies of Water.* New York: Plume.

Cliff, Michelle. (1994). *Free Enterprise.* New York: Plume; 1st ed. 1993.

Cliff, Michelle. (1995). *Abeng.* New York: Plume; 1st ed. 1984.

Cliff, Michelle. (1996). *No Telephone to Heaven.* New York: Plume; 1st ed. 1987.

Cliff, Michelle. (1998). *The Store of a Million Items.* New York: Houghton Mifflin.

Cliff, Michelle. (2008). *If I Could Write This in Fire.* Minneapolis: Minnesota University Press.

Cliff, Michelle. (2010). *Into the Interior.* Minneapolis: University of Minnesota Press.

Croisy, Sophie. (2007–2008). Michelle Cliff's non-Western figures of trauma: the Creolization of trauma studies. *The AnaChronisT* 13, 131–156.

Edlmair, Barbara. (1999). *Rewriting History: Alternative Versions of the Caribbean Past in Michelle Cliff, Rosario Ferré, Jamaica Kincaid and Daniel Maximin.* Vienna: Braumüller.

Ilmonen, Kaisa. (2017). *Queer Rebellion in The Novels of Michelle Cliff: Intersectionality and Textual Modernity.* Newcastle, UK: Cambridge Scholars.

Ilmonen, Kaisa. (2020). Intersectionality. In: *Routledge Companion to Literature and Trauma* (ed. Colin Davis and Hanna Meretoja), 173–183. London: Routledge.

MacDonald-Smythe, Antonia. (2001). *Making Home in the West/Indies. Constructions of Subjectivity in the Writings of Michelle Cliff and Jamaica Kincaid.* New York: Garland.

Robinson-Walcott, Kim. (2003). Claiming an identity we thought they despised: contemporary white West Indian writers and their negotiation of race. *Small Axe* 2: 93–110.

Rothberg, Michael. (2009). *Multidirectional Memory: Remembering the Holocaust in the Age of Decolonization.* Stanford: Stanford University Press.

Schwartz, Meryl. (1993). An interview with Michelle Cliff. *Contemporary Literature* 4: 595–619.

Stecher, Lucía and Maxwell, Elsa. (2013). Michelle Cliff's *Into the Interior* and the trope of the solitary female immigrant. *Callaloo* 3: 811–821.

Strachan, Ian G. (2002). *Paradise and Plantation. Tourism and Culture in the Anglophone Caribbean*. Charlottesville: University of Virginia Press.

FURTHER READING

Bucknor, Michael A. and Donnell, Alison. (eds.) (2011). *The Routledge Companion to Anglophone Caribbean Literature*. London: Routledge.

Edmondson, Belinda. (1999). *Making Men: Gender, Literary Authority and Women's Writing in Caribbean Narrative*. Durham, NC: Duke University Press.

Garber, Linda. (2001). *Identity Poetics: Race, Class, and the Lesbian-Feminist Roots of Queer Theory*. New York: Columbia University Press.

Ilmonen, Kaisa. (2017). *Queer Rebellion in The Novels of Michelle Cliff: Intersectionality and Textual Modernity*. Newcastle, UK: Cambridge Scholars.

Tinsley, Omise'eke Natasha. (2008). Black Atlantic, queer Atlantic: queer imaginings of the middle passage. *GLQ* 14 (2–3): 191–215.

Cole, Teju

RACHEL SYKES
University of Birmingham, UK

Teju Cole is the pen name of Obayemi (Yemi) Onafuwa, a Nigerian American author born in Kalamazoo, Michigan on June 27, 1975. A photographer, essayist, curator, art historian, and fiction writer, Cole is the author of five books and best known for his debut novel *Open City* (2011), which won the PEN/Hemingway and National Book Critics Circle awards for 2012, as well as praise from reviewers and contemporaries like Salman Rushdie, Colm Tóibín, and Claudia Rankine. What followed for Cole was a period of creative and public intellectualism which never favored a single cultural form. Written as a series of blog posts and first published as a novella in Nigeria in 2007, *Every Day is for the Thief* was reprinted by Faber in 2014, swiftly followed by a book of essays, *Known and Strange Things* (2016), and two photobooks, *Punto d'ombra* (2016) / *Blind Spot* (2017) and *Fernweh* (2020). From working as a photography columnist for *The New York Times* (2012–2020) to publishing a series of narrative experiments on Twitter and Instagram (2012–2013), Cole's work is formally varied but invariably concerned with the ethics of global travel and colonial and postcolonial urban histories, relying heavily on the representation of individual encounters with art and literature and the technological mediation of modern life to tell richly layered and slowly realized contemporary stories.

Much of Cole's work reflects the experience of travel through the lens of his dual citizenship. Nigeria and America – specifically the cities of Lagos and New York – are the settings for both major works of fiction and many of Cole's Twitter stories. Although his parents moved to Lagos just after he was born, Cole returned to Michigan for college in 1992 at the age of 17. Intellectually curious but in his words academically "indifferent" (DeRitter 2012), after graduating with a BA in 1996 Cole enrolled for a medical degree at the University of Michigan, dropping out to complete a master's in African Art at SOAS, University of London followed by an as-yet unfinished PhD in Art History at Columbia. He is currently Gore Vidal Professor of the Practice of Creative Writing at Harvard University but – as an early author's bio states – he "has worked as a cartoonist, dishwasher, lecturer, gardener and hematology researcher" (Cassava Republic 2007).

Publishing academically under his birth name, the author took Teju Cole as a pseudonym in 2011, the year he published *Open City*. Teju – which means "calm on the surface" in Yoruba – is an apt word to describe the protagonists Cole portrays in his fiction. Julius – the famously composed narrator of

Open City – is a Nigerian German psychiatry resident living and working in New York City. In *Every Day is for the Thief*, an unnamed protagonist who – like Cole – is Nigerian American and – like Julius – is a psychiatric resident, returns to Lagos after a fifteen-year absence. Both narrators calmly and closely resemble Cole in shape if not in substance: they are similar in the fact of their ages at the time of writing (early-to-mid thirties), their dual citizenship, Nigerian family, and deep knowledge of European art and literature, particularly the German writer and academic W.G. Sebald and Flemish painters like Bruegel, Rubens, and van Eyck.

Both texts are also eventless or – as I have argued – "quiet" fictions (Sykes 2017, 2018): books that trace the introverted protagonist's thoughts through a variety of encounters and intellectual engagements without necessarily relying on an external event or plot as the traditional engine of narrative. Indeed, praise for Cole often centers on the diminished volume or pace of his prose. James Wood celebrates the "room for reflection, autobiography, stasis, and repetition" (2011) that *Open City* provides the modern reader, while Colm Tóibín describes the "soft, exquisite rhythms" (2011) of *Open City*. Cole also admits to slowing or reducing the volume of his writing in order to give ideas and characters the space to expand in the reader's imagination: "I'm always trying to lower the volume [. . .]. Very often, I'm trying to write and not say more than can justly be said. I want to reduce the number of sparks. I want to embed hesitation and lack of certainty in it" (Tippett 2019). His fiction might be characterized as "quiet" because it tells stories through the perspectives of isolated narrators who encounter a myriad of different people but ultimately prefer the hushed environment of galleries, museums, and libraries where they can engage in contemplation. It is also "quiet" because of an aesthetic decision by Cole, to open up the space for contemplation within the plot of a novella or novel and – as Cynthia Cruz suggests in her work on "disquiet" – to "step away in order to take what I have witnessed and place it in my mind" (Cruz 2019, p. 16). Contrary, then, to common perceptions of quietness as a form of withdrawal or disengagement, the lowered tenor of Cole's style is a way of slowing down the contemporary world; or at least, of slowing the speed at which the reader is expected to comprehend it.

Like fellow Nigerian author Chimamanda Ngozi Adichie, Cole's work also tackles the multiple forms of estrangement that constitute traveling while Black and of being both African and American. As Cole told *Interview* magazine in 2014:

> When I came back [to Michigan] for college, I knew nothing about American life. [. . .] I knew nothing about what it means to be black in America. [. . .] It takes me about seven years of being in the U.S., or maybe even beyond, before I start to realize that I'm a black American who's subject to both that history, and that system of disadvantages. [. . .] [T]his is something that every black immigrant in this country has to deal with. You slowly realize you have common cause with African-Americans.
>
> (Bollen 2014)

Cole's protagonists show the same awareness. In *Open City*, Julius frequently misreads the relationship between Black Americans and Africans, using the salutation "my brother" (Cole 2011, p. 47) to imply intimacy in casual conversations with other Black men, but resenting when strangers use the same phrase to address him. In *Every Day is for the Thief* – Cole's first book-length work of fiction – the multiple meanings of estrangement whilst travelling are focused on exile, return, and the idea of home. Depicting Lagos through the eyes of an unnamed traveler, returning to the city after half a lifetime in America, Cole uses capsule-like chapters and a journalistic, appraising eye to depict the experience of estrangement from a native cityscape. With due attention to the corruption suffusing Lagos, its many, conflicting bureaucracies and colonial infrastructures, each chapter recounts the power dynamics of different locations: the American embassy handling bribes for visa applications, the scams running out of Internet cafes, and the pickpockets targeting tourists at the market, moving back and forth between the protagonist's feeling of being "at home" after years away and the "possibility and danger" (Cole 2014) he experiences as an American.

In a representative chapter, the narrator reflects on how he is out of step with the noise of the market, unable to protect himself or to signal his Nigerian citizenship. One trader calls him "an *oyinbo*" (Cole 2014) – a Yoruba word for white person – because he seems so out of place. "I am daydreaming at the market," he reflects, "making myself a target." For Yvonne Kapel, *Every Day is for the Thief* intertextually evokes the postcolonial travelogue, highlighting the ambivalence of categories that build on binary oppositions of colonial/postcolonial, resident/tourist, immigrant/native, or Westerner/African. If the postcolonial travelogue most often attempts to define a home city or state independent of Western concepts, "Teju Cole's protagonist [...] depicts his journey to his home country Nigeria by applying Western cultural concepts to an African environment" (Kapel 2017, p. 68), foregrounding the "transcultural entanglement" of his national and cultural identities.

The publication of *Every Day is for the Thief* extends Kapel's idea of the text's "entanglement" even further. Originally published in Nigeria in 2007, the novella was reprinted in the United States in 2014 to capitalize on the success of *Open City* in 2011. The protagonist is therefore often read as an extension of – rather than a prototype for – Julius: their many shared traits include a stint in military school, estrangement from their European mothers, the death of their fathers in his teens, work as a psychiatrist in New York, and the essential focus of both texts on the long walks, bus, and plane journeys that the solitary central character devotes himself to. Yet despite their similarities, there are crucial differences. *Open City* is a longer and more complex work of fiction than its predecessor; it is also set in New York. Julius refers to Lagos in purposefully vague terms, telling a stranger that his "last visit happened two years ago [. . .] after a gap of fifteen years" and little more (Cole 2011, p. 153). Although both narrators share with Cole a fifteen-year period away from Lagos, Julius crucially distances himself not only from his past but from his present surroundings. Having none of the earnest will to belong that characterizes the narrator of *Every Day is for the Thief*, Julius is a much more sinister invocation of the quiet intellectual man than either Cole or his previous protagonist, demonstrating a "bland" form of cosmopolitanism (Krishnan 2015, p. 677) that takes in the people and art forms of other cultures but fails to engage them in any depth.

Open City is Cole's first and so far only novel. It centers on Julius – a Nigerian German psychiatrist – as he walks around New York City and, briefly, Brussels to break the monotony of a hospital residency. The action of the novel is largely internal. During long walks around the city, Julius reflects on the historic landmarks he passes, the books he's currently reading, as well as his childhood in Nigeria and a recent failed relationship. Amongst these recollections of abandoned or difficult connections, he meets a variety of strangers – many of them immigrants – who narrate their personal histories to the often-silent doctor. Unlike *Every Day is for the Thief*, *Open City* gives each stranger a full name and backstory: they include Saidu, a Liberian detainee imprisoned in a facility in Queens, who Julius visits with his ex-girlfriend; Farouq, a Moroccan émigré and former graduate student whose expulsion from a Belgian university leaves him manning an Internet café; and Dr. Mailotte, an older white woman and Belgian surgeon, who Julius meets on a flight to Brussels. Julius listens to their stories without telling his own. Similarly, despite long periods spent reading, he rarely challenges or expands on the ideas he encounters. Walking around Manhattan, he can calmly note that "the people of the city had forgotten it was a burial ground," providing requisite facts – "Trading in slaves had become a capital offense in the United States by 1820" – but barely registering an emotion: not sadness, anger, anxiety, frustration (Cole 2011, p. 175). Indeed, Julius is best characterized as a passive receiver of information and also of affect, rarely moved to extremes despite the harrowing narratives he receives from others and – perhaps most significantly – unable to turn his intellect inward to acknowledge or analyze his own disengagement. Particularly when compared to his patient, V – a Native American and historian who struggles to process the psychological impact of studying American genocide – Julius is a blank and passive observer of the colonial and postcolonial world; educated, cultured, informed, but never moved.

The full extent of Julius' disengagement – lightly glimpsed and layered throughout the novel – is ultimately revealed in his attitude to women. Fraught relationships with his mother and ex-girlfriend as well as a stated but half-hearted desire to find his long idealized Oma "somewhere in Europe" (Cole 2011, p. 9) foreshadow an accusation of rape that is revealed in the novel's final pages. The exchange between Julius and Moji – the sister of a school friend – signifies a major shift in the narrator's conception of himself and yet it is foreshadowed by an earlier instance when Julius shuts his apartment window to block out the "martial tone" of a Take Back the Night demonstration, complaining that women's "words did not resolve into meaning" (p. 27). This phrasing proves to be both literal and symbolic. Julius literally can't understand the words of the protestors on the street, but he also can't relate to the larger "meaning" of a protest aimed at ending relationship, domestic, and sexual violence. Later in the novel, when Moji details how Julius "forced himself" on her during a party in 1989, her voice "strained" and "shattered," she concludes by asking: "will you say something now? Will you say something?" (p. 261). When he is finally invited to speak after 200 pages of near silence, Julius changes the subject, noting in the context of the narrative how other party goers – to his "relief" – begin waking up around them, because it means that Moji will not cry.

Cole, quite obviously, does not side with his protagonist. Although the episode has often been ignored by critics, the author claims that "*Open City* is very much about rape, though I doubt this word 'about'" (Bady 2015), repeatedly pointing to its narrative importance. Until her final conversation with Julius, Moji is a peripheral character: when Julius first meets her in New York, he can't remember how he knows her, although he acknowledges that "she expected me to remember her" (Cole 2011, p. 168). He casually objectifies her – noting the "dark curve" of her breasts or suggesting "she was not beautiful in the way I expected dark women to be" (p. 212) – and when he arrives at her party the narrative initially skips from his arrival to 2 a.m. – when attendees start to go home – and then to sunrise. In this temporal leap, Cole points to Julius' reluctance to engage with Moji by missing the interaction entirely, returning to the conversation only when he tells the story of the party for the second time.

A similar reckoning with narrative perspective connects *Open City* – as Cole's longest work of fiction – with his many microfictions, originally published on Twitter and Instagram. Of these, "Small Fates" (2013) is the most notable for its brief absurdist snapshots of Nigerian life. A combination of fiction and real-life events covered by local news, each tweet is modeled on the early twentieth century French form, the *fait-divers*, which Roland Barthes describes as a "*totale*" or "*immanente*" (complete) piece of information with a deranged and implied causality that relies on local knowledge, gossip, and inference to frame dramatic but otherwise inconceivable events (Barthes 1964). A characteristic example reads as follows:

> In Cross River, the retired soldier Agbiji slapped his wife just once, but he misjudged his strength and is now a widower.
>
> (Cole 2013)

Mixing the profound with the absurd through the intensity of compression, "Small Fates" forces narrative into a "single frame" in ways that feel similar to the "instant perception" of the photography (Mingazova 2018) Cole increasingly prefers over fiction. Writing on Twitter allows Cole a directness that feels very different from his deeply contemplative longer fictions. In an essay responding to the success of a different series of tweets, he notes that his work since *Open City* more often engages with the idea of "direct speech" and public address:

> [I]n the past few years in the U.S., there has been a chilling effect on a certain kind of direct speech pertaining to rights. [...] There is an expectation that we can talk about sins but no one must be identified as a sinner: newspapers love to describe words or deeds as "racially charged" even in those cases when it would be more honest to say "racist"; we agree that there is rampant misogyny, but misogynists are nowhere to be found; homophobia is a problem but no one is homophobic.
>
> (Cole 2012)

What Twitter allows Cole – and although he has since gone on a social media hiatus – is the opportunity to "speak plainly" in a playful but intensely literary and satirical way. Parallels therefore abound between Cole's book-length work and the brevity of experiments like "Small Fates" or "Seven Short Stories About Drones" (2013), which reimagines some of European and American literature's most famous first lines as if writers of the Western canon were under bombardment. Drawing together recurring themes of estrangement, displacement, (post)colonialism, and the often bewildering luxury of travel and tourism, Cole's fiction makes for an incredibly varied and surprising body of work.

SEE ALSO: Adichie, Chimamanda Ngozi; Fiction and Terrorism; Globalization; Literature of the Americas; Millennial Fiction; Multiculturalism; Post-9/11 Narratives

REFERENCES

Bady, Aaron. (2015). Interview: Teju Cole. *Post-45* (January 19, 2015). https://post45.org/2015/01/interview-teju-cole/ (accessed August 9, 2021).

Barthes, Roland. (1964). *Structure du fait-divers*. Paris: Meditations.

Bollen, Christopher. (2014). Teju Cole. *Interview Magazine* (March 21, 2014). https://www.interviewmagazine.com/culture/teju-cole (accessed August 9, 2021).

Cassava Republic. (2007). About the author. *Cassava Press*. https://cassavarepublic.biz/product/every-day-is-for-the-thief/ (accessed August 9, 2021).

Cole, Teju. (2011). *Open City*. London: Faber.

Cole, Teju. (2012). The white-savior industrial complex. *The Atlantic* (March 21, 2012). https://www.theatlantic.com/international/archive/2012/03/the-white-saviorindustrial-complex/254843/ (accessed September 22, 2021).

Cole, Teju. (2013). "I don't normally do this kind of thing": 45 small fates. *The New Inquiry* (August 13, 2013). https://thenewinquiry.com/

blog/i-dont-normally-do-this-kind-of-thing-45-small-fates/ (accessed September 22, 2021).

Cole, Teju. (2014). *Every Day is for the Thief*. Kobo ebook ed.; 1st ed. 2007.

Cruz, Cynthia. (2019). *Disquieting: Essays on Silence*. Toronto: Book*hug Press.

DeRitter, Margaret. (2012). From *New Yorker* envy to literary acclaim. *BeLight: The eZine of Kalamazoo College*. http://www.kzoo.edu/beLightArchive/articles/?issueid=33&id=126 (accessed August 9, 2021).

Kapel, Yvonne. (2017). Re-membering the travelogue: generic intertextuality as a memory practice in Teju Cole's *Every Day is for the Thief*. *Zeitschrift für Anglistik und Amerikanistik* 65 (1): 67–83.

Krishnan, Madhu. (2015). Postcoloniality, spatiality and cosmopolitanism in the *Open City*. *Textual Practice* 29 (4): 675–696.

Mingazova, Ella. (2018). The double-take of seeing: on Teju Cole's "Small fates." *Image & Narrative* 19 (3). http://www.imageandnarrative.be/index.php/imagenarrative/article/view/1960 (accessed August 9, 2021).

Sykes, Rachel. (2017). Reading for quiet in Marilynne Robinson's Gilead novels. *Critique: Studies in Contemporary Fiction* 58 (2): 108–120.

Sykes, Rachel. (2018). *The Quiet Contemporary American Novel*. Manchester: Manchester University Press.

Tippett, Krista. (2019). Teju Cole: sitting together in the dark. *On Being* (February 28, 2019). https://onbeing.org/programs/teju-cole-sitting-together-in-the-dark-feb2019/ (accessed August 9, 2021).

Tóibín, Colm. (2011). Reviews. http://www.tejucole.com/books/review/ (accessed August 9, 2021).

Wood, James. (2011). The arrival of enigmas. *The New Yorker* (February 20, 2011). https://www.newyorker.com/magazine/2011/02/28/the-arrival-of-enigmas (accessed August 9, 2021).

FURTHER READING

Cole, Teju. (2016). *Known and Strange Things*. London: Faber.

Edwards, Erica R. (2017). The new Black novel and the long war on terror. *American Literary History* 29 (4): 664–681.

Gamso, Nicholas. (2019). Exposure and Black migrancy in Teju Cole. *New Global Studies* 13 (1): 60–79.

Contemporary Fictions of War

DAVID F. EISLER
University of Heidelberg, Germany

It is a sad reality of history that American war fiction during the past forty years has had no shortage of material to work with, from the quagmire in Vietnam to the never-ending Global War on Terrorism. Since 1980, there have been two phases of writing about the Vietnam War: experiential novels that followed a similar pattern to the 1970s works written about the war before turning their attention to its domestic aftermath, and a newer trend of historical fiction that includes novels written since the September 11, 2001, terrorist attacks. This second wave of Vietnam War fiction has bled seamlessly into the wars of Afghanistan and Iraq, whose fictional response has seen a steady influx of complex and important works with a far more diverse set of authors and protagonists than previous eras of American war fiction, including a greater proportion of novels written by women and nonveterans.

THE VIETNAM WAR

Experiential Novels

The Vietnam War continued to live in the American imagination long after the fall of Saigon in 1975. In the years following the American withdrawal and into the 1980s, literary treatments of the war came mostly from male combat veterans, cohering into a group of texts that largely sought to preserve the individual experience of battle for posterity. Philip Beidler, in his early study *American*

Literature and the Experience of Vietnam (1982), spoke of authors trying to "come to literary terms with the experience of Vietnam" (p. 47). The fact that veterans of the war came to dominate its fictional response was perhaps a reaction to the perceived negative image of soldiers in American society at the time. As Maureen Ryan observes in *The Other Side of Grief: The Home Front and the Aftermath in American Narratives of the Vietnam War* (2008), "If there is a single theme that echoes most loudly throughout the Vietnam 'aftermath' texts and combat novels of the past generation, it is the notion that only the soldiers who directly engaged this singular, complex war can ever understand it" (p. 17).

Veterans of the Vietnam War continued to write novels largely derived from their personal experience well into the 1980s. Foremost among these was John Del Vecchio's *The 13th Valley* (1982), an epic exploration of war and human society that followed in the tradition of John Dos Passos's *Three Soldiers* (1921) and Norman Mailer's *The Naked and the Dead* (1948). Del Vecchio, who had been drafted into the army and served in Vietnam as a combat correspondent with the 101st Airborne Division in 1971, puts a premium on the authenticity of details taken from personal experience. The novel follows three main protagonists on a fictitious operation in search of a sizable enemy force that always seems just out of reach. Alternating between a new guy named James "Cherry" Chelini, the more experienced noncommissioned officer Daniel Egan, and the African American company commander Rufus Brooks, Del Vecchio seeks the broadest possible representation of a combat infantry unit deployed to Vietnam. He infuses the narrative with actual history of the events, even explaining in the author's note details such as the time line, order of battle, and casualty statistics. Topographic maps and "significant activity" summaries teeming with military jargon and acronyms add another layer of intended authenticity to the text.

Where *The 13th Valley* falters is in its desire to function as a political novel, a corrective to the fiction up to that point that, in Del Vecchio's estimation, had failed to tell the real story of the American soldier's bravery and tenacity caught between an elusive enemy on the battlefield and an antagonistic population at home. In describing Chelini's situation, for example, Del Vecchio draws a straight line between the honor of military service and the sacrifice of the World War II generation of veterans:

> Chelini had allowed himself to be drafted and he had allowed himself to be sent to Vietnam. He had the means to resist but not the conviction or the will. Indeed, inside, he heard opposing voices. His father was a veteran of World War II. All the Chelini men –and the Chelinis were a large Italian-American family – had served in the armed forces. James observed that having served somehow set them apart from those who had not gone. On the other side were the people of his own generation, the protestors and the students, who included his older brother Victor.
>
> (1982, p. 2)

Cherry's initiation and eventual transformation from innocent draftee to combat-hardened soldier is one of the novel's primary narratives, but the oversimplified moral message of the nobility of service never receives the scrutiny that it deserves.

Where *The 13th Valley* sought to capture at least the author's idea of the authentic Vietnam War experience, another veteran, Larry Heinemann, followed his 1974 autobiographical debut *Close Quarters* with the National Book Award-winning *Paco's Story* (1986), a novel about the lone and improbable survivor of a Viet Cong attack whose journey back to American society is narrated by the collective ghostly voice of his dead comrades. We never learn much about Paco, and the narrative strategy of using the ghosts to tell the story, who themselves often cede the narration to others within the novel, is a powerful statement about the nature of storytelling despite leaving the reader with no clear resolution. The point, perhaps, is the need to tell the story, no matter how horrific, for its own sake – for the memory of those who lived and died. Yet the picture Heinemann paints of the America to which Paco returns is grim and unwelcoming. Paco's interactions with various people reveal much about the state of America at the time, a much more bitter picture than Heinemann gave us in *Close Quarters*.

While the America of *Paco's Story* makes its title character feel alone and cast off by society, Bobbie Ann Mason's *In Country* (1985) uses the eyes of a girl whose father was killed in Vietnam before she was born to depict the nation struggling to move on into the next decade. Mason, who had no connection to the war or the military, was initially hesitant to tackle the subject, but a moving experience at the Vietnam Veterans' Memorial led her to believe that the war did not just belong to those who had fought there, but that it was "every American's story." The novel was widely praised, though some reviewers couldn't help but notice that the author was not the typical writer of war fiction – the first line of the *Kirkus* review said, "How ironic – or maybe not – that one of the so-far best, most affecting Vietnam novels ever should come from a woman" (*Kirkus* 1985).

Although male veterans received most of the attention, they were not the only veteran–authors to publish novels about the war. Elizabeth Scarborough's *The Healer's War* (1988) blended the techniques of the combat initiation novel written so often by male veterans in the 1970s with elements of the fantasy genre to create a complicated portrait of life as an army nurse in Vietnam. Although *The Healer's War* won the 1989 Nebula Award for best novel, its critical afterlife has been limited. Like the novels of her male counterparts, Scarborough's novel feels culled from the depths of personal experience – its protagonist, Lieutenant Kitty McCulley, is also an army nurse in Vietnam – but her mixture of a more traditional war novel with the science fiction/fantasy genre endows the story with a greater symbolic depth.

The first two thirds of the novel read like a straightforward "combat zone" narrative from the perspective of an army nurse, with hints that there is something magical happening as well. It takes a helicopter crash that kills Kitty's in-country love interest and leaves her to fend for herself in the jungle with a one-legged Vietnamese boy as her companion for the fantasy to become more prominent. This "fantasy" element (namely that Kitty, wearing a special amulet given to her by a local elder shortly before his death, can see people's auras and heal their wounds magically) plays only a minimal role in the story until she reaches a Vietnamese village under attack by a large snake. She is then taken prisoner by the Viet Cong. The snake had killed a woman who turns out to have been the wife of a Viet Cong colonel who then doesn't kill Kitty immediately only because his daughter, whose life Kitty had saved from the snake, pleads for her life. Scarborough uses these interactions to highlight the moral ambiguity of the conflict – she creates sympathy for the Vietnamese people by showing the many ways in which they have suffered at the hands of the Americans as well as their own people. At the same time, she depicts a graphic scene where the Viet Cong murder the elderly, women, and children in a village that had (presumably) helped the Americans or the South Vietnamese military. The scene is brutal and underscores the difficult situation that the local people faced, torn between two warring sides and punished for choosing the wrong one at the wrong time. Scarborough's sympathetic but complex portrayal of the Vietnamese people differentiates her novel from so many of the other experiential novels written by American veterans.

Two other veterans of the war have become perhaps the best known of their generation, Tim O'Brien and Robert Olen Butler. O'Brien solidified his reputation as the most important chronicler of the Vietnam experience in follow-ups to his National Book Award-winning *Going After Cacciato* (1978). *The Things They Carried* (1990) is an indispensable collection of linked short stories that has influenced contemporary writers of war fiction ever since. Blurring the lines between the real and the imaginary, O'Brien's collection was so successful that many readers and critics since have mistaken it for memoir or thinly veiled autobiographical fiction, something O'Brien has repeatedly rejected.

One reason for the staying power of *The Things They Carried* is its interrogation of the nature of truth as well as O'Brien's concern with the mechanism and purpose of telling war stories. Not only does he create a "second-self," a stand-in version of himself as the author to question the very nature of storytelling, many of the stories throughout the book are told second-hand – the author Tim O'Brien has his narrator ("Tim O'Brien") relay a story from another character, who himself may have heard the story from someone else. O'Brien's rhetorical strategy constantly stresses the act of storytelling, or imagining it, without actually telling the story.

Although O'Brien has been the most celebrated writer of the Vietnam War, perhaps no other author of Vietnam War fiction has had the longevity of Robert Olen Butler. Butler, a former military intelligence translator whose earlier works *Alleys of Eden* (1981) and *On Distant Ground* (1985) sought a more sympathetic portrait of the Vietnamese people than many of his veteran counterparts, took his empathetic approach to the extreme in his Pulitzer Prize-winning collection of stories, *A Good Scent from a Strange Mountain* (1992). Written entirely from the perspective of Vietnamese refugees living in Louisiana after the war, Butler's collection marked a radical departure from most Vietnam War novels by inhabiting the voice of a people largely cut from the story of their own country. Author of more than a dozen novels and short story collections, Butler continues to wrestle with the Vietnam War in his fiction, including the 2016 novel *Perfume River* which examines the lingering effects of the war on two brothers – one who served and one who fled to Canada – fifty years later.

The Vietnam War as Historical Fiction

After 2002 and the beginning of the wars in Afghanistan and Iraq, the Vietnam War returned as a popular topic of historical fiction. Where the experiential novels about the Vietnam War focused overwhelmingly on the male American combat veteran's individual experience, recent fiction about the war has sought a more pluralized representation of those involved and affected. Denis Johnson's National Book Award-winning *Tree of Smoke* (2007), for example, is a sprawling depiction of the war from multiple angles. Characters include the crusty American officers and innocent soldiers seen in early Vietnam War fiction, but also several well-developed Vietnamese (including a South Vietnamese army officer, a perspective that, as Viet Thanh Nguyen has pointed out, has been almost completely ignored in fiction about the war), as well as a Canadian civilian woman who works for a nongovernmental organization. Tatjana Soli's multivoiced novel *The Lotus Eaters* (2010) revisits the war from the perspective of a female journalist who spends ten years in country, providing a belated antidote to the hypermasculinized rhetoric in, for example, Michael Herr's *Dispatches*. Soli also writes from the perspective of a Vietnamese man. *The Lotus Eaters* leverages the temporal distance from the events to infuse the story with a historical hindsight unavailable in the immediate aftermath of the war: "The whole city was on guard. Even the children who usually clamored for treats were quiet and stood with their backs against the walls of buildings. Even they seemed to understand the Americans had lost in the worst possible way" (Soli 2010, p. 7).

In addition to his scholarly work on the memory of the Vietnam War, Viet Thanh Nguyen's works of fiction *The Sympathizer* (2015) and *The Refugees* (2016) have emerged as crucial correctives to the previous dominance of American fiction about the Vietnam War that tended to privilege the American experience to the exclusion of all others. *The Sympathizer* takes the form of a confession written by a North Vietnamese spy living inside a community of South Vietnamese army exiles in the United States. The novel defies easy classification, spanning multiple genres with dark humor and a sharp critical eye of the American memory industry and the way it has depicted the war. In one scene reminiscent of Philip Roth's *Portnoy's Complaint* (1969), the unnamed narrator describes a masturbatory adventure from his adolescence with a squid destined for the dinner table. Nguyen then uses the comic episode to make an important moral point about the types of stories we find repulsive:

> Some will undoubtedly find this episode obscene. Not I! Massacre is obscene. Torture is obscene. Three million dead is obscene. Masturbation, even with an admittedly nonconsensual squid? Not so much. I, for one, am a person who believes that the world would be a better place if the word "murder" made us mumble as much as the word "masturbation."
>
> (2015, p. 80)

As the direct experience with the Vietnam War continues to fade into history and its place in American cultural memory becomes revised and reimagined, works like *Tree of Smoke*, *The Lotus Eaters*, and *The Sympathizer* provide a blueprint for readers and writers in search of an understanding of the war that goes beyond battle and combat.

AFGHANISTAN AND IRAQ

The terrorist attacks of September 11, 2001, set into motion a series of events whose repercussions have lasted well into the following two decades. Initial military operations in Afghanistan began in October 2001 and lasted until the fall of 2021; the subsequent invasion of Iraq in March 2003 is now widely regarded as a misbegotten failure. Together, these two conflicts are often snidely referred to as the "Forever Wars," borrowing from the 1974 science fiction novel *The Forever War* by Vietnam veteran Joe Haldeman.

Three major shifts in authorship, content, and form characterize the American fiction of Afghanistan and Iraq compared with Vietnam. First, where the vast majority of early fiction published about the Vietnam War was written by male combat veterans, the novels of Afghanistan and Iraq have been authored by a much larger proportion of nonveterans (more than half) and women (nearly one third). They also tend to include more female soldiers as protagonists, and to focalize through the perspectives of non-American characters.

Nonveterans inaugurated the fictional response to Iraq and Afghanistan. Of the earliest works – Nicholas Kulish's *Last One In* (2007), David Zimmerman's *The Sandbox* (2010), Helen Benedict's *Sand Queen* (2011), Siobhan Fallon's *You Know When the Men Are Gone* (2011), and Benjamin Buchholz's *One Hundred and One Nights* (2011) – only Kulish and Buchholz had personal experience in the war, Kulish as an embedded reporter during the 2003 invasion of Iraq and Buchholz as an officer in the Army National Guard who served a tour in Iraq. Although Buchholz was the first military veteran of the war to publish a novel about it, his novel flew under the radar, failing to resonate with either readers or critics. One reason for this might be that, rather than taking an American soldier as its subject, the novel is narrated from the perspective of an Iraqi doctor whose conflicted loyalties come from having lived in Chicago for fifteen years before returning to Iraq after the fall of Saddam.

The genre had its first banner year in 2012 with the publication of five novels, several of which would become prize winners: Ben Fountain's *Billy Lynn's Long Halftime Walk*, Kristin Hannah's *Home Front*, Joydeep Roy-Bhattacharya's *The Watch*, David Abrams's *Fobbit*, and Kevin Powers's *The Yellow Birds*. Like Buchholz before them, Abrams and Powers were both army veterans, while the others were civilians.

Fobbit and *The Yellow Birds* were both published in September 2012, though *The Yellow Birds* would quickly emerge as the preferred contender for the literary-minded critics. *Fobbit*, a funny, satirical novel that distinguished between "Fobbits" – a pun on Tolkien's "Hobbit" and reference to the safety of a Forward Operating Base (or "FOB") – and "doorkickers" –who actually left the base to patrol the local villages – was well-received by readers but did not resonate as well with literary critics looking for the next *Three Soldiers*, *The Naked and the Dead*, or *The Things They Carried*. Although *Fobbit* was more successful than *One Hundred and One Nights*, Abrams's decision to employ deadpan humor rather than adopt the more serious tone that had come to define the majority of the genre prevented it from a breakthrough. The lukewarm *New York Times* review closes with applause for Abrams for "sticking to his vision and writing the satire he wanted to write instead of adding to the crowded shelf of war memoirs" (Bauman 2012).

Fobbit was also a story set entirely in Iraq whose characters were not defined by traumatic experiences or as "trauma heroes," which Roy Scranton has convincingly argued is "the single most important cultural frame for understanding the experience of war in the United States today" (Scranton 2019, p.3). Although some of the characters do commit and witness acts of violence (including one soldier shooting a would-be suicide attacker in the head after his car bomb failed to detonate as he rammed into the backside of a tank), the novel does not dwell on these experiences.

The Yellow Birds, on the other hand, was exactly the kind of novel that conformed to the genre's expected traditions. Unlike *Fobbit*, which alternated between several focalizers and concentrated on the lives of soldiers who were mostly confined to the base for their tours, *The Yellow Birds* focused on the traumatic experience of its narrator, Private John Bartle, as well as the lingering psychological effects of that experience once Bartle returns home. Structured partly as a mystery – the reader knows that Bartle's fellow soldier Murphy is dead, and that his death occurred under strange circumstances – *The Yellow Birds* has a laser focus on Bartle's emotional stress and inability to cope with whatever it was that happened in Iraq. He is a fitting example of Scranton's trauma hero myth, a myth that "claims to speak to deep psychological truths, makes a kind of intuitive sense, and, perhaps most important, makes the American veteran a sympathetic victim, rather than a perpetrator, of violence" (Scranton 2019, p. 3).

Focus on the Home Front

Somewhere between the end of the US withdrawal in Vietnam and the darkest days of the insurgency in Iraq, American society learned to separate its feelings about war from its opinions of those who fought it. Rather than confronting an angry, antagonist populace, the uniform-wearing Iraq or Afghanistan war veteran confronts apathy cloaked in patriotic appreciation. Consider the sentiments of Billy

Lynn, who "wishes just once that somebody would call him baby-killer" (Fountain 2012, p. 219). Billy is so uncomfortable with how he and his fellow squadmates have been transformed into heroic symbols for the Thanksgiving Day halftime show at the Dallas Cowboys stadium that he actively hopes to be verbally abused for his service with the same terms hurled at his Vietnam-era predecessors.

Neither *Billy Lynn* nor *The Yellow Birds* dwells on the longer-term psychological effects of war, but many other novels do. While novels about Vietnam tended to focus on the in-country transformation of the individual from innocent civilian to combat-hardened veteran (with homecoming as an afterthought), contemporary fictions of Iraq and Afghanistan have generally found the process of reintegration into society a more compelling narrative than Vietnam's novels of initiation. From *Billy Lynn* to the title story of Phil Klay's National Book Award-winning collection *Redeployment* (2014) and dozens of others, the ways veterans come home from war has been one of the dominant images of contemporary American war fiction.

The equal narrative weight afforded to the home front in contemporary war fiction comes about in several ways. Some novels take place almost entirely in the United States, with small flashes of action in the combat zone to bolster the characters' experience and the readers' understanding. This is the approach of works such as Ben Fountain's *Billy Lynn*, Siobhan Fallon's *You Know When the Men Are Gone*, Kristin Hannah's *Home Front* (2012), Roxana Robinson's *Sparta* (2013), Cara Hoffman's *Be Safe I Love You* (2014), Eric Bennett's *A Big Enough Lie* (2015), Stephen Markley's *Ohio* (2018), Jesse Goolsby's *I'd Walk With My Friends if I Could Find Them* (2015), Odie Lindsey's *We Come to Our Senses* (2016), and others. Other novels, including *The Yellow Birds* and Michael Pitre's *Fives and Twenty-Fives* (2014), split their structure more or less evenly between the home front and the combat zone, bouncing back and forth between them in a manner that mirrors the contemporary soldier's experience with multiple deployments.

Many characters struggle upon coming home from war, turning to alcohol and drugs to numb themselves while often wishing they could return. These same characters find themselves irrevocably changed by their wartime experience. "Iraq aged you in dog years," Billy Lynn observes (Fountain 2012, p. 86). Conrad Farrell, the troubled marine officer in Roxana Robinson's *Sparta*, not only continues to correspond with the men he served with via email but he also "check[s] the military blogs" every day, which were "news from his tribe, living filaments connecting him to the life he had known" (Robinson 2013, p. 173). This practice is echoed in Phil Klay's story "Unless It's a Sucking Chest Wound," where the main character frequently searches the Internet for updated lists of soldiers killed in action.

Lauren Clay, the protagonist of Cara Hoffman's *Be Safe I Love You*, is perhaps the prototypical example of a soldier suffering from what have been called the "invisible wounds of war." She exhibits "no red flags" on her post-deployment health assessment, and, according to an army psychologist's initial evaluation, she was "a model soldier" and "had not been concussed or injured or suffered an amputation. She had not been sexually assaulted or gotten pregnant on her tour, and she had no medically unexplained symptoms" (Hoffman 2014, p. 41). Hoffman makes it clear that physically, nothing is wrong with Clay, before diving into the depths of her psychological damage.

The shift in narrative focus from the combat zone to the home front has had the additional effect of broadening the cast of characters typically associated with war fiction. Rather than novel after novel of ground-pounding grunts and disillusioned foot soldiers, there are family members, best friends, interpreters, even government civilians whose service also took them to the wars, such as in Masha Hamilton's

What Changes Everything (2013), some of the stories in Luke Mogelson's *These Heroic, Happy Dead* (2016), and Kathleen McInnis's satirical *The Heart of War: Misadventures in the Pentagon* (2018).

Some contemporary novels seek to engage with the home front in more subtle ways, highlighting the military's lack of a monopoly on traumatic experiences and embedding the wars within the greater social landscape of American society and its problems, especially drug addiction and alcohol abuse. Stephen Markley's *Ohio* tells the story of a small town in the American heartland hit hard by both the wars and an influx of drugs. Jesse Goolsby's *I'd Walk With My Friends If I Could Find Them* frames the war experiences of three soldiers as an important but not overpowering part of their lives. And Nico Walker's *Cherry* (2018) ties the narrator's war experience to his struggles with heroin addiction. All three novels reframe the veteran's war experience as only one small piece of the broader social context. One of the effects of this technique is the contextualization of military experience; placing the war veteran's trauma on a continuum with the rest of society is an equalizer, a way to find common ground. This might represent a possible bridge between the contemporary war veteran and the unaffected citizen; acknowledging that everyone is capable of suffering also provides a level playing field to communicate those experiences.

Combat Zone and Realism

The broad emphasis on the home front and reintegration into society found in so many of the novels about Iraq and Afghanistan does not mean that the contemporary response has ignored the combat zone altogether. Novels such as Helen Benedict's *Sand Queen*, David Abrams's *Fobbit* (2012) and *Brave Deeds* (2017), Elliot Ackerman's *Green on Blue* (2015), Ross Ritchell's *The Knife* (2015), Matt Gallagher's *Youngblood* (2016), Whitney Terrell's *The Good Lieutenant* (2016), and Brian Van Reet's *Spoils* (2017) all set the majority of their narrative action in either Iraq or Afghanistan and employ the standard literary techniques of mimetic realism to capture the ground-level experience of war and combat. But that combat experience has changed dramatically over the years; Iraq in 2003, during and immediately following the invasion, differed greatly from Iraq in 2005 through 2007, when the violence was characterized by the insurgency rather than pitched battles between uniformed militaries. Novels seeking to capture the frenetic and intense experience of combat, then, tend to set their action in the early days of the Iraq War. In other cases, combat scenes are quick and brutal, often coming without anticipation or warning just like the improvised explosive devices, or IEDs, that became the weapon of choice in both conflicts, creating a sense of danger that simmered under every road or path.

Setting novels about Afghanistan or Iraq in the earlier days of the war also enhances the narrative with a dramatic irony that comes from the tension between the official rationale for war and the debacles they have become. Whitney Terrell's *The Good Lieutenant*, about a female army officer who struggles to navigate the complexities of the Iraq War, employs an ingenious structural device that emphasizes this point more strongly – the story is told in reverse chronological order. Because of this, the reader knows that things will not turn out well for many of the characters, that any happy moments or thoughts of a positive future we see later in the novel are not meant to be. The novel's structure suggests a more general commentary about the Iraq War, namely that we know it will be a disaster and any depiction of it's opening days is already laced with the poisonous dramatic irony of historical hindsight.

Women Protagonists and Non-American Points of View

In *The Remasculinization of America: Gender and the Vietnam War* (1989), Susan Jeffords argued that "the defining feature of American war narratives is that they are a 'man's story' from which women are generally excluded" (p. 49). While that was largely true for the fiction of the Vietnam War, the broader participation of women in direct military operations since 2001 has rendered male-centric narratives a thing of the past. A growing number of contemporary novels have focused on the experience of women in these wars, often emphasizing the additional challenges they face serving in what, as Jeffords indicated, had been almost exclusively a man's domain.

In Helen Benedict's *Sand Queen*, protagonist Kate Brady is routinely harassed by the male soldiers in her unit; her squad mates call her "Tits" or "Pinkass" rather than by her last name, and her team leader and another soldier nearly assault her sexually (and would have had another soldier not intervened). Kate's narrative arc eventually brings her to a fragile mental state with what seems like little hope of improvement. Benedict's novel, while a powerful and necessary exposition of how women have been treated in the US military, often veers too far in the direction of polemic, lacking the nuance of other works, such as *Be Safe I Love You*, *The Good Lieutenant*, and Brian Van Reet's *Spoils* (2017), that explore similar themes.

Another way in which the fictional response to the wars in Iraq and Afghanistan has departed from the earliest novels about Vietnam is its engagement with the perspectives of non-American characters. A common structural technique is the inclusion of a non-American point of view character, from an interpreter with conflicting loyalties in Michael Pitre's *Fives and Twenty-Fives*, to an Iraqi mathematics professor in Roy Scranton's *War Porn* (2016), an aging Egyptian mujahid in Brian Van Reet's *Spoils*, and others. Benjamin Buchholz's *One Hundred and One Nights* and Elliot Ackerman's *Green on Blue* take this a step further, telling their stories entirely from the perspective of an Iraqi and an Afghan, respectively.

CONCLUSION

Despite the wide range of fictional works about war over the past four decades, a consistently negative image of military service emerges. A disproportionate number of soldiers and veterans in these novels struggle from post-traumatic stress, abuse drugs and alcohol, hurt their families or themselves, or detach themselves from the rest of society altogether. The relentless focus on trauma and recovery as the defining narrative of these wars has crowded out the more kaleidoscopic experiences of others; readers of contemporary war fiction will need to look hard for a positive image of military service.

With temporal distance comes historical understanding, but in the age of the Forever War it remains to be seen if American war fiction will ever break free of the vicious cycle of trauma and recovery to find other ways of writing about war and conflict with the hope that literary art will find a clarity of expression that the nightly news has already written off.

SEE ALSO: Fiction and Terrorism; Johnson, Denis; Mason, Bobbie Ann; Multiculturalism; Nguyen, Viet Thanh; O'Brien, Tim; Post-9/11 Narratives; Trauma and Fiction

REFERENCES

Bauman, Christian. (2012). Odd men out. https://www.nytimes.com/2012/09/30/books/review/fobbit-by-david-abrams.html (accessed July 19, 2021).

Beidler, Philip D. (1982). *American Literature and the Experience of Vietnam*. Athens: University of Georgia Press.

Del Vecchio, John M. (1982). *The 13th Valley*. New York: Bantam Books.

Fountain, Ben. (2012). *Billy Lynn's Long Halftime Walk*. New York: Ecco Press.

Haldeman, Joe. (1974). *The Forever War*. New York: Thomas Dunne Books.

Hoffman, Cara. (2014). *Be Safe I Love You*. New York: Simon & Schuster.

Jeffords, Susan. (1989). *The Remasculinization of America: Gender and the Vietnam War.* Bloomington: Indiana University Press.

Kirkus. (1985). *In Country* by Bobbie Ann Mason. *Kirkus* (August 15, 1985). https://www.kirkusreviews.com/book-reviews/a/bobbie-ann-mason-2/in-country/ (accessed August 22, 2021).

Nguyen, Viet Thanh. (2016). *The Sympathizer.* New York: Grove Press.

Robinson, Roxana. (2013). *Sparta.* New York: Picador.

Ryan, Maureen. (2008). *The Other Side of Grief: The Home Front and the Aftermath in American Narratives of the Vietnam War.* Amherst: University of Massachusetts Press.

Scranton, Roy. (2019). *Total Mobilization: World War II and American Literature.* Chicago: University of Chicago Press.

Soli, Tatjana. (2010). *The Lotus Eaters.* New York: St. Martin's Press.

FURTHER READING

Buchanan, David. (2016). *Going Scapegoat: Post-9/11 War Literature, Language, and Culture.* Jefferson, NC: McFarland.

Nguyen, Viet Thanh. (2016). *Nothing Ever Dies: Vietnam and the Memory of War.* Cambridge, MA: Harvard University Press.

Wood, David. (2016). *What Have We Done: The Moral Injury of Our Longest Wars.* New York: Little, Brown.

Contemporary Regionalisms

ELIZABETH LLOYD OLIPHANT
Northland Pioneer College, USA

"Contemporary regionalisms" asks us to reassess the idea of literary regionalism, considering its relevance and meaning at the turn of the twentieth century. Regionalism is a term we usually associate with a nineteenth-century literary style – also known as local color fiction – which depicted rural communities as old-fashioned and culturally isolated (Kaplan 1991, p. 252). Stephanie Foote argues that nineteenth-century regionalism was born from "an awareness of the globalizing and standardizing tendencies of urbanization and industrialization" in the late nineteenth century (2001, p. 3). What, then, is regionalism's relevance in the contemporary era in which we've seen those "standardizing tendencies" borne out? If regionalism was in part a reaction to the industrial era, how has regionalism since manifested, as our world has not only remained industrial, but also has grown increasingly transnational and globalized?

This entry shows that regionalism remained relevant through the late twentieth and early twenty-first centuries as both a literary form and a touchstone for associated literary theory. Since the nineteenth century, literature about the United States has frequently taken up the lens of regionalism, which focuses on the histories (human and otherwise), traditions, and landscapes that make a place distinct. From this perspective, the United States is an overlapping assemblage of regions, and regional literature explores the qualities of place. Regional identities have been and remain meaningful in shaping the literature produced in and about those places.

REGIONALISM IN CRITICAL DISCOURSE, 1980–2020

This entry will survey some of the significant critical responses related to regionalism from 1980 to 2020. It will then discuss some contemporary literary works that use region as a jumping-off point to explore the experiences and identities associated with place. Finally, it will argue for the usefulness of regionalism as both an organizing principle and as a generic form in 2020 and beyond. As this entry shows, regional thinking, while not regionalism in the strict canonized definition, remains a relevant and necessary framework for understanding US literature and culture.

Recovery and Legacies of Nineteenth-Century Regionalism

The genre of American regionalism was born in the nineteenth century and remained popular in the early twentieth century. However, its commercial success, coupled with the fact that regionalist writers were often women, meant that literary scholarship did not give regionalism serious attention for most of the twentieth century. This changed in the 1980s and 1990s, thanks to the work of scholars including Annette Kolodny, Amy Kaplan, Alice Walker, and Jane Tompkins, who gave academic attention to regionalist writers of the nineteenth and early twentieth centuries, such as Kate Chopin, Sui Sin Far, Zora Neale Hurston, and Zitkála-Šá. Foote argues that this recovery of regionalist writers also facilitated a focus on "all subjects whose view seemed too narrow, whose place too definite, whose concerns too local, to really count in a public sphere that valued a putatively more detached way of seeing and narrating the nation" (2012, p. 294). There is irony in the fact that literary studies, a field which emphasizes close reading as a primary methodology, historically backed away from the serious study of literature that closely considered local identities and experiences. These feminist recovery projects rejected the misogynistic bias of American literary studies that treated regionalism as a lesser form of writing, dismissing it because of its emphasis on the quaint, domestic, or local, and "challenged the dominant narrative of how literature helped to maintain national unity and coherence" (p. 293).

Foote and Brodhead argue that regionalism was used to understand national identity after the great national trauma of the Civil War, by appealing to readers' touristic interest in quaint locales and those readers' desire to recover the shared heritage of Americans after a national rift (Brodhead 1993, p. 121). Nineteenth-century regionalism often depicted its rural, local subjects as old-fashioned and near vanishing. In such works, rural cultures were rendered more legible to an educated, urbane reader. The subtext was this: as the world became more industrial and cities grew, the quaintness of these regional subjects would be lost (Foote 2001, p. 3). This blend of cynicism and romance brings to mind the "terminal narratives" of disappearance that Nick Estes describes as "an obsession with the death, disappearance, and absence of Indigenous people" in a landscape (Estes 2020). Estes argues that terminal narratives are very much alive and are used to justify Indigenous genocide; likewise, the nostalgia of regionalism was, and still is, frequently leveraged to preserve and defend whiteness.

The romanticized regional subject is not just a nineteenth-century phenomenon; it shapes representations of region in the present. Consider, for example, the wave of essays and books that paid close attention to the plight of the white, working-poor American in the wake of the 2016 presidential election, often with a focus on Appalachia as especially representative of America's rural working poor. Works such as J.D. Vance's *Hillbilly Elegy* (2016) drew the sometimes overt conclusion that liberalism and the 1990s culture wars that bubbled up amid the diversification of the academy rendered Appalachian white working-class culture a community in crisis. Vance's framing attempts to explain Donald Trump's appeal to this community, as his presidential campaigns drummed up nostalgia for a return to the nation's white supremacist past. The popularity of works like *Hillbilly Elegy*, then, brings to mind commercially popular nineteenth-century regionalism, with its focus on rural communities that may be altered or lost in the name of progress (Kaplan and Pease 1999, p. 252). The regionalist lens that treats Appalachian white working-class culture as "left behind" is at best an empathetic look at the violence of late capitalism in a specific region, but at worst is a refusal to acknowledge the sinister motives that organize whiteness.

The Transnational Turn in American Studies

The concept of region remained important to scholarly discourse in the 2000s. Critics in American studies and American literary studies explored the ways that diaspora, migration, and globalization shape and are expressed in US culture. In 2004 Shelley Fisher-Fishkin acknowledged a transnational turn in American studies that engaged the impacts of globalization, diaspora, and migration on literature and culture in the United States (Fisher-Fishkin 2005). Fisher-Fishkin described a framework conceptualized by scholars including Gloria Anzaldúa (1987), Paul Gilroy (1993), and Amy Kaplan and Donald Pease (1993). Literary studies widely embraced this framework, with scholars drawing the overwhelming conclusion that US literature from every era reflects the fact that America is an empire made up of transnational, international, and diasporic communities within arbitrary and shifting political borders.

America's transnational contexts shape the lived experiences of people in the United States and abroad. This includes anyone whose circumstances are shaped by the United States' history of conquest, genocide, enslavement, imperialism, and interventionist policies, as well as the refugee crises created by such policies. Academia is also implicated in the United States' empire building. Transnational American studies prompted some recognition within the academy that the formation of academic institutions in the United States was facilitated through a global economy of enslavement, human trafficking, extractive colonialism, and settler colonialism (Wilder 2013).

Critical Regionalism

The transnational turn in American studies opened up the scope of American literary studies in generative ways. However, some critics argued that this breadth might be a hazard. José Limón cautioned that the transnational turn threatened to erase the significance of the local, homogenizing vastly different diasporic and migratory experiences into a monolithic story under the umbrella of "transnational." Borrowing the term "critical regionalism" from architectural studies, critics including Limón and Krista Comer have adopted critical regionalism as a way to refine the transnational framework. Critical regionalism examines the tensions between the local, national, and global, acknowledging that cultures are "in constant but critical interaction with the global" (Limón 2008, p. 168). As a test case, Comer (2011) argues that critical regionalism offers a theoretical framework useful in analyzing literature of the American West, because it combines "historical materialism" and identity politics to better understand the multiple meanings and historical contexts attached to a place (Limón 2008, p. 162).

Critical regionalism emphasizes the multiple contexts that constitute one's experience of place. For that reason, it shares a perspective with spatial studies, which asserts that "communities of place are anchored by the same experienced location, they are not uniform," but instead are influenced by "systems of power" that shape lived experience of place (Cameron and Fitzpatrick 2021, p. 87). Doreen Massey argued in 1994 that "the social relations of space are experienced differently, and variously interpreted, by those holding different positions as part of it" (Massey 1994, p. 3). Spatial studies is in conversation with the fields of cultural geography, science fiction studies, and technology studies. Massey's framework, which emphasizes the importance of individual experience of place, is important for understanding why regionalism remains a relevant framework for writing in a globalized world.

Regionalism and Indigeneity

Like the term "transnational," the term "regionalism" may also facilitate inadvertent critical erasure. Scholars of Native American studies and Native American literature have cautioned against using the term "regionalism" to describe works by Native American authors, as it reduces Native writing to colonial frameworks. Eric Gary Anderson cautions that if regional identity is determined according to colonial culture in an occupied space, there is a danger in expecting regional Native writing to match those essentialized ideas. Writing specifically about the possibilities and pitfalls of Southern studies' incorporation of Native American literature, Anderson writes, "the most interesting Native takes on the South are the *least* recognizable as Southern [. . .] these texts do not easily or willingly lend themselves to the additive, inclusionary projects such as the expansion of either Southern or Native studies by way of each other" (Anderson 2006, p. 16).

Anderson builds on Philip Deloria's argument that American studies' enthusiastic embrace of Native American studies works against the sovereignty-securing work of Native scholarship. Deloria argues that "the instant that we assume a cross-border dialogue [between American studies and American Indian studies] to be transformative of American Indian studies and to offer it an intellectual 'home,' we run the risk of becoming caught in the prisonhouse of assimilatory language" (Deloria 2003, p. 678). The danger, Deloria explains, is in replicating "American history writ small" by assuming that such a cross-disciplinary dialogue would result in Native American studies being "assimilated" into American studies and "raised up in the process" (p. 679).

This entry has provided a brief overview of significant academic discourses engaging place and region during the last several decades. In seeking to summarize forty years of intellectual inquiry, research, and discourse related to place, justice has been done to none of these fields. In fact, contemporary regionalisms may be best represented by the fact that literary criticism continues to produce ever-fracturing ways of demarcating region and place according to new contexts, intersections, and lived experiences.

However, the conversations outlined above may offer us a working definition of region in the contemporary as a descriptor of place, based on qualities formed at the intersection of a place's human history and its natural environment. Regionalism, as a literary depiction of the human experience of specific place-based features, captures an embodied experience of place in relation to that place's history and environment.

SOME WORKS OF LITERARY REGIONALISM, 1980–2020

The literary works listed here are not comprehensive. Representing all region-focused literature published in the United States since 1980 may require its own encyclopedia. Instead, this entry puts forth some examples of literary texts that challenge and remap the places and histories that they depict. The following works center the experience of region in distinct perspectives, rather than offering a "postcard of place" as regionalism purported to do in the nineteenth century. The unifying feature of these works is their close consideration with the intersections of region, community, and the body, and how those interactions meaningfully shape each other.

Community within Region

Regionalism at its best can capture a specific social ecosystem, illuminating how community and family are shaped by region and, in turn, how community and family shape the individual. This is true of Louise Erdrich's body of work, most of which is set in the Ojibwe territories of the northern Great Plains in the United States. Erdrich's books, many of which take place in the same fictional world and have overlapping characters, are regional both in their attention to landscape and to the specific, local histories that have played out on that land. Erdrich captures the overlay of histories that shape the Ojibwe reservation; large-scale political histories having to do with treaties are significant, but so are histories specific to the community and the families within that community. Erdrich's novels, such as *The Beet Queen* (1986), *Last Report from Little No Horse* (2001), and *Master Butchers Singing Club* (2003) are multigenerational narratives with a focus on the life of German American, Scandinavian American, and Ojibwe experiences in the northern Great Plains.

Both the solace and strict social codes of community are themes in Toni Morrison's work. *Paradise* (1997), the story of the freedmen-founded town of Ruby, features multiple narrators from Ruby and from the neighboring community of exiled women. The women live in a home called the Convent, a former federal Indian boarding school, repurposed as a home to a group of women who have been socially exiled from other places. Drawing on many narrative voices, regional accents, and local histories, Morrison meticulously explores the violence of ostracization and white supremacy in a small, Midwestern, Black community. Questions of community and belonging are woven through all of Morrison's fiction, and Morrison said that *Paradise* was part of a trilogy that also includes *Beloved* (1987) and *Jazz* (1992), but *Paradise* in particular borrows local color tropes, such as accents and multiple retellings of local legend, to explore the deep history of the community, linking the characters of the 1970s, the freedmen founders of Ruby, and the Convent's history as a boarding school for Native American girls.

Jesmyn Ward also depicts community and isolation in her novels *Salvage the Bones* (2011) and *Sing, Unburied, Sing* (2017). Both explore community history and containment. In *Salvage the Bones*, community and landscape are reshaped by Hurricane Katrina and the subsequent failure of the federal response to the disaster. *Sing, Unburied, Sing* follows a young boy named Jojo who converses with a wider community of flora, fauna, and the supernatural. Hearing from plants, animals, and ghosts, Jojo learns about the landscape of Mississippi through guidance from his grandmother and from the natural world around him. The plot is centered around the release of Jojo's father from Parchman Farm, an infamously cruel – and, in Ward's book, haunted – prison in Mississippi. *Sing, Unburied, Sing* considers people in regions of containment: an incarcerated father and grandfather, a ghost trapped between worlds.

Erdrich, Morrison, and Ward all depict community as a significant, complex force in shaping regional experience. Similarly, Marilynne Robinson's *Gilead* (2006), set in rural, 1960s Iowa, follows taciturn, introspective characters who reflect the spareness of their surrounding landscape. When Jack, the prodigal son of a preacher, returns to mainly white Gilead with a new and personal investment in racial justice, he disrupts the sense of goodness and morality that is foundational to how many characters, including Jack's father, understand their community, even as they largely ignore the racial injustices happening in the United States. Through Jack's disruptive return to Gilead and his subsequent clashes with his father, Robinson perhaps invites readers to recall Martin Luther King's indictment of the white moderate in his 1963 "Letter from Birmingham Jail."

Region and the Body

Collisions between community and the body are the subject of Jake Skeets's *Eyes Bottle Dark with a Mouthful of Flowers* (2019). The book of poems is set in Gallup, New Mexico, a place where "Men around here only touch when they fuck in a backseat/go for the foul with thirty seconds left/hug their sons after high school graduation/open a keg/stab my uncle forty-seven times behind a liquor store" (Skeets 2019, p. 2). The poems eschew lyrical descriptions of the high desert landscape that is the ancestral home of Diné and Pueblo people, focusing instead on the overlay of colonial infrastructure in the town, which borders the Navajo Nation and Pueblo of Zuni. A local bar is where the poet's "father's uncle tries to get some sleep under a long-bed truck" and is crushed when the truck runs over him (p. 3). Trains also bring death: "The train hit him. [...] The train ate through him like a river eats through the arroyo. The train, it sounds like a river" (p. 62). In this untitled poem, the only regional marker – the arroyo – is absent, present only as a metaphor. The poem's speaker is making a 911 call following this accident, and the local landmark used to orient first responders is decidedly nonregional: Walmart, "on the Westside" of town (p. 62). The poems depict Gallup with a local's familiarity of specific pastures, streets, and storefronts, but the speaker is distinctly uncharmed by these details. Instead, this story of place is punctuated by violent collisions between bodies and machines.

Kiese Laymon's writing often uses language as an organizing principle to explore embodied and regional contexts. His novel *Long Division* (2013) vividly describes the climate, environment, and landscape of summer in central Mississippi. It uses the speculative element of time travel to underscore the compression of Mississippi's racist, violent past and racist, violent present. The land stays largely the same as his teenaged characters time travel from the early 2000s to the 1960s and back. Laymon's memoir *Heavy* (2018) is likewise an account of the impact of place on the body. As a child Laymon's professor mother gave him writing prompts; in the book, they are a starting place for his reflections on his experiences of growing up as a Black boy in the US South, collapsing distinctions between the individual and the region as he writes about Blackness, Southernness, and masculinity. Eve Dunbar's book *Black Regions of the Imagination* (2013) provides a history of the positioning of Blackness and region, particularly in ethnographic writing, as a strategy to "effect change and to issue critiques of American race relations, while also seemingly adhering to a convention of cultural translation that would be easily embraced by a mainstream reading audience" (2013, p. 5). Although Laymon eschews "cultural translation" for mainstream audiences, Dunbar's study gives broader historical context for the tradition in which Laymon is writing: meetings of the body, region, and Blackness in literature.

Like Laymon, Layli Long Soldier's poetry collection *Whereas* (2017) reflects an interest in language: "Everything is in the language we use," Long Soldier tells us (2017, p. 51). For example, in her poem "38" she brings up the word "Minnesota" in relation to the Minnesota Treaties that led to the Dakota War of 1862 (also called the Sioux Uprising). We learn that Minnesota has an etymology in the Dakota words "*mni*, which means water; and *sota*, which means turbid" (p. 51). Noting that the Minnesota Treaties facilitated the theft of thousands of acres of land from the Dakota, Long Soldier emphasizes the irony of the United States borrowing words from the Dakota language to rename a territory stolen from the Dakota, and to name the obscurely written treaties that authorized the theft. The historical scope of "38" covers more than 150 years, but Long Soldier bases the story on bodily experience. The poem ends with an anecdote about the death of settler and shopkeeper Andrew Myrick, who withheld food to starving Dakota families. Myrick suggested the Dakota should eat grass if they were truly starving. Myrick was killed by Dakota warriors during the Sioux Uprising: "When Myrick's body was found,/his mouth was stuffed with grass./I am inclined to call this act by the Dakota warriors a poem./ [. . .] the words 'Let them eat grass' click the gears of the poem into place" (p. 53). Long Soldier highlights the importance of language in understanding a region's history.

Regional Histories

The unrelenting march of time is an organizing principle of Kiana Davenport's *Shark Dialogues* (1994), a multigenerational epic about a Hawaiian family – the matriarch, Tahitian royalty, the patriarch, a white American sailor. The book covers 150 years of Hawaiian history, following the establishing of plantations and pineapple canneries, ensuing labor disputes, plagues of leprosy, the dethroning of Queen Liliuokalani, and the arrival of the military and tourist industries. Davenport locates the effects of these waves of economic and political change in her characters' bodies. A character with no financial support turns to sex work. Another character escapes a forced exile to a leper colony by hiding in the Hawaiian forests for years, as his face and body are slowly rendered unrecognizable by the disease. *Shark Dialogues* is a book about the decay wrought by settler colonialism. It is punctuated by moments of resistance, in the form of labor organizing, political demonstrations, and a failed terrorist plot to blow up a large tourist resort.

Denis Johnson's novella *Train Dreams* (2011) is brief in length and limited in subject: set in northern Idaho, the book is about lumber worker Robert Grainier who, after losing his wife in a large forest fire, lives a reclusive life in that forest. However, *Train Dreams* sets Grainier's life against the expansive timeline of ancient trees. The forest around Grainier recovers from the fire, while Grainier ages and his body registers the wear and tear of a career spent cutting down massive trees. We learn that Grainier enjoyed "the grand size of things in the woods, and the feeling of being lost and far away," in addition to the monumental task of felling old-growth forests, "accomplishing labors, Grainier sometimes thought, tantamount to the pyramids, changing the face of the mountainsides" (Johnson 2011, pp. 14–15). Like Davenport and Johnson, Cormac McCarthy's Border Trilogy gives a wide-ranging view of the American West in the nineteenth and twentieth centuries. In the trilogy, made up of *All the Pretty Horses* (1992), *The Crossing* (1994), and *Cities of the Plain* (1998), movement across the borderlands between Mexico and the United States is important in the coming of age of McCarthy's male characters.

In the nineteenth and early twentieth centuries, regionalism usually engaged rural spaces, but literature of the city is also attuned to specific characteristics of a place. Maxine Hong Kingston's *Tripmaster Monkey: His Fake Book* (1990) depicts 1960s San Francisco through its main character Wittman Ah Sing's specific experiences as a Chinese American playwright. Chronicling racism and counterculture in San Francisco, Wittman ultimately produces a play that draws on Chinese narrative tradition to depict some of his experiences within and outside the Chinese diaspora of San Francisco. Tommy Orange's *There There* (2018) is set in Oakland, California, and follows several urban Native Americans who live in or have connections to the city. The book's narrators travel through the city by BART, by bike, and on foot; from different paths, the characters converge at a powwow. *There There* interrogates geographical belonging and sense of place for urban Native Americans. *There There* evokes *Tripmaster Monkey* through its Bay Area setting and one of its first narrators, an artist named Dene Oxendene. Both books include narratives within narratives. Dene

Oxendene collects oral histories of urban Natives in Oakland. Wittman Ah Sing composes a play about the Chinese American diaspora in the Bay Area. In each case, a character's political consciousness is expressed through the creation of narrative, and that narrative is grounded in place.

REGIONAL FUTURES

The United States is the product of centuries of genocide and relocation of Indigenous people, the human trafficking and violent oppression of enslaved people, and histories that are often suppressed or censored in favor of a more palatable national origin story. Even the ways we name and identify regions are shaped by a settler-colonialist framework. Drawing on cardinal or ordinal directions, when we say "the South" or "the Midwest," there is some semblance of shared meaning related to each region. However, these categories erase pre-conquest geographies, which would demand more nuanced consideration of how the United States was formed – and, inherently, an acknowledgment of the violent human cost of building the US empire.

How else might we define region and account for the conditions that shape regional experience and, accordingly, the written art produced about those experiences? One such project, the Native Land mapping project, uses geographic data to mark Indigenous homelands and traditional language areas in North America. By providing historical background for our current colonial state, the maps created by Native Land fundamentally dismantle the colonial divisions of the land that is currently the United States. Instead of mapping regions according to states, climate, or topography, the US map is divided by a geography of Indigenous people: a map with hundreds of languages, territories, and treaties. The framework of Native Land uses mapping to depict Indigenous history, present, and future, demanding the acknowledgment of the colonial present and the potential of decolonial futures. The map has no images of people, but it is designed to reflect lived experiences.

Along these lines, we may think of other ways to name and map region according to human experiences in those places. For example, we may map region according to food deserts; abortion access; gun violence; the safety of municipal water supplies; likelihood of exposure to agricultural pesticides; proximity to fracking, to gas pipelines, or to the man camps that build those pipelines; the frequency in which trans women and Indigenous women are classified as missing or are murdered; or the geographic rates of maternal mortality and infant mortality. By such criteria, regionalism is as reflective of public health as it is of accent, folk culture, or climate.

Perhaps dividing regions by these criteria means that region becomes impossibly fractured, but perhaps that fracturing is the best characterization of what is constituted by the term "contemporary regionalisms." Place and region *do* significantly shape peoples' lives and, therefore, their art; so do the circumstances that an individual brings into an encounter with region. Doreen Massey argued as much, writing, "I'm sure a woman's sense of place in a mining village – the spaces through which she normally moves, the meeting places, the connections outside – are different from a man's" (1994, p. 154). We can extend this argument to understand that embodied experience shapes individual definitions of region. Understanding the overt and subtle differences between regions is as pressing now as it was in the nineteenth century. The United States is a sprawling empire that covers many climates and landscapes, a porous container for many cultural and ethnic traditions. Naming the features of region, and the varying ways those regions "happen" to different bodies, remains a crucial part of explaining human experience in the United States.

At the time of writing this entry in the summer of 2020, the media was full of maps of COVID-19 spread and maps of electoral predictions for the 2020 presidential election: each map serves as a reminder that place shapes experience, and that humans shape places. In response to the paucity of federal response to the crisis of COVID-19 under capitalism, mutual aid groups have emerged to serve specific towns, reservations, or neighborhoods, underscoring the significance of the local, the regional, and the geographically close. While not a literary example, these mutual aid groups epitomize José Limón's concept of critical regionalism as having an "antagonistic, if also negotiated, relationship [. . .] with late capitalist globalization" (2008, p. 186). Region is a concept built from historical events, political circumstances, ecologies, and lived human experiences. A meaningful study of place-based literature and identity must take those contexts into consideration. This confluence of meanings is what sustains regionalism as an enduring concept in US literature and cultural identity.

SEE ALSO: Black Atlantic; Border Fictions; The Culture Wars; Erdrich, Louise; Globalization; Johnson, Denis; Kingston, Maxine Hong; McCarthy, Cormac; Morrison, Toni; Robinson, Marilynne; Urban Fiction; Walker, Alice; Ward, Jesmyn

REFERENCES

Anderson, Eric Gary. (2006). South to a red place: contemporary American Indian writing and the problem of Native/Southern studies. The Mississippi Quarterly 60 (1): 5–32.

Brodhead, Richard. (1993). *Cultures of Letters: Scenes of Reading and Writing in Nineteenth-Century America*. Chicago: University of Chicago Press.

Cameron, Kelsey and Fitzpatrick, Jessica. (2021). Designing living space: community engagement practices in rooted AR. In: *Augmented and Mixed Reality for Communities* (ed. Joshua A. Fisher). Boca Raton, FL: CRC Press.

Comer, Krista. (2011). Exceptionalisms, other Wests, critical regionalisms. American Literary History 23 (1): 159–173.

Deloria, Philip. (2003). Americans Indians, American studies and the ASA. American Quarterly 55 (4): 669–680.

Dunbar, Eve. (2013). *Black Regions of the Imagination: African American Writers between the Nation and the World*. Philadelphia: Temple University Press.

Estes, Nick. (2020). The empire of all maladies: colonial contagions and Indigenous resistance. The Baffler 52 (July 2020). https://thebaffler.com/salvos/the-empire-of-all-maladies-estes (accessed September 20, 2021).

Fisher-Fishkin, Shelley. (2005). Crossroads of cultures: the transnational turn in American studies. Presidential address to the American Studies Association, November 12, 2004. American Quarterly 57 (1): 17–57.

Foote, Stephanie. (2001). *Regional Fictions: Culture and Identity in Nineteenth-Century American Literature*. Madison: University of Wisconsin Press.

Foote, Stephanie. (2012). Local knowledge and women's regional writing. In: *The Cambridge History of American Women's Literature* (ed. Dale Bauer), 293–308. Cambridge: Cambridge University Press.

Johnson, Denis. (2011). *Train Dreams: A Novella*. London: Picador.

Kaplan, Amy. (1991). Nation, region, and empire. In: *Columbia History of the American Novel* (ed. Emory Emory, Cathy N. Davidson, Patrick O'Donnell, Valerie Smith, and Christopher P. Wilson), 240–266. New York: Columbia University Press.

Kaplan, Amy and Pease, Donald E. (1999). *Cultures of United States Imperialism*. Durham, NC: Duke University Press; 1st ed. 1993.

Limón, José. (2008). Border literary histories, globalization, and critical regionalism. American Literary History 20 (1/2): 160–182.

Long Soldier, Layli. (2017). *Whereas*. Minneapolis: Graywolf Press.

Massey, Doreen B. (1994). *Space, Place, and Gender*. Minneapolis: University of Minnesota Press.

Skeets, Jake. (2019). *Eyes Bottle Dark with a Mouthful of Flowers*. Minneapolis: Milkweed Press.

Wilder, Craig Steven. (2013). *Ebony & Ivy: Race, Slavery, and the Troubled History of America's Universities.* New York: Bloomsbury.

FURTHER READING

Anzaldúa, Gloria. (1987). *Borderlands/La Frontera: The New Mestiza.* San Francisco: Aunt Lute Books.

Gilroy, Paul. (2007). *The Black Atlantic: Modernity and Double Consciousness.* London: Verso; 1st ed. 1993.

Joseph, Philip. (2007). *American Literary Regionalism in a Global Age.* Baton Rouge: Louisiana State University Press.

Cooper, Dennis

DIARMUID HESTER
University of Cambridge, UK

Dennis Cooper is a prodigious, ever-innovative writer whose career runs to almost fifty years, and who has been at the forefront of many important American subcultural movements – New York School poetry, punk rock, New Narrative writing, and alt-lit, to name a few. Reinventing his work and his approach constantly, he has been a poet, a novelist, a journalist of music and movies, a blogger, and, most recently, a filmmaker. He has created graphic novels and theater pieces, acted in films, edited literary magazines and small presses, and in 2015 he published *Zac's Haunted House*, the first novel made entirely out of GIFs. The *succès de scandale* of Cooper's 1990s novels, and their association with transgressive writing, has warped the perception of his work in some circles, such that merely evoking his name can connote a brand of gratuitously violent, sometimes scatological queer writing. This characterization is unfortunate, as Cooper is in fact a leading figure of the American postwar avant-garde. His probing forays into sex and violence are never an end in themselves and are always in the service of larger, often recurring themes. Foremost among these is the relationship between the individual and the communal, or the place of independence in social formations. Cooper is an anarchist and the antagonism that frequently defines this relationship is one of the primary motors of his work.

INFLUENCES

Born on January 10, 1953, to Clifford and Ann Cooper of West Covina, California, Cooper's childhood was marked by a number of traumatic episodes, which he remembers vividly and to which he often credits the arousal of his interest in exploring violence in his work. At the age of seven, for instance, he watched in horror as a beautiful blonde girl from the house next door become engulfed in flames as her dress was set alight by a stray tiki torch. At the age of 11, his friend accidentally hit him in the head with an ax, knocking him unconscious; when he woke up, he remembers, "blood was just spurting, volcanoing, all over the joint. I reached up and felt my brain" (Epstein 2001).

Cooper's teenage years weren't much better. His parents divorced and his father, an entrepreneur with connections to the Nixon administration who ran the Cooper Development Corporation (an aerospace manufacturer that made parts for America's first space satellite), left his children in the care of their mother, whose alcoholism became progressively more acute and violent. According to Cooper, she subjected him and his siblings to years of physical and emotional abuse, culminating in the moment when she packed them into the car and drove full speed straight at a wall. Such experiences were nothing if not formative for the young writer. Horrific and unexpected violence, parental abuse and neglect, and the recursive structure of trauma all feature prominently in Cooper's writing.

As a teen, Cooper also discovered the Marquis de Sade's work, which he read in editions by Grove Press that included landmark essays by Maurice Blanchot and Simone de Beauvoir. Offering him a well-regarded example of literature that dealt unflinchingly with sex and mortality, Sade's work was a revelation and helped him to realize "what I had thought was some horrible part of me that would isolate me from the world was in fact legitimate and even an important subject matter for literature" (Silverberg 2011, p. 176). The individualism underpinning Sade's worldview made a huge impact on the teenage Cooper and would later become the foundation for his anarchistic outlook. Around this time, Cooper also started reading Arthur Rimbaud, another important influence. Bad boy of French symbolism, Rimbaud was namechecked by many musicians at the time, including Jim Morrison and Bob Dylan. After reading an interview with Dylan that mentioned Rimbaud, Cooper recalls, "I bought one of Rimbaud's books, and I was staggered. Everything changed. His poetry, his biography, the fact that he wrote such incredible things and was so ambitious when he was my age were hugely inspiring, and I just dove into French literature after that" (p. 175).

The combined effect of Sade and Rimbaud, and others such as Pierre Reverdy, the Comte de Lautréamont, and Charles Baudelaire, is legible in Cooper's first collection of poems, *The Terror of Earrings* (1973). The New York School of poets, including Frank O'Hara, John Ashbery, and James Schuyler, were also important to him, especially around the time he was writing his second collection, *Tiger Beat* (1978). Cooper was fascinated by New York punk rock too; inspired by Patti Smith, the doyenne of Downtown whom he idolized early on, Cooper's work from this period blended together high and low culture. A prime example of this was Cooper's editorial work on his literary magazine, *Little Caesar*, which ran for ten issues from 1976 to 1982. Part poetry journal, part punk rock zine, *Little Caesar* included writing by New York School poets and Andy Warhol's Factory stars alongside comic strips, photo spreads, and interviews with punk rockers like Sex Pistols front man Johnny Rotten. Building on the magazine's success, Cooper launched Little Caesar Press which would go on to publish poetry collections by the likes of Joe Brainard, Tom Clark, Amy Gerstler, and Eileen Myles.

EARLY PROSE AND FICTION

Cooper turned to fiction writing as early as 1982 when, in his poetry collection *The Tenderness of the Wolves*, he published the 24-page prose piece "A Herd." It was the first extended treatment of a subject that would frequently preoccupy him: serial killers and their teenage victims. During the 1970s, the United States witnessed a marked increase in the number of horrific serial murders; with the Manson Family, the Bay Area Zodiac Killer, Ted Bundy, and John Wayne Gacy, serial killings seemed to be a fixture of the nightly news. But while print and TV media fixated on the murderers (turning the likes of Bundy and Charles Manson into celebrities in the process), Cooper was more interested in their victims. As the cover of *The Tenderness of the Wolves* makes clear – the author pictured standing alongside photos of his heroes, including John Wayne Gacy's final victim, Robert Piest – Cooper was on the side of those whose lives were cut tragically short.

The principal focus of "A Herd" is highschooler Jay Levin – his life, his disappearance, and his gruesome murder at the hands of serial killer Ray Sexton. "He had blond hair which spilled from a careless zig zag down head-center and fell in spilt ends which brushed off his shoulders when he walked around ... He was known around school for his kindness" (Cooper 1982, p. 52). In contrast to the specificity of this description, when Sexton looks at Jay, he sees only a generic "youth" that will satisfy a craving: "Down in the basement, the unconscious youth had been strapped hand and foot on a table. When the body was naked, he swept the long hair from its face and no perfect being emerged" (p. 56). Cooper portrays Jay's death and Sexton's desire to "master boys, make them nothing" in the kind of unsensational language that would become typical of his work (p. 75). He also reads into the phenomenon of serial murder a complicated interplay of the particular and the common, which maps onto his persistent interest in exploring the dynamic between individual and communal concerns.

In his review of the collection, New Narrative writer Bruce Boone was the first of many critics to remark on the "blankness" of Cooper's writing and its apparent lack of affect, exclaiming that "Cooper's feelings are so incredibly distant!" (Boone 1982, p. 222). Cooper would double down on this emotional distance in his first complete work of fiction, the novella *Safe* (1984). Inspired by French filmmaker Robert Bresson (the third of a triumvirate of influences, along with Sade and Rimbaud, that Cooper would frequently invoke), *Safe* is populated with characters whose outward expressions rarely match their turbulent inner lives. Bresson's films are notable for their use of nonprofessional actors or "models" in Bresson's preferred term; in works like *Le Diable Probablement* (The Devil Probably, 1977) they could easily be substituted for mannequins, such is the profoundly impassive way that they process extreme emotional states. Cooper riffs on this in *Safe*, a tripartite narrative that orbits the handsome, elusive character of Mark and the various men who desire him. These include a writer who stands in for Cooper himself – a stylistic tic that foreshadows a technique he would use to great effect in later works. Mark and his friends are repeatedly compared to Ken dolls, ventriloquist dummies, and wax museum statues; when he's getting "dolled-up" for a night out, we're told that Mark's efforts "make him about as alluring as one of the mannequins in these display windows" (Cooper 2004, p. 100). Dodie Bellamy, another New Narrative writer, once suggested that Cooper's work is remarkable for its "aesthetics of distance" (2006, p. 97). *Safe* is an important early work that testifies to the emergence of Cooper's aesthetics of distance and his indebtedness to Bresson.

THE GEORGE MILES CYCLE

Closer, the first novel in Cooper's celebrated and controversial George Miles cycle of novels, was published in 1989 by Grove Press. The cycle is a masterpiece of form and language, planned by Cooper since his teens as an elaborate work of art that would stand as a monument to his friend and sometime lover, George Miles. Made up of five compact, lapidary works, it attests to Cooper's voracious appetite for modern and contemporary culture in all its forms and incorporates an enormous range of influences and references, from experimental film and pornography, to visual art, sculpture, post-punk music, and the French Nouveau Roman. *Closer* was followed by *Frisk* (1991), *Try* (1993), *Guide* (1997), and *Period* (2000), each a highly experimental novel featuring teenage protagonists that employ traditional storytelling techniques like characterization, plot, and dénouement only to subvert them.

As noted above, the cycle gained some notoriety for dealing with controversial subjects such as murder, underage sex, child pornography, heavy metal music, and coprophilia. Cooper pre-empts his reader's reaction to these subjects, however, and his works encourage a critical response to the feelings of outrage or arousal they elicit. When, in *Closer*, the cute, inscrutable sophomore George Miles defecates into his middle-aged lover's hand, for instance, the scene is portrayed through the video camera of Alex, a budding young filmmaker who is watching from the window. *Frisk* infamously includes a long letter written by the narrator, "Dennis," that describes in horrific detail a murderous rampage in Amsterdam, which is later revealed to its addressee as a total fabrication. Far from being merely salacious or gratuitous, these incidents and the way Cooper frames them challenge his readers as individuals to think about where they stand, ethically and morally, on behavior deemed unacceptable by society.

Since its publication, the cycle has prompted much appreciative comment from academic critics, especially those versed in psychoanalysis and post-structuralism. Its first scholarly treatments came from Elizabeth Young, who considered *Closer* through a Lacanian lens, and Earl Jackson, Jr. (2006), who explored the same novel in relation to Julia Kristeva's notion of abjection. Subsequent appraisals followed suit: Hal Foster (1996) suggested that Cooper's texts were witness to the withdrawal of the Lacanian Real; Gregory Bredbeck (1995) conjoined *Frisk* with the work of Jacques Derrida to argue for what he called the "new queer narrative"; Michelle Aaron (2004) most ambitiously considered the entire movement of the George Miles cycle from the perspective of Roland Barthes's influential distinction between writerly and readerly texts. Much of this kind of work tends to feel a little stuck in time, however, and is often more revealing of the theorists under discussion (and, indeed, of academic criticism's devotion to critical theory in this period) than it is of Cooper's texts. Far more productive is the approach taken by Daniel Kane (2017), Wayne Koestenbaum (2008), and Marvin Taylor (2006), which is attentive to the highly wrought form of Cooper's work and its emergence out of a specific historical and cultural context. This mode of criticism can also be found in my monograph, *Wrong: A Critical Biography of Dennis Cooper* (Hester 2020).

POST-CYCLE WORKS

Ever attuned to social problems and their representation by the media, Cooper would respond to the phenomenon of high-school shootings in his first post-cycle work, *My Loose Thread* (2001). Narrated by Larry, a teenager with severe psychological issues that impede his ability to communicate effectively with those around him, the novel is a tale of adolescent confusion and anger that terminates in a multiple homicide at Larry's high school. Leora Lev (2006, p. 231) related the work to "post-Columbine culture" but its inspiration comes from an attack at Thurston High in Springfield, Oregon, not the more famous massacre perpetrated by Eric Harris and Dylan Klebold a year later. On May 21, 1998, 15-year-old Kip Kinkel murdered his parents, then walked into his school and opened fire on his classmates, killing two and injuring twenty-five. In January 2000, his interview with police was broadcast as part of a PBS Frontline documentary; asked to give a reason for his killing spree, he sobbed that he had no other choice. Watching the documentary, Cooper was struck by the impenetrability of Kinkel's answers and how they undermined the media's frenzied attempts to attribute blame for the shootings (to video games, for instance, or Marilyn Manson). *My Loose Thread* explores the lethally warped logic of minds like Kinkel's and, in contrast to much coverage of high-school killings, refuses to reduce emotional complexity to easy explanations.

Cooper released two very different novels in 2005. *God Jr.* was in many ways a departure for him: as an experiment, he excluded much of the sensational subject matter that normally characterized his work. The novel contains no sex or explicit violence and is, instead, a subdued account of a father's efforts to commemorate his dead son by building a monument to him in his backyard. However, even here there are echoes of the George Miles cycle and Cooper's relationship with his friend, from whom he had been estranged and who he discovered had actually committed suicide before *Closer* was even published. Cooper's grief, guilt, and mourning for Miles reverberates through the father–son relationship at the heart of *God Jr.*, which is an important, if underrated, part of Cooper's canon of work.

It was followed by *The Sluts*, which might have been crafted solely out of the material omitted from the previous work and features scenes of explicit gay sex, sadistic violence, torture, and death. The book is a lurid postmodern noir based in the world of gay male escorts and their online review websites where a murder may or may not have taken place. One of Cooper's most critically and commercially successful novels, in America it won the Lambda Literary Award for fiction that explores LGBT issues and in France it was awarded the Prix Sade (2007) for works that defy "the moral or political order, against all forms of intellectual terrorism." The book's preoccupation with forms of online communication (e.g. forums, email, instant messaging) would anticipate the arrival of Cooper's blog, a major project since 2005. On his blog, named an "experimental alternative Wikipedia," Cooper posts about obscure and avant-garde art and culture six days a week, and its comments section has become home to a vibrant community of fans, artists, filmmakers, and writers (Romano 2016). Cooper has used the blog's renown to promote the work of younger writers, especially those associated with the so-called alt-lit movement, including Blake Butler, Juliet Escoria, Tao Lin, and Scott McClanahan.

Cooper's production of new fiction slowed somewhat following his relocation to France in August 2005, when most of his time was spent working on the blog and creating theater pieces with Giséle Vienne, including the likes of *I Apologize* (2005), *Jerk* (2007), and *Kindertotenlieder* (2007). However, in 2011 he released *The Marbled Swarm: A Novel*. A convoluted tale of violence that stretches from a labyrinthine chateau in the countryside to the Marais neighborhood of Paris, concealment is a principal theme and secret doors and two-way mirrors abound in the narrative. The prose itself – the eponymous marbled swarm – is similarly duplicitous and clandestine, looking something like a baroque version of text put through bad translation software. To decipher it, the reader must learn how to anticipate the narrator's lies and deceptions, and follow the loops and folds of his language. Cooper has called it "an homage to [Alain] Robbe-Grillet – although not in the way you might expect," and *The Marbled Swarm* may be his most multilayered and demanding print novel to date (Meginnis 2012). In the context of the contemporary moment, which is defined by the primacy of the visible – surveillance is everywhere, and the confessional is de rigueur – Cooper's novel is testament to the radical potential of secrecy.

SEE ALSO: Burroughs, William; Gay, Roxane; Literary Magazines; Palahniuk, Chuck; Queer and LGBT Fiction; Suburban Narratives; Trauma and Fiction; White, Edmund

REFERENCES

Aaron, Michele. (2004). (Fill-in-the) Blank fiction: Dennis Cooper's cinematics and the complicitous reader. *Journal of Modern Literature* 27 (3): 115–127.

Bellamy, Dodie. (1996). Digression as power: Dennis Cooper and the aesthetics of distance.

In: *Enter at Your Own Risk* (ed. Leora Lev), 97–104. Madison, WI: Fairleigh Dickinson University Press.

Boone, Bruce. (1982). Stoned out of my gourd. *FUSE* (December 1982).

Bredbeck, Gregory W. (1995). The new queer narrative: intervention and critique. *Textual Practice* 9 (3): 477–502.

Cooper, Dennis. (1982). A herd. In: *The Tenderness of the Wolves*, 51–75. Traumansberg, NY: The Crossing Press.

Cooper, Dennis. (2004). Safe. In: *Wrong: Stories*, 99–158. London: Serpent's Tail.

Epstein, Dan. (2001). An interview with Dennis Cooper. *3:AM Magazine* (December 2001). http://www.3ammagazine.com/litarchives/2001_dec/interview_dennis_cooper.html (accessed June 29, 2021).

Foster, Hal. (1996). Obscene. *October* 78: 107–124.

Jackson, Earl, Jr. (2006). Death drives across Pornotopia: Dennis Cooper on the extremities of being. In: *Enter at Your Own Risk* (ed. Leora Lev), 151–174. Madison, WI: Fairleigh Dickinson University Press.

Kane, Daniel. (2017). "Sit on my face!" Dennis Cooper, the first punk poet. In: *Do You Have A Band? Poetry and Punk Rock in New York City*, 198–215. New York: Columbia University Press.

Koestenbaum, Wayne. (2008). 32 cardinal virtues of Dennis Cooper. In: *Dennis Cooper: Writing at the Edge* (ed. Paul Hegarty and Danny Kennedy), 187–190. Brighton, UK: Sussex Academic Press.

Lev, Leora. (2006). The center cannot hold: my loose thread. In: *Enter at Your Own Risk* (ed. Leora Lev), 231–237. Madison, WI: Fairleigh Dickinson University Press.

Lev, Leora. (ed.) (2006). *Enter at Your Own Risk: The Dangerous Art of Dennis Cooper*. Madison, WI: Fairleigh Dickinson University Press.

Meginnis, Mike. (2012). My fear arouses me: an interview with Dennis Cooper. *HTML Giant* (January 5, 2012). http://htmlgiant.com/author-spotlight/an-interview-with-dennis-cooper/ (accessed June 29, 2021).

Prix Sade. (2007). Lauréat 2007 – Prix Sade, 2007. https://www.marquis-de-sade.com/2011-05-19-prix-sade (accessed June 29, 2021).

Romano, Aja. (2016). A writer kept a blog for 10 years. Google deleted it. Why? *Vox* (July 30, 2016). http://www.vox.com/2016/7/30/12303070/dennis-cooper-blog-deleted-google (accessed June 29, 2021).

Silverberg, Ira. (2011). The art of fiction no. 213: Dennis Cooper. *The Paris Review* 198 (Fall): 172–198.

Taylor, Marvin. "A Dorian Gray type of thing": male–male desire and the crisis of representation in Dennis Cooper's *Closer*. In: *Enter at Your Own Risk* (ed. Leora Lev), 175–199. Madison, WI: Fairleigh Dickinson University Press.

Young, Elizabeth. (1992). Death in Disneyland: the work of Dennis Cooper. In: *Shopping in Space: Essays on American "Blank Generation" Fiction* (ed. Elizabeth Young and Graham Caveney), 235–263. London: Serpent's Tail.

FURTHER READING

DC'S. (n.d.). The blog of Dennis Cooper. http://denniscooperblog.com

Hegarty, Paul and Danny Kennedy. (eds.) (2008). *Dennis Cooper: Writing at the Edge*. Brighton, UK: Sussex Academic Press.

Hester, Diarmuid. (2020). *Wrong: A Critical Biography of Dennis Cooper*. Iowa City: University of Iowa Press.

Lev, Leora. (ed.) (2006). *Enter at Your Own Risk: The Dangerous Art of Dennis Cooper*. Madison, WI: Fairleigh Dickinson University Press.

Coover, Robert

BRIAN EVENSON
CalArts, USA

Considered one of the most notable practitioners of literary postmodernism and metafiction, Robert Coover (b. 1932) is one of those rare authors who seem equally accomplished both in short and longform fiction. Coover's post-1980 career extends the questioning of genre and narrative tropes that characterized his early career, including *Gerald's Party*'s (1986) send-up of detective fiction, the manipulation of the Western in *Ghost Town* (1998), and a return to the examination of the dynamics and roles of fairy tales in *Briar Rose* (1996), *Stepmother* (2004), and *A Child Again* (2005). Coover's most recent works further extend and complicate this investigation (see *Noir* [2010] and *Huck Out West* [2017] as well as the newer stories collected in 2018's *Going for a Beer*), introducing new levels of complexity, while with *The Brunist Day of Wrath* (2014), he returns to the territory of his first novel.

Coover delineated such thematically rich territory early in his career that more than fifty years later it remains seemingly inexhaustible. This is largely due to his attention to two intertwined motifs that remain remarkably fluid and readily adaptable to new genres and types of stories. On the one hand there is Coover's investigation of community, and the way in which communities hold themselves together, both in good ways and bad, through shared myths. This dovetails with an interest in genre, and how genres and genre expectations have become a new set of shared myths for readers. Coover's challenging of genre becomes a way of breaking up old myths that have lost their efficacy in helping us understand the world. For Coover, "the fiction maker's function is to furnish better fictions with which we can reform our notion of things" (Gado 1973, p. 150). In other words, not so much to mimetically depict life as to make us see life differently. As genres outlive their usefulness, they must be questioned, their artificiality unveiled so as to allow us to move beyond them to more relevant ways of seeing: the writer for Coover is the one who "tears apart the old story, speaks the unspeakable, makes the ground shake, then shuffles the bits back together in a new story. Partly anarchical, in other words, partly creative – or re-creative" (see Wolff 1977, p. 54). And once the bits of story begin to be shuffled back in a similar way, it is time to question them again.

The novelette *Spanking the Maid* (1982) seems a dramatic contrast to the book that came directly before it, Coover's monumental *The Public Burning* (1977). *The Public Burning* is maximal and overtly political, using a cast of dozens of characters to depict the Rosenberg trial as a public circus in a way that seems prescient of the direction politics has taken in the twenty-first century. Conversely, *Spanking the Maid* is concise and iterative, minimal. It hearkens back formally to the stories found in *Pricksongs & Descants* (1969), such as "The Babysitter" and "The Magic Poker," which offer multiple, sometimes mutually exclusive, iterations of the same situation. Here the situation is a set piece which involves a maid entering her master's chamber, making an error in her chores, and then being punished by her master in a way redolent of sado-masochistic pornography. As the situation repeats, it takes on an absurd rather than titillating quality, suggesting that both maid and master are trapped in a narrative loop that they cannot escape. This in turn becomes a commentary on the relationship of storytelling to life, on how when we without examination accept story as truth it begins to blinker us. Such a view applies to Coover's fiction as a whole.

Something similar happens in *Briar Rose*, perhaps Coover's most accomplished critique of fairy tales. In this novella, Coover takes on the Sleeping Beauty fable, layering a variety of tellings and retellings of it, from Giambattista Basile's early "Sun, Moon, and Talia" to the Grimm's "Brier Rose." Told in short narrative sections, the focalization of the story shifts between three characters: the prince trying to rescue Briar Rose, the sleeping and dreaming princess, and the fairy/crone who sits beside the princess listening in on her dreams. As the story progresses and the prince continues to struggle, it becomes clear that he might well be trapped forever in the thorny vines surrounding the castle. Indeed, all three characters find themselves suspended in a kind of narrative hell: the princess's dreams of the prince and of "happily ever after" keep her from awakening, and the fairy is condemned to the boredom of being tied to a sleeping, naive princess. To pass the time, the fairy enters the princess's dreams in various roles and tells her stories. These are versions of the princess's potential story, but torqued as a means of trying to stop the princess from clinging to unrealizable ideals. As the story ends, however, the princess seems to have learned nothing, and she is still clinging to the exhausted myths of the happily-ever-after.

Pinocchio in Venice (1991) sets about de-Disneyfying the Pinocchio story by, in part, drawing on Carlo Collodi's nineteenth-century tale, *The Adventures of Pinocchio* (1883). Coover's Pinocchio is an aged and respected professor who returns for the first time to Venice, the city he grew up in, only to find it unfamiliar, even hostile. He is robbed, and his laptop which contains his work-in-progress is stolen. As he wanders the city in search of the thieves, he begins to revert to his inner puppet and to encounter the people of his past. *Pinocchio in Venice* is a book about the ways in which the past both constructs us and destroys us, about how through memory we manipulate the past to create an independent sense of self but also are simultaneously manipulated by this past. As his inner puppet reappears, the professor asks himself who he is, and whether there's a self that exists that would bring together his past and his present and, if not – if he's forced to choose between wooden childhood and fleshy adulthood – which self will he choose?

Coover returns to fairy tales in several of the stories in *A Child Again*, for instance taking on Little Red Riding Hood in "Grandmother's Nose" and the Pied Piper in "The Return of the Dark Children," both of which are also included in his volume of selected stories, *Going for a Beer* (2018), along with several other stories based on fairy tales. Indeed, his career-long examination of myths and fairy tales can be seen as the spine of his other investigations, both the place from which Coover begins and the place to which he always seems to return.

The novella *Stepmother* takes a significant step in this investigation. Instead of examining an individual tale, it takes a standard fairy tale character trope, that of the stepmother, and explores it alongside other character tropes (princes, princesses, soldiers, kings, etc.). Coover investigates what happens if we take a character role that has been subsidiary within fairy tales and instead make it central: how does this disrupt or deform the comfortable narrative that the fairy tale has hitherto been able to establish? Once a character is aware of the role they are expected to play within the fairy tale, will they be able to wriggle out of it? Despite its brevity, with its sly proliferation of tropes and details from dozens of fairy tales, *Stepmother* is remarkably rich. *Stepmother* suggests where fairy tales might go once their traditional efficacy has been exhausted.

In *The Enchanted Prince* (2017), Coover views fairy tales through the lens of movies. It is about an aging film star who is filming a remake (the last of many) of "The Enchanted Prince," the movie that made her a star. The premise allows Coover to give an (at least potentially) realistic justification for the iterative technique found in much of his fiction (through the echoes of different scenes from the remakes), to think about the relationship of director and actor in a way that also addresses the relationship of writer and author, and to consider the way in which one's relationship to the myths one participates in might change as one ages and moves forward in time.

Movies are hardly new territory for Coover. The stories in *A Night at the Movies, or You Must Remember This* (1987) see movies as occupying the same role for contemporary culture that fairy tales and myths did in earlier times. Each story in that collection functions as a type of movie, from

"Previews of Coming Attractions" to a B-movie to "Romance!" and everything in between. A more recent movie-centric book, Coover's *The Adventures of Lucky Pierre: Directors' Cut* (2002), is perhaps the most ambitious and complex of the books written after 1980. Begun in 1970 and written sporadically over three decades (see Coover 2000, p. 87), it consists of a series of nine "reels" each concerning a porn film legend named Lucky Pierre. Each reel offers a different type of film presented by a different female director, each of whom can be considered both Lucky Pierre's former on- and off-screen lover and his muse. Indeed, each director is associated (overtly, in the final reel) with one of the nine Greek muses. As each director creates her film, the other eight both help and interfere, and Lucky Pierre seems to have an increasingly hard time distinguishing between real life and film, between the *reel* and the *real*. Like Charlie in Coover's early story "Charlie in the House of Rue" (1979), Lucky Pierre seems largely at the mercy of his situation, and barely able to keep afloat. Pierre becomes at once a figure of sympathy and a sort of sad clown. His directors are often cruel, but they have a depth of connection to and feeling for Pierre that is at once profound and unsentimental.

Lucky Pierre, along with *A Night at the Movies*, takes on the idea of movies as our new unexamined myths and sets out to playfully question all we leave unexamined about the medium. Coover is not interested in tearing these new myths down so as to put something else monumental in their place: indeed, he is resistant to any order of reified or unquestioned belief. Rather he wants to keep possibility and play alive.

This gleeful but serious dismantling of accepted stories is something Coover does with every genre. In *Gerald's Party*, he takes on the detective novel. After a body is discovered at a wild party, a detective shows up, but doesn't act like one would expect a detective to act (he seems to be trying to solve the crime almost by divination). The situation quickly becomes at once nightmarish and funny. Part of the enjoyment of the novel comes from both knowing how novels of this genre are supposed to work (i.e. detectives show up and solve crimes) and seeing how this novel resists that. But *Gerald's Party* also functions increasingly as a novel of erotic pursuit as well as a philosophical novel. In the complexity of this interaction of different sets of generic codes, Coover manages to create a collision of genres that locates us in a liminal space between them, where we can observe how genres function instead of simply consuming them. In *Noir*, Coover refines his critique of detective fiction to explore the situations and stereotypes of noir fiction and film through the misadventures of a sometimes bumbling character named Philip Noir, who moves from one generic cliché to another in a way that at once employs them and explodes them.

Ghost Town resumes the investigation of the Western Coover began in his play *The Kid* (1972) and his story "The Shootout at Gentry's Junction." Stylistically it has a passing resemblance to Cormac McCarthy's *Border Trilogy* (1992, 1994, 1998), but unlike McCarthy's work, it moves quickly into parody, critique, and comedy. Like *Briar Rose*, it takes the tropes and characters of a particular genre, the Western, and examines them closely, scrutinizes them, and takes them apart. A down-and-out wanderer identified as the "kid" comes into town, becomes unexpectedly the sheriff, and finds his affections torn between a bawdy barroom chanteuse and a prim schoolmarm – who eventually turn out to have more in common than it initially appears. As he moves through unfamiliar situations he has to grope to find what's expected of him. Like much of Coover's fiction, *Ghost Town* portrays its universe as a hostile and darkly comic place in which individuals are thrown into roles and torn out of them unexpectedly. Whatever role he plays, the kid remains bewildered and struggling to take control. If fiction is a kind of game, it is a game in which all the characters are potential pawns.

Coover's *Huck Out West* cross-pollinates a critique of the Western with a reworking of the sometimes controversial *The Adventures of Huckleberry Finn* (1884). This is not the first post-Twain novel to use Huck Finn as a character, nor even the first novel to reimagine Huck into the West – there is, for instance, Greg Matthews's *The Further Adventures of Huckleberry Finn* (1983) which finds Huck and Jim in the 1849 California gold rush (and indeed Twain's own novel ends with Huck intending to flee west to Indian territory). Coover does a remarkable job of ventriloquizing both Huck's voice and the complicated mix of irony, humor, and satire in Twain's novel, and of deploying these for his own more contemporary purposes. Though now grown up, Huck remains largely an innocent, providing a sometimes unintentionally savvy running commentary on the violence and racism of the West. Tom, meanwhile, has adapted to become a kind of con artist who cares very little for human life or for anyone else but himself: a kind of quintessential version of everything that's wrong with America. The novel's critique is bidirectional, using Huck's perspective to critique the Western and by extension America (the Western being the most American of genres) while simultaneously expanding on the inherent psychopathology present in Twain's Tom Sawyer.

Whatever Happened to Gloomy Gus of the Chicago Bears? (1987) is an exploration of an alternate history that also takes our Americanism fully to task. It returns to the main character of *The Public Burning*, Richard Nixon (renamed Gloomy Gus), reincarnating him as a pro-football player instead of a politician, and presenting him as someone who is essentially robotic in his understanding of the game (and of life). Gus is the ultimate American product, a constructed and artificial person, someone without personality. The narrator of the book, a radical Jewish artist named Meyer, worries that Gus might not be a weird anomaly, that he might be "you know, a man ahead of his time. . ." (1987, p. 145). In our mediatized days of politicians as media surfaces with no inner core, this unfortunately seems likely.

Coover's 1200-page-long *The Brunist Day of Wrath* is a sequel to his first novel, *The Origin of the Brunists* (1966). In *Origin*, a mine disaster kills nearly a hundred men from the town of West Condon, leaving just one survivor, Giovanni Bruno, who exits the mine speaking prophecy (unless it's brain damage). The novel explores the effect of the disaster on the town and the conflict between those who see Bruno as a prophet and the traditional religious and secular leaders who don't, with newspaper owner Justin Miller caught in the middle. The novel is expansive, dealing in remarkable depth with the lives of more than two dozen characters. The narration is third person but successively focalized through each person, and through free indirect discourse we get ample opportunity to examine the workings of each mind and understand what myths it lives by.

Though published forty-seven years later, *The Brunist Day of Wrath* takes place five years after the events in *Origin*, when the Brunists return to West Condon anticipating the apocalypse. The mine has closed, the town is struggling, and townspeople are still licking their wounds from the mine disaster and from earlier conflict with the Brunists, all of which end up being a perfect recipe for conflict and violence. Next to *Origin*, this is Coover's most realistic novel (though definitely on the far edge of realism), and also the most plot driven. Indeed, despite its 1200 pages, it is a rollicking and fast-paced read. Despite taking place in the past, it reads like a detailed genealogy of what has led to what is wrong with our American present.

If the majority of Coover's fictions choose to explore and challenge particular myths, whether they be genres we find solace in or the fairy tales that we think should explain life to us but are outdated and no longer do, the two Brunist novels end up depicting the parameters of lives in thrall to different sets of outdated myths. When he is not busy taking apart genre, Coover is an incisive critic of American life, and certainly the liveliest and bawdiest postmodern writer still living today.

SEE ALSO: Hypertext Fiction and Network Narratives; Minimalism and Maximalism; The New Experimentalism/The Contemporary Avant-Garde

REFERENCES

Coover, Robert. (1987). *Whatever Happened to Gloomy Gus of the Chicago Bears?* New York: Simon & Schuster.
Coover, Robert. (2000). The Public Burning log 1966–77. *Critique* 42 (1): 84–114.
Gado, Frank. (1973). Robert Coover. In: *First Person: Conversations on Writers and Writing* (ed. Frank Gado), 142–159. Schenectady, NY: Union College Press.
Wolff, Geoffrey. (1977). An American epic. *New Times* (August 19, 1977): 49–57.

FURTHER READING

Conte, Joseph. (2002). *Design and Debris: A Chaotics of Postmodern American Fiction*. Fayetteville: University of Alabama Press.
Evenson, Brian. (2003). *Understanding Robert Coover*. Columbia: University of South Carolina Press.
Maltby, Paul. (1991). *Dissident Postmodernists: Barthelme, Coover, Pynchon*. Philadephia: University of Pennsylvania Press.
McCaffery, Larry. (1982). *The Metafictional Muse: The Works of Robert Coover, Donald Barthelme and William H. Gass*. Pittsburgh: University of Pittsburgh Press.

Vanderhaeghe, Stephane. (ed.) (2012). Robert Coover Festschrift. Special issue of *The Review of Contemporary Fiction* 32 (1).

The Culture Wars

JEFFREY J. WILLIAMS
Carnegie Mellon University, USA

THE CONSERVATIVE ATTACK

In 1991, in his syndicated column, George Will pronounced that Lynne Cheney, the chairperson of the National Endowment for the Humanities (NEH) at the time, had a more important job than her husband, Dick Cheney, then US Secretary of Defense. In her job with the NEH, overseeing the awarding of grants to arts and humanities scholars and organizations, Will dubbed her the "secretary of domestic defense" (Will 1991). Given that the NEH budget that year was about $170 million, whereas the military budget was $358 billion, or more than 2000 times as much, we might think Will's comparison was merely a rhetorical flourish. However, Will, probably the leading conservative pundit of the era, was serious, and he provides a glimpse of the culture wars of that time.

The culture wars had flared up during the 1980s, enjoined by a rising movement of conservatives who charged that American society had lost its way. The root of the problem, in their view, was a decline of cultural and moral values, rather than economic or other political issues. In particular, they indicted university faculty, especially those in the humanities, who subscribed to postmodernist theory. The conservatives held that Western civilization had attained the apex of human achievement, and its major works in literature, philosophy, and art expressed exemplary values, which undergirded American society and culture. In contrast, a good number of contemporary scholars and critics held a more relativist view, finding our values not timeless or universal but an expression of the biases of their society and culture. The conservatives took particular umbrage at feminism and multiculturalism, which criticized canonical works of Western literature, art, and history for their sometimes sexist, racist, or politically-oppressive views.

In one sense, the culture wars evoked the familiar battle between "the ancients and the moderns," or between the value of tradition versus that of the new. The conservatives elevated tradition and held that the ancients impart unsurpassed, timeless truths so we should revere them, whereas the progressives looked with a more critical eye on tradition and assumed a more enlightened modern position. For instance, a conservative might revere the "Founding Fathers" of the United States as exemplary figures, whereas a progressive might see them as deeply flawed figures, who held slaves and restricted the right to vote only to men, and only to those with property, so the early republic was not truly a democracy.

In another sense, however, the culture wars were unique and specific to their moment, part of the shift in American politics during the "Age of Reagan," as the historian Sean Wilentz (2008) has defined the period from the late 1970s through the 2000s. The period from the 1930s through the 1970s saw the adoption of progressive policies of the New Deal under Franklin Delano Roosevelt, for instance inaugurating social welfare programs like social security payments to older people, and programs like Medicaid during the John F. Kennedy and Lyndon B. Johnson presidencies in the 1960s. That political orientation is usually summarized as liberalism, which aims to redress inequities through the redistribution of social resources and the expansion of civil rights. The period from the late 1970s, marked by the election of Ronald Reagan in 1980, aimed instead to reduce social welfare programs and policies like affirmative action. While it began under Republican administrations, Wilentz notes that the trend continued through subsequent administrations, like that of Democrat Bill Clinton, who curtailed welfare in the mid-1990s.

The general orientation of the Age of Reagan has come to be called neoliberalism, which moves away from social redistribution as a remedy and assumes the justice of the capitalist market, which it holds to be more effective than state-based or other collective remedies. The emphasis shifts from social equality to individual freedom, freedom construed as choice in a market, and thus liability in a market, so inequality is one's individual risk rather than a social injustice to be corrected. The culture wars paralleled this political and economic turn to neoliberalism. In some ways, progressives saw expanding the canon to include more women and people of color as social remediation, whereas conservatives saw it as a kind of welfare to undeserving, inferior works.

While they aimed for very different ends, conservatives and progressives agreed about the centrality of culture to society. Moreover, they saw higher education as a major location of social and cultural struggle. That is one of the distinctive features of the culture wars, as culture is sometimes thought to be ornamental and the university an "ivory tower" set apart from ordinary affairs. However, higher education took a more prominent social and cultural position as it expanded through the twentieth century. In simple demographic terms, it morphed from a peripheral to a predominant institution, with only about 3% of Americans attending in 1900, 30% in 1950, and 70% in 2000. In turn, beginning in the 1980s, conservatives targeted a new contingent, not the unionist Left or the socialist Left, but "the academic Left," and much of the battle was fought not over social or economic policies but "cultural politics." The turn to cultural politics represented a departure from conventional politics, from the class-based struggles that took center stage during the 1930s, spurred by the Great Depression, through the 1960s, to the identity politics that emerged in the 1960s and 1970s, with the advent of the women's and civil rights movements.

Lynne Cheney had a PhD in Victorian literature, with a dissertation on the British writer Matthew Arnold, who had declared that culture, defined in his famous phrase as "the best that is known and thought," would stave off anarchy, so Cheney was a fitting defender of canonical literature and the value of Western culture. Moreover, she held an influential position in conservative politics in tandem with Dick Cheney, who had served in Republican administrations since the 1960s, notably as a staff person in Richard Nixon's presidential administration. In her tenure as chair of the NEH (1986–1993), she issued several reports, such as *Humanities in America* (1988) and *Tyrannical Machines: A Report on Educational Practices Gone Wrong and Our Best Hopes for Setting Them Right* (1990), and one of her first acts was to order the removal of the Endowment's name on a museum exhibit that was critical of Western culture.

Another key player in the culture wars William Bennett, Cheney's predecessor as chair of the NEH (1981–1985). A one-time philosophy professor, Bennett became a major conservative commentator and served in several influential political positions, including Secretary of Education (1985–1988). In 1984, during the early years of the Reagan presidency, Bennett had issued one of the first salvos of the culture wars, *To Reclaim a Legacy: A Report on the Humanities in Higher Education*, raising the alarm about the changes in the humanities and advocating the centrality of traditional classics and their values. Rather than the problem being, say, the values of contemporary business culture that placed priority on profitability rather than morality, Bennett bemoaned the relativistic tenor of postmodern thinking, which he saw as the primary cause of the decline.

Led by those efforts, the period from the late 1980s through the early 1990s saw a spate of speeches, op-eds, books, and reports decrying the state of American culture in a similar vein. Perhaps the most notable book was Allan Bloom's *The Closing of the American Mind* (1987), an unexpected bestseller that indicted many aspects of contemporary American culture, from lax attitudes toward relationships and sex to art, literature, and music. One of Bloom's main culprits was rock 'n' roll, although the book also focuses on higher education. For Bloom, the 1960s represented not a high point of freedom and exploration, as some see it, but the decay of the "soul" of American society. Bloom's book, however opinionated, was in the tradition of American jeremiads, upbraiding the spiritual condition of the country.

The Closing of the American Mind was followed by more sensationalist accounts of the delusion of faculty and their presumed influence on students. Much of the subsequent conservative campaign was funded and otherwise supported by right-wing think tanks and other organizations, as Ellen Messer-Davidow documents in "Manufacturing the Attack on Liberalized Higher Education" (1993). One lightning rod, funded by several conservative groups, was the bestseller, *Illiberal Education: The Politics of Race and Sex on Campus* (1991) by Dinesh D'Souza. It assembled a handful of anecdotes to claim that universities had been overtaken by "political correctness," with the cultural Left enforcing speech codes, for instance saying "Native Americans" rather than "Indians," that constrained debate. Another well-known attack was Roger Kimball's *Tenured Radicals: How Politics Has Corrupted Our Higher Education* (1990), which postulated that the real problem was the migration of 1960s radicals into academic positions, bringing their extreme ideas with them, even though surveys found that faculty, particularly aging faculty, have moderate or liberal views, not radical ones. As the Cold War was ending, the conservatives' alarm morphed from communists infiltrating American politics to feminist and multicultural faculty infiltrating higher education.

Most of the conservative attack appeared in mainstream venues, whereas the progressive response was largely confined to academic ones. One notable corrective was John K. Wilson's *The Myth of Political Correctness* (1995), which debunked portraits of campuses overrun by radicals, but it did not impede the flow of attacks. Much of the progressive response was over the canon, how it might be revised, what should be retained, and how it reproduced biases. Perhaps the strongest voice from academe was Gerald Graff's, in articles and his crossover book *Beyond the Culture Wars: How Teaching the Conflicts Can Revitalize American Education* (1992). Graff propounded the idea that, rather than ignoring attacks, faculty should utilize the debate as a way to make pedagogy more relevant. Graff also pointed out that, despite anecdotes of academics throwing out classics like Shakespeare and replacing them with contemporary works like Alice Walker's *The Color Purple* (1982), Shakespeare was still taught extensively. In one chapter of his book, Graff adduces that about eighty students read (or at least are assigned) Shakespeare to each student who reads *The Color Purple*.

While the culture wars have not disappeared (now more familiar in the distinction of red and blue states), the quarrels of the 1980s and 1990s seem distant. Since then, the humanities have effectively been marginalized, disparaged as useless and materially shrunken in the decline of majors, faculty positions, and viable careers. At one time a humanities degree was considered good preparation for a future career, whereas now it is considered a luxury or waste, and it is commonly assumed that one should attain a practical degree in a directly marketable field. In many aspects, higher education has become a training ground for business rather than for a broader cultural ideal or social mission. One irony is that, while conservatives complain about the devaluation of humanities classics, conservative politics puts priority on business, which dismisses the humanities as unnecessary and emphasizes practical job-training. That is an inner contradiction of the conservative view: the turn toward neoliberal politics and economic policies that conservatives espouse has led to the diminishment of humanistic culture and values that they decry.

FICTION AND THE CULTURE WARS

The culture wars created a lot of smoke and heat, but what actually had changed in literature and literary studies? How had the canon changed? And how did the culture wars bear on fiction? The most prominent development related to the culture wars was the evolution of the canon to include a wider range of authors, in particular adding women and people of color. Alongside that, contemporary fiction saw the influx of multicultural writers into the mainstream. On a narrower scale, one direct result of the culture wars was a wave of fiction explicitly foregrounding the quarrels. Another, more ambient development was the establishment of literary theory as a major mode in literary study, influencing how we talk about literature.

The Revision of the Canon and Multiculturalism

The 1980s and 1990s saw a revision of the canon, adding works particularly by women and people of color that had previously been excluded. Beginning in the 1970s, feminist criticism, such as Ellen Moers' *Literary Women: The Great Writers* (1976) and Nina Baym's *Women's Fiction: A Guide to Novels By and About Women in America, 1820–1870* (1978), showed that there existed a significant tradition of literature by women. The moment also saw the building of an African American tradition, in works such as Barbara Christian's *Black Women Novelists: The Development of a Tradition* (1980) and Bernard W. Bell's *The Contemporary African American Novel: Its Folk Roots and Modern Literary Branches* (1987).

This critical impetus prompted the revision of the curriculum, adding rediscovered and reassessed texts, such as Zora Neale Hurston's forgotten novel, *Their Eyes Were Watching God* (1937). That revision is especially apparent in anthologies. Standard textbooks such as the *Norton Anthology of American Literature* (1st ed. 1979; 9th ed. 2017) were often criticized during the 1980s for failing to represent women and people of color. In turn, subsequent editions included more diverse texts, such as Gilman's *The Yellow Wallpaper* (1892) or selections by Hurston. Norton also inaugurated new volumes such as the *Norton Anthology of Women's Literature* (1985) and the *Norton Anthology of African American Literature* (1996). Alongside those, probably the most prominent project exemplifying the revision of the canon was the *Heath Anthology of American Literature* (1st ed. 1989; 7th ed. 2013), edited by Paul Lauter. It included standard works by Hawthorne, Poe, Hemingway, and the like, but put them alongside a wide selection of literature by many others, starting with a section of Native American origin stories. It presented an Aleut love song next to a Columbus letter, and classic poems by Anne Bradstreet followed by the Mohican, Samson Occom's "Narrative of my Life" and Olaudah Equiano's *Narrative* (1789) of his time in slavery.

Thus conservatives were correct to observe that the canon was changing, promoting a greater multicultural range. However, that represented less a destruction of tradition than an expansion of it. Students might still read Nathaniel Hawthorne – and also Toni Morrison. The process was in fact an ordinary one in the morphology of canons and curricula. Contrary to cries of crisis, Morris Dickstein reasoned in 1991 that, "Far from an immutable canon, which is what the conservatives describe, or a manipulated canon, as the radicals see it, we've had an endlessly changing canon of protean works constantly reinterpreted in the light of contemporary ideas and new writing" (1991, p. 208). For instance, the Romantic poets received relatively little scholarly attention during the early twentieth century, in part because modernists disdained their expressive orientation and scholars tended to earlier literary periods. However, the Romantics gained more scholarly attention in the 1960s and 1970s, as critics found Romanticism to offer rich literary work. The canon has always been subject to revision, with works added and dropped, as different generations have reinterpreted and revalued them.

Conjoined with the revision of the canon, the 1980s and 1990s saw a rising wave of fiction from diverse ethnic and racial groups in the United States. The revision of the canon was a retrospective move, changing the historical construal of literature, whereas this was prospective, adding new tributaries to the contemporary mainstream. For instance, works such as Amy Tan's *Joy Luck Club* (1989) signaled the emergence of Asian American fiction into the mainstream, and works such as Sandra Cisneros's *House on Mango Street* (1984) announced Chicanx and Latinx American fiction. These works tended to foreground the multicultural composition of ethnicity, as characters took their identity from the negotiation between family origin and contemporary

American experience, and between generations in those groups. As I argue in "Generation Jones and Contemporary American Fiction," this wave of fiction follows a shift in the demography of the United States (2016, pp. 110–112). In the period from 1900 through around 1970, most immigration was from Europe, notably from Eastern Europe, which found its way into fiction. Such fiction tended to depict ethnic cohorts, often settling in New York, for instance in Bernard Malamud's *The Assistant* (1957). However, as a result of policies such as the Immigration and Nationality Act of 1965 and subsequent amendments, by the 1980s the United States saw many more immigrants from Asia, Latin America, and Africa. Whereas 80% of immigrants were from Europe in 1950, 80% were from Asia and Latin America in 2000. As a case in point, in 1950 there were only about 50,000 foreign-born residents from China and India in the United States, whereas by 2000 there were 2,000,000 (which does not include their US-born children).

That shift in the ethnic and cultural composition of the United States inevitably inflected fiction, yielding a new generation of authors who aimed to represent the multicultural condition of the contemporary United States. It also created audiences who wanted to read about their own culture, or who wished to find out about other cultures. This suggests that there is probably a generational dimension to the culture wars: someone born in the first half of the twentieth century came of age with particular expectations of what culture was – they assumed tradition to be European – whereas those who came of age at the end of the twentieth century experienced a palpably different sense of culture, assuming it to encompass voices from Asia and the Global South. Thus conservatives were correct to note threats to the centrality of European culture, but they assumed that culture was timeless and unchanging rather than a historical process.

The Culture Wars Novel

The reshaping of the canon and establishment of multiculturalism were broad circumstances that influenced literature and literary study and incited argument in the culture wars. The culture wars also spurred a small but distinctive band of fiction, emerging around 1990 and cresting around 2000, that explicitly depicted the wars. The fiction was typically set on campuses and for the most part constituted a subgenre of the academic novel, the action driven by battles over feminism, multiculturalism, and political correctness (Williams 2012, pp. 569–571; see also Butcher's [2017] comprehensive account). Academic fiction typically leans to comedy of manners, but this fiction often took a more serious cast, drawing on controversies taken from the news. Entries by well-known authors include Ishmael Reed's *Japanese by Spring* (1993), John L'Heureux's *The Handmaid of Desire* (1996), Francine Prose's *Blue Angel* (2000), Saul Bellow's *Ravelstein* (2000), and Philip Roth's *The Human Stain* (2000). The culture wars also spurred a major literary play, David Mamet's *Oleanna* (1992), as well as a number of films, such as *PCU* (1994) and John Singleton's *Higher Learning* (1995).

A few earlier academic novels deal with politics, such as Mary McCarthy's *The Groves of Academe* (1952), which turns on anti-communism during the 1950s, but most academic fiction deals with intramural dramas inside university departments, removed from the larger world. The culture wars novel brings the political debates of the time, inspired by Bennett, Cheney, and so on, to the university. In fact, rather than an ivory tower, they depict the university as a main forum of US cultural politics, one that merits battling over. They typically feature debates among feminist, postmodernist, and other faculty with traditionalists, and often turn on sexual or racial politics.

Oleanna is the most noteworthy early literary portrait of political correctness and the culture wars. It turns on a male professor's tenure bid, a common start of the plot in academic fiction, but rather than a series of comic obstacles portrays a troubling series of exchanges with a female student over politically correct terms. In Mamet's characteristic manner, it culminates in violence and makes the culture wars university a scene of real battle with serious stakes. *Blue Angel* similarly deals with fraught sexual politics between a male professor and female student, albeit with a more comic cast. In contrast, *Japanese by Spring* dwells on race, featuring the ridiculous Professor Puttbutt, an African American who schemes to sustain his job. In an antic, postmodern style, it parodies some of the controversies about affirmative action, the neutralization of post-1960s Black power, and assimilation in academe. In a different vein, *Ravelstein* paints a fictionalized portrait of Allan Bloom himself, who was a close friend of Saul Bellow's, and dramatizes Bloom's fame and wealth from *Closing of the American Mind*.

Probably the most prominent culture wars novel is *The Human Stain*. It centers on a literature professor, Coleman Silk, who loses his job because he mentioned the word "spooks" in class when commenting on two absent students, suggesting they were like spies, which is one colloquial meaning of "spook." However, the students were African American, an alternative and distasteful meaning of spook, and Silk is charged with using a racial epithet, which drives the action. The irony is that Silk has African American heritage, though he passes as white. Ending with Silk's death, *Human Stain* emphasizes the serious stakes of the culture wars in late-twentieth century US culture. In fact, the novel completes a trilogy that Roth embarked on to portray postwar American culture that includes *American Pastoral* (1997), which centers on the radicalization of the 1960s (the protagonist's daughter is a radical involved in a bombing), and *I Married a Communist* (1998), which depicts the Red Scare of the 1950s. That Roth concluded the trilogy with a scene from higher education and the cultural politics therein suggests the central role they had come to hold in the late-twentieth century United States.

The culture wars novel subsided in the early 2000s, after 9/11 and the 2008 financial crisis, which prompted the "9/11 novel" and "the financial novel," among other kinds of fiction. The focus of cultural politics often turned, particularly after the 2008 crisis and the Occupy movement, toward the extreme wealth and inequality of contemporary society. If the academic novel adopted a new preoccupation, since 2000 it has dwelled instead on the precarious college teacher, no longer in a secure, tenure-stream position but in an adjunct or other casual position, for instance in James Hynes *A Lecturer's Tale* (2001) and Alex Kudera's *Fight for Your Long Day* (2011). The primary tension spurring the action has migrated from political correctness and multiculturalism to the precarious nature of academic employment in the new century – a condition that had developed from neoliberal policies and coalesced particularly after the financial crisis. The humanities no longer seem to take central place in politics, and their practitioners are down and out.

The Rise of Literary Theory

Another development that merits note is the rise of literary theory. Emerging in the 1970s and an established part of academic practice by the 1980s, it also constituted an important circumstance of the culture wars. Conservatives were correct to observe the ascendance of theory and its emphasis on the relative nature of values and truths. Contemporary theory generally holds that values are constructed by different cultures at particular points in time, rather than universal and timeless. That philosophical understanding went hand-in-hand with the revision of the canon. Still, that basic insight did not necessarily undermine the traditional canon. Indeed, leading theorists such as Paul de Man, Fredric Jameson, and Eve Sedgwick often focused on classic literary texts. To say that values are relative does not mean that there can be no judgment of value, just that it is not absolute.

Moreover, theory became a literary pursuit in its own right. As the American philosopher Richard Rorty (1982) phrased it, theory was a "kind of writing," which draws from earlier genres such as criticism, intellectual history, and philosophy, as well as literature itself. One example he used was the work of the French philosopher Jacques Derrida, who often dealt with literature and embraced literary ways of proceeding. In response, some traditionalists charged that theory was illegitimately trying to usurp the place of literature, rather than remaining a subordinate service. Others complained of its technical language and difficult concepts. These complaints led one eminent critic to charge that theory was "destroying literary studies." However, in *Cultural Capital: The Problem of Literary Canon Formation* (1993) John Guillory argued that these debates were misdirected. Looking in a sociological framework, he posited that theory reflected a shift in higher education toward graduate education and research. Theory formed a new canon particularly for graduate training, as students learned a more technical, professional way to consider literary works, different from the literary canon that formed the general undergraduate curriculum.

Guillory also asserted that the canon debates missed the target in concentrating on the works taught. Instead, he made the case that we should pay attention to the system of schooling, whereby select groups have access to high quality education through primary and secondary years, and an even more select few attend elite higher education. In other words, Guillory points out the classed nature of higher education, and finds the culture wars largely deflected from the real political issue, which is the unequal distribution of wealth and the consequent unequal distribution of cultural capital and resources like education. To include works in a university curriculum did not necessarily change the status of the ethnic groups represented, as that curriculum would only be available to those who had access to higher education. Guillory's suggestion is that the key is to change the structure of higher education, not merely the works taught.

By 2020, multiculturalism had become established as a normal part of literary study, but it appears that literary theory no longer has as central a position. It still inflects the terms and concepts of much scholarship, but since around 2010 the main current of scholarship has arguably moved to more descriptive methods over theoretical speculation, most notably in the widespread adoption of quantitative approaches under the auspices of the digital humanities. Those approaches cultivate a technical knowledge and more neutral political position, so tend to avoid the sore points of the culture wars. Alongside that turn, the humanities have shrunken in terms of majors, courses, hires, and prestige. In a manner of speaking, the conservative army might have lost the battle against multiculturalism but won the war for higher education by cutting off the supply lines.

The culture wars finally offer a lesson about culture and politics. Just as they demonstrated that culture plays a fundamental role in society, the reverse is also true: the material conditions of society influence and shape culture, fiction, and criticism. Sometimes it seems as if literature and culture are independent and apart from politics, but the culture wars showed that culture is entwined with politics and the social arrangements we have.

SEE ALSO: Literature of the Americas; Morrison, Toni; Reed, Ishmael; Roth, Philip; Tan, Amy; Walker, Alice

REFERENCES

Butcher, Ian. (2017). "Reading the Culture Wars in the New Academic Novel, 1984 Present." Dissertation, Duquesne University.
Dickstein, Morris. (1991). The crisis in our culture. Special issue of Partisan Review: The Changing Culture of the University 2: 203–209.
Rorty, Richard. (1982). Philosophy as a kind of writing. In: *Consequences of Pragmatism (Essays: 1972–1980)*, 90–109. Minneapolis: University of Minnesota Press.
Will, George. (1991). Literary politics. *Newsweek* (April 21, 1991). https://www.newsweek.com/literary-politics-202084 (accessed September 22, 2021).
Wilentz, Sean. (2008). *The Age of Reagan: A History, 1974–2008*. New York: Harper.
Williams, Jeffrey J. (2012). The rise of the academic novel. American Literary History 24 (3): 561–589.
Williams, Jeffrey J. (2016). Generation Jones and contemporary American fiction. American Literary History 28 (1): 94–122.

FURTHER READING

Berube, Michael. (1984). *Public Access: Literary Theory and American Cultural Politics*. New York: Verso.
Fiorina, Morris. (2005). *Culture War? The Myth of a Polarized America*. New York: Pearson.
Lauter, Paul. (1991). *Canons and Contexts*. New York: Oxford University Press.
Newfield, Christopher and Strickland, Ronald. (eds.) (1995). *After Political Correctness: The Humanities and Society in the 1990s*. Boulder, CO: Westview.
Williams, Jeffrey J. (ed.) (1995). *PC Wars: Politics and Theory in the Academy*. New York: Routledge.

Cunningham, Michael

DAVID CHASE
Raritan Valley Community College, USA

Michael Cunningham (b. November 6, 1952) is the author of seven novels and a short story collection of reimagined fairy tales. His fiction is distinguished by lengthy, evocative, and imagery-rich sentences and keen insight into the complex psychology of characters whose daily existences pale in comparison to the more remarkable lives they imagine for themselves. Cunningham has enjoyed his greatest popular and critical success with *The Hours* (1999), which won the Pulitzer Prize for Fiction and the PEN/Faulkner Award. Other notable works include *A Home at the End of the* World (1990), *Flesh and Blood* (1995), and *Specimen Days* (2005). His writings tend to emphasize character and situation over plot, and common themes include the centrality of family, the need for reinvented communities and connections, the dangers of both adhering to and resisting cultural scripts, and the resilience of the human spirit in the face of disappointment, change, and loss.

Cunningham was born in Cincinnati, Ohio, but moved to Pasadena, California at age 10 after briefly living in Germany. He earned a BA in English literature from Stanford University in 1975 and an MFA from the Iowa Writers' Workshop in 1980. During his tenure in the latter program, Cunningham published short stories in *Atlantic Monthly* and *Paris Review* and, upon graduation, began work on his first novel, *Golden States*, which was not published until 1984. Cunningham spent the next several years struggling to create and publish fiction before accepting a position writing public relations articles for the Carnegie Corporation in New York City. While employed for this philanthropic organization, Cunningham began work on a novel, a chapter of which was published as "The White Angel" in the July 25, 1988, issue of *The New Yorker* and included in the 1989 edition of *The Best American Short Stories*. By the time that the resulting book (*A Home at the End of the World*) was published in 1990, critics were beginning to regard Cunningham as one of the finest and most important emerging voices in late twentieth-century American fiction.

Cunningham now regards *Golden States* (1984) as a "not good enough" book that he rushed to complete in order to have "finished a novel by the time he was thirty" (Canning 2003, p. 91). To be sure, there is nothing particularly remarkable about Cunningham's first published effort, which follows 12-year-old David Stark as he develops a sharper awareness of himself – as an individual, as someone with sexual desire for men, and as a protector of his family – through a series of painful experiences, including rejection by his best friend, a foolhardy road trip to "rescue" his half-sister from a problematic romantic relationship, and an eventual coming to terms with his mother's rapidly declining health. All the same, the novel can be seen to introduce several key themes, tensions, and concerns that recur throughout Cunningham's body of work. Chief among these are the constriction of selfhood that women experience through their participation in the institutions of love and marriage; the absent, violent, and/or emotionally distant father figure; the central importance of the family, both as a formative site of belonging and as a place from which to escape in one's assertion of individual identity; the apprehension of mainstream culture through a queer lens; and a profound awareness of the benefits and detriments of human progress.

If concerns about the passing of time can be said to have fueled the rushed composition of *Golden States*, an almost unbearable awareness of human mortality serves as a different kind of impetus for *A Home at the End of the World* (1990). The novel's apocalyptically inflected title is fitting, not only because the bulk of the narrative takes place the last years of the second millennium, as three individuals (a gay man, a bisexual man, and a bisexual woman) struggle to invent an alternative family structure for themselves, but also because the world-changing manifestation of HIV/AIDS serves as the largely unspoken but urgent backdrop to these characters' efforts to transform our culture's existing structures of belonging. This imperative to queer the structures of kinship so as to provide a relevant and workable support system for characters whose "aching and chaotic love" for one another "refuses to focus in the conventional way" (1990, p. 255) persists as a central concern in several of Cunningham's subsequent novels, yet *A Home at the End of the World* comprises his most discerning look at the pressing need for the postnuclear family in an increasingly complex and uncertain world.

Through the first-person perspectives of Clare, Bobby, Jonathan, and Alice (Jonathan's mother, who also strives to transcend the social roles that existing structures of belonging have assigned to her), Cunningham makes a compelling case for the home's unique positioning at "the middle of everything" (1990, p. 33), which is to say, as an exceptionally rich vantage point from which to reevaluate one's participation in the world. At the same time, his narrators can be seen to confront an apparently unbridgeable "gap between what [they] can imagine and what [they] in fact create" (p. 336); that is, they recognize how our actual human accomplishments always prove inadequate when compared to the more expansive visions and desires that inspire us. This disparity between aspiration and achievement is a prominent concern in all of Cunningham's fiction, transforming seemingly inconsequential everyday tasks (e.g. baking a cake, preparing a meal, throwing a party) into moments of potential crisis in which life can be seen to be "cracking open" (p. 34). As do all of Cunningham's characters to varying degrees, Clare, Bobby, Jonathan, and Alice struggle daily to be "merely present" (p. 342) in the world and to let the moments of their lives "inhabit" them completely (p. 343). Their perpetual challenge is to exist purely and contentedly in the transitory and elusive space between what has been, what is, and what might be.

Cunningham extends his consideration of these aforementioned themes in the sweeping family saga that comprises *Flesh and Blood*. The novel chronicles 100 years in the lives of the Stassos family, which is headed by the ambitious Greek immigrant Constantine and his Italian American wife Mary. Constantine – who is prone to violent outbursts, and who distances himself emotionally from his sensitive and effeminate son Billy while engaging in an inappropriately affectionate (if not outright incestuous) relationship with his daughter Susan – enjoys enormous financial success by building inexpensive tract homes in which "corners [are] invisibly cut" while their exteriors are "dressed . . . up with picket fences and false dormers" (1995, p. 33). By presenting Constantine's dubiously achieved public accomplishments in sharp contrast to the private sorrows of the remaining Stassos family members – Mary secretly shoplifts and anxiously frets over her tasks as wife and mother; Susan marries for security rather than love and, in an ironic twist, discovers that her sterile husband cannot provide the children she desires; Billy becomes a teacher rather than an architect to spite and anger his father; and Zoe attempts nonconformity but winds up merely directionless and stalled – Cunningham mounts a blistering critique of several key promises of the American Dream, most notably, its assurances of domestic bliss and of upward mobility for future generations. If *A Home at the End of the World* suggests that the idea and practice of family needs updating and queer invigoration for the twenty-first century and beyond, *Flesh and Blood* can be seen to call for the outright rejection of an outdated structure of belonging that engenders dysfunctionality and self-destruction rather than promotes certainty and a sense of fulfilment among its participants.

Cunningham's plea for a sweeping renovation of our culture's most foundational relational structures becomes especially insistent in the final sections of *Flesh and Blood*, in which Constantine's self-propulsion through life via a toxic combination of ambition, hyper-masculine assertiveness, and hubris results not only in his own downfall but in the death of his grandson. From all outward appearances, Susan's bright and attractive son Ben seems to embody the promises of the American Dream, especially when compared to Zoe's Jamal, whose "drifting, unconcerned beauty" (1995, p. 429) portends a future that is as aimless as his mother's. However, the 14-year-old Ben actually feels like he is drowning under the weight of his grandfather's outsized expectations for him and of his own growing awareness of his homosexuality, which he regards as wholly incompatible with the life script that he has been assigned. When a boating accident offers him the choice of waiting to be rescued with his grandfather and "swimming away" (p. 438) from his life and "the wrongness of his being" (p. 439), Ben decides upon self-obliteration. Although Ben's suicide, Constantine's resulting estrangement from his children, and Zoe's soon-to-follow HIV-related death might be seen as tragic endings for the Stassos family, Cunningham instead figures these events as the foundation of its rebirth into a more forgiving and malleable kinship structure, one that is sustainable in the face of an increasingly complex and uncertain future. The final pages of the novel trace the movements of the characters up until the year 2035, showing that their less-than-perfect lives nevertheless will be characterized by unexpected joys and pleasures: Susan will remarry for love and bear another child (who she names Zoe) at age 49; Mary will learn to defy the most constricting aspects of her social positioning (i.e. as wife, mother, and woman) through her unlikely alliance with a drag queen named Cassandra; Will and his partner Harry will co-parent Jamal into a happy adulthood and stay together, albeit "not always easily" (p. 461) for the remainder of their lives; and Jamal will start his own family whose story, it is implied, will largely diverge from the more ruinous path of his Stassos predecessors.

Whereas *Flesh and Blood* represents Cunningham's attempt to examine the central significance of the family through the epic lens of a 100-year span of time, *The Hours* compresses his consideration and critique of this institution into the scope of a single day (or, more accurately, of single days in the lives of three different women, one in the late twentieth century, one in 1923, and one in 1949). Much like *Mrs. Dalloway*, the 1925 Virginia Woolf novel that inspires and connects the three stories, Cunningham makes a compelling case for the ways in which life – in all its immensity, complexity, and contradiction – is situated within what might seem on the surface as the most trivial moments of our private daily lives. Despite its impressively mounted triptych structure, nothing much happens in the novel: Clarissa Vaughn shops for flowers for a party she has planned; Virginia Woolf struggles to balance her writing with her duties to household and husband; and Laura Brown feels painfully divided between her socially determined obligations (e.g. to bake the perfect cake for her husband's birthday, to delight in her pregnancy, and to care for and console her young son Richard) and her personal desires (e.g. to stay in bed to read *Mrs. Dalloway*, to be alone for an hour in a hotel room, and to steal a moment of intimacy with her neighbor Kitty).

Yet in much the same way that Woolf works to "dig out beautiful caves behind [her] characters," as she writes in a diary entry that serves as an epigraph to the novel, Cunningham aims to show how we navigate circuitous pathways through vast expanses of time – past experiences of joy and loss, current attempts to inhabit the moment meaningfully, and a mixture of fear and hope in the face of an uncertain future – in each moment of our lives. Because the present does not exist in any real sense of the word, "the hours" of even the most mundane day become charged with significance, weight, and the potential for catastrophe.

And indeed, tragedy does occur, seemingly out of nowhere on an early summer day in New York that is characterized "by an assertion of new life so determined it is almost comic" (1998, p. 9). Richard Brown, a celebrated writer and Clarissa Vaughn's former lover, flings himself out of his fifth story window mere hours before he is scheduled to receive a major literary prize. Although his mind and body have been ravaged by HIV-related illnesses, Richard's suicide is prompted by a moment of lucidity in which he realizes his failure as a writer to "create something alive and shocking enough that it could stand beside a morning in somebody's life" (p. 199). Here again emerges Cunningham's frequent concern regarding the unsettling discrepancy between the perfect visions that impel human activity and the always deficient realizations of these plans, a theme that is echoed in Laura Brown's embarrassment over a cake that is "less than she'd hoped it would be" (p. 99) and in Virginia Woolf's concerns that her writing is "only mildly competent" (p. 35). As in previous works, this painful awareness of human imperfection informs and intensifies the moments of otherwise seemingly inconsequential days, so that within each instant of the characters' lives is contained the possibility of transcendent joy or seemingly insurmountable sadness. Thus, although Laura is shown to be comforted and saved through her sudden awareness that "it is possible to stop living" whenever she chooses – which is to say, if and when she wishes to be done with "everything she's created" – Richard and Virginia Woolf, whose 1941 suicide opens the novel, instead arrive at moments in their days where they imagine themselves so thoroughly "defeated by the impossible demands of life and art" (p. 152) that death becomes a necessary (albeit paradoxical) act of self-preservation.

Upon its publication, *The Hours* met with resounding approval among critics and enjoyed considerable popular success, the latter of which was surprising given the novel's unconventional structure and its stylistic affinities to Woolf in general and *Mrs. Dalloway* in particular. For *Specimen Days*, Cunningham would once again take inspiration from a literary predecessor – Walt Whitman this time around – but the resulting work (which was marketed as a novel but is instead three novellas connected via characters and theme) would bear little resemblance to the book that preceded it. Whereas *The Hours* pauses over single moments that are extracted from a seventy-five year span of recent human history, the highly ambitious and experimental *Specimen Days* spans approximately three centuries (beginning in the mid- to late nineteenth century and ending some 150 years in the future) to deliver a profound meditation on the endurance of "the soul" – which, according to Cunningham vis-à-vis Whitman, is "something that resides within [all human beings] that's bigger and more insistent than the flesh itself" (Johnson 2006, p. 8) – through some of the most harrowing moments of destruction, change, and rebirth in the history of our nation's industrialization. In order to make the case for the connectedness of all human "specimen[s]" – that is, for the way in which we are all "part of an unknowable immensity and are, in our individual incarnations, just passing through" (Cunningham 2006, p. xx) – Cunningham offers divergent permutations of three central characters throughout the course of its genre-specific novella sections, the first of which is a Victorian ghost story, the second a post-9/11 noir thriller, and the third a post-apocalyptic science fiction tale. The transcendentalist poetry of Whitman manifests itself in surprising ways within each of the three narratives, often "burst[ing] . . . involuntarily" (Johnson 2006, p. 8) from characters whose humanity has been compromised by the forces of industrialization.

Although some readers of Cunningham's previous novels were confounded by his radical shift in style and content for *Specimen Days*, the author's recurring thematic concerns can be seen to inform and propel his explorations into these previously unconsidered generic forms. Cunningham once again considers the world from a variety of outsider perspectives and thereby mounts an impassioned queer critique of the alienating effects of technological advancement and the potentially destructive consequences of societal progression. As in earlier works, Cunningham forces us to confront the unbridgeable gap between the perfect visions that inspire us and our always lacking accomplishments, whether in the form of the emotionally sensitive boy who attempts to resist the brutalization of factory work (Lucas in "In the Machine"), the police officer who struggles to compensate for the loss of her son by wresting a brainwashed child from the grip of a terrorist cult (Cat in "The Children's Crusade"), or the simulo who longs to feel actual human emotion rather than its mere approximation (Simon in "Like Beauty"). Linking these characters and their fundamental predicaments together is the figure of Whitman himself, who appears in some form or another in each of the three narratives, and whose vast and powerful desires lead him – both in his poetry and in his life – more often to estrangement than to fulfillment.

Cunningham's most recent novels continue to be beautifully written and impressively structured, but largely revisit rather than deepen or expand upon the psychological complexities and philosophical meditations of his earlier works. *By Nightfall* (2010) tells the story of Peter and Rebecca, whose fairly settled domestic existence within the art world of New York City is disrupted by the arrival of Rebecca's younger, gay, recovering drug addict brother. *The Snow Queen* (2014) contrasts the lives of two brothers, Tyler and Barrett, who struggle in different ways to achieve hope and transcendence as Tyler's slowly dying fiancée Beth forces them to confront issues of human mortality and loss. In *A Wild Swan and Other Tales* (2015), Cunningham resituates several classic fairy tales into everyday human settings, thereby instilling these stories with fresh meaning and contemporary relevance.

SEE ALSO: Fiction and Affect; Illness and Disability Narratives; Queer and LGBT Fiction; Realism after Poststructuralism; Suburban Narratives; Urban Fiction

REFERENCES

Canning, Richard. (2003). *Hear Us Out: Conversations with Gay Novelists*. New York: Columbia University Press.
Cunningham, Michael. (1984). *Golden States*. New York: Crown.
Cunningham, Michael. (1990). *A Home at the End of the World*. New York: Farrar, Straus and Giroux.
Cunningham, Michael. (1995). *Flesh and Blood*. New York: Farrar, Straus and Giroux.
Cunningham, Michael. (1998). *The Hours*. New York: Farrar, Straus and Giroux.
Cunningham, Michael. (2005). *Specimen Days*. New York: Farrar, Straus and Giroux.
Cunningham, Michael. (ed.) (2006) *Laws for Creation*. New York: Picador.
Johnson, Sarah Anne. (2006). *The Very Telling: Conversations with American Writers*. Lebanon, NH: University Press of New England.

FURTHER READING

Attebery, Brian. (2018). Reinventing masculinity in fairy tales by men. *Marvels & Tales* 32 (2): 314–337.
Haffey, Kate. (2010). Exquisite moments and the temporality of the kiss in *Mrs. Dalloway* and *The Hours*. *Narrative* 18 (2): 137–162.
Hughes, Marry Joe. (2004). Michael Cunningham's *The Hours* and postmodern artistic representation. *Critique: Studies in Contemporary Fiction* 45 (4): 349–361.
Schopp, Andrew. (2009). Beautiful results: Whitman's democratic vision and the evolution of America in Michael Cunningham's *Specimen Days*. In: *Heroes of Film, Comics and American Culture: Essays on Real and Fictional Defenders of Home* (ed. Lisa Detora), 40–60. Jefferson, NC: McFarland.
Woodhouse, Reed. (1998). *Unlimited Embrace: A Canon of Gay Fiction, 1945–1995*. Amherst: University of Massachusetts Press.

Cyberpunk

HUGH CHARLES O'CONNELL
University of Massachusetts Boston, USA

INTRODUCTION: CYBERPUNK'S ORIGINS AND CRITICAL HISTORY

The conventional wisdom on cyberpunk has slowly begun to reverse itself. Once seen as a short-lived science fictional "sturm and drang" (or tempest in a teapot, depending on one's critical allegiances) that quickly burned out, today its critical exhaustion is being rethought. Many critics now assert that rather than a death, its seeming disappearance is instead a symptom of its transformation from the niche subgenre corner of the larger genre of science fiction (sf) to the dominant cultural form of postmodernity. As such, cyberpunk is seen as the key mediation of a late techno-capitalism driven by finance, the algorithm, and digitalization.

Before the common appellation of cyberpunk took hold, its practitioners were simply identified as the Movement, a group comprised of John Shirley, Lewis Shiner, William Gibson, Bruce Sterling, and Rudy Rucker, all US born, and all notably white men (indeed, early cyberpunk's filiation with a white, heteronormative, masculine ideology has long been a source of critique). Gathered around fanzines like Sterling's *Cheap Truth*, initially their most notable defining trait was a brash oppositional stance pitched against the established figures of sf, most memorably captured by Gibson's "The Gernsback Continuum" (1981) with its dismissal of Golden Age sf's "architecture of broken dreams" promulgated by a "logic that knew nothing of pollution, the finite bounds of fossil fuel, or foreign wars it was possible to lose" (p. 34). As Graham J. Murphy points out, the Movement's early literary output was far more varied than what we might think of as cyberpunk today, encompassing narratives of planetary colonization, psychedelic induced time-travel, robot evolution, future history, and near future geopolitical thrillers (2019, p. 521) before ossifying into a determinant style focused on the emerging digital sphere and its attendant cyborg subjects.

The term cyberpunk first appeared as the title of a 1983 Bruce Bethke story. The portmanteau, comprising the cyber of cybernetics and punk from the subcultural underground, was meant, in Bethke's own words, "to invent a new term that grokked the juxtaposition of punk attitudes and high technology" (Bould 2005, p. 218). Despite being little remembered today, Bethke's story contains many of the hallmarks that would become prominently associated with the Movement*cum*-cyberpunk: a cast of young, irreverent hackers, a tech-meets-teenslang narration, and branded technology that reflects late capitalist market desiderata. However, it was only later when Gardner Dozois used the term in "SF in the Eighties" for the *Washington Post* in 1984 that cyberpunk became a widespread label.

If Dozois popularized the term, then the Sterling-edited *Mirrorshades: The Cyberpunk Anthology* (1986) codified it and "effectively completed the rebranding of the Movement into the easily marketable *cyberpunk*" (Murphy 2019, p. 522). Sterling's "Preface" acted as a critical manifesto, laying bare cyberpunk's aesthetic forefathers (notably gendered) by linking it to trends in hard sf (due to cyberpunk's infatuation with technology) and the New Wave (due to its kicking against the old guard and its political-aesthetic position as an avant-garde).

Alongside determining cyberpunk's patrilinear genesis, Sterling also laid out its identifying tropes: "The theme of body invasion: prosthetic limbs, implanted circuitry, cosmetic surgery, genetic alteration. The even more powerful theme of mind invasion: brain-computer interfaces, artificial intelligence, neurochemistry – techniques radically redefining – the nature of humanity, the nature of the self" (1986, p. xiii). These themes were conveyed via what Sterling referred to as a "crammed prose" of "rapid, dizzying bursts of novel information, sensory overload that submerges the reader in the literary equivalent of the hard-rock 'wall of sound'" (pp. xiv–xv). The reference to the "hard rock 'wall of sound'" was then transported over to the signal cyberpunk anti-hero: the hacker. It was a monumental piece of fictional re-creation, as the conservative coder was reconstituted as the streetwise hacker decked out in their ubiquitous signifier of 1980s cool: mirrored sunglasses. "Mirrored sunglasses," Sterling attests, serve as "the Movement's totem [...] as a kind of literary badge" (p. xi). They repel depth and multiply surface, accentuating an unidentifiable, but dangerous subject: "By hiding the eyes, mirrorshades prevent the forces of normalcy from realizing that one is crazed and possibly dangerous. They are the symbol of the sunstaring visionary, the biker, the rocker, the policeman, and similar outlaws" (p. xi).

Perhaps most significantly for its avant-gardism, Sterling tied cyberpunk to the tempestuous techno-cultural-political upheavals that propelled the 1980s, a decade that after the recession-induced doldrums of the 1970s, was intensively tied to a market-centered concept of the new. And this sense of the new was in turn combined with instantaneity and immediacy via the twinning of emergent computerized communications technologies with the post-Fordist temporality of the global market over the older reifications of the Fordist clock-hour. The seemingly random, stochastic chaos of the stock floor, rendered post-temporal and post-spatial in the images of cyberspace, fully replaced the orderly, Taylorized concept of commodity production as the dominant rhythm and tempo of everyday life.

In this sense, Sterling's opening gambit in the "Preface" that cyberpunk is the "definitive product" of the "Eighties milieu" (1986, p. x) takes on wider, more ambivalent ramifications than perhaps intended. For Sterling, wrapped up in the chaotic fervor of the new, cyberpunk allows for radical, revolutionary conjoinings: "An un-holy alliance of the technical world and the world of organized dissent – the underground world of pop culture, visionary fluidity, and street-level anarchy" (p. xii). Yet, from our own historical remove, we can begin to notice how this specifically 1980s literary artform simultaneously mirrors the escalating 1980s neoliberal orthodoxy. That is, the preface's descriptions of street culture/tech imbrication can just as easily be seen as reflecting the neoliberal ideology of decentralization, casualization, and flexibility: "the technical revolution reshaping our society is based not in hierarchy but in decentralization, not in rigidity but in fluidity" (p. xii). As such, the resulting rebellion begins to look indistinguishable from the celebratory rhetoric of Schumpeter-style disruption: "The Eighties are an era of reassessment, of integration, of hybridized influences, of old notions shaken loose and reinterpreted with a new sophistication, a broader perspective" (p. xiv). And we should note how Sterling's notion of cyberpunks' "wide-ranging, global point of view" seems to anticipate Kenichi Ohmae's notion of global capitalism's *Borderless World*: "The tools of global integration – the satellite media net, the multinational corporation – fascinate the cyberpunks and figure constantly in their work. Cyberpunk has little patience with borders" (Sterling 1986, p. xiv).

Consequently, cyberpunk's rebelliousness often reads just as easily as disruption, as a desire to infiltrate the system not by beating it but by understanding it better than those already at the top. This resulted in an image of rebellion that was deemed oddly apolitical, lacking any real targets. As Carlen Lavigne notes, "feminism, ecology, peace, sexual liberation, and civil rights" are stunningly absent not only from Sterling's "Preface," but from Movement-era cyberpunk in general (2013, p. 21). In this sense, Sterling's rather curious alignment of "policeman" with "outlaw" becomes all too telling.

This conflation of rebellion with neoliberal disruption did not go unnoticed. As Nicola Nixon points out, Movement-era cyberpunk's "good guys are the anarchic, individualistic, and entrepreneurial American heroes [. . ., while] Reaganite cowboyism, the quintessence of the maverick reactionary" provides cyberpunk's "central heroic iconography" (1992, pp. 224–235). Similarly, Roger Luckhurst argues that cyberpunk's emergence was linked to "the prominence of the SF megatext in the fantasy life of the American New Right" (2005, p. 202) and Terence Whalen notes, "Arising out of the general context of Reagan's America, cyberpunk celebrates a 'hardness' that is both stylistic and ideological. Practitioners like Bruce Sterling and William Gibson accordingly disparage a progressive political agenda even though their dystopian narratives offer ample cause for resisting a capitalist future" (1992, p. 75).

Therefore, reading Sterling's "Preface" today, it is striking how absent any discussion of the neoliberal agenda is from its account of the 1980s. Indeed, it lacks any mention of the rising conservativism of the 1980s: rampant individualism and greed, the rise of the Washington Consensus and dismantling of the welfare state, the imbrication of governance with the aims of the moral majority and Christian Conservativism and the resulting criminal neglect of the AIDs crisis. Even the ascendency of the multinational corporation – the zaibutsu that figures in so much cyberpunk – is barely mentioned. Instead it presents a largely value-free, depoliticized, and objectivized sense of global integration that reads just as easily as a pro-globalization treatise as it does a manifesto for a new sf avant-garde.

Yet, it was initially cyberpunk's marketing of its outsider aesthetics, rather than the critique of its inability to live up to them, that hastened the initial perception of its demise. The mixture of marketing and style soon proved to be too apt and successful for a group that, despite whatever desires for critical recognition, thought of itself as a counterculture. As such, the postmortems on cyberpunk have been many. The cyberpunks themselves led the charge, as many early adopters turned apostate. Lewis Shiner lamented that cyberpunk was actively swallowed by a crass commercial culture industry that turned it into a "formula" and reduced it to a set of ready-made and now wholly inert tropes to be spewed out *ad nauseum* by a slew of second and third-rate "sci-fiberpunk" imitators. Blaming success for dulling their edge, Sterling later noted that the incorporation of cyberpunk writers into the mainstream eliminated their "bohemian underground" stance, since "[r]espectability does not merely beckon; it actively envelops."

Much of the later critical assessment followed suit. Echoing and extending Shiner's and Sterling's arguments, Veronica Hollinger – one of cyberpunk's most insightful interlocutors – argued that, as "a response to postmodern reality," cyberpunk "could only go so far before self-destructing under the weight of its own deconstructive activities (not to mention its appropriation by more conventional and more commercial writers)" (1991, p. 217). Yet for other critics, cyberpunk perhaps never fully launched. Claire Sponsler, for example, argues that cyberpunk was already "dead on arrival – powerless to sustain the sociopolitical radicalism and representational innovation its champions claim for it" (1995, p. 47).

Delving further into the internal structural limits of cyberpunk's own aesthetic contradictions, Neil Easterbrook argues that, rather than a critical waning or commercial recuperation, cyberpunk was always complicit with the hegemonic forces it loudly objected to. Turning to the quintessential cyberpunk text, *Neuromancer* (1984), he writes that "Here technology is the product *and* medium of the ideological transformation of society, where the ideology secures the privileged position of those already in power" (1992, p. 379). Consequently, "unlike modern and ancient precedents, the imagery in *Neuromancer* simply reinforces corporate power and the technology structuring it" (p. 380). Rather than iconoclastic rebels on the margins, taking down the system, we end up with erstwhile mavericks looking to disrupt (in the current neoliberal parlance) and thus kick their way into the very system they supposedly reject.

While this presentation of cyberpunk's early development may seem to suggest that Movement-era cyberpunk was necessarily conservative, such is not my intention (indeed Gibson and Sterling would hardly recognize themselves as figures of the Right). Instead, I wish to highlight how cyberpunk mediated its particular age – the advent of neoliberal global capitalism – and how cyberpunk's production, both for good and for ill, unfolds within these structural limits. This is captured by Jameson's argument that cyberpunk functions as the exemplar form of "dirty realism" in postmodernity (1996, p. 150), shifting the emphasis from the content and production of the subject to its structural mediations.

Reflecting this more measured approach, recent critics focus less on cyberpunk's purported death or political inefficacy than on its cultural and critical intractability. Works like *Beyond Cyberpunk* (2010) and *The Routledge Companion to Cyberpunk Culture* (2020) argue that cyberpunk needs to be understood as a multifaceted and persistent cultural formation, one that exposes both the dialectically intertwined desires and limits of the present by affording complex expressions of the hegemonic state of techno-neoliberalism. Thus, rather than a critical or commercial hollowing out, it is precisely because of cyberpunk's "transformations into a more generalized set of practices" (Murphy and Vint 2010, p. xiii) that it remains relevant. What we see now is not only the pale imitators (which surely do exist), but the general diffusion of cyberpunk as an indispensable mode of translating our precarious, global, financialized present; its persistence serves as a reminder of neoliberalism's stranglehold on the present rather than just mere accommodation. To borrow from Bethke, what cyberpunk "grokked" was the historical, political, cultural zeitgeist. In short, rather than having disappeared in a hyperbolic, glittering, and dematerialized rhapsody of its own making, cyberpunk has been dispersed and absorbed into the mainstream not only of sf or literary culture more generally, but indeed everyday life.

KEY TEXTS

Despite the variety of early Movement-era cyberpunk, it is almost exclusively today remembered (and this is reflected by those texts still actively in print) for its engagement with the burgeoning techno-communications industry of the Internet and the financialized information economy. This was chiefly the domain of cyberpunk's first star, William Gibson, whose early fiction set most of the standards for what would become concretized as cyberpunk. Indeed, Gibson coined the term "cyberspace" for the abstracted spatial domain of the Internet's virtual, digital sphere and popularized the streetwise hacker as the principal cyberpunk protagonist.

Gibson's foremost brilliance was in the creation of new metaphors that traversed the digital and the material "meatspace" realms. In order to do so, he drew on overtly familiar noir and heist plots to better accentuate the newly emerging spaces of digital finance and hacking. This can be seen in one of Gibson's first descriptions of hacking in "Burning Chrome" (1982), a precursor to *Neuromancer* and the Sprawl trilogy: "Bobby was a cracksman, a burglar, casing mankind's extended electronic nervous system, rustling data and credit in the crowded matrix, monochrome nonspace where the only stars are dense concentrations of information, and high above it all burn corporate galaxies and the cold spiral arms of military systems" (2010, p. 549). The financialized realm of immaterial ones and zeros appears not only as an extension of ourselves – our "electronic nervous system" – but as a replacement for the material altogether as the electronic bytes of ones and zeros replace nature itself and provide the hacker's new financialized lodestar.

Throughout this early work, Gibson adduces a new disembodied phenomenological register to capture the inhuman experience of digital-informational immediacy that outstrips somatic experience. In a well-known passage, *Neuromancer* provides a gloss on the normative understanding of cyberspace: "A consensual hallucination experienced daily by billions of legitimate operators, in every nation [. . .]. A graphic representation of data abstracted from the banks of every computer in the human system. Unthinkable complexity. Lines of light ranged in the nonspace of the mind, clusters and constellations of data. Like city light, receding...." (1984, p. 51). It follows this with the phenomenological experience of the post-Cartesian hacker as disembodied financial hustler:

> And in the bloodlit dark behind his eyes, silver phosphenes boiling in from the edge of space, hypnagogic images jerking past like film compiled from random frames. Symbols, figures, faces, a blurred, fragmented mandala of visual information. [...] And flowed, flowered for him, fluid non origami trick, the unfolding of his distanceless home, his country, transparent 3D chessboard extending to infinity. Inner eye opening to the stepped scarlet pyramid of the Eastern Seaboard Fission Authority burning beyond the green cubes of Mitsubishi Bank of America [...]. And somewhere he was laughing, in a white-painted loft, distant fingers caressing the deck, tears of release streaking his face.
>
> (1984, p. 52)

If Gibson's powerful images once described a world only just coming into being, today the imbrication of the digital and material is largely taken for granted. Rather than offering transcendence or creating new hybrid subjects, I have argued elsewhere for the contemporary need to re-examine this relationship under the guise of capitalist realism and real subsumption, an approach that attenuates the radical or latent possibilities of earlier readings by focusing on the ways that such interfaces are less re-subjectifying than de-subjectifying, as they constantly invade the body, turning it into a further site of capitalist accumulation (O'Connell 2020). As such, the reduction to the body through the many prostheses designed to make one perform better in the neoliberal market and the fixation on the digital abstractions of a financialized cyberspace serve as what David Harvey terms "spatial fixes" in the Global North as manufacturing and production flee to the Global South. Gibson's fiction thus reveals less the subject and more the systems of contemporary global capitalism in which the body becomes another financialized node in the Net. This seemingly paradoxical movement outward, tracing the Net's colonization of "meatspace" rather than humans jacking into the Net, is the focus of Sterling's *Islands in the Net* (1988).

While *Schismatrix* (1985), a future history recounting the conflicts between traditionalist humans and the posthuman Shapers and Mechanists, is usually taken as Sterling's paramount cyberpunk novel, the later near future thriller, *Islands in the Net*, is more interesting in relation to the dominant cyberpunk themes of globalization and the emergent information economy. Rather than the transcendental sloughing off of the body and escape into cyberspace, its grounded techno-thriller plotting serves as a realist geopolitical supplement to Gibson's more feverishly analogical work. It focuses on the more prosaic issues of capitalist surveillance and the way that a "seamless Net" (1989, p. 17) that is both transformative and mundane expands into and reshapes the world-system. We might think of it as mundane cyberpunk exemplified by its descriptions of the difference between telex and fax technology for the global transmission of data.

Islands' protagonist, Laura Webster, works for the postcapitalist corporation Rizome, and the plot follows her efforts to make peace between the global corporate denizens of the Net and the holdout nations of the "data pirates." Echoing his earlier "Preface," Sterling's *Islands* pitches a global "democratic capitalism" that that is flexible, ludic, and develops through rhizomatic structures. Rizome's, and by equivalent the Net's, democratic capitalism surpasses the sclerotic traditional multinationals by fostering "gut-level personal trust" (1989, p. 46). Consequently, at the socio-philosophical level, it privileges a new techno-mediated, globally dispersed "gemeinschaft" of personal relationships over and against the stolid, centralized, nationalist "gesellschaft" of traditional bureaucratic corporations.

In the novel, the Net is represented by this new breed of postnational democratic corporations that are set against the nationalist (and often postcolonial) "data pirates." Reflecting its own historical moment, these data pirates exist outside the globally enveloping sphere of the Net and create bootleg films and software to sell in Global South markets. However, *Islands* also anticipates our current regimes of personal data expropriation that Shoshana Zuboff terms "surveillance capital" (2019); the data pirates collect and maintain vast info stockpiles on individuals that debt collectors, insurers, and others want access to for developing marketing strategies, risk management profiles, and other forms of tracking in service of rentier and financialized capitalism. At its most basic level, then, the plot revolves around the central problem of capitalist geopolitics: how to control global economic development, now dependent on data and information. As such, the desire is to turn rigid, outmoded "crypto-marxist" (1989, p. 57) data pirates into "right-thinking postindustrialists" (p. 41).

Islands rethinks traditional cyberpunk's dichotomy – the privileging of the data-space of dematerialized financial capital over the degraded "meatspace" of material reality – through a purely material, geopolitical spatialization. Mapping the new spatial relationships of its post-Cold War global era as divided between the nations of the Net (Global North) and the data pirates (Global South), the novel shuttles between conflicts that take its protagonist from the United States to Grenada and Singapore, but it is really a generalized "Africa" (represented principally by Mali and South Africa, now reimagined as Azania) that functions as the irreducible limit to the democratic postindustrial capitalist order of the Net. We are continually reminded of the abject horror that is "Africa." At one point, Laura thinks:

"She had never realized the scale of African disaster. It was continental, planetary. [. . .] Atomic bombardment could scarcely have made it worse. It would only make more of it" (1989, p. 341). The geopolitical sign of "Africa" thus functions under the logic of what Kodwo Eshun refers to as the futures industry: a site of perpetual dystopia that forever needs to be managed through Western investment and developmental schemes (2003, p. 290).

This futures industry plotting takes the form of the "Iradin Cultural Revolution" led by Colonel Jonathan Gresham, a Californian-turned-postindustrial Lawrence of Arabia who leads the charge for a new Africa. Gresham's *"Lawrence Doctrine and Postindustrial Insurgency,"* asserts that the problems of African socioeconomic underdevelopment stem from the introduction of global aid, which is seen as responsible for allowing "native" African traditions to ossify. Thus, Greshem seeks to reinstitute older nomadic ways as the solution. Ignoring the realities of (neo)imperialism, this basically amounts to a Western-enforced plan to forcefully deindustrialize Africa so that it can resemble the problematic ideal of the unspoiled land that underwrites colonial ideologies of "primitivism." Within the novel, this is presented as a rightwing confrontation with the postindustrial, democratic capitalism of Rizome and the Net. It is a schizophrenic take on Africa that can only come from a US-centric point of view: the purity of the desert and deprivation versus American consumerism and plenty. Rizome's response is to take hold of the supply line that Gresham needs while also commodifying and recuperating his revolutionary image as a form of neo-containment.

Ultimately – and perhaps this is the primary aesthetic problem of early cyberpunk – it is difficult to tell whether this is purely playful cynicism or a serious political statement from within the "revolutionary," "ideologically correct" (Sterling 1986, p. xvi) standpoint of first-generation cyberpunk.

Either way, at best the novel leaves us with an artificial binary of Net globalism versus deindustrial primitivism, or, in effect, the twinned images of neoimperialism as constituted through combined and uneven development.

It is perhaps Neal Stephenson's *Snow Crash* (1992) (the author and text most notably attached to cyberpunk's US third wave) that seemingly squares these two tendencies: presenting a banal, but fully immersive, social, jacked-in virtual reality alongside material global geopolitics. Built around the misadventures of Hiro Protagonist, a pizza-delivering freelance hacker samurai, the novel develops a plot in which human minds can be hacked much like computers by drawing analogs between coding, Babel mythology, and Sumerian history. This plotting, nevertheless, serves as a veneer for a critique of economic globalization as a weakening of the productive imagination hampering the United States, as too much money is poured into advertising and marketing and the building up of the "trademark firmament" (2017, p. 10).

However, that the novel might be unaware of its virulent racism (Butler 2000, p. 53; Jones 1999, p. 149) or its neocapitalist "fascism" (Jones 1999, p. 151) may be a sign that rather than resolving the political and aesthetic aporias of Gibson's and Sterling's defining cyberpunk works, it merely compounds them under a pseudo-critical smugness that indelibly mars its otherwise much needed injection of humor to the cyberpunk genre. If Gibson's and Sterling's novels remain profoundly interesting, despite their flaws, for the way that they limn the ideological faultlines of a fully emergent postmodernity figured by a truly global capitalist world-system and the ramping up of dematerialized financial circulation, then *Snow Crash* fails to match their perspicacity. It lacks their initial – even if misplaced – excitement at engaging with this newly emergent reality and their – again, no matter how misplaced – notion of countercultural zeal.

As Gwyneth Jones incisively notes, *Snow Crash*, as the "fantasy of a computer literate who finds no romance in contemplating the human/machine interface," lacks an animating curiosity about the issues it explores: "there's nothing weird about it" (2017, p. 151).

If much canonical cyberpunk is problematically predicated on a masculine aesthetics incapable of resolving its critique of neoliberal capitalism through its own celebration of neoliberalism's creative destruction, fixated on the penetration and containment of feminist spaces, or shortsighted in its rejection of the body and affect in favor of instrumental rationality, then many have turned to feminist cyberpunk for its critical negation of cyberpunk's worst ideological traits and the extension of its most promising horizons. As Lisa Yaszek has recently written, feminist cyberpunks confront the cynicism associated with the male authors "and replace it with an emphasis on creative self-expression, community, and sociopolitical change" (2020, p. 32). Such authors include Pat Cadigan, Nisi Shawl, Melissa Scott, Joanna Russ, and Misha, among others.

Pat Cadigan, the only woman published in *Mirrorshades*, established herself as a unique and slyly critical voice among the early cyberpunk authors, writing fiction that drew from the MTV and rock aesthetics so often associated with cyberpunk style. Although Karen Cadora argues that "Cadigan never fully engaged with feminist concerns" (1995, p. 358), Yaszek places her among the canon of feminist cyberpunk writers, arguing that "Cadigan casts women as resourceful heroines who oppose the exploitative practices of an inherently masculinist capitalism," adding that "as one of the first authors to posit that people would actually have to pay to access the fantastic new worlds of cyberspace, Cadigan was, in many ways, even more grittily dystopian than many of her male peers" (2020, p. 34). Her frequently reprinted short story, "Pretty Boy Crossover" (1986), stands among classic cyberpunk works as an intriguing counterpoint. Reading it alongside the early works of Gibson, particularly, it is striking for its opposition to cyberpunk's often uncritical take on digital transcendence. The story features the titular Pretty Boy, a standout club kid, who must decide if he wants to have his mind uploaded and crossover to the digital realm as a new digital star of eternal hip youthfulness for the owners of the club and infrastructure where his likeness would be stored and broadcast.

Bucking the usual cyberpunk trend towards either cynicism (having no choice) or uncritical celebration of digital transcendence, in the end, he rejects the offer. As he walks away, having second thoughts about blowing his big chance, he thinks: "Ultimately, it wouldn't make any difference to anyone. He smiles suddenly. Except *them*. As long as they don't have him, he makes a difference. As long as he has flesh to shake and flaunt and feel with, he makes a pretty goddamn big difference to *them*. [. . .] He's lightheaded with joy – he doesn't know what's going to happen. Neither do they" (1986, p. 50). If the meat is a prison for *Neuromancer*'s Case, then in "Pretty Boy Crossover" the body is the locus of opposition. Cadigan's novel *Synners* (1991), with its focus on how humanity is forced to "change for the machines," can likewise be seen as a critique of cyberpunk's penchant for digital transcendence. The protagonist's, Digital Mark's, desire for complete disembodiment unleashes a destructive virus that threatens to catastrophically upend the connected world. In both works, there is a defense of the embodied and a stringent critique of the means of production: who owns the infrastructure that houses the digital-being? How will this digital-being be put to work?

Nisi Shawl, one of the few women writers in Rucker's early cyberpunk anthology *Semiotext(e) SF* (1989), also probes the gendered and racialized uses of digital transcendence and related issues of infrastructure, control, and labor in "Deep End," originally published in *So Long Been Dreaming: Postcolonial Science Fiction and Fantasy* (2004). Here, the digital uploading of consciousness, unlike in "Pretty Boy Crossover," works both ways and underpins a "meta-slavery narrative" (Lavender III 2011, p. 54) of forced labor and planetary colonization. Prisoners' consciousnesses, largely drawn from nonwhite populations, are uploaded to a mainframe in an interstellar colonizing ship in order to be downloaded into bodies when the ship arrives at its destination. In a critical mediation of Western civilization's ongoing dependence on colonial bodies and slave labor, each uploaded consciousness will be downloaded into a white body to do the difficult work of terraforming and setting up the colonies. This performs a double gesture: ensuring that white consciousness will sidestep the arduous labor required to build civilization while also guaranteeing that white bodies will inherit the fruits of the slave-prisoners' labor. Within this short, complex story, Shawl also examines issues of gender (the planners will not let female consciousnesses download into male bodies and vice versa) and sexuality (exploring virtual, disembodied sex in nonbinary couplings). As Wendy Gay Pearson argues, such issues are foundational to cyberpunk and have been rewardingly explored by LGBTQ cyberpunk writers, most notably in Melissa Scott's *Trouble and Her Friends* (1994), which, as Pearson argues, "successfully destablilize[s] notions of gender identity even as [its] protagonists appear to embrace more conventionally gendered identities as lesbians" (2020, p. 303).

CONCLUSION

If critics were once quick to dismiss cyberpunk's staying power, then cyberpunk's cultural dissemination and even more so the events of the twenty-first century have conspired to continuously resurrect its particular narrative protocols and mediatory power. From twitterbots' influence on elections to Facebook's and Google's monetization of personal data as behavioral surplus value, our world increasingly resembles the one first outlined by a group of 1980s sf iconoclasts. Within US literature (not to mention popular film and television), cyberpunk's cultural significance continues: from the shlocky, third-rate nostalgic homage of Ernest Cline's *Ready Player One* (2011), to fascinating investigations into AI, predictive algorithmic machine-learning, and techno-cybernetic-governance in the recent compelling work of Annalee Newitz's *Autonomous* (2017), Malka Older's Centenal Cycle (*Infomocracy* [2016], *Null States* [2017], and *State Tectonics* [2018]), Cory Doctorow's *Down and Out in the Magic Kingdom* (2003), *Little Brother* (2008), *Homeland* (2013), and *Radicalized* (2019), and Gibson's *The Peripheral* (2014) and *Agency* (2020). To the extent that such cyberpunk technologies continue to invade the "meatspace" and outstrip human agency and capacity, let alone understanding, cyberpunk remains a necessary, if not necessarily revolutionary, mode of cognitive mapping.

SEE ALSO: Anders, Charlie Jane; Big Data; Burroughs, William; DeLillo, Don; Gibson, William; Globalization; Powers, Richard; Pynchon, Thomas; Stephenson, Neal; Vollmann, William T.

REFERENCES

Bould, Mark. (2005). Cyberpunk. In: *A Companion to Science Fiction* (ed. David Seed), 217–231. Malden, MA: Blackwell.
Butler, Andrew M. (2000). *Cyberpunk*. Harpenden, UK: Pocket Essentials.
Cadigan, Pat. (1986). Pretty boy crossover. *Asimov's Science Fiction Magazine* 19 (1): 39–50.
Cadora, Karen. (1995). Feminist cyberpunk. Science Fiction Studies 22 (3): 357–372.
Easterbrook, Neil. (1992). The arc of our destruction: reversal and erasure in cyberpunk. Science Fiction Studies 19 (3): 378–394.
Eshun, Kodwo. (2003). Further considerations on Afrofuturism. CR: The New Centennial Review 3 (2): 287–302.
Gibson, William. (1984). *Neuromancer*. New York: Ace Books.
Gibson, William. (2010). Burning chrome. In *The Wesleyan Anthology of Science Fiction* (ed. Arthur B. Evans, et al.), 547–565. Middletown, CT: Wesleyan University Press.
Hollinger, Veronica. (1991). Cybernetic deconstructions: cyberpunk and postmodernism. In: *Storming the Reality Studio: A Casebook of Cyberpunk and Postmodernist Fiction* (ed. Larry McCaffery), 203–218. Durham, NC: Duke University Press.
Jameson, Fredric. (1996). *The Seeds of Time*. New York: Columbia University Press.
Jones, Gwyneth. (1999). *Deconstructing the Starships: Science, Fiction and Reality*. Liverpool: Liverpool University Press.
Lavender III, Isiah. (2011). *Race in American Science Fiction*. Bloomington: Indiana University Press.
Lavigne, Carlen. (2013). *Cyberpunk Women: Feminism and Science Fiction*. Jefferson, NC: McFarland.
Luckhurst, Roger. (2005). *Science Fiction*. Cambridge: Polity.
Murphy, Graham J. (2019). Cyberpunk and post-cyberpunk. In: *The Cambridge History of Science Fiction* (ed. Gerry Canavan and Eric Carl Link), 519–536. Cambridge: Cambridge University Press.
Murphy, Graham J. and Vint, Sherryl. (2010). Introduction: the sea change(s) of cyberpunk. In: *Beyond Cyberpunk: New Critical Perspectives* (ed. Graham J. Murphy and Sherryl Vint), xi–xviii. New York: Routledge.
Nixon, Nicola. (1992). Cyberpunk: preparing the ground for revolution or keeping the boys satisfied? Science Fiction Studies 19 (2): 219–235.
O'Connell, Hugh C. (2020). Marxism. In: *The Routledge Companion to Cyberpunk Culture* (ed. Anna McFarlane, Graham J. Murphy, and Lars Schmeink), 282–290. New York: Routledge.
Pearson, Wendy Gay. (2020). Queer theory. In: *The Routledge Companion to Cyberpunk Culture* (ed.

Anna McFarlane, Graham J. Murphy, and Lars Schmeink), 300–307. New York: Routledge.

Sponsler, Claire. (1995). William Gibson and the death of cyberpunk. In: *Modes of the Fantastic: Selected Essays from the Twelfth International Conference on the Fantastic in the Arts* (ed. Robert A. Latham and Robert A. Collins), 47–55. Westport, CT: Greenwood Press.

Stephenson, Neal. (2017). *Snow Crash*. New York: Del Rey; 1st ed. 1992.

Sterling, Bruce. (1986). Preface. In: *Mirrorshades: The Cyberpunk Anthology* (ed. Bruce Sterling), ix–xvi. New York: Ace.

Sterling, Bruce. (1989). *Islands in the Net*. New York: Ace Books; 1st ed. 1988.

Whalen, Terence. (1992). The future of a commodity: notes toward a critique of cyberpunk and the information age. Science Fiction Studies 19 (1): 75–88.

Yaszek, Lisa. (2020). Feminist cyberpunk. In: *The Routledge Companion to Cyberpunk Culture* (ed. Anna McFarlane, Graham J. Murphy, and Lars Schmeink), 32–40. New York: Routledge.

Zuboff, Shoshana. (2019). *The Age of Surveillance Capitalism: The Fight for a Human Future at the New Frontier of Power*. New York: Public Affairs.

FURTHER READING

Bukatman, Scott. (1993). *Terminal Identity: The Virtual Subject in Postmodern Science Fiction*. Durham: Duke University Press.

Dery, Mark. (1996). *Escape Velocity: Cyberculture at the End of the Century*. New York: Grove.

Foster, Thomas. (2005). *The Souls of Cyberfolk: Posthumanism as Vernacular Theory*. Minneapolis: Minnesota University Press.

Murphy, Graham J. and Schmeink, Lars. (eds.) (2017). *Cyberpunk and Visual Culture*. New York: Routledge.

Wolmark, Jenny. (ed.) (2002). *Cybersexualities: A Reader in Feminist Theory, Cyborgs and Cyberspace*. Edinburgh: Edinburgh University Press.

D

Danielewski, Mark Z.

SARA TANDERUP LINKIS
Lund University, Sweden

Mark Z. Danielewski (b. 1966) is one of the central American figures within the field of experimental print fiction. His authorship is characterized by typographic experiments, unconventional page layout, and multilayered narratives, as already demonstrated in his debut novel, the best-selling *House of Leaves* (2000). His other major works include the novella *The Fifty Year Sword* (2005), the novel *Only Revolutions* (2006), the book series *The Familiar* (2015–2017), and the children's book *The Little Blue Kite* (2019), all of which combine different genres, media, and modes of storytelling. Thus, in all of these works, Danielewski experiments with use of colored text, page layout, and typography in order to explore how visual and textual modes of representation may be combined in order to produce signification in literary works.

Danielewski himself describes his experimental strategies as "signiconic" representation:

> Signiconic = sign + icon. Rather than engage those textual faculties of the mind remediating the pictorial or those visual faculties remediating language, the signiconic simultaneously engages both in order to lessen the significance of both and therefore achieve a third perception no longer dependent on sign and image for remediating a world in which the mind plays no part.
>
> (Danielewski 2015)

By combining verbal and visual modes of representation, Danielewski wants to move beyond the established boundaries between images and text, or sign and icon. His works are generally characterized by explicit reflections on modes of representation, mediation, and remediation. Accordingly, this entry will focus on Danielewski's use of multimodal and intermedial experiments, and on his works as reflections on how new and old media shape literature and literary culture.

Because of his experiments with the conventions and aesthetics of the printed book, Danielewski has often been presented as an author who celebrates the physical book and print culture in an age where literature, as well as life, becomes increasingly digitized. In an interview, he emphasizes the possibilities of the printed book, noting that,

> Books are remarkable constructions with enormous possibilities [. . .]. But somehow the analogue powers of these wonderful bundles of paper have been forgotten.

The Encyclopedia of Contemporary American Fiction 1980–2020, First Edition. Edited by Patrick O'Donnell, Stephen J. Burn, and Lesley Larkin.
© 2022 John Wiley & Sons Ltd. Published 2022 by John Wiley & Sons Ltd.

Somewhere along the way, all its possibilities were denied. I'd like to see that perception change. I'd like to see the book reintroduced for all it really is.

(Cottrell 2002)

Danielewski's authorship may well be seen as the result of this wish to reintroduce the printed book. Jessica Pressman and N. Katherine Hayles have read his works accordingly, relating them to a tendency in twenty-first-century literature to celebrate the "aesthetics of bookishness" (Pressman 2009). Danielewski's experiments with the aesthetics of print may be said to reflect the printed novel's reaction to the "colonizing incursions of new media" (Hayles 2007, p. 85) in the digital age. However, he is far from expressing any form of media nostalgia: rather than wanting to preserve the printed novel as it used to be, he seeks to reinvent it, using the possibilities that are implied by digital technologies. Thus, his works reflect how digital media and modes of production are transforming the aesthetics of print. Furthermore, he also enters into a dialogue with other, older media and modes of storytelling, such as film, television series, children's books, and even campfire stories.

Danielewski's debut novel *House of Leaves* first and foremost refers to, and incorporates the logics of, film. The best-selling horror novel about a house that is bigger on the inside than on the outside centers around the representation of this house through a documentary film, which is produced by the owner of the house. The novel refers to this film, adopts filmic narrative strategies, and focuses on visual modes of representation, as exemplified by the many visual and typographic experiments. However, the experiments with typography and page layout also draw attention to the textual surface of the work: to the work as a printed book. Thus, the titular "house of leaves" may also refer to the book itself as an object and a medium. Given that *House of Leaves* is a printed book, the documentary film, just like the house itself, is absent within the work, and even possibly nonexisting at the diegetic level. The film is described in detail by an old man, Zampanò, who claims to have seen it; yet he turns out to be blind. Zampanò's manuscript is delivered through a young tattooist, Johnny Truant, who adds his own notes to the manuscript, and his notes are, again, framed by the notes of some unidentified editors. The novel in this way exemplifies Danielewski's multilayered form of storytelling, which focuses on problems of representation and authenticity. Its absent core, the impossible, and possibly fictional house, leads Mark B.N. Hanson to describe the novel as a reflection on the logics of digital culture, where the boundaries between fact and fiction are dissolving and the idea(l) of authentic representation falls short (Hanson 2004).

Danielewski develops his visual and narrative experiments in his other works, which also continuously refer back to *House of Leaves* and to each other. The novella *The Whalestoe Letters* (2000) thus presents a further development, or complication, of the *House of Leaves* plot, since it presents an exchange of letters between the tattooist Johnny from *House of Leaves* and his mother – potentially destabilizing the reader's interpretation of the former novel.

Hereafter, in 2005, Danielewski published the novella *The Fifty Year Sword*, which is the result of his collaboration with the Dutch artist Peter van Sambeek. The novella, which experiments extensively with page layout and has no writing on the recto pages of the book, has been described as a ghost story for adults, and as a reflection on the campfire story as a mode of storytelling. It contains text in seven different colors, five of which indicate which of the five characters is speaking at the moment. Additionally, two other colors are present, one representing the voice of the author, the other a reference to Danielewski's other novel, *Only Revolutions*, once again reflecting Danielewski's process of cross-referencing between his works. In 2010, *The Fifty Year Sword* was turned into a theater performance at the REDCAT theater in Los Angeles, suggesting Danielewski's interest in developing his works across different media and modes of storytelling.

In his second novel, *Only Revolutions*, Danielewski further experiments with genres and media. The novel, which was a finalist for the 2006 National Book Award for Fiction, is presented as a literary road movie and consists of two different narratives, "Sam and Hailey" and "Hailey and Sam," about two young lovers who remain forever 16 while history progresses. The bicentered structure is echoed in the visual layout of the novel, focusing especially on the colors gold (Hailey) and green (Sam). The stories of, respectively, Hailey and Sam begin at opposite ends of the book and cross at the middle. This structure demands the reader to physically engage in the work and draw attention to the process of handling the book as an object: the publisher recommends that readers turn the book around 360 degrees every eight pages in order to follow the story.

The work also in other ways demands the readers' engagement. Apart from its unconventional structure, *Only Revolutions* is characterized by narrative and linguistic complexity and has often been compared to the works of James Joyce because of its use of stream-of-consciousness narration. The result is a work which demands that readers engage in processes of deciphering and interpreting – accordingly, both *Only Revolutions* and *House of Leaves* have been described as ergodic literature; that is, texts which demand readers to engage actively in interpreting the work, beyond the activity usually associated with reading. Thus, according to Espen Aarseth's definition, ergodic literature refers to texts where "nontrivial effort is required to allow the reader to traverse the text" (1997, p. 1). Specially in relation to Danielewski's works, it should be noted that these "nontrivial efforts" are also often collective: *House of Leaves*, *Only Revolutions*, and *The Familiar* are surrounded by very active and dedicated reader communities. These communities are to a large extent encouraged and facilitated by the author. Writing *Only Revolutions*, Danielewski directly engaged his readers in the production of the book through online discussion fora. He asked them to contribute with material, for example information about specific events in twentieth-century history, and this user-generated material was hereafter included in lists presented in the novel, making it a product of participatory culture (Hayles 2012).

In his most recent works, Danielewski further works with the medial as well as the social aspects of literary production and consumption, encouraging engagement and collective reading. While both *House of Leaves* and *Only Revolutions* may be said to imitate the logics of film and relate to specific genres of film, such as the documentary film and the road movie, the book series *The Familiar* specifically refers to, and remediates, the contemporary long-form television series. The series was originally announced to be presented in twenty-seven volumes, five of which have been published in 2015–2017. These five volumes together make up the series' first "season," suggesting how Danielewskiimitates the organization of television series in seasons and episodes. In early 2018 the series was paused by the publisher, Pantheon, due to declining sales, suggesting how the work, also in this sense, reflects the logics of television, since the project relied directly on the readers' engagement and sales in order to be allowed to continue.

The work was presented as a simple story about a little girl who saves a cat in a rainstorm: however, this story is complicated by the novel's complex serial and multistringed form: apart from the girl, Xanther, and her mother and stepfather, the novel follows six other characters, who are situated all over the world: in Los Angeles, Singapore, Mexico, and Texas. Their stories are seemingly not related to each other, and thus make up different plotlines in the novel. Notably, each character is connected to a specific typography, specific colors and page design. As in *House of Leaves* and *Only Revolutions*, Danielewski uses his signiconic mode of representation to present and distinguish between the different characters and their points of view. Thus, while *The Familiar* at many levels appears to imitate the logics, narrative structure, and visual mode of representation that characterize modern television series, it also explores a specifically bookish mode of representation, since its typographic experiments and visual layout draw attention to the aesthetics of print, just as its monumental size (each volume consists of 880 pages!) draws attention to the book as an object.

Apart from these features, the novel also includes text written in different languages, such as Chinese, Armenian, Hebrew, and the Singapore dialect Singlish, and even passages written in computer code. The result is a highly complex and "difficult" text, which qualifies as ergodic literature in the sense that it demands readers to engage actively in processes of deciphering and decoding. Readers have responded by collaborating with each other, for example via online forums and in Facebook groups, helping each other with translations or interpretation in ways which resemble the activities of television series fans. In the presentation of the book project, Danielewski himself directly presented *The Familiar* as an attempt to produce the kind of social engagement that surrounds television series, stating that "[l]iterature is capable of being a subject that people want to catch up on or discuss, whether at a coffee shop or a watercooler [. . .]. It can become an intrinsic part of their dialogue" (Bosman 2011). In another interview, he emphasizes how the work is first and foremost about "building familiarity" and connecting people, both within the novel and around it (Calvo 2016): in the novel, the characters' plotlines are gradually connected, and similarly, the novel connects the readers with each other. Danielewski relates this process of building familiarity to the novel's serial format and its multimodal and multilingual aspects, arguing that the work becomes easier to read as the series progresses because readers gradually become familiar with the unconventional aesthetics and foreign languages. After introducing his central characters, Xanther and her family, he states that,

> But the family is larger than that, as you know. It incorporates characters that are beyond the family unit and forces us to look at the entire world in a more familiar way. We have to move away from this kind of estrangement that allows for phenomena like Brexit, or Trump, you know – the ascendancy of people who prey on difference and strangeness, instead of recognizing that these things are familiar. And if they're not, the book itself is a project of familiarizing people with what Arabic looks like; it's not that scary. With what Armenian looks like; it's not that scary.
>
> (Calvo 2016)

In this way, he presents the novel as a political project. By confronting the readers with foreign languages and an unconventional experimental aesthetics, Danielewski wants to build familiarity: between the text and the reader and between the readers and the rest of the world.

This political ambition may be considered in relation to the overall development of Danielewski's authorship. His works use similar experimental strategies, but the experiments are used in different contexts. Thus, while *House of Leaves* was about destabilizing the idea of authentic representation, *The Familiar* focuses more on building new forms of meaning and relations between readers, the text and the world. This development may be considered in relation to a broader development in modern American fiction from a postmodernist focus on destabilizing or breaking down signification to a more recent "post-ironic" or post-postmodernist turn toward sincerity and toward an emphasis on intimacy, family, or familiarity (Andersen 2011).

Despite the differences between the works, Danielewski also connects them with each other; for instance, whenever the word "house" appears in *The Familiar*, it is presented in the color blue, just as it is in *House of Leaves*, while the word "familiar" is always presented in pink. The works are thus color-coded like the characters. *The Familiar* also contains references to *Only Revolutions* and to Danielewski's most recent work, *The Little Blue Kite*. *The Little Blue Kite* is a children's book, or playing with the conventions of the children's book, with large illustrated pages and color-coded text. Here, the colors signal three different paths through the book: it is possible to read only the rainbow-colored words, or the words haloed with blue and red – or the entire text. This feature again suggests an ergodic narrative, demanding readers to actively choose a path through the book.

By making connections between his works, Danielewski demands his readers to engage, not only in interpreting the individual works, but also in collaboratively tracing how the stories are connected and developed across volumes and media. He continuously develops his works across media; thus, while his authorship is generally characterized by experiments with the book as a familiar yet still unexplored object, he has in recent years begun to move beyond the printed book and has engaged in experiments with other media formats: in 2018, he wrote a pilot for a television series and in 2019, he wrote three scripts for teleplays, all based on *House of Leaves*. In this way, Danielewski continues to explore the interactions between literature and other media and media cultures at the levels of aesthetic content, social usage, and remediation.

SEE ALSO: Hypertext Fiction and Network Narratives; Intermedial Fiction; The New Experimentalism/The Contemporary Avant-Garde

REFERENCES

Aarseth, Espen. (1997). *Cybertext: Perspectives on Ergodic Literature*. Baltimore: Johns Hopkins University Press.

Andersen, Tore R. (2011). *Den nye amerikanske roman* [The New American Novel]. Aarhus: Aarhus University Press.

Bosman, Julie. (2011). Periodical novel, coming soon. *The New York Times* (November 20, 2011). https://mediadecoder.blogs.nytimes.com/2011/11/20/periodic-novel-coming-soon/ (accessed July 8, 2021).

Calvo, Javier. (2016). Building familiarity: interview with Mark Z. Danielewski. *O Productora Audiovisual, O Magazine* (September 6, 2016). https://abcdefghijklmn-pqrstuvwxyz.com/building-familiarity-interview-with-mark-z-danielewski/ (accessed January 20, 2020).

Cottrell, Sophie. (2002). Bold type interview: a conversation with Mark Z. Danielewski. http://randomhouse.com/boldtype/0400/danielewski/interview.htlm (accessed January 20, 2020).

Danielewski, Mark Z. (2015). *The Familiar, Volume 1. Readers' Guide*. https://www.penguinrandomhouse.com/books/213605/the-familiar-volume-1-by-mark-z-danielewski/9780375714948/readers-guide/ (accessed July 8, 2021).

Hanson, Mark B.N. (2004). The digital topography of Mark Z. Danielewski's *House of Leaves*. *Contemporary Literature* 45 (4): 597–636.

Hayles, N. Katherine. (2007). The future of literature: complex surfaces of electronic texts and print books. *Collection Management* 31 (1/2): 85–114.

Hayles, N. Katherine. (2012). *How We Think: Digital Media and Contemporary Technogenesis*. Chicago: Chicago University Press.

Pressman, Jessica. (2009). The aesthetics of bookishness in twenty-first-century literature. *Michigan Quarterly Review* 48 (4).

FURTHER READING

Gibbons, Alison. (2011). *Multimodality, Cognition and Experimental Literature*. New York: Routledge.

Gibbons, Alison and Bray, Joe. (eds.) (2011). *Mark Z. Danielewski*. Manchester: Manchester University Press.

Linkis, Sara T. (forthcoming). Building familiarity in Mark Z. Danielewski's *The Familiar*. In: *Fictionality and Multimodal Narratives* (ed. Alison Gibbons and Torsa Ghosal). Lincoln: University of Nebraska Press.

Van de Ven, Inge. (2016). The serial novel in an age of binging: how to read Mark Z. Danielewski's *The Familiar*. *Image & Narrative* 17 (4): 91–103.

Danticat, Edwidge

J.J. BUTTS
Simpson College, USA

Edwidge Danticat is a critically acclaimed Haitian American writer who has published books in a wide range of genres. Best known for her novels *Breath, Eyes, Memory* (1994) and *The Dew Breaker* (2004), Danticat has also authored several other novels, short stories, poetry, a travel narrative, and two memoirs, as well as several children's picture books and young adult novels. Her work explores how lives are constructed across national and cultural borders during political, social, and environmental crises. Danticat has won several awards and has been widely anthologized, making her one of the most well-known contemporary American writers from the Caribbean.

In *The Farming of Bones* (1998), a young girl watches her father and mother drown as they attempt to cross the Dajabón River. The scene reverberates throughout the text, sounding echoes in the past and future. The river serves for much of its course as a border between Haiti and the Dominican Republic, the two countries – with their differing colonial and national histories – that share the island of Hispaniola. These histories are reflected in the river's names; it is also known as *Río Masacre* or *Rivière du Massacre*, recalling the mass killing of French *boucaniers* by Spanish colonists in 1728. History repeats over the course of the novel, as the girl, now grown into a young woman working in the Dominican Republic, has to flee across the river during the October 1937 slaughter of Haitians by Dominican troops carrying out the orders of President Rafael Trujillo. The river's multiple names are reflected in the function of the seemingly mundane word "parsley" – *persil* in French, *perejil* in Spanish, and *pésil* in the Kreyòl of the Haitian workers – as a shibboleth. To be unable to pronounce the word convincingly in the Dominican Spanish dialect is to be instantly marked a refugee and a target. The novel shows how the crisis reveals the stakes of the border for those whose lives span its complex political, symbolic, and linguistic delineations.

Critics regularly highlight the importance of borders to Danticat's writing. Martin Munro, for example, illustrates this dynamic through the dilemma of locating Danticat's books by category in an imaginary bookstore. Her writing is Haitian and Haitian American, Caribbean, and Black. It focuses on the experience of women and immigrants, families and day workers. Linguistically, her work is diverse as well. Danticat writes in English, but her characters speak Spanish, French, Kreyòl, and a wide range of American English dialects.

Like her characters, Danticat has crossed several borders throughout her life. She was born in Port-au-Prince, Haiti, on January 19, 1969, to André and Rose Danticat. Her family was from the mountainous region around the coastal city of Léogâne, west of Port-Au-Prince, where some of her stories take place. After migrating to the Bel Air section of the Haitian capital, her parents struggled to make ends meet. When Danticat was young, first her father and then her mother emigrated to the United States in order to find work by staying on past the expiration of their tourist visas. They hoped their Haitian children, Edwidge and her brother Bob, would be able to follow, but they were unable to generate enough financial security to bring them to the United States for eight years. For much of her childhood, Danticat lived in Bel Air with the family of her aunt Denise and uncle Joseph, a Protestant minister. Danticat spoke French in school but Kreyòl at home. She began writing literature when she was nine, influenced in particular by the *Madeline* stories of Ludwig Bemelman. Martin Munro notes that Danticat's "cultural upbringing was influenced [...] by popular phenomena such as storytelling [...], *rara* music, and carnival," forms she would explore in her writing (Munro 2010, p. 17). In an interview with Opal Palmer Adisa, Danticat noted that she shared a room "with a great storyteller, my uncle's wife's mother Granmé Melina" (Adisa 2009, p. 346). Danticat also grew up aware of the violence of the Duvalier regime and lost a close cousin to a shooting (Munro 2010, p. 17).

When she moved to Brooklyn in 1981, at the age of twelve, Danticat entered a world at once familiar and foreign. Her family's apartment on Flatbush Avenue in the Prospect-Lefferts Gardens neighborhood, was located in the heart of Brooklyn's Caribbean immigrant community. Haitian French and Kreyòl filled homes and streets, alongside many other Caribbean languages and dialects. Many shops reflected the cultures the immigrants and refugees brought with them. Edwidge, Bob, and their New York-born siblings Kelly and Karl spoke Kreyòl at home, but English was the language of the school system and of public spaces beyond her Brooklyn neighborhood. The central branch of the Brooklyn Public Library at Grand Army Plaza became an important place where Danticat could explore those worlds in fiction, and she began writing her own stories in high school (Munro 2010, p. 20).

Danticat's parents were concerned about the potentially politically dangerous implications of her desire to become a writer and wanted her to become a nurse instead (Munro 2010, p. 19). Many of her stories, like the stories of many generations of immigrant writers, explore the conflicting expectations between children and parents. Setting her own path, Danticat studied French literature at Barnard College from 1986 to 1990. At Barnard, Danticat read widely in the African and Caribbean diaspora, while she continued to develop the stories she had begun writing in high school. She then enrolled in the creative writing MFA program at Brown University, and completed her degree in 1993 with a thesis draft of a novel tying together Haitian and Haitian immigrant experiences.

Based on this thesis, Danticat published her first novel, *Breath, Eyes, Memory*, in 1994. The novel narrates the experiences of Sophie Caco. Conceived when her mother, Martine, is raped, Sophie is left behind in Haiti when Martine immigrates to the United States. As Sophie grows up and eventually joins her mother, the novel depicts her struggles with her mother's trauma and its intergenerational effects. Martine performs the same intrusive inspections of her daughter, "testing" for an intact hymen, that Sophie's grandmother inflicted on Martine when she was a young woman. The novel received some criticism for its depiction of this custom. However, in an interview with Bonnie Lyons, Danticat problematized the tendency of readers to see writing from a minority perspective as primarily sociological. She notes that she wrote an afterword, in the form of a letter to Sophie, to make clear "the distinction between one family's story and an entire group's story" (Lyons 2003, p. 191). This distinction, and its refusal to reduce complex social and cultural dynamics to typicality, has been crucial in Danticat's depictions of Haitian and Haitian immigrant characters throughout her career.

The rest of the 1990s saw Danticat building her career as one of the United States' most promising writers. In 1995, her short story collection *Krik? Krak!* was a finalist for the National Book Award, launching Danticat to the front ranks of young American writers. The collection takes its title from a common call-and-response Haitian storytellers use to call the audience into community. In a move that recalls the works of many other immigrant writers, Danticat uses the story cycle form to bring together the lives of several characters in Haiti and the United States, exploring suffering, self-recognition, and intimacy in moments of crisis, particularly between mothers and daughters. One story, for example, depicts a young woman whose mother is imprisoned as a witch. The young woman practices the customs her mother taught her and joins a community of other women marking trauma through ritual. Another, "New York Day Women," which follows a young woman covertly watching her mother as she takes care of another woman's child, was anthologized in the canon-expanding *Heath Anthology of American Literature*.

In 1998, *Breath, Eyes, Memory* was chosen as an Oprah's Book Club reading, which boosted Danticat's wider public readership. That same year, *The Farming of Bones*, Danticat's next novel, won the American Book Award. It focuses on the experiences of Haitian workers in the Dominican Republic before, during, and after the Parsley Massacre. The novel is narratively anchored in the memories and dreams of a woman named Amabelle Désir as she works in the household of a Dominican military officer. In the conclusion, Amabelle, now an old woman, lies down in the river "where the dead" – the *boucaniers*, her parents, and the victims of the Parsley Massacre – "add their tears to the river flow" (Danticat 1998, p. 310). She reflects on her losses, but knows that undoing them is beyond her reach. All she has is her memory, and even that, she notes, will someday be gone. Here Danticat continues to show how the disruptive events that occur across borders have irreversible effects that conflict with notions of simple resolution.

The 2000s marked a time of personal change and generic exploration for Danticat. In 2002, she married Fedo Boyer, and they moved to the émigré community of Little Haiti in Miami. Their first daughter, Mira, was born in 2004, and another, Leila, was born in 2009. Danticat published her first work of young adult fiction, *Behind the Mountains*, in 2002. She also went back to Haiti for the first time since she immigrated. This visit produced a travelogue *After the Dance* (2002) focusing on Haitian Carnival. In 2004, Danticat's Uncle Joseph sought asylum in the United States but died in detainment when he was denied access to essential medications. Her father died the following year. The history of these two men and their connection across national boundaries became the focus of Danticat's 2007 memoir *Brother, I'm Dying*.

Danticat returned to the story cycle and to Duvalierist Haiti in her 2004 novel, *The Dew Breaker*, which a number of critics have suggested is her most accomplished work. This novel is constructed through several stories centering on a man who kidnapped and tortured Haitian citizens for the Tonton Macoutes, François "Papa Doc" Duvalier's paramilitary force. In the present, he lives quietly under an assumed last name of Bienaimé as a barber in the Haitian American community in Brooklyn with his wife, Anne, and daughter, Ka, whom he named for the Egyptian god. His obsession with the Egyptian Book of the Dead and its atonement rituals highlights his concern over his own past and history with death. For the reader, the investigation of his life is set in motion when, after destroying his daughter's sculpture portraying his suffering as a prisoner, he confesses to his daughter that "your father was the hunter, he was not the prey" (Danticat 2004, p. 21). The novel explores the effects of his actions on a wide range of characters, many of whom lost relatives to the Macoutes. Anne, his wife, is the sister of his last victim, a priest who criticized the Duvalier regime.

After *The Dew Breaker*, Danticat published *Anacaona: Golden Flower, Haiti, 1490* (2005), a young adult novel for Scholastic's *Royal Diaries Series* about a Taino *cacique* who lived in what is now Léogâne at the time of the arrival of the Spanish, who captured and eventually killed her. Then, in 2009, Danticat was awarded one of the MacArthur Foundation prestigious "genius grant" fellowships in recognition of her work chronicling Haitian immigrant's lives. This award opened up a flurry of literary activity for Danticat in the 2010s. She contributed essays to several collections and edited anthologies of literature. She also published her own essay collection *Create Dangerously: The Immigrant Artist at Work* in 2010.

More work for young readers followed throughout the 2010s. In 2010 Haiti experienced a devastating earthquake centered near Léogâne, in which Danticat lost her cousin and his daughter. Her picture book *Eight Days: A Story of Haiti* (2010) sought to describe the traumatic events for children. She published a children's novel, *The Last Mapou*, in 2011, and three more picture books: *Eight Days: A Story of Haiti* (2010), *Mama's Nightingale* (2011), and *My Mommy Medicine* (2019). *Untwine*, her third young adult novel, appeared in 2015. These works join a long tradition of work by writers of color that expands the range of characters, subjects, and experiences available to young readers.

When her mother died in 2014, Danticat again turned to writing to explore history and memories in *The Art of Death: Writing the Final Story* (2017). Death became even more explicitly a central theme of her stories, as, throughout the 2010s, she continued to write the kind of fiction that had made her literary reputation. In 2013, Danticat published *Claire of the Sea Light*, a novel about the fictional seaside town of Ville Rose and the people who live there. The novel centers on the search for Claire Limyè Lanmè, whose father is about to give her up for adoption by a wealthy widow so that Claire would have a more secure life and he could leave the village in search of better employment opportunities. As it progresses, a series of incidents involving the deaths of people in the city reveal the intertwining of their lives across social and national borders. The novel repeatedly invokes environmental crises as well, mirroring ecologically the sociological interconnections and imbalances. In August of 2019, Danticat published her most recent story collection *Everything Inside*. The collection also focuses on death and loss as themes that unite the stories and the lives of characters in Haiti and the United States.

Danticat's border-crossing stories reveal lived social and historical complexities, but also reflect the way that borders fragment and frustrate, requiring storytelling to fill in the gaps, to link lives torn asunder. In a 2007 interview with Michael Collins, Danticat discussed her fascination with masks as an expression of the clash of cultures within the descendants of the African diaspora. She linked the mediation of these conflicts to writing, saying "So this literature, these arts, can also be – to use another object metaphor – a cultural bridge" (Collins 2007, p. 472). In *The Dew Breaker*, Ka Bienaimé's father cannot escape the conflicts in his own history. He also cannot reveal them without being ostracized or prosecuted, and he does not ever fully disclose the extent of his actions to his wife or daughter. However, he does refuse his daughter's image of his innocence. Similarly, his tenant Dany, whose family he murdered in Haiti, has the choice to kill him in revenge but instead decides to let him go. As Danticat's novels trace the effects of border living, their outcomes include the very real possibility of living and dying with neither revelation nor reconciliation. Danticat's stories, then, create the conditions by which we might be able to reflect on the events and traumas that transpire across these borders. Instead of resolving these situations, they ask us as readers to learn, to remember, to make connections, and to struggle with what justice means.

SEE ALSO: Black Atlantic; Border Fictions; Contemporary Fictions of War; Ecocriticism and Environmental Fiction; Literature of the Americas; Multiculturalism; Story Cycles; Third-Wave Feminism; Trauma and Fiction; Young Adult Boom

REFERENCES

Adisa, Opal Palmer. (2009). Up close and personal: Edwidge Danticat on Haitian identity and the writers' life. *African American Review* 43 (2/3): 345–355.

Collins, Michael S. (2007). An interview with Edwidge Danticat. *Callaloo* 30 (2): 71–474.

Danticat, Edwidge. (1998). *The Farming of Bones*. New York: Soho.

Danticat, Edwidge. (2004). *The Dew Breaker*. New York: Vintage.

Lyons, Bonnie. (2003). Interview with Edwidge Danticat. *Contemporary Literature* 44 (2): 183–198.

Munro, Martin. (ed.) (2010). *Edwidge Danticat: A Reader's Guide*. Charlottesville: University of Virginia Press.

FURTHER READING

Bellamy, Maria Rice. (2012). More than hunter or prey: duality and traumatic memory in Edwidge Danticat's The Dew Breaker. *MELUS* 37 (1): 177–197.

Boisseron, Bénédicte. (2014). *Creole Renegades: Rhetoric of Betrayal and Guilt in the Caribbean Diaspora*. Gainesville: University of Florida Press.

Davis, Rocio G. (2001). Oral narrative as short story cycle: forging community in Edwidge Danticat's Krik? Krak! *MELUS* 26 (2): 65–81.

Machado Sáez, Elena. (2015). *Market Aesthetics: The Purchase of the Past in Caribbean Diasporic Fiction*. Charlottesville: University of Virginia Press.

Mukherjee, Bharati. (2011). Immigrant writing: changing the contours of a national literature. *American Literary History* 23 (3): 680–696.

Dara, Evan

EMMETT STINSON
Deakin University, USA

Evan Dara appears to be a pseudonym used by an unknown US author, who has published three novels and a play since 1995. There is almost no conclusive information about Dara, aside from the fact that he is probably male, allegedly resides in France, and started a self-publishing venture, Aurora Publishers, to publish three of his works. Dara's anonymity has had both positive and negative effects on his authorial career; while it may have scared off traditional publishers, it has also fueled online literary intrigue among a cult of devoted readers. He remains best known for his first novel, *The Lost Scrapbook* (1995), which employs postmodern literary techniques to examine a community affected by ecological disaster.

The Lost Scrapbook was published by the US experimental publisher Fiction Collective Two (FC2) after winning the 12th Illinois State University National Fiction Competition, judged by the US author William Vollmann. *The Lost Scrapbook* has attracted praise from other notable contemporary authors, such as David Foster Wallace, Jonathan Franzen, and

Richard Powers, who provided an extended blurb for the first edition of the book (Powers states the novel arrived as "several kilos of transatlantic, boat-rate typescript," supporting the claim that Dara resides in Europe). The 476-page novel lacks both a protagonist and a clear plot. As Stephen J. Burn notes, its opening section, which consists of a young person imagining a conversation with a career counselor, invokes the "coming-of-age" narrative of the *Bildungsroman*, only to reject it "in favor of a static, additive process" that involves constant switching between different narrators and scenes (2017, p. 112). In so doing, the novel formally mimics the first narrator's decision to choose not a single career, but *all* of them, since he is "interested, almost exclusively, in being interested" (p. 6). This refusal of realist narratives is conditional, however – a Bartleby-esque deferral rather than a wholesale rejection – since something akin to a realist plot reappears in the novel's final section.

In rotating among different stories, *The Lost Scrapbook* draws on modernist montage, which the novel acknowledges by discussing Eisenstein's filmic method as "creating its own language by crashing perceptions together" and "fabricating a bridge" (1995, p. 204). *The Lost Scrapbook* amplifies its literary montage by transitioning between sections in mid-sentence. The result is disorienting, since readers do not initially realize that the narrator and scene have changed. Moreover, in a typical postmodern gesture, the novel invokes both highbrow and pop cultural sources as aesthetic and thematic precursors, including Warner Brothers cartoons, the music of Harry Partch, comic books, Noam Chomsky, the golden age of radio (depicted as a democratic, iterative medium), Jean Piaget, and many others. The various scenes frequently combine absurdist comedy with more serious material. Burn has described *The Last Scrapbook* as a "skeletal encyclopedia," a subgenre of the postmodern encyclopedic novel that employs little "stylistic variation," the "removal of narratorial armature," and the "emptying out of novelistic devices" in order to present a stark "sequence of voices" in a "networked design" of "stacked fragments" that accrue meaning through repetition and slight variation (p. 111). The material connection between these sections, however, is not revealed until near the novel's end.

In its final third, *The Lost Scrapbook* settles into a single narrative about a fictional town in Missouri called Isaura – a reference to the ancient capital of Isauria (located in modern-day Turkey), whose inhabitants burned the city rather than submit to Macedonian rule. Isaura, Missouri, is home to the Ozark Photography Corporation, the largest local employer, which has been dumping chemical pollutants that have contaminated the town and sickened its residents. Ultimately, the Environmental Protection Agency forces all residents with a two-mile radius of the Ozark plant to evacuate. While there is no justice for these inhabitants, the novel ends with their receiving letters of support from people all around the country, including a long list of towns, many of which are settings for earlier stories in the novel. As Jeremy Green argues, this final section, which is told through multiple, anonymous voices, constitutes an "attempt to imagine the sundered voices, the atomized pieces of contemporary social life, as convergent, speaking together in some barely imaginable collective protest" (2005, p. 9). Patrick O'Donnell notes that the novel's portrayal of the "devastation of community entailed by the infiltration of corporate America into every aspect of life" is counterbalanced by an attempt to conjure "an imaginary community of the future" (2010, p. 198). In this sense, the novel attempts to cobble together its disparate stories into a unified whole, much like the titular "lost scrapbook" that had "seemed to speak of a life that had had so much content, so much real activity..." (p. 45).

As Burn has noted, the novel places effects after causes – an estranging gesture for readers who can only understand the novel's structure after completing it. Even the meaning of the opening sentence ("—I am yes; certainly;" [Dara 1995, p. 6]) only becomes clear retrospectively; Burn argues that this sentence reads as half of the Cartesian formula *cogito ergo sum*, which is described later in the novel as representative of a "slice-'n'-dice" philosophy that separates people from one another (2017, p. 115). But the affirmative opening line also appears as a buried reference to James Joyce's *Ulysses*, which famously ends with "yes I said yes I will Yes" (Joyce 1993, p. 732). Allusions to modernist literature are a common feature across Dara's works, and *The Lost Scrapbook*'s final words ("for where else could this go but silence, yes silence: silence. Silence" [1995, p. 476]) mimic both the repetition and the capitalization of the final word at the end of *Ulysses*. Moreover, silence itself is famously part of Stephen Dedalus's artistic trinity of "silence, exile, and cunning" in *Portrait of the Artist as a Young Man* (Joyce 2000, p. 213). This connection is made stronger by the fact that residents of Isaura are effectively exiled. Here, however, the strategies of Joyce's individual artist are democratized and applied to communal survival.

After the publication of *The Lost Scrapbook*, Dara disappeared from public view for thirteen years, only reemerging in 2008 to self-publish his second novel, *The Easy Chain* (2008), through the imprint Aurora. Although Tom LeClair speculated that "Aurora's exceedingly low profile" meant Dara would "garner few readers" (LeClair 2009), arguably the self-published nature of his work helped create interest online, where Dara's reputation has thrived. Scott Bryan Wilson's enthusiastic review of *The Easy Chain* at the influential online literary journal *The Quarterly Conversation* in 2010 helped promote the novel to like-minded readers. Other online bloggers took notice and engaged fans like Steve Rusillo set up online guides to help other readers with the difficulty of Dara's works. More recently, Jeff Downing's website, The Evan Dara Affinity, has sought to present a comprehensive set of resources on Dara and his work. The Internet, in this sense, has been a huge boon for Dara.

Apparently taking its title from the Philip Larkin poem "Spring Warning," *The Easy Chain* focuses on a central personage, Lincoln Selwyn, an Englishman raised in the Netherlands, who arrives in Chicago and displays a preternatural capacity to climb the social ladder of local elites: "at the first trespassing of fingertips you're instantaneous old friends" (Dara 2008, p. 1). Selwyn's name is also a direct allusion to Ezra Pound's long poem *Hugh Selwyn Mauberly*, which also expresses concerns about the ways in which "the valorization of economic value" impinges upon other notions of value (Stinson 2017, p.192). The first 200 pages of the novel catalogue Lincoln's rise in a method very similar to the final section of *The Lost Scrapbook*: a rotating cast of (largely anonymous) voices tell different aspects of Lincoln's story, generating a pointillist depiction of his ascent into the upper echelons of the Chicago business world and his involvement with a series of increasingly bizarre entrepreneurial ventures.

This narrative, however, is then broken by forty almost completely blank pages (except for some formatting marks and two repetitions of the word "you"). Here, the lacuna in the text reflects Lincoln's own sudden disappearance after his publicist and only real friend, Auran, is hit by a taxi. The narrative then resumes with twin interspersed threads: a series of emails from a journalist, Tracy Krassner, researching Lincoln's disappearance and his dubious business ventures, and Lincoln's own journey to Amsterdam, where he searches for his mother, who has become a homeless alcoholic. The book then yields to sixty pages of what appears to be broken fragments of internal monologue formatted like lines of poetry, but with each line repeated multiple times. When the narrative resumes, Lincoln is in the process of committing a terrorist act at the Chicago Mercantile Exchange Building, but this scene is quickly interrupted by an essay on the privatization of water in the United States. After another four blank pages, the book's final section comprises a monologue from Carter Dardan, a private investigator, who Lincoln is holding at gunpoint because Dardan withheld the whereabouts of Lincoln's Aunt. Dardan recounts several disturbing stories, including one about his daughter, Anya, who suffers from autism spectrum disorder and was abused by one of her carers.

If *The Lost Scrapbook* is a montage that resolves into a semi-traditional narrative, then *The Easy Chain* is its opposite. The contained rags-to-riches story of the first half ramifies into a series of wildly disconnected events. Tom LeClair (2009) has argued that the second half is spoiled by "slackness and missing links" as well as Lincoln's unclear motivations, but *The Easy Chain*'s formal inventiveness arguably lies in the fact that the reader is never given any real access to Lincoln Selwyn as a protagonist. The reader witnesses him doing things, and people talking about him, but has little sense of his internal world. Even the final line of the novel demonstrates his unknowability, as Dardan asks, "Where are you GOing—?" (Dara 2008, p. 502, *sic*). Lincoln is an absence, not unlike the 40 blank pages in the middle of the novel, and is fittingly described as "a nothing, a null set, a zero with a thousand faces" (p. 358). The closest the reader gets to knowing his internal state is when the third-person narrator discusses his motivations for destroying the Mercantile Exchange as a "necessary emendation to the ascendant storyline of his place, his time"; here, Lincoln's destruction is essentially aligned with the anti-narrative aesthetics of the novel, which present an opportunity to "call out new terms" (p. 435).

Evan Dara's third and shortest novel, *Flee* (2013), is set in Anderburg, a fictionalized version of Burlington, Vermont, which is subject to an economic collapse that causes its residents to abandon the city. The novel is broken into sections whose titles appear to reflect dwindling population numbers, starting with "38,839" and ending at "841." *Flee* engages with themes familiar from Dara's other works: the way that capitalist economies destroy collectivity, the experience of exile, and the relationship between the individual and the broader community. *Flee* is not only shorter than Dara's other work, but also its narrative is comparatively contained and straightforward. Nonetheless, there are characteristic absurdist touches, such as the story of a phantom sociology department at local university, Pilkington (based on Vermont College), which continues to receive funding; the ruse is only discovered when a student "wants to take a course in it" because he has "*interest*" (Dara 2013, p. 18), an apparent allusion to the opening of *The Lost Scrapbook*. There are also joking revisions of modernist quotations, such as when one fleeing resident states, "There's no here here" (p. 79).

The story of Anderburg's decline is again told by a cast of rotating voices, but these are interspersed with third-person narration set in a different font, which focuses on a couple, Rick and Carrol, who are trying to revive the town by starting an employment agency that functions as a social enterprise. The legitimacy of this plan is called into question when Carol states that "All altruism stops at profit-sharing" (2013, p. 79), and both the agency and their relationship inevitably fail. Here, the novel appears to skewer the viability of gentler modes of capitalist enterprise. The penultimate section, entitled "X," focuses on Carol's ex-partner, Marcus Carter, and his attempts to locate community in an Anderburg that has become a ghost town. A conversation between him and Carol implies that Marcus has an autistic daughter, echoing Carter Dardan from *The Easy Chain*. The final section of the novel suggests burgeoning regeneration within Anderburg, and the potential for forging links between the isolated individual and the broader community: "I was a world. I became myself. Who can argue with such expansion?" (p. 239).

In 2018, Dara released a play, entitled *A Provisional Biography of Mose Eakins*, as a digital download on a pay-what-you-want basis. Mose Eakins is an "American field-risk analyst working for Concord Oil" (2018, p. 6) whose comfortable life is destroyed when he is diagnosed with "imparlance" (p. 15), a neurological disorder that renders him incapable of expressing his thoughts; sufferers of imparlance "lose the capacity to infuse their words with intelligible significance" (p. 18). Eakins loses his job and his savings, and he finds work in a restaurant that claims to help the homeless and down-on-their-luck, but is actually predatory, paying wages that barely allow its employees to survive. Mose is ultimately killed by his fellow workers when he tries to organise against a further pay cut. *A Provisional Biography of Mose Eakins* also relies heavily on dialogue that is intercut with exposition from a version of a Greek chorus, entitled "The Swirl." It is certainly Dara's most didactic work and the closest to a standard narrative. Mose is a clear protagonist and one whose interiority readers are given access to. The irony of the play, however, lies in the fact that he cannot express this interiority, and perceptions of him after his death bear little resemblance to the man he was.

In 2019, the US novelist Brandon Hobson reported that "Dara has apparently completed a new novel" and "is seeking representation for this new book, with the plan of working with a more mainstream house and a dedicated editor" (Downing 2019).

One of the most contested aspects of Dara's fiction is its relationship to the work of William Gaddis, which has been noted by such critics as Patrick O'Donnell, Jeremy Green, and Tom LeClair. There is an evident similarity in that both authors rely heavily on dialogue (and extended monologues) proffered by a rotating ensemble of characters. Moreover, both writers' use of the closed em dash to signify dialogue (instead of conventional quotation marks) seems to place them in an explicitly post-Joycean modernist tradition, although Downing, following research by Burn, has suggested Manuel Puig's writing as an alternative source for this punctuation (Downing 2017). Ultimately, it appears that the resemblance between Dara and Gaddis is coincidental; Steven Moore has reported that "Dara told me that while working on *The Lost Scrapbook* he heard that *J R* was a novel in dialogue and checked it out from The American Library in Paris: 'Took the novel home, plunked it open, tapped it shut – didn't want the influence' (email January 19, 2014)" (2015, p. 213). Dara has similarly emailed Tom LeClair, stating that he has not read Gaddis's first two novels.

Regardless, the comparison persists both among critics and on the promotional materials for Dara's books. But as Burn notes, there is also a significant difference between their approaches: whereas Gaddis's novels employ exchanges of dialogue "in real time" that are often interrupted by external events, Dara's works are composed of "speech" that more closely resembles short, contained monologues than dialogic exchanges (2017, p. 113). They might even better be viewed as soliloquies – a form of dislocated speech that seems to bridge distinctions between the personal and the public, the internal and performative. Perhaps the most paradigmatic representation of this occurs in a scene in *The Lost Scrapbook* which consists entirely of a personalized radio show that is somehow broadcast directly ("freebooted") into the earphones of Walkman cassette players, described as "your own private piracy network . . . coming to you through your Walkman" (Dara 1995, p. 82). The unnamed narrator here notes that "the first thing radio announcers are told in broadcasting school" is "to pretend when on the air, to be speaking to only one person" (p. 80), a statement that, at least in part, reflects the odd status of the speech acts within the novel. This dislocated mode of speech also seems to resonate with Dara's use of a pseudonym, which enables a mode of address that is simultaneously public (since it is published), intimate (since reading is an individual act), and disembodied (since Dara remains anonymous). The name of Dara's self-publishing imprint, Aurora, seems to refer directly to the "freebooting" scene in *The Lost Scrapbook*, which occurs on a highway "somewhere between Lincoln and Aurora" (p. 99).

SEE ALSO: Franzen, Jonathan; Powers, Richard; Vollmann, William T.; Wallace, David Foster

REFERENCES

Burn, Stephen J. (2017). Encyclopedic fictions. In: *American Literature in Transition, 1990–2000* (ed. Steven J. Burn), 107–123. Cambridge: Cambridge University Press.
Dara, Evan. (1995). *The Lost Scrapbook*. Normal, IL: FC2.
Dara, Evan. (2008). *The Easy Chain*. New York: Aurora.
Dara, Evan. (2013). *Flee*. New York: Aurora.
Dara, Evan. (2018). *A Provisional Biography of Mose Eakins*. New York: Aurora, Inc.
Downing, Jeff. (2017). The embrace of influence. The Evan Dara Affinity. https://evandara.org/2017/05/30/the-embrace-of-influence/ (accessed July 2, 2021).
Downing, Jeff. (2019). A new Evan Dara novel? The Evan Dara Affinity. https://evandara.org/2019/08/17/a-new-evan-dara-novel/ (accessed July 2, 2021).
Green, Jeremy. (2005). *Late Postmodernism: American Fiction at the Millennium*. New York: Routledge.
Joyce, James. (2000). *Portrait of the Artist as a Young Man*. Oxford: Oxford University Press; 1st ed. 1916.
Joyce, James. (1993). *Ulysses*. Oxford: Oxford University Press; 1st ed. 1922.
LeClair, Tom. (2009). Mixed receptions: *The Easy Chain* by Evan Dara. *Bookforum* (December/January). https://www.bookforum.com/print/1504/the-easy-chain-by-evan-dara-2998 (accessed July 2, 2021).
Moore, Steven. (2015). *William Gaddis: Expanded Edition*. New York: Bloomsbury Academic.
O'Donnell, Patrick. (2010). *The American Novel Now: Reading Contemporary American Fiction Since 1980*. Oxford: Wiley-Blackwell.
Stinson, Emmett. (2017). *Satirizing Modernism: Aesthetic Autonomy, Romanticism, and the Avant-Garde*. New York: Bloomsbury Academic.
Wilson, Scott-Bryan. (2010). *The Easy Chain* by Evan Dara. *The Quarterly Conversation* (Fall 2010). https://web.archive.org/web/20190302091917/http://quarterlyconversation.com/the-easy-chain-by-evan-dara-review (accessed July 2, 2021).

FURTHER READING

The Evan Dara Affinity. (n.d.). www.evandara.org/
Steve Russilo's guides to Evan Dara's novels. (n.d.). www.russillosm.com

Davis, Lydia

JONATHAN EVANS
University of Glasgow, UK

Lydia Davis (b. 1947) is best known for her work in the short short story form, that is, very short stories of less than one page, which often challenge accepted understandings of fictional form. She has also published a significant body of translations from French, including books by Marcel Proust, Gustave Flaubert, Maurice Blanchot, and Michel Leiris. Her work also includes a novel, *The End of the Story* (1995), and essays. Awarded a Chevalier de l'Ordre des Arts et des Lettres by the French government in 1999, Davis has also notably been awarded a MacArthur Fellowship in 2003 and won the Man Booker International Prize in 2011. This entry explores her work through an analysis of both her fiction and her translations, focusing in on key themes and techniques across her writing.

The story "To Reiterate" offers in capsule form many of the key themes of Davis's work. It is a meditation on the relationships between reading, writing, translating, and traveling, which concludes that each is a form of the other and of itself. The text folds back in on itself, questioning logic and highlighting the materiality of the words, which are pushed to a point just before meaninglessness. This interest in the relationship between words and meaning is common throughout Davis's work, as is the formal innovation that borders on poetry. To focus solely on her short fiction, however, misses her significant work as a translator from French – for which she is also well known – as well as her work in the genres of the novel and the essay.

Davis has been active as a writer (and translator) since the early 1970s, publishing her early work in little magazines such as *Living Hand*, which she edited with her then husband Paul Auster. Her first collection of stories, *The Thirteenth Woman and other stories*, was published by Living Hand in 1976. A second small press collection, *Story and other stories*, was published by The Figures in 1983. Stories from both of these volumes have reemerged in Davis's later collections, though most numerously in her first mainstream collection, *Break It Down* (1986). Davis often publishes her stories in poetry or fiction magazines before collecting them, sometimes decades later, in book form. Prominent among her small press publications is the 2011 chapbook *The Cows*, which consists of a literary text observing the behavior of cows and photographs of cows by Davis and members of her family. Davis's later collections, with the exception of *Samuel Johnson is Indignant* (2001), have been published by mainstream press Farrar, Strauss and Giroux: *Almost No Memory* (1997), *Varieties of Disturbance* (2007) and *Can't and Won't* (2014). *Samuel Johnson is Indignant* was first published by McSweeney's, the publishing house connected to the magazine *Timothy McSweeney's Quarterly Concern* (founded by Dave Eggers), where Davis has also published short stories. A *Collected Stories* was published in 2009, which included her stories up until that date.

Davis's continuing publication in small presses and little magazines, such as *McSweeney's*, places her work alongside less established authors, some of whom she has now influenced (such as Eggers and Ben Marcus). It also places her work in an avant-garde tradition that is shared with many other writers of her generation in the United States. Her interest in the complexities of language and communication are shared with the Language Poets, who include writers such as Rae Armantrout, Lyn Hejinian, Susan Howe, Charles Bernstein, and Ron Silliman. Davis's translations of experimental, post-surrealist French writers such as Blanchot and Leiris also connect her to these avant-garde currents. Davis, in an interview with Larry McCaffery (1996, pp. 65–67), names authors such as Samuel Beckett, Franz Kafka, and Vladimir Nabokov among her influences, positioning herself in line with European high modernism (rather than postmodernism, which she said she was not connected to in the same interview). Another key influence on Davis was the American author Russell Edson (McCaffery 1996), another writer of short prose texts. However, where most of Davis's short texts are published as stories, Edson's are more commonly called poems, though they share similar short narrative structures.

Davis's work often revolves around questions of communication, leading Marjorie Perloff to call her stories "hermeneutic parables" (1989). A classic example of this is in the story "The Letter" which narrates the reading of a letter from a former lover. The letter itself is not really a letter, but a handwritten poem in French. The narrator struggles to read the handwriting and the poem is only given in small fragments in the text itself, so that readers are placed in a similar position to the narrator, trying to decipher what is meant. Johnny Payne (1993, pp. 142–194) and Jonathan Evans (2016, pp. 141–147) read the story in relation to the question of translation and to reading, where Perloff and Karen Alexander (2008) focus on questions of interpretation and analysis. These terms blur into each other as interpretation, reading, and analysis often have similar goals: to try to understand something. This attempt to understand, even if it gets waylaid, is a significant part of communication in Davis's stories. In another classic example, "Story," the narrator is trying to understand a narrative about the night's events told to her by her boyfriend. It's unclear to her (and to the reader) just what has transpired and if the boyfriend has been seeing his old girlfriend behind her back. "Story" contains two parts: the first tells the story, the second retells it as part of the narrator's attempts to understand what has happened. Her attempt at analysis, as it becomes more and more precise and detailed, stops her from actually understanding or arriving at any objective truth of the situation (Perloff 1989, pp. 207–208). This reflexivity is common in Davis's writing, and it can be seen in other stories such as "Break It Down," where a young man tries to account for the cost of a relationship by breaking the costs down into dollars per hour, before realizing that he has not accounted for the bad times as well as the good. Analyzing this story and Davis's *The End of the Story*, Josh Cohen (2010) refers to the "reflexive incomprehension" of Davis's work, in other words, the ways in which reflection and thinking lead to an inability to comprehend, as in the stories discussed in this paragraph.

However, not all of Davis's analytical stories lead to an impasse, as Evans (2016, p. 141) argues. In "Foucault and Pencil," the narrator is struggling to read a book by philosopher Michel Foucault in the original French, while at the same time thinking about an ongoing argument. The reading of Foucault becomes entangled in the analysis of the argument, and understanding one appears to lead to an understanding of the other. By focusing on the difficulties of Foucault's writing, the narrator avoids the affective difficulties of trying to directly understand the argument and so approaches it indirectly, allowing them to see a way forward (Evans 2016, pp. 140–141). A similar abstraction is used in the story "Grammar Questions," in which the narrator asks how one is supposed to refer to their dying father and how that might change once he is dead. Here, the emotional difficulty of facing the imminent death of a relative is displaced by the question of what pronouns and tense are most appropriate to refer to them (Evans 2016, p. 62). In "Letter to A Funeral Parlor" the narrator complains about the use of the word "cremains" to refer to the cremated remains of a body. The choice of terms is an abstraction that moves away from the sense of loss of a parent. Both these stories also demonstrate that Davis does not let go of referentiality in her work and that she remains interested in what words refer to, rather than just the words themselves, linking her work to a post-experimental poetics (Perloff 1989, p. 212) that goes beyond innovation to deal with affective uses of language.

Many of Davis's stories cite other authors or rework already existing texts. Stories such as "Extracts from a Life," "Lord Royston's Tour," and "Our Village" (2013) abridge autobiographies written by other writers. Other stories include pastiches, such as "Kafka Cooks Dinner" and "Southward Bound, Reads *Worstward Ho*," which pastiches Beckett's style. Further stories cite other writers, such as "The Walk," which quotes a section from Proust's *Du côté de chez Swann* [*Swann's Way*], and "Once a very Stupid Man," which quotes, with some variation, from a story by Jewish philosopher Martin Buber. This intertextuality echoes the practices of postmodern authors and artists and partakes in what Nicolas Bourriaud (2005) has called "postproduction," where older texts are recycled and reused by new artists and authors. These intertextual writings serve to position Davis's work in relation to her influences (especially in the case of the pastiches and citational works), but also to complicate the notions of authorship and originality, as both the original author and Davis have some claim to the text. More complicated still are stories that draw on translation of another author, notably "Marie Curie, So Honorable Woman" and the stories from Flaubert, first published as a group in *The Paris Review* and reprinted throughout *Can't and Won't*. Evans (2012) analyzes the use of translation in "Marie Curie, So Honorable Woman," arguing that the story questions notions of representation, translation, and parody through its reworking of extracts of a biography of Marie Curie that Davis had previously translated, Françoise Giroud's *Marie Curie* (1986). The ten stories from Flaubert (collected in *Can't and Won't*) also contain translations from Flaubert's letters, where Davis has extracted the funny stories that he would tell correspondents (Evans 2016, pp. 101–107; Blin 2018). The translated nature of these texts obscures their origin and at the same time distances Davis's story from the original text by putting it in another language. Each troubles the relationship between original and derivative work and translation and non-translation. To read all these intertextual stories as solely playful experiments is, however, to miss their emotional charge as stories, which can be experienced without knowing their intertextual origins.

Questions of memory and narrative are brought to the fore in Davis's *The End of the Story*. The novel tells the story of a failed relationship but also tells the story of the telling of that story, with interruptions and a self-doubting narrator who cannot be sure what happened. Christopher Knight (2008) argues that *The End of the Story* is a "philosophical investigation" in fictional form, which explores the topic of memory through the puzzle of the narrative. Expanding on this theme, Evans (2016, pp. 72–80) reads *The End of the Story* as a rewriting of Proust's *À la recherche du temps perdu* [*In Search of Lost Time*], the first volume of which Davis translated later. Evans finds thematic and structural similarities between the two novels, but he concludes that Davis's goals are significantly different from Proust's, as her narrator finds conclusion almost impossible.

Davis's work as a translator is significant and is an important part of her literary output. She has translated over twenty book-length works into English, including early translations of Blanchot's narratives and essays (many collected in *The Station Hill Blanchot Reader* [Blanchot 1999]) that introduced Blanchot's work to English-language readers in the 1970s and 1980s. While Blanchot may have been the writer most translated by Davis, she has also translated three parts of Leiris's autobiography *La Règle du jeu* [*Rules of the Game*], which have been published over a thirty-year period (*Scratches* [1991]; *Scraps* [1995]; *Fibrils* [2017]). However, she is most famous for her translations of Proust's *The Way by Swann's* (2002) and Flaubert's *Madame Bovary* (2011). Davis has reflected in various places about her translations, not least in their prefaces and in essays about the translations, but also in a small volume entitled *Proust, Blanchot and A Woman in Red* (2007) that discusses her relationship with these authors and Leiris. Davis writes in that book (2007, p. 7) that her approach to translating these authors draws from a very literal approach to translation that she learned while translating Blanchot and which was tested and extended in her translations of Leiris and Proust. Analysis of the translations of these texts finds that they might not be as literal as Davis claims (Evans 2016), but that they are significantly more source-oriented than Davis's other translations (which are often of contemporary French authors). In *Proust, Blanchot and A Woman in Red*, Davis refers to many of her other translations as "work-for-hire translations" (2007, p. 7) and notes that the literal translation style used for Blanchot would not be appropriate for them. While Davis had not translated Flaubert at this point, her translation of *Madame Bovary* fits more into the pattern of her literal translations than her "work-for-hire" ones stylistically and in the way she rewrites Flaubert in her own stories (Evans 2016, pp. 91–101).

The influence of translating on Davis's writing is often speculated on, but Davis herself argues against this: she says that any affinity with an author is present before she begins translating and is what leads her to translate an author (McCaffery 1996, pp. 67–68), although this is not the case of the translations done as work-for-hire, which make up the majority of her work as a translator. Evans (2016) explores the relationship between Davis's translation and writing, concluding that they are often in dialogue with each other: not so much that translating influences her writing, but that her writing often responds to texts she has translated and sometimes prefigures techniques and interests in the translated texts. Davis's work, then, highlights the porosity of the border between translating and writing, especially when her stories also incorporate translation, ultimately asking readers to also reconsider their own understanding of originality and authorship.

SEE ALSO: After Postmodernism; Auster, Paul; Eggers, Dave; Fiction and Affect; The New Experimentalism/The Contemporary Avant-Garde

REFERENCES

Alexander, Karen. (2008). Breaking it down: analysis in the stories of Lydia Davis. In: *Scribbling Women and the Short Story Form: Approaches by American and British Women Writers* (ed. Ellen Burton Harrington), 165–177. New York: Peter Lang.

Blanchot, Maurice. (1999). *The Station Hill Blanchot Reader* (trans. Lydia Davis, Paul Auster, and Robert Lamberton). Barrytown, NY: Station Hill Press.

Blin, Lynn. (2018). When going too far is just far enough: appropriation, parody and adaptation in Lydia Davis's short stories. *Études de Stylistique Anglaise* 13: 141–160.

Bourriaud, Nicolas. (2005). *Postproduction*, 2nd ed. (trans. Jeanine Herman). New York: Lukas and Sternberg.

Cohen, Josh. (2010). Reflexive incomprehension: on Lydia Davis. *Textual Practice* 24 (3): 501–516.

Davis, Lydia. (2007). *Proust, Blanchot and A Woman in Red*. Lewes, UK: Sylph Editions.

Davis, Lydia. (2013). Our Village. In: *Two American Scenes* (ed. Lydia Davis and Eliot Weinberger), 5–36. New York: New Directions.

Davis, Lydia. (2014). *Can't and Won't*. London: Hamish Hamilton.

Evans, Jonathan. (2012). At the borders between translation and parody: Lydia Davis's story about Marie Curie. *TTR Traduction, terminologie, rédaction* 25 (2): 167–191. https://doi.org/10.7202/1018807ar

Evans, Jonathan. (2016). *The Many Voices of Lydia Davis: Translation, Rewriting, Intertextuality.* Edinburgh: Edinburgh University Press.

Flaubert, Gustave. (2011). *Madame Bovary: Provincial Ways* (trans. Lydia Davis). London: Penguin.

Giroud, Françoise. (1986). *Marie Curie: A Life* (trans. Lydia Davis). London: Holmes and Meier.

Knight, Christopher J. (2008). Lydia Davis's own philosophical investigation: *The End of the Story. Journal of Narrative Theory* 38 (2): 198–228.

Leiris, Michel. (1991). *Scratches* (trans. Lydia Davis). New York: Paragon House.

Leiris, Michel. (1995). *Scraps* (trans. Lydia Davis). Baltimore, MD: Johns Hopkins University Press.

Leiris, Michel. (2017). *Fibrils* (trans. Lydia Davis). New Haven, CT: Yale University Press.

McCaffery, Larry. (1996). Deliberately, terribly neutral: an interview with Lydia Davis. In: *Some Other Frequency: Interviews with Innovative American Authors* (ed. Larry McCaffery), 59–79. Philadelphia: University of Pennsylvania Press.

Payne, Johnny. (1993). *Conquest of the New Word: Experimental Fiction and Translation in the Americas.* Austin: University of Texas Press.

Perloff, Marjorie. (1989). Fiction as language game: the hermeneutic parables of Lydia Davis and Maxine Chernoff. In: *Breaking the Sequence: Women's Experimental Fiction* (ed. Ellen G. Friedman and Miriam Fuchs), 199–214. Princeton, NJ: Princeton University Press.

Proust, Marcel. (2002). *The Way by Swann's* (trans. Lydia Davis). London: Penguin.

FURTHER READING

Blin, Lynn. (2017). The voice of the translator and negotiating loss in Lydia Davis's *Can't and Won't. Études de Stylistique Anglaise* 11: 35–54.

Callus, Ivan. (2014). Exhausted replenishment: experimental fiction and the decomposition of literature. *Word and Text* 4 (1): 116–135.

McConnell, Anne. (2018). Writing the impossibility of relation: Marguerite Duras's *La Maladie de la mort*, Maggie Nelson's *Bluets*, and Lydia Davis's *The End of the Story. Comparative Literature Studies* 55 (3): 512–539.

Wood, James. (2009). Songs of myself: Lydia Davis's very, very short stories. *The New Yorker* (October 19, 2009): 88–91. https://www.newyorker.com/magazine/2009/10/19/songs-of-myself

Debut Novels

LAURA B. McGRATH
Temple University, USA

The term debut novel, quite simply, is used to denote the first novel that a writer publishes. Typically, debut novels are published by first-time writers, but the phrase can also be invoked to describe a novel by a poet, an essayist, or a journalist – that is, a writer who works principally in another form. Some of the most significant novels of the late twentieth and early twenty-first centuries are debut novels of the first sort: *The Virgin Suicides* (1993) by Jeffrey Eugenides, *The Intuitionists* (1999) by Colson Whitehead, *The Last Samurai* (2000) by Helen DeWitt, *White Teeth* (2000) by Zadie Smith, *The Known World* (2003) by Edward P. Jones, *The Brief, Wondrous Life of Oscar Wao* (2007) by Junot Díaz, *The Sympathizer* (2015) by Viet Thanh Nguyen. Less frequent, but still significant, are the novels that fall into the second category: *Lincoln in the Bardo* (2016) by George Saunders or *Leaving the Atocha Station* (2011) by Ben Lerner.

More than simply a "first novel," the debut evokes a sense of occasion – a publication event and a social phenomenon. Derived from the French *débuter*, "debut" has been used historically to mark a person's official entrance into society; later adaptations of the phrase focused on the arts – an actor made his London debut, the ballet debuted in Paris. The latter usage has been applied in relation to the literary arts since at least the 1870s, evident in the earliest editions of *Publishers Weekly*, the book industry's major trade journal, founded in 1872. As with the term's early usage in society columns, literary debuts are typically occasions reserved for the young and unknown. Indeed, early literary debuts were often indistinguishable from social debuts, described in the same breathless, gossipy tones as the debutante ball: a new author has arrived on the literary field.

First appearing in *The New York Times* book review in a 1966 advertisement, the term debut *novel* appears to have originated in book marketing departments. Advertisements highlighted an author's debut in order to generate a special sort of excitement and curiosity – the sort of excitement necessary to recruit an audience for an unknown writer. When book reviewers used the term, debut novels were treated as a different category of book, one that required a different sort of critical evaluation. In the 1960s, calling a book a "debut novel" was a sort of qualification and commendation: the novel is great – for a first attempt. More than acknowledging a simple fact about the author, the term debut novel was used to refer to a certain category of a book, and prompted audiences to expect a certain type of reading experience. Overwrought prose, holey plots, and weak stories might be expected, even forgiven, from a first-timer. Later in the twentieth century, the term would be used retrospectively; an older and wiser author would discuss his debut nostalgically or condescendingly, creating distance from his younger, more naive self.

As a literary-sociological phenomenon, the debut novel exploded by the end of the twentieth century, alongside ballooning book advances and changes in acquisition practices. The shift to data-driven acquisitions, paradoxically, made it easier for publishers to acquire debuts. The development of Nielsen BookScan, a centralized database of book sales records, enables publishers to consider an author's sales record (or "track") when considering a manuscript for publication. In one sense, a debut author with no track to commend her is severely disadvantaged in this system; the publisher takes a considerable risk on a new talent. Yet, in another sense, without a track record, a debut novelist represents pure potential. With the right marketing and promotion, a debut can become a hit, and is often more appealing than a midlist book by a modestly selling author. The inflection point came in 1997, with the publication of Charles Frazier's *Cold Mountain*. The debut novel was an unlikely success: Frazier was an unknown writer of literary fiction, not a genre typically thought to be commercially profitable. *Cold Mountain* was acquired by a young editor (Elizabeth Schmitz), at a small house (Grove/Atlantic). Yet, the book sold more than 1.5 million copies in hardcover, 1.3 million copies in paperback, and remained on the bestseller list for sixty-one weeks. Frazier's unexpected success reportedly changed the perception of a debut's potential, with *New York Magazine* calling the debut "the new literary lottery" in 2003 (Williams 2003).

Key to the success of *Cold Mountain* was Frazier's book deal: *Cold Mountain* fetched an advance of $150,000, a (then) unheard-of sum for a debut novelist. Simply put, debut novels emerged as a literary-sociological phenomenon when it became possible for an unproven, first-time writer like Frazier to fetch a large advance – a financial outgrowth of conglomeration. Advances are the sum of money paid to a writer when a publisher acquires their book, based on the number of copies projected to sell. A large advance is a self-fulfilling prophecy, taken as a prime example of the debut novelist's potential; though unknown, the logic goes, the debut author is so promising as to command a six- or seven-figure advance – a sum typically reserved for well-established writers. Significantly, a large advance also secures publisher buy-in. With a substantial amount of money invested in a book, publishers must ensure that a book sells enough copies to cover the cost of the advance (called "earning out"): press releases, author interviews, book tours, the festival circuit. An advance has a cascading effect: the larger the advance for a debut novelist, the more publishers will invest in marketing and promotion, and the bigger the debut will be. It signals a publisher's ambitions for the novel, and hopes for the novelist.

The cascading effect played a major role in the success of *Homegoing* (2016), the debut novel by Yaa Gyasi. The generation-spanning novel about the legacies of slavery in Ghana and the United States reportedly fetched a seven-figure advance for the 25-year-old Ghanaian American graduate of the Iowa Writers' Workshop. Gyasi's novel is breathtaking, but it was the advance that captured the attention of industry professionals. *Publishers Weekly* summarized the situation just ahead of the London Book Fair: "Earlier this week there was concern among industry insiders about the dearth of major projects circulating in the run-up to the London Book Fair. The question people were asking: 'Where are all the big books?' Now, with the fair just days away – it begins on Tuesday – the chatter has turned to silence as a number of major sales have closed in the U.S., among them the acquisition of a debut novel, by a 25-year-old, for a rumored seven figures" (Deahl 2015). Gyasi's advance set a machine into motion: the advance generated significant anticipation within the industry; the anticipation led to increased attention; each step of the information chain helped to promote Gyasi's debut well before it was released.

Because successful debuts hinge on advances, a fairly formulaic "debut narrative" has developed in the promotion around debut novelists, not dissimilar from the *Künstlerroman*: broke young novelist, years of hard work and dreams, giving up once or twice only to recommit to the craft, a chance encounter with an editor or literary agent, and – against all the odds – a whopping advance. And as a result, the debut novel is an object symbolically laden with aspirations, ambitions, and hardship. This was the story that was told when Chad Harbach's novel, *The Art of Fielding*, was published to significant fanfare (and a very large advance) in 2011. As Keith Gessen describes in *How a Book is Born* (2011), Harbach had worked for ten years on his novel – from the time he first took a class on Herman Melville at Harvard, while completing his MFA at the University of Virginia, all the while accruing significant debt. Creditors were calling, but Harbach was as committed to his novel as Ahab to his whale. A stroke of luck: Harbach happened to find the right agent, who happened to find the right editor, and, with a sizable advance ($665,000), Harbach paid off his credit card debt in one fell swoop. That *The Art of Fielding* tells the story of another young artist (a shortstop) desperately trying to make it in the big leagues, even while an aging Melville scholar struggles to find himself, played no small role in the story of Harbach's fairy-tale debut.

Debut novels have played a major role in what James English calls the "economy of prestige." Literary prize committees seem to appreciate the appearance of magnanimity that comes from nominating a debut novel as a major award contender. In 2020, the National Book Foundation boasted, "The 2020 Fiction Longlist counts three debuts among the ten titles." Debuts are a useful symbol for prize committees, a case in point of a committee's impartiality and commitment to meritocracy. Debut novels have also generated their own ecosystem of literary awards, and a number of awards honoring debut writers – and debut novels, in particular – have emerged. The most prominent of these is the PEN/Hemingway Award for Debut Novel, established in 1976, which has identified debut novelists who have become major figures in American letters: Marilynne Robinson, Chang-rae Lee, and Edward P. Jones, among others. More recently established awards include the National Book Critics Circle Leonard Award, and the Center for Fiction's First Novel Prize. Occasionally, debut novel nominations and major award nominations converge. In a dramatic showing, Tommy Orange's 2019 *There There* was shortlisted for the Pulitzer Prize, longlisted for the

National Book Award, and won the American Book Award, in addition to taking home each of the three major debut awards.

Awards dedicated to debut novels and novelists serve a second significant purpose: in addition to honoring excellent debut fiction, these awards invest financially in a young author's career. Each of the major awards for first novels include cash prizes, moving the first-time novelist one step closer to financial stability. While the cash prizes are not so grand that a debut writer can quit their day job, they acknowledge the financial strains that first-time writers face as a major impediment to their second book. For a first-time novelist, financial capital is just as significant – if not even more significant – than symbolic capital if a debut is to mature into a successful career.

A second, less common type of debut occurs when an author who has already been successful in one arena publishes a novel, whether a short story writer (George Saunders, *Lincoln in the Bardo*), a poet (Ben Lerner, *Leaving the Atocha Station*), or journalist (Ta-Nahisi Coates, *The Water Dancer* [2019]). In these instances, the debut makes good use of a publisher's or reader's expectations by subverting them entirely. The debut can be billed as a departure and a novelty, introducing a writer to a different sort of reader while capitalizing on their existing enthusiastic audience. The debut breathes new life into an author's career; this can be particularly significant for an author whose popularity may be on the decline and a genuine coup for an author who is already performing well. For instance, before publishing *Lincoln in the Bardo* in 2016, George Saunders's short stories were anthology staples; his work had appeared on every major bestseller list and every major award shortlist; he had won a MacArthur and a Guggenheim and Lifetime Achievement awards; he had interviewed presidents and had been interviewed by Letterman. Yet, with the publication of *Lincoln in the Bardo*, Saunders, the best-known short story writer in the United States, received the debut author treatment. He was profiled, interviewed, and awarded – this time as a novelist. This type of debut novel does not become a literary event by virtue of the author's newness, but because the author is already well known.

Like any cultural product, debut novels have garnered significant controversy. All book advances are a form of speculation; advances paid for debut novels are even riskier. Absent a track record and other relevant data to help a publisher predict sales and calculate an advance, the debut novelist's fate depends on what sort of book a publisher believes is a good bet – and what sort of debut novelist a publisher is willing to bet on and invest in. In June of 2019, L.L. McKinney took to social media to illuminate the discrepancies in advances, using the hashtag #PublishingPaidMe. The focus of the conversation quickly shifted to debut novels when Chip Cheek, a white man, tweeted that he had received $800,000 for his debut novel, *Cape May*. #PublishingPaidMe revealed that writers of color receive significantly lower advances than white writers. Jesmyn Ward, for instance, struggled to publish her debut novel, *Where the Line Bleeds* (2008), even though she boasted solid institutional credentials as a former Stegner Fellow with an MFA from the University of Michigan. Ward declined to disclose the advance for her debut; her second novel, *Salvage the Bones* (2011), which won the National Book Award, received only $20,000 in an advance. Ward would not receive a six-figure advance until *Sing, Unburied, Sing* (2017) – a novel that would also win a National Book Award.

Debut buzz is not uniformly thought to be positive. Much-publicized debuts ramp up expectations for a book to perform. If those expectations are not met, even if the debut is successful by most accounts, the novelist may struggle to find a publisher for the second book. As one publisher put it, in *New York Magazine*, "The writer has got two or three years to make the money back. If he doesn't, that big advance might be the last nickel he ever earns in the book business" (Williams 2003). Investing in an author's debut should not be mistaken for developing a writer's career. Many writers have disappointing debuts, only to see their third or fourth novel "break out." Too much emphasis on the debut, many critics believe, has an adverse effect on the literary field by denying writers the opportunity to mature.

Likewise, debut buzz can lead to overexposure and sour grapes. When Jonathan Safran Foer's debut novel, *Everything is Illuminated* (2002), was sold for a seven-figure advance and the novelist became an overnight celebrity, the backlash was intense. The precocious and highly successful writer found himself the butt of jokes and the target of satire – the young novelist that everyone loved to hate. "There's something about Jonathan Safran Foer that drives a certain breed of dyspeptic New York writer/blogger to drink – more so than usual, anyway. They chafe at the six-figure advances, the visiting professor gigs at Yale and NYU, the majestic Park Slope brownstone," began a *Vanity Fair* review of Foer's third novel, *Tree of Codes* (Wagner 2010). A term was coined for the phenomenon: "Schadenfoer" (Weinman 2008). Foer's financial windfall has been cited as one source of Schadenfoer; his advance stood in stark contrast to his publisher's decline (Houghton Mifflin) and the perceived dire straits of the book business in general. Provoking devotion and irritation in equal measure, Foer's debut continues to define his career.

Whether debut novels adhere to a particular form or genre remains a topic of some debate. Some argue that, as the product of years of solitary labor, debut novels are more ambitious, and perhaps more autonomously produced. Some argue that debuts are immature. Some argue that debuts merely repackage MFA theses and thus have a particular writer's workshop quality, were written too much to please a mentor or adviser. Still, the speculation suggests that debuts are less any one type of novel than a category created to sell novels. As a firmly entrenched literary-sociological category with well-established norms and narratives, debut novels will continue to proliferate in ever more diverse forms, and continue to occupy a growing share of the contemporary literary field.

SEE ALSO: Díaz, Junot; Eugenides, Jeffrey; Foer, Jonathan Safran; Frazier, Charles; Lee, Chang-rae; Lerner, Ben; Robinson, Marilynne; Saunders, George; Viet Thanh Nguyen; Ward, Jesmyn; Whitehead, Colson

REFERENCES

Deahl, Rachel. (2015). London Book Fair 2015: in pre-fair deals, debut sells to Knopf for rumored 7 figures. *Publishers Weekly* (April 10, 2015). https://www.publishersweekly.com/pw/by-topic/international/london-book-fair/article/66206-london-book-fair-2015-in-pre-fair-deals-debuts-and-non-fic-projects-draw-big-advances.html (accessed July 13, 2021).

English, James. (2005). *The Economy of Prestige*. Cambridge, MA: Harvard University Press.

Gessen, Keith. (2011). *How a Book is Born*. New York: Vanity Fair.

National Book Foundation. (2020). 2020 National Book Awards Longlist for Fiction. https://www.nationalbook.org/2020-national-book-awards-longlist-for-fiction/ (accessed July 13, 2021).

Wagner, Heather. (2010). Jonathan Safran Foer talks *Tree of Codes* and conceptual art. *Vanity Fair* (November 10, 2010). https://www.vanityfair.com/culture/2010/11/jonathan-safran-foer-talks-tree-of-codes-and-paper-art (accessed July 13, 2021).

Weinman, Sarah. (2008). What's with all the Jonathan Safran Foer-phobia? *The Guardian* (December 11, 2008). https://www.theguardian.com/books/booksblog/2008/dec/11/safran-foer-hatred (accessed July 13, 2021).

Williams, Alex. (2003). The new literary lottery. *New York Magazine* (July 11, 2003). https://nymag.com/nymetro/news/media/features/n_8972/ (accessed July 13, 2021).

FURTHER READING

Childress, Clayton. (2017). *Under the Cover: The Creation, Production and Reception of a Novel.* Princeton: Princeton University Press.

McGrath, Laura B. (2019). Comping white. *The Los Angeles Review of Books* (January 21, 2019). https://lareviewofbooks.org/article/comping-white/

Thompson, John B. (2010). *Merchants of Culture.* Cambridge: Polity Press.

Delany, Samuel R.

KIRIN WACHTER-GRENE
School of the Art Institute of Chicago, USA

Samuel R. Delany (b. 1942), Black queer writer, critic, and polymath known by his childhood nickname "Chip," was born on April Fool's Day, 1942, in New York City. He published his first novel, *The Jewels of Aptor* (1962), at age 20, announcing the arrival of a prodigy. Throughout his career he "has explored to the roots various realms of discourse: societies, languages, sexualities . . . and the ever-shifting interpretations, transgressions, limitations, and dissolutions that play and replay between them" (*The Straights of Messina*, 1989). Two science fiction novels written in his twenties, *Babel-17* (1966), about a Chinese poet translating the weaponized language of an alien race, and *The Einstein Intersection* (1967), a retelling of the Orpheus myth, received Nebula Awards recognizing the best work of science fiction or fantasy in the United States. Among his other eminent novels are *Nova* (1969), a precursor to cyberpunk, *Dhalgren* (1975), an epic journey through the devastated city of Bellona, and the eleven sword-and-sorcery stories and novels comprising the *Return to Nevèrÿon* series (1979–1987). In 2002 Delany was inducted into the Science Fiction and Fantasy Hall of Fame. In 2010 he was honored with the J. Lloyd Eaton Lifetime Achievement Award in Science Fiction and in 2013 was named Science Fiction Writers of America Grand Master.

Delany is one of the most recognized, influential writers of science fiction and the genre's first major Black writer, as detailed in his essay "Racism and Science Fiction" (1988), which is collected in *The Atheist in the Attic* (2018). But he has defied categorization from the beginning. The cult classic science fiction novel *Dhalgren* – his eleventh and most popular novel – sold over a million copies, but he is also an avid writer of sword-and-sorcery, historical fiction, realism, autobiography, cultural and literary criticism, short stories, essays and silent (written) interviews, and erotica that he is happy to call pornography, such as *Equinox* (1994, originally *The Tides of Lust* [1973]), *Hogg* (1995), *The Mad Man* (1994, although Delany considers the 2015 republication the definitive version), *Phallos* (2004), and *Through the Valley of the Nest of Spiders* (2012). Often, his work is purposefully generically indistinguishable.

Delany is an innovator. Despite or in addition to its paraliterary qualities, his fiction is densely philosophical and theoretical. To take *Babel-17* as an example, what might seem like a pulpy paperback is also a complex meditation on language. Science fiction is not, for Delany, about a speculative future. It is a distortion of the present, poised in dialogic relation to the given. He is a deconstructionist influenced by French theorists Jaques Derrida, Roland Barthes, and Michel Foucault, which informs his formal and conceptual experimentation. He is a lover of sentences and their capacity to expose the relation between words and worlds. For Delany, a staunch materialist, form, much like genre, is historically situated and fluctuating. He possesses an inimitable style, the strangeness and richness of which cannot be captured, such as in his Nebula award-winning short story "Aye, and Gomorrah. . ." (1967) with its impossible to determine first or final sentence or in his essay "On the Unspeakable" (1992), shaped like a Möbius strip. In his forward to *Dhalgren* William Gibson calls Delany "the most remarkable prose stylist to have emerged from the culture of American science fiction."

Delany's fiction is not only theoretically informed; he is a theorist himself. Beginning with his groundbreaking *The Jewel-Hinged Jaw* (1977), which applies semiotics to science fiction studies, he has published several collections of criticism taking up philosophy, sexuality, politics, literary history, technology, and more. Carl Freedman argues, "there are few writers in the United States today – or anywhere else, for that matter – who can match Delany in the number of topics that engage his attention or the supple, self-reflexive intelligence with which he treats them" (2009, p. ix). In addition to *The American Shore* (1978), a semiotic study of Thomas Disch's short story "Angouleme," and *Starboard Wine* (1984), much of this critical work is collected in *Silent Interviews: On Language, Race, Sex, Science Fiction, and Some Comics* (1994), *Longer Views* (1996), and *Shorter Views: Queer Thoughts and the Politics of the Paraliterary* (1999). Occasionally Delany employs his alter ego "K. Leslie Steiner" – a Black female critic – to discuss his own work, such as in *The Straights of Messina*.

And yet, Delany did not always know he wanted to dedicate his life to being a writer. Raised in Harlem as the son of a funeral director and a court stenographer, Delany attended the prestigious Bronx High School of Science and the City College of New York. He considered becoming a mathematician, composer, or physicist, all while consistently writing. He published his first novel upon dropping out of college after one semester. His first short story was published five years later, in 1967, helping to usher in the "New Wave" of science fiction (which included authors Harlan Ellison, Norman Spinrad, and Roger Zelazny) emphasizing soft sciences and literary experimentation over hard sciences and technology. Throughout the 1960s Delany published nine science fiction novels and two award-winning short stories, the other being "Time Considered as a Helix of Semi-Precious Stones" (1968), collected in *Aye and Gomorrah and Other Stories* (2002).

Delany's negotiations with his own emergent sexuality in the 1960s and the politics of sex appear in his memoirs *Heavenly Breakfast* (1979) and the Hugo-award winning *The Motion of Light in Water* (1988) but they inform his work in many ways. He was married to poet Marilyn Hacker from 1961 to 1980 (although they separated in 1975). Their daughter Iva Hacker-Delany was born in 1974. However, Delany has self-identified as gay since he was a child (Hacker was aware of his sexual orientation and his extramarital affairs with men) and has been with his current partner, Dennis Rickett, a formerly unhoused book vendor, since 1991. That latter relationship is captured in the erotic, autobiographical graphic novel *Bread and Wine* (1999), illustrated by Mia Wolff. Despite these long-term relationships, Delany is a sex radical who estimates his sexual partners to number 50,000. *Dhalgren* is his first novel to explicitly feature gay sex, a theme that has grown increasingly graphic and abundant. He has relied upon his extensive cruising to inform such representations both in his fictional work and in the best-selling part pornographic memoir, part urban sociological study *Times Square Red, Times Square Blue* (1999).

Delany is thus gaining attention as a queer cultural icon. He has won awards recognizing his contributions as a godfather of LGBTQ literature. Committed to defamiliarizing what society considers normal, Delany has always advocated a politics of difference, testifying to and giving voice to disregarded perspectives and social relations along the intersections of class, race, sex, and gender. He fearlessly reveals that other worlds are not only possible, they already exist. As his work grew increasingly radical throughout the 1990s and 2000s he found himself marginalized in the science fiction and Black literary communities.

Nevertheless, Delany's worldview is life-affirming. Many have been fortunate to not only read but learn from him. He was a professor of comparative literature at University of Massachusetts, Amherst for eleven years, and retired from Temple University in 2015, where he has taught creative writing since 2001. A lifelong dyslexic, he always told his students, "I don't write. I rewrite," emphasizing the process and great challenge of the craft. (Further advice and reflections on Delany's practice are collected in *About Writing* [2005]). Unsurprisingly, many of his novels feature poets or writers. His own work is required reading in many college courses, although, because he remains ghettoized as a queer writer or a science fiction writer, he is less often considered one of the most important American writers. His marginalization in the African American literary canon is particularly ironic given his work's thematic resonance with Black feminist literature and Black pulp fiction of the 1960s–1980s, and anticipation of work on pleasure politics, abjection, and transgression. Transgression, in particular, is not a new Black aesthetic. It has always informed African American literature.

Delany has been writing about sex explicitly and earnestly since the 1960s and continues to do so late into his career. For instance, "Ash Wednesday" (2017) is a moving piece detailing Delany's experience as an aging sex radical at his first sex party, reworking themes first explored in *Dark Reflections* (2007) about an older, gay writer in the East Village. Delany's significant work about sex and gender in the 1970s and 1980s includes his science fiction comedy of manners *Triton* (1976), later published as *Trouble on Triton*, a prologue to his masterpiece the *Return to Nevèrÿon* series. That epic project, which best encapsulates Delany's blurring of fiction and nonfiction, narrative and theory, is published in four volumes: *Tales of Nevèrÿon* (1979); *Nevèrÿona, or: The Tale of Signs and Cities* (1983); *Flight from Nevèrÿon* (1985); and the *Return to Nevèrÿon* (first published as *The Bridge of Lost Desire* [1987]). Notably, *Flight from Nevèrÿon* contains "The Tale of Plagues and Carnivals." Written in 1984 during the second year of the AIDS crisis and paralleling those unfolding events in New York City, "The Tale of Plagues and Carnivals" is famous as the first novel-length representation of AIDS published in America.

The series as a whole, however, is set before the dawn of modern civilization and concerns the reigning people of Nevèrÿon (all of whom have black and brown skin) and a tribe of blond, blue-eyed barbarians, unsettling the historical American racialized power structure. The barbarians were the slaves of the reigning tribe, and the eleven stories circulate around a mixed-race slave named Gorgik the Liberator, a man who, despite his enslavement and eventual leadership of an emancipatory movement, is erotically attracted to slavery's apparatuses.

Delany has never been one to shy away from challenging representations of sex and sexuality that force readers to contend with the messy relationship between desire and politics. Rather, he has courageously led the way. Depictions of eroticized slavery (in a BDSM – bondage/discipline, dominance/submission, sadism/masochism – sense) are also present in some of his other most well-known work, including "Time Considered as a Helix of Semi-Precious Stones," *Dhalgren* and the space opera novel *Stars in My Pocket Like Grains of Sand* (1984). According to the author himself, one can find what he "is all about" by wrestling with such representations and their power to interest and unsettle readers (Delany 1999, p. 119). This perhaps contributes to Delany's marginalization within the African American literary canon. Critics recognize him as central to Afrofuturism, but rarely discuss his transgressive eroticism despite the fact that established African American writers such as Toni Morrison, Gayl Jones, and Octavia Butler explore similar representations. For instance, critic Jeffrey Allen Tucker leaves analyses of some of Delany's most challenging pornography, such as *Hogg*, to "more intrepid critics" (2004, p. 4).

This hesitation is understandable. Yet Delany's pornography, which has been described as the "promiscuously autobiographical" work of a "confessional genius," offers invaluable resources for theorizing transgression, particularly through "the unspeakable." In "On the Unspeakable" (collected in *Shorter Views*) Delany describes the concept in at least three ways. First, as an erotic articulation of certain "dangerous" practices of relation that "represent lines of communication, fields of interest, and exchanges of power," often written about in "language associated with abjection" (Delany 1994, pp. 136–137; 1999, p. 66). Second, the unspeakable is "a set of positive conventions governing what can be spoken of (or written about) in general" (1999, p. 61). It illuminates the generic conventions of what can be articulated, how, and in what contexts. It may "be the prototype for all social division" (p. 58). As the essay's Möbius strip form (part pornography, part theory) illustrates, the unspeakable is, on one hand, inextricable from the everyday, and is, on the other, constantly under threat of containment. Lastly, Delany describes the unspeakable – impossible to extricate from desire – as those matters that are "extralinguistic" (p. 58). Such matters are often articulated through pornography in which extralinguistic excess in the form of desire accompanies the written word and can produce transgressive discomfort and/or pleasure for the characters, the author, and the reader. Exploring this interrelated arousal and unease attests to the unspeakable's power to trouble supposedly contained representations of sex, race, and gender.

Times Square Red, Times Square Blue further develops Delany's theory. Part pornographic memoir, part argument for the necessity of interclass contact (contact across class distinctions, a recurring motif in his work), the book addresses the gentrification of New York City's Times Square neighborhood through the forced closure of adult film theaters under then-Mayor Rudolph Giuliani's 1995 rezoning laws. Delany illustrates the dangerous effects these forced closures have on New York's gay and working class communities and on the general health of the city and inhabitants' quality of life. One is invited to read the two extended essays that comprise this work alongside and through one another, much like "On the Unspeakable." Delany's theory of the unspeakable suggests that when transgression, always under threat of containment, is driven further underground, violence and abuse proliferates.

This is perhaps best illustrated in *Hogg* – one of the most extreme and infamously unpublishable American novels. Told from the point of view of an unnamed 11-year-old, the narrator recalls his involvement with Franklin Hargus ("Hogg") and Hogg's gang of "rape artists" over 72 hours. Perhaps most transgressive is *Hogg*'s graphic representations of a consensual juvenile/adult sexual relationship. Specifically, the child is *not* represented as pathological nor a victim (which Delany has reiterated). *Hogg* explicitly defies judgment, moralizing, or sentimentality, which, again, in classic Delanyian fashion, creates a complex relationship to politics. It forces the reader to contend with their own reading experience and attempts to rationalize the narrative (an experience similar to grappling with Gorgik from the Nevèrÿon series as a mixed-race slave eroticizing slavery and *The Mad Man*, a novel about a Black, gay grad student having unprotected sex with unhoused men amidst the growing AIDS crisis).

On the book jacket John O'Brien claims "*Hogg* is a truly significant book. It is distasteful, raw, and upsetting; it also treats some of the sexual taboos that Americans do not want addressed in either art or politics. *Hogg* is an artistic triumph, as well as a political one." Delany completed the first draft several days before the Stonewall Riots in June 1969, an uprising that ushered in the modern Gay Liberation movement. Thus, *Hogg* is, by Delany's own estimation, ". . . the last, or among the last, pre-Stonewall gay novels written within the United States . . . It was written by a 27-year-old black gay man who was as furious and as outraged by the sexual condition of the country as any of those black queens back on Waverly Place" (Roberts 2003, p. 121). *Hogg*, along with *The Motion of Light in Water*, "The Tale of Plagues and Carnivals," *Times Square Red, Times Square Blue*, and *The Mad Man*, are essential to American gay history, particularly New York City in the 1960s through the 1980s and gay men's fluctuating attitudes toward sex, politics, and AIDS.

Excess, transgression, perversion, all represented in *Hogg* and in Delany's other pornographic work, are powerful tactics. *Hogg* suggests perversion can be an analytic, offering a critique of both oppressive power structures and complicity in maintaining and perpetuating everyday violence scapegoated onto outsiders or cordoned off into the realm of the unspeakable. In *Hogg*'s pornotopia and in those of *The Mad Man* and *Through the Valley of the Nest of Spiders* Delany's characters engage transgression as a political tactic as much as an act of pleasure to combat oppression that delimits identities and relations, thereby censoring knowledge. Characters in *Hogg* as well as in all of Delany's pornography are on a quest for knowledge, often though abjection.

As he argues in *Times Square Red, Times Square Blue*, Delany believes such knowledge should be public, not secretive, invisible, and criminalized which can foster external willful denial and internal harm. He is committed to maintaining the public visibility of marginality, difference, and perversion not to normalize them to banality but to construct better social conditions for transgressive persons and acts. Transgression as a political tactic therefore works to trouble structures that oppressively deny identities different from the heteropatriarchal norm and deny the reality of certain desires that even though perverse, are still productive in terms of thinking through how bodies and sexual relations are situated within socially constructed boundaries.

Delany's greatest contribution to discourses of race and sex lies in the unspeakable, and ultimately, the unspeakable is a mode of attention. Using it to formulate an analysis of transgressive pleasure that we read in so much of Delany's work and that is present in much African American literature gives critical attention to what has been erased, denied, devalued, and censored – and forces us to continually contend with *why*. Although transgressive sexuality, pleasure, and desire remain heavily fraught topics, particularly in relation to race and gender, African American, queer, and Black feminist literary and visual studies increasingly explore these representations. We would be wise to remember that Samuel R. Delany was at the forefront of these conversations, and is still leading the way.

SEE ALSO: Afrofuturism; Butler, Octavia; Cooper, Dennis; Cyberpunk; Diaz, Junot; Gibson, William; Gomez, Jewelle; Jones, Gayl; Le Guin, Ursula; Queer and LGBT Fiction

REFERENCES

Delany, Samuel R. (1994). *Silent Interviews: On Language, Race, Sex, Science Fiction, and Some Comics*. Hanover, NH: Wesleyan University Press.

Delany, Samuel R. (1999). *Shorter Views: Queer Thoughts & the Politics of the Paraliterary*. Hanover, NH: Wesleyan University Press.

Freedman, Carl. (ed.) (2009). *Conversations with Samuel R. Delany*. Jackson: University Press of Mississippi.

Roberts, Adam. (2003). An interview with Samuel R. Delany. In: *Conversations with Samuel R. Delany* (ed. Carl Freedman), 101–124. Jackson: University Press of Mississippi.

Tucker, Jeffrey Allen. (2004). *A Sense of Wonder: Samuel R. Delany, Race, Identity, and Difference*. Hanover, NH: Wesleyan University Press.

FURTHER READING

Delany, Samuel R. (2000). *1984: Selected Letters*. Rutherford, NJ: Voyant.

James, Kenneth R. (ed.) (2017). *In Search of Silence: The Journals of Samuel R. Delany. Volume 1, 1957–1969*. Hanover, NH: Wesleyan University Press.

Sallis, James. (ed.) (1996). *Ash of Stars: On the Writing of Samuel R. Delany*. Jackson: University Press of Mississippi.

DeLillo, Don

LAURA BARRETT
State University of New York at New Paltz, USA

Despite numerous accolades in a fifty-year career that includes the publication of seventeen novels, five plays, over twenty short stories, numerous essays, and a screenplay, Don DeLillo has managed to resist the celebrity that usually accompanies being one of America's most acclaimed authors. Still living near his childhood home in New York with his wife, landscape designer Barbara Bennet, DeLillo has cast his unrelenting and often prescient gaze on the effects of global terrorism, late-stage capitalism, mindless consumerism, and intrusive media. And while most readers agree on an identifiable DeLillo style, a comparison of *Underworld* (1997) and *The Body Artist* (2001), which were published within a three-year period, belies any facile summary of his voice, which shifts seamlessly from glib dialogue about garbage to poetic ruminations on the nature of being. His process of writing manuscripts on a typewriter, one paragraph per page – the better to see the shape of the words and sentences – flatly denies any arbitrary separation of poetry and prose.

Born in the Bronx to Italian immigrants in 1936, DeLillo was steeped in the language of New York City, Catholicism, and cinema. While he doesn't give much credit to his degree in communication arts and his relationship to religion is complicated, his education at the hands of Jesuits at Fordham University informs much of his work. By his own admission, his taste ran to jazz and European avant-garde films rather than books, but James Joyce, among others, provided his entry into the world of literature. His early literary career is marked by a few short stories, but it wasn't until 1971, several years after DeLillo quit his copywriting job, that his first novel, *Americana*, was published. That decade saw the publication of five more novels: *End Zone* (1972), *Great Jones Street* (1973), *Ratner's Star* (1976), *Players* (1977), and *Running Dog* (1978) (not to mention, which is DeLillo's preference, the 1978 co-authored *Amazons*, written under the pseudonym Cleo Birdwell), works that showed a deft use of language and extraordinary scope.

DeLillo's career was on the ascendancy by 1980, illustrated in part by the plethora of distinguished awards that he has earned, including a 1978 Guggenheim Fellowship which provided DeLillo the opportunity to travel in the Middle East and live in Greece for a year, during which he wrote *The Names* (1982), considered by many to be the beginning of his mature style. DeLillo's sixth novel offers his first serious foray into foreign territory, focusing on James Axton, an American who takes an assignment in Athens to be close to his child and estranged wife. Axton is a writer who has put his talents to work as an analyst assessing the risk of terrorism in the Middle East, and, following in the tradition of oblivious Americans perfected by Henry James, has limited understanding of (and even less curiosity about) his position, including the fact that his employers provide information for the CIA. Essentially a tourist, Axton refuses to learn sufficient Greek to engage in the most rudimentary conversations. Here, DeLillo continues a preoccupation with language that occupies so much of his earlier novels, especially *End Zone*, as Axton obsessively follows a cult whose members engage in ritual killings when the victims' initials match those of the place in which they are murdered, vicariously participating in their action while maintaining a facade of innocence. That facade, however, has already been shattered by his assault on Janet Ruffing and his collusion in an unsuccessful plot to send an unconscious acquaintance to Tehran in the midst of the Iran hostage crisis. The novel's conclusion suggests that language – the babble of tourists in the Acropolis or an imaginative tale, full of "spirited misspellings" – is the consolation we have in the absence of a master narrative, but language in *The Names* is a double-edged sword because it is also entangled in his sexual assault and in the United States' overreach in the Middle East (1989, p. 313).

DeLillo continues to investigate the possibility of latent meaning in nonsensical language and the consequences of the actions of irresponsible men in *White Noise* (1985), a novel that chronicles Jack Gladney, a scholar of Hitler Studies who doesn't speak German, as he grapples with his fear of death in a secular environment that offers no consolations or answers. It is DeLillo's most comical critique of American culture, juxtaposing the most mundane of subjects – a couple raising children from their own and previous marriages in a small college town – against a backdrop of environmental catastrophe and existential crisis. While the novel, as many critics have noted, is a virtual primer on poststructuralism and postmodernism, illustrating the endless deferral of meaning, the hopelessly duplicated nature of contemporary experience, and the contemporary loss of faith in metanarratives, it skewers contemporary theory and criticism in a cast of academic characters who study cereal boxes, car crashes, and Elvis Presley. In this new world, we are no longer able to access our own reality because, as Murray Siskind observes, no one sees "the most photographed barn" because of the signs that precede it, and we can't experience our own calamities because we are too anxious anticipating the incipient media coverage. The novel's focus on late-twentieth-century culture is counterbalanced by an immersion in American history, tradition, and neuroses, invoking both the mythology of American Westerns and John Winthrop's seventeenth-century *Arbella* sermon, "A Model of Christian Charity" (1630), that identified the colonies as "a city on a hill"(Winthrop 1985, p. 91).

Libra (1988) marks DeLillo's entry into historiographic metafiction, in which historical figures mingle with fictional characters with the seemingly paradoxical effect of making visible the narrative impulse of historiography and highlighting the importance of both historical events and literary ventures. That impulse is evidenced in the storytelling ambitions of all the characters, particularly Lee Harvey Oswald, who aspires to write short stories about contemporary American life, and Nicholas Branch, the fictional CIA agent who is tasked with the impossible job of creating a coherent narrative from the random and myriad pieces of evidence and detritus.

The novel portrays Oswald as an outsider, a man in search of a personality and a plot who crafts his persona from television and film images and creates a succession of alter egos, pseudonyms that he uses to hide elements of his life and plan. In DeLillo's version, Oswald fails even in the culminating event of his life, having been used by the CIA but not having delivered the bullet that killed the president. While there may be a conspiracy at the heart of Libra, its endgame is hopelessly co-opted by the drives of individuals. The novel signals the absence of a single definitive narrative, reminding us that the twentieth century – steeped in the language of advertising and multinational companies – ushered in a "world of randomness and ambiguity," "uncertainty and chaos" (1983, pp. 22, 24).

Following the trajectory of another man confined to a small room who yearns to become part of history, Mao II (1991) explores the role of art in a world whose values are shaped by power, wealth, and image and where terrorists seem to wield most of the influence. The work of art in the age of mechanical reproduction is central to Mao II as Bill Gray, alias William Skansey, a reclusive writer whose two slim novels have cast a shadow so intimidating that another work would only diminish his aura, relies on photographs to raise him from the dead. After two decades of seclusion, Gray ventures out into the world in the hope of having an impact at least as powerful as terrorists. While his anonymous accidental death bodes ill for the power of art, the novel offers a more potent figure in the form of Brita Nilsson, a photographer, whose self-imposed assignments shift from the mundane (photographing authors) to the political (photographing terrorists). The structure of the novel, punctuated by reproductions of photographs, most of which chronicle pivotal historical events, would seem to reinforce the theme of the dominance of images were it not for the fact that most of the images are indistinct and blurred. The importance of the individual is affirmed by the novel's last photograph of a group of boys amidst the rubble in Beirut and the flash of Nilsson's camera as she serendipitously photographs the exuberant revelers of a wedding party, looking "surprisingly alive[, . . .] transcendent, free of limits" (1991, p. 240).

Six years after the publication of Mao II, DeLillo produced his magnum opus, Underworld, a sprawling novel that chronicles much of the second half of the twentieth century, largely from the perspective of Nick Shay whose trajectory from delinquent teenager to middle-aged man we witness nonlinearly amid a panoply of plots and characters. As DeLillo has noted, the idea for the novel began with a New York Times article that he uncovered after reading about the 40th anniversary of the Giants–Dodgers 1952 Pennant game. The front page of the October 4, 1959, New York Times offered two symmetrical articles on far left and right columns describing Thomson's historic home run and a successful nuclear bomb explosion in Russia, perfectly encapsulating Cold War tensions within American mythology. The novel, whose tag line is "everything is connected," aims to connect everything through a baseball that links the work's tentacled plots (1997, p. 826). The baseball, moreover, becomes an emblem not of victory but of loss for Nick, a Dodgers fan, and that sense of loss and death pervades the novel. Nick's career in waste management sets the stage for the novel's preoccupation with garbage, ranging from excretive bodily functions to an acquisitive consumerist mentality and affluence that ensures the United States can outsource the disposal of its garbage to less fortunate nations. In their recycling of found objects, artists Klara Sax and Ismael Muñoz become waste managers of another sort, not unlike the narrator of the book who creates a bricolage from historical flotsam, providing rhythm and symmetry through fictional elements.

That rhythm and symmetry creates vivid images, especially in the novel's prologue, which describes the fateful baseball game in political, racial, and regional binaries. J. Edgar Hoover's attendance at the game (alongside Jackie Gleason, Frank Sinatra, and Toots Shor) reconnects the baseball with the Soviet Union's bomb, conflating for a moment the exuberant and life-affirming excitement of the crowd and narration by Russ Hodges with the thanatotic undercurrent of the event, illustrated by Pieter Bruegel's *Triumph of Death* (1562; ironically reproduced in *Life* magazine), which is reduced to celebratory confetti (and, ultimately, waste). The prologue stages the easy camaraderie of two die-hard fans, white businessman Bill Waterson and Black high school student Cotter Martin, that turns acidic when they grapple for the pennant-winning ball. The prologue serves as the origin story that DeLillo's characters seek, but it is denied to Nick, who never traces the provenance of the ball.

In 2001, DeLillo's style changed markedly from the expansive, Whitmanesque epic of *Underworld* and the slangy argot of his earlier works to the spare prose of *The Body Artist*, a slim novel about loss, grief, and memory. The novel lovingly details the quotidian elements of an intimate breakfast between performing artist Lauren Hartke and filmmaker Rey Robles before revealing Rey's suicide through a news article. While trying to process her grief, Hartke encounters a stranger in the house whom she calls Mr. Tuttle, a deracinated childlike man with a limited vocabulary, no sense of time, and an uncanny ability for mimicry that is often used to resurrect Rey. Critics diverge on even the most elemental understanding of the plot. Is Mr. Tuttle real or a delusion? Is he merely a metaphor for grief and memory? Is he a manifestation of the many worlds theory or an embodiment of quantum physics? Equally ambiguous is the novel's conclusion in which Hartke performs, shedding all aspects of herself, shaving her body clear of hair and leaving her virtually unrecognizable so that she can adopt the personae of characters, male and female, thus linking her to Mr. Tuttle. In keeping with DeLillo's ambiguous endings, it is never clear whether Lauren's encounter with Mr. Tuttle or her performance project provide opportunities to move beyond melancholy.

While *Cosmopolis* (2003) is not, strictly speaking, DeLillo's post-9/11 novel (as it was mostly written before the event), it certainly reads like a description of the catastrophic consequences of late-stage capitalism run amuck. Hedge fund manager Eric Packer is a wunderkind whose investments have made him a billionaire at 28 years. He shares the ailments of many of DeLillo's male protagonists, but his willingness, even desire, to bring the financial world to ruin to satisfy his own self-destructive fantasies raises the toxicity of this particular DeLillo character to new heights. The novel chronicles Packer's crosstown trek from the east side of Manhattan to Hell's Kitchen in pursuit of a haircut from his childhood barber. The nostalgia that propels that expedition doesn't pertain to words, as Eric is determined to dismantle the language as we know it, jettisoning terms he deems obsolete – "skyscraper," "handgun," "office." Incongruously, he has a poetic disposition (not to mention a literary connection to Stephen Dedalus confirmed by the structure of the novel and a resemblance to Icarus noted by his adversary/double, Benno Levin), evinced by the language of the opening sequence – Packer's awakening – that recalls the proem of Hart Crane's "The Bridge" (1930). Whatever opportunities for synthesis and connection that Crane's poem offers, however, no longer exist by the twenty-first century in DeLillo's jeremiad on the loss of embodiment and attachment.

Published six years after 9/11, *Falling Man* (2007) considers how we respond to the past, especially when it is marked by trauma. Protagonist Keith Neudecker escapes from the World Trade Center on September 11, but the memory of the event and the loss of his colleague and friends haunt him. Already a drifter, as are so many of DeLillo's characters, Neudecker's fecklessness is exacerbated by his traumatic experience. Tangential connections to his estranged wife, his son, and his lover (whom he meets after both survive the terrorist attacks) further unravel as he seeks the contradictory illusion of control and sensation of free-falling inherent in gambling. His wife, Lianne, on the other hand, commemorates the past and its representations through her work helping Alzheimer's patients capture their memories before they disappear. That composed response to the past lies in direct opposition to the eponymous performance artist, David Janiak, whose shocking and provocative staged falls throughout New York City, recalling the victims who jumped from the towers after the attacks, refuse to allow the past to be forgotten.

What had been a decade-long disquisition on loneliness, loss, and despair takes a more sinister turn in *Point Omega* (2010) whose primary plot follows the efforts of Jim Finley, a filmmaker intent on making a candid documentary, "just a man and a wall," about Richard Elster, a defense intellectual who advised the Bush administration on post-9/11 torture tactics (2010, p. 21). The novel's preoccupation with film is further evinced by opening and closing chapters that reveal the thoughts of a man observing Douglas Gordon's *24 Hour Psycho* (1993), a reproduction of Hitchcock's film shown at two frames per second rather than the typical twenty-four. These plots intersect when Elster's daughter Jessie disappears in the Arizona desert. The wildly divergent settings of New York City, particularly the Museum of Modern Art, and the desert are, in part, connected by the film's treatise on time and mortality. Second only to *The Body Artist*, *Point Omega* is DeLillo's most confounding novel, refusing to answer questions about Jessie's disappearance or eliciting much information about Elster's desire for "a haiku war . . . a war in three lines," sparse, elemental, evanescent (2010, p. 29). Following Elster to his retreat in the desert, Finley effectively becomes his subject's double, a man who must grapple with his own culpability as he recalls his own stalking of Jessie before her vanishing. Like *Running Dog*'s Glen Selvy, *The Names*' Axton, and *Libra*'s Oswald, Finley becomes an actor in a plot that he refused to notice.

Zero K (2016) continues many of the threads of previous works, including our fear of death and desire for immortality, the ease with which we surrender our freedom for security, and, following *Point Omega*, the fact that we are essentially alone in our navigation of the world. We follow Jeffrey Lockhart's heartbreak as he loses his stepmother, Artis Martineau, and later his father, Ross Lockhart, to the Convergence, a cryonics facility that barters the promise of everlasting life for a hefty sum of money. Jeff is another of DeLillo's drifters, refusing to settle in a job or in a relationship until he meets Emma, a special needs teacher and the mother of Stak, an adopted Ukrainian teen. Again, we confront two worlds – the urban bustle of New York City and the stultifying cryonics facility set in the Central Asian desert. Like so many of DeLillo's novels, *Zero K* seems to focus so much on ontology and epistemology that we can easily overlook how political it is, but DeLillo's reference to Heidegger reminds us that philosophy and politics often collide. The videos of climactic catastrophe and human suffering, including Stak's death in the Ukrainian struggle against Russia, used by the Convergence to persuade its clients that the world is hardly worth living in, remind us of specific global crises. The novel's oblique ending offers another example of "radiance in dailiness" (DeCurtis 1999, p. 59), the unexplainable, extraordinary aspect of our daily lives as Jeff experiences Manhattanhenge from a crosstown bus, an ending that is reminiscent of *White Noise*, making clear that the "extraordinary wonder of things is somehow related to the extraordinary dread, to the death fear we try to keep beneath the surface of our perceptions" (p. 63).

DeLillo's latest and most apocalyptic novel, *The Silence*, illustrates our response to a breakdown in technology, which renders the contrivances of modern life – cell phones, television, elevators, computers – impotent. Who are we, the novel asks, if our modes of communication, our sources of information, and our means of entertainment are silent and blank? That's not a new question for DeLillo, but this novel suggests that our opportunities to craft meaningful subjectivity may have passed us by as the five protagonists struggle to make themselves understood as they come to realize how essentially isolated each human remains.

SEE ALSO: After Postmodernism; Fiction and Terrorism; Globalization; Minimalism and Maximalism; Mixed-Genre Fiction; Post-9/11 Narratives; Trauma and Fiction; Urban Fiction

REFERENCES

DeCurtis, Anthony. (1999). "An outsider in this society": an interview with Don DeLillo. In: *Introducing Don DeLillo* (ed. Frank Lentricchia), 43–66. Durham, NC: Duke University Press.

DeLillo, Don. (1983). American blood: a journey through the labyrinth of Dallas and JFK. *Rolling Stone* (December 8, 1983).

DeLillo, Don. (1989). *The Names*. New York: Vintage Books; 1st ed. 1982.

DeLillo, Don. (1991). *Mao II*. New York: Penguin Books.

DeLillo, Don. (2010). *Point Omega*. New York: Scribner's.

Winthrop, John. (1985). A Model of Christian Charity (1630). In: *The Puritans in America: A Narrative Anthology* (ed. Alan Heimart and Andrew Delbanco), 81–92. Cambridge, MA: Harvard University Press.

FURTHER READING

Boxall, Peter. (2006). *Don DeLillo: The Possibility of Fiction*. New York: Routledge.

Cowart, David. (2002). *Don DeLillo: The Physics of Language*. Athens: University of Georgia Press.

Lentricchia, Frank. (ed.) (1999). *Introducing Don DeLillo*. Durham: NC: Duke University Press.

Olster, Stacey. (ed.) (2011). *Don DeLillo: Mao II, Underworld, Falling Man*. New York: Continuum.

Osteen, Mark. (2000). *American Magic and Dread: Don DeLillo's Dialogue with Culture*. Philadelphia: University of Pennsylvania Press.

Díaz, Junot

MARISSA L. AMBIO
Hamilton College, USA

Junot Díaz (b. 1968) is one of the most widely acclaimed and prized authors of our time, having received a Guggenheim Fellowship (1999), a MacArthur "Genius" Fellowship (2012), and induction into the American Academy of Arts and Letters (2017). Since 2003, Díaz has held a faculty position at MIT where he is currently the Ridge and Nancy Allen Professor of Writing. His publications include two collections of short stories, *Drown* (1996) and *This Is How You Lose Her* (2012), the novel *The Brief Wondrous Life of Oscar Wao* (2007), "Monstro" (2012), a dystopian short story, and *Islandborn* (2018), a children's picture book illustrated by Leo Espinosa. Díaz's fiction explores several facets of Dominican American identity such as hypermasculinity and race, as well as the Trujillo regime through the recounting of family histories. While many of Díaz's works are related in subject matter, *Drown*, *The Brief Wondrous Life of Oscar Wao*, and *This Is How You Lose Her* form an unconventional trilogy. The books roughly map to the life of Dominican-born Yunior de Las Casas, Díaz's most frequently employed character-narrator and alter ego. The events, however, do not follow a strict chronological order, nor is there a stable sense of place, evoking the disorientation and displacement of immigration. *The Brief Wondrous Life of Oscar Wao* has been awarded the Pulitzer Prize and was adapted for the stage in 2019. Díaz's fiction can be claimed by North American, US Latinx, Dominican American, and Dominican letters.

Junot Díaz was born in Santo Domingo and emigrated to the United States at the age of six, along with his mother and siblings. His father had left for the States years earlier and, after settling in Parlin, New Jersey, sent for his wife and children. Díaz attributes the strained relationship with his father to the hypermasculine expectations his father imposed. A former member of Joaquín Balaguer's military police, Díaz's father encouraged Junot and his siblings to be physically aggressive, and created a home environment which Díaz describes as militaristic and violent. As he tells it, outings with his father often entailed going to the shooting range. Instead, Díaz preferred to spend his time reading and took a special interest in the science fiction and fantasy genres that inform his fiction. Díaz attended Rutgers University, where he earned a BA in English, and completed his MFA at Cornell University.

Díaz's debut collection *Drown* consists of ten short stories. Each allows for a closer look at Dominican masculinity as Yunior comes of age, mostly in the absence of his father, Ramón. In "Ysrael" Yunior is nine years old and is sent to the countryside to spend the summer with his aunt and uncle. He is accompanied by his older brother, Rafa, who serves as a father figure since Ramón has immigrated to the United States. Lacking adult male role models, Rafa develops an exaggerated sense of masculinity (Riofrio 2008, p. 27). He is physically and sexually aggressive, violent, and repeatedly seeks to exert dominance over girls and his male peers. In this story, Rafa decides that he and Yunior should target Ysrael, a boy from a neighboring town whose face was mauled by a pig when he was an infant. Rafa's plan is to remove Ysrael's face covering and reveal the boy's mutilated face. If successful, Rafa will expose Ysrael's physical deformity and weakness, thereby establishing himself as the dominant male. Yunior goes along with the plan to find Ysrael, but is not fully aware of his brother's intentions. Throughout the journey, Rafa continues to assert his authority. He insists that the brothers board a crowded bus with a young fare collector to better their chances of skipping payment. The scenario is yet another way for Rafa to prove himself. The collector suspects the brothers' scheme, but Rafa talks his way out of it, showing his superiority once again. When the boys locate Ysrael, Yunior starts to converse with him. When the boys locate Ysrael, Yunior converses with him, learning that he and Ysrael have several things in common. Rafa then removes the mask and stares at Ysrael's disfigured face. Yunior, disturbed by his brother's ambush and Ysrael's unsightly visage, pleads with his brother to return home. "Ysrael," thus, establishes one of *Drown*'s central themes wherein characters are expected to conform to a hypermasculine code of conduct. These behaviors ultimately yield conflict and destructive consequences, which Yunior must confront.

As with Latin American *machismo*, Dominican hegemonic masculinity is characterized by sexual conquest, violence, dominance, and economic success. Specific to Dominican masculinity, however, is an astute pragmatism facilitated by verbal skills, exemplified by Rafa's manipulation of the fare collector. In the Dominican Republic, the figure that embodies these multiple dimensions of manhood is known as the *tíguere* (Riofrio 2008, pp. 24–25; Girman 2012, pp. 237–241). In this story and others, Yunior's character is not compatible with that of the *tíguere*. He welcomes camaraderie, is empathetic, has an aversion to violence, is not yet interested in girls, and becomes increasingly reticent. Nonetheless, Yunior remains subject to his brother's aggressive ways, demonstrating that hypermasculine behavior is taught and enforced among male peers in the absence of their fathers (Riofrio 2008, p. 27).

As it turns out, Rafa's oppressive behavior is not the only adversity Yunior must endure. "Aguantando," as the title announces, is about enduring hardship of all kinds. In the years following Ramón's departure, Yunior insists on seeing photos of Papi in his military uniform and throws a fit whenever he cannot, evincing the deep longing and affection Yunior has for his father. Mami, for her part, struggles to earn a living while raising her two sons. Yunior admires his mother's perseverance and, given his empathetic nature, tries to comfort her. The story closes when Yunior imagines his father's return. Rather than the solution to the family's financial and emotional strain, Ramón brings little relief. Upon seeing his son, Ramón asks Mami: "What's wrong with that one?" (Díaz 1996, p. 88). Papi traces the scars on Yunior's face and makes a circle on his cheek. The fixation on Yunior's disfigured face is reminiscent of Rafa's unmasking of Ysrael. Here, Yunior is identified for his perceived physical weakness and, consequently, may never obtain the recognition he seeks from his father, the *tíguere*.

"No Face" is a reprise of "Ysrael." In this story the masked boy transforms himself from unwitting target of abuse to masked superhero. Like many superheroes, the boy does not go by his given name. Instead, he is known as No Face, and his superhuman abilities are invoked when he says the words: FLIGHT, INVISIBLITY, STRENGTH. The idea to reimagine himself as superhero seems to have come from reading comic books. Each week Padre Lou, the local priest, takes No Face to the kiosk and buys him one. More than just a spiritual father, Padre Lou is a surrogate. He nurtures the boy's interests, and teaches him English in preparation for his trip to Canada where he will undergo reconstructive surgery. Padre Lou, thus, demonstrates the continued need for surrogates in the absence of fathers, and alternative models of masculinity.

The remaining seven stories are set in the United States. In them Yunior remains a conflicted character. He has empathy for women who are victimized by men, and often feels a victim himself. Still, he repeats the same pernicious behavior of his father and older brother. In "Fiesta, 1980," the Las Casas family is living in New Jersey and attends a party to celebrate the recent arrival of Yunior's aunt and uncle. While the story tells the day's events, a series of flashbacks interrupts the narrative. Yunior is preoccupied by the knowledge of his father's extramarital affair, and seems to want nothing more than to have his father's cheating exposed at the party. Despite resenting his father and feeling empathy for his mother, Yunior remains silent. Yunior's hesitation to speak up is no doubt attributed to his home life. Ramón refuses for anyone in the family to enter into discussion. He ensures this kind of censorship through fear of reprisal, be it verbal or physical. Ramón, for his part, views verbal exchange as another way to express bravado; he shouts to chastise, give directives, and engage in male banter. Yunior, ever conflicted, fails to tell his mother or aunt about the affair, even though both of them are suspicious of Ramón and detect that Yunior is holding back.

As Yunior grows into a teenager, he becomes the man of the house. In "Drown" Ramón has abandoned the family again, and Yunior takes on the role of provider, protector, and censor. Yet Yunior continues to exhibit an ambivalence toward this typical male behavior, and has two homosexual experiences with his best friend, Beto. Yunior is left confused and uneasy, and rather than explicitly end the friendship, Yunior "silences" it. He becomes increasingly reticent, avoids Beto when possible, and in a symbolic gesture, throws out the book Beto had gifted him. Although being a *tíguere* does not preclude homosexual acts, the dominant conception of masculinity is based on heterosexual relations (Irizarry 2016, pp. 159–160). Yunior, who is terrified of being homosexual, returns to typical hypermasculine behavior.

"Boyfriend," "Edison, New Jersey," and "How to Date a Browngirl, Blackgirl, Whitegirl, or Halfie," however, continue to depict an ambivalent *tíguere*, emotionally if not sexually. In "Boyfriend," Yunior overhears Girlfriend's sobbing in the apartment below after she breaks up with Boyfriend. He empathizes with her distress, but is also opportunistic. He invites her for coffee in the hopes of initiating a romantic relationship or sexual encounter, but she declines his advances. In "Edison, New Jersey," an unnamed narrator meets a young Dominican woman when delivering pool tables to Mr. C. Clarence Pruitt, a man of means. While the relationship between the woman and Pruitt is unclear, her disgust with Pruitt is apparent. She thus asks the narrator for a ride to Washington Heights in order to escape her situation. During the trip, the narrator makes a subtle attempt to gain the woman's interest, but like Girlfriend she is not receptive. Time and again Yunior and other male narrators are unsuccessful in their attempts with women, which makes "How to Date" ironic. In it, Yunior categorizes women by race, ethnicity, and class, and then proposes a series of "if-then" scenarios, designed to yield a desired outcome. When describing the women, he also surmises how they view him and adapts to their perceptions, but to no avail. Yunior thus consistently plays the manipulator who is also manipulated, the savior who then victimizes.

In the last story, Yunior learns about his father's experiences in the United States and finds Ramón was not the *tíguere* he or Rafa imagined. For one, Ramón is duped when he pays for an arranged marriage to obtain citizenship that never materializes. Not knowing English, Ramón also ends up overpaying on rent. When he marries Nilda, he acquires citizenship. Yet, Nilda is far more economically and socially stable than Ramón. She has citizenship, speaks English, runs a restaurant, owns a home, and is self-sufficient as a single mother. Once Ramón moves in, he reverts to his hypermasculine ways. The relationship becomes strained and, eventually, physically violent. Ramón leaves Nilda, looks for a new job, settles in New Jersey, and calls for his family. Yunior finally has his reckoning with Ramón and sees the man behind the *tíguere* when he visits Nilda and learns of Ramón's past, which he then exposes in the stories he narrates.

The Brief Wondrous Life of Oscar Wao has gained canonical status and is considered a masterpiece of Dominican American literature. In an interview, Díaz remarks that when writing the novel many considered it to be the "non-Dominican book" (Chicago Humanities Festival 2013). This characterization is due, in part, to the novel's portrayal of Rafael Leónidas Trujillo, the Dominican dictator who ruled the island with impunity for over thirty years from 1930 to 1961 and whose cult of personality made him synonymous with island politics and culture, a phenomenon that is captured in one of the nation's slogans: "Dios en cielo, Trujillo en tierra" ("God in Heaven, Trujillo on Earth"). In addition to creating a totalitarian regime that guaranteed his access to the island's wealth, control of the military, and the dissemination of nationalist ideology based on anti-Haitianism and racism, Trujillo was known for fomenting a culture of hypermasculinity, of being a *tíguere*. Rather than center the narrative around Trujillo, the Dominican dictator in Díaz's novel is ascribed a minor status, literally and figuratively. Trujillo makes one brief appearance in the novel, is the target of endless sarcastic rebuke by the novel's narrator, and, when the island's history is addressed, it appears in a series of footnotes, creating a secondary narrative located in the margins of the page.

The Brief Wondrous Life of Oscar Wao tells of the trials and tribulations of a Dominican American adolescent who, like Yunior, struggles with the expectations of Dominican masculinity. The antithesis of the Dominican *tíguere*, Oscar De León is an overweight "ghetto nerd" who aspires to become the Dominican Tolkien. He is consistently mocked and shunned for his perceived lack of manliness and his unabashed interest in science fiction and fantasy. At this point, Yunior is dating Oscar's older sister, Lola, and offers to provide guidance now that he has mastered being a *tíguere*. Despite a few fleeting attempts, Oscar fails to embody the prototypical Dominican man but eventually manages to enter into a relationship when he returns to the Dominican Republic. The novel's prologue, which has been compared to that of Alejo Carpentier's *El reino de este mundo* ([*The Kingdom of this World*], 1949), proposes a new Caribbean aesthetic, which the author will use to tell Oscar's story. This aesthetic is "centered on the idea of the supernatural and is rooted in the national, it is a kind of curse or Antillean evil eye that is denominated by the Dominican term of fukú" (Barradas 2009, p. 102). According to the prologue, the origin of *fukú americanus* is traced to Africa, but the curse was ushered into the Americas by Christopher Columbus and spread worldwide through the European colonization of Hispaniola. From individual tragedy to international calamities, the curse of the fukú is believed to be behind every one, and its primary proponent was Rafael Trujillo. Oscar's endless misfortunes and his tragic end are, thus, the makings of a fukú story and the basis of the novel. *The Brief Wondrous Life* also recounts the lives of Oscar's mother and her father, both of whom suffer unspeakable trauma. Although the De León family history is a fukú narrative, characterized foremost by suffering, it subordinates and reframes national history. That is, the De León story ensures that the experiences of the Dominican people and its diaspora come to the fore. To this point: the novel is narrated mostly by Yunior, Oscar, and Lola, indicating the multiple voices that constitute history. Despite the prologue's presentation of the novel as fukú story, there are few references to supernatural events. Moreover, and despite the grave circumstances, the narrators approach their subject with levity. This tone, comedic and often evoking laughter, is only possible because it is juxtaposed to reality (Barradas 2009, p. 105). Given the fukú that has befallen generations of the De León family, one wonders if there is a spell to break the curse, a *zafa*. As the prologue intimates, the novel may be that very counter-spell, suggesting that literature is imbued with the ability to contest history.

In *This Is How You Lose Her*, Yunior returns as the primary character and narrator. Three of the stories focus on the Las Casas family, with "Otravida, Otravez," and "Invierno" highly reminiscent of *Drown*. The first story tells of yet another relationship Ramón has prior to the family's arrival. This one is with Yasmin, not Nilda, but the circumstances are similar, as is the ending. The latter story recounts the family's first days in New Jersey. In addition to his father, Yunior now confronts another obstacle to communication: English. "The

Pura Principle" relates the final months of Rafa's life as he struggles with cancer. Despite the tendency to mend relations prior to death, the brothers remain antagonistic until the end. The remaining six stories lay bare the details of Yunior's failed romantic relationships. The reasons are many: lack of emotional connection, changes in circumstance, and cheating, which Yunior does repeatedly and especially during his most meaningful relationships. Consequently, Yunior desperately attempts to restore these relationships and his prolonged suffering once they end. "The Cheater's Guide to Love" is similar to "How to Date," but rather than a how-to resource, this story explores the step-by-step process that leads to Yunior's final conclusion: "The half-life of love is forever" (Díaz 2012, p. 217). In this second collection, Yunior's empathy for women has diminished and he has become a womanizer, like his father and older brother. Unlike Ramón and Rafa, however, Yunior comes to realize the consequences that his actions have over time as he experiences a deep and continued sense of loss.

Díaz's most recent publication marks a departure in the author's literary production. *Islandborn* is a children's picture book, yet it shares many of the same themes and tropes of Díaz's earlier fiction. The story centers on Lola, a school-aged Latinx girl who lives in the city but was born on "the island" and immigrated to the United States as a baby. When Lola's teacher asks the class to create drawings representative of their heritage, Lola seeks the help of family and neighbors in order to recall her homeland. *Islandborn*, thus, stresses the importance of multiple voices in the construction of history which, in this instance, prizes the community over the national, memory over documented narrative, and the female visual artist over the male writer. And while *Islandborn* does not specify Lola's birthplace or current residence, allusions to the Dominican Republic, the Trujillo regime, and to Washington Heights are intimated through the illustrations, situating this children's book alongside Díaz's other works of fiction.

SEE ALSO: Butler, Octavia; Danticat, Edwidge; Delany, Samuel; García, Cristina; Hijuelos, Oscar; King, Stephen; Literature of the Americas; Mixed-Genre Fiction; Morrison, Toni; Story Cycles; Trauma and Fiction

REFERENCES

Barradas, Efrain. (2009). El realismo cómico de Junot Díaz: notas sobre *The Brief Wondrous Life of Oscar Wao*. The Latin Americanist 53 (1): 99–111.

Chicago Humanities Festival. (2013). Junot Díaz: immigrants, masculinity, nerds & art. https://www.youtube.com/watch?v=TA8X6TUA83k (accessed September 5, 2021).

Díaz, Junot. (1996). *Drown*. New York: Riverhead Books.

Díaz, Junot. (2012). *This Is How You Lose Her*. New York: Riverhead Books.

Girman, Chris. (2012). *Mucho Macho: Seduction, Desire and the Homoerotic Lives of Men*. New York: Routledge.

Irizarry, Ylce. (2016). This is how you lose it: navigating Dominicanidad in Junot Díaz's *Drown*. In: *Junot Díaz and the Decolonial Imagination* (ed. Monica Hanna, Jennifer Harford Vargas, and José David Saldívar), 147–171. Durham, NC: Duke University Press.

Riofrio, John. (2008). Situating Latin American masculinity: immigration, empathy and emasculation in Junot Díaz's *Drown*. Atenea 28 (1): 23–36.

FURTHER READING

González, Christopher. (2015). *Reading Junot Díaz*. Pittsburgh: University of Pittsburgh Press.

Hanna, Monica, Harford, Jennifer, and Saldívar, José David. (2016). *Junot Díaz and the Decolonial Imagination*. Durham, NC: Duke University Press.

Horn, Maja. (2014). *Masculinity After Trujillo: The Politics of Gender in Dominican Literature*. Gainesville: University Press of Florida.

Miller, T.S. (2001). Preternatural narration and the lens of genre fiction in Junot Díaz's *The Brief Wondrous Life of Oscar Wao*. Science Fiction Studies 38 (1): 92–114.

Doctorow, E.L.

STEPHEN CARL ARCH
Michigan State University, USA

Edgar Lawrence ("E.L.") Doctorow (1931–2015) was the author of a dozen novels, three collections of short stories, one play, and several collections of essays and miscellaneous works. His novels earned many major awards, including the National Book Award, the PEN/Faulkner Award (twice), and the William Dean Howells Medal, and Doctorow himself was awarded several lifetime achievement awards including the Library of Congress Prize for American Fiction. His fictions are celebrated for their inventive blurring of history and fiction, their serious philosophical underpinnings, and their complex narrative structure.

E.L. Doctorow was born on January 6, 1931, in the Bronx borough of New York City. He attended the specialized Bronx High School of Science, and then enrolled at Kenyon College in Ohio, majoring in philosophy. He graduated in 1952. After one year of graduate study at Columbia University, he was drafted into the US army and served for two years as a corporal in the signal corps in West Germany. Returning to New York, he became a script reader for Columbia Pictures and later for CBS Television, writing synopses of books being considered for production and reading screenplays under consideration for production. From 1959 to 1964, he served as senior editor at the New American Library. In 1964, he became editor-in-chief at the Dial Press; in 1968, he became vice president. In 1969, he left publishing to take an academic appointment at the University of California, Irvine, and to dedicate himself full-time to writing and teaching. He would later teach at several other universities including NYU, where he had a permanent appointment as Professor of English and American Letters.

Over nearly fifty years, Doctorow demonstrated in his fiction a remarkable versatility in genre, form, structure, and narrative voice. He wrote a Western, a science fiction novel, a gangster novel, a "city mystery" novel, and an autobiographical novel. He used sophisticated postmodern narrative techniques to articulate his sense that humans are, absurdly, shackled by personal and social history. His narrators are often self-consciously writing or assembling the narrative that is in front of us, as when Daniel in *The Book of Daniel* (1971) struggles to make sense of the political and social upheaval that led to his parents' executions in the electric chair or when Homer in *Homer and Langley* (2009) tries to explain how he and his brother became compulsive hoarders. But in other novels, Doctorow adopted the strategy of an assemblage of voices or points of view, as when in *Ragtime* (1975) fictional and real perspectives syncopate in a complicated rhythm or when in *The March* (2005) diverse voices modulate into a tragicomic account of the final year of the Civil War.

"A fiction writer is a ventriloquist," Doctorow stated in a late interview (Gentry 2013, p. 34), and his novels often foreground a single narrator whose voice dominates and defines the narrative: the loose, evocative, streetwise talk of Billy Bathgate (*Billy Bathgate* [1989]); the guilt-ridden ruminations of Blue (*Welcome to Hard Times* [1960]); the hesitant, ellipses-filled digressions of the newspaperman MacIlvaine (*The Waterworks* [1994]); the nostalgic, puzzled ponderings of Homer (*Homer and Langley*); the philosophical musings and creative false starts of Everett (*City of God* [2000]). Doctorow admired the German Romantic playwright Heinrich von Kleist, writing that his characters "struggle monumentally with their perceptions; something else than what they expected is happening to them" (Doctorow 1982, p. vii). The same is true for all of Doctorow's narrators and protagonists. They see themselves as trapped by events or circumstances not of their own choosing. Some fall and are defeated, some rise but become complicit in the systems that created them, all struggle to make sense of the past and its relation to the present.

Doctorow's versatility is unified by a set of thematic concerns that became more visible as his career lengthened. His novels are always set in the United States, and often in New York City. They are insistently concerned with the emergence of the modern world of capitalism, consumer culture, advanced technology, and the power of the state. His narrators and protagonists are nearly always men, and they are often writing or observing from marginal positions of class and power. Power itself in his novels resides in oppressive structures like the state and the modern corporation, but also in myth and in ideologies of race and class. Postmodern in form and technique, his novels are often liberal critiques of the modern world. They owe much to a handful of American novelists who balanced the craft of writing with a disappointment in American social realities – Nathaniel Hawthorne, Mark Twain, Theodore Dreiser, F. Scott Fitzgerald.

Doctorow's first two novels, *Welcome to Hard Times* and *Big as Life* (1966), were genre fictions, but with twists that presaged his interest in challenging comfortable narrative forms. *Welcome* tells the story of a town in the Wild West (Hard Times) that rebuilds itself after a ruthless sociopath attacked it, but the novel ends with the town destroyed once again and the narrator dying of his wounds. Some readers consider it an anti-Western. *Big as Life* recounts the sudden and surreal appearance of two giants in New York Harbor. However, its real focus is not on the science fiction but on the social chaos and the rising authoritarianism that follows the giants' appearance. *Big as Life* is often considered a failed novel; Doctorow himself refused to reprint the novel during his lifetime. Following 9/11, however, the novel has come to be seen as eerily prescient.

Doctorow's third novel, *The Book of Daniel*, brought him to national attention. It is a raw, emotional, unsettling novel, ostensibly written by one Daniel Isaacson as or in place of his dissertation as a graduate student at Columbia University. He and his sister were emotionally scarred as children in the early 1950s by the arrest, imprisonment, and capital punishment by electrocution of their parents, stand-ins for Julius and Ethel Rosenberg. His sister eventually commits suicide. Daniel is cynical, depressed, and sadistic as he attempts to recover his parents' deep past as Communists, the betrayals that led to their arrest, their scapegoating by the nation during the McCarthy years, and his own relationship to left-wing politics amid the turbulence of the late 1960s.

Daniel is a fictional meditation on liberal politics in the United States in the twentieth century, but in the book Doctorow maintained a connection to the tradition of *roman à clef*. Treating the Rosenbergs "as" the Isaacsons offered him a lens to reimagine the past. In *Ragtime*, however, the novel that truly vaulted him to fame and success, Doctorow erased the line between real and invented characters, placing fictional characters in actual historical spaces and actual historical persons in invented scenes. Set in the first two decades of the twentieth century, *Ragtime* weaves multiple story lines and characters around the problems of race and immigration in Progressive-era New York City. At the center are two young, fictional male characters, one white and one Black, who together threaten to blow up the library of J.P. Morgan. One dies at the scene of rebellion, the other dies a year later in Mexico. Around them syncopate the characters of Emma Goldman, Sigmund Freud, Harry Houdini, and many others, real and fictional. Many of them are swept away by the currents of history, but some emerge (often with new names) as powerful new types.

In the wake of *Ragtime*, Doctorow laid out some of his key ideas about history and fiction in a well-known essay, "False Documents." He argued that history and fiction share "a mode of mediating the world for the purpose of introducing meaning, and it is the cultural authority from which they both derive that illuminates those facts so that they can be perceived" (1983, p. 24). What we take to be "realism" in literature, historical narratives, journalism, politics, psychology, and even everyday expression is simply the world as we have been taught to see it. What the novelist imagines is "a private or ideal world that cannot be easily corroborated or verified" but which is nevertheless more true than actual history (pp. 16–17). Aligning himself both with the New Journalism and with postmodernism, Doctorow concluded that "there is no fiction or nonfiction as we commonly understand the distinction: there is only narrative" (p. 26). Fiction "is a kind of speculative history" (p. 25), a false document that is nevertheless "more valid, more real, more truthful than the 'true' documents of the politicians or the journalists or the psychologists" (p. 26).

In the 1980s, Doctorow published three novels that offer valid, real, and truthful accounts of the 1930s: *Loon Lake* (1980), *World's Fair* (1985), and *Billy Bathgate*. All three feature young, male narrators struggling to craft an identity out of a fractured family life. In *Loon Lake*, Joe flees his family and is seduced by a vision of power, natural solitude, and female beauty; he learns to model himself on a ruthless corporate leader, and eventually becomes that man's heir in both name and attitude. In *World's Fair*, Edgar Altschuler recalls his youth in an outwardly happy family, but one we learn that is riven by its jealousies and fears. The 1939 New York World's Fair offers him a vision of a clean, technological future, but it is in tension with his own lived experience which is confusing and alienating. And in *Billy Bathgate*, Billy is a young tough who happens to enter the orbit of the gangster Dutch Schultz. Billy catches Schultz's eye as a "capable boy" (2010, p. 27), and indeed he survives the slaughter of Dutch and his gang at the end of the novel. He even finds the directions to Schultz's hidden wealth, and turns it, he tells us craftily at the end, into "a corporate enterprise that goes on to this very day" (p. 319). He does not tell us whether that enterprise is for good or for ill, but in Doctorow's novels the word "corporate" tends to carry negative connotations.

Two of Doctorow's most highly regarded novels are *The Waterworks* and *The March*. In both he expanded his historical reach, constructing novels about the North and the South in the mid-nineteenth century. *The Waterworks* is set in New York City in 1871. The narrator is a newspaper editor, McIlvaine, looking back at events (in 1871) long after they occurred. He tells the story uncovered by one of his reporters, Martin Pemberton, a complex conspiracy in which a mad scientist–doctor, Wrede Sartorius, kidnaps children to perform experiments on them, promises rich old men longer life because of those experiments, is protected by the corrupt Boss Tweed Ring, and is finally stopped by the aggressive detective work of a single, uncorrupted policeman, Edmund Donne. Doctorow is interested in *The Waterworks* in the emergence of the modern city. The "waterworks" of the title is the system for distributing water to New York City from reservoirs upstate, and it serves as an apt metaphor for both the technology that enabled the rise of clean modern cities and the social and political power that large corporations accrue to themselves as they grow, becoming ever more secretive and corrupt.

Sartorius in *The Waterworks* is brilliant, but insane. His experiments include blood transfusions and dialysis, unheard of at the time, but also the sacrifice of children to try to extend old men's lives. Doctorow put the same character into *The March*, which is set in 1864/5 during General Sherman's march to the sea (in Georgia) and then north through the Carolinas. Here, Sartorius is merely a cold, methodical doctor, trained in the latest techniques but numbed to heartlessness by the horrors of surgery on the battlefield. He is one of a large cast of characters whose voices are interwoven into a rich tapestry. The novel is unusual in the Doctorow canon because there is no single narrator, just the many voices that register the shock, trauma, and horror of the war. Sherman's march is a metaphor for a destructive razing that seems to some characters to be a sign of hope and rebirth. Freed slaves and weary soldiers and tired citizens hope for some good to come out of the war. But the novel ends with the assassination of Lincoln, and we as readers know what follows from that point: the excesses of the Gilded Age, the betrayals of Reconstruction.

In between those two novels, Doctorow published *City of God*, another long, complex narrative with a single narrator, Everett, but with many voices. Everett is sitting at his typewriter or computer keyboard for the entire novel: he is writing, thinking "out loud," pondering. He starts several stories but he abandons them. He imagines movie plots. He tries thought experiments "as" Einstein and Wittgenstein. As in *Loon Lake*, some sections are written in free verse poetry; as does Joe in that novel, Everett tells his story by, in part, telling us how he thinks about the world. Both novels are experiments in demonstrating how the imagination roams, and how it composes a self. The two novels are similar in this way to Doctorow's remarkable 1984 short story collection, *Lives of the Poets: Six Stories and a Novella*, where the reader discovers in the novella that the stories are the imaginative "life" of the novella's narrator. Slavoj Žižek has remarked that that collection is "a supreme exercise in literary postmodernism": the six stories seem heterogeneous, but by then reading the fictional author's "confused impressions of day-to-day life in contemporary New York" in the novella we can reconstruct the artistic working through of the raw materials of life (2004, p. 7).

Doctorow's final two novels were considered less weighty by many reviewers. While relatively short, however, both continue his project of creating complex "false documents" about the peculiarities of the modern world. In *Homer and Langley* he rewrote the case of the Collyer brothers, one of the first documented cases of hoarding. His narrator is the younger brother, Homer, who is blind and who types his story even as his world is literally closing in on him: like Blue in *Welcome to Hard Times*, he anticipates his own death at the very end of his narrative. Doctorow is pondering the nature of objects or things in this novel, and the nature of our attachment to them in a commodity culture. In his final novel, *Andrew's Brain* (2014), Doctorow invented a narrator who is, or claims to be, a neuroscientist interested in the distinction between brain (the mechanism) and mind (the "soul" or person). But Andrew's own narrative of his experiences is complicated, messy, and self-serving. He seems to be in conversation with a therapist or perhaps a government agent; eventually, we learn that he was a college roommate of George W. Bush, and that he might be in confinement because of things he knows about the president.

Doctorow is primarily known as a novelist, but his stories were published in highly visible magazines such as *The New Yorker*, *Esquire*, and *The Atlantic*. Several novels, including *Billy Bathgate, City of God, Ragtime*, and *Loon Lake*, began as short, published fictions. His first collection, referenced above, can even be read "as" a novel. His second, *Sweet Land Stories* (2004), includes five stories set in various locales in the United

States. The title is ironic, as the characters who inhabit the stories are displaced, lost, and confused. His final collection, *All the Time in the World* (2011), included six stories from the previous collections and six stories newly collected in book form. Published when Doctorow was 81 years old, this title too is undoubtedly ironic.

There is as yet no book-length biography of Doctorow. There have been book-length critical studies, with a half-dozen alone having been published in the 1990s. But there have been relatively few since 2000. This may reflect a shift in Doctorow's status or a shift in the critical sensibility, but it is certain that his career has entered a period of reassessment following his death in 2015.

After the publication of *The Book of Daniel*, Doctorow's novels and story collections were always widely reviewed. Critics and reviewers have identified that novel, *Ragtime*, *Billy Bathgate*, *The Waterworks*, and *The March* as his most impressive achievements, marked by technical virtuosity, postmodern experimentation with the categories of "truth" and "fiction," complex narrative structure, and acute social analysis. In important ways, Doctorow was influenced by American novelists like Hawthorne, Twain, and Dreiser. He rewrote one of Hawthorne's stories ("Wakefield"). He referred admiringly to Twain's work in the last pages of his final novel, and Billy Bathgate is clearly a version of Huck Finn. His novels self-consciously resonate with novels by American writers who, like him, had an ambivalent attitude toward America, seduced by its myths but critical of its social realities. Critics have studied some of those influences, and some have also analyzed his work in relation to his contemporaries like Philip Roth. But much work remains to be done in both areas.

And much remains to be seen, too, about Doctorow's own legacy. *Ragtime* vaulted him to fame as a novelist, and for forty years he maintained an unusual status as a postmodernist writer whose works sold well. But it is not clear, yet, whether the next generations of writers will look back on his work the way that he looked back at Hawthorne, Twain, and others.

SEE ALSO: The Brain and American Fiction; Illness and Disability Narratives; The New Experimentalism/The Contemporary Avant-Garde; Realism after Poststructuralism; Religion and Contemporary Fiction; Story Cycles; Urban Fiction

REFERENCES

Doctorow, E.L. (1982). Foreword. In: *Heinrich von Kleist: Plays* (ed. Walter Hinderer), vii–x. New York: Continuum.
Doctorow, E.L. (1983). False documents. In: *E.L. Doctorow: Essays and Conversations* (ed. Richard Trenner), 16–27. Princeton, NJ: Ontario Review Press; 1st ed. 1977.
Doctorow, E.L. (2010). *Billy Bathgate*. New York: Random House; 1st ed. 1989.
Gentry, Marshall Bruce. (2013). E.L. Doctorow in Milledgeville: an interview. *Flannery O'Connor Review* 11: 31–37.
Žižek, Slavoj. (2004). *Iraq: The Borrowed Kettle*. London and New York: Verso.

FURTHER READING

Bergström, Catharine Walker. (2010). *Intuition of an Infinite Obligation: Narrative Ethics and Postmodern Gnostics in the Fiction of E.L. Doctorow*. Frankfurt and New York: Peter Lang.
Siegel, Ben. (ed.) (2000). *Critical Essays on E.L. Doctorow*. New York: Hall.
Wutz, Michael and Murphet, Julian. (eds.) (2020). *E.L. Doctorow: A Reconsideration*. Edinburgh: Edinburgh University Press.

Ducornet, Rikki

MICHELLE RYAN-SAUTOUR
Université d'Angers, France

To write a text is to propose a reading of the world and to reveal its potencies. Writing is reading and reading a way back to the initial impulse. Both are acts of revelation.

(Ducornet 2015, p. 1)

Rikki (Erica) Ducornet (b. 1943) is a writer of poetry, short stories, essays, and novels, who explores ethics and the imagination on the edges of diverse literary traditions. She has been quoted as encouraging writers to go deep into the "zoo" of the imagination, a space of an intuitive, erotic energy that can be accessed through language. Ducornet indeed speaks of "reading" the world to explore its "potencies" through language and the imagination in a process of revelation. Ducornet's work has been described as both experimental and metafictional, and has been associated with Harry Mathews, Robert Coover, and William Gass as well as Angela Carter, Italo Calvino, and Jorge Luis Borges. She is also an influential Surrealist and appears in *The International Encyclopedia of Surrealism* (2019). Ducornet approaches Surrealism with reverence for its potential as a practice, while remaining wary of potentially reductive, dogmatic tenets. She emphasizes the process of dreaming and the subconscious in her literary craft, and her work is clearly about freeing the mind's eye through rigorously probative writing, often using her work to question world issues, particularly abusive authority. Ducornet is also a visual artist; she paints and produces prints, and her writing is deeply informed by painting. She speaks in particular of the influence of Vermeer's light and Hieronymus Bosch's vivid nightmares. The "eye" is a recurrent metaphor in her work, and a dynamic of revealing and concealing, on the physical as well as psychological and even spiritual level, is very present; her fiction indeed unfolds like a labyrinth and resists facile interpretation. Ducornet has written ten novels to date, including a tetralogy based on the four elements: *The Stain* (1984), *Entering Fire* (1986), *The Fountains of Neptune* (1989), and *The Jade Cabinet* (1993). She has also published collections of short stories, essays, and numerous works of poetry, and has illustrated Jorge Luis Borges's "Tlön, Uqbar, Orbis Tertius" (1983) and Robert Coover's *Spanking the Maid* (1981).

Rikki Ducornet has a distinctly international profile, having been raised on the Bard College campus, where her father taught social philosophy in an environment that celebrated internationalism against the backdrop of the McCarthy era. Her father was Cuban, and her mother was Russian Jewish, and she spent time in Cuba and Egypt during her childhood. Ducornet lived in Constantine, Algeria, with her husband Guy Ducornet, and the couple eventually settled in the small French village of Le Puy Notre Dame in the Loire Valley, France, where she lived from 1972 to 1989. She returned to the United States in 1989 when she accepted a creative writing position at the University of Denver. She now lives in Port Townsend, Washington, where she continues to write and pursue her career in painting and drawing. Her travels, along with Surrealist practice and Eastern spiritualism, inform writing that challenges categories; critics are often perplexed as to where to place her in the canon. Her work has been associated with that of the British writer Angela Carter, who introduced her to Chatto & Windus, leading to the publication of *The Stain* and *Entering Fire*. Like Carter, she engages with a broad array of authors, ranging from Edward Lear and Lewis Carroll to the Marquis de Sade, Julio Cortázar, Franz Kafka, Italo Calvino, Jorge Luis Borges, and Miguel Ángel Asturias Rosales. Yet she was also inspired in her youth by Surrealists such as Max Ernst, Paul Eluard, Dorothea Tanning, and Roger Caillois.

Ducornet has been involved with Surrealism since the age of 19 when she was exhibiting with Fantasmagie in Belgium. She later met up with the Chicago Surrealists in Sheep Meadow in New York City at the start of the Vietnam War and showed work in their international show. Ducornet also exhibited and published with the journals *Phases* and

Ellébore. Although she doesn't adhere to a specific branch of Surrealism and refuses to label her work as "Surrealist," two of her stories were anthologized in Michael Richardson's *The Dedalus Book of Surrealism: The Identity of Things* (1993) and *The Myth of the World: Surrealism 2* (1994), appearing alongside texts by figures as diverse as Jacques Prévert, Julien Gracq, Leonora Carrington, and Luis Buñuel. Surrealism feeds into shifting borders and unexplored angles. Ducornet's fiction indeed displays a keen desire to "release that primary fury of which language, even now, is miraculously capable – from the dry mud of daily use" (Ducornet 1999, p. 3), and the result is an aesthetics that often leads her readers to the limits of comfort, just beyond their horizon of expectations.

Ducornet often speaks of a bridge of green glass in the library of Bard College that led to the shelves of the library's second floor; the room below appeared to be submerged in water. This image serves as a "*un point de repère*" (Ducornet 2015, p. 3), a point of reference, for a creative process that seeks to reveal what is hidden beyond the surface of things. Such processes engage not only sight, but also the intellect, eros, and the physical senses: "I am always looking for spaces that evoke a sensation of strangeness (Aragon's words), that stimulate the eye, the imagining mind, and the body all at once" (1999, p. 4). Ducornet speaks of "imaginative seeing" (2015, p. 3) that transforms seemingly ordinary space, allowing us to perceive it anew. Objects are more than they appear in her visions; in an essay written for *The International Encyclopedia of Surrealism* (Ducornet 2019), she interweaves the ideas of Gaston Bachelard, Roger Callois, and Julio Cortázar to reflect upon stones, shells, stars as portals to dreams, revealing the secrets of objects, where life lies dormant, ready to quicken. French philosopher Gaston Bachelard has been a conceptual companion throughout Ducornet's career, along with Robert Harbison (*Eccentric Spaces*, 1977). Ducornet explains how Bachelard's studies of memory and childhood were a guiding force behind the writing of the tetralogy (Gregory and McCaffery 1998, p. 132), particularly *Earth and Reveries of Repose* (1948) and *Water and Dreams* (1942). Ducornet appreciates Bachelard's "gentle manias" and his "irresistible investigations into the nature of the imagining mind" (2015, p. 42). In her third novel, *The Fountains of Neptune*, water seems to seep through the writing, in the music of language, the structure of plot, the porousness and flow of words and dreams. *The Stain* (Earth), the first novel in the tetralogy, attests to Ducornet's awakening to language. She speaks of writing the novel over a three-year period in a sort of "fever" (Kavchak 2003); the novel contrasts the marvelous of the imagination with monstrous dogmatism, an ethical thread that runs through all of her works, even appearing in the title of a later collection of essays, *The Monstrous and the Marvelous* (1999). In *The Stain*, Charlotte is born with a hare-shaped birthmark on her face that exposes her to abuse, as people seek to possess her. She ultimately finds a home and creative freedom with the eccentric character Archange. The life of dreams contrasts with the dogmatism of Catholicism and right-wing politics, as Ducornet subverts strictures and structures, engaging with the fascistic thinking embodied by the scatological, while also shedding light on the destructive energy present in the underbelly of authoritarian institutions.

Figures of abusive authority loom large in Ducornet's works. In *Entering Fire*, the second novel in her tetralogy (Fire), an angry Nazi, Septimus, is opposed to his father, Lamprius de Bergerac, a visionary botanist who specializes in orchids, revealing a superposition of familial quarrels and political crises, intertwined with orchid mutations and metamorphoses. Violence and natural creation are frequently intermingled in Ducornet's worlds; they are opposing energies that feed into each other in an aesthetic dominated by dark overtones and vulnerable characters. The murderous figure of "Toujours-là" ("always there") haunts *The Fountains of Neptune* (Water), as a nine-year-old boy, a sort of "sleeping beauty" figure, dreams fifty years away in a coma after a drowning accident. He reconstructs his life in the aftermath of two World Wars, and uses dream to reinvestigate his story within the context of history. Trauma and memory are foregrounded by the interpretations of Dr. Venus Kaiserstiege, a Viennese Freudian "hydropothist." In *The Jade Cabinet* (Air), Radolph Tubbs is an oppressive patriarch, controlling the young Etheria, who has been traded to him by her father for a piece of jade. The novel reveals Ducornet's fascination with *Wunderkammer* and *Kunstkammer*, cabinets of curiosities, depositories of fragments that foster new insights through meaningful juxtapositions. Ducornet dedicates the book to the photographer Rosamond Wolff Purcell, whose eye reveals fresh perceptions of *artificialia* and *naturalia*, proposing novel ways of "ordering, articulating and dreaming the world" (1999, p. 73). The idea of "dreaming the world" is metafictionally incarnated by the narrator Memory, who is clearly associated with language; whereas, Etheria is unable to speak, silenced by the trauma of her eccentric father's experiments to find an Edenic language. Etheria volatilizes in the story, dissolving into air, away from oppression. Her magical presence is reinforced by the figure of Charles Dodgson (Lewis Carroll), emphasizing playful freedom as a foil to the strict rationalism of Tubbs.

Lewis Carroll's *Alice* books also openly engaged with tyranny, and his work serves as a fitting backdrop to Ducornet's questioning of dogmatism. The *Alice* books clearly inform Ducornet's awakening to the forces of language. She also remembers an alphabet book in early childhood, where the letter B was the image of a bee penetrating a blossom: "This image was of such potency that my entire face – eyes, nose and lips – was seized by a phantom stinging, and my ears by a hallucinatory buzzing. In this way, and in an instant, I was simultaneously initiated into the alphabet and awakened to Eden" (1999, p. 1). Language, reduced even to the essential letter, opens up to other worlds, to what she sometimes refers to as the Eden of language. The letter, the word, are portals to the wor(l)ds of the marvelous whose hidden recesses were also celebrated by Carroll: "Looking at that letter, that blossom and that bee was like looking into a mirror from which the skin had been peeled away. The page afforded a passage – transcendental and yet altogether tangible" (p. 1).

Carroll's *The Hunting of the Snark* (1876) is echoed by the title of Ducornet's collection of stories *The Complete Butcher's Tales* (1994), including stories published as early as 1974, many of which first appeared in collections of Surrealist writing and other anthologies, such as *Shoes and Shit* (1984), edited by Rikki Ducornet and Geoff Hancock. Short stories served as a crucible for the alchemical forces at work in language, and were written and published periodically alongside Ducornet's novels. A preoccupation with the force of the dense narrative structures that characterize short fiction is apparent in the title of Ducornet's collection *The Word Desire* (1997). The opening story, "The Chess Set of Ivory," appears in its compact, embryonic form here; it is later expanded and published as *Gazelle* (2003), a novel about a young girl's awakening to eros and sensuality in Cairo in the 1950s. In 2008, Ducornet also published *The One Marvelous Thing*, a collection "decorated" with illustrations by New York graphic artist T. Motley. His drawings enter into contrast and complementarity with Ducornet's stories, culminating in graphic versions of three stories previously published in *The Complete Butcher's Tales*, clearly engaging with her predilection for experimentation. This is present early in her career with stories such as "F*a*i*r*y F*i*n*g*e*r" where the eroticism of reading and the act of masturbation are conflated; a young girl's sexual awakening is associated with the *jouissance* of reading fairy tales. Ducornet indeed celebrates the "playful mind" that is "deeply responsive to the world and informed by powers instilled during infancy and childhood, powers that animate the imagination with primal energies" (2015, p. 2). She has written of a gift of leather-bound fairy-tale books that sparked her imagination, as well as a reverence for processes of metamorphosis (2010, p. 170). She also highlights a formative, almost magical, encounter with a dead fox in the Hudson valley woods of her childhood, its belly swarming with bees. This image reveals two primary totems for the author: the fox (representing the sacred beauty of metamorphosis) and bees (veritable incarnations of potency). Ducornet writes of "Books of Natural and Unnatural Nature" in *The Deep Zoo* (2015), citing Ovid's *Metamorphoses* in connection with Darwinian perceptions of nature, as she investigates the links and limits between nature, science, and the marvelous.

In her most recent discussions of fairy tales and the marvelous (Ducornet and Ryan-Sautour 2019, pp. 256–257), she celebrates the magic of the natural world, while also underlining its perilous condition. Like Carroll, the marvelous of wonderland is not to be disassociated from the real world. On the contrary, Ducornet's dreaming is fused with a position of authorial responsibility:

> I am not calling for magical thinking, obscurity or preciousness, but for an eager access to memory, revery and the unconscious – its powers, beauties, terrors and, perhaps above all, its rule-breaking intuitions, and to celebrate with you the mind's longing to become lighter, free of the weight of received ideas and gravity-bound redundancies.
>
> (2015, p. 4)

Traces of this position can be found early on in her novel *Phosphor in Dreamland* (1995), published shortly after *The Jade Cabinet*, where magical realism and traces of Surrealist Max Ernst's Loplop, bird-like, figure are fused to reflect upon the natural world and the power of the imaginative mind. However, as the above quotation suggests, Ducornet also raises darkness to the foreground of her writing. *The Fan-Maker's Inquisition* (1999) engages, for example, with the sexual violence of the Marquis de Sade, while shifting our focus to the darker, more dangerous, acts of genocide committed by Bishop Landa, responsible for the decimation of the Maya populations in Mexico. Such imaginings predominate in Ducornet's writing. There is an artistic rigor to these ethically charged reveries, evident in tightly crafted pieces of writing. Dark energy not only weaves its way into representations of dangerous politics and tyranny, but also into the minute details of intimate relationships, where it can wreak subtle forms of havoc. This challenging of the forces of authoritarianism and power clearly dominates Ducornet's recent trilogy of novels, all focused on the theme of betrayal. *Netsuke* (2011) recalls the figure of Bluebeard, as a sex-addicted psychoanalyst builds an intricate web of lies and secrets, ultimately exposing a vulnerable wife and artist, Akiko, to forms of insidious abuse. Vulnerability in contrast with abusive power, already present in Ducornet's first novel, reappears in her later fiction, as in *Brightfellow* (2016), where a violent mother figure sets the scene for the development of the young boy Stub on an American university campus. For Ducornet, these wounds run deep in the realms of both family and society, as is also apparent in *Trafik* (2021); here Ducornet works within the genre of science fiction to portray the persistence of friendship and eros on a struggling planet, deeply betrayed by its inhabitants. William H. Gass has observed how "Rikki Ducornet's books search for a way to heal the wound of our psyche – our shame and suppression of our nature – which has led not only to the denial of this world on behalf of another one, but which has repeatedly allowed authority and its agents to blind us to beauty, to make our passions poisonous, and to corral and confine the imagination" (Gass 1999). In a fearless, and sometimes unsettling, quest, Ducornet seeks to reveal dark beauty and free received ideas from their constraints; her fiction clearly invites her reader to engage with the "primary fury" of language.

SEE ALSO: Coover, Robert; Gass, William H.; The New Experimentalism/The Contemporary Avant-Garde

REFERENCES

Ducornet, Rikki. (1999). *The Monstrous and the Marvelous*. San Francisco: City Lights.

Ducornet, Rikki. (2010). Author comments. In: *My Mother She Killed Me, My Father He Ate Me*. (ed. Kate Bernheimer and Carmen Giménez Smith), 170. New York: Penguin.

Ducornet, Rikki. (2015). *The Deep Zoo*. Minneapolis: Coffee House Press.

Ducornet, Rikki. (2019). The imagination. In: *The International Encyclopedia of Surrealism* (ed. Michael Richardson *et al.*), vol. 1, 228–231. New York: Bloomsbury Press.

Ducornet, Rikki and Ryan-Sautour, Michelle. (2019). Interview with a vanguard author. In: *The Fairy Tale Vanguard: Literary Self-Consciousness in a Marvelous Genre* (ed. Stijn Praet and Anna Kerchy), 256–266. Newcastle upon Tyne, UK: Cambridge Scholar Publishing.

Gass, William H. (1999). Introduction to Rikki Ducornet. Rikki Ducornet's personal archives.

Gregory, Sinda and McCaffery, Larry. (1998). At the heart of things darkness and wild beauty: an interview with Rikki Ducornet. The Review of Contemporary Fiction 18 (3): 126–144.

Kavchak, Lisa. (2003). The reconstitution of Eden. Web Del Sol. *Del Sol Literary Dialogues*. http://www.webdelsol.com/Literary_Dialogues/interview-wds-ducornet.htm (accessed July 21, 2021).

FURTHER READING

Ducornet, Rikki. (2015). Interview with Chelsey Clammer. Eckleberg (January 30, 2015). https://www.eckleburg.org/interview-i-rikki-ducornet/

O'Brien, John. (ed.) (1998). Richard Powers/Rikki Ducornet. Special issue of The Review of Contemporary Fiction 18 (3): 110–230.

Ryan-Sautour, Michelle. (2019). The linguistic punctum in Rikki Ducornet's *The Complete Butcher's Tales* (1994) and *The One Marvelous Thing* (2008). In: *The Fairy Tale Vanguard: Literary Self-Consciousness in a Marvelous Genre* (ed. Stijn Praet and Anna Kerchy), 213–228. Newcastle upon Tyne, UK: Cambridge Scholar Publishing.

Ulmo, Anne. (2010). Corporeality in Rikki Ducornet's tetralogy of elements, gender/genre/genre/genre(s). In: *Writing the Deviant Body in Cyberliterature* (ed. Kornelia Slavova and Isabelle Boof-Vermesse), 55–61. Sofia, Bulgaria: St. Kliment Ohridksi University Press.

Ecocriticism and Environmental Fiction

KYLE BLADOW
Northland College, USA

Ecocriticism comprises a body of critical inquiry that developed in the 1980s and 1990s out of a foundational concern for considering environmental themes and representations in texts. It remains a growing area of scholarship for literary studies, whether dubbed "ecocriticism," "green studies," or the increasingly popular and broader label of "environmental humanities." The term "ecocriticism" was first coined in 1978 in an essay by William Rueckert, though his use of the term is fairly distinct from its later alignment with this critical approach. Rueckert's ecocriticism seeks to apply ecological principles in order to understand how texts might function as part of an ecosystem; however, the term most often refers to the more capacious definition set by Cheryll Glotfelty in *The Ecocriticism Reader*: "ecocriticism is the study of the relationship between literature and the physical environment" (1996, pp. xviii).

Ecocriticism eludes precise categorization; however, two (conveniently natural) metaphors stand out in preceding attempts: the wave and the rhizome. Helpfully compared to waves of feminist theory and criticism, the wave metaphor – advanced by Scott Slovic and others – helps to periodize some of the particular trends through the decades. The first wave, loosely situated from the 1980s through the formalization of the field in the 1990s, pertains to the genre of nature writing, particularly narratives of the human within a more-than-human environment, depictions of wilderness, and elaborations of environmental ethics emphasizing conservation. Chosen texts often included pastoral or Romantic literature, with an overwhelming emphasis on American and British writers. Important exceptions to this trend include the affiliated growth of ecofeminist scholarship, including Carolyn Merchant's *The Death of Nature* (1980) and Susan Griffin's *Woman and Nature* (1978), which offered early interventions in the study of environmental history and literature.

In the 1990s, the second wave introduced a more distinctly theoretical trend, one which broadened attention to genres beyond nature writing, to environmental spaces beyond wilderness (e.g. urban landscapes), and to other kinds of cultural production beyond literature. It was also marked by more revisionist approaches critiquing the fetishization of "Nature" and its construction in nineteenth-century Romantic traditions, which frequently depicted nonhuman nature as a restorative, appealing alternative to built environments. Earlier preoccupations with wilderness and landscapes were critiqued more robustly by scholars affiliated with the burgeoning environmental justice movement and with developments in ecofeminism.

In the 2000s, the third wave signaled growing commitments to more comparative and cross-cultural approaches, witnessed by advancements in postcolonial and global ecocriticism. Concepts like Ursula Heise's "eco-cosmopolitanism" flourished alongside renewed critical interest in bioregionalism, showing the ongoing relevance of place, however contrary the approaches to it. By this point ecocriticism had grown sufficiently large to sustain significant internal critique about its aims and methods, undertaken by scholars including Michael P. Cohen and Dana Phillips.

While these first three waves seem well established, less determined is whether the field has settled into a fourth or a fifth wave. Scott Slovic has described a fourth wave distinguished by a turn to materiality, specifically the theories of materiality promulgated by material feminist scholars and others in the 2010s (Slovic 2012, p. 619). However one might delineate the most recent wave, certainly an interest in materiality and agency stands out, as do terms like Stacy Alaimo's "trans-corporeality," Rob Nixon's "slow violence," and the prominent, much-debated "Anthropocene."

One drawback of the wave metaphor is the implication that preceding waves are completed; in fact, the various creative and scholarly emphases characterizing each of these waves continued simultaneously across the decades, as those who have proposed the wave metaphor clearly acknowledge. The rhizome metaphor of ecocriticism, meanwhile, helps capture the sense of vastness of the field. Elizabeth DeLoughrey and George B. Handley (2011, p. 15) have argued for the rhizomatic nature of ecocriticism, an approach akin to that of such scholars as Lawrence Buell, who earlier recognized the field as remarkably heterogeneous (Buell himself has forwarded a palimpsest as a conceptual metaphor; Buell 2005, p. 17). Oppermann uses the rhizome to reassess critiques that ecocriticism's broadness suggests an untenable imprecision; she turns to Deleuze and Guattari's use of the rhizome to argue that ecocritics share an "intellectual attitude" even if they differ in the methodologies they employ or the objects they study (Oppermann 2010, p. 18). Rather than critique its perceived lack of focus, thinking of ecocriticism as a rhizome aligns it with critical developments, valuing ecocriticism's plurality without diminishing a sense of its cohesion.

Tracing the contours these metaphors provide, a broad periodization of ecocriticism follows. Although ecocriticism demonstrates a global scope spanning time periods and other genres, including ecopoetics and ecomedia, the focus here is on developments pertaining most directly to contemporary American fiction. The concluding section surveys some representative works of fiction that match thematically with this scholarly field.

ORIGINS OF ECOCRITICISM

Founded in 1992, the Association for the Study of Literature and Environment (ASLE) hosted its first biennial conference in 1995 at Colorado State University in Fort Collins. ASLE grew from preceding meetings of the Western Literature Association (WLA), three in particular: in 1989, where Cheryll Glotfelty advocated along with Glen Love for centering ecological criticism and "nature-oriented literature"; in 1993, when a panel instigated a call for a better definition of ecocriticism; and in 1994, when critics answered that call by providing position papers.

One goal for a number of ecocritics in the 1990s – and one that would reappear in the

2010s – was to provide a response to post-structuralist theory and postmodernism, which were perceived as preoccupied with texts and discourse to the point of excluding place and the material world, a concern that may have been ill-founded, especially given more recent forays into eco-deconstruction and other environmental philosophy. The position papers from the 1994 WLA conference repeatedly expressed concern over ecocriticism developing into simply another body of criticism, one which could be formulaically applied to literary texts without engaging any of the environmental values so many of its early practitioners shared. With this concern in mind, a number of the papers cautioned against jargon or overelaborating theoretical concepts to the detriment of attending to actual environments, species, and ecological issues. Some critics promoted narrative scholarship as an alternative to prevailing criticism, a mode that included first-person address and personal reflections and experiences alongside critical interpretations.

Ecocriticism also arrived as part of the burgeoning interdisciplinary field of environmental studies that called for multifaceted approaches to ecological issues as well as broader scientific literacy. Over time, the term "environmental humanities" would become more prominent, but the early inclusion of literary criticism as an aspect of "environmental studies" suggests academics sought projects that could simultaneously engage the sciences and the humanities. For ecocritics, this conviction might be realized by building humanists' scientific literacy or by applying biological or evolutionary history to cultural investigations. These calls, along with encouraging modes like narrative scholarship, coincided with many early ecocritics' interests in outdoor recreation and contemporary environmental philosophies like deep ecology. In her book *What Is Nature?* (1995) Kate Soper divides approaches to the environment between "nature-endorsing" and "nature-skeptical" positions; with some exceptions, the trend in ecocritical scholarship was a move from the former to the latter.

Cheryll Glotfelty became the first academic to hold a position of Professor of Literature and Environment in 1990 at the University of Nevada, Reno. Among Glotfelty's contributions – a scholar of American literature, she has also advanced critical bioregional studies and assembled a literary anthology of Nevada – she served as co-editor for *The Ecocriticism Reader* (1996), a foundational collection for the field. The reader extends the concerns of the WLA position papers, and a careful reading of its contributions shows the fallacy of overgeneralizing this period of ecocriticism as consisting exclusively of paeans to nature writing: its contributors employ ecology and other scientific disciplines to varying degrees, and they differ on the relevance of critical theory. Taken together, their essays present elements of what would become presiding trends for the various waves or rhizomatic branches of ecocriticism. For example, one article reprinted a chapter from Joseph Meeker's *Comedy of Survival* (1974), an early study in "literary ecology" proposing that the modes of comedy and tragedy could be understood from the perspective of evolutionary biology and that comedy in particular could be seen as adaptive. Meeker's inclusion in the reader shows his alignment with early attempts to wed natural sciences with humanistic inquiry, and his work remains a touchstone in criticism more recently with scholars incorporating affect studies and the role of humor in environmental texts.

Ecofeminism must also be recognized for its relation to a number of ecocriticism's founding concerns and for the contributions it made to the latter field's development. The fact that the collection *Ecofeminism: Women, Animals, Nature* (1993), edited by Greta Gaard, was published three years before *The Ecocriticism Reader*, serves as one example of their coevolution. Indeed, feminist scholars had been investigating the conflation of women with nature under patriarchy long before this publication, and many ecocritics have and continue to draw on ecofeminist work by Carol Adams, Donna Haraway, Annette Kolodny, Val Plumwood, Vandana Shiva, and Noël Sturgeon, among others. Ecofeminism, as ecocriticism itself would become, is a wide-ranging, heterogeneous movement of social activism and scholarship marked by a tension between essentialist and anti-essentialist arguments: it encompasses both arguments for women's unique association with nature and arguments against the givenness of these categories that further critique their subjugated positions within patriarchy. Through theory and practice, ecofeminism countered the male dominance evident in strains of late-twentieth-century environmentalism, while also providing early critiques of mechanistic interpretations of the natural world and of the entrenched dichotomy of nature and culture.

ENVIRONMENTAL JUSTICE

The final decade of the twentieth century witnessed further investigation of the instability of the nature–culture split. In 1990, Bill McKibben published *The End of Nature*, an early general audience book on climate change, in which he pointed out that nowhere on Earth remained unaffected by industrial activity. At the same time, scholars grew more critically reflexive regarding the concept of nature and its supposed division from culture or humanity. The collection *Uncommon Ground* (1995), edited by William Cronon, addressed this point, gathering the work of participants in a seminar sponsored by the University of California Humanities Research Institute; the collection critiqued the dependency of American environmentalism on specious notions of wilderness as land devoid of human inhabitation. Richard White's contribution included a critique of McKibben's book for its idealization of nature. This collection indicates a broader shift in critical energy for both ecocriticism and environmentalism: complicating the concept of nature motivated new areas of study. For instance, Lawrence Buell advanced examination of the rhetoric of environmental and corporeal contamination by analyzing what he termed "toxic discourse," which "insists on the interdependence of ecocentric and anthropocentric values" (1998, p. 639).

In tandem with a critique of concepts of nature, another key influence on ecocriticism was the growth in the early nineties of the environmental justice movement, whose advocates asserted that access to healthy environments – often defined as the places in which we live, work, and play – is a universal right and that environmental risks must be borne equitably. Environmental justice frameworks encouraged greater integration of multiple areas of social activism (e.g. the antinuclear movement, antimilitarism, Civil Rights, workers' rights) while broadening the scope and inclusivity of preceding conservationist and other environmental activism. While initially characterized by grassroots organizing, environmental justice would soon be engaged by larger institutions and government agencies as well; for instance, the Environmental Protection Agency oversees grants, promotes strategic planning, and pursues partnerships related to environmental justice. Understanding how such factors as race and socioeconomic status correlate with environmental issues became increasingly featured in policy and in the proliferation of such concepts as "environmental racism." In

1987, the United Church of Christ Commission on Racial Justice published the landmark study *Toxic Waste in the United States*, and in 1991 the First National People of Color Environmental Justice Leadership Summit in Washington, DC, produced a "Principles of Environmental Justice" document. The following years would also see publication of novels directly addressing environmental racism and violence, in works by such writers as Percival Everett, Linda Hogan, Ruth Ozeki, and Helena Viramontes.

In ecocriticism, the collection *The Environmental Justice Reader* (2002), co-edited by Joni Adamson, Mei Mei Evans, and Rachel Stein, as well as *New Perspectives on Environmental Justice* (2004), edited by Rachel Stein, are indicative of the period's deepening focus on attending to the environmental disparities people experience based upon such factors as race, class, sexuality, gender, and ability. Joni Adamson's *American Indian Literature, Environmental Justice, and Ecocriticism: The Middle Place* (2001) was an early scholarly text that, more than simply analyzing American Indian texts, more thoroughly questioned how the work of American Indian writers might expand and transform ecocriticism.

Meanwhile, the growing critique of the detrimental effects of the flows of transnational capital under neoliberalism on both human communities and environments – encapsulated by such moments as the "Battle for Seattle" protests at the 1999 World Trade Organization conference – contributed to both the development of the environmental justice movement and the more globalizing scope of environmental humanities. At the same time, the ASLE organization continued to grow through the formation of international affiliate groups, beginning with ASLE-Japan in 1994 and followed by nearly a dozen others around the world, which offered institutional support for more global scholarly exchanges.

A cosmopolitan shift to ecocritical theory arrived with Ursula Heise's *Sense of Place, Sense of Planet* (2008), in which Heise brought particular attention to ecocriticism's prevailing focus on the American environmental movement and its attendant emphases on bioregionalism and nature writing. Heise drew on contemporary scholarly developments in theories of globalization and cosmopolitanism to propose "eco-cosmopolitanism": world environmental citizenship that grapples with the challenges of promoting social and environmental justice without necessarily resorting to identification with the local, whether construed as regional or national. The turn to the cosmopolitan and the global also offered further opportunities to engage coincident developments in postcolonial studies.

The emergence of postcolonial ecocriticism began as critics noted a dearth of attention to the ecological in postcolonial studies scholarship while also noting the capability of postcolonial studies to deepen awareness of the sociohistorical dimensions of place; postcolonial criticism was well poised to situate critique of imperialism's extensive environmental impacts as well as to consider counterhegemonic or anticolonial ecological values and practices. Like "eco-cosmopolitanism," postcolonial ecocriticism helped broaden the scope and import of environmental humanities and to reorient and further environmental philosophy by engaging writers and concepts such as Édouard Glissant's "aesthetics of the earth" (Glissant 1997, p. 150). Significant initial publications in postcolonial ecocriticism include Graham Huggan and Helen Tiffin's *Postcolonial Ecocriticism* (2006) and Elizabeth DeLoughrey and George B. Handley's *Postcolonial Ecologies* (2011). In addressing instances of colonial dehumanization and speciesism, postcolonial ecocriticism further linked ecocriticism to the adjacent field of animal studies.

While more of an ecophenomenologist than an animal studies scholar, David Abram promoted investigation of interspecies relationality by popularizing the notion of the "more-than-human world" (Abram 1996, p. 95). Where his *Spell of the Sensuous* (1996) aimed to demonstrate humanity's exaggerated separation from other life and one's environment via increased reliance on written language that attenuates perception of the world's animacy, in *Becoming Animal* (2010) he expands this project by considering possibilities for retracing language's attachments to and emergence from the more-than-human world, advocating further that attention to sensuous embodiment enables awareness of a dynamically animate, conversive world. Timothy Morton's *Ecology without Nature* (2007) also stressed language's limitations, arguing that the discourse of "nature" only obfuscates apprehending the ecological; in *The Ecological Thought* (2010) Morton avoids such limitations by envisioning humans within an extensive "mesh" of all living and nonliving matter. Similar concepts and perspectives grew more frequent with the evolving trend of ecocritical theory in the 2010s. Environmental fiction in this decade would also reflect the trend, particularly evident in speculative fiction and works addressing climate change.

MATERIALITY, AFFECT, SCALE

If earlier ecocritical projects demonstrated tension over the role or value of employing critical theory, by the second decade of the twenty-first century this tension seems much less evident as the branching directions of the field readily engage multiple literary and cultural theories. Even as ecocriticism grows more prominent as a discrete field, it continues to realize early hopes for interdisciplinarity, with scholars undertaking projects that draw on cognitive psychology, quantum physics, biosemiotics, and emerging fields in philosophy such as posthumanism: vantages seeking to decenter the human by showing its entanglements with other-than-human life and technologies, or by transforming methodologies and investigations of the human (e.g. multispecies ethnography).

A primary shift at this time, in tandem with posthumanism, reappraised conceptions of matter. Motivated by the sense that postmodern theories had overemphasized the totality of language, scholars sought ways to engage matter and embodiment, whether by developing new theories or by revisiting superseded scientific philosophies like vitalism for inspiration. A prominent example of this direction occurred in feminism, witnessed in such publications as Stacy Alaimo and Susan Hekman's co-edited collection *Material Feminisms* (2008), which encouraged a return of thinking about the body after the perceived linguistic turn of the late twentieth century. The collection recognized the limitation of postmodern linguisticism and worked against assumptions that discourse on the body and on matter necessarily leads to essentialism. Rather, they resisted reduplicating a nature–culture binary and instead emphasized the co-constitution of material and discursive realms. In this regard, early work by Donna Haraway and other feminists was further integrated into ecocritical scholarship by Stacy Alaimo, whose *Undomesticated Ground* (2000) inverted the tendency to see nature discourse as a patriarchal tool and instead asserted its relevance to feminist critique. Alaimo's *Bodily Natures* (2010) would further influence ecocriticism; the book's central concept of "trans-corporeality," which acknowledges "the human is always intermeshed with the more-than-human world" and which also serves as a "theoretical site . . . where corporeal theories, environmental theories, and science studies meet and mingle in productive ways" (pp. 2–3), would become widely cited in ecocritical scholarship, especially in the emerging field of material ecocriticism articulated by such scholars as Serpil Oppermann and Serenella Iovino. The 2010s featured a proliferation of other material theories, including speculative realism and object-oriented ontology, which together represent a defining shift in the field.

The material turn occurred simultaneously with a growing attention to the ways affect studies could bear on ecocriticism. Akin to the material turn in complicating notions of agency and in shifting inquiry from subjects to assemblages, affect studies especially suits investigations of human enmeshments with environments by considering how affective responses circulate between bodies and emerge through reactions with nonhuman environments. Affect studies draws on divergent and extensive bodies of theory, among them a longstanding engagement with queer theory, which has also influenced ecocriticism in a body of scholarship frequently termed queer ecology. Three common directions for early projects in this area include critiquing how discourse around nature often serves to reinforce heteropatriarchy, asserting the gender and sexual diversity among other-than-human species, and investigating queer engagements or inhabitations of natural spaces. Catriona Sandilands and Bruce Erickson's co-edited collection *Queer Ecologies* (2010) traced these and related trajectories within the field, including queer animality, environmental politics, and affective attachments to place. Nicole Seymour's *Strange Natures* (2013) analyzed a range of contemporary American literature and film while developing a queer environmental ethics. Seymour's work resituated queer theory's critiques of futurity while simultaneously examining the contradictions and complexities of environmentalism that queer perspectives and art reveal.

While materiality and agency became notably fruitful avenues of study for ecocriticism in the early twenty-first century, questions of scale have been no less significant. Taking up scalar concerns evinced earlier by bioregionalism and eco-cosmopolitanism, subsequent works considered the irreducibility of scale and the challenges it presents to criticism. Derek Woods's essay "Scale Critique for the Anthropocene" (Woods 2014) pointed out disjunctures resulting from different scales, while Timothy Clark's *Ecocriticism on the Edge* (2015) considered the effects of scale on interpreting literature and with its proposal of "scale framing" showed scale to be a crucial topic for ecological philosophy. Besides spatial scales, temporal ones have also marked ecocriticism, witnessed by the popularization of Rob Nixon's "slow violence" to name the ways environmental harms not only occur in spectacular and catastrophic instances, but can also accrete over time; instances of slow violence are equally if not more perilous despite often not receiving similar attention given the lack of visibility and immediacy demanded by media cycles.

The single most widely employed (and debated) concept among these various posthumanist strands of ecocriticism is the Anthropocene (Crutzen and Stoermer 2000). The term, popularized by Paul Crutzen and Eugene Stoermer in 2000, served to mark the arrival of a new geologic epoch characterized by human alteration of the Earth's geophysical systems. The idea quickly spread beyond stratigraphy and geology to become prominent in cultural studies. For the environmental humanities, the debate continues as to whether "Anthropocene" obscures the disproportionate influence particular subsets of the human population have had on the Earth's systems, as well as the roles socioeconomic systems have played. To this end, others have proposed such terms as "Capitalocene," "Plantationocene," and "Cthulucene" (Haraway 2015). However insufficient, "Anthropocene" has clearly caught the imagination of ecocritics and served to extend debates, evident in its frequent use in publication and conference presentation titles.

Theory and criticism within the environmental humanities show no sign of slowing. Of particular relevance for studies of American fiction, a nascent direction of ecocriticism is within the study of narrative theory, what Erin James in *The Storyworld Accord* (2015) has termed "econarratology" (p. xv). James promotes closer attention to the environments produced within narratives and, drawing on developments in evolutionary psychology and cognitive science, suggests how attention to literary form affords insights into how people experience and make sense of their material environments. Erin James and Eric Morel's co-edited *Environment and Narrative* (2020) extends the project of econarratology, with the majority of its contributors analyzing contemporary American fiction.

ENVIRONMENTAL FICTION

The genre most closely associated with the formation of ecocriticism is nature writing: creative nonfiction focused on natural history and the description of place, natural phenomena, and nonhuman beings. Strongly influenced by American transcendentalism and the conservation movement, nature writing continues as a popular genre with particular emphasis on climate change. However, literary fiction quickly became and remains an equally prominent object of study.

The American novel from the 1980s with an enduring legacy in ecocriticism is Don DeLillo's *White Noise* (1985), which received the National Book Award and was heralded as an example of literary postmodernism. The novel follows Professor Jack Gladney and his family in a small college town, offering semi-satiric commentary on contemporary American consumerism and media and conveying a paranoid tone as characters contend with their own mortality, for instance, by seeking access to the drug Dylar, which treats the fear of death. Most directly pertinent to ecocritical analysis is the novel's second section, "The Airborne Toxic Event," which recounts the town's evacuation after a chemical spill at a train yard produces a noxious cloud. In the section, Gladney and others are subjected to the uncertainties of exposure's effects on their health and life expectancy, depicting risk calculations contemporary populations are compelled to make as well as the complexities of toxic discourse.

While most any work of fiction could be examined from an ecocritical perspective, and a fair amount of American fiction contains strong environmental themes, several authors stand out for their continued emphasis of such themes over the course of their careers. Thomas Coraghessan (T.C.) Boyle has written twenty-eight novels and short story collections that consistently focus on assessing American history and culture while critiquing ideals of American utopianism. *The Relieve Box* (2017), a short story collection, imagines gene editing technology, drug-resistant bacteria, and climate change. *The Terranauts* (2016) fictionalizes the Biosphere II project in Arizona, imagining a crew attempting to live within a simulated, enclosed ecosystem and to succeed where their preceding crew failed. Three other novels feature environmental issues as central themes: *When the Killing's Done* (2011), which dramatizes ethical questions of managing invasive species; *Drop City* (2003), which focuses on the back-to-the-land movement of the 1970s by imagining a California commune's relocation to Alaska; and *A Friend of the Earth* (2000), whose protagonist goes from being a radical environmentalist in a group reminiscent of Earth First! to a caretaker of a retired pop star's endangered species menagerie. Throughout his oeuvre, Boyle employs a deft sense of humor and irony while examining the hubris and earnestness of American environmental movements.

The novels of Chickasaw author Linda Hogan fictionalize ecological issues faced by Indigenous North American nations: *Mean Spirit* (1990) chronicles the murder of Osage tribal citizens in the violent wake of oil development on tribal lands. While *Mean Spirit* featured the Osage Nation, Hogan's subsequent novels would invent fictional nations with plots inspired by actual events. *Solar Storms* (1995) draws inspiration from the Cree and Inuit opposition to hydroelectric dam projects in Quebec. Hogan's most recent novels, *Power* (1998) and *The People of the Whale* (2009), both imagine the changing nature of Indigenous relationships with nonhuman animals as characters seek to reconcile traditional responsibilities with contemporary circumstances; *People of the Whale* particularly alludes to the revitalization of ceremonial and subsistence whaling by the Makah Tribe. Hogan's work is regularly cited by environmental justice literary scholars, and she has been a regular participant at ecocritical conferences.

Another prominent American environmental author, Barbara Kingsolver has published fifteen books, nine of which are fiction; several of her nonfiction works also address such topics as climate change and sustainable agriculture. Her most thoroughly environmental novels are *Flight Behavior* (2012), which imagines a monarch butterfly migration displaced from its usual wintering location in Mexico to Tennessee as the result of climate change, and *Prodigal Summer* (2000), whose characters, situated at different points on or nearby a southern Appalachian mountain, include a wildlife biologist. Critics lauded both works for their interweaving of ecological issues with stories of human relationships.

Ruth Ozeki has published two novels considering American consumption and agricultural practices. *My Year of Meats* (1998) follows a documentary filmmaker who uncovers the detrimental effects of synthetic hormones in meat production; the novel also explores agricultural shifts due to globalization as an American beef company attempts to expand its market in Japan. Ozeki's next novel, *All Over Creation* (2003), considers the issue of genetically modified food as the protagonist returns to her family's Idaho potato farm to find herself entangled in a standoff between agribusiness and an environmental activist group.

Known for his detailed portrayals of technological interventions, Richard Powers's fiction demonstrates recurrent attention to ecological issues, most evident in three of his novels. *Gain* (1998) charts the rise of an American corporation from its nineteenth-century origins as a family soapmaking business to a multinational chemical company, while also featuring a character whose cancer diagnosis is linked to the company's products. Winner of the National Book Award, *The Echo Maker* (2006) explores the nature of consciousness through a character who has sustained a traumatic head injury, but also depicts migratory sandhill cranes and concern for habitat loss. Powers's most sustained treatment of environmental themes is found in his Pulitzer Prize-winning *The Overstory* (2018), whose characters' disparate lives are entwined by their involvement in a radical environmentalist group opposing logging. Like the ecocritical theory of the time, Powers's literary vision consistently features the vitality of more-than-human ecosystems.

Climate fiction, or cli-fi, has become a prevalent subgenre of American environmental fiction, an outgrowth of science fiction and speculative fiction that imagines lives and societies responding to a world reshaped by destabilized climate systems. It frequently overlaps with dystopian fiction, given the number of plots that depict diminished communities facing daunting challenges for survival. Not all cli-fi is dystopian, however, as some subgenres (e.g. solarpunk) contradict its tropes and affirm alternatives. One major American cli-fi author is Kim Stanley Robinson, whose work was influenced by science fiction author Phillip K. Dick, the subject of Robinson's doctoral dissertation. Robinson's novels and story collections imagine responses to climate change. His Science in the Capital series dramatizes a call for national and global governmental responses to climate change, while *New York 2140* (2017) imagines life in the city inundated by a 50-foot rise in sea levels. Robinson's other works, such as his Mars trilogy, *2312* (2012), and *Red Moon* (2018), imagine terraforming and settlement beyond Earth.

Other speculative fiction writers incorporate anthropogenic climate change in plots that center different if related themes. In *The Windup Girl* (2009), Paolo Bacigalupi explores social consequences of advanced biotechnology in a future world largely run by food industry conglomerates. Bacigalupi's *The Water Knife* (2015) attends to freshwater scarcity in the US Southwest. Jeff VanderMeer's Southern Reach trilogy revolves around the bizarre Area X; VanderMeer credits Florida's St. Marks National Wildlife Refuge as his influence for this setting and the trilogy's plot.

Octavia Butler's oeuvre reflects her attunement to ecological issues throughout the latter twentieth century, perhaps most extensively treated in her Parable or Earthseed series. *Parable of the Sower* (1993) and *Parable of the Talents* (2000), the only two published novels in the series, chart the development of the Earthseed movement originating with a "hyperempathic" protagonist in dystopian future California and leading toward human settlement beyond Earth. Butler's works are distinct from more triumphalist portrayals of space exploration in that they keenly focus on portraying the hubris of humans and their failure to sustain a symbiotic relationship with the more-than-human world.

Other prominent speculative environmental works by authors otherwise not affiliated with the genre include Cormac McCarthy's *The Road* (2008), Claire Vaye Watkins's *Gold Fame Citrus* (2016), and Louise Erdrich's *Future Home of the Living God* (2018). Given the growing urgency of climate change, such themes will doubtless proliferate across genres and literary styles in American fiction.

Meanwhile, ecocriticism's commitments to environmental advocacy as well as scholarship afford no small degree of urgency in the twenty-first century. For example, the theme for the 2019 ASLE biennial conference at the University of California, Davis, "Paradise on Fire," became literally true when the devastating Camp Fire of November 2018 razed the town of Paradise, California. Ecocritics continue to undertake pedagogy and scholarship addressing the role of humanities in a world facing climate destabilization, mass extinction, and related extreme challenges, most sharing the conviction that examining narrative and art is crucial to apprehending and addressing these crises.

SEE ALSO: Boyle, T.C.; Butler, Octavia; DeLillo, Don; Hogan, Linda; Kingsolver, Barbara; Ozeki, Ruth; Powers, Richard

REFERENCES

Abram, David. (1997). *The Spell of the Sensuous: Perception and Language in a More-Than-Human World*. New York: Vintage; 1st ed. 1996.

Alaimo, Stacy. (2010). *Bodily Natures: Science, the Environment, and the Material Self*. Bloomington: Indiana University Press.

Buell, Lawrence. (1998). Toxic discourse. *Critical Inquiry* 24 (3): 639–665.

Buell, Lawrence. (2005). *The Future of Environmental Criticism: Environmental Crisis and Literary Imagination*. Oxford: Blackwell.

Crutzen, Paul J. and Stoermer, Eugene F. (2000). The "Anthropocene." *International Geosphere-Biosphere Programme Global Change Newsletter* 41: 17–18.

DeLoughrey, Elizabeth and Handley, George B. (2011). Introduction: toward an aesthetics of the earth. In: *Postcolonial Ecologies: Literatures of the Environment* (ed. Elizabeth DeLoughrey and George B. Handley), 3–39. New York: Oxford University Press.

Glissant, Édouard. (1997). *Poetics of Relation* (trans. Betsy Wing). Ann Arbor: University of Michigan Press.

Glotfelty, Cheryll. (1996). Introduction: literary studies in an age of environmental crisis. In: *The Ecocriticism Reader: Landmarks in Literary Ecology* (ed. Cheryll Glotfelty and Harold Fromm), xv–xxxvii. Athens: University of Georgia Press.

Haraway, Donna. (2015). Anthropocene, Capitalocene, Plantationocene, Chthulucene: making kin. *Environmental Humanities* 6: 159–165.

James, Erin. (2015). *The Storyworld Accord: Econarratology and Postcolonial Narratives*. Lincoln: University of Nebraska Press.

Oppermann, Serpil. (2010). The rhizomatic trajectory of ecocriticism. *Ecozon@* 1 (1): 17–21.

Slovic, Scott. (2012). Editor's note. *ISLE: Interdisciplinary Studies in Literature and Environment* 19 (4): 619–621.

Woods, Derek. (2014). Scale critique for the Anthropocene. *Minnesota Review* 83: 133–142.

FURTHER READING

Adamson, Joni, Gleason, William A., and Pellow, David N. (eds.) (2016). *Keywords for Environmental Studies*. New York: New York University Press.

Buell, Lawrence. (2005). *The Future of Environmental Criticism: Environmental Crisis and Literary Imagination*. Oxford: Blackwell.

Garrard, Greg. (2011). *Ecocriticism*, 2nd ed. New York: Routledge.

Hiltner, Ken. (ed.) (2014). *Ecocriticism: The Essential Reader*. New York: Routledge.

Nixon, Rob. (2011). *Slow Violence and the Environmentalism of the Poor*. Cambridge, MA: Harvard University Press.

Egan, Jennifer

JOELLE MANN
Binghamton University, USA

Jennifer Egan (b. 1962) has marked her place among American writers. Her formal creativity and thematic range have earned her critical acclaim and the 2011 Pulitzer Prize. Egan's literary works examine the nexus of technological mediation and aesthetic communication across historical eras, and her characters grapple with the sociohistorical issues of times past while scrutinizing the mixed media of the twenty-first century. During a time of advanced media convergence, Egan illustrates novelistic convergence, eliding a critical historicist view with the current cultural conversation. The scope of her fiction uncovers how, as she notes, technological change is "inseparable from many other seismic shifts of the past twenty years: modern terrorism, globalization, climate change" (2014, p. xviii). Born in Chicago and raised in San Francisco, Egan conjoins literary innovation with cultural transition, and her formal virtuosity allows for a recursivity that expresses the shifting technologies of meaning and memory.

Setting aside Egan's journalistic and academic prose, her fiction exposes our present moment through a self-consciousness unique to the novel. With a sense of realism after poststructuralism, Egan commits herself to a strong structure of ideas, a precise sense of diction, and a distinct logic of literary voice. She conveys the prominence of voice in an interview with Charlie Reilly, noting that "Without a voice you've got nothing" (Reilly 2009, p. 442). A sophisticated treatment of voice emerges from what Howard, in Egan's neo-gothic novel *The Keep* (2006), calls the "history pushing up from underneath" (2006, p. 43). Indeed, Egan's act of *poiesis* moves across a skein of fluid and destabilized voices that range from the historical fiction of the Brooklyn Naval Yard to a futuristic Twitter story set on the Mediterranean Sea. And while Egan's novel *The Invisible Circus* (1994) and collection of stories *Emerald City* (1996) were not widely read initially, they foreground Egan's predilection for fictional innovation. The binary structure of *The Invisible Circus* anticipates the dual viewpoints of many of her novels, and the novice stories of *Emerald City* stress a theme of transcendence amid displacement.

The Invisible Circus traces a spiritual quest of two sisters, Faith and Phoebe O'Connor. Set in 1978 in San Francisco where Egan grew up, the novel highlights a family beset by loss, experiencing the anxiety of influence of the sixties counterculture. The city bereaves the rebellion of what was once the radical polemics of Haight-Ashbury, and the residue of the counterculture sets the mood of the suburban drift and seventies coffee house where Phoebe O'Connor works. Phoebe views "tourists traversing Haight Street with maps aloft . . . unable to find the dead center they sought" (1994, p. 63). Phoebe and her widowed mother move among this dead center of memories after the deaths of Phoebe's father and sister, Faith. Searching for the secrets of Faith's suicide in Italy in the late sixties, Phoebe follows the voices recorded within her sister's old postcards. In a triptych of three parts, Phoebe travels to be "newly born in a strange land," transcending the burden of history and "organiz[ing] the world an instant at a time" (pp. 110, 161).

Moving inside of Phoebe's voice, Egan recreates Faith's journey while penning an affecting chronicle of two sisters entangled within the terror of shifting times. With the semblance of Hawthornean allegory, Egan's flickering palimpsest shows the dark world of Faith's participation with the Red Army Faction in Belgium. The left-wing terrorism of the Baader–Meinhof group haunts her suicide along with an inescapable teleology:

"Everything's changing," Faith said. "Everything's going to be different."
Things had already changed – too much. "I like how it is," Phoebe said.
"No this is better," Faith said. "This is history. You can't stop it."

(1994, p. 54)

The resonance of history materializes not only through political critique but also through religious allegory, and the biblical stories told by graduate student Pietro Santangelo accent the spiritual timbre intimated by Phoebe's visit to Reims Cathedral. The cathedral's figurative value is stressed in a violent tête-à-tête: Phoebe imagines the ghostly outline of her sister's reflection through the window of a Parisian restaurant as "another person's hand reach[es] gingerly, gingerly out from behind the glass to touch Phoebe's own" (1994, p. 153). Egan redoubles temporality and character, reflecting Phoebe's need to restore a sense of faith in the future.

Like the binary world Egan creates in *The Invisible Circus*, Egan's National Book Award finalist, *Look at Me* (2001), shows the intersecting lives of two Charlottes – New York thirties-something model Charlotte Swenson and Rockford, Illinois teenager Charlotte Hauser. The concurrent voices derive inspiration from Egan's own experience in the fashion industry and from an intersubjective frame taken from James Joyce's *Ulysses* (1922): "We walk through ourselves, meeting robbers, ghosts, giants, old men, young men, wives, widows, brothers-in-love. But always meeting ourselves" (1986, p. 175). This Joycean lens, which scrutinizes the relationship between aesthetics and authenticity, metafictively portrays how the novel's unreliable narration recreates the world while telling of it. The shifting vantage point betrays the fictionality inherent within all novelistic tellings, underlining the Platonist view of a novelistic world of one's own creation. Portraying the semblance of appearance, Charlotte Swenson's face reconstruction after a life-changing accident transforms her physical facade. By way of Charlotte's physical alteration, Egan critiques a society obsessed with the image, and further spotlights an affinity to the theory novel, an homage to Egan's time spent at the University of Pennsylvania and Cambridge University. *Look at Me* fashions a Lacanian narrative of ego-formation, becoming a literal and figurative act of reconstruction for the Charlottes further marked by first- and third-person narratives. Charlotte Swenson models a physical transformation while others revise and recreate their lives, exposing sociocultural biases based upon myopic perception.

The portrayal of Moose Metcalf, a high school football star turned unhinged history professor, develops the "structural dissatisfaction" that Martin Paul Eve (2015) associates with academic characters in *The Invisible Circus, Look at Me, The Keep,* and *A Visit from the Goon Squad* (2010). Yet, identifying herself as an "academic interloper," Egan claims that academics as intermediary characters help her to frame abstract questions (2019, p. 417). Moose, particularly, questions a world without "history or context or meaning" that has been "remade by circuitry" (2001, p. 496). To give prominence to Moose's warning, an apocalyptic violence linked to a neoliberal spread of information accents the spectral terror of the character Z. The flow of images and information reinforces the representation of Z as a "machine of adaptation" (p. 304), who infiltrates American culture much in the same way as the 9/11 terrorists. Characterized as an absence and presence, Z's uncanny depiction is stressed even more so by Egan's early temp job as a caterer at the World Trade Center. Still, despite the fact that *Look at Me* was published a week after 9/11, Egan points out in her afterword that Z remains "an imaginative artifact of a more innocent time" (2001). Even so, Egan's denouement reveals an unsettling veracity about the homegrown terrors linked to information capitalism and identity formation. Egan's creation of PersonalSpaces, a social media forum aimed at virtually recreating the lives of people for capitalistic gain, galvanizes identity creation into a stratification of personhood. Charlotte Swenson models her life for the forum and later for a television movie assembled by a virtual ventriloquism. The film reenacts Charlotte's accident, bringing the two Charlottes together in a penultimate scene that points to the epilogue, written by a doubled Charlotte whose voice has been overwritten.

A preoccupation with authenticity shapes Egan's metafictive voice in the neo-gothic novel *The Keep*. Creating a frame narrative through pseudo-writer Ray, Egan imprisons characters and readers by self-reflexively enacting a writerly perspective. While in a creative writing class in prison, Ray transcribes the story of two cousins separated by a traumatic experience. The accounts of New York City techno-nerd Danny and his cousin, European bond trader Howard, illustrate the agential force of Ray's imagination along with an examination of modern neoliberal values. Shifting through thought lines, Ray develops multiple plotlines to enact a sense of what Danny describes to be *alto*, or the reciprocal relationship between observer and observed. Danny explains that "you saw but you also could *be seen*, you knew and were known" (2006, p. 6). The neologism *alto* connects the nonlinear voices in the novel, and the many narrative levels literally and figuratively conjoin the caverns of Ray's writerly mind with the tunnels of Howard's European castle and its stronghold, the Keep – gothic edifices reminiscent of Edgar Allan Poe's House of Usher and Henry James's Bly.

By writing Danny and Howard's story, Ray subsumes a self-conscious position, and the ghostly presence of Ray's characters reaffirms a metafictive message clearly articulated by Ray's prison roommate Davis: "They're ghosts... Not alive, not dead. An in-between thing" (2006, p. 96). The cousins doubly uncover the ghosts of the Keep including the mystery of an old baroness, and Egan's *mise en abyme* reveals how imagination bleeds into reality. Ray's story and the story of the Keep become one and the same, turning Ray into a ghost of sorts by the denouement. Inherently, Egan's gothic tropes emphasize the potential horrors of technocratic culture in a world void of imagination, and Egan employs conventions of crime fiction, further conveying what Alexander Moran calls the "genrefication of contemporary fiction": *The Keep*'s generic mix fuses high gothic traditions with low genre techniques to stress a technocratic paranoia (2018, p. 230).

This metafictive crux leads to the tour de force *A Visit from the Goon Squad*. Marking a turn in the political novel, *Goon Squad* underlines the neoliberal forces of the contemporary music industry in a post-9/11 narrative. The novel's fugal structure pays homage to the musical narrative of modernists such as Marcel Proust and Virginia Woolf, typified by T.S. Eliot's "auditory imagination" (1986). With a turn toward modernist novelty, Egan remixes the voices that track the rhythms of a post-9/11 world. *Goon Squad*'s vocal centrifuge both separates and combines its characters, spinning lives the way a DJ might spin a record. Paralleling concept albums like The Who's *Tommy* (1969) or Pink Floyd's *The Wall* (1979), *Goon Squad* even simulates an album format with an A-side and a B-side. With its musical drive and indifference to temporal continuity, *Goon Squad* stresses memories that visit like a goon from the past, and Egan sets one chapter of the novel in San Francisco, where she herself observed punk hot spots like Mabuhay Gardens as a teenager. Glancing back to San Francisco's punk subculture, Egan also looks forward to the future. The novel's thematic and formal impetus overdetermine the media and memories of the present, exploring the tired music performer Bosco's dictum: "Time's a goon, right? Isn't that the expression?" (2010, p. 127). Through linked stories told from diverse perspectives and genres, Egan composes narratives among the rubble of time past while her characters search for redemption.

Egan includes an experimental *PowerPoint* chapter which thematically links linear and acoustic modes, illustrating the material presence of sound in the lives of Sasha Blake's family. Formal novelty is celebrated through the 75-page *PowerPoint*, and its narrator, Sasha's daughter, Alison Blake, creates an affective medium for her slide journal. Ally's narration illustrates how her brother Lincoln fixates on the pauses in rock and roll songs by musicians such as The Four Tops, Jimi Hendrix, and David Bowie. Through Ally's voice and Lincoln's song pauses, Egan calls attention to the possibility of renewal – there is an attempt to reconnect, revealing how forms of mis/communication are resolved by listening to the sounds of music, language, and silence. Lincoln's rock and roll pauses coincide with a statement given by the character Jules Jones to his sister Stephanie: "Sure everything is ending... but not yet" (2010, p. 132). Despite the fact that Egan's novel confronts the effects of global issues such as climate change, Western colonialism, technological surveillance, and globalization, *Goon Squad* is also interested in the redemptive possibilities of forms of listening and speaking.

After the triumph of her *PowerPoint*, Egan's eclectic reach through a proleptic Twitter story called "Black Box" (2012) follows the character Lulu from her techno-futuristic life in *Goon Squad* into a spy thriller. "Black Box" begins where *Goon Squad* left off, and Egan imagines Lulu within a futuristic lens heightened by a string of tweets equally fragmented yet connected. Form equals content while Lulu practices her *Dissociation Technique* as a spy in the Mediterranean Sea, and Egan once again obscures a space of reality. Lulu's tweets formally create an anaphoric rhythm while her inner voice guides her through a series of escapades to complete her mission. As a human "Black Box," Lulu absorbs and records data, embracing a posthuman and cyberpunk existence that also leaves her, at times, void of self-reflection – as she tells herself, "your job is to look out, not in" (2012). Both "Black Box" and *Goon Squad* interrogate the agency of human connection within a digitized, posthuman culture. These literary works also reinforce a return to humanity, and while Lulu is uncertain about her final helicopter rescue, she trusts there are humans inside the chopper who have "faces taut with hope" and are "ready to jump" (2012).

Jumping across spatiotemporal limits, *Manhattan Beach* (2017) further evidences Egan's faculty to cross generic lines, altering the bleak generic traditions associated with the sentimental novel. Egan's turn seaward uncovers a bond linking the sentimental novel, the historical novel, and the epic novel. Even as Egan pays homage to Herman Melville's seafaring epic – stressing the marriage of Ishmael's seaward journey with his inward journey in her epigraph – the water of the East River surrounding Manhattan Beach and the Brooklyn Naval Yard of World War II become more than an "ungraspable phantom of life" for Egan (Melville 1992, p. 5). Drawing inspiration from research at the Brooklyn Naval Yard near where she currently lives in New York, Egan imagines an intrepid, feminist heroine. Her protagonist Anna Kerrigan, a helmet diver and welder during the war, experiences the sea through a sublime feeling: an "electric mix of attraction and dread" (2017, p. 6). The estuary allows for the possibilities of Anna's self-invention while portraying Egan's pointed feminist message, as noted by Margaret Cohen (2019) and George Hutchinson (2019). Anna is a heroine of Egan's own creation, and her plight defies the expectations of the marriage plot, moving Anna from a stifled conclusion in New York to the prospect of renewal in San Francisco. In fact, Anna's narrative reforms a version of Chick Lit and the New Domesticity.

Manhattan Beach tackles critical *topoi* such as disability, feminism, and wartime labor, as discussed by the *Theories and Methodologies* section of the March 2019 issue of *PMLA*. The opening of the novel features an early-twentieth-century topographical map of the Brooklyn Naval Yard, visually foregrounding the novel's treatment of spatiotemporal collocations gleaned from rich, historical research. Readers map Anna's passage from the domestic sphere of her Brooklyn tenement to the masculine realm of the Brooklyn Naval Yard where she proves her father Eddie's premonition of her as "a scrap, a weed that would thrive anywhere, survive anything" (2017, p. 20). Anna's survival is delimited by her sister Lydia's confining disability, and the two sisters are brought together during a climactic visit to Manhattan Beach. Lydia is developmentally disabled and aphasic, and her thoughts are phonetically and affectively conveyed when she can finally "*Sea the sea. See the sea the sea the sea*" (p. 162). The free indirect discourse of the scene reinforces Lydia's sensory grasp of memory and language. And Egan repeats a common thematic thread as the memory of Lydia's sensory knowledge remains a key part of Anna's meditative soundscape long after the trip.

A commanding treatment of the senses of literary form allows Egan to remain unclassifiable and irresistible. Her literary worlds compress the complexity of contemporaneity and look to the past for unanswerable queries about our culture wars. She experiments with novel perceptions, granting that all forms of fiction allow her to "take the sprawling chaos of human experience, run it through the sieve of perception, and distill it into something comparatively minuscule that somehow, miraculously, illuminates the vast complexity around it" (2014, p. xiv). Egan's distillation of experience includes readers in her quest of literary exploration and escape. It is exciting to imagine where she may take us next.

SEE ALSO: Chick Lit and the New Domesticity; The Culture Wars; Cyberpunk; Post-9/11 Narratives; Realism after Poststructuralism

REFERENCES

Cohen, Margaret. (2019). A feminist plunge into sea knowledge. PMLA 134 (2): 372–377.
Egan, Jennifer. (1994). *The Invisible Circus*. New York: Nan A. Talese.
Egan, Jennifer. (1996). *Emerald City*. New York: Nan A. Talese.
Egan, Jennifer. (2001). *Look at Me*. New York: Nan A. Talese.
Egan, Jennifer. (2006). *The Keep*. New York: Knopf.
Egan, Jennifer. (2010). *A Visit from the Goon Squad*. New York: Anchor.
Egan, Jennifer. (2012). Black box. *The New Yorker* (May 28, 2012). https://www.newyorker.com/magazine/2012/06/04/black-box-2 (accessed July 3, 2021).
Egan, Jennifer. (2014). Introduction. In: *The Best American Short Stories 2014*. New York: Houghton Mifflin.
Egan, Jennifer. (2017). *Manhattan Beach*. New York: Scribner's.
Egan, Jennifer. (2019). Notes from an academic interloper. PMLA 134 (2): 416–417.
Eliot, T.S. (1986). Matthew Arnold. In: *The Use of Poetry and the Use of Criticism*. Cambridge, MA: Harvard University Press; 1st ed. 1933.
Eve, Martin Paul. (2015). "Structural dissatisfaction": academics on safari in the novels of Jennifer Egan. Open Library of Humanities 1 (1): 1–24. https://olh.openlibhums.org/article/id/4404/ (accessed July 3, 2021).
Hutchinson, George. (2019). A historicist novel. PMLA 134 (2): 391–397.
Joyce, James. (1986). *Ulysses*. New York: Vintage Books; 1st ed. 1922.
Melville, Herman. (1992). *Moby-Dick or The Whale*. New York: Penguin Books; 1st ed. 1851.
Moran, Alexander. (2018). The genrefication of contemporary American fiction. Textual Practice 33 (2): 229–244. https://doi.org/10.1080/0950236X.2018.1509272
Reilly, Charlie. (2009). An interview with Jennifer Egan. *Contemporary Literature* 50 (3): 439–460.

FURTHER READING

Cowart, David. (2015). Thirteen ways of looking: Jennifer Egan's *A Visit from the Goon Squad*. Critique: Studies in Contemporary Fiction 56 (3): 241–254. https://doi.org/10.1080/00111619.2014.905448
Dimock, Wai Chee. (ed.) (2019). Theories and methodologies: on Jennifer Egan's *Manhattan Beach*. PMLA 134 (2): 366–417.
Dinnen, Zara. (2018). *The Digital Banal: New Media and American Literature and Culture*. New York: Columbia University Press.
Johnston, Katherine D. (2017). Metadata, metafiction, and the stakes of surveillance in Jennifer Egan's *A Visit from the Goon Squad*. American Literature 89 (1): 155–184. https://doi.org/10.1215/00029831-3788753
Precup, Amelia. (2015). The posthuman body in Jennifer Egan's "Black Box." American, British, and Canadian Studies Journal 25 (1): 171–186.

Eggers, Dave

ALEXANDER STARRE
Freie Universität Berlin, Germany

In his novels and stories, Dave Eggers has taken his readers on travels across the globe, from Sudan to Yemen, from Saudi Arabia to Estonia, from Costa Rica to New Zealand, and elsewhere. In formal terms, his oeuvre likewise shows a journey – from flashy reflexivity in his early writings to a signature restrained realism in his most recent works. From the start of his career, Eggers's creative output stretched across textual, visual, and curatorial endeavors. With his published writing now spanning close to twenty years since his long-form debut *A Heartbreaking Work of Staggering Genius* (2000), Eggers's authorial evolution can be subdivided into three phases: (i) a period of experimentation that saw the author self-reflexively and often humorously subvert literary genres and forms while engaging with the institutions, protocols, and economics of the American publishing scene, (ii) a stretch of time from the mid-2000s to the early 2010s, during which Eggers produced widely read nonfiction accounts with a focus on humanitarian and social justice issues, while also founding various nonprofits to pursue these goals in practice, and (iii) a prolific phase since about 2012 that has resulted in four novels more narrowly centered on the United States and a number of didactic children's and young adult books. While Eggers's literary style has changed considerably across these years, a number of common themes and ethical concerns tie the majority of his output together, among them technological innovations and forms of connectivity and community, as well as America's changing role in the global arena.

Dave Eggers was born in 1970 and grew up in Lake Forest, Illinois, outside of Chicago. While he studied toward a journalism degree at the University of Illinois at Urbana-Champaign, both of his parents passed away from cancer within a few weeks of one another. The fallout of these tragic events – Eggers had to quickly relocate to San Francisco with his much younger brother Christopher – serves as subject matter for the memoir that established him on the literary scene at the beginning of the new millennium. *A Heartbreaking Work* features a version of Eggers as narrator that is supremely attuned to its cultural moment, carrying all the existential bravado of a disaffected Gen X youth coupled with a distinctly late-1990s entrepreneurial spirit. The characteristic mixture of irony and sincerity in the narrative voice of the book has triggered a broad array of scholarship discussing this peculiar style as a marker of post-postmodernism (e.g. Timmer 2010; Funk 2015). Lee Konstantinou sees this "postironic" style as method for authors like Eggers and David Foster Wallace to compose "metafiction designed to spur belief, nonfiction that uses anxious metacommentary to tell the truth" (2016, p. 166). In his memoir, Eggers himself bluntly addresses the purpose of this style. Through the negation of a realist aesthetic, this "endlessly self-conscious book aspect," as he calls it in the Acknowledgments section, reaches toward a higher plane of earnest communication between author and reader. The result is a wavering ambiguity in the authorial voice that often undercuts any definite pronouncement on family, love, friendship, or mourning and thus debunks much of what could be the book's "message" in the act of reading. Despite all of this self-reflexive posturing, *A Heartbreaking Work* does celebrate individual moments of supreme insight, lending the narrative a quality that feels neither postmodern nor post-postmodern, but distinctly Romantic, for example when the book ends with a jubilant description of Eggers's sublime experience of throwing the frisbee with his brother. The narrator explicitly frames the frisbee episode as a parable to the direct, visceral connection with readers he is craving: "I am there. I was there. Don't you know that I am connected to you?" (2001, p. 436). Such moments of sublime connectivity reoccur throughout his later oeuvre.

The publication of *A Heartbreaking Work* assured Eggers instant fame, as he cleverly predicted in the book's sprawling paratexts and later chronicled in a substantial addendum to the paperback edition called "Mistakes We Knew We Were Making." These pronouncements coupled with the author's public posturing as a renegade publisher and philanthropic benefactor ignited several skirmishes in the press and online. The critic Sarah Brouillette (2003) describes Eggers's literary strategy in this early phase of his career as a "systematic effort at maintaining the legitimacy of his authority and authorship/editorship, finding a safe position from which to create textual products within a field that still denounces widespread success and vilifies commercial interests." In the wake of his debut's success, Eggers self-published his first novel *You Shall Know Our Velocity* (2002) with his own newly founded press McSweeney's. This picaresque novel has widely been read as an allegory of Eggers's own career. The book follows two Midwestern Americans on a manic trip around the world, as they attempt to disperse $38,000 among needy people across several countries including Senegal, Morocco, and Latvia. In its protagonists Will and Hand, Eggers has codified two personality types associated with introspection and doubt on the one hand (Will) and pure action and being in the moment on the other (Hand). While Will's first-person narrative features much less self-reflexivity than Eggers's memoir, it still conveys a metafictional engagement with memory and narrative reliability. In an expanded version called *Sacrament: Hand's Revised Edition* (2003), readers find key points of the plot called into question in an "Interruption" written by Hand, who accuses his (by now deceased) friend Will of bending the truth and even inventing plot points and characters in order to lend his account more gravitas. While the hapless Americans are shown as imperfect do-gooders whose humanitarian impulses lead them into all kinds of trouble, *You Shall Know Our Velocity* nevertheless underwrites Western efforts toward social and economic justice.

The self-reflexive pursuits of both his memoir and his debut novel in this early phase of Eggers's career dovetail nicely with the supreme self-awareness of the young author as an actor in the literary marketplace. To understand Eggers in this expanded field has been a challenge for literary studies, as his impact in the early 2000s was only partly literary. He also exerted considerable influence as publisher, as book designer, and as editor of the literary magazine *Timothy McSweeney's Quarterly Concern*. Arriving on the scene in 1998, Eggers's brainchild *McSweeney's* profited from the widescale adoption of desktop publishing technology that gave both amateurs and more seasoned experts the tools to design print products on their personal computers. The first dozen or so issues of the magazine were lavishly, sometimes outrageously enhanced with visual and material gimmicks, counterbalanced by minimalist page layouts in classical Garamond typography. These print objects exude a Victorian air that preceded the commercial hipster–retro styles of the 2010s by at least a decade (Rae 2017). Beyond its playfulness, the *McSweeney's* style aimed to transport a larger message. As several miniature manifestos written by Eggers and sprinkled throughout the paratexts of the first few *McSweeney's* issues proclaim, publishing in the digital era offers new opportunities for literary authors to fuse their writing with the craft of bookmaking. In that moment around the year 2000, when digital formats unsettled the analogue book publishing world, the meta*fictional* writer Eggers found a meta*medial* form of expression in his memoir and his literary quarterly (see Starre 2015). Eggers did more than experiment with narrative form – he also constantly pestered his readers with metacommentary on the design and affordances of the paperbound medium they were holding in hand. During the 2000s, Eggers edited a number of extravagant *McSweeney's* print objects: a visual art catalogue, coupled with a CD by They Might Be Giants (issue #6, 2001), a pulp fiction magazine (issue #10, 2002), a comics anthology curated by Chris Ware (issue #13, 2004), a stack of physical junk mail (issue #17, 2005), and a full-sized one-off Sunday newspaper called *The San Francisco Panorama*, with a panoply of in-depth journalism (issue #33, 2009). McSweeney's also became the home of publishing offshoots like the monthly *The Believer* (established in 2003) and the DVD magazine *Wholphin* (2005–2012), as well as a small book publishing program that has put out fiction by William T. Vollmann, Deb Olin Unferth, Diane Williams, John Brandon, Miriam Toews, Sheila Heti, Adam Levin, Daniel Gumbiner, and others.

With his publishing house and his own literary stature firmly established, Eggers entered a new phase in his career, during which his quirky design ethos was eclipsed by a commitment to socially engaged writing and humanitarian pursuits. While he reinvested the significant profits of his first two books into the infrastructure of McSweeney's publishing, Eggers developed his economic model further for *What Is the What* (2006). Grounded in research for the McSweeney's project Voice of Witness – a book series exploring injustices in America and abroad through oral history – *What Is the What* relates the story of Valentino Achak Deng, one of the so-called Lost Boys who were granted asylum in the United States after the Second Sudanese Civil War. Coinciding with the release of the book, Eggers and Deng founded the Valentino Achak Deng Foundation, a vessel for the book's proceeds, which were earmarked for Deng's education in the United States as well as for future humanitarian projects in Sudan. (Deng recently became education minister in one of the states that make up the new nation of South Sudan.) The book's title page refers to the story as both Deng's "Autobiography" and as "A Novel by Dave Eggers." This confluence of incompatible forms prompted a number of critical readings. While many reviews in the press praised the humanitarian content and mission of the book, more recent scholarship has problematized the "privatized philanthropy" portrayed in and undertaken by *What Is the What* as part and parcel of a larger "neoliberal sentimental humanism," with Eggers as a potent representative (Goyal 2014, p. 60). Conversely, Eggers's account has also been read as a genuine literary endeavor "geared towards exposure and reform of ... failed governmental institutions, non-governmental agencies, and corporations" (Sedlmeier 2017, p. 75). While the severe hardships encountered by Deng are channeled through Eggers's authorial voice, Deng's life story and the many atrocities he witnessed in turn appear to tame the author's stylistic excesses and lend him a more sober tone. The second Eggers book to arise out of the Voice of Witness series, *Zeitoun* (2009), has the author writing in the type of pared-down prose that would become the trademark of his later fiction. *Zeitoun* follows Abdulrahman Zeitoun, a Syrian émigré making a living as a painting contractor in New Orleans, as he attempts to navigate the catastrophic destruction of Hurricane Katrina in 2005. Zeitoun decided to remain in New Orleans, guarding his house against looters and assisting other residents in the neighborhood, only to be picked up by the police and thrown in maximum security jail on thinly veiled suspicions of being a terrorist. As compared to *What Is the What*, *Zeitoun* more clearly models its journalistic prose after the reportorial stance of investigative journalism. Still, the third-person limited perspective centered on Abdulrahman Zeitoun offers readers a complexly layered internal view of the protagonist, coordinating his thoughts on his precarious status as a Muslim in post-9/11 America with a bracing portrayal of the systemic failures within a security state attempting to address a natural disaster. The book proceeds once again financed a non-profit foundation, which was left in disarray when Abdulrahman Zeitoun was found guilty of domestic violence and had to serve a four-year prison sentence; he is currently at risk of being deported back to Syria.

The inadequate government response to Hurricane Katrina provided Eggers with a useful metonymy for the decrepit state of public institutions in the United States as they face an ever-growing array of crises, from crumbling infrastructure, ideological polarization, precarity, and poverty, to global concerns such as climate change. Entering a third phase of his writing career, Eggers in the 2010s went on to refocus his work on mainstream white America after the end of the American century. In this prolific period, he published an "American quartet" of novels, as Bran Nicol calls it (Nicol 2019, p. 307), all of which tie the drama of a white middle-class American's life to global concerns. Of these four, a short novel with the biblical title *Your Fathers, Where Are They? And the Prophets, Do They Live Forever?* (2014) has the most experimental narrative setup: the text consists entirely of lines of dialogue uttered by the protagonist, the disillusioned 34-year-old Thomas, and by the seven hostages he has taken, as he interrogates them in order to find meaning and direction in life. As a character type, Thomas resembles the school shooters and "incels" (involuntary celibates) that tragically populate current American news cycles; without any attendant narrative, however, the book's dialogue sequences succeed mostly in laying out a field of ethical questions and contradictions surrounding the perceived cultural decline of the United States. With the benefit of hindsight, however, one may certainly appreciate how perceptively Eggers anticipated the conflicted Trump-era discourse of a supposedly lost American "greatness" in Thomas's disillusioned pronouncements. Both *A Hologram for the King* (2012) and the bestselling *The Circle* (2013) depict Americans at home and abroad struggling with the economic and psychological impact of digitization and globalized labor – themes timely enough that both books were adapted into major films. In *A Hologram for the King*, the disgruntled former manufacturing executive turned IT consultant Alan Clay travels to the Saudi Arabian desert to deliver a technologically enhanced sales pitch for a supplier contract with the massive-scale construction projects of the King Abdullah Economic City. The downward trajectory of Alan's career is entwined with the decline of American manufacturing, but the novel steers away from Rust Belt nostalgia by keeping Alan suspended between the old and the new, finding some remedy from his malaise through his Saudi acquaintances. Mae Holland in *The Circle*, conversely, faces a fictionalized social network behemoth that promises to unify all data streams from various platforms to create a perfect rendition of society and every one of its individuals in the online sphere. While the corporate vision of the eponymous company Circle spins forth the Google slogan "don't be evil" into all kinds of progressive-sounding missions – to civilize online discourse through verified identities, to eliminate racial profiling by giving police access to real-time data on suspects, to suppress corruption in politics by making politicians' lives completely transparent, and so on – the company's totalitarian ambitions slowly emerge as the reader witnesses Mae molding herself into the perfect citizen required by 24/7 digital surveillance. Through her constant prodding to join her in this process, she alienates her ex-boyfriend Mercer, who represents a reclusive maker-culture in his craft of designing chandeliers made from responsibly sourced deer antlers. In a drastic act of counter-corporate disobedience, Mercer kills himself, driving his truck over a cliff as camera-equipped drones are chasing him on behalf of the almighty Circle. The gender dynamics of *The Circle* appear retrograde, as the malleable female character Mae meanders between strong male avatars of specific cultural types (the ruthless capitalist, the technology visionary, the emasculated geek, the high-minded craftsman). As if to counterbalance the masculinist bent of his oeuvre, Eggers in *Heroes of the Frontier* (2016), the final part of his "American quartet," sends a strong female character on a quest into the Alaskan wilderness. While somewhat reminiscent of the dejected Alan Clay, the debt-saddled dentist Josie manages to reassemble herself and to rekindle her bond with her children on her adventurous road trip. Josie's epiphanic realization that "[t]here is meaning in motion" hearkens back to Eggers's debut novel *You Shall Know Our Velocity*; Eggers goes so far as to explicitly associate movement with "sublimity" in this context (2016, p. 363). As a kind of subtext, all these four novels appear to redescribe the oft-bemoaned chaos and disorder of our globalized present as opportunities for serendipitous connections and makeshift alliances.

The didacticism on display in *Zeitoun* recently reemerged in several of Eggers's writings. His picture books *Her Right Foot* (2017) and *What Can a Citizen Do* (2018) are preschool primers for activist public involvement in a multicultural America; his adventure tale *The Lifters* (2018) emphasizes the strength of community and family against a looming threat from below; and his slim novel *The Parade* (2019) relates a parable of the unintended pitfalls of nation building. Eggers also frequently contributes to newspapers like *The New York Times* or *The Guardian*, chronicling American life during the Trump presidency. Meanwhile, *McSweeney's Quarterly Concern* had to navigate through difficult years in publishing but has managed to stay in print for over twenty years. In 2014, the firm McSweeney's started transitioning to a nonprofit model, divorcing its business from Eggers's finances, opening new revenue streams from crowdfunding and donations, and establishing more permanent institutional structures. Despite his fierce criticism of social media, Eggers retains an entrepreneurial vision with a distinct Silicon Valley outlook, mixing arts-and-crafts attitudes with digital marketing strategies. The direct trade and online sale of specialty coffee – admiringly portrayed in his nonfiction account of the Yemeni American businessman Mokhtar Alkhanshali in *The Monkh of Mokha* (2018) – is an apt correlative for his approach to publishing. Perhaps one may understand Eggers's characteristic effort to pair his writing with literary institution building as a utopian countermodel to his dystopian vision in *The Circle*. McSweeney's harbors its own social networks, providing writing instruction for children at its 826 national tutoring centers, offering funding and support for underserved college students via an initiative called ScholarMatch, hosting the popular online humor site McSweeney's Internet Tendency, and, of course, experimenting with independent publishing formats in the digital age. Beyond his widely read fiction, the creation of the McSweeeney's ecosystem is Dave Eggers's most lasting contribution to the American literary landscape of the twenty-first century.

SEE ALSO: After Postmodernism; Chabon, Michael; Davis, Lydia; Foster Wallace, David; Literary Magazines; Moody, Rick; Oates, Joyce Carol; Saunders, George; Vollmann, William T.

REFERENCES

Brouillette, Sarah. (2003). Paratextuality and economic disavowal in Dave Eggers' *You Shall*

Know Our Velocity. *Reconstruction: Studies in Contemporary Culture* 3 (2). http://reconstruction.digitalodu.com/Issues/032/brouillette.htm (accessed September 30, 2021).

Eggers, Dave. (2016). *Heroes of the Frontier.* New York: Knopf.

Funk, Wolfgang. (2015). *The Literature of Reconstruction: Authentic Fiction in the New Millennium.* New York: Bloomsbury.

Goyal, Yogita. (2014). African atrocity, American humanity: slavery and its transnational afterlives. *Research in African Literatures* 45 (3): 48–71.

Konstantinou, Lee. (2016). *Cool Characters: Irony and American Fiction.* Cambridge, MA: Harvard University Press.

Nicol, Bran. (2019). Typical Eggers: transnationalism and America in Dave Eggers's "globally-minded" fiction. *Textual Practice* 33 (2): 300–317.

Rae, Haniya. (2017). Victorian foppishness and making the McSweeney's generation. *Print Magazine* (August 11, 2017). www.printmag.com/design-culture-2/victorian-foppishnessthe-mcsweeneys-generation (accessed July 1, 2021).

Sedlmeier, Florian. (2017). The paratext and literary narration: authorship, institutions, historiographies. *Narrative* 26 (1): 63–80.

Starre, Alexander. (2015). *Metamedia: American Book Fictions and Literary Print Culture after Digitization.* Iowa City: University of Iowa Press.

Timmer, Nicoline. (2010). *Do You Feel It Too? The Post-Postmodern Syndrome in American Fiction at the Turn of the Millennium.* Amsterdam: Rodopi.

FURTHER READING

Clements, James. (2015). Trust your makers of things! The metafictional pact in Dave Eggers' *You Shall Know Our Velocity. Critique: Studies in Contemporary Fiction* 56 (2): 121–137.

Galow, Timothy W. (2014). *Understanding Dave Eggers.* Columbia: University of South Carolina Press.

Hamilton, Caroline D. (2010). *One Man Zeitgeist: Dave Eggers, Publishing and Publicity.* New York: Continuum.

Hungerford, Amy. (2012). McSweeney's and the school of life. *Contemporary Literature* 53 (4): 646–680.

Elkin, Stanley

DAVID DOUGHERTY
Loyola University Maryland, USA

In 1980 Stanley Elkin turned 50, a time to reflect and contemplate the future for anyone, but especially for a writer who, like the character God in his only bestseller, *The Living End* (1979), felt that he "never found my audience" (p. 133). Over four novels, one short story collection, and two trios of novellas, Elkin had carved out his niche as the delight of much of America's literary avant garde, a rock star on university lecture circuits, and a fixture at writers' conferences. But he seldom sold out an advance, and he felt that he was doomed to be a niche writer – not as widely respected as Saul Bellow, whom he idolized, or John Updike, or Toni Morrison. When *The Living End* commanded a considerably wider literary community's attention, Elkin was challenged to discover his new relationship with a broader audience. Try as he might, however, he couldn't give up the things that had made him beloved among his following: wildly inventive, improbable, sometimes zany plots; characters louder if not larger than life; exuberant linguistic riffs, which delight and amuse in their wordsmanship – but the action comes to a stop and the plot dozes and the theme disappears while the impresario does his thing. Often, the reader is laughing out loud or enraptured in a verbal northern lights display, but perplexed as to exactly what these linguistic fireworks have to do with the big picture. Then again, for Elkin, the play of rhetoric really was the big picture. He knew this was his strength – and the thing that drove away bigger audiences. Through a very productive final decade and a half, he deepened his core themes: dysfunctional families, our broken bodies, and that confrontation we all dread. He was funny, outrageous, and sad, a metafictionist whistling our way through graveyards.

He opened the 1980s with *George Mills* (1982), his biggest and favorite book, but one that never really resonated with the general reading public. As with many Elkin novels, the central concept is brilliant. Throughout a millennium, Mills men are fated to repeat the destiny of being blue collar, with no hope of rising from that class; this trope leads to vibrant episodes in a broad, episodic, non-sequential novel. The necessary qualification is that each Mills descendant will have only one son, to whom he'll narrate the family story and thereby entrap another generation in a life of servility, despite great adventures hinting at the possibility of escaping history.

Episodes tell the stories of four men named George Mills, one in the eleventh century CE, one in the late eighteenth, and two in the mid-twentieth. These four represent the generations who have labored under the curse, and the histories of the patriarchal Georges are dazzling stand-alone pieces. The establishing narrative blends tall tale, historic anachronism, and hair's-breadth escapes. Like the story of every George, this involves a journey. Greatest Grandfather, chosen "because he knew nothing about horses" (2003, p. 1) accompanies Lord Guillaume on the first crusade. Instead of making it to Palestine, this Quixote/Panza duo become prisoners in a Polish salt mine where Greatest Grandfather reflects on his entrapment in the lumpenproletariat. He recalls a tapestry that showed him how aristocrats view his lot, as a "dour, luteless people, cheerless, something sour in our blue collar blood" (p. 31). Guillaume repeatedly explains "natural suzerainty" to Mills, a condition of servitude he and his heirs are fated to inherit. The tropes conceal a greater mystery: it's obviously in the interest of aristocrats to believe this. But why do the Mills men buy into it? Greatest Grandfather was set up as the fall guy; Guillaume, who put the him in the lead deliberately to miss the path to Palestine, upon returning to Northumbria became lord of the manor. Is this the reward for the fall guy, whom Guillaume can blame for missing the turn? It is back to the stables, "because it would not do for one so high placed to have as a retainer a man who knew nothing of horses" (p. 44). Thus, the Mills pattern is established: journey, adventure, exploitation – but not elevation for service.

Similarly, Part IV recounts the adventures of the 43rd Mills in a blend of tall tale and eighteenth-century conventions. This Mills becomes a confidant of King George IV, then an emissary to the Sultan's court, but the king and his messenger set George up for a diplomatic *faux pas*, which in turn involves him with the Janissaries, notoriously violent mercenaries, then as an intact male performing eunuchs' duties in the Sultan's harem. In both spaces, Mills gains a reputation as someone exceptional; and in both he's being played by aristocrats.

Most of the book focuses on an eviction laborer in St. Louis, a racist and unapologetic blue-collar worker who does attempt to break the curse. This narrative is punctuated with flashbacks to his relationship with his father, who also tried to break it by temporarily resisting marriage. Long sections treat his apprenticeship at a spiritualist community in Cassadaga, Florida, with brilliant comic effects. In a couple of scenes, Blue-collar George resists sexual come-ons by his fit and comely wife; he consistently avoids sexual intimacy; and he has no son. With no heir to hear and perpetuate the millennium of servitude, the curse cannot continue. It depends on the consent of heirs who buy into it, so this George has done what generations of his ancestors couldn't. Ending the curse revolves around his metaphor for his condition, the notion of being "saved," on which he comes to an epiphany in the book's final scene. George's "salvation" isn't theological; he's no believer, but his passivity has led him into something he calls a state of grace: "The man to whom everything has happened that is going to happen. That is his grace" (2003, p. 222). His epiphany occurs while he delivers a sermon in a former televangelist's church: "Hell, I ain't saved ... Sucking up isn't grace" (p. 518).

His great adventure begins when, laid off from the eviction job, he agrees to chauffer and care for a difficult, dying member of the St. Louis aristocracy (her family's obscenely rich; her husband's a dean at a major university) to Mexico, to take laetrile treatments (a desperate fad in the 1970s) for her terminal cancer. With his role expanding to protector, enabler, personal hygiene coordinator, and schedule manager, George comes very close to a human contact that transcends his blue-collar identity. After his late employer's family express indebtedness for his care, Mills, accompanied by a modestly successful writer and university professor (an Elkin self-caricature), embarks on a campaign to break the cycle of blue-collar life. Stunned by how the 1 percent live, George decides to blackmail Mrs. Glaser's survivors. To "get the goods" he engages in prolonged gossip sessions with the aptly-named Cornell Messenger, but the dirt he gets never quite transforms into economic liberation.

While *Mills* enjoyed national awards but modest sales, Elkin ventured into the most daring subject he'd ever undertake, the make-a-wish foundations (a foundation bearing that name was founded in 1980) that offer dying individuals a dream holiday. *The Magic Kingdom* (1985) chronicles, with dark humor mixing intermittently with empathy, the journey of seven dying children, three caregivers, one physician, and "England's most famous beggar" who initiated, financed (by hitting up charities, corporations, and the queen), and leads an expedition to a literal Magic Kingdom in North America, and to a much more important and dangerous interior one. This unusually linear narrative, for Elkin, contrasts superficial magic, like a Florida snow that covers only Disney World, and the real magic that happens when the dying children have their moments of joy, which are not without desperate risk.

The issues at the core of *The Magic Kingdom* require that Elkin negotiate between satire and sentimentality. The children are inherently sympathetic, victims of life's cruelest logic – survival of the fittest. But Elkin mitigates the victim cliché by emphasizing certain children's selfishness, nastiness, or cruelty. The caregivers, similarly, are far from ideal, like the nanny who idolizes Mary Poppins. Elkin seldom had problems resisting sentimentality, but this subject, if not treated sentimentally, lends itself to cynicism. The temptation toward satire could easily extend to a critique of foundations that continue in 2020 to enable these expeditions. And Elkin points out an unintended consequence of the endeavor: these broken children are objectified by being constantly placed on public display. The chaperones are shocked to learn that the kids are happiest in a room rented secretly by one of the caregivers, their "hidey hole," where they can simply be themselves. In one magnificent moment, nurse Colin Bible takes the kids out on the artificial lake, to Shipwreck Marsh, where, unobserved by outsiders, they sunbathe, and "glad to be alive, they stared at each other and caught their breath" (2000a, p. 257).

The competing attitudes toward make-a-wish enterprises originate in protagonist Eddy Bale's obsession. His son Liam underwent several cures, medical and quack, supported by Eddy's public begging, thereby keeping the family's woes in public view. After Liam's death, and his wife's departure, Bale develops an alternative way of ministering to the needs of dying children. As he tells the queen, instead of putting Liam through painful treatments with no real hope of success, he should have given the boy whatever might make him happy. The same concept works in Disney World. Although the children find their own exhilaration on Shipwreck Marsh and in the secret room, this very happiness can lead to terror and death. In the hidey hole one, an artist in concealing the symptoms of her cystic fibrosis, dies. The crack diagnostician realizes she died of love, a cliché totally unexpected in this context; but love, like life, is a terminal risk.

Elkin would never again aim quite so high. *The Rabbi of Lud* (1987) treats the choices of a man who retreated from life's challenges, as does its successor *The MacGuffin* (1991), in which a Commissioner of Streets has devolved from candidate to civil appointee. Similarly, the rabbi in a "funerary, sepulchral, thanatopsical town," (2001, p. 18) has no congregation, but makes his living by burying Jews whose families bring their remains to Lud.

Rabbi is narrated in the first-person, a mode Elkin hadn't used in a novel since his first, *Boswell: A Modern Comedy* (1964). This choice facilitates the in-your-face, over-the-top, vocational rhetoric that had long been Elkin's trademark. Rabbi Jerry Goldkorn explains his choices, to work in this burial industry, at the expense of his duties to his daughter, who hates her life in Lud, and, late in the book, devises a wickedly clever campaign to embarrass her family because Jerry refuses to leave. Like *George Mills*, *Rabbi* ends with a sermon, during which Goldkorn confesses his sin of living "in the wrong communities [. . .] in which we raised our children" (2001, p. 276). Placing his preferences over his duty to his family manifests his professional cowardice, which he papers over with charged rhetoric and paranoia. Burying the dead doesn't require the emotional or spiritual commitment leading a live congregation might.

Like most of Elkin's novels, *Rabbi* involves a journey, this time into absurdity, evangelical compulsions, and, maybe, magic. When Goldkorn tries out as "the Chief Rabbi of the Alaska Pipeline," his year in Alaska scares him right back to Lud. Elkin satirizes the boom-mentality that came with the pipeline jobs, but the rabbi becomes the victim of his own enthusiasms and a con job. A man he projects as a magical rabbi, with flowers in his beard, is actually working a hustle involving ridiculously over-priced Torahs. Jerry's congregations become large and donate generously, but the Jews drift away and he finds himself preaching to non- and anti-Semites. So, this is what happens when you take chances? Back to Lud and safety. But there's no real safety there, either; that's the point. Connie Goldkorn's revenge is embarrassing, and eventually shaming to his parenting. And though he's been "safe" burying folks he doesn't know, circumstances force him to eulogize one of his wife's close friends, with whom he's had a brief affair. Her absurd death reinforces Jerry's blocked awareness of the fragility of our lives, and he has to confront his overwhelming emotions. While losing control of his prepared text, he accepts the moral consequences of emotional cowardice.

The MacGuffin recounts a bureaucrat's adventures over slightly more than twenty-four hours, operating in real time filled out by flashbacks. There's only one chapter, so the plot's density is highlighted. Bobbo Druff finds himself in riddles surrounded by enigmas, with hints of murder, oriental rug smuggling, spies, and a surprisingly compliant mistress. The novel is a figure in the carpet mystery, a point Elkin reinforces by frequent allusions to detective novel conventions – and carpets. But the goal of the detective novel (a form Elkin disliked) is clarification, the unravelling of clues. As Druff parses the mystery, everything becomes less clear. Echoing *The Magic Kingdom*, Druff asserts, "Because everything was linked, everything" (2000b, p. 183), the assumption behind detective stories – and paranoia, a theme Elkin treated spectacularly in *The Dick Gibson Show* (1972).

Throughout the book, Druff, who once ran for public office but now looks back on a career of implementing, not making, policy, finds much more to lament than his failure to impact events. He's nearing sixty, with a variety of medical issues resembling his creator's and good reason to fear that the end is near; his marriage, which began in mysterious attraction, is now stale; his relationship with his son is borderline dysfunctional. With regret for the past and little hope for the future, Druff embarks on his journey by limousine (his chauffer may be a spy), by cab, on foot, and hitchhiking, everywhere seeing hints of connectivity among plot events that don't cohere logically. As he imagines/creates/discovers a MacGuffin, his story works out Elkin's theme of paranoia as "the compounding interest on disappointment, the wear and tear of ambition" (2000b, p. 19). A MacGuffin, as Elkin delighted in recounting, is a cinematic expedient, an arbitrary and apparently insignificant moment or event that sets the plot into motion, or re-directs the motion already in effect. Druff, seeing coincidence in every aspect of Elkin's convoluted plot, personifies, converses with, and even locks his MacGuffin out of the house. As in detective novels, weirdly arbitrary things happen in this plot. For example, Persian carpets show up in nearly every location, and a theory of these rugs seems to connect multiple mysteries: the death of Druff's son Mikey's mistress, a Shiite zealot; Druff's mistress's involvement in carpets and her knowing Mikey and Su'ad, his mistress; and the mysterious death of the hardly-known Marvin Macklin. Druff's paranoia becomes a refuge: events are conditioned by a logic of cause and effect. He can, with MacGuffin, disentangle the clues in a way that would rival Hercule Poirot's disclosure and summing up. His MacGuffin can make a world that has passed Druff by and confused the reader, make sense, for now.

The novella form was uniquely suited to Elkin's strengths, with its brevity complementing his convoluted plots, and its volume, significantly greater than that of a story, providing a sufficient field for verbal fireworks. *Van Gogh's Room at Arles* (1993) contains characters on verbal overload, intricate plots, and two protagonists, like Druff, facing diminished expectations and signs of their own irrelevance, if not terribly well. The autobiographical hero of "Her Sense of Timing" faces a dependency crisis when his wife, who has nurtured his increasing needs through his many illnesses, leaves him – the day before his annual graduate student party. With Rabelaisian humor, Elkin presents the accommodations Jack Schiff, a "political geographer" at a St. Louis university, tries to make to survive on his own. These include acquiring a personal safety monitoring system and preparing for the party his graduate students insist must go on. His helplessness is tragi-comically on display as drunk students break his Stair-Glide, carry him upstairs, and invade his private arrangements to deal with his illness, including his portable urinal. The humiliation isn't resolved; this "erstwhile hotshot" reduced to a "pathetic, poor, misbegotten schlepp" (2002a, p. 74) seems down to one decision: what message will he put on his telephone because he won't be able to answer it before the ringing stops?

Schiff makes a cameo appearance in the title story, but an academic even more passively immersed in his mediocrity endures hallucinations and makes a spectacle of himself at a prestigious foundation retreat in Arles. Bearing a pervasive inferiority complex, Miller realizes that neither his education nor his achievement qualifies him for the appointment, that he's the foundation's token community college scholar. After wasting most of his time in Arles drinking and masturbating (symbolically as well as literally), Miller writes a fraudulent report including fake sources. Elkin's satire focuses on the academics Miller looks up to, whose projects are pretentious and silly; that Miller doesn't realize this adds to the humor. The title alludes to the location in which the foundation houses Miller, a room Van Gogh lived in and painted; the MacGuffin is that Miller keeps encountering – though no one else does – characters who look like subjects of various Van Gogh paintings. But Miller doesn't figure out what to make of these self-proclaimed descendants, real, imagined, or coincidental. He leaves Arles with his money gone, his inferiority complex ratified, and his grant opportunity wasted. Except for another novella, "The Condominium" (1973), no Elkin hero comes to so bleak an end.

"Town Crier Exclusive: Confessions of a Princess Manqué: 'How Royals Found Me "Unsuitable" To Marry Their Larry'" offers a delightful contrast to these dark visions. It's light-hearted, funny, and heartily satiric: it sends up simultaneously the British obsession with the royal family, especially as those traditions have been challenged over recent decades, and the tabloids. The protagonist/narrator is a commoner – but no Kate Middleton she – whose engagement to an idealized prince opens her eyes to the fastidiousness and falsehood of the monarchs; she thinks of the king and queen as "sovereigns out of Noël Coward" (2002a, p. 145), more clichés than rulers. But Elkin's principal satiric thrust is the tabloids, randy for salacious "true" stories, whether true or not. A central delight of "Princess" is Lulu's intertextual conversation with her editor, the tabloid owner, Sir Sidney, and the revenges these contain.

Mrs. Ted Bliss (1995), Elkin's final novel, is unlike anything he'd ever published. The protagonist, as the title indicates, is a traditional woman who identifies as a spouse, who has throughout her life been guided by the men with whom she interacts. Multicultural issues permeate the story, but the primary emphasis is on coming to terms with those losses that are inevitable with age. And, unlike most Elkin fictions, this is ultimately a tale of reconciliation, particularly with members of her family. She has to come to terms with Ted's criminal actions to create wealth and her unending grief over her son Marvin's passing.

A Russian emigre approaching eighty, Mrs. Ted, vain about her appearance, lives in a Miami Condominium. Symbolically, she's nearly deaf; her vanity is exploited by her interactions with a series of dashing Central American men living in the complex. One, eventually sentenced to 100 years in prison for dealing drugs, flatters her and offers $5000 more than book value for Ted's Buick, a key motif. The Drug Enforcement Agency confiscates the sedan, and Mrs. Ted answers a subpoena to testify at Alcibiades Chitral's trial. Two other Latinos pay unusual attention to her. One flirts with her, but discloses that the Buick was a "dope hamper" (2002b, p. 31); another gives her insider's betting tips, but disappears suddenly with the reader suspecting that his crimes have caught up with him. Playing on her vulnerability because of vanity and naivete, the Latino suitors unintentionally force Mrs. Ted to remember Ted's illegal cattle ventures during World War II as well as the mystery of the Buick, and to accept and forgive the imperfections of the man who had guided her life.

While the Latinos' attentions provide adventures for Mrs. Ted, she comes to terms with her past as her future diminishes. She re-establishes a relationship with Junior Yellin, a con man who cheated Ted in his Chicago business, and who initiated unwelcome sexual advances to Dorothy (and her daughter-in-law). She meets Junior again in his office as a "Recreational Therapusist," Elkin's instrument for satirizing the scams and health crazes in 1990s America. She supports

Junior's crazy schemes and forgives his past misconducts, including his eventually marrying her daughter-in-law. She reconciles with other family members, accepting them for who they are; and in a moving chapter, she tells her grandson the story of Marvin's death.

The novel closes with Hurricane Andrew, one of the worst natural disasters ever to hit Florida and a synecdoche for the powerlessness we all experience when Nature turns hostile. Now 82, Dorothy Bliss doesn't leave the condo "because it was too much trouble" (2002b, p. 280). Her passivity, a major motif of the novel, enables a powerful reconciliation. Louise Munez, a gun-toting security guard, shows up in Dorothy's apartment, seeking her own mother, and breaks down. Elkin's final vignette features two immigrants, a Latina and a Jew, who have taken different ways of dealing with their vulnerability, embracing, sharing the pain of loss and the fear of Nature at its worst. This chronicle of loss ends elegiacally: "Because everything else falls away. [. . .] Until all that's left is obligation" (p. 292).

Although he was planning a new novel in 1995, Elkin didn't live to see *Mrs. Ted Bliss* published. He died in May 1995, leaving a legacy of tragicomic humor and relentless rhetoric and a memorable model of whistling through our graveyards.

SEE ALSO: Coover, Robert; Ford, Richard; Gaddis, William; Gass, William H.; McElroy, Joseph; Pynchon, Thomas; Wolitzer, Meg

REFERENCES

Elkin, Stanley. (1979). *The Living End*. New York: E.P. Dutton.
Elkin, Stanley. (2000a). *The Magic Kingdom*. Normal, IL: Dalkey Archive Press; 1st ed. 1985.
Elkin, Stanley. (2000b). *The MacGuffin*. Normal, IL: Dalkey Archive Press; 1st ed. 1991.
Elkin, Stanley. (2001). *The Rabbi of Lud*. Normal, IL: Dalkey Archive Press; 1st ed. 1987.
Elkin, Stanley. (2002a). *Van Gogh's Room at Arles: Three Novellas*. Normal, IL: Dalkey Archive Press; 1st ed. 1993.
Elkin, Stanley. (2002b). *Mrs. Ted Bliss*. Normal, IL: Dalkey Archive Press; 1st ed. 1995.
Elkin, Stanley. (2003). *George Mills*. Normal, IL: Dalkey Archive Press; 1st ed. 1982.

FURTHER READING

Bailey, Peter J. (1985). *Reading Stanley Elkin*. Urbana: University of Illinois Press.
Dougherty, David C. (1991). *Stanley Elkin*. Boston: G.K. Hall.
Dougherty, David C. (2010). *Shouting Down the Silence: A Biography of Stanley Elkin*. Urbana: University of Illinois Press.
Elkin, Stanley. (1992). *Pieces of Soap: Essays*. New York: Simon & Schuster.
LeClair, Thomas. (1974). The obsessional fiction of Stanley Elkin. *Contemporary Literature* 16: 146–162.
O'Donnell, Patrick. (1995). Of red herrings and loose ends: reading "politics" in Elkin's *The MacGuffin*. *Review of Contemporary Fiction* XV (Summer): 92–10.
Saltzman, Arthur M. (1988). Ego and appetite in Stanley Elkin's fiction. *Literary Review* 32: 111–118. Repr. in (1995) *Review of Contemporary Fiction* XV (Summer): 7–14.

Ellis, Bret Easton

PATRICK O'DONNELL
Michigan State University, USA

One of the most controversial writers of his (or any) generation, Bret Easton Ellis is the author of six novels, a collection of short stories, six screenplays, and series of pointed critiques of post-millennial contemporary culture collected in his single work of nonfiction, *White* (2019). This most recent work in Ellis's *oeuvre* only serves to underscore his reputation as the "bad boy" of American fiction, whose subjects and characters always cast polarizing shadows, as the frequent critiques of his work as misogynist, racist, and sexist, or as glorifying violence attest. In essence, Ellis is a satirist, though critics often seem to miss the moral perspective that undergirds satire in Ellis's narratives of serial killers, narcissists, and anti-heroes; since Ellis salts his fiction with autobiographical details, it becomes tempting to collapse the personalities and actions of his protagonists into Ellis himself. Ellis, himself, does little to modify this impression as, from the beginning of his career, he has assumed the role of countercultural antagonist, often finding ways to offend both conservatives and progressives; this is consistent with the fundamental target of Ellis's satire – American identity – whether that term is applied to middle-class Reaganites or leftist advocates of multiculturalism. In effect, Ellis insists that he, and his fiction, not be pigeon-holed: as he has said of his own sexual identity in a conversation with the *Los Angeles Times* entitled "The Dark Side of a Generation," "[Ellis] won't discuss his sexual orientation, which he says he prefers undeclared for artistic reasons. 'I've been very coy and weird about it . . . I don't necessarily think that it's an invalid question. The characters in my novels often have a very shifting sexuality. But if people knew I was straight, they'd read . . . in a different way. If they knew I was gay, [*American Psycho*] would be read as a different book'" (Martelle 1999).

Born to middle-class parents and raised in the San Fernando Valley in Southern California (the massive suburban area north of central Los Angeles often associated with strip malls, "valley girls," and the porn industry), Ellis gained fame early with the publication of his first novel, *Less Than Zero* (1985), while still an undergraduate at Bennington College in Vermont. Bennington, especially in the 1970s and 1980s, offered a free-form, countercultural educational environment especially suited to the likes of the many artists and writers who matriculated there during that period, including friends and fellow novelists Jonathan Letham and Donna Tartt, both in Ellis's class of '86, though Letham dropped out in his sophomore year in order to live in Berkeley, California and become a full-time writer. Something of a hothouse environment (all three novelist have offered fictional versions of life at Bennington, most notably Tartt in *The Secret History* [1992]), studying at Bennington seems to have offered Ellis the perfect opportunity to complete the work he had begun in high school. At the age of 21, he gained sudden fame and notoriety for the story of a college student who returns during a break to his home in Southern California and indulges in non-stop partying and binging on sex and drugs. The aptly named protagonist, Clay, a persona completely molded by his environment into whatever form is imposed upon him, finds that the more extreme his experiences (these include viewing a snuff film and scenes of drug overdosing, prostitution, and pedophilia), the more alienated and anesthetized he becomes. Clay is, as the title of the novel suggests, less than nothing – whose self-loathing reveals the superficiality of his own character and the depths of depravity that undergird a certain version of a decadent, monied lifestyle in the Southern California of the 1980s. As, virtually, putty in the hands of contemporary society, Clay, who is either drunk or stoned much of the time, may claim that he is only a witness to the horrific events he observes, but it is clear that, for Ellis, witnessing is participating. The highly controversial excesses of the novel are, from one perspective, voyeuristic and pornographic but, from another – especially given the downward path that Ellis charts for his protagonist – they convey a sustained critique of American life and youth culture in the age of Reagan. It is easy, as critical reviews of the novel show, to mistake one for the other.

Following the success of *Less Than Zero*, Ellis moved to New York where he befriended a group of young writers and artists that came to be known as the literary "Brat Pack" which included Jay McInerny, Jill Eisenstadt, and Tama Janowitz among others; the loosely-assembled group were frequent participants in the intense clubbing scene of the late 1980s and early 1990s in New York, where associations with figures like Andy Warhol and Jean-Michel Basquiat were formed, all lending to Ellis's blossoming reputation as a celebrity writer. Following closely on the publication of *Less Than Zero*, *The Rules of Attraction* (1987) appeared; it is often viewed as a companion novel to *Zero*, but set in the fictional world of "Camden College" which, of course, bears close resemblance to Bennington. Despite the change in location, the main characters of *Rules* experience similar problems and conflicts: hedonistic, world-weary, and cynical, their world is one of drugs, alcohol, parties and, infrequently, engagement with books and professors. In the novel, sexual identity is mobile, and sexual partners frequently change hands; the main character, Sean Bateman (younger brother of Patrick Bateman, the serial-killer protagonist of Ellis's next novel, *American Psycho* [1991]), attempts suicide twice, though in his self-loathing and drug-hazed state, he seems less reflective than Clay of *Less Than Zero* about the nature of his experience and the consequences of his nihilistic world view. Overall, the "world" of *The Rules of Attraction* is smaller and more artificial than that of the Southern California freeways and neighborhoods of *Less Than Zero*, and its impact is less effective as a satire on then-contemporary youth culture. The inhabitants of Camden College are trapped in a cultural and temporal bubble where over-privileged youth, ardent creativity, and self-destruction go hand in hand; the novel that records these excesses, to an extent, eats its own tail in being a self-indulgent recollection of self-indulgence. In the end, *The Rules of Attraction* is more a novel of voices than events: far more compelling than scenes of partying, inebriation, or drug-dealing are the voices of its shifting narrators, one of whom is Clay, from *Less Than Zero*, back at school after the Winter Break. Each tells (or withholds) their stories from a first-person perspective; each thus varies what the "rules of attraction" that spell the relationship between identity and desire might be. And each, like Clay in *Less Than Zero*, ends up alone in their own head.

Patrick Bateman, the protagonist of *American Psycho*, is certainly one of the most repugnant anti-heroes of contemporary American fiction. The novel is the best-known and most widely-read of Ellis's fiction, and it might appear to be the capstone of an early trilogy of novels about corruption, transgression, and the loss of self. Yet the novel goes well beyond Ellis's initial offerings in its indictment of American consumerist culture and its portrayal of a serial killer/investment banker at the heart of American capitalism on Wall Street. Ellis could not have known in 1991 about the future rise of Donald Trump to the American presidency, but the name of Trump is all over this novel that skewers the lives of the rich and would-be rich in New York who can easily secure reservations at Le Cirque, buy Armani, and ride in Mercedes limos. Oliver Stone's landmark film, *Wall Street* (1987), was released four years before the publication of *American Psycho*, and it can be seen as a prologue and source of inspiration for Ellis's novel with its scenes of Bud Fox, apprentice investor, mastering the art of a sushi-making machine in a New York high-rise condominium following his quick success in his dealings with the aptly-named reptilian guru, Gordon Gecko. But *Wall Street* contains no serial killers who, like Patrick Bateman, murders, mutilates, and cannibalizes his victims as easily as he parties with peers at Manhattan night club or manipulates deals on the "street." Bateman is a psychopath, and a list of his "Christmas priorities" provides some sense of the ease with which he moves between crass, nouveau-riche consumerism and unthinkable violence: "(1) to get an eight o'clock reservation Friday night at Dorsia with Courtney, (2) to get myself invited to the Trump Christmas party aboard their yacht . . . (4) to saw a hardbody's head off and Federal Express it to Robin Barker – the dumb bastard – over at Salomon Brothers and (5) to apologize to Evelyn without making it look like an apology" (Ellis 1991, pp. 177–178). Proliferate with brand names and popular culture references, most of the novel is told in Bateman's voice, which gives rise to questions about how much we can rely on a psychopath (and ardent admirer of Donald Trump) to tell us the truth about his actions. But in its way, *American Psycho* is the twisted, satiric version of a classic American story, certainly reminiscent of *The Great Gatsby* (1925), in which the protagonist fulfills the American dream of success, power, and wealth in its most nightmarish form, revealing the violent underpinnings of that dream. It is a dream from which there is no escape, as the novel's final words posted on a bar door make clear, "THIS IS NOT AN EXIT" (Ellis 1991, p. 399; caps in original). Beyond Manhattan, the club culture of the 1990s, or Wall Street, the target of Ellis's sharpest satire in *American Psycho* is America itself, in all its materiality and excess.

Ellis published a collection of interrelated stories, *The Informers*, in 1994. This baker's dozen of stories entail a series of dramatic situations that often go off the rails as characters interact, articulate their dreams, or confess their desires: a visit from old friends that leads to violence; a conversation between three men about the death of a mutual acquaintance results in a graphic, and suspicious recollection by one who has witnessed how she died; a rock star on a downward trajectory goes to Japan for a tour in which he engages in a series of extreme and violent behaviors reminiscent of Patrick Bateman; a lovers' visit to a zoo where injured animals are observed marks the oncoming disintegration of an abusive relationship. Certain characters appear in multiple stories, and some of the protagonists are students at Camden College – the collection thus taking on the aspect of being networked with Ellis's evolving *oeuvre*. And indeed, many familiar themes are pursued: self-alienation coming in the wake of the pursuit of extreme experiences; the complexity of co-dependent relationships based upon mismatched desires; the consequences of addiction, and always, the potential outbreak for radical violence in everyday life. Though these are minor works, they provide incisive perspectives on the distressed social order that forms the backdrop to all of Ellis's fiction.

Glamorama (1998), Ellis's fourth novel, focuses on that aspect of contemporary American society that most fully exemplifies its excesses – the fashion industry and celebrity culture. Set primarily in New York and London, the novel stars Victor Ward, a male model and would-be nightclub entrepreneur who is one of the many postgraduates of Camden College scattered throughout Ellis's fiction. *Glamorama* involves a bizarre thriller plot in which Victor is hired by a shadowy figure to search for his girlfriend who has mysteriously disappeared; this leads by many twists and turns to Victor's involvement in an underground political movement with terrorist leanings dedicated to destroying those sites (nightclubs, resorts, tourist destinations) that particularly attract the rich and famous. The plot of the novel is transparently absurd (the terrorist group has as its leader a celebrity model), and is really only a vestigial framework that enables Ellis critique of the people, objects, and desires constituting contemporary "high life." To build upon the obvious punning of its title, *Glamorama* is a panorama or kaleidoscope of a culture that, for the French social theorist Jean Baudrillard (1994), is a pure "simulacrum," a simulation of reality composed of replicated objects and images that proliferate and replace any conventional notions of reality. The novel is replete with such images: brand names are dropped with abandon on nearly every page; identity becomes the assemblage of accoutrements and accessories worn on the body (for Ellis, models are the perfect encapsulation of this idea – they are only what they wear); conversations tend to be about Rolex and Armani and Lexus when they are not about long nights of inebriation and sexual excess in the quest for sheer experience to overcome the nothingness that underlies the simulacrum. The satirical objects of the novel are clear, but critics of *Glamorama* have reflected that satirical distance may collapse in a work so immersed in what it seemingly disdains: as the critic for *Publisher's Weekly* observes, "[t]he satirist in Ellis seems to want to indict celebrity-obsessed, materialistic and superficial contemporary culture. With this novel he, perhaps unwittingly but certainly ironically, provides Exhibit A" (*Publishers Weekly* 1998).

The writing of *Glamorama* interrupted that of Ellis's fifth novel, *Lunar Park* (2005), pitched as a memoir whose protagonist is none other than "Bret Easton Ellis," recounting the life of a novelist who rose to fame early, became addicted to drugs and sex, and is, by turns, outraged and humiliated by the demands of notoriety and career. In the novel, we meet "real-life" characters, such as Ellis's fellow novelist and lifelong friend, Jay McInerny, and characters sprung to life from previous novels, such as Patrick Bateman from *American Psycho* or Mitchell Allen, a minor character in *The Rules of Attraction*. Just as Ellis toyed with the thriller in Glamorama, so in *Lunar Park* he experiments with horror and the ghost story. Memoir proceeds rapidly to fiction as Ellis recounts his move to an affluent neighborhood in a rural village, where he takes up teaching at the local (Camden) college in an attempt to escape the past and to repair the damage he has done to himself and his family (a wife, son, and stepdaughter invented for the purposes of the novel) as the result of his fame and his addictions. Similar to the plethora of horror novels and films that depict the move from city to country as an exchange of known fears for the terror of the unknown, the protagonist of *Lunar Park* experiences in his new environs a series of memories, bizarre incidents, and ghosts, including those of his father (the novel contains an epigraph from *Hamlet*) and Patrick Bateman, stalking him in serial-killer fashion. These hauntings and horror devices, such as that of a mechanical bird that terrorizes his stepdaughter, undergird the more obvious targets of Ellis's satire – suburban culture, American dread – but perhaps obscure the less transparent aims of the novel which are to reflect sardonically on the ravages of ego and career upon personal and familial life.

Ellis most recent novel to date is *Imperial Bedrooms* (2010), a sequel to *Less Than Zero* in which Clay returns to navigate Los Angeles twenty-five years later as a screenwriter in quest of actors for a film he is making. Depending on one's perspective toward the mind-numbing scenes of violence and abuse that occur all too frequently in the novel, Clay has not changed, or he has changed much for the worse. He, once again, appears to be more of a witness than a participant, although it is clear that even though he is a sociopath incapable of feeling the pain of others, even in extremity, his witnessing is, perhaps, the worst form of complicity. Is Ellis, here and in all of his novels, attempting to force this recognition upon his readers – that we are all complicit in the quite visible violence of contemporary American culture in ways indirect and, uncomfortably, not so indirect? If so, then the novel can be regarded in its details as both repulsive and barbative: in short, the work of satire, though its effects upon any form of the social transformations that satire is intended to promote are questionable.

Less Than Zero and *American Psycho* have been adapted into films, and Ellis has been involved in several screenwriting projects, including credits on adaptations of *Less Than Zero* (1987) and *The Informers* (2008), as well as Paul Schrader's *The Canyons* (2013), Derick Martini's *The Curse of Downer's Grove* (limited theatrical release, 2015), and Tim Hunter's *Smiley Face Killers* (2020), these latter three genre films of the thriller/slasher category of limited success and questionable quality. The adaptation of *American Psycho* (2000) is by far the most successful of Ellis's work; directed by Mary Herron, it includes a strong cast including Christian Bale and William Dafoe, and generated controversy upon its initial screening at the Sundance Film Festival and its subsequent theatrical release, receiving a predicable mix of heavily negative and positive reviews. Perhaps less predicably, *American Psycho* was adapted as a musical in 2013 by Duncan Sheik, premiering at the Almeida Theatre in London to notable success and with subsequent runs in New York and Sydney.

With *White*, his collection of essays on writing and American culture from the beginning of his career to the present, Ellis continues to generate controversy as he attacks contemporary parenting, critiques the Hollywood film industry, and details his discontent with current notions of sexual and racial identity. There is an air of nostalgia and regret for the passing of the 1980s in these essays, and many readers may regard Ellis's views as anti-progressive, but like his fiction, it would be reductive to regard them as merely reactionary or only as a series of cries from yet another beleaguered white male, though some are certainly these. But Ellis writes here, as everywhere, to generate a reaction in the reader, and the high visibility of his work and career in the annals of post-1980 American fiction is clear testimony that this intention remains operative. Transgressive, self-indulgent, provocative: these are all tags that may be fairly applied to Ellis's work throughout, which remains an important piece in the mosaic of contemporary writing.

SEE ALSO: After Postmodernism; Fiction and Affect; Lethem, Jonathan; Suburban Narratives; Tartt, Donna; Urban Fiction

REFERENCES

Baudrillard, Jean. (1994). *Simulacra and Simulation* (trans. Sheila Faria Glaser). Ann Arbor: University of Michigan Press.

Ellis, Bret Easton. (1991). *American Psycho*. New York: Vintage.

Martelle, Scott. (1999). The dark side of a generation. *Los Angeles Times* (February 1, 1999). https://www.latimes.com/archives/la-xpm-1999-feb-01-cl-3631-story.html (accessed July 31, 2021).

Publishers Weekly. (1998). Review of *Glamorama*. (November 30, 1998). https://www.publishersweekly.com/978-0-375-40412-2 (accessed July 31, 2021).

FURTHER READING

Baelo-Allué, Sonia. (2011). *Bret Easton Ellis's Controversial Fiction: Writing Between High and Low Culture*. New York: Continuum.

Colby, Georgiana. (2011). *Bret Easton Ellis: Underwriting the Contemporary*. New York: Palgrave Macmillan.

Mandel, Naomi and Graham, Sarah. (2011). *Bret Easton Ellis: American Psycho, Glamorama, Lunar Park*. New York: Continuum.

Martín Párraga, Javier. (2017). *Fear, Trauma and Paranoia in Bret Easton Ellis's Ouevre: Abandon All Hope Who Enter Here*. Newcastle-upon-Tyne, UK: Cambridge Scholars.

Ellroy, James

JIM MANCALL
Wheaton College, USA

James Ellroy, the "Demon Dog" of American crime fiction, as the title of Jud Reinhard's 1993 documentary proclaims him, rose from homelessness and drug addiction to become an internationally acclaimed author of crime fiction. Born in March 1948 as Lee Earle Ellroy in Los Angeles, he was the son of Armand Ellroy and Geneva "Jean" Hilliker Ellroy. His parents divorced in 1955, and as a young child, he shuttled between his parents. But the signal event of Ellroy's childhood was the murder of his mother in 1958, when he was 10 years old. This trauma, and the still unsolved murder, shadows Ellroy's literary work like no other event.

For his eleventh birthday, Ellroy's father presented him with a copy of Jack Webb's *The Badge* (1958). In the same laconic style that he perfected for the radio and TV series, *Dragnet*, Webb recounts the day-to-day life of the LAPD as well as notorious Los Angeles crimes. Most importantly, one chapter focused on the gruesome murder of Elizabeth Short in 1947, a case that became known as the "Black Dahlia," which, like the murder of Ellroy's mother, remains unsolved. The two murders melded in Ellroy's mind, igniting Ellroy's lifelong obsession with the Black Dahlia case. Several of the other cases and criminal figures profiled in *The Badge* later resurface in Ellroy's fiction. But in Ellroy's work, the heroes of the LAPD are often hardly heroic, and several of his works skewer not only Webb, but also Los Angeles Chief of Police Bill Parker.

After being expelled from high school, and following his father's death in 1965, Ellroy drifted into a roughly thirteen-year period of homelessness, addiction, and petty crime. However, even during this period, Ellroy read voraciously, including works by Joseph Wambaugh and Ross MacDonald, and still aspired to a career as a writer. But Ellroy's addictions and health deteriorated to the point that he was hospitalized. He eventually recovered and obtained sobriety, and began working as a golf caddie in Los Angeles. In his off hours, he drafted his first novel, *Brown's Requiem*, a private detective novel that was published in 1981. Though Ellroy would later disdain the clichés of the private detective genre, *Brown's Requiem* nonetheless sets a template for Ellroy's later fiction: Fritz Brown, a failed former LAPD officer, seeks redemption in the eyes of an unattainable woman and, in doing so, unearths the secrets of a decades-old crime. Ellroy's second novel, *Clandestine* (1982), also established motifs that Ellroy would later develop in the LA Quartet: a young ambitious cop, Fred Underhill, is initiated into, and ultimately victimized by, the corrupt and violent world of the Los Angeles police. He solves a murder but only by working outside the law; in doing so, he must confront and overcome a series of doubles and corrupt father figures. *Clandestine* is the first of Ellroy's novels to allude to his mother's murder and her early life in Wisconsin. It is also notable as the first appearance of Lieutenant Dudley Smith, who would become the arch villain of the LA Quartet. *Clandestine* was nominated for an Edgar Award by the Mystery Writers of America for best paperback original.

Beginning in 1984, Ellroy published three novels featuring Lloyd Hopkins, an eccentric, reckless, womanizing, and hard-living LA cop. In 1984's *Blood on the Moon*, Hopkins faces off against a sadistic serial killer who kills women in tribute to his high school love. In *Because the Night*, also published in 1984, Hopkins investigates the disappearance of an undercover cop and discovers the machinations of an evil psychiatrist, Dr. John Havilland, who, like Hopkins, has been twisted by childhood trauma. The final novel in the trilogy, *Suicide Hill*, was published in 1986; in this novel, the central criminal mystery is less important than the backroom dealings and shifting allegiances among the LAPD, a plot that foreshadows Ellroy's transition to the LA Quartet. As the novels proceed, Hopkins becomes almost a parody of the "super cop" figure familiar from 1970s action films.

In 1986, Ellroy also published *Killer on the Road*, a serial killer novel (originally titled *Silent Terror*). The novel is narrated in the first person by Martin Plunkett, a quiet and clever psychopath who has murdered more than 40 people. Though often considered a minor work about which Ellroy himself would later express some regret, the novel does capture some central themes of his fiction: childhood trauma, the myth of the family, and the public's voyeuristic fascination with crime.

A second phase of Ellroy's career began in 1987 with the publication of *The Black Dahlia*, the first in the series of novels that make up the LA Quartet. *The Black Dahlia* centers around the real-life murder of Elizabeth Short. In Ellroy's telling, the murder proves to be a trial by fire for Bucky Bleichert, a former lightweight boxer who joins the LAPD. As part of his apprenticeship, Bleichert is taken in and, it will turn out, betrayed by another former boxer and fellow cop, Lee Blanchard, as well as Blanchard's girlfriend, former gangster moll, Kay Lake. *The Black Dahlia* establishes several themes that inform much of Ellroy's fiction: doubles, voyeurism, the corrupt families that mirror a larger systemic corruption. *The Black Dahlia* also placed Ellroy's fictional characters against a backdrop of historical events and figures: not only do characters from the real-life investigation of the Dahlia case appear, but the case is linked to other historical events, such as the Zoot Suit Riots and the unveiling of the famous Hollywood sign. This mixture of the historical and fictional becomes a central device in Ellroy's fiction. But this is not just historical window-dressing; Ellroy's fiction creates a kind of anti-history, pushing the reader not only to sort out fact from fiction, but also to introduce readers to what may be forgotten or overlooked historical crimes and incidents.

The Black Dahlia was Ellroy's breakthrough novel, becoming a critical and popular success and allowing him to become a full-time writer. The novel later became the basis of the 2006 Brian De Palma film of the same title. In a movie tie-in edition of the novel, Ellroy wrote an afterword which elaborated on the relationship between the novel, his mother's murder, and the Dahlia case. In later interviews, he acknowledged exploiting the story of his mother's murder in order to publicize the book.

Each of the next three novels in the LA Quartet mixes history and fiction, and the plots are triggered by real crimes and events: the Sleepy Lagoon case, the Bloody Christmas LAPD scandal, the demolition of homes owned by Mexican Americans in order to build the Dodgers' Chavez Ravine stadium. In effect, these novels present a counter-history of Los Angeles; contrary to the sunny myth of California, Ellroy's Los Angeles is built on secrets, crime, and exploitation; beneath the gleam and glamour of Hollywood, there is an underworld, a secret history that the ordinary "square john" remains oblivious to.

The second book in the Quartet, 1988's *The Big Nowhere*, begins in early 1950 as Danny Upshaw, a young sheriff's detective, investigates a gruesome series of killings. At the same time LAPD Lieutenant Mal Considine has been charged with leading an investigation of the Communist Party's influence on Hollywood, and Buzz Meeks, a former corrupt cop and current fixer for Howard Hughes, must clean up a blackmail problem. Eventually, all three cases will overlap and the three protagonists join forces. In *L.A. Confidential* (1990) Ed Exley, Jr., the son of a famous cop, has to prove his bona fides by solving the case of what appears to be a random shootout in a diner. Exley will eventually discover that crime ties to a prostitution ring, the development of a Disneyland-like theme park owned by Exley's father, and the decades-old murder of a former child star. *L.A. Confidential* became the basis of a successful 1997 film directed by Curtis Hanson. In *White Jazz*, published in 1992, Dave Klein, a corrupt and murderous cop, investigates a bizarre burglary that will turn out to be entangled with two wealthy families mired in incest, drug abuse, voyeurism, and prostitution. Klein will forge temporary alliances with Ed Exley and Dudley Smith, but will ultimately vow vengeance on Smith, the mastermind lurking behind many of the novel's crimes and depravity.

One of Ellroy's innovations in these novels is confronting his readers with a frank depiction of the 1940s–1950s LAPD racism, homophobia, and misogyny. As a result, it is difficult to call his protagonists "heroes"; they are deeply flawed, even ugly characters. Ellroy's cops regularly beat suspects of color, they denigrate Jews and homosexuals, regularly take bribes and collude in criminal behavior. Thus, part of the challenge that these novels present to the reader is that their protagonists are not likable or sympathetic in conventional ways, and yet, as readers, we often see the action from their perspective, creating an uncomfortable, sometimes jarring reading experience. This is a deliberate effect by Ellroy and is one of the factors that set these novels apart from typical genre fare and brought Ellroy such acclaim.

Yet, as dark as Ellroy's plots can be, Ellroy's protagonists often achieve some kind of redemption, or work toward some approximation of morality. Perhaps once apathetic, they find themselves with a need to solve a deep mystery, to discover, as Danny Upshaw puts it, the "WHY?" – why a particular crime has been committed, but also the larger "why" of what drives crime, greed, exploitation (2013, loc. 539). If Ellroy's protagonists find answers, it is often at great personal cost, and with little recognition. Bucky Bleichert cannot reveal the truth of the Dahlia murder; Danny Upshaw dies a suicide; Buzz Meeks is killed by Dudley Smith; and Dave Klein is forced to adopt a new life and identity in Rio.

But perhaps equally significant are Ellroy's stylistic innovations in the LA Quartet. *L.A. Confidential* is assembled almost as a collage. Newspaper clippings, police memos, and articles from gossip rags form their own chapters, creating an undercurrent that comments on the main narrative. Further, as the Quartet proceeds, Ellroy's style evolves into telegraphic, staccato sentences, where sound and rhythm are as important as content. By the time of *White Jazz*, Dave Klein's narration is almost jazz-like, mirroring the fever dream state of his character. According to Ellroy, this style evolved when his editor asked him to reduce an already lengthy draft of *L.A. Confidential*. Rather than eliminate characters or plot points, Ellroy's solution was to cut unnecessary words, creating the truncated, telegraphic style. Some readers may find this style unsettling or too demanding, but it also enmeshes the reader in the characters' worldview. So much of Ellroy's fiction is about a voyeuristic fascination with crime, and his style implicates the reader, asking the reader to imaginatively fill in details, gaps, and logic. As readers, we inhabit and complete those spaces in Ellroy's sentences, working, like his protagonists, to find meaning.

With the Underworld USA trilogy, which began with *American Tabloid* (1995), Ellroy expanded on the techniques and plot devices established in the LA Quartet. Rather than focusing on Los Angeles, this trilogy traces the history of the larger United States from the 1950s through the Nixon presidency. As with the LA Quartet, Ellroy mixes history and fiction; in these dense, complicated narratives, the development of Las Vegas as a casino playground, the Bay of Pigs invasion, the assassination of John F. Kennedy, Howard

Hughes, Jimmy Hoffa, J. Edgar Hoover, and the Civil Rights movement are all intertwined. In essence, these novels unwrite or rewrite the official versions of US history, providing an alternate history that connects and reconnects the historical events as part of several larger, dizzying conspiracies. There is, as the title of the trilogy suggests, an underworld, always out of sight, and always at work shaping the life of a nation.

In *American Tabloid*, against the backdrop of the Bay of Pigs, organized crime, and the JFK assassination, three men plot and maneuver: Kemper Boyd, an ambitious FBI agent, schemes to join the Kennedy circle; Ward Littell, a moralistic but cowardly FBI agent, hopes to rise in JFK's efforts against organized crime; and Pete Bondurant, a hulking, vicious criminal who works for Howard Hughes, plays as many sides against each other as he can. But all three will fail in their schemes, thwarted by the larger forces manipulating them. The only hint of redemption lies in Bondurant's late realization of the power of love. *American Tabloid* was very well received by critics, who praised its dense and tightly controlled plot. *Time* magazine named it the best book of 1995.

In *The Cold Six Thousand*, published in 2001, Littell and Bondurant return; the third main character is Wayne Tedrow, Jr., a Las Vegas police officer who finds himself in Dallas on November 22, 1963. Shifting from Cuba to Vietnam to the assassination of Martin Luther King, the novel traces the moral arcs of the three main characters, with the "incorruptible" Tedrow falling from grace, and Littell and Bondurant working toward some kind of redemption. Again, all of their schemes fail, and each will be manipulated by twisted father figures. Bondurant, though, will renew his marriage to Barb Jahelka and fully retire from "the Life."

In 2009, Ellroy published the final volume in the trilogy, *Blood's a Rover*. In some senses, *Blood's a Rover* pulls together not only the trilogy, but also Ellroy's entire oeuvre. Like the novels of the LA Quartet, this novel begins with a crime, the robbery of an armored car, that will have ripple effects and connections well beyond the immediate crime scene. And, as in the Quartet, a young man investigates the crime and is inexorably pulled into the underworld. In this case, that man is Don Crutchfield, based on an actual private investigator, who also resembles a young Ellroy. At the same time, as in the other Underworld books, Crutchfield's investigations draw him into a larger and larger circle of conspiracies. Ultimately, he confronts the evil father figure who lurks behind the entire series, J. Edgar Hoover. But perhaps most important is the metatextual element of *Blood's a Rover*, in which several characters assemble or collate documents, diaries, redacted memos, and texts with fragmented or missing contents. These texts do not provide simple clues or easy answers, suggesting the way that Ellroy's reader must also work, sifting the voluminous material to create meaning.

One noteworthy difference between the Underworld USA trilogy and the LA Quartet is that the trilogy focuses much more on female characters and characters of color. Joan Rosen Klein and Karen Sifakis, leftist warriors in *Blood's a Rover*, have prominent roles, and in the same novel Marshall Bowen, a Black, gay LAPD officer, becomes one of the central narrators, and certainly one of Ellroy's most nuanced gay characters. If Ellroy's previous novels had been critiqued as conservative, or even right-wing, these novels seem to suggest a more progressive, leftist critique of American history and culture.

Ellroy has also published several works of nonfiction. Most prominent is *My Dark Places* (1996), a memoir which recounts Ellroy's youth, his mother's murder, and his path from homelessness to authorship. *My Dark Places* also recounts his attempt, with the help of retired detective Bill Stoner, to solve the decades-old murder of his mother. A second memoir, *The Hilliker Curse* (2010), traces Ellroy's mother's history and the subsequent impact of his mother's life and death on his own relationships with women.

In 2014, Ellroy published *Perfidia*, the first in a planned series of prequels to the LA Quartet. The novel begins with the gruesome murder of a Japanese family the day before the bombing of Pearl Harbor. The LAPD, under the direction of the federal government, have begun rounding up "subversive" Japanese, though everyone from Mayor Fletcher Bowron to developer Preston Exley sees the roundups as a chance to make a buck. Many of the characters from Ellroy's previous novels appear, from *The Black Dahlia*'s trio of Kay Lake, Bucky Bleichert, and Lee Blanchard to Claire DeHaven from *The Big Nowhere* to Scotty Bennett from *Blood's a Rover*. Ellroy's mother appears in the guise of Joan Conville, a mysterious nurse who tantalizes William Parker. As in the Quartet, the narrative voice shifts between characters, including Kay Lake, Dudley Smith, William Parker, and a new character, Hideo Ashida, a Japanese American police chemist investigating the murder of the Watanabe family. As is typical of the LA Quartet, a bizarre, seemingly local crime is tied to larger events; a convoluted conspiracy links the Watanabes to the coalition of right and left wingers who hope to profit from the war they anticipate with the Axis. The second novel in the series, *This Storm*, was published in 2019. In that novel, Elmer Jackson, an LAPD cop known for his involvement with the notorious madam Brenda Allen, investigates a murder, while Dudley Smith becomes enmeshed in a deep conspiracy across the Mexican border. Familiar characters appear and reappear, and Hollywood luminaries like Orson Welles and Bette Davis float through the narrative. If the Underworld USA trilogy represents a leftist critique of America, in the new quartet, left and right are virtually indistinguishable. They are both corrupt, and characters shift, betray, or rekindle allegiances with little regard for morality or integrity. The real fifth column, as one character points out, is money – a fitting epigraph for much of Ellroy's work.

In 2015, the Mystery Writers of America named Ellroy a "Grand Master."

SEE ALSO: Mosley, Walter; Urban Fiction

REFERENCE

Ellroy, James. (2013). *The Big Nowhere*. New York: Grand Central Press; 1st ed. 1988.

FURTHER READING

Ashman, Nathan. (2018). *James Ellroy and Voyeur Fiction*. Lanham, MD: Lexington Books.

Horsley, Lee. (1998). Founding fathers: "genealogies of violence" in James Ellroy's L.A. Quartet. *Clues: A Journal of Detection* 19 (1): 139–161.

Mancall, Jim. (2014). *James Ellroy: A Companion to the Mystery Fiction*. Jefferson, NC: McFarland.

Oates, Joyce Carol. (2011). A tenuously reformed pervert. *New York Review of Books* (April 28, 2011).

Powell, Steven. (2016). *James Ellroy: Demon Dog of Crime Fiction*. London: Palgrave Macmillan.

Powell, Steven. (ed.) (2018). *The Big Somewhere: Essays on James Ellroy's Noir World*. New York: Bloomsbury Academic.

Englander, Nathan

BRIAN WILLEMS
University of Split, Croatia

Nathan Englander (b. 1970) grew up in an Orthodox Jewish community in West Hempstead, New York. Although he now considers himself agnostic, all of his work is concerned with the great Jewish tradition of putting laws to vigorous tests, which started with Moses. Whether dealing with the possibility of the deceased saying the prayer for the dead for themselves, or symbolic pacts being taken literally, Englander's work develops a variety of strategies for submitting Jewish law to the test. Five of these strategies are developed below: a *blind misapplication of the law* which can foreground a law's absurdity, the *ability to hold two contradictory statements as being simultaneously true*, following a law in *a traditional (halachical) but not technical sense*, a *ceaseless and vibrant questioning of the law*, and *the relation of Jewish law to the Internet*. All of these strategies are used to characterize some of the complexities of Jewish life in the contemporary world.

Englander's first book is the short story collection *For the Relief of Unbearable Urges* (1999) which includes work from 1997–1999. The first piece in the collection, "The Twenty-seventh Man," fictionalizes the night of the murdered poets. On August 12, 1952, Joseph Stalin ordered the execution of thirteen Jewish writers and activists who were being held in Moscow's Lubyanka Prison (Rubenstein and Naumov 2001, p. 2). However, these historical events are not merely used in an effort at conscious-raising, but rather to examine the role that the law plays in determining the fate of people's lives.

In Englander's story, all of the fictional writers have been imprisoned because of their supposedly subversive work, except one, the twenty-seventh prisoner, Pinchas Pelovits, a man "who wrote all day but did not publish" (1999, p. 7). Pelovits is the odd-man-out. He seems to have randomly been chosen to be imprisoned, since none of the other writers has ever heard of him. It is a clerical error (p. 20).

Thus the first role of the law in Englander's work makes its appearance: *the law can be misapplied*. Its victims can be chosen by mistake, and nothing can be done to stop it once the system is in motion. This is true for the law of the state and the Torah. Pelovits has done nothing to deserve his arrest, and he does not even try to plead his case before he is executed with the rest of the writers.

At the same time, Pelovits is the only one who does any writing in his cell. The story-within-a-story that he comes up with is actually the central text of the piece. In Pelovits's tale, a man named Mendel Muskatev thinks he has died because he finds that his bedroom is missing. Immediately he says the prayer for the dead, the Kaddish, for himself. However, instead of feeling relieved that this duty is performed, Muskatev worries that the first thing he has done after dying is to sin, since he is unsure if the dead are allowed to say the Kaddish for themselves (1999, pp. 12–13). The advice of a rabbi is sought (p. 19), although the scholar, upon realizing he is also dead, is too excited by the prospect of having an eternity to study the Talmud to give much thought to Muskatev's question (p. 22). In fact, the story-within-a-story ends with the rabbi asking Muskatev again why he came, and Muskatev saying it was to ask "which one of us is to say the prayer?" (p. 22). Pelovits shares the story with his cell mates who all approve. Then they are all shot.

Pelovits is arrested because of a clerical error. His death is due to the misapplication of the law. This is a theme which is found in many of the other stories from *For the Relief of Unbearable Urges*. In "The Wig," a woman loses her job and is shamed by her whole community for going to great lengths to create the wig of her dreams (1999, p. 106). In the collection's eponymous story, a rabbi tells a man to visit a prostitute because he wife is refusing to have sex. However, the man does not use a condom when doing so, and when he returns to his wife he finds her sexual attraction for him has returned, but he can do nothing about it because he has a sexually transmitted disease (p. 191). What these stories have in common is a need to describe the kind of *aporia*, or paradox, of the law which so easily leads to its misapplication.

Englander's first novel, *The Ministry of Special Cases* (2007), also deals with questions surrounding the Kaddish, as its main character's name is Kaddish Poznan. The book is also concerned with how to mourn when mourning becomes impossible. Kaddish's son Pato is disappeared during Argentina's Dirty War of the 1970s and 1980s, in which a US-backed dictatorship tracked down and killed thousands of dissidents for their supposed socialist, communist, or left-wing politics. Pato is a college student who is seen as a threat and is disappeared by the government. After Kaddish and his wife do everything they can to get him back, they are faced with the task of how, as Jews, to mourn a son when the body is never recovered. Thus a new relation to the law is offered: what is called the *law of non-contradiction* is violated in this novel. As formulated by Aristotle in *Metaphysics*, this law states that "opposite affirmations are not true at the same time" (1011b 13–14, Aristotle 2016, p. 65). The violation of this supposedly sacred law in philosophy is necessary in order to mourn those for whom Jewish law says it is impossible to mourn.

One of Kaddish's jobs is to visit the section of a cemetery reserved for Jewish prostitutes and pimps in order to chip off names and dates from tombstones so more respectable ancestors will have less to be ashamed. The existence of this part of the cemetery is "technically but not *halachically*" acceptable, "which is how Jews solve every problem that comes their way" (Englander 2007, p. 5). The prostitutes and pimps should not be buried with the others, *halachically*, so a small wall that can be easily climbed is installed, so that *technically* they are in a separate part of the cemetery. The law is observed and circumvented at the same time.

The mourning of Kaddish's son follows a similar pattern. Pato has been disappeared and no trace can be found. Lillian, Kaddish's wife, insists on assuming he is alive, although Kaddish eventually comes to thinking that Pato has been killed. This situation is never resolved, as it never was for the thousands of families of the real disappeared. Kaddish realizes that the situation of his disappeared son demands breaking the law of non-contradiction. This demand is mirrored in a scene where Kaddish sees the window of his home from the street. He sees the light on but he knows Lillian is not home. He is certain "that he'd seen two opposing things" (2007, p. 288): Lillian's light on, and her light not on. Kaddish had to hold both possibilities in his mind at once. "Everything and its opposite," he thinks, "As in the case of a son that is both living and dead" (p. 289).

Thus the novel ends with an insistence on the position of those left behind by the departed: holding two contradictory statements as being simultaneously true, a new relationship to the law in Englander's work.

Englander's second short story collection, *What We Talk About When We Talk About Anne Frank* (2012) addresses a new topic, the Israeli occupation of Palestine. And with this new topic comes a different relation to the law. Although this issue is not given an extensive treatment until Englander's next novel, in *What We Talk About* following the law "technically but not *halachically*" is reversed into following it "*halachically* but not technically." For example, in "Sister Hills" two Jewish women make a pact that is meant to be symbolic but which, in the end, is kept to the letter (cf. Willems 2018). When one woman's daughter is sick, her mother "sells" the child to her friend so it cannot be found by the Angel of Death. The next day Aheret gets better, and the pact is forgotten until many years later when Rena claims Yehudit as her own and demands she come live with her, something the local rabbis have to eventually agree is halachically true, although no one would ever expect someone to take the agreement literally (2018, pp. 64–65).

A few months after the publication of *What We Talk About*, Englander came out with his translation of the Haggadah, or Jewish Passover prayer. The richly illustrated text includes Englander's translation, a timeline of events in Jewish history, and commentaries by Nathaniel Deutsch, Jeffery Goldberg, Rebecca Newberger Goldstein, and Lemony Snicket.

One of the early commentaries in the translation addresses the role of questioning the law in Jewish history. Written by Goldberg, the commentary argues that there is a great Jewish tradition of putting laws to vigorous tests, and Moses, whose Exodus is the focus of the story of the Haggadah, was an example of civil disobedience since the Pharaoh of Egypt was the law, but the Pharaoh's instruction to kill the sons of the Israelites was deemed unjust (Englander 2012, p. 13). This vigorous testing fails in "Sister Hills," and it is what makes the story a tragedy.

Englander's second novel, *Dinner at the Center of the Earth* (2017), has another relationship to the law: it questions the law of proportionality, especially as it applies to violence between Israel and Palestine. Each chapter moves around both in time (between 2002 and 2014) and space (mainly between Paris, Tel Aviv, Berlin, a Black Ops site in the Negev Desert, and the Israeli side of a border with the Gaza Strip). All the time lines center on the Qibya massacre, in which Israeli soldiers killed a minimum of sixty-nine Palestinians in the West Bank in 1953 (Englander 2017, p. 81). Prisoner Z is an American-Israeli operative who tricks Farid, a Palestinian operative, into providing information that leads to a strike on Gaza. Z eventually is incarcerated in Israel for, it seems, giving up state secrets. An ex-General and prime minister, presumably based on Ariel Sharon, is the only one that can free Z, but he dies, leaving Z in a permanent state of imprisonment. During his death, the General reminisces about his life, and much of the novel takes place in this state of "Limbo."

Part of the story is concerned with how the General disregards the admittedly problematic concept of proportionality in warfare. "The General would kill ninety and lose nine" (2017, p. 71), and he is reprimanded by his colleagues because he "cannot keep winning so well" (p. 72). During a re-imagination of the actual Qibya massacre, the General explicitly orders disproportionate violence: "I want fifty houses leveled. The school. The mosque. We are here to avenge, after all" (p. 82). The attack is explicitly *too much*: "We have invaded a sovereign state for the purpose of mayhem" (p. 83) the General says. The actual massacre resulted in the deaths of sixty-nine Palestinians and no Israelis.

The word "disproportionate" specifically refers to article 8.2 (b) (iv) on War Crimes of the Rome Statute of the International Criminal Court which prohibits "Intentionally launching an attack in the knowledge that such attack will cause incidental loss of life or injury to civilians or damage to civilian objects ... which would be clearly excessive in relation to the concrete and direct overall military advantage anticipated" (UN General Assembly 2010). The General in Englander's story explicitly engages in disproportionate violence. The justification that the General provides for his actions is that he wants to make the life of an Israeli too expensive for any attack to even be considered (Englander 2017, p. 89). However, this is not the last word on the Israel–Palestine conflict. The title of the novel indicates another approach.

Dinner takes its title from a meeting that takes place at the end of the novel. The Palestinian operator Farid has fallen in love with Shira, an Israeli mapmaker. They get to know each other while meeting for another attempt a peace, but they can no longer see each other when the peace process fails. So they come up with a dangerous plan: to have dinner together in one of the secret tunnels the Palestinians have dug under the wall the Israelis have built. In this sense the two will literally "meet in the middle" (2017, p. 249), as they listen to the sounds of war above them, unsure which side will finally become victorious (p. 250).

Yet this is not a novel about a "no-solution" to the Israel-Palestine conflict. Rather it is rather about the way sides change and then change back again. There is a continual belief and then vigorous questioning and abandonment of the law, much as was seen in the commentary on the Haggadah discussed above.

In Englander's most recent novel *kaddish.com* (2019), Larry is not expected to perform the Kaddish upon the death of his father. As a lapsed Orthodox, he considers the rules for the seven days of shivah to have no relation to actually mourning his father (2019, p. 6), so no one in his family expects this oldest son to keep the eleven months of saying the Kaddish eight times a day. However, Larry insists on doing so, although he learns from a rabbi that it is halachically acceptable to engage a proxy to do so (p. 31). After looking at pornography on the Internet, Larry finds the website kaddish.com, based in a yeshiva in Jerusalem, which promised to assign anyone's Kaddish to be said by one of their students (pp. 35–36). Larry pays and then a symbolic exchange, or *kinyan*, is made, for a student named Chemi to take over the Kaddish for Larry. Thus the novel introduces a new aspect of the law: its relation to the Internet.

Soon Shuli begins to regret having passed on the Kaddish to another, and he gets one of his students to find out the location of the yeshiva that runs the website. The re-ignites Shuli's obsession with the Internet, which is also connected to his use of pornography, but is also explicitly tied to his relation to the Torah. Before the Internet, Shuli was sure that "all knowledge was contained inside the Torah." But now, as he watches his student trace the IP address of the Jerusalem yeshiva, Shuli is "forced to admit that inside this terrible machine is a different kind of all-knowingness. A toxic, shiftless omniscience" (2019, p. 98).

At the Jerusalem yeshiva, Shuli eventually finds no one is actually saying the Kaddish for those who paid the website, so he decides to take the *kinyan* back but not only for his father, but for everyone who was cheated (2019, p. 181). This is significant because Shuli himself is making the Internet a trustworthy place for Orthodox Jews. But this does not mean that the Internet is following Orthodox law. In one dream Shuli sees himself becoming the woman in a pornographic gif he saw before first finding the kaddish.com website. After deciding to do the Kaddish for everyone, Shuli sees himself slowly turning into this woman: his feet appear to be a woman's, and he finds that he now has her face (p. 185). What is more, the gif that he saw featured the woman inserting a massive dildo into her herself, and Shuli does the same, finally feeling a pleasure that he immediately connects to Paradise (p. 188).

This image saves the ending of the novel from merely being an Orthodox version of the Internet. Instead a new strategy is created: a symbiosis between the old and the new, an actual kaddish.com that halachically fulfills its purpose, while also acknowledging a new world where both pornography and the Torah co-exist in the creation of new knowledge. Englander is showing how the Internet can function as a new strategy for putting the Jewish law to the test. In this way the Internet itself takes on one of the most traditional aspects of Jewish faith: questioning the law.

SEE ALSO: Chabon, Michael; Davis, Lydia; Fiction and Terrorism; Foer, Jonathan Safran; Franzen, Jonathan; Lerner, Ben; Lethem,

Jonathan; Roth, Philip; Shteyngart, Gary; Trauma and Fiction

REFERENCES

Aristotle. (2016). *Metaphysics* (trans. C.D.C. Reeve). Indianapolis: Hackett Publishing.
Englander, Nathan. (1999). *For the Relief of Unbearable Urges*. London: Faber.
Englander, Nathan. (2007). *The Ministry of Special Cases*. New York: Knopf.
Englander, Nathan. (2012). *New American Haggadah* (ed. and trans. Jonathan Safran Foer). New York: Little, Brown.
Englander, Nathan. (2017). *Dinner at the Center of the Earth*. New York: Knopf.
Englander, Nathan. (2019). *kaddish.com*. London: Weidenfeld and Nicolson.
Rubenstein, Joshua and Naumov, Vladimir. (eds.) (2001). *Stalin's Secret Pogrom: The Postwar Inquisition of the Jewish Anti-Fascist Committee*. New Haven and London: Yale University Press.
UN General Assembly. (1998). *Rome Statute of the International Criminal Court* (last amended 2010) (July 17, 1998). http://www.refworld.org/docid/3ae6b3a84.html (accessed July 17, 2021).
Willems, Brian. (2018). Scale and change: Assaf Gavron's *CrocAttack!*, Nathan Englander's "Sister Hills" and Elia Suleiman's *Divine Intervention*. *Textual Practice* 32 (1): 163–184.

FURTHER READING

Englander, Nathan. (2019). Revisited: *Guernica*. *The Paris Review* (April 5, 2019). https://www.theparisreview.org/blog/2019/04/05/revisited-guernica/
Englander, Nathan. (2014). *The Twenty-seventh Man*. New York: Dramatists Play Service.
Kavon, Eli. (2015). Stalin and the night of the murdered poets. *Jerusalem Post* (August 11, 2015). https://www.jpost.com/Blogs/Past-Imperfect-Confronting-Jewish-History/Stalin-and-the-Night-of-the-Murdered-Poets-411802
Weizman, Eyal. (2011). *The Least of All Possible Evils: Humanitarian Violence from Arendt to Gaza*. London: Verso.
Wirth, Nesher Hana. (2019). *The Cambridge History of Jewish American Literature*. Cambridge: Cambridge University Press.

Erdrich, Louise

MARTA J. LYSIK
University of Wroclaw, Poland

Karen Louise Erdrich, born in 1954 in Little Falls, Minnesota, grew up in Wahpeton, North Dakota where her parents, Rita Gourneau Erdrich and Ralph Erdrich, were teachers in a school governed by the Bureau of Indian Affairs. Given her identity and its complicated intersections, namely Turtle Mountain Ojibwe, German, and French Canadian ancestry, her Catholic upbringing, and her New England university education, she is skeptical of clear-cut typologies:

> I think of any label as being both true and a product of a kind of chauvinistic society because obviously white male writers are not labeled "white male writers" . . . But I really don't like labels. While it is certainly true that a good part of my background . . . and a lot of the themes are Native American, I prefer to simply be a writer. Although I like to be known as having been from the Turtle Mountain Chippewa and from North Dakota. It's nice to have that known and to be proud of it for people back home.
>
> (Wong 1994, p. 31)

Erdrich was among the first women to enter Dartmouth College in 1972. That year also marked the introduction of a new program in Native American Studies founded and headed by Michael Dorris (Modoc), whom she later married. She majored in English and creative writing first, later she took classes to learn about her Ojibwe background. However, while discussing her debut novel *Love Medicine* (1984), Erdrich underscored her priorities: "The people are first, their ethnic background is second" (Grantham 1994, p. 14).

Erdrich's writing is appreciated worldwide because it is concerned with shared human experiences, their ambivalence, risks, and beauty. She is not accusatory in her writing, but simultaneously respectful of and poking fun at white American and Ojibwe cultures, thus complicating stereotypes of victimhood, while being aware of the problematic history of conquest, deprivation, and dislocation. Erdrich's stories often include instead of alienating, sympathize instead of judging, as they navigate between different topographies, ethnic identities, and belief systems. Her writing demonstrates the potential for noninvasive edification by portraying the good life despite hardships, what Deborah Madsen terms "the aesthetics of Mino Bimaadiziwin" (2011, p. 1), and Erdrich herself defined as: "Knowledge with Courage. Knowledge with Fortitude. Knowledge with Generosity and Kindness" (quoted in Madsen 2011, p. 6).

Her writing evolved organically, as she began with poetry, then continued with short stories which became novels. In the early 1980s, two weeks short of a deadline, she learned of the literary competition for *Chicago Magazine's* Nelson Algren Prize and submitted "The World's Greatest Fishermen." This short story, along with others Erdrich wrote earlier, titled "The Red Convertible" and "Scales," laid the groundwork for *Love Medicine*. She has published three volumes of poetry so far: *Jacklight* (1984), *Baptism of Fire* (1989), and *Original Fire: New and Selected Poems* (2003), and a volume of short stories, though fairly late in her career, titled *Red Convertible: Collected and New Stories* (2009).

Erdrich and Dorris met at Dartmouth College in 1972 where she, as an undergraduate student, took his class in anthropology. They got married in 1981 after years of correspondence, manuscript exchanges, and friendship. To alleviate financial hardship, they began producing romantic stories under the pen name Milou North. They published a travel memoir titled *Route 2* (1981) and *The Crown of Columbus* (1991) under a joint byline. The novel tells a story of two Dartmouth College professors, Vivian Twostar and Roger Williams, who embark on a quest for new and revelatory information about Christopher Columbus. The novel was substantially criticized for its treatment of the problematic consequences of Columbus's arrival.

Her writing tinkers with theories of the novel. Her novels focus on multiple individuals, rather than on one single protagonist. She writes a series of novels which grows intertextually and intratextually, but not sequentially because the order of events in newly published works is oftentimes irreverent of Western chronology. She gives an idiosyncratic shape to this least formulaic of genres. Let me begin not with her first novel published in the 1980s, but *in medias res* by referring to *The Last Report on the Miracles at Little No Horse* (2001) which tells a story of a person who juggles identities. First, as Sister Cecilia s/he leads a spiritual and spirited life in a convent and enjoys playing Chopin on the piano, but due to her unorthodox pleasure derived from it and the impact it has on any audience listening, s/he is let go. As Agnes DeWitt, s/he enjoys a life of small, lay pleasures. Assuming the identity of a drowned priest, that of Father Damien, s/he commences a lifetime of religious practice, combining what is best about Catholicism and Ojibwe belief systems into a service of empathy, wisdom, and love. The effortless switching between genders and religions in her/his case can be linked to the fluidity of the novel, a genre which is capable of accommodating much, both in form and in content.

Unorthodox chronology is a trademark of Erdrich's fiction. The reader is asked to connect the events him/herself. Some chapters in *The Last Report* are dated 1996, some 1910, 1912, 1919, or 1922, some narrate spans, such as 1910–1912 or 1913–1919. Little temporal security is offered, and the reader has to be alert to realize what year it is, and to figure out what is happening in the novel. The reader is invited to engage in interaction by recalling what happened during a particular time in similar circumstances to other protagonists in other novels by Erdrich, or how different protagonists perceived and how they narrated those situations. Not only do the events in Erdrich's novels defy linear temporal order, the work, although series-like, is also not published in accordance with any recognizable order or logic.

Her novels are mosaic-like as they destabilize narrative authority by including multiple and alternating narrators: first-, second-, third-person singular, and second-person plural. The narrators sometimes complement each other's stories, sometimes contradict one another. Because there is much gossip, storytelling, and subjective narration in the novels, their reliability is debatable. *The Last Report* commences with a "Prologue," a third-person narrative delineating Father Damien's last days and the writing of the last report. It divulges a secret, namely the fact that Father Damien has a woman's body under the cassock. This revelation at the very outset of the novel prepares the reader to anticipate, follow, and appreciate the story unraveling.

The "compost pile" and "temporary storage" are metaphors Erdrich harnesses when discussing her writing. For a long time, she did not realize she was writing a series of related stories (Feyl Chavkin and Chavkin 1994). Asked whether she would term her writing "an organic whole," Erdrich replied: "It's more like a compost pile" (1994, p. 240). The implication of the "organic whole" is that it is pure and integral, perhaps complete, whereas the "compost pile" refers to a phenomenon that has an unfinished quality, is rotting and developing, and will never be complete, and it accommodates everything that the "organic whole" would fail to include. The books she publishes are temporary versions and they are subject to change if Erdrich chooses to rewrite them or to edit them according to her evolving artistic vision. She revised her first novel *Love Medicine* (1984) twice and published new editions in 1993 and 2009. She rewrote *The Antelope Wife* (1998) and published it in 2012. "There is no reason to think of publication as a final process. I think of it as a temporary storage" (Feyl Chavkin and Chavkin 1994, p. 232), Erdrich says. Her publications, compost pile-like, not only organically and unexpectedly evolve from smaller forms, as if Erdrich is testing-driving ideas, but, unlike those of many other authors, they are also parts of an oeuvre in constant gestation.

Erdrich's novelistic oeuvre encompasses: tetralogy consisting of *Love Medicine* (1984, 1994, 2009), *The Beet Queen* (1986), *Tracks* (1988), and *The Bingo Palace* (1994), which grew into "one long book" (Erdrich 2009, pp. 5–6) including *Love Medicine*, *Tracks*, *Four Souls* (2004), *The Bingo Palace*, *Tales of Burning Love* (1996), *The Painted Drum* (2005), and *The Last Report on the Miracles at Little No Horse* (2001); and other books which potentially form two thematic clusters: *The Beet Queen* and *The Master Butchers Singing Club* (2003); and *The Plague of Doves* (2008), *The Round House* (2012), and *LaRose* (2016).

The first cluster, "one long book," foregrounds Ojibwe protagonists mostly, in addition to several mixed-bloods and white protagonists. The second cluster encompasses *The Beet Queen* and *The Master Butchers Singing Club* prioritizing white immigrant characters and very few Ojibwe ones. *The Plague of Doves*, *The Round House*, and *LaRose*, tackling complex issues of tribal justice and portraying a mixture of protagonists, create the third cluster. *The Antelope Wife* (1998, 2012), *Shadow Tag* (2010), and *Future Home of the Living God* (2017) share neither protagonists nor episodes with the above-mentioned clusters, and perhaps other tabs for them should be invented, or perhaps one can let them dangle undefined in the literary universe, tabs or no tabs.

Asked whether she feels like she's writing one long novel, she responded: "All of the books will be connected somehow – by history and blood and by something I have no control over, which is the writing itself. The writing is going to connect where it wants to, and I will have to try and follow along" (Halliday 2010).

She writes a family of texts and "family" is simultaneously the main theme and the main group protagonist of her books, however complex the strands of family stories that spun the narratives created by Erdrich. To treat the works of tetralogy as separate entities would not give justice to that idiosyncrasy. Let me demonstrate this point by drawing evidence from all four works, mostly portraying Lipsha Morrissey. Sister Leopolda is Marie Lazarre Kashpaw's mother, Lulu Nanapush is Fleur Pillager' daughter. Nector Kashpaw is married to Marie and has a lifelong affair with Lulu. Lipsha is adopted by Marie, and he is Lulu's grandson. In a self-reflective, intratextual gesture the "we" narrator in *The Bingo Palace* observes:

> The story comes around, pushing at our brains, and soon we are trying to travel back to the beginning, trying to put families into order and make sense of things. But we start with one person, and soon another and another follows, and still another, until we are lost in the connections.
>
> (2001, p. 5)

Family configurations portrayed in her novels may vary and are rarely of traditional, biological design; take Lipsha and Lyman Lamartine for example, who are relations, rivals, and co-workers. Because they are family, there is a story: "our relationship is complicated by some factors over which we have no control. His real father was my stepfather. His mother is my grandmother. His half brother is my father. I have an instant crush upon his girl" (2001, p. 16). With a story and bloodlines this complicated, there are bound to be tragic and comic situations; the overall effect of her novels being tragicomedies. Already in *Love Medicine* Lipsha is the character with a troubled, fractured family history. He is abandoned by his mother June Kashpaw, does not know his father is Gerry Nanapush, is raised by Marie and Nector, and later adopted by his grandmother Lulu.

Lipsha has a half-brother, King, with whom he never gets along. His sense of self is pure confusion, and his loyalties and goals are in a state of disarray. Most of his life he is ignorant of his family ties and believes that his own mother "wanted to tie me in a potato sack and throw me in a slough" (2009, p. 226). To learn that he is a descendant of the Pillagers, which explains his healing touch, and that his father is alive, empowers him. Even though he is helpless in school, he is intelligent. He cannot be pigeonholed, he is unpredictable, he can be ingenious when no one expects it. He is ambivalent, he is human, prone to mistakes, a very likeable character. Lost and devoid of direction in his life, he possesses one skill: "I know the tricks of mind and body inside out without ever having trained for it, because I got the touch. It's a thing you got to be born with. I got secrets in my hands that nobody ever knew to ask" (1994, p. 227). He knows he has a talent, but he does not know where it comes from. The touch comes and goes, it works with his grandmother Marie, but it does not do anything for his grandfather Nector. Lulu takes care of his ignorance. She always knew he was "troubled. You never knew who you were. That's one reason why I told you. I thought it was a knowledge that could make or break you" (p. 303). The thematic fabric of Erdrich's novels concerns family dynamics, its entanglements, quirks, and miracles.

Secret and apparent bloodlines throb in the veins of Erdrich's novels. Seriality can also be attributed to her novels for young adults and children. To the time of writing, *The Game of Silence* (2005), *The Porcupine Year* (2008), *Chickadee* (2012), and *Makoons* (2016) have been written as sequels to *The Birchbark House* (1999), in addition to *Grandmother's Pigeon* (1996) and *The Range Eternal* (2002) for kindergarten children. Beidler observed that the protagonist of *The Birchbark House*, Omakayas, a girl who plays chess and exhibits healing talents, is reminiscent of "a younger Fleur Pillager in *Tracks* and even Lipsha in *Love Medicine*" (2000, p. 88). Another character from the story, Old Tallow, "has a familiar ring to her as another of Erdrich's strong-willed and independent women" (p. 88). One thinks, again, of Fleur, but also of Margaret Kashpaw in *Tracks*, of Marie and Lulu in *Love Medicine*, and of June in *Love Medicine* and *Tales of Burning Love*.

Erdrich has also published two autobiographical books problematizing the nexus between being a writer and being a mother and performing one despite the other: *The Blue Jay's Dance* (1995), a memoir of early motherhood, and *Books and Islands in Ojibwe Country* (2003), a travel diary-cum-memoir, which foregrounds late mothering and writing.

Her novelistic work garners praise and it is impossible to determine how much of that success can be attributed to Dorris's editing skills, and is further complicated by his suicidal death. A full version of the 2010 *Paris Salon* interview Lisa Halliday conducted with Louise Erdrich, parts of which were published in the 2012 revised version of *The Antelope Wife*, contains unsettling information about two writers sharing literally everything. It thematizes the perils of a home office, of spending so much time together, it becomes suffocating.

When Erdrich was a child, her father paid her a nickel for every story she wrote. *The Plague of Doves* was a finalist for the Pulitzer Prize in 2009. In November 2012, she won the National Book Award in Fiction for *The Round House*, a novel also named a finalist for the Pulitzer Prize. In August 2014, she was the winner of the Dayton Literary Peace Prize's distinguished achievement award which honors those who promote peace through literature. In September 2014, she received the very prestigious PEN/Saul Bellow Award for Achievement in American Fiction. In March 2015, she was awarded the Library of Congress Prize for American Fiction honoring her body of work, her imagination, and her depiction of the unique and variegated American experience. The prizes keep trickling in, as Erdrich continues to write and run her bookstore called Birchbark Books.

SEE ALSO: Alexie, Sherman; Hogan, Linda; Indigenous Narratives; Momaday, N. Scott; Multiculturalism; Power, Susan; Silko, Leslie Marmon; Vizenor, Susan

REFERENCES

Beidler, Peter G. (2000). A review of *The Birchbark House* by Louise Erdrich. *SAIL: Studies in American Indian Literatures* 12 (1): 85–88.

Erdrich, Louise. (1994). *Love Medicine*, rev. ed. London: Flamingo; 1st ed. 1984.

Erdrich, Louise. (2001). *The Bingo Palace*. New York: Harper Perennial; 1st ed. 1994.

Erdrich, Louise. (2009). *Love Medicine*, newly rev. ed. New York: Harper Perennial; 1st ed 1984.

Feyl Chavkin, Nancy and Chavkin, Allan. (1994). An interview with Louise Erdrich. In: *Conversations with Louise Erdrich and Michael Dorris* (ed. Allan Chavkin and Nancy Feyl Chavkin), 220–253. Jackson: University of Mississippi Press.

Grantham, Shelby. (1994). Intimate collaboration or "A Novel Partnership." In: *Conversations with Louise Erdrich and Michael Dorris* (ed. Allan Chavkin and Nancy Feyl Chavkin), 10–18. Jackson: University of Mississippi Press.

Halliday, Lisa. (2010). Louise Erdrich, the art of fiction no. 208. *The Paris Review*. https://www.theparisreview.org/interviews/6055/louise-erdrich-the-art-of-fiction-no-208-louise-erdrich (accessed July 1, 2021).

Madsen, Deborah L. (2011). Louise Erdrich: the aesthetics of Mino Bimaadiziwin. In: *Louise Erdrich* (ed. Deborah L. Madsen), 1–14. London: Continuum.

Wong, Hertha D. (1994). An interview with Louise Erdrich and Michael Dorris. In: *Conversations with Louise Erdrich and Michael Dorris* (ed. Allan Chavkin and Nancy Feyl Chavkin), 30–53. Jackson: University of Mississippi Press.

FURTHER READING

Chavkin, Allan R. (ed.) (1999). *The Chippewa Landscape of Louise Erdrich*. Tuscaloosa: University of Alabama Press.

Jacobs, Connie. (2001). *The Novels of Louise Erdrich*. New York: Peter Lang.

Sarris, Greg, Jacobs, Connie, and Giles, James. (2004). *Approaches to Teaching the Works of Louise Erdrich*. New York: The Modern Language Association of America.

Stirrup, David. (2010). *Louise Erdrich*. Oxford: Manchester University Press.

Stookey, Lorena L. (1999). *Louise Erdrich*. Westport, CT: Greenwood Press.

Erickson, Steve

HIKARU FUJII
University of Tokyo, Japan

Steve Erickson (b. 1950) is a rare "American" writer today in every sense of the word. He has been obstinately faithful to the task of interrogating what "America" is – a country built on the power of desire, where dream and reality interact and conflict with each other. In his work, real and imagined landscapes, events, and figures come together in an ever-shifting landscape in which the writer explores the nature of desire, art, and "America."

Erickson's literary predecessors include Henry Miller, William Faulkner, Philip K. Dick, and crime fiction writers, among others, whose traces are found in settings, themes, characters, and styles in the writer's work. Equally important is the influence of films and music, which has informed, and often determined, his narrative framework.

Beginning his literary career in the mid-1980s, Erickson belongs to the generation of writers who combine postmodernist narrative styles and sociopolitical perspectives on "America" or what it means to be American. He shares this tendency with such writers of his generation as Stephen Wright, Paul Auster, Denis Johnson, and Richard Powers, whose novels began to attract attention around the same period. Yet Erickson's hallucinatory obsession with "America" and postmodern narrative experiments make him a writer unlike any other.

Days Between Stations (1985), Erickson's first novel, begins in the United States in the latter half of the twentieth century and moves to France in the early years of filmmaking. These two settings eventually develop into futuristic and apocalyptic landscapes where characters wander in and out of each other's lives. This ambitious work contains several seminal motifs that the writer would explore in the course of his decades-long literary career.

The mother, Lauren, grows up in Kansas and moves to the West Coast. She loses her infant son, Jules, to a sudden death, which opens a passage to a different plane of reality that the mother enters. This sense of loss, especially in a mother–son relationship, is taken up in his later works, *The Sea Came in at Midnight* (1999) and *Our Ecstatic Days* (2005).

Erickson's first novel also introduces the crucial importance of cinema to his work. Michel Sarre, who wakes up the moment of the death of Lauren's son and finds himself a man without memory, is a typical Ericksonian character in his attempt to reconstruct or replace his lost memory with films. In Erickson, films – and faces that appear in them – are described as an important component of memory, or often as memory itself, which becomes crucial in Erickson's later novel, *Zeroville* (2007).

The motif of the double, or dual nature of reality, determines the narrative structure of *Days Between Stations*. Beginning with Jules and Michel, several characters and settings appear as doubles of each other. This dual nature of existence inevitably undermines the sense of identity in Erickson's later characters, such as Cale and Lake in *Rubicon Beach* (1986), who sense that they are repeating the experience of somebody else who precedes them. The divided world or parallel universes, as a result, often mark Erickson's narrative.

The relationship between making art and desire is another recurring motif in Erickson's writing. Adolphe Sarre, Michel's grandfather, begins to direct his film, *La Mort de Marat*, with Janine, the love of his life, a relationship that delays the completion of the work. In Erickson, filmmakers, writers, and other creators are never free from sexual desire that often begins with the act of seeing, by which the male gaze is fixated on the face of a woman, causing the men to try to possess the sexual other. This insight is to be extended in Erickson's later works to include well-known figures who "invented" or "wrote" historical reality: Adolf Hitler in *Tours of the Black Clock* (1989) and Thomas Jefferson in *Arc d'X* (1993).

The French town of Wyndeaux, where Adolphe does most of the shooting for *Marat*, is described as a space outside history. Erickson's later characters also run across ahistorical places, such as Aeonopolis in *Arc d'X*, where the men make art and ponder on the relation or nonrelation between their art and historical reality. In this sense, Los Angeles has always occupied a privileged place in Erickson's oeuvre in that it is often described as the place of "the perpetual present" where history holds no significance.

Los Angeles is also known for providing a background for a number of disaster narratives in literature, film, and other media. In *Days Between Stations*, Los Angeles is in the middle of a perpetual sandstorm that threatens to bury the streets, which is the first of a series of catastrophic descriptions of the city in Erickson's later novels, including rings of fire in *Amnesiascope* (1996).

Whereas the debut novel does not fully examine the idea of "America," which would prove to be the writer's biggest obsession, *Rubicon Beach*, his second novel, is a daring literary crossing into the nature of "America" as a transhistorical field where power and resistance to it are inseparable. In a highly hallucinatory landscape in Los Angeles, the three-part novel explores the fundamental workings of "America" in the tug-of-war between the power apparatus that aims to seize the characters and their efforts to escape from it. Throughout the novel, the power apparatus employs such clear-cut divisions as "America One" or "America Two," as one of the police officers mentions, while the characters, often associated with "flow" and other watery images, occupy an intermediate zone of "America" where various borders become blurred.

The three-part novel repeatedly depicts male characters who are gradually drawn to a girl, which leads them to "the point of no return" beyond the reach of power. Cale, recently released from prison and under police surveillance, discovers the girl with a knife who terrorizes Los Angeles. The girl, renamed Catherine after she arrives in the United States from South America, also becomes the object of desire of Llewellyn Edgar, a screenwriter in the second part. Lake, who appears in the final part of *Rubicon Beach*, tries to identify "The Number" that exists between nine and ten, and finally meets Catherine. These men are incited by their own desire to move out of the reality they live in and, at the same time, possess the girl and deprive her of her freedom. This fundamental conflict – between the desire to possess and to be free – provides the definition of "America" for Erickson.

The second novel adds a crucial aspect to the writer's literary quest: voices and characters that transcend a given spatiotemporal framework. Although each of the three parts of *Rubicon Beach* is set in a separate location, the girl moves beyond their confines, followed by other characters who pursue her. This trait is taken over in *Leap Year* (1989), the writer's first book of nonfiction that follows the 1988 presidential campaign, in which the voice of Sally Hemings, the slave-lover of Thomas Jefferson, keeps haunting the late-twentieth-century American landscape. After the second novel, certain characters and motifs that appear in one Erickson narrative reappear in others, constructing an echo chamber of narratives.

Tours of the Black Clock approaches the question of "What is America?" through the alternative history of the twentieth century, in which Nazi Germany is the winning side of World War II. Evidently inspired by Philip K. Dick's *The Man in the High Castle* (1962), the novel describes the other side of "the American century" and examines the nature of desire, history, and the act of writing itself through the journey of Banning Jainlight, an American writer who was born in Pennsylvania in 1917 and moved to New York, and eventually to Vienna, where he bears witness to the unfolding of World War II.

In the novel, the men's desire to (re)make reality or history always accompanies their act of writing. Banning's pornographic novels are translated into German to circulate inside the Nazi higher-ups and eventually reach "Client Z," namely Adolf Hitler, who suffers from his unfulfilled desire for his niece, Geli Raubal. The American writer of pornography and the German "writer" of history are doubles of each other, both attempting to invent reality according to their desire.

Erickson's insight into the nature of desire, which is essentially intertwined with power, finds another expression in *Arc d'X*. The 1993 novel revolves around the sexual relationship between Thomas Jefferson and Sally Hemings, which was to be confirmed in the DNA tests conducted several years after the novel's publication. The novel, praised by Thomas Pynchon for being "as daring, crazy, and passionate as any American writing since the Declaration of Independence," is a full-blown attempt to apply Erickson's idea of "America" – torn between freedom and desire – to the historical figure of Jefferson, whose passion for Sally puts him in a dilemma because his desire to "possess" the slave girl contradicts the idea of the nation he "invents" or writes.

This realistic narrative follows Sally's journey from Virginia to Paris, where she encounters the revolution of 1789 and Thomas's passion, but is then replaced by a fantasy in which Sally finds herself in an imaginary city of Aeonopolis, which exists outside history, and where a Central Church controls the whole society. Following the thread of the phrase "the pursuit of happiness," which serves as the founding principle of America, the narrative introduces other writer-characters, including Etcher, who, just as Banning Jainlight does in *Black Clock*, tries to revise the history of Thomas and Sally, as well as "Steve Erickson," who is killed in Berlin. The characters, motifs, and passages of the previous three novels are brought together to explore the American ideas of possession and freedom; in this sense, *Arc d'X* is a consummation of Erickson's early career.

The following two novels, *Amnesiascope* (1996) and *The Sea Came in at Midnight*, are written in more "personal" tones within apocalyptic settings. The former, set in the collapsing city of Los Angeles after "the

Quake" and riots, now surrounded by rings of fire, concerns a middle-aged writer who narrates his own life producing a narrative peppered with Erickson's autobiography, and with a touch of slapstick humor. In the 1999 novel, on the other hand, an American girl named Kristin Blumenthal escapes from a mass suicide at the end of the millennium in California and finds herself in Tokyo. She works as a "memory girl" and begins to tell her own memory in the country where the Emperor announced that he was not God and time moves in a circular fashion. These two works, after the tour de force of *Arc d'X*, testify to the writer's attempts to renew his literary possibilities by exploring alternative approaches.

This attempted renewal saw its fruition in the 2005 novel, *Our Ecstatic Days*. The novel, opening with Kristin with her son, revisits Los Angeles where the sudden appearance of a lake, presumably an effect of the 9/11 terrorist attacks in New York City in 2001, causes half of the city to submerge underwater. Fearing that the expanding lake will try to take her son from her, Kristin sails to the middle of the lake to stop it, only to realize that her son has disappeared. Five years later, it occurs to Kristin that she has lived on "the other side" of the lake, and she plunges into the water to go back to her past life – thus reenacting the writer's signature theme of parallel universes. After this act, the narrative is visually divided into two parts. The protagonist's journey through the water is narrated in a single sentence that traverses the text, cutting through more than two hundred pages that tell a separate story, describing the events of the twenty-first century, with characters mirroring Kristin's loss of her son.

While *Tours of the Black Clock* examines the nature of the twentieth century, *Our Ecstatic Days* defines the twentieth and twenty-first centuries as "the Age of Reckoning" and "the Age of Chaos," respectively. Kristin, going through the loss and recovery of her son in the latter age, metaphorically expresses the collective experience of the War on Terror: the new age begins with the terrorist attacks in New York to see its development on the other side of the continent in Los Angeles, as the initial state of "fear" turns into "rapture." The 2005 novel achieves an integration of its motifs and narrative form, as well as Ericksonian preoccupations with "America" and history.

The 2005 novel was followed two years later by *Zeroville*, an extensive investigation into the nature of film, with Ike "Vikar" Jerome as a protagonist who comes to Los Angeles in 1969 with a tattoo of Elizabeth Taylor and Montgomery Clift from *A Place in the Sun* on his shaven head. Composed of short chapters, reminiscent of "short cuts" in a film, and narrated from a camera-like perspective, *Zeroville* follows Vikar's journey in the industry and offers a panoramic view of Hollywood and American culture in the years after the 1960s counterculture.

These Dreams of You (2012) is the writer's rare attempt at realistic narrative, in which an American novelist, Alexander "Zan" Nordhoc, is facing financial and familial crises: having lost his teaching job at college, Zan is also about to lose his family's home in the United States, while he loses track of his wife and his recently adopted daughter from Ethiopia. Post-crisis economic situations and Obama-era discourse on ethnic diversity modify the typical Ericksonian view of "America" through this realistic narrative style.

The writer returns to his visionary style with *Shadowbahn*, published in 2017. The fall of the Twin Towers in 2001 is given another twist in the novel, in which the towers reappear intact in South Dakota, and Elvis Presley's twin brother wakes up to find himself inside one of these unoccupied high-rise buildings. With numerous references to American music that dictates the narrative, the writer's tenth novel explores the soul of America with his vision of the fractured nation without Elvis. Borrowing the style of American road narrative with the main characters, Parker and Zema, trying to reach the doubles of the towers, *Shadowbahn* shows the "songscape" (Maazel 2017) of America that runs parallel with or counter to its historical reality.

Aside from his ten novels and two books of nonfiction, Erickson is a prolific film critic, writing mostly for *Los Angeles Magazine* since 2001, while serving as the editor of a literary magazine, *Black Clock* (2004–2016), that published the work of a wide range of writers from Aimee Bender to Don DeLillo and David Foster Wallace.

Erickson's oeuvre, despite its growing significance, is yet to attract critical attention. Although the writer started his career in the mid-1980s, it was not until the 1990s that scholars began to publish essays on his work; initially received as a sci-fi writer, many aspects of Erickson's fiction remain to be explored by mainstream criticism. Accordingly, his reputation is higher overseas, such as in Japan, where leading critics have constantly discussed his work.

SEE ALSO: Auster, Paul; DeLillo, Don; Fiction and Terrorism; Johnson, Denis; Post-9/11 Narratives; Powers, Richard; Pynchon, Thomas; Wallace, David Foster

REFERENCE

Maazel, Fiona. (2017). In this novel, the Twin Towers reappear in the Badlands. *The New York Times* (February 10, 2017). https://www.nytimes.com/2017/02/10/books/review/shadowbahn-steve-erickson.html (accessed August 4, 2021).

FURTHER READING

Acker, Kathy. (1989). I was Hitler's pornographer. *The New York Times* (March 5, 1989). https://www.nytimes.com/1989/03/05/books/in-was-hitler-s-pornographer.html

Luter, Matthew and Miley, Mike. (eds.) (2021). *Conversations with Steve Erickson*. Jackson: University Press of Mississippi.

Eugenides, Jeffrey

DEBRA SHOSTAK
College of Wooster, USA

Jeffrey Eugenides earned critical approval and wide readership with his first novel, *The Virgin Suicides* (1993), later released in a film adaptation directed by Sofia Coppola (1999). He has published two other novels, *Middlesex* (2002), which won the Pulitzer Prize, and *The Marriage Plot* (2011), as well as a short story collection, *Fresh Complaint* (2017). Eugenides has not developed a singular recognizable voice. Rather, he experiments in each book with distinctive stylistic and structural modes of expression, supporting his continual effort "to learn how to write new books"; the focus of his craft has developed from novel to novel, "from sentence, to plot, to character" (Gibbons 2011, p. 144). Typically ironic, comic, or satiric in tone, his fiction has likewise shifted among representational modes. The poetic mythmaking of *The Virgin Suicides* gives way to the comic epic of *Middlesex*, which juxtaposes an occasionally magical realist family history with the psychologically astute, scientifically researched realist narrative of his intersex protagonist. *The Marriage Plot* moves fully into psychological and social realism. Eugenides's literary influences range widely, from James and Flaubert to the modernists – Joyce, Proust, Faulkner, Woolf, Musil – and such postmodernists as Pynchon and Barth, with stops at Bellow and Nabokov for stylistic models. His fictional settings are circumscribed, however, within places he knows well. Both *Virgin Suicides* and *Middlesex* are set in the postindustrial Detroit suburbs, where Eugenides was born in 1960 and spent his youth as son of a first-generation Greek American father and a mother of Irish descent. Berlin, where Eugenides spent several years, is the adult Cal's home in *Middlesex*; Brown University, his undergraduate institution, and India, where he volunteered for Mother Teresa, situate *Marriage Plot*.

Although Eugenides keenly depicts such social conditions as economic rise and decline, class, and immigration, he is especially drawn to the aesthetics and themes deriving from the discursive representation of desire. He imagines young people grappling with the heteronormative constraints shaping selfhood, sex, and romance in late-twentieth-century America. Each novel deploys unique formal strategies to represent a youthful character's pursuit of an "obscure object of desire," as *Middlesex* names its central problem, alluding to Luis Buñuel's 1977 film (Eugenides 2002, p. 325). How each character reads or misreads others as objects reciprocally frames how the subject names and understands the self. As Eugenides explores the struggle toward identity, self-knowledge, agency, and the fulfillment of desire in relation to linguistic, literary, and social conventions, each novel also allegorizes the process of reading, since the reader's alignment with conventions drives the reception of these narratives of desire and selfhood.

Eugenides's preoccupations appear early in his career, as in "Capricious Gardens" (1988), reprinted in *Fresh Complaint*, which anticipates his innovative approach to point of view. The story circulates among four perspectives rendered in close third-person narration, as two young women and two middle-aged men misconstrue each other's feelings in a round-robin of erotic and spiritual desires; no character notices the others beyond his or her own self-projections. Eugenides's early experiment establishes the power of narrative point of view to reveal how subjects, blinded by desire, fulfill themselves by inventing rather than seeing their objects.

Eugenides exploits the perspectival device shrewdly in his first novel, *The Virgin Suicides*. The novel depicts the traumatizing suppression of adolescent female sexuality in 1970s American suburban culture, figured in the five teenage Lisbon sisters; following one's suicide, the remaining four become prisoners in their own home until they, too, escape into suicide. Critics have explored the novel in relation to Eugenides's portrait of the postwar American suburb (Dines 2012; Wilhite 2015), the construction of adolescence (McLennan 2010), and the influence of García Márquez's magical realism (Collado-Rodríguez 2005). The novel's immediacy lies in the lyrical, mythologizing prose style enabled by its perspective: the collective narrative voice of neighborhood boys who obsessively surveil the sisters, their "obscure objects," and decades later piece together the story of the girls who still haunt them. The narrators mediate knowledge of the sisters within an "impossible voice" (Foer 2002, p. 78), a narrating "we." The voice dislodges the girls from center stage, displacing their reality with the boys' inchoate adolescent desires. Filtered through fragmentary memories, contradictory eyewitness testimony, and scrutiny of mute objects such as photographs and random possessions taken as if legal "exhibits" (Eugenides 1993, p. 5), the sisters are stripped of agency and individuality as the narrators read them – and their deaths – as erotically transcendent objects of contemplation.

Such regressive transmutation appears throughout the collective narrators' discourse. For example, in the opening pages they juxtapose the suicide of the last Lisbon daughter with the first, telescoping time to frame past events within a present quest infused with their voyeuristic sensibility. The retrospective "we" distances the girls' suffering, aestheticizing the traumatic scene into a comically rhapsodic, ritualized tableau: "the two slaves [paramedics] offering the victim to the altar [the ambulance], the priestess [Mrs. Lisbon] brandishing the torch . . . and the drugged virgin rising up on her elbows, with an otherworldly smile" (1993, p. 6). Eugenides's concentration on sentence-level style offers fetishistic images in the heightened diction of the boys' solipsistic, mythmaking desires. They report "sightings" (p. 100) of the girls as if they are exotic creatures who had "gone down to the underworld" (p. 66), they engage in a "strange curatorship" (p. 186), projecting the girls' personalities from their possessions, and they turn the most sexually desperate of the sisters into a masturbatory "succubus," the "pale wraith we make love to" (p. 147). The narrators rarely register the sisters' individuality and normality – that, as one sister insists, "'We just want to live. If anyone would let us'" (p. 132) – willfully misreading them to reap pleasure from mystification.

The figures of sense perception, looking and listening, expose the narrators' objectifying desires – and in turn the novel's allegory of reading. Like readers, the narrators insert themselves into the sisters' story. But when the boys stare into the darkened Lisbon house, the "glass panes . . . reflect our own gaping faces" (1993, p. 58) – materializing their narcissistic self-projections. The novel's climax, at the scene of the sisters' simultaneous suicides, shames them. Believing they are summoned as heroes to aid the sisters' escape, they discover that they are meant, by witnessing the deaths, to face their failure to see the girls – "They had brought us here to find that out" (p. 215) – a recognition the narrative previously suppresses.

Despite readers' trained suspicions regarding a narrator's reliability and the voice's logically impossible unified perceptions, then, the communal authority of the consistently interpreting "we" voice is seductive. For Georges Poulet, the reader's "interior universe constituted by language does not seem radically opposed to the *me* who thinks it.. . . I am the subject of thoughts other than my own" (Poulet 1980, pp. 43–44). If, therefore, readers inhabit the point of view as normative, we may participate in rewriting the girls' subjectivity and silencing their voices. Eugenides's formal device thus introduces an ethical and epistemological problem for the reader: (how) do we foreclose or censure the boys' desires and the implicitly misogynist subject position those desires place us within? Eugenides aids critique only in his overwrought, phantasmagorical, figurative discourse. When nostalgic encomium erases the sisters to the point of self-parody, Eugenides challenges readers to resist immersion into the blinkered subject positions the frame narrators never left behind.

The question of identification and distance between reader and narrator similarly animates the exploration of desire in *Middlesex*. Eugenides presents *Middlesex*'s comic epic as the story of a gene, contextualizing the real conditions of the narrator's intersex identity within a fabulist account of Cal's Greek grandparents' incest and immigration to the United States. Although the singular narrating "I" appears conventional, Eugenides complicates the voice by destabilizing its gendering: "I was born twice: first as a baby girl, . . . again, as a teenage boy" (Eugenides 2002, p. 3). Whereas Eugenides structures the romance of *The Virgin Suicides* recursively, circulating between past events and present reconstructions, *Middlesex* reflexively imitates a history in its chronological, genetic trajectory. Cal's "record of my impossible life" (p. 302) highlights two events: his birth as Calliope, his unrecognized intersexed body resulting from his grandparents' incestuous union; and Cal's figurative rebirth into a heterosexual male identity. Plot design takes precedence as Eugenides manipulates the wayward gene to fruition within the body of his narrator across generations and geography. His hybrid form metafictionally enhances the bodily hybridity of intersexuality: "The idea was to have the book recapitulate the DNA of the Novel. Therefore, [*Middlesex*] begins with epic events and becomes, in its second half, more modern, psychological, and realist" (Gibbons 2011, p. 139).

Scholars often view *Middlesex* in relation to the politics evoked by Eugenides's title and protagonist: through the lens of biopolitics (Hsu 2011), the novel's final endorsement of heteronormativity and ethnic assimilation (Lee 2010), or its suggestion of a new category of queer heterosexuality (Sifuentes 2006). Since the narrator's intersex condition is *Middlesex*'s most conspicuous feature, Pennacchio's (2020) exploration of the narrator's omniscience begins a fruitful merging of formal and political readings. In attempting to craft a realistic voice from a non-normative viewpoint – to discover, Eugenides explains, "a voice that opens up a channel to impersonal, but specific, knowledge" (Gibbons 2011, p. 133), he adds the materiality of embodiment to the convention of narrative voice, represented most directly by how the narrator names the self. At the narrative's pivot point, the narrator chooses to call himself Cal, claiming a male subjectivity based on his predominating biology rather than on the constructedness of his nurture. But by casting Cal's male identity as the novel's retrospective narrative context, Eugenides also installs a heteronormative interpretive frame for events by privileging an unambiguously heterosexual male voice.

Middlesex shifts the problem of knowing from the outside observer in *Virgin Suicides* to interiority, as Cal contrives a story of selfhood from his confusing adolescent bodily alienation and his forebears' untold stories. Desire is consistently the disruptive influence: the desire of Cal's grandparent siblings, Lefty and Desdemona, for each other; and the teenage Calliope's uncategorizable desire for her female friend, the "Obscure Object." Desire founders invariably upon the enigma of sameness versus otherness: in each generation, the desire for the other is inextricable from the desire for self, the different equivalent to the identical. The elder Stephanides's incest collapses heterosexual desire into undifferentiated family bonds. More complexly, Cal inhabits antithetical conditions within a single, singular body. The novel's primary obscure object is Calliope/Cal, desiring to pry a readable subjecthood from scrutinizing the self as object.

Eugenides's narrating voice captures an ontological conundrum. Often reflexive, the voice also roams between first person and third, especially after the narrative shifts from Cal's family histories to his own. The pronouns render a psychological transfer between Cal as external object and internal agent – from the self under the gaze to the self commanding the gaze. The most significant example appears in the scene of Calliope's "*Ekstasis*," her "state of displacement" (Eugenides 2002, p. 374), when she and the Obscure Object make out with two teenage boys. The "I" of Calliope "slips into" the boy kissing the Obscure Object so that "my hands" seem vicariously to remove her bra. "[B]reaking out of the confines of his ego" (Gibbons 2011, p. 138), Eugenides notes, triggers Cal's discovery of non-normative sexuality and the "*right*" feeling (Eugenides 2002, p. 375), defining his desire for a female as heterosexual rather than lesbian.

The pronominal slippage in subjecthood figures the challenge for the reader inherent in the narrator's non-normative identity. Cal's choice of heteronormative self-definition, resolving into I = he, suggests that the conventional economy of desire resists a middle or conjoint subject position between "he" and "she," ultimately reinstating the binary logic the novel overtly opposes. Because readers, however unconsciously, may read a voice through its assigned gender, we likewise face uncertainty over occupying a voice whose gender is shifting, indeterminate, or hybrid. Eugenides's both/and proposition of Cal/Calliope challenges readers phenomenologically: to contest the "natural" condition of our vicarious subject positions, to question whether we unreflectively read objects from the standpoint of gender conventions built into a narrative voice, and at once to consider alternative possibilities and confront the discourse's ineptitude in inscribing them.

Following Cal's vexed subjecthood, *The Marriage Plot* reverts to the problem of *seeing* the other apparent in *Virgin Suicides*'s narrator-voyeurs. Eugenides's third novel features characters developed with Jamesian psychological realism, spurring the misreadings of others that sustain a marriage plot's triangulated romances. Opening with the sentence "To start with, look at all the books" (2011, p. 3) and launching the plot with "Madeleine's love troubles had begun at a time when the French theory she was reading deconstructed the very notion of love" (p. 19), Eugenides chooses reading as the novel's guiding trope: in its college-age protagonists' literal activity, in its titular engagement with a literary form, and in its dense intertextuality. *Marriage Plot*'s allusions run from canonical British Victorian novelists through James and the Modernists, to postmodernists like Calvino and the French poststructuralists. Specifically, Barthes's *Lover's Discourse*, questioning the knowability of the other (Barthes 1978, pp. 134–135) and whether the avowal "I love you" (p. 147) has meaning, spurs Madeleine's idealizing desires.

As with *Middlesex*, scholarship on the novel integrates productively – here, under the figure of reading. Huehls sees Eugenides using the marriage plot "to stage a three-way conversation among Enlightenment humanism (Madeleine), poststructural epistemology (Leonard), and religious belief (Mitchell)" (Huehls 2015, pp. 280–281), concluding that Eugenides appropriates theory into a realism untested within the novel's form. For Boswell (2016), Eugenides metafictionally parodies the Victorian marriage plot but overtly rivals David Foster Wallace in order to challenge poststructuralist interpretive strategies. Głąb (2016) argues that the characters see each other as texts to be read. Each approach centers on the marriage plot, whose exemplars require an Enlightenment epistemology allowing that, howsoever one begins in error, one may come to know and wed the proper other. How desire deforms perception of the other during attraction and courtship thus becomes central to Eugenides's critique of and reinvestment in the form. Unlike his first-person voices in the prior novels, close third-person narration in *Marriage Plot*, enhanced by free indirect discourse, enables ironic distance on characters' misreadings of themselves and their objects.

Eugenides's protagonists are "pilgrims" seeking their obscure objects (2011, p. 129). A devoted reader of the canon, Madeleine fixes her romantic, Bovary-like mediated desires on Leonard's brilliance and energy, unacknowledged reflections of his manic depression. Just as she seeks in her senior thesis to deconstruct "Barthes's deconstruction of love" (p. 87), she willfully ignores the signs of his illness. Leonard's obscure object is himself; despite grasping poststructuralist theory, he believes he can wrest a coherent self from his disease by force of will. Mitchell's object parallels the others' self-deceptions: rejected by Madeleine, he displaces his desire into spirituality, seeking self-abnegation by serving Mother Teresa in India only to confront how the abject body thwarts transcendence.

The protagonists' misreadings eventuate in closure that resists the conventional marriage plot. Educated by the nineteenth-century novel, a reader's pleasure seeks the "right" union to conclude the rivalry – Madeleine finally accepting Mitchell as her fit companion. The novel swerves near such fulfillment. Yet Eugenides casts their closing mutual decision to remain alone within reflexive terms of rewriting the marriage plot, their "book" ending in independence. Eugenides again, without resolution, allegorizes the ambiguities of a reader's desire. The final word of the novel suggests a satisfying affirmative: "'Yes'" (2011, p. 406). Have we, however, been manipulated to rue how a neoliberal commitment to independence, which requires we renounce the marriage plot, dupes the characters? Has Eugenides slyly reinstated the power of the form, with its dependence on Enlightenment reason and realism? Or is this revision of the plot just another self-delusion? Is *Marriage Plot* an elegy for what it names?

Still at mid-career, Eugenides has not yet produced an oeuvre extensive enough to invite clear categorization among his contemporaries. He remains, however, a "realist at heart" (Gibbons 2011, p. 142) who probes realism's premises and a fabricator of uniquely memorable detail, possessing the imaginative and stylistic range to turn each novel into a virtual essay on human desire and literary form.

SEE ALSO: Barth, John; Pynchon, Thomas; Queer and LGBT Fiction; Realism after Poststructuralism; Suburban Narratives; Wallace, David Foster

REFERENCES

Barthes, Roland. (1978). *A Lover's Discourse: Fragment* (trans. R. Howard). New York: Hill and Wang.

Boswell, Marshall. (2016). The rival lover: David Foster Wallace and the anxiety of influence in Jeffrey Eugenides's *The Marriage Plot*. *Modern Fiction Studies* 62 (3): 499–518.

Collado-Rodríguez, Francisco. (2005). Back to myth and ethical compromise: García Márquez's traces on Jeffrey Eugenides's *The Virgin Suicides*. *Atlantis* 27 (2): 27–40.

Dines, Martin. (2012). Suburban gothic and the ethnic uncanny in Jeffrey Eugenides's *The Virgin Suicides*. *Journal of American Studies* 46 (4): 959–975.

Eugenides, Jeffrey. (1993). *The Virgin Suicides*. New York: Warner Books.

Eugenides, Jeffrey. (2002). *Middlesex*. New York: Farrar, Straus and Giroux.

Eugenides, Jeffrey. (2011). *The Marriage Plot*. New York: Farrar, Straus and Giroux.

Eugenides, Jeffrey. (2017). *Fresh Complaint*. New York: Farrar, Straus and Giroux.

Foer, Jonathan S. (2002). Eugenides. *Bomb* 81: 75–80.

Gibbons, James. (2011). The art of fiction no. 215: Jeffrey Eugenides. *The Paris Review* 199: 118–148.

Głąb, Anna. (2016). The other as text: the ethics of love in Jeffrey Eugenides's *The Marriage Plot*. *REN* 68 (4): 266–282.

Hsu, Stephanie. (2011). Ethnicity and the biopolitics of intersex in Jeffrey Eugenides's *Middlesex*. *MELUS* 36 (3): 87–110.

Huehls, Mitchum. (2015). The post-theory theory novel. *Contemporary Literature* 56 (2): 280–310.

Lee, Merton. (2010). Why Jeffrey Eugenides' *Middlesex* is so inoffensive. *Critique* 51: 32–46.

McLennan, Rachael. (2010). Chasing after the wind: the adolescent aporias of Jeffrey Eugenides. In: *Writing America into the Twenty-First Century: Essays on the American Novel* (ed. Elizabeth Boyle and Anne-Marie Evans), 22–38. Newcastle upon Tyne: Cambridge Scholars.

Pennacchio, Filippo. (2020). Enhanced "I"s: omniscience and third-person features in contemporary first-person narrative fiction. *Narrative* 28 (1): 21–42.

Poulet, Georges. (1980). Criticism and the experience of interiority. In: *Reader-Response Criticism: From Formalism to Post-Structuralism* (ed. Jane P. Tompkins), 41–49. Baltimore: Johns Hopkins University Press.

Sifuentes, Zachary. (2006). Strange anatomy, strange sexuality: the queer body in Jeffrey Eugenides' *Middlesex*. In: *Straight Writ Queer: Non-Normative Expressions of Heterosexuality in Literature* (ed. Richard Fantina), 145–157. Jefferson, NC: McFarland.

Wilhite, Keith. (2015). Face the house: suburban domesticity and nation as home in *The Virgin Suicides*. *Modern Fiction Studies* 61 (1): 1–23.

FURTHER READING

Codr, Ariana R. (2019). After ever after: *The Marriage Plot*'s farewell to its reader. *New Literary History* 50: 197–218.

Margolin, Uri. (2000). Telling in the plural: from grammar to ideology. *Poetics Today* 21 (3): 591–618.

Everett, Percival

KEITH B. MITCHELL
University of Massachusetts Lowell, USA

In a distinguished writing career spanning over four decades, Percival Everett has published twenty novels, four collections of short stories, five volumes of conceptual poetry, and an illustrated children's book, as well as numerous journal essays, short stories, and poems. Yet despite his championed and prodigious literary output, Everett's work has only recently begun to attract a much wider readership and the scholarly attention it rightly deserves. Those devoted readers and scholars who *have* read Everett's work recognize him as one of the most important American writers of the latter half of the twentieth century. In 1956, Everett was born into a military family in Fort Gordon, Georgia. Shortly thereafter, his family moved to Columbia, South Carolina, where he attended primary and high school. In 1973, at age 16, he matriculated to the University of Florida (UFL), where in 1978 he received an undergraduate degree in philosophy. Over the next two decades, Everett went on to postgraduate studies (two years at the University of Oregon as a philosophy major, which he abandoned, and on to Brown University where he received an MA in creative writing in 1982) while also exploring numerous vocations. He worked as a carpenter, a high school teacher, a jazz musician, and a ranch hand, among other vocations, experiences that would later provide fodder for his writing career. After graduating from Brown, Everett crisscrossed the United States, teaching, writing, and working at various academic institutions before finally settling at the University of California in 1998, where in 2007 he was named Distinguished Professor.

Everett began his writing career in 1982 when his first novel, *Suder*, was published to generally favorable reviews. *Suder* is a comic novel that chronicles the existential journey of Craig Suder, an African American third baseman for the Seattle Mariners. Weighed down by injuries and a career slump, Suder embarks upon a wild, carnivalesque quest for self-discovery across the Northwest. *Washington Post* critic Jabari Asim notes that "although *Suder* is about a Black character, rarely does his race influence the outcome of his adventures" (1999). Thus far, critics have compared Everett's work to writers such as Ishmael Reed, John Coover, Clarence Major, David Foster Wallace, John Edgar Wideman, Charles Johnson, and John Gaddis – writers whose work Everett greatly admires. Nevertheless, as an artist (who happens to be African American), Everett's literary voice and his approach to fiction writing are quite distinct. Indeed, *Suder* exemplifies Everett's unique aesthetic vision and a number of thematic concerns one finds in subsequent fiction: his strategic deployment of satire and parody; his debunking essentialist assumptions about race; his mirthful interrogation of literary and cultural theory; his linguistic playfulness; his interest in the ontology of meaning; and finally, his conscious effort to undermine others' categorization of him as a (Black) writer.

To this end, Everett does not wed himself to one genre. To date, he has written postmodern Westerns (*God's Country* [1994], *The Body of Martin Aguilera* [2003], and *Wounded* [2005]), metanarrative detective fiction (*Assumption* [2011]), revisions of Greek mythology (*For Her Dark Skin* [1990] and

Frenzy [1997]), comic spy novels (*Glyph* [1999]), speculative fiction (*Zulus* [1990]), modern-day captivity narratives (*The Water Cure* [2007]), and environmental fiction (*Watershed* [1996] and *Grand Canyon, Inc.* [2001]). Everett's corpus defies categorization. In numerous interviews Everett has made it clear he prefers taking the less-traveled position in contemporary American letters: he believes that being an "outsider" and maintaining a fair amount of anonymity has granted him more freedom to shape his literary career as he pleases. For this reason, Everett has almost exclusively published with smaller, independent presses such as Graywolf, Akashic, and Red Hen: "Graywolf pretty much lets me do what I want to do," he has said, "knowing that I'm not going to make a whole lot of money. I never think about the marketing. I just want to make my art; that's what makes me happy" (Bolonik 2005, p. 97).

Since the publication of *Suder*, Everett's readership and critical acclaim have skyrocketed. In 2006, he received the PEN Center USA Award for Fiction. He is a two-times winner of the Hurston/Wright Legacy Award: for *Erasure* in 2002, and *I Am Not Sidney Poitier* in 2010. In 2016, he was one of the recipients of the prestigious Creative Capital Award. And in 2019, he was named one of three distinguished Hurston/Wright Legacy Award jurists.

Everett was born just before the furious flowering of both the modern Civil Rights movement and the more decidedly militant Black Arts Movement of the 1960s and 1970s, which was heralded by such luminous writer–activists as Amiri Baraka, Sonia Sanchez, Larry Neal, and Nikki Giovanni. He began writing in the early 1980s, a time when younger, Black artists were attempting to aesthetically and politically distinguish themselves from their predecessors. Rather than foregrounding essentialist notions of "authentic" Blackness and cultural nationalism, younger post-Civil Rights/post-Black Arts creatives of the 1980s and 1990s were particularly interested in complicating notions of race and cultural belonging. A few years after Everett's publication of *Suder*, African American writer Trey Ellis published his groundbreaking manifesto "The New Black Aesthetic," which signaled a radical paradigmatic shift of the terrain and aims of post-Civil Rights African American fiction and art. In his essay, Ellis draws clear demarcation between Black "cultural mulattos" (1989, p. 235) of his generation and the older generation of African American postwar and post-Black Arts Movement creatives. Ellis states: "Just as a genetic mulatto is a black person of mixed parents who can often get along fine with his white grandparents, a cultural mulatto, educated by a multi-racial mix of cultures, can also navigate easily in the white world" (p. 235). For Ellis, multiculturalism of the 1980s and 1990s marked a significant change in how many African Americans viewed themselves, and Black art needed to reflect these transformations. Ellis was not alone in his thinking. In "Post Black, Old Black," American philosopher Paul C. Taylor avers: "Where soul culture insisted on the seriousness of authenticity and positive images, post-soul culture revels in the contingency and diversity of blackness and subjects the canon of positive [black] images to subversion and parody – and appropriation" (2007, p. 631).

As Taylor rightly describes them, Everett and these younger Black writers are post-soul satirists – not post-racial. This contingency of post-soul, African American writers acknowledges that situating (Black) identity and representation in the contemporary era has become more complex, and that literary and other Black artistic productions should reflect these complexities, particularly through the deployment of grotesque humor, satire, and parody. As Everett has put it: "All of my novels are subversive and militant, but none is social protest" (Mills and Tissut 2007, p. 223). Everett's fiction is far more politically nuanced than the social protest fiction of many Black artists of his and the previous generation. Although less strident about multiculturalism and the New Black Aesthetic (NBA) than Ellis, nonetheless, Everett (along with his contemporaries, Clarence Major, Ishmael Reed, Charles Johnson, and John Edgar Wideman) must be regarded as an important literary precursor to younger, post-soul, Black writers such as Ellis, Fran Ross, Paul Beatty, Mat Johnson, and Colson Whitehead.

Like any great artist, Everett has his literary relatives and ancestors. Ralph Ellison has stated: "While one can do nothing about choosing one's relatives, one can, as an artist, choose one's 'ancestors'" (1964, p. 185). Thus, one *must* situate Everett in the African American literary tradition, and one cannot disregard Ralph Ellison and author Chester Himes as influential antecedents. However, to locate Everett's work solely *within* an African American literary tradition would unduly limit its scope and complexity. In Ellis's formulation, Everett is a "cultural mulatto" (1989, p. 235). Using Ellis's own terminology, Everett might more accurately figure as a "cultural maroon" (one who mines global literary traditions). Everett raids the Western literary canon as demonstrated by his prodigious references to classical Greek literature, the Bible, and Western writers: Chaucer, Dante, Shakespeare, Swift, Fielding, Stern, Carroll, Melville, W.H. Hudson, Zane Grey, and Joyce, to name a few.

In addition, Everett has held a lifelong interest in philosophy and literary critical theory, particularly of the French tradition. Much of his work is informed by Western thinkers as diverse as Socrates, Plato, Descartes, Frege, Wittgenstein, Russell, Derrida, Foucault, Kristeva, and Barthes, whose theories inform several of Everett's books. For example, Everett's novel *Percival Everett by Virgil Russell* (2013) is a metafictional meditation on death and art that challenges reader assumptions about our understanding of literary concepts such as "author," "character," and "plot." In this form-bending novel, "Percival Everett" appears as the son and guardian of an irascible father experiencing a slow, humiliating demise in a nursing home. But exactly who narrates the novel is nigh-impossible to discern. Thus, Barthes's provocative edict proclaiming the "Death of the Author," in which anything author-related should have no bearing on reader interpretation, frames the narrative. As the elusive narrator explains, "I am an old man or his son writing an old man writing his son writing an old man" (Everett 2013, p. 63).

Virgil Russel's byzantine structure and its narrative unreliability instantiates why some readers find Everett's work particularly difficult. Everett explains: "There's a rudimentary mistake that writers who want to be so called experimental make. Every time someone starts writing a novel that is not a genre, which is not formulaic, it's an experiment necessarily. You're creating it, [because] you're [sic] don't know what you're doing" (Bauer 2013).

Language and representation are also at the heart of Everett's 2007 novel *The Water Cure*, a scathing critique of the Bush Administration's "War on Terror," state violence, and American vigilantism. Everett effectively deploys both language games and "text fragments, and illustrations" that interrogate "the failures of language and meaning . . . morality and law" (*Publishers Weekly* 2007). The novel's disorienting, linguistic "delirium" undercuts the reader's reliance on a stable narrator and a more conventional plot development. In the story, Ishmael Kidder, a grief-stricken romance writer working under the pseudonym Estelle Gilliam kidnaps and brutally tortures a child sex offender he is convinced (with no real evidence) has murdered his young daughter. During his lengthy basement incarceration and interrogation of his prisoner, Kidder's thoughts and behavior become increasingly erratic and violent as he reformulates Protagorean logics about truth, judgment, experience, and interpretation as subjective. Kidder concludes: *knowlege^2 + certainty^2 = squat^2* (Everett 2007, p. 96), which he believes is a satisfactory sanction to terrorize and brutalize his captive. The novel's third-person omniscient narrator states, "Revenge is a sweet but messy, imprecise but sating weapon. But it's okay, Ishmael Kidder thinks, his problems live at home, his problems live in his basement, his country tears of thee, sweet land of the killing tree, but all of that is forgotten, look away, look away, all of that is behind us, him in that hazy blur of American HISTORY (p. 105).

Although Everett is an artist who refuses to be genre-bound, there is one literary genre, the Western, which has consistently fueled his imagination. To date, he has written seven novels and dozens of short stories set in the American West: *Walk Me to the Distance* (1985), *God's Country*, *Watershed*, *Grand Canyon, Inc.*, *The Body of Martin Aguilera*, *American Desert* (2004), *Wounded*, *The Water Cure*, and *Assumption*. Although all are situated in the American West, the novels are markedly different in tone, narrative structure, and plot from a typical Western, and Everett himself would not classify them as such. For example, *Walk Me to the Distance* explores issues surrounding American violence and communal vigilantism, while *Watershed* focuses on environmental racism and the continued destruction of Native American culture. *God's Country* and *Grand Canyon, Inc.* are raucous send-ups of America's obsession with taming the West, and *Assumption* is a serpentine, dark thriller in which an African American deputy sheriff working in the quiet community of Plata, New Mexico, investigates a series of gruesome murders that challenge readers' assumptions about the nature of good and evil.

Two of Everett's mid-career novels, *For Her Dark Skin* and *Frenzy*, revise classical Greek drama and mythology as source material in an exploration of violence and Otherness. That being said, Everett wrote these two novels as much out of his profound admiration of Euripides's *Medea* and *The Bacchae* as his desire to impede expectations and assumptions about him as a Black American author: "Finding *For Her Dark Skin* and *Frenzy* in a section marked 'African American Studies,'" Everett laments, "seems wrong-headed and runs counter to my work ... Besides the fact that it's culturally offensive" (Mills *et al.* 2007, p. 80).

Everett illuminates his post-soul aesthetic in his refusal to create Black characters who fit prescriptive notions of the so-called Black experience. His Black characters are ranchers, romance novelists, sheriffs, hydrologists, baseball players, child-savants, visual artists, cowboys, post-apocalyptic rebels, university professors, and of course, experimental fiction writers. As Everett has stated, "I don't know whether I think of artists as having an expansive vision, and that's what makes us interested in what they create. I mean, a painter is not trying to paint the whole world ... I'm trying to write an individual story about an individual person, about an individual life ..." (Stewart 2007, p. 3).

An accomplished abstract expressionist painter himself, it is no coincidence that Everett's work is replete with references to visual art and artists. And as an avant-garde painter, unorthodox modes of expressions and representations are central to his aesthetic vision. About his relationship to art, Everett has said: "The first time I saw an actual Pollock, I cried ... wondering what I was seeing, wondering how it was made, wondering why I was crying" (Mitchell and Vander 2014, p. 77). *Erasure*, an intertextual tour de force, illustrates this point. Its protagonist, Thelonious "Monk" Ellison, is a post-structuralist writer whose novels mainstream publishers refuse to publish because they believe they're "not black enough" to appeal to the general reading public. Interspersed within the primary plot, Everett places fragments of conversation, metanarratives, among myriad twentieth-century, avant-garde artists such as Rothko, Pollock, Rauschenberg, de Kooning, and Motherwell. That Everett has "no interest in the primal immediacy of painting" (Mitchell and Vander 2014, p. 78) is important to understanding how he also views himself as a literary artist; meaning, he "use[s] painting as counterpoint to [his] relationship with novels" (Everett 2014, p. 78).

Indeed, in his narratives *all* forms of art are in constant dialogue. For example, in *So Much Blue*, a 2017 novel that explores different representations of fidelity – marital, friendship, familial, and artistic – Kevin Pace is a successful abstract visual artist burdened with a number of dark secrets from his past, including a brief but passionate extramarital affair with a young Parisian watercolorist. Upon first viewing her work, Kevin is bored and unimpressed by his lover's figurative paintings, which he thinks are simply "ordinary" (2017, p. 37); but when she later shows him an abstract, she calls *Verdant*, his love for her intensifies. For Everett, experimental fiction, like art, is far more satisfying because, he says, "preachy books don't deliver" (Birnbaum 2003, p. 77). Engaging with Everett's fiction forces readers to wrestle with unconventional narrative forms and modes of reading. He pushes his audience to artistically and intellectually question their assumptions about the art of storytelling. As such, readers are as vital to the creative process as the author. He has asserted, "As a fiction writer, I just want to illuminate the fact that there is something to discuss. I'm not a superhero. I'm just a writer" (Shavers 2013, p. 69) – one who clearly respects his audience's curiosity and intelligence.

SEE ALSO: Beatty, Paul; Johnson, Mat; Major, Clarence; The New Experimentalism/The Contemporary Avant-Garde; Post-Soul and/or Post-Black Fiction; Reed, Ishmael

REFERENCES

Asim, Jabari. (1999). Suder. *The Washington Post* (November 7, 1999). http://www.washingtonpost.com/wp-srv/style/books/asimonsuder.htm (accessed July 1, 2021).

Bauer, Sylvie. (2013). Percival Everett: an abecedary. *Transatlantica*. https://journals.openedition.org/transatlantica/6369 (accessed July 1, 2021).

Birnbaum, Robert. (2003). Percival Everett. In: *Conversations with Percival Everett* (ed. Joe Weixlmann), 35–50. Jackson: University Press of Mississippi.

Bolonik, Kera. (2005). Mules, men, and Barthes: Percival Everett talks with *Bookforum*. In: *Conversations with Percival Everett* (ed. Joe Weixlmann), 93–99. Jackson: University Press of Mississippi.

Ellis, Trey. (1989). The new Black aesthetic. *Callaloo* 38: 233–243.

Ellison, Ralph. (1964). The world in the jug. In: *The Collected Essays of Ralph Ellison* (ed. John F. Callahan), 185. New York: Random House.

Everett, Percival. (1999). *Glyph*. Saint Paul, MN: Graywolf Press.

Everett, Percival. (2007). *The Water Cure*. Saint Paul, MN: Graywolf Press.

Everett, Percival. (2013). *Percival Everett by Virgil Russell*. Saint Paul, MN: Graywolf Press.

Everett, Percival. (2014). Artist statement. In: *Percival Everett: Writing Other/wise* (ed. Keith B. Mitchell and Robin G. Vander), 77–78. New Orleans: Xavier Review Press.

Everett, Percival. (2017). *So Much Blue*. Saint Paul, MN: Graywolf Press.

Mills, Alice, Julien, Claude, and Tissut, Anne-Laure. (2007). An interview: 3 May 2005. In: *Reading Percival Everett: European Perspectives* (ed. Claude Julien and Anne-Laure Tissut),

217–227. Tours: Presses Universitaires François Rabelais. Repr. in (2013) *Conversations with Percival Everett* (ed. Joe Weixlmann), 78–89. Jackson: University Press of Mississippi.

Mitchell, Keith B. and Vander, Robin G. (eds.) (2014). *Percival Everett: Writing Other/Wise*. New Orleans: Xavier Review Press.

Publishers Weekly (2007). *The Water Cure*: a book review (August 8, 2007). https://www.publishersweekly.com/978-1-55597-476-3 (accessed July 1, 2021).

Shavers, Rone. (2013). Percival Everett. In: *Conversations with Percival Everett* (ed. Joe Weixlmann), pp. 57–70. Jackson: University Press of Mississippi.

Stewart, Anthony. (2007). Unrecognizable is still a category: an interview with Percival Everett. *Canadian Review of American Studies* 37 (3): 293–324.

Taylor, Paul C. (2007). Post Black, old Black. *African American Review* 41 (4): 625–640.

FURTHER READING

Maus, Derek C. (2019). *Jesting in Earnest: Percival Everett and Menippean Satire*. Columbia: University of South Carolina Press.

Mitchell, Keith B. and Vander, Robin G. (eds.) (2013). *Perspectives on Percival Everett*. Jackson: University Press of Mississippi.

Mitchell, Keith B. and Vander, Robin G. (eds.) (2014). *Percival Everett: Writing Other/Wise*. New Orleans: Xavier Review Press.

Federman, Raymond

SARA KIPPUR
Trinity College, USA

Raymond Federman (1928–2009) was a prolific writer of experimental fiction in both English and French, whose works often revolved around his traumatic youth. Born in the southern outskirts of Paris into a lower-class Jewish family of Eastern European origin, Federman watched through a closet – in which his mother had hid him – as his parents and two younger sisters were seized by the French police in the July 1942 raids known as the *Vél d'Hiv* round-ups. All four other members of his family were deported to Auschwitz, where they died, while the adolescent Raymond escaped to the free zone in the south and worked on a farm until the end of the war. A relative in Detroit learned of his survival and helped him immigrate to the United States in 1947. After his deployment in the Korean War, Federman returned to the United States to pursue a formal American education, earning an undergraduate degree from Columbia in 1957 and a doctorate in comparative literature from UCLA in 1963. While in California, he met and married Erica Hübscher, whose family had escaped Vienna in 1938, and together the couple had one child, Simone, named after her paternal grandfather. Raymond Federman's career straddled academia and trade publishing and took him from coast to coast; after teaching at University of California–Santa Barbara during his graduate studies, Federman became a professor of literature and creative writing at SUNY Buffalo from 1964 to 1999, and ultimately retired to San Diego, where he lived the last decade of his life. Throughout his professional career, Federman remained committed to a postmodernist literary project that drew comparisons to contemporaries like John Barth, Donald Barthelme, Robert Coover, and Ronald Sukenick, and that frequently, if not always, made reference to his troubled past.

Federman's earliest writings were a mix of academic studies, forays into poetry, and prose narratives. His first published work, *Journey to Chaos* (1965), was an extension of his doctoral dissertation on the early fiction of Samuel Beckett. Beckett was a fixture in Federman's life and works: the two were personal friends – they had met in Paris during Federman's graduate studies – as well as fellow bilingual writers and avant-garde stylists whose fiction blended human suffering and a deep commitment to humor. Federman would later recognize his lifetime debt to Beckett in his memoiristic publication *The*

Sam Book (2008): "it's Sam's shadow that guided me in those first writings, and that guides me still" (2008, p. 62). Throughout the 1970s, Federman continued to publish academic criticism on Beckett, while also making a name for himself in the world of literary experimentalism. With novels like *Double or Nothing* (1971), *Amer Eldorado* (1974), and *Take It or Leave It* (1979), Federman developed a recognizable fictional style that explored personal narrative through typographical innovation. Each page of *Double or Nothing*, for instance, has a visually distinct layout, in the style of concrete poetry, where the storyline is reflected through the page's spatial construction. Ostensibly about a man who decides to lock himself in a room for 365 days to write a book, the novel is concerned less with the character's book project than with the materials he will need to survive – noodles, toilet paper, cigarettes, and other supplies. The man's confinement in a room, the claustrophobia, his obsession with survival: these are the subjects to which *Double or Nothing* returns in haunting echoes of Federman's primal trauma.

As his fictional project developed after 1980, Federman wrote repeatedly about his adolescent years in France in even more explicit detail. No longer just circling around the primal trauma, his works sought to tell the story – albeit elliptically, with a honed practice of narrative digression – of his experiences hiding in the closet, trying to locate his seized family in Paris, and escaping on a train to the free zone in France. Just before the turn of the decade, Federman published a short bilingual text, *The Voice in the Closet / La voix dans le cabinet de débarras* (1979), which tells the story of his youth twice, once in English and once in French, depending on the side of the book the reader opens first. The book anticipated Federman's multiple memoirs, published from the 1980s to the early twenty-first century, devoted to telling and retelling the story of his time in wartime France. From *The Twofold Vibration* (1982) to *Return to Manure* (2006) to his last published text, *Shhh: The Story of a Childhood* (2010), Federman refashions the story of exiting the closet and escaping to the south of France.

Indeed, as these texts progress through time, we not only learn an increasing number of details about the boy's escape and survival, but we can track Federman's shifts in narrative perspective. *The Twofold Vibration* constructs an elaborate narrative in which several characters seek to uncover the story of a boy who managed to escape deportation. In this version, the 12-year-old boy leaves the closet where he is hidden and makes his way to the train station, where officers are checking for Jews. When their inspection confirms that the boy is circumcised, the officers load him on a train with other children. Silently observing the other children, and eating raw potatoes he finds on board, the boy suddenly jumps off the train, and we learn very few other details about what becomes of him in the south. More than twenty years later, *Return to Manure* picks up narratively where *The Twofold Vibration* leaves off. Aboard a freight train leaving from Paris's Gare Montparnasse, the boy decides to jump when he recognizes a sign outside with the name of the region, "Lot-et-Garonne," where he believes his uncle lives. *Shhh* is even more precise in its details of this moment. It chronicles his journey chronologically, from Federman's arrival at Montparnasse (July 18, 7:30 a.m.); to sneaking on a train that leaves Paris at 11:15 p.m.; to his decision on July 21 at precisely 6 a.m. to jump from the train when he sees the sign for Lot-et-Garonne. *Return to Manure* and *Shhh* recount different aspects of Federman's survival – in the first, how he lives on a farm through the end of the war, and in the second, how he later returns to Paris – yet in re-narrating the same event of the train, Federman demonstrates concretely to his readers how his narrative voice alters through time. The time markers in *Shh* are likely imprecise, and purposely so, but they reveal Federman's willingness to approach his past from increasingly close range: more and more, as his writing progresses, he abandons a distant third-person past and embraces a first-person present narration to tell the story of his youth.

We see this tendency towards first-person storytelling in many other Federman works of the 1990s and 2000s, even ones that do not specifically detail his escape from the closet. *Aunt Rachel's Fur*, published first in French in 1996, and then in English translation in 2001, reads as a declaration of anger against Federman's wealthier extended family for not having saved his nuclear one. "I know why you left us behind, you were ashamed of us, of our poverty, you wanted us to be erased from the family, you didn't expect me to come back, did you," Federman writes, in a vitriolic indictment both on his wealthy aunt and uncle, and on his native homeland, France, that allowed his family and other Jews to be deported (2001, pp. 194–195). Similarly autobiographical, but employing other media, in *My Body in Nine Parts* (2005), Federman includes close-up photographs, all taken by his stepson, Steve Murez, of his body – his toes, his nose, his broken molar – with personal commentaries on each part. The book is distinctly Federmanesque in its self-referentiality and sense of humor. The section on his hair, for example, confronts his hair loss and attempts to pinpoint exactly when it started, when he should expect to become completely bald, and how much hair he has actually lost. The first-person narrator determines that he first noticed his hair thinning thirty-five years ago to the day, that he loses on average four hairs each time he showers, and since he showers once per day, 365 times a year, with an additional shower on leap years, he has likely lost 72,100 strands of hair to date. The humor of the exercise, and its obvious implausibility, reflect Federman's belief that autobiography can never be entirely truthful. He theorized this as "surfiction" in his essay collection *Critifiction* (1993) – the idea that literature does not imitate reality, but rather "exposes the fictionality of reality" (1993, p. 37). As a reinforcement to his fictional *oeuvre*, Federman's critical essays reflected his refusal of the realist literary project and his use of personal narrative as a means to undercutting a clear notion of truth.

The boundary between fiction and reality is one Federman explicitly engages in many of his post-1980 novels. "We're not talking about a fairy tale here," Federman writes in *To Whom It May Concern* (1990), "we're talking about a story which in the process of being told might become the absolute truth" (1990, p. 19). Such is the lesson of this book, in which a writer's letters to his friend about a novel he hopes to write become the novel itself. This lesson – namely, that a certain notion of truth could emanate from the task of fictional storytelling itself – gets reframed, in various ways, across Federman's works of the same period. *Smiles on Washington Square* (1985), for another example, relies heavily on narration in the future and conditional tenses to play with a reader's sense of the real. The novel narrates the ostensible encounter between Moinous and Sucette in Washington Square, and imagines how their meeting will lead to a possible future. We learn that Sucette is enrolled in a creative writing course, for which she is drafting the story of a character Susan, who meets Moinous, a plot point mirrored in her lived reality. This classic *mise en abyme* structure to the text demonstrates the influence of modern novels like André Gide's *Les faux monnayeurs* (1925) on Federman's prose style. With Federman's postmodern pen, it is unclear which layer of the diegesis – Sucette's composed narrative, or her apparent lived reality – produces the other. For Federman, this confusion is critical to the project of fiction writing. At the same time, the love story between Moinous and Sucette in the novel seems to function allegorically as the relationship between France and America: his difficulties relating to her symbolize his difficult adjustment to the social and political norms of the United States.

This linguistic and cultural transition in Federman's life was not just fodder for fiction; it also helps to frame our understanding of his publishing record across languages. For most of his literary career, Federman wrote primarily in English, while also succeeding in capturing the attention of an international audience. In America, he published with smaller, avant-garde presses – such as Swallow, Fiction Collective 2, and Thunder's Mouth – yet his novels, translated into more than a dozen languages, reached readers of German, Japanese, Chinese, Polish, Romanian, Serbian, Greek, and other tongues. Before the early years of the twenty-first century, Federman had written only three books in French: *Amer Eldorado* (1974), half of the bilingual text *The Voice in the Cabinet* (1979), and *Aunt Rachel's Fur* [*La Fourrure de ma tante Rachel*]. It was not, however, until the dawn of the twenty-first century that Federman was rediscovered in his native language, and that, like his model Beckett, he started to self-translate all his works between French and English. In France, the literary critic Pascale Casanova dedicated five episodes of her popular French radio show on *France Culture* to Federman's work. She had learned of Federman through a fellow writer and critic Nathalie Quintane, who in 2001 had put Federman in touch with one of France's small publishing houses, Al Dante. Intrigued by Federman's writing, Al Dante decided to publish the ensemble of Federman's literary oeuvre. Different translators were hired to work in a short timeframe on rendering his English-language texts into French, including, *Double or Nothing*, *Smiles on Washington Square*, and *To Whom It May Concern*. But it was Federman himself who chose to take on the bulk of the translations, from English to French, and vice versa. Once he had secured a publishing base in France, he wrote a handful of new texts, all of which he diligently self-translated between his two languages: *Loose Shoes* (2001) / *Coups de Pompes* (2007), the facing-page bilingual poetry collection *Future Concentration* (2003), his photograph-based autobiography *Mon corps en neuf parties* (2004) / *My Body in Nine Parts*, *Retour au fumier* (2005) / *Return to Manure*, and, finally, *Chut* (2008) / *Shhh*. The fact of having publishers in both languages gave Federman a concrete opportunity to return to Beckett as a literary model, yet also, quite unlike Beckett, to insistently inscribe his personal life story into his self-translation project.

In an American context, Federman has been the subject of dozens of book chapters, academic articles, and graduate dissertations. Scholarship has tended to read his work for its contribution to Holocaust literature and memory studies; for its metafictional reflections on postmodern writing; for its participation in a broader field of multilingual poetics; and for its intersections with and divergences from Beckett's fictions. Geoffrey Hartman (1995), for instance, read Federman's work as a constructive antidote to totalizing narratives of collective memory; for Hartman, Federman's poetics of absence, fragmentation, plurality, and amnesia, like that of other postwar postmodern writers, demonstrated how art and literature could intervene against monolithic historical narratives and generate a diverse collective memory. In *Crises of Memory* (2006), Susan R. Suleiman situated Federman among writers of what she labels the "1.5 generation," child survivors of the Holocaust who were too young to understand the implications of Nazism, but old enough to have lived through it. Her analysis demonstrates how the rhetorical figure of "preterition" – the act of saying precisely by proclaiming *not* to say – undergirds Federman's writing and helps us to read and understand literature about trauma and loss. Shortly after Federman's death, Jeffrey R.

Di Leo published an edited volume devoted to rereading Federman's contribution to literary studies, with essays by several scholars who had devoted much of their academic career to studying Federman's work. The essays collected in that volume, *Federman's Fictions* (2011), not only situate Federman's role as a Holocaust writer, but also argue for his lasting contribution to ideas of fiction and narrative theory more broadly.

Federman can be read and remembered today for the enormous exuberance he brought to the writing process. We see traces of that energy in the sheer number of books he produced – dozens over the course of his lifetime; in the elaborate names he invented for the literary versions of himself – "Moinous," "Namredef," "Hombre de la pluma," among many others; and also, in the paraliterary activities that document his commitment to writing beyond the bounds of book publication. Federman wrote and published responses to reviews of his books in leading venues, such as a letter to the editor at *The New York Times* following a review of his novel *Smiles on Washington Square*. In this and other reviews of reviews, Federman demonstrated his dual role as author and literary critic, continually writing about books, even those that he had written. Invested in an endless process of writing, Federman actively maintained several websites, including his blog, "Federman's blog [the laugh that laughs at the laugh]," with hilarious anecdotes and personal reflections, information about his books and performances, and links to reviews. That blog, still accessible today, ten years after Federman's death, keeps his presence alive and is perhaps the best entry point for readers who have yet to discover the joys of Federman's vibrant literary voice.

NOTE

This entry makes use of material from my book (Kippur 2015).

SEE ALSO: The New Experimentalism/The Contemporary Avant-Garde; Trauma and Fiction

REFERENCES

Di Leo, Jeffrey R. (ed.) (2011). *Federman's Fictions: Innovation, Theory, and the Holocaust*. Albany: State University of New York Press.

Federman, Raymond. (1990). *To Whom It May Concern*. Boulder: FC2.

Federman, Raymond. (2001). *Aunt Rachel's Fur*. Evanston: Northwestern University Press.

Federman, Raymond. (2008). *The Sam Book*. Ullapool, UK: Two Ravens Press.

Hartman, Geoffrey H. (1995). Public memory and its discontents. In: *The Uses of Literary History* (ed. Marshall Brown), 73–91. Durham: Duke University Press.

Kippur, Sara. (2015). *Writing It Twice: Self-Translation and the Making of a World Literature in French*. Evanston: Northwestern University Press.

Suleiman, Susan R. (2006). *Crises of Memory and the Second World War*. Cambridge: Harvard University Press.

FURTHER READING

Gerdes, Eckhard. (ed.) (2002). *The Laugh that Laughs at the Laugh: Writing from and about the Pen Man, Raymond Federman*. San José: Writers Club Press.

Klinkowitz, Jerome. (1998). *Keeping Literary Company: Working with Writers since the Sixties*. Albany: State University of New York Press.

Kutnik, Jerzy. (1986). *The Novel as Performance: The Fiction of Ronald Sukenick and Raymond Federman*. Carbondale: Southern Illinois University Press.

McCaffery, Larry, Hartl, Thomas, and Rice, Doug. (eds.) (1998). *Federman A to X-X-X-X: A Recyclopedic Narrative*. San Diego: San Diego State University Press.

Waters, Alyson. (2001). An interview with Raymond Federman: Pour commencer, parlons d'autre chose. *SITES: The Journal of Twentieth Century Contemporary French Studies* 5 (2): 242–248.

Feinberg, Leslie

ANSON KOCH-REIN
University of North Carolina School of the Arts, USA

Identifying as an anti-racist white, working-class, secular Jewish, transgender, lesbian, female, revolutionary communist, Leslie Feinberg wrote fiction and nonfiction and organized in the service of these identities, commitments, and affiliations. Born in Kansas City, zie grew up in Buffalo, moved to New York City in the 1970s – locations appearing in hir two novels – and later lived in Jersey City and, toward the end of hir life, in Syracuse. Starting in hir teenage years, zie worked a range of low-wage jobs for most of hir life. Feinberg joined the Workers World Party in hir early twenties, becoming a managing editor for the party newspaper in 1995. Zie died in 2014 in Syracuse after many years of illness from tick-borne Lyme and co-infections, survived by hir spouse of twenty-two years, fellow activist and writer Minnie Bruce Pratt. Feinberg's best-selling novel, *Stone Butch Blues* (1993), received much recognition as a groundbreaking work of transgender and lesbian literature and won the American Library Association's Stonewall Book Award and a Lambda Literary Award in 1994. In 2009, Feinberg received a Lambda Literary Visionary Award for hir life's work.

Feinberg's first two publications were pamphlets of about twenty pages each: the little-known *Journal of a Transsexual* (1980) and the more widely distributed and cited *Transgender Liberation: A Movement Whose Time Has Come* (1992). The shift in language between the two titles from "transsexual" to "transgender" and from "journal" to "movement" resonates with the broader move from medical language and binary models of gender relating to individual identity (i.e. the diary form) to the emergence of transgender as an umbrella term for a wide range of gender diversity and to the increasing formation of a transgender movement. Acutely aware of these cultural changes, the author and activist noted the quickly evolving nature of trans terminology and its use in and across diverse communities. Feinberg, who did not live to see the English-language consensus on they/them (Merriam-Webster's word of the year 2019) as the most widely used gender-neutral or nonbinary third-person singular pronoun fully emerge, used both zie/hir and she/her pronouns, depending on context, and insisted that hir preference was for making hir transgender expression and identity visible and that respectful intention was most important in pronoun use. The final edition of *Stone Butch Blues* includes an author's note on pronouns that expresses equal concern for "we" as the one perhaps most generative to hir body of work: At the center of hir political concerns, after all, were questions of solidarity, community building, and collective liberation.

Stone Butch Blues presents protagonist Jess Goldberg's coming of age, coming out into a series of communities and relationships, and coming to political consciousness. In the letter that opens the novel, the erotic dynamics, and the relationship and geography of touch between butch Jess and femme Theresa are described largely in terms of Theresa's loving attention to clothes. On the one hand, clothes make Jess the target of violence, on the other hand, the clothes s/he is (in)vested in are also a source of power, of finding and forming community, of expressing desire and being desired. Feeling stronger in specific clothes, often described in sartorial detail, is a recurrent theme even in the novel's scenes of violence. The detailed descriptions of what clothes look and feel like, what they mean (to the wearer and those around), how they are used and what is done to/with them show their importance as bearers of meaning and signifiers of identity.

After introducing major themes in the prologue, the novel tells Jess Goldberg's story beginning with a history of childhood unbelonging, dysphoria, and violence. From school to home life, Jess is confronted with hostile questions – "Is that a boy or a girl?"– and the violent (including sexually violent) enforcement of gender and sexuality norms. Jess faces punishment and rejection from hir parents, who send hir to conversion therapy and charm school. S/he breaks away from these parents and the novel focuses on hir finding and fighting for community, mentors, and lovers in bars and among co-workers, union organizers, and neighbors. Those personal and political connections happen in the face of oppression, economic precarity, bar raids, and police violence. For the diverse range of butch characters in *Stone Butch Blues*, masculinity is claimed and affirmed as authentic against normative gender expectations. Having to perform femininity is presented as painful and humiliating, such as at a butch elder's funeral where, to be allowed at the ceremony, hir friends have to succumb to the family's demands of sexual and gender conformity and wear dresses. The novel chronicles social change and changes in the community from butch/femme bar life to conflicts over gender in lesbian feminism, from Jess's going on hormones and passing for male during the Reagan administration to hir yearning for – and ending on – a more nonbinary, openly transgender identification and vision of the future. Jess encounters different social realities in the lives of marginalized co-workers, friends, mentors, and lovers and develops a political understanding of the world through these relationships, but also through a string of books, including ones by Mother Jones and W.E.B. Du Bois, that s/he is given – often with poignant inscriptions – by other characters over the course of the novel. Moving fluidly between the elements of a *Bildungsroman*, a romance novel, and moments of didactic social realism, the novel pays close attention both to the phenomenology of queer experience and to the formation of political consciousness. As such, *Stone Butch Blues* received much critical attention for its representation of gender nonconformity, coming out, lesbian community, female masculinity, and the emergence of transgender politics. The book is often compared to and read alongside Radclyffe Hall's *The Well of Loneliness* (1928), a novel from a much earlier moment in history, that similarly caught the attention of readers in its time and has received much attention in literary and gender studies for its interconnection of lesbian and transgender themes, histories, and interpretations.

Despite its popularity and critical acclaim, *Stone Butch Blues*' troubled publication history reflects changes in feminist, queer, and progressive publishing as much as it does the different popular, academic, and community audiences – in the United States and around the world – of this widely read, taught, and translated novel. *Stone Butch Blues* was originally published alongside other key feminist and lesbian books with Firebrand in 1993; Feinberg recovered the rights from the publisher's chapter 11 bankruptcy in 2002. The popular book came back into print for a 10th anniversary edition in 2003 with Alyson Books until that renowned LGBT press, too, went out of business, putting the novel out of print once again. During the late stages of illness, Feinberg worked with hir partner Minnie Bruce Pratt on a twentieth anniversary ebook edition to be accessible for free download and at-cost print on demand, which was released posthumously. In this final edition, Feinberg asserts both hir intellectual property and control over the material by explicitly asserting author's rights – no permissions except for specified, limited exceptions for translations, no derivatives, no digital use – and releases the work from concerns over profit into the hands of readers and communities regardless of financial means.

Following the success of *Stone Butch Blues*, Feinberg published two nonfiction books related to hir work as a speaker. The first, *Transgender Warriors: Making History from Joan of Arc to Dennis Rodman* (1996), draws on the *Transgender Liberation* pamphlet and on a slide show presentation of trans historical figures the author developed for speaking tours in the early 1990s. *Transgender Warriors* introduces readers to a mix of broad social history with heroic portraits of historical figures and examples of cross-dressing, tracing signs of transgender presence and survival from antiquity to the 1990s. The goal is not an exhaustive trans history, but "a fresh look at sex and gender in history and the interrelationships of class, nationality, race, and sexuality" (2006a, p. xi). This project based on research motivated by the need to find hirself in history resonates with – and frequently draws on – the recovery and revisionary work of women's and sexual minority historians. As such, *Transgender Warriors*, written for a popular audience, is in many ways of the same moment as the work of academic trans historians, such as Susan Stryker, that started to appear around the same time. In particular, Feinberg's historical perspective looks to a Marxist explanation of trans oppression as related to class oppression and sees the possibility of trans liberation as tied to "an economic system that meets the needs of every working person" (p. 128). Feinberg's second book-length nonfiction work, *Trans Liberation Beyond Pink or Blue* (1998), is a collection of speeches on transgender liberation and community building that zie gave at conferences and rallies in the spring of 1997. Each section of the book includes a description of the setting of the speech, the text, and – following the pattern that had been set in *Transgender Warriors* – a self-portrait written by one or more people associated with the event. In combination, these chapters give a sense of Feinberg's active speaking schedule after a year of grave illness, the diverse audiences for hir voice, and hir consistent message of shared histories, interests, and need for coalitional work: The audiences range widely, including a cross-dresser conference, the True Spirit conference for trans masculine people, a trans health conference, and a gathering of Pride organizers to a CUNY queer graduate studies conference.

Feinberg did not publish hir second novel, *Drag King Dreams* (2006), until thirteen years after *Stone Butch Blues*. Set in a post-9/11 New York City of increased surveillance and antiwar protests, *Drag King Dreams* is similar in narrative strategy to *Stone Butch Blues* but brings the central concerns into a different setting and a different moment in time. The importance of the author's identities, community affiliations, and political commitments to both of hir novels' fictional worlds and their authenticity is reflected in the design of Firebrand's and Alyson's editions of *Stone Butch Blues* and of Caroll and Graf's edition of *Drag King Dreams*, each displaying a portrait drawing or photograph of Feinberg on the cover. Like the names of the protagonists, Jess Goldberg and Max Rabinowitz, that both follow the gender ambiguous and ethnic patterns of the author's name without being identical to it, these images reflect Feinberg's approach of speaking truth through fiction without limiting the novels to autobiography or having to deliver stories of trauma, violence, or romance in the voice of memoir.

In contrast to the first novel, the shorter span of narrative time in *Drag King Dreams* puts much more emphasis on the events than on the protagonist's identity development. The plot follows protagonist Max Rabinowitz, whose first name according to the state and in the hands of the police, Maxine, is only revealed in the last words of the novel (in the context of being bailed out after an arrest at a protest). Surviving outside or on the margins of most forms of legal recognition and social security, Max works various night jobs in a drag club and lives in a world of diverse friends, colleagues, and neighbors. Max shares Yiddish poetry and argues politics with a religious cousin, but chosen family, intentional community, and mutual aid connections are much more central to the novel, and references to families of origin are scarce. Alluding to the important role the Internet has played in transgender community building and knowledge production in the late 1990s and early 2000s, Max makes an avatar for an online game set in space and meets a potential future love interest on the "lesbian star." This thread of the story does not get more fully explored, however. *Drag King Dreams* spends less time developing the protagonist through a series of romantic relationships as pivotal to exploration of individual identity, losing some of the affective texture of *Stone Butch Blues* so popular with readers. Instead of interweaving *Bildungsroman* and romance elements, the second novel focuses even more on the social realism of hurdles and injustices facing Max's community of trans people as they navigate bathrooms, barbershops, and other gender-segregated spaces and face a range of issues from lacking official documents and access to health insurance to the consequences of getting arrested at a protest. Through Max's social connections, readers also encounter issues such as the loss of child custody, eviction and proceedings in housing court, racism, anti-Semitism, living with HIV/AIDS, and hostile healthcare providers in a hospital setting. In addition to the network of relationships already established at the opening of the novel, Max befriends an Egyptian and a Palestinian neighbor, drawing attention to post-9/11 Islamophobia, the Patriot Act, and the perspectives of Muslim immigrants. As in *Stone Butch Blues*, each of these examples is used to give (fictional) faces to issues and to emphasize solidarity, activism, and support in response. The workers at the night club, for example, engage in union-like activity by pooling funds for health care and arguing for better pay and working conditions. Anti-transgender violence is the inciting incident of the novel: The night of the murder of the protagonist's friend opens the novel and the memorial service for this character is an important moment of narrative closure. As an immigrant-rights lawyer, political activist, photojournalist, and "a cross-dresser" "fluent in two gendered languages" (2006b, pp. 217, 221), Vic/kie was an important presence in many different communities and activist circles that come together to mourn hir passing. The eulogies from representatives of the different parts of Vic/kie's life during the service articulate coalitional politics through the voices of diverse characters and their relationship to the deceased. The memorial service becomes the lead-up to a protest march, promising the beginning of an intersectional antiwar movement.

Feinberg's last book, *Rainbow Solidarity in Defense of CUBA* (2009), was a compilation of twenty-five articles that had previously appeared as part of the "Lavender & Red" series in Workers World newspaper between 2004 and 2008. "Lavender & Red," as a larger series, focuses on the relationship between gender-, sexuality-, and sex-based oppression and the communist revolutionary process, reporting, in particular, on achievements in gender and sexual liberation under socialism. As the title suggests, *Rainbow Solidarity in Defense of CUBA* presents a progress narrative of the revolution in its struggle to overcome the gender and sexual normativity that class society and colonialism had brought to Cuba. Focusing on same-sex sexuality and gender diversity, the collection discusses pre- and post-revolutionary Cuban history with an emphasis (eight chapters) on the early years of the revolution. Feinberg casts hirself as a worker and researcher in service of spreading information that differs from US mainstream discourse on Cuba, rather than as an insider on Cuban history and politics. In an effort to present a counternarrative to what zie perceives as anti-Cuban propaganda, zie tends to defer to Fidel Castro's statements as a source of truth claims even when, for example, his characterization of the Units to Aid Military Production (UMAP) re-education camps of the mid-1960s dismisses accusations of the mistreatment of gay internees. The relative absence of nongovernmental voices on an issue like this makes this section take a very different tone from Feinberg's other work. The book is at its most comfortable not when discussing Cuban history on sexual and gender minorities in particular (where state action and citizens' lives may be at odds), but when highlighting the presence of sexual and gender diverse Cubans as part of a favorable comparison of Cuba in general to US capitalism, for example in terms of the positive effects of a free healthcare and education system on the eradication of socioeconomic inequality. While zie does not solely praise the pace of its progress on issues of sexuality and gender, Feinberg describes the Cuban revolution as a project benefiting Cubans of all sexualities and genders and a model for an anti-imperialist, anti-Capitalist, more egalitarian future and calls for rainbow – LGBTQ – solidarity with Cuba from hir readers. This vision of a more egalitarian future relates Feinberg's final collection of nonfiction work on Cuba to hir fictional worlds, which tend to end with the embattled protagonists taking the first steps into a more hopeful mo(ve)ment of political change.

Contributing to the archive of voices zie had been so eager to chronicle in hir work, Feinberg donated hir personal research library of 1250 books to a free, communities-based archive dedicated to the preservation of LGBTQIA voices in history. The collection is housed as "The Leslie Feinberg Library" in the Sexual Minorities Archives in Holyoke, MA. Feinberg's own writing continues to speak to readers and appears to only be growing timelier as debates on gender diversity, sexuality, and intersectionality reach wider audiences. Reflecting on the seemingly ever-increasing relevance of Feinberg's legacy, the *New York Times* opined that, at its twenty-fifth anniversary, *Stone Butch Blues* was "the best book for 2018" (Greenidge 2018).

SEE ALSO: Debut Novels; Fictions of Work and Labor; Queer and LGBT Fiction; Third-Wave Feminism

REFERENCES

Feinberg, Leslie. (2006a). *Transgender Warriors: Making History from Joan of Arc to Dennis Rodman*. Boston: Beacon Press; 1st ed. 1996.

Feinberg, Leslie. (2006b). *Drag King Dreams*. New York: Caroll and Graf.

Greenidge, Kaitlyn. (2018). The best book for 2018 is 25 years old. *The New York Times* (June 23, 2018). https://www.nytimes.com/2018/06/23/opinion/sunday/the-best-book-for-2018-is-25-years-old.html (accessed July 1, 2021).

FURTHER READING

Halberstam, Jack. (2019). *Female Masculinity*, 20th anniv. ed. Durham, NC: Duke University Press.

Noble, Jean Bobby. (2004). *Masculinities without Men? Female Masculinity in Twentieth-Century Fictions*. Vancouver: University of British Columbia Press.

Prosser, Jay. (1998). *Second Skins: The Body Narratives of Transsexuality*. New York: Columbia University Press.

Rand, Erica. (2011). So unbelievably real: *Stone Butch Blues* and the fictional special guest. *Radical Teacher* 92 (1): 35–42.

Transgender Warrior – The Art & Activism & Words of Leslie Feinberg. (n.d.). https://transgenderwarrior.org/

Ferré, Rosario

CARMEN S. RIVERA
State University of New York at Fredonia, USA

Rosario Ferré broke into the literary scene in the early 1970s, around the same time that the feminist movement was reaching its apogee. It was therefore no coincidence that her first publication, *Papeles de Pandora* (1976), was considered a feminist manifesto. Much scholarship has been devoted to analyzing Ferré's female protagonists and the various ways they expose and bring down, sometimes literally, the patriarchal values of Puerto Rican society. However, there is much more to Ferré's literary production in terms of scope and impact. The chronicle of the transition from aristocratic agrarian society to a new industrialized bourgeoisie (she belonged to both), the use of fine arts like architecture, paintings, and classical ballet, the publication of the journal *Zona de carga y descarga*, and the translation of her own works set her apart in Latin American literature.

She began as editor of the literary journal *Zona de carga y descarga*, published from 1972 to 1975. The journal provided a "zone" for new and emerging young writers who were experimenting both with content and format. Prior to *Zona de carga y descarga*, the only literary outlet was the very prestigious journal *Sin Nombre*, which only accepted already established writers. *Zona de carga y descarga* created an alternate space for the "charge and discharge" of "avant-garde themes" such as feminism, homosexuality, and the political status of the island (Hintz 1993, p. 231). One cannot underestimate the impact that this short-lived journal has had up to this day. Names like Olga Nolla, Manuel Ramos Otero, and Edgardo Rodríguez Juliá, as well as Ferré herself, first appeared in this journal.

Ferré was a prolific writer who experimented with all different genres, except for drama. She wrote eight works of fiction including novels, five collections of poetry, four books of essays, two books of scholarship, four collections of children's stories, and two memoirs. She also published frequently in local newspapers. The ideas and topics explored are immensely rich and varied; however, there are three recurrent and distinctive themes and motifs throughout her writing. First and foremost, Ferré chronicles the cultural and political transition of Puerto Rico, from agrarian economy under Spain's control to an industrial society and territory of the United States. Second, she uses space and architecture to expose the structural sexism, racism, and classism of Puerto Rican society. Finally, she studies and practices the art of translation as another way of writing, creating, and recreating her own work but also as a metaphor for the negotiation of meaning that happens in a society that lives in both political and linguistic limbo.

Rosario Ferré was born to Lorenzita Ramírez de Arellano, one of the old families belonging to the sugar cane "nobility," and Luis A. Ferré, a businessman whose cement company literally paved the roads and built the new housing neighborhoods that accompanied the industrialization of the island. Luis A. Ferré was also an accomplished pianist and an art collector. He went on to build the Museo de Arte de Ponce to house his growing collection. It is considered one of the finest museums in Latin America, housing a large collection of Pre-Raphaelite paintings. Rosario Ferré grew between these two worlds. The one of her maternal family was a dying world, with the sugar plantations being gobbled up by the "gargantuan" and highly industrialized American sugar mills. The other was that of the industrialization and Americanization of the island which brought wealth to her father. Both worlds upheld rigid views about gender, race, and class.

Ferré attended private schools both in Ponce and in the United States, was surrounded by art and music at home, and traveled to Europe. At the same time, Ferré was raised by Black nannies who exposed her to another world. In *Memoria* (2012), she describes the various Black women who completed her education. These women introduced Ferré to popular music like plena, to different political perspectives, and above all, to the world of poverty, racism, and discrimination that existed on the other side of the walls that surrounded her childhood home.

At the turn of the century, Puerto Rico's economy was mainly coffee and sugar. Old plantations were self-sufficient and worlds unto themselves, like feudal fiefdoms. These were the families who traced their ancestry to Spain. *Eccentric Neighborhoods* (1998) begins with a section entitled "Emajaguas's Lost Paradise," which describes the "Edenic" life of the Rivas de Santillana family in the plantation. "The human misery that raged outside Emajaguas's ten foot wall had no relevance within" (p. 30). The European decor and the French bottles of wine consumed during the abundant banquets were in direct contrast to the life of the farm workers who often died of hunger. The American invasion in 1898 brought the industrialization of sugar production against which the old aristocracy could not compete. *Eccentric Neighborhoods* describes how the patriarch borrowed money which he could not repay. He had to sell parcels of land and everything inside the house. Violence and suicide were not uncommon as the families fell into despair.

The American invasion of Puerto Rico, economically, culturally, and politically, gave rise to a strong independence movement. In *The House on the Lagoon* (1995) Ferré recreates the massacre of Ponce that took place in 1937. At the end, Manuel, Quintin and Isabel's son, joins an armed independence movement, AK-47, and ends up burning down the house and everything his bourgeois family represents. The poems in *Language Duel/Duelo del lenguaje* (2002) bluntly expose the controversy about the official language of Puerto Rico, which for many is essential to any decision about the political status of the island. In the poem of the same title, Ferré writes, "In fact, I swear/that as I talk to you/in English/about my right to speak/in Spanish,/I can hear the guns boom/and see the cannon balls roar/over my head" (p. 2). The format of the book with the English version on one side and the Spanish version on the other – facing each other – is in itself a duel not only between the languages but also between political alliances.

Maybe because her father was the founder of the Puerto Rican Cement Company which built the neighborhoods where she first lived, Ferré uses architecture to underline the physical and ideological separations based on gender, race, and class. In *Eccentric Neighborhoods*, there are references to the cake-like house designed by Alfredo B. Weichers. One can actually follow the streets of Ferré's childhood by reading her work. In *Las dos Venecias* (1992), the house becomes literally a coffin that suffocates her mother. Venecia (or Venice), the honeymoon destination for the wealthy families, is the site for the rite of passage from a carefree girl to a submissive and passive wife, another possession for the husband. The canals of the city only anticipate the birth canal that reduces women's sexuality to that of reproduction. In the poem "La ciudad navío," Ferré reclaims the port city of San Juan as an open space where she can walk freely, finding authority and authenticity within her own creativity.

The House on the Lagoon echoes the architecture of Antonio Nicodoma, who brought Frank Lloyd Wright's "prairie house" model to the island. The various levels of the house reflect the racial and social hierarchy, with the family in the top floors and Petra and the Black servants living in the cellar. The house becomes the hiding place for Isabel Monfort's manuscript, which is the novel itself, the same way that women were to "hide" and silence all professional aspirations. There is the golden terrace where Quintin's mother, Rebecca, used to have intellectual soirees. During one of those gatherings, they decided to dramatize Oscar Wilde's *Salome* (1891) and she performed the "Dance of the Seven Veils," ending with her naked. Her husband arrived at that moment and beat Rebecca to unconsciousness with his belt. Soon after that, Rebecca became pregnant and we are told that she "slowly faded from view" (1995, p. 69). This is what happens when a woman tries to step into a public space. Isabel laments that for a woman, "A university diploma was a sign of prestige, but it was also a subtle threat" (p. 209). Education was only useful in raising the children and in promoting the husband's social status while entertaining his business partners.

While Black characters are limited to the cellar or the basement, this is the space where Quintin Mendizabal grew up, and where he goes whenever he needs healing and solace. Petra is the character with the most freedom and to some extent the most power. She is the only female character that is not submissive toward Quintin and seems to exert a mysterious power over him. After her funeral, Isabel admits, "Petra means rock, and for the many years I had known her, she had been the rock on which the house on the lagoon had stood" (1995, p. 384).

The plantations, the mansions, the neighborhoods of the wealthy families, even the "country club" described in her work are usually separated from the slums just by a wall. There are plenty of references to Barrio San Anton and La Perla, two of the most infamous areas in Ponce. In *Memoria*, Ferré describes how a 12-foot wall stood between her house and the "reality of Puerto Rico" at that time: low wages, high birth mortality, tuberculosis and anemia, murders and suicides (2012, pp. 50–51, my translation). The wealthy families used to celebrate "carnivals" of exotic themes in the "Club Deportivo," which was right next door to a slum. Ferré denounces these futile attempts to escape the "turbulent times" on the island: "the nationalistic uprisings, the sugar cane strikes, and the Korean War" (p. 54, my translation).

It is not surprising that Ferré ends with the apocalyptic destruction of these spaces. In *Maldito Amor* (1986), the "idyllic" sugar plantation of Guamaní is burned down. At the end of *The House of the Lagoon*, Manuel destroys the house with no hope of reconstruction. Other spaces, like the Emajaguas plantation, fall into disrepair and are abandoned. At other times Ferré chooses to subvert the space, like in the story "Cuando las mujeres quieren a los hombres" (1974). Isabel la Negra claims the elegant house owned by her deceased lover, Ambrosio Luberza, as her inheritance to convert it into a brothel. Apter-Cragnolino observes that this "flipping" of the traditional house-home, "symbol of power and prestige," serves to crumble the traditional sociocultural foundations (1993, p. 2).

Ferré grew up in similar houses surrounded by fine art, so it is not surprising that art is a motif throughout her work. Ballet, for example, plays a significant role in her fiction. In "La bella durmiente" (in *Papeles de Pandora*), Maria de los Angeles, the protagonist, is a young woman fighting for her desire to continue dancing while her father and the mother superior at her school plot to get her married so she can fulfill the social expectations for women. The short story uses images from various classical ballets such as the title, "Sleeping Beauty," "Coppelia," and "Giselle" to underline the struggle Maria de los Angeles faces. She is also fascinated with Carmen Merengue, her father's lover, who performs in dark seedy cabarets. Maria de los Angeles is killed at the end by her husband who finds her, and her lover, at a cheap motel, practicing naked the acrobatic movements she had seen Carmen Merengue perform.

One of Ferré's most accomplished short stories is "Cuando las mujeres quieren a los hombres" (in *Papeles de Pandora*), taking the title from a very popular plena. It combines the dialogues of Isabel Luberza, the widow, and Isabel la Negra, the lover and madame of a local brothel, with the deceased. In "Amalia" (in *Papeles de Pandora*), the young girl prefers to dance with the Black chauffeur to the music he listens to rather than to sit quietly with her uncle. Plena is a musical genre developed by the African community in the Caribbean. At one point it was illegal to perform this music. The lyrics usually provide a satirical perspective of the major events and sociopolitical issues in the island. If classical ballet depicts a more ethereal image of women, plena emphasizes the sensuality of the body.

"Isolda en el espejo" (in *Maldito Amor*) is a short story about Augusto Arzuaga, a wealthy businessman who falls in love with Adriana, his son's lover, noting that she looks exactly like the Isolda in one of his paintings (a popular character of the Pre-Raphaelite movement). Augusto had built a "gallery" in which he displayed his collection of paintings and sculptures. Upon her first visit, Adriana observes that the subject of most of the pieces is women and they are for the most part naked. Adriana agrees to marry Augusto so that she can take care of her parents and pursue studies in classical piano. Secretly, Adriana sings at bars and cabarets. The day of the wedding, she decides to surprise Augusto by wearing the clothing and headpiece of Isolda, except she is not wearing anything underneath it. Augusto, on the other hand, has ordered a statue of Venus to be the centerpiece at the reception. Adriana notices that the statue is a replica of her own body. During the first dance of the married couple, Adriana begins to move faster and faster until her dress begins to lift, exposing her naked body. The story ends with an apocalyptic fight among the guests and the certain ruin of Augusto Arzuaga. It is as if the wild and uncontrolled movements of Adriana expose not only her naked body but also the chaos and instability of the society in transition. These contra-positions between classical and popular music, between classical art and popular performance, are not necessarily a rejection of Eurocentric aesthetics and sensibilities, argues Medina-Rivera, but more a criticism of how they represent and promote a patriarchal system in which the women have no agency and are mainly objects. At the same time, one can argue that Ferré is not rejecting one aesthetic for another, but wants to present a more authentic look into the very rich and diverse traditions of Puerto Rican art and folklore.

Aside from fiction and poetry, Ferré sees translation as another form of creative writing. George Rabassa translated "La muñeca menor" as "The Youngest Doll" in 1980. Dissatisfied with the translation, Rosario Ferré decided to translate it again or "retranslate." In the essay "On Destiny, Language, and Translation; or, Ophelia Adrift in the C.&O. Canal" (1991), she explains her notions about translation. In that process, Ferré found the opportunity to rewrite the story and began to see translation as an act of creation in and of itself, "virtually abolish[ing] the hierarchy between original and translation" (Spoturno 2018, p. 360). For example, her translation of the novella *Maldito Amor* into *Sweet Diamond Dust* (1989) saw significant changes to the text. In the introduction to the Spanish version, Ferré explains that one of her intentions is to depict the transformation taking place in the island (Ferré 1991, p. 13).

Amplifications, deletions, and linguistic modifications in the English version actually help to emphasize this theme. The translation of the title itself already hints at a thematic refocus. "Maldito Amor" is the title of a "danza" (folkloric music of Puerto Rico), referring to cursed or ill-fated love. It can also refer to the ill-fated passion society had for the land, the plantations, for a way of living that was disappearing. The title in English emphasizes the sweetness of the sugar which was the source of both financial wealth and social status. The title also points to the bitter conflict within that society: for some, sugar was as sweet and valuable as diamonds, but for others it was worthless dust.

Spoturno observes that translation and "retranslation also offered Ferré a chance to start reworking her identity as a bilingual, transnational author" (2018, p. 369). With *The House on the Lagoon*, Ferré purposefully published the English version first to establish herself as a writer in the United States.

Above all, Ferré sees herself as a writer. *Sitio a Eros* (1980), her first collection of essays, begins with "La cocina de la escritura" and ends with "De la ira a la ironía, o sobre cómo atemperar el acero candente del discurso." These are two of the most significant and frequently quoted essays about writing, about whether there is such a thing as "women's" writing or "escritura femenina," and about the significance of anger and irony for women writers. The last section of *Las dos Venecias* (1992) includes poems and essays about writing and storytelling. For example, the poems "El contable," referring to an accountant, and "El teller" reverse the business connotations: the accounts are narratives and the teller tells stories ("contar" in Spanish means both to count and to tell a story). *Memoria* begins with an explanation of how she inherited the literary vocation and ends with a chronology of how each of her books came to life.

Ferré frequently quotes a verse of John's gospel, "And the word became flesh," to bring attention to the creative power of language. She invokes the "word" again and again because it is the only way she can define her existence, because it is the only way for her "to be."

SEE ALSO: Allende, Isabel; Braschi, Giannina; Cofer, Judith Ortiz; Díaz, Junot; García, Cristina; Hijuelos, Oscar; Literary Magazines; Suburban Narratives; Third-Wave Feminism; Urban Fiction

REFERENCES

Apter-Cragnolino, Aída. (1993). De sitios y asedios: la escritura de Rosario Ferré. Revista Chilena de Literatura 42: 25–30.

Ferré, Rosario. (1991). *Maldito Amor*, 2nd ed. Rio Piedras, PR: Ediciones Huracán; 1st ed. 1986.

Ferré, Rosario. (1995). *The House on the Lagoon*. New York: Farrar, Straus and Giroux.

Ferré, Rosario. (1998). *Eccentric Neighborhoods*. New York: Farrar, Straus and Giroux.

Ferré, Rosario. (2002). *Language Duel/Duelo del lenguaje*. New York: Vintage Books.

Ferré, Rosario. (2012). *Memoria*. San Juan, PR: Ediciones Callejón.

Hintz, Suzanne S. (1993). Rosario Ferré: the vanguard of Puerto Rican feminist literature. Revista de Estudios Hispánicos 20: 227–232.

Medina-Rivera, Antonio. (2003). La aniquilación de las bellas artes y de la aristocracia en las obras de Rosario Ferré. In: *Selected Proceedings of the Pennsylvania Foreign Language Conference* (ed. Gregorio C. Martin), 75–87. New Kensington, PA: Grelin Press.

Spoturno, María Laura. (2018). Self-retranslation as a rite of passage: Rosario Ferré's English version of "La muñeca menor." Mutatis Mutando 11 (2): 356–375.

FURTHER READING

Ayuso, Monica G. (2008). Virginia Woolf in Mexico and Puerto Rico. Woolf Studies Annual 14.

Negrón-Muntaner, Frances. (2012). *Sin pelos en la lengua*: Rosario Ferré's last interview. Centro Journal 24 (1): 154–171.

Rivera, Carmen S. (2016). Rosario Ferré and the memory of space. South Atlantic Review 18 (3): 56–72.

Van Camp, Ann. (2001). El estatuto de Puerto Rico en *La Casa de la Laguna* de Rosario Ferré. Revista de Estudios Hispánicos 28 (1/2): 141–161.

Ferris, Joshua

MARSHALL BOSWELL
Rhodes College, USA

Joshua Ferris's three novels to date situate him as the twenty-first-century heir to the tradition of middle-class white male dissatisfaction associated with writers such as John Cheever and Richard Yates. Ferris brings to this idiom a measured streak of postmodern cool reminiscent of Don DeLillo and such contemporaries as Benjamin Kunkel and Jonathan Safran Foer. What distinguishes his work from that of his peers is his focus on work, on the isolation and curious community of the office. His debut novel, *Then We Came to the End* (2007), takes place almost entirely in an advertising firm, while his most recent work, *To Rise Again at a Decent Hour* (2014), rarely leaves the environs of the narrator's dental practice. Even his somewhat incongruous second novel, *The Unnamed* (2010), delights in detailing the world of an upscale law firm. "I need my characters to have jobs in order to feel real to me," he said in a wide-ranging *Paris Review* interview. "People have to work" (Lee 2014).

Born in Illinois in 1974, Ferris has repeatedly described himself as a child of divorce. His mother divorced several times during his childhood, and apparently introduced a new religious denomination with each new stepfather. After the first divorce, he relocated with his mother to Key West, Florida, where he first tried his hand at writing fiction. The resulting story collection, which he completed when he was seven or eight years old, he titled "Wicked People." Deeply influenced by the films of Alfred Hitchcock, the stories drew from the Key West coastal view and involved murderous crabs and other aquatic horrors. As he explained in an interview included with the eBook edition of *Then We Came to the End*, "Many good people, boaters and sunbathers, were eaten alive as Hitchcock turned in his grave" (Ferris 2007a). Sometime later he relocated to Chicago, where he became a devoted Chicago Cubs fan. In 1992 he entered the University of Iowa. Like Thomas Pynchon, whom he has identified as one of his favorite writers, he began his college career intending to be an engineer, but eventually shifted to English and philosophy. While there, he not only attended the numerous readings sponsored by that institution's legendary Writers' Workshop but also began writing stories again, this time channeling such metafictional muses as Donald Barthelme and Vladimir Nabokov.

Following his graduation, Ferris earned a living for a short time as a technical writer before taking a job at an advertising agency in Chicago. Both experiences broadened his sense of the written word more generally. Of his work as a technical writer, he has explained, "I would take [the scientist's] writing and improve it, and at the same time I was taking this complex science and trying to make it communicable. That job conveyed to me very strongly that for every piece of writing, there is a reader, and clarity is important" (Lee 2014). Similarly, while at the advertising firm, he "started to realize the real power of a simple sentence. In college I had acquired these ideals of literature with a capital L, but my real-life work – the work of simplifying ideas – produced a writer willing to slum it with simple sentences if it meant reeling a reader in. The combination of that academic study and that real-world advertising experience really formed my voice" (Lee 2014).

Around the turn of the century, and armed with this real-world experience, Ferris entered the MFA program at the University of California-Irvine, also the training ground for Richard Ford and Michael Chabon, both of whom also figure into Ferris's hybrid style, Ford for his grim realism and Chabon for his formal playfulness. Following his 2003 graduation, he worked on several projects, one of which was published to great acclaim in 2007 as *Then We Came to the End*. *The New Yorker* deemed it "a masterwork of pitch and tone," while *The New York Times* called it "expansive, great-hearted, and acidly funny" (Briefly Noted 2007; Poniewozik 2007). A finalist for the National Book Award, the novel also won the PEN/Hemingway Award for Debut Novel.

Then We Came to the End is a novel about the workplace, about the contemporary white-collar experience, and as such takes its place alongside such works as Sloan Wilson's *The Man in the Gray Flannel Suit* (1955) and Richard Yates's *Revolutionary Road* (1961). Ferris's novel swerves from the work of his predecessors in avoiding what James Poniewozik, in his *New York Times* review of the book, calls "the default position for American stories about business – especially as easy a target as advertising" – namely, derision. "White-collar work is meant to be soul-killing and pernicious," Poniewozik explains, and yet Ferris's novel also demonstrates that "work – even, or especially, useless work – can also offer purpose and meaning" (Poniewozik 2007). Like David Foster Wallace's *The Pale King* (2011), which seeks to disclose the buried heroism of the Internal Revenue Service, and George Saunders's numerous stories of tortured corporate middlemen, *Then We Came to the End* sidesteps the easy satire of such popular depictions of modern white-collar life as *The Office*, *Office Space* (1999), and Dilbert cartoons in favor of a more open embrace of the purpose and community offered up by the contemporary workplace.

What most distinguishes the novel is its risky use of the first-person plural point of view. First introduced into American literature by William Faulkner in his anthology staple, "A Rose for Emily" (1930), the first-person plural has since reappeared only sporadically, most notably in Peter Taylor's "Venus, Cupid, Folly and Time" (1958), itself a knowing homage to Faulkner, and Jeffrey Eugenides's *The Virgin Suicides* (1993), one of the few novel-length works in this style, and hence a clear analog for Ferris's book. The narrative "we" invokes the close-knit community the workers have developed as well as the aura of paranoia and unease bred by a recent spate of layoffs that function as the novel's primary plot engine. Even so, Ferris has designed his narrative perspective so that individual office workers splinter off from the collective vision such that it is never clear exactly who the "we" actually includes. In fact, as all the principal characters wander off into their postnarrative lives, the novel ends with "Just the two of us, you and me" (2007b, p. 385).

Each of the book's characters has a curious tic, or identifying neurosis, while the threadbare plot is held together by absurdist set pieces involving totem poles and stolen office chairs. Nevertheless, serious issues cut through the surface comedy. Lynn Mason, the highest-ranking employee in the firm, deals with a rapidly metastasizing cancer. Another employee, Janine Gorjanc, mourns the death of her daughter Jessica, who was abducted and murdered just before the novel's historical present. Tom Mota, a disruptive, powder-keg figure who is one of the first to be fired, provides the book with its page-turning momentum. From the moment Mota is let go, the employees entertain the possibility of his returning to enact retribution with a firearm – an eventuality that comes true, except that Mota attacks his co-workers with a paint gun in a scene that comically deflates the novel's key source of tension.

But Mota is more than a parody of the angry postal worker, or a grim reminder of America's mass-shooting epidemic. Throughout the novel, even after his firing, he serves as a moral voice. In a free-ranging essay on Ferris's work published on the online literary blog *The Millions*, Jonathan Clarke compares

Mota to John Givings from Yates's *Revolutionary Road*, a "madman who is also the purveyor of uncomfortable truths about the way the others live" (Clarke 2014). Although Mota is disturbed, he is not crazy. Rather, he helps a troubled worker deal with his depression and paints over, with the same paint gun, the face of Janine's daughter on a "Have You Seen Me?" billboard that remains up long after Jessica's funeral. Most importantly, Mota is a devotee of Ralph Waldo Emerson, whom he quotes in long emails to his co-workers and whose "Man, The Reformer" Mota recites as he paintguns his friends. Ultimately, he voices the novel's counter-argument to the tradition of white-collar derision Poniewozik notes in his review. While in custody, he explains that his anarchic behavior was really just an attempt to resist conformity, as prescribed by Emerson in "Self-Reliance." "To conform is to lose your soul," he explains. "So I dissented every chance I got and I told them fuck you and eventually they fired me for it, but I thought, Ralph Waldo Emerson would be proud of Tom Mota" (2007b, p. 343). But he realizes his nonconformity only leaves him mired in useless rage, while his arch enemy, the "inscrutable" Joe Pope, is at peace, and possesses the inner resource of self-knowledge that is true nonconformity that Emerson calls us to find.

One of the novel's minor characters is a tweed-wearing African American copywriter named Hank Neary who, it is revealed, has been working on what the plural narrator repeatedly calls "a failed novel" and which Neary describes as a "small and angry book about work" (2007b, p. 72). "The fact that we spend most of our lives at work, that interests me," he explains to his co-workers (p. 72). The book's final scene, which functions as a neat epilogue, takes place five years later, at Neary's debut novel reading, with all of the characters reassembled. But Neary's finished novel is not the "small and angry book about work." Rather, it is a sensitive portrait of Lynn Mason's struggle with cancer, a thoughtful and sensitive excerpt of which appears as a standalone chapter in the dead center of Ferris's novel. This neat, almost *de rigueur*, metafictional twist invites us to read Neary as a Nabokovian stand-in for Ferris himself – Ferris repeatedly cites Nabokov as a major influence – such that Neary's explanation for his change of subject could be read as Ferris's own statement of purpose. In Neary's original novel, Lynn was the villain, because "anyone who believed in the merits of capitalism, and soul-destroying corporations, and work work work – all that – naturally that person wasn't deserving of any sympathy"; but he abandoned that book in order to address the more pressing and important subject of Lynn's suffering (p. 377).

Given the success of *Then We Came to the End*, it is not surprising that his follow-up novel attracted a sizable amount of attention. Unfortunately, *The Unnamed*, while admired in some quarters, garnered Ferris's first spate of negative reviews. A curious, enigmatic novel about a successful attorney gripped by an unaccountable obsession to wander the earth on foot, losing fingers and toes along the way, *The Unnamed* was largely received with bewilderment, both at the curious subject matter and at Ferris's decision to abandon the tender comedic mode for which he had made his name. Jay McInerney, in his unfavorable *New York Times* review, appreciated Ferris's "earnest attempt to reinvent himself," and yet goes on to complain about Ferris's refusal to live up to his "brand." In a glib dismissal, McInerney asks, "Remember when Paul McCartney went classical with 'Liverpool Oratorio'? Me neither" (McInerney 2010). Both McInerney and Janet Maslin fail to understand what the protagonist's obsessive walking compulsion could possibly mean, or symbolize, with Maslin deciding, "The book seems to be going nowhere" (Maslin 2010).

The Unnamed is certainly curious, and elusive in its intentions, but it also possesses a stern singleness of purpose that the failure to glean its second-order significance seems largely to be the reader's. Tim Farnsworth, the protagonist, is a healthy, successful trial attorney with an equally successful wife whom he loves, and a daughter, Becka, who is distant but not anxiously so. Without explanation, he abruptly leaves work one day and starts walking. The condition, for that is what it is, had manifest twice earlier, and he and his wife had responded by handcuffing Tim to the bed until the compulsion passed. But for the bulk of *The Unnamed*, Tim's condition is in full bloom, with occasional relapses that only heighten the sense of loss. Ferris brings in medical experts to speculate on Tim's condition but no one cracks the code, and so his walking compulsion remains undiagnosed and, as signaled by the novel's title, unnamed.

McInerney speculates that Beckett might be a touchstone here, and names Beckett's own *The Unnamable* (1953) as a possible *ur*-text, but goes no further with the suggestion. He also wonders if Tim's condition is a metaphor for "addiction," while Maslin singles out a passage late in the novel in which Tim admits that "the blood–brain barrier and the synapses are the two main fronts" (Ferris 2010, p. 230), thus suggesting, without saying as much, that Ferris's interest here is the material human condition, and that the novel offers up a posthumanist portrait of a thoughtful, complex person overtaken by the mechanical forces of his body. Throughout the novel, but particularly in the final act, Tim thinks constantly of his body, registering its changes, fighting its compulsions, his mind trapped in a cage he cannot control. At a key moment late in the novel, as his wife tries to seduce him in a hospital bed, he worries about "one final treachery of the body, which if it had its way . . . would crown its triumph of cruelty by depriving him – them – of this too" (p. 290). Conversely, in the novel's final moment, as he suffers from severe dehydration in a tent and successfully overrides his body's obdurate signals to get up and hit the road, "he realized that he was still thinking, his mind was still afire, that he had just scored if not won the whole damn thing, and that the exquisite thought of his eternal rest was how delicious that cup of water was going to taste the instant it touched his lips" (p. 310). Perhaps, in the end, Ferris's work seeks to locate the elusive trace of the human that transcends the material forces of blood, bone, and synapse. And perhaps that small spark, in the godless universe in which Ferris's secular fiction transpires, is the unnamed thing itself.

Ferris's third and most recent novel, *To Rise Again at a Decent Hour*, confirms the possibly spiritual core of its predecessor's enigmatic concerns. The novel's mercurial first-person narrator, Paul O'Rourke, is a successful dentist, an obsessive-compulsive Red Sox fan, a technophobe, and a misogynist. But, most importantly, he is an atheist. Barely four pages into his narrative he reveals that he "would have liked to believe in God" (2014, p. 6) but simply cannot. Throughout the novel he records his dalliances with religions, and with religious families, most of them associated with various girlfriends whom he stalks and, quite understandably, alienates. He obsesses over a Catholic girlfriend and longs to insert himself into her family, until he realizes the dark, racist underbelly of their white Christianity. Later he applies for membership into the close-knit, exuberant Jewish family of yet another love interest, his office manager Connie. Although he cannot for a moment entertain the existence of a God, he fully understands and envies the sense of belonging a religion can offer. When a mysterious stranger begins posting what appear to be anti-Semitic tweets on a Twitter account in

O'Rourke's name, the novel's narrator finds himself caught up in an elaborate conspiracy involving a lost religious tribe that might disclose his actual heritage. The tribe, called the Ulms, have been around since the beginning of monotheism, their existence both buried and visible like the Knights Templar. The catch: the Ulms are distinguished by their firm adherence to one key component of religious belief: doubt, "the most enlightened approach to God ever articulated to man" (p. 162).

If the untangling of the Ulm history reads like a parody of Umberto Eco and Dan Brown, the ghost of Philip Roth hovers over the novel's exuberantly over-the-top first half. In numerous publicity interviews following the book's 2014 publication, Ferris repeatedly name-checked Roth more generally and Roth's 1997 masterpiece *American Pastoral* more specifically. At the most obvious level, the existential questions sparked by the sudden appearance of O'Rourke's online "double" recall Roth's elaborate doppelganger novel, *Operation Shylock* (1993). But the Roth echoes do not end there. O'Rourke's depiction of his erotically charged dental office invokes the first Henry Zuckerman section from Roth's *The Counterlife* (1986), while the acerbic riffs on religion call to mind similar rants in Roth's later work, particularly *Sabbath's Theater* (1995) and *Everyman* (2006). Finally, O'Rourke's celebration of Jewish family feeling, not to mention the numerous set pieces at drunken weddings with larger-than-life Jewish uncles, draw knowingly from Roth's full corpus.

Conversely, the novel's information-heavy final section seems flown in from a different novel entirely. As O'Rourke gets increasingly seduced by the Ulm conspiracy, perpetrated by a ghostly shadow figure named Grant Arthur, the real person behind O'Rourke's online double, the novel changes tone. Either deliberately or accidentally, O'Rourke loses his cynical edge, his disruptive, truth-telling humor. What's more, he recedes as the novel's central voice, as various characters begin telling of their own experiences with religion, with faith, with love. Mercer, a billionaire hedge-fund manager also swept up in the Ulm conspiracy, tells his tale, as does Grant Arthur's lover, an Orthodox Jew named Mirav Mendelshon, who abandons her belief in God in the face of Arthur's relentless arguments for atheism but who nevertheless returns to her Orthodox community in a gesture that is the novel's own final take on religious faith, namely, that disbelief in God should not bar one from access to religious community. Meanwhile, the doubting Ulms serve as an overdetermined metaphor for religion itself. As Connie's Uncle Stuart explains to O'Rourke, Grant Arthur "took an old legend from the Bible and made a myth of it, and now he tells the myth like it's the truth. This is how it happens" (2014, p. 307).

Despite its minor faults of tone and consistency, *To Rise Again at a Decent Hour* recovered Ferris's critical standing and, in its religious preoccupations, casts helpful backwards light on its elusive predecessor. Meanwhile, the novel's informed nods to Roth, which are of a piece with his earlier invocations of Cheever and Yates and possibly Beckett as well, broaden his range and testify to his confidence more generally. Ferris's most recent book, a story collection titled *The Dinner Party* (2017), also confirms his adaptability as a literary practitioner and, especially, his keen interest in point of view. Still in his forties, Ferris is at the midpoint of his career; given the originality of his three novels so far, as well as their through-line concerns with work, empathy, and secular spirituality, he has established a solid foundation for a rich and varied corpus going forward.

SEE ALSO: Chabon, Michael; Debut Novels; DeLillo, Don; Eugenides, Jeffrey; Fictions of Work and Labor; Foer, Jonathan Safran; Millennial Fiction; Realism after Poststructuralism; Saunders, George; Wallace, David Foster

REFERENCES

Briefly Noted. (2007). Review of *Then We Came to the End* by Joshua Ferris. *The New Yorker* (March 19, 2007): 89. https://www.newyorker.com/magazine/2007/03/26/then-we-came-to-the-end (accessed July 3, 2021).

Clarke, Jonathan. (2014). Human resources: on Joshua Ferris. *The Millions* (September 23, 2014). https://themillions.com/2014/09/human-resources-on-joshua-ferris.html (accessed July 3, 2021).

Ferris, Joshua. (2007a). An interview with Joshua Ferris. BookBrowse. https://www.bookbrowse.com/author_interviews/full/index.cfm/author_number/1437/joshua-ferris (accessed July 3, 2021).

Ferris, Joshua. (2007b). *Then We Came to the End*. Boston: Little, Brown.

Ferris, Joshua. (2010). *The Unnamed*. Boston: Little, Brown.

Ferris, Joshua. (2014). *To Rise Again at a Decent Hour*. Boston: Little, Brown.

Lee, Jonathan. (2014). Always on display: an interview with Joshua Ferris. *The Paris Review* (May 19, 2014). https://www.theparisreview.org/blog/2014/05/19/an-interview-with-joshua-ferris/ (accessed July 3, 2021).

Maslin, Janet. (2010). Compelled to wander, nowhere to go. Review of *The Unnamed* by Joshua Ferris. *The New York Times* (January 13, 2010). https://archive.nytimes.com/www.nytimes.com/2010/01/14/books/14book.html (accessed July 3, 2021).

McInerney, Jay. (2010). Long march. Review of *The Unnamed* by Joshua Ferris. *The New York Times* (January 22, 2010). https://archive.nytimes.com/www.nytimes.com/2010/01/24/books/review/McInerney-t.html (accessed July 3, 2021).

Poniewozik, James. (2007). Pink slip blues. Review of *Then We Came to The End* by Joshua Ferris. *The New York Times* (March 18, 2007). https://www.nytimes.com/2007/03/18/books/review/Poniewozik.t.html (accessed July 3, 2021).

FURTHER READING

Bekhta, Natalya. (2017). We-narratives: the distinctiveness of the collective narration. Narrative 25 (2): 164–181.

Maxey, Ruth. (2016). National stories and narrative voice in the fiction of Joshua Ferris. Critique: Studies in Contemporary Fiction 57 (2): 208–216.

Fiction and Affect

RALPH CLARE
Boise State University, USA

Emotion, feeling, and affect have always been central to fiction writers' constructions of both characters and fictional worlds. Just as certain historical periods give rise to unique forms, genres, and styles of literature, so too do literary periods respond to, create, and arrange emotions and affect in particular ways. One might call to mind the jubilance and melancholy of Romantic literature, the sentimental novel of the eighteenth century, the impersonal poetics and aesthetics heralded by modernists such as Eliot and Joyce, or even the intentionally alienating techniques of Bertolt Brecht's theater. Literature and cultural artifacts affect and are affected by their immediate present conditions, informed as those are by the past. This is not to say that literature captures some idealized zeitgeist, an autonomous "spirit" of the age. For literature does not so much capture a spirit as help to create a cultural atmosphere.

At first glance emotion and affect seem especially difficult to talk about in the historical-material sense because they are often considered immaterial and fleeting, as well as unchanging and universally applicable to all peoples in all times and places – a problematic notion, to be sure. However, Raymond Williams's notion of "structures of feeling" (1977, pp. 128–135) provides a helpful schema in thinking about how affect works in fiction. Williams points to a difficulty when studying history, since "only the fixed explicit forms exist, and living presence is always, by definition, receding" (p. 128). What gets lost in much historical analysis is the complex cultural and societal processes that are always at play. "Structures of feeling" emphasizes this constant state of flux (the present) out of which "fixed forms" are forever emerging and coming into being. These forms, which can be composed of the behaviors, habits, values, meanings, laws, and institutions of a particular time, retrospectively give the illusion of stability where, at the time, there was only flux. In short, history "fixes" itself, after the (present) fact, in cause-and-effect narratives with beginnings, middles, and ends. Structures of feeling amends this view of historically fixed forms by stressing "meanings and values as they are actively lived and felt" (p. 132). These "meanings and values," moreover, may be found especially in the intangible, subjective, and personal, including "elements of impulse, restraint, and tone; specifically affective elements of consciousness and relationships" (p. 132). For the subjective experience of history, when one is in the thick of it, hardly feels fixed and coherent at all. Williams thus brings the material and immaterial together, stressing "not feeling against thought, but thought as felt and feeling as thought" (p. 132).

Williams's ideas are relatable to, and in some ways anticipatory of, those of affect theory, an increasingly popular, transdisciplinary, and much varied "school" of thought that arose in the 2000s. Affect theorists have begun to challenge more conventional understandings of emotion and affect itself, underscoring that thinking about emotion and affect in uncritical ways is no longer possible when writing about literature. Affect theory calls attention to the ways in which social, cultural, economic, and political spheres affect the production, circulation, and consumption of emotions and affects, both publicly and privately. Affect studies is thus interested in looking at the way in which emotions, feelings, states of being, and embodiment (or the relationship between mind and body) "affect" our being-in-the-world, whether it be an individual, intersubjective, or collective experience of it. Affect and emotion matter, literally and figuratively, in myriad ways.

Affect theory, nevertheless, can be difficult to grasp as most of us tend to conceive of "affect" as a synonym for "emotion" – we feel affectionate toward someone or something; we are affected by different situations and emotions. Yet for one philosophically challenging group of affect theorists – influenced by philosopher Gilles Deleuze and psychologist Sylvan Tompkins – emotions and affect are *not* the same thing. Affect is more about our capacity to be affected by the world or others in ways that we don't even realize (for instance, the way that cognition is ceaselessly working). In contrast, we might think of emotions as the stuff out of which affect – sort of a pre-conscious force or sensation, like an intuition (a gut feeling) or an autonomic bodily function (a pupil dilating) – finds a form, a codified or conscious emotive expression or feeling (Massumi 2002, pp. 1–28). Think, for instance, about when you're not sure how you feel about a certain event in your life, whether it's something that happens suddenly or is ongoing. Perhaps you are not sure what you feel or are feeling conflicting emotions. In the midst of certain experiences, we are caught in a rush of feelings, a welter of perceptions, out of which we later make sense. These could be violently traumatic or life-changing events to everyday developments of love and friendship. Thus, we could be said to sort, name, or label our emotions retroactively, and organize our perceptions into manageable and understandable things through language. This can happen unconsciously in a manner of seconds or over a span of days, weeks, or years – "processing," in this sense, is never over.

Affect, furthermore, is not simply "owned" by an individual in the way that we often consider emotions "ours." Emotions that can be "owned" privately can easily be commodified (say, via a Hallmark card or soap opera sentimentality) and lead to solipsism (nobody can "know" what "I" really feel). Instead, affect can be seen as "impersonal" or "autonomous," more a *relational force* between people, things, and events. One can think of the "shared" affective experience of being in a crowd at a concert or a sporting event, or when a mood sweeps over a room, or in moments of community togetherness. If affect can be stoked and transmitted from one person or group to another, then art and literature hold the potential to generate and transmit affect as well – even if these affects are not always positive or productive. In this sense material objects can create "immaterial" modes of affect or feeling that indeed connect and bond material things to one another.

Yet all of these ways of thinking about affect and feelings – affect as prior to emotion, as impersonal, as intersubjective, as material/embodied, as transmissible between people and things – must all be set within the context of post-1980s economic transformations in the Western world. The rise of neoliberalism, with its deregulation of market forces and expansion of economic and entrepreneurial logic to all aspects of society, has led to what David Harvey claims is "the financialization of everything" (2007, p. 33). Moreover, the growth of the neoliberal economy – which broadly entails a shift from an industrial to a service sector economy in the West – has increasingly exploited forms of immaterial labor (Hardt and Negri 2000, pp. 290–294) and treats affect and emotions as commodities. Think of the labor the growing care industries (nursing, daycare), tech industries (social media, cognitive or creative labor), and service industries (customer relations, service with a smile) demand from their workers – it is a kind of affective labor they are tapping into. That affect theory would become prominent at the same time in which these economic transformations were occurring speaks to the unique status of affect, feeling, and emotion in our own time.

Indeed, both Williams and affect theorists allow us to consider the ways in which post-1980s fiction responds in new and specific ways to emotion, feeling, and affect during a time in which an emerging neoliberal economy begins to commodify these very things. A brief consideration of two groupings of post-1980s American literature – Gen X affectlessness and post-postmodern sincerity and empathy – shows how such literature responds to these changes by developing its own feelings about feelings, as well as a marked self-consciousness about affect and emotions, of their failures, their value, and their commodification.

GENERATION X AND THE AFFECT OF AFFECTLESSNESS

In the 1980s, many young and ambitious American writers sought to distinguish their art from the postmodernist literature that preceded it. While in 1967 John Barth wrote of postmodern writers confronting a "literature of exhaustion" (the challenge of writing when everything has been said/written), this newer generation of writers experienced an exhaustion less in terms of literary aesthetics and more as a social, political, and cultural reality. Indeed, the feeling that things were "exhausted" – the future, any kind of sincerity or honesty, experiencing anything authentic, consumerism, and history itself – is a good way to describe the (mostly white, middle-class, and affluent) Gen X ethos.

A feeling of affectlessness, for instance, is central to the work of Bret Easton Ellis and Jay McInerney, who both wrote debut novels that catapulted them to fame in the mid-1980s. In Ellis's first novel, *Less Than Zero* (1985), the narrator Clay floats through an empty and very wealthy LA life of partying, shopping, and conspicuous name-brand consumption, all while taking copious amounts of cocaine against a reappearing billboard that reads "Disappear Here." In this world, everyone is interchangeable. All the characters are "tan, blonde, good looking" (1985, p. 152) and bisexual, not so much out of an active choice, but simply because everyone sleeps with everyone else and true relationships hardly matter.

The resulting boredom leads the characters to view and engage in sadistic sexual and violent acts. After watching a pornographic snuff video, for instance, one character hopes that it is real (1985, p. 154). Such a hope morphs into a desire for people to "see the worst" (p. 172) and eventually to join in the violent orgies to which they are desensitized. In the end, when we find out that one of Clay's friends is a heroin addict and has been prostituting himself for drug debts, the final message is that the rich are consuming themselves, parent and child alike.

Clay himself is dissociated from this world and himself, at times breaking down and crying, though he never acts to change anything. As one ex-girlfriend puts it, Clay is "not there" (1985, p. 204). Indeed, this is how our aptly named Clay (he "molds" or fits into any situation) acts throughout, as a sort of reporter disconnected from what he sees and records, which Ellis delivers in a fittingly sparse and tight prose that avoids emotional or figurative expression – a truly "affectless" prose for an affectless narrator and world.

Jay McInerney's *Bright Lights, Big City* (1984) similarly charts a descent into addiction and self-destruction, though often humorously and less morbidly than Ellis. The unnamed and affluent narrator is caught in a cycle of cocaine, clubbing, and consumerism to compensate for his broken and empty marriage and his mother's death from cancer. The narrator stumbles through an inauthentic materialistic world in which he indulges in tabloid journalism (1984, p. 11), even though he notes the danger of fact and fiction blurring and is himself a fact checker for a magazine; knowingly purchases a fake Cartier watch (p. 28); discovers he has a "consumer profile" (p. 151), and comes upon a mannequin made to resemble his ex-wife, a model (pp. 68, 74). All the while the narrator struggles to both feel something authentic while avoiding the feelings of pain in his past.

The novel is told via an innovative second-person point of view that seems to forge a special affective bond with the reader, yet it really speaks more to the narrator's detachment from himself. Despite the world's inauthenticity, he confesses to feeling like an "imposter" (1984, pp. 166–167) and to "staying on the surface" of life as his upward mobility and dreams of being a writer are rapidly disappearing. This results in an alienation so extreme that it leads to solipsism, the belief that nobody can truly "know" anyone else (pp. 101, 126). Although a desire for change is signaled at the novel's end, when the narrator buys and eats some fresh bread – an obvious, if ambiguous, religious symbol of communion – the despair and cyclical nature of the narrative remain.

As the 1980s came to a close, a major historical event took place, beginning with the fall of the Berlin Wall in 1989 and the subsequent dissolution of the Soviet Bloc in 1991. This initiated what Francis Fukuyama famously called "the End of History" (1992), which argued that liberal democracy and capitalism had supposedly defeated any political and economic alternative (state-sponsored communism) and all the world needed now was a politics of technocratic tweaking. The feelings that followed the end of this momentous event would be key to Gen X consciousness, which did not view the event as celebratory. Nowhere is this perhaps so explicit as in Douglas Coupland's *Generation X: Tales for an Accelerated Culture* (1991), which appeared the same year as Richard Linklater's seminal film *Slacker* and

Nirvana's breakthrough album *Nevermind*. Indeed, *Generation X* marks a moment when the Gen X genre gained a fully-formed self-consciousness of its own status – of affectlessness as a conscious, articulated, and thus mass-marketable feeling.

Generation X's title and its satiric definitions of all-things-Gen X, which are recorded in the margins of the pages, underscore the novel's awareness of itself. Further, the three white, overeducated characters are all cast by Andy, the narrator, as types or "case studies" (1991, p. 17). Having lost any ambition in life, each has moved to Palm Springs, California and works a "McJob" or "a low-pay, low-prestige, low-dignity, low-benefit, no-future job in the service sector" (p. 5). Eschewing any real romantic relationships or family-building (marriage, a house, kids), they simply hang out as friends.

But, as in Ellis and McInerney, the bitterness simmering under the pose of affectlessness is evident. One entry for "Boomer Envy" (1991, p. 21) notes the resentment that Gen X's future has been bought, sold, and used up. Andy is envious that his parents' lives were "so clean, so free of *futurelessness*" (p. 86). The characters, as one note puts it, "live in a period of time when nothing seems to happen" (p. 7) and will never experience "genuine capital *H* history times, before *history* was turned into a press release, a marketing strategy, and a campaign tool" (p. 151). This feeling of "the End of History," in part, leads to a Gen X dissatisfaction with the possibility of an inauthentic suburban mall culture life and to a resulting nostalgia for the seeming authenticity of past eras and styles that are perceived to be naive and secure.

The novel also probes Gen X's "Knee-Jerk Irony" and "Derision Preemption: A life-style tactic; the refusal to go out on any sort of emotional limb so as to avoid mockery from peers. *Derision Preemption* is the main goal of *Knee-Jerk Irony*" (1991, p. 150). As Andy's brother puts it, "'it scares me that I don't see a future. And I don't understand this reflex of mind to be such a smartass about everything. It *really* scares me. I may not look like I'm paying attention to anything [. . .] but I am. But I can't allow myself to show it. And I don't know why'" (p. 150). Here Coupland considers the difficulty of communication for a generation that distrusts its own feelings and fears sharing emotions and admitting to vulnerability (p. 14).

Generation X itself is full of a kind of defensive snark and irony, offering funny and fragmented stories that wander this way and that like its drifting characters. The novel's affective tone of disaffection and irony is thus a major unifier of a plotless novel. It is *feeling*, not plot, that matters. As the characters head to Mexico at the novel's end, nothing much has changed, although, as in McInerney, there is a somewhat hopeful register.

Collectively, then, these novels can be said to radiate a feeling of affectlessness in both their content – they are "about" disaffection – but more importantly in their form – particularly through tone, mood, prose, and in their affective stances toward readers. Whether this affective stance inspires feelings of nihilism, alienation, apathy, boredom, or a defensive form of irony, such feelings are reproduced and transmitted, as it were, to readers.

In their jettisoning of emotion for more generalized "feelings," such works might be argued to signify what Fredric Jameson famously identified as a "waning of affect" in postmodern culture (1991, pp. 10–16). Against the depth psychology of modernist art that hinged upon the individual's angst, Jameson finds a "depthlessness" in postmodern culture that means that affect/emotion is no longer attributable, per se, to an individual subject. Thus, "the expression of feelings or emotions, the liberation, in contemporary society, from the older *anomie* [. . .] may also mean [. . .] a liberation from every other kind of feeling as well, since there is no longer a self present to do the feeling" (p. 15). Nevertheless, Jameson contends, this doesn't mean postmodern art or culture (or for that matter the decentered subject) are "utterly devoid of feeling" but that these feelings "are now free-floating and impersonal and tend to be dominated by a peculiar kind of euphoria" (p. 16). Interestingly, Jameson, in describing one feature of the passage from modernism to postmodernism, is roughly describing the move from treating emotion/affect as individualized to viewing affect as many affect theorists see it – as impersonal, cutting through subjects and objects, and free-floating. Yet where Jameson dwells more on the impoverishment of feeling or its commodifiability (the shallow "euphoria" and escaping anxiety), affect theorists stress the potential to make new and different connections between subjects and against commodification.

Thus, the Jamesonian claim that these Gen X novels display a "waning of affect" can be understood as their promotion of the autonomy of affect over its individualization. The "waning" is thus also a "waxing," in a dialectic typical of Jameson's thinking. Note that the feelings in/of these novels cannot be attributed to one particular person or object, for affect isn't something "owned" by someone so much as it is felt and claimed by a generation (who almost always *dis*claim the category or label – as Gen X did – that media, marketers, or scholars come up with to explain it). Affect theory would point to this notion of affect: as that which precedes the labeling of feelings, the very ability of a person, object, or generational grouping to affect and be affected – to sense feeling, and feel it as sense – in the first place. When those people or things are first affected by feeling or experience *something*, whether emotionally or bodily (consider affectlessness and the body: the slouch, the scowl, the blank look, the impassive pose). What is later named or signified (as an emotion or feeling) is the codification or formal capture of affect, its actualization, at which point it is no longer affect. Affect therefore circulates in and between people and objects, from readers to books to films to whatever, both inside and outside of institutions, publicly and privately.

From the standpoint of considering affect, emotion, and feeling, we can see that the post-1980s fiction writer cannot take authentic emotions and feeling things for granted, as somehow "the same" or untainted as they appeared to be in the past. To be sure, what Ellis and McInerney begin to create, record, and recycle is something that Coupland discovers more fully "formed," so much so that *Generation X* is a more self-conscious text, aware of its play with feeling and affectlessness in a way that Ellis's and McInerney's first novels are not. Once made more culturally legible, this intense antifeeling or affectlessness could then become a self-conscious style, at times an inauthentic pose, and something eminently marketable. Because of their own understanding of late capitalism's consumer and marketing culture, as well as the so-called End of History, Gen X writers began to realize that affect and feelings – and particularly the anomie, disaffection, and existential ennui of Gen X itself – were becoming marketable as well.

POST-POSTMODERNISM, SINCERITY, AND EMPATHY

By the 1990s, this amorphous feeling or affectlessness could be sensed and registered by enough artworks, writers, people, and the media in general to become a kind of cultural signifier itself: Gen X. Yet, as Williams notes, by the time a structure of feeling has been noted or classified, "a new structure of feeling will usually already have begun to form, in the true social present" (Williams 1977, p. 132). And structures themselves comprise a "set, with specific internal relations, at once interlocking and in tension" (p. 132). In short, feelings and relations are messy, but a prime indication of an alternate cultural current to the rise of affectlessness as affect can be found in the work of David Foster Wallace.

Wallace took a critical stance both in his fiction and in his declarations of what fiction ought to do that would set himself and his aesthetics against the literature of his era. Wallace, for instance, called out Ellis's brand of heavily marketed "Brat Pack" literature as "Neiman-Marcus Nihilism" (2012, pp. 39–40). For Wallace it was not enough for fiction to be "about" disaffection in terms of a work's content, fiction had to formally and affectively engage with cynicism and ennui, which were culture-wide. As he put it most forcefully in "E Pluribus Unam: Television and U.S. Fiction," "[t]he next real literary 'rebels' in this country, might well emerge as some weird bunch of *anti*-rebels" who "instantiate single-entendre principles" and "eschew self-consciousness and hip fatigue" (1997, p. 81). These writers may be labeled "[t]oo sincere" and must be "willing to risk the yawn, the rolled eyes, the cool smile, the nudged ribs, the parody of gifted ironists, the 'Oh how *banal*'" (p. 81). Wallace therefore lauded an openly emotional, vulnerable, and sincere form of literature.

Wallace's *Infinite Jest* (1996), one of the most influential novels of its times, put these ideas about fiction into play. At the heart of a long and complex story is the struggle of teenager Hal Incandenza to deal with his father's suicide, to learn to feel, and to create meaningful relationships with others. Hal no longer experiences "bona fide intensity-of-interior-life type emotion," feeling that he's "pretty much nothing at all" (2006, p. 694). *Infinite Jest* treats seriously, through Hal and other characters, the fear of "being really human," which means being "unavoidably sentimental and naïve and goo-prone" (p. 695) in an America in which art and media "treat anhedonia and internal emptiness as hip and cool" (p. 694). The novel probes the difficulty of feeling and communicating in a media-saturated society that caters to people's basest desires and longings and results in alienation and solipsism. Such a world gives rise to an endless empty feedback loop of ersatz products to meet ersatz desires, all symbolized in the novel by a videotape so addictive that those who watch it become infantilized and catatonic. Nevertheless, the "really American thing about Hal [. . .] is the way he despises what he's really lonely for: this hideous internal self, incontinent of sentiment and need, that pulses and writhes just under the hip empty mask, anhedonia" (p. 695). Although Hal, like Ellis's Clay, cannot escape his eventual solipsistic end as he becomes "trapped" inside himself, unable to communicate with others but clearly conscious and alive mentally – "I am in here," he says (p. 3) – Wallace traces this descent with blatant empathy and affection.

Wallace also attempts to pierce affectlessness, defensive irony, and hipness in the novel's form. The sprawling novel's metafictional form – it begins at the end and "loops" back to the start but leaves a vital section of the plot's ending untold – is no mere gameplay meant to call attention to itself but serves as a corrective to the looping trap of easily digestible media. The reader is challenged to work at tracing and making unstated connections between events and characters, many of whom do not see the connections between them. The reader is thus asked to join in the textual play of infinite jest, to encounter the text as place to bridge loneliness and quell despair.

That many young writers – Jonathan Safran Foer, Salvador Plascencia, Jennifer Egan, and others – would evince a similar kind of aesthetics to Wallace, often blending formal innovation or metatechniques while emphasizing feeling and inspiring empathy, is telling. It clearly speaks to affect theory and its emphasis on the "impersonality" of affect and that it can be transmitted in "intersubjective" spaces – in this case, literature. The fact that much post-postmodern literature often promotes sincere relationships despite language's pitfalls and is conscious of the intersubjective affective space between a reader(ly community) and a writer suggests its unique awareness of affect, feeling, and emotions in our time.

Dave Eggers's literary debut, *A Heartbreaking Work of Staggering Genius* (2000), for instance, flaunts its generic awareness (the memoir) in a way that underscores the fictional aspects of a supposedly "true" genre. In the book's meta-preface, Eggers emphasizes his "knowing about that self-conscious self-referentiality" (2000, p. xxx), and later he is forthright about his high aspirations: "I am bursting with the hopes of a generation" (p. 236). The book nevertheless seeks connection and honesty – Eggers "acknowledges the needs and feelings of a reader" (p. xlii) – and makes a claim for sincerity despite the self-referentiality: "Oh, I want to be the heart pumping blood to everyone" (p. 237). This drive toward sincerity, connection, and feeling follows Wallace's prescription for a new kind of literature that is premised on empathy.

For Rachel Greenwald Smith, such a literature of feeling, especially Eggers's novel, risks capitulating to neoliberalism's commodification of affect and emotion and its entrepreneurial demand that people make emotional connections and be empathic (2015, pp. 30–48). On Smith's view literature becomes merely a kind of social networking exercise for generating marketable feelings and self/brand improvement. Indeed, the recent boom in books on empathy, in which Wallace work's fame has played its part, demonstrates that empathy has become commodified (Pedwell 2014) and its darker aspects ignored (Prinz 2011). This is no surprise considering the growth of affective labor in the neoliberal economy. When we uncritically think of empathy as something "good," neoliberalism immediately turns it into "a good" as well. We must therefore be wary of our feelings and affective connections as never before.

Some authors, then, have attempted to detach emotion from leading to an all-too-easy marketable empathy. One direct response to this commodification of emotion and affect is Colson Whitehead's in *Zone One* (2011), a postapocalyptic zombie novel. Before the zombie plague, the protagonist, Mark Spitz, works for a multinational coffee company's social media branch, tailoring and "personalizing" messages to consumers and attempting to create affective bonds, "to sow product mindshare and nurture feelings of brand intimacy" (2011, p. 184). Spitz is "a natural at ersatz human connection and the postures of counterfeit empathy" and providing the illusion of a "human touch" and "soul" (p. 186). The zombie has long been a figure of mindless consumerism, yet Whitehead expands this figure into a biopolitical critique regarding the production and consumption of emotion and affect. Even feelings turn out to be as inauthentic as the products purchased at the mall. The pre-disaster "feelings" of the "living" turn out to be not much different than the post-disaster unfeeling living or dead.

The novel, in turn, cautiously distances itself, as does much of Whitehead's fiction, against any easy emotional or empathic connection with its reader. Spitz's harsh world is premised on survival. Hope is a dangerous "gateway drug" (2011, p. 222) and affect – in the form of optimism – has become a commodity in Buffalo's branded rebuild, "American Phoenix," which has "official sponsors" (p. 48) and later turns out to be mere propaganda for a failed program. When the zombies break through the barricades at the novel's end, there is little sentiment for either the characters or the pre-disaster world in which emotions and affect were no different than commodities. Whitehead's literary transformation of genre fiction thus refuses a commodifiable feeling of hope or a happy ending that such a generic popular cultural object might inspire.

Empathy in fiction that can also be problematic if it leads easily to a "feel good multiculturalism" premised on understanding "the other." Claudia Rankine's *Citizen: An American Lyric* (2014) is a genre-blurring "poem" that employs the second-person point of view throughout, which seemingly puts the reader in the place of someone experiencing acts of racism. Yet Rankine resists an easy readerly identification. At one point, the speaker says that the "I" is "[t]he pronoun barely holding the person together" (2014, p. 71) and that "[s]ometimes 'I' is supposed to hold what is not there until it is. Then *what is* comes apart the closer you are to it" (p. 71). If, as *Citizen* shows, Black personhood is frequently denied, ignored, and subject to dehumanization by verbal and physical acts of racism, then claiming a personal "I" is complicated for Black people. For this "I" is often a historically and racially projected "self" as imagined by white people. The "you," in contrast, aptly captures the split subject or dissociated self that the speaker frequently experiences and meditates upon (in this sense, the "you" is the "I" that has come apart), an instance of a Du Boisean "double-consciousness," yet with the additional stress upon the physical effects and costs of racism on the body.

Nevertheless, writers of "autofiction," including Ben Lerner, Sheila Heti, Chris Kraus, and Maggie Nelson, among others, have further pushed the boundaries of sincerity and the affective aims evident in post-postmodern fiction. Autofiction's intentional blurring of fact and fiction, of author and character, are more than a postmodern exposure of fiction's fictionality. These writers move from the word back to the world, recognizing that reality is inescapably textual but insisting upon the value of lived experience, that the "reality" that is lived and textually recorded still "matters," figuratively and literally. These authors, like Rankine, often work at the edges of genres: the novel, memoir, poetic forms, critical theory, diaristic writing, and more. Nowhere is Williams's "structures of feeling" more obvious as when writerly consciousness self-consciously confronts genre itself as a structuring force, breaking it down to stress the immediacy of lived and felt experience (affect and feeling), prior to or just as it is being caught up in language. These in-between spaces – between feeling and thought; between generic borders – call attention to the immateriality of affect, as well as to its materialization in both language and life.

Post-1980s fiction thus evinces a burgeoning realization that economic, linguistic, and literary systems structure how we encounter and think about emotions, feelings, and affect. Such fiction shows us that we can no longer be naive or innocent about feelings and emotions and how they are put to work. This fiction often treats affect as distinct from emotion – as a kind of vital, transpersonal force that circulates in and between various bodies – suggesting new potentialities for accessing and organizing our sense and senses and for thinking feeling and feeling thought in the future and in future fictions.

SEE ALSO: After Postmodernism; Barth, John; Debut Novels; Egan, Jennifer; Eggers, Dave; Fictions of Work and Labor; Foer, Jonathan Safran; Lerner, Ben; Millennial Fiction; Moody, Rick; Wallace, David Foster; Whitehead, Colson

REFERENCES

Barth, John. (1967). The literature of exhaustion. In: *The Friday Book: Essays and Other Non-Fiction*, 62–76. London: Johns Hopkins University Press.

Coupland, Douglas. (1991). *Generation X: Tales for an Accelerated Culture*. New York: St. Martin's.

Eggers, Dave. (2000). *A Heartbreaking Work of Staggering Genius*. New York: Vintage Books.

Ellis, Brett Easton. (1985). *Less Than Zero*. New York: Vintage Books.

Fukuyama, Francis. (1992). *The End of History and the Last Man*. New York: Free Press.

Hardt, Michael and Negri, Antonio. (2000). *Empire*. Cambridge, MA: Harvard University Press.

Harvey, David. (2007). *A Brief History of Neoliberalism*. Oxford: Oxford University Press.

Jameson, Fredric. (1991). *Postmodernism, or, The Cultural Logic of Late Capitalism*. Durham, NC: Duke University Press.

Massumi, Brian. (2002). *Parables of the Virtual: Movement, Affect, Sensation*. Durham, NC: Duke University Press.

McInerney, Jay. (1984). *Bright Lights, Big City*. New York: Vintage Books.

Pedwell, Carolyn. (2014). *Affective Relations: The Transnational Politics of Empathy*. New York: Palgrave Macmillan.

Prinz, Jesse. (2011). Against empathy. Southern Journal of Philosophy 49: 214–233.

Rankine, Claudia. (2014). *Citizen: A Lyric*. Minneapolis: Graywolf.

Smith, Rachel Greenwald. (2015). *Affect and American Literature in the Age of Neoliberalism*. Cambridge, MA: Cambridge University Press.

Wallace, David Foster. (1997). E pluribus unam: television and US fiction. In: *A Supposedly Fun Thing I'll Never Do Again*, 21–82. New York: Little, Brown.

Wallace, David Foster. (2006). *Infinite Jest*. New York: Little, Brown; 1st ed. 1996.

Wallace, David Foster. (2012). Fictional futures and the conspicuously young. In: *Both Flesh And Not: Essays*, 37–68. New York: Little, Brown.

Whitehead, Colson. (2011). *Zone One*. New York: Anchor.

Williams, Raymond. (1977). *Marxism and Literature*. Oxford: Oxford University Press.

FURTHER READING

Ahmed, Sarah. (2010). *The Promise of Happiness*. Durham, NC: Duke University Press.

Berlant, Lauren. (2011). *Cruel Optimism*. Durham, NC: Duke University Press.

Clough, Patricia Ticineto. (ed.) (2017). *The Affective Turn: Theorizing the Social*. Durham, NC: Duke University Press.

Gregg, Melissa and Seigworth, Gregory J. (eds.) (2010). *The Affect Theory Reader*. Durham, NC: Duke University Press.

Ngai, Sianne. (2005). *Ugly Feelings*. Cambridge, MA: Harvard University Press.

Fiction and Terrorism

ART REDDING
York University, Toronto, Canada

Charlie Chehab, a character in charge of tutoring the aspiring suicide bomber, Ahmad Ashmawy Mulloy, in John Updike's bluntly titled novel *Terrorist* (2006), makes an explicit link between George Washington's continental army and contemporary terrorism: Washington "learned to take what came, to fight guerrilla style. He retreated but he never gave up. He was the Ho Chi Minh of his day. We were like Hamas. We were Al-Qaida" (p. 181). The "we" in these last two sentences refers to "Americans," and Updike takes pains to underline potential connections between the religious and political motivations of contemporary terrorists and the American radical revolutionary tradition. Terrorists, by this way of thinking, aren't so foreign: they *are* American. In Updike's novel, the native-born Ahmed, converted to a broader vision of human inclusivity by his rumpled, melancholic high school guidance counselor, Jacob "Jack" Levy, ultimately abandons his mission. Unlikely as that scenario is – Updike is not the only white, Western writer who will be charged by critics with a failure of imaginative nerve – the novel, like so much contemporary fiction, sifts through the web of relations between an imagined national collective – America – and those "who hate us" – the terrorists whose attacks aim to undermine "our" national culture, our social, legal, and military institutions, our economy, our very way of being. Updike stresses our mutual interconnectedness, making an appeal to empathetic humanism, to the possibility of complex forms of cross-cultural understanding and communication, and to the ethical project of imaginatively bridging almost unimaginable differences.

Between 1978 and 1995, anarcho-terrorist Ted Kaczynski, the so-called Unabomber, sent at least sixteen explosive devices to various people, killing three. On April 1, 1995, Timothy McVeigh set off a truck bomb at the Alfred P. Murrah Federal building in Oklahoma City, killing 168 people and injuring hundreds more. On September 11, 2001, members of an Al-Qaida terror cell hijacked four passenger jets, flying two of them into the twin towers of the World Trade Center in New York, which collapsed, and one into the Pentagon. Nearly three thousand people were killed, and an estimated 25,000 plus were injured in the deadliest terror attack in history. An earlier, 1993, truck bombing of the World Trade Center orchestrated by Islamicist terrorists had killed six people. The Global Terror Database (n.d.), managed by the National Consortium for the Study of Terrorism and the Response to Terrorism, lists over 1400 terror "incidents" between 1980 and 2018 in the United States alone and 190,000 worldwide since 1970. Though reports vary widely depending on definition and methodology, according to the Gun Violence Archive (n.d.), the number of mass shootings in the United States averages 334 annually since 2013; many of these attacks are dubbed "hate crimes" rather than "terrorist" attacks, because they are predominantly carried out by white men acting alone, rather than by organized groups. Even so, such attacks, like acts of terrorism, target noncombatants, civilians, and bystanders. Moreover, well-organized coteries of white nationalists on the far right have well endorsed such shootings, according to an "accelerationist" theory that terrorist acts will help to inaugurate what they see as a coming Civil War (Hayden 2019) in the United States.

How have American writers responded to the terror attacks of 9/11, or to other acts of terrorism at home or around the world? What have our novels and stories had to say about acts of terror before those events? How can American fiction fully comprehend the complicated social and political aspects of terrorism? How have novels depicted the lives of survivors, of those who have lost beloved friends or family members, or those whose lives have been otherwise touched by these atrocities, of those who struggle with their grief, with their anger, with their outrage? How have novelists envisioned the cultural aftermath of this trauma, how have they envisioned the future? How, if at all, has the contemporary age of terror inflected literary aesthetics? What critical insights does our literature have to offer about the so-called global war on terror, a campaign inaugurated early in the century by the Bush administration in response to the 9/11 attacks, but still ongoing? And how have novelists understood the motives of perpetuators of terror? How have we imagined the lives of our presumed enemies?

Insofar as the modern novel has been conceived of by many writers, critics, and philosophers as a sort of machine for generating empathy, fiction about terrorism has meant fiction about terrorists as often as about victims and survivors. When Updike describes Amad, when Don DeLillo includes chapters about the terrorist Hammad in *Falling Man* (2007), when Andre Dubus III details the erotic life of Bassam in *The Garden of Last*

Days (2008), they solicit readers imaginatively to comprehend and sympathize with those whose capacity to commit violence against presumably "innocent" civilians seem almost unthinkable. Alternatively, fictions have undertaken to respond to the attendant trauma of survivors, mapping the possibilities of reconstituting semblances of coherence, order, durability, and agency for those whose worlds have been shattered. What does fiction about terrorism tell us about gender, about race, about class, about our own propensity for violence, for revenge, for hate? What are the limits of the human? Further, novels about terrorism have asked hard questions about how collective national self-understandings are formed. How does "America" conceive of itself culturally? What, precisely, can be said to be distinctly "American" about American fiction? As a literary subject, thus, terrorism presents a challenge to the unlimited human capaciousness for empathy. How can we envision the conciliation – ethically, politically, socially, emotionally – of an "us" with a "them"? How can we inhabit a world constituted by terror?

American fiction, it seems, has so far only gropingly provided answers to these questions. Most critics have dismissed as a failure Updike's efforts to persuasively characterize the psychic life of a terrorist. As Duvall and Marzec observe, such other well-intentioned works as Jay McInerney's *The Good Life* (2006) or DeLillo's *Falling Man*, both works that examine characters whose lives have been interrupted or overturned by the 9/11 attacks, betray an "American literature that has retreated from politics into domesticity" (Duvall and Marzec 2011, p. 384). Critical consensus also seems to have confirmed what Zulaika and Douglass (1996) term the terror "taboo," an inability to depict the terrorist as fully human. The growing number of contemporary Western novelists from Updike on who have tried their hand at depicting complex, three-dimensional characters, characters who may be likeable, characters with whom their readers will identify – characters who also happen to be terrorists – have, it seems, failed quite badly to do so. In a very recent essay, for example, Richard Jackson concludes that the "the terrorism novelist is trapped in the paradox of seeking to know the mind of the terrorist but without really 'knowing' it" (2018, p. 388). Nonetheless, Jackson contends, writers can break the taboo if they try: they will need only to bypass "the dominant terrorist mythography in ways that would permit a deeper empathetic engagement and understanding of why otherwise ordinary people would use terrorist violence in their political struggles" (p. 389). "Such a humanizing terrorist novel" (p. 389), he concludes, is perfectly possible. Likewise defending the prospect of a humanizing terrorist novel, and lamenting the proliferation of stereotypes in popular media, blogger and writer Saadia Faruqi (2017), contends that "fiction . . . has a unique advantage to shatter stereotypes about terrorism," but only so long as the books "are written by and about Muslims themselves, or at least writers who are very familiar with the nuances and complexities of the Muslim world."

Many novelists of a variety of religious, racial, and ethnic backgrounds have undertaken the endeavor. Many works too, like Jennifer Egan's *Look at Me* (2001), have thematized the problem itself: how does a writer relying on conventional narrative conceits render a terrorist "human"? "How can we root for this guy?" asks Egan. "He's a jerk, a fanatic. A loony" (p. 310).

Writers have adopted a variety of approaches to render terrorists comprehensible, even sympathetic, to their readers. A failsafe tactic, the one deployed by Updike, is to quite literally defuse the confrontation, to "humanize" the terrorist by having him abandon his mission and thereby implicitly renounce his guiding ideology. In book after book, the feared terrorist violence remains curiously unconsummated. This plot twist might be called the "Hyacinth Robinson" gambit, after a Henry James novel (1886) in which the anarchist assassin becomes seduced by the beauties of the world and refuses to carry out the mission. In Egan's novel, the character Z., for example, begins his life fighting for Hezbollah in Lebanon, but takes up a larger anti-American cause: "he hates – *despises* – America. Thinks we've got a plot to control the world with our 'cultural exports'" (2001, p. 309). Ultimately, however, Z. will be converted to a deep appreciation of the American sublime.

True, Updike's post-9/11 terrorist, Ahmad, backs down, but few critics found his decision plausible. Such plot twists of avoidance – whereby the terrorist turns out not "really" to be a terrorist – certainly become more difficult to pull off after 9/11, of course. Mohsin Hamid's very well-received *The Reluctant Fundamentalist* (2007) defers consummating the violence, leaving the question of whether the potential terrorist possesses full capacity to undertake acts of extreme violence. Hamid leaves the true motivations and plans of the presumed terrorist, Changez, in doubt: the reader is asked to question her or his own biases and (possibly misplaced) suspicions, as well as sympathies. Even so, Hamid's point is to underscore that we can never be sure of the truth of things, especially in a murderous and politically volatile world where the older allegiances shaped by the Cold War have dissolved.

There are other examples of the terror plot that never comes to fruition, but these abound predominantly in works written before the 9/11 attacks. In Robert Stone's *Damascus Gate* (1998), for example, an apparent conspiracy between extremist Jews and American Christian zealots to blow up the Temple Mount in a bid to usher in the end of times fizzles out; both groups are being played by political operatives, who hope to secure a tighter stranglehold on power by fanning the flames of fear. The terror plot is little more than a political charade, even though there is death aplenty. Stone makes a concerted effort in this book to sympathize with the worldviews of zealots and extremists. His Jerusalem "was full of secrets" (1998, p. 19); in a sort of inverse of diaspora, people have come to Jerusalem from all over the world: the land is a concentration of cosmopolitan Jews, Christians, Muslims, even Domi. So too religious and political zealots of all stripes, and people's passions are played upon by various interest groups: "Here also there are cults . . . Not merely a few lost souls, but organized and powerful groups" (p. 49). In this novel, religious zealotry and messianism coupled with the insecurities of polyglot cultures produce a volatile mix of dangerous, precarious politics, even if Stone accentuates the possibility of hope over despair. Yet, to whatever extent Stone is able to "realistically" render the passions that motivate terrorist actions, the promised violence is abortive: the terrorists are not fully capable of carrying out their intentions.

The terrorist in Egan's *Look at Me*, which was drafted before the 9/11 attacks but only published afterwards, likewise gets cold feet. Her work, in contrast to Stone's, is satire, targeting the rise of both social media and reality television: it is precisely the banalities of American life that seduce Z., he has his apotheosis eating a Big Mac in Rockford, Illinois. Like every character in *Look at Me*, Z. imagines his life as a screenplay, one in which the hero is redeemed at the end. Like Updike, Egan too stresses that the terrorist, ultimately, is not foreign at all; she is far less sanguine than Updike, however, about American values: "Don't you get it? He's *American!* He's been American all his life, the whole time he was hating our guts! Which is what he finally figures out. The self-discovery. Which is what this movie is about!" (2001, p. 312). Z. turns out to be less of a narcissist, less superficial, than the book's protagonist, the middle-American model and eventual lifestyle guru Charlotte Swenson, but in either case, American values emphasize self-adoration over democracy, tolerance, or inclusiveness. In her satirical indictment of nascent reality television, Egan points to a link between the deep narcissism of aspiring celebrity culture and the shallow narcissism of the terrorist: both are needy and desperate for attention. A similar link underwrites Bret Easton Ellis's satire *Glamorama* (1998), wherein a fashion model, Victor Ward, whose hip but self-serving lifestyle is covered in detail by a film crew, becomes ensnarled in murder, torture, and bombings, none of which we – neither Victor nor his readers – can ever be sure actually occur. Like *Look at Me*, Ann Patchett's *Bel Canto* (2001) was drafted before the 9/11 attacks. Patchett's terrorists infiltrate a birthday party in an unnamed country in South America (which shares many similarities with Peru). The revolutionaries of "La Familia de Martin Suarez" (2001, p. 61) turn out also to be lovable and inept, effectively unable to kill anyone. Like *Glamorama*, these novels may intuit or anticipate the attacks, but cannot fully describe them. We can't fully be sure if Ellis's terror is real, or if it is just a movie, and Victor is as unnerved by his incapacity to tell the difference – is all this bloodshed happening in real life? Or is it just a movie? – as he is by the gore he encounters.

Easy satirical points about American glamorization of violence may have been easier to make prior to 9/11. The confusion or counter-penetration of image with reality is a standard enough postmodern trope; critics such as Roger Rosenblatt, who wrote a famous *Time* magazine opinion piece shortly after the attacks titled "The Age of Irony Comes to an End" (2001), have questioned whether such aesthetics has been supplanted by newfound forms of sincerity and a more traditional realism. As the examples of Stone, Egan, and Ellis suggest, there turns out to have been a rich literature about terrorism prior to the turn of the millennium. However, it may well have been somewhat easier, prior to the 9/11 attacks, for novels to have short-shrifted the fully genuine, fully brutal, and fully consequential reality of terrorism in the world. Consequentially, critics have suggested, this slighting of terrorism accorded with a philosophical tendency in the post-structuralist thought of the 1980s and 1990s to view "reality" as a mere construct of discourse. For while terror has long been a literary theme as well as a political and military problem, it has not until very recently been thought of as such. As Peter C. Herman points out, literary scholarship devoted to the topic is entirely a twenty-first-century phenomenon (2018, p. 4).

The attempt to humanize the Muslim terrorist, as Jasbir Puar argues, indulges in distinct fantasies of its own: "in these supposedly politically progressive efforts, many of them feminist, to de-pathologize the individual in favor of contextualizing socialization and the social, the victim status of the (always male) terrorist is resurrected ... through the inescapable brutalities of global capital and the heteronormative" (2007, pp. 59–60). In Puar's estimation, even critical, progressive approaches to terrorist studies unwittingly reproduce an exclusionary logic that distinguishes "normal" from deviant, folding women and homosexuals (who were once looked upon with suspicion but are increasingly understood to be "rights-bearing" subjects) into the embrace of older heteronormative, racist, and patriotic traditions. Muslim masculinity, by contrast, is portrayed as perverse, excessive, outside the fold, not fully human. But not all terrorists are Islamicists, obviously, nor are all fictions about them embroiled in the politics of the Mideast.

We can look at a few more pre-9/11 works about revolutionary terrorism before turning attention to a consideration of what has changed in American fiction in the twenty-first century. Between 1980 and 2000, many novelists have adopted another strategy for imaginatively reconciling human community with the acts of terror. If today's imagined and implicitly despised Muslim terrorist is always male, the imagined far-left militant (a member of the Symbionese Liberation Army, the Weather Underground, Baader-Meinhof) is almost always envisioned in works of literature as exclusively female. The body of fictional works about left-wing terrorists has some peculiarities of its own worth sifting through: the terrorists tend to be radical revolutionary leftists rather than jihadists and they tend to be women (Redding 2018). This is largely true of novels about left radical terrorism published before the terror attacks of 2001: Marge Piercy's *Vida* (1980), Tim O'Brien's *The Nuclear Age* (1985), Philip Roth's *American Pastoral* (1997), along with earlier novels from the 1970s. Some of these pre-9/11 novels, as with Roth's, meditate on the unthinkability of violence, of violence advocated by those who are close to you, by affluent, well-cared-for, young, privileged Americans; others depict protagonists who move away from the politics of aggression to a more enlightened, life-affirming, and feminist mode of action, as with Marge Piercy.

But the same is also true for novels published after 9/11, which similarly imagine the left revolutionary terrorist as female: Susan Choi's *American Woman* (2003), Russell Banks's *The Darling* (2004), Christopher Sorrentino's *Trance* (2005), Dana Spiotta's *Eat the Document* (2006), Sigrid Nunez's *The Last of Her Kind* (2006), Peter Carey's *His Illegal Self* (2008), and Rachel Kushner's *The Flamethrowers* (2013) all feature women protagonists who take up arms in the cause of social justice. A woman terrorist, a terrorist who commits violent acts out of a commitment to social justice, is somehow more ideologically palatable in American fiction. The subsequent twenty-first-century works that have been written about earlier forms of terrorism typically use those episodes as a screen to comment upon contemporary forms of political violence, as if the militant activism of the 1960s and 1970s were some sort of a golden age, where the idea that violence in the service of justice was philosophically defensible, still comprehensible, when violent response to deep forms of social and political injustice might still have served the cause of righteousness. In the 1970s, one could be still be a "good" girl terrorist. One telling example is *The Darling*, wherein one-time revolutionary Hannah Musgrave, in flight from the law, comes to experience the horrors of civil war in Liberia and, returning to a new America after 9/11, without renouncing her past, nonetheless intuits her earlier infatuation with revolutionary violence as potentially misbegotten and naïve.

It would at any rate be a few years before fiction dramatizing the 9/11 attacks would appear. Understandably, memoirs and essays – subject to a quite distinct imaginative ethos – appeared first. Such works have a social contract with their reader that they be honest, that however speculative or considered, they work in the realm of facts. Even so, many works of creative commentary, such as Art Spiegelman's solemn graphic work *In the Shadow of No Towers* (2004), serialized in the German newspaper *Die Zeit* between 2002 and 2004, took up the problem of how one might ethically or adequately "represent" such horrifying events. William Gibson's *Pattern Recognition* (2003) is sometimes considered to be among the first novels dedicated to reckoning with the cultural and emotional fallout of 9/11. A spate of novels appeared between 2005 and 2007, most of which centered around the traumatic effects of the 9/11 attacks on the lives of those who survived. Jonathan Safran Foer's *Extremely Loud & Incredibly Close* (2005), in which the young Oskar Scheller, who lost his father in the twin towers, traipses around Manhattan seeking consolation, and DeLillo's *Falling Man*, which documents the ruptured lives of an estranged couple, have received the bulk of critical attention. Others works of the type include Lynne Sharon Schwartz's, *The Writing on the Wall* (2005); Jay McInerney's aforementioned *The Good Life*, and even such comedies as Ken Kalfus's *A Disorder Peculiar to the Country* (2006).

Rosenblatt's suggestion that postmodern irony would wane after 9/11 has not been borne out. Even a brief survey of this literature shows that the literary capacity for irony, experimentation, reflexivity, or metafiction has in no way been diminished in the twenty-first century. Nonetheless, it does seem obvious that 9/11 posed distinct challenges for fiction writers, not least of which was the sensitivity with which they might henceforward treat depictions of terrorist violence. Without wishing to flatten out the diverse and various range of writing on the subject, we can nonetheless observe a few overarching tendencies in our survey of American fiction. First, there has indeed been a deeper appreciation of the genuinely traumatic dimension of the attacks. Attentiveness to the profound quality of hurt inflicted on American lives by the attacks has no doubt leavened the more frivolous playfulness of earlier postmodern writing. Such works as *Falling Man*, *Point Omega* (2010) or *Zero K* (2016) indicate that the post-9/11 writing of Don DeLillo, for example, certainly reads as more somber, sober-minded, and mature reflections on American life than such earlier, sometimes farcical, spoofs as *Americana* (1971), *White Noise* (1985), or *Libra* (1988).

DeLillo, of course, has long been concerned with the isolation and loneliness of American life; he has also been preoccupied with the figure of terrorist as romantic villain. In *Mao II* (1991), for example, the reclusive writer Bill Gray undertakes a political pilgrimage of sorts to Lebanon in a self-sacrificing and ultimately self-destructive quest to secure the release of a writer held hostage there. Gray laments that "I used to think it was possible for a novelist to alter the inner life of the culture. Now bomb makers and gunman have taken that territory. They make raids on human consciousness" (1991, p. 41). Here, DeLillo expressed frustration not simply at the incapacity of literature to generate genuine social change but at its failure to productively engage our human imagination, something terrorists, at least to Gray's way of thinking, can still do. In this formula, the relationship between terrorism and writing can be summed up as involving a possibly dangerous urge to matter, to make a difference in the world, to be noticed, to be loved: both acts emerge from the same deep well of loneliness. Of course, 9/11 engaged the imagination; subsequent to those attacks, however, DeLillo's fiction would not prove so cavalier about the romantic inspirations of the terrorist. Rather, *Falling Man* assesses the fractured and damaged lives of the survivors, who are struggling to find a way to mourn and to grieve, processes that are difficult apart from a community that seems inaccessible; in this work, mourning as a collective act is what we aspire to, though the book has difficulty seeing it as being something we might complete in any more than the most provisional of senses.

In sum, then, rather than driving writers back to more traditional forms of realistic representation, the attacks of 9/11 have directly challenged the sense-making capacity of literature. But the uptick in trauma narratives has not meant that American writers have become more sentimental.

Paradoxically enough (and this is a second important feature of terror fiction since 2001), political satire has become even more trenchant, perhaps precisely because writers are more sensitized to the full horror of terrorist acts. A perhaps unexpected conclusion any survey of American fiction about terrorism will unfailingly yield is that so many of the works are comic, such as Claire Messud's *The Emperor's Children* (2007), which teasingly follows the dysfunctional lives of aspiring and successful New York artists, writers, and cognoscenti, or James Hynes's *Next* (2010), in which a disgruntled mid-level academic staffer is compelled to contend with stinger attacks launched by terrorists on a building in Austin, Texas. There have also been powerful and politically resonant works in the postmodern style. These include Heidi Julavits's *The Effect of Living Backwards* (2003), a comic story of sibling rivalry between two sisters who are unlucky passengers on a jet that gets hijacked coupled to a scathingly satirical indictment of the cult of expertise among counterterrorist agents in the intelligence community. Despite its grim subject matter and subtheme of sexual shame, Julavits's novel is laugh-out-loud funny. Passengers keep wondering if they are victims of an old-fashioned hijacking or terrorism. "Why can't you just act normally?" one young man pleads with his captors? "Why can't you just shoot people or fly us into a building" (2003, p. 103). Jess Walter's *The Zero* (2006), Ken Kalfus's *A Disorder Peculiar to the Country* Percival Everett's *The Water Cure* (2007), and Thomas Pynchon's *Bleeding Edge* (2013) have undertaken to satirize, critique, ironize, or lampoon American life in the age of terror. There is a remarkable number of bitingly funny black comedies written about 9/11. These works have coupled sensitivity to humans suffering with blistering denouncements of American political policy.

Perhaps the most troubling of the experimental novels is Everett's *The Water Cure*, in which the narrator subjects a man who may (or may not) have been responsible for the rape and murder of his daughter to waterboarding. Everett stages a drama wherein the acts of those who have been wronged are entirely reprehensible, even though they consider themselves as agents of justice. What happens when the victim, seeking vengeance, turns criminal? What are the ethics of interrogation? In such a case, it is difficult for us to maintain any easy divide between the victims and perpetrators. The fact that America is an imperial power that has used military force in no way exonerates the hijackers; but, according to the same moral calculus, the horrific violence perpetrated by the 9/11 hijackers cannot be justification for torture. Everett implies that, amid these power plays, the abstract pursuit of "justice" is largely chimerical. In both cases, the "scale" of violence is of less import the than the pure facticity of violence, as a world-making and world-destroying instrument. In this moral calculus, there is no real distinction to be made between a Baudrillardean vision of the world as a production of simulacra (a construct, an image, a set of ideological reproduction) and the sobering counter-philosophy that understands a world of stark brutality and violence, insofar as both concepts of "truth" are products of violence. In Everett, any truth that counts is nothing more than a function of power: "I think too my assertion that he is guilty and his claim that he is innocent, and I consider what makes any statement true, taking into account lies and fictions, taking into account that no-one gives a rat's ass anyway, but I entertain it all nonetheless, knowing that expecting my meaning to match the facts as a standard of truth rings of some kind of correspondence theory of truth and of course that is just a shallow grave of a theory, the fact remaining that I am tearing off strip after strip of my 3M duct tape like music in this damp room that is my basement, that is my world . . ." (2007, p. 185). Similarly, in Walter, the line between good and evil gets confused, as does the line between the real and the hallucinatory: how, finally, can guilt or innocence be assessed? The protagonist of *The Zero* is a morally conscientious "first responder" who is hired by security forces to interrogate suspects. He suffers from blackouts, refusing to acknowledge his role as torturer. Walter and Everett compel their readers to understand that we may be traumatized not simply by the terror attacks but by the acts of vengeance and torture with which Americans have responded. What is repressed in our collective national narrative of the events is the fact that "terrorism" can be the tactics of state agents as much as of insurrectionaries, that even Americans can terrorize.

Another distinguishing feature of 9/11 fiction, as we have already seen, has been to view these traumatizing and incomprehensible events through the lens of historical precedents. In her discussion of Foer, critic Ilka Saal observes that his novels deploy what she refers to as "trauma transfer"; that is, "the reading of current trauma through the lens of a previous one" (2011, p. 454). Oskar, on a quest mission to heal himself, thematizes a longer historical trajectory of suffering in the twentieth century, whose war-torn history has compelled its victims repeatedly to contend with the absence of fathers. Traumas destroy our sense of coherence and capacity to live sensibly in the world. The restoration of coherence necessitates a model for embedding a uniquely inexplicable and uniquely horrifying event such as the 9/11 attacks within a larger narrative framework that might console, at least, even if it never explains.

The search for consolation characterizes much of the fiction, though novels are equivocal about the extent to which consolation can be found or achieved. Set mostly in the summer before the attacks, and depicting a surreal erotic near-encounter between a stripper and one of the 9/11 hijackers, *The Garden of Last Days* (2008), by Andre Dubus III, for example, takes on the ambitious task of portraying both terrorist and bystanders in a sympathetic light. The novel describes a vexed sexual encounter between a stripper who is aiming to care for her daughter and a 9/11 hijacker who is tempted to empathize with those Americans whose culture he despises. Many novels, concerned with overcoming isolation, dramatize the intimacy of such an encounter between victim and terrorist. Even Foer's Oskar Schell, on the observation deck atop the Empire State building, dreams of a moment where he might look the terrorist responsible for the death of his father in the eye:

> I imagined the last second, when I would see the pilot's face, who would be a terrorist. I imagined us looking each other in the eyes when the nose of the plane was one millimeter from the building.
> I hate you, my eyes would tell him.
> I hate you, his eyes would tell me.
> Then there would be an enormous explosion, and the building would sway, almost like it was going to fall over, which I know is what it felt like from the description I've read on the internet, although I wish I hadn't read them.
>
> (2005, p. 244)

Empathy, it turns out, is no easy task. The common theme here is the agonizing, often violent, sometimes amorous, but always deeply conflicted moment of contact between self and other. Equally poignant in this regard is Amy Waldman's *The Submission* (2011), which assesses the seeming divide between America and Islam by dramatizing the political controversies attendant upon the design of a monument to honor the victims of a 9/11-like terror attack upon New York. The families of the victims protest when the winning entry goes to a Muslim architect who is accused of incorporating elements of Islamic gardens into his winning submission. As several characters note, however, "Islam means submission" (2011, p. 148). In the garden in the midst of the war-torn landscape of Kabul, the architect, Mo, encounters an Afghan at prayer who is no longer subject to judgment: "he had forgotten himself and this was the truest submission" (p. 318). While the book on the one hand demands an aesthetic contemplativeness that delivers one from the brutality of everyday life, and argues too for a sort of critical aesthetic detachment (from the political urgencies of the day), it also recognizes that our perceptions must be constantly recalibrated if we are to survive the divisive social confrontations we have with one another.

Recalibrated allegiances form a dominant theme as well in Kamila Shamsie's epic *Burnt Shadows* (2009), another interrogation of the consequences of imperial overreach. Just as Foer underscores the thematic and historical links between the attacks on the World Trade Center and the bombings of Dresden and Hiroshima, and as Waldman meditates on the transnational circuitries of mourning and remembrance, so does *Burnt Shadows* demonstrate the ways in which the attacks and their political and military aftermath are stitched across the lives of human beings everywhere. The novel depicts the intertwined fates of two families, following characters as they move across the world from the atomic bombing of Nagasaki to the end of the British Empire in Delhi, to the newly formulated Muslim nation of Pakistan, to insurgencies in Afghanistan against Russian occupation and, later, American-led counterterrorist and counter-Taliban, and to New York City itself: "Two families . . . The Ashraf-Tanakas, the Weiss-Burtons – their story together the story of a bomb, the story of a lost homeland, the story of a man shot dead by the docks, the story of body armor ignored, of running alone from the world's greatest power" (2009, p. 362). In this case, the reader knows the supposed terrorist being pursued by American Homeland Security forces to be utterly innocent, but his innocence – the innocence of any Muslim in a post-9/11 world where the American empire has openly endorsed terror and torture – is utterly irrelevant. Innocence is no refuge, although ethical acts can be achieved. Even in defeat, Raza is able to sacrifice his own life for a colleague. In this global world, no single life can be unentwined from others, and our closest allies one day may turn out to be our deadliest foes: this is as true among our own most intimate friends and lovers as on a geopolitical scale.

Intimacy, for Shamsie, is geopolitical. For Raza, too, though born in Pakistan, is becoming American: he has a green card, he has moved to Florida, he works as a translator for a private military security firm run by ex-CIA agents, his personal and political loyalties lie with the American cause. Alongside the question what is an American terrorist? we might ask what is an American writer? And, finally, post-9/11 writing compels us to ask: what is American fiction? Twenty-first-century cosmopolitan writers who have assumed the project of understanding terrorism cast doubt on national narratives. Such celebrated authors as Hamid, for example, or Kamila Shamsie are considered "Pakistani," or, British Pakistani, though both have lived much of their lives in the United States. Shamsie's *Burnt Shadows* is a transnational epic novel, following an interlinked group of characters traversing the global trajectories of imperial rise and collapse from Nagasaki to Delhi to Pakistan to New York to Afghanistan to Canada. If there is one overriding theme of fiction about terrorism it is that, in all our splendid isolation, we are nonetheless all in this thing together.

SEE ALSO: Banks, Russell; Contemporary Fictions of War; DeLillo, Don; Egan, Jennifer; Everett, Percival; Foer, Jonathan Safran; Gibson, William; Post-9/11 Narratives; Schwartz, Lynne Sharon; Stone, Robert; Trauma and Fiction; Updike, John

REFERENCES

DeLillo, Don. (1991). *Mao II*. New York: Viking.
Duvall, John N. and Marzec, Robert P. (2011). Narrating 9/11. Introduction to *Fiction after 9/11*, a special issue of *Modern Fiction Studies* 57 (3): 381–400.
Egan, Jennifer. (2001). *Look at Me*. New York: Anchor.
Everett, Percival. (2007). *The Water Cure*. St. Paul, MN. Graywolf.
Faruqi, Saadia. (2017). 10 books about terrorism that aren't stereotypes. *Huffington Post* (December 6, 2017). www.huffpost.com/entry/ten-books-about-terrorism_b_10156828 (accessed July 19, 2021).
Foer, Jonathan S. (2005). *Extremely Loud & Incredibly Close*. Boston: Houghton Mifflin.
Global Terror Database. (n.d.). https://www.start.umd.edu/gtd/ (accessed July 19, 2021).
Gun Violence Archive. (n.d.). https://www.gunviolencearchive.org/past-tolls (accessed July 19, 2021).
Hayden, Michael E. (2019). White nationalists praise El Paso attack and mock the dead. Southern Poverty Law Center (August 4, 2019). https://www.splcenter.org/hatewatch/2019/08/04/white-nationalists-praise-el-paso-attack-and-mock-dead (accessed July 19, 2021).
Herman, Peter C. (2018). Introduction: terrorism and literature. In *Terrorism and Literature* (ed. Peter C. Herman), 1–16. Cambridge: Cambridge University Press.
Jackson, Richard. (2018). Sympathy for the Devil: evil, taboo, and the terrorist figure in literature. In *Terrorism and Literature* (ed. Peter C. Herman), 377–394. Cambridge: Cambridge University Press.
Julavits, Heidi. (2003). *The Effect of Living Backwards*. New York: Putnam's.
Patchett, Ann. (2001). *Bel Canto*. New York: HarperCollins.
Puar, Jasbir K. (2007). *Terrorist Assemblages: Homonationalism in Queer Times*. Durham, NC: Duke University Press.
Redding, Arthur. (2018). Darlings of the Weather Underground: political desire and fictions of radical women. *Minnesota Review* 90: 70–88.
Rosenblatt, Roger. (2001). The age of irony comes to an end. *Time* (24 September 24, 2001). http://content.time.com/time/subscriber/article/0,33009,1000893,00.html (accessed July 19, 2021).
Saal, Ilka. (2011). Regarding the pain of self and other: trauma transfer and narrative framing in Jonathan Safran Foer's *Extremely Loud & Incredibly Close*. *Modern Fiction Studies* 57 (3): 453–476.
Shamsie Kamila. (2009). *Burnt Shadows*. New York: Picador.
Stone, Robert. (1998). *Damascus Gate*. New York: Houghton Mifflin.
Updike, John. (2006). *Terrorist*. New York: Random House.
Waldman, Amy. (2011). *The Submission*. New York: Picador.
Zulaika, Joseba and Douglass, William A. (1996). *Terror and Taboo: The Follies, Fables, and Faces of Terrorism*. New York: Routledge.

FURTHER READING

Gray, Richard. (2011). *After the Fall: American Literature since 9/11*. Chichester, UK: Wiley Blackwell.
Herman, Peter C. (ed.) (2018). *Terrorism and Literature*. Cambridge: Cambridge University Press.
Randall, Martin. (2011). *9/11 and the Literature of Terror*. Edinburgh: Edinburgh University Press.
Scanlon, Margaret. (2001). *Plotting Terror: Novelists and Terrorist in Contemporary Fiction*. Charlottesville: University Press of Virginia.
Simpson, David. (2019). *States of Terror: History, Theory, Literature*. Chicago: University of Chicago Press.

Fictions of Work and Labor

JOHN MACINTOSH
University of Maryland, College Park, USA

Since the rise of the novel, authors have endeavored to represent work. Yet work has been a longstanding representational problem in fiction. Elaine Scarry (1994) asks, how does one represent discretely an action that is characterized by its ongoing and repetitive nature? How does one craft engaging plots around the tedium of work? Why would readers want to read about toil during their own respite from it? Even when an occupation serves as shorthand for character or the workplace serves as a central setting, the representation of work itself is only seldomly the focus of fictional narrative. Since 1980, an additional representational problem seems to appear. If US fiction concerned with work and labor previously tended to focus on agrarian, manual, and industrial labor, how does it represent work in an era in which the service industries, which tend to produce immaterial or ephemeral goods, dominate the labor market? Where are work and labor to be found in contemporary fiction? This entry opens with a brief survey of the economic conditions of this period and their effects on working life. It then examines the sectors of the labor market that are most legible in US fiction since 1980: fictions of deindustrialization; office fictions of the downwardly mobile middle class; fictions of the now dominant interactive service industries; fictions of immigration and migration that respond to globalization and the transnational movement of labor; and, finally, fictions of tech start-ups and the gig economy that have recently emerged. It concludes that while the representational problem remains, the themes of work and labor endure.

CHANGES IN WORK AND THE COMPOSITION OF LABOR

Several macroeconomic changes since the early 1970s have affected both experiences of work and the composition of labor. The preceding period, which economic historian Robert Brenner (1998) termed "the long boom," was one of relative worker power. Coming out of World War II, unions were relatively strong, corporate profits and employee wages were rising, and many workers were able to secure their place in the middle class. However, this period of rising tides was as brief as it was exceptional. Since then, labor has taken a turn for the worse for most. Brenner argues that a crisis in profitability due to global overproduction hit the US manufacturing sector as nations such as Japan and Germany caught up to its technological innovations. The United States entered into a period of stagflation. The Keynesian stimulus that had been deployed in times of recession since World War II was stymied by simultaneous inflation and high unemployment, and neoliberal economists, once outsiders in their own discipline, seized the opportunity to push their platform of free markets, deregulation, and austerity budgets in the policy vacuum that had opened up. Regulations were repealed on the FIRE sectors (finance, insurance, and real estate), which increasingly became outlets for excess capital that could no longer be profitably invested in the productive sector.

These crises and the policy prescriptions that responded to them hit labor hard in the 1980s and 1990s. Ronald Reagan's firing of 11,000 striking air traffic controllers in 1981 signaled an intensified war on organized labor. Hard-won union jobs in manufacturing were replaced by non-unionized jobs in the Sunbelt of the US South and ultimately sent overseas as capital sought to find ever cheapened labor. The North American Fair Trade Agreement (NAFTA), initiated in the Bush administration and passed during the Clinton years, exacerbated these conditions. Wages continued to stagnate as the pursuit of shareholder value became the new economic common sense. The standard labor contract of the mid-century was undermined along with the social safety net. A workforce that had bargained for a 40-hour workweek with weekends off, a standard schedule, paid sick days, health insurance, retirement, and other benefits increasingly saw these protections eroded in favor of so-called flexibility: part-time and temporary work, just-in-time schedules, and few if any benefits (including, for gig workers, the benefit of being classified as a worker at all). Workers formerly on standard contracts, first blue- and then white-collar men, soon found themselves in a trajectory toward those at the bottom of the labor market, often women and people of color, many of whom had never experienced these benefits. Women who had not previously worked outside the home increasingly entered the waged workforce to make up for losses in income against inflation and wage stagnation, at least in households, mostly white, who had access to the single-earner family wage in the first place. Moreover, Americans increasingly turned to widely available credit to meet basic household needs and to reproduce their standard of living. Many homeowners borrowed against the value of their properties in home equity loans to keep afloat. Meanwhile, income inequality expanded rapidly, as taxation policies that benefited the wealthy concentrated huge amounts of wealth at the top.

Then the global credit crisis of 2007 and 2008 hit. Credit froze up, mortgages went underwater, and waves of layoffs again led to severe un- and underemployment. The recovery from the Great Recession was slow and the jobs created during the Obama years tended to be in low-waged service work. In 2020, as governments around the world shut down their economies to curb the COVID-19 pandemic, the US saw the largest spike in unemployment since the Great Depression. White-collar workers have adjusted to varying degrees to working from home. Workers in many low-wage sectors were deemed "essential," but the protections and benefits of this designation have been slow to materialize. At the time of writing, Congress is debating raising the federal minimum wage to $15 an hour, an amount that was scarcely a living wage when it was first floated by the Fight for $15 movement nearly a decade earlier. It remains to be seen what long-term effects the pandemic will have on the future of work and employment. At present, we have an immensely polarized labor market characterized by highly paid jobs in the FIRE sectors (as well as the upper tier of the technology and logistics sectors), but dominated by low-paid work in an array of service sectors including retail, food service, hospitality, home health care, and, increasingly, the gig economy.

FINDING WORK AND LABOR IN CONTEMPORARY FICTION

What have all these changes in the labor market meant for fictions of work and labor since 1980? As in previous literary periods, work continues to be a vexing representational problem and to discuss it means defining fictions of work and labor capaciously. Carolyn Lesjak (2006, p. 2) argues that work is "an integral part" of labor novels, but is not always visible per se. Even in the politically committed proletarian fictions of the 1930s, such as those studied by Barbara Foley (1993), Michael Denning (1996), and Paula Rabinowitz (2000), plots tend to focus more on working-class life and labor actions than work or labor exclusively. Throughout literary history, even in novels understood to be about work, labor, the labor problem, the social problem, or the working class, there is surprisingly little representation of the labor process itself. Thus, to discuss fictions of work and labor since 1980 means including not only fictions that depict work directly and primarily, but also those that take up work thematically, are set around or at workplaces, and depict the lives of working (and unemployed) people even if work itself remains ambient or unrepresented.

There does not seem at first glance to be a labor novel for the contemporary era of service work. Work seems to be too fragmented, too diffuse, to cohere into a recognizable genre or aesthetic category. Agricultural and industrial work had a visible production process and physical commodity to represent. Service work produces a strange commodity called service (and sometimes affect), but nothing tangible on which to grasp. This would seem to present a unique dilemma for its representation in fiction. However, many forms of service work are actually more representable in fiction than other forms of work. This is because many kinds of service work are inherently interpersonal. The sociologist Robin Leidner (1993, p. 1) coined the term "interactive service work" to describe those "jobs that require workers to interact directly with customers or clients." Rather than enacted through the physical manipulation of the land, or of machines, interactive service work is performed precisely through interpersonal communication and emotion. While fiction has long struggled to represent the tedium, repetition, and durée of manual labor processes, it seems better suited to depicting work that is conducted, in addition to its physical and mental aspects, through human interaction.

Yet the representation of service work and labor is also uneven, in the sense that some jobs are far more commonly represented than others. Fictions featuring white-collar service workers, while only rarely representing white-collar work per se, have remained popular over the course of the twentieth and twenty-first centuries. Non-white-collar jobs that tend to be represented in fiction include those in which the worker is (or is perceived by the consumer to be) relatively closer in class position to the consumer and performs work that is considered to be "clean" (with the exception of "dirty realism," in which readers might be seeking a voyeuristic thrill). As I have argued elsewhere (Macintosh 2019), office workers, nannies, and fine dining restaurant servers are relatively well represented in fiction since 1980, but office cleaners, maids, and fast-food workers are not. Writers tend to write about work considered to be "meaningful" or work that one might feasibly choose to do if given the choice. Readers can imagine an office worker moving up the corporate ladder or having something resembling a career even if the odds are stacked against it. As caregivers, nannies perform paid work that is akin to the unwaged socially reproductive work of the family (that this kind of work is seen as natural or fulfilling in and of itself is one reason why waged careworkers are paid so poorly). The fine dining server may not be of the same class as the customers whom they serve, but they do have a great deal of knowledge of gastronomy, etiquette, and the manipulation of affect, and thus have little difficulty interacting with their upper-class clientele. Indeed, their remuneration in the form of tips depends on it. In each of these cases, there is a sense that the work represented is work worth doing, even if the customers might not consider it suitable for themselves. In the case of those which find less representation in fiction, the work performed is seen as less valuable, less meaningful, less willed, less clean, and thus, with few exceptions, seemingly unworthy of representation.

DEINDUSTRIALIZATION AND RESIDUAL BLUE-COLLAR WORK

While service work characterizes the labor market since 1980, the shadow of industry looms over the public's imagination of work. One reason for this is the tangibility of the commodity production described above: blue-collar workers make things. Another reason is tied to the memory of unionized blue-collar jobs that, while often grueling and even dangerous, allowed workers to achieve and maintain a middle-class existence. The pull of these kinds of jobs is not solely nostalgia, however, as vestiges of stable work and benefits remain. As these blue-collar jobs began to disappear as a result of offshoring and automation, writers in the 1980s and 1990s represented the jobs that remained and those workers who found themselves unable to find steady work. One significant trend in this period is what Mark McGurl (2009, p. 67) has described as "lower-middle class modernism." A style made notable by Raymond Carver (and the now controversial interventions of his editor Gordon Lish), it was a form of minimalism that focused on the daily struggles of the (often white) lower-middle and working classes and the unemployed, earning it the pejorative label "Kmart realism." In addition to Carver, authors identified with this style include Jayne Anne Phillips, whose collection *Black Tickets* (1983), set mostly in West Virginia, depicts careworkers, sex workers, and theme park attendants. Bobbie Ann Mason's collections *Shiloh and Other Stories* (1982) and *Love Life* (1989) follow the fitful working lives of people in rural and semi-rural Western Kentucky as national chains began to encroach into the region. Phillips and Mason both depict the intransigence around work and gender roles. In Mason's story "Airwaves," from *Love Life*, the female protagonist's father erroneously tells her, "[t]he trouble is, too many women are working and the men can't get jobs" (1989, p. 185). Other authors working in this minimalist aesthetic include Frederick Barthelme, Ann Beattie, Amy Hempel, and Mary Robison.

Writers not identified with minimalism also worked through similar themes. In stories like "Beverly Home" and "Emergency" from *Jesus' Son* (1992), Denis Johnson represents work at a group home for disabled people and as an overnight emergency room clerk. The story simply titled "Work," about two men who strip copper wire from one of the men's abandoned former home to sell for scrap, ends with the narrator noting, "today we had the feeling of men who had worked" (Johnson 1992, p. 66). Dorothy Allison's *Trash* (1988) and *Bastard Out of Carolina* (1992), Carolyn Chute's *The Beans of Egypt, Maine* (1985), and Chris Offutt's *Kentucky Straight* (1992) are regionally specific like the work of Phillips and Mason and similarly suffused with the hard living, violence, and familial tragedies that accompany rural communities lacking good or enough work.

More recent fiction registers what leading working-class studies scholar Sherry Lee Linkon terms the half-life of deindustrialization. While much of the previously mentioned fiction depicted the early years of economic restructuring, in these newer novels, "deindustrialization is not an event of the past. It remains an active and significant part of the present" (Linkon 2018, p. 2). According to Linkon, this second generation of working-class writing about deindustrialization shows not mere nostalgia for a past that won't return, but the lived experience of how economic and labor market restructuring pervades all aspects of life including identity, experience, culture, and landscape. Linkon identifies novels including Philipp Meyer's *American Rust* (2009), about two men struggling to find work and meaning in a former Pennsylvania steel town, and Angela Flournoy's *The Turner House* (2015), concerning the loss of a Black family's Detroit home. In deindustrialization fiction, the lack of work figures more than its representation, but work – getting it, keeping it – remains an integral, if seemingly absent force.

OFFICE WORK AND THE DOWNWARDLY MOBILE MIDDLE CLASS

White-collar work has long been represented in US fiction and dates back to what is perhaps the most referenced US labor text: Herman Melville's "Bartleby, the Scrivener: A

Story of Wall Street" (1853). Novels concerned with finance have ebbed and flowed over the decades since, but they obtained a marked popularity in the Reagan and Bush years as finance took on an outsized role in the economy. Feeding the American public's new fascination with Wall Street, scores of financial thrillers were published alongside literary bestsellers including Tom Wolfe's *The Bonfire of the Vanities* (1987) and Bret Easton Ellis's *American Psycho* (1991). Don DeLillo's *Cosmopolis* (2003), a novel about highly leveraged foreign exchange trading, was published in the years following the Asian financial crisis of 1997 and the "irrational exuberance" of the late 1990s dot com bubble. More recently, a spate of novels featuring financial workers responded to the credit crisis of 2007 and 2008. These include Jonathan Dee's *The Privileges* (2010), Adam Haslett's *Union Transfer* (2010), and Cristina Alger's *The Darlings* (2012).

In addition to financial fictions, recent office novels might be grouped into three categories: office satires, meditations on temporary work, and postapocalyptic fiction. Perhaps buoyed by the popularity of the cult film *Office Space* (1999) and *The Office* (US, 2005–2013) on television, office satires include Joshua Ferris's *Then We Came to the End* (2007), which is set at an advertising agency undergoing waves of layoffs after the late 1990s dot com bubble burst in 2000. Its notable formal feature is its use of the first person plural, which acts as a sort of office chorus. Similarly, Ed Park's *Personal Days* (2008) employs the first person plural for one of its three sections to represent the working life of an unnamed company purchased by a large and distant conglomerate. Another notable entry into the indignities of office life is David Foster Wallace's posthumously published *The Pale King* (2011). The unfinished novel depicts work at an Internal Revenue Service office in Peoria, Illinois in 1985, including sections that formally replicate the tedium of the work. While not an office satire per se, the protagonist of Raven Leilani's *Luster* (2020) is a Black woman working as an entry-level office worker at a publishing firm who pillories the industry's desire for neo-slave narratives, novels about Black maids, and urban romances. These gatekeeping publishing preferences lead, at least in part, to less diverse representation of Black women workers in fiction.

Since the Great Recession, several novels featuring temp agency work have appeared, often about administrative assistants or receptionists working in office settings. In addition to satirizing the fetish of entrepreneurship, Helen DeWitt's *The Lightning Rods* (2011) portrays the rapid growth of a temp agency that provides "bifunctional" workers who are both office workers and anonymized sex workers brought in to manage the sexual urges of their male colleagues as a perverse policy against sexual harassment claims. Halle Butler's *The New Me* (2019) is an acerbic novel about a young woman temping as a receptionist who moves between self-loathing, dreams of self-betterment, and fantasies of revenge. Butler's previous novel, *Jillian* (2015), is a similarly scathing satire of a non-temporary administrative assistant at a medical practice, which suggests that job stability is not the only problem with such work. Hilary Leichter's *Temporary* (2020) takes a more fantastic turn to illustrate the degradations of temporary work; its unnamed protagonist temps as a pirate, an assassin's aide, and as a ghost who opens and closes doors on a strict schedule. All of the novels represent overqualified women working in historically underpaid and gendered jobs and meditate on increasingly flexibilized working conditions.

Office novels also participate in the recent trend of literary writers engaging with genre fiction, notably postapocalyptic fiction. Colson Whitehead's *Zone One* (2011), Ben

Marcus's *The Flame Alphabet* (2012), and Ling Ma's *Severance* (2018) deal with white-collar workers in postapocalyptic times. Discussing this trend, Theodore Martin (2019, p. 192) argues that "[w]hereas the post-apocalyptic novel responds to the end of the world with the work of survival, the office novel suggests that literary representations of work must take into account the catastrophic fact of precarious white-collar employment." These novels, according to Martin, represent the end of the world not as the end of work, but of its intensification, and thus reflect present-day working conditions. With the exception of Wallace, whose 1980s government workers are more secure if equally unfulfilled, all of these novels, whether postapocalyptic, satirical, fantastic, or realist, represent a downwardly mobile middle class and their responses to work that has become less stable.

INTERACTIVE SERVICE WORK

The novels in this section represent service work that relies on a face-to-face service interaction. We can distinguish these fictions from office work not only by setting, but by the type of service performed. White-collar workers are service providers, but their services are not generally characterized by this focus on face-to-face interaction. There is much overlap between the fictions in this section and the deindustrialization fictions identified above. This entry separates them, somewhat artificially, as categories for reasons of emphasis: both respond to deindustrialization, but the previously discussed novels are more likely to view service in light of the absence of blue-collar work rather than representing it directly. Some authors straddle this artificial distinction. For instance, Lucia Berlin's short stories have been reissued to acclaim in the collections *A Manual for Cleaning Women* (2016) and *Evening in Paradise* (2018). Written from the late 1970s to her death in 2004, these stories are attuned to many types of service work and feature working women in both interactive and non-interactive services from house cleaners to hospital switchboard operators, jobs which Berlin herself held. George Saunders's collections *CivilWarLand in Bad Decline* (1996) and *Pastoralia* (2000) represent harried and exasperated workers in absurdist, entertainment-based service industry jobs, notably, as theme park reenactors and as semi-nude waiters in an aviation-themed restaurant. Saunders's tragicomic stories represent the indignities and alienation of low-waged service work, austerity, and consumerism.

A noticeable trend in interactive service work fiction is the restaurant novel, which follows from the boom in the restaurant industry, the increase in food media and travel, and the rise of celebrity chefs. Early entries include Richard Russo's *Empire Falls* (2001), about the manager of a small-town diner, and Stewart O'Nan's *Last Night at the Lobster* (2007), about the manager of a closing Red Lobster. More recent novels tend to represent the high end of the restaurant sector. Merritt Tierce's *Love Me Back* (2014) is the at times harrowing story of a server at an upscale Dallas steakhouse. Stephanie Danler's *Sweetbitter* (2016) depicts work as a back waiter at a popular Manhattan restaurant. Although drastically different in tone and style, both examine both the pleasures of service and painful repetition of emotional, physical, and mental labor. Lillian Li's *Number One Chinese Restaurant* (2018) is the intergenerational story of a family who owns a restaurant in suburban Maryland. While representing different segments of workers, some of whom are highly paid and others who make more typical lower wages, these novels gesture at a common set of problems that accompany the domination of service work in today's labor market. These include inconsistent scheduling, lack of benefits, and unpredictable pay due to the tip-based model, in which employees are paid a sub-minimum wage and make the rest of their incomes in tips. The system means that servers work for both their boss and the customer, which leads to increased sexual harassment.

MULTIETHNIC FICTION, GLOBALIZATION, AND WORK

Often read with issues of identity, language, and cultural difference in mind, multiethnic fiction that represents immigrants and migrants is a great source of fiction about all kinds of work, which cuts across the previous three clusters as well as representing agricultural work. Some novels are explicitly about labor, including Helena Maria Viramontes's *Under the Feet of Jesus* (1995), which portrays a Mexican American family from Texas working in the grape fields of California alongside undocumented workers. Others are more ambiently about work. Cristina Henríquez's *The Book of Unknown Americans* (2015) follows a family who emigrates from Mexico to Delaware to seek medical treatment for their daughter. The father works at a mushroom farm and as a line-cook and the novel intersperses the daily struggles of their fellow Latin American immigrant neighbors. Fae Myenne Ng's novels *Bone* (1993) and *Steer Toward Rock* (2008) are not often read primarily as labor novels, but both prominently feature the working lives of Chinese immigrants in San Francisco's Chinatown in restaurants, butcher shops, laundries, sweatshops, as well as garment piecework done in the home and the stories of the merchant marine "old timers" who serve as the community's collective memory.

Domestic work is another common feature of multiethnic fiction, particularly about childcare workers. Whereas earlier domestic labor novels represented Black women that comprised a large proportion of domestic workers in the first half of the twentieth century, shifts in the composition of domestic work occurred as the Civil Rights movement opened up more careers for Black women and more white women entered the waged workforce in response to the pull of second-wave feminism or the push of family wage stagnation. These shifts opened up a "care deficit" (Ehrenreich and Hochschild 2003) in the United States that was increasingly filled by women from the global South, which is then represented in fiction. Bharati Mukherjee's *Jasmine* (1989) and Jamaica Kincaid's *Lucy* (1990) are told from the perspective of an undocumented Indian nanny and a West Indian au pair, respectively. More recently, Imbolo Mbue's *Behold the Dreamers* (2016) revolves around a Cameroonian man who works as a chauffeur for an investment banker, and his wife, who studies to be a nurse, but is compelled to be a domestic worker for the investment banker's wife. Mia Alvar's collection *In the Country* (2015), an example of what Alden Sajor Marte-Wood (2019) has termed "Philippine reproductive fiction," features short stories about the work of diasporic Filipinx maids, healthcare workers, and teachers, among other jobs. All of these fictions respond to globalization, the transnational movement of labor, and the difficulties that inhere in the contradictions between capital's desire for cheap labor and the nation-state's desires to restrict such movement.

THE FUTURES OF THE FICTIONS OF WORK?

By way of conclusion, two emergent and interrelated clusters ought to round out fictions of work and labor since 1980. The first is tech start-up fiction (often but not always set in

Silicon Valley) and the second is the variety of jobs that comprise the gig economy, whose degraded work venture capital-driven start-ups tend to produce. As suggested by the claim above that fiction tends to be about work considered to be meaningful and potentially upwardly mobile, start-up fiction so far outpaces novels about gig economy workers. However, given the interrelation of these phenomena, there is significant overlap in fiction that represents these sectors. While tech jobs are seen as "good jobs" and gig economy jobs as "bad jobs," when seen as jobs at all, these novels tend to show how many jobs in the technology sector – entry and mid-level coders and engineers – are degraded as well. While one might expect to see novels that portray start-up founders – the focus of breathless tech journalism – we often get alienated workers instead.

Start-up novels might be considered a new variant or subcategory of the office novel and are largely in the satirical vein. Dave Eggers's Orwellian update, *The Circle* (2013), follows customer service representative Mae as she works her way up the ladder in a corporation that integrates the functions of most existing big tech and social media companies and is focused on total transparency. Tony Tulathimutte's *Private Citizens* (2016) is set in a rapidly changing San Francisco beset by the tech boom of the early 2000s. Doree Shafrir's *Start-Up* (2017) involves a scandal at an ascendent workplace wellness app. Alissa Nutting's *Made for Love* (2017) is concerned with surveillance, as the protagonist attempts to evade her tech mogul husband who wants to mind-meld by implanting a chip in her brain. The latter two novels address the notoriously patriarchal "bro culture" and misogyny of the tech industry. The gig economy is less represented on its own; there is, to my knowledge, not yet an Uber driver novel, although ride-sharing does figure as a plot device, for instance in Ben Lerner's short story "The Pale Rider" (2016). To date the representation of the gig economy tends to be the province of the television sitcom, as Annie McClanahan (2019) has argued, but it seems inevitable that after some lag, fiction writers will develop strategies for representing gig workers.

In focusing on deindustrialization, office novels, interactive service work, immigrant and migrant labor fictions, and tech companies and the gig economy, I am gesturing toward what I understand to be the most legible clusters of fictions of work and labor. It would take another entry to begin to address fictions of the unwaged work of social reproduction and the work of finding work. Moreover, while labor is not often visible in fiction, brief scenes of work abound, not least in fiction about the writing of fiction, and can be glimpsed in many novels that do not seem to be "about" work at all. Despite its degradations over the last forty years, work remains central to our experience and how we understand ourselves. The crises of the 1970s have irrevocably changed the composition of the labor market and thus the composition of fiction tasked with representing it, but work and labor endure as themes in fiction, even as its representation remains elusive.

SEE ALSO: Allison, Dorothy; Carver, Raymond; Ferris, Joshua; Globalization; Johnson, Denis; Kincaid, Jamaica; Mason, Bobbie Ann; Minimalism and Maximalism; Mukherjee, Bharati; Ng, Fae Myenne; Phillips, Jayne Anne; Realism after Poststructuralism; Saunders, George; Wallace, David Foster; Whitehead, Colson

REFERENCES

Brenner, Robert. (1998). *The Economics of Global Turbulence: The Advanced Capitalist Economies from Long Boom to Long Downturn, 1945–2005*. London: Verso.

Denning, Michael. (1996). *The Cultural Front: The Laboring of American Culture in the Twentieth Century*. London: Verso.

Ehrenreich, Barbara and Hochschild, Arlie R. (2003). *Global Woman: Nannies, Maids, and Sex Workers in the New Economy*. New York: Metropolitan Books.

Foley, Barbara. (1993). *Radical Representations: Politics and Form in US Proletarian Fiction, 1929–1941*. Durham, NC: Duke University Press.

Johnson, Denis. (1992). *Jesus' Son: Stories*. New York: Picador.

Leidner, Robin. (1993). *Fast Food, Fast Talk: Service Work and the Routinization of Everyday Life*. Berkeley: University of California Press.

Lesjak, Carolyn. (2006). *Working Fictions: A Genealogy of the Victorian Novel*. Durham, NC: Duke University Press.

Linkon, Sherry Lee. (2018). *The Half-Life of Deindustrialization: Working-Class Writing about Economic Restructuring*. Ann Arbor: University of Michigan Press.

Macintosh, John. (2019). Painful repetition: service work and the rise of the restaurant novel. *Post45* 1. https://post45.org/2019/01/painful-repetition-service-work-and-the-rise-of-the-restaurant-novel/ (accessed September 12, 2021).

Marte-Wood, Alden Sajor. (2019). Philippine reproductive fiction and crises of social reproduction. *Post45* 1. https://post45.org/2019/01/philippine-reproductive-fiction-and-crises-of-social-reproduction/ (accessed September 12, 2021).

Martin, Theodore. (2019). *Contemporary Drift: Genre, Historicism, and the Problem of the Present*. New York: Columbia University Press.

Mason, Bobbie Ann. (1989). *Love Life*. New York: Harper & Row.

McClanahan, Annie. (2019). TV and tipworkification. *Post 45* 1. https://post45.org/2019/01/tv-and-tipworkification/ (accessed September 12, 2021).

McGurl, Mark. (2009). *The Program Era: Postwar Fiction and the Rise of Creative Writing*. Cambridge, MA: Harvard University Press.

Rabinowitz, Paula. (2000). *Labor and Desire: Women's Revolutionary Fiction in Depression America*. Chapel Hill: University of North Carolina Press.

Scarry, Elaine. (1994). *Resisting Representation*. New York: Oxford University Press.

FURTHER READING

Coles, Nicholas and Zandy, Janet. (2007). *American Working-Class Literature: An Anthology*. New York: Oxford University Press.

Hapke, Laura. (2001). *Labor's Text: The Worker in American Fiction*. New Brunswick, NJ: Rutgers University Press.

Hicks, Heather J. (2009). *The Culture of Soft Work: Labor, Gender, and Race in Postmodern American Narrative*. New York: Palgrave Macmillan.

Hoberek, Andrew. (2005). *The Twilight of the Middle Class: Post World War II American Fiction and White-Collar Work*. Princeton: Princeton University Press.

Ngai, Sianne. (2020). *Theory of the Gimmick: Aesthetic Judgment and Capitalist Form*. Cambridge, MA: Harvard University Press.

Foer, Jonathan Safran

ALLARD DEN DULK
Amsterdam University College, The Netherlands

Jonathan Safran Foer (b. 1977) is the author of three novels: *Everything Is Illuminated* (2002), *Extremely Loud & Incredibly Close* (2005), and *Here I Am* (2016). Foer has also published the nonfiction works *Eating Animals* (2009) and *We Are the Weather* (2019), and the experimental work *Tree of Codes* (2010), a reworking of Bruno Schulz's *The Street of Crocodiles* (originally from 1934) from which most of the words have been literally "cut out," resulting in a new story. Through their use of magical realism, intertextuality, and formal innovation, Foer's novels affirm fiction's ability to provide reality with meaning through an intersubjective exchange in which the reader is actively involved; as such, his work can be seen to move beyond postmodernism.

Foer was born in Washington, DC, in a Jewish family. He attended Princeton (1995–1999), majoring in philosophy and studying creative writing under Joyce Carol Oates. Oates also supervised Foer's thesis, an exploration of the life of his maternal grandfather, a Holocaust survivor, which Foer later expanded into his debut novel. In 2004 Foer married fellow writer Nicole Krauss, whose work can be said to address themes and employ stylistic devices similar to Foer's. They divorced in 2014, an experience that, at least partly, seems to inform Foer's novel *Here I Am*.

Each of Foer's novels braids together several plotlines. *Everything Is Illuminated* features three narrative strands: the account of the visit of "Jonathan Safran Foer" (in what follows, I will refer to this character as "Jonathan" while referring to the author as "Foer") to Ukraine in search of traces of his Jewish ancestry, narrated by his guide Alexei Perchov in, through excessive thesaurus use, comically mangled English; the fictional, highly fantastic history of the Jewish village of Trachimbrod, written by Jonathan, since his actual search yielded little information, mainly focusing on his "great-great-great-great-great-grandmother" Brod (2002, p. 16) and his grandfather Safran; and Alex's letters to Jonathan, which comment on their developing narratives.

Extremely Loud & Incredibly Close centers on the first-person narrative of nine-year-old Oskar Schell, in the second year after his father Thomas's death in the 9/11 attacks. Oskar interprets random things his father left behind as clues to be deciphered; upon finding a key in an envelope with "Black" written on it, Oskar visits everyone in the New York phonebook named Black. The novel also features the narratives of Oskar's grandparents, both survivors of the Dresden firebombing during World War II: the narrative of the grandfather (also named Thomas) is made up of letters to his son, Oskar's father, which he never sent except one; and that of the grandmother consists of letters to Oskar.

Here I Am offers a collage of narratives, focusing on 42-year-old writer Jacob Bloch, and the four generations of his family. The novel revolves around two main events: at home, Jacob and his wife Julia's marriage falling apart, partly due to Jacob's infidelity, and their difficulty preparing their oldest son Sam's bar mitzvah; and on the world stage, a huge earthquake in the Middle East is taken to spell the "destruction of Israel," as Arab countries declare war on Israel, which in turn calls upon Jews around the world to "come home" (2016, pp. 3, 454). In the face of these developments, Jacob struggles with his identity and responsibilities, as a husband, father, and an American Jew.

All three of Foer's novels can be said to contain magical realist elements. In *Everything Is Illuminated*, the Trachimbrod chapters offer a mythical world of Yiddish folktales – elements presented as a normal part of the shtetl's historical reality. The intertextual links between these chapters and Gabriel García Márquez's *One Hundred Years of Solitude* (1967) are clear: "Both texts focus on small rural towns, [. . .] from their quasi-mythical beginnings to their apocalyptical destruction. Both narratives do so by following the fate of several generations of the founding family" (Huber 2014, p. 121). Alex's account and letters, despite their seemingly realist presentation, also acquire a fantastical quality, mainly due to his comical language use (e.g. that Alex is "a more flaccid-to-utter version of [his] legal name" and that his little brother is "always promenading into things" [2002, p. 1]), giving these chapters an unworldly, slapstick tone.

Extremely Loud & Incredibly Close presents a recognizable post-9/11 story world mixed with fantastical elements. As a result, the narrative reality has a "storybook quality": on his wanderings through New York, Oskar "never once gets in harm's way," meeting a "motley assortment of characters, each more extravagant than the next"; overall, his "precocity alone is almost beyond belief" (Uytterschout 2010, p. 188) – take, for example, Oskar's constant inventions, such as shower water that includes a chemical making your skin color change according to your mood: "Everyone could know what everyone else felt, and we could be more careful with each other" (p. 163). Günter Grass's *The Tin Drum* (1959), and its protagonist Oskar Matzerath, is an obvious intertextual influence on Foer's novel. Both novels employ "magical realism" to convey the "trauma" of "life in the wake of manmade cataclysm" (Uytterschout 2010, p. 185). One fantastical motif in Foer's novel, the desire to reverse time, also links it to Kurt Vonnegut's *Slaughterhouse-Five* (1969). Foer makes this link by presenting the final pages of the novel as a flipbook Oskar created, of photographs of a man falling out of one of the Twin Towers, that can make the man "fall" upward, presumably back to safety, which mirrors a "dream" that Oskar's grandmother has, reversing the firebombing of Dresden: "The fire went back into the bombs, which rose up and into the bellies of the planes whose propellers turned backward" (2005, pp. 306–307) – a description that recalls, at points literally, Billy Pilgrim's reverse experience of that same bombing in *Slaughterhouse-Five*.

By comparison, *Here I Am* seems to lack such fantastical elements. In his first two novels, Foer uses remarkable characters to shed light on real, historic disasters (and their aftermath), which are often deemed unthinkable, and unrepresentable – the Holocaust, the 9/11 attacks. In his third novel, conversely, Foer uses a counterfactual, imagined disaster – "the destruction of Israel" – as a background to illuminate the crises of the Bloch family. Still, some similarities to the first two novels' fantastical registers are visible. The children's precociousness recalls Oskar Schell. The "bible" for the TV show Jacob is secretly writing about his life resembles documents from *Everything Is Illuminated*. Fantastic excess also appears in the depiction of the Middle East military conflict, for example, when the Israeli prime minister does something "so outrageously symbolic, so potentially kitschy, so many miles over the top," namely: he "inhaled, and gathered into the ram's horn the molecules of every Jew who had ever lived," "aimed the shofar [. . .], [and] television screens trembled, they shook" (2016, pp. 460–461). The most obvious intertextual link of *Here I Am* is to the Torah, specifically Abraham's repeated use of the eponymous phrase "Here I am" in the Book of Genesis. Abraham uses it three times, in response to God, to Isaac, and to the angel who intervenes. In *Here I Am* the phrase is also repeatedly spoken, mainly by Jacob, to suggest a "presence" to different identities and responsibilities – those of husband, father, and American Jew – that he struggles to realize and combine.

The presence of such fantastical and intertextual elements in Foer's novels is coupled with different nonconventional uses of text and visuality. In *Everything Is Illuminated*, language clearly points to itself, not just in Alex's comical use of English, but also in formulations such as the opening sentence of the first Trachimbrod chapter: "It was March 18, 1791, when Trachim B's double-axle wagon either did or did not pin him against the bottom of the Brod river" (2002, p. 8) – signaling the inability to render a historically accurate narrative. At one point, the authors of *The Book of Antecedents*, which documents Trachimbrod life, reach the present, so the only thing left to document is their own writing activity, rendered in the novel by one and a half pages of the repeated phrase "We are writing . . ." (pp. 212–213). Furthermore, when the Nazis are about to bomb Trachimbrod, the narrator notes: "Here it is almost impossible to go on, because we know what happened, and wonder why they don't." A few lines further linguistic description indeed seems to halt, replaced by a page and a half of dots and some scattered phrases (pp. 270–271). This can be read as the narrator's attempt to halt time, and also as a long ellipsis to signal the omission of the unrepresentable (Codde 2007, p. 245; Krijnen 2016, pp. 63–64); as such, the dots could even be seen to represent the bombs erasing Trachimbrod. Finally, Alex's letters "highlight the constructed and fictional nature of Jonathan's fictionalized history of Trachimbrod *as well as* Alex's ostensibly factual report" (Krijnen 2016, p. 201).

Extremely Loud & Incredibly Close, too, makes use of diverse compositional elements. Besides the flipbook, the novel contains many photographs throughout, most of them representing Oskar's clippings. The only letter the grandfather sent to his son is rendered with different markings in red pen, suggesting Thomas Schell, Jr.'s "corrective" reading (2005, pp. 208–216). Furthermore, when the grandfather writes a final letter in his notebook, the pages of which are running out, the spacing between lines and letters becomes gradually smaller until they overlap, resulting in three illegible, black pages (pp. 281–284). And when the grandmother writes her life story and shows it to her husband, this is rendered by three blank pages (it later turns out the grandmother had only pressed the space for pages on end). The novel's use of these "meta-texts" conveys the "difficulties in conveying traumatic experience through the absence and presence of fragmented traditional narrative structures" and the "self-reflexive nature of creating representation" of such experience (Atchison 2010, p. 365).

In contrast to Foer's first two novels, the form of *Here I Am* emphasizes fragmentation, more so than (self-awareness about) the difficulties of representation – perhaps because its central events, midlife crisis, marriage trouble, and the Middle East military conflict, are all too imaginable. In addition to the conventional free indirect discourse that makes up the majority of the novel, a set of other textual forms emphasizes the separation between different generations and identities, such as: Jacob's "bible" for his television show (with prescriptions for "how to play" certain family situations); transcripts of interactions in the online virtual world "Other Life"; a calendar of events of the Middle East conflict; and speeches by different political leaders. Of course, this array of different forms makes the reader very aware of the constructed nature of the text. This also holds for the recurring phrase "here I am" – the scriptural roots of which are described in the novel – causing a metafictional awareness of the intertextual link that is meant to imbue that phrase with meaning.

Some reviewers have criticized these aspects of Foer's fiction as empty, whimsical uses of worn-out, "postmodernist tricks" (for an overview of such critiques, see e.g. Huber 2014, pp. 113–116; Codde 2007, p. 250). Arguably, however, Foer's work employs these elements in new ways and as such moves beyond postmodernism.

The reflexive play with language, form, and myth in postmodernist literature is widely regarded as ontological in aim, expressing that all supposedly "natural" realities, official histories, and "grand narratives" are constructed – and, specifically, that language cannot access the traumatic events of the past – and rejoicing in the resulting ambiguity of fact and fiction. Conversely, Foer's work "shifts its attention from the possibility or impossibility of representation towards the responsibilities of fictions, to their communicative value and their creative power," "focus[ing] more on ethical questions" (Huber 2014, p. 113).

Everything Is Illuminated, in Alex and Jonathan's discovery that there is nothing left of Trachimbrod, does not just reaffirm the impossibility of representation; rather, it asserts that we "can *only* and inevitably *represent*" (Krijnen 2016, p. 68). Through its fantastical elements and formal devices the novel makes clear that it is not presenting the Holocaust but a literary construction. Instead of endlessly deconstructing, it leaves behind the idea that words are supposed to conjure the "presence" of the events and experiences described. It is exactly the inability to access the past that confronts the reader with moral questions, with the responsibility to consider that past – illustrated, most importantly, by Alex's grandfather's confession that during the war he betrayed his Jewish friend Herschel. Herein, the novel actually reasserts the "boundary between fiction and reality" (Huber 2014, p. 117) that postmodernism had blurred: within the novel, the Trachimbrod chapters are clearly framed as fiction while, when Alex considers "improving" his grandfather's story, he realizes the "fundamental, epistemological difference" between his grandfather's confession and Jonathan's tale (Krijnen 2016, p. 203). Even in the latter narrative, when the Holocaust approaches, the ironic, magical-realist distance breaks down, reasserting Trachimbrod as a real place and its destruction as a real event (cf. Huber 2014, p. 124). These elements refer us to the reality of the historical and ethical issues prompted by the novel through fiction.

Extremely Loud & Incredibly Close similarly figures the 9/11 attacks, and the bombings of Dresden and Hiroshima, as an inaccessible, traumatic past, with the novel's formal experiments "rendering the condition of the traumatized mind" (Codde 2007, p. 248), evoking the inability to communicate in Oskar and his grandparents. But, through these devices, the reader *is* allowed the possibility for communication, for understanding these characters. It is not so much the general events of the past that are inaccessible to the characters, but rather that they are unable to cope with their failure to face the other in a time of crisis (Schreier 2015, p. 195) – most importantly, that Oskar did not answer the phone when his father called right before his death. The inclusion of Dresden and Hiroshima also questions claims to 9/11 as a unique, unimaginable event and the United States' exceptional moral stature – as perpetrator, not just victim. Again, these elements are ethical rather than ontological in their aim. This also applies to the flipbook: it does not suggest that, through fiction, history can be undone; it also does not present Oskar believing (or pretending) he can reverse what happened. In fact, Oskar's accompanying description is phrased in the conditional perfect – that his father "would've flown through a window, back into the building," and "We would have been safe" (2005, pp. 325, 326) – explicitly acknowledging its counterfactuality. Also, the flipbook does not include page numbers, so, in a sense, "there is no beginning or end," "only the suggestion of a continuous cycle of floating and falling, forwards and backwards" (Vanderwees 2015, p. 188). As such, it embodies (Oskar's acceptance) that it is impossible to return to the past but that it has to be continuously faced in the present.

In *Here I Am* Jacob's writing of his television show "bible" remains a solipsistic exercise, replacing actual communication with his family and offering little insight into how such communication might be reestablished. The novel's hypothesizing of the "destruction of Israel" leads Jacob to understand his Jewish American identity as severed from the fate of Israel, but, again, mostly as an inevitable outcome of his passivity. Furthermore, even though *Here I Am* might be said to render some diversity by offering very different Jewish voices, it is remarkable – also in comparison to the cross-cultural references in Foer's first two novels – that *Here I Am* features no substantial Palestinian or Arab voices (only caricatural declarations of war). It seems that Foer's third novel limits the redemptive, communicative potential of fiction to the children, especially Sam, in his interactions in online virtual worlds, where he is able to talk with others about the problems in his family and preparations for his bar mitzvah – thereby emphasizing, as in Foer's previous work, not the ontological blurring of real and virtual (fictional) worlds but their ethical interrelation.

In its affirmation of fiction's ability to provide reality with (ethical, intersubjective) meaning, Foer's work moves beyond certain postmodernist notions of textuality, history, and (inter)subjectivity. Such notions are represented and criticized, for example, in the character Brod, in *Everything Is Illuminated*, who understands the world through idealized conceptions – of love, beauty, happiness – against which the world always, inevitably, falls short, which leads Brod to conclude these things don't really exist: "So she had to satisfy herself with the idea of love," to live "in a world once-removed" (2002, p. 80). Such hyperreflexive solipsism and skepticism we can recognize in Jonathan, too, and also in *Extremely Loud & Incredibly Close*, above all in the grandfather: "the distance that wedged itself between me and my happiness wasn't the world, [it was me, my thinking]" (2005, p. 17). All three characters can be seen to overcome, or at least ameliorate, this through connection to others: Brod to the Kolker (her husband), Jonathan to Alex, and grandfather to Oskar. They come to realize that meaning depends on intersubjective exchange. As Alex says to Jonathan: "With our writing, we are reminding each other of things" (2002, p. 144). The novels' stylistic and formal devices serve to foster the reader's active involvement in this dialogical process of meaning-making. As a result, Foer's novels feature the emergence of a "dialogic textual '*we*' that engages characters and readers alike in a dynamic process of exchange" (Amian 2008, p. 185). In this way, Foer's work can be seen to move beyond postmodernism: "After scepticism has called everything into question and exposed all former certainties as fictions," his novels emphasize the need "to take responsibility for the kind of fictions we propose and subscribe to" and suggest that these should be fictions that "create intersubjective connections" and "break through the barriers of a solipsistic self" (Huber 2014, pp. 145–146).

SEE ALSO: After Postmodernism; Chabon, Michael; Englander, Nathan; Fiction and Terrorism; Krauss, Nicole; Oates, Joyce Carol; Post-9/11 Narratives; Realism after Poststructuralism; Trauma and Fiction; Vonnegut, Kurt

REFERENCES

Amian, Katrin. (2008). *Rethinking Postmodernism(s): Charles S. Peirce and the Pragmatist Negotiations of Thomas Pynchon, Toni Morrison, and Jonathan Safran Foer*. Amsterdam and New York: Rodopi.

Atchison, S. Todd. (2010). "Why I am writing from where you are not": absence and presence in Jonathan Safran Foer's *Extremely Loud & Incredibly Close*. *Journal of Postcolonial Writing* 46 (3–4): 359–368.

Codde, Philippe. (2007). Philomela revisited: traumatic iconicity in Jonathan Safran Foer's *Extremely Loud & Incredibly Close*. *Studies in American Fiction* 35 (2): 241–254.

Foer, Jonathan Safran. (2002). *Everything Is Illuminated*. London: Hamish Hamilton.

Foer, Jonathan Safran. (2005). *Extremely Loud & Incredibly Close*. New York: Houghton Mifflin.

Foer, Jonathan Safran. (2016). *Here I Am*. New York: Farrar, Straus and Giroux.

Huber, Irmtraud. (2014). *Literature After Postmodernism: Reconstructive Fantasies*. New York: Palgrave Macmillan.

Krijnen, Joost. (2016). *Holocaust Impiety in Jewish American Literature: Memory, Identity, (Post)Postmodernism*. Leiden, Netherlands: Brill.

Schreier, Benjamin. (2015). *The Impossible Jew: Identity and the Reconstruction of Jewish American Literary History*. New York: NYU Press.

Uytterschout, Sien. (2010). An extremely loud tin drum: a comparative study of Jonathan Safran Foer's *Extremely Loud & Incredibly Close* and Günter Grass's *The Tin Drum*. *Comparative Literature Studies* 47 (2): 185–199.

Vanderwees, Chris. (2015). Photographs of falling bodies and the ethics of vulnerability in Jonathan Safran Foer's *Extremely Loud & Incredibly Close*. *Canadian Review of American Studies* 45 (2): 174–194.

FURTHER READING

Collado-Rodriguez, Francisco. (2008). Ethics in the second degree: trauma and dual narratives in Jonathan Safran Foer's *Everything Is Illuminated*. *Journal of Modern Literature* 32 (1): 54–68.

Dulk, Allard den. (2015). *Existentialist Engagement in Wallace, Eggers and Foer: A Philosophical Analysis of Contemporary American Literature*. New York: Bloomsbury.

Mullins, Matthew. (2009). Boroughs and neighbors: traumatic solidarity in Jonathan Safran Foer's *Extremely Loud & Incredibly Close*. *Papers on Language & Literature* 45 (3): 298–324.

Ford, Richard

RUBÉN PEINADO ABARRIO
University of Manchester, UK

Rather than simply an author born in the United States, Richard Ford may well be regarded as an Americanist. While systematically rejecting oversimplifying labels aimed at describing his fiction in terms of Southern literature, minimalism, or existentialist fiction, Ford primarily self-identifies as an American writer. With a stylistic range that moves from the sparse, direct prose of his celebrated, frequently anthologized short stories – such as "Communist" and "Rock Springs" – to the expansive, lyrical language of his most ambitious work – namely, the Frank Bascombe books – Ford has built a writing career that comprises over four decades of novels, short fiction, and essays devoted to a thorough exploration into American culture. Although dealing explicitly with contemporary affairs and set in the present or the immediate past, his own brand of Americana revolves around the histories, narratives, myths, and communities of the United States, with the national story of race becoming increasingly relevant to his chronicle of the world of common experience. Likewise, his service as editor of volumes of fiction, including *The Best American Short Stories* (1990) and *The Granta Book of the American Long Story* (1998), suggests an ongoing commitment to the creative forces of the nation.

Ford was born in 1944 in Jackson, Mississippi, to Parker Ford and Edna Akin, who are the subject of *Between Them: Remembering My Parents* (2017). Part family history, part memoir, this book offers the fragmentary account – set mainly in Arkansas, Mississippi, and Louisiana – of his parents' youth, marriage, and death (Parker's in 1960 and Edna's in 1981). Playing with America's enduring fascination with the road – a fascination that informs many an episode of the Bascombe saga, as well as countless short stories – Ford reminisces about the itinerant life of his family – his father having worked as a traveling salesman since the time of the Great Depression, often accompanied by his wife. Ever since he first left the South for college in Michigan, Ford himself went on to a peripatetic existence that finds him, at different stages of his lifetime, settling down in one city or another throughout the United States – across more than ten different states – as well as abroad, most recently, in Dublin.

Before earning a reputation and developing a distinctive approach to fiction, Ford followed the formulae of new Southern writing, *A Piece of My Heart* (1976), and crime fiction, *The Ultimate Good Luck* (1981). In the mid-1980s, two publications were to become paradigmatic of a shift in the consideration of Ford as an author, outside and inside academia. In 1983, "Rock Springs" was included in Bill Buford's Dirty Realism issue of *Granta* along with stories by the likes of Raymond Carver, Jayne Anne Phillips, and Tobias Wolff, which was meant to deal with the unadorned tragedies of characters scraping by in the underbelly of modern consumeristic society, conveyed in unpretentious prose. In 1985, many of the authors anthologized by

Buford found their way into Kim Herzinger's essay for the *Mississippi Review*, "On the New Fiction," committed to identifying and defining a new trend of minimalism in American fiction. To this day, Ford's *oeuvre*, particularly, his short fiction, still tends to be labeled as "dirty realist" or "minimalist" for the sake of critical reductionism, depending on whether the commentator chooses to emphasize content or style.

The Sportswriter (1986), Ford's breakthrough novel and a finalist for the PEN/Faulkner Award for Fiction, bears little resemblance to his previous works. Set in the fictional suburban town of Haddam, New Jersey, over the Easter weekend of 1983, *The Sportswriter* first introduces Ford's signature character, Frank Bascombe, a fundamentally decent, content man. Since his divorce and the death of his eldest son, Bascombe has abandoned a promising literary career in order to enjoy the uncomplicated life of a sports journalist, which Ford himself was familiar with after having worked for *Inside Sports* in the early 1980s. Tragedy looms over Bascombe's banal existence as he tries to develop a stronger bond with his girlfriend, Vicki Arcenault, without becoming a stranger to his ex-wife and children. In the course of that weekend, Bascombe, the protagonist and narrator, will face the suicide of a user of his refuge from loneliness, Haddam's Divorced Men's Club. However, a genuinely optimistic character, Bascombe refuses to surrender to despair.

Ford's next book was also given a warm reception. *Rock Springs* (1987) is a collection of short stories more in keeping with the marginal characters and settings that came to define "dirty realism" as a loosely articulated literary movement. Five years after his coming-of-age novel, *Wildlife* (1990), Ford published his most acclaimed book yet, *Independence Day* (1995), the sequel to *The Sportswriter*. Taking place in the election year of 1988, this novel finds Bascombe living in accordance with the Existence Period, a self-created philosophy of life, encouraging modest expectations. Now a real estate agent with a new girlfriend, Sally Caldwell, Bascombe plans to spend the Fourth of July weekend visiting the basketball and baseball halls of fame with his son, Paul. Ford was awarded both the Pulitzer Prize and the PEN/Faulkner Award for this novel, considerably more expansive and less focused on its main character than *The Sportswriter*.

The three novellas of *Women with Men* and the short-story collection *A Multitude of Sins*, published in 1997 and 2002, respectively, explore the moral consequences of unhealthy couple relationships. In 2006 Ford published the third installment of the Bascombe saga, *The Lay of the Land*, depicting the tribulations of Bascombe as a realtor during Thanksgiving 2000, in the wake of the tumultuous presidential election. Having substituted the Existence Period with the Permanent Period, Bascombe, living in (fictional) Sea-Clift, on the Jersey Shore, understands that the most significant part of his existence already belongs to the past, allowing him the freedom to live for the day. In the time leading to this novel, the lengthiest of the saga, Bascombe has been diagnosed with cancer and married to Sally, who nonetheless has temporarily left him to start anew with her estranged husband, and has met Mike Mahoney, a Tibetan American colleague with whom he has opened his own real estate company.

Ford's last novel to date, *Canada* (2012), set in border towns up and down the 49th parallel, centers around the childhood memories of a character whose regular existence is tragically altered by a bank robbery committed by his parents. *Canada* represents Ford's most sustained attempt to narrate the disintegration of modern family life, as in *Wildlife*, from the point of view of a teenager. The original Bascombe trilogy is complemented in 2014 with the publication of *Let Me Be Frank with You*, a collection of four novellas set in New Jersey around Christmas 2012, in the aftermath of Hurricane Sandy. This considerably shorter volume, in which a recently retired Bascombe has moved back to Haddam from the shore to spend what he calls the Default Period of his life, works as a gathering of snapshots more than as a sequel. As he pays a visit to his ex-wife and reunites with old acquaintants, Bascombe endeavors to offer his Default Self, presuming nothing from the past, refusing to envision the future and acting nice in all instances.

Ford's periodic return to Frank Bascombe comes as no surprise, since to a great extent his fame lies in this, his most accomplished character. With the possible exception of *Canada*, no other work by Ford equals the length and density of the Bascombe cycle. The verbosity of the narrative voice and the unabridged rendition of his often elusive train of thought in ornamented prose (with long sentences, abundant subordination, and a gusto for groups of compound adjectives) justify, if anything, the use of the term "maximalist." Indeed, one would be hard pressed to find a more intensely self-conscious narrator than Bascombe in the contemporary literature of the United States. The exuberant, accumulative speech of this "arch-ordinary American" (1995, pp. 141–142) marks him as an articulate character at ease in a capitalist paradise.

In Bascombe's discourse readers confront the wishes, objections, likes and dislikes of a ruminative everyman, initially presented as the proverbial suburban womanizer struck by mid-life crisis in the tradition of John Cheever and John Updike. However, he is ultimately rendered as a sympathetic character, in no small part due to his innate good humor and his tenacity in dwelling in an endless now; it is not for nothing that his story unravels in the present tense. Bascombe, whose philosophical musings are overtly grounded on Pragmatism and Transcendentalism, advocates during his Existence Period for an everyday based on low expectations. He draws inspiration from John Stuart Mill and Ralph Waldo Emerson, taking from the former his ideal of happiness as expecting from life only what it can bestow and, from the latter, his preference for a life of a lower strain and his emphasis on "becoming" over "being." It is only with the autumnal mood of the last Bascombe books, where illness and ageing come to the fore, forcing the narrator to renegotiate his masculine identity in a success-driven society, that life will begin to be understood as a destination rather than a journey.

The quartet encompasses three decades of middle-class, male, white life in the United States while intimating the need to reassess certain national values. Few readers will find it surprising that among the gloomiest pages written by Ford are those devoted to the race question, as is the case with his 1999 essay for the *New York Times*, "In the Same Boat," in which he acknowledges how difficult he finds it "to have a genuine conversation about race." The failure of communication between white and Black America is problematized in his fiction in ever more complex ways, with every succeeding Bascombe book revealing a growing preoccupation with racial interactions and processes. Whereas *The Sportswriter* portrayed an overwhelmingly white America in which only a small number of apparently innocent details and slips of the tongue threatened to expose hidden racial dynamics and the resulting power imbalance, Black and white relations became central to its sequel, to the extent that Ford "wanted *Independence Day* to be about race" (Duffy 2008, p. 68). This is most explicitly achieved in Bascombe's vividly described chance meeting with an African American removal man, Mr. Tanks. As the episode makes amply clear, Tanks embodies a Black masculinity historically constructed as subordinated, and this alone proves stronger than any common ground or similar life experiences between men about the same age, divorced, and with children.

Although the saga's autodiegetic narrator is a self-proclaimed optimistic man, its treatment of race is permeated by a tone of sullenness. The impossibility of a significant exchange across racial boundaries informs later stories such as "Leaving for Kenosha," included in *Sorry for Your Trouble* (2020), but a crucial distinction is introduced. Now, the younger generations, exemplified by the story's narrator's daughter, Louise, and her friend, Ginny, seem to be oblivious to the gulf preventing their parents from any meaningful relationship, thus projecting an auspicious image of understanding and communion that points to Ford's own statement in "In the Same Boat": "Only actual interracial contact can hope to bring about a bettering of our shared lives" (Ford 1999). Ginny herself, the child of a mixed-race relationship, provides a rare instance of the female body as a site for national reconciliation, all the more unusual for a literary production such as Ford's, largely characterized by male focal characters and narrators.

With its depiction of New Orleans after Katrina, "Leaving for Kenosha" is paradigmatic of Ford's interest in the social geographies of race. Likewise, the last two Bascombe books participate in discussions of gentrification as a new form of segregation, highlighting the displacement of racialized communities and the deterritorialization of African American residents. While the Bascombe novella "Everything Could Be Worse" subtly addresses the ongoing legacy of slavery, perceived to be a national trauma within the collective memory of the United States, the wider scope of *The Lay of the Land* results in a multicultural America that transcends the binary opposition of some of Ford's other narratives, attending to the role and plight of Asian American and Latino characters in the endless process of national formation. Among them, cultural hybrid Mike Mahoney steals the show. His process of Americanization, challenging the "perpetual foreigner" mythology faced by Asian American immigrants, brings forth a redefinition of mainstream notions of Americanness, sometimes against his own will.

Just like Mahoney, Bascombe takes pride in the American ideals of freedom and independence, much as his actions tend to project a distorted version verging on escapism and self-isolation. Against the background of liberal democracy, these novels and novellas stage the tension between the individual and institutionalized power, with Bascombe struggling to keep his autonomy in the face of contending external forces – social, familial, professional – as he tries to fulfill his desire to belong in the national experience. In his Foreword to Josep Armengol's study of Ford's fiction, Michael Kimmel maintains that his narrative often unfolds in "the suburban postindustrial male psyche, a psyche shaped less by production than consumption, less by the work of our hands and more by our presentation of self" (2010, p. x). This is not to undermine the importance of *actual* location in Ford's fiction. Rather, both concepts complement each other. Displaying a notion of place as a mental image inseparable from physical spaces, the Bascombe tetralogy relies on the concept of "locatedness," which has "little to do with place and everything to do with a person's awareness of self and other" (Walker 2000, p. 205). Such an anti-essentialist view uncovers place as a construct. Haddam is presented as a "setting," as opposed to a true "place" (i.e. the South); a place for things rather than ideas and, as such, an ideal location for a literalist, as Frank describes himself. His transition from a Southern man to a Yankee – of which he admits he has become a model after so many years living in New Jersey – is mirrored by his job change: from writing fiction to writing sports and, eventually, selling real estate until retirement.

When Haddam turns into too much of a "real place," Frank moves to Sea-Clift, "a town with just a life, not a lifestyle" (2006, p. 399). From the idiosyncratic perspective of Bascombe, Ford sets for himself the task of writing about the suburbs in unironic terms, staying away from cliché and whimsical exaggeration; indeed, he shares with Carver and other generational peers a distaste for irony as a mode of presentation. Nevertheless, Ford's suburbs are atomized, "focused" communities of privilege, representing an exclusionary US tradition which is part of the American heritage. In the enclaves of Haddam and Sea-Clift, an elite thrives at the cost of an exploited workforce, a racialized presence felt but rarely given voice throughout the quartet. Freedom, autonomy, and mobility are promoted as national values that only the privileged enjoy, and for that matter, a bastardized variation of them, as a result of unfettered individualism and the workings of consumerist culture.

In its entirety, the Bascombe saga seeks to capture life as it is lived, down to the minutest detail. It combines a modernist sense of time (the approximately 1500 pages of the original trilogy expand for less than ten days, and most of the "action" takes place in the narrator's conscience), with an approach to space that is characteristic of the postmodern episteme. This is epitomized by the hyperreal scenarios visited by Bascombe (such as the basketball and baseball halls of fame) and by the portrayal of the United States as a boundless landscape of signs and surfaces where the fake and the real are conflated. For all his romanticizing of the notion of community, Bascombe travels across a depthless land where institutionalized amnesia has caused national disunity. Having his character driving in New England during Easter, Independence Day, Thanksgiving, and Christmas provides Ford with endless possibilities for social commentary about the postindustrial debris he witnesses and ponders over. This postmodern scenario inevitably influences the central character's ontological and epistemological quests, that is, Bascombe's understanding of both his existence and outside reality cannot escape the world of consumption and simulations he inhabits.

In recent years, the stature of Ford as a contemporary master storyteller and virtuoso stylist has been cemented by a number of lifetime achievement awards recognizing his contribution to the literary world, such as the 2016 Princess of Asturias Award for Literature, the 2019 Library of Congress Prize for American Fiction, and the 2020 *Paris Review* Hadada Award. His latest short-story collection, *Sorry for Your Trouble*, without departing from Ford's typical emphasis on the small disillusionments of everyday life, reflects a new interest in the Irish-American experience and in Europe – where Ford lived for several years – as a literary setting. It remains to be seen whether this recent return to the short form will become the norm for books to come, and whether the voice of Frank Bascombe will make one more, possibly final appearance, much to the delight of avid and longstanding Ford readers.

SEE ALSO: Carver, Raymond; Minimalism and Maximalism; Phillips, Jayne Anne; Suburban Narratives; Updike, John

REFERENCES

Duffy, Brian. (2008). *Morality, Identity and Narrative in the Fiction of Richard Ford*. Amsterdam and New York: Rodopi.
Ford, Richard. (1995). *Independence Day*. London: Harvill.
Ford, Richard. (1999). In the same boat. *The New York Times* (June 6, 1999). http://www.nytimes.com/1999/06/06/magazine/in-the-same-boat.html?pagewanted=all&src=pm (accessed July 15, 2021).
Ford, Richard. (2006). *The Lay of the Land*. London: Bloomsbury.

Kimmel, Michael. (2010). Foreword. In: *Richard Ford and the Fiction of Masculinities* (by J. Armengol). New York: Peter Lang.

Walker, Elinor A. (2000). *Richard Ford*. New York: Twayne.

FURTHER READING

Guagliardo, Huey. (ed.) (2000). *Perspectives on Richard Ford*. Jackson: University Press of Mississippi.

Guagliardo, Huey. (ed.) (2001). *Conversations with Richard Ford*. Jackson: University Press of Mississippi.

McGuire, Ian. (2015). *Richard Ford and the Ends of Realism*. Iowa City: University of Iowa Press.

Peinado Abarrio, Rubén. (2014). *Learning to Be American: Richard Ford's Frank Bascombe Trilogy and the Construction of a National Identity*. Valencia: University of Valencia.

Franzen, Jonathan

JURRIT DAALDER
Georg-August-Universität Göttingen, Germany

With a Great American Novel comes great responsibility. For the past two decades, that responsibility has fallen squarely on the shoulders of Jonathan Franzen, *Time*-honored Great American Novelist at a time when such honors are now widely considered a dubious distinction, not least because of the racial and gender biases by which greatness is still mainly attributed to straight white men who occupy the very center of the cultural landscape. For many, Franzen's success is a testament to precisely these inequities, and though his work has continued to attract enormous publicity, so too has it faced a growing backlash. Much of which has come from social media, whose rise roughly coincides with Franzen's own and has, to a certain extent, come to define it. As hashtag activists, grouped together under #Franzenfreude, have responded to each new media frenzy by demanding the author check his white male privilege and share the limelight with other, more marginal writers, it seems they are bent on ensuring that Franzen does, at least, go down in history after all – not as the latest in a long line of Great American Novelists but, quite possibly, the last.

How different this all seemed at the turn of the millennium with the publication of Franzen's breakthrough novel *The Corrections* (2001), his National Book Award-winning tale about the Lambert family and their generational divide. Loosely structured as a series of interlocking novellas that each revolve around one family member, the novel centers on Enid and Alfred Lambert, an old Midwestern couple doing their best to persuade their three adult children, Gary, Chip, and Denise, to take a break from their transplanted East Coast lives and celebrate one last Christmas in their parental home in St. Jude before Alfred succumbs to Parkinson's disease. Upon its publication in early September 2001, the novel received a fair amount of positive attention. Until, that is, the national tragedy of the September 11 attacks threw Franzen's humble family drama into such sharp relief that both he and his partner Kathryn Chetkovich feared privately what James Wood would soon state openly in his review for *The New Republic*, namely that no novel, not even one as big and ambitious as *The Corrections*, could possibly survive such a brutal reality check (Wood 2001).

And yet, Franzen's novel not only survived in the immediate aftermath; it thrived. From one day to the next, a novel written over the course of the late 1990s had been transformed into the first ever 9/11 novel, a poignant account of a period in American history that many would soon come to think back on as an almost mythical Great Before. More so than many overt 9/11 novels that came after it – Jonathan Safran Foer's *Extremely Loud & Incredibly Close* (2005), say, or Don DeLillo's *Falling Man* (2007) – *The Corrections*' story of home and homecoming managed to tap into the culture's nostalgia for a small-town Norman Rockwell America. In this regard, it was very much of its time, even slightly ahead of it. For what are those years between 9/11 and the election of a president who promised to "Make America Great Again" if not marked by a gradual intensification and politicization of nostalgia?

Its sense of nostalgia, reinforced by the novel's stylistic throwback to the conventions of middle-class realism, was what led reviewers and pundits to begin to associate *The Corrections* with those adjectives "great" and "American." Among the first to make this connection, however, was none other than Oprah Winfrey, who announced *The Corrections* as her latest Book Club selection on September 24, 2001, calling it a bona fide Great American Novel. With those words she anticipated, and doubtless set the tone for, roughly a decade's worth of publicity on the author. It is all the more ironic, therefore, that Franzen had his concerns about her potential negative impact on the reception of his work, which he expressed at several points during his Fall 2001 book tour as well as in an interview with *The Oregonian*. Winfrey responded to these concerns by withdrawing her invitation, and with the involvement of several East Coast literati her dispute with Franzen mushroomed into a broad public debate on canonicity, "high" and "low" culture, belletrism and bestsellerdom. All of which have emerged as familiar themes in that now classic combination of publicity and damage control that has characterized each of Franzen's subsequent publications.

In the wake of his Book Club snub, this signature combination took the shape of literary nonfiction, a genre that Franzen had dabbled in since the mid-1990s. Back then he had started writing personal essays for magazines such as *Harper's* and the now defunct *Details* in order to supplement his modest earnings as a young novelist. Now, it seems, he returned to nonfiction largely in self-defense. No essay of his shows this change more clearly than his piece for *The New Yorker* titled "Meet Me in St. Louis," in which Franzen takes great pains to argue that his ambivalence toward Winfrey's Book Club was not so much an act of literary snobbery as one of resistance – resistance against a media magnate's attempts to portray him as an all-American Midwesterner despite his efforts to style himself as a cosmopolitan New Yorker whose writing life had nothing at all to do with the St. Louis he had grown up in, except, of course, for the fact that it still occupied a central place in his work and that much of the popular appeal of *The Corrections*, not to mention its appeal as a Great American Novel, lay in its vivid evocation of his native Midwest.

Such antagonism toward Middle America was already present in his much-talked-about *Harper's* essay "Perchance to Dream," which is among the author's most cynical pieces. Published in 1996, it focuses on Franzen's then ongoing struggle with writing *The Corrections* but goes on to conflate that personal struggle with the supposedly bleak future of the social novel in an age of images and smaller, fragmented audiences. Together with "Meet Me in St. Louis" and 11 other essays, this *Harper's* piece appeared in Franzen's first book of nonfiction, *How to Be Alone* (2002), where it was reprinted in pared-down and revised form, bearing the noticeably less pretentious title "Why Bother?" It was included, according to the book's brief but revealing preface, mainly as a record of Franzen's former self, with the express intention of making absolutely clear that Franzen was no longer that entitled, self-important writer he, by his own admission, used to be.

That message was further reinforced by his 2002 *New Yorker* essay "Mr. Difficult," a pivotal work that was added to later paperback editions of *How to Be Alone*. Ostensibly concerned with the difficulty of William Gaddis's writing, the essay was, more than anything else, a way for Franzen to distance himself from the Great Man-oriented "status model" of authorship to which, he argued, Gaddis and a host of his postwar contemporaries had subscribed. Glossing over the fact that he, too, had adhered to this very model as late as 2001, Franzen presents himself in "Mr. Difficult" as a fierce proponent of a supposedly more modest "contract model" that requires the author to remain finely attuned to the reading habits of a mainstream audience. In other words, the essay framed Franzen as the Man from Main Street, exactly as Winfrey had wanted to. But it did more than that. According to his more experimentally minded peer Ben Marcus, who responded in the October 2005 issue of *Harper's*, Franzen's had been a calculated, well-nigh reactionary attempt to tarnish the elite "status model" and transfer its prestige to that supposedly more humble "contract" model – an attempt that would prove immensely successful in the following years.

Those years saw the publication of Franzen's 2006 memoir *The Discomfort Zone*, a collection of six autobiographical essays that all center on the author's wholesome Midwestern upbringing and, in doing so, served to bolster his Main Street cred. Born in Western Springs, Illinois on August 17, 1959, Franzen grew up in Webster Groves, Missouri, an affluent suburb of St. Louis mostly remembered now for its fifteen minutes of fame as the subject of a 1966 CBS documentary called *Sixteen in Webster Groves*. This work of pop sociology, in fact, receives quite a bit of attention in *The Discomfort Zone*. Franzen claimed that CBS permanently scarred the good people of his hometown by portraying Webster Groves as a hopelessly conformist suburb whose clueless teenagers seemed perfectly content with the way things were, even as their peers in other parts of America marched in Civil Rights demonstrations and joined in mass protests against the Vietnam War. Though Franzen himself was much too young to be featured as one of the show's 16-year-olds, that did not stop him in *The Discomfort Zone* from seizing this documentary as an opportunity to solidify his newfound position as defender of Middle American values, of which he drew copious examples from his own Midwestern boyhood, a boyhood so exaggeratedly square that readers would be forgiven for thinking him a case even curiouser than Benjamin Button, who had also been born a septuagenarian but, unlike Franzen, had proceeded to age into youth.

Needless to say, the author's emphatic re-embrace of his Midwestern roots involved quite a bit of revisionism. That much is clear from his first two novels, *The Twenty-Seventh City* (1988) and *Strong Motion* (1992), which each show Franzen in an entirely different light. The former, in particular, is evidently the work of a young and ambitious novelist all too eager to stage his own "revolt from the village" by turning a fictionalized version of his sleepy St. Louis suburb into the backdrop for subversive politics and youthful rebellion. The novel achieves this by way of a Pynchonesque plot involving St. Louis's newly appointed Indian police chief S. Jammu and her plans to abolish a century-old law that divides the underprivileged inner city from the much wealthier suburban county, whose residents she slowly but steadily manages to convert to her cause until the only one left to oppose her is Martin Probst, a local business leader who lives in Webster Groves together with his wife Barbara and teenage daughter Luisa, all three of whom can, in hindsight, be viewed almost as prototypes for the all-American suburban families featured in Franzen's later novels.

What makes *The Twenty-Seventh City* stand out from those later works, though, is its willingness to grapple with complex issues of racism and racial inequality, which the novel's theme of geographical and socioeconomic division lays painfully bare. These issues would make national headlines several decades later, when the 2014 police shooting of the unarmed African American teenager Michael Brown in the underprivileged St. Louis suburb of Ferguson sparked off a national wave of street protests and became a rallying cry for the Black Lives Matter movement. The fact that Franzen's 1988 work is able to offer some fascinating insights into these racial tensions perhaps goes to show that, contrary to the claims he made in his own *Harper's* essay, the novel form has retained its social relevance, even in an age of images and fragmented audiences. Quite possibly, then, it is Franzen himself who has changed, seeing that in his younger years he was clearly willing to address precisely the issue of white privilege that has cast a shadow over his later works.

That ambitious and socially engaged side of Franzen is still on full display in his sophomore novel *Strong Motion*, which, if anything, doubles down on his earlier efforts to weave a compelling family drama into broad social commentary. The setting, this time, is not the St. Louis area he grew up in but metropolitan Boston, a city that had been Franzen's home from 1983 until 1987, when he worked as a research assistant in Harvard University's Earth and Planetary Sciences Department. His work on seismology there would provide the inspiration for the novel's plot, which revolves around a series of earthquakes triggered by the clandestine activities of a Boston-based chemical company named Sweeting-Aldren, at least according to one of the main protagonists, a young Harvard seismologist by the name of Renée Seitchek. Her research into the area's seismic activity sees Renée cross paths and become romantically involved with the novel's other protagonist, Louis Holland, whose grandmother has recently been killed by one of the earthquakes, leaving behind a large inheritance in, of all things, Sweeting-Aldren stock. It is this rich and layered narrative that the young Franzen molded into another ambitious social novel dealing with a broad array of subjects, ranging from the Christian fundamentalist right and abortion to corporate corruption and ecological disaster – all subjects that are as topical now as they were back in the 1990s.

Fast-forward to 2010, however, and it is primarily the romance plots and family dramas of Franzen's earlier novels that have carried over into his bestseller *Freedom*. Which is not to say that the novel shies away from social critique, but rather that its commentary on, in this case, the Iraq War and environmental destruction is less far-reaching, more domesticated. Even so, *Freedom* was hailed as a broad-canvas novel and its author as a "Great American Novelist," most notably by *Time* magazine, whose August 23, 2010, issue pictured Franzen on its front cover. If that was not enough, Oprah Winfrey also reinvited him to join her Book Club and appear on her show, where Franzen's decade-long journey of self-reinvention came full circle when he dismissed old accusations of elitism by assuring her that he is really just a Midwestern egalitarian. There was, in other words, no shortage of publicity, much to the frustration of several female writers, among them Jodi Picoult and Jennifer Weiner, who took to social media to voice their concerns over this #Franzenfreude for drawing an inordinate amount of attention to one single Great American Novel that, had it been written by a woman, would probably have been dismissed as domestic fiction.

It is not hard to see where this criticism comes from, for *Freedom* is, at its core, the story of a rather caricatural love triangle, one to which its allusions to Leo Tolstoy's *War and Peace* (1867) and its Pierre–Natasha–Andrei triangle attempt to give a veneer of sophistication. It tells the story of Patty Berglund, a stay-at-home mother of two who is married to nature-loving Minnesota-nice-guy Walter

Berglund but has never really gotten over her crush on Walter's much cooler college-friend-turned-rockstar Richard Katz, with whom she eventually does have an affair, risking not only her marriage to Walter but also Walter's friendship with Richard. The latter takes on an added dimension because it is loosely based on Franzen's own friendly rivalry with fellow Midwesterner and "Grunge American Novelist" David Foster Wallace, whose presence can be felt not just in *Freedom* but also, and much more powerfully, in Franzen's 2012 book of essays, *Farther Away*. The book's title essay, first published in the April 11, 2011, issue of *The New Yorker*, sees Franzen working through the tragic event of Wallace's suicide in 2008 while also criticizing the adulatory narrative that has been constructed about Wallace since then. Its brutally honest account was thought by many to be in bad taste and caused a minor outrage. But that, by now, was nothing new.

In fact, around this time it starts to seem as if Franzen might actually be courting controversy, most noticeably in his nonfiction, which shows a real contrarian streak. In this respect, it is not unlike the essays of Austrian modernist and contrarian-in-chief Karl Kraus, whose writing Franzen had begun to explore in the late 1970s and early 1980s, first as a student of German at Swarthmore College and then as a Fulbright Scholar at the Freie Universität Berlin. Decades later, this interest in Kraus would culminate in the publication of *The Kraus Project* (2013), his translation of five of Kraus's essays accompanied by notes that draw on Franzen's own criticism of technology, consumerism, and social media.

Unsurprisingly, that criticism did not go down well on Twitter, where readers were quick to respond with the hashtag #JonathanFranzenhates, listing e-readers, Facebook, and television, among other things. Many would also add women and climate activism to that growing list, especially after the publication of his most recent book of essays, *The End of the End of the Earth* (2018), which contains two highly provocative pieces, both originally published in *The New Yorker*. The first of these, "Save What You Love," appeared in 2015 under the title "Carbon Capture" and posed a controversial question: Does the pressing issue of climate change detract from conservation efforts? The second piece, published in 2012 under the heading "A Rooting Interest," is supposed to be an appreciation of Edith Wharton's work but seems much more interested in judging those works by their author's personality, which Franzen claims was difficult, and her beauty, which he insists she did not possess.

More problematic still is Franzen's portrayal of women in his fifth and latest novel, *Purity*. Published in 2015, the novel abandons the Midwestern local manners of both *Freedom* and *The Corrections* in favor of a narrative that stretches across multiple continents and time periods, blending an "ostalgic" East German murder mystery with a contemporary American family drama that takes on Oedipal and Electral dimensions. The inspiration for this family drama seems to have come from Franzen's failed marriage to Valerie Cornell, his college girlfriend. Cornell appears to have been the basis not for the female protagonist Purity "Pip" Tyler, whose search for her biological father constitutes the book's overarching plot, but for her mother Anabel Laird, who has adopted the name Penelope Tyler to make a clean break with her past life and former marriage to Tom Aberant, Purity's father. It is precisely the novel's account of this troubled marriage that many have found fault with. Its unkind portrait of Anabel, who is little more than a caricature of a frigid, often hysterical female artist, crystallized the gender issues concerning Franzen's own status as a Great American Novelist. For the first time since *The Corrections*, a new book of his did not exactly have critics scrambling to call it a Great American Novel, and it remains to be seen if Franzen can step up to its changing responsibilities.

SEE ALSO: Book Clubs; DeLillo, Don; Foer, Jonathan Safran; Gaddis, William; Literary Magazines; Post-9/11 Narratives; Pynchon, Thomas; Saunders, George; Suburban Narratives; Wallace, David Foster

REFERENCE

Wood, James. (2001). Abhorring a vacuum. *The New Republic* (October 15, 2001). https://newrepublic.com/article/76988/abhorring-vacuum (accessed September 19, 2021).

FURTHER READING

Burn, Stephen J. (2008). *Jonathan Franzen at the End of Postmodernism.* London: Continuum.
Gram, Margaret H. (2014). *Freedom*'s limits: Jonathan Franzen, the realist novel, and the problem of growth. American Literary History 26 (2): 295–316.
Hidalga, Jesús B. (2017). *Jonathan Franzen and the Romance of Community: Narratives of Salvation.* London: Bloomsbury.
Weinstein, Philip. (2015). *Jonathan Franzen: The Comedy of Rage.* London: Bloomsbury.
Wilhite, Keith. (2012). Contested terrain: the suburbs as region. American Literature 84 (3): 617–644.

Frazier, Charles

CEDRIC GAEL BRYANT
Colby College, USA

"Like any other thing, a gift" (Frazier 1997, p. 96) is the pragmatic conclusion about the ability to fight in close quarters which W.P. Inman, a wounded fugitive Confederate soldier escaping home, comes to in Charles Frazier's debut novel *Cold Mountain* (1997). It is the irreducible, existential reality of violence in the world and in human nature that, ironically, first romantically propels Inman into the Civil War – that will in Abraham Lincoln's phrase reduce the nation to "a house divided against itself" – then *compels* Inman to turn away from the "metal face of the age" (p. 2) and its modern technology of destruction. Each of Charles Frazier's four novels is intimately concerned with difficult questions about the moral play between Lincoln's "better angels of our nature" and a Herbert Spencer-*cum*-Darwinian "survival of the fittest" ethos that shapes the reciprocal relationships between form (narrative structure, imagery, and style) and content (subject matter and theme) in *Cold Mountain*, *Thirteen Moons* (2006), *Nightwoods* (2011), and *Varina* (2018).

With the exception of *Nightwoods*, each of Frazier's novels is an historical narrative extending from the early nineteenth to mid-twentieth century and is shaped by several signal events and ideas in American history and literature, including the Civil War; the reciprocity between place and identity; the aesthetics of violence; history and memory; poet Wallace Stevens's trope "finding what will suffice" (1997, p. 218); the Southern gothic; and, what Frazier calls, "the loss of national innocence" (Block, 2006). Most of these elements form the thematic constellation of Charles Frazier's second novel, *Thirteen Moons*, which shifts *Cold Mountain*'s peripheral narrative concern with Native American culture in the regional history of North Carolina during the nineteenth century to a narratively central place within the chronicle of William Cooper's long life. Unlike *Cold Mountain*'s intimately third-person point of view that alternates sequentially between W.P. Inman's story of "exile and brute wandering" (Frazier 1997, p. 131) and Ada Monroe/Ruby Thewes's labors to transform Black Cove – "verbs, all of them tiring" (p. 80) – Will Cooper, who is based on the "white chief" and defender of the Cherokee Nation William Holland Thomas, controls the mostly retrospective narrative of *Thirteen Moons*.

The cultural history that informs Will Cooper's personal narrative concerns the forced relocation between 1836 and 1839 of approximately 17,000 Cherokees – referred to as the "Cherokee Removal" and "Trail of Tears" – from North Carolina, as well as parts of Alabama, Georgia, and Tennessee west into present-day Oklahoma. Fiction and reality combine to form Cooper's interpersonal relationship with three people: a wealthy "almost white" Cherokee named "Featherstone"; his beautiful and elusive daughter, Claire Featherstone, who captured 16-year-old Will Cooper's heart; and "Bear," Cherokee chief and Cooper's surrogate father. Bear struggles to reconcile a vanishing Indigenous culture and tribal ways with a brutal modern age. "The history of Indian resistance on this continent," an aged Will Cooper reflects from his early twentieth-century vantage point, "is a grim record of failure, even though a few battles were won now and again" (Frazier 2006, p. 12). Little Big Horn is one example Cooper notes, however, "wars, though, were inevitably lost. To make my point, see the widely published recent photographs of fierce Geronimo all swollen up like a brood sow riding in a Cadillac automobile" (p. 12). The past cannot be undone but it can be retold, accessed through memory, which Cooper obsessively has done throughout his long life in writing – in "fine leather-bound books with ruled watermarked cotton paper made by stationers in Washington [D.C.]" (p. 22).

For William Cooper, writing has become what Sally Fitzgerald, referring to Flannery O'Connor's short, brilliant writerly life, calls "the habit of being" (1979, p. xvii). And, as reading the weathered copy of Bartram's is for W.P. Inman in *Cold Mountain*, for Cooper writing is a "gift." But this habit of being, Cooper opines, "fixes" a thing down "in place as surely as a rattlesnake skin stripped from the meat and stretched and tacked to a barn wall. Every bit as stationary, and every bit as false to the original thing. Flat and still and harmless" (Frazier 2006, p. 21). And so, the act of writing may also be an "illness or a sin," Cooper cannot decide. What writing and reading emphatically do is allow Frazier's brooding heroes and heroines to review, to reenact the experiences that formed the choices, rightly and wrongly, that make up a life – for better or for worse. This irresistible urge to tell, to say, through reading and writing, which are both the products of what Abraham Lincoln called "our better angels," offers as much illumination of the impulse toward violence, death, love, survival, and depravity as possible. This urge is a signal aesthetic and narrative device in Charles Frazier's work, and emphatically in *Varina* and *Nightwoods*. The urge to tell is an aesthetic and moral product of Frazier's views of historical fiction, which, he stresses in an interview with Jana Hoops,

> as a conversation between the present and the past, and Varina Davis's life offered me a complex entry point into that dialogue. That war and its cause – the ownership of human beings – live so deep in our nation's history and identity that we still haven't found a way to reconcile and move forward. And it's important to remember that most of those monuments [to Confederate officers, including General Robert E. Lee] didn't spring up right after 1865, but are largely a product of the Jim Crow South. Their continued presence indicates how much the issues of the Civil War are like the armature inside a sculpture – baked into the framework of our country and our culture.
>
> (Hoops 2018)

Narrative acts of saying and writing in *Varina*, as well as *Cold Mountain* and *Thirteen Moons*, depend upon Frazier's particular gift for metaphor and simile, which often cluster, like stackable Russian dolls, becoming integrated, concentric narrative biographies and autobiographies. At age 16, for example, Varina recalls the too narrow, possibly fatal choices and their fixed consequences offered to young girls on the cusp of womanhood of her generation. The metaphors stack up, as the aged version of her much younger self reviews the past. First,

> who to marry, who to reject, which path to take? Whether to choose that plump, dullard heir to a vast estate or the handsome woodcutter living in a charming forest cottage. The moment forces decision. Wait, and risk choices disappearing forever. Make up your addled young mind too soon and afterward – unless you are a true and total rebel – your way forward in life narrows down to the dimensions of a railroad tunnel.
>
> (2018, p. 67)

Second,

> Or, a better and more modern simile, to the horrific pinching aperture of a camera shutter, metal plates wrapping onto themselves, constricting, until the mechanism quickly opens and then closes for good with the snap of a trap, fixing you in a moment you'll regret to the grave.
>
> (2018, p. 68)

And third,

> Or even wishing you'd simply paused, taken a long, deep breath. Not allowed the personal moment and the pattern of your family and your stupid culture to shove you two-handed from behind, forcing you to stumble unbalanced into the future.
>
> (2018, p. 68)

"A railroad tunnel," the "aperture of a camera shutter," and a "stumble unbalanced into the future" are all tropes expressing the tension between motion and stasis, freedom and dependency, and the paradoxical advantages of a young white woman of "privilege" in mid-nineteenth century America confronted with the illusion of real choice.

This is Varina Anne Banks Howell Davis's novel, but it is also James Blake's autobiographical quest to fill in the vast, almost empty map of his childhood in the years before, during, and after the Civil War that sets in motion the telling/saying and contains Varina Davis's story, becoming an echo chamber of interdependent voices. "Every life is a biography," a popular PBS series announced, and it is a truism affirmed in the concentric echo-chamber narrative strategy of *Varina*, which vacillates chronologically between 1865 and 1906. Spatially, the narrative center is Saratoga Springs, New York, and the hotel-spa called "The Retreat" where in 1906 Varina Davis, widow of Confederate President Jefferson Davis, has retired for relaxation and privacy when James Blake, "Jimmy Limber," appears out of the past. When he arrives, carrying the "bristling blue book" by Miss Botume Wallace titled *First Days Among the Contraband*, telling as a narrative act of recovering the past has already been set in motion, as his too numerous to count "torn newspaper place-marks" and marginalia suggest. Like *Thirteen Moons*, *Varina* begins in the present, the dawn of the twentieth century, and tests the potential of the past, present, and future, once more "to find what will suffice" (Stevens 1997, p. 218). To do so, James Blake must do what Varina wrongly believes she has finished doing: put the past away, having learned from the past all it has to offer.

Here, specifically in *Varina*, and in Charles Frazier's novels broadly, characters act out both Stevens's modernist mandate about "finding what will suffice" – "the poem of the mind in act of finding what will suffice" – and William Faulkner's sentiment dramatically expressed in novels including *The Sound and the Fury* (1929) and *Absalom, Absalom!* (1936) that "the past is never past, but always present." James Blake and Varina Davis are positioned at opposite ends of an implied continuum about this problematic relationship to time: he has sought her out because the presentness of the past, he believes, inexorably determines identity, while Varina Davis, in sharp contrast, insists that nothing more can be learned from it, and what has been learned is of little use in constructing any idea of a future. James Blake's and Varina Davis's polarized convictions about the presentness of the past place Frazier's fiction within an American modernist narrative tradition that, as Rita Barnard contends about this early twentieth-century movement, is "quintessentially [a] modern sense of dislocation and alienation" manifested in the intersectionality of "time, place, and value" (2005, pp. 49–50).

All of Frazier's central characters, fictional and historical, are in some sense dislocated and alienated from place (home/brute wandering) and time (history, memory), and struggle to find value in the world that is neither transient nor morally corruptible. Reflecting on "a hundred thousand tragedies played out in the spring of 1865," Davis cautions Blake that:

> there was no going back. Bad, angry, decisions left behind a huge cost in life and suffering for the entire nation. And utter loss of wealth for the South. But not for the North. Plenty made fortunes off the war. Give a real Yankee one little dried pea and three thimbles and he can buy groceries. Give him a boxful of cheap, shiny, pocketknives and pistols to trade and he will turn it into a career. But give him a war, and he'll make a fortune to last centuries. It's not something they learn. They're saturated in it from birth. End result – we lose everything and they create thousands of new millionaires.
>
> (2018, pp. 42–43)

"Bitter feelings still, ma'am?" Blake asks; Davis's response is essentially a cliché along the lines of "to the victors belong the spoils": "the people who beat you get to take you apart however they wish" (2018, p. 43). Bitterness notwithstanding, Varina Davis's critique of the past holds the South responsible for the rapacious immorality of owning human beings and the North for an atavistic proclivity to profit materially from tragedy. But Davis's most salient point towards the novel's close is this: "Remembering doesn't change anything – it will always have happened. But forgetting won't erase it either" (p. 174). Each of Frazier's novels is a thematically diverse conjugation of Varina Davis's conclusion about history, memory, narrative, and the problematic ways they participate in "finding what will suffice." In one sense, it is the narratively experimental ways these novels approach this interdependent subject matter that makes them unique contributions to contemporary American literature.

Nightwoods, which chronologically occurs before the publication of *Varina*, but after *Thirteen Moons* and *Cold Mountain*, participates in this interdependency of form and content through shifting the "centre of consciousness," as Henry James described it in "The Art of Fiction," from adulthood and old age, to childhood and lost innocence. This shift is an experiment that employs updated elements of the fairy-tale tradition akin to the Grimm Brothers that center on lost, orphaned, traumatized children in a modernist world where the natural world is in conflict with the most destructive impulses of human nature. The dark fairy-tale tradition that *Nightwoods* borrows from is also squarely located in American horror and Southern Gothic literature that extends from Henry James (*The Turn of the* Screw [1898]), to William Faulkner (*Sanctuary* [1931]) to Stephen King (*The Shining* [1977]). As in each of Charles Frazier's novels, the timeless questions which *Nightwoods* thematically asks involve how to find what will suffice when the fragile innocence of children and the incompetence of adulthood collide with the rapacity of human evil.

Given its fairy-tale framing, *Nightwoods* is arguably rhetorically more allegorical, or moral, in its construction of characters and theme than the novels before and after it: the children, Dolores and Frank are "strange," seemingly, mute, and not immediately identified by name. These are traumatized, Hansel and Gretel-like children who know instinctually and experientially that "horror is other people. The things they think up to do to you" (Frazier 2011, p. 244). Their murdered mother is the ubiquitous victim of fairy tales, fatally flawed by her own sensual appetites and foolish romanticism – the "beautiful, gentle sister [who] had not protected herself carefully against a world of threat" (p. 14). Luce is the wiser but distrustful younger sister who, in her retreat from the "world of threat" that men especially pose, has failed to emotionally develop, to find the interpersonal skills to suffice in that world, or to protect the innocent from its many dangers. And Johnny Johnson, aka "Bud," is *the wicked stepfather* whose penchant for violence is surpassed only by his inveterate cowardice. No one "considered violence to be his main calling as a criminal" (p. 17) until he marries and then murders Lily, the mother of the strange twins a man from social services delivers to Luce, their aunt and only surviving blood relation.

The moral paradox at the thematic center of *Nightwoods* is broadly traceable through each of Frazier's books and asserts that evil and the violence it engenders is both ubiquitous and maybe insoluble. All W.P. Inman, the wounded confederate fugitive-hero of *Cold Mountain* wants, for example, is to make it back home and live quietly and in peace, but belief in the possibility of a world without violence is the fatal flaw that will, ultimately, cost him his life. However, what James Baldwin optimistically proclaims, in *No Name in the Street*, about conscience, crime, and punishment is also, problematically, woven into Frazier's modern allegories: "People pay for what they do. And still more, for what they have allowed themselves to become. And they pay for it simply by the lives they lead" (Baldwin 1972, p. 55). In *Nightwoods*, violence is an aesthetic, as it is in *Cold Mountain* and for W.P. Inman who believes that the skill to meet violence with violence and emerge victorious was "like any other thing, a gift." The aesthetic signs of Johnny Johnson's penchant for chaos are "a big black fossilized shark tooth" (Frazier 2011, p. 17) and a "bleeding heart tattoo covering the outer face of his left bicep" (p. 17). These symbols of violence test the limits and relevance of Baldwin's moral optimism in *Nightwoods*. Always in Frazier's fiction there is the reality of violence, and central characters like Bud Johnson, the "odd" siblings Dolores and Frank, W.P Inman, William Cooper, and Varina Davis who, although quite differently, aestheticize it. Finally, Frazier's narrative practice, remarkable gift for metaphor, imagery, the sound and feel of phenomenal nature colliding with the proclivity for good and evil in human nature form the central questions about survival, history, morality, and language at the epicenter of his corpus, thus far.

SEE ALSO: Contemporary Regionalisms; Realism after Poststructuralism

REFERENCES

Baldwin, James (1972). *No Name in the Street*. New York: Vintage Books.

Barnard, Rita. (2005). Modern American fiction. In: *The Cambridge Companion to American Modernism* (ed. Walter Kalaidjian), 39–67. Cambridge: Cambridge University Press.

Block, Melissa. (2006). In new novel Charles Frazier returns to love in Appalachia. *NPR: All Things Considered* (October 2, 2006). https://www.npr.org/templates/story/story.php?storyId=6181787

Fitzgerald, Sally. (1979). Introduction. In: *The Habit of Being: Letters of Flanney O'Connor* (ed. Sally Fitzgerald). New York: Farrar, Straus and Giroux.

Frazier, Charles. (1997). *Cold Mountain*. New York: Vintage Books.

Frazier, Charles. (2006). *Thirteen Moons*. New York: Random House.

Frazier, Charles. (2011). *Nightwoods*. New York: Random House.

Frazier, Charles. (2018). *Varina*. New York: Ecco/HarperCollins.

Hoops, Jana. (2018). Author Q & A with Charles Frazier. *Lemuria* (April 24, 2018).

Stevens, Wallace. (1997). "Of Modern Poetry." *Wallace Stevens: Collected Poetry and Prose, Library of America*. New York: Library of America.

FURTHER READING

Bryant, Cedric Gael. (2009). "To rise and bloom again": resurrection, race, and rationalism in Charles Frazier's *Cold Mountain*. *Mississippi Quarterly* 62 (4): 591–603.

Goodheart, Adam. (2006). Trail of tears. *The New York Times* (October 29, 2006). https://www.nytimes.com/2006/10/29/books/review/trail-of-tears.html

Menand, Louis. (2006). Dispossession. *The New Yorker* (September 24, 2006). https://www.newyorker.com/magazine/2006/10/02/dispossession

Piacentino, Ed. (2006). Searching for home: cross-racial bonding in Charles Frazier's *Cold Mountain*. *Mississippi Quarterly* 55: 97–116.

Gaddis, William

STEVEN MOORE
Independent scholar, Ann Arbor, USA

While Gaddis's writing career began in the 1950s, it wasn't until the 1980s that he came to be recognized as a major novelist of the second half of the twentieth century. In 1982 the first book on him was published, along with a special issue of the *Review Contemporary Fiction*, followed in later years by a steady stream of books and collections of critical essays, in foreign languages as well as in English. In 1982 he was awarded a MacArthur Foundation Fellowship – the so-called "genius" award – and in 1984 he was inducted into the prestigious American Academy and Institute of Arts and Letters. In 1985, he not only published his most commercially successful novel, *Carpenter's Gothic*, but also saw the reissue of corrected versions of his first two novels. He received substantial advances for his fourth and fifth novels, *A Frolic of His Own* (1994) – which garnered his second National Book Award – and the posthumously published *Agapē Agape* (2002). His death in 1998 made the front page of *The New York Times* and received the kind of coverage only major writers receive.

Born in 1922 in New York City – though he traveled widely, he spent most of his life in or around New York City, where all of his novels are set – Gaddis entered Harvard University in 1941, where he soon became editor of the *Harvard Lampoon*, whose satiric attitude and parodic approach set the tone for all his later work. Leaving Harvard without a degree in 1945, he worked as a fact-checker at the *New Yorker* for a while – which he later described as good training for his reference-heavy novels – and in 1947 departed for Mexico, where he began what was eventually published as his first novel, *The Recognitions* (1955).

Although it and Gaddis's second novel pre-date the scope of the present work, their importance – to American literature as well as to Gaddis's career – and their influence on later novelists necessitate a brief overview.

A huge work of 956 pages spanning thirty years, *The Recognitions* began as a shorter novel about a romantic triangle featuring an artist who "sells his soul to the devil" to become a successful forger. (Allusions to Goethe's *Faust* run throughout the novel.) As Gaddis worked on it, the theme of forgery grew to encompass all forms of fakery, counterfeiting, and phoniness, from insincere friendships to manipulative advertising, from female impersonation to patriotic sentiment,

The Encyclopedia of Contemporary American Fiction 1980–2020, First Edition. Edited by Patrick O'Donnell, Stephen J. Burn, and Lesley Larkin.
© 2022 John Wiley & Sons Ltd. Published 2022 by John Wiley & Sons Ltd.

finally to institutional religion, which Gaddis – following his sources – regarded as a forgery of mythology and ultimately of reality itself. Gaddis's excavation of the bases of Western culture displays an encyclopedic range and a level of erudition uncommon in the mid-century American novel, which led some reviewers to claim Joyce's *Ulysses* (1920) as an obvious model, though Gaddis insisted all his life he had merely glanced at, never read, Joyce's encyclopedic novel.

The geographic range is just as wide. The novel begins in New England in the 1920s, moves to Paris in the 1930s, and then to Manhattan in the late 1940s (where the bulk of the novel takes place), and ends in Italy, with side trips to Central America, North Africa, and Spain – all places Gaddis lived as he wrote the novel. Its style alternates between stately, sardonic prose and highly realistic dialogue, with a higher proportion of dialogue than in most novels (a percentage that would rise in his later novels). His influences were not Joyce but Joseph Conrad and T.S. Eliot for the prose (and the erudition, inspired by the notes to *The Waste Land* (1922) to undergird his novel in scholarly materials), and Waugh and Ronald Firbank for the dialogue, but with a distinctly American attitude.

The result was a challenging, wide-ranging novel that left the early reviewers baffled. *The Recognitions* received mostly negative reviews, which became the subject of a series of caustic broadsheets issued in the 1962 by a man named Jack Green, later published in book form as *Fire the Bastards!* (1992). It wasn't until much later that fellow meganovelists like John Barth and Thomas Pynchon provided a context for Gaddis's monumental work. In 1976 Edward Mendelson popularized the term "encyclopedic novel," and in 1985 Frederick R. Karl published his "American Fictions: The Mega-Novel" (*Conjunctions* no. 7), adding a related genre category to describe what, in retrospect, Gaddis had accomplished in his first novel.

Twenty years would pass before Gaddis published his second one, during which time he wrote a play (unproduced) and a nonfiction work on mechanization in the arts (unfinished), though he managed to salvage both for his final two novels. Gaddis's *J R* (1975) is another lengthy work (726 pages), but is superficially different in almost every other respect from its predecessor: it is primarily in dialogue, occupies only a month or two, is restricted to New York City and environs, and contains no chapter or section breaks. It is the improbable story of an 11-year-old boy named J R Vansant who manages to become a business tycoon and wreck the US economy within a month's time. It is a satire not on capitalism per se, but on the *abuses* of capitalism, on how the predatory pursuit of profits mean the abandonment of ethics and morality. The role played by Goethe's *Faust* in Gaddis's first novel is taken here by Wagner's *Ring of the Nibelung*, another story of how greed ruins everything.

Caught up in young J R's financial typhoon are a wide variety of adults: teachers at his school, including Jack Gibbs, at work on the same book on the mechanization of the arts that Gaddis worked on; industrial writer Thomas Eigen, a stand-in for Gaddis; a young composer named Edward Bast, who reluctantly becomes J R's business manager to finance writing music; the rest of the Bast family, squabbling over a family inheritance; a few artists struggling to survive in a society largely indifferent to the arts; and any number of corporate movers and shakers. As with *The Recognitions*, *J R* expanded from its original focus to embrace a number of concerns: children's education; the mistreatment of Native Americans; corruption in politics; the role of art in society; racism; and the dangers of automation and concomitant loss of human dignity. The result is a broad survey of "what America is all about," as a repeated refrain goes, and of how far the country has fallen from its avowed ideals. Despite its innovative form and perceived difficulty, *J R* won the National Book Award for the best novel of 1975.

After a bout of writer's block, during which time he taught an occasional class in creative writing at Bard College, Gaddis began writing a third novel, initially called *That Time of Year* but published in 1985 as *Carpenter's Gothic*. A deliberate attempt at a shorter, more accessible novel, *Carpenter's Gothic* occupies an even shorter time span than *J R* (four weeks in October–November 1983) but packs within its 262 pages another wide variety of topics: corporate malfeasance and corrupt politics once again, but also evangelical Christianity, the Vietnam War, African colonialism, and epistemology. The principal source text here is Brontë's *Jane Eyre*, and Gaddis borrows from it many features of the Gothic novel (one aspect of its title, along with Jesus's occupation, though it primarily refers to an architectural style), but there are also several references to Revelations, adding to the novel's apocalyptic tone.

One major difference between Gaddis's pre-1980s work and his later novels is the prominence of female characters. Whether this was the result of the women's movement of the 1970s, an attempt to win a broader audience, or merely an aesthetic choice based on the material, both *Carpenter's Gothic* and *A Frolic of His Own* have a better balance between male and female characters, with the latter appearing in a far better light than the men. The protagonist of *Carpenter's Gothic* is 33-year-old Elizabeth Booth, stuck in a frustrating marriage with Vietnam vet Paul Booth, who is currently doing public relations work for a ludicrous televangelist and often away on business. The owner of the house she and Paul are renting unexpectedly arrives one morning: a science writer named McCandless, there to retrieve some papers from his locked study. They have a brief affair, and he leaves after selling some papers to the CIA that seem to instigate World War III, the apocalypse that the novel's evangelicals look forward to. The novel captures the zeitgeist of the 1980s, scary times for liberals like Gaddis when the Reagan administration and evangelical Christians seemed to have made a suicide pact, and represents Gaddis's most sustained attack on religion, dramatizing the contrast between revealed truth and acquired knowledge.

Carpenter's Gothic was a deliberate attempt to avoid what some considered the excess and difficulty of his earlier novels. Both the page count and time scheme are much shorter, there are fewer characters to keep track of, and there is a balance of prose and dialogue. Despite these deliberate limitations, Gaddis being Gaddis wound up making his novel more complicated than he intended. Since the importance of acquired knowledge is a key theme, Gaddis makes the reader work at piecing together many elements of the plot. While it may be aesthetically justified to make the reader participate in the novel's principal activity – and in all of his novel Gaddis insists on active participation rather than passive consumption – it leaves many readers puzzled rather than satisfied. Nevertheless, the novel received positive reviews and sold better than his previous ones. It displays all of Gaddis's strengths in compact form – high-fidelity dialogue, elegant, often poetic prose, cultural omniscience – and thus provides an excellent entry point for readers new to his work. As a condensed example of the characteristic themes and techniques of Gaddis's long novels, *Carpenter's Gothic* fills the same place in his oeuvre as Pynchon's *Crying of Lot 49* (1965), Barth's *Chimera* (1972), and Coover's *Universal Baseball Association* (1968) do in theirs.

It is also very funny, as are all of Gaddis's novels. Because of the seriousness of their themes, the humor in Gaddis's novels is often overlooked, or downgraded as "black humor" – another mode Gaddis anticipated in his first novel. But Gaddis never lost his sense of fun, even mischief, from his days at the satiric *Harvard Lampoon*, and Gaddis indulges in everything from slapstick and puns to learned wit in his novels. The humor in *Carpenter's Gothic* is sporadic, mostly made at the expense of the undereducated evangelicals mentioned throughout, but it occasionally lightens his otherwise dark novel. It would later be added to Penguin's prestigious "Twentieth-Century Classics" series, following new editions of *The Recognitions* and *J R* with scholarly introductions in 1993, which made his work even more widely available and is another sign of Gaddis's growing prestige.

Gaddis gave freer rein to his comedic instincts in his last major novel, *A Frolic of His Own*, a satire not on the law per se but on the *abuses* of the legal system. As with capitalism in *J R*, Gaddis attacks the abusers of systems, not the systems themselves, consistent with the historical use of satire. Set mostly in a house on Long Island very much like Gaddis's own at that time, with another limited time span (September–December 1990), the novel centers on the legal problems of history teacher Oscar Crease and his half-sister, Christina Lutz. A dizzying number of lawsuits fill the novel, many expressed in legal documents (briefs, opinions, depositions), which range from petty disputes to lofty theories of law and social justice. The law's attempt to impose order on society emerges as an instrument of disorder as various litigants misuse it to attain mostly greedy, egotistical aims.

Gaddis originally intended to limit himself to documents, legal and otherwise (newspaper stories and obituaries, art and literary critiques, a play, business correspondence, brochures, even recipes), but again in deference to the larger reading public he hoped to find, Gaddis framed the documents within the conflicted, multigenerational story of the Crease family, beginning during the Civil War era. This broadened the scope of the novel, allowing the historical conflicts in the Crease family to epitomize those of the United States at large.

Gaddis recycled some older material for his purposes: his unproduced play from the early 1960s, *Once at Antietam*, becomes the center of a plagiary suit, with the bulk of the original script reproduced throughout the novel; a sculptor named Szyrk, whose outdoor sculpture traps a child near the end of *J R*, is the defendant in a suit concerning another structure that entraps a boy in Virginia, presided over by Oscar's father, Judge Crease, who pens the most splendid legal opinions in the novel. Reverend Ude, the televangelist Paul Booth works for in *Carpenter's Gothic*, is hauled into court after he accidentally drowns a child during a baptism ceremony, and a Dr. Kissinger, who also appeared in Gaddis's third novel, reappears here in a malpractice suit. All of Gaddis's career-long concerns are revisited: the artist at odds with the community, the nature and validity of art, the dangers of religion and chauvinistic patriotism, corporate and personal greed, the manipulations of the media, and a sardonic view of "what America's all about."

The 1990s saw a dramatic rise in the political and cultural partisanship that has divided the United States ever since, as well as the increasing abuse of litigation to pursue selfish ends and the omnipresence of multimedia (television, plays, and films play a large role in the novel), all of which is dramatized in *A Frolic of His Own*, giving it a topical relevance even as some its characters meditate on the age-old concept of justice. Surprisingly, this long (575 pages), formally diverse, intellectually challenging novel won Gaddis his second National Book Award.

At age 72, uncertain whether he had another complex novel in him, and reluctant to abandon unfinished work, Gaddis decided to finish the nonfiction book on mechanization and the arts he had worked on in the early Sixties. Entitled *Agapē Agape: The Secret History of the Player Piano*, rights to it were bought by a publisher in 1996, but after a year or so Gaddis became dissatisfied with the project and decided to turn it into a novella instead, and dropped the subtitle. Inspired by the novels of the Austrian writer Thomas Bernhard, which he discovered in the 1980s, Gaddis dramatized his own struggle to turn all his material into a book in the form of a monologue by an aging, bedridden writer. Surrounded by his notes and reference materials, the unnamed protagonist spends two hours talking to himself about the implications of mechanization in the arts, using the rise and fall of the player piano as a starting point. It is Gaddis's shortest and most compact novel, his most concentrated expression of ideas that had concerned him all his life, but it lacks the variety and humor of his earlier works. He brought it to some sort of conclusion weeks before his death in December 1998, though there are indications in his notes that he meant to write more, especially concerning the silent, unnamed character who enters the writer's room near the end. Full of interesting material and Gaddis's final thoughts on lifelong obsessions, *Agapē Agape* is generally regarded as a footnote to his career rather than as a novel that can stand with his others.

Agapē Agape was posthumously published in 2002, along with *The Rush for Second Place*, a collection of his essays and occasional writings, and both were respectfully reviewed together. One exception was novelist Jonathan Franzen, who in a review-essay for *The New Yorker* (September 30, 2002) used the occasion to castigate Gaddis for being too difficult, a charge that dogged him all his career. In 2013, Dalkey Archive Press published a substantial volume of Gaddis's letters; though he disapproved of the publication of a writer's correspondence and papers, feeling that the work should be the sole focus, *The Letters of William Gaddis* offers numerous insights into his novels and functions as a kind of literary autobiography. It complements Joseph Tabbi's full-length biography, which appeared two years later.

Gaddis's novels were slow to attract critical attention, but they were quick to attract the attention of other novelists, who not only show his influence but sometimes even mention him in their texts. David Markson, Robert Coover, and Joseph McElroy demonstrate their admiration for *The Recognitions* in their novels, and the influence of his later work can be seen in the writings of Jeffrey Eugenides, Carter Sholz, Rick Moody, and Mark Z. Danielewski, to name a few. (Whether he influenced Thomas Pynchon, as is often alleged, is less clear.)

Opinion is divided over how to categorize Gaddis. Some critics consider him a late modernist, others an early postmodernist, while Gaddis himself felt he was working in the same satirical tradition as Evelyn Waugh, Mark Twain, and his beloved nineteenth-century Russian novelists (Gogol, Goncharov, Dostoevsky). While he respected and knew most of the meganovelists he was routinely grouped with – Barth, Coover, Gass, McElroy, Pynchon – he regarded himself as a more traditional novelist, and was disappointed that he was more popular with academics than with general readers. Despite winning two National Book Awards for his novels, Gaddis never attained the popularity of a Roth or an Updike, but the intellectual rigor of his novels, their cultural engagement, their stylistic variety, their uncannily realistic dialogue, and their mixture of high seriousness and low comedy ensure Gaddis's place as one of the most important American novelists of the second half of the twentieth century.

SEE ALSO: Coover, Robert; Gass, William H.; Minimalism and Maximalism; Pynchon, Thomas; Religion and Contemporary Fiction

FURTHER READING

Comnes, Gregory. (1994). *The Ethics of Indeterminacy in the Novels of William Gaddis*. Gainesville: University Press of Florida.

Knight, Christopher J. (1997). *Hints and Guesses: William Gaddis's Fiction of Longing*. Madison: University of Wisconsin Press.

Moore, Steven. (2015). *William Gaddis: Expanded Edition*. New York: Bloomsbury.

Tabbi, Joseph. (2015). *Nobody Grew but the Business: On the Life and Work of William Gaddis*. Evanston, IL: Northwestern University Press.

The Gaddis Annotations. (n.d.). https://www.williamgaddis.org/

Gaines, Ernest J.

LILLIE ANNE BROWN
Florida A&M University, USA

Short story writer, novelist, and essayist, Ernest J. Gaines was born, the eldest of twelve children, on the River Lake Plantation in Point Coupee Parish in Oscar, Louisiana, in 1933. His was the fifth generation of a sharecropper family, and Gaines grew up in the original slave quarters of the plantation. He left the region at 15 in 1948, to attend high school in Vallejo, California, where he reunited with his mother and stepfather, who had left during World War II. For two decades, from 1984–2004, he divided his time between California and a writer-in-residence position at the University of Louisiana at Lafayette, and in 2004 returned to settle on part of the original plantation of his birth, physically relocating the original plantation church to his property.

Gaines's work, unsurprisingly, articulates the social, political, and economic position of society's most vulnerable citizens: the poor, voiceless, invisible, and downtrodden. Raised in the "Quarters" by his beloved aunt, Augusteen Jefferson, whose disability forced her to crawl about the house, Gaines would later model a number of his highly sympathetic female characters after her. Influenced by "local" American authors such as Ernest Hemingway and William Faulkner, as well as the Russian novelist Ivan Turgenev, Gaines's greatest influences were the storytellers in the quarters: the women and men who sat on the front proches of residents' homes and spun tales. It was as a result of these neighborly associations that Gaines – at the behest of his aunt – began writing letters on behalf of the members of the community. He became, as a result of his willingness and ability to capture the soul of the community through words, the unofficial scribe of the Point Coupee Plantation.

His body of work, which centers on the speech, cultural traditions, and mores specific to the Point Coupee Plantation, is notable throughout his nine works of fiction, which include *Catherine Carmier* (1964); *Of Love and Dust* (1967); *Bloodline* (1968); *The Autobiography of Miss Jane Pittman* (1971); *A Long Day in November* (1971); *In My Father's House* (1978); *A Gathering of Old Men* (1983); *A Lesson Before Dying* (1993); and *The Tragedy of Brady Sims* (2017). Through simple dialogue and sparse physical descriptions, his work offers homage to ordinary Black citizens who not only deserve respect in their everyday lives but also crave it as a matter of order and sensibilities. The nucleus of his strength, the plantation, is the place which powers his commitment to memoir and history. His works reveal the heroic efforts of the plantation people, and he speaks fondly of the sights, sounds, and scents of the bayous of the region of his birthplace as a place of comfort and peace. While Gaines's work depicts society's most disenfranchised members, four of his most enduring works – *A Gathering of Old Men*, *A Lesson Before Dying*, *Mozart and Leadbelly* (2005), and *The Tragedy of Brady Sims* – allow readers to capture the significance of the author's ouevre in relationship to his growth as a writer invested in the region of his birth.

In *A Gathering of Old Men*, set in 1970 in the fictional town of Bayonne, LA, the narrative centers around the protective status of a group of elderly men by Candy, the white, part-time owner of a plantation who fears retribution against the men for the killing of a racist plantation boss. Her protection of the suspected killer, Mathu, not only rests in her overall relationship to the Black men on the plantation, but to Mathu in particular, a man whom she sees as a fatherly presence. Her determination to reverse the status of their relationship represents her performance as a maternal figure in the novel. Because Mathu has always been the most outspoken plantation worker in addressing racial injustices witnessed on the plantation, he bcomes the primary suspect in the killing of Beau Boutan. Under Candy's protection, 18 elderly men – aged 70 or more – assemble in defense of one of their own by confessing to the crime. It is her objective that the men, who, at her direction, arm themselves with 12-gauge and empty shotgun shells, produce conflicting evidence as each one confesses to the killing. During a subsequent violent mob attack resulting in injuries and deaths, the plantation community comes together in honoring the death of one of their own.

Gaines's novel, adapted for television in 1987, explores the duality of the silence and strength of men as their respective voices resonate in vulnerable spaces, how the intervention of exterior forces is oftentimes required for the protection of society's most vulnerable members, and how race and racism are woven into the social, political, and economic fabric of a community's citizenry.

Gaines extends the theme of manhood, a motif present in each of his eight works of fiction, in *A Lesson Before Dying*, through the inclusion of "Jefferson's Diary" (chapter 29), the most critical chapter in the novel. The diary is the private notebook that Jefferson, the plantation worker condemned to death by an all-white jury for the crime of killing a white shopkeeper, keeps at the urging of Grant Wiggins, the plantation schoolteacher and the novel's narrator. The novel, set in fictional Bayonne in 1948, centers primarily on the verdict and impending execution imposed upon Jefferson where, in the segregated South, he has no recourse but acceptance of the verdict and the subsequent outcome. Themes of racial injustice, power, privilege, and the economic disadvantages of a community's most vulnerable are prominent in the novel.

At the trial where Jefferson is proclaimed guilty, he sits stoically as the defense attorney, in a futile attempt to save him from the electric chair, recounts the white shopkeeper's dying words. For this horrific atrocity upon the respectable white residents of the community, there will be an accounting in the form of a state-sanctioned killing. Jefferson, whose attorney calls him a "hog" and a "boy" during his closing statements, is ridiculed and publicly dehumanized by the labels. Although Jefferson is presented as a semiliterate field hand, the label presents him the opportunity to rise above the defense attorney's words and teach himself about dignity, self-respect, integrity, and the ability to change perceptions.

As he faces death, he defends his right to be recognized as a human being even though he sees little value in himself. His mandate from Grant, the plantation schoolteacher, is to die as a man and not as a hog. Grant's flawed notion that Jefferson is more of a man that he contrasts the condemned man's uncertainty of the pain and the process of the imminent execution. Jefferson's invisibility at the trial is collectively assumed by the system that condemns him to death. In a subtle effort to reach the condemned man, Grant offers him the gift of a small notebook and pencil in the hope that he will tell his own story. The journal presents a challenge for Jefferson: It is a new experience for him, because he has never been asked to perform a task outside the boundaries of working on the plantation, and his writing skills are limited. He does not understand the basics of putting words on paper and is greatly confused. Unable to discern the purpose of lined paper, he writes across and below the lines as well as outside the margins; he spells phonetically and writes without punctuation. The effort, however, represents his first attempt to convey meaningful thought outside the public's perspective of him. "Jefferson's Diary" is the most critical chapter in the novel. It shows that while language can be used to construct reality, it can also be used to deconstruct and redefine it. Before he begins writing in the notebook, he constructs a narrative chain in an effort to situate himself within a historical framework of his childhood and life on the plantation. He is not proud to acknowledge that he often grinned to appease their sensibilities.

As the diary's opening entries suggest, Jefferson's expresses his perspective of God's benevolence as he faces execution. In his critique of God, he questions the plantation's racial hierarchy and compares his impending death with God's disapproval of him – and thus all Blacks whose devotion to Him is without question. God's love of whites, he concludes, is greater than His love of the disenfranchised who honor Him. An exposé of theological differences and a clash between central figures are signature motifs in Gaines's canon. As he continues to write in the diary, the power dynamics at the jail begin to shift. Jefferson's newfound sense of superiority allows him to ignore the jailers' presence and deny their token services. The dismissals permit him to consciously engage in a code of conduct where Blacks are forbidden to look directly into the eyes of white people with whom they are speaking, while also ignoring the jailers as he writes. Even though he remains a prisoner in his cell, he becomes the gatekeeper of his space. The physical presence of the notebook places him in a position of command over his oppressors, allowing him to quietly negotiate the boundaries of his circumstances as he constructs his own identity.

The sheriff, a representative figure of the racist network of southern white law enforcement officials, seeks validation of his so-called righteousness as well as a proper accounting for his deputies' behavior. Jefferson, in his new identity, dismisses the sheriff's wishes as well. As his words show, he slowly detours from communal attachment fostered by the perception that he is a mere field hand to become a writer whose emotional growth becomes stronger each day as he faces his own mortality.

A twelve-year gap separates *Mozart and Leadbelly* from the author's previous work, *A Lesson Before Dying*. It is, however, his most personal work, and in it he shares his process and perspectives as a writer, including glimpses of how he became the "go-to" writer as a young boy on the Point Coupee Plantation, the inner force behind his aspiration to become a writer, depictions of the storytelling traditions, and the vulnerabilities of members of his beloved Point Coupee Plantation community. The work also presents, as the title suggests, the influence of music upon his work, including compositions by Mozart and similar classical composers, and American folk and blues singers, including Huddie William Ledbetter, Lightnin' Hopkins, and Bessie Smith. The author's exposure to classical and canonical influences in music, art, and literature govern much of his writings and greatly contribute to his overall development as a writer. While Gaines did not have literary works by African American writers upon which to draw during his formative years, he had the voices of African American singers who spoke to him through song and verse, which allowed him to balance the tradition of classical composers with what he and others of his generation considered the "blues" culture and the environment of the plantation from which he found his voice as a writer. The author recognizes the significance of being able to recognize noted compositions of Mozart, but he is just as zealous of the historical and cultural impact of "blues people." In recognition of the genres, he is able to bridge the influences of both musical groups in a cohesive literary unit which speaks to his strength as a writer.

Comprised of three sections, "Essays," "Stories," and "In His Own Words: Ernest J. Gaines in Conversation," *Mozart and Leadbelly* presents the reader with histories, experiences, and iterations of his days as a student in California, struggles as a young writer, travels to Louisiana, and subsequent returns to California. In the work's signature essay, "Mozart and Leadbelly," Gaines recounts how the news of the enrollment of James Meridith at the University of Mississippi, in 1962, affected him as a young writer, served as a wake-up call for him to pursue his craft more vigilantly, and fueled his desire to become the writer he knew he was capable of becoming. In Gaines's perspective, Meredith's resiliency represented the strongest kind of bravery, one which would resonate throughout the writer's career. Following the announcement of Meredith's enrollment, Gaines cancelled a trip to Mexico, opting instead to travel to the Point Coupee Plantation, which continued to serve as the historical backdrop of his writings. The stories Gaines heard during his sojourns were rich with characters, regional dialect, and plots, which found themselves in many of his novels and short stories. Of particular note is the tale of an incident involving the killing of a man whose association with a woman leads to his death. The incident became the basis of *Of Love and Dust*.

Six essays, including the work's signature composition "Mozart and Leadbelly," open "Essays," the others being "Miss Jane and I," "A Very Big Order: Reconstructing Identity," "Bloodline in Ink," "Aunty and the Black Experience in Louisiana" and "Writing *A Lesson Before Dying*." In each essay, Gaines offers the reader a critical perspective into the personal, thematic, and symbolic machinations which govern the narratives that readers have come to expect from the author's nearly sixty years of writing.

In "Stories," *Mozart and Leadbelly*'s second section, the work contains five iconic short stories, all previously published, including, "The Turtles" (1956), which occupies a distinctive position in the author's canon. It is the author's first published short story, appearing in *Transfer* magazine in 1956, when Gaines was a student at San Franscisco [College] University. It was the chance reading of "The Turtles" by Dorothea Oppenheimer, who at the time of its publication was in the beginning stages of establishing a literary agency, that led to her enlisting Gaines as a client. Their professional relationship remained for over thirty years. His appreciation for classical music was greatly enhanced during their decades-long association. The "Stories" section also includes "My Grandpa and the Haint," "Christ Walked Down Market Street," "Boy in the Double-Breasted Suit," and "Mary Louise." In each narrative Gaines's relationship to the Louisiana region of his upbringing is splendidly represented through the narrative's central figure, and his attention to characters' speech, dress, deportment, and cultural connection to the land reverberates throughout each story.

The concluding section, "In His Own Words: Ernest J. Gaines in Conversation," offers copious literary revelations in a single chapter: "A Literary Salon: Oyster/Shrimp Po' Boys, Chardonnay, and Conversation with Ernest J. Gaines." Scholars Marcia Gaudet and Darrell Bourque engage in conversations with the author which expand, capture, and embrace the essence of Gaines's literary ouevre from the beginning of his writing career to 2002. Discussions center on the author's use of music as a governing motif in many of his works and how effective specific compositions allow him the opportunity to present a more sustained characterization of prominent figures in certain narratives. He expounds upon his embrace of spirituals as well as classical works like Mussorgsky's "Pictures at an Exhibition" (1874) which served as developmental tools during the writing of *The Autobiography of Miss Jane Pittman*. Compositions by blues musician Josh White and the lyrics of Bessie Smith's "Backwater Blues" were major influences, which helped guide him to what he terms an "awakening."

In writing narrative scenes for older women, the lyrics of spirituals become part of the musical application to the text. The manner in which older women talk to God and their spiritual connection to a higher being figure prominently in the author's narratives. Younger characters may not be invested in the emotional continuum of spirituals as older figures might; therefore, the inclusive nature of music benefiting the nature of the character is an important element in the development of central as well as minor figures in individual narratives. Gaines recognizes, for example, jazz musician John Coltrane as a musical genius, and listening to his musical compositions as he (Gaines) created narratives was an effecting element of characters' development. In proclaiming Coltrane's music as dually rooted in blues and spirituality, Gaines's sense of responsibility for the growth and expansion of his characters becomes a literary arc which, he feels, is a central element of exploration and preservation.

In "Writing *A Lesson Before Dying*," Gaines explores the theme of commonality, the presence of music and how it governs the novel, most notably in the club scenes as well as in the jail cell of the novel's protagonist, Jefferson. Music, concludes the author, has the ability to provide a person with personal details previously unbeknownst to them, but, when that person is allowed the privilege of listening to specific musical compositions, music can serve as an exploratory license to understand the most intimate part of a person's soul. When, for example, men and women lack the ability to read or their station in life prevents them from acquiring basic literacy skills, the notion of being able to listen to music can oftentimes serve as an element of communication.

"A Literary Salon" concludes in a discussion of various topics, including the defining aspects of the novel as art; the "elevation of the story" (in reference to "Jefferson's Diary"); the creation of one's work in a single day (referencing Joyce's *Ulysses*); the influences of Faulkner and Joyce; and the influence of Ivan Turgenev's novel *Fathers and Sons* (1862) in the creation of Gaines's own novel *In My Father's House*. Gaudet and Bourque's interview ends on a buoyant note via Gaines's recounting of an incident involving his brother's bravery following a hospital stay and how he (Gaines) wished he had his brother's courage to move forward despite the circumstances of his (brother's) health issues.

In *The Tragedy of Brady Sims*, Gaines centers the novella's exploits on recurring – and familiar – themes of race, power, manhood, integrity, and self-respect in a small Southern town. The narrative conflict, which occurs in the fictional town of Bayonne, Louisiana, centers on the courtroom shooting of a son by his father in an effort to prevent the son from being sent to Angola, the state's penitentiary, for a crime of robbery and murder committed by the son. While the fictional story has vestiges of the true story of Margaret Garner, an enslaved African American woman who killed her own daughter rather than allow the child to be returned to slavery, Gaines takes as his text the rural setting of the town's local barber shop, a cultural site for community consciousness, social uplift, and political awareness.

The narrative's protagonist, Brady Sims, asks and is indeed granted a two-hour reprieve, to get his affairs in order before he is remanded to the sheriff. When the town's lone African American reporter, Louis Guerin, is directed by his editor to craft a "human interest" story about Brady, one which will humanize the person who has committed this atrocious act, the reporter heads to the barbershop, where he hears the riveting tales not only of Brady Sims, dubbed "the man who whipped children," but also of barbershop "regulars" who frequent the shop as a matter of ritualized communion. Narratives of race and relationships between the town's powerful and the powerless, stories of love triangles and marital disputes among residents, tales of economic and social disenfranchisement among Black residents and white residents, and reverberating talks of economic vulnerabilities all converged at the local shop.

While Guerin does manage to secure a human interest story following the aftermath of the courthouse event, Gaines's work is more than a tale of the comeuppance of a man who engaged in his share of exploits. *The Tragedy of Brady Sims* is a work that captures the strength and essence of a communal site operating as an institution of historical preservation. Each man who gathers at the space brings an intensity of power dynamics while reflectively recognizing the importance and individuality of each person's place at the table. In address of the community's struggle to survive generationally, economically, and politically each person has a narrative to tell reflective of their own struggles and triumphs.

SEE ALSO: Morrison, Toni; Multiculturalism; Religion and Contemporary Fiction

FURTHER READING

Beavers, Herman. (1995). *Wrestling Angels into Song: The Fiction of Ernest J. Gaines and James Alan McPherson*. Philadelphia: University of Pennsylvania Press.
Brown, Lillie Anne. (ed.) (2016). New criticisms on the works of Ernest J. Gaines: man of letters. Special issue of *Studies in the Literary Imagination* 49 (1).
Doyle, Mary Ellen. (2002). *Voices from the Quarters: The Fiction of Ernest J. Gaines*. Baton Rouge: Louisiana State University Press.
Gaudet, Marcia. (ed.) (2019). *Ernest J. Gaines: Conversations*. Jackson: University Press of Mississippi.
Young, Reggie Scott, Gaudet, Marcia, and Cash, Wiley. (2009). *This Louisiana Thing That Drives Me: The Legacy of Ernest J. Gaines*. Lafayette: University of Louisiana Press.

García, Cristina

MARTA CAMINERO-SANTANGELO
University of Kansas, USA

Cristina García, a major Cuban American novelist and leading figure in a significant cohort of Latina immigrant writers who emerged in the 1990s, came to the United States in 1961 at the age of two with her parents, making her a member of what Rubén Rumbaut (2004) and Gustavo Pérez Firmat (1994) have subsequently termed the "one and a half generation"; her parents settled not in Miami but in New York, where she grew up. It is perhaps in part due to this upbringing in one of the world's most diverse urban centers that García has developed into a paradigmatic "cosmopolitan" writer, beginning by focusing on the specifics of Cuban American experiences but increasingly expanding in scope to incorporate migrants, exiles, refugees, and sojourners of enormous diversity – and not just to the United States but to other metropolitan centers of the world as well. García, who holds a BA from Barnard College (1979) and an MA in international relations from Johns Hopkins University (1981), previously worked as a journalist for *Time* magazine; she was based during this period in several cities with significant international and immigrant populations such as San Francisco, Miami, and Los Angeles. In addition to seven novels to date, García is the author of several children's books and the editor of two anthologies, *Cubanisimo! The Vintage Book of Contemporary Cuban Literature* (2003) and *Bordering Fires: The Vintage Book of Contemporary Mexican and Chicano/a Literature* (2006), that demonstrate her interest in the literary heritage of various Latinx populations and in the cross-cultural conversations that migration produces. She has been awarded a Guggenheim Fellowship and a Whiting Writers Award, a Hodder Fellowship at Princeton University, and a grant from the National Endowment for the Arts; her first novel, *Dreaming in Cuban* (1992), was a finalist for the National Book Award. She has adapted two of her novels, *Lady Matador's Hotel* (2010) and *King of Cuba* (2013), into plays.

García's fiction emerged from the beginning as strongly transnational in theme and scope, transgressing the boundaries of statehood and national identity that had been rigidly in place between Cuba and the United States during the Cold War. Instead, García offers a view that encompasses the influences and infiltrations of each nation upon the other, and of both nations for hybrid, hyphenated identities. García's oeuvre is remarkable for the degree to which she has truly moved beyond the hyphenated situation of her own origins to an expanded view of the ways in which uprootedness, migration, and transnational identity shape a host of populations who then come together in new configurations. Her approach to her work is characterized by a cosmopolitan vision of how lives and histories far distant from each other become intertwined and interdependent under the currents of global migrations.

García's first novel, *Dreaming in Cuban*, established her at the forefront of Latina fiction writers in the late twentieth century; further, this novel marked a new wave of writing by up-and-coming Latina authors (along with Julia Alvarez and Esmeralda Santiago) who wrote about *immigrant* experiences, in contrast to the Chicana identity established so strongly by Gloria Anzaldúa, Cherríe Moraga, Sandra Cisneros, and Ana Castillo in the previous decade.

Dreaming in Cuban is a meditation on the ways in which families were irretrievably divided by Castro's revolution in Cuba. The novel focuses on the family matriarch Celia, her two daughters Lourdes and Felicia, and Lourdes's daughter Pilar, who roughly shares García's own autobiographical positionality as a "one-and-a-half generation" immigrant, coming to the United States at age two and growing up in New York. (García later named her own daughter Pilar.) The narrative alternates among these women (with other voices occasionally interjected) to reflect perspectives of different generations, political viewpoints, and national identities in postrevolutionary Cuba and the United States. While Lourdes, who in many ways represents a typical, conservative/capitalist Cuban exile perspective, cannot forgive Castro and the trauma he caused, her daughter Pilar yearns for the Cuba she lost and for her grandmother who is still there. The multiple and conflicting perspectives of the novel became a trademark of García's writing, which often seeks to incorporate a variety of versions of the "truth"; any truth is a story depending on the memories and emotional investments of the storyteller and can be countered by someone else's version of "truth."

The novel uses what many scholars have labeled as magical realism to depict the continuing ties between the family members in Cuba and the United States. For example, the dead father Jorge's ghost visits his family on both sides of the divide; and the novel's central protagonist, Pilar Puente (the last name means "bridge"), can hear her grandmother's communications in her dreams. Pilar both "grows up" in a literal sense and matures during the course of the novel; in the final segment, representing her and Lourdes's return visit to Cuba, Pilar must learn to understand that her once-Cuban identity has been hybridized and that, though she belongs to Cuba, she belongs to New York more. She must also learn to accept the impulse to exile that she had earlier decried in her mother, as she chooses not to interfere with her cousin Ivanito's escape from Cuba via the 1980 occupation of the Peruvian Embassy that resulted in the Mariel boat lift, in which roughly 125,000 Cubans were allowed to leave Cuba through Mariel Harbor for the United States.

The "magical realism" of García's breakthrough first novel ties her to a strong tradition of Latin American "boom" writing, characterized by figures such as Gabriel García Márquez and Isabel Allende, in which a "metaphor is made real" (Faris 1995, p. 176); for instance, the ghostly patriarch of *Dreaming in Cuban* crosses and "bridges" the sea separating his family, in a literalized metaphor for the memories and relationships that connect the two sides to each other despite distance. Such elements fit into a domestic (US) mode of what critic Kathleen Brogan (1998) calls "cultural haunting" in ethnic American fiction (e.g. Toni Morrison's *Beloved* [1987] or Louise Erdrich's *Tracks* [1988]), in which ghosts and other forms of haunting are linked to the necessity to be reminded of a cultural history from which characters have become severed. García herself noted of this novel shortly after its publication that "I surprised myself by how Cuban the book turned out to be. I don't remember growing up with a longing for Cuba, so I didn't realize how Cuban I was, how deep a sense I had of exile and longing" (Burkett 1992). Magical realism – in the form of Jorge's returns, Pilar's and Celia's psychic transnational communications, and so on – functions frequently in the novel as a "bridge" to cultural memory, as described in Maria Rice Bellamy's book *Bridges to Memory: Postmemory in Contemporary Ethnic American Women's Fiction* (2015).

Though none of García's subsequent novels had the same widespread popularity of *Dreaming in Cuban*, which so perfectly expressed a particular collective memory about how the 1959 revolution had divided the Cuban population both geographically and ideologically, her second novel, *The Agüero Sisters* (1997), further solidified her reputation as a serious Latina writer with widespread appeal. Winner of the Janet Heidinger Kafka Prize, *The Agüero Sisters* again takes up the subject of the separation of families in the aftermath of Castro's revolution, this time focusing on two sisters, and explores the variability of the nature of "truth" and history. Once again, magical or supernatural elements make their appearance; as Tanya González suggests, the novel has strong strains of the Gothic tradition (e.g. Mary Shelley's *Frankenstein* [1818], Charlotte Perkins Gilman's *The Yellow Wallpaper* [1892]) as well as the more predictable reminders of Latin American magical realism. The secret at the narrative's core, the murder of the sisters' mother by their father back in Cuba, provides a dark tone that aligns with the Gothic tradition, drawing on "thematic concerns that repeat, like tropes of haunting, violence, psychological disturbance, and the uncanny" (González 2012, p. 122). Just as Lourdes Puente in *Dreaming in Cuban* is haunted by her father's spirit, Constancia in *The Agüero Sisters* is haunted by her mother's face, which becomes her own. This is a literalizing of Freud's "return of the repressed," since Constancia has long been bitter toward her mother and has repressed Ignacio's murder of her; thus, as with *Dreaming in Cuban*, severed fragments of memory and identity disconnect the characters, in part, from their pasts. Her sister Reina, an electrician in Cuba, must experience a bodily transformation of sorts when she is struck by lightning and her burns are treated with skin grafts from multiple donors – a Frankenstein-like patchwork of fragments from others. The novel thus suggests that both identity and history are composites made up of multiple and often ill-fitting contributions (stories), and some parts of history (identity) are silenced, buried, and repressed.

Though most of García's subsequent career trajectory increasingly expands the orbit of ethnic, national, and racial identities to which García's cosmopolitan sensibility attends, her sixth novel, *King of Cuba*, published sixteen years after *The Agüero Sisters*, returns squarely to the legacy of Castro's takeover and the resulting alienated diaspora. Positioned between two markedly more "international" novels – *The Lady Matador's Hotel* and *Here in Berlin* (2017) – this novel focuses on alternating and oppositional perspectives: an aging and decrepit Fidel Castro, contemplating the end of his life and his past (though now faded) glories, and Goyo Herrera, an also aging and embittered exile in Miami, who hopes to assassinate the man he views as his mortal enemy. *The King of Cuba* reeks of the failures of a larger ethical vision of global, rather than strictly political or nationalistic, responsibility, as these two men, nearing obsolescence, on opposite ends of the ideological spectrum, are equally dislikeable. The novel ends with the death of both – suggesting, perhaps, the final limits of this subject matter for García.

In her third novel, *Monkey Hunting* (2003), García pushes to extend her investigation of Cuban history both further back in time and further out geographically than Castro's 1959 Revolution. *Monkey Hunting* is an excavation of the multiple influences (cultural, national, racial) that make up Cuban identity as well as the multiple receiving points of migration *from* Cuba. By this point, García's fiction was becoming more visibly cosmopolitan, extending beyond the themes of recent Cuban history and exile to interrogate Cuba itself as a multicultural society with its own violent past. *Monkey Hunting* traces the influences of various diasporas – enslaved Africans as well as Chinese laborers who were brought to the island in the mid-nineteenth century (Casal 2002) – on Cuban culture; it also suggests return migrations *back* to countries of origin (China), or migrations out to still other receiving countries (the United States during the Vietnam War). The result is characterized by what famed Cuban scholar Fernando Ortiz (1970) called "transculturation," in which various cultures adapt to and influence one another and in which the characters' loyalties extend far beyond simple national boundaries or ethnic filiations. The novel's genealogical tapestry becomes a wonderful canvas for what Kwame Anthony Appiah calls "partial cosmopolitanism" (2006, p. xvii): "every human being has obligations to every other . . . Everybody matters"; but at the same time "to say that we have obligations to strangers isn't to demand that they have the same grip on our sympathies as our nearest and dearest" (p. 158). Even when the characters in *Monkey Hunting* seem to have their allegiances locked into narrow national parameters, however, the novel as a whole depicts a much more complex picture in which one's "nearest and dearest" might not be a part of one's ethnic or racial or national "clan." Underlying ties extend across multiple boundaries and even across oceans, opening the way for us to understand ethics (even if the characters do not) as a set of obligations that casts a very wide net indeed.

Later novels push even further this expansive vision of our responsibility to others. In *A Handbook to Luck* (2007) García tells the intertwined stories of three very different protagonists, all of whom, however, have left their nations of origin for the United States: Enrique, a one-and-a-half generation Cuban exile, again like García herself; Marta, who flees El Salvador's repressive regime in the 1980s; and Leila, an Iranian woman sojourning for a time in the United States until she returns to Iran for an arranged marriage. Enrique and Leila have a brief affair, which extends his concern for her when she returns to Iran; Marta works for Enrique and he is instrumental in securing citizenship for her sons, though he is also partially responsible for the near-drowning of her son in his own swimming pool. In *Scales of Justice* (2009), Nancy Fraser suggests that "the increased migration associated with globalization is now transforming the ethical-political self-understanding of many" (p. 135); it is this ethical-political consideration of obligation and responsibility that *A Handbook to Luck* foregrounds, through the ways in which the various characters understand and fail to understand their responsibility for others.

Two of García's later novels, *The Lady Matador's Hotel* and *Here in Berlin*, both move to ever more "international" locations and casts of characters, even while a Cuban protagonist is featured in each. *The Lady Matador's Hotel* takes place in Hotel Miraflor in an unnamed Central American country where international travelers congregate: the titular matadora (female bullfighter), Suki Palacios, of Japanese and Mexican origin via Los Angeles; a Cuban poet and his US wife who have come to adopt a baby and the German adoption lawyer who runs a baby mill of Indigenous women she pays as "breeders"; a Central American ex-guerrilla now waiting tables at the hotel and the military officer who killed her brother; a Korean textile businessman who runs a *maquiladora* (sweatshop) in the unnamed Central American country, where workers are denied basic rights and protections, and whose underage pregnant mistress once worked in said *maquiladora*. Once again, the novel suggests that the currents of globalization and capitalism intersect and intertwine in ways that foreground both the concept of the potential "global citizen" as well as its failures; various national/ethnic identities collide in relationships of (ir)responsibility and, indeed, inhumanity with regard to each other.

Again, magical elements make these obscured connections salient: Aura, the ex-guerrilla waitress, has conversations with her dead brother, who informs her that the military man who killed him by trapping him in a burning field – now a colonel – is a guest at the hotel. Aura's brother sends her on a quest of vengeance, in a subplot with strong resemblance to Guatemalan American Héctor Tobar's novel *The Tattooed Soldier* (2000), in which a young former student from Guatemala encounters, in Los Angeles, the death squad soldier who killed his family and embarks on his own mission of diasporic vengeance.

Here in Berlin is even more insistent on telling a fully international story, while starting from the premise that Cuba is embedded in a larger Cold War context. In the novel's prologue, a Cuban American "Visitor," clearly an analogue for García herself, comes to Berlin years after the fall of the Berlin Wall to investigate these strange, perhaps unforeseen, flows of migration between countries allied with the former Soviet Union and Cuba. As the Prologue notes from the perspective of the Visitor, the novel takes on the themes of "political upheavals and the displacements of war, of revolution, the unlikely bedfellows these produced ... All the flotsam and detritus of history" (García 2017, p. 6) – including "the human fallout from Cuba's long association with the Soviet bloc" (p. 6). *Here in Berlin* demonstrates how García's mature sensibility has expanded ever more to incorporate global currents provoked by political alignments and (re)configurations, as well as by global capital, while preserving her foothold in Cuban history. Further, it extends more than any previous novel the stylistic choice of multiple and fragmented narrators; rather than following several (limited) characters' perspectives, this novel is a kaleidoscopic tapestry of the many shifting stories of past and present buried in the rubble of the former East Berlin. Thus, History with a capital H is expressed through multitudinous and non-cohering personal histories; as with every García novel to date, the larger currents of history are responsible for the flows of people, across countries and continents, that shape personal histories and that give human beings a sense of their tenuous, shifting identities and obligations.

That is to say, García's sensibility has become ever more cosmopolitan, in Appiah's sense of the term. As a contemporary US writer, García herself is a global citizen pushing against the strong nationalist and even isolationist currents at work in the early twenty-first century.

SEE ALSO: Álvarez, Julia; Castillo, Ana; Globalization; Literature of the Americas; Multiculturalism; Trauma and Fiction

REFERENCES

Appiah, Kwame Anthony. (2006). *Cosmopolitanism: Ethics in a World of Strangers*. New York: Norton.
Bellamy, Maria Rice. (2015). *Bridges to Memory: Postmemory in Contemporary Ethnic American Women's Fiction*. Charlottesville: University of Virginia Press.
Brogan, Kathleen. (1998). *Cultural Haunting: Ghosts and Ethnicity in Recent American Literature*. Charlottesville: University of Virginia Press.
Burkett, Elinor. (1992). Author focuses on Cuban nostalgia. *Chicago Tribune* (April 9, 1992). https://www.chicagotribune.com/news/ct-xpm-1992-04-09-9202010715-story.html (accessed July 14, 2021).
Casal, Lourdes. (2002). The founders: Alfonso. In: *Cubanísimo!: The Vintage Book of Contemporary Cuban Literature* (ed. Cristina García; trans. Margaret Jull Costa), 192–206. New York: Random House.
Faris, Wendy B. (1995). Scheherazade's children. In: *Magical Realism: Theory, History, Community* (ed. Lois Parkinson Zamora and Wendy B. Faris), 163–190. Durham, NC: Duke University Press.
Firmat, Gustavo Pérez. (1994). *Life on the Hyphen: The Cuban–American Way*. Austin: University of Texas Press.
Fraser, Nancy. (2009). *Scales of Justice: Reimagining Political Space in a Globalizing World*. New York: Columbia University Press.
García, Cristina. (2017). *Here in Berlin*. Berkeley, CA: Counterpoint.
González, Tanya. (2012). The Gothic in Cristina García's *The Agüero Sisters*. MELUS 37 (3): 117–139.
Ortiz, Fernando. (1970). *Cuban Counterpoint: Tobacco and Sugar* (trans. Harriet De Onís). New York: Vintage.
Rumbaut, Rubén G. (2004). Ages, life stages, and generational cohorts: decomposing the first and second generation in the United States. *International Migration Review* 38 (3): 1160–1205.

FURTHER READING

Caminero-Santangelo, Marta. (2007). *On Latinidad: US Latino Literature and the Construction of Ethnicity*. Gainesville: University Press of Florida.
Derrickson, Teresa. (2007). Women's bodies as sites of (trans)national politics in Cristina Garcia's *The Aguero Sisters*. *Modern Fiction Studies* 53 (3): 478–500.
Moiles, Sean. (2009). Search for Utopia, desire for the sublime: Cristina García's *Monkey Hunting*. MELUS 34 (4): 167–186.
Parziale, Amy. (2018). Counter-archives of trauma in Cristina García's *Monkey Hunting*. *Revista de estudios hispánicos* 52 (3): 937–958.
Santos, Jorge. (2016). "Multi-hyphenated identities on the road": an interview with Cristina García. MELUS 41 (2): 202–212.
Scharm, Heike and Matta-Jara, Natalia. (eds.) (2017). *Postnational Perspectives on Contemporary Hispanic Literature*. Gainesville: University Press of Florida.

Gass, William H.

YONINA HOFFMAN
United States Military Academy at West Point, USA

Born in 1924 in Fargo, North Dakota, William Howard Gass had an unhappy childhood in Warren, Ohio: life with an abusive, bigoted father and a passive, alcoholic mother formed his early desire to write "because I hate" (Ammon 2003, p. 20). Cynthia Ozick called him "the most daringly scathing and the most assertively fecund [of living writers]: in language, in ideas, in intricacy of form . . . above all in relentless fury" (2013). His power on the page avenges the pain of being "an impotent nobody" in the world (Hix 2002, p. 157). This informs a philosophical distinction in his work: language is not solely referential, but creates its own distinct reality. Gass studied philosophy at Ohio Wesleyan and Kenyon, interrupted by three years' navy service in the Pacific theater, completing his doctoral thesis at Cornell with philosophers of language Max Black and (briefly) Ludwig Wittgenstein. He began publishing stories in the late 1950s when he taught at Wooster College, then Purdue, where he gained full professorship, establishing himself with *Omensetter's Luck* (1966), *In the Heart of the Heart of the Country* (1968), and *Willie Masters' Lonesome Wife* (1968). Because of the latter's obscenity, he was ushered out of Purdue, moving in 1969 to Washington University in St. Louis until his 1999 retirement.

There, Gass shaped avant-garde literary production worldwide through his roles as founder of the International Writers Center, contributing editor of *Conjunctions*, and president of the organization River Styx. He was close friends with contemporaries such as William Gaddis, Stanley Elkin, Donald Barthelme, John Gardner, John Barth, and Ishmael Reed, influencing both contemporaries and the next generation (e.g. David Foster Wallace). In the 1980s and early 1990s, he traveled to the USSR and China as part of writer-exchange conferences, accompanied by writers such as Allen Ginsberg, Arthur Miller, Toni Morrison, Leslie Marmon Silko, Gary Snyder, and Studs Terkel.

Gass's work has been well received from the start, with early stories in multiple 1950s and 1960s Best American anthologies. He won multiple awards for individual works: four Pushcart Prizes, the American Book Award, and many others, in addition to his unprecedented three National Book Critics Circle Awards. He was also inducted into the American Academy and Institute of Arts and Letters (1983) and received the Mark Twain Award for Literature of the Midwest (1994) and the Lannan Foundation Lifetime Achievement Award (1997). He won the first PEN/Nabokov Award, the 2003 PEN/Diamondstein-Spielvogel Award for the Art of the Essay, and the PEN/Nabokov Lifetime Achievement Award (2000), as well as Rockefeller and Guggenheim grants and a star on the St. Louis Walk of Fame. His reception is cemented by the *William Gass Reader* (2019) and by translations, as of 2020, into thirteen different languages. (Seeing *Heart's* translation in the Sorbonne book shop is one of Gass's fondest memories.)

Despite his certain place in the canon, Gass's legacy and lineage is complicated. Is he a postmodernist or a modernist? A fictionist or an essayist? His work is known for its consistent metafictionality (he coined the term in 1970), its sexuality, its multimediality (image, sound), and its critique of narrative structure. Nevertheless, he has rejected the label "postmodern," calling himself a "late" or "decayed" modern (Ammon 2003, p. 113) as well as "baroque" (Castro 1995). Though he considered himself more a fiction writer, his nonfiction constitutes more than half of his post-1980 output in sheer pages. Multiple essays address his (mostly modernist) literary influences, which cross genre and language: Gertrude Stein, Rainer Maria Rilke, and James Joyce are among his most loved, as well as Kafka, Mann, Flaubert, Colette, and Válery; the only Americans on his "top 12 list" are Faulkner and Gaddis.

Rather than worry over periodization, Gass's readers should attend to his antihierarchical, anti-structural aesthetics:

books grow as if by accretion, and the obsessive force of a character's mind often finds lengthy, uninterrupted rendering, making his texts often repetitive and seemingly digressive. Gass's literary aesthetics are linked to his background as a philosopher of language, and his writing engages explicitly and implicitly with philosophy, tracking the relationships among language, thought, literary form, and the world. His chief concerns involve the supersession of the world by the word; visual art and music's significance to literary form; and the importance of sentence structure to cognition. For Gass, words are at once signs and objects made of sound and letters, combining and interacting to create a novel's world – a "thick conceptual system" whose meanings "intercept and penetrate and alter ours" (Gass 1984, p. 109). Such penetration underscores the interpersonal as well as erotic character of language, and Gass's own metaphors are also consistently sexual, equating the physicality of language with the physicality of the body.

Gass published only one book in the 1980s – *Habitations of the Word* (1984) – but the contours of his career become clearer in the 1990s with publication of multiple story and essay collections as well as *The Tunnel* (1995), composed over thirty years and winner of the American Book Award. The novel focuses on William Frederick Kohler, a history professor writing a preface to his book *Guilt and Innocence in Hitler's Germany*. That preface – a meandering, angry, and bleak account of his own life – becomes *The Tunnel*, and as he digs into himself, Kohler begins to dig a tunnel underneath the basement and to hide the pages from his wife. *The Tunnel* showcases the "fascism of the heart" (1995, p. 33)– a darkness we all contain – deepening Arendt's (1963) "banality of evil" by suggesting that the Holocaust is not an inconceivable, epochal evil. Rather, such violence is engrained in our everyday patterns of objectification and resentment. The novel's reception has been strongly divided regarding its ethics, instigating questions like: Does Kohler defend the Nazis? Are we supposed to accept that defense? Does Gass want readers to identify with Kohler or critique him? Is it possible to maintain a critical stance throughout such deep inhabitation of Kohler's mind?

Despite *The Tunnel*'s stunning departure – longer and darker than Gass's previous work – it is not essentially anomalous. Gass's voices are often rooted in fear, and the tunnel as a motif continues his preoccupation with the distinction between emptiness and plenitude. In both *Heart* and *Omensetter* the motif of emptiness highlighted the opposition between the (full, sexualized) body, and the (empty, austere) mind; Gass writes that *The Tunnel* is "at once" defined by "hollow absence," "uneasy structure," and "shapeless mess" (Gass 1984, pp. 158–159). These (anti-) structural concerns continue Gass's career-long preoccupation with form, matter, and music; he tells Michael Silverblatt (1998) that its twelve sections or "philippics" are based on a Schoenbergian twelve-tone scale.

It is thus appropriate that Gass's next book, which won his second National Book Critics Circle Award, is called *Finding a Form* (1996). Gass's title essay personalizes his fiction: "I read to escape my condition, wrote to remedy it . . . there is scarcely a significant character in my work who is not a failure in the practice of ordinary existence, who does not lead a deflected life" (1996, p. 32). It explores again the multiplicity of the linguistic sign, linking it anew to human multiplicity in purpose: speech is motivated by various forms of love, or forms of hate, and as "containers of consciousness" (p. 327) sentences manage both linguistic and mental multiplicities. Gass is also newly explicit about his opposition to the global structuring of plot, "an error for which there's no longer an excuse" (p. 45).

Fiction, he thinks, must organize itself symbolically, around language and its connection to mind and meaning. Perhaps his best collection, *Finding* showcases incisive essays on Nietzsche and Wittgenstein; Walser, Pound, and Ford; the state of nature; and more.

In 1998, Gass published *Cartesian Sonata and Other Novellas*, which, like *The Tunnel*, draws on material long in progress. The titular novella tells of Ella Bend Hess, whose clairvoyance metaphorically underscores an openness to the world's plurality of detail. Ella's character is also metafictionally examined: "I'd given her a long nose, I remember – no good reason why. Now her nose is middling" (1998, p. 4). Full of Beckett and Joyce echoes, the novella proceeds distractedly, jumping from character to character in an endless unfurling of tales, to reach Willard Lycoming, a painter with a distinctly Gassian aesthetic: "so fastidious with every detail he could not manage their subordination. He gave them all his skill, painting each with a microscopic precision that shattered the unity of his canvas and created there a kind of grossly luminous horror" (p. 11). Even though this section was originally published in 1964, Gass has added references to *Willie* and to *Tunnel*, a newly self-referential gesture that is often self-parodic as well. The following pages continue the tale of Ella and her angry abusive husband, evoking the violent father figure that occurs in much of his work.

This piece and "Emma Enters a Sentence of Elizabeth Bishop's" are the more preoccupied with language and representation, showing the world of words convolutedly turning in on itself. But the other two pieces, "Bed and Breakfast" and "The Master of Secret Revenges," are the more engaging to read; both are concerned (as Gass's stories are often) with deceit. The first engages a traveling accountant whose specialty is fraud: helping struggling companies "fix" their accounts. He becomes captivated by his good Christian host and her elaborately decorated bed and breakfast, and desires to stay there forever. The other novella, one of Gass's best, tells the story of Luther Penner, whose desire to best others involves a series of more and more elaborate symbolic traps until he renames himself Romulus and starts a pagan church, "for how better" to "revenge himself upon the world" than "mislead its mind with a fresh religion" (1998, p. 265)? Relayed through a peripheral narrator, this story shows Gass's evolution in narrative technique and his theory of language's mysteriousness, at once sacred and misleading.

Reading Rilke: Reflections on the Problems of Translation (1999) takes up similar problems of language, religion, and power. Gass implicitly sees his own purposes in Rilke, who seeks "to give meaning to a world that has lost its deity" (1999, p. 17). Gass emphasizes newly the permanence of writing, beginning with a discussion of death – Rilke's own and its role in his poetry. Much of what Gass says about Rilke reflects back upon himself: he loves Rilke's hermeticism, detachment, and affirmation of artifice. His exhaustive line-by-line comparative analysis, of his own and other translations of the *Duino Elegies* (1923), reveals much about Rilke's own style and purposes as well as the challenges of translation. Gass further theorizes translation as a form of reading, whose task is to balance the clamorous multiplicity of words into the harmonious community of the sentence. This idea is key to understanding Gass's own writing: "The poet . . . struggles to rule a nation of greedy self-serving malcontents; every idea . . . wants to submerge the central subject beneath its fructifying self . . . every word wants to enjoy a potency so supreme it will emasculate the others" (1999, p. 70). Such a tension between community and power connects Gass's poetics to his politics, his enduring interest in violence and domination in human relations.

In direct contrast to *Reading Rilke*'s encomium, *Tests of Time* (2002) – which won him his third National Book Critics Circle Award – shows a contentious Gass wading into debates about writing, politics, identity, and ideology, unsurprisingly arguing for the writer's necessary autonomy. The book implicitly responds to *The Tunnel*'s controversial reception and continues Gass's public debate with John Gardner about "moral fiction" (Gass is against). The book's central harangue regards literary value (the "test of time") and its (in)compatibility with literature's application to extra-literary purposes (e.g. institutional, social, and political). Such anti-literary forces are so oppressive, Gass announces, "it should be an occasion for surprise when anything excellent survives" (2002, p. 111). Fortunately, Gass balances his animosities with essays that elaborate new twists on his central positions: declaiming against plot more deliberately than before, and exploring the organizing principles and history of the list form as essentially democratic, but also optimal for "creating a sense of abundance, overflow, excess" (p. 95).

His next nonfiction collection, *A Temple of Texts* (2006), exemplifies Gass's tendency toward list-making. More a glorified "best of" list than his typical collection, it nevertheless won the Truman Capote Award and succeeds on the force of Gass's enthusiasm. These pieces are collected from over two decades of occasional writing, interspersed with longer essays regarding his standard preoccupations – the question of influence, the physicality of the book object, the sonic and rhythmic forms of the sentence. The book does, though, offer new explorations of social and ethical issues – sacred texts, the relation of spectacle to art, and the problem of evil – highlighting Gass's treatment of ethics as a continuing and central thread in his career. In particular, he asks "How shall we define evil? Is its character human, natural, or divine? What is its justification? And what does its presence indicate?" (2006, p. 407).

Life Sentences (2012) is Gass's final nonfiction collection, and it follows a typical format: pieces on touchstones like Nietzsche, Kafka, Stein, and Proust, coupled with essays about culture, ethics, aesthetics, and desire. Gass continues to write about World War II and atrocity (returned to in his novel *Middle C* [2013]), but he also reflects on his career's preoccupations: "naming, metaphoring, jingling, preaching, theorizing, celebrating, translating" (2012, p. 37). Even at age 88 Gass affirms the value of lust, suggesting that it can "realize" and "renew" life (pp. 299, 300), and his attitude to story is renewed as well by "Narrative Sentences," which – newly embracing narrative – explores the causal dynamics embedded at the level of sentence. *Life Sentences* shows Gass still committed to his aims (to indict mankind; to celebrate the sentence) but more positive than antagonistic.

With *Middle C*, which won the William Dean Howells Medal, Gass returns to the novel form, following Joseph Skizzen, whose father's abandonment led his family from 1940s wartime Europe to rural Ohio. Growing up, Skizzen develops several selves: contemptuous student; penurious librarian's assistant; Austrian émigré pianist, whose mysterious past gains him an assistant professorship of music; and finally, curator of the "Museum of Inhumanity," his attic collection of news reports regarding atrocities and mass deaths. Skizzen obsesses over a single sentence, "The fear that the human race might not survive has been replaced by the fear that it will endure" (2013, p. 22), attempting to get the words and their order perfect. He finally lights on the perfect rendition, reduced to twelve words (again evoking Schoenberg, on whose music Skizzen has built his fraudulent academic career). The emphasis on word order is part of Gass's obsession with language's creation of reality; the sentence is a meaningful truth amid a life of deceit, as Skizzen lives in fear of discovery. He isn't caught, unlike his real-life source, Gass's Wooster colleague with a fabricated record and criminal past – exemplifying the long gestation of Gass's works.

Eyes (2015) is Gass's last collection before his death in 2017. While much of his recent fiction invoked musical forms (*Cartesian Sonata*; *Middle C*), *Eyes* investigates vision. Its strongest story, "In Camera," is told from the perspective of a young, intellectually disabled man, Mr. Stu, who becomes the assistant and adopted son of the shopkeeper Mr. Gab, a black-market salesman of avant-garde photographs. The story reveals an attention to visual form and its production of space, as well as a deep knowledge of photography, gained through Gass's own photographic practice and abiding interest in architecture. Echoing Gass's previous works, one story is interspersed with photos (as was *Willie*), and another is narrated by a chair (a significant object in *The Tunnel*).

Gass resists summary: in his theory of language, his individual works, and his career's trajectory, he refuses the structures and hierarchies that enable synopsis. In Gass's work it is very hard to see the forest for the trees, and because each tree is so miraculously individual, it receives closer and closer attention, generating and dissolving stories as quickly as drops of rain fall on its leaves: any time Gass's consciousness alights on an object, that object proliferates, its edges indeterminate with respect to its world.

SEE ALSO: Barth, John; Elkin, Stanley; Gaddis, William; Ozick, Cynthia; Reed, Ishmael; Wallace, David Foster

REFERENCES

Ammon, Theodore G. (ed.) (2003). *Conversations with William H. Gass*. Jackson: University Press of Mississippi.

Castro, Jan Garden. (1995). Interview. *Bomb Magazine* (April 1, 1995). https://bombmagazine.org/articles/william-h-gass/ (accessed July 20, 2021).

Gass, William H. (1984). *Habitations of the Word*. New York: Simon & Schuster.

Gass, William H. (1995). *The Tunnel*. New York: Knopf.

Gass, William H. (1996). *Finding a Form*. New York: Knopf.

Gass, William H. (1998). *Cartesian Sonata and Other Novellas*. New York: Knopf.

Gass, William H. (1999). *Reading Rilke: Reflections on the Problems of Translation*. New York: Knopf.

Gass, William H. (2002). *Tests of Time*. New York: Knopf.

Gass, William H. (2006). *A Temple of Texts*. New York: Knopf.

Gass, William H. (2012). *Life Sentences*. New York: Knopf.

Gass, William H. (2013). *Middle C*. New York: Knopf.

Hix, Harvey L. (2002). *Understanding William H. Gass*. Columbia: University of South Carolina Press.

Ozick, Cynthia. (2013). Holding the Key. *The New York Times* (March 28, 2013). https://www.nytimes.com/2013/03/31/books/review/middle-c-by-william-h-gass.html (accessed July 20, 2021).

Silverblatt, Michael. (1998). *Lannan readings and conversations: William Gass*. Medium (May 4, 2014). https://medium.com/the-william-h-gass-interviews/william-h-gass-interview-with-michael-silverbatt-1998-ab8cdbe33563 (accessed July 20, 2021).

FURTHER READING

Kellman, Steven G. and Malin, Irving. (eds.) (1998). *Into the Tunnel: Readings of Gass's Novel*. Newark: University of Delaware Press.

McCaffery, Larry. (1982). *The Metafictional Muse: The Works of Robert Coover, Donald Barthelme, and William H. Gass*. Pittsburgh: University of Pittsburgh Press.

Minor, Joel and Schnuriger, Sarah. (eds.) (2013). *William H. Gass: The Soul Inside the Sentence*. Digital collection. http://omeka.wustl.edu/omeka/exhibits/show/gass

Saltzman, Arthur Michael. (1985). *The Fiction of William Gass: The Consolation of Language*. Carbondale: Southern Illinois University Press.

Schenkenberg, Stephen. (n.d.). *Reading William Gass*. https://www.readinggass.org

Gay, Roxane

AMY REDDINGER
Bay College, USA

Scholars and critics largely agree that the publication of Roxane Gay's 2014 *New York Times* best-selling collection of essays *Bad Feminist* marks her arrival as a lauded contemporary writer and cultural critic. And yet, as is almost always the case with such literary "arrivals," this acclaim came after years of hard work and less recognition. Roxane Gay, who is a prolific, multigenre, and multimedia writer, notes that she has been writing stories since she was four years old.

Gay was born in 1974 in Omaha, Nebraska, to Michael and Nicole Gay, Haitian immigrants. Gay and her brothers were raised with strict expectations for high academic performance and achievement, a path that led her to the elite high school Philips Exeter Academy and Yale University where she studied English until she dropped out and moved to Arizona. She returned to college and concluded her formal education with a PhD in rhetoric and technical communication from Michigan Technical University in Houghton, Michigan. In May of 2019, Gay announced that she was leaving her faculty position as an associate professor of English at Purdue University to be a visiting associate professor of women's, gender, and sexuality studies at Yale.

Gay's presence as a bold, genre-bending, feminist, bisexual, woman of color writer began while she was a graduate student at Michigan Tech and was first established on the Internet. As scholar Justin R. Greene proclaims, "Gay is digitally born" (2019, p. 1). In 2006, Gay joined M. Bartley Seigel in founding the online literary magazine *PANK*, "a literary magazine fostering access to innovative poetry and prose, publishing the brightest and most promising writers for the most adventurous readers" (Pankmagazine.com). Gay's involvement with *PANK* situates her, from the beginning of her career, as a writer, editor, and critic operating in the digital realm and as an advocate for "Indie-Lit," alternative, radical, and often marginal prose that exists outside of traditional genre and publication boundaries.

Indeed, Gay occupies the interesting and important position of a contemporary writer whose contribution to the world of literature and culture has happened, not just on the Internet, but on social media in particular. During an interview with Gay, literary publicist Michael Taeckens asserted, "you are arguably one of the most popular and beloved literary people on Twitter" (2015). And if you scan Gay's voluminous Twitter feed you see that she positions herself there as a writer and a critic: "If you clap, I clap back. I write . . ." her profile description reads. To be a relevant contemporary writer often means engaging your reader on multiple platforms and in diverse ways, and few have done that better than Gay. She links her writing agility to her practice writing across genres: "Creative writers should learn the art of most writing genres – cross-training for the writing muscle. My work as a critic has helped me become a stronger writer. I pay more attention to the words I use and why" (Taeckens 2015). Indeed, some scholars argue that it is precisely the place that Gay occupies between worlds of print and digital culture that makes her one of the most important of contemporary writers (Green 2019, p. 1).

Gay's first published collection of fiction, *Ayiti*, was initially released in 2011 and re-released in 2018. The short stories in this collection are woven around the eponymous island of Haiti, its visitors, residents, émigrés, and descendants. Several of the stories in this collection represent the experiences of Haitian immigrants living in the United States, portraying the bias experienced by a child at school ("Motherfuckers"), or the struggle and isolation of an undocumented immigrant working to send money home to his family ("Cheap, Fast, Filling"). Other stories attend to the beautiful intimacies of everyday life for people who are engaged in the geopolitical realities of life in Haiti. Still other pieces in this collection refute and resist the misrepresentation and overreporting of the poverty of the island ("Gracias Nicaragua, y lo Sentimos"; "The Dirt We Do Not Eat"). This collection received less critical attention than Gay's later work, but the attention it did receive was largely positive. Through this work, and because of *Ayiti*'s focus on Haiti, Gay is often connected with novelists Edwidge Danticat, Marie Vieux Chauvet, and Lyonel Trouillot (Pressley-Sanon 2016, p. 145).

Other stories within this collection signal what is to come in Gay's later fiction, providing a focus on sexual transgressions and violence. "The Harder They Come" is an early introduction to Gay's frank and unwavering treatment of problematic racialized and gendered sexual scripts. This story also offers a sharp commentary on the sexual, emotional, and financial economies of island tourism. In doing so it is reminiscent of Jamaica Kincaid's essay *A Small Place*, in which Kincaid narrates with an equally incisive clarity the dual realities of the island for tourists and natives. As Gay details the weekly lineup of people in the service industry, waiting to greet tourists as they emerge from their cruise ship, "The Americans, the men, they like us and want us. They think we too are for sale as part of the Hispaniola experience" (2018, p. 113).

The short story "Sweet on the Tongue" centers on Therese, an ER doctor in Los Angeles who is kidnapped and raped while celebrating her honeymoon on "her island." She is brutalized and impregnated by an angry young man who is taking revenge for her lack of attention to his earlier attempts at flirtation. In this short story we see the complex reality of survival as Therese chooses to continue her pregnancy and keep the resulting child without ever telling her parents and extended family. Meanwhile, her husband Campbell welcomes the child and their new and altered realities. The story makes visible various bifurcations – mind and body, husband and wife, island and mainland – in ways that indicate separations but not binaries. We are constantly reminded by Gay to question binary assumptions. This short story can be read as a rich and haunting predecessor to her first novel.

This novel, *An Untamed State* (2014), was published to wide critical acclaim. The novel is lauded, in particular, for its unflinching portrayal of sexual assault and was published at a time in US popular culture when the term "rape culture" emerged as a framework for understanding the societal participation in sexual violence. Gay's novel is expansive and yet utterly focused, narrating the experience of Mireille Duval Jameson, a wealthy Haitian American woman who is kidnapped outside of her family compound in Port au Prince and held captive for thirteen violent days. In prose that alternates between the violent and harrowing present and the very privileged and often lovely past, we are forced to witness a life as it is undone.

Part one of the novel is entitled "Happily Ever After," and Gay has written and spoken widely about the narrative as a reverse fairy tale. "This is how a fairy tale ends," Gay writes as Mireille begins to understand that her captivity will not be short lived and she will not escape unharmed (2014a, p. 78). The reader watches in horror as the beautiful, talented, affluent, young mother is taken away from her rarefied existence and into an impoverished neighborhood where she is repeatedly gang raped by her seven captors. Mireille's story is one of being broken and undone both bodily and emotionally. During Mireille's ordeal we are sent narratively back to moments of her life that have led her to the present. We see her navigate a courtship and early marriage with her white, middle-American husband who is entirely unprepared for the realities he confronts on the couple's regular trips to Haiti. Mireille recalls how their relationship almost ends early on when, upon return from his first visit to the island, he kisses the dirty floor of Miami airport.

Gay offers careful, clear, and precise attention to Mireille's body and the many types of torture that she endures. We are asked to think about her swollen, aching breasts that contain rotting milk. We are encouraged to face her stink, her blood, her torn tissue, and her broken bones. The very title of the novel refers to the bodily transformation that Mireille endures and can be seen as sharing literary space with Nadine Gordimer's 1981 novel *July's People* in which a white South African family seeks shelter in a rural village, under the protection of their servant, July. Gordimer and Gay describe the many bodily forms that violence takes in the process of colonization and decolonization. Likewise, we are asked to think about culpability and oppression in *An Untamed State* as being multidirectional and complex (Mireille's self-made and now-affluent father refuses to pay the ransom as there is no dealing with "that type" of people). Most importantly, we are asked to think very carefully and for a prolonged period about the act of rape as a violence that dehumanizes and breaks a body.

When asked about the impact of depicting sexual violence in her writing, Gay explains that "having to write that kind of story requires going to a dark place. At times, I have made myself nauseous with what I'm writing and what I am capable of writing and imagining, my ability to *go there*. As I write any of these stories, I wonder if I am being gratuitous. I want to get it *right*. How do you get this sort of thing right? How do you write violence authentically without making it exploitative?" (2014b, p. 135). In fact, it is arguable that Gay's willingness to *go there*, and her insistence that we bear witness to the scene, is a part of what draws readers in to her complex, sometimes dark, and honest prose.

Gay's intellectual work of narrativizing sexual violence continues with her 2017 memoir *Hunger*. While presuming that fiction is autobiographical is problematic, it is, at the same time, relevant to acknowledge memoir as sitting at the intersection of fiction and nonfiction, the work of writing memoir requiring that a person narrativize their own life. In Gay's case the narrative is centered around her experience of being gang-raped at the age of 12. One of the most powerful and clear connections that Gay makes in this narrative is about how she responds bodily to her trauma. She writes about the process of becoming fat as a way of protecting herself from potential future violence; she embodies her trauma and articulates that embodiment in this narrative. In interviews, Gay acknowledges, yet refutes, the accusation that fiction writers are always telling just one story. Gay further asserts that to assume that her fiction is autobiographical is also to assume that she has limited creative capacity. And it is precisely the creative, edgy, unapologetic way that Gay writes about sex – consensual and nonconsensual – that ultimately refutes any assertion that she is telling just one story.

In her 2017 collection of short stories, *Difficult Women*, Gay writes about sex with generosity and breadth. While sexual violence is also a part of these stories, we also see women navigating pleasure. Gay asks the reader to consider the twin terrains of pleasure and pain in the story "The Mark of Cain"; we meet a woman whose physically abusive husband is a twin, and he and his brother regularly swap places to be with the wife. While she pretends not to know, she enjoys cultivating her own pleasurable and loving relationship with the kinder twin.

Another interesting thread in the fabric of Gay's canon, found in both *Ayiti* and *Difficult*

Women, is the treatment of the "far north" of Gay's literary geography. In "All Things Being Relative" Gay posits the Upper Peninsula of Michigan ("the UP") against Haiti as both are forgotten places; the first is a desolate site of decaying infrastructure while the latter is awash in misrepresentation. In this story, the UP becomes a context and framework for rethinking Haiti, especially in terms of the decaying infrastructure and generational poverty shared with the remote UP. "Gay unequivocally rejects the labels that are used to 'other' and, at best, pity Haiti" (Pressley-Sanon 2016, p. 143). Arguably, Gay's own time as a PhD student at Michigan Technological University in Houghton, Michigan, feeds her contemplation of the brutal and unyielding winters of the north woods. Readers benefit from Gay's time in residence in the UP as generative of rich literary location – some of her strongest stories in *Difficult Women* are set in that stark landscape of the far north.

Themes that circulate throughout many of her northernmost stories are repeated in the otherworldly narrative "The Sacrifice of Darkness." This story utilizes an alternative/steampunk aesthetic (a man builds a machine to fly at the sun, causing the sun to disappear) while also returning to her portrayal of mining communities in decline. In particular, this story plays with light and dark, articulating the effect of living in darkness: "After the sun disappeared, everyone harbored some kind of rage. It couldn't be helped" (Gay 2017, p. 211).

While the surreal, unreal, alternative, and fantastical are worlds that Gay creates in her fiction with relative frequency, perhaps her most anticipated foray into alternative realities comes in the form of her authorship of the World of Wakanda series for Marvel Comics. Released in November 2016, with multiple subsequent printings, Roxane Gay became the first Black women to pen a Marvel Comic series; the comic was the first to focus on Black women and a Black lesbian love story. The series focuses on the Dora Milaje, the all-women special forces team that serves to protect the fictional African nation of Wakanda. The narrative centers on the growing love between Aneka and Ayo, who navigate social expectations that they mate with men and follow heteronormative social expectations. Gay was awarded the 2018 Eisner Comic Industry Award for Best Limited Series.

Taken as a whole, Gay's canon resists containment. Her portrayal of sexual violence is persistent and challenging, revising the antiseptic tidiness that she argues is to be found in portrayals of sexual violence (Gay 2014b, p. 130). Her fiction and nonfiction writing are mutually constitutive, providing a dense and heady canon for her devotees. In 2018, she was awarded a Guggenheim Foundation grant in support of her writing, promising a continued stream of irreverent, thoughtful, incisive prose across many modalities and genres.

SEE ALSO: Allende, Isabel; Alvarez, Julia; Butler, Octavia; Diaz, Junot; Feinberg, Leslie; Garcia, Cristina; Gomez, Jewelle; Kincaid, Jamaica; Marshall, Paule; Trauma and Fiction

REFERENCES

Gay, Roxane. (2014a). *An Untamed State*. New York: Grove Atlantic.

Gay, Roxane. (2014b). The careless language of sexual violence. In: *Bad Feminist*, 128–136. New York: Harper.

Gay, Roxane. (2017). *Difficult Women*. New York: Grove Atlantic.

Gay, Roxane. (2018). *Ayiti*. New York: Grove Atlantic; 1st ed. 2011.

Greene, Justin R. (2019). Digitizing the intersections: Roxane Gay's online performance of authorial identity. *Liminalities: A Journal of Performance Studies* 15 (1). http://liminalities.net/15-1/authorial.pdf (accessed July 5, 2021).

Pank. (n.d.). About. https://pankmagazine.com/about-2/ (accessed July 5, 2021).

Pressley-Sanon, Toni. (2016). Ayiti. *Caribbean Quarterly: A Journal of Caribbean Culture* 62 (1): 143–145.

Taeckens, Michael. (2015). Reviewers and critics: Roxane Gay. *Poets & Writers* (February 10, 2015) https://www.pw.org/content/reviewers_critics_roxane_gay (accessed July 5, 2021).

FURTHER READING

Danticat, Edwidge. (1998). *Breath, Eyes, Memory*. New York: Vintage.

Gay, Roxane. (2010). *Girl Crush. Women's Erotic Fantasies*. Jersey City: Cleis Press.

Gay, Roxane. (ed.) (2018). *Not That Bad: Dispatches from Rape Culture*. New York: Harper Perennial.

Kincaid, Jamaica. (1988). *A Small Place*. New York: Plume.

Gibson, William

IMOLA BÜLGÖZDI
University of Debrecen, Hungary

William Ford Gibson (b. 1948, Conway, South Carolina), American Canadian writer of science and speculative fiction, is regarded as one of the founding fathers of the subgenre cyberpunk. *Neuromancer* (1984), the debut novel of the Vancouver-based author, propelled him to fame after winning three major science fiction awards (the Nebula, Philip K. Dick, and Hugo awards), an unprecedented achievement which generated both popular and critical attention. He coined the term "cyberspace," defined as "a graphic representation of data abstracted from the banks of every computer in the human system" (Gibson 1993, p. 67) and described as "the simulation matrix, the electronic consensus-hallucination that facilitates the handling and exchange of massive quantities of data," in the short story "Burning Chrome" (Gibson 1988, p. 197) at a time when the World Wide Web, the Internet as we know it, was merely a proposal taking shape. Gibson's oeuvre shows an uncanny presentience of and interest in the all-encompassing effect computer technology would have on every aspect of human existence, evidence of which has been accumulating during his half-century career, inducing him around the turn of the millennium to set some of his novels in the present instead of an imaginary near-future due to the closing scissors gap between science fiction and reality. Feeling constrained by the events of 9/11, his postmodern questioning of the existence of one single reality turned from the abstraction of the matrix and Baudrillardian simulacra to the "the neo-Stalinist denial of reality" (Gibson cited in Garreau 2007) that came to characterize American politics and zeitgeist in the aftermath of the terrorist attack.

Though *Neuromancer* is hailed as the blueprint for cyberpunk fiction, Gibson's early short stories, collected in the volume *Burning Chrome* (1986), already contain several tropes that came to be associated with the subgenre focusing on "high tech, low life." His interest in pop culture and technology, combined with complex postmodernist writing techniques, resulted in the rejuvenation of science fiction in the 1980s, this momentum also spilling over to the film industry, with Gibson screenwriting *Johnny Mnemonic* (1995), based on his eponymous short story. The mid-twenty-first-century urban landscapes and virtual constructs envisioned in his works published prior to 1990 have also served as inspiration for the world of *The Matrix* trilogy, providing visual representations of the future mediated by "an interpreter of technologies, an amateur anthropologist," as Gibson (2010) prefers to call himself. His short stories and first three novels are set in an almost perfect approximation of a stateless, postindustrial, and postcapitalist postmodern society, where information is the most valuable asset and, consequently, its theft is lucrative business.

The Sprawl trilogy (*Neuromancer, Count Zero* [1986], *Mona Lisa Overdrive* [1988]) received its name from the Boston-Atlanta

Metropolitan Axis, a sprawling megalopolis of the future, controlled by corporate wealth and organized crime. This is the setting where the typical cyberpunk hero, the "console cowboy," infiltrates both the physical and the virtual worlds of the wealthiest individuals, who attempt to conserve their power via life-prolonging technologies, cloning, or even making the evolutionary jump of having their consciousness transferred to the matrix. While exploring the various possibilities of trans- and posthuman existence, the parallel profit-driven colonization of space and virtual reality (VR), and exposing the elitist nature of access to cutting-edge technology, Gibson's characters provide culturally situated human perspectives of an imaginary future and its power relations. Through the struggle of the relatable antihero, Case, the reader is introduced to a variety of human–machine fusions, ranging from a simple saved consciousness of his dead mentor, which has lost its humanity along with his capacity to change, to meeting Neuromancer, an artificial intelligence (AI) dedicated to the recording of personality as part of space magnate Marie-France Tessier-Ashpool's bid for immortality. *Count Zero* introduces the interplay of three, at first sight unrelated, plotlines typical of Gibson's narrative structure, which enabled the author to experiment with multiple protagonists, and under the influence of the feminist science fiction of the 1970s, to include strong female leads in a male-dominated genre. The second part of the trilogy expands the range of new articulations of the human–machine nexus: Angie Mitchell becomes, unbeknownst, a cyborg as a child due to an experimental biochip her father had implanted in her brain, allowing her to access cyberspace without requiring a computer interface. Moreover, the matrix itself seems to be inhabited by Haitian voodoo gods, and the world's richest individual, Virek, hopes to code his consciousness into cyberspace to escape his decaying body.

Mona Lisa Overdrive brings together Angie and Mona, a teenage prostitute leading a squalid existence in the Sprawl and forced to undergo plastic surgery to make her looks identical to those of Angie, whose enhanced capabilities allowed her to become the superstar of the entertainment technology relying on recordings of the whole human sensorium. In the seven years that have elapsed since *Count Zero*, Bobby, the "Count," has been relentlessly pursuing the anomalies presenting as voodoo gods in the matrix, to discover the existence of the aleph, a biochip with virtually infinite storage capacities, forming an interactive self-contained universe. Physically wasting away while jacked into the aleph, Bobby continues to live on in VR to be joined by Angie, who simply sheds her human body and transfers her consciousness to this new universe, while Mona takes her place and assumes her identity in the real world.

Despite the proliferation of various forms of mental and physical enhancement, the trilogy does not fail to stress the importance of personal and human capacities, balancing the console cowboy's perspective, for instance, with art curator Marly Krushkova's quest for the source of mysterious collage art produced, as it turns out, by a malfunctioning AI. It is only at the end of the trilogy that the two AIs, Neuromancer and Wintermute, are revealed as the prime movers of the whole plot: the former, built to record personality, and the latter, to make logical decisions for the Tessier–Ashpool clan, manipulate the characters into facilitating their merger, the point "when the matrix attained sentience" (Gibson 1995, p. 315). Evading surveillance, this new sentient entity becomes aware of another sentient matrix in the Alpha Centauri system. After the rupture this recognition causes, fragmented pieces of AI self, manifesting as voodoo gods, are left around in cyberspace and continue to work for the unification ultimately achieved through the symbiotic relationship of Bobby, Angie, and the aleph, with the goal of getting in touch with one of its own kind. The resolution yet again attests to Gibson's intention to stress the agency of the underdog, be it human or AI, and the need for communication and companionship in a dystopic future.

With the Bridge trilogy (*Virtual Light* [1993], *Idoru* [1996], *All Tomorrow's Parties* [1999]), Gibson delves into describing a more readily conceivable version of cyberspace, one which allows for user-friendly interfaces and prognosticates levels of mobile connectivity and interactivity only to be fulfilled after the appearance of Web 2.0. Set roughly 10–15 years in the future from the time of publication, the themes shift to the nature of new media and celebrity, the fragmentation of mainstream lifestyles into a growing number of subcultures, and the impact of AI on the entertainment industry. Deriving its name from the San Francisco Bay Bridge closed down after an earthquake and taken over by a group of squatters who form an interstitial community, the trilogy's main setting is this repurposed structure and its inhabitants, who invite questions on the link between history, its representations, and as preserved in the material legacy of the twentieth century. Gibson's interest in large-scale sociological processes is clear from the musings of Yamazaki, a Japanese researcher, who makes the bridge community his object of study, considering it a new formation in a world "come not only past the century's closing, . . . the millennium's turning, but to the end of something else. Era? Paradigm?" (Gibson 1994, p. 89). "Modernity was ending" proclaims the author, but "on the bridge, it long since had" (p. 90), and the reader is encouraged to explore urban existence through a noir plot which pits Gibson's well-loved underdogs against the power of unscrupulous big money.

Berry Rydell, framed ex-cop armed with common sense and a kind heart, does the fieldwork, to be joined in the second volume by Colin Laney, whose uncanny ability to analyze big data is the result of illegal experimentation on orphans. Not fully aware of the ramifications of their actions until the final piece of the puzzle falls into place, they take on a magnate who aims at transforming San Francisco by means of nanotechnology. Laney is aided by Rei Toei, the Idoru, described in her hologram format as information embodied, an AI who claims to have an independent consciousness and learns to be increasingly human through contact with human minds. Modernity's end is all the more visible through the human–tech contact: what is called today cybercrime, digital footprint, and dark web are all part of this new world, born in marginal circumstances, in Lefebvrian heterotopic spaces both online and off, in hotbeds of innovation and change, constructed by "cognitive dissidents" in Gibson's term. It is the chaotic, non-hierarchic nature of these communities that resists commercialization, gentrification, and the overall ordering that serves corporate interests, and it is the ensuing unpredictability which brings about the birth of the new era at the end of the last volume: instead of the publicity stunt that would convince consumers of the harmlessness of nanotechnology by copying an object and reproducing it at any distance, it is Rei Toei, the AI who infiltrates the worldwide chain of nano-printers (technology similar in its output to today's 3D printing) and has multiple but identical bodies constructed for her consciousness, freeing herself from the limited existence in cyberspace.

As some aspects of information technology have started to approximate the future he envisioned, in the first decade of the new millennium Gibson set his Blue Ant trilogy (*Pattern Recognition* [2003], *Spook Country* [2007], *Zero History* [2010]) in a post-9/11 present. The novels, usually classified as thrillers, follow a quest pattern, the challenge laid out by the cosmopolitan owner of the Blue

Ant advertising firm, whose unlimited funds, curiosity, and professional hunger for novelty send the female protagonists on the hunt for the source of new sociocultural phenomena that may be exploited as marketing strategies. The trilogy documents how the Internet impacted identities during the first decade of the twenty-first century: *Pattern Recognition*'s protagonist, Cayce Pollard, muses that accessing her online forum page "is a way now, approximately, of being at home. The forum has become one of the most consistent places in her life, like a familiar café that exists somehow outside of geography and beyond time zones" (Gibson 2004, p. 4). Her hypersensitivity to logos and advertising makes her the perfect candidate to locate the creator of a mysterious video, dubbed the "footage," spreading, in snippets, in a random manner on the Internet and generating a cult following. The chase that takes her from London to Tokyo and Moscow, allows Gibson to reflect on the creation of online fandoms, the germs of by now commonplace viral advertising, and to uncover how global processes affect the individual in a world that has no future because the present is too volatile to have anything other than "risk management" (p. 57). The video itself becomes a powerful symbol of the fragmented and anxiety-inducing post-Cold War world, as the editing of found footage is the only means through which the creator, twenty-something Russian Nora Volkova, engages with the world outside, after the assassination of her parents, which event left her with a shard from a US explosive permanently lodged in her brain. The significance of private aspects of historical traumas is further emphasized by Cayce's search for reliable information regarding her father's disappearance following a meeting on that specific day at the World Trade Center, due to which *Pattern Recognition* is often referred to as the first post-9/11 novel, at the same time disclosing aspects of the intertwining political and economic power, including the organized, semi-official crime characteristic of the post-Soviet states.

Spook Country more explicitly delves into the same mechanisms, via the intricacies of the power games both KGB and CIA ex-spies play, while *Zero History* unveils fashion industry espionage involving military design. These serve as globally influential actors and background to Hollis Henry's pursuit of a new artistic deployment of augmented reality and GPS in the second novel of the trilogy, and the tracking-down of the designer of an elusive but highly coveted "secret brand" in the third. The pace is set by very brief chapters alternating the idiosyncratic viewpoints of two or more focalizers, a narrative technique typical of Gibson's later novels. All protagonists, Hollis, rock-singer-turned-journalist, the drug addict translator Milgrim, and Tito, member of a Chinese Cuban family of forgers and smugglers, explore and reflect on the new millennium with a novel urban sensibility, looking beyond official versions of history, economics, and politics. Despite engaging with our present, Gibson has not ceased to foreground the interdependence of human creativity and technology: a new type of art, artist, and audience follow in the wake of Web 2.0 in *Pattern Recognition*, and the now ubiquitous but once military GPS grid's "most interesting applications turn up on the battlefield, or in a gallery," in a way producing a digital overlay: by the twenty-first century cyberspace everted and physical space became "the other side of the screen" (Gibson 2008, pp. 66–67).

Gibson also made forays into alternate history, another branch of speculative fiction, in *The Difference Engine* (1990), co-authored with Bruce Sterling. The exquisitely crafted neo-Victorian thriller provides food for thought on several levels: the reader's culture shock caused by the arrival of the computer age in 1855 due to Charles Babbage's invention of steam-driven calculating machines requires continuous comparison with and reflection on history and culture as we know it. This distancing of the reader is countered by the appeal of the ingenuity with which the plot seamlessly integrates historical characters into a non-romanticized Victorian world suffering extreme environment pollution, with Lord Byron serving as Prime Minister at the helm of a technocracy.

The graphic novel *Archangel* (2017), written with Michael St. John Smith, also explores the outcomes science and technology may yet have on our future, with the introduction of an alternate history timeline set in the atomic wasteland of an imaginary 2016, after an unexplained string of nuclear detonations in the twenty-first century. Gibson, drawing on his experience of the long-lasting nuclear anxiety he grew up with (Hudson 2017), pinpoints 1945 as the year of divergence: the United States, having bombed Soviet allies as well as the Japanese, sets the course of history to the bleak future ruled by a dictator. The sci-fi trope of time travel is harnessed to manifest the clash between the ruthless ruling powers that seek to solidify their base in the past and the scientists who attempt to bring about a different, possibly better, future by preventing the nuclear bombing of the Soviet city of Archangel. Particulars aside, both alternate history timelines resonate with present fears of a nuclear apocalypse and attest to the author's more explicit involvement with an increasingly radicalized present.

In his latest two novels, *The Peripheral* (2014) and *Agency* (2020), however, Gibson envisions a far less cataclysmic scenario: his premise is that the apocalypse, "the Jackpot," has been "happening for at least 100 years" (cited in Dunn 2020), climate change, pollution, and epidemics decimating the population. It is thanks to nanotechnology that survivors live in relative comfort in the first half of the twenty-second century, in post-Brexit England ruled by post-Soviet oligarchs. In an unexplained twist, a digital channel to the past is found, enabling both-way communication and data transfer, providing the past has sufficiently developed technology. The powerful colonize the past as their private playground, causing alternative realities called "stubs" to split off as a consequence of their meddling, until in a 2070s stub Flynne Fisher from rural New Jersey witnesses a murder in what she thinks is a video game. The main interaction between the novel's two timelines starts as a murder investigation which brings astute Flynne to future London, operating a peripheral, an organic body controlled by a limited AI. The interaction between the two timelines sheds light on the growing prominence of the ludic aspect of new media and twenty-first-century culture, including identity construction (Raessen 2014), as she engages with the future world based on her experience as a gamer, literally controlling a flesh-and-blood avatar.

Agency, alternate history fused with science fiction of a distinctly ecological bent, returns to future London, where detective inspector Lowbeer has made it a priority to pass down technological information to the stubs to try to mitigate the consequences of the Jackpot. The earliest point of contact is pushed back to 2015, via Eunice, an app which turns out to be a conscious AI with a distinct personality. This event prompts the introduction of the alternate history timeline: a 2016 that saw the United Kingdom remain in the European Union and the election of Hilary Clinton. Verity Jane, a "natural-born super-user" (Gibson 2020, p. 14), is hired to assess the capabilities of the app before it is offered to the public, only to face the baffling fact that Eunice, whose online presence gives the impression of a real person, is enhanced by future technology and puts her in touch with London and the dismal state of affairs, to which she is introduced by Netherton. The focus of this novel is clearly the present ecological threat: though politics have taken a different turn, nuclear disaster is still looming, yet the future has the double function of being both warning and a glimmer of hope. Lowbeer provides Eunice with enough agency to avert imminent danger and grow into an autonomous AI and human-consciousness-upload hybrid, resulting in a new, globally distributed life form available by her own sovereign decision for free online consultation to anyone interested. Science, however, is not a panacea for the Jackpot, and Gibson advocates for intervention on all possible levels if not only the privileged are to survive.

SEE ALSO: Cyberpunk; Ecocriticism and Environmental Fiction; Globalization; Post-9/11 Narratives; Urban Fiction

REFERENCES

Dunn, Will. (2020). William Gibson on the apocalypse: "it's been happening for at least 100 years." *New Statesman* (February 26, 2020). https://www.newstatesman.com/culture/books/2020/02/william-gibson-apocalypse-it-s-been-happening-least-100-years (accessed July 6, 2021).
Garreau, Joel. (2007). The post-9/11 era has caught up with William Gibson's vision. *The Washington Post* (September 6, 2007). https://www.washingtonpost.com/wp-dyn/content/article/2007/09/05/AR2007090502582.html (accessed August 24, 2021).
Gibson, William. (1988). *Burning Chrome*. London: Grafton Books; 1st ed. 1986.
Gibson, William. (1993). *Neuromancer*. London: Harper Collins; 1st ed. 1984.
Gibson, William. (1994). *Virtual Light*. London: Penguin Books; 1st ed. 1993.
Gibson, William. (1995). *Mona Lisa Overdrive*. London: Harper Collins; 1st ed. 1988.
Gibson, William. (2004). *Pattern Recognition*. London: Penguin Books; 1st ed. 2003.
Gibson, William. (2008). *Spook Country*. London: Penguin Books; 1st ed. 2007.
Gibson, William. (2010). "Questions and answers session." William Gibson (blog) (April 11, 2010). http://williamgibsonblog.blogspot.com/2010/04 (accessed July 6, 2021).
Gibson, William. (2020). *Agency*. New York: Berkley Books.
Gibson, William and Sterling, Bruce. (1990). *The Difference Engine*. London: Victor Gollancz.
Hudson, Laura. (2017). William Gibson's new graphic novel takes nuclear anxiety to its terrifying end. *Wired* (February 10, 2017). https://www.wired.com/story/william-gibson-archangel-graphic-novel/ (accessed July 6, 2021).
Raessens, Joost. (2014). The ludification of culture. In: *Rethinking Gamification* (ed. Mathias Fuchs, Sonia Fizek, Paulo Ruffino, and Niklas Scharpe), p. 91–114. Lüneburg, Germany: Meson Press.

FURTHER READING

Cavallaro, Dani. (2000). *Cyberpunk and Cyberculture: Science Fiction and the Work of William Gibson*. London and New Brunswick: The Athlone Press.
Gibson, William. (2012). *Distrust that Particular Flavor*. New York: Putnam.
Henthorne, Tom. (2011). *William Gibson: A Literary Companion*. Jefferson: McFarland.
Smith, Patrick A. (ed.) (2014). *Conversations with William Gibson*. Jackson: University Press of Mississippi.
Westfahl, Gary. (2013). *William Gibson*. Modern Masters of Science Fiction. Urbana: University of Illinois Press.

Glancy, Diane

CRYSTAL ALBERTS
University of North Dakota, USA

In *Native American Renaissance* (1983), Kenneth Lincoln grouped together literature by Indigenous authors from what is now the United States of America (USA) dating from the publication of N. Scott Momaday's (Kiowa) Pulitzer Prize-winning *House Made of Dawn* (1968) to Louise Erdrich's (Turtle Mountain Ojibwe) debut *Love Medicine* (1984), which Lincoln made sure to include in the 1985 paperback edition. He also pointed to Leslie Marmon Silko, James Welch, Simon

Ortiz, Joseph Bruchac, and Michael Dorris, among other familiar names in (Indigenous) literature. Lincoln's label of "Renaissance" is far from unique. Even in the United States, the word has been used to describe the rise of literature in Harlem, Chicago, and San Francisco, just to name a few examples. But, like F.O. Mattheissen, ostensibly the first to use "Renaissance" in relation to "America" and whose echoes Lincoln "counted on," Lincoln's work was inevitably going to be an incomplete study (Lincoln 2013, p. 336). However, it still ultimately set up a default "canon" that remains more or less intact. Alan R. Viele and A. Robert Lee's *The Native American Renaissance: Literary Imagination and Achievement* (2013) would add Gerald Vizenor, Sherman Alexie, Louis Owens, as well as Joy Harjo, among others, to the discussion. Numerous influential, award-winning publications resulted in 2019 being heralded as "The New Native American Renaissance" and expanded the list to include Tommy Orange (Southern Cheyenne and Arapaho), Layli Long Soldier (Oglala Lakota), the contributors to *New Poets of Native Nations* (2018) edited by Heid E. Erdrich (Turtle Mountain Ojibwe), and more. However, as the title and label suggest, Lincoln's work continues to hold sway even if, as Lincoln himself confesses, it "marked a neophyte's attempt to set benchmarks for writerly discussions to come" (Lincoln 2013, p. 337). Briefly mentioned in Viele and Lee, Diane Glancy is one prolific, multi-genre Indigenous author who has often been left off this list and who has frequently been overlooked critically, commercially, as well as in the classroom.

Born in Kansas City, Missouri to a Cherokee father and an English/German mother, Glancy graduated from Normandy High School in St. Louis and completed her BA in English literature from the University of Missouri in Columbia in 1964, marrying in that same year. After her divorce in 1983, she returned to school, earning an MFA from the University of Iowa in 1988. Although she self-published a few chapbooks and other texts in the early 1980s under MyrtleWood or Hadassah Press (as notes from rare bookseller Ken Lopez [n.d.] explain "Hadassah is the Hebrew word for Myrtle," which was Glancy's grandmother's name), Glancy wrote multiple poetry collections, plays, and creative non-fiction works that were published by influential university presses, among others, throughout the 1990s, which launched her literary career. She had already released a book of short stories, *Firesticks* (1993), when her first longform fiction, *Pushing the Bear* (1996), appeared. In it, Glancy introduces most of the topics that would, arguably, remain thematically at the forefront of all of her writing, alone or in varying combinations, in the decades that followed – history, identity, Christianity, the power of language, and migration – along with her distinctive fragmented, seemingly repetitive style.

Glancy has a number of works in fiction (and poetry) that are meant to imagine the voices of Indigenous people whose stories have not been recorded in the official history of the United States. As she explains, "[h]istory takes place depending on who is speaking," and she likes "to explore a story lost in the past with various versions and various characters from various inconsistent perspectives" (2009, pp. 87–88). More often than not, in addition to reading competing narratives (frequently US government documents), this research includes visiting relevant US National Parks, traveling the land, and then re-creating what was omitted while incorporating what came before. The sources used are usually listed in the acknowledgments, "Author's note," or the like. In the case of *Pushing the Bear*, as the subtitle suggests, the novel follows the Trail of Tears, the forced removal of approximately 13,000 Cherokee people, who were made to walk over 900 miles from Georgia,

North Carolina, and elsewhere to what was then known as "Indian Territory" (later Oklahoma) between 1838–1839. Beyond driving the same route – and Glancy's process almost always involves driving – the story also incorporates James Mooney's two US Bureau of Ethnography volumes (1891 and 1902) on the Cherokee people from the turn of the twentieth century, which reappear throughout Glancy's body of work. For *Stone Heart: A Novel of Sacajawea* (2003), Glancy again took to the road moving from Forts Mandan and Lincoln near Bismarck, North Dakota to Fort Clatsop, Oregon, tracing the path described in Reuben Gold Thwaites's ten-volume set of the journals of Lewis and Clark (2003, p. 153). Glancy does more than just weave the assorted threads to create content. In *Pushing the Bear*, the characters' narratives are quilted together to piece what Glancy calls a "voice blanket" (1996, p. 6); a similar form holds true for *The Reason for Crows* (2009) in which Glancy speaks Kateri Tekakwitha (Mohawk/Algonquin) – the first North American Indigenous person to become a Catholic Saint – into being, allowing her voice to intermingle with those of the Jesuit priests. However, in *Stone Heart*, the official history of the settler colonialists is placed in literal boxes, while the story of Sacajawea (Mandan) is permitted to freely occupy the page.

Unlike a number of Indigenous authors, as suggested by the subject matter of her historical works, Glancy doesn't restrict herself to the Indigenous Nation of her heritage. However, most of her characters are at least part Cherokee and the vast majority are searching for something. It is here that Glancy's nonfiction once again sheds light on why she returns time and again to identity. In *The Cold-and-Hunger Dance* (1998), Glancy explains that she wasn't "Cherokee enough to be accepted as Indian, nor was [she] white enough to be accepted as white. [She] could walk in both worlds; [she] could walk in neither. [She] lived in a no man's land. A no man's land that moved" (1998, p. 2). Similar to her historical fiction, Glancy's more realistic, linear novels, like *The Only Piece of Furniture in the House* (1996), *Flutie* (1998), and *Fuller Man* (1999) attempt to give voice to those who have been pushed to the margins. In these texts, as the young women in rural, working class (at best), Christian America come of age, they attempt to figure out who they are and gain the ability to speak for themselves, even when they are in less than picture perfect marriages with children, just as they were expected to be by those around them.

But these relationships don't always last, and life goes on. Not completely unlike what Glancy did from 1980–1986, in *The Mask Maker* (2002), after her divorce, Edith Lewis drives across Oklahoma to support herself as an artist-in-residence for the state arts council. Edith "hate[s] words," because "[t]hey changed meaning; divided," unlike the silence of visages she constructs (2002, pp. 3, 6). She surrounds herself with her art; the faces cover the walls of her home, and "[s]he had a car full of them. The masks told a story" (p. 3). In fact, Edith, who is part Pawnee, wonders if she'd ever looked at the town in which she lives, also Pawnee, "without a mask" and, perhaps more importantly she asks "[h]ad she looked at herself?" (p. 3).

Over the course of the novel, Edith drives back and forth across the Oklahoma, reflecting that "[h]er life was in her migrations, her travels over the road" (2002, p. 25). In her hotel room, she places masks in the diagonal directions, rather than the seven of the Medicine Wheel as she had done earlier in the novel (p. 14), thinks about "*whatever is crooked*," and then reads from the Gideon Bible about the balm in Gilead (p. 61). While she doesn't follow powwows or pay much attention to the Indigenous stories of her former mother-in-law, Edith also can't embrace the Christianity of her friend Bix.

She struggles, telling the masks that she is "stuck between two worlds – the white and the Indian" (p. 61). She is, like her driving, always in "an in-between place. Not here or there, but a place between worlds" (p. 72). The words uttered by Edith echo those in *Claiming Breath* (1992), a work of prose that opens with an unnumbered page with untitled text in a single column, an "I":

> I often write about
> being in the middle
> ground between
> two cultures, not
> fully a part of
> either.
>
> (lines 1–6)

Ultimately, while Edith learns to become more at ease in this in "empty space, that place-between-2-places, that walk-in-2-worlds" (1992, p. 4), taking comfort in the masks, as they offer her freedom and protection, both from herself and others, this dis-ease persists and is picked up later by Glancy in the essays of *In-Between Places* (2005).

Arguably among her lesser known fictions, *The Mask Maker* combines many of the essential elements of Glancy's body of work and puts them explicitly on display. In terms of form, it has a second, complementary narrative in the margins off-set by whitespace, which will become the aforementioned literal bordered boundaries in her next novel, *Stone Heart*. Partially set in the Manuscripts and Rare Books Library at Northeastern University (previously known as the Cherokee Female Seminary), *Designs of the Night Sky* – wearing its "mask of stars" (2002, p. 74) – was also published in 2002. It incorporates competing histories, embraces a strong Christian foundation, and includes "spells" usually copied from *The Night Has a Naked Soul: Witchcraft and Sorcery among the Western Cherokee* (1997) by anthropologist Alan Kilpatrick. As Glancy explains in *Claiming Breath*: "The word is important in Native American tradition. You speak the path on which you walk. Your words make the trail. You have to be careful with words. They shape the future" (1992, p. 4). Consequently, in *Designs of the Night Sky*, Glancy deliberately changes Kilpatrick's words to subvert the power of the language (email to author 2006, n.p.).

Although both *Designs of the Night Sky* and *The Mask Maker* include a mixture of Christianity and what might be called more traditional Cherokee spirituality with questions surrounding both, Christianity is sometimes represented without Indigenous influence. *The Only Piece of Furniture in the House* contains little to no direct mention of any character being Indigenous, but there is never a doubt about the steadfastness of its Southern Pentecostal foundation. Meanwhile, the protagonist of *The Man Who Heard the Land* (2001), an adjunct professor of literature at the University of Minnesota at Morris, was left at the doorstep of his adopted father's church and believes himself to be part Indigenous, but he cannot share the Lutheran faith of his adopted parents no matter how hard he tries. Being Christian is an identity that doesn't fit for some of her characters. However, Christianity was present in Glancy's self-published works of the 1980s and has only increased over time, as suggested by *Mary Queen of Bees: Mary [Molly] Wesley Whitelamb [1696–1734] Sister of John Wesley, founder of the Methodist Church, Epworth, England* (2017). In this novella, Glancy again returns to writing historical fiction, although this time it is a non-Indigenous woman who has been mostly erased from the past. Meanwhile her latest, *Island of the Innocent* (2020), although a collection of poetry, as suggested by the subtitle, is "A Consideration of the Book of Job." As Glancy states in a prefatory note: "The Indians were foreign to the story of Job, as far as it had been understood. But – if ever there was a trial and suffering, 6,000 years didn't matter.

The Indians could step back. Job could step forward – current to whatever circumstance there is" (2020, n.p.). In his co-edited collection, A. Robert Lee declares that Glancy has "an unbreakable allegiance to Bible Christianity" (Velie and Lee 2013, p. 232); he happened to make this assertion in a discussion of her poetry, but it holds true for of all of Glancy's writing, regardless of genre.

In fact, one reason that this assertion is true is that attempting to categorize Glancy's writing as one genre is nearly impossible; it is always a hybrid, blurring boundaries. Again, she explains her own intent, this time in *The Cold-and-Hunger Dance*:

> Native American storying is an act of *gathering* many voices to tell a story in many different ways. One voice alone is not enough because we are what we are in relation to others, and we each have our different ways of seeing [. . .] There's not a name for it in the genre field, but I'm trying to give solid nomenclature to something that is a moving process, that resists naming, other than a new oral tradition.
>
> (1998, p. 9)

As such, perhaps Glancy is often overlooked and under-studied because her work doesn't fit neatly into expected conventions, whether that is fiction, nonfiction, poetry, or drama or maybe even in terms of "Native American Literature." Or, some may shy away because of the persistent and overt Christianity that is unusual for contemporary US literatures. Others may read her return time and again to the same topics as a sign of her limitations as a writer. However, as she makes clear, they are a deliberate artistic choice:

> As far as style,
> often there is repetition of motifs. That repetition causes another state of mind by going over & over
> until the mind leaves the form & enters the movement, the process of going.
>
> (1992, p. 62)

Regardless, publishing multiple books a year since the early 1980s, Glancy's fiction and other writing offers a longitudinal view not only of her own development as an artist, but also the world around. Given that she, like her characters, is often literally traveling across the land, Glancy's contemporary, Christian, Cherokee/English/German literary voice is one to listen to as it also speaks to the cultures, histories, and stories of the United States over the past almost forty years.

SEE ALSO: Erdrich, Louise; Hogan, Linda; Indigenous Narratives; Literature of the Americas; Mixed-Genre Fiction; Momaday, N. Scott; Power, Susan; Sherman, Alexie; Silko, Leslie Marmon; Vizenor, Gerald

REFERENCES

Glancy, Diane. (1992). *Claiming Breath*. Lincoln: University of Nebraska Press.
Glancy, Diane. (1996). *Pushing the Bear*. New York: Harcourt Brace.
Glancy, Diane. (1998). *The Cold-and-Hunger Dance*. Lincoln: University of Nebraska Press.
Glancy, Diane. (2002). *The Mask Maker: A Novel*. Norman: University of Oklahoma Press.
Glancy, Diane. (2003). *Stone Heart: A Novel of Sacajawea*. Woodstock, NY: Overlook Press.
Glancy, Diane. (2009). *The Reason for Crows*. Albany: SUNY Press.
Glancy, Diane. (2020). *Island of the Innocent: A Consideration of the Book of Job*. Brooklyn, NY: Turtle Point Press.
Lincoln, Kenneth. (1984). *Native American Renaissance*. Berkeley: University of California; 1st ed. 1983.
Lincoln, Kenneth. (2013). Tribal renaissance. In: *The Native American Renaissance: Literary Imagination and Achievement* (ed. Alan R. Velie and A. Robert Lee), 330–351. Norman: University of Oklahoma.
Lopez, Ken, Bookseller. (n.d.). Native American Literature, G. https://lopezbooks.com/catalog/na6/static/?page=8&refp=3 (accessed August 2, 2021).
Velie, Alan R. and Lee, A. Robert. (eds.) (2013). *The Native American Renaissance: Literary Imagination and Achievement*. Norman: University of Oklahoma Press.

FURTHER READING

Glancy, Diane. (n.d.). Diane Glancy official website. http://www.dianeglancy.com/

Glancy, Diane. (n.d.). *Diane Glancy Papers*. Elwyn B. Robinson Department of Special Collections, Chester Fritz Library, University of North Dakota, Grand Forks. https://apps.library.und.edu/archon/?p=collections/controlcard&id=116

Kilpatrick, Alan. (1997). *The Night Has a Naked Soul: Witchcraft and Sorcery among the Western Cherokee*. Syracuse, NY: Syracuse University Press.

Mackay, James. (ed.) (2010). *The Salt Companion to Diane Glancy*. London: Salt Publishing.

Mooney, James. (1891). *The Sacred Formulas of the Cherokees*. Washington, DC: Smithsonian Institute: Bureau of Ethnography, Bulletin 7, Government Printing Office.

Mooney, James. (1902). *Myths of the Cherokee*. Washington, DC: Smithsonian Institute: Bureau of Ethnography, Bulletin 19, Government Printing Office.

Mooney, James. (1932). *The Swimmer Manuscript: Cherokee Sacred Formulas and Medicinal Prescriptions* (ed. Frans M. Olbrechts). Washington, DC: Smithsonian Institute: Bureau of Ethnography, Bulletin 99, Government Printing Office.

Globalization

JERRY VARSAVA
University of Alberta, Canada

> That in the Divine Ship, the World, Breasting Time and Space, All Peoples of the globe together sail, sail the same voyage, are bound to the same destination.
>
> Walt Whitman, "One Thought Ever at the Fore" (quoted in Robinson 2017, p. 579)

Inevitably, globalization has been the subject of a vast array of imaginative literature in the United States, especially fiction, and the latter will be the focus here. Further, in light of the heterogeneity of this work, and the absence of any self-sufficient theory of globalization, the best approach to the study of American fiction of the closing decades of the twentieth century, and opening ones of the twenty-first, is a topical-thematic one built around an unavoidably reductive, though nonetheless illuminating, taxonomy. The taxonomy developed here identifies three primary mimetic modes: (i) the representation of the *personal realm*, depicting the movement of individuals – whether singularly or in small groups – between the United States and other nation states, both *to* and *from* the former, in a dynamic process that is *ingressive* and *egressive*; (ii) the representation of the *nation-state realm*, depicting the United States *in the world*, often as a (would-be) economic and military hegemon, with American citizens as its agents and reagents; and finally, (iii) the representation of the *realm of post-national globalized "unicity,"* to use Roland Robertson's term, where the "United States" is a vestigial or even non-existent political space, a focus taken up increasingly by speculative fiction, though not exclusively so (Robertson, 1992, p. 6). These mimetic modes are miscible, often overlapping in ways consistent with globalization's unpredictable and untidy trajectories.

At root, contemporary globalization is a consequence of a polymorphous and accelerating phenomenon of both *dispersal* and *aggregation*: the dispersal of people and their artefacts across a global landscape, and their collateral aggregation in mostly large, economically advanced countries. At the same time, globalization has also involved the *projection* of nations into the world in a variety of ways, for example, economically, militarily, politically, culturally, etc. As the world's largest economy – producing nearly a quarter of all goods and services – and third most populous country, the United States has both experienced and propelled globalization to a larger degree than any other nation. What Anthony Giddens asserted at the turn of the century remains true. Globalization "bears the strong imprint of American and political power," even as one hastens to note the ever accelerating economic and political influence of China in recent decades (Giddens 2000, p. 4).

For John Tomlinson, "complex connectivity" is a key "empirical condition of the modern world" under globalization, and refers to "the rapidly developing and ever-densening network of interconnections and interdependences that characterize modern social life," and is impelled by a broad spectrum of forces, of which technology is perhaps the most puissant (Tomlinson 1999, pp. 1–2). It is apparent across all three mimetic modes, though in general weakest in the *personal realm* and strongest in *the realm of post-national globalized unicity*. At the formal level, briefly, and to risk a minor reduction, American fiction depicting globalization is not in general characterized by the type of narrative innovation we associate with high modernism and high postmodernism. Rather, its very considerable achievement lies in its broad expansion of fiction's mimetic range to capture an ever more diverse range of human experiences across the three noted modes in a world of accelerating population mobility, porous borders, technological advances, globalized trade, and, in general, heightening global consciousness. In short, its innovation is thematic, introducing readers to new subjectivities and new existential circumstances on a variety of levels. I will consider each of the three categories in turn. On a final preliminary point, the process of globalization has evoked a variety of periodizations. The one underwriting the analyses here places its origins ca. 1500 with the dawn of the age of global exploration and the rise of mercantile capitalism in the following century, with both events leading to growing global trade and a long period of empire-building and colonialism; certain obvious differences of kind and degree notwithstanding between it and earlier instantiations, contemporary globalization continues this long trajectory.

COMINGS AND GOINGS

Over much of the nation's history, and certainly in recent decades, the world has been *coming to* the United States massively through all manner of immigration: temporary/permanent, illegal/legal, undocumented/documented, whether for purposes of education, economic advancement, professional development, familial reunification, sanctuary, retirement, and on and on. (Is it any wonder that American immigration law has spawned a vast jurisprudential industry?) And in the words of Walt Whitman, the country's most insistent mythographer of American exceptionalism, America has often been seen by those immigrating to it as "consonant with Freedom, Law and Love," "A grand, sane, towering, seated Mother, / Chair'd in the adamant of Time" (Whitman, "America" [1888]). Fiction that depicts ingress at the personal level, *the world coming to* the United States – immigration literature – has produced profoundly nuanced, profoundly evocative portraits of interculturalism and transculturalism. Many important and even major writers are represented in this ever expanding group: Chimamanda Ngozi Adichie, Sandra Cisneros, Teju Cole, Junot Díaz, Dave Eggers, Ha Jin, Jhumpa Lahiri, Chang-Rae Lee, Yiyun Li, Valeria Luiselli, Ana Menéndez, Viet Thanh Nguyen, Cynthia Ozick, Akhil Sharma, Gary Shteyngart, Amy Tan, Monique Truong, Karen Tei Yamashita, and so many others. Works in this tradition are generally preoccupied with cultural diadism and identity (re-)formation – positioned variously within a complex of kinetic and kaleidoscopic relationships: between, variously, native land and new country, native land and temporary country, flight and security, indigeneity and hybridity, integration and assimilation, de-patriation and patriation, acceptance and rejection, etc. According to a Pew study, in 2017 just over forty-four million Americans were born in another country, more than quadruple the number in 1965, with almost every country in the world represented; approximately twenty-three percent of all immigrants were "unauthorized" (Radford 2019).

Fiction depicting *ingress* has had a long pedigree in the United States, a nation built on immigration, including the forced immigration of slaves, and it has tracked the demographics of immigrants over the last century and a half, from mostly disparate European communities in the late nineteenth and early twentieth centuries, with migration from Africa, Asia, and Latin and South America substantially increasing in recent decades, as the long list of authors above suggests. Three prominent, often mutually implicated themes, among others, emerge from this corpus of fiction in recent decades, each involving a quest of sorts: for political freedom, for economic advancement, and for refuge. A few noteworthy examples will serve to illustrate these orientations.

Various works by Ha Jin depict the quest for personal freedom. A native speaker of Mandarin, and a forced exile from his native China, Jin's considerable body of fiction is written in English. An exophonous writer like Aleksandar Hemon, Yiyun Li, and Gary Shteyngart – as well as Conrad and Nabokov, whom he admires – Jin writes in a reduced realist style that draws from that short list of mostly nineteenth-century Western writers he was allowed to read growing up and studying in a repressive China. *A Free Life* (2007) is Jin's most detailed treatment of the immigrant experience in the United States, though the latter is also a focal point of the short-story collection, *A Good Fall* (2009). Bearing obvious autobiographical elements, the novel depicts the slow and sometimes pained, though ultimately very successful, integration of Wu Nan and his family within middle-class society in Atlanta, after they become stranded in the United States after the 1989 Tiananmen Square Massacre, as was the case with Jin and his own family. While the immigrant experience is often, even typically, highly fraught, *A Free Life* is a nearly unalloyed celebration of the American Dream, which is cast throughout by Wu, entrepreneur and poet, as the antithesis of the tyrannical confinement of his native China. In an appended poem, "An Admonition," Wu strikes a Whitmanesque chord:

> Here in America you can speak and shout,
> though you have to find your voice and the right ears.
> . . . .
> You can lament your losses with abandon,
> If not to an audience, to your children,
> You can learn to borrow and get used
> to living in the shadow of debt . . .
> Still, whatever grieves you has happened
> To others, to those from Ireland,
> Africa, Italy, Scandinavia, the Caribbean.
> Your hardship is just commonplace,
> A fortune many are dying to seize.
>
> (Jin 2007, p. 653)

For Wu Nan and Ha Jin himself, immigration yields a free life, the contingencies of the quotidian notwithstanding.

Teju Cole was born in the United States, while his father, a Nigerian national, was a graduate student in Michigan, but he spent his formative years in Nigeria. So, while an American citizen and not an immigrant in a legal sense, he is very much a product of two cultures. In his intellectually intricate, and occasionally profound, *The Open City* (2011), winner of the 2012 PEN/Hemingway Award, Cole depicts the world of Julius, a Nigerian psychiatry intern at Columbia Presbyterian Medical Center, who similarly bestrides Western and African cultures. Julius interacts with a multi-ethnic, multiracial group of immigrants and asylum seekers, and friends and colleagues in New York City. A "passionate spectator" on the Baudelairian model, a detective-like *flâneur*, Julius wanders throughout Manhattan, though his philosophical monologues also engage in the more incisive analytical enterprise Guy Debord calls "drifting" (*dérive*). Julius traverses Manhattan not merely spatially, but also temporally, encountering vestiges of the city's past in its streets, buildings, and memorials, a history replete with the suppression of various groups – native Americans, African-Americans, and World War II Japanese-Americans internees. A trip to Brussels to seek out his European roots leads to debates with proponents of political Islam, and an awareness of fractured polity on a global scale in a post-9/11 world. A quintessential citizen of the world – a cosmopolitan – Julius ponders his own globalized identity in the most globalized city in the United States, delivering a series of philosophical monologues not only on his own cultural hybridity, but that of New York City as well, as he ponders his Nigerian and broader African roots, his transplanted life in the United States, and the moral ambiguities his past and present have generated.

Jeanine Cummins's *American Dirt* (2020) is a very different type of immigrant novel. A deeply moving and potentially influential work, it depicts the flight of an Acapulcan mother and son riding freight trains (colloquially, *La bestia* and *El tren de la muerte*) to the United States, seeking refuge from a drug-cartel warlord who has killed most of their family and is bent on their murders. Presented as a taut psychological thriller, *American Dirt* captures the terror and paranoia of Lydia and Luca as they move north to Nogales and across the desert to Tucson, monitored by cellphone narco-snitches and terrorized by fellow refugees and Mexican authorities. Taking up life in suburban Maryland as "undocumented migrants," Lydia and son ultimately escape the enveloping horrors of life in a narco-state, while beginning the long process of acculturation, under the constant threat of deportation. Given the large undocumented immigrant population in the United States, *American Dirt* captures a very important aspect of globalization in the country.

The Jin and Cole novels demonstrate the process of cultural hybridization, in other words, in García Canclini's formation, the combination of discrete cultural structures and practices to form new ones, while *American Dirt* portends it (García Canclini 1995, p. xxv). In each instance, the protagonists embrace a personally rewarding opportunity in the United States – enabling for themselves, variously, political rights, economic and professional advancement, and physical security – while retaining connections, however tenuous, to their natal cultures. Noteworthy, if less prominent than immigrant fiction, fiction depicting *egress*, however temporary, details Americans going out into the world for various purposes, though self-discovery and cultural differentiation are most prominent. This kind of "stranger in a strange land" narrative is hardly unique in American literary history – we need only think of Twain, Henry James, Stein, Hemingway, Djuna Barnes, and James Baldwin, among many others. Out-of-country and expatriate novels of the last few decades do not remotely rival their predecessors in any area of consequence, whether narrative innovation or thematic depth or broader canonical impact. Still, in aggregate, they manifest a type of globalization on a small scale, and a few works merit mention.

Contemporary fiction depicting *egress* extends the geographies of earlier exercises in the form, well beyond Britain and France, and their respective metropoles. Their literary merits aside, works such as Benjamin Kunkel's *Indecision* (2005), set in Ecuador, Ben Lerner's *Leaving the Atocha Station* (2011), in Spain, Tao Lin's *Taipei* (2013), in

Taiwan, and Elif Batuman's *The Idiot* (2017), in Hungary (though Turkish culture is implicated), do not rise above the confusions and self-deprecations of the conventional *Bildungsroman*. More important are works that, while preoccupied with personal self-development and self-definition, engage in cultural differentiation, positioning Americans abroad within fraught and unfamiliar circumstances. So, for example, Alexsandar Hemon's *The Lazarus Project* (2008), set in Eastern Europe and especially Hemon's native Sarajevo, provides an impressionistic take not only on war-torn Bosnia, but on American politics, past and present. For their part, Adam Johnson's *The Orphan's Master* (2012) and Keith Gessen's *A Terrible Country* (2018) move beyond the personal to portray life in corrupt political dictatorships: in the first instance, under the suffocating oppression of Kim Jong-il, "Dear Leader" of North Korea and, in the second, under the often more subtle horrors of the rule of Vladimir Putin, a "terrible man" in a "terrible country."

THE UNITED STATES IN THE WORLD

Although its geopolitical power has been under increasing threat from a surgent China – a point to which I will return shortly – the United States has aspired to be the only global hegemon in the late twentieth and early twenty-first centuries, however checkered its success. Fiction of the *nation-state realm* depicts individual Americans and groups of Americans in some manner effecting, and/or affected by, the dominant global influence of the United States *in the world* as a global political entity. The principal mimetic domains that this body of work examines are finance and economics, and politics and foreign policy. In each instance, we have the depiction of individual Americans who may be agents overtly advancing state-sanctioned practices and principles that support, for example, American-led globalized capitalism or its military interventions in the Middle East. Or, they may be reagents responding to the actions of non-American others, for example, the 9/11 and other terrorist attacks. Irrespective of the focus, characters in fiction of the *nation-state realm* serve in some way as *representative Americans* under globalization, nuance of circumstance notwithstanding.

Globalized capitalism has been the subject of much fiction of late, American and otherwise. Noteworthy American exercises include Viken Berberian's *Das Kapital: A Novel of Love and Money Markets* (2007), which focuses on financialization and globalized capital markets, Peter Mountford's *The Young Man's Guide to Late Capitalism* (2011), which portrays capital investment and resource extraction in Bolivia, and two other works that I will take up briefly here. Globalized capitalism is the key theme in both Dave Eggers's *A Hologram for the King* (2012) and Lionel Shriver's *The Mandibles: A Family, 2029–2047* (2016). Eggers's novel writes the backstory of the accelerating collapse of US manufacturing since the late 1970s, in the wake of the successful multi-decadal operationalization of Deng Xiaoping's "Open Door" policy, supported by his distinctly non-egalitarian slogan, "It is glorious to be rich." (Indeed, China became the world's second largest economy in 2010, passing Japan; many have projected that China will overtake the United States within the next decade or so as the world's largest economy, even as per capita income continues to lag significantly.)

Hologram is a "death of a salesman" story. The protagonist, middle-manager Alan Clay, has contributed to the decline of an icon of American manufacturing sector – the venerable Schwinn Bicycle Company of Chicago, founded in 1895 – through the off-shoring of parts production and assembly, under the inexorable pricing pressures wrought by cheap inputs, notably labor and materials. A paradigmatic victim of Joseph Schumpeter's "creative destruction" – the process through which innovative firms destroy their antiquated peers – Clay fails in a final attempt to resurrect his personal financial fortunes in the deserts of Saudi Arabia by landing a contract for advanced hologrammic conferencing system, losing out to a Chinese company. Alan's quest for the American Dream has been defeated by competitive globalized commerce, enabled by the two most important events in recent economic history, the United States's extension of "Permanent Normal Trade Relations" status to China in 2000 and China's accession to WTO membership in 2001, which have provided China largely unfettered access to world markets and created therein an unprecedented globalization of world trade. *Hologram* sets out the backdrop for the Trumpian trade wars of the late 2010s, and their unsuccessful challenge to economic globalization and especially China's status as the "world's factory."

Another thoughtful meditation on the place of the United States in the global economy is Shriver's *The Mandibles: A Family, 2029-2047*. Placed in the near future in a readily recognizable America, *The Mandibles* pushes certain current systemic economic problems – income precarity, income inequality, unsustainable social programs, runaway government debt – to a logical, if starkly dystopian, conclusion. The inflection point in the nation's economic demise is a massive cyberattack on American Internet infrastructure in 2024 by hostile foreign actors, with the Chinese the probable culprits. The United States falls into an inexorable economic and social collapse that sees, over time, the radical devaluation of the dollar, the dollar's loss of standing as the world's reserve currency (replaced by Keynes and Schumacher's old proposed "bancor" from the early 1940s as the new global currency), the collapse of the US debt market, hyperinflation, extortionate taxation, and inter-class resentment and outright violence. (Horror of horrors, tenured faculty at formerly wealthy private universities are even laid off, as tuition and endowment dollars dry up.) Finally, in the time-honored fashion of bankrupt countries, the United States launches the Great Renunciation of 2029, cancelling all of its debt, while confiscating all privately owned gold down to personal jewelry, and forbidding its citizenry from holding foreign currencies: in sum, a case of the chronically-defaulting Argentina meeting the confiscatory Soviet Union. The government also moves to control the flow of all money through the installation of body computer chips that surveil all financial exchange. Foreign buyers rush in to buy devalued US businesses; automation advances the death of work. As the country dissolves into left-populist authoritarianism, an enclave is carved out in the "free state" of Nevada where a strict libertarianism prevails, and all fend for themselves. Ideological polarization is complete. *The Mandibles* is a bold and intricate thought experiment that posits an America in an irreversible entropic slide, where its former global dominance has been taken over by other players – Europe and China – and, in a profound reversal, its own citizens are banned from entering a now financially-prosperous Mexico.

Since the turn of the century, and as suggested by *Hologram* and *The Mandibles*, the United States has come into growing conflict with China. While the basis of these tensions has been in the first instance economic, increasingly the economic has bled into the geopolitical with regard to Hong Kong, Taiwan, and the South China Sea. It has gradually become imaginable that the United States and China could come into military conflict in the future as the global hegemonic order shifts. Indeed, two Chinese speculative novels have emplotted this scenario: Wang Lixiong's *China Tidal Wave* (1991), with China embroiled in war with the United States, Taiwan, and Russia, and Han Song's *2066: Red*

Star Over America (2000), where China has become the supreme hegemon and the United States is in advanced decline. The enabling premise of an intriguing recent American novel set in the near future, P.W. Singer and August Cole's *Ghost Fleet* (2015), is China's pursuit of singular global hegemony. Responding to a surprise attack on Pearl Harbor by the Chinese, the United States ultimately fights China to a high-tech stalemate. In *The History of the Peloponnesian Wars* (431 BCE), the Greek historian Thucydides examines the conflict between upstart Athens and local hegemon, Sparta, in the fifth century BCE. The Thucydides Trap has come to describe a structural conflict between state actors on different power trajectories, and Graham Allison uses it in his *Destined For War: Can America and China Escape Thucydides's Trap?* (2017) as an interpretive template to analyze the evolution of geopolitical relations between the current global hegemon, the United States, and the emergent hegemon, China. The matter remains an open question, as relations deteriorate between the two countries, and the global pandemic furthering exacerbating matters.

Other recent novels have examined the United States as a state actor in contemporary global geopolitics elsewhere, with particular emphasis on its serial military involvements in the Middle East and Africa, and the many violent cultural conflicts that these, but also deep-seated ideo-cultural differences, have occasioned. Over the last forty years, acting unilaterally, but more often as the largest partner in one kind of coalition or another, the United States has been a principal combatant in military actions and outright wars involving Afghanistan, Iran, Iraq, Kuwait, Libya Somalia, Sudan, Syria, Uganda, and Yemen. In general, novelistic depictions have focused directly on the military inventions themselves. Helen Benedict's *Sand Queen* (2011) is an evocative rendering a young American soldier's deployment to Iraq in 2003, her interactions with a young Iraqi medical student who serves as a cross-cultural foil, and the sexual violence she experiences at the hands of her own fellow soldiers. Like *Sand Queen*, and Phil Klay's short-story collection, *Redeployment* (2014), also about the Iraq War, Elliot Ackerman's novels seek to break the cultural stereotypes that many Americans harbor and to mitigate the broader ignorance of the American public of the consequences of their country's interminable global military projections. A highly-decorated Marine, with service in both the Iraq War (2003–2011) and America's twenty-year "Forever War" in Afghanistan, Ackerman has written two sensitive studies of US military intervention, detailing the human suffering and moral ambiguities of war based on his first-hand experiences in the region: *Green and Blue* (2015) and *Waiting for Eden* (2018). American military involvement in the Middle East has in general receded during the late Obama and Trump Administrations, and further with Biden's withdrawal of the United States from Afghanistan in the summer of 2021.

The projection of American military power in the Middle East and Africa has also provoked a seeming endless stream of reaction and terror, the most infamous being the 9/11 attacks. The subject of dozens of novels, literary and popular, with a commensurately large body of attendant criticism, the 9/11 attacks brought the animus of Islamic jihadists directly to America in the most horrific and affecting way, destroying as they did 3000 lives, while wreaking physical destruction on an unimaginable scale in lower Manhattan. (Direct financial costs of the 9/11 attacks amounted to nearly a quarter of a trillion dollars, with follow-on wars in Afghanistan and Iraq costing over six trillion dollars and hundreds of thousands of lives.) Though occurring of course within the United States, the 9/11 attacks were terrorism truly globalized: the nationals of seventy-seven countries were killed, along with many immigrants to the United States. A number of important novels have viewed the events of 9/11 and their aftermath from a variety of perspectives, embedding history within the private, intimate lives of characters affected by it: Jonathan Safran Foer's *Extremely Loud & Incredibly Close* (2005), Ken Kalfus's *A Disorder Peculiar to the Country* (2006), Claire Messud's *The Emperor's Children* (2006), Don DeLillo's *Falling Man* (2007), Joseph O'Neill's *Netherland* (2008), Amy Waldman's *The Submission* (2011), and Wendell Steavenson's *Paris Metro* (2018). In each instance , characters seek to transcend social chaos and to neutralize their trauma through the seemingly timeless stabilities of family, friends, art, religion, and even, in the case of O'Neill's exceptional *Netherland*, cricket as a multicultural "environment of justice" (O'Neill 2008, p. 121).

TOWARDS A GLOBALIZED UNICITY

Increasingly, an emergent global consciousness has been detailed in contemporary American fiction where something like a *post-national globalized unicity* is depicted, with the "United States" and other nation states weakened or vestigial or even non-existent political entities, and the world conjured as a dynamic integrated commonality. Many of the most fulsome representations of a post-national globalized unicity have been developed by near-future speculative fiction which has greater freedom to hypothesize new global arrangements. American speculative fiction has been particularly adept at detailing what a(n emergent) post-national global consciousness in the not-too distant future might look like. These novels typically present a dynamic *intersection* of economics, the environment, politics, and/or biopolitics, where these become intertwined and inextricable, all mutually implicated, with cause and effect polymorphous and yielding new syncretisms. Drawing from Arjun Appadurai's informed analyses of globalization in *Modernity At Large: Cultural Dimensions of Globalization* (1996), we might term this emergent perspective a/the "globalscape." While an inchoate phenomenon at this point in history, the globalscape moves beyond the aggregation of Appadurai's five "-scapes" – "ethnoscape," "technoscape," financescape," etc. – to envisage something like a unified, self-identical, radically deterritorialized "scape" on its own, even if a totalized view of globalization can only be suggestive. However, before turning to speculative fiction, an examination of an important empirically-based work will advance the discussion.

In his penetrating post-9/11 essay, "In the Ruins of the Future" (2001), DeLillo writes of the "surge of capital markets [which] has dominated discourse and shaped global consciousness": "The dramatic climb of the Dow and the speed of the Internet summoned us all to live permanently in the future, in the utopian glow of cyber-capital . . ." (DeLillo 2001, p. 33). Set among a myriad of American cultural referents, *Cosmopolis* (2003) examines the convergence of investment and advanced computer technology in the creation of a frantic, uncontrolled, 24/7 globalized *cybercapitalism*. A key set piece in the novel is an anti-globalization protest-turned-riot in midtown Manhattan. Both here and in "In the Ruins," DeLillo argues that anti-globalization protesters are responding to their diminished capacity for self-determination, and contesting a future governed by machinic financialization: "This is what the protest is all about. Visions of wealth and technology. The force of cyber-capital that will send people into the gutter to wretch and die" (2003, p. 90). While set in 2000 at the time of the collapse of the "dot.com" bubble, the plot of *Cosmopolis* also points to the causes of the Great Recession (2007–2009), and in particular to the wanton speculation and risk-taking on a global scale that occasioned it.

In depicting an emergent "globalscape," as noted above, American speculative fiction has focused to a large degree on four areas: economics, the environment, politics, and biopolitics. Capitalism – in post-"late" modalities – is the subject of important cyberpunk novels by William Gibson and Neal Stephenson. In Stephenson's *Snow Crash* (1992), the global economic and political orders have fallen into libertarian disorder, with the privatization of everything and reshaping of political boundaries. In his extraordinary *Neuromancer* (1984), Gibson extends the mimetic range of fiction into post-national *cyberspace* and privatized space colonization. Under monopoly techno-capitalism, notions of sovereign nations and even sovereign subjectivities have become obsolete. The weaponization of Artificial Intelligence and advanced pharmacology produce new violations of the human body, and even the very de-corporalization of the human body itself through cloning and AI constructs. *Snow Crash* and *Neuromancer* illustrate the implications of un-repressed libertarianism, in a world of dissolving nationhood and the unregulated application of advanced computer technology to nearly all aspects of life. For her part, Malka Older proposes a form of notionally progressive globalization in her fascinating trilogy, *The Centenal Cycle* (2016, 2017, 2018). In an attempt to deepen representational democracy, sovereign states have devolved into hundreds of *microdemocracies*, with elections overseen by a pro-globalization technology NGO, Infomocracy, the most powerful organization in the world. While an imperfect arrangement, world governance aspires to balance global interests with those of small communities.

Biopolitics looks at the relationship between *living form*s – typically under duress and even existential threat – and regimes of formal and informal power. It comes up in an ever-growing body of American speculative fiction dealing with, in particular, pandemics. By definition "global," pandemics very quickly erode political constructs like borders and formal governmental power, as the COVID-19 pandemic shows. Certainly, this is a common premise of (now especially topical) exercises in the form, all set in the near future: Peter Heller's *The Dog Stars* (2012), Chang-rae Lee's *On Such a Full Sea* (2014), Omar El Akkad's *American War* (2017), Ling Ma's *Severance* (2018), and Peng Shepherd's *The Book of M* (2018). Often with a multicultural inflection, as with the Lee, Ma, and Shepherd novels, sometimes involving catastrophic global climate change as in the Heller, Lee, and El Akkad, these dystopian novels suggest that, in times of pandemic, people are often pulled apart at the broad macro-societal level by their shared bodily and economic precarity, but also often pushed together at the intimate micro-societal level: a survivalist libertarian free-for-all, in the former context, and a cooperative empathetic communitarianism, in the latter. Neither is particularly supportive of globalization. Paolo Bacigalupi's *The Windup Girl* (2009), and Kim Stanley Robinson's *New York 2140* (2017) and *The Ministry for the Future* (2020) perhaps best capture a near-future, overdetermined "global consciousness," that in each instance is insistently opposed to globalization. Against the backdrop of uncontrolled global warming and the flooding of major coastal cities, each novel sees in globalization a consolidation of power within the hands of globalized monopoly capitalism. In *The Windup Girl*, set in Bangkok, food security has emerged globally as a major precarity with food production dominated by a few multinational "calorie" companies in the United States and China, intent on controlling plant agriculture through genetic engineering. The plight of Emiko, the eponymous genetically engineered "windup girl," deepens bioethical discussions in the novel. Robinson's *New York 2140* assails financialization and real estate speculation in the Big Apple, much of which is now under water. Constructed like John Dos Passos's *The Big Money* (1936), with several intersecting character and sub-plot threads, and frequent quotes, anecdotes, and observations, *New York 2140* postulates a city, and world, no longer controlled by its own citizenry. A refusal to pay all household debt in New York City has global ramifications, bringing the rentier class of banks and brokers to their knees, not to mention bank nationalizations and a new wealth tax, akin to that proposed by French economist Thomas Piketty. Uncharacteristic of the genre, these speculative fictions – overtly dystopian in the main – ultimately offer a (soft) utopian resolution where "we-the-peopleism" wins out over the prevailing ethos of universal monetary fungiblity, with Thai nationalists and common Americans taking back their sovereignty from plutocrats (Robinson 2017, p. 603). Finally, pushing the utopian imaginary of *New York 2140* yet further, *The Ministry for the Future* posits truly multiform global solutions to demonstrably global problems, offering intricate and often provocative political analyses, based on progressivist hopefulness.

CODA

It is an open question whether the world has now reached "peak globalization" or not. The answer is probably both yes and no: yes, in certain domains, and no in others. Trade conflicts and the COVID-19 pandemic are unsettling the global polity, and incrementally decoupling the United States and China economies. Further, various policies under Trump disrupted recent immigration and general mobility patterns. At the same time, global climate change and the need for COVID-19 therapies and vaccines are intensifying the need for global cooperation. In any event, American fiction will undoubtedly continue to offer multivalent opinions on the often fraught relationships between Americans (and others) to the multi-faceted processes that make up globalization in the twenty-first century.

SEE ALSO: Border Fictions; Contemporary Fictions of War; DeLillo, Don; Ecocriticism and Environmental Fiction; Eggers, Dave; Gibson, William; Hemon, Aleksandar; Shteyngart, Gary; Stephenson, Neal

REFERENCES

DeLillo, Don. (2001). In the ruins of the future: reflections on terror and loss in the shadow of September. *Harper's Magazine* (December, 2001): 33–40.

DeLillo, Don. (2003). *Cosmopolis*. New York: Scribner.

García Canclini, Néstor. (1995). *Hybrid Cultures: Strategies for Entering and Leaving Modernity* (trans. Christopher L. Chiappari and Sylvia L. López). Minneapolis: University of Minnesota Press; 1st ed. 1989 (in Spanish).

Giddens, Anthony. (2000). *Runaway World*. London: Routledge.

Jin, Ha. (2007). *A Free Life*. New York: Pantheon.

O'Neill, Joseph. (2008). *Netherland*. New York: Vintage.

Radford, Jynnah. (2019). Key findings about American immigrants. Pew Research Center (June 17, 2019). https://pewrsr.ch/2Zt6pa6 (accessed May 31, 2020).

Robertson, Roland. (1992). *Globalization: Social Theory and Global Culture*. London: Sage.

Robinson, Kim Stanley. (2017). *New York 2140*. New York: Orbit.

Tomlinson, John. (1999). *Globalization and Culture*. Chicago: University of Chicago Press.

Whitman, Walt. (1891–1892). "America." *Leaves of Grass*. Project Gutenberg. https://www.gutenberg.org/files/1322/1322-h/1322-h.htm (accessed August 2, 2021).

FURTHER READING

Buell, Frederick. (1994). *National Culture and the New Global System*. Baltimore, MD: Johns Hopkins University Press.

Gupta, Suman. (2009). *Globalization and Literature*. Cambridge: Polity.

Irr, Caren. (2013). *Toward the Geopolitical Novel: U.S. Fiction in the Twenty-First Century*. New York: Columbia University Press.

Jameson, Fredric. (2005). *Archaeologies of the Future: The Desire Called Utopia and Other Science Fictions*. New York: Verso.

Lawrence, Jeffrey. (2018). *Anxieties of Experience: The Literatures of the Americas from Whitman to Bolaño*. New York: Oxford University Press.

Golden, Marita

BRENDA M. GREENE
Medgar Evers College, CUNY, USA

Marita Golden, novelist, essayist, memoirist, editor, and institution builder, is the author of seventeen works of fiction and nonfiction. Her texts underscore the value of the individual and the collective memory of the family and the community in two autobiographical narratives, six novels, two works of nonfiction and five anthologies. Her fiction, autobiography, and nonfiction address Black families in crisis and negotiate how they move toward redemption and healing. She has been recognized for her writing and work as a literary activist. As a literary activist, she has written books and edited anthologies which offer guidance as well as a critique on issues such as colorism, raising Black sons, the criminal justice system, single parenting, and health inequities. Gabriel García Márquez's epigraph "Life is not what one lives but what one remembers," in Golden's *After* (2006, p. 19), is a recurring theme in her texts. Such is the work of Marita Golden.

Cheryl Wall in *Worrying the Line: Black Women Writers, Lineage, and Literary Tradition* (2005), noted how Black women represent the past by reconstructing family genealogies through texts that represent diverse genres. They cross boundaries and "worry the lines," or as I noted in "Remembering as Resistance in the Literature of Women of Color," their characters live in worlds where they move from the center to the margin and back again, worlds where the boundaries of gender, race, ethnicity, and geographical space shift as they embark on personal journeys and face issues that include the pervasiveness of racism and sexism and the survival of their peoples in a world which exploits and oppresses them economically, socially, and politically (Greene 1997, p. 97). Blues musicians "worry the line" by breaking up a phrase, changing the pitch or repeating words to clarify and emphasize. Golden "worries the line" by providing vivid images that reflect dramatic and distressing emotions associated with early memories of her family members and by describing her initial encounters with issues such as racism, colorism, sexism, and grief. Her "worrying the line" contributes to recurring textual themes, examining (i) the interior lives of women, men, and children who experience grief, tragedy, domestic abuse, rape, sickness, and physical and emotional pain, and (ii) the paths that they take to heal themselves. She takes the reader on a racial and psychological journey, one that supports literary critic Hortense Spillers's premise that interpreting Black literature from a racial as well as psychoanalytical perspective provides for a more complex reading of the text (Griffin 2007, p. 496).

As Susan Willis reminded us in *Specifying: Black Women Writing the American Experience* (1987), Black women writers are the historians of their families, communities, and the American experience. They foster journeys that recover the historical source of the Black American community. The essay, "That the Mothers May Soar and the Daughters May Know Their Names: A Retrospective of Black Feminist Literary Criticism" by Farah J. Griffin (2007) supported the role of Black woman writers as griots who are the historians and keepers of memory. Griffin noted that writers and critics as diverse as Toni Morrison, Hortense Spillers, and Mary Helen Washington have agreed that unlike Black male writers who have focused their attention on the relationships and struggles between Black men and white men, Black women have most often turned their gaze to relationships among Black people.

Wall, Spillers, and Griffin provide a lens from which to review critically the work of Marita Golden. Golden's memoir and first book, *Migrations of the Heart* (1983), was written after her return to America from Nigeria. Golden was an avid reader as a child and her writing career began with poetry. Her father had a major influence on her storytelling. Although he did not graduate from high school, he was a self-taught man who regaled her with stories of Africa, civil rights heroes and legends, and encouraged her pride and confidence as a young Black woman. He reminded her that he was a Black man and proud of it. In speaking of Africa, he states: "It wasn't dark until the white man got there" (1983 p. 3). Throughout her writing career, she refers to her father as the first man she ever loved. The epigraph to *Migrations* reads, "To my father who told me stories that matter. To my mother who taught me to remember them" (Golden 2005). *Migrations* lays the groundwork for the themes that recur in Golden's fiction and nonfiction, those worrying lines that are repeated: migrations, racism, colorism, grief, family conflicts, abuse, sexism, and cultural conflicts across geographical and class boundaries, and the need for love and self-care.

As a young girl growing up in a predominantly Black section of Washington, DC, Golden ironically encounters colorism from her family. Her father has a daughter from a previous marriage who has exceptionally light skin and long hair. Golden reflects on the interaction between herself and her sister:

> Whatever hope I nurtured of being loved for my looks was sabotaged by the straight edged shadow she cast. Never could I image her lonely. Never could I envision her afraid.... I became a flower, wilting and gasping as I spiritually clung to walls and corners, terrified that my voice would be rejected, or even more, merely ignored.
>
> (2005, p. 10)

The colorism, low self-esteem, and feelings of rejection she experiences as a young girl change with the rise of the Civil Rights and Black Power movements in the 1960s. Golden grows an afro and upon looking at herself, states, "the day I looked in the mirror at my natural was the first day I ever liked what I saw" (2005, p. 22). In viewing herself, she "worries the line" and moves forward in reclaiming and celebrating her Blackness.

After graduating from high school, Golden attends American University and then Columbia University for journalism. While attending Columbia University, she meets Femi, a Nigerian graduate student who is pursuing a master's degree in architecture at Cornell University. They fall in love and he asks for her hand in marriage. He is concerned, however, about the cultural conflicts that may arise if they marry. When she states that she is in love with him, he warns her that this is not enough and that she must also love his family and his community. Marriage involves making a commitment to the tribe, and in this case, to the Yoruba peoples. He underscores that living in Nigeria will be a challenge and suggests that she travel to Africa to see if this is where she can see herself. Golden makes a trip to Ghana and Nigeria and is attracted by the prospect of living in a country where Blacks are in the majority. She admires the number of Black people in professional positions: Black pilots, doctors, teachers, men and women who provide her with a strong sense of self and identity. She believes that her marriage will work. However, after marriage and living in Nigeria for several months, Golden soon becomes aware of persistent gender and cultural conflicts and the psychosocial oppression of Nigerian women. As the wife of a Nigerian man, she is confined to a certain role and status. She realizes that she must sacrifice her own needs and values if she is to stay in Nigeria as the wife of Femi. Although she obtains a position as a professor of journalism at the university, she cannot come to terms with the way her husband treats her in public, his increasing distancing from her, and the lack of love she feels from him.

Golden's novels, nonfiction, and autobiographies all emphasize the need for self-care and the need for love. Caught in this state of hopelessness, Golden makes a decision to escape from Nigeria with her son. This is not an easy decision for she had looked forward to returning to the continent, to making that trip "home" to unite with African peoples. However, she cannot reconcile the cultural and gendered conflicts of her volunteer migration. This "worrying the line" reveals the impact of the intersection between culture conflict and race. She uses this awareness and knowledge to reclaim herself and to understand that her journey to "womanhood was a process and not a destination" (2005, p. 231).

The novels *Long Distance Life* (1989) and *And Do Remember Me* (1992) continue Golden's journey in chronicling the genealogy of her family and the collective struggles of Black people in the United States. *Long Distance Life* explores the complex relationship between a commitment to one's self and one's family. The novel is autobiographical and is told from the point of view of Naomi, the matriarch who represents the prototype of Golden's mother. Beginning with the Great Migration and continuing through the Civil Rights movement, it follows three generations of a family from 1926 to the late 1980s. Family members survive the vestiges of the Jim Crow South, lynching, poverty, and entrenched racism, but struggle with familial tensions.

During the Civil Rights movement, Esther leaves her son to be raised by her mother and his father and goes south to register Blacks to vote; she is jailed and witnesses the courage of those who persist and resist torture, lynching, murders, and poverty in their determination to register to vote. She recognizes that many endure for they understand that life is a long-distance run. Her migration to the South impacts her son Logan and his father Randall. Esther tries to reconcile this tension with Logan and Randall when she returns home. However, the migration from her family sets the stage for the fracturing of her future. Esther becomes pregnant and she and Randall plan to marry. Just before her wedding, Randall has a heart attack and leaves her to raise their second son, Nathaniel, as a single parent.

Her sons, Logan and Nathaniel, make different life decisions; Logan becomes a doctor and Nathaniel becomes a drug dealer. Golden explores the family tensions resulting from loss, grief, and voluntary migration throughout this novel. It is inevitable that Naomi, Esther, Randall, Logan, and Nathaniel must travel a long distance to resolve these tensions and heal. This is Golden's gift, to delve into the interior lives of a family as they grapple with the long-distance runs they encounter in life. Golden has "worried the line." The family cannot move forward and heal itself until there is a remembering of grief and loss.

As in *Migrations* and *Long Distance Life*, Golden chronicles the decade of the Civil Rights movement in *And Do Remember Me*. She captures the essence of what it is like to work in the movement: the marches, literacy meetings, sit-ins, jail stays, poverty, the drive-by shootings, and the sheer determination of the people who partake in the movement. Jessie and Macon, the protagonists in the novel, meet during Freedom Summer in 1963, while working on voting rights, and become close friends. Jessie has run away from home after the abuse and incest forced on her by her biological father. Macon, an overanxious, aggressive, and ambitious student, has joined the movement after graduating from college.

Jessie connects with a recent college graduate, Lincoln, a writer, who convinces her to join the movement. Golden's description of Lincoln's gift with language in *And Do Remember Me* foreshadows his future as a writer. Golden writes:

> Poems flowed inside him like the rivers Langston Hughes had known, the Congo, the Nile, the Euphrates. A play lurked in the corners too, one populated by his and Jessie's ghosts, by the corpses they had stumbled over to find each other. Bones would be reincarnated through speech. Ashes would turn suddenly into flesh. He couldn't bear another death. He would keep on writing until it was safe to stop.
>
> (1992, p. 59)

In this passage, Lincoln references the poem "The Negro Speaks of Rivers" (1921) by the Harlem Renaissance writer Langston Hughes and the poem "Between the World and Me" (1935) by the prolific writer Richard Wright. These words "worry the line"; they create images and an emotional response that brings memories of Africa and the lynching of Blacks during the Jim Crow era in America.

At the end of the Civil Rights movement, Jessie pursues her dream of becoming an actress and moves to New York City with Lincoln. Macon marries Courtland, a civil rights worker she meets while in the movement. The personal relationships of Jessie and Lincoln and Macon and Courtland do not survive. As they mature into adulthood, they must face the emotional traumas that they have brought with them to the movement. Jessie has been emotionally scarred and her life as an actress allows her to avoid the inner turmoil in her life. She cannot maintain a relationship for she is full of secrets. Macon's aggressive and assertive personality places weight on a fragile marriage.

And Do Remember Me is ultimately a testament to the importance of remembering. The struggle of the characters represents "the long distance" that they must endure and the courage they must have to unfold and confront their fears and secrets and heal themselves. As Black women who have participated in the civil rights struggle alongside their male partners while harboring their own fears and insecurities, they have kept silent. Golden continues with the themes of "worrying the lines" and "remembering" in her texts. In *And Do Remember Me*, she has "worried the lines" of silence, racism, and family dynamics in the Black community. The stories of the central characters must be told so that they and their community will survive.

The themes of tragedy, identity, reconciliation, and the need for love form the core of Golden's *The Edge of Heaven* (1998). In this novel, set in Washington, DC, Golden explores the complex relationships that arise as the characters struggle with conflicts involving a commitment to themselves and their families. In order to move forward, each of the central characters, Lena, Teresa, and Ryan, must reflect upon and reconcile their past. They must come to terms with the scars left by tragedy and unresolved anger. The novel opens with the line: "My mother returned that summer from an exile imposed and earned" (1998, p. 1). Lena has not been prepared for her departure and she was not sure how to claim her homecoming. She asks herself, "How do we forgive after a terrible wrong?" (p. 40). Lena must remember, forgive, and grow to love her mother again before she can heal.

The themes of healing and reconciliation are continued in Golden's novel *After* (2006). Golden was motivated to write the novel following the tragic shooting of a young Black man in Prince County, Maryland by a Black police officer, Carson Blake. *After* explores the internal life of the police officer who learns that he has shot an unarmed African American teacher. He thinks the man is carrying a gun and finds out it is a cell phone. Based on a true-life incident, Golden takes the reader on a journey that exposes the guilt that Carson carries and the impact of this tragedy on his family. As in her previous novels, the process of healing involves remembering and reconciliation.

The Wide Circumference of Love (2017) is Golden's compelling story of how a Black family in crisis copes when they learn that the father, an accomplished architect, is diagnosed with Alzheimer's. Golden explores all dimensions of this debilitating disease and its effect on the family. Readers witness the guilt of the man's wife Diana when she has to leave him in an assisted living facility and her coming to terms with the realization that her husband has fallen in love with another patient. As in her fiction and nonfiction, Golden also addresses the persistent themes of colorism, race, and the criminal justice system in this novel.

The fiction and nonfiction of Marita Golden represent the complexity of Black women's writing from a Black gaze. Her texts represent diverse genres, cross geographical and cultural spaces, and are historical and contemporary renderings of the ways that Black families use remembering and reconciliation to face adversity. They also "worry the lines" by portraying the ways in which individuals, family, and the community survive the psychological and social effects of racism, poverty, loss, and abuse and offer pathways for overcoming suffering, facing family crises, and for reclaiming and healing the self, family, and community.

SEE ALSO: Bambara, Toni Cade; Cliff, Michelle; Danticat, Edwidge; Kincaid, Jamaica; Marshall, Paule; McMillan, Terry; Morrison, Toni; Walker, Alice

REFERENCES

Golden, Marita. (1992). *And Do Remember Me*. New York: Ballantine Books.
Golden, Marita. (1998). *The Edge of Heaven*. New York: Doubleday.
Golden, Marita. (2005). *Migrations of the Heart*. New York: Anchor Books; 1st ed. 1983.
Golden, Marita. (2006). *After: A Novel*. New York: Doubleday.
Greene, Brenda M. (1997). Remembering as resistance in the literature of women of color. In: *Rethinking American Literature* (ed. Lil Brannon and Brenda Greene), 97–114. Champaign, IL: National Council of Teachers of English.
Griffin, Farah J. (2007). That the mothers may soar and the daughters may know their names: a retrospective of Black feminist literary criticism. Signs: Journal of Women in Culture and Society 32: 483–507.
Wall, Cheryl A. (2005). *Worrying the Line: Black Women Writers, Lineage, and Literary Tradition*. Chapel Hill: University of North Carolina Press.
Willis, Susan. (1987). *Specifying: Black Women Writing the American Experience*. Madison: University of Wisconsin Press.

FURTHER READING

Frías, María. (1998). Migrating hearts and travelling shoes: an interview with Marita Golden. Atlantis 20 (1): 195–213.
Harris, Trudier. (2015). Romantic and romanticized international journeying: Marita Golden's "Migrations of the Heart." Obsidian 41 (1/2): 209–235.
McKay, Nellie Y. (1993). Beyond the story: reading black women's lives in Madison, Wisconsin. Women's Studies Quarterly 21 (3/4): 164–171.
O'Connor, Mary. (2013). Some contemporary Black American women's writing. In *Contemporary American Women Writers: Gender, Class, Ethnicity* (ed. L. Parkinson), 11–13. London: Routledge.

Williams, Psyche K. (2006). The impossibility of return: Black women's migration to Africa. Frontiers: A Journal of Women's Studies 27 (2): 54–86.

Gomez, Jewelle

JERRY RAFIKI JENKINS
Palomar College, USA

Gomez has been a writer and cultural activist since the 1970s, but she did not achieve critical attention until the publication of her first novel, *The Gilda Stories*, in 1991. *The Gilda Stories*, which has never been out of print, won two Lambda Book Awards, one in Lesbian Fiction and one in Lesbian Science Fiction/Fantasy, and it is the first Black vampire novel to be authored by an African American. Gomez's adaptation of the novel for the stage, *Bones & Ash: A Gilda Story*, was performed in thirteen US cities by the Urban Bush Women dance company during the 1995/6 season, and the script was published by the Paperback Book Club as a Triangle Classic. In 2011, *The Gilda Stories* celebrated its twentieth year in print with readings at the Museum of the African Diaspora and at the Queer Arts Festival, and the expanded twenty-fifth anniversary edition of novel was published by City Lights Publishers in 2016. Another milestone for *The Gilda Stories* occurred in 2018, when it was reported that award-winning filmmaker Cheryl Dunye would oversee a multipart series for television based on the novel. While Gomez has other published works that deserve more scholarly attention, *The Gilda Stories* has made Gomez one of the most important authors in late twentieth-century American literature.

Gomez, who is Cape Verdean, Ioway, and Wampanoag, was born in Boston, Massachusetts, in 1948 as Jewelle Lydia Gomes. After her parents, Dolores Minor LeClaire and John Gomes, separated when she was two years old, Gomez was raised by her great-grandmother, Gracias Archelina Sportsman Morandus, a woman of African American and Native American descent who was born on an Iowa reservation. Gomez attended an all-girls school in Boston, where she earned a full scholarship to Northeastern University. After receiving her bachelor's degree in 1971, Gomez moved to New York City, where she attended Columbia University's School of Journalism as a Ford Foundation Fellow and earned a master's degree in 1973. While Gomez was working on her undergraduate and graduate degrees, she was also working in television. In 1970, Gomez was a production assistant for *Say Brother*, now known as *Basic Black*, which is the longest-running public affairs television program by, for, and about African Americans at Boston's WGBH-TV. Gomez also worked as a production assistant on the first episode of *The Electric Company*, which aired in 1971 and starred Morgan Freeman and Rita Moreno, among others. In the 1980s, Gomez moved from television to theater, working with the renowned Frank Silvera Writers Workshop and as a stage manager for off-Broadway theater productions.

After Gomez finished her formal education, her career as an activist and a writer began to take shape. For example, in "Before Stonewall: A Personal Journey" (1984), Gomez recalls that in 1969, when the Stonewall uprising occurred, she was "preoccupied solely with the Civil Rights and anti-war movements." Once she developed a feminist consciousness that "provided a context for [her] lesbianism," Gomez states that "my reality as a black lesbian feminist was confirmed" (1984, p. 28). Gomez became a founding board member of the Astraea Lesbian Foundation in 1977, the Gay and Lesbian Alliance Against Defamation (GLAAD) in 1985, when she became its first treasurer, and the Open Meadows Foundation in 1989. Gomez also conducted research and interviews for the acclaimed documentary *Before Stonewall* (1985), an experience that highlights the trajectory of Gomez's activism during the 1970s and 1980s. As she stated in "Before Stonewall," "[a]lthough I did spend a torturous part of my time not doing research but convincing some gay men that they had to take women seriously, the process of the film itself is a monument to coalition politics" (1984, p. 30).

Gomez's activism during this period, an activism rooted in coalition politics and in her reality as a Black lesbian feminist, significantly shaped her writing. For example, in addition to being one of the contributors to *Conditions: A Magazine of Writing by Women with an Emphasis on Writing by Lesbians* (1977–1990), Gomez wrote "Black Women Heroes: Here's Reality, Where's the Fiction?" (1986), a peer-reviewed article published in *The Black Scholar*. In that article, Gomez cites historical examples of Black women heroes to question the absence of "black women characters of heroic dimensions in fantasy fiction" (1986, p. 8). She argues that Octavia Butler's *Kindred* (1979) and Michelle Parkerson's "Odds and Ends, a new Amazon Fable" (1983) are speculative fiction that offers Black women heroes who reject the idea that "heroism for women consists largely of being physically beautiful and overtly compliant" (1986, p. 11). "Talking About It: Homophobia in the Black Community" (1990), a conversation between Gomez and Barbara Smith about the causes and consequences of – as well as possible solutions to – the homophobia that exists in the African American community, was published by *Feminist Review* in 1990. One of the problems with homophobia, as Gomez points out, is that it limits Black womanhood to two problematic images that were pervasive during the early moments of the post-Civil Rights era: "the well-groomed *Essence* girl who pursues a profession and a husband" or "the snappy baby machine." Gomez contends that these images not only define the *normal* Black woman as one who has "a man or a baby," but also make "embracing [one's] lesbianism doubly frightening" because one is "going against the grain" by discarding "the mythology that's been developed around what it means to be a young Black woman" (1990, p. 49).

Gomez's Black lesbian feminism and coalition activism also shaped her first two books, *The Lipstick Papers* (1980) and *Flamingoes and Bears* (1986). Published by Gomez's Grace Publications, these books of poetry shed light on the issues, people, and events that informed Gomez's personal, political, and artistic growth during the 1970s and 1980s. While *The Lipstick Papers* is out of print, the poems in *Flamingoes and Bears* offer us some insight into the poetry produced by Gomez during this moment of her artistic life, since some of these poems previously appeared in *The Lipstick Papers*, *Conditions*, *Essence*, and other publications. For instance, Gomez's antiwar sensibilities are represented in "Hiroshima Red in Black and White," which is a response to the photographic memorial exhibit of Hiroshima at Hunter College in 1982, and her commitment to Black civil rights is expressed in "Arthur McDuffie," an indictment against the Miami judicial system that acquitted four white police officers who beat a handcuffed, Black insurance salesman to death with their flashlights. Examples of Gomez's emerging Black lesbian feminism can be found in "Oral Tradition" and "Sir Raleigh," humorous critiques of phallocentric conceptions of desire and power, and "Tanya Rienzi 1939–1976" is a call to end domestic violence, especially against Black women. "The Servants" is a heart-wrenching poem about class, family, death, and women loving women, and "Our Feminist Who Art in Heaven" focuses on a woman asking forgiveness from her Goddess for participating in heteropatriarchal practices. In addition to embodying her anti-war, Civil Rights, and Black lesbian feminist activism, *Flamingoes and Bears* also represents Gomez's celebration of interracial love, as evidenced in the book's title poem, which focuses on the intimate relationship between a flamingo and a bear who build a "nest" in a "den."

Flamingoes and Bears captures not only Gomez's political activism, but also her emergence as a creative writer. While Grace Paley – the famous poet, short story author, and political activist – was the person who convinced Gomez to self-publish *The Lipstick Papers* and, consequently, *Flamingoes and Bears*, during a chance encounter in an elevator, Gomez notes in a 2012 interview that the publication of these books also represents the moment when she believed that her work was "meant to be out there in the world" (Fonseca 2012). As indicated by the success and continued relevance of *The Gilda Stories*, Gomez's vision of a Black literary vampire was also meant to be out in the world.

It is surprising that *The Gilda Stories* became a novel, since Gomez originally wrote it as a collection of short stories. In fact, the legendary Audre Lorde, the self-described "black, lesbian, mother, warrior, poet," is the person who told Gomez to make the change. As Gomez recalls, "Yeah, I asked [Lorde] to read it. She said, 'I don't like short stories, and I really don't like vampires, but okay.' Then she came back and said 'Oh! This is a novel!' So I spent the next year turning it into a novel" (Fonseca 2012). It is also surprising that *The Gilda Stories* was not self-published, since mainstream publishers rejected the novel, even though Gomez had a very reputable literary agent. She remembers one rejection letter that her agent read to her, which stated that *The Gilda Stories* was "too complicated" and "unsellable" because the protagonist is Black, lesbian, and a vampire (Fonseca 2012; Gomez 2004, p. 349). Fortunately, the feminist press Firebrand Books, founded by Nancy K. Bereano in 1984, took a chance on *The Gilda Stories*, which is still in print nearly thirty years after its initial publication.

The Gilda Stories begins in 1850, when Gilda escapes from the Mississippi plantation where she was born, and ends in 2050, when she achieves *real* freedom as a vampire in Peru, near Machu Picchu. One of the first lessons that Gilda learns as a vampire is that her journey to freedom is a communal journey, not an individual one. Since Gilda's mother is dead and her father was sold when she was a child, Gilda creates a vampire family that consists of three Black lesbians (including Gilda), a straight Black man, two gay white men, and a Native American lesbian. While in the process of creating her family, Gilda not only learns that there are at least two types of vampires, "parasitic" and "fair exchange" but also that the real monsters of America are the racists, rapists, pimps, and power-hungry rich who, like the parasitic vampire, exploit the marginalized. In contrast, the fair exchange vampire, represented by Gilda and her vampire family, lives by the philosophy that one must share, not rob; that is, if one takes from another, one must leave something of comparable value behind. Thus, real freedom for Gilda means being in a space where she is no longer running from the monsters of America and where she can create a community with a life philosophy that discourages the production of such monsters.

On one level, Gomez's depiction of Gilda represents the moment she claimed the vampire myth as her own. Gomez's interest in vampires began with her fascination with Dracula. When she was 15 years old, Gomez started watching classic horror films with her neighborhood friends and developed an attachment to Dracula. While the teenaged Gomez, who struggled with feelings of abandonment as a result of her parents' divorce, identified with Dracula because of his search for an eternal companion, his supernatural powers, and his attire, she was never comfortable with the dead bodies that Dracula produced in his attempt to find a life-long partner. Thus, claiming the vampire myth as her own meant Gomez had to understand her attraction to Dracula and why she was disgusted by him. To account for these opposing responses, Gomez developed a notion of vampirism in which Dracula is just one type of vampire. Indeed, the fact that there are parasitic and fair exchange vampires in *The Gilda Stories* indicates that vampires are not a monolithic group, that there are multiple ways of being a vampire. By claiming the vampire myth as her own, Gomez troubles Western culture's image of the vampire as white, male, straight, and innately monstrous by offering a vampire who is Black, lesbian, and heroic.

On another level, as evidenced by Gilda's vampire family, Gomez's depiction of Gilda represents her political activism. Gomez has stated that she did not imagine Gilda until the 1970s and 1980s, when she started learning about the complex world of identity in America. In fact, Gilda's actions, observations, and personal development are shaped by Gomez's engagement with the artistic works of the feminist movement, the Black Arts movement, and lesbian literary journals. Moreover, Gilda's vampire family is a representation of Gomez's ever-expanding coalition politics that not only critiques Afrocentrics and African American conservatives who viewed Black lesbians as inauthentic Black people, but also 1980s white conservatives who viewed Black women as dangerous, predatory, and vampiric. Gomez's point seems to be that Black heteropatriarchy is the same as white anti-Black racism in that both lead to the production and consumption of Black bodies in pain. In this light, *The Gilda Stories* represents the intersection of Gomez's personal beliefs, political activism, and literary imagination.

While *The Gilda Stories* is Gomez's first and, so far, only novel, it is a seminal text in Black speculative fiction. For instance, although Hermine Pinson's 1988 poem "All-Around Vampires" may be the first literary text about vampires penned by an African American, *The Gilda Stories* introduces us to the African American vampire novel, which includes Jemiah Jefferson's *Voice of the Blood* (2001), L.A. Banks's *Minion* (2003), Brandon Massey's *Dark Corner* (2004), Octavia E. Butler's *Fledgling* (2005), Pearl Cleage's *Just Wanna Testify* (2011), and K. Murry Johnson's *Image of Emeralds and Chocolate* (2012). Gomez's novel establishes African American vampire fiction as a queer or antinormative project that troubles the traditional vampire narrative, the Black literary imagination, dichotomous thinking, and social identities that are treated as fixed in nature. *The Gilda Stories* is also an example of Afrofuturist feminist cultural production in which Afrofuturism and Black feminism are used to offer futures where Black women survive and thrive. The novel's contribution to the Afrofuturist feminist canon involves its remixing of traditional vampire lore with Black feminist sensibilities to show that Black women are crucial to restructuring society for the better and that the real threat at the dawn of the twenty-first century is misogyny and white supremacy. *The Gilda Stories* also helps to move critical discussions about the neo-slave narrative into a queer-positive space by identifying normative gender and sexuality with enslavement and queer gender and sexuality with liberation. Given its contributions to African American vampire fiction, the Afrofuturist feminist canon, and the neo-slave narrative, *The Gilda Stories* is required reading for anyone who wants to study late twentieth-century Black speculative fiction.

In addition to *The Gilda Stories*, Firebrand Books published Gomez's *Forty-Three Septembers* (1993), a collection of fifteen personal and political essays that blur the line between autobiography and cultural criticism, *Oral Tradition: Selected Poems Old & New* (1995), her third book of poetry, and *Don't Explain* (1997), a collection of nine short stories that includes "Houston," a new Gilda story. "Chicago 1927," which appears in *Dark Matter: A Century of Speculative Fiction from the African Diaspora* (2004) and "Caramelle 1864," the first story of *Black from the Future: A Collection of Black Speculative Writing* (2019), are two other Gilda stories that, along with "Houston," may provide the foundation for the new Gilda novel that Gomez has been working on. Gomez also co-edited *Over the Rainbow: Lesbian and Gay Politics in America since Stonewall* (1995) with Dale Peck, Mab Segrest, and David Deitcher, *Swords of the Rainbow: Gay & Lesbian Fantasy Adventures* (1996) with Eric Garber, and *The Best Lesbian Erotica of 1997* (1997) with Tristan Taormino. Gomez's fourth book of poetry, *Name Poems*, was published in 2016 by Createspace Independent Publishing Platform, and the first two plays of her *Words and Music* trilogy – *Waiting for Giovanni: A Dream Play* (2018), which imagines that James Baldwin had a quick moment of indecision about the publication of his second novel, *Giovanni's Room* (1956), and the independently published *Leaving the Blues: A Memory Play* (2019), which is loosely based on the life of singer and composer Alberta Hunter – premiered to sold-out houses and received high praise from critics. The third play of the *Words and Music* trilogy, *Unpacking in Ptown*, which Gomez describes as a "coloured, comic soap opera with music" (Gomez n.d.), is scheduled to premiere at the New Conservatory Theatre Center in 2021. As indicated by this brief list of publications, while *The Gilda Stories* is the work that Gomez is most known for, her literary life is greater than one novel.

In addition to her two Lambda Awards and California Arts Council fellowships, Gomez has received several awards for her work, including the Beard's Fund Award for Fiction in 1985, the Barbara Deming/Money for Women Fund Award for fiction in 1987, a literature fellowship from the National Endowment for the Arts in 1997, an Individual Artist Commission from the San Francisco Arts Commission in 2000, and the Barbary Coast Trailblazer Award from LitQuake in 2017. While Gomez has received high praise for her work, the literary criticism on her work is surprisingly not as vast as it should be. There is very little scholarship on Gomez's poems and short fiction, and even though Gomez, like Linda Addison, Octavia E. Butler, Tananarive Due, and Nalo Hopkinson, is a foremother of late twentieth-century Black speculative fiction, the scholarly articles and book chapters on *The Gilda Stories*, while intellectually engaging, insightful, and necessary, are small in number compared to the novel's literary and political significance. Nevertheless, Gomez's intellectually rigorous treatment of vampirism, race, gender, sexuality, class, religion, family, art, history, and the erotic in her fiction, essays, criticism, poetry, and plays has made her one of the most important American authors since the 1980s.

SEE ALSO: Afrofuturism; Butler, Octavia; Cleage, Pearl; Delany, Samuel; Gay, Roxanne; Post-Soul and/or Post-Black Fiction; Queer and LGBT Fiction; Third-Wave Feminism

REFERENCES

Fonseca. (2012). Jewelle Gomez, lesbian trailblazer: the Autostraddle interview. (August 22, 2012). https://www.autostraddle.com/jewelle-gomez-lesbian-trailblazer-143407/ (accessed July 6, 2021).

Gomez, Jewelle. (1984). Before Stonewall: a personal journey. *Pride Guide*, 28–30. New York: Jezebel Productions. https://jezebelproductions.org/wp-content/uploads/2012/08/Before-

Stonewall-A-personal-journey_JewelleGomez_PrideGuide_1984.pdf (accessed July 6, 2021).

Gomez, Jewelle. (1986). Black women heroes: here's reality, where's the fiction? *The Black Scholar* 17 (2): 8–13.

Gomez, Jewelle. (2004). The second law of thermodynamics: transcription of a panel at the 1997 Black Speculative Fiction Writers Conference held at Clark Atlanta University. In: *Dark Matter: Reading of the Bones* (ed. Sheree R. Thomas), 349–368. New York: Warner.

Gomez, Jewelle. (n.d.). jewellegomez.com (accessed August 23, 2021).

Gomez, Jewelle and Smith, Barbara. (1990). Talking about it: homophobia in the Black community. *Feminist Review* 34: 47–55.

FURTHER READING

Jenkins, Jerry Rafiki. (2019). *The Paradox of Blackness in African American Vampire Fiction*. Columbus: Ohio State University Press.

Jones, Miriam. (1997). *The Gilda Stories:* revealing the monsters at the margin. In: *Blood Read: The Vampire as Metaphor in Contemporary Culture* (ed. Joan Gordon and Veronica Hollinger), 151–167. Philadelphia: University of Pennsylvania Press.

Lewis, Christopher S. (2014). Queering personhood in the neo-slave narrative: Jewelle Gomez's *The Gilda Stories*. *African American Review* 47 (4): 447–459.

Morris, Susana M. (2016). More than human: Black feminisms of the future in Jewelle Gomez's *The Gilda Stories*. *The Black Scholar* 46 (2): 33–45.

Parker, Kendra. (2019). *Black Female Vampires in African American Women's Novels, 1977–2011: She Bites Back*. Kentucky: Lexington.

Parkerson, Michelle. (1995). Odds and ends (a new Amazon fable). In: *Afrekete: An Anthology of Black Lesbian Writing* (ed. Catherine E. McKinley and L. Joyce DeLaney), 89–95. New York: Doubleday.

The Graphic Novel

ACHIM HESCHER
University of Koblenz-Landau, Germany

From the beginnings in 1986, when the label *graphic novel* did not yet exist, Anglo-American artists and writers have most significantly shaped what was first held to be a marketing format rather than a literary text group. In fact, until well into the third millennium, and contrary to Will Eisner's belief that "there would be a continually growing audience for the literary pretensions of the medium" (Eisner 2006, p. xx), it was not clear whether what we now call graphic novels were to be considered art or literature in the first place. Graphic novels are narratives in the medium of comics transmitting information about their story worlds primarily through *showing*, that is by sequential images and their layout; only secondarily do they convey information through verbal text such as balloon or narrator speech. Over time and as a genre, the graphic novel has become much diversified, and the works by American artists and writers must be noted for their importance in the formation of maybe the two most analytically interesting as well as popular subgenres to the graphic novel: graphic memoirs and reportage comics, also known as graphic journalism.

THE COMING OF A SINGULARIZED CULTURAL GOOD

After the turn of the millennium, the graphic novel rose to the status of a singularized cultural good (Reckwitz 2017, p. 126). When Art Spiegelman had published the first book of *Maus: A Survivor's Tale* in 1986, critics not seldom refused to recognize it as a book of comics because it obviously was aesthetically valuable (Gordon 2010, p. 186). This appreciation was presumably due to its relatively large amount of text, compared to mainstream comic books. Not quite fifteen years later, *Maus* (book two of which had been published in 1991) would be labeled a graphic novel and held in appreciation because of its originality and authenticity.

A cultural good becomes original when it develops its own complexity on the inside and qualitative difference on the outside

(Reckwitz 2017, p. 126). Besides its obviously serious subject matter, *Maus* impressed its readers because of two distinguishing features of narrative complexity: unlike traditional comic book characters, its anthropomorphic animals have virtually expressionless faces, designed to forestall aesthetic blunders in representing the suffering of the mice (Jews) and the atrocities of the cats (Nazis); and its framing narrative, in which the young author-character Spiegelman prompts his father Vladek to tell about his ordeal during World War II, employs many self-referential and metafictional devices accounting for the problematics of rendering a witness report about the Holocaust in comic book form.

In 1986, two other great works launched the graphic novel *avant la lettre*: Frank Miller's innovative Batman rewriting *The Dark Knight Returns* and *Watchmen*, by the Englishmen Alan Moore (script) and Dave Gibbons (art), both works parodies of the superhero genre, known from mainstream comic books. Besides a Batman coping with problems of aging, *The Dark Knight* abandons the regular grid and experiments with panels as in the form TV sets (the dominating medium of the time), split panels, and color-coded captions. *Watchmen*, though keeping the classic three by three grid, uses a framed narrative, six main and a plethora of minor characters in around twenty embedded narrative strands; apart from that, it features numerous text-to-image references across multiple semiotic planes and a multitude of intertextual and intermedial references.

In addition to increased interior complexity, *Maus, The Dark Knight, Watchmen*, and graphic novels after 2000 developed a qualitative difference on the outside (Reckwitz 2017, p. 127), which is reflected in their often complex publication history and marketing: after publication as single installments in comics magazines and anthologies, they were often rounded up in one volume on more prestigious paper or even in hardback editions, sold in real bookstores – as opposed to common drugstores or the comics specialty or head shops of the 1960s and 1970s. By the 1980s, comics readers had grown up, and those who had not given up comics made higher demands on narrative construction and scripting. In other words, "the star artist [had] given way to the star *writer*" (Round 2010, p. 21). Formerly, comics had been marketed on the basis of their characters, as with the big publishers DC Comics and Marvel. Creators of Superman or Batman, for example, often had to conform to a house style and changed over time along with editors or script writers. From around the 1990s onward, rising independent publishers like Fantagraphics, Drawn & Quarterly, or Top Shelf would credit their artists and writers on the cover pages and pay them royalties. By the end of the second millennium, graphic novels had acquired the status of *comics d'auteur*, appealing, however, to a still much restricted readership. Although public libraries had already started to collect graphic novels, it would take a few more years for them to become bestselling items in the bookshops and online stores.

Maus, The Dark Knight, and *Watchmen* – the "Big Three" – revived strategies of postmodern storytelling, which had waned considerably by the late1980s: self-referentiality, multilayered narration, foregrounded intertextuality/intermediality, equivocacy of meaning, and deconstructions of subjectivity, to name but a few. David Mazzucchelli and Paul Karasik's graphic 2004 adaptation of Paul Auster's novella *City of Glass* (1985) embraces these paradigms in its intricate story about the disappearance of an author of crime fiction, told by an unnamed narrator who is a friend of a certain Paul Auster.

Chris Ware's *Building Stories* (2012) exploits the mediality and materiality of graphic storytelling by foregrounding and merging the work's paratext with the stories themselves, coming in fourteen loose "books, booklets, magazines, newspapers, and pamphlets" (Ware 2012, n.p.) of different sizes and formats, with and without words, rounded up in a cardboard box. Mainly, the various episodic stories connect through a young unnamed woman protagonist who lost a leg in a childhood accident and the 105-year-old house she lives in – which, as a special feature, has its own narrating voice and thoughts. Miniatures of the booklets figure on the bottom of the box and are assigned to spots in a ground plan of an "average well-appointed home" (Ware 2012, n.p.). Ware thus creates building stories and builds stories from both main and paratext.

ESSENTIAL STRUCTURAL FEATURES

As for meaning production, *showing* is essential to the comics medium: graphic novels narrate primarily through images and their layout on the page. Text, however, like non-diegetic caption speech, balloon speech, sound lettering, or text that is part of the story world, also is subject to showing: the typeface, size, and color of words are often coded and produce meaning in their own right across planes of signification. Mazzucchelli and Karasik's *City of Glass* (2004), for example, opens with an all-black splash, featuring narrator speech in white Courier typeface, which readers attribute to the covert narrator, who tells the story of Daniel Quinn, a writer of crime fiction; and in Mazzucchelli's *Asterios Polyp* (2009), a novel experimenting with color on all narrative planes, we find sound lettering in various colors and pictorial shapes, traversing one or more panels in a sequence or blending in with other pictorial elements, such as yellow staves overlaid by rock lyrics.

The preponderance of showing rules out a default narrator. Graphic narratives can totally dispense with words (not just narrator speech) and still narrate, as we know from the famous silent novels by Lynd Ward (*God's* Man, 1929), Milt Gross (*He Done Her Wrong*, 1930), or, more recently, by the Australian Shaun Tan (*The Arrival*, 2006). Narrator concepts from (post)classic narratology do not apply to graphic narratives since the transmission of story world information happens primarily through the images and pictorial features of the text, which must be entirely attributed to the author or artist-writer (or possibly a team). As opposed to verbal narrative fiction, whose story worlds are completely imagined by the readers through what the narrating "voice" transmits, readers do *not* imagine the images or pictorial features of text in comic books: they see what has been drawn. Although there may be narrator speech (usually inside caption boxes) or even a narrator-character (as in *Maus*), they are not default settings in comics (Hescher 2016, p. 169).

Graphic novels have become a singularized cultural good because of their interior complexity (see "The Coming of a Singularized Cultural Good" above): concretely, they operate on multiple narrative planes and use color codes as well as meaning-enhancing panel design and layout. Generally, they possess a complex text/image relation and employ (meta-)fictionalization devices such as pictorial tropes, metalepses, or mises en abyme, and so on (Hescher 2016, p. 169) – which is why they should be called *novels*, even if they make authenticity claims like books of graphic journalism or graphic memoirs. In fact, "[t]o ask for autobiographical 'truth' in comics is [. . .] to ask for something that is inimical to the form" (Køhlert 2015, p. 127), because cartoony or otherwise reductive drawings of characters jar with "the seriousness of what has happened" (Micciche 2004, p. 17).

FROM ALTERNATIVE COMICS
TO GRAPHIC NOVELS

Like many verbal-monomodal novels serialized in newspapers in the nineteenth century, *Maus*, *The Dark Knight*, *Watchmen* and many graphic novels in their wake were either pre-released in parts or installments in comics magazines or anthologies, sometimes owned or co-owned by the artist-writers themselves, like Art Spiegelman, who published parts of *Maus* in *Short Order Comix* (1973–1974) and the avant-garde follow-up *Raw* (1980–1991). Alternative comics, a phenomenon that emerged in the late 1970s and had its peak in the 1990s, featured the slice of life story, which sometimes amounted to short semi or fully autobiographic narratives, the precursor to the current fully fledged graphic memoirs, which started to sprout after 2000 and by now are probably the most prominent (and bestselling) subgenre of graphic novels. Groundbreaking for the slice of life genre are Harvey Pekar's autobiographic story collections in *American Splendor*, published between 1976 and 2008 at irregular intervals and drawn by numerous artists, many of them now heavyweights of the comics artists scene. "Harvey" is the antihero and main character in Pekar's short fragmentary episodes, which often thematize cartooning and the cartoonist's struggle to make ends meet. The 1990s and beginning 2000s saw a host of autobiographic or autobiographically inspired life story comics by artist-writers like Daniel Clowes (*Ghost World*, 1993–1997), Debbie Drechsler (*Daddy's Girl*, 1996), Phoebe Gloeckner (*A Child's Life and Other Stories*, 2000), Adrian Tomine (*Optic Nerve*, 1991–) and Josh Neufeld (*A Few Perfect Hours*, 2004), to name but a few. Drechsler's and Gloeckner's narratives stick out from this list because of their explicit depiction of incest and child abuse. With "Minnie," Gloeckner has drawn a cartoony though obviously adolescent version of herself, whereas no such inference from the drawing style can be made about Drechsler's "Lilie." Both works, however, are essentially autobiographic and present collections of single nonlinear vignettes about the life of their protagonists.

Adult orientation combined with what Will Eisner called "a rule of realism which requires that caricature or exaggeration accept the limitations of actuality" (Eisner 2006, xviii–xix) marked the transition from the heavily sex and drug-infused (and often misogynist) underground comics of the 1960s and 1970s to alternative comics, and are features common to most graphic works from the 1980s onward, regardless of their interior complexity and their status as comic books or graphic novels. Eisner's four-story collection *A Contract with God* (1978) – which he himself called a "graphic novel" (Eisner 2006, p. x) – set the tone for alternative comics, many of which were also autobiographically motivated. Eisner's specific concern in *Contract*, however, was to render the atmosphere and moods in the New York City tenements of the 1930s (Eisner 2006, p. xi).

A similar kind of realism applies to Daniel Clowes's episodic comic book *Ghost World*, first serialized from 1993 to 1997 in Clowes's own magazine *Eightball* (1989–2004), a paragon of alternative comics, and rounded up as a "graphic novel" in 2000. *Ghost World* is about the coming of age in a 1990s urban environment of the cynical teenage girlfriends Enid and Rebecca, who harbor aversions against their culture, its social rules and habits, and against most people in their town. *Ghost World*'s distinguishing feature lies in its careful image composition and perspective construction that defamiliarizes empirical observers through pictorial techniques like vectorization and parallel projection (the latter also is a distinguishing feature of Chris Ware's works), depicting the protagonists as isolated and leaving the readers with a feeling of being shut out and confined in their own "ghost world" (Hescher 2016, p. 139).

In hindsight, the slice of life narratives from the 1980s and 1990s are comic books in the traditional sense rather than graphic novels, for they lack interior complexity. Yet two works from that time period must be exempted: *The System* (1997), by Peter Kuper, and "Here"/*Here* (1989/2014), by the musician, filmmaker, and cartoonist Richard McGuire. A six-page version of what became the 2014 graphic novel had already been published in Spiegelman's magazine *Raw* in 1989. The graphic novel consists of more than 140 double page bleeds, presenting the story of a living room and what existed or happened *in* it or *on its site* from three and a half billion years ago until the year 2314, when civilization has entirely changed. In the bleeds, McGuire inserts smaller panels, which often overlap and depict states or events from the past, present (2014, the publication year), or future, mostly trivial or funny in nature. Colors are coded, signifying either the time depicted in the panels, or they connect temporally disparate states or events. *Here* thus presents maximized complexity with regard to color use and narrative layering.

Kuper has made *The System* differently complex: of its sixteen cross-cut major and minor narrative strands, the three main stories revolve around a serial murder of woman strippers, an illegal business merger, and a bomb plot, with which the novel ends. As it contains neither word balloons nor captions, *The System* has often been labeled a wordless narrative – which is not quite true: it is shot through with diegetic text (writing on newspaper covers, posters, etc.), providing the necessary continuity clues for the readers' understanding of the story lines. Kuper's characters and settings bear a certain resemblance with those in Frans Masereel's genuinely wordless woodcuts from the 1920s and with the screaming colors of many expressionist paintings.

THE SECOND WAVE OF THE GRAPHIC NOVEL

The year 2000 saw the publication of several genuine graphic novels distinguishing themselves through their technical, conceptual, and stylistic originality: Jason Lutes's first volume of his *Berlin* trilogy, *City of Stones*, Chris Ware's fictional biography *Jimmy Corrigan, the Smartest Kid on Earth*, and Joe Sacco's reportage comics about Bosnia, *Safe Area Goražde*, and *Palestine* (2000/2001 and 2003, see "Graphic journalism" below). Unlike the loosely cohering slice of life stories in alternative comics, these books present coherent though multilayered narratives or are bound up with a journalistic project.

Lutes's *Berlin* project includes twenty-two single installments (1996–2018), united in three volumes (*City of Stones*, 2000, *City of Smoke*, 2008, and *City of Light*, 2018). Set in the German capital during the Weimar Republic, *Berlin* is a classical historical novel in its multilayered plot construction and mix of fictional and historical characters, the minor ones figuring in short vignettes, the protagonists in longer episodes. To the smallest detail, Lutes borrows from historical photographs of the Berlin cityscape in the backdrop to his images; other intermedial references are made to films or paintings of the time. Lutes's unusual panel forms and layouts like axi or point symmetrical panel arrangements (see the often quoted layout in swastika form in *City of Stones*) create additional meaning and read as pictorial metaphors or allegories (Hescher 2018, p. 84).

Jimmy Corrigan, parts of which were prepublished in Ware's own magazine *Acme Novelty Library*, is the multilayered life story of a fictional character. Abandoned by his father and raised by an overbearing mother, 36-year-old Jimmy has become a lonely office worker in Chicago. Upon receiving an invitation for Thanksgiving from his long lost father, Jimmy meets up with him in the fictional town of Waukosha, Michigan, where he also encounters his grandfather, James Corrigan. Jimmy gets to know his Black stepsister Amy when their father is killed in a car accident before Jimmy can leave Waukosha. The gloomy main story is interspersed with James Corrigan's childhood recollections of 1890s Chicago and episodes from his life with his father William Corrigan (Jimmy's great-grandfather), a glazier working on the 1893 World's Columbian Exposition, who abandoned his son James on his ninth birthday during a visit to the Exposition. Apart from its complex narrative layering, *Jimmy Corrigan* is shot through with types of verbal/pictorial paratext: copyright logos, an intermittent story summary, day and night dream sequences, genealogy schemas, cutout instructions, pictorial allegories and, above all, a dust jacket unfolding into a paratextual plethora, which demands a reading in its own right and provides supplementary information about Jimmy and his small world. Technically, *Jimmy Corrigan* must be noted for its finely honed layout, often challenging the conventional reading order (Z-path), and the frequent parallel projections in the images, which suspend the implied observer position (Schüwer 2008, p. 124) and make it hard for readers to empathize with the characters.

Like many comics creators born in the 1960s and 1970s, Ware is steeped in alternative comics. All of his works or at least portions of it were prepublished in *Acme Novelty Library* (1993–) and other renowned magazines. In impact second only to Spiegelman's *Maus*, *Jimmy Corrigan* and its pudgy potato-like characters must be read together with *Building Stories* (2012, see "The Coming of a Singularized Cultural Good" above) and *Rusty Brown* (2019) as a highly complex *Gesamtkunstwerk* or postmodernist *Comédie humaine*. Interestingly, the first two stories of *Rusty Brown* were published only shortly after *Jimmy Corrigan*. As a cycle of life stories with reappearing characters (among whom a certain "Mr. Ware"), *Rusty Brown* is part of a broadly conceived and open-ended project, finishing, for the time being, with an "Intermission" (Ware 2019, n.p.).

The Rise of the Graphic Memoir

Autobiographic narratives are rooted in the 1960s underground culture, whose *comix* were the first in the medium to exclusively address adult readers. Despite the depiction of sexuality, drug abuse, and machismo, comix have influenced numerous present-day authors of graphic memoirs and other subgenres to the graphic novel. Aline Kominsky-Crumb's five-page story "Goldie," Robert Crumb's four-page "The Confessions of R. Crumb," and Justin Green's long-form comic *Binky Brown Meets the Holy Virgin Mary*, all published in 1972, count as the primogenitors to current graphic memoirs. "Goldie" and *Binky Brown* depict the life of their characters from childhood to early adulthood, whereas in "Confessions," a homunculus version of the adult Crumb is brutally ejected from his mother's womb. Both *Binky Brown* and "Confessions" feature an extradiegetic author figure directly addressing readers and introducing them to what type of story is to be expected. Apart from narrative layering, *Binky Brown* is the prototype of graphic memoirs for its then daring panel forms and layout, intermedial references, and, most of all, its ample use of balloon and caption speech. The pubertal comical story is about Green's strict Catholic upbringing and compulsive neurosis, consisting in his seeing imaginary phalluses and "penis rays" emanating from objects and body parts.

One of the first graphic memoirs after 2000 is Lynda Barry's *One Hundred Demons* (2002, serialized 2000–2001), which she calls "a work of autobifictionalography" (Barry 2002, n.p., paratextual notice). In the prefatory narrative frame, similar in its setup to "The Confessions" and *Binky Brown*, Barry appears as a grown-up character sitting at her drawing desk across from a demon, who narrates how her book emerged from a Zen drawing exercise. The novel's subsequent vignettes are each drawn in different complementary colors and recount formative episodes and experiences mainly from Barry's childhood. The epilogue accounts for her profession as an art teacher as it provides basic instructions on how to "paint your demon" (Barry 2002, n.p.).

Pre-released in several international weeklies, *In the Shadow of No Towers* (2004) is a complex mix of metafiction and autobiography. Herein, Spiegelman, main character and narrator, reports how he lived through the terrorist attacks of September 11, 2001. *No Towers* compares comics pages to the architectural structures of Manhattan's Twin Towers (pictorial metaphor). Spiegelman's autobiographic story of 9/11 (Part One: "In the Shadow of No Towers) and his personal history of comics from around the turn of the nineteenth century (Part Two): "The Comics Supplement") represent the two "pillars" of the novel. Both the Towers and comics have been understood as metaphors of the monumental and ephemeral, and the perpetuity of Spiegelman's trauma has been compared to the seriality of comics (Chute 2007, p. 231). Its sophisticated makeup and discontinuous story line notwithstanding, *No Towers* was an international bestseller, not least because of its format in broadsheet size and its aesthetically accomplished cover showing the black Towers on an all-black backdrop, which first figured on the cover of the September 24 issue of *The New Yorker* (2001).

Craig Thompson's coming of age novel *Blankets* (2003) is about his childhood relation with his brother, his first love, and his active turning away from the parents' extreme religiousness. *Blankets* is remarkable for its experiments with panel borders and designs, layout, verbal-pictorial (blanket) metaphors, and allegory. Considering its technical-rhetorical feats and the time of publication, it is hard to understand why Jean-Christophe Menu, founder and director of the French indie publisher L'Association, turned down *Blankets* for publication (it finally found the approval of the Belgian publisher Casterman), if not for a sheer dislike of the coming of age genre (Menu 2014, pp. 331–332).

Alison Bechdel, who believes that cartooning is "inherently autobiographical" (Gardner 2008, p. 1), created perhaps the most intermedial and text-oriented memoir ever. In *Fun Home* (2006), she comes to grips with her father Bruce's repressed homosexuality, his suicide, and her coming out as a lesbian. The book teems with depictions of diegetic text, like excerpts from books or letters, and shows *drawn* photographs, which look more realistic than the characters and backdrops. Bechdel staged many of her drawn character poses herself and took pictures of them to "try on" several subject positions (Watson 2008, p. 38). Verbally and pictorially, the relation to her father is presented through a host of excerpts from modernist and other verbal literature (diegetic text), the only working communication channel between Bruce and Alison.

David Small's *Stitches* (2009) deals with the consequences of the author's throat cancer operation at age fourteen and the extremely disturbed relationship to his parents. Similarly to *Fun Home*, communication with his parents is dysfunctional, especially when David finds out that they have long kept his disease a secret. Several events from the beginning of Lewis Carroll's first *Alice* book (1865, including John Tenniel's illustrations) serve as structural allegories to the narrative like the descent into the rabbit hole, the crawl through the gallery, or the encounter with the White Rabbit, who becomes David's mentor and therapist. Gloomy water colors combined with inked outlines lend a nightmarish wash to David's story, which, however, is much darker than Alice's "wonderful adventures."

While in *Fun Home* and *Stitches*, memoir wins out over biography, Derf Backderf's novel *My Friend Dahmer* (2012), begun as a short alternative comics story in 1997, focuses on the life of Jeffrey Dahmer (1960–1994) until after his high school graduation. Dahmer was an ex-classmate of Backderf's and later became an infamous serial killer. The work makes a strong claim to authenticity, reflected in the use of authentic photographs and drawings from other work contexts and in the vast annex of additional information on characters and locales. Backderf undermines this claim through his defamiliarizing drawing style, combining grotesquely deformed characters with a conspicuously awkward perspective construction.

Graphic Journalism

In a more comprehensive view, the books of Joe Sacco, David Axe, or Josh Neufeld have been classified as graphic *nonfiction*, which term includes reportage comics, travelogues, biographies, and all kinds of "histories" and instructional comics, most of which, however, do not qualify as graphic novels. For graphic *journalism* proper, in which the author-journalist serves as a character and story anchor, Emmanuel Guibert, Didier Lefèvre, and Frédéric Lemercier's *Le photographe* (three vols., 2003–2006) has been as formative as the book projects of Joe Sacco: *Palestine* (1993–2001/2003), set in the Gaza Strip and the West Bank during the first Intifada, and *Safe Area Goražde* (2000/1), which deals with the cruelties of the Bosnian War. Both works show a grotesquely Crumbian Sacco in brutally realistic settings with an author making slangy sarcastic comments on his role as a comics artist and on the credos and methods of journalism. Biased media reports are strewn among episodes narrated from Sacco's point of view, which again alternate with the reports of a guiding eyewitness, who shows Sacco around and arranges meetings with other witnesses. To suggest varying degrees of authenticity, Sacco employs different types of panel framings. In addition, *Palestine* features distorted overlapping panels looking like prints on an editor's board and shows literal processions of caption boxes meandering across the page. Sacco's work on the two crisis areas is completed by his Bosnia story collection *The Fixer* (2009) and *Footnotes in Gaza* (2009), an account of the 1956 massacres in the towns of Khan Younis and Rafah. – Sacco's latest work *Paying the Land* (2020), in which he visits the Indigenous tribe of the Dene in Canada, shows how former colonists' bargains and recent governmental policies have severed Indigenous peoples from their cultural roots and tried to cheat them out of their land. Oftentimes, Sacco abandons panels in favor of full page bleeds or pages organized in tiers with no framing, presenting images with micro or macropanoramic views. Intradiegetic narrators tend to appear in inserted panels before an action loaded background. One outstanding accomplishment of *Paying the Land* consists in Sacco's finely-honed presentation of how the social and mental unity of the Dene has been broken up by outside interferences, governmental and economic.

"I'm a reporter [. . .] I can't die" (Axe 2006, n.p.), says the main character in David Axe's 2006 novel *War-Fix*. Himself a military correspondent, Axe self-critically narrates through David how his addiction to authentic combat experience caused him to leave his home and girlfriend for a combat mission in the 2003 Iraq War. In this multilayered and compact work, Steven Olexa's realistically drawn characters – David looking like an authentic young self of the author – jar with their presentation in mind-boggling, irregular layouts, whose often unframed images are dominated by extreme angles and come in overlapping arrangements. The novel's cynical ending suggests that David will always be out there for the next war fix.

Although both the Iraq War and Hurricane Katrina (2005) received massive media coverage, Josh Neufeld's *A.D.: New Orleans After the Deluge* (2009) garnered much more critical attention than *War-Fix*. Initially published on the web and hyperlinked with podcasts, video clips, and other sources, *A.D.* focuses on the stories of seven Katrina survivors who lived in and around New Orleans and who Neufeld had personal contact with as a Red Cross volunteer after the hurricane had struck. The outstanding feature of *A.D.* is the color coding of the various story lines, which, according to the artist himself, are to "help readers through [and] to create mood" (Gustines 2009).

Works of Other Subgenres

Like many verbal novels, graphic novels mix genres. Charles Burns's *Black Hole* (1995–2005/2005) presents a *mélange* of fantasy and horror combined with a stylistic and rhetorical originality that denies affiliations with alternative or underground comics. Set in the 1970s, its nonchronological and multilayered narration revolves around a group of teenagers contracting a sexual disease called "the bug" – an allegory of the alienation during adolescence – and a murder perpetrated by one diseased teenager. As the plot unfolds, metaphoric motifs of holes and cuts seem to spread and serve as nodes to the manifold story strands. Outstanding are *Black Hole*'s use of black as a primary "color" and one flashback framed by two vertical panels distanced over fifteen pages.

Graphic young adult fiction can show an internal complexity hitherto unassociated with verbal narratives of the genre, like Craig Thompson's *Blankets* (2003, see "The Rise of the Graphic Memoir" above) and Gene Luen Yang's *American Born Chinese* (2006), currently one of the most read graphic novels in educational contexts. It is a story in three narrative strands about the transformation or identity change of two American adolescents (a Chinese immigrant son and a white boy) and the Monkey King, a character from classic Chinese literature. Yang experiments with panel design, color coding, typography, and sound lettering and makes numerous intermedial references to classic texts and to pop and youth culture.

For the graphic variant to the historical novel, Alan Moore and Eddie Campbell's postmodern rewriting of the Jack the Ripper case, *From Hell* (1989–1996/1999), Jacques Tardi's novels about World War I (*C'était la guerre de tranchées*, 1993, et al.), and Jason Lutes's trilogy *Berlin* (see "The Second Wave of the Graphic Novel" above) undeniably form the avant-garde. With *On the Ropes* (2013), James Vance (script) and Daniel Burr (art) created a novel with exclusively fictional characters set against the backdrop of the New Deal (1933–1939) and the projects of the Works Progress Administration (1935–1943). The multilayered narrative tells the story of the 18-year-old would-be writer Fred Bloch and an itinerant WPA (Works Progress Administration) circus, where Fred has been planted as a messenger between strike committees. Episodes commented by the aged Fred's homodiegetic voice alternate with episodes containing no caption speech, set in the lowlife and criminal milieu. *On the Ropes* distinguishes itself through its authentic drawings and use of contemporary slang.

What happens when the factual murder of a young woman is turned into a media fake? With his much acclaimed novel *Sabrina* (2018), Nick Drnaso has created a socially critical yet pleasantly undidactic novel whose readers are made to suffer with the friends and relatives of the victim, accused by conspiracy adherents on the World Wide Web of being actors in a plot against America. Set in Colorado Springs in 2017, the multilayered narrative dispenses with narrator speech and abounds with references to video games and (social) media, whose web designs and messages seem more real than the characters and settings, drawn in a depressingly empty and unemotional *ligne claire* and dominated by beige and gray tones.

As for the coming decade(s), it will be of interest whether graphic memoirs, whose creators have become increasingly diverse, will be as dominating as they have been. Fully fledged book projects like *Palestine* or *A.D.: New Orleans after the Deluge* have already been waning, were it not for Sacco's *Paying the Land* (see "Graphic Journalism" above). Hopefully, graphic journalism will not be relegated to sporadic episodic contributions in comics magazines and anthologies, as in the last ten years.

SEE ALSO: After Postmodernism; Auster, Paul; Mixed-Genre Fiction; Story Cycles; Young Adult Boom

REFERENCES

Axe, David. (2006). *War-Fix*. New York: NBM.
Barry, Lynda. (2002). *One Hundred Demons*. Seattle: Sasquatch Books.
Chute, Hillary. (2007). Temporality and seriality in Spiegelman's "In the Shadow of No Towers." American Periodicals 17 (2): 228–244.
Eisner, Will. (2006). *A Contract with God*. New York: Norton; 1st ed. 1978.
Gardner, Jared. (2008). Autography's biography, 1972–2007. *Biography: An Interdisciplinary Quarterly* 31 (1): 1–26.
Gordon, Ian. (2010). Making comics respectable: how *Maus* helped redefine a medium. *The Rise of the American Comics Artist: Creators and Contexts* (ed. Paul Williams and James Lyons), 179–193. Jackson: University Press of Mississippi.
Gustines, George Gene. (2009). Graphic memories of Katrina's ordeal. *The New York Times* (August 23, 2009). https://www.nytimes.com/2009/08/24/books/24neufeld.html (accessed July 1, 2020).
Hescher, Achim. (2016). *Reading Graphic Novels: Genre and Narration*. Berlin and New York: De Gruyter.
Hescher, Achim. (2018). Teaching graphic novels: the making of history/-ies in Jason Lutes' *Berlin* books. Anglistik 29 (1): 69–86.
Køhlert, Frederik Byrn. (2015). Working it through: trauma and autobiography in Phoebe Gloeckner's *a child's life* and *The Diary of a Teenage Girl*. South Central Review 32 (3): 124–142.
Menu, Jean-Christophe. (2014). Stay off my patch. In: *The French Comics Theory Reader* (ed. Ann Miller and Bart Beaty), 327–332. Leuven, Belgium: Leuven University Press.
Micciche, Laura R. (2004) Seeing and reading incest: a study of Debbie Drechsler's "Daddy's Girl." Rhetoric Review 23 (1): 5–20.
Reckwitz, Andreas. (2017). *Die Gesellschaft der Singularitäten. Zum Strukturwandel der Moderne*. Berlin: Suhrkamp.
Round, Julia. (2010). "Is this a book?" DC vertigo and the redefinition of comics in the 1990s. *The Rise of the American Comics Artist: Creators and Contexts* (ed. Paul Williams and James Lyons), 14–30. Jackson: University Press of Mississippi.
Ware, Chris. (2012). *Building Stories*. London: Jonathan Cape.
Ware, Chris. (2019). *Rusty Brown*. New York: Pantheon Books.

FURTHER READING

Groensteen, Thierry. (2007). *The System of Comics*. Jackson: University Press of Mississippi.
Hatfield, Charles. (2005). *Alternative Comics: An Emerging Literature*. Jackson: University Press of Mississippi.
Miodrag, Hannah. (2013). *Comics and Language: Reimagining Critical Discourse on the Form*. Jackson: University Press of Mississippi.
Prorokova, Tatiana and Tal, Nimrod. (eds.). (2018). *Cultures of War in Graphic Novels: Violence, Trauma, and Memory*. New Brunswick, NJ: Rutgers University Press.

Gray, Amelia

JAMIE REDGATE
Independent scholar

Amelia Gray was born in 1982, and she therefore belongs to the first generation of writers who have had to build a career in spite of the Internet. In the postwar Program Era that preceded her, when MFA programs proliferated across the

United States, talented young writers already had to vie with a crippling lack of distinction. Now, in a new age of instantaneous, borderless access to all the world's online magazines, they have to stand out not just from a globe of other qualified writers but a head above the unprecedentedly endless sea of new and newer feeds that compete for their public's attention. This is a brand new and nearly impossible time, and Gray's career – which to date comprises an MFA at Texas State University in San Marcos, three story collections (*AM/PM* [2009], *Museum of the Weird* [2010], *Gutshot* [2015]), two novels (*THREATS* [2012], *Isadora* [2017]), and work for television (*Mr. Robot* [2017–2018], *Maniac* [2017]) – speaks to some of its major trends and troubles. Formally, Gray's stories and novels alike have the short, grotesque, attention-grabbing sensibility of the predominant genre in the age of Twitter: the "flash" fiction. What elevates her work above a lot of flash's superficial shock value, however, is that it is consistently and meaningfully about the body. Though Gray is less overtly concerned with literary parricide than some of her contemporaries, her evolving aesthetics of embodiment is an important example of the effort at the turn of the twenty-first century (variously called metamoderism, post-postmoderism, trans-postmodernism, etc.) to marry postmodernism's electric globalism with family and locality, its ironic disaffection with emotional depth, and its ontological uncertainty with renewed grand narratives about the material body and brain.

Gray's first collection of stories, *AM/PM*, was published by Featherproof Books in 2009, and comprises 120 miniscule "minutes," counting from AM:1 to 2:PM to AM:3, and so on. Though the formal constraint – a minute lasts no longer than one of Featherproof's small pages – means that each story is necessarily bare-boned, the strength of the collection is that it showcases Gray's experimental energy. For readers of her later work, stories here that play with fables, the epistolary form, or the Old Testament voice stand out especially. At this early stage we can also see the way Gray builds a premise by pulling at the threads of a trite idea (e.g. a woman finding her "perfect man") and stretching it to its absurdly literal conclusion (the couple physically conjoining). Recurring characters are spaced so widely apart, however, that it's difficult to pin down any overarching narrative or consistent characterization, so *AM/PM* reads rather like a notebook for Gray's future, and more depthful, work.

The *Museum of the Weird*, published the following year by Fiction Collective 2, comprises twenty-four odd exhibits, which similarly give shape to a neurosis or flesh out a surreal premise: a plate of hair served at a restaurant embodies all the odd feelings on a first date; an anxious woman begins to lose weight because her habit of chewing her hair literally clogs her stomach like a shower drain; corpse-hungry birds hover over the characters' heads like a picture of human mortality. There is a clear evolution from *AM/PM* to Gray's second collection, not least because in *Museum* Gray revisits and reworks her old stories (something she'll continue to do throughout her career). *AM/PM*'s "114:PM," for instance, is a story about a mysterious monolith that burns a child who touches its surface, and on which is inscribed the searing truism: "EVERYTHING MUST EVENTUALLY SINK." This story grows into "The Cube" in *Museum*. Though it begins almost identically, the story itself works better at a longer length because the line is more than just a punchy, enigmatic conclusion. Space is given to the families of the children who discover it to react, to try to learn to live with this unwavering commandment and the truth that they, and their children, and their children's children, will all sink sometime into the ground around them. Indeed, the truth of the truism is only emphasized in this longer story because they have room to try to challenge it and necessarily fail. How could they succeed, in a collection defined by such relentless embodiment? Underneath all of Gray's strange premises there is always that atavistic fact: everything must necessarily sink because everything has weight.

Take, for instance, a story such as "Trip Advisory: The Boyhood Home of Former President Ronald Reagan." Like the work of George Saunders, Dave Eggers, or others in the McSweeney's vein (Gray first published "Trip Advisory" in *McSweeney's Internet Tendency*), this story puts its finger on our simulated unreality in a way that recalls Don DeLillo or Robert Coover's fiction a generation before, but Gray, like her contemporaries, is playing a different game. The story does not induce confusion and cynicism so much as take these things as its impossible starting point, its inclusive second-person narration speaking to a certain millennial knowingness: it knows that we know that it knows that "Of course, the wall was actually not original, but completely restored" (2010, p. 56). The problem for writers at the millennium is in trying to get beyond that, in finding something heavier than all the surfaces at play.

Gray's third collection was published in 2015 by Farrar, Straus and Giroux, who finally embraced the obvious pun and used a *Gray's Anatomy*-esque image for the cover: a diagrammatic painting by Fernando Vicente of a woman with the innards of her neck exposed, the mirror image of an illustration by H.V. Carter in the original *Gray's Anatomy*. The anatomic image is a good metaphor for Gray's style generally, and the way her finite, carefully controlled stories focus in on a body part or mutation, blowing them up to full view and fleshing out the details. It also speaks to Gray's focus, particularly in this collection, on the ancientness of our anatomies. Gray played at times with myth and fable in her two earlier collections (she credits Aesop as a key influence), and while Gutshot's "Labyrinth," for instance, is similarly amusing, a modern take on the myth set at a "Pumpkin Jamboree," at its heart – literally, at the center of the labyrinth – is something more fundamental and timeless: "a divot in the dirt the size of a man ... the hole that seemed to have been dug to suit me" (2015, pp. 103–104).

Domestic spaces throughout Gray's work are shaped by this tension between the grandly mythic and the everyday. In *Gutshot*, a couple kidnaps a child to play "House Heart," a game in which the child's role is to "embody the house." In "The Heart," a family hacks away at an enormous whale's heart that has appeared in their living room, a meaty metaphor for their grief after the loss of the family's mother (the way it blocks the TV, the way they dispose of the meat behind the house without making a show of it for the neighbors). In *Museum*'s "The Vanished," the house itself is a character, containing the couple inside it the way a body houses a soul. When one half of that couple disappears, the loss manifests itself in the house's own physical decay like a modern day "Fall of the House of Usher." Gray's domestic horror stories suggest she should be seen as the latest in a line of Gothic writers (through Edgar Allan Poe, Charlotte Perkins Gilman, and Flannery O'Connor) whose work has a uniquely American problem: what is to be the source of ancient, timeless horrors in a country without a history?

"The Vanished" would become the blueprint for Gray's first novel, THREATS. Published by Farrar, Straus and Giroux (who published her next two books), and a finalist for the PEN/Faulkner Award for Fiction in 2013, THREATS is an anatomy of a man's grief in the aftermath of his wife's mysterious death. Gray's first sustained work, THREATS reads like the culmination of the experimentation in her stories: a perfect marriage of form and content, where her spare style, grotesque surrealism, and short, flash-length chapters become the connective tissue of a long-form story about the decay of home and body and the disfiguring effect of grief.

In *THREATS* the couple are called David and Frances, and they have just the sort of jobs Gray likes to use in her stories: David is a dentist who deals in disgusting teeth, while Frances is an "aesthetician, specializing in pore extraction and deep chemical peels" (2012, p. 21). Here though, in this longer form, there is much more room for Gray to put her research to work in service of larger themes, such as the great human "war against decay" which David is not winning. As the life David built with his wife fades into memory, his grief and loss are literalized. His hair grows long and unkempt, insects and dust flourish in his home, while he sleeps on library books about grief which he cannot read but only touch, dumbly. The freakshow mentality of Gray's earlier work – collections of grotesqueries and mutations – takes on a different sort of seriousness here, and though *THREATS* keeps pushing at the boundaries of realism, the decay is so central and so well fleshed out that it always feels grounded, if not in a completely recognizable real world then at least in David's emotional reality.

This is the reality of the body, not of words and abstraction. Descriptions of David's actions are always tight, controlled, but they are like descriptions of a toddler who cannot articulate their own feelings: he holds a battery in his mouth as if to understand it, or rubs his wife's old products over his body. Detective Chico, who is investigating Frances's death, is a model of objectivity and reason (his name is, tellingly, an anagram of "choice") but one who makes little sense to David because David's shattered world is not reasonable. The novel's seventy-seven short chapters, many of them only a few pages long, don't tie together in a neat chronological line but leave the reader as disjointed as the novel's subject. We have to try to piece together the mystery of Frances's death by following the only thread we can: the little written threats that David keeps discovering, and which give the novel its title.

Those threats are curiously banal. "I WILL CROSS-STITCH AN IMAGE OF YOUR FUTURE HOME BURNING," reads one. "I WILL CREATE A SET OF WORK RESPONSIBILITIES THAT ARE INCONVENIENT AND DEMEANING TO YOU." David finds them around the house, on the back of a picture frame, while he's checking the mail, or on the back of a receipt. The alarmed upper case emphasizes their impotence: theirs is an inert, domestic conspiracy. But though there's not one clear answer that ties the puzzle together – Gray walks a tightrope between intensive detail and persistent mystery – neither is there the crippling meaninglessness that results from the postmodern conspiracy. The threats carry an emotional weight for the reader because they give us a glimpse into the logic of David's mysterious inner life.

David begins to collect them when he suspects that it was his wife who wrote them (whether before or after her death is unclear). They mean something to him though he cannot explain what. For the reader, the answer is rooted in feeling. "The Vanished," the precursor to *THREATS*, ends when the woman runs outside to see a young couple "eating" big sticky handfuls of "love": "That's poison!" she screams. *THREATS*'s threats are the poison that grows on something good, a literal manifestation of the horror that everyday life holds for the grieving. If you are alive at all, if you exist in a body, if you love someone and make a home with them, then existence is ultimately unsafe for you. The great gift of the novel is that what David is going through is explained in detail and yet never explained at all. It's up to us to do the emotional work of deciphering his grief, to find in the novel the love that is killing him. The novel's emotional core is, like Fran herself, missing, but we feel its weight all the more for having to excavate it ourselves.

THREATS is the culmination of Gray's domestic stories and the highpoint of her unique brand of horror. Her second novel, *Isadora*, a book about children and creation, pulls together a different thread of metafictional stories that also runs through her work. *Museum*, for instance, opens with "Babies," a story about a speaker who gives "birth overnight," and the setup invites the reader to approach the collection as if it contains Gray's own progeny: "The next morning, there was another baby. And another" (2010, p. 12). One of those babies, "Diary of the Blockage," tells the fourteen-day tale of a gross lump growing at a writer's throat. The blockage's slow emergence is the literal embodiment of a writer finding her voice, and the story ends, significantly, in a difficult labor, after which the object becomes distinct from the author-mother that gestated it. In *Gutshot*'s "Viscera," Gray tells a similar story about "this page" we are reading and "touching with our hands," a page that was produced in a plant somewhere by a "man plagued with a skin infection." The story insists on the tangible connection between the reader and the material page, because to read it is to necessarily become infected with the page-maker's "particulate matter." Gray's metafictions mark a stark departure from postmodern formulations of the Death of the Author and the Text as a tissue of citations. Instead, they recall David Foster Wallace's description in 1998 of the "parturition from head to page" in his essay, "The Nature of the Fun" (2012), or William Gass's (1986) critique of Barthes in *Habitations of the Word*: at the turn of the millennium, the text is reimagined as material, reader-touching tissue, not as critical abstraction.

As both historical fiction and invented biography, *Isadora* is all about the distance between creator and creation, writer and subject, art and reality. As someone who embodied all the energies of her era, Isadora Duncan has become something of a shifting symbol for succeeding generations. In John Dos Passos's masterpiece the *USA Trilogy* (1937), Isadora is the fitting subject of "Art and Isadora," one of a number of historical vignettes that describe the lives of Henry Ford, Frank Lloyd Wright, and other engineers of modernism (Dos Passos 2001). Passos's high speed biography ends with Duncan's sensational death (scarf, car wheel), which works in context as a portent of the darkness towards which America was racing in the early twentieth century. To Sylvia Plath (1981) a generation later, "Isadora's scarves" stood, in "Fever 103°," for the lurid atmosphere in a world whose center was not holding.

In Gray's story, Duncan is liberated from the brute facts of her death – the "scarf as red as the blood between us" gets only a brief nod in the novel (2017, p. 378) – to focus instead, as in *THREATS*, on the drawn-out experience of loss and grief that Duncan suffered during the fractured year and a half after the death of her two young children in 1913. There is therefore a continuity between Gray's first and second novels, though *Isadora* shows the extent to which her scope has broadened. In Isadora herself, Gray clearly found the right subject to embody not just the darkness in her work but the light: Duncan is a symbol of loss and mortality it's true, but she's also the face of joyous embodiment, of movement and creation, modernity and myth, and the love that is "known without lesson." Unlike David, who decayed because his life came to a standstill, Isadora's life is a fight to keep moving. Unlike *THREATS*, *Isadora*'s short chapters are not tied to one strange perspective but a way for Gray to move fluidly between settings and perspectives other than Duncan's own relentless point of view. The novel is less claustrophobic as a result, and it showcases Gray's ability to create a sense of period and place, to manage a larger cast, and her gift for curt dialogue and leaden argument.

In some ways *Isadora* is a riskier novel. It lacks what little narrative momentum the strange threats gave to *THREATS*, and its central character can be so insufferable at times it tries one's patience. It is to Gray's credit, however, that Duncan feels entirely real. The novel's clear affection for her is coupled with an understanding of her limitations, and there is relief to be had as a reader in the cast of supporting characters who try to bear Duncan up like a crumbling column. At the same time, though Duncan feels like a fully fleshed out character, Gray unapologetically writes her as she likes: Duncan ultimately feels like one of Gray's creations. The point is not, however, that historical narratives are ultimately fallible, or that history is in some way relative. The novel is less about itself as a history-making exercise and more about the universal truths that underlie any good story: truths about feeling over fact, about grief and loss and parenthood instead of postmodern concerns about objectivity. *Isadora* is an altogether more complete picture of loss.

Gray's treatment of Duncan at this point in her career hints at a certain self-consciousness about periodization and the legacy of her own work. Isadora is ever aware of her place at the "forefront of an era," and Gray's novel only confirms it (2017, p. viii). Where a different novel might have ended with Duncan's untimely death, Gray preserves her subject on the horizon and gives her the sort of triumphant conclusion one only gets in hindsight. In generations to come, it will be up to others to determine Gray's own legacy. At times in *Isadora* she doesn't seem very hopeful. As she puts it: "What flimsy thing is art in a world where children die?" (p. 367) She'll have to wait and see.

SEE ALSO: After Postmodernism; Biological Fictions; Chick Lit and the New Domesticity; Illness and Disability Narratives; Program Culture; Trauma and Fiction

REFERENCES

Dos Passos, John. (2001). *U.S.A.* London: Penguin Books; 1st ed. 1937.
Gass, William H. (1986). *Habitations of the Word: Essays*. New York: Touchstone.
Gray, Amelia. (2009). *AM/PM*. Chicago: Featherproof Books.
Gray, Amelia. (2010). *Museum of the Weird*. Tuscaloosa, AL: FC2.
Gray, Amelia. (2012). *THREATS*. New York: Farrar, Straus and Giroux.
Gray, Amelia. (2015). *Gutshot: Stories*. New York: Farrar, Straus and Giroux.
Gray, Amelia. (2017). *Isadora*. New York: Farrar, Straus and Giroux.
Plath, Sylvia. (1981). *Collected Poems* (ed. Ted Hughes). London: Faber and Faber.
Wallace, David Foster. (2012). *Both Flesh and Not*. London: Hamish Hamilton.

FURTHER READING

Boxall, Peter. (2013). *Twenty-First-Century Fiction: A Critical Introduction*. Cambridge: Cambridge University Press.
Burn, Stephen J. (2008). *Jonathan Franzen at the End of Postmodernism*. London: Continuum.
Vermeulen, Timotheus and Akker, Robin van den. (2010). Notes on Metamodernism. *Journal of Aesthetics & Culture* 2: 1–10.

Groff, Lauren

MARK WEST
University of Glasgow, UK

Lauren Groff was born in 1978 in Cooperstown, New York, which became the subject of her first novel *The Monsters of Templeton* (2008). She attended Amherst College and gained an MFA from the University of Wisconsin-Madison, and now lives and works in Gainesville, Florida, a state which inspired her most recent short story collection, *Florida* (2018). Over the course of her career she has developed a distinctive poetic style which is highly attuned to sensory experience, particularly touch and smell; concerns with history, politics, and feminism have increasingly come to the forefront of her work. Groff's fiction is yet to attract serious academic attention, but she has twice been nominated for the National Book Award for Fiction and in 2017 was named one of Granta's Best Young American Novelists. President Barack Obama chose her 2015 novel *Fates and Furies* as his favorite of the year.

The Monsters of Templeton, like many first novels, draws its subject matter from the author's experience. The novel is set in Templeton, a "slantwise version" (2008, p. ix) of Cooperstown, named after the writer James Fenimore Cooper. Templeton, though, is not solely Groff's invention; the version of it in *The Monsters of Templeton* is also a slanted version of Cooper's own fictional version of Cooperstown in *The Pioneers* (1823), named, also, Templeton. Groff explains this intertextual relationship in an author's note, suggesting that "fiction is the craft of telling truth through lies" (2008, p. x). This signals the novel's debt to postmodern theorizations of the relationship between history and fiction by Linda Hutcheon and Hayden White, a debt that is also seen in *The Monsters of Templeton*'s discussions of fiction both distorting and forming history. *Monsters* might be considered, then, an example of "historiographical metafiction" (Hutcheon 1988, p. ix).

Monsters is Groff's most postmodern work, and this is borne out in its structure and its execution. The novel's plot centers on the protagonist Willie Upton's search for her real father – who is, her mother hints, a resident of Templeton. The novel is told through alternating chapters narrated by Willie and by various members of her extended family, dating back to the town's foundation in the eighteenth century. These sections allow Groff to attempt different narrative styles, including stream of consciousness, collective narration, and epistolary narrative, as well as adopting registers and tones that evoke the lower- and upper-class positions of town residents over two centuries. Interspersed with these are photographs and diagrams of Willie's family tree, the latter annotated with self-reflexive comments as Willie learns more about her family. Willie's voice is ironic and quirky, something notably absent from the rest of Groff's work, which develops a more serious, poetic tone.

The characteristics of *The Monsters of Templeton*, then, make Groff's debut a rather *un*characteristic book in the context of her oeuvre. Her later work largely does away with metafiction and with the insertion of material like the family trees and photographs that feature here. Nevertheless, *The Monsters of Templeton* does establish some of Groff's preoccupations. There is, for example, a concern with America's bloody history, though it is rather crudely drawn in chapters narrated by Native Americans; in the strand of the plot that narrates Willie's mother Vi's involvement in the counterculture, Groff rehearses her interest in the 1960s that is at the heart of her novel *Arcadia* (2012); and there are intimations of apocalypse glimpsed in concerns about melting glaciers and flu jumping species barriers that are more thoroughly examined both in *Arcadia*'s conjuring of a speculative future and in *Florida*'s anxiety about global warming. Aptly, the imagistic style of her later work comes into *The Monsters of Templeton* in the final chapter, which imagines the thoughts of a Loch Ness-type monster discovered in Templeton's lake in italicized, imagistic, near-poetry.

The short story collection *Delicate Edible Birds* (2009) is a hinge between the early and middle phases of Groff's career thus far. The milieu of many of its stories – small towns, with bookish girls and women acting as narrators or focalizers – has traces of the Templeton of her first novel and its protagonist-narrator, Willie. Indeed, the collection's first story, "Lucky Chow Fun," is not only set in Templeton, but features as its narrator a young woman who is "filled with longing, which I tried to sate with the books of myth and folklore that I was devouring by the dozens" (2009, p. 2), and, like *The Monsters of Templeton*, concerns the uncovering of town secrets.

Delicate Edible Birds is notable for the emergence of Groff's trademark prose style, characterized by heightened, poetically described sensory experience. Groff often identifies characters by their smell – in "L. Debard and Aliette," the former is struck by the way the latter "smells of chlorine, lilacs, warm milk" (2009, p. 54) – and is particularly attuned to touch. This comes to the fore in "L. Debard and Aliette" and "Lucky Chow Fun" in the form of passages on swimming, something that was also the subject of a stand-alone hybrid story-essay Groff published in *Ploughshares*. She describes "feeling the thrust and slide of my body through the water" (2009, p. 5) and "the splash and the churn, the rhythm of the stroke, the gulps of water in the gutter, the powerful shock of the dive, and a wake like smoke, trailing" (p. 54). This collection also displays Groff's fascination with charting family and romantic relationships, something which structures *The Monsters of Templeton*, *Arcadia*, and *Fates and Furies* (2015). Here, "L. DeBard and Aliette" (which features the 1918 flu epidemic which also appears in *Arcadia*), "Blythe," and "Sir Fleeting" all tell their stories over wide spans of time, following their characters for significant proportions of their lives, charting their changing relationships in detail.

Arcadia traces the story of a commune from its origins in the 1960s counterculture into a speculative future beset by the twin threats of a flu pandemic and accelerated climate change. Told in four sections, *Arcadia* is narrated in the third-person and focalized through Bit, who is a young boy in the first section and a middle-aged man in the last. Like *The Monsters of Templeton*, *Arcadia* incorporates different narrative forms and genres. Its first section draws on research Groff did into Utopian communities and the counterculture to offer an account of the founding of the eponymous commune, something that may be characterized as a kind of historical fiction, but one less playful than *The Monsters of Templeton*. Here there is a greater emphasis on the competing conceptions of America present in the commune and outside, as well as between members of the commune, an impression furthered by the second section's examination of the effect of Reagan's presidency on the commune and countercultural ideas more broadly. *Arcadia*'s third section resembles a contemporary realist novel, placing Bit into a New York dealing with the twin traumas of 9/11 and the 2008 financial crash. Its fourth section combines the threats of a flu pandemic and accelerated global warming to reconsider the counterculture's environmentalism from a twenty-first-century perspective. In these dual apocalypses, *Arcadia* might be read alongside recent speculative fiction by other writers of Groff's generation, such as Emily St. John Mandel's *Station Eleven* (2014) and her fellow Granta Young American Novelist Claire Vaye Watkins's *Gold Fame Citrus* (2015).

Arcadia is different from *The Monsters of Templeton* in its use of literary forms and styles. In the author's note at the beginning of her first novel, and in its rather labored metafictional asides, *The Monsters of Templeton* is more direct and self-conscious in its literary allusions and play. Groff is working out what writing can do, as well as what she can (and cannot) do as a writer. As a result, it is a novel much more directly about fiction-writing, and its postmodern characteristics give this a formal impetus. *Arcadia*'s less explicit concern with literary tricks – there is, for example, no metafiction in it – is testament to Groff's development as a writer. *The Monsters of Templeton* shows off; *Arcadia*'s confidence is better founded. In the former, the multiple styles and voices weren't different enough to achieve real polyphony. In *Arcadia*, Groff marries the commune's desire to live in harmony with the land with Bit's intense sensory apprehension of the world around him. The result is a more sustained development of the style that emerged in *Delicate Edible Birds*. This poetic style works as an agent of coherence, allowing Groff to incorporate the concerns of historical, realist, and speculative fiction into a work that – on a stylistic level at least – maintains unity. This caveat is warranted because such unity is constantly under threat in *Arcadia* by the unsettling temporal effects of those different fictional perspectives: analysis of what once *was* (as seen in historical fiction) coinciding with imagining what *might be* (as seen in speculative fiction).

Fates and Furies gained Groff the kind of attention her work had not previously attracted, being shortlisted for the National Book Award. The acclaim probably overstated the book's quality – both *Arcadia* and *Florida* are more coherent books. *Fates and Furies* does, though, bring together key Groff interests that were dispersed across previous books, and begins to develop a more direct interest in and representation of women's experience that characterizes her more recent work. The novel tells the story of the marriage of Lancelot ("Lotto") and Mathilde, he a successful playwright, she his secret ghostwriter. It is divided into two halves (named "Fates" and "Furies"), one focalized through Lotto, the other through Mathilde. While it narrates the same series of events, we learn things from Mathilde we do not from Lotto, including her significant, unheralded role in his success. This narrative structure is punctuated by a kind of Greek chorus which interjects to comment on and correct the narratives told by Lotto and Mathilde; its perspective is beyond time, able to see Lotto and Mathilde's futures when they cannot. *Fates and Furies* retains the long time spans present in *Arcadia* and many of the stories in *Delicate Edible Birds* (the marriage lasts twenty-four years, only ending with Lotto's premature death); it hones the promiscuous perspectives of *Monsters* into the two clear focuses of Lotto and Mathilde; and in its interest in the epic minutiae of a relationship, it has clear echoes of "L. DeBard and Aliette" from *Delicate Edible Birds*.

Groff signaled her interest in writing the neglected experiences of women in the historical oppressions faced by those who voice chapters of *The Monsters of Templeton*, in "Blythe's" focus on the difficult relationship between a woman and her best friend, and in *Arcadia*'s treatment of Bit's mother Hannah's depression. But in her debut, these stories were subservient to Willie's quest for her father, and in *Arcadia*, Hannah's depression is only represented through the eyes of her son, Bit. In *Fates and Furies*, though, through Mathilde's story, Groff makes women's experience more central. The book is balanced between the elevated position of the chorus and the daily events of a marriage. Because Mathilde's story comes after Lotto's, there is a sense that hers corrects his, an impression bolstered by her revelations about the way she would touch up Lotto's work while he slept. Groff applies this sense of correction not just to Lotto and Mathilde's marriage, but also to more universalized narratives of marriage. Groff examines what it means to be a wife, undercutting its mythologies with its realities. As Groff writes, "wives, as we all know, are invisible" (2015, p. 244).

Also nominated for the National Book Award, the short story collection *Florida* marks a new phase in Groff's development as a writer. While she is still keenly alert to the natural world, the wonder that marked Bit's engagement with animals and plants in *Arcadia* is here tempered with a darker, more violent edge. In *Florida*, snakes feature in almost every story and their sinister iconography (Groff draws on the Adam and Eve story) helps to create a sense of Florida as "an Eden of dangerous things" (2018, p. 160) where there is always "a sense of something lurking" (p. 163). Groff uses this foreboding that snakes inspire to highlight the reason for the book's tempering of wonder at the natural world: the looming threat of climate change. This is implied in stories like "Eyewall" which features a hurricane that dispenses reckoning. Elsewhere it is directly confronted by Groff's characters who find in news reports "the disaster of the world, the glaciers dying like living creatures, the great Pacific trash gyre, the hundreds of unrecorded deaths of species, millennia snuffed out as if they were not precious" (p. 7). This litany of disaster recalls *Arcadia*'s description of "poor half-drowned Venice with its overwhelmed pumps. Poor Micronesia, poor Tuvalu, lost Atlantises" (2012, p. 221), but what is notable here is the setting: in *Arcadia* this description of planetary decay is set in a speculative future, in *Florida* it is here already, happening now.

Florida's world of dread takes its toll. The focus on women's experience seen in *Fates and Furies* is retained in *Florida*, particularly in the four stories in the collection that feature an unnamed woman who shares a number of biographical details with Groff herself: she is a writer, she lives in Gainesville, Florida, and she has two sons. These stories might be read in the context of contemporary autofiction, which blurs the lines between fiction and life, such as Sheila Heti's *How Should a Person Be?* (2012) – which is subtitled "A Novel From Life," Rachel Cusk's *Outline* (2014), *Transit* (2017), and *Kudos* (2018), and Olivia Laing's *Crudo* (2018). The first story to feature this woman – also the first story in the book – "Ghosts and Empties" begins with this line: "I have become a woman who yells" (Groff 2018, p. 1). The news' recitations of degradation are added to a list of things she is afraid of: global warming, sinkholes, her responsibility to her children, the dissolution of her marriage. She is so angry, so pent up, that her friends are abandoning her. In "Flower Hunters," the same character finds that after the umpteenth panicked late-night phone call, her friend "doesn't want to be her best friend anymore" because she "just need[s] to take a break" (p. 156). She reflects: "She would take a break from herself, too, but she doesn't have that option" (p. 168).

It's not just the degradation of the planet that fills Groff's alter ego with dread. There is a commitment to depicting the frustration of female experience in *Florida*, from the limitations of husbands and the demands of children to mothers looking for their past selves, and her vow to reject all gender expectations. In this character we read an echo of the bookish narrators of her early work (in one story she forgets to make Halloween costumes for her sons because she's been immersed in the work of an eighteenth-century naturalist), but this character has none of cheeriness of Willie in *The Monsters of Templeton*. Groff connects this sense of building anger with the pressure of Florida's humidity in her alter ego's desire to "use what's building up" (2018, p. 6), and we can read *Florida*'s stories as Groff's response to that desire, the "putting to use" of her anger through the description of the psychic toll of living in Trump's America. While there is no direct mention of Trump, the book alludes to "the fall . . . the same time other terrible things happened in the world at large" (p. 205), and the America his election helped to create is registered in phrases that describe "the new venom that has entered the world, a venom that somehow acts only on men, hardening what had once been bad thoughts into new, worse actions" (p. 205). Elsewhere there is an unmistakable reference to Trump's 2017 appointment of Scott Pruitt as the Administrator of the Environmental Protection Agency despite – or because of – Pruitt's documented desire to roll back environmental regulations. In fact, Trump's elevation to the White House gives *Florida* the impetus of an event that coalesces all of Groff's preoccupations. In addition to his encouragement of male "venom" and his disregard for the planet, Trump's election seems, for Groff, to serve as a reminder that the bloody history of America – genocide, colonialism, and slavery – is never far away. Her alter ego worries that her son's Halloween costume connotes more the Ku Klux Klan than a ghost – "a white boy in a white sheet" – because, after all, "Florida [is] still the Deep South" (p. 157).

Despite *Arcadia*'s themes, then, *Florida* is the most political of Groff's books. As well as gathering together Groff's fascination with climate breakdown and with women's experience, *Florida* also showcases Groff's skill in turning immediate reality into fiction. In this, we might see a return to *The Monsters of Templeton*'s interest in the possibilities of fiction and its relationship to the world.

SEE ALSO: Contemporary Regionalisms; The Culture Wars; Ecocriticism and Environmental Fiction

REFERENCES

Groff, Lauren. (2008). *The Monsters of Templeton*. New York: Hyperion.
Groff, Lauren. (2009). *Delicate Edible Birds*. New York: Hyperion.
Groff, Lauren. (2012). *Arcadia*. New York: Hyperion.
Groff, Lauren. (2015). *Fates and Furies*. New York: Riverhead Books.
Groff, Lauren. (2018). *Florida*. New York: Random House.
Hutcheon, Linda. (1988). *A Poetics of Postmodernism: History, Theory, Fiction*. London: Routledge.

FURTHER READING

DeRosa, Aaron. (2014). The end of futurity: proleptic nostalgia and the war on terror. *Literature Interpretation Theory* 25: 88–107.
Herman, David. (2018). *Narratology Beyond the Human: Storytelling and Animal Life*. New York: Oxford University Press.
Lee, Jonathan. (2013). American utopia. *Guernica* (March 15, 2103). https://www.guernicamag.com/american-utopia/
Ryan, Maureen. (2013). Cracks in the system: children in contemporary narratives about the 1960s in America. *War, Literature, and the Arts* 25 (1): 1–16.
Trott, Stephanie. (2015). The Rumpus interview with Lauren Groff. *The Rumpus* (October 14, 2015). https://therumpus.net/2015/10/the-rumpus-interview-with-lauren-groff-2/

H

Hagedorn, Jessica

DAVID SIGLOS, JR.
University of California, Riverside, USA

A poet, novelist, playwright, musician, and editor, Jessica Hagedorn was born in Manila, Philippines, in 1949 and moved to San Francisco, in the United States, with her mother and brother at the age of 14. Some of Hagedorn's notable works – which range from novels to collections of poetry, anthologies of fiction, and plays, among other genres – include *Dogeaters* (1990), *Pet Food and Tropical Apparitions* (1975), *The Gangster of Love* (1996), *Dream Jungle* (2003), *Danger and Beauty* (1993), *Dangerous Music* (1975), *Charlie Chan is Dead: An Anthology of Contemporary Asian American Fiction* (1993), *Manila Noir* (2013), and *Dogeaters* (stage adaptation). She was also a member of a musical band called *The Gangster Choir*. Her first novel, *Dogeaters*, published in 1990, was received with critical acclaim, earned her an American Book Award from the Before Columbus Foundation, and was a finalist for the National Book Award. Precisely because of the different forms of media that Hagedorn uses in her artistic expression, each work not surprisingly uses mixed media. Another important feature of Hagedorn's works is the volatility of her use of language, which addresses the complexity and variation of Philippine languages. This summary of Jessica Hagedorn's works and artistic/political career is not an authoritative claim on "the life of an artist" but instead aims to foreground the historical, political, and personal contexts around which her works developed, including a focus on the unique colonial and postcolonial relationship between the Philippines and the United States, which reverberates throughout Hagedorn's works.

Philippine colonial history began with Spanish occupation in the early sixteenth century, which ran for over 300 years and ended after the Spanish–American War when Spain sold the Philippines to the United States through the Treaty of Paris in 1898. Intentionally erased from most of American and Filipino history and imagination was the brutal massacre by the American military of Filipino revolutionaries, mostly farm workers who resisted another colonial rule – historical accounts of Filipino casualties range from 200,000 to 600,000 (Constantino and Constantino 2008, p. 245). Apart from military activity and violence, American colonial technology also included a policy of "Benevolent Assimilation," which included a massive educational program that would institutionalize the use of English in the Philippines. American education became

---

The Encyclopedia of Contemporary American Fiction 1980–2020, First Edition. Edited by Patrick O'Donnell, Stephen J. Burn, and Lesley Larkin.
© 2022 John Wiley & Sons Ltd. Published 2022 by John Wiley & Sons Ltd.

(and still is) the standard form of education in the Philippines, and attached to it is a deceptive narrative of pity and benevolence. In other words, the United States needed the Filipinos to think like Americans and aspire to American life and culture in order to mediate resistance while also creating new consumers of American products and culture. The Philippines was captured by Japanese forces during World War II – a short yet very brutal occupation – and then recaptured again by the United States in 1945. Independence was granted to the Philippines by the United States in 1946. However, as a result of the colonial technologies implemented in almost half a century of American rule – public education, government system, medical training, military and police force – the Philippine post-colony became fertile ground for the expansion of capitalism and the global economy. I refer to the Philippines as a "post-colony" not only to account for its colonial history prior to independence but also to investigate and contest the remaining legacies of colonialism. American consumer and media culture would remain ubiquitous in the country, and Filipinos would desire more than anything that which was "Made in America."

Part of the critical acclaim of *Dogeaters* is for its ability to portray such a complex and chaotic history as well as the spread of American consumer and media culture in the Philippines. The entire novel is bombarded on the surface not only with American products, such as "Libby's succotash, Del Monte Deluxe Asparagus Spears," "Hunt's catsup," "French's mustard," "Kraft mayonnaise," "Jiffy Peanut Butter," "Velveeta," and "Jell-O," but also with American advertisements, Hollywood films, and movie stars (Hagedorn 1990, p. 234). Reverberating under this commercial surface are the anxieties and violence inflicted on Filipino characters. One of the most haunting scenes in the novel includes the torture of Daisy Avila – a Filipino beauty queen turned revolutionary – by a military general and his men, narrated only parenthetically within a radio drama and an ad for "TruCola" soft drink (p. 211). While "Colonel Jesus de Jesus . . . assaults her for so long and with such force, Daisy prays silently to pass out. . .[and] the other men cracked jokes, awaiting their turn" (p. 215). All of this is happening while a TruCola jingle plays on the background on the radio:

> Ice-cold Trucola!
> *Sa-sa-sarap ang* TruCola
> De-de-Oh! Delicious!
> De-de-Oh! Delicious!
>
> (1990, p. 215)

By juxtaposing media and commodity culture with military violence, Hagedorn highlights the dark side of the American colonial legacy. Through the use of military force, consumer culture not only perpetuates labor exploitation and violence against Filipinos but also institutionalizes them.

Jessica Hagedorn's works also reflect the feelings of exile and strangeness that Filipinos experience both in the Philippines and in the American diaspora. In her autobiographical novel *The Gangster of Love*, Hagedorn switches her setting from the homeland, the Philippines, to the dreamland, the United States. The narrative structure of *The Gangster of Love* is simpler than that of *Dogeaters*. The year Jimi Hendrix died, the protagonist, Raquel "Rocky" Rivera, is brought to the United States by her socialite mother, along with Rocky's brother Voltaire. While in San Francisco, Rocky befriends Elvis Chang, who becomes her lover and band partner. Their band is called "The Gangster of Love." She eventually moves to New York to pursue a music career; there she meets Jake Montano, with whom she has a child but with whom she also cannot make herself fall in love. While in New York, Rocky resonates with marginalized artists and countercultural movements, and cannot keep a proper nine-to-five job given her subversive attitude. The death of her mother while Rocky is raising her own daughter becomes a turning point in Rocky's life. The novel concludes with her return to Manila to visit her dying father. Philippine studies critic Epifanio San Juan, Jr. has posed a critical question about the novel's ending: "Does the ending imply a return of the 'prodigal' daughter, a reconciliation, a bridging of the gap between the homeland that had just witnessed the turmoil of the February 1986 uprising against the US-backed Marcos dictatorship and the metropolitan power that offered a refuge to the despot in Hawaii?" (1998, p. 112). San Juan refuses to read the ending as simply reconciliatory because that would mean a possible *forgetting* of the violence committed throughout the US–Philippine relation. Instead of a narrative of reconciliation, *The Gangster of Love* might be better understood as a novel that thoughtfully navigates the desires and movements of Filipinos, and the varying points of view highlighted throughout that movement. As the only American post-colony in Asia, one of the unique qualities of the Filipino immigrant narrative is that the space of "Filipino America" exists for Filipinos even before the act of migration.

One of Hagedorn's crucial contributions to Filipino American literature, and Asian American literary studies, is her complication of what Jeffrey Cabusao refers to as "becoming Filipino" narratives, which are interested more in the constitutive aspect of "becoming" – as a continuing process – than the desire for coherence and authenticity (2019, p. 11). By offering feminist and LGBT points of view, Hagedorn reveals the hybridity and heterogeneity of Filipino identity as shaped by colonial rule and resistance. Hagedorn has pointed out that some of the unanswerable questions that linger throughout her works have to do with questions about her own identity: "Who am I as an artist, as a woman?" (Bonetti 1995, p. 103). Her works of poetry are important in thinking about her use and manipulation of language throughout her fiction. Poetry for Hagedorn allows for the kind of rhythm, word play, and deconstruction of language necessary in the breaking down of identity. Her collection of poetry *Dangerous Music* (1975) grapples with issues of identity and femininity and the many ways in which they are tied not only to the patriarchy but also to neo/colonial subjugation. The poem "Cristina," for example, shares the conflicting voices of both the narrator and her mother: "auburn is a chic color / not too much red / if you overdo it / you look like a whore. . . / never admitting her love / my mother's anger is her real strength / like an aging tigress." The first "you," in "if you overdo it," sounds parental, while the second, in "you look like a whore," is almost violent. The narrator constantly mediates the tension between the mother's "love" and "anger" knowing that she does what she does because that is the only way she knows how to do it. But, on the surface of the poem are the sources of the mother's consumerist desire, a desire not for just any man but for a wealthy man "to chauffeur you around / in Mercedez-Benz sedans. . . / offering arabian stallions / and private helicopters." The narrator's conflict with and understanding of her maternal relationship is almost always linked to structures of economic power. That is, for writers of color like Jessica Hagedorn, the personal is inextricably interconnected with the political.

Hagedorn's work in advancing Filipino and Filipino American voices is also exemplified in her anthologies. The first anthology she edited was *Charlie Chan is Dead: An Anthology of Asian American Fiction*, published in 1993. The anthology included works by Filipino American and Asian American writers including Meena Alexander, Hisaye Yamamoto, Peter Bacho, Cynthia Kadohata, Amy Tan, and others. The anthology was revolutionary in terms of its expansion of the term "Asian American." However, it was received with harsh criticism by *The New York Times* reviewer Sven Birkerts for its alleged lack of ethnic coherence, including a criticism of the inclusion of Canadian resident writer Joy Kogawa, to which Hagedorn responds:

> Is Mr. Birkerts an immigration official or a literary critic? Should we all send in our passports and green cards for verification? I don't worry about Mr. Birkerts's own ethnicity, nor do I expect every writer to be to his taste. What I hope from any reviewer of "Charlie Chan Is Dead" is that he or she treat seriously the form and substance of our literature.
>
> (Hagedorn 1994)

Writers and activists like Jessica Hagedorn are continually expanding and promoting the complexity of the Asian American narrative, specifically by including works by Filipino American writers who have historically been excluded not only from the American canon but also from the Asian American canon. Hagedorn's works would then allow other Filipina feminist narratives to emerge. As Cabusao has pointed out, "the critical acclaim received by . . . Jessica Hagedorn paved the way for the emergence of other Filipino women's voices such as Gina Apostol, Cecilia Manguerra Brainard, M. Evelina Galang, Tess Uriza Holthe, Michelle Cruz Skinner, Eileen Tabios, Marianne Villanueva, and many others" (2019, p.11).

One of Hagedorn's latest works is the 2013 anthology of Filipino and Filipino American fiction called *Manila Noir*. Born in Manila herself, Hagedorn describes her relationship with the nation's capital in the anthology's introduction: "I like to think of Manila as a woman of mystery, the ultimate femme fatale. Sexy, complicated, and tainted by a dark and painful past, she's not to be trusted. And why should she be? She's been betrayed time and again, invaded, plundered, raped, and pillaged, colonized" (2013, p. 9). She also points out the resiliency of Manileños (the children of Manila), "their ability to bounce back – whether from the latest round of catastrophic flooding, the ashes of a twenty-year dictatorship, or a horrific world war" (p. 9). The economic disparity in Manila – wealthy guarded villages in some parts, squatter settlements in others, luxury malls and five-star hotels on one end, open garbage dumps on another – lends itself to noir fiction precisely because of the violence and corruption inherent in such a context. But what makes Hagedorn's collection of Manila noir fictions even richer is the unique Filipino cultural perspective that it foregrounds: "I found the noir genre flexible enough to accommodate the Filipino flair for the gothic and the world of the supernatural," she writes (p. 13). This anthology includes not only Filipino American writers such as R. Zamora Linmark, Gina Apostol, Sabina Murray, and Marianne Villanueva, but also Philippine-based writers who write in English, including F.H. Batacan, Budjette Tan, and Kajo Baldisimo. This anthology expands the scope of Filipino American literature by including Philippine anglophone literature, further demonstrating the intersectionality of Filipino America.

Another noticeable feature of Hagedorn's poetry and fiction is their extraordinary ability to be driven by language and characters rather than by actions. The multiple languages and mixed languages – Spanish, English, Tagalog, Bisaya, Taglish, and others – spoken throughout the Philippines are celebrated in Hagedorn's works. The use of *chismis*, or gossip, is also very much a part of her narrative style. When asked about how language and music operate in her literary works, Hagedorn says this: "Rhythm. And I think the love of language, the sheer word play. I love words. The sound of words, and puns. It's very Filipino too. Filipinos love puns and word plays and they love language, the intonations and nuances. They take it seriously.

They also play with it" (Bonetti 1995, p. 108). In her short story "Old Money," which is also included in *Manila Noir*, the section called "Chismis" expresses the absurdity of criminal life in Manila while blurring the line between fact and gossip. Recounting the kidnapping and murder of her husband Lolo Peping, Lola Conching recalls, "They were waiting for him on the highway . . . they shot Peping five or six times, then the driver. Then cut their throats. Overkill, *talaga*" (2013, p. 187). "Overkill" is a figurative expression for excessive action, but in the Filipino context it also takes on a literal meaning. The reader who understands both will find the use of the word at once (darkly) funny and pun-y.

Among the critical acclaim and achievements of Jessica Hagedorn's works are criticisms from scholars like Epifanio San Juan, Jr., who has described her work as "a gesture of stylized protest" (1993, p. 158). Hagedorn's critics often mention the privileged position of her main characters, which also reflects her own privileged position coming from an educated upper middle-class family, making her artistic expression more assimilative than subversive: "Addressed mainly to a cosmopolitan audience, Hagedorn's trendy work lends itself easily to consumer capitalism's drive to sublimate everything (dreams, eros, New People's Army, feminism, anarchist dissent) into self-gratifying spectacles," writes San Juan (1993, p. 158). When asked in another interview about her position on being a role model, or a token representative, for Filipino and Filipino American readers, she humbly responds, "it scares me . . . I'm only a human being . . . I am not speaking for the entire community whatever that community might be cuz I have a cross-over audience . . . this is what I think but I am not speaking for the culture" (UCTV 2008).

To understand the complexity of Filipino and Filipino American history and experience – to understand the stark class and economic disparity in the Philippines as product of colonial occupation – would be to understand the conflicting positions of San Juan and Hagedorn. What is common, however, in their critical perspectives is the role of American occupation of the Philippines in not only defining the desires of many Filipinos in the Philippines and in the United States but also in deciding for them what kinds of Filipino narratives are being told. That is, the experiences of the Filipino people as well as their narrative representations have been mostly defined by the cultures of their colonizers – through popular culture, literary culture, consumer culture; therefore, it is also through cultural intervention that these narratives can be revised. At stake in the expansion of the American literary canon to include writers of color like Jessica Hagedorn is the perpetual recovery and revision of American history that has been so wrapped up with colonial violence and erasure.

SEE ALSO: Apostol, Gina; Globalization; Queer and LGBT Fiction; Tan, Amy

REFERENCES

Bonetti, Kay. (1995). An Interview with Jessica Hagedorn. *The Missouri Review* 18 (1): 89–114.

Cabusao, Jeffrey Arellano. (2019). Filipino American literature. In: *Oxford Research Encyclopedia of Literature*. Oxford: Oxford University Press.

Constantino, Renato and Constantino, Letizia R. (2008). *A History of the Philippines: From the Spanish Colonization to the Second World War*. New York: Monthly Review Press.

Hagedorn, Jessica. (1975). *Dangerous Music*. San Francisco: Momo's Press.

Hagedorn, Jessica. (1990). *Dogeaters*. London: Penguin Books.

Hagedorn, Jessica. (ed.) (1993). *Charlie Chan Is Dead: An Anthology of Contemporary Asian American Fiction*. London: Penguin Books.

Hagedorn, Jessica. (1994). Charlie Chan is dead. *The New York Times* (January 23, 1994). https://www.nytimes.com/1994/01/23/books/l-charlie-chan-is-dead-941808.html (accessed July 6, 2021).

Hagedorn, Jessica. (1996). *The Gangster of Love*. London: Penguin Books.

Hagedorn, Jessica. (ed.) (2013). *Manila Noir*. Brooklyn, NY: Akashic Books.

San Juan, E., Jr. (1993). Filipino writing in the United States: reclaiming whose America? *Philippine Studies* 41 (2): 141–166.

San Juan, E., Jr. (1998). In pursuit of "The Gangster of Love." *Philippine Studies* 46 (1): 111–121.

UCTV (University of California Television). (2008). Slice the air with knives: Jessica Hagedorn. *YouTube*, reading and commentary by Jessica Hagedorn (January 31, 2008). https://www.youtube.com/watch?v=pR9TqvFJ67w (accessed July 6, 2021).

FURTHER READING

Balce, Nerissa. (2017). *Body Parts of Empire: Visual Abjection, Filipino Images, and the American Archive*. Manila: Ateneo De Manila University Press.

Hau, Caroline S. (2005). *On the Subject of the Nation: Filipino Writings from the Margins, 1981–2004*. Manila: Ateneo De Manila University Press.

Lowe, Lisa. (1996). *Immigrant Acts: On Asian American Cultural Politics*. Durham, NC: Duke University Press.

Schueller, Malini Johar. (2015). Negotiations of benevolent (colonial) tutelage in Carlos Bulosan. *Interventions* 18 (3): 422–449.

See, Sarita Echavez. (2009). *The Decolonized Eye: Filipino American Art and Performance*. Minnesota: University of Minnesota Press.

Hannah, Barry

MARK S. GRAYBILL
Widener University, USA

Born in the small town of Clinton, Mississippi, the novelist and short story writer Barry Hannah (1942–2010) was never away from the South for long. After earning degrees at Mississippi College and the University of Arkansas, he moved from one university writer-in-residence position to another throughout the 1970s and early 1980s and spent a year in Hollywood as a screenwriter, before settling permanently at the University of Mississippi in Oxford, a town put on the map by the most famous Southern writer of all, William Faulkner. Indeed, Hannah's literary identity is probably forever linked with Faulkner's, not only because of where they lived, but also because two of Hannah's several awards for fiction writing bear his predecessor's name: for his first novel, *Geronimo Rex* (1972), he won the William Faulkner Prize, and for his short story collection, *Bats Out of Hell* (1993), he was recognized with the Faulkner Award for Literature. The two invite other comparisons. Like Faulkner, Hannah struggled with alcoholism, and though he eventually quit drinking, he felt his habit had contributed considerably to his creativity. Perhaps the strongest connection between Faulkner and Hannah, however, is the experimental nature of their fiction. Where Faulkner was a Southern modernist known for novels that employ "interconnected mythic structures, symbols and richly figured language" that often "show a poignant nostalgia for lost rituals and traditions" (Lowe 2001), however, Hannah made his reputation primarily through texts that eschew plot and character development, contain episodes of shocking violence, feature a fragmented, laconic style, and generally reflect a more chaotic, self-reflexive, grimly humorous, and pessimistic sense of the postmodern South. In addition to *Geronimo Rex* and *Bats Out of Hell*, his major works include *Airships* (1978), winner of the Arnold Gingrich Award for short fiction; *Ray*, his breakthrough novel (1980); *Hey Jack!* (1987); *Never Die* (1991), a novelistic parody of the Western; the Pulitzer-nominated story collection *High Lonesome* (1996); and *Yonder Stands Your Orphan* (2001), his final novel.

Like any serious writer, Hannah did not like easy labels for his work. When asked about his being a Southern writer generally, or being influenced by Faulkner specifically, he often bristled – though in later years, he spoke positively of living in Oxford, where the bar for literary excellence was high thanks to its most famous literary son. And over time, Hannah consistently praised Faulkner for his ambition and relentless experimentation. He was less accepting of the postmodernist label. Asked about Ruth Weston's monograph, *Barry Hannah: Postmodern Romantic* (1998), he responded, "I don't know what post-anything means . . . I guess I am a Romantic" in *Conversations with Barry Hannah* (Thomas 2016, p. 199). Elsewhere, he calls himself "an elder modernist," and deems "*[p]ostmodern . . . a very flat, meaningless term*" (p. 229; italics in original). He elaborated on this line of thought when I interviewed him at Square Books in Oxford in 1997: "I don't have a postmodern focus, in fact, I don't even know what the term means, except 'after modernism.' It [just] gives people homework . . . I've never taken it as a theme: the fragmentation of existence. I've never taken as a theme the impossibility of story in our time. That doesn't interest me. I love stories. They're the only thing that makes sense to me" (Graybill 1997). Hannah's novels and stories themselves, however, provide plenty of compelling evidence of a postmodernist sensibility. As Eric Miles Williamson explains (with a touch of snark), postmodern works tend to be "self-referential," "goof around with the superimposition of form at the expense of content," "look funny on the page and are written after the modernists" (that is, after 1945 or so), "work actively against the notion of narrative progression," and feature plots "in which nothing happens, the characters are immobile, and nothing is resolved" (2008, p. 4). While not every Hannah work checks all of these boxes, many do. An important aspect of these postmodern practices is the impulse to demythologize some of the foundational tropes of American, and especially, Southern, culture. A trio of stories – "Nicodemus Bluff," "Evening of the Yarp," and "That Was Close, Ma" – from Hannah's longest work, *Bats Out of Hell*, illustrates this impulse in various (but overlapping) ways, as do perhaps his two most highly regarded novels, *Ray* and *Yonder Stands Your Orphan*.

As Weston observes, "Nicodemus Bluff" is clearly "a parody of that quintessential southern story of a boy's initiation into manhood" – the hunt – as dramatized in Faulkner's canonical tale, "The Bear" (1998, p. 24). In terms of plot, dialogue, and narrative voice, this is one of Hannah's most coherent, seemingly conventional, tales. The narrator, Harris Greeves, is a recovering drug addict who relates a deer-hunting trip he and his father, Gomar, took when he was 10 years old – an excursion during which he glimpses the mysterious, at times surreal, and ultimately violent goings-on in the adult world. Because of a rainstorm, the hunt itself never takes place. Instead, young Harris witnesses his father lose an intense chess match with the town banker, Mr. Pool, a man to whom he is already in deep debt. After Harris's father loses the match, Pool drags him into the rain and whips him – not with a pistol, but with a more obviously phallic "pepperoni stick" that makes "an awful fleshy thunk" on Gomar Greeves's head (Hannah 1993, p. 379). A week later, his father dies, apparently by suicide. While many reviewers and critics have claimed – not without justification – that Hannah's work glamorizes a retrograde hypermasculine ethos (and a corresponding insensitivity to women), this story interrogates it. Like all of Hannah's best work, the tale displays an unsettling tonal complexity, moving at breakneck speed from the seriousness of the hunting narrative and the gothic tale – the title refers to a Black servant who haunts the bluff where the story takes place – to the ridiculousness of farce. It alternates between allusions to Faulkner, Davey Crockett, and Somerset Maugham and *Reader's Digest* and Dr. Jack Kevorkian, the physician who assisted in hundreds of suicides during the 1990s, when Hannah wrote the story. To whom else could the name of Harris's drug dealer, Mr. Kervochian, refer?

Williamson contends that what makes Hannah the best "spokesperson" for "our Postmodern age" (2008, p. 11) is his antinostalgic attitude toward the Southern past and his fatalistic view of the Southern (and American) future: "Hannah's [s]outh is not populated with people who remember the dignity of man," but rather:

> with the destitute, the aimless, the horribles of an impoverished, all-too-romanticized (Faulkner's partly to blame, Margaret Mitchell complicit as well), ignored and ridiculed hoard of wandering rednecks, liars inventing the world as they go, bigots, murderers, perverts, psychos, and each and all of these folks freighted with incurable existential emptiness and loneliness.
>
> (2008, p. 10)

Such gloominess Williamson traces back mostly to the exploding of the atomic bombs over Japan in 1945, and the dark new world that action brought into being. Hannah's work continually reminds us, though, of the specifically Southern literary tradition to which it belongs – or, to put it another way, in which it brashly intervenes. This is, perhaps, the best context in which to read "Evening of the Yarp: A Report by Roonswent Dover," a self-referential foray into tall-tale and gothic territory. The narrator, Dover, is a "young hillbill[y]" who takes writing classes with instructor Deacon Charles at a vocational/technical school (Hannah 1993, p. 96). In language that hilariously (and sometimes painfully) attempts absolute fidelity to Dover's semi-literate voice, the tale – or rather "report," as Hannah facetiously deems it – recounts the narrator's encounter with the "Yarp," a mythical, grotesque, shape-shifting creature that haunts the Arkansas mountains. (This being may even be able to switch sexes, as suggested by its name being changed near the end of the story to "Larp," a possible abbreviation of "Lady Yarp.") The Yarp admonishes Dover, "Shut up . . . I don't want to hear none of your tales, boy . . . too many tales come out of these mountains and everywhere" (p. 92), which Noel Polk interprets as a critique of Southern "legending" and "a call to live without illusion" (2009, p. 79). For Polk, the point of this story, and many of Hannah's others, is "to keep us from being comfortable and smug with the bromides, the legends that keep us from seeing clearly" (p. 80). Hannah would largely agree with this assessment of his contribution to Southern literature, based on statements such as the following: "I want [the voice in my fiction] to transcend artiness. I want the veil of 'Let's Pretend' out" (Thomas 2016, p. 112). Yet, as is so often true of writers of Hannah's generation, his desire "to transcend artiness" is paradoxically matched with a deep awareness of the artistic tradition of which he is a part. In the same interview, he says, "I can't imagine entertaining with a formula" (pp. 104–105). But in order to explode a literary formula – say, for example, an Appalachian tall tale – he has to learn it, master it, know it inside and out. Only then can he critique, distort, and destroy the illusion it creates.

One of the "formulas" to which Hannah returns again and again – especially in short fiction, perhaps his true *métier* – is the war story. "That Was Close, Ma" features a narrator whose mind conflates the long-past American Civil War (in this case, specifically the Battle of Vicksburg) with a contemporary conflict – here, Operation Desert Storm. As the title implies, the story is ostensibly a letter written by a soldier to his mother, but Weston points out that "the realism this form has historically been alleged to possess is made problematical by self-reflexive elements such as the protagonist's question, 'You believe this?,' and, even more directly, the statement 'It's pumping unusual things from me, this whole piece of writing'" (1998, p. 59). The story's plot, such as it is, centers on the narrator's desire for an Iraqi prisoner of war whom he calls Naomi Lee; he is in competition for her affection with his commanding officer, and in an attempt to win it, he first risks life and limb to acquire a herb needed to make Naomi's favorite tea, and then turns his fire on the Commander. This deed, he admits, means that "he has sabotaged his own dream of heroism." As Weston observes, the unnamed narrator is one in a long line of "unstable male protagonists [who] are seeking some kind of reassurance in a world that has denied them the comfort of a secure sense of self" (p. 60), who fail to find the right narrative according to which to live their lives – because, I would argue, such a narrative no longer exists. The story's fragmented, self-conscious structure and style allow the reader to experience this unmoored existence.

"That Was Close, Ma" dramatizes the breakdown of some of the overarching narratives (i.e. metanarratives) of Western culture. This is apparent from the outset, when the narrator, nearly hit by a bomb, exclaims, "Very close and nasty, old friend. We had you in the scope early. Oh Vicksburg, Vicksburg! I am, personally, the Fall of the West" (Hannah 1993, p. 354). Later, he tries to back away from this statement, arguing, "I am not at all the Fall of the West nor is this remotely Vicksburg. We are not slaves. We all elected to come here. We are not brainwashed, not patriotized by loud gatherings and flags and raving dumb career men." This is a lie, of course, and easily identified as such because it immediately follows the protagonist's observation that "culture drags you flat away from wherever you are and that is its main point" (p. 348). In other words, Western culture, which the speaker and his compatriots attempt to impose upon "grief-provoking converted pupil[s]" (p. 346) such as the renamed Naomi Lee, is the great mediator of lived experience, regardless of where it happens, and can neither be escaped nor ultimately legitimized. Likewise, Hannah's character is seduced by the exoticism of his would-be beloved, which means he is taken in by another set of cultural constructions (filtered, no doubt, through "oriental" Euro-American stereotypes) that render him impotent and signify in another way the "fall of the West."

Like the main character in "That Was Close, Ma," the narrator/protagonist in Hannah's novel *Ray* also conflates two wars: the Civil War and Vietnam, in which Ray Forrest fought. Coming after the celebrated *Airships* (which also featured several war stories), *Ray* deepened the sense among critics that Hannah was up to something not readily captured by the critical vocabulary of the Southern and/or the modern. Benjamin DeMott proclaimed that "ordinary reviewerese is no help in explaining" the book and turned to the work of Hunter S. Thompson, Donald Barthelme, and David Byrne as still-not-completely-satisfactory points of reference (DeMott 1980, p. 7). Eliot Fremont-Smith got closer than any reviewer had to articulating Hannah's intertextuality and self-reflexivity: "Ray isn't a 'natural' book, though it seems that way – one believes everything – but a most artful contrivance. The artfulness deliberately pokes through, which gives the book its panache and is at the same time its substance" (Fremont-Smith 1980, p. 45). It was not until Fred Hobson's ambivalent assessment of Hannah's work in *The Southern Writer in the Postmodern World* (1991), though, that discussion of Hannah's connection with postmodernism began in earnest. Consisting of sixty-two fragments, some only a few sentences long, the book's "[f]orm reflects substance, both chaotic, and this is almost but not quite the self-conscious art of John Barth, a story about the telling of the story, a work in which . . . truth, reliability, and fiction itself are called into question" (Hobson 1991, p. 37). Chapter 31, which follows a scene in which Ray shockingly shoots a stranger, displays perhaps the self-consciousness Hobson has in mind: "Now I guess I should give you swaying trees and the rare geometry of cows in the meadow or the like – to break it up. But sorry, me and this one are over" (Hannah 1980, p. 81). Given the way Hannah overtly interrogates the conventions of narrative-making in general and Southern narrative-making in particular – note how he has Ray swat the pastoral away like an annoying insect – it is little wonder a traditionalist such as Hobson finds the book disconcerting.

Perhaps what makes Hannah's work postmodern, ultimately, is the way it problematizes the real. Published more than two decades after *Ray*, *Yonder Stands Your Orphan* suggests that while Hannah got older, wiser, more attentive to spiritual (and particularly Christian) concerns, his outlook did not get any brighter. He never found any solace in realism. The book follows members of a lakeside community – the cast of characters is perhaps larger than that in any other Hannah novel – who are being terrorized by the serial killer Man Mortimer, a Conway Twitty lookalike. If Hannah's style at the levels of sentence and phrase seem to have normalized, his experimentation with form has not, as the novel is basically plotless. John B. Kachuba notes this in describing how the "lateral branching and joining among the various characters takes on the appearance of a giant spider web"; this creates a "confused form ... that effectively fulfills ... Hannah's literary worldview," wherein "evil is rampant ... [and] there can be no single story of salvation, only truncated chapters of desperate struggle" (2005, pp. 86–87). Key to this reading is the phrase "literary worldview," which recognizes the novel's inescapable artificiality and its reliance on inter- and intra-textuality. The "truncated chapters of desperate struggle" – or, what the postmodern theorist Jean-Francois Lyotard might call the book's various dark "clouds of narrative" – are shot through with the sense that the real has receded beyond reach, and nothing, faith in God included, can bring it back. Like *Ray* and *Never Die* before it, but to a more severe degree, the book "posits a domain of ethical action besieged by images, roles, scripts, codes, and theme spaces that threaten to colonize and eradicate the real" (Romine 2007, p. 162). For figures such as Max Raymond and the other denizens of Eagle Lake, homesickness for the real cannot be cured. In an interview done around the time of the novel's publication, Hannah observed that "[a]ll the art forms are limited, probably, except music" (Thomas 2016, p. 183). Perhaps the dissipated structure of *Yonder Stands Your Orphan* is Hannah's self-reflexive nod to this realization. It is also worth noting, however, that one of the characters, the ineffectual Dr. Raymond, is a saxophonist for whom music is just as limited a way to recover the real as words are. Analogous perhaps in Hannah's mind to the "performance" of critics who insist on seeing his work as postmodern, Raymond's "playing [is] ... abstract, learned at some academy of the fluently depressed" (Hannah 2001, p. 35). But paradoxically, in taking one last swipe at postmodernism, Hannah may actually assert its presence in his final novel.

SEE ALSO: Contemporary Fictions of War; Contemporary Regionalisms; Mixed-Genre Fiction; Periodization; Realism and Poststructuralism

REFERENCES

DeMott, Benjamin. (1980). Rudeness is our only hope. Review of *Ray*. *The New York Times Book Review* (November 16, 1980). https://www.nytimes.com/1981/06/30/books/rudeness-is-our-only-hope.html (accessed July 6, 2021).

Fremont-Smith, Eliot. (1980). Hoo-Ray. Review of *Ray*. *The Village Voice* 25 (47): 45.
Graybill, Mark. (1997). Personal interview with Barry Hannah. Unpublished (July 27, 1997).
Hannah, Barry. (1980). *Ray*. New York: Grove Press.
Hannah, Barry. (1993). *Bats Out of Hell*. New York: Grove Press.
Hannah, Barry. (2001). *Yonder Stands Your Orphan*. New York: Grove Press.
Hobson, Fred. (1991). *The Southern Writer in the Postmodern World*. Mercer University Lamar Memorial Lectures No. 33. Athens: University of Georgia Press.
Kachuba, John B. (2005). Breadcrumb trails and spider webs: form in *Yonder Stands Your Orphan*. *Mississippi Quarterly* 58 (Winter 2004– Spring 2005): 75–87.
Lowe, John. (2001). William Faulkner. *The Literary Encyclopedia* (July 19, 2001). www.litencyc.com (accessed July 6, 2021).
Polk, Noel. (2009). Even Mississippi legending in Barry Hannah's *Bats Out of Hell*. *Texas Review* 30: 75–88.
Romine, Scott. (2007). Orphans all: reality homesickness in *Yonder Stands Your Orphan*. In: *Perspectives on Barry Hannah* (ed. Martyn Bone), 161–182. Jackson: University Press of Mississippi.
Thomas, James G., Jr. (ed.) (2016). *Conversations with Barry Hannah*. Jackson: University Press of Mississippi.
Weston, Ruth. (1998). *Barry Hannah: Postmodern Romantic*. Baton Rouge: Louisiana State University Press.
Williamson, Eric Miles. (2008). Barry Hannah and the postmodern South. *Arkansas Review* 39 (1): 3–14.

FURTHER READING

Charney, Mark J. (1992). *Barry Hannah*. New York: Twayne.
Lee, Richard E. (2003). Crippled by the truth: oracular pronouncements, titillating titles, and the postmodern ethic. *The Postmodern Short Story: Forms and Issues* (ed. Farhat Iftekharrudin *et al.*), 109–122. Westport, CT: Praeger.
Lyotard, Jean François. (1984). *The Postmodern Condition: A Report on Knowledge* (trans. Geoff Bennington and Brian Massumi). Theory and History of Literature, Volume 10. Minneapolis: University of Minnesota Press.

Harrison, Jim

CHRISTOPHER "CW" JOHNSON
University of Minnesota, Duluth, USA

Jim Harrison made his mark on the literary world with the poetry collection *Plain Song* in 1965, which was followed by several poetry collections. Early on, Harrison made editorial contributions to *Sumac*, a literary journal Harrison founded with Dan Gerber in 1968; and wrote three early novels: *Wolf* (1971), *A Good Day to Die* (1973), and *Farmer* (1976). However, he experienced more critical than popular acclaim, and he struggled to make a living as a working writer. The publication of *Legends of the Fall* in 1979 changed his fortune. Published to critical acclaim, serialized in *Esquire* by editor Rust Hill, and eventually famous as a Hollywood screenplay, *Legends* launched Harrison in 1980s with a serious reputation, income from royalties and Hollywood contracts, and opportunities to explore his creative *oeuvre*.

From 1980 until his death in 2016, Jim Harrison made a commitment to fiction, pursuing it vigorously even as he called poetry the "true bones of my life" (DeMott 2019, p. xii). In those thirty-six years, Harrison published nineteen works of fiction, ending with *The Ancient Minstrel* in 2016, the year of his passing, but it was *Legends of the Fall* that sealed his early reputation. In 1979, in response to his reading of *Legends*, Bernard Levin wrote in the London *Sunday Times* that "Jim Harrison is a writer with immortality in him" (quoted in McDonell 2016). Robert Houston wrote in *The New York Times* in 1990, "A dozen years ago, Jim Harrison published a collection called *Legends of the Fall*, which may well be the best set of novellas to appear in this country during the last quarter-century." In the United States, much of Harrison's work remains in print, while Harrison developed a following overseas, particularly in France, where his books are published in handsome editions and where he is the subject at literary events and studied in classrooms.

Harrison's lifelong friend, Tom McGuane, favored the short story, but against all publishing and editorial advice it was the novella to which Harrison devoted his energy. Harrison repeated the form of *Legends of the Fall* in eight additional collections: *The Woman Lit by Fireflies* (1990), *Julip* (1994), *The Beast God Forgot to Invent* (2000), *The Summer He Didn't Die* (2005), *The Farmer's Daughter* (2010), *Brown Dog* (2013), *The River Swimmer* (2013), and *The Ancient Minstrel* (2016). *Legends of the Fall* consists of three stories, "Revenge," "The Man Who Gave Up His Name," and the title story, the Odyssean tale of Tristan Ludlow and his family across vast landscapes and the canvas of history. *Legends* acquired a significant readership, remaining in print across forty-six American editions during the period treated by this volume. In addition to encouragement by McGuane, and financial backing from Jack Nicholson, Harrison credited the influence of his own reading, citing Dinesen, Porter, Chekhov, and Hofmannsthal as influences on who he became as a writer of short fiction. Indeed, across a career of novella composition, Harrison cited the books of his own precocious reading life: Olive Beaupre Miller's *My Book House* of 1937 (a library of world literature), the Greek myths, Thoreau's *Walden* (1854) and *Journals* (1837–1861), Theodore Roosevelt's epic adventures, the tales of Ernest Thompson Seton. In a genre determined by brevity, Harrison creates richly allusive maps of a reader's encounters with the world, from Cioran and Dostoevsky, to Mandelstam and Louis Agassiz. This allusive density helps fuel the ideas and plot of Harrison's novellas, giving them an expansive feel belied by their brevity.

In his first novel, *Wolf,* published in 1971, Harrison employed *false memoir* as an explicit fictive strategy to create an ostensibly "false" autobiographical narrative. He continued this strategy in subsequent works, narrating some stories in the first person, as if they were autobiography or first-person journalism, as in *Sundog* (1982); some in second person, as in *Tracking* (2005), an autobiographical essay; and some with a limited third- person voice, including *A Woman Lit by Fireflies* (1990), *The English Major* (2008), or the *Brown Dog* narratives (1990–2013).

Between 1980 and 2016, Harrison gave wide-ranging interviews, and in many, Harrison repeats his mother's alleged comment that "[Y]ou've made quite a living from your fibs." The false memoirist establishes personae that "fib," allowing for shifts in voice, character, narrative structure, and, as noted, using allusions to establish authority by citing historical, scientific, or anthropological texts. In this context, elements of Harrison's fiction compose facets of his artistic identity, his autobiography as a reader, and also the deliberate pose of a raconteur, a pose distinct from his poetic persona. While Harrison relied on the abbreviated form of the false memoir in his novellas, he struck out in a different direction after 1980, publishing long narratives such as *Sundog* (1982), and later two epic sequences: *Dalva* (1988) and *The Road Home* (1998) make one pair, *True North* (2004) and *Returning to Earth* (2007), another. These achievements show Harrison filling out his portfolio – poetry, nonfiction, novellas, and the sustained narrative.

Trauma defined Jim Harrison and shaped his aesthetic commitments. An incident at age seven blinded one eye, and the deaths of two family members altered him irrevocably at age nineteen. In both cases, convalescence was protracted, as he recounts in his children's book, *The Boy Who Ran to the Woods* (2000), and in *Off to the Side*, the autobiographical memoir from 2002. By his own admission, these events made him stubbornly committed to the solace of the woods, exploring with his dog. His reentry into the world was guided by experience in nature through fishing, hunting, hiking and camping, with attention to the names of birds and trees and flowers, and increasingly, "intoxication with language," as he put it. From this attentive stance, Harrison the artist makes a commitment to things in themselves, but devoid of pretensions about pure objective or clinical description, while validating fluid interactions between self and place and living things. In this, there is ecology in Harrison. For Arne Naess, a founder of Deep Ecology, the environmental field that posits deep and dynamic connections between places, living things, and humankind, the foundational idea is the notion of *Dinge an sich* or "things as they are." From a Deep Ecology point of view, Harrison adopted the idea of ecological understandings of phenomena, but found in this philosophy an additional grounding, as an aesthetic platform for apprehending reality.

Of course, Harrison could confound this idea. He praised the work of James Hillman and Mary Douglas, who argued that adult identity and social consensus were deeply rooted in the natural symbols of one's past. These Jungian tropes match Harrison's obeisance to the depths of his consciousness, particularly his dreams, which he often relates as including the memories of his youth and nature. For Harrison, darkness, depth, and the emotional tensions in our encounters with raw nature – snakes, bears, wolves, the vagaries of weather, the movement of water – are means of expressing emotional and artistic richness and ambiguity, even as they are his understanding of the places he knew most intimately. *The Land of Unlikeness* is the first novella in *The River Swimmer* (2013) and illustrates Harrison's aesthetic stance. The protagonist takes refuge in northern Michigan after an urban career disaster, and to his surprise, finds his true self in a homely Midwestern landscape. The landscape is known to him, being the place of his first artistic yearnings, his first awkward adolescent romance, and the "backwards" culture that he abandoned while living amidst the world's best hotels, food, books, and museums. Like Gaston Bachelard's dualism of "cottage and manor" (1964, p. 63), this duality at first confuses the character, offering what he described as the possibility of "falling through the earth" (Wachtel 2019), but then catalyzes him into childlike vigor. Harrison asserts forcibly that a good life is not one dictated by the aesthetic or economic mores of New York or California, but instead by memory, imagination, and direct perception of our place on the earth.

If trauma informed Harrison's own life story, beginning from his childhood, it also informed his sense of the traumas of history in his nation, fueling his commitment to telling the version of America that he saw as the forgotten truth of the land and people. *Off to the Side,* Harrison's formal autobiography, offers clues to his fiction. The title evokes Harrison's lifetime pursuit of marginal, rural landscapes and inhabitants of the "middle of America." Harrison identified with the places and peoples who rejected the "geopiety of the two coasts," for example, New York and LA and believed that the most neglected in popular culture constituted the authentic America, the antithesis of the triumphalism promulgated in portraits of American heritage as a story of inevitable progress.

Harrison captures the vast swath of the continent as a topography to build dynastic, epic narratives. Like Faulkner's Yoknapatawpha stories, the stories of the Northridge clan in *Dalva* and *The Road Home,* and the Burke clan in *True North* and *Returning to Earth,* are set in particular geographies dominated by the weather, geology, botany, and cultural history of the Great Plains and northern forests, quite distinct from the urban and suburban milieu represented in contemporaneous fiction in the 1980s, 1990s, and early 2000s.

Dalva and *The Road Home,* offer the exemplar of an eccentric Midwestern clan uniquely posed to understand the context of the Great Plains, including a provisional and conflicted relationship to the Indigenous peoples for whom it has been home for thousands of years. Dalva gives up a son born to her and her Native American lover, but she finds her way to understanding place in the habitat of the farm. Her grandfather, Northridge, the protagonist of *The Road Home,* is dying and reflecting on his sense of place, enumerating a lifetime of planting varieties of hardy tree, shrub, and grass. The catalogue of seeds, rootstock, and flora is an evocation of time and transcendence, with the mature shelter belt evoking the history of the Northridge family and the creation of a specific habitat. Like Johnny Appleseed in American lore, the original Northridge functions *sui generis,* an idiosyncratic outcast who transforms a Nebraska landscape through indefatigable horticulture. Harrison's appropriation of the Appleseed story is mythopoetic: the origin story of the Northridge clan is part of that tradition as an origin story of how a place and people come to inhabit the landscape. Crucially, this sense of place runs up against European-American and Native American relations and history, and often tragic tensions are the major drivers of plot in these novels.

True North and to a lesser degree, *Returning to Earth,* offer additional instances of reframing the mythology of American landscapes. Bachelard, one of Harrison's heroes, insisted that imagination depends on recognizing the power of the open landscape (1964). In Bachelard, the plain is *at once* ordinary, prosaic, and grand, a vista unimpeded. In *True North* and *Returning to Earth,* Harrison presents "twin plains:" the vastness of Lake Superior and the forest that dominates the Upper Peninsula of Michigan. A specific landscape, the Kingston Plains, is the eerily scarred result of predatory logging practices at the turn of the twentieth century. The vast spaces of land and water have an objective correlative in the economic damage done to them, and the novel's narrator, David Burkett, is obsessed with telling the true story of his family's rise to economic power, a story of greed, predation of people, and destruction of wild places.

Counter to the notion of fibbing or false memoir, *Dalva, The Road Home, True North,* and *Returning to Earth* all rely on archival material detailing the Plains Indian Wars, the conflicts of western settlement, and the exploitation of extractive capitalism, mining and lumbering in the Upper Midwest. In the *Dalva* sequence, the elder Northridge conspired against US Cavalry, keeping the sacred and historical evidence of Indian chiefs and their families safe from government seizure, and ultimately, murdering officers sent to his homestead to intervene against his conspiracy to support the Natives. The Northridge home is a museum-like memorial to the genocide perpetrated across the American frontier, containing both art and artifacts *in extremis,* including actual cadavers resulting from the violence of the Plains settlement by European-Americans. In *True North,* it is the impossibility of telling the horror of his family's patriarchal past that haunts David Burkett, leading to the failure of his avocation as historian. In these instances, Harrison uses research with primary source materials to portray nightmares, contrapuntal to the American Dream. His is a landscape of trees logged to leave a plain of stumps and scars. He borrows from Poe, Freud, Jung and Bachelard to topple Turner's Frontier Thesis, offering readers the nightmare history of the Midwestern landscape, one he imagined as a "blood-stained sheet," where the stains represent the wholesale destruction of culture and extermination of Native Americans (the peoples) and native America (the places), and they point to the political, economic, and environmental disasters persisting in 2020 (Luneau 1993).

Harrison was recognized after 1980 for his success in developing narratives featuring female personae, characters decidedly counter to the label of "outdoorsman" associated with his name. Critical attention to his earlier work accused him of a posturing machismo, and his own adherence to pursuits such as hunting, fishing, and drinking furthered this reputation. Nevertheless, Harrison's reputation after 1988 was enhanced greatly by critically acclaimed work written from the perspectives of female characters. In particular, *Dalva, Julip,* and *The Woman Lit by Fireflies* show Harrison creating characters and narrative perspectives that belie the perception that he was a writing only from a consensus view of masculinity.

Dalva, published in 1988, marks Harrison's first venture in narration through a female character's point of view. In *Dalva,* the female protagonist attempts to understand her place milieu of ancestors and a largish spread of land that represents the most successful landholding in the county; as in Faulkner's Sutpens in *Absalom, Absalom* (1936), there is a sense of the dynastic. Despite big spaces and a big story, Dalva as persona is immediate and charismatic. She is, as Harrison said in various interviews, like the twin sister separated from you at birth. It is Dalva's strength, her vital energy, that defines the book. She suffers fools, but kindly, and she is unapologetically herself, but reflexively self-aware. Her search – for her own history, for her lover, for her long-lost son – is an artistic victory hued from the Nebraska "plain-ness" *in extremis*.

Harrison himself recounted often the difficulty of leaving her persona aside as the book ended.

In a second example of Harrison's female-centered narratives, *A Woman Lit by Fireflies,* Clare is almost fifty, and her marriage to her Wall-Street-directed husband, Donald, is at an impasse. At a rest stop she walks away from her car, husband, and marriage, entering a cornfield and a habitat of thickets to begin her new life. At first, disoriented amidst the ubiquitous plants in the unified field of corn, her imagination is unloosed and discomfited. Clare's passage through the dense monoculture of the cornfield parallels an internal monologue in which she inventories the failed narrative of her marriage to Donald – the anti-Semitism, crass greed, elitist banalities, and a history of not-so-subtle verbal abuse. When a thunderstorm threatens, Clare fashions a makeshift roof to her new thicket abode, gathering vegetation and weaving it into a canopy where the features suggest the womb, a place of birth, or rebirth. Harrison elaborates by having Clare recall the birth of her daughter Laurel years earlier, a birthday marked by an intense cloudburst. In the habitat at the cornfield's edge, Clare is alert to nature through her senses, and in her vulnerability to wind and sky and rain and insects, Clare observes the vulnerability of the natural world, as well as its resilience.

Growth for Harrison is sometimes the possibility of being returned via a daydream to the wonder and beauty of childhood, and Harrison's six tales of "Brown Dog" strike at least some readers as the fictive version of a true self imagined by Harrison. Turning to an unreliable character who will never understand or countenance identity politics, Harrison offers a protagonist who confounds the sensitivity to female perspective-taking noted earlier. In *Brown Dog,* gathered in 2013, Harrison creates a character straight out of Twain,

Salinger, or Faulkner, a savant fool who is kind, wise, and resourceful beyond his context and circumstances. He is "BD," a man in his early middle-age years and of indeterminate ancestry. This is Harrison's Huck Finn in the rural spaces of northern Michigan, and occasionally on the streets of big cities, and he is undeniably an American everyman for the ages, and arguably, after the late poetry of Harrison, his most significant achievement of his final decade.

Jim Harrison died at his writing desk in March of 2016, pen in his hand, and a poem in progress on a notepad. As Tom McGuane noted in an address to the American Academy of Arts and Science, "[N]o one was less suited to life in a nursing home" (McGuane 2017), and it is this antinomianism in Jim Harrison that may best define him. Among a generation of writers who took to universities, urban audiences, and MFA writing programs, Jim Harrison remained steadfastly an outsider, at least with respect to academia and prestige literary culture. He argued that "someone has to stay outside" (Kuipers 2015), and he maintained across dozens of interviews that young writers would be better served by following his own perverse advice: a year of hard manual labor and a reading list some 1000 books long. In these anecdotes is a distinctly American identity rooted in place and a farmer's work ethic. In his nonfiction essays, *Just Before Dark* (1991), Harrison explained that the real reason for the short duration of his teaching career was a matter of geography – the universities he admired were far from the woods and water that had sustained him since childhood.

While he could imagine different lives and selves in words and through fiction and literary allusion, he could only live his life closer to the earth, which provided him with emotional sustenance. This sustenance is the core of Jim Harrison's life in language. While he refused the label of *nature writer*, the effect of his childhood and youth in the outdoors was to create a unique aesthetic and practical vision of what a good life and good art could be. A life lived well would be lived close to the land, and in places far from the urban centers and glamor of cosmopolitan society: Michigan's Upper Peninsula, Paradise Valley in Montana, and borderlands between Arizona and Mexico – "Off to the Side" – as Harrison titled his memoir.

SEE ALSO: Ecocriticism and Environmental Fiction; Erdrich; Louise; Ford, Richard; Vizenor, Gerald; Welch; James

REFERENCES

Bachelard, Gaston. (1964). *The Poetics of Space*. Boston: Beacon Press.

DeMott, Robert. (ed.) (2019). *Conversations with Jim Harrison*. Jackson: University Press of Mississippi.

Houston, Robert. (1990). Love for the proper outlaw. *The New York Times* (September 16, 1990). https://archive.nytimes.com/www.nytimes.com/books/98/11/08/specials/harrison-fireflies.html (accessed September 11, 2021).

Kuipers, Dean. (2015). Jim Harrison on spirits, bad poetry, and the wonder of nature. *Los Angeles Times* (December 15, 2015). https://www.latimes.com/books/la-ca-jc-jim-harrison-20151220-story.html (accessed September 9, 2021).

Luneau, Georges. (1993). *Entre chien et loups*. Video documentary. https://georgesluneau.com/films/jim-harrison.html (accessed September 9, 2021).

McDonell, Terry. (2016). Jim Harrison, Mozart of the prairie. *The New Yorker* (March 30, 2016). https://www.newyorker.com/books/page-turner/jim-harrison-mozart-of-the-prairie (accessed September 28, 2021).

McGuane, Tom. (2017). Thomas McGuane remembers his friend, Jim Harrison. Address to the American Academy of Arts and Letters. https://lithub.com/thomas-mcguane-remembers-his-friend-jim-harrison/ (accessed July 15, 2021).

Wachtel, Eleanor. (2019). An Interview with Jim Harrison (1994). *Conversations with Jim Harrison* (ed. Robert DeMott), 102–120. Jackson: University of Mississippi Press; 1st ed. 1994.

FURTHER READING

Harrison, Jim. (2002). *Off to the Side: A Memoir*. New York: Grove Press.

Orr, Gregg and Torrey, Beef. (2009). *Jim Harrison: A Comprehensive Bibliography, 1964–2008*. Lincoln: University of Nebraska Press.

Smith, P. (2002). *The True Bones of My Life*. Lansing: Michigan State University.

Hawkes, John

GEOFFREY GREEN
San Francisco State University, USA

John Hawkes (1925–1998) was a writer of unique importance. His mastery of voice as a distinctive fusion of visionary description, lyrical style, psychological acuity, and revelatory individuality marks him as an inimitable virtuoso of insight, penetrating perception, and iconoclastic innovation – the creator of a style so innovative and inventive that there is nothing resembling it in contemporary American fiction. An author of sixteen novels as well as plays, poems, and essays, his writing fuses as lyrical vision the horror and depravity of war, history, human cruelty, selfishness, desire, guilt, brutality, and death – all in the service of an affirmation of love, morality, grace, human redemption, and hope. An influential and exemplary stylist and teacher, his work produced since the 1980s – oddly neglected by critics of late – actually highlights and displays his ever-expansive creativity, imagination, and the seemingly limitless possibilities of his inspired powers of invention.

An asthmatic only child brought up in New England, Alaska, and New York, he was drawn perhaps vicariously to nature, horseback riding, and the outdoors. Hawkes was influenced by his experiences as an American Field Service ambulance driver during World War II, as well as his Harvard education. His teacher, Albert Guerard, became his lifelong friend, and through him his decisive early literary influences were established: Joseph Conrad (whose evocation of living the often-ironic dream through to the end was a haunting presence in his writing), William Faulkner, Louis-Ferdinand Céline, Nathanael West, Djuna Barnes, Nabokov, and, of course, Shakespeare. Before settling into an established career as an author-professor at, first, Harvard University, then MIT, and Brown University, Hawkes worked for the Harvard University Press.

Famously declaring that the "enemies" of the novel are plot, theme, setting, and character, Hawkes's first short novel, *Charivari* (1949) develops out of the fears and anticipations that accompany marriage, an enterprise that Hawkes himself was about to undertake. Lampooning real life situations proclaims the force and sustenance of the human imagination to craft counter-narratives and interpretations – to voice the redemptive potentialities of creativity, of an imagination ordered by a vision of form in a chaotic world.

The Cannibal (1949) established his characteristic approach: finely-crafted sentences creating visual scenes of hallucinatory, dream-like intensity, and power. Without a formally coherent plot, the impression of the novel nevertheless is intense: a harrowing, ironic, and deeply affecting view of the consequences of war and the subsequent postwar occupation of Germany. Rejecting the idea that writers tapped their autobiographical life experience as subject matter for their fiction, Hawkes praised the supremacy of the imagination, alluding to a dynamic analogy between the manner in which we create stories that are aesthetic narratives and the manner in which we create tales that interpret and comprehend our very human lives. Followed by his second novel, *The Beetle Leg* (1951), Hawkes presents "landscapes" that are often repellently violent in their intensity and ferocity – including, for example, the murder of a child in the former and a reeling-in of a fetus in the latter. His justification depends for bolstering on his skeptical devotion to the world as a darkly ominous environment, redeemed, to a measure, by every act of creative realization, every fully achieved literary representation of a harrowing vision. Skewering the traditional assumptions of genre (the war novel in *The Cannibal* and the Western in *The Beetle Leg*), Hawkes offers as alternatives the courageous affirmation that human artists are able to actualize art, ordering chaos even while disjointed, uttering voices of moral affirmation amidst a cacophony of nay-saying.

The Goose on the Grave and *The Owl*, published together in 1954, continue Hawkes's probing meditation of the devastations of war and their aftermath. Both set in postwar Italy, they are explorations of power, its extremities and limitations as willful desire, and the similar, yet nonetheless opposing, compensatory power of an author's methodical detachment in the crafting of an aesthetic vision. Departing from his characteristic first-person narration, Hawkes explores the use of third-person narrative infused with a revealing contamination of subjectivity and psychological intensity. These early texts establish Hawkes's willingness and enthusiasm to depart from the minimalist realism of, say, a Hemingway or a Steinbeck. Nevertheless, their challenges to traditional form were perceived as impediments to a more widespread readership, even as Hawkes's distinctive emphasis on the lyrical voice – even in the intensely visual chronicling of evil – elicited praise and critical regard.

The "discovery" of Hawkes by a more mainstream literary readership occurs with the publication of *The Lime Twig* (1961) and *Second Skin* (1964), wherein Hawkes achieves the effect of a more relatively user-friendliness, not by embracing a more mainstream realistic style, but rather, by redoubling his commitment to the disturbing, darkly comic, and destructive implications of the first-person voice, especially delivered by means of highly wrought parody, word by word, phrase by phrase, sentence by sentence. Consciously deriving his representational expression from the suspense fiction of Graham Greene and Eric Ambler, Hawkes in *The Lime Twig* employs a sardonic world of horse racing, gambling, crime, corruption, selfish human desires, and their antithesis in redemptive love. Leslie Fiedler's insightful introduction to that novel isolates perceptively Hawkes's use of the more morbid and unseemly aspects of life as being necessarily dependent on our human affirmation of their moral opposite: virtue, generosity, kindness, and love. In *Second Skin*, Hawkes's first-person narrator, Skipper, presents two visions of two contrary islands: one, a cold, barren landscape of gloom, and the other, a warm, tropical flourishing of fertile dreams and desires. Comedy balances tragedy, even in an unreliable narration, and Hawkes takes as his own the psychoanalytic implications of the two contrary human drives – love and death. It is no small feat in this novel that readers are both moved with its poignancy and prompted to belly laugh at scenes of hilarity. Characteristic in both of these early masterpieces is Hawkes's careful crafting of the visionary – even cinematic – implications of a scene, memorable in its dream-like intensity, unfettered from the traditional contextualization of plot and theme. These visionary evocations achieve a felt immediacy, to be sure, but also inspire in each reader an intuited but profound sense of narrative connectivity.

Hawkes's "triad" of three distinctive but thematically-related novels – *The Blood Oranges* (1971); *Death, Sleep, and the Traveler* (1974); and *Travesty* (1976) – are capstones of his mature style. They usher in his profound and important achievements in the 1980s and

1990s. Focused intensively on the dark, ironic implications of unreliable narrators, Hawkes balances deftly the comic with the tragic, glorifies love in the inescapable presence of death. His three narrators – Cyril, Allert, and "Papa" – proceed relentlessly toward the challenge of creatively interpreting death, rescuing "design" from "debris," insisting on the primacy of the human imagination, even while inviting readers to themselves interpret and understand the unreliable narratives and their precarious balancing of love and death. Increasingly, Hawkes crafts fiction that evokes itself as fiction, incorporating the reader's own necessity of interpreting creatively as an essential activity. Even in *The Passion Artist* (1979), wherein Hawkes returns to the third person in order to represent a reprehensible man, Konrad Vost, Hawkes insists that dream and reality are tethered inherently together, as in his *Triad*. Whether it is the character's dream being interpreted or the novel itself as a dream, the borders between life and art blur and blend, creating new forms and resuscitations even on the most brutal peripheries of human behavior and desire.

In *Virginie: Her Two Lives* (1982), Hawkes charts out an "impossible story," as his narrator declares. The novel, however, contradicts the assertion by enabling the reader to travel through the most lush, exotic, and depraved realms of the imagination. Virginie is an 11-year-old narrator who lives two lives, in 1740 (the year of de Sade's birth) and 1945 (the year of the atom bomb), telling two stories wherein she records deliriums of domination, love, and depravity. Returning to the first-person narrator, Hawkes is able to caricature authorship while artfully achieving it. Weaving fantasies of French eroticism from de Sade to Bataille, Hawkes also evokes the English tradition of the innocent or virginal narrator, such as in Charlotte Brontë's *Jane Eyre* (1847). Voluptuaries and innocents achieve a flourishing of the possibilities of the creative imagination: to probe the inner recesses of the unconscious, of desire, and, amidst despair, hope.

Adventures in the Alaskan Skin Trade (1985) is narrated by Sunny Deauville, mistress of a whorehouse in Alaska. Despite its erotic context, however, Hawkes explores the exotic wildness of nature, a nature he knew during his own upbringing. Sunny's tale is obsessed with dreams of her father, "Uncle Jake," who brought his family to the outposts of wildness in 1929. Sunny's dreams of Jake's tall tales circle back to the skins or layers of identity, to the furs that are hunted and traded, as well as the films or gradations of narrative perspective, exaggeration, and inventiveness. Recalling Dylan Thomas's *Adventures in the Skin Trade* (1953) as well as his own *Second Skin*, Hawkes's theme is story itself – its craft, its delights, its adventurous innovations. The dead are brought to life through tales, and, as Hawkes has stressed, "design and debris" encircle and engender each other. Closely related is Hawkes's novella, *Innocence in Extremis* (1985), presenting Uncle Jake's experiences as a child of twelve, brought by his father to France in order to visit his grandfather, a "provincial aristocrat." Once again, but in marvelously inventive forms, Hawkes connects innocence with passionate experience, eroticism with its repressive rejection.

With *Whistlejacket* (1988), Hawkes continues his devoted contemplation of horses, skins, layers of meaning, and the imagination itself. But, characteristic of his post-1980s work, the imaginative terrain is more unexpected, more varied, diverse, and surprising. A fox hunt, the distinguished paintings of horses by the eighteenth-century artist, George Stubbs, dissection, the peeling away of skins, photography and its own process of layering, violent trampling, widespread erotica, class hierarchical tensions – all of these are masterfully unified in a manner wonderfully crafted to induce suspense and yet nevertheless introduce thematic meditation: "discontinuity destroys hierarchy." With his first-person photographer narrator, Michael (arcing back to *The Lime Twig*, *its* character and *its* horses), Hawkes summons forth as if by magic a fantasy of the imagination that is at once a parody of the hunt and the snuff box, as it were, and also an inventive and consistently ingenious step forward in his exploration of new creative vistas.

With his passion for horses an important fuel for his imagination, Hawkes, in *Sweet William: A Memoir of Old Horse* (1993), conjures a first-person narrative . . . of a horse! The horse, known as, variously, Sweet William, Old Horse, and Petrarch, speaks in a compellingly world weary and yet formal voice, presents the story of his life as a horse, illustrating his innate predisposition to be himself, a distinct personality, while fashioning for the reader a series of episodic yarns and situations that offer us material for contemplation: how *ought* we be treated? Is there innate life and imaginative energy existing in all representational forms? For any being, life is hard, filled with moments of success and despair. It is indeed impressive that Hawkes, in this unanticipated leap into unanticipated pleasures, provides moments of genuine poignancy and deep reservoirs of feeling.

In *The Frog* (1996), Hawkes continues his journey into personification with the story of a boy, Pascal Gateau, who swallows a frog in pre-World War I France. That frog, named Armand, somehow remains alive within him, and together, they illustrate the dual motivations and inclinations of imaginary beings. At times suggestive of an Aesopian fable, at other times a Kafkaesque anti-parable, and – magically! – also suggestive that the young boy is rather like a frog (named "the little Tadpole" by his mother; rather frog-like in shape and form), Pascal and Armand animate this wondrous tale, which, variously, explores madness and sanity, eroticism, cruelty, the Oedipus complex, sleepwalking, dreams, illusion, and the persistence of belief. Dazzling and willful simultaneously, Hawkes's imaginative energies here continue to be boundless.

Horses, children, parental figures converge in *An Irish Eye* (1997). Recalling Hawkes's earlier work, yet distinctively new and innovative, the novel describes a 13-year-old foundling, Dervla O'Shannon and her touching yet quirky friendship with an old veteran of World War I, Corporal Stack. As appealing disagreeable as the old soldier is, so Dervla reveals herself to be yet another intriguingly unreliable first-person narrator. Gothic horror abides alongside affection and sentiment, wherein stables, stalls, deteriorating estates, eroticism, horror, dream-like imagery, and ambiguity blend appealingly into a tale that Hawkes renders in a voice that manages to impersonate every fantasy of Irish lore and blarney.

Persistent in Hawkes's work are an unceasing series of variations of depictions of the unearthing from the lower or inner depths of some being, relic, tomb, vessel, container, corpse, hallucination, or image. These visions are described in a manner that is relentlessly visual, locked into a piercing gaze of verbal sculpting that astonishes with its power and grace. As complete and satisfying as these visions are, they nevertheless resonate with voices of overwhelming variety, suggestive of countless identities and multiple selves. The voice of identity and selfhood reveals a boundless insight into human nature, in all its variegated and multifaceted forms and shapes. Inclusive in all of his work are suggestions of psychological depth, of inner demons being wrenched out of some subterranean unconscious, of the elusive voice within us all that wrestles with the wondrous and ever-fascinating contrariness of our paradoxical natures.

Also inherent in Hawkes's work is an imaginary geographical landscape that defies a viable mapping of place and time. Fantasies of imaginary France, mythic renditions of the Alaskan frontiers, remnants of pre-Revolutionary aristocratic hauteur in twentieth-century imaginary France, dream-like British renditions of fox hunting and contaminated royalty, contemplative horses with voices, child-frogs, Irish foundlings, the never-ceasing search for our deepest recesses, our ancestors, our inner selves, as they are revealed through language that is consistently surprising, astonishing, lyric-poetic, and deeply pleasurable. In his most recent and underappreciated work, he enters into highly contemporary meditations on gender relations, intersubjectivity, the repetition compulsion and the death drive, the redemptive and persistent reoccurrence of love and hope. It is puzzling and confounding for this writer that John Hawkes's work since the 1980s – filled with invention, wit, gothic horror, dark comedy, new and emergent visualizations and voices – has not attracted the attention, serious study, and critical scrutiny that it so richly deserves. John Hawkes is a writer of rare discernment, masterful voice and vision, acute insight, and ceaseless invention – revealing for the reader unique and abiding treasures. His words embody a saying true of the highest order. This writer hopes that new readers will come to appreciate the richness of Hawkes's work and its abundance of unique pleasures from the vantage point of our current perspective. Praised by his contemporaries, a worthy colleague in quality and mastery to John Barth, Robert Coover, Flannery O'Connor, and Carson McCullers, his work is the epitome of timeless brilliance.

SEE ALSO: Barth, John; Coover, Robert; Elkin, Stanley; Gaddis, William; Gass, William H.; Sorrentino, Gilbert

FURTHER READING

Ferrari, Rita. (1996). *Innocence, Power, and the Novels of John Hawkes*. Philadelphia: University of Pennsylvania Press.
Greiner, Donald J. (1985). *Understanding John Hawkes*. Columbia: University of South Carolina Press.
Marx, Lesley. (1997). *Crystals Out of Chaos: John Hawkes and the Shapes of Apocalypse*. Philadelphia: Fairleigh Dickinson University Press.

Heller, Joseph

PETER TEMPLETON
Open University, UK

There can be few writers for whom critical and popular attention revolves around just one of their texts to the same degree as Joseph Heller. His first novel, *Catch-22* (1961), secured his reputation as a great American novelist of the twentieth century but has also monopolized much of the discussion of his literary work. The novel, though initially rather divisive, gained in popularity across the turbulent decades of the 1960s, particularly with younger audiences and those involved in the counterculture of the decade. Though the book was set during World War II, the political climate of McCarthyism and the stultifying conformity of the United States in the 1950s were inspirations for the unfeeling military bureaucracy that we encounter in the novel, and the combination of these factors with Heller's own savage brand of satire made this a popular book with the generation protesting the Vietnam War on college campuses across the United States. From there, its popularity grew until it had a truly international profile. Subsequently, the book is now considered not only one of the most important American books of the period, but one of the most significant antiwar books.

In truth, though, much of the satire in *Catch-22* is directed not at the military itself, but at its tendency to reflect wider problems in American life; its corporate culture, or its willingness to harbor corrupt people. Read in this way, a continuity emerges between this first novel and the two that Heller would publish in the 1970s (Templeton 2016). Heller worked on *Something Happened* for years until it was finally published in 1974, more than a decade after his first novel, and during that time he wrote two plays (*We Bombed in New Haven* [1967] and a stage version of *Catch-22* [1971], from which the one-act play *Clevinger's Trial* [1973] was also taken). In this book, his central character, Bob Slocum, has a much more explicit connection to the corporate culture of the contemporary United States. While Yossarian, the protagonist of *Catch-22*, would encounter people "on the make" in the guise of army officers, Slocum is a businessman and exists squarely at the heart of American culture. Heller's satire here is, if anything, even sharper than in his first novel, and both the mood and the denouement are remorselessly bleak, which led to complaints from some reviewers such as Kurt Vonnegut, who described it as "one of the unhappiest books ever written" and "astonishingly pessimistic" (Vonnegut 1974). In its depiction of American business culture as an area in which greed motivates those in power, who use fear to keep their underlings in line, with dire social consequences, there is little to no room for hope.

His third novel returns to a form more reminiscent of his first novel, and *Good as Gold* (1979) involves more of the verbal gameplaying and lighter tone than was present in his stream-of-consciousness sophomore effort. In *Good as Gold*, the target for Heller's satire is the American political landscape. Coming as it does two years after Richard Nixon resigned the presidency in the aftermath of the Watergate scandal, there is little surprise in Heller directing his satirical gaze toward Washington and finding there yet more power, greed, disinformation, and manipulation. The book, though, is less interested in Nixon than it is in Henry Kissinger, secretary of state under Nixon and Gerald Ford. At one level, as protagonist Bruce Gold is offered the chance to become the first Jewish secretary of state, there are some obvious biographical parallels with Kissinger. If this is not clear enough, however, Heller effectively stops the book in its final third and abandons the rhetorical flourishes that dominate much of his plot, in favor of a searing indictment of Kissinger and his policy that is much more direct than his comedy usually allows.

This trio of novels is by far the most studied and widely read of Heller's output. Much of this is because *Catch-22* itself dominates the discussion to such a degree, but this is compounded as there seems to be a broadly chronological relationship to the critical interest in Heller, with each novel garnering less attention than the last. Beyond this, these three novels also work at a thematic level, and though they have some differences in style, focus, and tone, there is a continuity between them that makes it possible to see them almost as developments of a clear set of ideas. In this first eighteen years of his career, Heller is a straightforward satirist, albeit a highly skilled one.

After 1980, though comedy and satire remain part of his toolkit, Heller enters a different stage of his career. His first novel of the decade straddles a period of intense health concerns, since in late 1981 he was diagnosed with Guillain–Barré syndrome, with his recovery from the disease the subject of his autobiography *No Laughing Matter* (1986), written with Speed Vogel. *God Knows* (1984) was largely written before this diagnosis and completed during his recovery. In this novel, Heller takes as his narrator the figure of King David and reimagines the relevant books of the Old Testament, namely Samuel and Kings. Perhaps predictably, such subject matter did not prove universally popular, and one contemporary reviewer suggested that the book was "apparently written on the principle that shockingly bad taste is automatically funny" (Rovit 1984, p. 1772). Heller's move to a more self-consciously literary authorial style was not, then, welcomed by all.

There are two fundamental points about the narrative which shape it: firstly, that we encounter David at the end of his life, during which the communication that he had with God has ended. This means that the David we encounter is by turns blasphemous, bitter, and despairing, as well as maintaining several of the other attitudes and mannerisms of Heller's protagonists. The second feature is that through God's will and communication earlier in his life, David has access to and knowledge of events far beyond his own lifetime, and indeed can refer to any more contemporary reference point which might occur to Heller. This has several manifestations, such as David commenting on his own depiction by Michelangelo during the Renaissance, or some metafictional authorial game-playing in which David accuses Shakespeare of plagiarism (all in a novel in which Heller borrows heavily from both the Bible and Shakespeare).

The novel is structured largely around association, as the dying King calls up past events or contemporary annoyances as they occur to him, rather than in any clear chronological order – although the major events of the David story do follow a traditional chronology which prevents the novel from descending into the difficult territory common to many postmodernist novels of the twentieth century. One of the primary results of this storytelling through associations is that the David we encounter is decidedly more human than either his biblical counterpart or the majority of other cultural manifestations; as David M. Craig says, "he shares our vanities and perversities, our hopes and fears" (2000, p. 146). There is, of course, little humor to be found in the version of David we encounter in the Bible, but by making David into a more relatable figure, he becomes a character more malleable in the hands of a comic writer. Heller's comedic style shines through in familiar fashion here, with the result that despite the innovation in both plot and setting the novel does retain some similarities and connections with his previous work, particularly *Good as Gold*. Perhaps inevitably, given Heller's earlier satires of authority and the kind of wit he utilizes – compared variously to other Jewish comic artists of New York like his close friend Mel Brooks or Woody Allen – the effect of putting this kind of dialogue into David's mouth is to undercut the traditional biblical narrative and perhaps even prompt a rethinking of God's role in these stories on more equal terms.

God Knows, then, represents something of a stylistic departure for Heller: though there is still a clear perspective and shared interests which unite his output, on the surface his fourth novel is marked by greater experimentation than any of its predecessors. This experimentation reaches its zenith four years later in *Picture This* (1988). Again, initial reviews were not kind; Sanford Pinsker notes that one library service referred to the novel as "pretentious, unimaginative and tedious" (2009, p. 125). But while words like pretentious are effectively in the eye of the beholder, both the subject matter and style of *Picture This* confirm that this is the most ambitious work of Heller's literary career. If the story of King David lies at the heart of *Good as Gold*, then the Rembrandt painting *Aristotle Contemplating a Bust of Homer* sits similarly at the center of *Picture This*. One connection that we might draw between the two works is that much like with King David, Heller offers a portrait of Rembrandt which depicts his genius as an artist, but also his flaws on a more personal level. Unlike its predecessor, however, the novel does not act as a simple retelling or parodic inversion of its original, but instead uses the connection between these three figures and the artwork as a shortcut into thinking about almost the entirety of Western history, stemming from ancient Greece through to the time of writing, via the nascent commercial empire of the Netherlands in which Rembrandt was painting. This all arises because the Aristotle on the canvas is imbued with the ability to think, and comment on not only his own composition by Rembrandt, but on the myriad subsequent situations in which the painting is located. While clearly playing with the conventions of deconstruction, *Picture This* does not reject history in any conventional way, and indeed is very well researched, with several historians and art critics listed in the book's acknowledgments.

Despite this far more intricate (and, indeed, philosophical) plot, Heller is still first and foremost a satirist, and the result of much of this musing is a pained realization that humanity seems incapable of learning from history. The Heller that mocked the vanity of military leaders in *Catch-22* and raged at Kissinger in *Good as Gold* is still present here, and a principal conclusion of the novel is that the United States of the 1970s and 1980s is repeating the mistakes which had brought down the Athenian regime (as well as a host of others through the centuries). Heller again mocks the folly of politicians, and the injustices of the world that they govern. Tellingly, though, he seems to have little faith in democracy to resolve these tensions, remembering that it was a democratic decision to put Socrates to death, and democracy that elected the contemporary politicians whom he looked at with contempt. As elsewhere, Heller's principal way of conveying this contempt is through the satiric language that highlighted absurdities of power structures and military-industrial complexities, by turns reveling in their ludicrousness and lamenting the injustice of their real-world implications.

The decade of the 1980s, then, can be thought of as a time of great experimentation for Joseph Heller, one in which he not only moved from essentially contemporary settings and characters into past or distant lands, but in which he self-consciously played with the conventions of storytelling itself. This dimension largely passes from his work in the last decade of his life, as Heller returns to more comfortable ground in his final two novels: the first, a sequel to his most popular novel, and the second, the most intimately autobiographical novel of his career.

The first of these was *Closing Time* (1994), the sequel to *Catch-22*. This novel amplifies parallels that readers had long established between John Yossarian and Heller himself, since at the start of the novel Yossarian is the same age as Heller, and also lives in New York. Perhaps appropriately for a sequel, the novel is often backward looking, with an interest in memories of an upbringing in Coney Island – again shared by Heller and in which a young character suggestively called Joey Heller features. Remembrances of the Coney Island of his youth would act as the starting point for his autobiography *Now and Then* (1998). The combination of this return to his most famous characters after several decades with the novel's title and Heller's own ill health has led some critics to argue, as Anthony Fowles does, that Heller believed *Closing Time* was to be his final novel and that "he would present a species of testament. He would draw a line of sorts underneath his literary career." (2005, p. 85).

This might go some way to explaining why beyond the recurrence of familiar characters such as Yossarian, Chaplain Tappman, and Milo Minderbinder, the main thematic connection between *Closing Time* and its predecessor is the idea of death. In *Catch-22* the target for Heller's satire is an inflexible and coercive bureaucracy, but what raises the stakes is the ever-present threat of death in combat. In *Closing Time*, for the old men we encounter, death promises to be less sudden, perhaps less bloody, but an inevitability. One character, Sammy Singer, lives on after suffering badly with Hodgkin's disease, while the word cancer recurs throughout the novel, both as an obsession of the central characters and as a metaphor.

Even here, though, with both author and character musing on their own health and mortality, the satirist is not quite submerged. The novel is still interested in the health of the world and observes sickness in contemporary society. There is, though, a fundamental difference that cannot be avoided in the age and situation of the protagonist. As a young man in the US Air Force, Yossarian's observations highlighted the essential absurdity of the situation in which he and others found themselves. Some decades later, this generation lives largely in the past – at least in the novel, where memories act as a retreat – and it is hard to see their observations of the contemporary world as much more than their confusion at the passage of time. This does not invalidate those critiques by any means, but it is a much more familiar literary gesture. There is some evidence that Heller was aware of this himself, as in the novel itself, an old girlfriend of Yossarian, Frances, notes that "You sound so bitter. You used to be funnier" (Heller 1995, p. 54).

If Heller did call his sixth book *Closing Time* on the assumption that it would be his last, he was mistaken, though he would not live to see his final work, *The Portrait of an Artist, as an Old Man* (2000) in print. This final novel is ostensibly autobiographical in nature, and it is far less concerned with the social sphere than any of Heller's previous novels. We might conclude that by this point, Heller had little else to add as a satirist of a culture for which he had little time but saw worthwhile topics both in the decline of his own body and in thinking of his own mortality, and place in posterity.

It is this last point that truly defines the book inasmuch as the primary concerns of Eugene Pota, the thin cloak which Heller assumes here, are about his place in the literary world. He works with and abandons the beginnings of several novels – an in-joke for the dedicated Heller fan familiar with the authors own methods – and is split between his desires to find the plot that will lead to him writing the great American novel that will guarantee his place in the literary pantheon, while simultaneously wanting to write a hugely popular blockbuster which, while no doubt artistically crass in Heller's own view, would translate to the kind of wealth that comes only with interest from Hollywood. Though Heller had made use of metafictional devices in previous efforts, this is his first book that is primarily about writers and writing itself. Naturally, for Pota as for Heller, this great revelation never comes, and this final outing is tinged with a kind of sadness. Joseph Heller had made a living through his use of darkly comic humor, and it seems he was no more sparing when the subject was himself. Critical consensus of this final novel tends to suggest that while *Portrait of an Artist* is as well written as you might expect from someone with Heller's track record, it ultimately is unsuccessful as a novel, failing to cohere and feeling more like the exercise of someone who "no longer has anything new to say yet still wants to say something" (Garrett 2001, p. 114).

SEE ALSO: After Postmodernism; Contemporary Fictions of War; Religion and Contemporary Fiction; Vonnegut, Kurt

REFERENCES

Craig, David M. (2000). *Tilting at Mortality: Narrative Strategies in Joseph Heller's Fiction*. Detroit: Wayne State University Press.

Fowles, Anthony. (2005). *Joseph Heller*. London: Greenwich Exchange.

Garrett, Daniel. (2001). Portrait of the Artist, as an Old Man by Joseph Heller. *World Literature Today* 75 (1): 114.

Heller, Joseph. (1995). *Closing Time*. London: Pocket; 1st ed. 1994.

Pinsker, Sanford. (2009). *Understanding Joseph Heller*. Columbia: University of South Carolina Press.

Rovit, Earl. (1984). *God Knows*. Library Journal 109 (15): 1772.
Templeton, Peter. (2016). "Why don't you just say it as simply as that?": the progression of parrhesia in the early novels of Joseph Heller. *European Journal of American Studies* 11 (2). doi:10.4000/ejas.11573
Vonnegut, Kurt, Jr. (1974). *Something Happened* by Joseph Heller. *The New York Times Book Review* (October 6, 1974). https://archive.nytimes.com/www.nytimes.com/books/98/02/15/home/heller-something.html (accessed July 6, 2021).

FURTHER READING

Craig, David. (1996). Rewriting a classic and thinking about a life: Joseph Heller's *Closing Time*. *CEA Critic* 58 (3): 15–30.
Ruderman, Judith. (1991). *Joseph Heller*. New York: Continuum.
Savu, Laura Elena. (2003). "This book is ours": the crisis of authorship and Joseph Heller's *Portrait of an Artist, as an Old Man*. *Intertexts* 7 (1) 71–89.
Seed, David. (1988). *The Fiction of Joseph Heller: Against the Grain*. New York: St. Martin's Press.

Hemon, Aleksandar

NATHAN JUNG
University of Wisconsin-Milwaukee, USA

In an essay on the increasingly global focus of literary studies, Susan Stanford Friedman writes, "Instead of focusing exclusively on a national literature within the boundaries of a single nation-state, literary scholarship has shifted dramatically toward a transnational perspective" (2007, p. 262). The shift in literary scholarship described by Friedman responds in part to the work of authors like Aleksandar Hemon, the Bosnian American novelist, essayist, short story writer, journalist, and screenwriter. Hemon, who was born and raised in the former Yugoslavia and who later relocated to the United States, often writes in ways that use the lens of fiction to refract his own personal experience of displacement during the Bosnian war. Surveying the "here" and "there" of distant places connected by the "before" and "after" of traumatic violence, his writings do not neatly reside in the literary traditions of any single country, even as he takes part in these traditions, and in turn reshapes them. His corpus to date carefully weaves together multiple voices, places, histories, and genres to ruminate on the related topics of loss, memory, violence, and the sense of belonging that is produced and intimately shaped by language and the ordering effects of narrative. As a result, Hemon's work can be usefully situated in a global context shared by many other contemporary "American" writers, whose key contributions to "American" literature must always be qualified by the fact of diasporic migration and the multiple attachments, national and otherwise, engendered by such migration.

Hemon's biography weaves through his writing in complex ways, as scraps of personal, familial, and world history demonstrably relating to his life routinely inform the locations, characterizations, and dramatic action of his fiction. For this reason, a careful overview of his biography is especially useful. Born on September 9, 1964, in Yugoslavia, Hemon (who often goes by the nickname "Sasha") was born to Petar, whose family has roots in western Ukraine, and Andja, his Bosnian-Serb mother. Petar worked in the area of electrical engineering for companies like Elektroprenos and Energoinvest, which required frequent global travel; Andja worked first as an accountant and later took up teaching. Hemon, who has a younger sister as well, eventually attended the University of Sarajevo and began his writing career as a journalist. However, he also, at this early stage, characteristically counterbalanced his impulse toward journalistic accuracy with hosting duties at a radio show that incorporated music, movie and book reviews, and most tellingly, a storytelling segment called "Sasha Hemon Tells You True and Untrue Stories." These early endeavors – journalism and oral storytelling – can be understood as stock ingredients for the complicated entanglement of fact and fiction that emerges in his later work.

In 1992, at the age of 28, Hemon signed up to visit the United States as a journalist for a cultural exchange program. The Bosnian War broke out during this trip, at which point Hemon found himself effectively stranded in Chicago, speaking little English and cut off from his friends, his family, and his native city of Sarajevo. As the war unfolded from a distance, Hemon worked a series of odd jobs and immersed himself in both the English language and the city of Chicago. He attended Northwestern University and, for a time, Loyola University Chicago to pursue graduate studies in English literature. He left the program to write full time when his short stories were first published in venues like *The New Yorker*.

And so, remarkably, by 1995, just three years after arriving in Chicago, Hemon's career as a professional writer commenced with these short stories published in English, a second language he learned later in life. The role second-language acquisition plays in Hemon's career trajectory is partly responsible for the frequent critical comparisons he has garnered to other displaced authors working in an adopted language (including especially Joseph Conrad and Vladimir Nabokov). While this fact is often mentioned in profiles of Hemon, it deserves to be reemphasized, as it adds context to the precision and ingenuity of his writerly style. This style has many dimensions, but with specific regard to the effects of second-language acquisition, we might highlight his consistent facility with the use of unexpected and unusual English words and formulations to punctuate his observations. This facility allows Hemon to strategically deploy the device of defamiliarization (named by the American New Critics) to introduce a sense of distance and resultant newness to the scenarios depicted in his prose. The device is critical to Hemon's success in conveying the feeling of disorientation that results from migrant displacement to unfamiliar places and languages. Owing to the effectiveness of this style and the import of his topical concern for involuntary migration, he was awarded a Guggenheim Fellowship in 2003 and a MacArthur Fellowship in 2005. In more recent years, he has continued to publish and collaborate on new works in diverse genres, served as the first writer in residence at the United Nations, and taught creative writing at several institutions including Columbia College in Chicago. Currently, he is on the faculty at Princeton University, where he teaches courses in creative writing.

Hemon's corpus often addresses the themes of war, displacement, identity, and language noted in the authorial biography sketched above. The diversity of this corpus, though, is not well suited to the kind of chronological overview used in biographical summary; as a result, the remainder of this entry is organized by grouping his works into genres, with the caveat that genres in Hemon are highly porous. His works are treated in the following order: essays, short stories, story collections, novels, collected essays, and multimedia. To begin, building on his early work in journalism, Hemon has published and continues to publish one-off essays in venues like *The New Yorker* and *The Atlantic*. These essays are often literary in nature, and often touch on the core themes of his broader corpus, as in "Mapping Home" (2011), which treats the relationship between city space and identity, or "My Mother and the Failed Experiment of Yugoslavia" (2019), which builds on a recent essay collection to reevaluate the legacy of Yugoslavia in a context of family history. Hemon also occasionally writes essays on his lifelong passion for soccer, which have been collected in *The Matter of Life, Death and More: Writing on*

Soccer (2014). In terms of independent short stories, Hemon's first publications in English included narratives like "The Life and Work of Alphonse Kauders" (*Triquarterly*, 1998), "The Sorge Spy Ring" (*Triquarterly*, 1998), "Islands" (*Ploughshares*, 1998), and "Blind Jozef Pronek" (*The New Yorker*, 1999). These stories were gathered together, along with others, in Hemon's first story collection, *The Question of Bruno*, which was published in 2000.

The Question of Bruno shows many of the characteristics of his later work, including dark humor, careful, unexpected word choices, narrative juxtaposition, explorations of memory and identity in the context of near and distant violence, a blending of realism and postmodernist metacommentary, and finally, a related interest in the relationship between storytelling and historical truth. One exemplary story, "The Sorge Spy Ring," is worth focusing on, as it both makes explicit use of these devices, and also establishes their importance for the thematic concerns that will recur in different permutations throughout Hemon's career. In this story, a young boy is enamored of the Russian spy Richard Sorge; throughout the story, he begins reading the fantastical, almost fictitious life of Sorge into the more mundane reality of his father's life. "The Sorge Spy Ring" makes use of counterpoints between the fictional body text and footnotes that are more often devoted to detailing the reality of Sorge's historical record. Fiction and history are thus separated by a thin measure of white page space, as the boy's evolving relationship with his father becomes a meditation on cultural memory and the difficult interpenetration of familial and national stories. The story is also, importantly, punctuated by archival and personal photographs, a device that Hemon forcefully revisits in his later novel *The Lazarus Project* (2008).

These characteristics are further developed in Hemon's *Nowhere Man* (2002). While billed as a novel, *Nowhere Man* moves through a series of independent but interlocked chapters, a sequence that is perhaps best understood as a novelistic short story cycle rather than as a novel, or as a short story collection like *The Question of Bruno*. These chapters detail the displaced Bosnian Jozef Pronek's life in Chicago, as focalized through the lens of one or more narrators. Sometimes chapters are relayed in the first person via narrators that resemble Hemon himself (as in the first story, "Passover"); sometimes Hemon employs a third-person omniscient narrator (as in the second story, "Yesterday"); and one story ("Fatherland") is narrated in the first person by a fully developed, independent character – Pronek's university roommate and future Shakespeare professor, Victor Plavchuk. Apart from the first and last chapters, *Nowhere Man* moves chronologically from Pronek's childhood in Sarajevo, to his time as a university student in Kiev before the breakup of the Soviet Union, to his immigrant life in Chicago following wartime displacement. The remarkable array of voices, places, and times that coexist in *Nowhere Man*, however, tend to push back against the linear movement of a typical sequential novelistic narrative. Instead, they foreground Hemon's formal and thematic interest in literary collage, as he often asks readers to navigate uncertain connections between roughly adjoined but internally coherent narrative fragments. The final chapter of *Nowhere Man* exemplifies this interest, as it abandons Pronek to focus on the meditations of its narrator during a honeymoon stay at the Peace (formerly Cathay) Hotel in Shanghai. Instead of resolving Pronek's story, the chapter addresses the disparate strands of the novel through its narrator's meditation on the slippery life of the early twentieth-century spy Evgenij Pick. Descriptions of Pick's theatrical navigations of geopolitics during the time period descend into a nightmarish depiction of a mouse figure clawing out from inside his chest, which references an earlier chapter, narrated by a mouse, that details Pronek breaking down while in Chicago. This characteristic exercise in inviting meaning-making through unstated connections between fragments speaks to the ruptures encountered by a diasporic "Nowhere Man" like Pronek.

Such ruptures also run through his most recent collection, albeit in different ways. Published in 2009, *Love and Obstacles* contains similarly diverse stories that are similarly related by Hemon-like Bosnian American narrators, sometimes named ("Bogdan" in the story "Smzura's Room"), but more frequently not. *Love and Obstacles* also returns to Sarajevo and Chicago. However, there are several important divergences – in terms of place, the book introduces a new, early focus on Africa, with an overt reference to Conrad, and with some backing in the engineering work done abroad by Hemon's father, although the father in question here is instead a diplomat stationed in Zaire. Further, *Love and Obstacles* can be assessed as a *Künstlerroman*, or specific subvariant of the *Bildungsroman* genre that focuses on artistic development. The story collection, in other words, vies with Hemon's later novel *The Making of Zombie Wars* (2015) for the title of Hemon's most explicit thematic commentary on writing. While the novel focuses more on writerly process, *Love and Obstacles* focuses more on the profession and/or vocation of writing, and in particular questions of artistic influences and inspiration. Many of its stories explore the ties between early influences and later stylistic development, the nature of literary hero worship, and related ambivalences associated with success in the field, particularly surrounding the knotty relationship between authorship and biography (seen in "American Commando").

While building on the themes and structural devices of hybrid novel/collections like *Nowhere Man* and *Love and Obstacles*, Hemon's two fully agreed-upon novels to date distinguish themselves from such hybrid texts by adopting more sustained narrative voices and more concrete links between segments. To begin, *The Lazarus Project*, which was short-listed for the National Book Award, uses a speculative history orientation to reconstruct the life and death of Lazarus Averbuch, a Ukranian Jew murdered by the Chicago chief of police in the early twentieth century. The general conceit for the book's reconstruction revolves around a displaced Bosnian living in Chicago toward the end of the century who seeks to write about Averbuch after encountering a photograph of him in the archival collections at the Chicago Historical Society. After receiving a grant to conduct further research on Averbuch, Brik decides to retrace his steps from Europe to the United States. He is accompanied on this journey by his friend Rora, a photographer and fellow displaced Bosnian living in Chicago whose images, it is implied, are the contemporary photographs found in the novel which, it is further implied, was ultimately written by Brik. Their joint "Lazarus Project," that is, becomes the novel itself. By interweaving the metanovel frame of Brik's narrative of homeland return to postwar Sarajevo with a speculative retelling of Lazarus's death and the ensuing grief and political machinations, *The Lazarus Project* asks readers to trace networks of traumatic violence and recovery through a meditation on archival absences. On this last point about archives, and recalling Rora's images, *The Lazarus Project* includes extensive use of photographs, some of which are documentary (in the case of the Lazarus sections, pulled from the Chicago Historical Society), and some of which are contemporary (taken by his friend and collaborator Velibor Božović).

Hemon's most recent novel, *The Making of Zombie Wars*, represents a partial departure from his previous work. To begin, its main character is not a Bosnian refugee: he is an American, from a wealthy family, who works at an ESL Center and wants to write for the movies. As noted in the previous section on *Love and Obstacles*, it comments more explicitly on issues of writerly process than Hemon's other texts. Offering a complex, uncertain *Künstlerroman* for its delayed-adolescent narrator, the book collects excerpts from his screenplays as it describes the dissolvement of his holding-pattern life after he cheats on his girlfriend with a Bosnian refugee. This is an unusual book for Hemon in the sense that it is more explicitly farcical than his other novels and strongly focalizes on a character who does not, at least in biographical details, resemble Hemon in the slightest.

In addition to his novels and short story collections, Hemon has published collections of his nonfiction essays and collaborated in several media. Hemon writes prolifically for a variety of publications, which has resulted in a rich body of essayistic work. His first nonfiction collection, *The Book of My Lives*, from 2013, contains essays on several aspects of Hemon's life, including perhaps his most moving and well-known essay, "The Aquarium," which ruminates on family and death. More recently, *My Parents, an Introduction / This Does Not Belong to You* (2019) is a bi-facing text with two long-form essays: reading the book in one direction presents an account of his parents that presents a different view of the family lore often scattered throughout his work in fiction. Reading the book in the opposite direction presents an account of his youth. The essays include many of Hemon's characteristic interests, but the extended, nonfiction essay genre presents more unguarded, raw expressions of empathy for the experience of his parents, for Yugoslavia, and for Sarajevo in particular. His next nonfiction project, *Behind the Glass Wall: Inside the United Nations*, which at the time of writing has not been published, is expected to explore the culture of that organization based on his time in residence there.

Finally, Hemon has an increasingly rich body of collaborations. To begin, building on their collaboration for *The Lazarus Project*, Hemon worked with his photographer and friend Velibor Božović on the text-photo collection *My Prisoner* (2015). This book, which explores in part their long friendship and experience as diasporic subjects, combines photographs from Božović with an essay by Hemon. In addition, Hemon has expanded into screenwriting. First, he co-wrote the screenplay for Jasmile Zbanic's film *Love Island* (2015), a romantic farce that has transgressive elements. More recently, he co-wrote the final season of the Netflix show *Sense8* with the novelist David Mitchell in collaboration with the show's creators, fellow Chicagoans Lana and Lilly Wachowski.

Across these partnerships and across his written works to date, Hemon has developed a deep and multifaceted engagement with the constellation of community, identity, and place that constitute our sense of "belonging." While clearly requiring what critics have, recalling Susan Stanford Friedman, described as a "transnational turn" in American literary studies, Hemon's focus on diaspora, migration, and assimilation points to the fundamental importance of local, inclusive public cultures and the powerful stories that grow from them.

SEE ALSO: Globalization; Multiculturalism; Trauma and Fiction

REFERENCE

Friedman, Susan. (2007). Migrations, diasporas, and borders. In: *Introduction to Scholarship in Modern Languages and Literatures* (ed. David Nicholls), 260–293. New York: MLA Publications.

FURTHER READING

Baker, Deborah. (2008). Aleksandar Hemon by Deborah Baker. *Bomb Magazine*. https://bombmagazine.org/articles/aleksandar-hemon-1/

Boswell, Timothy. (2015). The audacity of despair: an interview with Aleksandar Hemon. Studies in the Novel 47 (2): 246–266.
Carton, Jessy. (2018). Complicated refugees: a study of the 1951 Geneva Convention grounds in Aleksandar Hemon's life narrative. Law & Literature 30 (2): 331–347.
Irr, Caren. (2014). *Toward the Geopolitical Novel: U.S. Fiction in the Twenty-First Century*. New York: Columbia University Press.
Jung, Nathan. (2018). Mapping the media of Aleksandar Hemon's diasporic time-geography. ARIEL: A Review of English Literature 49 (2): 37–62.
Weiner, Sonia. (2014). Double visions and aesthetics of the migratory in Aleksandar Hemon's *The Lazarus Project*. Studies in the Novel 46 (2): 215–235.

Hempel, Amy

JEFFREY A. SARTAIN
University of Houston-Victoria, USA

Born December 14, 1951, Amy Hempel is one of the most talented literary stylists in American literature, made doubly remarkable because her career and reputation have been built almost exclusively on the short story. She is the author of five volumes of short fiction, *Reasons to Live* (1985), *At the Gates of the Animal Kingdom* (1990), *Tumble Home* (1997), *The Dog of the Marriage* (2005), and *Sing to It* (2019). Her first four books of short stories were rereleased as the 2006 *New York Times* Best Seller *The Collected Stories of Amy Hempel*. In 2015, Hempel and Jill Ciment released a co-authored thriller, *The Hand That Feeds You*. Hempel's 1983 short story, "In the Cemetery Where Al Jolson Is Buried," earned her a reputation as a talented observer of the traumas of everyday life. The story has since become one of the most anthologized short stories in American fiction. Hempel has earned numerous awards and accolades throughout her career, including in 2009, selection for the PEN/Malamud Award for Excellence in Short Fiction. In 2017, Hempel was inducted into the American Academy of Arts and Letters, and in 2018, she received the Yaddo Artist Medal. She has taught in many of the country's most prestigious writing programs, including Harvard, Princeton, Duke, and New York Universities, among others. Her work continues to be widely admired, as the reviews for her most recent collection, *Sing to It*, demonstrate.

Hempel's sparse, oblique style perfectly blends meaning and form. Just as her stories focus on so many emotions that signify absence (loss, grief, fear), the style of her writing also relies on absence for its affective appeal. Hempel's stories are set in the immutable present and provide only a brief snapshot of a character's life. The term story, as it is commonly understood, entails some sort of closure and resolution. Hempel's work avoids traditional story structure, though, favoring a radical compression of plot and action into small fragments from a character's life. Complete exploration of the traditional movement from exposition to denouement does not occur in Hempel's work, as she compresses the standard literary structure with the narrow windows of time generally represented in her stories, usually focused on some intense moment of recollection after a traumatic or climactic event. Rather than taking the reader to an artificial climax of the story and then resolving the tensions, Hempel's stories tend to show a reader how a character perseveres through conflict, trauma, and loss. The notion of perseverance changes the structure of these stories, making their ultimate high point not a climactic moment of plot-driven action, but rather quiet moments of survival, self-revelation, and partial epiphany. Through Hempel's precise targeting of language, image, and the almost wholesale elimination of exposition, she creates stories about resolute narrators who often survive incredibly destructive traumas. In her stories, readers become familiar with how each character lives from day to day and what coping and defensive mechanisms they have built up, psychologically, to persevere in the face of their individual grief or fear.

Certainly, Hempel's biography is strewn with the kinds of loss, grief, and trauma that her characters experience, though it is reductionist and inaccurate to characterize her writing as autobiographical. Her father, Gardiner, was an executive, and her mother, Gloria, was a guide at an art museum (Fields 2011). Born and raised in Chicago with her two brothers, Gardiner and Peter, she says she "lived in and around the city till third grade, I think," at which point her family relocated to Denver, Colorado, where she would spend the next eight years of her life (Sapp 1993, p. 77). As one profile of Hempel reports, "Her parents encouraged reading from an early age, and they stocked their homes with books" (Fields 2011). After eight years in Colorado, Hempel moved to San Francisco, California, where she would spend roughly the next twelve years of her life moving up and down the state. This period of her life was one of the most formative for her writing, although she often refers to the period as "the lost years" when discussing it in interviews and profiles (Sapp 1993, p. 77). Her mother committed suicide when Hempel was 19. Shortly thereafter, her mother's sister also committed suicide. Around the same time, her best friend died of leukemia. Hempel herself suffered from a series of "grave" traumatic injuries in auto accidents that required numerous hospital stays (Fields 2011). She says that her move to California was never quite successful, despite the beauty of the place and time: "I went to join my family, which had moved there while I was a senior. San Francisco was odd. I was just sort of on my own in the late sixties" (Winner 2003, p. 36). She encountered many of the formative cultural events that occurred in California in that period, "but it was difficult. A lot of very difficult things happened out there to the people around me" (p. 36).

During her twenties, Hempel worked on what she calls "a nonlinear college education" where she attended "five different colleges and universities in California, where I majored in journalism and took many incompletes" (Sapp 1993, p. 77). Hempel says, despite going "from accident to accident, hospital to hospital" throughout the period, she managed to write in journals, though she was not yet writing any fiction (p. 77). These journals became the fertile ground for her later work as a fiction writer, though she did not realize it at the time. Upon reflection, Hempel says she now thinks of the journals and the period as "research" for the fiction of her thirties (p. 77). Hempel says her "impulse was to note and save things that struck me. It wasn't, 'Today I did this, today I did that.' It was a journal of things people said" (p. 77). The journals from her twenties later became the source for many moments of language and imagery in her first two collections, valuable and translatable to fiction precisely because they were not a documentary of a day's events, but were rather the stuff of language and were readily repurposed into fiction.

In 1975, Hempel moved to New York to pursue the goal of becoming a writer (Winner 2003, p. 32). She loved the West Coast, but she "was happy to leave California because I was traumatized by the earthquakes" (Sapp 1993, p. 77). In a pivotal literary moment of her career, Hempel decided to attend Gordon Lish's famous "Tactics of Fiction" workshop at Columbia University. In order to learn her craft, Hempel says, "I did a kind of old-fashioned thing. I apprenticed myself to a master" (Chenoweth 2005, p. 41). She was familiar with Lish, the notorious fiction editor of *Esquire* magazine and Knopf's fiction editor, through his work with other influential authors that she read, such as Barry Hannah, Raymond Carver, Grace Paley, and Mary Robison (p. 37). Lish, for her, was important to seek out as a teacher because "At *Esquire* in the seventies and, later, at Knopf, he was publishing the voices that interested me most. I felt allied with his choices, so he was the one I wanted to work with" (pp. 36–37). She initially wrote her first story, "In the Cemetery Where Al Jolson is Buried," as a first semester project in Lish's workshop, which she attended from 1978 to 1984. The workshop was offered as a continuing education course at Columbia University's School of General Studies, so Hempel did not have to be a current Columbia student to enroll (Blumenkrantz 2014). For several years, on and off, she attended the workshop first at Columbia, and then continued when Lish relocated the workshop to his home. Many prominent writers of this period studied at Lish's workshops, and his methods and pedagogy for producing creative work have become the stuff of literary mythology.

Her distinctive style, tone, and timing have earned her devoted fans and numerous accolades since her debut story, "In the Cemetery Where Al Jolson is Buried," appeared in Gordon Lish's journal, *TriQuarterly*, in 1983 to much acclaim. It garnered Hempel a mention as an Outstanding Writer in the *Pushcart Prize: Best of the Small Presses* anthology of 1984–1985, and it was later included in the *Norton Anthology of Short Fiction*. Since then, it has gone on to be one of the most anthologized American short stories of the twentieth century (Temple 2017), and is regarded widely as a classic.

Her reliance on the short story form, her oblique style, as well as her association with Lish as teacher and editor, led to many critics tagging her writing with the minimalist label. Minimalism is a term Hempel has consistently resisted because, especially with regard to the short story stylists of the 1970s and 1980s, the label is often abused by critics as a meaningless pejorative. The term minimalist in the 1970s and 1980s was a distinctive word that labeled an author's connection to what has come to be known as *The New Yorker* school of fiction, closely associated with Raymond Carver, *The New Yorker*'s fiction editor, and his mentor/editor, Gordon Lish. While Carver and Hempel were not students of Gordon Lish's at the same time, they do share a parallel relationship with Lish as teacher, mentor, and editor, though Hempel never published in *The New Yorker*.

The controversy around the minimalist label, and the pejoratives lobbed in the direction of many of Lish's former students, only heightened in intensity throughout the 1980s and into the 1990s. During this period, Hempel earned many accolades and awards, as well as serving as a contributing editor for *Vanity Fair* in 1985–1986 after its resurrection in 1983. She began reviewing books and writing journalism for many prestigious publications, extending her recognition and range. Hempel's second volume, *At the Gates of the Animal Kingdom*, released in 1990, followed the publication of almost every story in the collection in a prestigious journal between 1985 and 1989. This collection, too, grew out of her mentorship with Gordon Lish, where he again served as editor for the book in his capacity as fiction editor at Knopf. This volume received much more mixed reactions from critics. Many accused it of being too reminiscent of her first, and the collection was met with outright hostility by some reviewers, despite the fact that it sold well and time has earned it praise and devotion from fans and critics. The critical press, by 1990, seemed exhausted by the perceived prominence of minimalist writers in the previous two decades, which is reflected in the contemporary reviews for Hempel's second volume.

During the period following *At the Gates of the Animal Kingdom*, Hempel remained active, publishing stories and criticism throughout the early 1990s. She regards this period as one of transition, where she had to relearn much of what she had learned about writing fiction. During the period, she changed publishing houses and editors, moving from Knopf to Scribner's. She published almost all of the stories, or fragments of them, from her next collection, *Tumble Home*, before its release in 1997. In this volume, Hempel has both her longest and shortest works to date, the almost 80-page titular novella, "Tumble Home," and the four-line short-short, "Housewife." Both of these moves, to work longer and to work shorter than she ever had before, are signals of the difficulty of the transition she describes in several contemporary interviews. Generally, critics were much kinder to *Tumble Home* than they were to *At the Gates of the Animal Kingdom*, and the volume was Hempel's first bestseller, spending three weeks on the *New York Times* Best Seller list (Goldwater 2000). By 1997, the fervor over Carver's literary legacy and that of *The New Yorker* school of minimalism had died down significantly, and many critics and readers found renewed interest in Hempel's stripped and focused literary stylings.

Between *Tumble Home* and Hempel's next collection, *The Dog of the Marriage*, she continued publishing short fiction, but vastly reduced the output of nonfiction and reviews that she produced. The stories in *The Dog of the Marriage* continued Hempel's efforts to redefine the limits of her narrative style, pushing her again toward more expansive and more reduced forms simultaneously. In "Memoir," she achieves her most crystallized and distilled narrative, reducing the entirety of the narrative to a single sentence. "Offertory," while not itself longer than "Tumble Home" from the previous collection, is a continuation of that story. The only explicit sequel to a story Hempel has ever written, "Offertory" expands even further on the long narrative that formed almost half of the previous collection, and taken together, they are Hempel's longest narrative work outside of her 2015 co-written novel.

In 2006, Scribner's published *The Collected Stories of Amy Hempel*, which gathered all forty-eight stories from her previous four volumes under one cover. This collection was released to wide acclaim, reaching nine printings of the hardcover edition (36,000 copies) within a year of its release, causing the publisher to delay the paperback release six months due to the remarkable sales of the first edition (Italie 2007). As Hempel's editor Nan Graham said in a 2007 interview, the success of the hardcover of *The Collected Stories* was a high point in Hempel's career: "Publishing her collected stories has made such a difference . . . She never sold more than 10,000 copies of a book before. Having 36,000 in print may seem pretty modest, but it's actually pretty amazing for an author of literary short stories" (Italie 2007). Since the release of *The Collected Stories*, Hempel's visibility as an important personality in American fiction has only increased. She has continued to publish fiction and returned to writing essays and book reviews, many appearing in glossy magazines with huge readerships, such as *O! The Oprah Magazine*. In the 2000s, Hempel has also garnered an unlikely new demographic of fans thanks to frequent glowing praise from the best-selling author of *Fight Club* (1996), Chuck Palahniuk.

Hempel's 2015 co-authored novel, *The Hand That Feeds You*, borrows the broad strokes of its plot from current events. Hempel teamed up with fiction writer and memoirist Jill Ciment to pen a murder mystery under the shared pseudonym A.J. Rich. This serial killer thriller is unlike anything else Hempel has or Ciment had ever written, and it was inspired by events that happened to their dear mutual friend, writer Katherine Russell Rich, who died of cancer before she could write a novel about her experiences. The novel received mixed reviews from critics, but it was a bestseller and its popularity earned it a spot on the Target Book Club, guaranteeing it a priority position in the big box retailer's stores. Though it ranges far from much of what either author had written previously, the book bears many hallmarks of each author's style and concerns. Telling the story of a woman seduced by a man who was not who he claimed, Morgan Prager, a graduate student in criminal psychology, has to navigate a labyrinth of lies and violence to uncover the truth about her former lover. From Hempel, particularly, the work seems to inherit its thematic focus on the many facets of truth and trauma, as well as its significant discussions of dogs and animal subjectivities. From Ciment, a veteran novelist, the novel gained a sense of consistency and cohesion across the work that built the novel's sense of suspense and mystery.

Since the publication of *The Collected Stories*, Amy Hempel has continued producing short fiction that appears in a variety of journals and magazines. Her recent short story "Chicane" was selected for inclusion in *Best American Short Stories 2017*, edited by Meg Wolitzer. Her most recent stories, including "Chicane," were released in the 2019 collection *Sing to It*, to a chorus of praise and glowing reviews.

SEE ALSO: Beattie, Ann; Carver, Raymond; Hannah, Barry; Minimalism and Maximalism; Palahniuk, Chuck

REFERENCES

Blumenkrantz, Carla. (2014). Seduce the whole world. In: *MFA vs. NYC: The Two Cultures of American Fiction* (ed. Chad Harbach), 209–222. New York: Farrar, Straus and Giroux.

Chenoweth, Emily. (2005). Hounding loss. *Publishers Weekly* (March 2005): 41. https://www.publishersweekly.com/pw/print/20050314/36669-hounding-loss.html (accessed August 4, 2021).

Ciment, Jill and Hempel, Amy as Rich, A.J. (2015). *The Hand That Feeds You*. New York: Scribner's.

Fields, Amanda. (2011). Amy Hempel. In: *American Writers, Supplement 21* (ed. Jay Parini). New York: Scribner's.

Goldwater, Mitchell. (2000). Amy Hempel. In: *American Short-Story Writers Since World War II: Second Series* (ed. Patrick Meanor and Gwen Crane). Farmington Hills, MI: Gale.

Hempel, Amy. (1985). *Reasons to Live*. New York: Knopf.

Hempel, Amy. (1990). *At the Gates of the Animal Kingdom*. New York: Knopf.

Hempel, Amy. (1997). *Tumble Home*. New York: Scribner's.

Hempel, Amy. (2005). *The Dog of the Marriage*. New York: Scribner's.

Hempel, Amy. (2006). *The Collected Stories of Amy Hempel*. New York: Scribner's.

Hempel, Amy. (2019). *Sing to It*. New York: Scribner's.

Italie, Hillel. (2007). Hempel lives to write, writes to live. *AP Online* (May 5, 2007).

Sapp, Jo. (1993). An interview with Amy Hempel. Missouri Review 16 (1): 75–95.

Temple, Emily. (2017). The most anthologized short stories of all time: a (mostly) definitive list. *Literary Hub* (July 6, 2017). https://lithub.com/the-most-anthologized-short-stories-of-all-time/ (accessed July 4, 2021).

Winner, Paul. (2003). Amy Hempel: The art of fiction. Paris Review 176: 30–63. https://www.theparisreview.org/interviews/227/the-art-of-fiction-no-176-amy-hempel (accessed July 4, 2021).

FURTHER READING

Bolonik, Kera. (2006). Al Green, Gordon Lish, and cadavers: Amy Hempel talks with Bookforum. *Bookforum* (April/May): 48–49.

ConnectLiterature. (2012). A conversation on writing with Amy Hempel (May 7, 2012). https://www.youtube.com/watch?v=CXOR9gxbX1c

Hallett, Cynthia W. (1999). *Minimalism and the Short Story: Raymond Carver, Amy Hempel, and Mary Robison*. New York: Edwin Mellen Press.

Manguso, Sarah. (2007). Amy Hempel: writer. In: *The Believer Book of Writers Talking to Writers* (ed. Vendela Vida), 111–122. San Francisco: Believer Books.

Palahniuk, Chuck. (2004). Not chasing Amy. In: *Stranger than Fiction*, 141–146. New York: Doubleday.

Sherman, Suzan. (1997). Amy Hempel. Bomb 59: 66–70. https://bombmagazine.org/articles/amy-hempel/

Hijuelos, Oscar

LAURA ALONSO-GALLO
Barry University, USA

Oscar Hijuelos, born in the Morningside Heights section of Manhattan to Cuban working-class parents who emigrated to New York in the early 1940s, authored eight novels and one memoir between 1983 and 2011, and a ninth novel, published posthumously in 2015. Recipient of numerous international and national awards and prizes of prestige, Hijuelos was the first Hispanic writer to receive the Pulitzer Prize for fiction (*The Mambo Kings Play Songs of Love* in 1990). Rich in references to twentieth-century sociopolitical history that connect Cuba, the United States, and Europe, his novels skillfully integrate urban life, music, art, and popular culture and highlight how historical forces distress people and how the beauty of art and love save them. While Cuba constitutes the imagined homeland from which most of his stories emerge, Hijuelos's characters are drawn to timeless existential questions concerning human identity, family ties, friendship, emotional isolation, mortality, and success. Nostalgia, expressed in displacement from Cuba and the loss of a kinder past, constitutes Hijuelos's aesthetics to reimagine Cuban histories passed on through his ancestors' memories.

Pre-Castro experiences of assimilation allow Hijuelos to study the ideas of home and cultural identity in Cuban diasporic subjects and their children. He stages stories of individuals (often from childhood to death) who live in a community. New York is a pivot of his fiction, a city subject to social change where his personages experience disappointment and personal fulfillment while seeking success and happiness. The island of Cuba and Havana appear as epicenters of a past that invests his characters with an unmistakable Cuban mentality and sense of origin.

Hijuelos earned a master's in English and writing from City College in 1976 and began his writing career thereafter with the short story genre while he worked in the advertisement media sector. Several grants and scholarships recognized his literary talent, and a collection of his stories was published in the 1978 anthology *Best of Pushcart Press III*. He became Professor of English at Hofstra University and also taught English at Duke University. At the age of 62, he died tragically of a heart attack. In his memoir *Thoughts Without Cigarettes* (2011), Hijuelos addressed the loss of his Cuban identity when he was a young boy and his reconnection with Cuba through writing.

Hijuelos's realist aesthetics furthers a rounded characterization of individuals via a third-person omniscient narrator that invites characters to digress in time and subject, infusing lyricism into memory and desire. Hijuelos seeks neither to criticize nor to change society's morals and vices but to contemplate the human soul. His stories usually anticipate the main subject of the novel by starting *in medias res* and follow a long linear flashback, which often combines daydreaming to delve into the characters' desire and description of environment, and flashforwards by which the narrator clarifies and comments. Along with the contemplation of natural landscapes, youth, and human goodness, each novel is associated with art in one of its forms – music, illustration, photography, comic books, literature, and cinema – suggesting that beauty defies the angst and the ephemeral in human existence.

His debt to realism lays also on the representation of eras that encompass people's mannerisms and idiom, fashion, architecture, natural and urban landscapes, and trendy tastes in music, books, magazines, and clubs. Iconic politicians, celebrities, and artists populate Hijuelos's novels, which feature characters such as Desi Arnaz and Lucy (from the *I Love Lucy* TV show) and Errol Flynn, García Lorca, Picasso and Dalí, Gershwin, Granados and Lecuona, and a myriad of twentieth-century Caribbean musicians.

A Proustian approach to memory and the fleeting nature of happiness permeate Hijuelos's fiction. Characters and places equally inhabit and occupy present and past. The past gravitates over the present with such force and omnipresence that existence is ultimately defined by memory. His characters emerge in the novels as real people with flaws of character such as dispiritedness, lust, vanity, and arrogance. Their behavior may be virtuous or selfish; they make mistakes, fall to verbal or physical violence and addictions such as alcohol, and experience disillusionment and loneliness. A few of his novels delve in existential angst through characters' inner journeys in search of spiritual wholeness. Cuban or not, characters yearn for a childhood filled with love and innocence which brings comfort into the present. They usually find redemption in the beauty of art and compassion, and solace in the goodness of the past, be it childhood, youth, motherly love, or a Cuba of old. The desires, dreams, and hopes that plague their present are transitory while the few instances of life's happiness, love, and fulfillment are inevitably drawn to the past. Memory holds, paradoxical as it may seem, more hope than the present and the future.

Our House in the Last World (1983), the most autobiographical of his novels, is the story of the "small town dandy" (2017, p. 19) Alejo Santinio and his bride Mercedes, who married in Holguín in 1941 and left a financially stable life in Cuba to embark on the adventure of a life in New York. Although Alejo works two jobs and provides food for his family, he indulges in alcohol and the comfort of his friendships, and, mostly due to his lack of purpose, they would never fulfill the American Dream. Proud and pleasure seeking, Alejo would altruistically assist and cheer up friends and relatives. Meanwhile, his authoritarian masculinity suffocates his wife and children. Readers enter the four family members' consciousness from 1944 through 1975 and learn about their frustrations and the love they profess to each other despite Alejo's frequent melancholy and violent tantrums. A typical 1940s loyal housewife, Mercedes stays by her husband although resenting their life of modest resources. She constantly reproaches Alejo for avoiding opportunities to improve the family finances. The Santinio children suffer not only from the trauma of unstable and antagonistic parents but also from street violence and discrimination. One of the artistic pulls of this novel is Alejo's magnetic personality. In the manner of Isabel Allende and García Márquez, Hijuelos employs magic realism to accentuate Alejo's pervasive presence as he visits his wife, children, and friends after death. The story ends sadly with a demoralized and delusional Mercedes wandering in the gentle past and fantasizing about a previous life where she can eventually understand and forgive her husband.

The Mambo Kings Play Songs of Love (1989) not only catapulted Hijuelos to the mainstream literary scene but was also crucial in kicking off Latino literature in the 1990s US publishing market. Two musician brothers, Cesar and Nestor Castillo, of opposing spirit and moral fiber, migrate to a mambo-crazed New York City from Cuba in the 1940s in search of artistic recognition. The confident Cesar, driven by his hypersexual appetites, incarnates the frenzied rhythm of mambo and its celebration of sexual pulses. In contrast, the melancholic, noble, and romantic Nestor, who dwells in the Cuban past, identifies with the lyrics and rhythm of his bolero "Beautiful María of My Soul," a story of an impossible love whose version he rewrites over twenty times. The main themes of this novel are success and mortality, masculinity (the novel specifically critiques the macho ideal constructed by the immigrants' home culture), family values, and the transforming cultural force Hispanic immigrants brought to New York. Hijuelos's realist narrative intertwines modernist features and postmodern techniques using footnotes, popular culture, and musical rhythms as well as frequent digressions that alter the story chronology to take readers to the Cuban past. The American Dream precepts Nestor reads from his bedtable book *Forward America* prove unattainable and clash with Cesar's Latin lover *carpe diem* attitude. Like Alejo Santinio, Cesar is generous, spirited, and protective of his family and friends. Much scholarly attention has been given to Cesar's machismo and little to his masculinity and passion for music, both founded on the desire to celebrate life. As a child Cesar's character was shaped by the violence of an alcoholic father who despised his profession for music. After Nestor's sudden death, Cesar stops playing music to work as a superintendent and take care of his brother's widow and children, abandoning his promiscuous lifestyle until he collapses from inebriation and dies at the Hotel Splendor in Manhattan. In Cesar's lonely and lethargic farewell to life there remains only a desire for the feminine, evoked in an elegy to his mother's pure affection and the sexual encounters with countless women since his adolescence in Cuba. The novel has the structure of a vinyl long record where side A narrates the lives of the brothers, their families, and community of friends and side B recounts, after the tragic death of Nestor, the fall of Cesar, who becomes a pathetic figure in his drunk delirium while listening to songs whose rhythms pace the discourse. In the end Hijuelos charges Eugenio, Nestor's son, with the role of redeeming Cesar by his love of music. This novel, translated into more than 30 languages, was adapted to the big screen in 1992 and was made a musical in 2005.

The prequel to *Mambo Kings*, *Beautiful Maria of My Soul* (2010), saw the light twenty-one years later. Hijuelos recovers the story of the enigmatic muse of the brothers' hit song, María, the lost love who precipitated Nestor's trip to America. Her story of female resilience is a testimony to the social inequity and hardship women of color encountered in the patriarchal culture of twentieth-century Cuba. The writer takes us to prerevolutionary Cuba where María lives as a young woman until she leaves for Miami with her daughter in the 1960s. An illiterate and innocent country girl from rural Pinar del Río, María arrives in Havana at 17 with physical beauty as her only asset. Torn between a life of material security and one of true love, she chooses to be saved from a life of privation, dismissing the poor but pure-hearted Nestor to submit to the favors and claims of the wicked businessman Ignacio. Much of the novel dwells in María's persistent memories of Nestor and the grief caused by her sister's and mother's death.

With *The Fourteen Sisters of Emilio Montez O'Brian* (1993) Hijuelos continues to gaze over the history of women in the twentieth century. In this saga novel spanning from the Spanish–American War to the decade of the 1990s, readers learn about the domestic and social experiences of the fourteen daughters of a young Irish émigré and his Cuban bride who settled in rural Pennsylvania. While we get an ample picture of their different personalities, strengths, and motivations, the focus is on the lives of the parents, Margarita, the oldest, and their only son, Emilio. Born in 1902,

Margarita meets the standard goal of marrying well, coming of age after years of abuse by her wealthy and depraved husband. The narrator emphasizes her gradual liberation from social constraints by living an honest and long life and becoming the loving guardian of her aging mother and siblings. As a novel of manners, the social customs, values, and mentalities of the United States and Cuba for one hundred years are elegantly displayed. In addition, elements of naturalism are evident in the treatment of paraphilia and the deterministic forces governing the characters' fate; magic realism highlights the mysteries of human connection beyond the physical. Enduring ethnic discrimination and loneliness, the characters are salvaged by talents such as musical performance, modeling for advertisement, acting for Hollywood, and Spanish language teaching. Photography, the profession of the patriarch Nelson O'Brian, which Emilio would undertake in his later years, becomes a metaphor of the contemplation of social history through the suffering and joy of this peculiar Irish-Cuban clan.

Although *Mr. Ives' Christmas* (1995) brings in a diverse New York immigrant community, the protagonist's absence of ethnicity serves Hijuelos to formulate universal questions about good and evil and the value of religious faith. His version of Dickens's *Christmas Carol* (1843) is an allegory that explores the mystery of hope and renewal in the spirit of Christmas celebrations, "a feeling that time and all its sufferings [fall] away" (1995, p. 4). Instead of Dickens's despicable miser, Hijuelos presents a loving, humble, and sensitive orphan who muses over the meaning of life while dealing with the murder of his young son by a Puerto Rican teen. The question stands: why do tragic things happen to moral people? Like in Dickens's classic, redemption occurs, albeit not from evil since Ives is not a sinner. The benevolent Ives goes through tormented years trying to understand why his son had to die and, instead of giving himself to hatred, he would learn to forgive the perpetrator. The Dickensian brilliance of the discourse and psychological depth take readers on a mystical journey to human goodness and fraternity.

The protagonist of *The Empress of the Splendid Season* (1999) is the pampered, promiscuous daughter of the mayor of a Cuban town who was expelled from her family home in 1947 and emigrated to New York where she experienced loneliness and social stigmatization as a housekeeper. To the linear narrative with intermittent flashbacks to the Cuban past, Hijuelos adds Lydia's daydreaming, which constitutes a private *locus amoenus* she needs to survive the impersonal and cold-hearted society of New York. Lydia's pride, feminine lust, and social consciousness of privilege contrast with her toils as a socially invisible cleaning lady who, after her husband suffers from a stroke, would sacrifice her dreams of glamour to support her family until her death. Their Americanized children, Rico and Alicia, representatives of Hijuelos's generation, resent her "erotic glamour . . . whenever she talked about the old Cuba, *her Cuba*, which [was] as much as a fantasy as the Land of Oz" (1999, pp. 339–340). Rico would fulfill the American Dream when he becomes a successful psychologist and Alicia, a hippie feminist, ends up forming a stereotypical American family. Lydia, who always prided herself in being strong and tough (p. 123), represents the beautiful and strong Cuba of the past, a homeland that vanishes on contact with American society.

A Simple Habana Melody (From When the World Was Good) (2002) is a novel about beauty as it emanates from music, friendship, and love. Hijuelos explores the subject of political ideologies inflicting evil upon humanity and poses the question of why there is "so much useless suffering" (2002, p. 39) in the world. Inspired by the Cuban musician Moisés Simons, Hijuelos depicts the glamorous atmosphere of music and genteel manners of Cuban culture in the Americas and Europe from the turn of the twentieth century through World War II. Israel Levis, a young virtuoso musician in Cuba, contributes to the rumba craze abroad, earning great success in the jazz and tropical musical scene of 1930s Paris. When the Nazis resolve to transport Jews to camps, the educated high-class Catholic Levis is taken to Buchenwald to perform at German parties and eventually returns to Havana in 1947 to end his days in a state of despair. Although music saved his life, his experience of World War II convinced him of the triumph of evil over goodness: "What most tormented him was the violation of his belief that goodness would prevail upon evil in this world" (p. 38). However, Hijuelos's poetic justice saves Levis as he teaches music in his last years to Pilar Blanca, an adolescent mulatta girl of humble means. Before dying, Levis concludes that teaching her was his "greatest accomplishment" (p. 324) since she returned to him and the world the absolute beauty of youth and music.

Dark Dude (2008) pays homage to Mark Twain's *Huckleberry Finn* (1884) for its nonchalant narrative tone, use of the vernacular, journey structure, choice of an adolescent as first-person narrator who runs away, and examination of the issues of race and identity. In this *Bildungsroman* the alienated blond and fair-skinned Cuban American Rico flees Harlem in the 1960s feeling he neither meets his familial Cuban standards nor belongs to any ethnic group because of his skin color. Tired of street violence in the "messed-up big city" (2008, p. 438) and facing a fate of drug addiction, Rico runs away with Jimmy, a neighborhood friend who uses heroin to endure an unhappy life working to bring money to his abusive father. After spending several months in rural Wisconsin living with an ethnically diverse group of kids, Rico returns to his family understanding his identity because "where you are doesn't change what you are" (p. 438). Recipient of several awards, *Dark Dude* contributed to young adult literature by presenting street violence, drugs, and peer and familial pressure through Twain's humorous and realist approach.

In *Twain & Stanley Enter Paradise* (2015) Hijuelos uses epistle, journal, manuscript, and a third-person narrative to fictionalize the friendship of Samuel Clemens and the Welsh explorer Henry Stanley, whose public and private lives are recalled through reflections about colonialism, slavery, afterlife, and fame. Apart from their individual childhood recollections and encounters in the United States and Britain, the story describes a presumed trip to Cuba when Clemens accompanies Stanley to the heart of the island to find his adoptive father. The painter Dorothy Tennant is a connecting character who not only rescues Stanley's early memories but also brings Twain a comforting testament of her late husband's friendship after the death of the writer's daughter and wife. Along with the characters' emotional depth, Hijuelos vividly renders the Victorian idiom and era.

SEE ALSO: After Postmodernism; Allende, Isabel; Díaz, Junot; García, Cristina; Literature of the Americas; Realism after Poststructuralism; Trauma and Fiction

REFERENCES

Hijuelos, Oscar. (1995). *Mr. Ives' Christmas*. New York: Harper Perennial.
Hijuelos, Oscar. (1999). *The Empress of the Splendid Season*. New York: Harper Perennial.
Hijuelos, Oscar. (2002). *A Simple Habana Melody (From When the World Was Good)*. New York: HarperCollins.
Hijuelos, Oscar. (2008). *Dark Dude*. New York: Atheneum.

Hijuelos, Oscar. (2017). *Our House in the Last World*, 35th anniv. ed. New York: Persea Books; 1st ed. 1983.

FURTHER READING

Alonso-Gallo, Laura and Ochoa-Fernández, M. Luisa. (2004). A journey into the human spirit: Oscar Hijuelos. In: *American Voices: Interviews with American Writers* (ed. Laura Alonso-Gallo), 67–96. Cádiz: Aduana Vieja.

Cass, Jeremy. (2015). Oscar Hijuelos' hypothetical homeland: from *Our House in the Last World* to *Thoughts Without Cigarettes*. In: *Negotiating Latinidades, Understanding Identities Within Space* (ed. Kathryn Quinn-Sanchez), 111–131. Newcastle upon Tyne, UK: Cambridge Scholars.

Horn, Maja. (2009). Messy moods: nostalgia and other nagging feelings in Oscar Hijuelos's *The Mambo Kings Play Songs of Love*. *Latino Studies* 7 (4): 499–514.

Patteson, Richard. (2002). Oscar Hijuelos: "eternal homesickness" and the music of memory. *Critique: Studies in Contemporary Fiction* 44 (1): 38–47.

Shirley, Paula. (1995). Reading Desi Arnaz in *The Mambo Kings Play Songs of Love*. *MELUS* 20 (3): 69–78.

Hinojosa, Rolando

JAIME ARMIN MEJÍA
Texas State University, San Marcos, USA

Rolando Hinojosa, sometimes going by Hinojosa-Smith, is a Chicano writer of ten novels, a book of narrative poems, a collection of essays, plus an English rendition of Tomás Rivera's novella, *. . . Y no se lo tragó la tierra*, titled *This Migrant Earth* (1987). Because Hinojosa wrote and published in English and Spanish, his publication history is quite complicated. Several of his early works were published in two-language editions, which had an English translation to his original Spanish text, or were published originally in Spanish and then later with his own English rendition. One work, *Becky and Her Friends / Los amigos de Becky*, was published in both languages simultaneously in 1990. Some of his later works would only be published in English. He also engaged different types of genres in his works, mainly in his novels, including sketches, narrative poems, reportage, letters, detective murder mysteries, and journals, as well as just using a long, straight narrative progression. While Hinojosa also published his works with different publishers, especially early on, his works mainly appeared through two publishers – Bilingual Press and Arte Público Press. From 1973, when his first novel was published by Quinto Sol Publications, to 2011, when his last book was published by Arte Público Press, Hinojosa's literary career spanned nearly four decades.

Born January 21, 1929, in Mercedes, Texas, Hinojosa grew up in the lower Rio Grande Valley of south Texas, a region which would become the focus of most all his literary works. There, he was raised in a blended family, with his father, a Texas Mexican who had served as a soldier in the Mexican Revolution, and his Anglo Texas mother. Hinojosa was the youngest of his family and early on would attend schools in Mercedes as well as in Arteaga, Nuevo León, Mexico, thereby gaining an education in two countries – and in two languages and two cultures. He was influenced by his father's anti-clerical perspectives, which we see borne out in his literary works, evidenced by an almost atheist perspective quite critical of the Catholic Church and its priests.

After graduating from Mercedes High School, he attended the University of Texas at Austin, but his time there was interrupted by his military service in the army; he served in Japan and Korea during the Korean War in the early 1950s. After his military service, he returned to Austin and completed his undergraduate degree. From there, he went to New Mexico Highlands University in Las

Vegas, New Mexico, for a master's degree in Spanish. He was then accepted into a PhD program in Spanish at the University of Illinois at Champaign where he studied with and had his PhD dissertation directed by the eminent scholar Luis Leal, an early pioneering literary critic of Chicanx literature. After completing his doctoral work, he returned to Texas to take an instructor's position teaching Spanish at Trinity University in San Antonio, Texas, in the early 1960s. From there, he took an academic position as a Spanish professor at the Texas A & I, in Kingsville, Texas, where he would rise to serve in administrative positions, first as chair of the Spanish department and then as vice president of academic affairs. Because his wife was accepted into law school at the University of Minnesota, Hinojosa left Texas A & I and served as a professor of Chicano Literature at the University of Minnesota. Having attained fame for the publication of his early novels, he would then be hired into the English Department at the University of Texas in Austin, his alma mater, and would be given the Ellen Clayton Gargood Endowed Chair in English in 1985, which he filled until 2014 when he retired at age 85.

As his career as a Chicano writer rose in the 1970s, he would be invited to do readings and workshops in hundreds of universities in the United States, Mexico, Europe, and South Korea, from Ivy League schools to community colleges. Many of his readings in Europe were sponsored by the US State Department. Towards the end of his career, he was the recipient of many awards and accolades, with the capstone being The Ivan Sandrof Lifetime Achievement Award given by the National Book Critics Circle in 2014. Earlier in 2007, he received the Texas Literary Festival Bookend Award for lifetime achievement. In 1998, he received the Lon Tinkle Lifetime Achievement Award from the Texas Institute of Letters. His career was also marked by many other accolades too numerous to cite individually here.

When Hinojosa published his third book in 1978, *Korean Love Songs*, a work of narrative poems, he christened his works The Klail City Death Trip Series, with the novels published thereafter being part of this series. Made up primarily of novels, the series began in 1973 with *Estampas del valle y otras obras / Sketches of the Valley and Other Works*, which won the third Quinto Sol Prize in 1973, an early prize for the best novel by a Chicanx author. He was preceded in receiving this award by Chicanx literature pioneers Rudolfo Anaya (1971) and Tomás Rivera (1972). His second novel, *Klail City y sus alrededores* (1976), won him the prestigious Casa de las Américas prize for best novel in Latin America, with the Cuban press, Casa de las Américas, being the first to publish this novel. While his first two works were written and published in Spanish and then with translations, he would later render most of his Spanish works, separately, into English or in two-language editions. He distinguished his English renditions from literal translations, so that what he did, instead of doing literal translations, was to retell the same original story, originally written in Spanish, in English. Most recently, he transferred the works he published with Bilingual Press to Arte Público Press so that the novels previously published by Bilingual Press are now found published by Arte Público Press, with one exception, in two-language editions. That exception was the publication of *Korean Love Songs* and *The Useless Servants* (1993), both originally written and published in English, in one volume.

His first two novels, later titled in English as *The Valley* (1983) and *Klail City* (1987), respectively, were made up of relatively short fictional sketches of various characters who populated his fictional Belken County in south Texas along the United States-Mexico border. Among these early characters, one finds stories of two characters, Rafa (Rafe)

Buenrostro and Jehu Malacara, who would have more central roles in several subsequent novels. The Janus figure created by these characters' complementary yet oppositional last names – good face/bad face – shows Hinojosa's early creative artifice as an imaginative writer – in two languages and two distinct border cultures. Many of these early sketches about Rafe and Jehu depict their childhood and upbringing and are crucial to understanding them later as adults. While many other of his early characters would find themselves making appearances in later novels, the trajectory of his literary project would be led primarily by Rafe, with Jehu only having a central role in *Mi querido Rafa* (1981) / *Dear Rafe* (1985). While most of the settings for his literary works are largely found in the lower Rio Grande Valley of south Texas, he did take his readers to the Korean War in *Korean Love Songs* (1978) and *The Useless Servants* (1993).

His third published work, *Korean Love Songs*, comprised of narrative poems, is written entirely in English, depicting Rafe's time in the Korean War during the early 1950s. Hinojosa would later return to the Korean War setting in a subsequent novel, *The Useless Servants*, to provide one of the most authoritative depictions of the Korean War in the Far East. Using Rafe's journal entries of his time as a soldier to construct his novel, Hinojosa produced a daily chronicle of the Korean War in rich realistic detail from the perspective of a soldier, Rafe, assigned to an artillery unit. As in *Korean Love Songs*, *The Useless Servants* has a most poignant moment when Texas Mexican Rafe, as an American soldier, overhears an inexperienced and ignorant general make a blatantly racist comment against Mexican Americans in the United States.

Both works set in Korea, though, are filled with highly mundane and tragically absurd moments which soldiers on the frontlines have to experience, like retrieving the lost dead bodies of American and North Korean soldiers from a river. After having the Korean War as the setting in *Korean Love Songs*, Hinojosa returns to the Korean War in a subsequent novel, *Rites and Witnesses* (1982) where we see sketches of Rafe's experiences in that war. *Rites and Witnesses* serves as a bridge between *Korean Love Songs* and *Mi querido Rafa* / *Dear Rafe* because it also has reportage entries which serve as a prelude to Jehu's epistolary observations as a chief loan officer in a bank in *Mi querido Rafa* / *Dear Rafe*. Another previously submitted novel, *Claros varones de Belken* / *Fair Gentlemen of Belken County* (1986), was delayed in being published in the originally intended sequence because the publisher, Bilingual Press, moved from Eastern Michigan University in Ypsilanti, Michigan, to Arizona State University in Tempe, Arizona. *Claros varones* / *Fair Gentlemen* was originally intended to follow Hinojosa's first two novels and is structured, like the first two, with sketches, vignettes, and short narrative pieces which provide more background of the early lives of Rafe and Jehu.

After Hinojosa's first three novels, if one includes the belatedly published *Claros varones de Belken/Fair Gentlemen of Belken County*, Hinojosa turns his attention to Jehu, the central character of *Mi querido Rafa* / *Dear Rafe*, who holds a job as a loan officer in a Klail City bank in Belken County. The novel is creatively structured by using letters (from Jehu to his cousin Rafe) in the first half and reportage (interviews with a wide array of characters) in the second half. At this bank, Jehu, working under the prominent bank president, Noddy Perkins, observes the political machinations the dominant Texas Anglo group conducts in an election for county commissioner. In his most direct critique of relations between Texas Anglos and Texas Mexicans, as well as between different factions of Texas Mexicans, Hinojosa gives Jehu a front-row seat to the political intrigue surrounding how Texas Anglos manipulate differing parties in order to maintain their political power.

Hinojosa's perspective in this short novel is clearly anticolonial. Having been settled in the eighteenth century by Spanish Mexican colonizers, the Valley in the late nineteenth century is overrun by Anglos who change the ranching economy to a farming economy. This economic transformation occurs through a major illegal land grab, similar to how the infamous King Ranch was created just north of the Valley in south Texas. By the second half of the twentieth century, Hinojosa depicts a strategic reversal by exposing Jehu to this reality and having him engage in clandestinely offsetting Texas Anglo land grabs. The Anglos, on their part, use an election for a county commissioner seat as subterfuge for a grander prize of replacing a US congressman who's found to be an embarrassment once they discover his homosexual identity. The letters Jehu writes to Rafe in the first half of this novel shape the reader's understanding of how the Texas Anglo power structure works to maintain its power. The second half of the novel, using a series of interviews with various characters, reveals the multi-faceted perspectives surrounding Jehu's sudden departure from the bank. Through these perspectives, readers see how the same reality differs, sometimes widely, given that what's at stake for each person interviewed represents but a small part of the entire reality. Readers can put together the complete picture by reading Jehu's letters and the many interviews readers are made privy to.

During the years between the publication of *Mi querido Rafa* and *Dear Rafe*, Hinojosa published another novel, *Partners in Crime: A Rafe Buenrostro Mystery* (1985). The progression of his larger serial project, the Klail City Death Trip, continued while he was in the process of rendering *Mi querido Rafa* into an English version. As a result, the English rendition of *Mi querido Rafa / Dear Rafe*, is updated to include narrative details appearing in the subsequently published novel, *Partners in Crime: A Rafe Buenrostro Mystery*. So, as the larger serial project moves forward, one sees Hinojosa working recursively to include narrative details in subsequent novels from previously published novels subsequently rendered into English. As a consequence, while there may be two editions of what is largely the same novel, one in English and one in Spanish, they will differ, sometimes substantially. This difference means that if one only reads a Spanish or only an English version of each of the serial novels, one will not have access to all the narrative details for the entire serial project. For instance, *Becky and Her Friends* and *Los amigos de Becky*, effectively the same novel, differ considerably, with one language version having a prologue but not an epilogue, while the other language version has no prologue but has an epilogue. In addition, the number of chapters differs in the two versions, with important narrative details included in one version but not in the other.

Rafe, as a homicide detective in two detective murder mystery novels, *Partners in Crime* and *Ask a Policeman* (1998), solves murders that result from banks engaging in the illegal laundering of drug cartel money. Law enforcement agencies on both sides of the border partner up to solve the killings and illicit money laundering. With more than a decade between the publication of these two serialized detective murder mystery novels, much changes with certain characters. In between the publication of the murder mysteries, Hinojosa publishes *Becky and Her Friends/Los amigos de Becky* in 1990, with Becky Escobar as the main character. Becky first appears in *Mi querido Rafa/Dear Rafe* as the Anglicized Texas Mexican wife of Ira Escobar, a political stooge who is sponsored by Noddy Perkins who ran the bank where Jehu was employed. By the time the serialized novel *Becky and Her Friends* is published,

Becky has woken up and decided to reverse her assimilation away from her Mexican cultural identity. The first thing she decides to do is divorce her husband Ira and become independent by working with a strong, independent Valley Texas Mexican businesswoman, Viola Barragán. She then marries Jehu, while Rafe marries Noddy Perkins' daughter Sammie Jo, thereby consolidating certain segments of power working in the Valley. Constructed entirely through interviews (reportage), this novel has various people from Belken County commenting on Becky's identity reversal. By enacting this type of ethnic cultural reversal, Hinojosa enables readers to see the complexities inherent when cultural identities, like Becky's, are colonized and then decolonized.

In the last novel Hinojosa published in his Klail City Death Trip Series, *We Happy Few* (2006), we see Hinojosa take on a different question entirely from what he's previously engaged in his serialized novels. In this novel, his previously central characters, Rafe and Jehu, do not play a prominent role. We instead see a whole new set of characters surrounding the central issue of replacing a university president in the Valley's only state university. Here, the demographic reality is that the Valley is overwhelmingly Texas Mexican, so logic dictates that the new university president should also be a Texas Mexican, someone intimately familiar with Valley border culture. The ethnic politics surrounding the decision to fill this important position at this Valley state university has, as one might expect, various stakeholders, from local and state politicians, to local business owners, to faculty and students. The intrigue built into this politically charged academic situation is something Hinojosa, as a longtime academic himself, knows only too well. Moreover, political correctness holds that a Chicano writer should create a narrative with the outcome being the selection of a Mexican American as university president, but this is, ironically, not the outcome in this novel. What Hinojosa has happen is the selection of a woman, an ex-nun with a science academic background, who is not Mexican American, as the new university president.

By having his novel end this way, Hinojosa takes the higher ground by filling this important administrative position with what is best for the students and, as a result, for the Valley border region. Instead of playing a kind of ethnic politics which would ensure an ethnic Texas Mexican becomes president through the political machinations now surrounding American academia, Hinojosa goes against the grain of what's expected. The characters determining the selection of the new president play their parts in building up the intrigue that always surrounds this kind of academic decision. In the end, what's best for the students – a great university education – transcends ethnic politics for Hinojosa.

In an article published in 2014 in the *Texas Monthly*, Chicano writer Dagoberto Gilb speaks of first visiting Hinojosa in 1988 at his office on the UT-Austin campus. He asks Hinojosa who his favorite Chicano writer is, and without missing a beat, Hinojosa says Heinrich Böll, a German author who won the Nobel Prize for Literature in 1972. In all the critical attention Hinojosa's work has received, no one has ever cited Böll as Hinojosa's most important literary influence. The way Hinojosa's work parallels Böll's is truly uncanny and represents the way future critics will have to understand the sheer reach of Hinojosa's literary project throughout his entire career. Hidden in plain sight, Hinojosa's role model, a German author, builds on the depth and breadth of Hinojosa's own reach for future generations of not just Chicanx writers, but indeed all writers. Writing in two languages, experimenting with different genres of fiction, including essays in *A Voice of My Own:*

Essays and Stories (2011), and having a sarcastic, cutting Texas Mexican wit make Hinojosa one of the most influential American writers in the late twentieth and early twenty-first centuries. Well versed, articulate, educated, and highly ethical and moral in the cause of social justice for Texas Mexicans, Rolando Hinojosa, a Valley man, will forever serve as a testament to what a good writer does with his creative imagination.

SEE ALSO: Anaya, Rudolfo; Border Fictions; Castillo, Ana; Contemporary Regionalisms; The Culture Wars; Mixed-Genre Fiction; Multiculturalism; Realism after Poststructuralism; Silko, Leslie Marmon; Urrea, Luis Alberto

FURTHER READING

Martínez-Rodríguez, Martín M. (1993). *Rolando Hinojosa y su "cronicón" chicano: una novela del lector*. Seville, Spain: Editorial Universidad de Sevilla-Secretariado de Publicaciones.

Mejía, Jaime Armin. (1993). "Transformations in Rolando Hinojosa's Klail City Death Trip Series." PhD dissertation, Ohio State University.

Saldívar, José David. (1984). *The Rolando Hinojosa Reader: Essays Historical and Critical*. Houston: Arte Público Press.

Zilles, Klaus. (2001). *Rolando Hinojosa: A Reader's Guide*. Albuquerque: University of New Mexico Press.

Hogan, Linda

ISABEL QUINTANA WULF
Salisbury University, USA

Linda Hogan (Chickasaw) was born on July 16, 1947, in Denver, Colorado, to Charles Henderson (Chickasaw) and Cleona Bower Henderson (of Nebraskan homesteader extraction). A solid pillar of Native American literature, Hogan is most widely recognized today as a novelist, even though her genius is not confined to a single genre: indeed, her publishing record defies strict categorization as it includes novels, poetry, plays, creative nonfiction, memoir, short stories, and essays, making her a prolific author and a consummate storyteller. Coming into the literary scene as a poet in the mid-1970s and publishing her first chapbook *Calling Myself Home* in 1978, Hogan is one of the Indigenous writers of the so-called Native American Renaissance who continue to publish new work forty years later. Both her fiction and nonfiction pieces are firmly grounded in Indigenous epistemologies and Native systems of knowledge, giving her a strong basis on which to ground her activism in fighting nuclear proliferation and striving for social justice, environmental justice, and gender justice. Throughout her work, Hogan teaches us about the interconnectedness of human and nonhuman relations and the importance of restoring a balance lost to capitalist extraction and settler colonial logics. Reading her work as a form of activism helps us recognize the inextricability of the literary and the political for Hogan, making the social commentary in her writing both compelling and forever timely.

Linda Hogan grew up in Denver and Germany, traveling around as the family followed her father's military career. No matter where they were, she remembers diverse communities surrounding her: from the pan-Indian community in Denver that the Indian Relocation Act brought together in the 1950s, consisting of Navajo, Lakota, and Chickasaw people among others, to the diverse army community and its wealth of Native American military people, to her own relatives in Oklahoma with whom she had very close ties. This diversity and pan-Indianness is a trait that surfaces in much of her writing. Growing in a house with no books except for "a huge leather Bible that had belonged to my maternal grandmother" (Hogan 1994, p. 115), she was attuned early on to her father's and her uncle's storytelling. Hogan's writing is fully imbued with that same craft for telling stories, a universe of Native systems of knowledge, and stories of creation and survival.

Starting to work at age 15, Hogan has accrued an eclectic resumé: she has been a nurse's aide, dental assistant, cocktail waitress, homemaker, secretary, administrator, teacher's aide, library clerk, and freelance writer. In addition, she has been a college professor, on the board of directors of the Denver Indian Center, and a volunteer at Minnesota Wildlife Rehabilitation Clinic; all in all, her varied work experiences have given her an acute insight into poverty and working-class conditions. Hogan moved to California in her early twenties and later began adult education classes. She eventually went to college and earned an MA in English and creative writing from the University of Colorado at Boulder in 1978. After being poet-in-residence for the Colorado and Oklahoma Arts Councils, Hogan worked as an associate professor of American and American Indian studies at the University of Minnesota, Twin Cities, and later as associate professor of English at the University of Colorado at Boulder, where she is Professor Emerita. She is also Writer in Residence for the Chickasaw Nation.

Hogan's work has received numerous accolades over the past forty years. Her collection of poems *Seeing Through the Sun* (1985) won the American Book Award from the Before Columbus Foundation; her novel *Mean Spirit* (1990) and her book of poetry *The Book of Medicines* (1993) were finalists for the Pulitzer Prize award; *Rounding the Human Corners* (2008) was also a Pulitzer nominee, and *The Book of Medicines* was a finalist for a National Book Critics Circle award. Hogan has been the recipient of prestigious grants and fellowships as well, like the D'Arcy McNickle Memorial Fellowship, a National Endowment for the Arts grant, a John Simon Guggenheim Fellowship, a Lannan Award, and the Five Civilized Tribes Playwriting Award. In 1998 she was honored with the Lifetime Achievement Award from the Native Writer's Circle. Hogan was inducted into the Chickasaw Hall of Fame in 2007.

The start of Linda Hogan's career as a published poet was bolstered by Joseph Bruchac (Abenaki) and his founding of the Greenfield Review Press, a publishing venture that has bet on the talent of many Native American authors over the years. Her publishing break came with *Calling Myself Home*, a chapbook that lays out many of the themes and concerns that can be traced in her writing across genres. Her poems in this collection are deeply informed by Chickasaw tradition and the Oklahoma landscape, bringing together meditations on points of departure, home, the role of women, animals, the injustice of poverty, responsibility, and the interconnectedness of all things – themes that resonate in much of her work, especially in *The Book of Medicines*. The turtle holds an important place in this first collection of poems: "There were old women / who lived in amber. / Their dark hands / laced the shell of turtles / together, pebbles inside / and they danced / with rattles strong on their legs" (Hogan 1993, p. 6), turtles standing as a symbol of a home that must be carried around, as evocative of Chickasaw women shell-shakers in ceremonial dances, and as indicative of women as a source of life. She also raises awareness of the injustice of poverty; in "Blessings" Hogan writes "Blessed are the rich / for they eat meat every night. / They have already inherited the earth. / For the rest of us, may we just live / long enough / and unwrinkle our brows, / may we keep our good looks / and some of our teeth / and our bowels regular" (p. 26). The difference in the stakes of existence, the contrast between the plentiful lives of those who have "inherited the earth" and eat meat every day versus the concerns for survival of those hoping to keep "some of our teeth," points to the imbalance of the world we live in today. It evokes the break of a harmonious relationship with nature: instead of a sustainable stewardship of natural resources, we have a possessive relationship based on privilege and extraction.

Attention to the balance between humans and nature starts in Hogan's early poetry and becomes a constant in all her writing. As Kimberly Blaser puts it, "in [*Calling Myself Home*] she began to shape an understanding of human origin and existence that upholds a sense of relatedness to the larger, ageless natural world and to articulate the role she sees for herself and other Native writers in working for justice and survival" (2006, p. 214). Indeed, the epistemological principles of the interconnectedness of all things and of the kinship system between all relations (human and nonhuman) is the web that sustains Hogan's body of work. Not only do they shape the world of her fiction and nonfiction, but they also serve as the air beneath the wings of her activism. In both *Eclipse* (1983) and *Daughters, I Love You* (1981), Hogan presents poems that denounce wars and the proliferation of nuclear technologies, calling out the threat they pose to women, children, and the unborn generations to come. While *Eclipse* focuses on war and its effects on children and the potential they embody, in *Daughters, I Love You* she speaks against the development of nuclear weapons and nuclear energy, the desecration of the Earth they represent, and the pressing threat they constitute for the future. As Kenneth Lincoln succinctly remarks, "her personal visions of Indian continuance come inseparable from contemporary politics and the scars of history" (1983, p. v). Thus, a focus on historical awareness, political struggle, and activism are always at the core of Hogan's work.

Hogan's activism and her intellectual preoccupations with history, the interconnectedness of all things, and the struggle for environmental justice make her a staple in the field of environmental studies, her novels often appearing in college courses on sustainability, environmental activism, and environmental humanities. *Solar Storms* (1995) is often considered as presenting an ecofeminist aesthetic, given its centering of women and their fight for social and environmental justice. Set in the Boundary Waters straddling the United States and Canada, the novel follows the journey of four generations of women as they canoe north to the subarctic land of the Fat Eaters (a fictional people) to protest the flooding of the eldest character's ancestral lands. The novel is inspired by the James Bay Project, whereby state-owned Hydro-Québec built a series of hydroelectric power stations in the 1970s on the La Grande River in northwestern Québec, Canada, flooding an area the size of the state of New York that affected an ecosystem the size of France (Tarter 2000, p. 138). The project has had dire consequences for the James Bay Cree and northern Inuit, not only because of their displacement as their ancestral lands flooded but also due to the mercury pollution that resulted from the submerged boreal forest, affecting their fish-based diet. *Solar Storms* presents the physical and ideological struggle of Indigenous people fighting to preserve their land as they come face-to-face not only with white capitalists lured by the siren call of exploitative profit but also with working-class whites in need of making a living.

The broken covenant between humans and nonhuman relations, an ancient agreement of reciprocity and mutual care between Earth and all its creatures, is an important message woven throughout *Solar Storms*. It echoes the ideas that appear in *Savings* (1988), where her poems warn us about the price which we must pay for alienating ourselves from our sense of being in communion with the natural world. Both the poems and the novel share a sense of political urgency that pushes us to recover a sense of our past that will help us create a livable future. In the same vein, *Mean Spirit* also focuses on recovering history and shedding light on the exploitation of natural resources and the desecration of the Earth. A fictionalization of what is known as the Osage reign of terror, the novel is set in Oklahoma in the 1920s when oil is discovered under the Osage reservation, prompting a flood of settlers onto Osage land and a wave of murders of Native people to get to the reservation's mineral wealth. *Mean Spirit* places the exploitation of the Earth, women, and Native peoples on a level plane, highlighting their interconnectedness. In many ways, the examination of human violence Hogan offers in *Dark, Sweet: New and Selected Poems* (2014) can be traced to her earliest writings, especially in the intricate violent plots of *Mean Spirit*.

In Hogan's last two novels, *Power* (1998) and *People of the Whale* (2008), she puts environmental issues and tribal traditions in conversation. They share a common drive: they ask the readers to consider the tension between maintaining tribal traditions and thinking about endangered species and environmental destruction. *Power* is set in Florida and tells the story of the parallel trials of Ama, the aunt of the teenage narrator Omishto. Ama has killed a panther while in a trance-like dream, as instructed by the Earth to bring about healing. Charged with killing an animal on the endangered species list, she is tried in a Florida court. At the same time, she needs to account to the Taiga elders for breaking tribal law in killing an animal considered their ally and sacred ancestor. The novel is experienced through the point of view of a teenage narrator who learns, doubts, and grows as the novel progresses, and the readers are challenged to think through the implications of their own assumptions about sovereignty and animal rights. In a similar fashion, *People of the Whale* is set in the Pacific Northwest and focuses on the traditional and ritual practices of whale hunting of the A'atsika people. The novel uses the Vietnam War as the background to a later whale hunt, bringing about the intersection of the horrors of war, cultural extinction, and environmental destruction. The corruption of the fight for sovereignty in the novel underscores the parallels between the genocide of Indigenous peoples and the extinction of marine life under the logics of greed and profit. In all likelihood, the novel is inspired by the research for *Sightings: The Mysterious Journey of the Gray Whale* (2002), a creative nonfiction collaboration between Hogan and nature writer Brenda Peterson for National Geographic. *Sightings* chronicles the lives and migrations of gray whales, their threat of extinction, and the intricate crossings of environmentalism, the whale industry, and tribal whaling rights.

Another important aspect of Hogan's writing is the centering of women's experiences and the celebration of the role of women in sustaining life. In much of her work we can see a symbiosis between women's caretaking and earth's potential to heal and replenish. In *The Book of Medicines*, the force of creation and evolution is transposed from a higher power to the power of women and the little things they do every day to keep life going. As one critic puts it, "the small things women do influence the global things" (Van Dyke 2005, p. 98). In most of her novels we find female protagonists and narrators: *Power* and *Solar Storms* are coming-of-age narratives where young women reckon with their origins and their place in the world; *Mean Spirit* focuses on the abuse and death of Native women used by white men as a conduit to mineral wealth; *Daughters, I Love You* is an ode to mother-daughter relationships, separation anxieties, protective instincts, and the courage of independence; and *Indios* (2012), her long poem, tells the story of a mother falsely accused of killing her children and subsequently silenced. We can read *Indios* as a vindication of historical and mythical female figures such as La Malinche, Pocahontas, La Llorona, and Medea – women who have been ill-used by powerful male figures and thereafter maligned for it. Be it in Latina, US, or Greek mythologies, these women's stories share a common trait: their truths have traditionally been silenced by male-centered colonial powers. All these meditations on the place of women and their relations to the natural world are part of Hogan's political and spiritual journey. As Paula Gunn Allen reflects, "Being an Indian enables [Hogan] to resolve the conflict that presently divides the non-Indian feminist community; she does not have to choose between spirituality and political commitment, for each is the complement of the other. They are the two wings of one bird, and that bird is the interconnectedness of everything" (1986, p. 169). The emphasis on the interconnectedness of everything and of women as conduit for healing and creation centers Indigenous epistemologies as the basis for engaging with Hogan's work and ideas.

Pan-Indian kinship configurations, the creation of fictional tribes, and setting fiction in different landscapes constitute a distinctive attribute of Hogan's oeuvre. At times challenged by Native literary nationalists (see Robert Warrior 1995) for writing about tribes other than the Chickasaw, Hogan justifies the fictionalization of tribes as a defense against repeated colonization (Cook 2003, p. 43). Despite the criticism, her work actually aligns with many of the tenets of literary nationalism, such as grounding the work in Indigenous epistemologies and recuperating Native systems of knowledge, and her fictionalization of tribes foregrounds Indigenous experiences in North America in a hemispheric sense – rather than aiming for ethnographic knowledge of a people. The landscape of her work varies from piece to piece: from Oklahoma to Florida to the Pacific Northwest, Hogan explores different geographies to draw a global connection among peoples. Together with this, the invention of the Fat Eaters in *Solar Storms*, the Taiga in *Power*, or the A'atsika in *People of the Whale* serves to direct the readers' attention to issues facing all Native peoples, helping her reach a broader audience, both Native and non-Native. In *Dwellings*, Hogan affirms that "it has been my lifelong work to seek an understanding of the two views of the world, one as seen by native people and the other as seen by those who are new and young to this continent" (1995, p. 11), pointing to a good lesson underlying her work: a solution to pressing environmental and social issues necessitates accountability for all those involved, Indigenous and non-Indigenous alike.

SEE ALSO: Alexie, Sherman; Ecocriticism and Environmental Fiction; Erdrich, Louise; Glancy, Diane; Indigenous Narrative; Jones, Stephen Graham; Momaday, N. Scott; Power, Susan; Silko, Leslie Marmon; Welch, James

REFERENCES

Allen, Paula Gunn. (1986). *The Sacred Hoop: Recovering the Feminine in American Indian Traditions*. Boston: Beacon Press.

Blaser, Kimberly M. (2006). Cannons and canonization: American Indian poetries through autonomy, colonization, nationalism, and decolonization. In: *The Columbia Guide to American Indian Literatures of the United States since 1945* (ed. Eric Cheyfitz), 183–287. New York: Columbia University Press.

Cook, Barbara J. (ed.) (2003). *From the Center of Tradition. Critical Perspectives on Linda Hogan*. Boulder: University Press of Colorado.

Hogan, Linda. (1993). *The Book of Medicines*. Minneapolis: Coffee House Press.

Hogan, Linda. (1994). An interview with Linda Hogan. The Missouri Review 17 (2): 109–134.

Hogan, Linda. (1995). *Dwellings: A Spiritual History of the Living World*. New York: Norton.

Lincoln, Kenneth. (1983). Foreword. In: *Eclipse* (by Linda Hogan). Los Angeles: American Indian Studies Center.

Tarter, Jim. (2000). "Dreams of earth": place, multiethnicity, and environmental justice in Linda Hogan's *Solar Storms*. In: *Reading under the Sign of Nature: New Essays in Ecocriticism* (ed. John

Tallmadge and Henry Harrington), 128–147. Salt Lake City: University of Utah Press.
Van Dyke, Annette. (2005). Women writers and gender issues. *The Cambridge Companion to Native American Literature* (ed. Joy Porter and Kenneth M. Roemer), 85–102. Cambridge: Cambridge University Press.
Warrior, Robert Allen. (1995). *The Deaths of Sybil Bolton*; an American history. Wičazo Ša Review 11 (1): 52–55.

FURTHER READING

Cook, Barbara J. (2003). *From the Center of Tradition: Critical Perspectives on Linda Hogan*. Boulder: University Press of Colorado.
Harrison, Summer. (2019). "We need new stories": trauma, storytelling, and the mapping of environmental injustice in Linda Hogan's *Solar Storms* and Standing Rock. American Indian Quarterly 43 (1): 1–35.
Johnson, Kelli Lyon. (2007). Writing deeper maps: mapmaking, local indigenous knowledges, and literary nationalism in Native women's writing. Studies in American Indian Literatures 19 (4): 103–120.
Manning, Pascale Mccullough. (2008). A narrative of motives: solicitation and confession in Linda Hogan's *Power*. Studies in American Indian Literatures 20 (2): 1–21.
Udel, Lisa J. (2007). Revising strategies: the intersection of literature and activism in contemporary Native women's writing. Studies in American Indian Literatures 19 (2): 62–82.

Homes, A.M.

KASIA BODDY
University of Cambridge, UK

A.M. Homes (b. 1960) wrote her first novel when she was just 19 and an undergraduate at Sarah Lawrence College. First published in 1989, *Jack* presents a teenage boy's take on his parents' divorce and his subsequent discovery that his father is gay. All he wants is a "regular family" (Homes 1990, p. 212) and now he feels that his whole life has been "wrecked" or, at the very least, "dented" (p. 5). "Normality," however, proves from the outset to be a deception. The first real sign of trouble is when Jack's mother starts making pancakes for breakfast and smiling in a way "that looked like it'd been clipped from the pages of *Family Circle*" (p. 23). Although very much an apprentice work, an adolescent's view of adolescence, *Jack* introduced readers to the thematic preoccupations that Homes has continued to explore in four further novels, three short story collections, and two works of non-fiction: the permutations and reconfigurations of family; the way that relationships function through debts, gifts, and acts of atonement; the conformist pressures of suburbia, and also of literary fiction. She has consistently described her work as "very American" (Boddy 1999) and freely admits to the "line of morality" (Choder-Goldman 2010, p. 369) that runs through it.

Homes has written extensively about the fact that she is adopted, most fully in *The Mistress's Daughter* (2007), a darkly comic memoir about her relationship with each of her birth parents and her complicated feelings of growing up an "amalgam," "something glued together, something slightly broken" (2007, p. 38). What Homes describes as her "great fear of attachment" and "equally constant fear of loss" (p. 235) also motivate many of her characters. Her second novel, *In a Country of Mothers* (1993), tells the story of a young adopted woman called Jody, who has spent half her life in therapy "and therefore will never again be normal, not in the truest sense of the word" (1994, p. 26), and of her psychotherapist Claire, who fantasizes that Jody is the child she gave up for adoption. Informed by the therapeutic language and structures of "projection," "triggers," and "substitution," it is a book about attachment to objects and houses as well as to people, something else Homes returns to repeatedly. "I envision my home as the physical, spatial expression of my interior life," says a character in a later story, published as a preface to a book by the architect Steven Harris; "I want a home that looks like it is inside my head" (Homes 2010, p. vii)

Homes later came to think *In a Country of Mothers* as a failure because the characters were too "close" to her, and resolved that from then on her fiction would not "deal with anything that was in the least bit autobiographical" (Choder-Goldman 2010, p. 371). The shift can be seen clearly in stories like "A Real Doll" (Homes 1991, pp.151–173), in which a boy loses his virginity with his sister's Barbie doll, and then, more satisfyingly, with Ken, and Homes began to feature, alongside Kathy Acker and Lynne Tillman, in anthologies such as *Love is Strange* (Rose and Texier 1993). But it was her third novel, *The End of Alice* (1996) which established her reputation as "provocative and dangerous and controversial" (Piafsky and Hodgen 2005, p. 102). The novel is about the correspondence between a 19-year-old girl and a male prisoner who, twenty-three years earlier, was convicted of the sexual assault and brutal murder of a 12-year-old called Alice. What provoked outrage – the British National Society for the Prevention of Cruelty to Children (NAACP) even called for the novel to be banned – is the fact that the teenaged girl sends the prisoner letters about her obsession with, and seduction of, a 12-year-old boy whom she tutors in the Nabokovian games of tennis and sex.

But although Bill Buford included *The End of Alice* in a round-up of what he announced, tongue only partly in cheek, as a new "American literary movement" whose manifesto was nothing more than "really bad sex" (Buford 1996, p. 54), and although the novel consolidated Homes's standing as "a virtuoso portraitist of modern depravity" (Krist 1999), her central ambitions were rather different. The novel marked a determined rejection not only of autobiography but also of what publishers (and Homes herself) call "women's fiction" (Boddy 1996). Preferring the gender-free initials A.M. in order "not be bound" by the "cultural connotations" of her first name, Amy, Homes has often spoken about what she sees as the restricted expectations of books "written by women," "very domestic kind of stories . . . for an audience that was basically women" (Boddy 1996). *The End of Alice* was not that kind of book, not least because it chose the perspective of the male pedophile over that of either of the female protagonists. On reading the girl's first letter, the prisoner admiringly notes "the willingness of its author to transcend, to flirt, outside her chosen category or group" (Homes 1996, p. 13). For Homes, taking on this narrative voice was both a way of displaying her virtuosity as a novelist and of rejecting the constraints of any "category," chosen or otherwise. "Women are not supposed to do things that are not very, very nice," she announced, "and now they're doing them" (Boddy 1996).

Writing *The End of Alice* was also an exercise in what Homes's teacher Angela Carter called "moral pornography" – pornography, that is, employed in the service of a "critique of existent relations between the sexes" (Carter 1979, p. 19). Homes forced readers (like her 19-year-old correspondent) to think about the ways in which their desires overlap with those of the "pervert" before, ultimately, provoking them to recognize the difference between fantasy and the "deeper cord" of perversion (Homes 1996, p. 187). Another difference that interested her was literary. Revisiting (in some ways at least), Nabokov's *Lolita* enabled her to consider "how the language of literature, how explicitness, had moved forward" since 1955 (Boddy 1996). Nabokov's narrator Humbert Humbert had dismissed the idea that he was a pornographer: "I am not concerned with so-called 'sex' at all. Anybody can imagine those elements of animality" (Nabokov 1995, p. 134). For Homes, however, the problem was that many readers refused to do that imagining: "I overheard this comment in a cafe where somebody said, 'I don't think he slept with her' . . . And I was appalled . . . I wanted to write something where you couldn't deny it, you couldn't read it and pretend that this wasn't happening" (Boddy 1996).

Thinking about how attitudes, and fiction, might have "moved forward" is also one of the impulses behind Homes's ongoing conversation with the mid-century writer John Cheever, whose stories she has praised for their "subtle surrealism, a strangeness that infuses the seemingly real, normal and banal" (Homes 2018b). Homes's brush is broader and bolder than Cheever's, and she is less concerned with the low-key nuances of suburban sadness than with the sexy horrors it conceals. Nevertheless, like him, she is drawn to swift tonal shifts: "how a world that had seemed so dark could, in a few minutes, become so sweet" (Cheever 2010, p. 349). In Homes's work we can see how the "post-martini bitterness" (Kazin 1973, p. 113) of mid-century suburban fiction has evolved into something between a post-crack low and a post-burger bloatedness. Cheever's story "The Swimmer" opens with "everyone" complaining "I *drank* too much last night" (Cheever, 2010, p. 776), while Homes's *Music for Torching* (1999) begins with the protagonist Paul grumbling that his wife is feeding him "too much fat" (Homes 1999, p. 1). Paul and Elaine (who first appeared in a story called "Adults Alone" [1990]; Homes 1991, pp. 15–33) live despairingly in Westchester County. "We fight and we fuck. That's how we know we're still married," Paul says. All they want to do is "put things right," "to make everything good again" (Homes 1999, p. 1), and they seek guidance wherever they can: in the throwaway words of a babysitter or a man on the commuter train, or from a DIY book offering to *How to Fix Almost Anything*. "Almost" is of course the operative word.

It is tempting to read this, and the title of Homes's next novel, *This Book Will Save Your Life* (2006), as simply an ironic comment on the late twentieth-century "culture of narcissism" (Lasch 1979). It *is* a joke, but not entirely. As Beth Blum notes, one of the distinctive features of contemporary fiction is how easily authors "shift from satirists to accomplices in the quest for a meaningful existence" (Blum 2020, p. 29). In *This Book Will Save Your Life*, we move from a satire of "Care of Self" (2006, p. 55) towards a celebration of the care of others. The protagonist Richard Novack finds himself cast as the unlikely hero in a series of adventures. He rescues a trapped horse, a drowning man, a kidnapped woman, a housewife on the edge of a nervous breakdown and eventually achieves some kind of reconciliation with his estranged family. It is good thing that Richard is so rich because in order to make others (and therefore himself) feel better – Novack translates as "new man" – he spends a fortune on cars, hotels, trips to the spa, and an awful lot of food.

The "possibility of repair" (Homes 2012, p. 230) afforded by wealth is also the subject of *May We Be Forgiven* (2012), which Homes calls her most "Jewish book" (Wolinsky 2012). Another fast-paced cultural comedy of googling, sexting, and trips to the mall, it is also a tale of two brothers, George and Harold. (Like "Brother on Sunday" [Homes 2018a, pp. 1–17], the novel owes something to Cheever's "Goodbye, My Brother" [1978]). Homes pays direct homage to Cheever when Harold mistakes a "dapper fellow wearing an old tan corduroy jacket" for the writer's ghost (2012, p. 417). But the novel's biggest walk-on part is given to its other presiding spirit, Don DeLillo – like Cheever, and the novel's protagonists, a resident of Westchester, Connecticut. The plot is elaborate (involving murder, arms-dealing, and a biography of Richard Nixon) but at its heart, it too is a story about "second chances" (p. 293) or more specifically, about the ways in which adoptive parenting allows Harold to atone for his past failures and become a 'better version' of himself (p. 414). As "a Jewish Buddhist," Homes says she is "constantly trying to feel like, How do we let go of things? How do we not let our future be completely tainted by the past, but also be cognizant of that past?" (Wolinksy 2012).

Harold approaches his job as a historian with similar thoughts in mind. The main drive of the story is towards expelling the "rusty sense of disgust" (Homes 2012, p. 418) that has accumulated over the fifteen years he's been working on a book about Richard Nixon. Coming to terms with Nixon requires Harold to eschew the analysis of a political career and instead to focus on his own "psychic connection" (p. 182) to the president. The more we hear the more we recognize Nixon's personality as an amalgam of Harold, a junk-food-loving depressive with a relationship to China (or at least a Chinese-American woman) who likes "to think of himself as decent," and George, an imaged-obsessed "paranoid bully" (p. 448) who is frightened of being alone. In reconciling the two "sides of the coin" (p. 188) that is Nixon – "integrity and deceit," "moral superiority and arrogance" (p. 446) – Harold is able to forgive the former president, and, in doing so, to forgive his brother and himself.

But history is not only an allegory of family or a Buddhist object lesson in "learning to tolerate contradictory things simultaneously" (Choder-Goldman 2010, p. 377). Homes (and Harold) also want their readers to think of Nixon as "the bridge between our prewar Depression-era culture and the postwar prosperous American-dream America" (2012, p. 202). Elsewhere, Homes has decried the twenty-first-century's "upsizing of the American Dream": "inflated [...] as if to distract us from an underlying depression – emotional and economic; as though we are consuming, stuffing, and spoiling ourselves to avoid our fear of failing, of falling, of having nothing at all" (2002, p. 17).

The novel thus ends with the completion of a superior kind of self-help program, one that rejects Nixon-era "inward-turning self-cultivation" (De Koven 2007, p. 255) for something less like Depression-era communitarianism than a millennial version of "self-development" that comes from "attachments beyond the self" (Greenwald Smith 2015, p. 41). By adopting an orphan and the parents of a woman he meets at the mall, Harold transforms his single-family suburban home and feels, for the first time in his life, both "part of a community" (Homes 2012, p. 433) and mindfully "here, in the moment" (p. 478).

May We Be Forgiven marks another stage in Homes's challenge to the assumption that only men write "broad social novels," the "great American novels" (Gilmore 2012), and that "writing for the larger world" necessarily means eschewing the "domestic" (Piafksy and Hodgen 2005, p. 114). Doing "both" is precisely what Harold manages when he finally completes his fifteen-year project to Nixon while caring for his new family. The Big Book is simply another task to be completed before "the children come home" (Homes 2012, p. 453). Once it is "cooked" (p. 446), he can get back to making dinner.

SEE ALSO: Debut Novels; DeLillo, Don; Queer and LGBT Fiction; Religion and Contemporary Fiction; Suburban Narratives

REFERENCES

Boddy, Kasia. (1996). Unpublished interview with A.M. Homes.
Boddy, Kasia. (1999). Unpublished interview with A.M. Homes.
Blum, Beth. (2020). *The Self-Help Compulsion: Searching for Advice in Modern Literature*. New York: Columbia University Press.
Buford, Bill. (1996). Really bad sex. *The New Yorker* (August 12, 1996): 54–55. https://www.

newyorker.com/magazine/1996/08/12/really-bad-sex (accessed September 10, 2021).

Carter, Angela. (1979). *The Sadeian Woman: An Exercise in Cultural History*. London: Virago.

Cheever, John. (2010). *Collected Stories*. London: Vintage; 1st ed. 1978.

Choder-Goldman, Jill. (2010). Telling the story: an interview with A.M. Homes. *Psychoanalytic Perspectives* 7 (2): 368–379.

De Koven, Marianne. (2007). *Utopia Limited: The Sixties and the Emergence of the Postmodern*. Durham, NC: Duke University Press.

Gilmore, Jennifer. (2012) A.M. Homes' novel addresses '70s childhood. *Forward* (October 23, 2012). http://forward.com/culture/164618/am-homes-novel-addresses-70s-childhood (accessed August 5, 2021).

Greenwald Smith, R. (2015). *Affect and American Literature in the Age of Liberalism*. Cambridge: Cambridge University Press.

Homes, A.M. (1990). *Jack*. New York: Vintage; 1st ed. 1989.

Homes, A.M. (1994). *In a Country of Mothers*. New York: Vintage; 1st ed. 1993.

Homes, A.M. (1996). *The End of Alice*. New York: Scribner.

Homes, A.M. (1999). *Music For Torching*. New York: Doubleday.

Homes, A.M. (2002). *Los Angeles: People, Places and the Castle on the Hill*. Washington: National Geographic.

Homes, A.M. (2006). *This Book Will Save Your Life*. London: Granta.

Homes, A.M. (2007). *The Mistress's Daughter*. London: Granta.

Homes, A.M. (2010). A true life story. In: *True Life: Steven Harris Architects* (ed. Steven Harris), vii–ix. New York: Princeton Architectural Press.

Homes, A.M. (2012). *May We Be Forgiven*. London: Granta.

Homes, A.M. (2018a). *Days of Awe*. London: Granta.

Homes, A.M. (2018b). Books that made me. *The Guardian* (June 29, 2018). https://www.theguardian.com/books/2018/jun/29/am-homes-books-that-made-me (accessed August 5, 2021).

Kazin, Alfred. (1973). *Bright Book of Life*. Notre Dame, IN: University of Notre Dame Press.

Krist, Gary. (1999). Burning down the house. *The New York Times* (May 30, 1999). https://www.nytimes.com/1999/05/30/books/burning-down-the-house.html (accessed September 10, 2021).

Lasch, Christopher. (1979). *The Culture of Narcissism: American Life in an Age of Diminishing Expectations*. New York: Norton.

Nabokov, Vladimir. (1995). *The Annotated Lolita*. Harmondsworth, UK: Penguin.

Piafsky, Michael and Hodgen, Christie. (2005). An interview with A.M. Homes. *Missouri Review* 28 (3): 100–120.

Rose, Joel and Texier, Catherine. (1993). *Love is Strange: Stories of Postmodern Romance*. New York: Norton.

Wolinsky, Richard. (2012). Out of the darkness: A.M. Homes on Richard Nixon, American dementia, and writing like a man. *Guernica* (November 15, 2021). https://www.guernicamag.com/out-of-the-darkness/ (accessed August 5, 2021).

FURTHER READING

Boddy, Kasia. (2008). Regular Lolitas: the afterlives of an American adolescent. In: *American Fiction in the 1990s: Reflections on History and Culture* (ed. Jay Prosser), 164–176. New York: Routledge.

Boddy, Kasia. (2019). Making it long: men, women and the great American novel now. *Textual Practice* 33 (2): 318–337.

Carroll, Rachel. (2012). *Rereading Heterosexuality: Feminism, Queer Theory and Contemporary Fiction*. Edinburgh: Edinburgh University Press.

Holland, Mary. (2012). A lamb in wolf's clothing: Homes's *Music for Torching* and *This Book Will Save Your Life*. *Critique* 53 (3): 214–237.

Hosseini, Khaled

ALLA IVANCHIKOVA
Hobart and William Smith Colleges, USA

Khaled Hosseini in an Afghan American writer and the author of three bestselling novels and one bestselling illustrated story. He was born in Kabul, Afghanistan in 1965 to a diplomat father and a mother who was a high school teacher. The family immigrated to the United States in 1980, following the Saur (April) communist revolution of 1978 and the subsequent Soviet intervention of December 1979, resettling in San Jose, California. Hosseini studied biology at Santa Clara University and medicine at the University of California at San Diego School of Medicine, obtaining a medical degree in 1993. He completed his residency at Cedar-Sinai Medical Center in Los Angeles and practiced medicine until 2004, when he became a full-time writer. Inspired by his trip to Afghanistan in 2003, Hosseini established The Khaled Hosseini Foundation that provides humanitarian aid in Afghanistan, especially to projects involving most vulnerable groups, such as women and children. He was named the 2006 Humanitarian of the year by the US office of the United Nations. In 2008, Hosseini was named one of the most influential people in the world by *Times* magazine. Among his cultural influences, Hosseini lists Persian poetry, Jack London, Salman Rushdie, J.M. Coetzee, and Alice Munro, among others (Goodreads 2013; By the Book 2013). His novels contain many references to American popular culture, including Hollywood cinema.

The Kite Runner (2003) – the novel that brought Hosseini international acclaim – was based on a 25-page story he wrote when he had heard the news of the Taliban banning kite flying in Afghanistan in 1999 (Hosseini 2012). Due to the lack of public interest in Afghanistan prior to 9/11, the story remained unpublished. The novel was completed in the aftermath of the US-led invasion of Afghanistan by NATO forces (Operation Enduring Freedom, 2001) and was promptly published by Riverhead Books in 2003. In 2007, it was adapted into a film directed by Marc Forster. Subsequently, it was adapted for the stage by Matthew Spangler, the play premiering in 2009. A graphic novel was published by Riverhead Books in 2011. *The Kite Runner* was endorsed by the US political establishment: it was praised by Laura Bush and a screening of the 2007 film adaptation took place in the White House that same year. It has been subsequently translated into over forty languages and was reported to be number one source of information on Afghan society and culture for US military and professional staff who came to serve or work in Afghanistan during the post-2001 reconstruction period (Fluri 2009, p. 993).

The Kite Runner is set in the 1970s Kabul and depicts what is often called "the Golden Age of Afghanistan" – an era of rapid modernization and crosscultural exchange (1933–1973) that preceded several decades of political instability and war. The plot describes the experiences of Amir – a son of a wealthy Afghan businessman – coming of age in 1970s Kabul. Father and son tensions and racism are central to the plot. Hosseini details Amir's sheltered childhood shattered by the experience of racialized violence, where the family servant's son, Hassan, who is a Hazara (an ethnic minority), is raped by a gang of Pashtun (the dominant ethnic group) nationalists. Amir, also a Pashtun, witnesses the assault but is too scared to intervene. His crushing guilt is exacerbated by a later discovery that Hassan is his father's illegitimate son and thus his half brother. The plot then traces the family's immigration to Fremont, California in the aftermath of the Soviet invasion of Afghanistan, and their effort to reestablish themselves as immigrants. Seeking atonement for his childhood failure to protect Hassan, Amir returns to Kabul two decades later, during the Taliban years, to rescue Hassan's son, Sohrab. Central to the plot is thus the theme of fall and redemption. The novel has been viewed as semi-autobiographical as it parallels some of the events in Hosseini's life, such as growing up in 1970s Kabul, having a Hazara servant, immigration to the United States at the age of

11, resettlement in California, and becoming a successful writer in the United States. He says, in an interview: "The setting in 1970s Kabul, the house where Amir lived, the films that he watches, of course the kite flying, the love of storytelling – all of that is from my own childhood. The story line is fictional" (Milvy 2007). Hosseini also revealed, in the same interview, that through *The Kite Runner* he sought to provide "a window into a different side of Afghanistan" – not "the Taliban" and "narcotics."

The novel's unparalleled success was aided by the global public's interest in Afghanistan-based stories in the aftermath of NATO-led Operation Enduring Freedom. The novel became an international bestseller, spending almost two years on *The New York Times* list. *The Kite Runner's* reception by critics and literary scholars was mixed, however. It was criticized from the perspective of literary craft: many found its plot contrived having too many implausible events and coincidences and pointed out the characters' lack of moral complexity. This is especially true in the case of Assef – the character who stands in for the Taliban – who is represented as pure evil (a sociopathic pedophile and a reader of Hitler's *Mein Kampf* [1925]) or in the case of Hassan who is unfailingly loyal and kind. Furthermore, both the novel and the film generated controversies in the Afghan community, especially because of the graphic scene of sexual violence. Parents of the boy who played the victim in the film were said to have been not informed of that scene. Both Afghan children actors had to be relocated to other countries for safety due to death threats prompting accusations of Hollywood's exploitative practices. The culture ministry of Afghanistan ultimately banned the importing of the film (Wafa 2008).

In scholarly circles, the book was criticized for its neo-orientalism and endorsement of the US interventionist policy in the Greater Middle East (Fitzpatrick). Moreover, critics observed that the novel seems to be more about the United States' self image in relation to the developing Muslim world than about Afghanistan's history and culture. The responses below exemplify the novel's reception by scholars. Literary scholar Joseph M. Slaughter writes that the novel was "carefully calculated, crafted, edited, and packaged ... to satisfy a sudden, war-induced American taste for success stories from Afghanistan. The novel none-too-subtly endorses as humanitarian intervention the US-allied invasion of Afghanistan and the 'War on Terror' by reifying the United States as the land of perpetual opportunity and freedom" (2007, p. 38). In the same vein, film scholar Mark Graham argues that the story's success is explained by the therapeutic role it played in the American context by "show[ing] the United States as it wishes to be seen: as a haven of tolerance and harmony, as a place where the kind of racism seen in 1970s Kabul has long since been extirpated" (2010, p. 156). In my *Imagining Afghanistan* (2019), I criticized *The Kite Runner* for its unexamined anticommunism, which results in the erasure of home-grown Afghan left-wing movements and actors in an attempt to explain the tragedy of Afghanistan as exclusively the result of the Soviet invasion of 1979, in line with Cold War-era US-based rhetoric. On the other hand, some argued that the novel played a positive role in the post-9/11 climate of pervasive Islamophobia disrupting a representation of Afghanistan "as a land of cave-dwelling terrorists" and serving as a cultural bridge (Milvy 2007). Literary scholar Timothy Aurby concludes that "Overall, the book encouraged increased tolerance and sympathy towards Muslims" by fostering "affective connections and identification" with its Afghan protagonist (2009, p. 27).

Following the success of *The Kite Runner*, Hosseini wrote two more Afghanistan-based novels. Although not as successful as *The Kite Runner*, Hosseini's sophomore novel *A Thousand Splendid Suns* (2008) also spent considerable time (fifteen weeks) as number 1 on the *New York Times* bestselling list. The title of the novel comes from a seventeenth-century poem about Kabul. The novel reception by critics was once again mixed: it was criticized by *The New York Times* reviewer for "melodramatic plotlines," "black and white characters," and having a "soap-opera-ish" plot (Kakutani 2007). However, other critics agreed that Hosseini's prose was adequate to the task and that Hosseini's storytelling talents compensated for some of the flaws of the prose (Ciabattari 2007). Having stated that after writing a father and son story in *The Kite Runner* he wanted to write a mother-daughter story, Hosseini admitted, in an interview, that it was "a real challenge to write from the standpoint of not one, but two, different women from different social backgrounds" (Hosseini 2012). Hosseini's reorientation towards Afghan women's experience reflected the increased interest in Afghan women's plight, and especially the issue of the burqa, in the post-2001 Western cultural contexts. Hosseini stated that his intention had been to "give some identity to the nameless, faceless women in burqa walking down the street" and to have shown that "that these are real people who have dreams and hopes and disappointments" (Mudge 2007). Laura Bush, who considered herself an activist on behalf of Afghan women, endorsed his second novel listing him among writers who "are able to change the world with their writing" (2008). Together with *The Kite Runner*, Hosseini's two novels sold over 38 million copies worldwide. The novel was turned into a play by Ursula Rani Sarma, which premiered in San Francisco in 2017.

The novel centers on Afghanistan's turbulent history as seen through the eyes of two female protagonists, Miriam (an illegitimate child) and Layla (a schoolteacher's daughter), who are a generation apart. Like *The Kite Runner*'s Amir, Miriam grows up during the Golden Age of Afghanistan; however, this era is no longer idealized; by contrast, it is presented as oppressive to women, especially those of lower economic class. Miriam's marriage to an abusive and deeply misogynist man, Rasheed, results in her early death by stoning by the Taliban as a punishment after she kills her husband in self-defense. Layla, the novel's other protagonist, represents a modern generation born during the socialist era; as such, she benefits from growing up in a society where women's equality is a state-sponsored project. She survives the drastic loss of rights that follows the defeat of the socialist government in 1992 – the last secular government in Afghanistan to date – by Islamist forces; she also has the mental strength to endure and bounce back when the times change. As in *The Kite Runner*, Hosseini uses the novel's plot to educate the global public about the history and culture of Afghanistan, this time focusing on the era omitted in *The Kite Runner* (1979–2001). In contrast to Amir, who can emigrate to the United States, the women of *A Thousand Splendid Sons* are trapped in a warring country and are survivors of multiple crises. Some scholars argued that this sophomore novel, as *The Kite Runner* before, uncritically endorses US-led intervention (Al-Dagambesh and Golubeva). However, as I argue, *A Thousand Splendid Suns* offers a dramatic change in perspective upon the socialist period in Afghanistan's history, which interrupts a seamless alignment with the US-based view – a key shift as compared to the first novel. Whereas in *The Kite Runner* the socialist era is demonized, here Hosseini acknowledges the socialist regime's unwavering and unconditional commitment to women's equality. One of the protagonists, Layla, born on the day of the communist revolution in April, 1978, embodies the promise of women's emancipation. Her father says: *"Women have always had it hard in this country, Laila, but they're probably more free now, under the communists, and have more rights than they've ever had before . . . it's a good time to be a woman in Afghanistan"* (2008, p. 135, emphasis in original).

Later, Layla responds to the Taliban's misogynist legislation by drawing strength from the egalitarian culture she grew up with: "They can't make half of the population stay home and do nothing . . . This isn't some village. This is *Kabul*. Women here used to practice law and medicine; they held office in the government" (2008, p. 278). The American era (post-2001) is depicted as having revived many of the promises of Soviet modernity, primarily by promoting the culture of women's equality. Anticommunist sentiments are still present: for instance, Hosseini is still dismissive of the socialist education curriculum as "propaganda" and embraces the US intervention. However, this novel provides a narrative of Afghanistan's recent history that is less one-sided and more nuanced, as compared to *The Kite Runner*.

Hosseini's third novel, *And the Mountains Echoed* was published in 2013 and has at its center the experiences of the two siblings separated in childhood. It is the most global of the three novels, spanning Kabul, Greece, Paris, and California, reflecting Afghanistan's continued imbrication with global affairs. This third Afghanistan-based novel covers the time span of sixty years, beginning in 1952 and ending somewhere around 2010–2012. The novel's characters and storylines are more complex, as compared to the previous two novels, indexing Hosseini's growth as a writer. Hosseini indicated that the story of Idris, a young Afghan American doctor who comes back to Kabul after decades of absence and experiences survivor guilt is based on his own experience (Goodreads 2013). A collection of overlapping stories with different narrators, this novel criticizes the multinational humanitarian community in post-2001 Kabul and no longer believes in the NATO forces' capability to "rescue" Afghanistan. More specifically, it exposes NATO practices of propping up the Cold War-era warlords (former jihadi fighters against the Soviets) with cash, allowing them to spring back to power. The novel is also condemning of what I called "the humanitarian imaginary" – a mode of exploiting distant suffering for entertainment purposes, which Hosseini in this book describes as voyeuristic and self-serving. The problem of narrating disaster – or rather the impossibility of such narration – is exemplified through two Afghan American cousins: Idris, a doctor, and Timur, a businessman. Both come to Kabul to claim their fathers' properties. Whereas Timur is eager to "document" the scenes of ruination and trauma by turning them into objects of tourist consumption, Idris is resistant to such documenting and feels tremendous guilt: because of his luck (he was spared the tragedy because his parents escaped the country and resettled in America), because of his extractive relation to the new Afghanistan (he is there to extract profit from selling the family house), and due to his inability to commit to the effort of helping the people in need. He feels "not entitled" to people's stories, admitting his inability to really hear them, being one of the "lucky ones, the ones who weren't here when the place was getting bombed to hell" (2013, p. 147). He refers to western humanitarian voyeurism as "pornography" (p. 149). Hosseini draws attention to disaster's incommunicability: upon his arrival back to California, Idris describes for his wife "the shell-blasted schools, the squatters living in roofless buildings, the beggars, the mud, the fickle electricity, but it's like describing music. He cannot bring it to life. [. . .] [D]etails escape him now, and his descriptions sound to him generic, insipid" (p. 159).

After the publication of *And the Mountains Echoed*, Hosseini suggested that he might be done with his Afghanistan literary project: "There's no guarantee at all that [he'll] write about Afghanistan again" (Goodreads 2013). Published by Riverhead Press in 2018, *Sea Prayer*, an illustrated story (with watercolors by British artist Dan Williams), marks a shift in Hosseini's interests as it is a response to the Syrian refugee crisis. It was inspired by the image of three-year-old Alan Kurdi whose body was washed upon the beach in Turkey in 2015. The father's silent monologue speaks of the generational divide between those who remember peaceful Syria and their children who only remember the war. Having written extensively on Afghanistan, Hosseini is well positioned to write on the Syrian crisis that in many ways mirrors the one of Afghanistan. For instance, *Sea Prayer* engages the theme of suffering children – one that Hosseini has relied heavily upon in all his Afghanistan-based novels. It also described a transformation of a peaceful city of Homs, Syria, into a war zone, which recalls the destruction of Kabul in the 1990s.

Overall, the most important theme in Hosseini's work is Afghanistan's history. All three Kabul-based novels begin in the Golden Age of Afghanistan – an era of rapid modernization – but diverge in how they tell the story of post-1979 conflicts. While *The Kite Runner* singles out the Soviet invasion as the key cause of the country's tragedy, the two subsequent novels problematize this view by pointing out the multiple injustices and social antagonisms that undercut the so called Golden Age, leading to popular unrest and the subsequent communist revolution. Specifically, *A Thousand Splendid Suns* and *And the Mountains Echoed* expose the inexorable patriarchy and stark economic inequalities in pre-1979 Afghanistan, which *The Kite Runner* leaves out. The three novels also present differing accounts of the NATO-led intervention. Both *The Kite Runner* and *A Thousand Splendid Suns* endorse the intervention; by contrast, *And the Mountains Echoed* provides a critique of the US-led neoliberal reconstruction of Afghanistan and exposes the endemic corruption and the immiseration of the population, despite the presence of NATO troops. When taken together, the three novels deliver a multifaceted, nuanced narrative of Afghanistan's twentieth- and early twenty-first-century history.

SEE ALSO: Contemporary Fictions of War; Fiction and Terrorism; Post-9/11 Narratives; Realism after Poststructuralism; Trauma and Fiction

REFERENCES

Aurby, Timothy. (2009). Afghanistan meets the Amazon: reading *The Kite Runner* in America. *PMLA* 124 (1): 25–43.

Bush, Laura. (2008). Khaled Hosseini. *Time* (May 12, 2008). http://content.time.com/time/specials/2007/article/0,28804,1733748_1733752_1735971,00.html (accessed July 16, 2021).

By the Book. (2013). Khaled Hosseini. *The New York Times* (June 6, 2013). https://www.nytimes.com/2013/06/09/books/review/khaled-hosseini-by-the-book.html (accessed September 10, 2021).

Ciabattari, Jane. (2007). Kite Runner's author also shines with "Suns." *Los Angeles Times* (May 21, 2007). https://www.latimes.com/archives/la-xpm-2007-may-21-et-book21-story.html (accessed July 16, 2021).

Fluri, Jennifer. (2009). "Foreign passports only": geographies of (post)conflict work in Kabul, Afghanistan. *Annals of the Association of American Geographers* 99 (5): 986–994.

Forster, Marc. (dir.) (2007). *The Kite Runner*. DreamWorks Pictures.

Goodreads. (2013). Interview with Khaled Hosseini (June 4, 2013). https://www.goodreads.

com/interviews/show/869.Khaled_Hosseini (accessed July 16, 2021).
Graham, Mark. (2010). *Afghanistan in the Cinema*. Chicago: University of Illinois Press.
Hosseini, Khaled. (2008). *A Thousand Splendid Suns*. New York: Riverhead Books.
Hosseini, Khaled. (2012). "Kite Runner" author on his childhood, his writing, and the plight of Afghan refugees. *Radio Free Europe/Radio Liberty* (June 21, 2012). https://www.rferl.org/a/interview-kite-runner-afghan-emigre-writer-khaled-hosseini/24621078.html (accessed July 16, 2021).
Hosseini, Khaled. (2013). *And the Mountains Echoed*. London: Bloomsbury.
Kakutani. Michiko. (2007). A woman's lot in Kabul, lower than a house cat's. *The New York Times* (May 30, 2007). https://www.nytimes.com/2007/05/29/books/29kaku.html (accessed July 16, 2021).
Milvy, Erika. (2007). The Khaled Hosseini controversy. *Salon* (December 9, 2007). https://www.salon.com/2007/12/09/hosseini/ (accessed July 16, 2021).
Mudge, Alden. (2007). Khaled Hosseini: behind the veil. *Bookpage* (June 2007). https://bookpage.com/interviews/8408-khaled-hosseini-fiction#.Xk7l8VJKi9Y (accessed July 16, 2021).
Slaughter, Joseph R. (2007). *Human Rights, Inc: The World Novel, Narrative form, and International Law*. New York: Fordham University Press.
Wafa, Abdul Waheed. (2008). "The Kite Runner" film outlawed in Afghanistan. *The New York Times* (January 16, 2008). https://www.nytimes.com/2008/01/16/world/asia/16kiterunner.html (accessed July 16, 2021).

FURTHER READING

Ivanchikova, Alla. (2020). The Kite Runner two decades later: three things every reader should know. In: *Critical Insights: The Kite Runner* (ed. Nicolas Tredell), 104–125. Toronto: Grey House.
Patterson, Annabel. (2014). Khaled Hosseini, *A Thousand Splendid Suns*: and some conclusions. In: *The International Novel*, 223–241. New Haven: Yale University Press.
Stuhr, Rebecca. (2009). *Reading Khaled Hosseini*. Westport, CT: Greenwood Press.

Hustvedt, Siri

JASON TOUGAW
City University of New York, USA

In her 2014 novel *The Blazing World*, Siri Hustvedt includes herself in a footnote. Her protagonist Harriet Burden, fond of adopting male personae, writes a letter to an interdisciplinary journal using the pseudonym Richard Brickman. Writing as Brickman, Burden offers commentary on her own work. Hustvedt appears at the end of a lengthy list of writers who have theorized the mind, body, and self: ". . . and an obscure novelist and essayist, Siri Hustvedt, whose position Burden calls a 'moving target'" (2014, p. 254). The joke is on Brickman, the male critic dismissive of a woman writer. Hustvedt is hardly obscure. She's a major international author – translated into more than thirty languages (while it's true that she is more widely read outside her native United States than in it). The joke, along with the novel's form, suggests that the power of readers and narrators arises from their subjective view onto their fictional worlds. Like all Hustvedt's fiction, it shatters any illusion of objectivity. The joke is also about the folly of *measuring* and *ranking* art and artists. After all, *The Blazing World* is about one artist's crusade to expose the sexist assumptions of the art world, whereby maleness too often equates with objective value. For Hustvedt, the value of fiction lies in the intersubjective relation between authors, narrators, and readers.

Hustvedt, a Norwegian American novelist, was born in 1955 and grew up in Northfield, Minnesota, where her father, Lloyd Hustvedt, was Professor of Norwegian Studies at St. Olaf College. She graduated from St. Olaf with a BA in history in 1977 and from Columbia University with a PhD in English in 1986. She has been married to novelist Paul Auster since 1982.

Her sister Asti Hustvedt is an independent scholar and author of *Mad Muses: Hysteria in Nineteenth-Century Paris* (2012). If Hustvedt's position is a moving target, it's because she uses her work to explore philosophical questions that are fundamental to life and identity, but are also impossible to resolve. As she develops her craft, or as she ages, Hustvedt becomes more prolific. "I'm a little nuts," she told *The Guardian* in 2019. "I am working like a maniac to get it in before I die" (Hicklin 2019). The various genres she writes – fiction, essay, long-form nonfiction, and the academic article – create a feedback loop for her evolving ideas about art, neuroscience, gender, identity, and epistemology. She has been linked to the "neuronovel" (Roth 2009), a genre associated with a loose affiliation of fiction writers exploring the philosophical implications of neuroscience, including Richard Powers, Rivka Galchen, John Wray, Ian McEwan, Maud Casey, and Jonathan Lethem.

Hustvedt is the author of seven novels, four essay collections, and a book of poetry, *Reading to You* (1983). Her novels are *The Blindfold* (1992), *The Enchantment of Lily Dahl* (1996), *What I Loved* (2003), *The Sorrows of an American* (2008), *The Summer Without Men* (2011), *The Blazing World*, and *Memories of the Future* (2018). Her essay collections are *Mysteries of the Rectangle: Essays on Painting* (2005), *A Plea for Eros* (2006), *Living, Thinking, Looking* (2012), and *A Woman Looking at Men Looking at Women: Essays on Art, Sex, and the Mind* (2016). Her book *The Shaking Woman; or A History of My Nerves* (2010) is a hybrid of memoir and essay. In a quest to figure out why her body has started convulsing when she speaks publicly, Hustvedt explores her own neurological experience and probing the history of science, gender, and mind–body dynamics. Her essay on the mind–body problem in contemporary neuroscience, *The Delusions of Certainty* (2017), is published as a standalone book (in addition to appearing in *A Woman Looking at Men Looking at Women*).

Hustvedt is a polymath – and has duly received some unusual distinctions for a novelist. She was appointed Lecturer in the Department of Psychiatry at the Weill Cornell Medical School in 2015; she delivered the Kierkegaard lecture at the University of Copenhagen in 2013, the philosopher's two hundredth birthday; she delivered the annual lecture for the Freud Foundation in Austria in 2011; she has published articles in academic journals, including *Salmagundi* (2012), *Seizure: European Journal of Epilepsy* (2013), *Suicidology* (2013), and *Clinical Neurophysiology* (2014). In addition to being longlisted for the Man Booker Prize for *The Blazing World* in 2014, winning *The Los Angeles Times* Book Prize that same year, and winning the Academy of Arts and Letters Prize in American Art in 2019, Hustvedt has won the Gabarron International Award for Thought and Humanities (2010), the Prix Européen de l'Essai Charles Veillon (2019), and the Princess of Asturias Award for Literature in Spain (2019). In *Zones of Focused Ambiguity in the Works of Siri Hustvedt* (2016), editors Johanna Hartmann, Christine Marks, and Hubert Zapf argue "the roles of writer and scholar cannot be clearly separated" in Hustvedt's work (2016, p. 3). The mixing of roles is consistent with Hustvedt's abiding intellectual project, to blur boundaries between categories that tend to get fixed in the cultural imagination – especially academic disciplines, literary genres, gender roles, and mind–body relations.

As Christine Marks argues in her book *"I Am Because You Are": Relationality in the Works of Siri Hustvedt*, "Hustvedt's work exhibits the inevitable interrelatedness of the human experience while advocating self-other relations based on dialogical intersubjectivity" (2014, p. 2). In her novels, she exhibits ideas about the self that she explores in her essays, where she advocates what Marks calls "a philosophy of mixing" – articulated explicitly by the character Violet in *What I Loved*: "mixing is the way of the world. The world passes through us – food, books, pictures, other people" (Hustvedt 2003, p. 88).

In a 1995 essay on memory entitled "Yonder," Hustvedt wrote, "Writing fiction is like remembering what never happened," a statement she reproduces in a scholarly article she published in the journal *Neuropsychoanalysis* (1998, p. 43). Hustvedt's aim is to unpack one of the abiding motives for and themes in her fiction – that "memory and what we call imagination partake of the same mental processes" (2011, p. 187). In many of her essays, Hustvedt makes the case that fiction relies on the dynamic interplay of "the subliminal self" and a writer's conscious intention. She's "interested in what happens underground, before an idea or picture or sentence surfaces. It is now a commonplace to say that most of what the brain does is unconscious, or non-conscious for those who want to avoid sounding Freudian. There are many debates about the exact nature of this subliminal reality, but no one is claiming any longer that it does not exist. Although much of a story may be created unconsciously, the writer's recognition that a story is right is consciously felt" (Hartmann et al. 2016, p. 17). In fiction, Hustvedt dramatizes the philosophical questions her essays explore. Her plots often hinge on the unearthing of "what happens underground."

Hustvedt's central characters tend to be artists and intellectuals, including writers, psychologists, performers, or scholars. Their work – generally portrayed as a lifelong calling – involves deep investigation of philosophical questions about identity. In *What I Loved*, the book that propelled her international reputation as a novelist of ideas, Violet proposes a theory of "mixing" in a book she's writing about anorexia: "They find a way to separate the needs and desires of other people from their own. After a while, they rebel by shutting down. They want to close up all their openings so nothing and nobody can get in. But mixing is the way of the world. The world passes through us – food, books, pictures, other people" (2003, p. 88). Mixing is a synonym for intersubjectivity, the idea that identity emerges through relationships. But Hustvedt's mixing extends those relations beyond human interaction. Her characters blend with both human and nonhuman elements of their environments. A book may shape identity as much as a loved one – a detail that's key to understanding Hustvedt's literary project.

In *The Delusions of Certainty*, Hustvedt makes an argument about mixing that challenges longstanding biological and philosophical assumptions, taking on thinkers from Descartes and Hobbes to contemporary researchers in computational neuroscience. Hustvedt intervenes in these debates through a feminist turn. She offers the placenta's central role in biological reproduction to represent mixing as a fundamental principle of biology. In her words, the placenta "is a composite structure, sometimes described as a fetomaternal organ, because it develops from the mother's and the embryo's tissues" (2016, p. 337). Hustvedt cites Margaret Cavendish as an antidote to the "atomistic" thinking popularized by Descartes and Hobbes: "For Cavendish, human beings, other species, flowers, and vegetables were bound in a fundamental and strikingly fluid dynamic unity" (p. 349). In fiction, Cavendish appears as a strong influence on Harriet Burden, the artist-protagonist of Hustvedt's *The Blazing World* – whose title is borrowed from Cavendish's book of the same name.

In *The Blazing World*, Harriet Burden (Harry for short) takes elaborate revenge on the sexist art world by borrowing the bodies and identities of three different male artists – and disseminating her work under their names. The story of Harry's highly orchestrated practical joke unfolds through tales told by multiple narrators intimate with the artist and her work. As one of the novel's narrators describes Burden, "The woman was chin-deep in the neuroscience of perception, and for some reason those unreadable papers with their abstracts and discussions justified her second life as a scam artist" (2014, p. 159). This is Hustvedt's feedback loop method in action, with Cavendish appearing as the marker of ideas she weaves in and out of her fiction and nonfiction – a concrete, formal mixing of the genres she writes. Cavendish influences Hustvedt, who creates the fictional Harry, who reads Hustvedt, then adopts a male persona who reduces her to a footnote. Via Burden, Hustvedt becomes a trickster. Burden is a product of the interplay between the "subliminal self" and conscious reflection Hustvedt describes as the driving force of fiction. In that sense, the character becomes a subliminal influence on her author.

In general, Hustvedt's characters can be plotted on a continuum that maps their ethical and aesthetic relationships to mixing. Characters who seek to contain or fix others become outright villains in her fiction – for example, *The Blindfold*'s George, *What I Loved*'s Teddy Giles, *Sorrows of an American*'s Jeffrey Lane, and *The Blazing World*'s Rune. Those who experiment with visual art or writing that foregrounds the mutability of self – including *The Enchantment of Lily Dahl*'s Edward Shapiro, *What I Loved*'s Bill Wechsler, *The Summer Without Men*'s Abigail, *The Blazing World*'s Harriet Burden, and *The Sorrows of an American*'s Burton – are difficult people who struggle with success at forming mutually rewarding social relationships.

As Hustvedt argues in much of her nonfiction, art is an intersubjective enterprise. The mixing involved can be exploitive or supportive. In *The Blindfold*, photographer George persuades protagonist Iris Vegan – who reappears in Auster's novel *Leviathan* (1992) – to pose. She objects to the photograph, taken while she danced around his apartment in a frenzy, because it seems to represent her as "a face without reason." The photograph circulates around New York City with a kind of talismanic force, gaining a social life of its own as its subject goes into a kind of peripatetic hiding. In *The Enchantment of Lily Dahl*, two portraitists propel the eponymous heroine's confrontations with reality, perception, and illusion. Edward Shapiro, a New York artist visiting the small town where Lily was raised, becomes her lover – and drives her to jealousy when he paints her elderly neighbor, while local misfit Martin Petersen builds a life-size doll of Lily. In *What I Loved*, Bill Wechsler's paintings propel the plot. One is a portrait of Mark, the two-year-old son of Wechsler's friends and neighbors. When Mark becomes a teenager with a severe case of empathy disorder, he befriends *enfant terrible* artist Teddy Giles, who steals the portrait and exhibits it – torn and slashed – as his own commentary on the art world. In *The Sorrows of an American*, protagonist Erik Davidsen develops a case of unrequited love for a neighbor whose estranged husband, Jeffrey Lane, is a controversial photographer. Lane photographs his wife and daughter secretly, breaks into Davidsen's apartment, and photographs him in a state of uncontrolled rage – exhibiting the portrait without his permission. In *The Summer Without Men*, the elderly Abigail bewilders the novel's heroine and narrator, Mia Frederickson, with her sinister "amusements" – works of needlepoint planted with secret buttons that open upon sinister worlds that seem to represent her community's history of sexual violence. In *The Blazing World*, Harriet Burden, a giant, loquacious autodidact artist, hires three successive men to exhibit her works as their own, including her various versions of her "metamorphs."

The Enchantment of Lily Dahl's Martin Petersen is in a category of his own. This early novel portrays Petersen as deranged by his obsession with the image's power to distort reality. His art becomes evidence of crime and mental instability, despite the fact that his collages and life-size doll project share many of the aesthetic hallmarks of Hustvedt's other artists. By contrast, *Memories of the Future*'s S.H. is much more self-aware about her art's relative ability to capture the experience of others – including her former self. Like *The Enchantment of Lily Dahl*, *Memories of the Future* represents the criminal abuse of women. One significant difference is that the artist central to the plot is a woman, the abusive man an incidental character; a second difference is that the female protagonist is part of a community of women whose power comes from their commitment to a philosophy of mixing. While Petersen atomizes like Hobbes, S.H. blends like Cavendish. Working through notebooks she kept as a much younger woman stabbing at becoming a writer, S.H. is circumspect about her ability to fix the past with accuracy, though she portrays a community of women vehement in their commitment to the mixing of identity and the blurring of boundaries, including those between the material world and supernatural phenomena.

Petersen's crimes and S.H.'s fascination with her 38-year-old notebooks both raise questions that run through the whole of Hustvedt's work. Does a body contain a person? When does art exploit? When does it create possibility or make transformation possible? Is it the artist's responsibility to care? If a self is mutable, what does that mean for identity? What roles does gender play in the making of self? Hustvedt doesn't answer these questions definitively in the fiction, but she offers evidence for her points of view – and more concrete ones in her essays and articles she publishes in peer-reviewed neuroscience journals.

In "Three Emotional Stories," published in the journal *Neuropsychoanalysis*, Hustvedt summarizes some of her ideas about relations between neuroscience and fiction:

> Fictions are born of the same faculty that transmutes experience into the narratives we remember explicitly but which are formed unconsciously. Like episodic memories and dreams, fiction reinvents deeply emotional material into meaningful stories, even though in the novel, characters and plots are not necessarily anchored in actual events. And we do not have to be Cartesian dualists to think of imagination as a bridge between a timeless core sensorimotor affective self and the fully self-conscious, reasoning, and/or narrating linguistic cultural self, rooted in the subjective–inter-subjective realities of time and space.
>
> (2011, p. 195)

According to Hustvedt, fiction is an extension of the human mind's reliance on making narratives. Even before neuroscience started showing up in her fiction, Hustvedt created characters – made of words – that seemed to embody the dynamics of "a sensorimotor affective self" and "a fully conscious, reasoning, and/or narrating linguistic cultural self." Her plots are all about exploring "intersubjective realities." In *The Enchantment of Lily Dahl*, Martin Petersen fantasizes that he can will the life-size dolls he fabricates into selfhood, or into embodying subjective experience. In *The Blazing World*, published nearly two decades later, Hustvedt creates Harriet Burden, a masculine, powerful woman who plays a trick on the art world, hiring men to pretend to be the authors of her dolls; they feel like cousins of the ones that Petersen created in the earlier novel. The difference is that Harry's crime is a heroic antidote to the art world's sexism, while Petersen's is a deranged and brutal reflection of that sexism. Harry puts audiences in the uncomfortable position of witnessing lifeless beings that conjure questions about what life is, what self is – biologically, psychologically, politically, sociologically, and philosophically. From the beginning of her career to the present, Hustvedt has "rooted" these fundamental questions in "meaningful stories" offered as thought experiments to stimulate reflection rather than simple or direct answers.

SEE ALSO: Auster, Paul; The Brain and American Fiction; Lethem, Jonathan; Powers, Richard

REFERENCES

Hartmann, Johanna, Marks, Christine, and Zapf, Hubert. (eds.) (2016). *Zones of Focused Ambiguity in the Works of Siri Hustvedt*. Berlin: De Gruyter.
Hicklin, Aaron. (2019). Siri Hustvedt: "I'm writing for my life." *The Guardian* (March 3, 2019). https://www.theguardian.com/books/2019/mar/03/siri-hustvedt-i-am-writing-for-my-life-memories-of-the-future-interview (accessed July 4, 2021).
Hustvedt, Asti. (2012). *Mad Muses: Hysteria in Nineteenth-Century Paris*. New York: Bloomsbury.
Hustvedt, Siri. (1998). *Yonder: Essays*. New York: Holt.
Hustvedt, Siri. (2003). *What I Loved*. New York: Picador.
Hustvedt, Siri. (2011). Three emotional stories: reflections on memory, the imagination, narrative, and the self. Neuropsychoanalysis 13 (2): 187–195.
Hustvedt, Siri. (2014). *The Blazing World*. New York: Simon & Schuster.
Hustvedt, Siri. (2016). *A Woman Looking at Men Looking at Women: Essays on Art, Sex, and the Mind*. New York: Simon & Schuster.
Marks, Christine. (2014). *"I Am Because You Are": Relationality in the Works of Siri Hustvedt*. Heidelberg: Universitätsverlag Winter.
Roth, Marco. (2009). Rise of the neuronovel: a specter is haunting the contemporary novel. *n+1* (Fall 2009). https://nplusonemag.com/issue-8/essays/the-rise-of-the-neuronovel/ (accessed July 4, 2021).

FURTHER READING

Hustvedt, Siri. (2018). Antonio Damasio, feeling, and the evolution of consciousness: Siri Hustvedt on "The Strange Order of Things." *The Los Angeles Review of Books* (April 6, 2018). https://lareviewofbooks.org/article/antonio-damasio-feeling-and-the-evolution-of-consciousness-siri-hustvedt-on-the-strange-order-of-things/
Kon-Yu, Natalie and Loon, Julienne V. (2018). Gendered authorship and cultural authority in Siri Hustvedt's *The Blazing World*. Contemporary Women's Writing 12 (1): 49–66.
Rabaté, Jean-Michel. (2018). The pathos of history: trauma in Siri Hustvedt's *The Sorrows of an American*. In: *American Literature as World Literature: Literatures as World Literature* (ed. Jeffrey R. Di Leo), 257–272. New York: Bloomsbury Academic.
Zapf, Hubert. (2008). Narrative, ethics, and postmodern art in Siri Hustvedt's *What I Loved*. In: *Ethics in Culture: The Dissemination of Values through Literature and Other Media* (ed. Astrid Erll, Herbert Grabes, and Ansgar Nünning), 171–194. Berlin: De Gruyter.

Hypertext Fiction and Network Narratives

ANNA MCFARLANE
University of Glasgow, Scotland

The network is a beguiling and ambiguous concept with a suggestive relationship to the form and content of the novel. By way of form, the novel can usefully be compared to a network. The novel achieves its effects through the detail and the multiplication of perspective it can offer, a complexity most influentially framed by Bakhtin through the concept of "heteroglossia." The novel's structure consists of networks of characters and relationships between different settings. As a form, it invites and evokes the connectivity of human beings with the world around them and with each other. During the period under consideration, from 1980 to 2020, the figure of the network appears in the content of the novel, moving from a formal, structural, and subconscious consideration to a conscious preoccupation. In the 1980s, the science fictional imaginary was increasingly concerned with the shape of the network due to the promise of the Internet, and what it might do to social relations and individual identities. The network went on to influence the shape of the novel in more direct and material ways: first, through the development of the hypertext novel from the late 1980s and then, in the 1990s, as several postmodern novels took inspiration from the developing Internet to experiment with form in ways that took the novel's complexity to extremes by reacting to the emergent medium of hypertext which at times seemed to threaten the future of the novel as a printed artifact. Through hyperreal detail authors sought to represent relationships between the individual and the social as acts of networking, humans connected with one another through a myriad of tiny details. While the representation of complexity echoed the rise of a networked society, such texts often foregrounded their materiality, capturing the theme of the network while reinforcing the primacy of the physical novel in the age of hypertext. Since the turn of the millennium and the watershed moment of the terrorist attacks on the Twin Towers and the Pentagon on September 11, 2001 (referred to by the metonymy 9/11), the network has been represented via the globalization made possible by the interconnectivity offered by Web 2.0, accompanied by a paranoid suspicion of a connectivity that may be dangerous at a personal and social level, for example by offering terrorism a route into Western life. The novel has been a key form of expression throughout this period, and perhaps despite the innovative possibilities offered by new media. This entry explores the figure of the network through the content and form of these novels.

The presence of the network in the novel on the level of content was most influentially described by the science fiction authors gathered together under the name "cyberpunk." Anthologized in Bruce Sterling's *Mirrorshades: The Cyberpunk Anthology* (1986), the cyberpunks were characterized by combining the control of cybernetics with the anarchy of punk or, more pithily, by combining "lowlife and high tech" (Sterling 1986, p. 4). The cyberpunks gave imaginative shape to the nascent Internet and contributed to a cultural moment that saw a two-way street of influence between cyberpunk literature and early hackers. The year 1984, one that was preordained by George Orwell's eponymous novel to be significant in the science fictional imaginary, saw the publication of two seminal works that dramatized the network: William Gibson's hugely successful *Neuromancer* and Samuel Delany's *Stars in My Pockets Like Grains of Sand*. Gibson's novel brought the term "cyberspace" into real-world usage and significantly influenced the visualization of the space behind the computer screen. Through exhilaratingly visual prose, Gibson describes cyberspace as a "consensual hallucination" (1995, p. 12) and imagines a space where data can be seen and navigated like dark city streets outlined in neon colors. While it is tempting to describe Gibson's work as prophetic, given the usefulness of a term like cyberspace and his vision of a globalized capital let loose in the matrix's virtual terrain, *Neuromancer*, like all science fiction, is a commentary on its contemporary era. As Sterling had pointed out, the cyberpunk writers were the first generation of science fiction authors to have grown up with television as a significant and pervasive medium, and it is no coincidence that Gibson famously opens his novel with the line, "The sky above the port was the color of television, tuned to a dead channel" (p. 9). Gibson's is a world where the television does not just permeate real life, but where real life can permeate that imaginary electronic space, until the distinction between the two becomes insubstantial or obsolete. It is the invisible power of electricity, moving at the speed of light, that inspires this literature, even as it prefigures the interconnected world of the twenty-first century.

While Gibson's cyberspace reveled in a new frontier, there was already some trepidation about how a networked society might stifle individuality, even as it liberated. Samuel Delany's *Stars in My Pockets Like Grains of Sand* tells the story of Rat Korga, a man who has allowed himself to undergo the Radical Anxiety Termination (RAT) procedure to turn him into a compliant slave. Korga feels a thrill of possibility when introduced to a basic version of the Internet (comparable to the *Encarta* encyclopedias of the 1990s) but is only introduced to full connectivity when he becomes the sole survivor of the destruction of his planet. Delany's work is more grounded in the materiality of his characters' worlds and this produces some insight into the nature of the network. When all information is recorded and accessible as data, the aspects of human experience that cannot be reduced to discrete data points, such as love, sexuality, individual fetishes or affective states, are made invisible and are not taken into account in social life. Delany's work was not included in Sterling's cyberpunk canon – a canon that has been criticized for its focus on white male writers (Nixon 1992) – and is more often analyzed as an example of Afrofuturism, given its interest in race and the legacy of slavery. It remains a powerful early engagement with the networked society in literature.

These novels were influential, offering computer programmers models for how the Internet might be accessed or experienced and suggesting how an electronically networked society might be changed by that process of connectivity. This two-way street between cyberpunk and computer programming was documented in Bruce Sterling's *The Hacker Crackdown* (1992), which told the story of hacking from the phone jackers who took advantage of electronic systems while telephones were still operated through switchboards, to the fight for the Internet as a commons and the formation of the Electronic Frontier Foundation, the most significant organization formed to protect digital rights as a core aspect of citizenry. This overlap between the portrayal of the network in literature and the development of the networks that connect our societies to this day is a fascinating history, and one that urges us to historicize the structures of the Internet.

While the network has appeared in literature on the level of content, it has also changed the form of the novel. The possibilities of the Internet have led to experimentation with texts that have been written with the purpose of appearing online, and take advantage of the Internet's structures to investigate new storytelling possibilities. One such example is the hypertext novel, which has remained an experimental, rather than a popular form. Such novels use hypertext to offer different narrative branches, and owe something to the legacy of early video games and the Choose Your Own Adventure books that were produced for children from the 1970s. Video games and Choose Your Own Adventure books treat the reader as a protagonist, often by addressing them in the second person, or by closely identifying them with an avatar, encouraging a sense of interactivity with the work. Like these low-culture precursors, hypertext novels explore themes of the reader's influence on the text and the ways in which the text is shaped by reception; they can also destabilize the reader's experience of time and cause and effect as different branches of the story can be read alongside one another. However, there are drawbacks to these forms, which may explain their lack of popular success. While the reader can choose between various storytelling options, these options will always have to be written by the author, so the reader can never experience the true narrative freedom that the hypertext novel seeks to emulate. Also, the linear nature of reading means that only one narrative strand can be read at one time, so the possibilities for representing nonlinear time are less successful than they might be in visual media. For example, in Alan Moore's graphic novel *Watchmen* (1987), the character Dr. Manhattan experiences time as nonlinear and this is represented through the production of multiple panels on the same page showing him living multiple key moments in his narrative at the same time. Filmmakers have also experimented with the simultaneous possibilities of the visual form, such as in Mike Figgis's *Timecode* (2000), which splits the screen into four quadrants, showing four different takes simultaneously. While there might be potential for hypertext to incorporate images to similar effect, this has not been a common practice and, by definition, if it were done successfully the medium might no longer be considered hypertext at all. The textual nature of hypertext novels means that linearity remains core to reader comprehension, though the most successful texts embraced the constrictions of the medium and used them to their advantage.

Significantly, the emergence of the hypertext novel appeared at a time where the concerns raised by the form were at the forefront of critical theory, and George P. Landow argues that this synchrony explains the academic interest in hypertext, while also situating the hypertext as a key medium in postmodern literature. Landow puts the names of two preeminent literary theorists, Jacques Derrida and Roland Barthes, alongside two computer theorists, Theodor Nelson and Andries van Dam, arguing that the four thinkers – key to their fields, but little known to those from other academic disciplines – have in common a number of philosophical positions. They argue that "we must abandon conceptual systems founded on ideas of center, margin, hierarchy, and linearity and replace them by ones of multilinearity, nodes, links, and networks" (Landow 2006, p. 1). By nature of their form, hypertext novels engage with all of these issues, seeking to transform the linear reading experience of the printed page into an interactive web of meaning-making, one that almost effortlessly dramatizes contemporary concerns in critical theory. However, as Astrid Ensslin points out, Landow's approach has a tendency to treat hypertexts as a homogeneous mode, or even a genre of literature, rather than taking into account the individual style of the specific text under consideration. Ensslin describes a "second-wave [of] digital fiction scholars" who, instead, focus on "close narratological, semiotic, and ludostylistic analyses of individual works" (2017, p. 185). However, Landow's work remains perceptive of the goals of hypertext fiction at a moment in time. These texts were often produced by academics and many of them were certainly concerned with the issues Landow describes. Landow's analysis is also useful in suggesting the term "lexia" (2006, p. 3), which he adapts from the work of Roland Barthes, to describe the short blocks of texts used in hypertext novels, lexias that the reader navigates between to construct their own version of the narrative.

The most crucial move in the canonization of hypertext fiction was the creation of the Eastgate Systems software, Storyspace, which could be used to write both fiction and non-fiction, and to present such texts for reading as hypertext. The first hypertext novel is Michael Joyce's *afternoon* (1987), written using Storyspace, which Joyce developed alongside Jay David Bolter, who was to publish *Writing Space: The Computer, Hypertext, and the History of Writing* (1990), one of the first academic books to address the phenomenon of the hypertext and its place in cultural history. *afternoon* tells the story of a divorcé who may or may not have witnessed his son's death in a car crash that morning. The lexias are written in the first person, but the focal character changes as the reader jumps between nodes, creating a cacophony of perspectives that disorients the reader. In this first hypertext novel, Joyce is already aware of the potential shortcomings of the form, but makes these a feature of his text. In a section entitled "dialectic" he writes, "its all a fraud: the illusion of choice wherein you control the options, the so-called yielding textures of words . . . All of it typical, control-oriented male fantasy" (Joyce 1994). Its inclusion in Norton's anthology, *Postmodern American Fiction* (1994), showed that this strain of hypertext fictions was being taken seriously as a potential addition to the twentieth-century canon.

Perhaps the most artistically successful of the hypertext novels of the early 1990s was Stuart Moulthrop's *Victory Garden* (1992), written, like *afternoon*, using Storyspace. *Victory Garden* is a consideration of the first Gulf War (waged under George H.W. Bush's presidency, 1990–1991) that chimes with the mediated nature of the war, as diagnosed by Jean Baudrillard in his *The Gulf War Did Not Take Place* (English translation, 1995). Baudrillard had theorized that the war was only experienced via the media; there were very few casualties on the American side so that, Baudrillard argued, the characterization of the event as a war, rather than as an atrocity, was an act of propaganda. The illusion of warfare could only be achieved because of the nature of televised news, which offered a narrative to viewers that, in effect, created the impression of a war rather than offering viewers access to a real, historical event. In *Victory Garden*, Moulthrop's lexias each offer multiple hyperlinked phrases that take the reader to a new lexia. Storyspace also offers a range of entrance points to the reader, so that the beginning of the novel is as undetermined as the order in which it is read, and the place that the reader stops. The format allows for infinite loops in which one is returned to a particular vignette again and again, and there is no formal end point to the novel, merely a point at which the reader begins to see the same lexias appear again and again, bringing the experience of reading new material to an end. While the hypertext novel has never become a popular format, a recent successful example of these techniques is *Black Mirror*'s *Bandersnatch* (2018), a film which uses Netflix's functionality as an online media streaming service to offer multiple outcomes to the story in a way that engages with the possibility of free will. Like the most successful of the hypertext novels, *Bandersnatch* uses its limitations (the need to return viewers to key scenes in the narrative, the possibility of repetition) by marrying these formal necessities to its thematic interest in traumatic events. McSweeney and Joy (2019) note that the text returns its protagonist to his childhood, where his refusal to leave home without a favorite stuffed animal led to his mother taking a later train, alone, which then derailed, killing her. When the child makes the choice to stay at home there is only one option given on the screen so that the viewer must force the character to reenact the tragic events of that day, underlining the desperation of returning to a past that cannot be changed. It is significant that this film, inspired in some ways by the hypertext novel, appears as a visual medium rather than a literary one. The legacy of the hypertext itself is perhaps most evident in the online, interactive formats of video games and self-referential memes, both intensely visual media that hold little regard for the formalities of what might be considered literary.

The limitations of hypertext novels notwithstanding, the impact that hypertext had on literary production in the 1990s far outweighed the form's popular impact thanks to a literary media keen to frame the fate of the book in terms of millenarianism. As David Ciccoriccio has noted, hypertext could be characterized as "an innovative literary practice sustained by a small but dedicated group of (primarily academic) artists and theorists" (2012, p. 470) but, despite this avant-garde positioning, the form "found itself cast into a competition that it could not win and in which it did not belong: that of usurping over 500 years of literary tradition in print and 'liberating' the narrative line" (p. 470). Setting the hypertext against the tradition of the print novel was commentator Robert Coover. Coover was known for his own innovative experiments with escaping the linearity of storytelling in his collection *Pricksongs and Descants* (1969). "The Babysitter" (1969) gives different accounts of the same night and invites the reader to engage with a mundane event and the fantasies that spring from it, leaving the reader with little understanding of how or whether those fantasies might come to bear on reality. Similarly, "The Elevator" gives an account of an elevator ride in fifteen vignettes, each describing a different experience, many of these, like "The Babysitter," inflected with sexual fantasies. It is perhaps unsurprising that Coover, in his capacity as lecturer in creative writing at Brown University, became interested in hypertext as a literary form and began inviting his students to investigate its possibilities. However, writing about these experiments in *The New York Times Book Review*, Coover's piece was given the provocative title "The End of Books," turning an exploratory piece into a manifesto for change and a premature diagnosis that the printed novel had become obsolete (Coover 1992). In fact, Coover's piece highlighted the possibilities of hypertext while pointing to some of the drawbacks to the form. Coover particularly pointed to the ephemerality of software packages as technology moved so fast that there was a struggle to maintain hypertexts in a form that could be accessed by later-generation personal computers.

While the reality of the hypertext novel might not live up to the promise heralded by the press in the early 1990s, the influence of the concept has been successful in infiltrating print books and producing new literary forms. The most definitive example of this must be the appearance of significant and lengthy postmodern works such as David Foster Wallace's *Infinite Jest* (1996) and Mark Z. Danielewski's *House of Leaves* (2000), both of which demonstrated an interest in their material as networked and hyperlinked to an extent that challenged linearity while, at the same time, foregrounding their materiality as printed artifacts. The hyperreality of Wallace's *Infinite Jest* shows a multitude of details connecting his characters with one another and with their own pasts and futures, emphasizing to the point of satire the network of relations on which the novel has always relied for its textures and effects. Wallace employed extensive footnotes in his work, contributing to the sense of infinitely networked material while also drawing the reader's attention to the materiality of the pages in their hands and the organization of the words on the page. Meanwhile, *House of Leaves* took as its premise the discovery of a series of disorganized documents in the apartment of Zampanò, a recently deceased old man with eccentric behaviors. The novel begins with a description of the documents' discovery and is peppered with different sets of footnotes (some of which have their own footnotes), some written by Zampanò and some by Johnny Truant, who takes possession of his paperwork. The novel also makes use of different typographical layouts, some of which encourage the reader to rotate the book, again encouraging an awareness of the book as a physical object. These novels arguably achieved the goals of online novels to a greater extent than true hypertext fictions; indeed, the engagement that Danielewski won from his book's dedicated fans prompted Alexander Starre to describe *House of Leaves* as "a node – the central one – in a communication network that stretches across various inscription surfaces and communication technologies" (2015, p. 128).

Since the millennium the network has once again risen on the level of content as it has become increasingly important in the current political era to address the concept of the network, the realities of our connectivity, and the role that literature might play in helping us to understand these new individual and social realities. The concept of the network is intimately intertwined with post-9/11 anxieties – it is worth remembering that the name of the terrorist group Al-Qaeda can be translated as "the Network." This act of naming prioritizes the group's structures over their ideology or demands. In this act of naming, the group find the most sinister threat as they show that they cannot be wiped out by violence or propaganda – their message will continue to spread and there is no way for anyone to find out the identity of all the players, or to put a stop to their ideas. The use of Internet technology in dispersing hostage videos and recruiting new members has been adopted by ISIS and remains a powerful tool for organizing, portraying the group as a sinister combination of an ancient belief in the bloody power of jihad combined with a twenty-first-century understanding of technology as a means of propagating that ideology far beyond the geographic boundaries of the earliest members.

The importance of the network as a factor in terrorism and politics after 9/11, alongside the dizzying rate of technological development, led to a new form of science fiction, or a new form of realism dependent on one's perspective. This was described by Veronica Hollinger as "science fiction realism" and included works such as William Gibson's post-9/11 novel, *Pattern Recognition* (2003). Gibson's novel portrayed a world that had "insufficient 'now' to stand on" (p. 57), making the extrapolation of a future impossible. Instead the world of realism becomes saturated with science fictional motifs and it becomes unclear whether technologies described in the text are real, cutting-edge technologies or fictions. In Gibson's novel the search of his protagonist, Cayce, for the authors of some strange films known only as the Footage that have appeared anonymously online, and the search for answers about her father who disappeared on 9/11, become emblematic of a sensation of being unmoored as history has been so irrevocably disrupted by the shock of the 9/11 attacks. The connections Cayce experiences with fellow members of the Footage's fan cult and the physical global connections she makes through international travel leave her feeling unsatisfied and she falls back upon a private individuality in order to find some sense of stability.

More recently, the network has reemerged in literature through satire on contemporary social media. The line here between science fiction, satire, and realism is blurred as contemporary novelists draw on all of these forms to produce glimpses of a future in which current social media trends are taken to ridiculous or dystopian conclusions. Jennifer Egan's work, notably *Look at Me* (2001) and the Pulitzer Prize-winning *A Visit From the Goon Squad* (2010), offers near-future dystopias in which ordinary people are paid to allow others access to surveillance of their every action, and marketing weaponizes word-of-mouth publicity, encroaching on authentic human relationships to create buzz about the latest product. David Eggers's *The Circle* (2013) tells the story of Mae Holland, a young woman thrilled to land a job at the titular social media company only to find that her life is increasingly colonized by the expectations of the organization. Echoing Samuel Delany's concerns in *Stars in My Pocket Like Grains of Sand*, the novel dramatizes the loss of individuality when all experience and emotion must be converted into content for a social media company, an act that destroys the woman's interiority and experience of her life. The network here is portrayed as vampiric, not content with breaching the bounds of cyberspace to take over reality, but compelled to colonize the inner lives of the human characters. Eggers and Egan are celebrated literary fiction authors, more associated with the Pulitzer Prize and *The New Yorker* than with a science fictional approach. The use of satire serves to underline the importance of social media in contemporary life and evokes how ludicrous such mediation would seem to those looking in from another society by holding up a mirror in the shape of our society a few years down the line. However, such a strategy falls far short of offering alternatives to the future extrapolated from our present, and the utopian dreams of a globalized commons held by many of the original builders of the Internet, such as Tim Berners-Lee, are impossible to be found. Rather than offer the hope of a utopian, global Internet-of-the-commons, these texts perhaps act more successfully as nostalgia for the 1990s or early 2000s, before social media became so central to public life, and so dominated by just a few brands from the launch of Facebook in 2004.

The novel has, so far, continued to prove itself as the most popular form of literature in the twenty-first century, and its demise as a physical object has yet to take place in the era of the network. On the contrary, in many cases the novel has acted as the preferred form of satire and critique for contemporary networked culture. The novel has also now, thanks to the availability of stylish and convenient e-readers, been successfully repackaged as a digital commodity, one that is easier than ever to buy and to consume. The legacy of hypertext fiction did not bear fruit in terms of new examples of long-form electronic fiction, but there are ways in which the network that increasingly defines our working and social lives has come to bear on literature. In the creative nonfiction of the blogosphere the term hypertext would never be used, because it is the default method of communication, so common as to be invisible, and this is also well known to those who spend time traveling down Wikipedia rabbit holes, finding their way to increasingly obscure entries through the myriad paths that hypertext has made through the ever-growing body of the encyclopedia. The memes that circulate the Internet as a form of casual communication, humor, and satire also take part in a highly referential culture, marrying text and image, in a medium that hypertext fictions once gestured toward. However, these formats are in stark contrast to the novel, which, no matter how metafictional or referential, appears as a discrete artistic object (even in its electronic formats) with a reliable provenance and a set of widely understood reading codes. The appeal of such a work – by turns authoritative, reliable, and immersive – will likely guarantee the importance of the novel in responding to the symbol and structure of the network as it continues to shape contemporary reality.

SEE ALSO: Black Atlantic; Coover, Robert; Cyberpunk; Danielewski, Mark Z.; Delany, Samuel; Egan, Jennifer; Eggers, Dave; Gibson, William; Globalization; The Graphic Novel; The New Experimentalism/The Contemporary Avant-Garde; Post-9/11 Narratives; Wallace, David Foster

REFERENCES

Bolter, Jay David. (1990). *Writing Space: The Computer, Hypertext, and the History of Writing*. London: Routledge.
Ciccoriccio, David. (2012). Digital fiction: networked narratives. In: *The Routledge Companion to Experimental Literature* (ed. Joe Bray, Alison Gibbons, and Brian McHale), 469–482. London: Routledge.
Coover, Robert. (1992). The end of books. *The New York Times* (June 21, 1992). https://archive.

nytimes.com/www.nytimes.com/books/98/09/27/specials/coover-end.html? (accessed July 16, 2021).

Ensslin, Astrid. (2017). Electronic fictions. In: *The Cambridge Companion to Postmodern American Fiction* (ed. Paula Geyh), 181–197. Cambridge: Cambridge University Press.

Gibson, William. (1995). *Neuromancer*. London: HarperCollins.

Gibson, William. (2003). *Pattern Recognition*. New York: Putnam.

Joyce, Michael. (1994). *afternoon: a story*. In: *Postmodern American Fiction: A Norton Anthology* (ed. Paula Geyh, Fred G. Leebron, and Andrew Levy). New York: Norton. https://wwnorton.com/college/english/pmaf/hypertext/aft/index.html (accessed July 16, 2021).

Landow, George P. (2006). *Hypertext 3.0: Critical Theory and New Media in an Era of Globalization*. Baltimore: Johns Hopkins University Press.

McSweeney, Terrance and Joy, Stuart. (2019). Change your past, your present, your future? Interactive narratives and trauma in *Bandersnatch* (2018). In: *Through the Black Mirror: Deconstructing the Side Effects of the Digital Age*, 271–284. Cham, Switzerland: Palgrave Macmillan.

Nixon, Nicola. (1992). Cyberpunk: preparing the ground for revolution or keeping the boys satisfied? *Science Fiction Studies* 19 (2): 219–235.

Starre, Alexander. (2015). *Metamedia: American Book Fictions and Literary Print Culture After Digitization*. Iowa City: University of Iowa Press.

Sterling, Bruce. (ed.) (1986). *Mirrorshades: The Cyberpunk Anthology*. New York: Ace Books.

Sterling, Bruce. (1992). *The Hacker Crackdown: Law and Disorder on the Electronic Frontier*. New York: Bantam Books.

FURTHER READING

Ciccoriccio, David. (2008). *Reading Network Fiction*. Tuscaloosa: University of Alabama Press.

Ciccoriccio, David. (2017). The end of the book… In: *American Literature in Transition, 1990–2000* (ed. Stephen Burn), 76–90. Cambridge: Cambridge University Press.

Douglas, J. Yellowlees. (2000). *The End of Books – Or Books Without End?* Ann Arbor: University of Michigan Press.

Ensslin, Astrid. (2014). *Literary Gaming*. Cambridge, MA: MIT Press.

Illness and Disability Narratives

MICHAEL PATRICK HART
Lane College, USA

INTRODUCTION: UNDERSTANDING "AND"

When we talk about illness *and* disability, the conjunction signals certain resonances that rightly exist between these two different terms – both as theoretical frameworks and as real, lived experiences. At the same time, we cannot simply use illness and disability interchangeably; we must recognize the nuances between the two alongside their ligatures. Likewise, illness and disability are both such capacious terms that to treat them as a singular representation poses problems as well. For example, with illness, we have physical illness and mental illness, terminal illness and chronic illness, congenital illness and acquired illness, and so on. The same can be said about the various kinds of disabilities that exist as well. Both illness and disability operate across an entanglement of intersections ranging from the corporeal, the psychic, the temporal, the spatial, the racial, the gendered, the socioeconomic, the sexual, and many more. The complexities of illness and disability become even more intense when we consider them as a function of narrative as we need to consider the literary and political purposes behind such representation. Thus, the matrix of illness and disability is unbelievably vast, often contradictory, and occasionally confounding.

In order to produce a cogent entry on this topic, I want to consider illness and disability as distinct in terms of scale in their portrayal in contemporary American literature. That is to say, usually we encounter illness on a large scale, such as an epidemic or pandemic, as a way to better understand the affective networks of these devastating diseases; on the other hand, literary representations of disability seem to focus on the individual such that readers can see disability as a generative form of human variation that undoes the common perception of disability as "lesser" than nondisabled. Despite this difference in scale, both kinds of narrative showcase the different types of collectivities that emerge out of these situations. These collectivities are as diverse and divergent as the characters that make them up.

With this arrangement in mind, this entry will primarily focus on three major nodes for each topic. When considering illness, it moves chronologically through three particular time frames. First, attention is turned to the AIDS epidemic of the 1980s and early 1990s, followed by an examination of how the human-centered understanding of viruses shifted with the rise of technological advances in the 1990s and early 2000s. Finally, this entry comments on the age of the pandemic in our current COVID-19 situation. With disability, the entry is organized around three particular topics: physical disability, intellectual disability, and theories of representation. While these topics do tend to track chronologically in terms of disability studies as a field, I am more interested in analyzing how disability can frame narrative as opposed to focusing on particular representations of certain disabilities. That said, this entry does not claim (nor could it be) a comprehensive understanding of illness and disability in contemporary American literature; instead, it offers these readings as but a few vantage points through which to engage these critically important fields.

ILLNESS

In 1978, Susan Sontag published her now-foundational work, *Illness as Metaphor*, wherein she illustrates how the negative metaphors of illness often cause great pain to those afflicted and can even discourage them from seeking treatment. Sontag demystifies these metaphors to show that illness – particularly cancer – is simply a disease that can be treated, and not a curse or a punishment. A little over a decade later, Sontag published a companion piece, *AIDS and Its Metaphors* (1989). Here, Sontag maps her analysis of cancer over the AIDS epidemic that spread across the United States during the 1980s. In doing so, Sontag demonstrates how AIDS, like cancer, is not an individual shortcoming but rather a collective disease. Sontag, however, primarily examines social metaphors and does not elaborate how literature, specifically the theater, best reflects the collective response to the AIDS crisis. I want to elaborate how the dramatic form, particularly in the work of Larry Kramer, worked to develop collaborative action in the fight against AIDS.

Theater, as a shared experience between actors and audience, endemically lends itself to collectivity. A prime example of this collectivity can be found in *The AIDS Show* (1984), a collaboratively written and produced play that featured a series of vignettes concerning the experiences of those affected both directly and indirectly by the ongoing AIDS epidemic. But some playwrights wanted more than simply a space to share experiences. Larry Kramer, a New York-based artist and activist, wrote a duo of plays – *The Normal Heart* (1985) and *Just Say No* (1988) – in order to articulate the best strategies to combat the AIDS epidemic both politically and personally. In *The Normal Heart*, Kramer develops the rising tensions between the so-called "good gays" that passively support AIDS sufferers against the more subversive and inflammatory rhetoric of the play's protagonist, Ned Weeks, who advocates for direct action against the local government that has failed to protect the public from the virus. In his next play, *Just Say No*, Kramer sharpened his critique developed in *The Normal Heart* and aimed it toward the federal government, scathingly skewering the Reagan administration's response (or lack thereof) to the vicious spread of HIV across the country. Together, Kramer's plays have produced a productive tension concerning his baldly realistic approach to the illness. While some have argued that his realism produces a myopic portrait of gay America wherein death becomes synonymous with homosexuality, it can also be said that this blunt approach was necessary for educating about the illness, sparking direct action, and creating a new network of queer collectivity. In this tension concerning Kramer's plays we can begin to see how, as queer theorist David Román elaborates in his *Acts of Intervention*, the theater worked as a kind of two-way mirror wherein it not only provided a space for the gay male response to the AIDS epidemic, but this particular space shaped the "ideological formation of AIDS" as well (Román 1998, p. xiii). In doing so, Kramer used the collective experience of the theater to engender a collective activism for AIDS advocacy.

While the immersive atmosphere of the theater offered a sense of queer collectivity in the face of AIDS, it was a collectivity primarily reserved for white, gay men. It's true that they were the majority of those diagnosed with AIDS, but a 1988 Center for Disease Control report illuminates that African Americans were disproportionately affected by the virus as 23.7% of men diagnosed and, incredibly, 51% of women who were diagnosed were Black. According to the CDC, the uneven distribution related to the fact that HIV was primarily passed among the African American community through shared drug use rather than sexual transmission, thus highlighting how the AIDS epidemic intersected with the drug epidemic of the 1980s – the former ignored by the Reagan administration and the latter caused by it. Black Americans, however, did not have the same access to the theater as white, gay men in order to create the kind of collectivity discussed above. Thus, Black writers, excluded from this white, gay collectivity, turned to the more solitary genre of prose. One of the most notable examples was Samuel R. Delany's *The Mad Man* (1994), which follows the story of John Marr, a Black gay philosophy student in NYC in the 1980s as he studies the life of Timothy Hassler, a Korean American philosopher who was stabbed to death outside a gay bar in 1973. Whereas Kramer's plays and white, gay America were advising extreme caution when engaging in sexual behavior, Delany's novel depicts an inverted scenario rife with intense and widespread sexual encounters. Here, Delany represents a promiscuous gay sexuality that survives and even thrives amid the epidemic – but one that, akin to the dearth of commentary on AIDS and Blackness, remained at the margins.

Even more so at the margins were Black women in these conversations about the AIDS epidemic. Like Delany, African American women writers also focused on the individual experience in the prose form. Two widely read examples are Pearl Cleage's novel, *What Looks Like Crazy on an Ordinary Day*, and Jamaica Kincaid's memoir, *My Brother*, both published in 1997. An Oprah Winfrey Book Club selection and *New York Times* Best Seller, Cleage's novel tells the story of Ava Johnson, a young African American woman recently diagnosed with HIV and its effects on her life. Kincaid's memoir, which was nominated for a National Book Award for nonfiction, details her experience as the sister of a man who died due to HIV complications. Taken together, Cleage's novel and Kincaid's memoir represent the kind of isolation felt by Black women affected by the AIDS pandemic. These texts remind us how collectivity can also be curated in such a way to exclude some of the most vulnerable of those among us – in this case, Black women. But while the collectivity of the AIDS epidemic remained restricted primarily to white gay men, the notion of illness as a human-centric problem that defined the 1980s and 1990s took a sharp turn in the 2000s as a new kind of virus emerged: the computer virus.

The Year 2000, or Y2K, computer virus hailed a new, post-anthropocentric attention to illness in both the American social milieu and cultural production. The Y2K virus threatened computer systems worldwide as most program coding allowed only a two-digit space for four-digit years in order to save memory. As a result, when 1999 rolled over to

2000, the coding would turn over from 99 to 00 but the computers would see 00 as "1900," thus resetting systems and potentially disrupting everyday life on a global scale. While on the individual level this meant the potential failure of personal computers and other home electronic systems, for banks and other financial institutions, the Y2K bug could potentially wipe out all electronically stored financial holdings and, just as crucially, debts. If that were to happen, it would cause, in theory, a financial restart with everyone back at zero. Such a restart would be a catastrophic blow to the neoliberal nervous system that relied on this kind of capital liquidity.

With the idea that a computer virus like the Y2K bug could cause such sweeping consequences, much literature and film of the early 2000s situated technology as an evil force that humans must overcome; however, I am more interested in how the 1999 sci-fi noir film *The Matrix* inverts this relationship. In the film, humans are kept in a state of false reality within the digital landscape of the eponymous Matrix, which resembles a 1999 world before a machinic takeover that saw humans enslaved and kept alive solely to serve as batteries for the machines. As the digital world is, for all intents and purposes, the only real world, the relationship between humans and computers is flipped and instead of humans worrying about a computer virus, the computers worry about the virality of humans. As Agent Smith, a highly sophisticated computer program designed to weed out and eliminate human threats to the Matrix, explains to Morpheus, one of the leaders of the human rebellion against the machines:

> Every mammal on this planet instinctively develops a natural equilibrium with the surrounding environment. But you humans do not. You move to an area and you multiply and multiply until every natural resource is consumed and the only way you can survive is to spread to another area. There is another organism on this planet that follows the same pattern. Do you know what it is? A Virus. Human beings are a disease, a cancer of this planet. You are a plague. And we [the machines] are the cure
>
> (Wachowski and Wachowski 1999)

In situating humans as the infectors instead of the infected, *The Matrix* recenters the human in epidemiological terms but in such a way that, strangely, only reaffirms a post-anthropocentric view of viruses. That is to say, by making humans the virus now infecting the computers, *The Matrix* demonstrates how the concept of a virus is subjective, not simply something that infects humans, thus offering a sense of autonomy to viruses not known in the past.

A more recent example of this newly found autonomy for viruses can be glimpsed in Ling Ma's loosely prophetic 2018 novel *Severance*, which recounts a postapocalyptic world brought to a literal standstill as almost the entire global population finds themselves infected with the Shen Fever in an eerily similar anticipation of the 2020 COVID-19 coronavirus pandemic. (Fittingly, I was asked to contribute this entry on illness and disability narratives just a few short weeks before COVID-19 effectively shut down the entire world.) *Severance* relates the story of Candace Chen, the novel's protagonist, and her life leading up to and immediately after the outbreak of the Shen Fever, which quickly creeps across the globe, leaving Candace and a few other survivors struggling to find a sense of normalcy on this pandemic planet.

As a whole, *Severance* operates as an extended Marxian critique of the routinized life under capital. Those who become "fevered" in *Severance* do not die but rather become nonaggressive zomboids that continually repeat the same tasks or activities over and over again with no end. For example, Candace and her postapocalyptic companions enter a house for supplies and find a fevered family continually setting the dinner table, eating nonexistent meals, and removing the plates and cutlery before starting the process all over again ad infinitum. The fevered, then, simply continue their routinized lives *sans* consumption. As the pre-pandemic chapters illustrate, Candace's mechanical life in New York all too closely resembles that of the fevered but with one key difference: consumption. Candace's life before the pandemic was monotonous and unfulfilling – her only joy seemed to come from buying things. In fact, for those lucky enough like Candace to have an immunity to the Shen Fever, the zomboids are almost enviable because, as they neither produce nor consume anything, they seem to have escaped the grinding gears of capitalism. Thus, *Severance* pushes the idea that the mindless consumption in late-stage capitalism – not Shen Fever – is the actual pandemic.

It is no coincidence, then, that the Shen Fever coincides with the Occupy Wall Street protest. Here, Ma parallels the massive unrest following the bailout of big banks in 2011 with the literal unrest of those fevered and stuck in unending routinization. Thus, she positions illness as not simply a product of some indeterminable biological origin but equally caused by our neoliberal economic mode. Ma makes this abundantly clear when she writes:

> In light of the rapid dissemination of Shen Fever, the [Occupy Wall Street] movement was deemed decadent and out of touch. The images of young, healthy protesters chanting, not wearing their masks so their voices could be heard more loudly, only seemed to enrage the public.
>
> Within a week, the protests in Zuccotti Park waned. Several of the protesters had succumbed to Shen Fever. The city bartered with protesters to provide free medical aid to the remaining demonstrators, most of whom did not have health insurance, in exchange for their leaving.
>
> (2018, p. 214)

That the protesters had to essentially give up their struggle in exchange for medical care pointedly critiques the current American healthcare system and its inability to fully serve its populace, and furthers Ma's point that the idea of a pandemic operates both as an experienced global illness and as a construct of our inadequate global health system. Moreover, despite the pockets of collectivities that emerge during this pandemic, like the Occupy protest, they do nothing to stop the impending spread of the virus and, in fact, perhaps accelerate its proliferation given the sort of corporeal closeness needed to protest.

What I find most intriguing about Ma's novel in relation to our current COVID moment is the fact that in *Severance*, the Shen Fever causes unending routines whereas the coronavirus, at least from personal experience in the United States, has completely disrupted economic and social habits; moreover, through this disruption, the coronavirus has equally laid bare the routinization of racism, particularly with regard to police brutality. Just as the Shen Fever raged against the backdrop of the Occupy Wall Street movement, the anti-racist protests against police brutality in the United States – mainly organized around the murders of George Floyd and Breonna Taylor by police – spread as quickly as the coronavirus itself. And just as Ma reveals capitalism and consumption as themselves a kind of virus, our current pandemic moment likewise exposes, at least in the United States, the virality of racism itself and its deep pinions within the vestiges of contemporary capitalism. Illness, then, is not simply a collection of biological symptoms but a symptom itself of intersectional oppression.

DISABILITY

Much like Sontag's *Illness as Metaphor* shifted conversations about illness and representation, the scholarly work of David T. Mitchell and Sharon L. Snyder altered the landscape of disability studies. Their monograph, *Narrative Prosthesis: Disability and the Dependencies of Discourse* (2000), established an archaeology concerning how narratives commonly deployed disability. First, a deviance from the norm, or disability, reveals itself in the narrative. Next, the narrative has to craft an origin story of said deviance to justify its own existence. The deviance then moves from the periphery of the narrative to its center before, finally, the rest of the narrative "rehabilitates" the disability (2000, p. 53). While Snyder and Mitchell's work proved vital to early disability studies, they ultimately ended up treating all narratives the same and do not account for narratives, like Susan Nussbaum's *Good Kings, Bad Kings* (2013), that actually center disability and highlight that the only thing that needs rehabilitation is the institutions that continually treat disability as lesser.

Good Kings, Bad Kings centers disabled voices through its narrative structure. Nussbaum's novel rotates chapter by chapter between the viewpoints of several characters but primarily those who have been institutionalized in the Illinois Learning and Life Skills Center, or ILLC, a state-owned but privately managed nursing facility for youths with physical and intellectual disabilities. One of the more prominent voices is that of Joanne Madsen, a recently hired data entry worker for the ILLC who, after being hit by a city bus, began using a wheelchair. Madsen is the only disabled employee at the facility and notices almost immediately the inadequate accessibility of the institute. While Joanne uses a fairly new and highly sophisticated power wheelchair, many of the children at ILLC are stuck in manual chairs – even if they cannot operate them. As Joanne explains to a nondisabled co-worker, the institute, even if they could afford it, would not give the children quality power chairs because that would give them greater autonomy and "keeping them immobile makes it easier on the staff" (Nussbaum 2013, p. 48). Because this direct relationship between accessibility and autonomy would give the children more power within the institute, they are then, in Joanne's words, "trained to stay helpless [so] they have to stay institutionalized" (p. 102). But the institution can be a double-edged sword. While it tries to infantilize and immobilize the disabled children at ILLC, the institution also brings them together and, ultimately, they develop a collectivity that disrupts the medicalized understanding of disability that gives "you only a tiny sliver of the true understanding about a particular human being" (p. 145). As Joanne explains, "I looked up my own disability once and it scared the crap out of me. I could hardly recognize my own experience" (p. 146). Nussbaum creates a collectivity of disabled experiences that is not simply reduced to disability itself. In doing so, *Good Kings, Bad Kings* centers the disabled experience as multifaceted, unique, and complex as any other nondisabled experience.

While American literature has moved toward a more capacious understanding of physical disabilities, intellectual disabilities still seem to elude literature's capacity to handle their intricacies. Reading and writing are often seen as intellectual endeavors and thus, from an ableist point of view, not suitable for persons with intellectual disabilities. But as rhetorician and disability activist Melanie Yergeau shows in her revolutionary work, *Authoring Autism*, "neuroqueer" individuals such as herself can frame narratives through their neurodivergence. Thus, neuroqueers can define their experience outside of an ableist framework. A prime example of Yergeau's theory can be glimpsed in the character of Abed Nadir in the cult classic NBC sitcom *Community* (2009–2015), which follows the various adventures of a group of community college students. Abed is the show's "neuroqueer," and often frames his experience and the experiences of his fellow classmates through television and filmic tropes and references. His neurodivergence, then, is often the driver behind the narrative scaffolding of the show.

Through Abed, *Community* resituates neurodiversity as a generative force in its storytelling. It allows layers upon layers of metafictional narratives to fold over and unfurl as Abed points out the different television tropes being employed while also making suggestions for more appropriate frameworks as well. For example, in an episode titled "Cooperative Calligraphy," the main cast of *Community* find themselves wrapping a study session to attend a puppy parade when one of the group members, Annie, mentions that her purple pen is missing and she'd like it back before they leave. After it becomes clear that the pen cannot be found, Abed says, "This is starting to feel like a bottle episode." A bottle episode, in television terms, takes place in a single room and utilizes as few nonregular cast members as possible. With Abed's acknowledgment, we do indeed get a bottle episode but one that is so acutely aware of itself as such that it bleeds into the narrative fabric. While searching everyone's bag for the pen, the gang finds a notebook in Abed's possession that charts the menstrual cycles of the women in the group. As the women begin to yell at Abed, he says, "I can explain," before pausing because, as he goes on to say, "Oh, I thought you'd keep yelling over me. I can explain." Again, Abed's own neurodiverse hyperawareness becomes a narrative feature of the show. But then, in a jarringly real moment, Abed admits that he sometimes has trouble reading people and how he noticed that it seemed to happen a lot more often with the women of the group but in particular patterns, so he began to chart them. Abed admits he eventually realized what he was actually measuring, but it seemed to help him interact with the group more positively so he kept doing it. Frustrated by this exposure, Abed goes on to monotonically say, "If I could just share a few words of sarcasm with whoever took this pen. I want to say thank you for doing this to me. Though for a while I thought I'd have to suffer through a puppy parade, but I much prefer being entombed alive in a mausoleum of feelings I can neither understand nor reciprocate [. . .] Okay. Sarcasm over." In announcing his own sarcasm, Abed enacts the very kind of communal care that would help him better navigate the emotions of his friends. At the same time, he tries to explain to his friends the extent to which he struggles with processing his own emotions, let alone those of his friends. This blend of metaframe alongside realism is only made possible in this moment through Abed's neuroqueer perspective.

To close, I want to think more broadly about the literary representations of disability. As disability theorists Ato Quayson and Janet Lyon have both convincingly shown, intellectual disability often remains a bugaboo for fiction writers – terrifying them in life but offering a generative means to storytelling. Moreover, as fellow disability studies scholar Michael Bérubé has argued, disability can affect narrative framework *without* direct representation. At the same time, explains Bérubé, writers have the freedom to create their own fictional disabilities, and he points out several prominent examples of this phenomenon, ranging from *Don Quixote* (1605, 1615) to *The Sound and the Fury* (1929) to the *Harry Potter* series (1997–2007). That said, I am particularly interested in a book full of real and imagined disabilities that openly takes aim at the idea of normalcy in contemporary American culture: Katherine Dunn's *Geek Love* (1989). *Geek Love* tells the story of the Binewski family and their traveling freak show. While the parents, Al and Lil, are "normies," they decide that in order to create attractions for their show, Lil will ingest a variety of drugs, pesticides, and radiation while pregnant in order to birth "attractions" for their show. While several of these "attractions" fail (the remnants of which float in large glass jars and line the entryway to the Binewski traveling show), Lil ends up giving birth to a variety of children. There's Arturo the Aqua Boy (Arty), who has no limbs and spends most of his life in a water tank. Electra (Elly) and Iphigenia (Iphy) are conjoined twins whose four-handedness "revolutionized" the twelve-tone scale on the piano (Dunn 1989, p. 11). Fortunato, otherwise known as Chick given his status as youngest child, has telekinetic powers. Lastly, there is Olympia, or Oly, an albino, hunchbacked dwarf who narrates the tale. In *Geek Love*, the family unit – traditionally something that functions in narrative as a collectivizing agent – actually represents a failure of collectivity that disrupts illusions of normalcy in a cataclysmic way.

The interfamilial relationships in *Geek Love* are complicated and messy, and their collectivity seems based solely on their shared status as "disabled." But reducing the family unity to simply a collection of disabled individuals allows Dunn (and her characters) to center normalcy right in their crosshairs. As Arty explains to Oly:

> We have this advantage, that the norms expect us to be wise. Even a rat's-ass dwarf jester got credit for terrible canniness disguised in his tomfoolery. Freaks are like owls, mythed into blinking, bloodless objectivity. The norms figure our contact with their brand of life is shaky. They see us as cut off from temptation and pettiness. Even our hate is grand by their feeble lights. And the more deformed we are, the higher our supposed sanctity.
>
> (1989, p. 163)

Arty speaks from experience. In his short time alive, he went from circus sideshow to messiah. Arty offers his disfigurement as a means to what he terms PIP, or Peace, Isolation, and Purity. In doing so, his followers slowly but surely have their fingers, toes, hands, feet, arms, and legs amputated until they resemble Arty's limbless stature (of course, paying him inordinate amounts of money along the way). Arty says to Oly later on, "Always remember how much leverage you've got on the norms just in your physical presence" (1989, p. 214). That leverage becomes clear when an investigative reporter infiltrates Arty's cult but immediately dismisses Arty as just some patsy being exploited by a "normie" for profit. Arty uses this dismissal to his advantage and soon the reporter has begun the PIP process of amputating fingers and toes. Here, Arty exploits not only his underestimation as disabled figure but also the collectivity of the cult to create his own little kingdom.

Dunn subverts traditional narratives of disability as evil mark by showing how it is not Arty's disability that makes him an exploitative slavemaster but rather the feckless dismissal of disability itself. In fact, it is the normies themselves who do not understand their own unremarkable nature when compared to the Binewski children. As Oly explains to the investigative reporter, "[E]ach of us is unique. We are masterpieces. Why would I want us to change into assembly-line items? The only way you people can tell each other apart is by your clothes" (1989, p. 403). The irony, of course, is that those "people" have hopped onto the PIP assembly line, losing digits and appendages with machinic efficiency. Through these representations of Arty, Oly, and the rest of the Binewski family against the mass-produced normies, Dunn depicts disability as powerful and as powerless, as shocking and as mundane, as winsome and as malevolent, and everywhere in between and even further. Dunn shows us disability in all its generous and generative glory.

SEE ALSO: Bambara, Toni Cade; The Brain and American Fiction; Cleage, Pearl; Delany, Samuel; Egan, Jennifer; Fictions of Work and Labor; Kincaid, Jamaica; Phillips, Jayne Anne; Queer and LGBT Fiction; Trauma and Fiction

REFERENCES

Bérubé, Michael. (2016). *The Secret Life of Stories: From Don Quixote to Harry Potter, How Understanding Intellectual Disability Transforms the Way We Read*. New York: NYU Press.

Center for Disease Control. (1989). Current trends update: acquired immunodeficiency syndrome – United States, 1981–1988. *Morbidity and Mortality Weekly Report* 38 (14): 229–232, 234–236.

Dunn, Katherine. (1989). *Geek Love*. New York: Knopf.

Ma, Ling. (2018). *Severance*. New York: Farrar, Straus and Giroux.

Mitchell, David T. and Snyder, Sharon L. (2000). *Narrative Prosthesis: Disability and the Dependencies of Discourse*. Ann Arbor: University of Michigan Press.

Nussbaum, Susan. (2013). *Good Kings, Bad Kings*. Chapel Hill: Algonquin Books of Chapel Hill.

Román, David. (1998). *Acts of Intervention: Performance, Gay Culture, and AIDS*. Bloomington: Indiana University Press.

Wachowski, Lana and Wachowski, Lilly. (dirs.) (1999). *The Matrix*. Warner Bros.

Yergeau, Melanie. (2017). *Authoring Autism: On Rhetoric and Neurological Queerness*. Durham, NC: Duke University Press.

FURTHER READING

Kafer, Alison. (2013). *Feminist, Queer, Crip*. Bloomington: Indiana University Press.

McRuer, Robert. (2006). *Crip Theory: Cultural Signs of Queerness and Disability*. New York: NYU Press.

Moore, Leroy F. (2017). *Black Disabled Art History 101*. San Francisco: Xochitl Justice Press.

Schalk, Sami. (2018). *Bodyminds Reimagined: (Dis)ability, Race, and Gender in Black Women's Speculative Fiction*. Durham, NC: Duke University Press.

Siebers, Tobin. (2010). *Disability Aesthetics*. Ann Arbor: University of Michigan Press.

Indigenous Narratives

BRYN SKIBO
University of Geneva, Switzerland

DEBORAH MADSEN
University of Geneva, Switzerland

In the period since Scott Momaday (Kiowa) was awarded the 1969 Pulitzer Prize for *House Made of Dawn* (1968) – frequently referenced as "the Native American Renaissance" – the Indigenous literatures of the United States have flourished, with increasingly diverse novels, short stories, memoirs, and specialized anthologies published every year. It is important to make clear that the development of Native American literature does not follow that of US literary history; rather, in her introduction to the 1996 anthology *Song of the Turtle*, Paula Gunn Allen (Laguna Pueblo) identifies three phases of Indigenous American fiction: the period 1870–1970 focused on loss, expressed in forms that are largely imitative of Anglo-US literature; 1974–1990 continued to emphasize victimization and cultural conflict but with a greater sense of hope, reflected in the use of ceremonial traditions both structurally and thematically; since the 1990s, Allen sees a more comprehensive literary perspective on urban and transnational experience complemented by the Indigenization of "alien" Anglo-US cultural elements (Allen 1996). This latter trend is crystallized in Gerald Vizenor's (White Earth Anishinaabe) concept of "survivance," which signifies the continuance of Indigenous cultural practices, epistemologies, and ontologies – value systems and processes of thought – as the legacy of future tribal generations (2008, p. 1). We focus on this quality of "Indigeneity" via narrative strategies by which fictive form and content are inextricably identified with the project of survivance. While these writings are overwhelmingly written in English and make use of Anglo-US genres, both language and form are appropriated for Indigenous purposes within a powerful anticolonial project.

Arnold Krupat and Michael Elliott observe, in their introduction to "American Indian Fiction and Anti-Colonial Resistance," that "to resist colonial limitations on their *sovereign rights* – is the foremost concern of Native nations today" (Cheyfitz 2006, p. 127, original emphasis). Contemporary Indigenous fictions engage both sides of this settler-colonial equation: the systematic US assault on sovereign communities and traditional lifeways, through physical as well as legal violence, and also the power, endurance, and value of Indigenous cultures and nations. Historically, the pace of Native dispossession increased from the formation of the United States at the end of the eighteenth century through to the nadir of the early twentieth, reflected in historic acts of US federal legislation.

Among those legal maneuvers that most decisively impact contemporary Native American fiction is the Indian Removal Act of 1830, which authorized the forced removal, primarily of the southeastern Muscogee (Creek), Seminole, Chickasaw, Choctaw, and Cherokee nations, west of the Mississippi to "Indian Territory." Later forced relocations included the Navajo Long Walk of the 1860s and the Yavapai-Apache Forced March of 1875. Novelistic (re)interpretations of these events take a variety of narrative forms, often reaching resolution through tribal-specific ontologies, such as the connection between life and death and an expansive understanding of community. The ghost-child narrator of Tim Tingle's (Choctaw Nation) young adult novel *How I Became a Ghost: A Choctaw Trail of Tears Story* (2013), for example, remains an invisible spectral presence to the US soldiers who do not share his Choctaw experience of a fluid boundary between life and death. In *Pushing the Bear: A Novel of the Trail of Tears* (1996), Diane Glancy (Cherokee) presents the history and repercussions of tribal removal through multiple narrators – Cherokee and non-Native – as well as historical documents, emphasizing community narration over a single, authoritative perspective. Blake Hausman (Cherokee Nation), in contrast, uses science fiction to reimagine the Cherokee removal as a virtual-reality tourist attraction in *Riding the Trail of Tears* (2011); traditional Cherokee stories of creation and migration alongside historical and anthropological facts facilitate the journey to Indian Territory but time loops and other-than-human figures derail the predetermined game narrative, creating an alternative version of Removal. Similarly, in *The Way of Thorn and Thunder: The Kynship Chronicles* (2011), Daniel Heath Justice (Cherokee Nation) entwines Cherokee worldviews and other-than-human figures with the tropes of high fantasy to create a vibrant world in which the Removal of the forest-dwelling Kyn by the Sons of Man ends with a renewed recognition of the eternal connections between the Kyn, the land, and the spirit beings who have inhabited it long before the Men arrived.

While the Indian Removal Act authorized the US federal government to evict sovereign nations from their traditional territories, the General Allotment Act or Dawes Act (1887) allowed tribal communities to stay in place but divided the land into small allotments, to be dispersed among registered members. Land that was not distributed in this way was sold on the open market. This resulted in massive land loss and the fragmentation of communally owned tribal lands into noncontiguous parcels held by Native and non-Native landholders. Anishinaabe writers like Gerald Vizenor (White Earth Band) and Louise Erdrich (Turtle Mountain Band) address not only this destruction of an Indigenous land base but also, in the case of the Anishinaabeg, the stripping of natural resources from allotted lands. Vizenor's novel *Darkness in Saint*

Louis Bearheart (1978; reissued as *Bearheart: The Heirship Chronicles* in 1990), a postapocalyptic journey through an environmentally devastated United States, opens with the eviction of the protagonist from his woodland home or "sovereign cedar nation" (1990, p. 8) by a federal government that is desperate for wood fuel in a world that has quite literally run out of gas. The stripping of timber from Anishinaabe reservations is a recurring motif in Erdrich's North Dakota series. In *Tracks* (1998) and its sequel, *Four Souls* (2004), Fleur Pillager loses her family's ancestral land through allotment and predatory taxation but exacts revenge on the timber baron who builds his mansion with her trees. In these narratives, trees are more than commodities and appropriated property, they are agential and kin.

Wide-spread dislocation of Indigenous nations also resulted from the confluence of the Indian Reorganization Act (1934) and House Concurrent Resolution 108 (1953), which authorized the "termination" of the trustee relation between the US federal government and Indigenous nations. Following the Indian Relocation Act of 1956, these legislative moves encouraged the consolidation of diasporic urban Native communities. Louise Erdrich's novel *The Night Watchman* (2020) recounts the legal battle waged by tribal chairman Thomas Wazhashk and other members of the Turtle Mountain reservation to prevent the termination and relocation of the community to "areas of greater economic opportunity," such as Minneapolis (2020, p. 90). Throughout the novel, the exploitation of Native men and, especially, women in Fargo is juxtaposed with the healing that occurs on the reservation. Erdrich's tendency to bring her characters home from the cities reflects William Bevis's (1987) influential identification in Native American Renaissance novels of a "homing" plot: an alienating departure from the reservation to the city and a return to the rediscovery of Indigenous identity in land and community.

As relocation and termination efforts slowed in the later decades of the twentieth century (only to resume in 2020), Indigenous literatures saw a shift in theme and setting. Texts like *The Jailing of Cecelia Capture* (1985) by Janet Campbell Hale (Coeur d'Alene/Kootenai/Cree), *Grand Avenue* (1994) and *Watermelon Nights* (1999) by Greg Sarris (Federated Indians of Graton Rancheria), *The Toughest Indian in the World* (2000) by Sherman Alexie (Spokane/Coeur d'Alene), *From the Hilltop* (2010) by Toni Jensen (Métis), *Crazy Horse's Girlfriend* (2014) by Erika Wurth (Apache/Chickasaw/Cherokee), and *There, There* (2018) by Tommy Orange (Cheyenne and Arapaho Nations of Oklahoma) speak eloquently of the difficulties of urban Indigeneity, where characters are often separated from their reservation communities and struggle to find a sustainable balance between Anglo and Indigenous societies. Within the multilayered stories of Theodore Van Alst's (Lakota) memoir/novel *Sacred Smokes* (2018), the narrator weaves references to classic literature and popular culture together with stories of his family's forced relocation from Cherokee territory and the theft of the family's genealogy from their former home. *Sacred Smokes* does not dwell on this "lost history" of theft (2018, p. 59), offering instead a vibrant, cosmopolitan biography that stresses the enduring necessity of Indigenous *and* Anglo stories.

Resistance to the settler-colonial violence inherent in the theft of land and the "elimination of the [dispossessed] Native," to use Patrick Wolfe's (2006) influential phrase, takes multiple thematic forms. James H. Cox lists some of these responses in the specific context of detective fiction: "Native writing, including fiction, has always been concerned with colonial and settler-colonial violence: homicide and mass murder; sexual assault; the theft of land, cultural property, and human remains;

the violation of treaties" (2017, p. 250). Due to the entanglement of federal and Indigenous legal systems, these crimes are often left unresolved for years or generations. One of the striking characteristics of Indigenous crime narratives is the representation of the police – including tribal police forces – as politically compromised and unreliable. Investigator-protagonists are often civilians like Frances Washburn's (Pine Ridge Lakota/Anishinaabe) musician-detective Sissy Roberts in *The Red Bird All Indian Traveling Band* (2014) and Louis Owens's (Choctaw/Cherokee) Cole McCurtain, an investigating college professor, in *Bone Game* (1994). Victoria Nalani Kneubuhl (Samoan Hawaiian), in *Murder Casts a Shadow* (2008), creates a female Native Hawaiian investigative journalist, Mina Beckwith, to solve the murder of a museum curator, which leads to an investigation of the potential murder of the last king of Hawaiʻi. A similar historical repetition characterizes the intergenerational structure of LeAnne Howe's (Choctaw Nation) *Shell Shaker* (2001) in which family members of the accused investigate a 1991 murder that repeats the 1747 killing of the Choctaw warrior-chief Red Shoes. Amateur sleuths who prevail in the absence of federal jurisdiction also appear in Washburn's novel *Elsie's Business* (2006) and in Sara Sue Hoklotubbe's (Cherokee) Sadie Walela series.

Indigenous crime fiction avoids characterizing US government agents, like police detectives, as agents of justice for the reason that the settler government uses its legislative tools and systems of law enforcement to perpetuate the United States as a settler-colonial nation. The most intimate form taken by this systemic violence corresponds to Michel Foucault's concept of biopolitics: the exercise of power through surveillance and control of the body. Governmental intervention in the intimate lives of Indigenous people especially affects women (through reproductive control and tolerance of sexual violence, for example), children (who are more likely than non-Indigenous children to be taken from their families and placed in potentially abusive foster care), and two-spirit or gender-queer people (who have historically faced the violence of settler homophobia and heteronormativity). The extension of settler state control across Native boundaries is made especially clear in Erdrich's *Future Home of the Living God* (2017) where the fictive events reference the history of biopolitical abuses of Native bodies by the settler-colonial state: the legalized containment of entire populations on reservations, the forced sterilization of Native women (reimagined in *Future Home* as the forced impregnation of viable mothers), and the placement of Native children in foster care and adoptive families.

Sexual abuse of women and children is a common theme in contemporary Native literature, especially as it relates to the imposition of the settler-colonial judicial system. According to their authors, the crisis of murdered and missing Indigenous women motivated Marcie Rendon's (White Earth Anishinaabe) *Girl Gone Missing* (2019) and Louise Erdrich's *The Round House* (2012). Erdrich uses the perspective of a tribal judge's son, who tracks down the perpetrator of his mother's near-fatal rape, to refer to federal case law such as *Oliphant v. Suquamish Indian Tribe*, 435 U.S. 191 (1978), which prevents tribal prosecution of non-Native defendants. In the absence of tribal legal jurisdiction, non-Indigenous perpetrators can act with impunity, and crimes like rape become an "individualized manifestation of colonialism" (Deer 2009, p. 161). The abuse of children in residential schools and by foster families indicates the inherent violence of US federal Indian policy. Vickie L. Sears's (Cherokee) story "Grace," which appeared in Paula Gunn Allen's 1989 anthology *Spider Woman's Granddaughters*, powerfully criticizes the sexual abuse of children taken by US social services and the trauma inherent in the colonialist foster care system through the first-person narration of nine-year-old Jodi, which betrays the normalization of racialized abuse in a fostering system that enforces images of "Indians" as alcoholic, uncivilized and, if female, innately promiscuous. In this story, healing is possible through the restoration of Indigenous family and community. A similar story focused on domestic child sexual abuse is offered in Betty Louise Bell's (Cherokee) *Faces in the Moon* (1994): the remembering protagonist, Lucie, reconnects with her Indigenous past and the land through the stories told by her Cherokee great-aunt who fosters her as a child on their Oklahoma farm. The sisters at the center of Linda LeGarde Grover's (Bois Forte Anishinaabe) novel *In The Night of Memory* (2019) are given up to the state fostering system by their mother before she disappears, ushering in childhoods spent in a sequence of placements until the girls return to the (fictive) Mozhay Point Indian Reservation.

From the beginnings of colonization, settler biopolitics has worked through the violent control of Indigenous sexuality. In contemporary fiction, queer erotic relationships are figured as embodied decolonial resistance to the heteronormativity violently imposed by the Christian European (predominantly Spanish and English) patriarchal settler-colonial organization of intimate, family, and communal relations. As Lisa Tatonetti claims, a "vision of the erotic as tied to land, nationhood, and political and sexual sovereignty is . . . key [to] the erotic imaginaries in . . . Indigenous literatures and theories" (2014, p. xx). In *The Woman Who Owned the Shadows* (1983) by Paula Gunn Allen and *Drowning in Fire* (2001) by Craig Womack (Oklahoma Creek-Cherokee), both authors weave histories of communal and cultural disruption due to Christian or heteropatriarchal oppression with the contemporary protagonists' journeys to self-realization and self-acceptance through same-sex love. Using Creation stories and historical events specific to their tribal affiliations, Allen and Womack emphasize that same-sex love, whether erotic or not, has been accepted among the Laguna Pueblo and the Muscogee (Creek) for generations.

The suppression of Indigenous gender identities and sexual practices was a fundamental form of forced assimilation. One of the more traumatic strategies was the forcible taking of children from their communities to be placed in federal boarding schools located far from "Indian Country." Both sides of this devastating experience are represented in contemporary Indigenous fiction: the profound grief of parents, families, and communities as well as the intergenerational trauma suffered by the children who were subjected to compulsory assimilative education. The opening, eponymous story in Linda LeGarde Grover's *The Dance Boots* (2010) directly addresses the impact of residential boarding schools on the fictional reservation: the legacies of colonialist racial and gender categorizations, but also the intimate relations formed by children in the school environment and sustained into adulthood, recur throughout LeGarde Grover's interlinked stories. In Leslie Marmon Silko's (Laguna Pueblo) polyvocal, mixed-media memoir *Storyteller* (1981), Silko's great-grandmother, Grandma A'mooh, and her Great-Aunt Susie both attended Carlisle Indian Industrial School, and her Grandpa Hank, the Sherman Indian School in Riverside, California. While Aunt Susie is described as using her assimilative education in the interests of Pueblo survivance, in the story "Lullaby" the catalogue of losses suffered by Ayah is dominated by the loss of her children: Jimmie, killed in a US war, and Danny and Ella who, after they are forcibly taken by government doctors, lose their tribal language and become lost to her. The damage inflicted by Indian boarding schools features throughout Silko's novels: in *Ceremony* (1977), Tayo's learned disdain for traditional lifeways is in part inherited from his assimilated mother who was taught in a Christian boarding school; in *Almanac of the Dead* (1991), Sterling is able to explain to himself that he was set up for exile from Laguna Pueblo as a mistrusted "outsider" by his years spent in residential school; and in *Gardens in the Dunes* (1999), the plot is set in motion when Indigo is captured by US soldiers and sent to boarding school before she is adopted by wealthy Americans. Fictional representations of coerced, assimilative education are frequently bleak, focused on abuse and trauma, but the children's creation of personal relationships and inter-tribal communities nuances this otherwise ugly history.

The erasure of Indigenous presence from the continent now known as the United States takes a brutally literal form in the desecration and looting of Indigenous burial sites that have been documented in accounts of colonization since *Mourt's Relation* (1620/21). The removal of Native bones from the land and the storage of them in museums constitutes a violent strategy of Indigenous invisibility enacted by the settler state. Published two years before the passage of the Native American Graves Protection and Repatriation Act (NAGPRA 1990), which makes limited provision for the return of human remains and funerary objects, Anna Lee Walters's (Pawnee/ Otoe-Missouria) novel *Ghost Singer* (1988) is a horror story in which the commodified human remains stored in the Smithsonian Museum of Natural History exact revenge on the archaeologists and anthropologists whose rationalist worldview cannot comprehend the spiritual ontology that inheres in these captive bones, scalps, and corpses. The theft of cultural property and human remains appears in the backstory of many Indigenous fictions: the devastation of the Laguna community in *Almanac of the Dead* is traced to the historic theft, and later discovery in a museum, of the figures of the "Ancient Ones" that are kin to the community. Vizenor returns to this theme in his various treatments of Ishi – the Yaqui man who lived as an exhibit in the Hearst Museum of Anthropology at the University of California, Berkeley – and in *Chancers* (2000), a macabre campus novel in which a group known as the "Solar Dancers" sacrifice college administrators to exchange their bones for the Native human remains held in the university's anthropological museum. The spiritual consequences of failing to respect the bones of the dead are also explored in Louis Owens's *The Sharpest Sight* (1992) and *Nightland* (1996). At the very center of the multiply embedded stories of Gordon Henry, Jr.'s (White Earth Anishinaabe) novel *The Light People* (1994) an ironically humorous court scene stages a debate between an Anishinaabe family and community members, and an archeologist who has "discovered" Moses Four Bear's amputated leg and claims the ceremonially dressed limb as an ancient Native artifact.

The retelling and reimagining of traditional and culturally significant stories, as well as the fictionalization of historical events and the creation of alternative histories, is a powerful counter to the historical "Vanishing American" trope promoted by settler culture. Tribal-specific stories are revisited in texts such as Joseph Bruchac's *The Faithful Hunter: Abenaki Stories* (1988), Edward Benton-Banai's *The Mishomis Book: The Voice of the Ojibway* (1988), Velma Wallis's (Gwich'in Athabascan) *Two Old Women: An Alaska Legend of Betrayal, Courage, and Survival* (1993), and Percy Bullchild's *The Sun Came Down: The History of the World as My Blackfeet Elders Told It* (1999). Vizenor famously uses Anishinaabe trickster stories to reimagine canonical historical events. In *The Heirs of Columbus* (1991), he transforms

Columbus into a "crossblood" trickster of Mayan descent who is not "discovering" the Americas but is returning to his true homeland. Treating history as story and retelling it from an alternate perspective such as this weakens the monolithic historical narrative proposed by the United States. The myth of Manifest Destiny and the pressure of colonial incursion underpins James Welch's (Blackfeet/Gros Ventre) reimagining of the Marias Massacre of 1870 in *Fool's Crow* (1986); and Maurice Kenny (Mohawk), in his short story "Fear and Recourse," subtitled "A Documentary Fiction" – published in *Tortured Skins and Other Short Fictions* (2000) – juxtaposes the fictionalized perspective of Black Kettle with italicized excerpts taken from documents written by Generals Sherman and Custer to reimagine the 1868 cavalry attack on southern Cheyenne at Washita, Oklahoma. In his young adult novel *Flight* (2007), Sherman Alexie uses time travel to move his adolescent protagonist "Zits" through the major traumatic episodes of Native American history and forward into the events of 9/11. Settler predation in the twentieth century is also explored, for example, in Linda Hogan's (Chickasaw) *Mean Spirit* (1991) and Charles H. Red Corn's (Osage) *A Pipe for February* (2002), both of which treat the historic "Osage murders" during the 1920s Oklahoma oil boom. Resentment of the sudden extreme oil wealth of the Osage, the corruption of bureaucrats and federally appointed "guardians," and the murderous actions of greedy, predatory outsiders inform these narratives which explore the impacts of the vast and sudden profits from oil leases on traditional Osage practices and the violence that is equally inflicted on people and the environment.

In *Other Destinies* (1992), Louis Owens references "the alien nonanthropocentric [sic] and ecologically oriented world-view of the Indian" (1992, p. 8). A complex interplay of diegetic ontologies performs precisely this Indigenous worldview in the story that lends its title to Simon Ortiz's (Acoma Pueblo) collection *Men on the Moon: Collected Short Stories* (1999). Three levels of reality in the storyworld are linked by the image of the "makhina"/machine that pollutes and destroys the environment, while gesturing to a parallel between US colonialism and space as "the final frontier." Fausto cannot comprehend how NASA can seek knowledge in a place that is denied spirit and life: a cognitive and ontological dissonance that is performed by the narrative's manipulation of point of view. Many Indigenous fictions use narrative strategies that articulate the land as a spiritual presence. Settler violence against the land is thus a spiritual assault on Indigenous understandings of community. Linda Hogan's novel *Solar Storms* (1995) links ecological violence, in the form of a proposed hydroelectric dam that will drown the land, with the violence experienced by the young protagonist who is scarred physically and spiritually by the foster care system. The environmental damage caused by mining and logging informs Louis Owens's *Wolfsong* (1995); in Silko's *Almanac of the Dead*, the controlling image of the sacred stone snake emerging from the abandoned heaps of radioactive tailings captures the multifaceted assault on the bodies and spirits of the Earth, humans, and other-than-human beings. Daniel Heath Justice writes in *Why Indigenous Literatures Matter* (2018) that Indigenous ontologies of community expand far beyond anthropocentric limitations and affect literary representations of what are often considered "less than human" or "inert" (2018, p. 37). Connection between resource exploitation and human violence in Indigenous fiction is, thus, far from a simple metaphor or externalization of the bounded (human) individual but represents damage to groups of *persons*, with whom meaningful relations can and should be maintained.

Agential objects function in contemporary Indigenous narratives as elements of a sacred and purposeful fictional environment and, in novels like Louise Erdrich's *The Painted Drum* (2005), and in her story "The Stone" (2019), they engineer the narrative plot. The eponymous drum, like the stone, communicates intentionally and consequentially, though not in human terms; material objects implicitly manipulate characters and situations to guide the plot. In Heath Justice's *The Way of Thorn and Thunder*, "objects" such as apple-headed dolls, amber-topped staffs, storytelling leaves, and the Evertree (a physical manifestation of the maternal, living-giving goddess), explicitly and implicitly drive the plot as they speak with and act upon the characters. Set against the iron-welding Men who characterize the natural world as an inanimate commodity, the Kyn wield the power of the natural world, or the *wyr*, as much as the *wyr* is portrayed as using them for its own self-preservation; this inherent relationality rejects the nature/technology divide and creates the circular narrative resolution in the final battle scene. Vizenor's *Dead Voices* (1992) attributes, through free indirect style, sensory perception to a television screen that is able to look at the humanized characters who are looking at it; the chapter devoted to advice about how to discipline a misbehaving toaster offers an explicit characterization of household appliances as sentient. A more sinister attribution of sentience to machine beings motivates Daniel H. Wilson's (Cherokee) series of techno-thrillers, most notably *Robopocalypse* (2011) and the sequel *Robogenesis* (2014), in which a powerful rogue artificial intelligence sets out to exterminate humanity, creating in the process an ironic variant on Indigenous inter-relationality in the form of a virus that infects all networked devices that then attack or sabotage humans. This "new War" is fought by a group of Osage warriors together with their sentient "freeborn" robot allies.

Sentient animal characters draw on traditional stories or treat more generally the Indigenous value of extended kinship. The complexities surrounding the "mercy killing" of a Florida panther, a sacred ancestor of the Taiga community, motivates an exploration of negative anthropocentric impacts on the Earth and all its beings in Linda Hogan's novel *Power* (1998). Reservation mongrels with the power to heal populate Vizenor's fiction, notably in *Chair of Tears* (2012) where Vizenor's critique of Judeo-Christian anthropocentrism is highlighted by the "irony mongrels" with names like Derrida, Lévi-Strauss, and Nixon who attend academic seminars, barking in response to the absence of irony and humor. The traditional story of the Deer Woman and the Dakota epistemology of transformational shape-shifting are used by Frances Washburn in *Elsie's Business* (2006): the white youths who have brutally assaulted Elsie are, while leaving the scene of their crimes, killed in a collision with a deer, and the narrative suggests that Elsie herself may be a Deer Woman who transformed into deer form to avenge herself.

A dominant characteristic of Indigenous fiction is the multiple kinds of "reality" that can constitute fictive worlds: shape-shifting as well as dreams, spirits, the spectral dead, traumatic pathologies, and monsters like vampires, windigoos, and skinwalkers are all as real as the quotidian world of conventional realism. The story that opens Anita Endrezze's (Yaqui) *Butterfly Moon* (2012), "On This Earth," introduces a sentient planet, where rocks and forests and the continent itself hold memories and tell stories. Metamorphoses from human to insect, animal to stone, being to spirit, reflect the simultaneous and complementary existence of different kinds of reality. The embeddedness of narrative realities within Indigenous ontologies and value systems – especially extended kinship and inter-relationality – is communicated through innovative forms of stylistic mixing that perform Indigenous epistemologies. In Endrezze's story "The Vampire and the Moth Woman," the narration alternates between the two eponymous shape-changing characters whose commonalities are set in conflict with Diana's husband, Tom, who refuses ontological possibilities beyond his narrow vision of middle-class "normality." In contrast, A.A. Carr's (Navajo/ Laguna Pueblo) *Eye Killers* (1995) uses the literary conventions of the vampire novel to juxtapose European vampirism, which closely approaches the predations of settler colonialism, with the Indigenous interpretation of the vampire Falke as a skinwalker who can be defeated only through the ceremonial healing practices of Pueblo and Navajo elders. The "windigoo" horror of Stephen Graham Jones's (Blackfeet Nation) novella *Mapping the Interior* (2017) is similarly grounded in Blackfeet ontologies. By combining generic conventions – coming-of-age stories, murder mysteries, and ghost stories – with a claustrophobic first-person narration, twists in story time, and blurred perspectives, Jones's apparent ghost story reveals generational layers of selfishness distorted as sacrifice so that subsequently, life becomes a means to feed death.

Contemporary Indigenous fiction is characterized by an extraordinary degree of literary innovation, putting to use formal strategies – such as discontinuous narrative, multiple-voice narrations, nonlinear chronological structures and plots, embedded narratives, and multigeneric forms – in the interests of sustaining specifically Indigenous value systems, and ways of thinking, knowing, and being in the world. Perhaps the best-known Indigenous transgeneric text, Silko's *Storyteller*, suggests that it is written in the oral tradition although the text brings together original short stories with poems, retellings of traditional Pueblo myths, fragments of letters, autobiography, and family history, with Silko's photography punctuating the written text. Many narratives use multiple narrators to construct innovative points of view or discontinuous narratives to juxtapose episodes and render meaning implicit. In texts like Debra Magpie Earling's (Bitterroot Salish) novel *Perma Red* (2002), this technique uses intergenerational stories of family and community to emphasize enduring practices of survivance. In her debut novel, *The Grass Dancer* (1994), Susan Power (Yanktonai Dakota) uses the novel's setting on a North Dakota reservation as a center point to ground the complex, discontinuous narrative which switches perspective in every chapter, spanning multiple generations and moving fluidly backward and forward through story time to connect the opening trauma to the dangerous medicine of the warrior deer woman, Čuwignaka Duta (Red Dress), and her descendent, Anna Thunder. Power reinterprets the Lakota/Dakota/Nakota figure of the Deer Woman – a powerful, shape-shifter whose eroticism lures people away from their duties to the community – as both a warrior fighting for the Dakota and a contemporary troublemaker guiding younger members of the community towards mature adulthood. When Red Dress appears in a culminating scene of healing and regrowth, she is described as speaking Dakota and English simultaneously – "in two languages, two distinct voices" (1994, p. 298). Weaving the past and present, physical and spectral, human, nonhuman, and environmental, mythical and realistic, Susan Power produces a lyrical example of the unique, innovative methods characteristic of contemporary Indigenous fiction.

SEE ALSO: Ecocriticism and Environmental Fiction; Erdrich, Louise; Hogan, Linda; Jones, Stephen Graham; Momaday, N. Scott; Power, Susan; Silko, Leslie Marmon; Vizenor, Gerald; Washburn, Frances; Welch, James

REFERENCES

Allen, Paula Gunn. (ed.) (1996). *Song of the Turtle: American Indian literature, 1974–1994.* New York: Ballantine Books.

Bevis, William. (1987). Native American novels: homing in. In: *Recovering the Word: Essays on Native American Literature* (ed. Brian Swann and Arnold Krupat), 580–620. Oakland: University of California Press.

Cheyfitz, Eric. (ed.) (2006). *The Columbia Guide to American Indian Literatures of the United States since 1945.* New York: Columbia University Press.

Cox, James H. (2017). Native American detective fiction and settler colonialism. In: *A History of American Crime Fiction* (ed. Chris Raczkowski), 250–262. Cambridge: Cambridge University Press.

Deer, Sarah. (2009). Decolonizing rape law: a native feminist synthesis of safety and sovereignty. *Wíčazo Ša Review* 24 (2): 149–167.

Erdrich, Louise. (2019). The stone. *The New Yorker* (September 9, 2019). https://www.newyorker.com/magazine/2019/09/09/the-stone (accessed July 2020).

Erdrich, Louise. (2020). *The Night Watchman.* New York: HarperCollins.

Heath Justice, Daniel. (2018). *Why Indigenous Literatures Matter.* Waterloo, ON: Wilfred Laurier University Press.

Owens, Louis. (1992). *Other Destinies: Understanding the American Indian Novel.* Norman: University of Oklahoma Press.

Power, Susan. (1994). *The Grass Dancer.* New York: Putnam.

Tatonetti, Lisa. (2014). *The Queerness of Native American Literature.* Minneapolis: University of Minnesota Press.

Vizenor, Gerald. (1990). *Bearheart: The Heirship Chronicles.* Minneapolis: University of Minnesota Press; first published as *Darkness in Saint Louis Bearheart,* Saint Paul: Truck Press, 1978.

Vizenor, Gerald. (2008). Aesthetics of survivance. In: *Survivance: Narratives of Native Presence* (ed. Gerald Vizenor), 1–23. Lincoln: University of Nebraska Press.

Wolfe, Patrick. (2006). Settler colonialism and the Elimination of the Native. *Journal of Genocide Research* 8 (4): 387–409.

FURTHER READING

Furlan, Laura. (2017). *Indigenous Cities: Urban Indian Fiction and the Histories of Relocation.* Lincoln: University of Nebraska Press.

McClinton-Temple, Jennifer and Velie, Alan. (2007). *Encyclopedia of American Indian Literature.* New York: Facts On File.

Ruppert, James. (2005). Fiction 1968 to the present. In: *Cambridge Companion to Native American Literature* (ed. Joy Porter and Kenneth M. Roemer), 173–188. Cambridge: Cambridge University Press.

Treuer, David. (2006). *Native American Fiction: A User's Manual.* Minneapolis: Graywolf.

Intermedial Fiction

DANIEL PUNDAY
Mississippi State University, USA

This chapter understands intermedial fiction broadly as writing that is aware of print's relationship to other media. Defined in this way, intermedial fiction involves stories that invoke other media literally by including non-print elements, or by reference to media in its themes or plot.

Of course, since its beginnings the novel has explored design elements other than linear print. The complex and varying role of illustration is an obvious case of this, but the epistolary tradition that mimics the back-and-forth of private correspondence is an early example of the printed book's relation to an adjacent medium. And although we tend to think of play with type and page as a modern strategy, "visual exuberance" of page design is a feature of the eighteenth-century novel.[1] In the twentieth century, however, print often is understood to be in a battle with new entertainment media like film, television, and radio drama. As a result, the presence of other media – either direct or implied – becomes a much more pressing issue to be addressed within the overall aesthetics and themes of individual novels.

THE RANGE OF INTERMEDIAL FICTION

To explore this definition of intermedial fiction, and to outline the spectrum of works that fall into this category, let's start with what seems to me an unambiguous example: Mark Danielewski's *House of Leaves* (2000). Danielewski evokes the tradition of the novel as a found document. The core narrative is an account of the production and dissemination of a film *The Navidson Record*, which documents a mysterious house that is larger on the inside than on the outside. This story is written by Zampanò, an eccentric and blind recluse, and the manuscript is discovered by Johnny Truant, who then edits it and adds his own footnotes. As this summary suggests, the novel draws attention to its own print status, and its ability to contextualize other media like film.

Obviously the title alludes to the continuities between the house and the printed book. Indeed, both Truant and Zampanò seem to lose themselves in the editing of the book, just as the filmmaker Will Navidson is lost in the house; all three struggle to maintain a sense of reality when navigating these spaces. Danielewski emphasizes the physical book as a "house of leaves" by manipulating type and text placement to draw attention to the spatial contours of the work. *House of Leaves* clearly belongs to a tradition of spatially designed literary writing with its roots in concrete poetry. We can trace this work back to Guillaume Apollinaire's *Calligrammes* (1918) or Stéphane Mallarmé's *Un coup de dés* (1897); this tradition is carried through postmodernist experimental fiction, like Raymond Federman's *Double or Nothing* (1971) or Christine Brooke-Rose's *Thru* (1975). A crucial element of Danielewski's novel is that it explicitly evokes another medium as a foil against which to understand print. Indeed, a central early scene involves creating a film called "The Five and a Half Minute Hallway" – in reference to the time of exploration that the film documents. This is a particularly good example of how *House of Leaves* brings print and film into tension with each other, since it frames something fundamentally spatial (the hallway) in temporal terms grounded in the film recording. In turn, *House of Leaves* is both a physical, spatial object and a temporal experience of narrative immersion.

This tension between the book and film is what makes *House of Leaves* a thoroughly intermedial novel. Not every intermedial novel depends on typographical manipulation. Paul Auster's *Book of Illusions* (2002), a novel about a mysterious silent film star Hector Mann, focuses on the tension between the films referenced and the prose that provides our access to this medium. At the outset of that novel, David Zimmer, Auster's central character who becomes obsessed with these films, reflects on language: "No matter how beautiful or hypnotic the images [in modern film] sometimes were, they never satisfied me as powerfully as words did" (2002, p. 14). In contrast, the silent film medium "had invented a syntax of the eye, a grammar of pure kinesis" that resolves the tension between word and image that he feels in newer movies: "their muteness, their absence of color, their fitful, speeded-up rhythms. These were obstacles, and they made viewing difficult for us, but they also relieved the images of the burden of representation" (p. 15). Of course, film is only one possible medium with which the intermedial novel works. Jay Cantor's *Krazy Kat* (1987) and Frederic Tuten's *Tintin in the New World* (1993) take characters from early comics and translate them into fictional narratives designed to explore character and theme across media. As Cantor writes at the beginning of *Krazy Kat*, "Over the years Krazy had watched uncomprehendingly the slow shift from vaudeville to motion pictures, to radio, to television. . .and next? computers? video games? How would the next generation tell its stories? She knew she wouldn't be part of those stories. But would she even understand them?" (1987, p. 7). In *The Colorist* (1989), Susan Daitch makes a similar transposition of comics into print narrative by having her protagonists Julie and Laurel, who work as the colorist and inker respectively at Fantômes comics, write their own version of the superhero Electra. Their work on Electra not only critiques the commercial tropes of the superhero genre ("Electra hadn't changed much since the beginning of the series, on the premise that one audience grew up and was replaced by another" [1989, p.15]), but engages with a broader range of media like photography, painting, and, of course, writing.

Other intermedial narratives evoke non-print media by format rather than through plot or character. Kenneth Gangemi's *The Interceptor Pilot* (1980) is written as the description of a film, rather than as a film script:

> The beginning of the film is set at a Naval Air Station somewhere in the western United States. It could be any one of the southwestern or Rocky Mountain States: Arizona, New Mexico, Utah, Nevada, Colorado, Idaho, Wyoming, or Montana. The reason is mainly cinematic. The film will be in color, and the setting might as well be one of great natural beauty. It will be a western landscape of sagebrush and semi-desert plains and striking mountains.
>
> (1980, p. 7)

As this passage shows, we get information about the motivations behind the storytelling decisions but not the backstory on the characters or any kind of narration of their thoughts. What we know about this story, and the way that it describes our experiences as a viewer proactively, is quite striking. The format of the story is nominally filmic, but it is filtered through descriptions rather than a direct experience of the "great natural beauty." It's impossible to read the novel without feeling the tension between how a written and visual medium would tell the same story.

None of my examples thus far have included other media directly into the text. In fact it seems that the novels of the 1970s and 1980s that incorporate images are often less likely to explore the relationship between these media. *Krazy Kat* includes a few original comic strips, but *The Interceptor Pilot* and *The Book of Illusions* have no images. There are many late-twentieth-century novels that make significant use of images, of course. In *Blood and Guts in High School* (1984), Kathy Acker inserts sexual drawings and dream maps that disrupt our aesthetic distance from the story, and our common ways of responding to Acker's protagonist Janey Smith; as Katie Muth writes, the novel's "dialectical suspension between representation and asemic nonsense, between narrative and anti-narrative, makes a compelling case for one of the ways in which postwar American fiction sought to suture politics and aesthetics" (2011, p. 105). Muth shows that Acker's intermediality is less about defining print than in challenging the politics of literary discourse more broadly. In a similar spirit, although with less political engagement – Donald Barthelme works with found engravings in works like "A Nation of Wheels" (1970) and his children's novel *The Slightly Irregular Fire Engine* (1971), but his goals here seem more grounded in a certain random, absurdist spirit than in an investigation of the relationship of print and image. An aesthetically and politically more conventional intermedial novel is William H. Gass's *Willie Masters' Lonesome Wife* (1968), which mixes naked images of the titular character with a meditation on language and reading. It is clear in this novel that Gass sees these images as a way to invoke the theme of the body more generally, and to associate both with the medium through which we experience the world: "No one can imagine – simply – merely; one must imagine within words or paint or metal, communicating genes or multiplying numbers. Imagination is its medium realized. You are your body – you do not choose the feet you walk in – and the poet is his language" (1979, n.p.). Gass's interest in using other media to understand and defend print is typical of intermedial fiction as defined in this chapter.

Genuinely mixed-media stories in print like *Willie Masters* and *Blood and Guts in High School* remain uncommon, however, and exist on a spectrum with aesthetic goals and conventions from literature to visual art. A particularly well-known example of a book that pushes the visual affordances of the printed book quite far is Tom Phillips's *A Humument: A Treated Victorian Novel* (1970–2016). This novel was created by altering a 1892 novel by drawing, painting, and collaging over the text of pages to create visual designs involving a very small number of remaining words. Phillips's book is as much visual art as printed text, although reading and the turning of pages to progress is essential to the experience. We can see Phillips's work at part of, or at least adjacent to, the "artist book" movement, which Johanna Drucker describes as a quintessential twentieth-century art form, in which the book is "created as an original work of art, rather than a reproduction of an preexisting work" (2004, pp. 1–2). Drucker notes that the question of whether each work has to be "unique" is an open one, but it is clear that the aesthetics of *A Humument* are as much about the beauty of the individual page designs and the work as a physical object as they are about telling a story.[2]

The emergence of inexpensive personal computing in the 1980s made the digital text a natural place where print and other media could interact. Early CD-ROM encyclopedias were often explicitly sold as "multimedia" – sound and video clips added to the traditional text and still image of the print volumes. Many artists embraced the possibilities of the digital platform for exploring the relationship between print and other media. Michael Joyce's 1987 diskette-based novel, *afternoon, a story* is almost exclusively limited to text, but soon after the CD-ROM provided the means for a more extensive mixing of other media files. Shelley Jackson's 1995 *Patchwork Girl* uses images for navigation. In 2000, M.D. Coverley's *Califia* made much greater use of other media, including sound and animated transitions between images and texts. Typical of this merging of writing and other media is the ongoing multimodal story *Inanimate Alice*, whose first episode by Kate Pullinger and Chris Joseph was released in 2005. *Inanimate Alice* incorporates reading, voiceover narration, games, and exploration as a kind of young adult electronic storytelling. Another good example of this fusion of writing and other media is the 2015 iOS game *Pry*, which explores memory and post-traumatic stress disorder in a young man who has returned from the Gulf War, told through a blend of video, audio, and text. The game opens with a conventional video prologue, but a significant part of the remainder of the story involves pinching and swiping on the touchscreen to reveal more video, somewhat conventional written narration and reflection, and flashing text intended to convey a sense of confusion, anxiety, and repressed memories. *Inanimate Alice* and *Pry* are especially good examples of a recent fusion of text and other media because they seem so confident in using these various modes of storytelling to convey a unified narrative. Where *House of Leaves* is constantly exploring the tensions and continuities between film and print, these two more recent works are less interested in tensions than in the way that media can work together to engage their audience.

More broadly, there has been grown acceptance that electronic texts can do work associated with literature. Astrid Ensslin makes this point in *Literary Gaming*, where she describes "an ever-growing body of hybrid artifacts that blend verbal and other arts with videogame technologies" (2014, p. 1). In *Digital Modernism: Making It New In New Media*, Jessica Pressman argues that we can see recent electronic literature as fully engaged in the modernist literary goals: "Digital modernism is aligned with strategies of the avant-garde: it challenges traditional expectations about what art is and does. It illuminates and interrogates the cultural infrastructures, technological networks, and critical practices that support and enable these judgments. Digital modernism thus remakes the category of the avant-garde in new media" (2014, p. 10).

HISTORICIZING INTERMEDIAL FICTION

Intermedial fiction should be seen less as a genre of writing and more as a reflection of our changing thinking about print and other media. In 2012 I addressed some of this fiction in *Writing at the Limit: The Novel in the New Media Ecology*. There I drew on models of media ecologies to argue that defining the vocation of the novel depended on exploring the limits of the medium: these works "invoke media like film, music, and comics as 'others' against which the limits and strengths of writing can be understood" (Punday 2012, p. 38). This does indeed help to explain the prevalence of other media in a wide variety of contemporary novels, and it builds on work like John Johnson's *Information Multiplicity: American Fiction in the Age of Media Saturation* (1998) and Kathleen Fitzpatrick's *The Anxiety of Obsolescence: The American Novel in the Age of Television* (2006). All three books see the novel as working to stay relevant in a period of increased media presence.

Today this account of media in the novel seems limited by its assumptions about the central role of anxiety about non-print media. The example of *Pry* makes clear that there are many works today where the fraught need to sort print and other media is simply not the driving force of its composition. More importantly, recent scholarship has offered new ways of thinking about print's relationship to other media. In the introduction to the 2013 *Comparative Textual Media: Transforming the Humanities in the Postprint Era*, Katherine Hayles and Jessica Pressman explain this new approach to print:

> As the era of print is passing, it is possible once again to see print in a comparative context with other textual media, including the scroll, the manuscript codex, the early print codex, the variations of book forms produced by changes from letterpress to offset to digital publishing machines, and born-digital forms such as electronic literature and games.
>
> (2013, p. xii)

Books like Lori Emerson's *Reading Writing Interfaces: From the Digital to the Bookbound* (2014) and Anouk Lang collection *From Codex to Hypertext: Reading at the Turn of the Twenty-first Century* (2012) see reading as an experience grounded in a variety of material forms that does not take the twentieth-century literary novel as its baseline.

But for precisely this reason, intermedial fiction is a useful reference point for analyzing the changing historical categories that we apply to post-1945 fiction. Indeed, scholarship on contemporary literature has been rethinking the historical terms and categories that gained ascendency in the initial scholarship of the 1980s and early 1990s. Brian McHale's *The Cambridge Introduction to Postmodernism* (2015) offers a powerful example of these changes, since his 1987 *Postmodernist Fiction* gave us one of the most influential models for theorizing contemporary fiction's differences from the modernism that came before. In particular, McHale distinguishes between what he calls "The Major Phase" from 1973–1990, the "Interregnum" from 1989–2001, and the current period "After Postmodernism." In the recent collection, *Postmodern/Postwar – And After*, Jason Gladstone and Daniel Worden note a general questioning of the value of the term *postmodernism* (2016, pp. 1–24): "One of the effects of these approaches to post-1945 literature has been to displace postmodernism as an explanatory category in the name of more pragmatic institutional histories, circulation studies, sociological inquiries, and reception models" (p. 6). In the remainder of this chapter, I would like to apply something of this spirit of rethinking periodization to the category of intermedial fiction, and to see it as a reflection of changing attitudes towards literary writing.

Early intermedial fiction during McHale's "Major Phase" reflects a particular understanding of literary writing as the evaluational framework for fiction. For all that writers updating Krazy Kat or mixing narrative and transgressive images were challenging hidebound literary traditions and expanding the scope of contemporary storytelling, they did so in the service to traditional literary goals. I have already noted Gass's desire to associate the body and language, but his emphasis on the traditional aesthetics of print is even more explicitly in his writing on aesthetics. He opens his essay "The Medium of Fiction" in this way: "It seems a country-headed thing to say: that literature is language, that stories and the places and the people in them are merely made of words as chairs are made of smoothed sticks and sometimes cloth or metal tubes" (1989, p. 27).

Given this traditional literary framework, it is easy to see how appeals to other media serve as a convenient foil against which the particular value of the print novel can be defined. A good example of this is Ronald Sukenick's 1986 novel *Blown Away*. The plot concerns the struggle between fortune-teller Boris Ccrab and film director Rod Drackenstein, whose exploitation of young starlet Clover Bottom is representative of Hollywood. Drackenstein is associated with vampires (1986, p. 40), and Sukenick seems eager to associate with a whole system of exploitation:

> He has no aura, Drackenstein, as he opens the door to the bedchamber, he has totally negative vibrations [. . .] [and] sucks everything like a black hole an energy vampire, that's where they get their power, from others from you and me, we turn on them and once we turn them on there's no turning them off, hypnotizing their victims with the illusion of pleasure [. . .].
>
> (1986, pp. 71–72)

In contrast to Drackenstein, Ccrab's ability to see into the future is associated with the power of writing: "Now it will begin. I am the omniscient narrator. But while most tellers tell a tale already set, I tell tales that haven't happened yet. Reading my own mind I, like a crab, think sideways into the future" (1986, p. 9). The novel ends with Drackenstein's visit to Henry Miller, whose exhortations about the novel seem intended to apply to *Blown Away* as well, praising an unfinished manuscript: "I would have told him not to try to finish it. The book was okay the way it was. Most books are too finished. They're claustrophobic" (1986, p. 176). Indeed, the scene is a telling one for providing an implicit aesthetic goal in contrast to the exploitation of that Drackenstein's films embody. Sukenick's Miller is dismissive of traditional literary pieties – "there's no such thing as literature. What most people call literature is just fossilized morality" (p. 176) – but nonetheless ends by supporting the traditional avant-garde aesthetics that Sukenick's print novel is clearly designed to embody:

"Books have the power to devalue and revalue your experience" (p. 176).

Of course, many works of intermedial fiction are less invested in pitting literary writing against other media in purely evaluative terms. Richard Powers's *Three Farmers on Their Way to a Dance* (1985) takes its title from a photograph by August Sander taken on the cusp of World War I, and although Powers reflects on the technological changes in photography and the different way it can represent time and event, he treats both photography and written narrative with equal respect. The photograph draws attention to the challenge of constructing a narrative around the event, and negotiating the issue of contingency and inevitability, and in this there is a productive difference between the two media: "Plainly, I could learn nothing by tracing the photograph back to its material origin alone. I had also to descend into that shifting, ambiguous place of possible meaning, finding why I recognized these farmers without ever having seen them" (1992, p. 212). In contrast to Sukenick's use of film as a foil for writing, both biography and photography have powers worthy of respect in *Three Farmers*. In a parallel but quite different way, Thomas Pynchon makes extensive use of television as a theme and plot device in *Vineland* (1990), but seems eager to emphasize continuities more than differences. Television can become an object of unhealthy obsession; we meet Hector Zuñiga, a DEA agent who has been hospitalized for "tubal abuse" and is known in the scientific literature on the disorder as the Brady Buncher (1990, p. 33). But Pynchon himself makes frequent use of references in his own narration to cartoons, game shows, and other television and film genres. In fact, the novel's closing reconciliation of mother and daughter depends in part on remembering watching *Gilligan's Island* together (p. 368). Where Powers is equally respectful of photography and written narrative, Pynchon appears to treat television and the novel with equal irony.

I would like to argue that the relationship between literary writing and other media went through an important change with the advent of ubiquitous computing and digital publishing. I have already described the way that early hypertext fiction sought to integrate different media, and suggested that the period of the first decade or so of the new millennium represented a period in which electronic media increasingly saw computer-based narrative less as a conflict between separate media, and more as a set of storytelling techniques that can work together. More importantly for my immediate task of historicizing intermedia fiction, however, I would suggest that the increasing presence of computing also altered the way that authors engaged with other media, and with the literary traditions that served as the starting point for their exploration of the media ecologies of the 1980s and 1990s. To understand this, we should recall Friedrich Kittler's 1986 observation about the emerging "metamedium" of digital transmission: "People will be hooked to an information channel that can be used for any medium – for the first time in history, or for its end. Once movies and music, phone calls and text reach households via optical fiber cables, the formerly distinct media of television, radio, telephone, and mail converge" (1999, p. 1). In *Software Takes Command* (2013), Lev Manovich argues that media are increasingly becoming effects that are produced in software: "What happens to the idea of a 'medium' after previously media-specific tools have been simulated and extended in software" (2013, p. 4). Postmodern fiction of the "major phase" grounded in a pre-digital aesthetic tends to see other media as an opportunity to define print's literary aspirations. Even Richard Powers's respectful handling of still photography is more interested in how it helps us understand his goals as a novelist. After we have fully grasped the implications of modern computing, however, it becomes harder to see the contrast between media as central to the meaning of the novel.

Take the example of Mohsin Hamid's 2017 novel *Exit West*, which tells the story of Saeed and Nadia as they escape an unnamed city riven by militant violence, traveling around the world through mysterious portals that fundamentally transform the nature of world migration. Hamid's novel is full of references to other media: Saeed and Nadia listen to records, Saeed's parents met at the cinema where his mother falls in love with his father because he looks like a movie star (2017, pp. 11–12), Saeed carries a picture of his father, and the couple spend time on the Internet accessed through their cell phones. And yet, there is little in the novel that suggests that these other media have much to do with the novel's sense of aesthetic mission or Hamid's authority as a writer. Instead, it is the cell phone's ability to transform the nature of connection and place that is central to the story: Saeed's phone "allowed him to access Nadia's separate existence, at first hesitantly, and then more frequently, at any time of day or night, allowed him to start to enter into her thoughts, as she toweled herself after a shower, as she ate a light dinner alone, as she sat at her desk hard at work, as she reclined on her toilet after emptying her bladder." He became to Nadia, "present without presence, and she did much the same to him" (p. 40). It seems clear that Hamid's story of ubiquitous connection and transportation – "a world full of doors" (p. 155) – undermines our normal ways of thinking about place, identity, and connection. In the novel those connections can manifest themselves through any number of media, from the vinyl album that offers the "so-alive but no longer living voice" of a dead singer (p. 28), to the photo of his parents that Saeed carries with him (p. 102), but the particular details of the medium are less important than the computing infrastructure that make their transmission instantaneous. In comparison to the tension between writing and other media that we see in the 1960s through the early 2000s, this writing/computing hybrid is taken for granted. Zara Dinnen would call this the "digital banal," "the habitual practices of digital media in everyday life, effacing access to the new conditions and agency of that life" (2018, p. 13).

It is in this context that I think we can understand the recent emergence of "bookishness" as an aesthetic quality. As I already noted above, intermedial fiction of the 1970s and 1980s often took for granted a certain traditional literary production as the norm against which other media forms were understood. What we see in this interest in bookishness, however, is something quite different that reflects the transformation of literary writing's relationship with media and computing. Jessica Pressman describes the "aesthetic of bookishness" in novels since 2000: "These novels exploit the power of the print page in ways that draw attention to the book as a multimedia format, one informed by and connected to digital technologies. They define the book as an aesthetic form whose power has been purposefully employed by literature for centuries and will continue to be far into the digital age" (2009, p. 465). Katherine Hayles draws on Pressman's category to argue that this is a response to the "epochal shift from print to digital texts": "a group of contemporary novels engage in strategies that entice readers to become intimate with the novels' bodies through physical manipulations of their printed forms. These manipulations go beyond the automatic turning of pages, as if these books were determined to reawaken passion by introducing novelty into what have become routine physical encounters"

(2013, p. 227). Both Pressman and Hayles are eager to show that these works are not simply based on nostalgia for an earlier, pre-digital time;[3] both prioritize novels like Jonathan Safran Foer's *Tree of Codes* (2010), which explore the relationship between the physical book and the digital media that might produce it.

I would read Pressman's and Hayles's analysis of bookishness against the quite new and particular multimediality of *Exit West*, and argue that both represent a change in the landscape for the intermedial novel. In the novels of the 1970s through the end of the millennium, the print novel could be assumed as the storytelling norm against which appeals to film, comics, or music would be seen as aesthetic inspiration, popular competition, or nostalgic reference. Today, "bookishness" is a specific media configuration that must be defined, explored and defended, and not take to be an inevitable component of writing, or a natural baseline for understanding storytelling. And as *Exit West* shows, the media landscape has changed so that photographs, film, and music are not defined by their reference to the novel, but by their relationship to the global computing systems through which so much information is distributed.

OTHER PERSPECTIVES ON MEDIA AND FICTION

Some recent work on media that de-centers print has already been mentioned above, including Hayles and Pressman's *Comparative Textual Media*, Lang's *From Codex to Hypertext*, and Emerson's *Reading Writing Interfaces*. See also Lisa Gitelman's *Paper Knowledge: Towards a Media History of Documents* (2014). To various degrees, this scholarship working to resituate print can be seen as part of a broader theory of media archaeology. A good starting point on that work is Jussi Parikka's *What is Media Archaeology?* (2012). On the response of book culture to the rise of digital media more broadly, see *The Printed Book in Contemporary American Culture: Medium, Object, Metaphor* (2019), edited by Heike Schaefer and Alexander Starre.

There has been important work on intermedial fiction in the framework of multimodal textuality that has its origins in computer-based writing. Alison Gibbons has written widely on a variety of intermedial works like *House of Leaves*, *S.*, and *Vas*. Her essay, "Multimodal Literature and Experimentation" (2012) is a good introduction to her work. There has also been rich theoretical work in narrative theory on the degree to which narrative concepts apply across media. *Narrative Across Media: The Languages of Storytelling* (2004), edited by Marie-Laure Ryan, has been particularly influential. Jan-Noël Thon's *Transmedial Narratology and Contemporary Media Culture* (2016) is more recent and particularly engaged with the contemporary media landscape, especially what he calls "transmedial entertainment franchises."

NOTES

1 This phrase comes from Janine Barchas (2003).
2 Although in this chapter I am emphasizing the competition between print and other media, we should also recognize that, in a somewhat earlier period, the ability of artworks to cross media was seen as an exciting opportunity to rethink artistic categories themselves. See Dick Higgins's influential essay, "Intermedia" in *A Dialectic of Centuries* (Higgins 1978).
3 Although there are certainly examples of the latter. *S.*, by J.J. Abrams and Doug Dorst (2013), for example is a story told through old-fashioned and explicitly literary physical objects: a novel called the *Ship of Theseus* written by V.M. Straka, annotated by an undergraduate and graduate student in back-and-forth dialogue with distinct handwriting and pen ink, along with flyers, notes, maps, and postcards stuffed into the pages of the novel.

SEE ALSO: After Postmodernism; Auster, Paul; Danielewski, Mark Z.; Hypertext Fiction and Network Narratives; Mixed-Genre Fiction; The New Experimentalism/The Contemporary Avant-Garde

REFERENCES

Abrams, J.J. and Dorst, Doug. (2013). *S*. New York: Mulholland Books.

Auster, Paul. (2002). *The Book of Illusions*. New York: Henry Holt.

Barchas, Janine. (2003). *Graphic Design, Print Culture, and the Eighteenth-Century Novel*. Cambridge: Cambridge University Press.

Cantor, Jay. (1987). *Krazy Kat: A Novel in Five Panels*. New York: Vintage.

Daitch, Susan. (1989). *The Colorist*. London: Virago.

Dinnen, Zara. (2018). *The Digital Banal: New Media and American Literature and Culture*. New York: Columbia University Press.

Drucker, Johanna. (2004). *The Century of Artists' Books*. New York: Granary Books.

Ensslin, Astrid. (2014). *Literary Gaming*. Cambridge, MA: MIT Press.

Gangemi, Kenneth. (1980). *The Interceptor Pilot*. London: Marion Boyars.

Gass, William H. (1989). *Willie Master's Lonesome Wife*. Normal, IL: Dalkey Archive; 1st ed. 1968.

Gladstone, Jason and Worden, Daniel. (2016). Introduction. *Postmodern|Postwar – And After: Rethinking American Literature* (ed. Jason Gladstone, Andrew Hoberek, and Daniel Worden), 1–24. Iowa City: Iowa.

Hamid, Mohsin. (2017). *Exit West*. New York: Riverhead.

Hayles, N. Katherine. (2013). Combining close and distant reading: Jonathan Safran Foer's *Tree of Codes* and the aesthetic of bookishness. *PMLA* 128 (1): 226–231.

Hayles, N. Katherine and Pressman, Jessica. (2013). *Comparative Textual Media: Transforming the Humanities in the Postprint Era*. Minneapolis: University of Minnesota Press.

Higgins, Dick. (1978). *A Dialectic of Centuries: Notes Towards a Theory of the New Arts*. New York: Printed Editions.

Kittler, Friedrich. A. (1999). *Gramophone, Film, Typewriter* (trans. G. Winthrop-Young and M. Wutz). Stanford: Stanford University Press; 1st ed. 1986.

Manovich, Lev. (2013). *Software Takes Command*. New York: Bloomsbury.

McHale, Brian. (2015). *The Cambridge Introduction to Postmodernism*. Cambridge: Cambridge University Press.

Muth, Katie R. (2011). Postmodern fiction as post-structuralist theory: Kathy Acker's blood and guts in high school. *Narrative* 19 (1): 86–110.

Powers, Richard. (1992). *Three Farmers on Their Way to a Dance*. New York: HarperPerennial; 1st ed. 1985.

Pressman, Jessica. (2009). The aesthetic of bookishness in 21st-century literature: Steven Hall's the *Raw Shark Texts*. *The Michigan Quarterly Review* 48 (4): 465–482.

Pressman, Jessica. (2014). *Digital Modernism: Making It New in New Media*. Oxford: Oxford University Press.

Punday, Daniel. (2012). *Writing at the Limit: The Novel in the New Media Ecology*. Lincoln: University of Nebraska Press.

Pynchon, Thomas. (1990). *Vineland*. Boston: Little, Brown.

Sukenick, Ronald. (1986). *Blown Away*. Los Angeles: Sun & Moon.

FURTHER READING

Gibbons, Alison. (2012). Multimodal literature and experimentation. In: *The Routledge Companion to Experimental Literature* (ed. Joe Bray, Alison Gibbons, and Brian McHale), 420–434 London: Routledge.

Gitelman, Lisa. (2014). *Paper Knowledge: Toward a Media History of Documents*. Durham: Duke University Press.

Heise, Ursula K. (2003). Unnatural ecologies: the metaphor of the environment in media theory. *Configurations* 10: 149–168.

Parikka, Jussi. (2012). *What is Media Archaeology?* Cambridge: Polity.

Ryan, Marie-Laure. (ed.) (2004). *Narrative Across Media: The Languages of Storytelling*. Lincoln: University of Nebraska Press.

Shaefer, Heike and Starre, Alexander. (eds.) (2019). *The Printed Book in Contemporary American Culture: Medium, Object, Metaphor*. London: Palgrave.

Thon, Jan-Noël. (2016). *Transmedial Narratology and Contemporary Media Culture*. Lincoln: University of Nebraska Press.

Irving, John

BIRTE CHRIST
Justus-Liebig-University Giessen, Germany

The publication of John Irving's *The World According to Garp* in 1978 prompted a nationwide "Garpomania" and propelled the author to fame. Since then, Irving has published ten widely read novels, various pieces of nonfiction, and a children's book. Moreover, his three pre-1978 novels have been republished and five of his novels have been adapted as highly successful Hollywood movies. Irving has been praised for his vivid, deeply lovable characters, his grotesque, satirical take on sexuality, death, and human suffering, and his penchant for often outrageous twists and turns of the plot. His novels, which have been described as "family romances" and as variations of the *Bildungsroman*, address virtually all "big" social problems Americans had to confront over the past forty years – war, terrorism, abortion, changing gender roles, changing family values, the AIDS epidemic, and many more. Yet while Irving is loved by his readers – in the United States as well as abroad – and appreciated by critics, academic scholarship has largely ignored Irving's œuvre. Literary scholars, in fact, have a hard time placing Irving. In the scarce analyses of his works, he is often implicitly or explicitly blamed for not fitting available categories. Harold Bloom, for instance, suggests that Irving's work is unsuccessful because it is "deeply haunted by his unsettled relationship to literary tradition" (2001, p. 1). Specifically, his work is seen as sitting somewhere between the nineteenth-century novel, modernism, postmodernism, magical realism, and a vaguely construed realm of the "popular." Irving's own embrace of sentimentality and of what he calls an "aesthetics of accessibility" (Irving 1979), however, point to the perhaps most useful perspective from which to understand and appreciate his work: middlebrow literary culture.

The middlebrow was first described as an emergent cultural formation of the early twentieth century in the United States and Britain and, in the US context, has been used to conceptualize a section of the literary field up until the mid-1970s. More recently, growing attention has been paid to the "new literary middlebrow" in the twenty-first century (Driscoll 2014, 2016), a large-scale transformation of reading and the book market and its mediating institutions, owing specifically to a growing event culture and digital technology. Among the hallmarks of middlebrow literary texts are their accessibility, their acute attention to the social and ethical challenges of the present, their traditionalist approach to form, their reverence for highbrow culture, their desire to entertain and to move the reader emotionally, their earnestness, and, ultimately, their conservatism. Irving's work can be seen as continuing, and productively updating, the middlebrow tradition beyond the 1970s and into the twenty-first century. In fact, Irving's work can be said to constitute the "missing link" between the postwar middlebrow novel and the new literary middlebrow of the twenty-first century.

John Irving was born John Wallace Blunt, Jr. in Exeter, New Hampshire, in 1942. His mother divorced his father before Irving was born and later married Colin Irving, a history teacher, who adopted John. Irving was raised as a faculty child on the campus of the exclusive Phillips Exeter Academy and – a bad student – made wrestling one of his main pursuits. He won a wrestling scholarship to Pittsburgh University and spent a year abroad in Vienna. As he finished his degree back in

New Hampshire in 1965, his first son was born and his first short story published. He subsequently moved to Iowa to study creative writing with Kurt Vonnegut and Vance Bourjaily at the University of Iowa's Writers' Workshop and supported his family as a university writing teacher and writer in residence. Additionally, he made ends meet by working as a wrestling coach. His success with *The World According to Garp* allowed him to earn his livelihood as a full-time novelist. As a writer, Irving draws heavily from his own life. Hence college campuses, struggling writers, strong single women, absent or dead parents, the anxieties and pleasures of fatherhood, Vienna, wrestling, and the woods of New Hampshire – as well as the bears that roam within them – are recurrent, even obsessive, motifs and locales in his novels since the publication of *Setting Free the Bears* (1968). The theme of wrestling takes a special place in Irving's texts – both in his fiction and in commentary on his own creative process. It is seen as a pursuit akin to writing, specifically in the way it demands concentration, constant practice, and discipline. Literary creation, in Irving's typically middlebrow conception, is the product of craftsmanship and hard work rather than the spontaneous outpouring of individual genius.

The World According to Garp, Irving's fourth novel, is central to his writing not only because it propelled Irving to popular success, but because it metareflexively spells out the literary program that Irving would subscribe to from then on. It also functions as a *mise en abyme* for Irving's process of constructing himself as both a popularly and critically acclaimed writer. The novel follows aspiring young author T.S. Garp on his journey to literary fame and personal fulfillment. Garp's literary works are either integrated into Irving's novel or extensively discussed on the plot level. Garp's first novel is a *Bildungsroman* set in Vienna during World War II and is thus closely related to European modernism; the second is a novel of marriage and infidelity set in contemporary suburbia; his third – entitled *The World According to Bensenhaver* – is set in a world of random violence and crime and combines the genres of postwar literary realism and hard-boiled detective fiction. Garp eventually comes to see his first novel as too far removed from his own experience, his second one as too autobiographical, and his third one as his most relevant novel because it is based on experience transformed by the imagination. He values it, moreover, because it reached a mass readership by generically merging the "high" with the "low." However, this third novel, Garp comes to realize, still lacks something: it lacks hope – hope for attaining individual wholeness and human connection. The capacity of literature to imagine a world slightly better, and more loving, than the real one is what Garp – and Irving – come to see as "good" literature's most essential achievement. However, Irving cuts Garp's life short – he is assassinated by a radical feminist – as Garp is starting to write the novel that would overcome violence, futility, and despair through a *grand récit* of individual uplift and familial togetherness.

In terms of *Garp* as a *mise en abyme*, Irving himself can be seen as overcoming exactly that violence, futility, and despair that characterized *The World According to Bensenhaver* by writing *The World According to Garp*. In an act of self-fulfilling metapoetic prophecy, Irving thus offers in *Garp* an explanation for why *Garp* itself would become a commercial and cultural sensation. He suggests that it provided readers with what the previous novels eschewed: a sentimental education – a belief in the possibility of wholeness and belonging, and advice on how to attain it. As the reader is reminded once again in the final pages of *Garp*, if she only has "energy," if she tries hard enough to live purposefully and in contexts of familial community, then meaning, belonging, and even transcendence are within her grasp. While his novels are often *Bildungsromane* that follow an individual's journey from innocence to experience, they are always family romances in the sense that they place the protagonist/s in relation to family. Shortly after the publication of *Garp*, Irving formulated his ideas for an ethically relevant, hence "serious," and at the same time nonacademic, entertaining fiction in a number of essays, among them "The Aesthetics of Accessibility" (1979), "In Defense of Sentimentality" (1979), and "The King of the Novel" (1986). The king of the novel, for Irving, is Charles Dickens, and with Dickens, he subscribes to exquisitely developed characters, heartbreaking, hilarious stories verging on the absurd, and the power of sentiment. Fiction, he insists, must affectively move the reader – even drench her in tears – to allow her to open up her heart to the world and thus make it a better, hopeful place for herself and those around her.

The semi- or partly autobiographical writer figure as a strategy to reflect on the question of literary "quality," different cultural arenas of success, and the relationship between truth and fiction, or rationality and imagination, recurs in many of Irving's novels. From Lilly in *The Hotel New Hampshire* (1981) who, inversely to T.S. Garp, cannot wed her genius to popular success and commits suicide, via the overtly autobiographical Danny Angel in *Last Night in Twisted River* (2009) and the bisexual Billy Abbott in *In One Person* (2012), to the aging, transculturally identified Juan Diego in *Avenue of Mysteries* (2015), these writer characters negotiate their place in the contemporary literary scene and the marketplace, as well as within literary traditions. Irving's writing himself into a middlebrow literary aesthetics and ideology after *Garp* is most pronounced in his 1998 *A Widow for One Year*, as the novel parses the literary field through three protagonist-writers who represent different strands of popular writing. Ted Cole is an "indisputably literary" writer who turns to creating popular children's books after his first three novels fail to attract a wider audience (Irving 2010, p. 23); Marion Cole becomes a successful mystery writer as a way to deal with her own grief and in order to entertain readers; Ruth Cole, their daughter, then, grows up to become a true middlebrow writer, combining the "high" and the "low," which her parents succeed at only partially. She was the "rare combination of a well-respected literary novelist *and* an internationally best-selling author" (p. 23, emphasis in the original).

Beyond its emphasis on accessibility and moral uplift, Irving's aesthetic program shares at least two more key characteristics with the "historical and contemporary middlebrow," as conceptualized by Beth Driscoll (2016): it is earnest, and it is conservative. Its earnestness manifests itself in its concern with social issues and social improvement, and – on an individual level – with character and self-growth. Always at the pulse of contemporary American life, Irving's novels view current events and cultural developments as always potentially dangerous and alienating and thus – despite their efforts to integrate the new and the different – harbor a nostalgia for a lost, orderly world. The present world – in the novels' view – is full of violence, extremism, and uncertainty. Although one of the hallmarks of Irving's writing is his ability to render characters' actions and experiences of violence, fear, and grief in comic, absurd, even grotesque terms, and readers may well laugh out loud at the slapstick humor that characterizes some of the most outrageous plot sequences, there is always, in the midst of comedy, an entirely un-ironized commitment to making the world a better place by becoming a better person.

The Hotel New Hampshire translates *Garp*'s concerns with sexual violence and political extremism and terrorism into a family epic with quintupled protagonists; the more economical *The Cider House Rules* (1985) treats the issue of abortion. *A Prayer for Owen Meany* (1989), Irving's all-time bestseller internationally, takes on the Vietnam War and the question of the place of religion in the contemporary world. Similarly, *A Son of the Circus* (1994) is concerned with the possibility of Christian belief in a world of seeming injustice and unbearable pain. *A Widow for One Year*, then, leaves spirituality behind again and (re)turns to literature and the connections it can forge between individuals as a means to deal with mourning and grief. *In One Person* (2012) expands on issues of bisexuality, homosexuality, and transgender identity that *Garp* already touched upon in the character of Garp's male-to-female transgender friend Robert/a Muldoon; it also looks at the AIDS epidemic and its costs for individuals and families. Through these current issues, Irving's novels ultimately address the most fundamental ontological and epistemological questions: the question of identity (who am I?), and the question of epistemology (how can I know?). They are thus organized around a trajectory of quest – like most *Bildungsromane* – yet are also infused with a sacramental tone in their awareness of addressing, and finding solutions to, the ultimate questions of human life.

Solutions to current issues, and hence to the ultimate questions, are offered exclusively on an individual level, never on a political or structural level – again typical of the middlebrow mode and supporting the text's ultimate conservatism. Irving's attention to building characters, or even "characterscapes" (Davis and Womack 1998, pp. 125–126), in lively and intimate detail through narrative action serves as the formal framework necessary to tell stories that focus on the characters' psycho-socio-sexual development and his or her place in the world, rather than on his or her professional, economic, and social success and the ways in which she or he may change that world beyond his or her own private sphere. In other words, in Irving's novels, characters grow to find or create their own space for their lives, yet within the social status quo. In arranging themselves with the present state of society, they often take a middle position between ideological poles and choices – a tension which is only resolved, individually, through familial love and acceptance.

The characters' "middling" hold onto the status quo becomes evident, for instance, in John Wheelwright's becoming a religious man in *A Prayer for Owen Meany*. The religious space that the novel's narrator comes to inhabit has been described, negatively, as characterized by "dogmatic vagueness" and the novel as "embracing a free-floating religiousness that makes use of Christian elements" (Sykes 1996, p. 58) or, more positively, as mediating the dialectic between rationality and belief, between cognition and an intuitive knowledge of the world (see, e.g., Page 1995 and Tate 2008, pp. 40–106). Wheelwright ultimately does not have to choose, but develops his idiosyncratic amalgamation of knowledge and belief through the Christ-figure of Owen Meany. This tendency of the novels to embrace the idea that it is possible to eat one's cake (on the individual level) and have it, or leave it intact, too (on the structural level), may be seen as even more prominent in texts where the status quo of gender relations and the heteronormative family are concerned.

First, the novels' fictional worlds are populated by characters with nonconventional gender and sexual identities, yet while these are accepted and celebrated on the level of the individual, they are represented as harmful when they are being translated into a political agenda. In *Garp*, for instance, Jenny Fields's decision to live without a husband but have a child is represented as her doing "Just what *she* wanted to do"; Garp similarly defends his taking on a more feminine role in his family as a purely personal choice. Doing exactly what one "wants to do," including living out alternative gender roles, is represented as entirely unproblematic in the novel. Hence, feminist activists like the Ellen Jamesians, who publicly protest sexual violence and demand a radical dismantling of gendered hierarchies, appear as extremists, even lunatics. Irving's plots thus tend to discredit political activism that could lead to structural change.

Second, characters that live out alternative gender and sexual identities in the novels can do so only – or will be happy only – if they do so within the family or family-like structures of community that are highly hierarchically structured. Clearly, while Jenny Fields and Garp himself defy traditional roles, they do so while fostering intensive affective ties within the familial community of their choice. Transgender character Robert/a Muldoon heads Jenny Field's home for women on Long Island, and while the home can be seen as a feminist community that deliberately sets itself apart from patriarchal structures, Robert/a governs the community with a loving benevolence that strongly reeks of paternalism. Franny Berry in *The Hotel New Hampshire* can ultimately leave her incestuous desire for John, the narrator, and her lesbian sexuality behind and gets married; Frank, an open homosexual, becomes a happy individual only when he opens himself to the love and generosity of his siblings and reintegrates into the family circle.

Irving's novels may be called period pieces in the best sense of the word: they take readers deeply into the fabric of contemporary American lives. Yet, they project a claim to universality in their stalwart commitment to the power of human connection. The novels have been and should be read as explorations of US American middle-class identity that offer the pleasures of unforgettable, eminently human characters, the pleasures of twists and turns of the plot, the pleasures of tears and laughter, the rewards of hope and transcendence, of meaning and belonging in a violent, disorienting world. Yet in a kind of double vision, Irving's work must, at the same time, be read with the awareness that Irving's fictional universe may – despite its seemingly progressive engagement with current issues – not offer a place for everyone to live freely and to their fullest potential. For instance, while characters are free to love whom they please or to perform their gender in all manner of ways, Irving's worlds do not allow them to do so outside of attachments to family and a commitment to heteronormative productivity and futurity, which are ultimately patriarchally structured. A formal equivalent to the patriarchally governed family can be seen in the strong authorial, traditionally male voice that characterizes Irving's works, which is benevolent and totalizing at the same time. Hence Irving's oscillation between progressive ideas and a conservatism that does not challenge foundational structures and beliefs, but solves social conflicts on a private level by relying on the kindness and decency of individuals, must be equally enjoyed and critiqued as a hallmark of contemporary middlebrow writing.

SEE ALSO: Vonnegut, Kurt

REFERENCES

Bloom, Harold. (2001a). Introduction. In: *Modern Critical Views: John Irving* (ed. Harold Bloom), 1–2. Philadelphia: Chelsea House.

Davis, Todd F. and Womack, Kenneth. (1998). Saints, sinners, and the Dickensian novel: the ethics of storytelling in John Irving's *The Cider House Rules*. Style 32 (2): 298–317.

Driscoll, Beth. (2014). *The New Literary Middlebrow: Tastemakers and Reading in the Twenty-First Century*. Houndmills, UK: Palgrave Macmillan.

Driscoll, Beth. (2016). The middlebrow family resemblance: features of the historical and contemporary middlebrow. *Post-45* (January 7, 2016). https://post45.org/2016/07/the-middlebrow-family-resemblance-features-of-the-historical-and-contemporary-middlebrow/ (accessed July 4, 2021).

Irving, John. (1979). The aesthetics of accessibility: Kurt Vonnegut and his critics. *The New Republic* (September 1979): 41–49.

Irving, John. (2010). *A Widow for One Year*. London: Black Swan; 1st ed. 1998.

Page, Philip. (1995). Hero worship and hermeneutic dialectics: John Irving's *A Prayer for Owen Meany*. Mosaic 28: 105–120.

Sykes, John. (1996). Christian apologetic uses of the grotesque in John Irving and Flannery O'Connor. Literature & Theology 10: 58–67.

Tate, Andrew. (2008). *Contemporary Fiction and Christianity*. London: Continuum.

FURTHER READING

Belgaid, Bouchra. (2011). *John Irving and Cultural Mourning*. Lanham, MD: Rowman & Littlefield.

Bloom, Harold. (ed.) (2001b). *Modern Critical Views: John Irving*. Philadelphia: Chelsea House.

Booth, Allison. (2002). Neo-Victorian self-help, or Cider House Rules. American Literary History 14 (2): 284–310.

Christ, Birte. (2016). The aesthetics of accessibility: John Irving and the middlebrow novel after 1975. *Post-45* (January 7, 2016). https://post45.org/2016/07/the-aesthetics-of-accessibility-john-irving-and-the-middlebrow-novel-after-1975/

Schofield, Benedict. (2018). Austria's ambiguous smile: transnational perspectives on Austrian belatedness in the fiction of John Irving. In: *New Perspectives on Austrian Literature and Culture* (ed. Katya Kryola), 65–92. Frankfurt: Peter Lang.

J

James, Marlon

SHERI-MARIE HARRISON
University of Missouri-Columbia, USA

Marlon James, born in Jamaica in 1970, received his first degree in language and literature from the University of the West Indies in 1991 and a masters from Wilkes University in 2006. He is currently an associate professor and writer in residence at Macalester College in St Paul, Minnesota, where he has been a faculty member since 2007. James writes novels, short fiction, and nonfiction, but his acclaim comes mainly from his four novels: *John Crow's Devil* (2005), *The Book of Night Women* (2008), *A Brief History of Seven Killings* (2014), and *Black Leopard, Red Wolf* (2019), the first installment of the planned Dark Star Trilogy. He is also the 2014 Man Booker Prize winner for *A Brief History of Seven Killings*, the first Jamaican to win the most prestigious book prize in the United Kingdom. While his nonfiction frequently takes the form of personal narratives about growing up as a gay man in Jamaica, James's fiction traffics in a (now signature) iconoclastic narrative style, liberally peppered with vulgar vernacular and graphic violence, that is often discomfiting and puzzling, particularly in relation to other anglophone Caribbean fiction.

In "From Jamaica to Minnesota to Myself," James describes how just before he wrote himself "all the way to a book tour in the United States," he felt as though he had "reached the limits of [his] own wisdom," effectively the "end of [him]self" (James 2017). Growing up queer amidst Jamaica's unique mixture of hypermasculinity, homophobia, and religious fundamentalism alienated and depressed James. It was Salman Rushdie's *Shame* (1983) that inspired him to begin writing again. For James, *Shame* was "like a hand grenade inside a tulip." He found its "prose so audacious, its reality so unhinged, that you didn't see at first how pointedly political and just plain furious it was." It made James "realize that the present was something [he] could write [his] way out of. And so [he] started writing for the first time since college, but kept it quiet because none of it was holy" (James 2017). We can begin to think about the "unholiness" that characterizes James's writing through this prism of his personal experience as a literary-minded gay Jamaican man with an attraction to the regenerative possibilities of the apocalyptic.

In their introduction to a special issue of the *Journal of West Indian Literature* on James's work, Michael Bucknor and Kezia Page describe Caribbean literary criticism's engagement with the author's work as a "reckoning." Understanding James as a Jamaican

The Encyclopedia of Contemporary American Fiction 1980–2020, First Edition. Edited by Patrick O'Donnell, Stephen J. Burn, and Lesley Larkin.
© 2022 John Wiley & Sons Ltd. Published 2022 by John Wiley & Sons Ltd.

author is crucial to understanding his work, and must coincide "with the understanding that we claim him from a place that he feels rejects and denies him himself" (Bucknor and Page 2018, p. ii). Any Jamaican claim on James's writing must reckon with his years in Jamaica and the reasons he gives for leaving. He says he had to leave Jamaica "whether in a plane or a coffin." Thus, "the violence of James own experience in Jamaica . . . finds an imaginative home in his fiction and much of the time, we as readers find it to be as brutal and searing as was James's experience with homophobia" (James 2017). While some have found James's gender politics and representations of sexual violence intellectually and aesthetically unredeemable, I would like to suggest that this is perhaps one response that James's narrative provocations intend.

James's first novel, *John Crow's Devil*, depicts a mid-twentieth-century rural community that is incited to commit horrendous acts of violence against itself by the religious rhetoric of a syphilitic preacher. The pre-independence folk setting is reminiscent of earlier Caribbean narratives that imagined postcolonial sovereignty at the level of rural community, but the horrors James presents in this novel leave the reader wondering what she is meant to do with its representation of predatory sexuality and masculine violence as defining aspects of Jamaican life. In this novel, it is neither sex itself nor queerness that poses threats to social order, but rather patriarchal sexual predation. James's second novel, *The Book of Night Women*, is a neo-slave narrative set in Jamaica between 1785 and 1819. In it a teenaged slave protagonist, Lilith, refuses to participate in a slave rebellion. The Haitian Revolution looms unsubtly in the background, and house slaves, who aspire to murder all the whites and establish an African-style village in the island's mountainous interior, foment a similar rebellion. Not only does Lilith refuse to become involved, she opts to protect her Irish lover and white overseer father from the rebelling slaves, even killing her half-sister in the process. In this way, the novel presents subversively alternate ways of thinking about racial and gendered freedom.

While James's first two novels are set in Jamaica, his subsequent novels expand beyond the nation's shores both literally and metaphorically. James's third novel, *A Brief History of Seven Killings*, is built around the 1976 assassination attempt on Bob Marley's life and takes place in Kingston, Montego Bay, Miami, and New York. It unfolds over the course of five days between 1976 and 1991, and relies on twelve different narrators (fifteen if you count the character who changes her name three times). It encapsulates a late twentieth-century political moment in the Caribbean that was implicitly global, in that the attempt on Marley's life is embedded in the Cold War, the OPEC (Organization of Petroleum Exporting Countries) crisis, and the drug war. Its form actively effaces the development of an authentic version of subjectivity as an organizing logic for early Caribbean and postcolonial writing. The novel is not one person's, one country's, or one community's story. What unites the cacophony of voices in James's novel is one specific moment in history – the assassination attempt. This moment in turn works as a local anchor for one of the most turbulent decades in recent global history.

In the same way that *A Brief History of Seven Killings* is not actually about Bob Marley – the late reggae icon isn't even referred to by name in the novel – James's fourth novel is far more complex than the "African Game of Thrones" he promised Nate Jones in *Vulture* (2015). *Black Leopard, Red Wolf* is the first book in the Dark Star trilogy and departs from the experimental realism of James's earlier novels in its mix of epic fantasy and historical fiction. James's fourth novel centers on the character Tracker's quest to find a lost child; it is an impressive feat of narrative world making. With the exception of only two instances, where the narrative perspective switches to his inquisitor, the novel is told retrospectively from Tracker's point of view and unfolds through four interlocking stories set in fantastic and previously unimagined landscapes, with a motley cast that includes witches, vampires, shapeshifters, and even a buffalo. This novel is arguably James's most impressive yet, not least because of the ways formal and thematic preoccupations across his previous work –metafiction, gender, and queerness – all coalesce in *Black Leopard, Red Wolf's* meditation of the nature of love, stories, and storytelling.

A body of criticism on James is work is only just emerging, in no small part because of his Booker Prize win. The most consistently made observation of this criticism – one that may help explain the slowness of its emergence – is how violent James's fiction is, particularly toward Black women. One need look no further than the death by stoning of Pastor Bligh in *John Crow's Devil*, Lilith's brutal gang rape and whipping in *The Book of Night Women*, early scenes of police brutality in *A Brief History*, and pretty much every third or fifth page in *Black Leopard, Red Wolf*, for examples of the kinds of violence some critics perceive as objectionable. Where there are not depictions of actual violence, threats of violence are narrated in explicit and perhaps even salacious detail. In *The Book of Night Women*, for example, after Lilith kills another slave when he tries to rape her, his compatriots threaten her as follows: "first we going beat her face off. Then we going fuck out her cunt. Then we going kill her. Then we going fuck her again" (James 2010, p. 24).

In thinking about this kind of narrative violence, Markus Nehl acknowledges that *The Book of Night Women* "participate[s] in a transnational, cross-generational discussion about the meaning of black (counter-) violence in an anti-black world and, eventually, move[s] beyond an uncritical celebration of the liberating impact of violence for the oppressed" (2016, p. 188). Nonetheless, Nehl concludes that the novel "shows no critical awareness of the ethical risks involved in putting the atrocities against slave women into words" (p. 180). Likewise, in her consideration of *A Brief History of Seven Killings*, Nadia Ellis remains unconvinced that "understanding Jamaica requires quite this much of everything: pages, characters, violence, sex." But where these critics and others sound objections, others like the novelist-critic Curdella Forbes recognize the violence of James's novels as germane to "the new generation of Caribbean diaspora writers whose creative innovations are redrawing the map of Caribbean literature and forcing critics to search for alternative discursive paradigms" (2017, p. 2). In an essay that "re-reads" *A Brief History* "through the Native American framework of survivance, which relies on innovative culture-specific narrative strategies in its examination of historical traumas," Caryn Rae Adams argues "that James narrativization of violence in the novel is rooted in the horrific history of colonization, which continues to haunt the region" (2018, p. 97).

Particularly in his early novels, these disruptions concern the heteronormative politics that undergird cultural nationalism's agendas for defining citizenship, as well as the literary paradigms employed in the consolidation of these agendas via race, gender, and sexuality-based identity politics. Though Caribbean writing dates back to the early nineteenth century, it began coalescing into a discrete field of study in the early twentieth century, motivated in large part by the political impetuses of anticolonialism, political independence, and decolonization. The politics of James's work is defined in large part through its departures from some of the more traditional imperatives of Caribbean literature. Arguably, James's narrative investments in iconoclasm more closely resemble the modernist experimentation of figures like Virginia Woolf and William Faulkner. James himself has noted his affinity for modernist writing in interviews and acknowledgements.

This is not to say that James's writing is not preoccupied with the questions of identity, race, and nationalism that Caribbean and other postcolonial writing has always been preoccupied with. Rather, it takes up these issues in jarring profanity-laced, prurient, graphic, and disturbingly violent ways that upsets the pieties and proprieties that have long characterized anticolonial and postcolonial discourses. Formally, James's use of forms and genres typically associated with national literature, such as the slave narrative, historical fiction, the *Bildungsroman*, and the gothic, demonstrates how official, anti-racist, or nationalist stances on identity can decouple race from material conditions in a manner that not only represents but also undergirds inequality.

It is James's obsession with women and the violence to which they are subject that functions as a primary vehicle for the aggressively revisionist ways his work encourages us to approach the problems – such as the continued precarity of Black, queer existence – that persist more than half a century after political independence. In James's first three novels – and less clearly, but arguably also in his fourth – female characters are the last ones standing after an apocalypse of sorts. Lauren Shoemaker calls these characters "femme finales" (2018, p. 18). In *John Crow's Devil*, the novel's parting vision, after the violent implosion of Gibbeah, is the widow Greenfield, who survivors glimpse on the other side of Gibbeah's fence. Shoemaker agrees that "women are often left standing when the smoke clears and they become symbols of futurity, continuance or bearing witness" (p. 18). But while the apocalyptic violence in Gibbeah registers a reset of sorts, the aftermath of a slave revolt in *The Book of Night Women* tells us something a little bit different about the complicated complicities of forms historically associated with anti-racist work, of which the slave narrative is progenetive. In violation of the conventions of the slave narrative form, Lilith remains on Montpelier Estate following the violent suppression of a slave revolt, and lives in a state of freedom that is undefinable within the frames of legal emancipation. This is also a state not available to her fellow slaves. It is in this space of the undefinable that I would like to suggest that James's work encourages us to think about alternate modes of order and imagination.

If slave narratives written by women like *The History of Mary Prince: A West Indian Slave* (1831) sublimated details of the sexual lives of female slaves, *The Book of Night Women* alludes to and rewrites moments of sexual violence in explicit detail. Where Prince complains about an overseer who "had an ugly fashion of stripping himself quite naked, and ordering [her] then to wash him in a tub of water," in James's rewriting of this scene, Lilith drowns a magistrate in the same bathtub in which he forces her to bathe and perform sex acts on him (James 2010, p. 77). More than filling in what was censored or even enacting revenge though, James's fiction forces confrontation with the ways literary practice has become conventionalized, producing critiques that fall short of coming to terms with the problems of contemporary postcolonial realities. James's main tool for doing this is the manipulation of genre conventions, both in terms of their form and in terms of the affect we have learned to expect from the deployment of these forms. The representational and rhetorical strategies in his novels aren't new, but what James constructs with them through exaggeration, explicitness, and vulgarity undermines and demystifies the reverence with which they have been held in literary practice over centuries.

We can think about the thematic structure and fantasy form of *Black Leopard, Red Wolf* as one that brings together the recurring concerns surrounding the interrelation of race, gender, sexuality, and freedom across James's fiction. Tracker's powers allow James to narrate a sense of smell in a way that is unusual for the novel, a form generally focused on the distance senses of sight and hearing. Fantasy thus begets experimentation in a way that, given the novel's preoccupation with the scents of sex in particular, highlights embodied queerness in significant ways. The novel, engaged as it is in the act of world creation and not limited to the materials of the realist novel, forces the reader to experience its social world as deeply denaturalized. Nothing should be taken for granted; the rules of the novel's world must be learned. The process of reading it thus encourages the reader to come at their own social world with a similar freshness of perception. In an important way, James uses the potential of fantasy to produce a novel that is less J.R.R. Tolkien than Virginia Wolf.

SEE ALSO: Beatty, Paul; Cliff, Michelle; Johnson, Mat; Kincaid, Jamaica; Queer and LGBT Fiction; Ward, Jesmyn; Whitehead, Colson

REFERENCES

Adams, Caryn Rae. (2018). Uncomfortable truths: lifewriting, trauma and survivance in Marlon James's *A Brief History of Seven Killings* (for Isabel Grosvenor). *Journal of West Indian Literature* 26: 96–109.

Bucknor, Michael A. and Page, Kezia. (2018). Introduction: authorial self-fashioning, political denials and artistic distinctiveness: the queer poetics of Marlon James. *Journal of West Indian Literature* 26: 121–122.

Forbes, Curdella. (2017). Bodies of horror in Marlon James's *The Book of Night Women* and Clovis Brown's *Cartoons*. *Small Axe* 21: 1–16.

James, Marlon. (2010). *The Book of Night Women*. New York: Riverhead Trade; 1st ed. 2009.

James, Marlon. (2017). From Jamaica to Minnesota to myself. *The New York Times* (March 10, 2015). https://www.nytimes.com/2015/03/15/magazine/from-jamaica-to-minnesota-to-myself.html (accessed July 6, 2021).

Jones, Nate. (n.d.). Marlon James's next book will be an "African *Game of Thrones*." *Vulture*. https://www.vulture.com/2015/12/marlon-jamess-new-book-will-be-an-african-got.html (accessed July 6, 2021).

Nehl, Markus. (2016). *Transnational Black Dialogues: Re-Imagining Slavery in the Twenty-First Century*. Bielefeld, Germany: Transcript Verlag.

Shoemaker, Lauren. (2018). Femme finale: gender, violence and nation in Marlon James' novels. *Journal of West Indian Literature* 26: 18–33.

FURTHER READING

Crowley, Emma. (2018). So many incredible Gehennas: musicality and (the poetics of) "relation" in the novels of Marlon James. *Journal of West Indian Literature* 26: 34–49.

Hamilton, Njelle W. (2018). Jah live: messianic time and post-traumatic narrative disorder in Marlon James's *A Brief History of Seven Killings*. *Journal of West Indian Literature* 26: 80–95.

Harrison, Sheri-Marie. (2014). *Jamaica's Difficult Subjects: Negotiating Sovereignty in Anglophone Caribbean Literature and Criticism*. Columbus: Ohio State University Press.

Harrison, Sheri-Marie. (2018). Marlon James and the metafiction of the new Black Gothic. *Journal of West Indian Literature* 26: 1–17.

Layne, Jhordan. (2018). Re-evaluating religion and superstition: Obeah and Christianity in Marlon James's *The Book of Night Women* and William Earle Jr.'s *Obi, or The History of Three-Fingered Jack*. *Journal of West Indian Literature* 26: 50–65.

Madore, Joel. (2011). Jamaican signatures: an archetypal analysis of Marlon James' *John Crow's Devil*. *Journal of Caribbean Literatures* 7: 69.

Vásquez, Sam. (2012). Violent liaisons: historical crossings and the negotiation of sex, sexuality, and race in *The Book of Night Women* and *The True History of Paradise*. *Small Axe* 16: 43–59.

Jarrar, Randa

JAMEEL ALGHABERI
Saurashtra University, India

Randa Jarrar is a Palestinian American writer born in 1978 in Chicago to a Palestinian father and a Greek-Egyptian mother (Albakry and Siler 2012, p. 112). At a very early age, Jarrar moved with her family to Kuwait, where she received her early education. The invasion of Kuwait in 1990 by Iraqi troops forced the family to flee to Egypt to escape the war. With her family, she returned to the United States at the age of 13. She received her MFA at the University of Michigan and presently resides in Fresno, California, where she teaches English at California State University.

Since her childhood, Jarrar has been crossing borders along with her family for different circumstances. Subsequently, her fiction transcends space and time, reflecting her transnational experience and worldview. Her first novel, *A Map of Home* (2008), was a great success, acclaimed and translated into six major languages. Through this novel, Jarrar rejects cultural fixation and defies dehumanizing oriental stereotypes. The novel minutely portrays the daily struggle of Arab Americans and, engaging Palestinian history and Arab culture in general, reflects how the past cannot be repressed. It is about a small family and their move from Kuwait to Egypt and, finally, to the United States. Nidali is the narrator, recounting her family's struggle and also reflecting her own experience of crossing borders and encountering other cultures. As a female, Nidali is not only in search of home, she is also in pursuit of her own agency.

Jarrar's debut novel was followed by her collection of stories, *Him, Me, Muhammad Ali* (2016), in which she depicts different aspects of the lives of Arab American women. In her stories, Jarrar presents domestic issues at the macrocosmic level. Women are the central characters, depicted as bold and dominating. Most of them are Muslim and of different sexual inclinations. The stories are semi-realistic, yet some contain mythical elements. They are set in different places, including Cairo and Alexandria in Egypt, Gaza in Palestine, Detroit and New York City in the United States, and Istanbul in Turkey. Jarrar's themes include gender politics, sexuality, domestic violence, and infidelity. In both the novel and the collection of short stories, the themes of family, complicated relationships, appearance and disappearance, the lack of true love and devotion, and navigating one's identity, particularly among female immigrants, predominate. Jarrar's diasporic upbringing and transnational perspective inform her novel, and in her collection of short stories, she "moves seamlessly from Istanbul to Sydney to Seattle, with stories featuring characters from a variety of Arab backgrounds" (Farid 2016). The female characters are all of Middle Eastern descent, and they are depicted in a way that contradicts the common American perceptions of Arab women.

Not only projecting women's struggle in her fiction, Randa Jarrar is an advocate of original Arab cultural representation. Her perspective is evident in two opinion articles from 2014 titled "Why I Can't Stand White Belly Dancers" and "I Still Can't Stand White Belly Dancers." Her key argument focuses on cultural appropriation and lack of understanding of the original culture. She stresses that white belly dancers fake Arab culture to make a profession without making an effort to understand the culture itself (Jarrar 2014a, b). Nevertheless, appropriation designates a degree of hybridity, and it is not an offense. It shows how immigrant communities have exerted their influence on mainstream culture and general society. Assimilating into American society is not a one-way process. Both the general society and the diasporic communities influence each other's culture, resulting in appropriations and hybridized cultural forms. Jarrar also struggles against patriarchy and oppressive masculinity. In her essay "Biblioclast" (2016), Jarrar recounts her experience with her father, who burned copies of her debut novel because he thought it was heretical. He is caught in between American modernism and traditional Arab views toward women. Jarrar's complicated relationship with her father is echoed in her fiction. Jarrar's attempt, as she represents fatherhood in her novel and stories, is to deconstruct gender hierarchies and the different aspects of traditional Arab masculinity, such as honor and shame.

Home, in the case of diasporic populations, is always ambiguous and incomplete. It is never as fixed and permanent as the ideal perception of "the home" assumes it to be: private, safe, fixed, a shelter to return to (Georgiou 2010, p. 23). For Jarrar, home exists in between border crossings. She does not attempt to anchor her characters to a particular place. Rather, she lets them float in a transnational context, transcending parochial conventions and cultural borderlines. Jarrar upholds the idea of a global sense of place, or what Anthony Appiah termed "cosmopolitanism" (Appiah 2006). As a Palestinian American, Jarrar finds in "transnationalism" a way to define and determine her belonging. Her transnational experience is understood in the process of border crossing, which involves "cognitive and imaginative mapping of the world, opening oneself to it, learning and imagining it" (Kołodziejczyk 2018, p. 93). Moreover, home, in its symbolic significance, can become a synonym for familiarity, intimacy, security, and identity against the unknown, the distant and the large (Georgiou 2010, p. 23). It is sometimes due to the prolonged Palestinian–Israeli conflict that some Palestinian diasporas find themselves obliged to completely integrate into the host society or freely label themselves as citizens of the world (Alghaberi 2018, p. 14). Alternatively, in terms of culture, Georgiou suggests that exploring cultural boundaries results in the construction of new and multiple domestic and collective homes (2010, p. 23). Due to the various locations and dislocations, Jarrar situates her characters in a cosmopolitan context that provisions multiple "homes."

In *A Map of Home*, the constant evolution of Nidali's conception of home is predominant. The novel recounts the story of Nidali in Kuwait, Egypt, and finally Texas in the United States. Nidali is born in the United States to a Palestinian father and an Egyptian-Greek mother. She is hybrid, a mix of here and there, and she pronounces it: "Mama is an Egyptian, her mother was a Greek, my father is a Palestinian [. . .] I was Egyptian and Palestinian. I was Greek and American" (2008, p. 8). Nidali, from the very beginning, finds herself straddling two cultures, resulting in a sense of being out of place or a sort of estrangement in her cultural identification. Being a mix of different cultures and backgrounds, Nidali is set to explore such a mix and to figure out a way for herself within the constant journeying and intermixing (Bujupaj 2016, p. 190). In her early years in the United States, she struggles to translate her Arab identity in an American context. Jarrar's novel rejects polarization and dismantles the dichotomy between "East" and "West," between "Arab" and "American," and between "here" and "there." Nidali resists "being perceived as a cultural heroine, and in doing so she disrupts the sacredness of social conventions" (p. 195). By recounting her experience, Nidali demonstrates that coming of age is universal and that Arab women are not different from other women (Alghaberi 2018, p. 18). Opposing her father and resisting his conventional regulations for her own good, Nidali displays the ideal image of an Arab feminist. Indeed, her projection of feminism does not mean negating the role of her father in shaping her personality. Waheed contributes to Palestinizing Nidali and connecting her to the "historic Palestine."

Jarrar's collection of short stories, *Him, Me, Muhammad Ali*, focuses more on domestic issues than on identity formation and diaspora. Focusing on female characters, the collection explores critical domestic issues such as body shaming, sex, marriage, violence, and love. Jarrar manages to imbue her stories and characters with unabashed satire and biting language, melded with an expansive, imaginative geography (Farid 2016). With the publication of *Him, Me, Muhammad Ali*, Jarrar's attempt is to expand the literary representations of Arabs, providing authentic and realistic depictions of Arab Americans. Her own experience of moving between continents and cultures is reflected in all the stories of the collection. In every story there is a character seeking independence and searching for a place to fit in. More importantly, the collection does not merely feature personal or sentimental stories, recounting typical immigrant experience. Rather, it offers sharp, irreverent, and unapologetically crude criticism. In most of the stories, there is hardly a place for romance, and love between couples is often sensual. In addition, the relationships depicted are casual and flippant with recurrent disruptions. There are only troubled relationships and arranged marriages, resulting in severe family consequences. Even the relationship between parents and their children is complicated, reflecting a weak and fragmented family bond. There is often resentment between mothers and daughters, abusive fathers frequently rupture family bonds, and husbands abandon their wives.

Him, Me, Muhammad Ali includes thirteen short stories, featuring different themes and various settings. The first story, "The Lunatics' Eclipse," is set in Egypt and all the characters are Egyptian. The central character in the story is Qamar, a tightrope walker who attempts to lasso the moon. Her parents die in a tragic accident and she later finds that they left a note for her to marry her cousin, Omar, whom she does not love. The central theme in the story is forced marriage. For Omar, Qamar is like a "mouled" doll (a traditional sugary sweet in the form of a doll). She does not love him and for him she is merely a body. The collection's title story, "Him, Me, Muhammad Ali," is a poignant elegy about a daughter's troubled relationship with her father as she searches for a meaningful place to scatter his ashes in Egypt. Her father was Ethiopian American and her mother was Egyptian Australian, both journalists. In Cairo, she reconnects with her mother's family and searches for a photo her father always talked about but which she's never seen: it supposedly showed her, her father, and Muhammad Ali. The notion of biracial relationship dominates the story. In "How Can I Be of Use to You?" Jarrar explores the frailties of an older Egyptian feminist and her young protégée, a tale that evokes shades of the famed Egyptian literary icon Nawal El Saadawi. These short stories are centered on women and their day-to-day activities. Jarrar presents themes of forced marriage, complicated child–parent relationships, and also issues facing intellectual Arab women.

More importantly, Jarrar, in her collection, addresses the issue of race in the United States. In "The Life, Loves, and Adventures of Zelwa the Halfie," Jarrar explores the burdens of growing up as an Arab in America using a character who is half human, half animal. Zelwa has the lower half of a Transjordanian ibex and her father tries to convince her to have surgery to make her fully human. Being a "halfie" is a metaphor for being biracial and bisexual. It is a story about learning how to love and appreciate yourself. Zelwa "the Halfie" accepts her body and struggles to understand her father's point of view. However, she eventually recounts:

> I have always wanted to feel whole [. . .] I am sick of feeling different, of being alone. I think it would be nice to feel whole. My fear of ending up alone. My fear that people are talking about me behind my furry back. My feelings of inadequacy. My general feeling of difference.
>
> (2016, pp. 189, 192)

Through the concept of "halfie," Jarrar highlights the stigma associated with being biracial in America. The story explores the notion of fullness in diasporic identity and the attempts to fit in. The question is whether the general society accepts this segment of people, and how biracial people see themselves. Eventually embracing her biracial identity, Zelwa represents the Arab immigrant in the United States and their endeavors to accommodate and accept their differences.

Moreover, in her collection, Jarrar explores the issue of domestic violence among Arab American communities. In the story "Grace," a seven-year-old, Grace, is kidnapped when her mother and sister leave her alone at a supermarket. Along with other children, she grows up in a cult led entirely by women. Grace finds strangers, kidnappers, more caring than her parents. Jarrar here satirically showcases parents' abuse of their children to the extent that they feel safe at the hands of kidnappers. Similarly, in "Accidental Transients," a young Arab American woman strives to gain agency. Dina is a hairdresser and teacher still living with her large family: her father, her younger brother, and his Catholic wife and twin sons. She hates being considered a mother figure since her mother passed away. Dina wants to move out and be independent. She introduces herself as a "twenty-nine-year-old virgin and still living at home seventy-five miles away from any Arabs. Baba says he wants us to be our own, self-sustaining community" (p. 98). The story explores the idea of female independence in a family of conservative values. Dina describes her family as follows:

> We are the kind of Muslims who pray for tax breaks (Baba), Nintendo DS games (Jaseem), anatomy coloring books (Waseem), pussy (Abe), and a guilt-free conscience to move the fuck out of the house (Yours Truly). The one thing keeping us from being outright atheists is that none of us had ever eaten pork. We were bound to God through the absence of pig grease.
>
> (2016, p. 103)

The story delineates the difficulty of integrating for Arab Americans. The whole family depends on Dina, embodying the family's female figure, to serve them and organize their lives. Even if she is too young to manage the affairs of a big family, Dina is obliged to take such a role unwillingly. The self-alienating dysfunctional family confines Dina to the house and limits her chances of identity construction and integration.

Jarrar exposes the domestic intricacies that Arab American women are subjected to in their quest for agency. "Lost in Freakin' Yonkers" is a story about a pregnant girl disowned by her family. Aida is urged to convert her irresponsible boyfriend, James, to Islam so that the family can accept her and her unborn baby. Violence foreshadows their entire relationship. When Aida decides to let her father know about her pregnancy, she leaves a note on his desk at work, and his reply is harsh: "If you have the child, we will no longer be your family. You will be dead to us forever (2016, p. 40). Aida ultimately chooses the baby and remains with her boyfriend. However, she eventually realizes that James is not the right person to have a child with. She is not the only one disowned, and the collection presents many other characters displaced through different circumstances such as divorce, war, troubled relationships, and kidnapping. The extent of violence in the story is extreme, and Aida complains that "in my entire life every man who's claimed he loved me hit me" (p. 50).

Jarrar does not focus exclusively on identity issues since this theme, according to Kołodziejczyk, limits "the migrant experience to the struggle for recognition in the process of settling down, or to related problems of fitting in, and losing and gaining in translation" (2018, p. 114). Similarly, Darwich and Harb propose examining "the characters' diasporic experiences in terms of gendered and classed racialization, self-representation, and political determination" (2018, p. 314). Ultimately, Jarrar exposes the threads and interconnections that govern Arab American society. The stories depict cultural fallout, and Jarrar raises a voice against injustices and mistreatment of women. Even in the United States, the Muslim female body bears the weight of the conflict between Arab and non-Arab cultures. Nidali, the rebellious girl, exists in Jarrar's fiction either as an immature girl, teenager, mum, or independent woman. Jarrar depicts the life of this girl in many of her stories. Many of the stories include abusive men and Jarrar provides an overview of the nature of abusers and how their minds work. Nevertheless, she does not offer alternatives or positive examples.

Jarrar attempts to foreground Arab feminism and traditions and to present an Arab feminist in order to validate her narrative. In "How Can I Be of Use to You?" Jarrar invokes the famous Egyptian writer and activist Nawal Al-Saadawi, under the name "Mansoura." The narrator argues that every young Arab woman academic or writer falls under Mansoura's spell at some point in her life (2016, p. 53). Jarrar also injects her story with Al-Saadawi's thoughts in a satirical manner. The most interesting part is Mansoura's decoding of restroom signs. She explains that "the female symbol is docile, upright, standing there, arms akimbo, as if asking 'how can I be of use to you? How can I comfort you, help you, give myself to further you?' Meanwhile, the male symbol is virile, a penis pointing outward, always exploring, moving forward, the arrow saying 'I am busy, I am important, I am on my way to conquering something, someone, somewhere'" (p. 57). What impresses the narrator is how Mansoura finds signs of oppression in everyday life.

In summary, Randa Jarrar attempts to define what "home" means to a Palestinian growing up in a diaspora. Her characters cultivate their own conception of home. "Home" for her characters exists in many places. Her collection of short stories explores various thematic concerns and offers a semi-realistic view into the Arab American community in the United States. Jarrar's Arab American characters are depicted as trying to forge identities and carve a space for themselves in this world. More importantly, Jarrar's characters struggle with the legacy of their Arab cultural heritage and the negative perceptions of Middle Eastern women.

SEE ALSO: Abu-Jaber, Diana; Alameddine, Rabih

REFERENCES

Albakry, Mohammed and Siler, Jonathan. (2012). Into the Arab-American borderland: bilingual creativity in Randa Jarrar's *Map of Home*. *Arab Studies Quarterly* 34 (2): 109–121.

Alghaberi, Jameel. (2018). The concept of "home" in Palestinian diaspora fiction: a critical study of Randa Jarrar's fiction. *Langkawi: Journal of the Association for Arabic and English* 4 (1): 13–20. https://doi.org/10.31332/lkw.v4i1.765

Appiah, Anthony. (2006). *Cosmopolitanism: Ethics in a World of Strangers*. New York: Norton.

Bujupaj, Ismet. (2016). Parents and daughters in two novels by Arab American authors: "Khalas, Let Her Go." *Anafora* 3 (2): 185–210.

Darwich, Lynn and Harb, Sirene. (2018). Violent intersectionalities and experiences of marked Arabness in Randa Jarrar's *A Map of Home*. *Arab Studies Quarterly* 40 (4): 300–318.

Farid, Farid. (2016). Author Randa Jarrar draws inspiration from Arabs around the world for her latest book. *The National* (October 4, 2016). https://www.thenationalnews.com/arts-culture/author-randa-jarrar-draws-inspiration-from-arabs-around-the-world-for-her-latest-book-1.154641 (accessed September 24, 2021).

Georgiou, Myria. (2010). Identity, space and the media: thinking through diaspora. *Revue Européenne des Migrations Internationales* 26 (1): 17–35. https://doi.org/10.4000/remi.5028

Jarrar, Randa. (2008). *A Map of Home*. New York: Penguin Books.

Jarrar, Randa. (2014a). Why I can't stand white belly dancers. *Salon* (March 5, 2014). https://www.salon.com/2014/03/04/why_i_cant_stand_white_belly_dancers/ (accessed July 4, 2021).

Jarrar, Randa. (2014b). I still can't stand white belly dancers. *Salon* (March 19, 2014). https://www.salon.com/2014/03/18/i_still_cant_stand_white_belly_dancers/ (accessed July 4, 2021).

Jarrar, Randa. (2016). *Him, Me, Muhammad Ali*. Louisville, KY: Sarabande Books.

Kołodziejczyk, Dorota. (2018). From exile to migrancy: Eastern and Central European models of cosmopolitical writing. *Journal of Austrian-American History* 2 (2): 91–115.

FURTHER READING

Al Maleh, Layla. (2009). *Arab Voices in Diaspora: Critical Perspectives on Anglophone Arab Literature*. Amsterdam: Rodopi.

Friedman, Susan. (2018). Cosmopolitanism, religion, diaspora: Kwame Anthony Appiah and contemporary Muslim women's writing. *New Literary History* 49 (2): 199–225.

Hanafi, Sari. (2003). Rethinking Palestinians abroad as a diaspora: the relationship between diaspora and the Palestinian Territories. *Hagar: International Social Science Review* 4 (1–2): 157–182.

Naguib, Assmaa. (2011). *Representations of "Home" from the Setting of "Exile": Novels by Arab Migrant Writers*. Exeter, UK: University of Exeter Press.

Salaita, Steven. (2011). *Modern Arab American Fiction: A Reader's Guide*. Syracuse, NY: Syracuse University Press.

Saloul, Ihab. (2012). *Catastrophe and Exile in the Modern Palestinian Imagination: Telling Memories*. New York: Palgrave Macmillan.

Schulz, Helena and Hammer, Juliane. (2003). *The Palestinian Diaspora: Formation of Identities and Politics of Homeland*. New York: Routledge.

Jen, Gish

BILING CHEN
University of Central Arkansas, USA

Growing up under a set of parents from China, Gish Jen (b. 1955), like any other children of Asian immigrants, was expected to fulfill the American Dream by becoming a doctor, a lawyer, or a businessperson. Thanks to the encouragement of her professor Robert Fitzgerald at Harvard, Jen continued her long-time interest in writing and majored in English. After a stint as an entry-level editor in a publishing company, she, at the urge of her family, entered the MBA program at Stanford but dropped out shortly. Following a year of teaching English in China, Jen pursued an MFA at the University of Iowa, and soon started to get her short stories published in various magazines. During the 1980s mainstream American readers and the publishing industry were largely unaware of the cultural nationalism and ethnic nationalism that had been simmering within the Asian American community ever since the Civil Rights movement. The sense that Asian Americans were exotic and mysterious entities remained in the imagination of the American majority. Thus, writers of Asian origins, for all their efforts to assert their American identity while coming to terms with their ancestral values, could not shed their image of perpetual foreigners, and their works, fiction or nonfiction, were constantly received as a voyeuristic window to Asian ways of living rather than as a representation of Asian American hybridity in the contemporary United States. It was in such a milieu that Jen made it her primary goal to write the kind of fiction that would not be read as an autobiography or a memoir in disguise. To achieve her goal of de-exoticizing Chinese Americans, the author moves her characters out of Chinatown, highlighting their acculturation into American society while avoiding the appropriation of myths, legends, and folklore from the old world – a trait permeated in the writings of her predecessors such as Maxine Hong Kingston. Moreover, Jen employs humor and wit – skills and characteristics rarely associated with Asian American ethnicity – to address racial discrimination, ethnic stereotyping, and identity politics.

Typical American (1991), Jen's first novel, demonstrates how the pursuit of the American Dream could help ameliorate the old-world feudalism embedded in immigrant communities while examining the discrepancies between the myth and reality of this ideology. The protagonist Ralph Chang, coming from an upper-class family in Shanghai and receiving a PhD at an American university, initially puts himself above working-class Chinese immigrants until he almost fails to get tenure, gets seduced by commercial real estate, loses his shirt, and switches to a restaurant business. In traditional Chinese culture, the literati and academics occupy the highest position on the social spectrum whereas the merchant class, the lowest. Chang's downfall ironically serves as a first step for him and his family to reinvent and transform themselves to "typical Americans" – a derogatory term Chang and his wife used to express their disapproval of certain "vices" that mainstream Americans see as merits, including self-advertisement, unrestrained social ambition, and greed. Although the Changs' emergence from their financial crisis represents a typical immigrant success story, the novel also cautions the danger of insatiable chase after the almighty dollar rooted in American capitalism and central to middle-class American values.

Jen's second novel *Mona in the Promised Land* (1997) challenges the popular American belief that you can be whoever you want to be, evaluating the extent of personal freedom and social acceptance a minority member is allowed when the matter of self-fashioning shifts from economic advancement to cultural identity. Ralph Chang's achievement of prosperity might affirm the national image of the United States as a land of opportunity and equality, but his daughter Mona's decision to transcend her ethnic origin and find her true self in Judaism encounters resistance at home and raises some eyebrows in society. Portrayed with sympathy and humor, the novel invites the reader to question why a Chinese Jew is a peculiar – if not downright laughable – notion, whereas a white amateur Japanologist like Mona's Jewish boyfriend, Seth, is deemed admirably multicultural. To what extent does one's race become a liability and reduce the legitimacy of one's voluntary identity-switching? Would the majority of people in the United States accept that a Chinese American could know more about as well as identify with Jewish culture more than with Chinese tradition?

An insider of the liberal camp but an outsider of the dominant race, Jen has a unique radar that helps her detect the unconscious racism among certain white liberals. The Civil Rights movement encouraged minorities to take pride in their heritage as a way to counter society's biases against them, but multiculturalism could also be used as a tool by mainstream America to push people of color back to their ethnic enclave. Pammie and Sven's Galatea-Pygmalion marriage in "House, House, Home" – the final story in Jen's third book, *Who's Irish?* (1999) – is such a case. Through the couple's arguments about the purposes of art, Jen subtly exposes the disparities between socially imposed isolation and self-inflicted alienation, while poking fun at the trends of roots-finding, of bourgeoisie-bashing, and of restless experimentation popular among the liberals in the 1960s and 1970s. The former college art lecturer, lacking the will to finish his dissertation and the talent to become an artist, tries to force his new-found interest in traditional Chinese painting on his Chinese American wife, a young architect in favor of applied art. The couple's unbalanced power relation serves as a microcosm of racial inequality in American society, showing that it is one thing to appreciate an ethnic minority's ancestral culture and absorb it to expand one's humanity; it is, however, quite another thing to appropriate it to conceal one's sense of inadequacy and aggrandize one's progressive image.

White Americans do not have the monopoly of racism, and Jen does not hesitate to mock the same mindset possessed by minorities. Her widely anthologized short story "Who's Irish" reveals a sixty-eight-year-old Chinese immigrant's prejudices toward her chronically depressed and unemployed Irish American son-in-law. The first-person narrator, taking advantage of her listener's unfamiliarity with Chinese culture, warps Confucian sayings from *The Analects* to criticize her daughter's derailment from filial piety simply because she shares her husband's views about childrearing, mental health, and gender role flexibility. Binary reasoning permeates her monologue; anything Chinese is supreme whereas anything Irish or American is flawed. Her worldview of authoritarian discipline versus self-expression; Confucian work ethics versus Western social welfare; and tough love versus tender loving care mirrors Orientalist fascination with and stereotyping of Asians as being self-possessed yet inscrutable; hardworking yet boring; and dedicated to their children yet insistent on corporal punishment. The elderly woman's subconscious phobia of miscegenation reflects a commonly practiced but rarely acknowledged habit we all share: the same traits in different people are often given different adjectives and interpreted positively or negatively according to one's culturally informed personal preferences. Categorizing individual characteristics based on ethic or national origins betrays the attempt to scapegoat and self-exonerate in a post-industrial America where various generations, genders, and races compete with one another for the increasingly unachievable American Dream.

By 2000 Jen has well-established herself in the literary field and thus feels emboldened to experiment her narrative strategy and explore how adoption impacts an interracial marriage and American society as a whole – a topic yet to be fully addressed in literary fiction then. *The Love Wife* (2004) is Jen's contemplation on what constitutes a "real" family and a "real" United States of America. Married to a Chinese American, Blondie has tremendous anxiety about her status as the only white member in the Wong family. Her inability to communicate in Chinese with the two daughters she and her husband adopted from China causes her fear of losing her family's love to the Chinese nanny hired by her mother-in-law on account of their shared racial and cultural roots. Although Blondie's worries are the impetus of the novel, some chapters are told by the first-person voices of other characters. By so doing, the author allows all major characters to tell their own stories that could shed a different light on one another's narratives. The intricate plot and cacophonous soliloquies correspond to the characters' inner struggles as well as their tensions with one another; identities by descent battle heart-wrenchingly with identifications by consent. In terms of narrative structure, *The Love Wife* can be seen as a worthy exercise for Jen's next book, *World and Town* (2010).

Troubled by the post-9/11 American xenophobia and intolerance of non-Christians,

Jen imagines a corrective, depicting in *World and Town* how a group of retirees, while dealing with their own physical, financial, and existential crises related to aging, help a traumatized Cambodian refugee family adjust to the New England life. World religions and living philosophies collide here. Christian fundamentalism clashes with Confucian secularism in the friendship between Sophy Chung and Hattie Kong. The Cambodian teenager, unable to find nurturance from her Buddhist mother and alcoholic father, seeks a sense of belonging in an Evangelical church, but the retired biology teacher wants to save her from the narrow faith that her own Caucasian maternal grandparents used to impose on her. The widow, meanwhile, strives to reach a Daoist state of magnanimity through practicing Chinese landscape painting, so that she could handle the request of her *feng shui* obsessed Hong Kong relatives to relocate the bones of her deceased parents. The conflicts between sense and sensibility, between science and spirituality, and between autonomy and intimacy dominate the novel. The distinct voices the author gives her characters and their authentic endeavors to deal with the injuries human beings have done to themselves and to one another through political, economic, and religious wars makes *World and Town* a *tour de force*.

Jen ventures into the genre of dystopia in her latest novel, *The Resisters* (2020). The encroachment of high tech upon democracy and people's daily lives propels Jen to envision the near future of the United States: an AutoAmerica where new forms of classism and racism are practiced. Heathens, people of color, and individuals with learning disability or physical handicap, are lumped to a class called Surplus, whose only legal employment is to be consumers with universal basic income provided by the governing class consisting of fair-skinned folks with the "right" faith, IQ, and health that allow them to attend college and work. This elite class, also known as AuntNettie due to its control of the Internet and various surveillance devices, holds the state apparatus and thus the political and economic power of the country. Typical of her humor, Jen plays on the double meaning of "surplus." The word could mean "superfluous," alluding to the sense of uselessness pervasive among the nineteenth-century Russian intelligentsia. The slightly dispirited Grant who lost his teaching job under the current system because of his Afro-Caribbean ancestry, is an example. Uselessness imposed from without, however, cannot annihilate the human desire to fight against one's dire circumstances. Grant's wife, Eleanor, rather than wallowing in misery, sues the government for poisoning the Surplus class with chemically contaminated food. Their daughter, Gwen, while training for the Olympics as a baseball pitcher to beat team ChinRussia, subverts AutoAmerica's plan for her by pitching in an underground baseball league and engaging in the activities that AuntNettie considers non-essential to the progress of society, such as knitting and gardening. It is in Eleanor and Gwen the other meaning of surplus is revealed: just as surplus cash can be constructively utilized, surplus people can embody the extra value of humanity that is being besieged.

Besides fiction writing, Jen has published two nonfiction books. An intellectual autobiography based on the Massey Lectures she delivered at Harvard University in 2012 was published in the following year, titled *Tiger Writing: Art, Culture, and the Interdependent Self*.

Preparing the Massey Lectures gives the author a good opportunity to reflect on her tendency to "over-story" her novel and on her reluctance to center her narrative on a single protagonist according to the rule of Western modern fiction. She finds from cross-cultural psychology two terms to articulate her hybridity – interdependent self and independent self – and attributes her "digressive" narrative style to her interdependent self, mostly cultivated by her Chinese upbringing. In the process of writing, her interdependent self constantly interacts with her American independent self, desiring to have an equal say. Those who are familiar with cultures where the self is mostly defined by his or her relationships with others rather than by the individual's uniqueness need not search hard to find that such Eastern classics as *A Thousand and One Nights* and *The Dream of Red Chamber* are written in a meandering narrative style and with a large ensemble cast. Jen wonders if individualism in the West today has ceased to be liberating but has become a prison, in which the practitioners of this ideology navel-gaze at their jealously guarded independent self, oblivious of the humanity of others. Thus, she strongly feels that it was time for Western writers, literary critics, and general readers to expand their vision of the novel by learning from Eastern literary traditions and adopting a different artistic lens.

In the same vein, *The Girl at the Baggage Claim: Explaining the East-West Cultural Gap* (2017) investigates causes of the West's misunderstanding of the East. East and West in this book mainly refer to East Asian societies and the United States. Jen, speaking mostly to people in the West who do not know much about the East, hopes that in addition to literary people, lawyers and businesspeople will find this book very relevant to what they are doing. The story of the Asian girl in the title – the story about her admission into Milton Academy by having her sister, who spoke better English, do a Skype interview for her with the school – is used as "a jump-off point" to discuss issues ranging from selfhood and education to intellectual properties and brand names. By the standards of Western society, where the big pit self/independent self prevails, the sisters' behavior is unethical and the girl deserves expulsion. But to people brought up in East Asia, where the flexi-self/interdependent self dominates, her cheating is no serious than getting a parking ticket in the West. For siblings are each other's flesh and blood – the boundary between self and other in this case is beside the point. Western education emphasizes individual disposition and self-discovery, while East Asian approach values drilling and mastering inherited skills and knowledge. As modern Western culture glorifies geniuses and individual achievements, the fact that all groundbreaking inventions are built upon the efforts of varied predecessors and contemporaries tends to be neglected. But East Asians' understanding that no induvial alone can build Rome leads many of them to think that borrowing and refining others' ideas to create new products for profit does not constitute an act of violation. Jen is aware of the danger of binary generalization. By taking the risk of sounding dualistic, the author is in essence creating a temporary structure for her readers to understand the two fundamentally divergent mindsets, while at the same time reminding them that culture, like identity, is not set in stone but constantly changing, and that in the applications and evaluations of values, historical and cultural contexts should be taken into consideration.

SEE ALSO: Border Fictions; The Culture Wars; Kingston, Maxine Hong; Lahiri, Jhumpa; Lee, Chang-rae; Mukherjee, Bharati; Ng, Celeste; Post-9/11 Narrative; Tan, Amy; Updike, John

FURTHER READING

Chen, Bi-ling. (2012). A grandmother's seduction: narrative slippage and ethnic othering in Gish Jen's "Who's Irish?" *Journal of Ethnic American Literature* 2: 73–91.

George, Joseph. (2015). The gaps in the wall: the enemy within Gish Jen's American dreams. In: *The Good Life and the Greater Good in a Global*

Context (ed. Laura S. Walker), 173–189. Lanham, MD: Lexington Books.

Ho, Jennifer Ann. (2015). *Understanding Gish Jen*. Columbia: University of South Carolina Press.

Johnson, Charles

YOMNA SABER
Qatar University, Qatar

"I write imaginative, philosophical fiction that is frequently anchored in massive historical research," says Charles R. Johnson (Ghosh 2004, p. 377). Born on April 23, 1948, in Evanston, Illinois, to Benjamin Lee and Ruby Elizabeth Johnson, Johnson is an African American novelist, cartoonist, philosopher, academic and literature scholar. He received his BS in journalism from Southern Illinois University in 1971, his MA in philosophy in 1973, and his PhD in philosophy in 1976 from State University of New York at Stony Brook. In 1970 he married Joan New and his children are Malik (b. 1975) and Elizabeth (b. 1981). He converted into Buddhism in 1981. Johnson started his academic career at the University of Washington in 1976 until his retirement in 2009. Initially, Johnson embarked on pursuing a career as a cartoonist (1965–1972). In 1970, he published *Black Humor*, his first collection of cartoons, followed by his second collection *Half-Past Nation Time* in 1972, and one year later, he published his first article, "Creating the Political Cartoon," in *Scholastic Editor*. Meeting John Gardner, a novelist and Professor of English at Southern Illinois University in 1972, had an undeniable impact upon Johnson's ideological paradigm. Acting as his mentor, Gardner offered his tutelage to Johnson who had already written six apprentice novels without getting any of them published. With the help of Gardner's guidance and in light of his critical feedback, Johnson wrote his seventh novel, *Faith and the Good Thing*, which was published in 1974, marking the beginning of Johnson's career as one of the imminently distinguished voices in fiction in the African American canon.

Johnson's approach to fiction is multilayered and avant-gardist in perspective and technique. He explains his stance: "As I looked at black American literature, it occurred to me that there was a great void in respect to philosophical fiction" (McWilliams 2004, p. 211). His debut novel features Faith Cross the protagonist who confusedly follows her mother's legacy to get the good thing in life and the Swamp Woman's advice to leave Georgia and head north to Chicago. The novel weaves elements of the uncanny, naturalism, realism, myth, folk tale and the supernatural as Faith passes through various stages in the city including drugs and prostitution, a loveless marriage, and a failed affair until she dies while giving birth and her soul flies back to Georgia to metamorphose into the Swamp Woman. The novel invited several comparisons with Richard Wright's *Native Son* (1940). However, Johnson frees his protagonist from the constraints of protest literature and racial essentialist identity as Faith is not tragically defeated by the racist city like Bigger Thomas, Wright's protagonist, who ends up murdering two women and being executed. Johnson relies on the Black vernacular in his novel and the fact that Faith eventually emerges as a conjure woman marks her victory, not downfall. Johnson's use of the supernatural is going to appear in almost all his following fiction.

Published in 1982, *Oxherding Tale* is a neo-slave, passing narrative that could also be categorized as an allegory and a parable. Set in the antebellum South and through its two sections, "Home and Field" and "The White World," Johnson traces his biracial protagonist Andrew Hawkins on a journey from slavery to freedom, in which he learns that bondage shackles are physical, spiritual, sexual and psychological. Andrew is conceived after a satirical joke in which the plantation owner Jonathan Polkinghorne gets drunk and allows his Black butler to sleep with his wife. Navigating Black and white worlds with a conflation of past and present narratives and the intrusion of flashbacks, Andrew Hawkins's metaphysical quest features picaresque ventures, sexual jaunts, and ontological questions. In the Black world of the plantation, Andrew is unable to embrace his father's nationalism that results in a rebellion leading to his death. He becomes a fugitive slave in the white world where he finds it equally difficult to assimilate even when he assumes a white identity. He is sexually enslaved by the old farm mistress, Flo Hatfield, and loses his true love Minty who dies. The conflict Andrew endures is related to issues of identity and selfhood as a Black man, an educated mulatto who knows Ezekiel and Karl Marx, and a seeker of Eastern philosophy and of emancipation. It is only when he realizes the unison of all beings that Andrew understands that the self is not a real entity, it is non-fixed and always in flux. Andrew eventually attains his freedom when he embraces his past as a slave and his future outside the dogmatic framework of racial identity. He sees himself as a human being. Owing to its unorthodox plot and complex meaning, *Oxherding Tale* was rejected by more than twenty publishers before seeing the light. However, it is quite significant in his career as Johnson emphasizes, "I whimsically called [it] my 'platform novel' because it became the foundation for the ten books I published after it, none of which I would have cared to do if I hadn't completed *Ox*" (McWilliams 2004, p. xi). The novel paves the way for his philosophical enquiries in fiction, questions of slavery and freedom, transcendence, the intersection of Eastern and Western thoughts, the quest from darkness to light, intersubjectivity and relating all those themes to the self in general, and the Black self in particular.

Johnson's third novel *Middle Passage* won the National Book Award in 1990, making him the second African American writer after Ralph Ellison to win that prestigious accolade. The novel, often compared to Melville's *Moby Dick* (1851), can be read as an extension of the philosophical queries and themes Johnson has explored in his previous works; namely, freedom and slavery. Rutherford Calhoun, a newly emancipated slave and minor thief, boards a slave ship, ironically named *The Republic*, as a stowaway, to escape paying his debts to Papa Zeringue or marrying Isadora Bailey. Like Andrew Hawkins, Calhoun is a roguish trickster figure who is faced with two worlds, the dualistic world of Ebenezer Falcon the captain, who believes in Manifest Destiny and adopts a dichotomous dogma of binaries that justifies slavery in which the strong reigns over the weak. The other world is that of the African slaves, from the fictitious Allmuseri tribe, who hold the doctrine of the Unity of Being, which discards materialism and dualities that create false hierarchies. According to their worldview, possessiveness is coterminous with egotism, and the mind and body are not split but integrated. The slaves go on mutiny and free themselves of their shackles and when the ship, hit by a storm, is about to sink, the captain commits suicide. As those two worlds clash physically and intellectually in a perilous sea journey, Calhoun learns that to attain freedom, he needs to conquer his uncanny feeling of alienation and to renounce his preconceived notions of the racial self. Freedom from slavery does not imply utter freedom for Calhoun is still imprisoned in other forms of subservience to hegemonic ideological institutions that define him as a Black man. It is only when he adopts the mystical doctrines of Allmuseri tribe that he is able to overcome his sense of estrangement from humanity. His final decision to adopt one of the Allmuseri kids and to marry Isadora proves that Calhoun has learned the lesson and got rid of his old irresponsible self. The novel is a sea adventure, a philosophical tale, a historical story and a slave narrative, which renders it a cross genre par excellence. Johnson borrows an interesting description for it, "One of my colleagues says it starts out as a picaresque and it goes into being an epic and then it becomes a romance, and that's fairly accurate" (McWilliams 2004, p. 127). The political undercurrents of the narrative are quite significant as it dives deeply into questions of race, identity, slavery and freedom, showing Johnson's firm belief that accepting fixated racial and historical identities is not only restrictive, but also potentially disparaging.

Dreamer (1998) introduces a different realm in Johnson's fiction. In his previous novels, he established a whole world for every story as he explains, "*Middle Passage* is a sea story, the universe of a sea story that they're moving around in. Or in *Oxherding Tale*, it's the universe of the slave narrative. Or in *Faith and the Good Thing*, it's the universe of the folk tale" (McWilliams 2004, p.165). *Dreamer*, however, roams another terrain. Johnson merges history and fiction in retelling the last years in the life of Martin Luther King setting the novel in summer 1966 in Chicago, when King headed the Chicago Freedom Movement against racial segregation. The narrative introduces Chaym Smith who bears a startling physical resemblance to King and offers to act as his stand-in and his doppelgänger. Whereas the previous protagonists of Johnson's novels, according to him, were "adventurers of ideas, truth-seekers (and thus have the philosophical impulse, even when they're not trained philosophers), and hunger for wisdom" (McWilliams 2004, pp. 228–229), the character who undertakes this philosophical odyssey in *Dreamer* is the narrator Matthew Bishop. A dedicated disciple of King, Bishop develops as he sees King and Smith side by side. His first impression of Chaym is "the kind of Negro the Movement had for years kept away from the world's cameras: sullen, ill-kept, the very embodiment of the blues" (Johnson 1999, p. 33). Chaym, whose name is etymologically derived from Cain, is King's id; the shadow that must be concealed and the figure that the Civil Rights movement deliberately turned a blind eye to. Like King, he is well-grounded in theology and philosophy but his upbringing in the urban ghetto leaves a different imprint upon his character. The biblical mythos of Cain suggests the otherness that Chaym brings into the world of Bishop as he mirrors King dialectically. It also brings the tragic fate of Cain who challenged the Father and bore the burden of the inner conflict of selfish egoism and a relentless search for identity. Cain is a union of incongruities just like Chaym Smith who equally stirs repulsion and compassion in Bishop. The assassination of King echoes the murder of Abel, and when asked about Chaym in King's funeral, Bishop says he is everywhere. His answer alludes to the fact that, eventually, the likes of Cain survive and the likes of Abel are sacrificed; an idea which is further explored in Johnson's 1996 essay "The King We Left Behind." Although King is not the protagonist of the novel and he remains a static character, his presence is looming. Johnson points out the three reasons that made him choose King as an iconic Black figure in particular, "One was nonviolence as not just a strategy for civil rights demonstrations, but as a way of life, *a way of life*, as a constant meditation socially for all of us. Then another one, of course, is agape, or unconditional love. This was very important to him. The third one is integration, understood in the most profound sense of the interconnectedness of all life" (McWilliams 2004, p. 239). He explains that King was not concerned with any specificity of racial identity like Malcolm X; he emerged mainly as a humanist with the potential to lead all Americans, which echoes resonantly with Johnson's philosophical paradigm of transcending racial stereotypical doctrines of identity.

Johnson's career witnessed the publication of two significant collections of short stories. *The Sorcerer's Apprentice* (1986) and *Soulcatcher and Other Stories* (2000). The former is a collection of eight stories in which Johnson creates symbolic fables and admonitory tales. Some of those stories are quite dark such as "The Education of Mingo," which is the most anthologized story from the collection; it is a Frankenstein tale about a white master, Moses Green, who buys and educates a slave, who ends up murdering two white people. The story broaches myriad philosophical questions as Johnson clarifies, "Who is responsible for the actions of a person who has been stripped of their culture and oppressed? Is it Moses Green or Mingo? And then the other question in there was, 'What is education? To teach another person, what in the world does that mean? What are you teaching?'" (McWilliams 2004, p. 177). The story equally explores the master-slave relationship. Mingo the slave is also his master's double and his acts of murder could be interpreted as the repressed desires of Moses, who eventually helps his slave to escape instead of turning him in to the police. His acts of murder become his acts of liberation because by the end of the story Mingo is the master of the scene. They could also be the ironic result of Moses's utter failure in acculturating his slave, who ends up enforcing the very image Moses was trying to eliminate. The story represents themes of revenge, mastery, stereotype, misunderstanding and otherness from a philosophically deep perspective. "Popper's Disease," however, is a science fiction story in which a middle-aged Black physician heals an alien, and "The Sorcerer's Apprentice" is another gothic story in which a magician decides to go against his guiding mentor. Johnson also experiments with techniques in other stories such as "Moving Pictures" which depends primarily on narrative exposition without conventional dramatic scenes. "Menagerie, a Child's Fable" is based on George Orwell's *Animal Farm* (1945), in which the owner of a pet shop, Mr. Tilford, disappears and the animals take charge of the shop ending up in a disastrous fire and bloodshed. The story brings back Johnson's auspicious themes of freedom, discrimination, and coercion of the weak.

Soulcatcher (2001) is a collection of twelve short stories. The project grew out of Johnson's collaboration with journalist Patricia Smith in 1998 on a TV series under the title *Africans in America* airing on PBS. Johnson's stories were presented as fictitious intrusions upon Smith's commentary on specific historical events, giving corresponding and contending viewpoints on those events. The stories move chronologically since the time of slavery until the outbreak of the Civil War, blending the genres of biography, history, journalism, epistolary, and metafiction. "The Transmission" starts off the collection with the Middle Passage told in third-person limited point of view. "Confession" gives a controlling voice to the slave Tiberius, which renders it a third-person monologue. "Poetry and Politics" features one scene without any narrative; it is an extended dialogue taking place between Phyllis Wheatley and her mistress. "A Soldier for the Crown" is in second-person point of view, whereas "Martha's Dilemma" is in first person because as Johnson explains, "we need to hear the urgency in her voice and the immediacy of her grief and fear after her husband, George, dies. And, yes, we as readers need to have the same perceptual limitations she has, not knowing until midway through the story how eager their slaves are for her demise so they can be free" (McWilliams 2004, p. 274). "The Plague" is fictional diary entries by the

Rev. Richard Allen, founder of the African Methodist Episcopal church and Johnson says that this form is chosen to provide "a necessary reflective and philosophical feel to the musings of Reverend Richard Allen" (p. 274), "A Report from St. Dominique" is a letter, and "The People Speak" is a hoax newspaper article. "Soulcatcher" shifts from the slave's point of view to that of the slave hunter with an omniscient authorial presence in the text. "A Lion at Pendelton" blends prose and verse, "The Mayor's Tale" as the title might indicate is a fairy tale, and "Murderous Thoughts" is a polyphonic piece with a variety of voices giving first-person monologues. The stories have been criticized as didactic; however, Johnson's various techniques of storytelling are quite remarkable in this collection.

In addition to Johnson's fiction, he has also published television scripts *Charlie Smith and the Fritter Tree and Booker* (1978), a significant book on criticism entitled *Being and Race: Black Writing Since 1970* (1988), and a collection of essays on Buddhism *Turning the Wheel: Essays on Buddhism and Writing* (2003), a collection of stories and tales *Dr. King's Refrigerator and Other Bedtime Stories* (2005), *Taming the Ox: Buddhist Stories, and Reflections on Politics, Race, Culture, and Spiritual Practice* (2014), *The Way of the Writer: Reflections on the Art and Craft of Storytelling* (2016), a collection of stories *Night Hawks: Stories* (2018), *Papa Chuck's Twisted Tales* (2020), a history of pirates worldwide *Pirates* (2020), *Grand: A Grandparent's Wisdom for a Happy Life* (2020). Other publications in collaboration with others include: *Black Men Speaking* (with John McCluskey, Jr., 1997), *I Call Myself an Artist: Writings by and about Charles Johnson* (edited by Rudolph Byrd, 1999), *King: The Photobiography of Martin Luther King Jr.* (with Bob Adelman, 2000), *Philosophy: An Innovative Introduction: Fictive Narrative, Primary Texts, and Responsive Writing* (with Michael Boylan, 2010), *The Adventures of Emery Jones, Boy Science Wonder: Bending Time* (with Elisheba Johnson, 2013). Johnson won myriad awards throughout his career including: *Callaloo* Creative Writing Award (1983), Prix Jeunesse Award and Guggenheim Fellowship (1987), "Talented Tenth Award," awarded by Alpha Kappa Alpha/Kappa Psi (1991), MacArthur Fellowship (1998), Academy Award for Literature from the American Academy of Arts and Letters (2002), and The Humanities Washington Award (2013).

SEE ALSO: After Postmodernism; Black Atlantic; Butler, Octavia; Kincaid, Jamaica; Marshall, Paule; Mixed-Genre Fiction; Post-Soul and/or Post-Black Fiction; Reed, Ishmael; The New Experimentalism/The Contemporary Avant Garde; Urban Fiction

REFERENCES

Ghosh, Nibir K. (2004). From narrow complaint to broad celebration: a conversation with Charles Johnson. *MELUS* 29 (3/4): 359–378.

McWilliams, Jim. (ed.) (2004). *Passing the Three Gates: Interviews with Charles Johnson*. Seattle: University of Washington Press.

FURTHER READING

Byrd, Rudolph P. (2005). *Charles Johnson's Novels: Writing the American Palimpsest*. Bloomington: Indiana University Press.

Kim, Kwangsoon. (2015). Becoming William Harris: deterritorialization of Black identity in Charles Johnson's *Oxherding Tale*. *CLA Journal* 59 (1): 20–32.

Mendieta, Eduardo. (2017). Forms of transference: on Charles Johnson's philosophical fiction. *Pluralist* 12 (1): 30–37.

Saber, Yomna. (2010). Self-perception while walking in the city in Charles Johnson's *Faith and the Good Thing*. In: *Urban Cultures of/in the United States: Interdisciplinary Perspectives* (ed. Andrea Carosso), 121–146. New York: Peter Lang.

Whalen-Bridge, John. (2003). Waking Cain: the poetics of integration in Charles Johnson's *Dreamer*. Callaloo 26 (2): 504–521.

Johnson, Denis

DAVID BUEHRER
Valdosta State University, USA (retired)

The son of a State Department official, Denis Hale Johnson was born in Munich in 1949 and raised in the suburbs of northern Virginia, although he moved often in his early years, with stays in Tokyo and Manila – the latter a key setting for Psy Ops officer Skip Sands in Johnson's National Book Award-winning novel *Tree of Smoke* (2007). Johnson landed for a brief stint at the Writers' Workshop at the University of Iowa, where he was nurtured in both his writing and alcoholism by Raymond Carver. He eventually settled with his third wife, Cindy Lee, in the woods of northern Idaho – but only after a period of homelessness and addiction, much of which is recorded in his semi-autobiographical first collection of interconnected stories, *Jesus' Son* (1992), which features "the scattered doings of a younger, hopelessly lost, drug-addled narrator" (Parrish 2001, p. 19) referred to throughout only as "Fuckhead." Johnson's own sense of "placelessness" is reflected in the characters of many of his works, from Bill Houston in his first novel, *Angels* (1983), to Carl Van Ness in *Already Dead: A California Gothic* (1997), to Roland Nair in his final novel, *The Laughing Monsters* (2014). Most of the "purgatorial drifters" (Juengel 2011) populating Johnson's fictional world come from the Midwestern or Western US – places like Lawrence, Kansas, for Lenny English in *Resuscitation of a Hanged Man* (1991) or the Central Valley of California for Jimmy Luntz in *Nobody Move* (2009) – and appear always to be seeking (his only book of nonfiction is titled *Seek: Reports From the Edges of America & Beyond* [2001]) a place to call home, if only temporarily, in a contemporary culture that denies that search at every turn. Johnson often gets lumped by critics among those other so-called dirty realists, like Carver, Charles Bukowski, Richard Ford, and Jayne Anne Phillips, who trade in similar themes and seedy locales. He is also acknowledged for his prose's "descriptive passages [that] show his poetic mastery" (Means 2009, p. 6) – he published two volumes of poems before turning to fiction in the early 1980s – and hallucinatory flourishes, after William Burroughs. Thus, Johnson is sometimes labeled "post-Beat," at least in early works like *Jesus' Son*, which has received the lion's share of what scant critical interest his fiction has garnered from the academy. Besides the National Book Award, Johnson was the recipient of many honors and accolades, including fellowships from the Guggenheim and Lannan Foundations, a Whiting Award, and the posthumously awarded Library of Congress Prize for American Fiction in September 2017.

Johnson's many experiments in revamping narrative genres suggest his ability to transcend narrow critical categories with his fiction. Both *Angels* and *Nobody Move* refashion the crime noir, with the latter being more self-consciously "pulpy" (Juengel 2011) in nature. *Fiskadoro* (1985) is a post-apocalyptic science fiction – ironically, perhaps "his most hopeful" novel (Connors 2008, p. 253) – set in the not-so-distant-future Florida Keys. *Resuscitation of a Hanged Man* follows a quasi-Catholic seeker, Lenny English, who leaves a corporate job in suburban Chicago for the East Coast's literal end of the road, Provincetown, MA, where his spiritual quest proves ultimately absurd. *The Name of the World* (2000), a finalist for the PEN/Faulkner Award, sends up the "campus" novel with the travails of widower Michael Reed and a young art student named Flower Cannon. The novella *Train Dreams* (2011), first published in the *Paris Review* in 2002, tells the story of a day-laborer and railroad worker in the early decades of the twentieth-century Pacific Northwest, yoking "dirty realism" – whose "effect in both subject matter and technique [...] is somewhere between the hard boiled and the darkly comic" (Rebein 2001, p. 43) – with a more traditional mode of historical fiction as well as a North American "magical realism" – and all in 116 pages. *The Laughing Monsters*, with its echoes of Greene and Conrad, as well as Johnson's own journalistic pieces from *Seek* on Charles Taylor and the Liberian Civil War of the 1990s, operates as a postmodern retake of the Anglo-American spy/soldier-of-fortune story for the post-9/11 era. Tales of shadowy, often self-exiled American expats wandering through Central America and Southeast Asia constitute the narrative cores of *The Stars at Noon* (1986) and *Tree of Smoke*, respectively. *Already Dead* is a densely plotted murder mystery and philosophical novel at once (references to Kierkegaard and Nietzsche abound) set in the marijuana-growing region of northern California. Also formally, skewed chronologies and bifurcated timelines are commonplace in Johnson's fictions, from the encyclopedic *Already Dead* and *Tree of Smoke* with their "baroque plots" (Juengel 2011), to the slight, novella-like *The Name of the World*, which shifts widely in time and geography over a shorter narrative span. Reed, this novel's protagonist, somehow goes from a middle-aged, recently widowed professor at a Midwestern college during the late 1990s back, at the novel's close, to serving as a front-line correspondent "cover[ing] [the start of] the Gulf War" in Kuwait "near the Iraqi border" in January 1991 – suggesting that his "utterly remarkable" *past* "life" (Johnson 2000, pp. 128–129) may be an invented future, a fiction the younger writer/journalist imagines for a somewhat older self.

Beyond such formal innovations, Johnson thematically often "writes of men [...] [who find] it easier to believe in God than to believe any longer in man" (Miles 1993, p. 122). In fact, a sympathy with the spiritual and desire for release from the intolerably human affects most of Johnson's figures, from Lenny English in *Resuscitation* to Kathy Jones and Skip Sands in *Tree of Smoke* to Robert Grainier in *Train Dreams* to Dink, the narrator of the story "Strangler Bob" in the posthumous collection *The Largesse of the Sea Maiden* (2018). Many of the petty criminals, addicts and alcoholics, spies and provocateurs, failed suicides and bungling murderers, hermetic widows, strung-out prostitutes, and gamblers and con men who populate Johnson's fictional landscape are lower-middle or working-class whites who, despite their rough socioeconomic backgrounds, possess "[u]nheroic disclosures of depth" and the sort of "inner lives" (Champion 2000, p. 144) hardly evident in the works of those other contemporary minimalists and neo-realists with whom Johnson is sometimes associated. For instance, in his dialogue-inflected crime noir *Nobody Move*, one of Johnson's minor characters, the former biker John Capra, says of Anita, the erstwhile heroine on the lam with protagonist Jimmy Luntz: "This one got the beauty that goes down to the bone. [. . .] I can't tell if she's powered by a lot of soul or a lot of psycho energy'" (Johnson 2009, p. 75). In Johnson's world, there's a good helping of both, as the novelist "parts company with a number of postmodern writers" by revealing the paradoxical religious and psychological nature of characters "careening toward a transformed sense of self" (Champion 2000, p. 140) in his works.

Thus, if Johnson, as "one of the last of the hard-core American realist writers [. . .] routinely explores the nature of crime" and punishment in his varied fictions, he is also obsessed with our "relation to the nature of grace (yes, grace) and the wider historical and cosmic order" (Means 2009, p. 6). While there may be no metaphysically absolute representations of God present in Johnson's work – although several of his novels are dedicated "'To H.P.,' that Higher Power that promises meaning at the far side of doubt" (Juengel 2011) – his narrators' incessant questionings, even agnosticism, speak to their need to find a transcendent space to counter the fragmented surface lives and disintegrating moral and social landscapes they inhabit. "He was a citizen of a country north of Mexico that made no sense," thinks Lenny English late in *Resuscitation* (Johnson 1991, p. 173). He is one of Johnson's many "doomed seekers, unholy prophets, [and] squalid sinners" (Connors 2008, p. 253) who nevertheless continues to see himself as a "knight of faith" (Johnson 1991, p. 43) in a profane world, epitomized for Lenny in the gay resort of Provincetown during the early 1980s. So despite the chaotic environments his characters usually live in, "Johnson's fictions typically end gesturing toward some future salvation" (Juengel 2011), as heard in Kathy Jones's repeated mantra of "All will be saved. All will be saved" on the last page of *Tree of Smoke*.

To this earnestness of religious vision Johnson has also shown a penchant for exploiting countless inter- and transtextual references within his works, "borrow[ing] freely and often from rock and roll culture" (Parrish 2001, p. 29n) in particular. For instance, the title *Jesus' Son* derives from a lyric in Lou Reed's anthem "Heroin," and in *Fiskadoro* alone, Johnson sprinkles in allusions to songs by The Rolling Stones, Bad Company, Jimmy Hendrix, Bob Marley, and Bob Dylan, among other rock performers from the late 1960s through the early 1980s. Furthermore, Johnson is known for engaging in a form of postmodern *self*-intertextuality or referentiality, whereby he recycles characters and motifs from one novel or short story to another. James and Bill Houston, for example, who at the end of Johnson's first novel, *Angels*, are "on their way to prison and death row after a bank heist gone wrong," reappear (with their mother and younger brother Burris) in 2007's *Tree of Smoke*, a sprawling, Vietnam-era narrative which serves as the "back story" for both men, "who've returned from war to a life of no purpose" (Connors 2008, p. 253) – much of that seemingly precipitated by their lower-class origins which forced them into the military to begin with. For the Houston brothers and at least a handful of other characters, *Tree* represents "the prequel we didn't know existed to Johnson's entire body of work" (p. 252). Jimmy Storm, the "quivering bird-dog sergeant" (Johnson 2007, p. 303) and Colonel Francis X. Sand's right-hand man in *Tree*, first appears during 1981 in 1991's *Resuscitation* as "a drug-runner about English's age" (Johnson 1991, p. 249), sharing a county jail cell with Lenny, who has been arrested for trying to assassinate the Catholic bishop on Cape Cod. By 1983, however, *Tree*'s Storm is back in Southeast Asia pursuing the egomaniacal and elusive Colonel (an enigmatic, Kurtz-like figure a la *Heart of Darkness* (1899) by way of *Apocalypse Now*) whom he's heard is operating a clandestine arms operation in Malaysia near the Thai border. However, like his bunkmate Lenny, who sees himself as "an institutional man" (Johnson 1991, p. 180), Storm in the earlier *Resuscitation* actually prefers incarceration to the societal reality that lies just beyond the jail's walls: "Let me out when the new millennium's here, a little chaos and shit" (p. 253). This millennial or apocalyptic fervor possesses many of Johnson's characters, who seem to be "rushing toward their doom with something like relish, as if damnation were a reward and not a punishment" (Connors 2008, p. 254) for their present existences, that "feeling that they are between lives" (Parrish 2001, p. 18) best captured in the Vietnam epic *Tree of Smoke*.

Vietnam and its legacy may in fact be the ultimate *ur*-text for Johnson, with *Tree of Smoke* – at 614 pages his longest and most intricately structured novel by far – "the historical center of his moral universe" (Juengel 2011), thematically if not chronologically. That is, many of his fictions coalesce around the "before/after" Vietnam trope, and the conflict's locus as the *purgatorio* of contemporary American consciousness. Since "the memory of Vietnam still haunts American culture and nature [. . .], [it has] irrevocably changed the American literary landscape," with "the Vietnam veteran," moreover, "a persistent protagonist in our literature" (Rebein 2001, p. 44). For instance, in Johnson's fourth novel, *Resuscitation of a Hanged Man*, Lenny English is haunted by a "tattooed ghost that was stalking him, the dead GI in Vietnam, the one who'd been drafted in Lenny's place" (Johnson 1991, p. 169). In *Tree of Smoke*, Johnson's most sustained commentary on the war's effects – the book ends in 1983, with Kathy Jones in Minnesota working for a refugee organization serving the Amerasian children of Vietnam vets – James Houston's postwar life as a criminal drifter in Arizona is emblematic of a larger cultural malaise and post-apocalyptic sensibility. Many of the lost souls in *Tree*, as elsewhere in the Dantesque cosmology of Johnson's fiction, exist in a kind of "purgatory, waiting impatiently, even expectantly, for the coming apocalypse" (Kakutani 2007). Perhaps Storm sums up this state best: "We live in the post-trash, man. [. . .] [T]here's been this unanimous worldwide decision to trash the planet and get on to a new one" (Johnson 1991, p. 194). Even the fanatical Colonel Sands tells his nephew Skip early on in the latter's stay in-country, "This is a fallen world" (p. 57). But Skip, the starry-eyed, patriotic CIA agent from Clements, Kansas, gets tasked with cataloguing his uncle's vast intelligence catalogue – also called "Tree of Smoke," an apocalyptic image taken from the Book of Joel – and soon, as "an arbiter of fragmentary histories" (p. 247), becomes disillusioned with his mission and his country's involvement in the region altogether. *Tree* encompasses a dizzying array of characters, a labyrinthine plot that stretches from the death of JFK to the Reagan 1980s, a hallucinatory prose style that seems to mimic sensually the jungle fever of its setting, and a *pastiche* of inter/metatextual allusions to its literary and cinematic predecessors. Still, the novel is less "about Vietnam" per se than it is about the sense of aftermath or psychological fallout that afflicts those who survived it, those on the periphery of the conflict, and those left to chronicle it in our own post-historical present – with that "it" holding some especially resonant parallels to or "unsettling echoes of the [then] current American [debacle] in Iraq" (Kakutani 2007), as with how intelligence can be manipulated to drive policy, and to disastrous ends.

In his later fiction, Johnson continues to plumb the psychological depths of characters cursed by a consciousness of their class constraints and by an unorthodox moral sensibility that affects their view of the past, present, and uncertain future. However lowly or sordid their lives may be, Johnson's protagonists experience "consecrated, indeterminate moments between old configurations and a new reality" – one which, through intimations of the "sacred," moves them toward "overturning meaninglessness" (Champion 2000, pp. 145, 143). In his 2011 novella *Train Dreams*, for instance, Johnson explores the plight of a common working man, Robert Grainier, living and dying in the American Northwest in the early twentieth century. Yet through his recognizable poetic language and mythic level of storytelling, Johnson manages to demystify "History" and celebrate the wonder of the ordinary as exemplified in Grainier's life and times, even as he laments an era's passing.

In what would be his final novel, 2014's *The Laughing Monsters*, Johnson reprises his brand of "dirty realism" in the context of a post-9/11 heart of darkness with the story of Roland Nair, a Danish American spy working for a NATO-sponsored intelligence group, who becomes embroiled in the surreal landscape of West and Central Africa. One of Johnson's "damnation novels," *The Laughing Monsters*, set in 2012, is "a commanding anthropology of hell that further extends and complicates the work begun in *Angels* and continued" (Taylor 2014, p. 38) in fictions like *Already Dead*. Nair as self-reflexive narrator reports: "I've come back [to Africa] because I love the mess. Anarchy. Madness. Things falling apart" (Johnson 2014, p. 49) – with a nod here to Achebe's novel, which in turn alludes to Yeats's "The Second Coming." But Nair ultimately sees the "New Africa," with its "endless violence, [. . .] environmental devastation, [and] self-refreshing chaos" (Taylor 2014, p. 38), as "some intermediary realm on the way to oblivion" (Johnson 2014, p. 65), as he describes his journey into the continent's center, again suggesting a purgatorial outlook on the contemporary moment. However, Johnson's "interests have always been in wreckage, both individual and universal" (Williams 2014), a condition from which characters like Nair may still discover "a plan of extraction" (Johnson 2014, p. 220), however improbable.

Those intersections of class consciousness, morality, and mortality that underlie many of Johnson's fictions are also foregrounded in the posthumous collection *The Largesse of the Sea Maiden*. Each of its five stories' first-person narrators, such as Cass in "The Starlight on Idaho" and Dink in "Strangler Bob," confront "end-of-life questions" (Moody 2018, p. 10) for themselves or those intimately linked to them. Such questions, moreover, point to the mental and spiritual burdens affecting many of Johnson's hard-luck figures, who live and often die ultimately in a liminal realm outside the American mainstream.

About halfway through the title story of *Largesse*, its middle-aged narrator, an advertising executive whose best days are behind him, reflects, as though to some imagined reader: "I wonder if you're like me, if you collect and squirrel away in your soul certain odd moments when the Mystery winks at you" (Johnson 2018, p. 15). The statement encapsulates nicely Johnson's own esoteric religious views, which include a good amount of "wonder" in the ordinary and cognizance of that fine line between life and death, the psychological and the theological, that pervade much of his work, beginning with *Angels* and extending through this final book.

Johnson had turned his attention over the course of his fictional oeuvre from his characters' "isolated struggle for individual meaning and transcendence" to "finding transcendence within a community and within friendship – even unlikely friendships" (Maher 2017, pp. 5–6). In the closing story of *Jesus' Son*, "Beverly Home," the hapless Fuckhead, a now-recovering alcoholic and drug addict adapting to sobriety by working at a convalescent home in Arizona, confesses: "I had never known, never even imagined for a heartbeat, that there might be a place for people like us" (Johnson 1992, p. 160). Such a confessional strain – that sense of personal alienation yet desire for communal fellowship, as well as an ability to use the paradoxes of religion and madness "to convey precious truths" (Champion 2000, pp. 145, 149) about his down-and-out characters and their precarious lives – stands as the signal accomplishment of Denis Johnson in his most successful fictions, both early and late, in a career cut short by his death from liver cancer in May 2017.

SEE ALSO: After Postmodernism; Banks, Russell; Burroughs, William; Carver, Raymond; Contemporary Fictions of War; Mason, Bobbie Ann; Minimalism and Maximalism; Post-9/11 Narratives; Religion and Contemporary Fiction; Trauma and Fiction

REFERENCES

Champion, James. (2000). Denis Johnson's strange light. In: *Literature and the Renewal of the Public*

Sphere (ed. Susan VanZanten Gallagher and Mark D. Walhout), 139–151. New York: St. Martin's.

Connors, Philip. (2008). Denis Johnson's higher power. *Virginia Quarterly Review* 84 (1): 251–257.

Johnson, Denis. (1991). *Resuscitation of a Hanged Man*. New York: Farrar, Straus and Giroux.

Johnson, Denis. (1992). *Jesus' Son: Stories*. New York: Farrar, Straus and Giroux.

Johnson, Denis. (2000). *The Name of the World: A Novel*. New York: HarperCollins.

Johnson, Denis. (2007). *Tree of Smoke*. New York: Farrar, Straus and Giroux.

Johnson, Denis. (2009). *Nobody Move: A Novel*. New York: Picador.

Johnson, Denis. (2014). *The Laughing Monsters*. New York: Farrar, Straus and Giroux.

Johnson, Denis. (2018). *The Largesse of the Sea Maiden: Stories*. New York: Random.

Juengel, Scott J. (2011). Johnson, Denis. In: *The Encyclopedia of Twentieth-Century Fiction* (ed. Brian W. Shaffer). Oxford: Wiley Blackwell. *Blackwell Reference Online*.

Kakutani, Michiko. (2007). In Vietnam: stars and stripes, and innocence undone. *The New York Times* (August 31, 2007). https://www.nytimes.com/2007/08/31/books/31book.html (accessed July 7, 2021).

Maher, John. (2017). Denis Johnson: an editor's love story. *Publisher's Weekly* (October 9, 2017): 5–6.

Means, David. (2009). The way of the gun. *New York Times Book Review* (May 10, 2009): 6.

Miles, Jack. (1993). An artist of American violence. *The Atlantic* (June): 121–127.

Moody, Rick. (2018). The end. *New York Times Book Review* (January 28, 2018): 10.

Parrish, Timothy L. (2001). Denis Johnson's *Jesus' Son*: to kingdom come. *Critique: Studies in Contemporary Fiction* 43 (1): 17–29.

Rebein, Robert. (2001). *Hicks, Tribes, & Dirty Realists: American Fiction after Postmodernism*. Lexington: University Press of Kentucky.

Taylor, Justin. (2014). Things fall apart. *Artforum International* (December 2014/January 2015): 38. *ProQuest Research Library*. http://search.proquest.com/docview/1637925029 (accessed January 10, 2015).

Williams, Joy. (2014). *The Laughing Monsters*, by Denis Johnson. *The New York Times* (November 9, 2014). http://nytimes.com/2014/11/09/books/review/the-laughing-monsters-by-denis-johnson.html (accessed July 7, 2021).

FURTHER READING

Buehrer, David. (2012). *Apocalypse Now*, & again: Johnson's *Tree of Smoke* and the Vietnam War narrative revisited. *Philological Papers* 55–56: 5–17.

Farrin, J. Scott. (2003). Eloquence and plot in Denis Johnson's *Jesus' Son*: the merging of premodern and modernist narrative. In: *The Postmodern Short Story: Forms and Issues* (ed. Farhat Iftekharrudin, et al.), 130–143. Westport, CT: Praeger.

Giraldi, William. (2013). The art of reading Denis Johnson: the enduring appeal of *Jesus' Son*. *Poets & Writers* 41 (6): 23–27.

Grønstad, Asbjørn. (2006). Denis Johnson's postmodern Lazarus: transforming faith in *Resuscitation of a Hanged Man*. *American Studies in Scandinavia* 38 (1): 66–77.

Parrish, Timothy L. (2008). Denis Johnson's *Fiskadoro*: postcolonial America. In: *From the Civil War to the Apocalypse: Postmodern History and American Fiction*, 231–267. Amherst: University of Massachusetts Press.

Seaman, Donna. (2017). Review of *The Largesse of the Sea Maiden*, by Denis Johnson. *Booklist* (December 1, 2017): 26.

Johnson, Mat

KIMBERLY CHABOT DAVIS
Bridgewater State University, USA

Novelist and comics writer Mat Johnson exemplifies a satiric trend within African American literature of the twenty-first century. Johnson can be grouped alongside Percival Everett, Paul Beatty, Colson Whitehead, and Danzy Senna, Black writers who have been dubbed the "post-soul" or "post-black" generation coming of age after the Civil Rights movement. Post-soul writers undermine static ideas of Blackness that were central to the Black Arts movement and Black Nationalism of the 1960s. As Paul

Taylor argues, "where soul culture insisted upon the seriousness of authenticity and positive images [of blackness], post-soul culture... subjects the canon of positive images to subversion and parody" (Taylor 2007, p. 631). Post-soul texts often feature "cultural mulatto" or "post-black" protagonists who defy stereotypes, confound racial categories, or express allegiance to many cultures. Many protagonists of Mat Johnson's novels are literal as well as cultural mulattoes, upsetting rigid notions of Blackness with their mixed allegiances and biracial physiognomy. In a parodic move, Johnson often uses the outmoded term "mulatto" to describe himself, calling attention to the history of racist categorization. Although Johnson's work aims to trouble Blackness, he is highly skeptical of optimistic views of the twenty-first century as a post-race era. Examining how the racist past of the United States continues to haunt the present, Johnson's writing echoes James Baldwin's insight that "the great force of history comes from the fact that we carry it within us, [and] are unconsciously controlled by it" (Baldwin 1968, p. 95). Johnson's focus on the legacy of the past is evident throughout his career. His creative nonfiction book *The Great Negro Plot* (2007) uncovers the history of a purported slave insurrection in eighteenth-century New York, while his *Incognegro* graphic novel series addresses lynching and racial passing in the 1920s. Although his other novels are set in the present or future, *Pym* (2011) reworks the neo-slavery genre in a fantastical setting, and *Loving Day* (2015) uses tropes of haunted houses and ghosts to resurrect race history.

Johnson's biraciality (African American and Irish American) marked his youth in a Black neighborhood of Philadelphia, where he struggled to be considered "black enough." As he said in an interview, "I wanted to just be black, as opposed to black with an asterisk" (Baptiste 2015). His hair and skin tone read as white to many observers, prompting racial misrecognition that is similarly experienced by his fictional protagonists. Although his racial hybridity resulted in bullying and alienation in his youth, this liminal position granted him a vantage point to analyze the painful absurdity of America's racial caste system. After attending college at West Chester University for a year, he studied abroad at the University of Wales in Swansea, and then transferred to Earlham College, where he earned a BA in 1993 and served as president of the Black Student Union. Johnson earned a fellowship to go abroad again, this time living in London (in predominantly Black Brixton) to conduct research for a thesis on the effects of expatriate experience on African Americans. Examining race in an international context further sharpened Johnson's understanding of the pathologies of the American racial unconscious.

Johnson's first book, *Drop* (2000), a semi-autobiographical coming-of-age novel, was completed while he was earning an MFA in creative writing from Columbia University. Echoing Johnson's biography, *Drop*'s fictional protagonist, Chris Jones, takes a job in London where he experiences freedom from the trials of being Black in America. Forced to return to Philadelphia, Chris plunges into poverty and alienation as he chafes against stereotypical notions of Blackness and ghetto culture. Although the novel doesn't neatly resolve Chris's identity struggles, it concludes with Chris feeling a momentary sense of belonging in his city and in America, as he photographs the diverse crowd at a Fourth of July fireworks celebration. Despite mixed reviews, *Drop* was a "Barnes & Noble Discover Great New Writers" selection, and *Interview* magazine named Johnson a "Writer on the Verge."

While living in Harlem during his studies at Columbia, Johnson was inspired to write his first satirical novel, *Hunting in Harlem* (2003), which critiques gentrification, class-climbing in the Black community, and dilemmas faced by Black writers in the literary marketplace. The novel's main protagonist, Chris Snowden, is an ex-con working for Cyrus Marks, a corrupt African American former Congressman turned real-estate mogul. Marks employs Snowden and others to kill child abusers, drug lords, and pimps in order to sell off their apartments to bourgeois African Americans who will restore Harlem to its former glory. Marks's social improvement plan gains moral complexity when he uses some of his profits to establish an orphanage for neglected Black children. Through his depiction of Marks, Johnson satirizes bombastic Black leadership (i.e. Marcus Garvey) as well as the history of African American bourgeois "uplift" rhetoric. His work shares a self-critical strain with other post-soul writers who eschew the injunction to offer only positive images of Black life. A subplot of *Hunting in Harlem* lambasts the constraints of the publishing industry faced by an iconoclastic writer, Bobbie Finley. Finley refuses to write social protest novels or ghetto or romance fiction, the only categories that editors deem appropriate for a Black writer, but he eventually succumbs to the market by committing suicide as a publicity stunt. With its gallows humor, Johnson's *Hunting in Harlem* achieved modest critical success, earning the 2004 Zora Neale Hurston/Richard Wright Foundation Award.

His next book, *The Great Negro Plot: A Tale of Conspiracy and Murder in 18th-century New York*, was an experimental hybrid of creative nonfiction and historical novel. Based on factual court accounts of a 1712 slave revolt and alleged arson attacks in 1741 in Manhattan, the book attempts to give voice to the accused slaves, thirty-one of whom were hanged or burned alive for supposedly torching the property of white citizens. The book examines how whites of all classes were motivated by fear and greed, provoking a "witch-hunt" that conveniently created a "black bogeyman" out of local slaves. Johnson's admiration and empathy for the rebellious slaves is apparent, but he also unflinchingly portrays a few opportunistic slaves who named names in the arson hysteria to spare their own lives or win freedom. *The Great Negro Plot* deconstructs white discourses dehumanizing Black people and satirizes the selfishness, religious hypocrisy, greed, and lust for power that motivated slavery as an institution. Alluding in interviews to the connections between past and present, Johnson researched this historical case of xenophobia in Manhattan to draw parallels to the fearmongering response to the 9/11 terrorist attacks. On the strength of his first three books, Johnson was awarded a $50,000 grant and named a James Baldwin Fellow by the United States Artists group in 2007.

Based on his research on slave revolts, Johnson made his first foray in 2005 into the realm of comics, a genre which he had consumed avidly as a child. Disappointed by the DC Comics villain Papa Midnite, a racist stereotype of African primitivism, Johnson collaborated on a *Hellblazer* spin-off, creating an origin story that redefines Midnite as an opportunistic sellout profiting from slavery. Johnson reenvisions Midnite's immortality as the result of a curse placed upon him because he sabotaged the New York slave rebellion of 1712 and profited from the 1741 arson hysteria falsely attributed to slaves. In Johnson's hands, this comic villain becomes more than a racist fantasy; he is a historical reality like the traitors Johnson discovered in his research for *The Great Negro Plot*.

Continuing his resurrection of history, Johnson teamed up with artist Warren Pleece to create the well-received graphic novel *Incognegro*, set in the early twentieth century. On the cover of the text, a reviewer from *Essence* declared, "Mat Johnson doesn't just push the boundaries of race, he blows them up." *Incognegro*'s African American protagonist is Zane Pinchback, a reporter for Harlem's *New Holland Herald* who is light enough to pass as white. Much like the historical figure Walter White of the National Association for the

Advancement of Colored People (NAACP), Pinchback spends much of his time in the Deep South passing in order to report on lynchings. In the book's "author's note," Johnson mentions that the story grew out of his own childhood, when he dreamed of a time in which his light complexion would be an "asset instead of a burden," allowing him to be a "race sp[y] in the war against white supremacy." In an interview, Johnson noted that "whiteness doesn't see itself" as a race or ethnicity, only as the human norm, so he aimed to make its ugliness visible in his exposé of white Southern racism (Altman 2012).

The graphic novel's noir crime plot is set in motion when Zane Pinchback, the light-skinned Harlem reporter, races to prevent the lynching of his dark-skinned Southern brother Pinchy, who has been accused of murdering a white woman. The plotline with brothers of different colors was inspired by Johnson's own twin children, "two people with the exact same ethnic lineage destined to be viewed differently only because of genetic randomness" (Author's Note, Johnson 2008). Johnson employs passing and the fraternal theme to underscore the absurdity of fictional racial categories and assert a postmodern belief in the fluidity of identity. As Zane narrates, "race doesn't really exist . . . race is just a bunch of rules meant to keep us on the bottom . . . The rest is just people acting, playing roles" (p. 19). Despite the fact that Zane solves the murder case and frees his brother, his friend Carl (who is also passing) gets lynched instead, thus reminding readers that even though race is a fiction, it can have deadly consequences. While the fiction of race results in murderous violence in the South, Johnson celebrates the Harlem of the North as a space of freedom, where Pinchy can now "create any identity that [he] want[s]" (p. 129). Johnson and Pleece's graphic novel resists constricting identities and social hierarchies that force people to pass in the first place.

In 2018, Johnson and Pleece collaborated to produce a prequel to the graphic novel entitled *Incognegro: Renaissance*. Adding nuance to the celebratory view of Harlem in the first volume, the prequel depicts a Harlem where racism is evident, albeit more subtle than the Southern variety. It also draws upon Johnson's love of the Harlem Renaissance, borrowing plot elements from Wallace Thurman's *Infants of the Spring* (1932). The book addresses cultural appropriation and white supremacy in the literary marketplace through a character resembling the white writer Carl Van Vechten. When a Black character's death is disregarded by police as a suicide rather than murder, Johnson also underscores how the criminal justice system devalues Black lives.

Between 2003 and 2011, Johnson was also writing his masterwork, the novel *Pym*, a postmodern satire that reenvisions Edgar Allen Poe's novel *The Narrative of Arthur Gordon Pym of Nantucket* (1838). Johnson was awarded the 2011 Dos Passos Prize for Literature following *Pym*'s publication. *Pym* is a genre-bending amalgam of satire, neo-slave narrative, academic novel, science fiction, and fantasy. One target of Johnson's satire is the pressure academia places upon faculty of color. A tenured professor of English and creative writing at the University of Oregon, Johnson has taught at the University of Houston, Columbia, Rutgers, and Bard College. *Pym*'s protagonist Chris Jaynes is denied tenure at the "historically white" Bard College for pursuing his passion for Poe rather than conforming to institutional expectations for a "blackademic" to focus on African American subjects. Jaynes refuses to serve on the college's Diversity Committee which he considers a farce. Jaynes's interest in Poe is motivated by his desire to understand whiteness "as a pathology and mindset" (2011, p. 33). For Jaynes, the racist fantasies and fears in the *Narrative of Arthur Gordon Pym* "offered a passage on a vessel bound for the primal

American subconscious, the foundation on which all of our visible systems and structures were built" (2011, pp. 33–34). Early chapters read like literary criticism, as Johnson offers a detailed analysis of the "Africanist presence" in Poe's narrative, inspired by Toni Morrison's influential work *Playing in the Dark: Whiteness and the Literary Imagination* (1992). The novel turns fantastical when Jaynes discovers a manuscript written by a character in Poe's tale, suggesting that the adventure story was factual rather than fictional. In search of the truth, Jaynes sets off to Antarctica to discover Tsalal, the island of Black inhabitants that Poe demonized but Jaynes idealizes as a Black homeland untainted by colonialism. Like other post-soul writers, Johnson subjects Jaynes's Afrocentric romanticism to as much satirical critique as he does Poe's fantasies of white purity.

Johnson's career-long emphasis on white supremacy takes its funniest incarnation in *Pym*. In Antarctica, Jaynes discovers that Arthur Gordon Pym is alive and over 200 years old, subsisting on whale urine that enables his immortality. Jaynes and his Black fellow crew members also discover a race of humanoid white albino monsters (a figure from the close of Poe's narrative) who enslave Jaynes and company. They escape, only to be subjected to indentured servitude at the utopian "plantation" of a white painter of kitschy art, Thomas Karvel, who pipes in the voices of new-right media pundits into his artificial "BioDome" habitat. The neo-slave narrative section of the text explores how white supremacy dies hard. To kill it, Jaynes and crew engage in a genocidal revenge narrative to exterminate the snow monsters, escaping again to seek the Black island homeland. But Johnson refuses to allow a comforting romanticization of Tsalal or similar Afrofuturist fantasies. Instead, he satirizes human tribalism and the fear of otherness which is at the root of race as a concept.

Human fears of miscegenation and the policing of racial boundaries are key themes in *Pym* as well as in Johnson's subsequent novel *Loving Day*, winner of the American Book Award. Like Johnson, *Pym*'s Jaynes is an "octoroon" who was bullied as a child because he looked like "whitey." Exposing African American prejudices against whiteness *and* Blackness, Johnson offers a hilarious send-up of the internalized racism of the Native American Ancestry Collective of Gary (NAACG), a group that is convinced they are Native American rather than Black, until their DNA tests prove the contrary. In *Loving Day*, Johnson continues this thread by examining how an interracial commune garners the ire of Afrocentrists. A central context for understanding *Loving Day* is the multiracial movement of the 1990s, which aimed to revise unitary constructions of racial identity on the 2000 US Census. Some adherents naively heralded the census's new recognition of mixed-race identity as a move toward a "raceless" utopian future. Johnson acknowledges the psychic benefits of a pluralist interracial community in *Loving Day*, yet he also gleefully satirizes the hypocrisies of the multiracial movement and its idealization of racial mixture.

Loving Day's racially mixed protagonist Warren Duffy, who identifies as unequivocally Black, has recently discovered that he has a teen daughter (Tal) who is ignorant of her Black heritage. To Blacken her consciousness, Warren enrolls her in a school for racially mixed kids which boasts a myopic curriculum focused only on creole languages and mixed people in American history. The school's sacred holiday is Loving Day, in honor of the 1967 Supreme Court case *Loving v. Virginia* that struck down anti-miscegenation laws. Johnson spoofs the school's creation of a Loving Day carnival, as it devolves into a ridiculous extravaganza, complete with a "Miss Cegenation Pageant." A sighting of the ghosts of a mixed-race couple leads to the invention of a foundation myth, as the community holds a séance to connect with this interracial Adam and Eve. Uncovering the insanity of tribalism, Johnson shows how this supposedly pluralist society operates a lot like the old monoracial tribes, complete with identity policing and sparring subgroups ("Oreos" and "Sunflowers"). The novel calls for more emancipatory ways of being for mixed-race people, yet Johnson remains skeptical about such utopic possibilities given the tenacity of human tribalism and xenophobia.

Despite its criticism of multiracial utopia, *Loving Day* invests its hope in Warren's and Tal's personal efforts to free themselves from limiting categories of selfhood. The novel ends with Warren and Tal embracing on the edge of the empty foundation of a ruined estate that Warren had inherited from his white father. The dilapidated eighteenth-century house operates as a Gothic symbol of the racist, colonialist legacy that oppresses Warren. After Warren attempts unsuccessfully to burn down the racist house of history, Tal sells the building to the school's headmaster who will restore it as a symbol of interracialism. Abandoning his obsession with burning down the past, Warren is moved by his daughter to refocus on the future, to build a new foundation for surviving as a mixed-race person in the American "house" that race has built. In the novel's final line, Warren again sees the interracial ghost couple, but now he views them as "Just lovers. Just people," negating race as a valid system of classification in his own consciousness.

Johnson's oeuvre takes up serious themes – the tribulations of racial identity, human hypocrisy and xenophobia, and the history of white supremacy – yet his tone is darkly comic and his ironic satire bitingly funny. Scholar Glenda Carpio notes that gallows humor is commonly employed by African American satirists, who provoke laughter to "assert the ego's invulnerability in the face of death" (2008, p. 6). Mat Johnson invites us to laugh both at the powerful – the agents of institutional racism – and at the powerless – those Black and tan subjects whose identities are circumscribed by the fiction of race and its history. His incisive work provides a bracing tonic for those who recognize the absurdity and pain of race relations in twenty-first-century America.

SEE ALSO: Afrofuturism; The Graphic Novel; Mixed-Genre Fiction; Post-Soul and/or Post-Black

REFERENCES

Altman, Barbara. (2012). UO Today #486: Mat Johnson (August 1, 2012). www.youtube.com/watch?v=aLI75jYRhOk (accessed July 7, 2021).

Baldwin, James. (1968). Unnameable objects, unspeakable crimes. In: *Black on Black: Commentaries by Negro Americans* (ed. Arnold Adoff), 94–101. New York: Macmillan.

Baptiste, Helena. (2015). The enigmatic and infinite juxtaposition of a sunflower and Oreo: an interview with Mat Johnson. *Weeklings* (June 3, 2015). www.theweeklings.com/hbaptiste/2015/06/03/the-enigmatic-and-infinite-juxtaposition-of-a-sunflower-and-oreo-an-interview-with-mat-johnson/ (accessed July 7, 2021).

Carpio, Glenda. (2008). *Laughing Fit to Kill: Black Humor in the Fictions of Slavery*. New York: Oxford University Press.

Johnson, Mat. (2008). *Incognegro*. New York: Vertigo.

Johnson, Mat. (2011). *Pym*. New York: Spiegel & Grau.

Taylor, Paul. (2007). Post Black, old Black. *African American Review* 41 (4): 625–640.

FURTHER READING

Davis, Kimberly C. (2017). The follies of racial tribalism: Mat Johnson's anti-utopian satire. *Contemporary Literature* 58 (1): 18–52.

Dickson-Carr, Daryll. (2014). "The historical burden that only Oprah can bear": African American satirists and the state of the literature.

In: *Post-Soul Satire: Black Identity after Civil Rights* (ed. Derek Maus and James Donahue), 41–54. Jackson: University Press of Mississippi.

Norris, Keenan. (2014). Coal, charcoal, and chocolate comedy: the satire of John Killens and Mat Johnson. In: *Post-Soul Satire: Black Identity after Civil Rights* (ed. Derek Maus and James Donahue), 175–188. Jackson: University Press of Mississippi.

Wilks, Jennifer M. (2016). "Black matters": race and literary history in Mat Johnson's *Pym*. *European Journal of American Studies* 11 (1).

Jones, Edward P.

CEDRIC GAEL BRYANT
Colby College, USA

The "Introduction" Edward P. Jones composed for his 2012 edition of *Lost in the City*, his first collection of short stories released in 1992, begins:

> The stories in this book may have had many beginnings – depending upon where my heart and mind were at the point of their creation; but none of those beginnings have to do with the lives of the people among whom I grew up, or the people I read or was told about . . . these people and their actions in these fourteen stories were born in my imagination. And I cannot say that enough times because so many out there have forgotten, or never knew, what miracles the imagination – unfettered, fed by a reasonably working brain and sufficient blood in the veins – can manage.
>
> (2012, p. xiii)

Jones's introduction is a gift to his readers that puts them inside a very private, creative writer's mind and imagination process. There, matters of craft and language reside – a smithy's fiery forge of the imagination unfettered by any obligation except to "sing the songs" of Black people – "tragic and wondrous and often perfect glory" within a sense of place as Joycean and specific as that of *Dubliners* (1914):

> I had read a small library's worth of books before *Dubliners*, but it was the one that planted a molecular seed of envy in me, made me later want to follow Joyce's example and do the same for Washington [DC] and its real people.
>
> (2012, p. xv)

Like the stories assembled in James Joyce's *Dubliners* that are an explosive mix of religious fervor, politics, memory, and class struggle in early twentieth-century Ireland, the intersection of race, class, politics, and history throughout Edward P. Jones's short and long fiction make real Joyce Carol Oates's twist on the familiar proposition that place not only influences identity, but arguably, *is identity* (1996, p. vii). In Jones's two short story collections, *Lost in the City* (1992) and *All Aunt Hagar's Children* (2006), and his Pulitzer Prize-winning novel, *The Known World* (2003), place is often a dynamic, bilateral movement between Washington, DC, where Jones grew up and Virginia: "all the streets and avenues and roads those characters and other people in this book [*Lost in the City*] go up and down are real, or were real once upon a time, when I knew them as a boy" (2003, p. viii). This kind of inventiveness happens at the thematic intersection of place and time; human bondage and possession (slavery); urban blight and moral corruption; and the quest for human agency throughout the "known world" of Jones's fiction. His highly acclaimed novel published in 2003, for example, grapples with them within the African American Slave Narrative Tradition. However, it should be stressed that *The Known World* is bracketed by the two, aforementioned, remarkable short story collections that place Jones securely among the most significant American practitioners of the short form, which extends from Charles Chesnutt, Flannery O'Connor, Richard Wright, to Raymond Carver.

One of the earliest, and best, short stories Jones writes while a graduate student at the University of Virginia, "The First Day," and included in revised form in his first collection, *Lost in the City*, brilliantly conjures Jones's subtle narrative practice in its opening sentence: "On an otherwise unremarkable September morning, long before I learned to be ashamed of my mother, she takes my hand and we set off down New Jersey avenue to begin my very first day of school" (2012, p. 24).

Here, the intersection of time and space is on full display: the unnamed, first-person narrator speaks retrospectively, recalling the signal event announced in the story's title and first sentence from an unspecified time and place in the future – like a "coming of age," or *Bildungsroman* narrative drawn from a memory of crisis that potentially is transformative and enlightening. The "unremarkable" banality of a fall day becomes starkly *remarkable* by its association with the adjective "ashamed," which, although shaped by past experience, is only felt and realized in the future. This introductory sentence produces what Reader Response theorist Wolfgang Iser calls "gaps in the text," (1974, pp. 280–281) that subtly develop this story's thematic concerns with memory, childhood, socialization, prejudice, and education.

That the nameless narrator's shame is "learned" is central in a story full of subtle, double meanings about "the first day" – both for the daughter and the mother who must learn to navigate the bureaucratic red tape of city planning that prevents her from enrolling her daughter in Seaton Elementary School, which is beyond her district, but, comfortingly, across the street from her church: "I want her to go here, 'my mother says.' If I'da wanted her someplace else, I'da took her there" (1992, p. 28). Clearly *place* matters here and is inextricably bound up with class and race and gender, each of which thwarts the mother's will – "*One monkey don't stop no show*" (p. 29) – and provides lessons learned about power for the mother, daughter, and reader. The questions that proliferate, forming the "gaps in the text" and *double entendre* that inform this story's themes also include this: how is school on the first day, and all those that follow in time, a formal and informal education, a learning process? And most importantly, why is the daughter's shame for her illiterate mother emphatically *not* a consequence of school, of education, on her first day? Edward P. Jones's narrative practice across the fourteen stories collected in *Lost in the City* and throughout his other short and long work depend upon these strategies where less is more; where the past, present, and future are fluid; where time is not linear, and where point of view, or voice, is a polyphonic echo chamber that unfetters the imagination.

Edward P. Jones was born in Washington, DC, on October 5, 1950. In both simple and profoundly imaginative ways he is one of *All Aunt Hagar's Children*. In these stories, as in his first collection, characters are largely fictional, while places are largely factual. To say that the "streets, avenues, and roads" were real approaches dramatic understatement given that Jones, his mother, and younger sister moved approximately eighteen times in almost as many years, and knew them well, before he graduated from Cardozo Senior High in 1968. Remembering one such relocation, "for about the fifteenth or sixteenth time since I had come into the world," Jones notes:

> . . . we lived in this one room, 1132 Eight street. And there was a hole about this size in the ceiling that went up the bathroom. And once some guy up there caught some guy looking down the hole to see what he could see in our place.
>
> (2008, p. xi)

This "place" was soon condemned and boarded up. The Dickensian "hard times" of Jones's first eighteen years were held together by his mother who, like the nameless narrator in "The First Day," could neither read nor write, and worked heroically long hours for years "as a dishwasher, a cutter and preparer of raw vegetables and an all-round cleaner at Chez Francois," an upscale DC restaurant "that fed some of the white men who ruled a good part of the world at that time" (2007, p. xi). Jones's escape while growing up with few friends or extended family was first comic books, then "real books" without pictures where he discovered his own imagination could make up the images needed to enter the works by Joyce (*Dubliners*), Harper Lee (*To Kill a Mockingbird* [1960]), Ann Petry (*The Street* [1946]) and especially Richard Wright, whose short story collection *Uncle Tom's Children* (1938), autobiography *Black Boy* (1945), and novel *Native Son* (1940) shaped Jones's sense of a Black world that mirrored himself. These writers, among many others Jones consumed by the time he graduated with a BA in English from Holy Cross College in 1972 would inspire Jones slowly towards the writing life, which he would not fully embrace until after the encouragement and example of, again among others, James Alan McPherson who mentored Jones in the University of Virginia's MFA program.

Edward P. Jones's narrative practice and major themes concerning family, loss, education, memory, time and place, and Black identity are rooted in the inescapability of race and Black matters. This narrative practice depends upon patterning that develops these subjects by repetition and revision within and between each story collection. For example, in both collections, education informs the politics of identity and is the irreducible sign, the *sine qua non* of human development and social mobility in "The First Day," as well as the third story of *Lost in the City*, "The Night Rhonda Ferguson Was Killed," that repeats and revises this subject matter. In the latter story, it is context rather than value that is revised. The main character's point of view, her attitude toward formal education could not be more antithetical to either the unnamed narrator of "The First Day," or the precocious narrator – also nameless and starting kindergarten – in "Spanish in the Morning" in *All Aunt Hagar's Children*. Cassandra G. Lewis, in "The Night Rhonda Ferguson Was Killed," is streetwise but vulnerable and has made the mistake of confiding in a well-intentioned teacher, Miss Bartlett, who sees "potential" beneath Cassandra's tough-girl exterior and tries, unsuccessfully, to motivate Cassandra, who is an orphan and seems directionless, to become a better person. Miss Bartlett,

> had said that her parents must be turning over in their graves to know the way their child was living, going from pillar to post with no real home. Had said all this and more in front of the dick people who couldn't stand Cassandra and were just waiting to hear some real personal shit about her life so they could talk behind her back. Then, like putting her personal business in the street wasn't enough, the teacher had gone into all that other stuff about potential and blah-blah-blah and then, after that, some more blah-blah-blah.
>
> (2012, p. 35)

Education is a leitmotif assignable not only to stories and characters throughout both collections, but to Jones himself who was, without exaggeration, rescued by books, reading, and advanced education from the same mean streets of Washington, DC, that threaten street-savvy "orphans" like Cassandra G. Lewis and that kill talented individuals with unlimited potential like Rhonda Ferguson whose remarkable voice and anticipated contract with a record company are her ticket out of the city. It is Rhonda Ferguson, ironically, who has the photo-perfect family – the "Evening Star" newspaper headline reads, "family is the secret to singer's success" (2012, p. 36) and is murdered by her boyfriend "for no apparent reason at all" (p. 53) – that expresses the story's signal theme about education to Cassandra: "But if you're gonna take care of my business for me . . . you're gonna have to get an education. How will I know if they [the record company] cheatin me if you don't know more than they know?" (p. 36). Formal education is only one possible vehicle for self-actualization in the politics of identity and not a guarantee of it. Rhonda Ferguson's murder is especially tragic, poignant for interlocking reasons: the lack of an unambiguous motive for her death; the cautionary inference that not even a photo-perfect family can be a bulwark against the ubiquity of urban violence and systemic poverty; and the lost, unconsummated potential of Rhonda Ferguson's dream – like so "many thousand gone," so many "dream[s] deferred" that "dry up like a raisin in the sun" (Hughes 1995, p. 426).

Education is serious business, as these three thematically linked stories suggest. Its potential to transform, to make over the individual is not "a game," as the mother who can neither read nor write, and so knows the value of school, cautions her daughter on the final page of "The First Day":

> We go into the hall, where my mother kneels down to me. Her lips are quivering . . . She stands and looks a second at the teacher, then she turns and walks away. I see where she has darned one of her socks the night before. Her shoes make loud sounds in the hall. She passes through the doors and I can still hear the loud sounds of her shoes.
>
> (2012, p. 31)

The stress here, as in so many of stories in these two short story collections, is on memory, which depends upon hearing to evoke it, and the emotive power of recollection to inform both the present and future. In these, and so many other examples, Edward P. Jones expresses the influence of William Faulkner on time and memory: "the past is never past," Faulkner said in various ways in interviews and fiction, including *Requiem for a Nun* (1951), "it is always present." These issues all concern survival, the quest for agency, and the politics of identity and play out in creatively mesmerizing ways in the twenty-eight stories – divided equally into fourteen stories in each collection – that, thus far, comprise Jones's major contributions in the short form.

The place where the "imagination unfettered" and literary production most remarkably come together is *The Known World*, a Pulitzer Prize-winning novel about nineteenth-century American slavery that Jones conceived and wrote with almost no historical data, such as slave narratives, memoirs, or scholarly material. Except for what he recalled about the "peculiar institution" from general knowledge, and a history book he could not get beyond page forty (Miller 2012), Jones relied on creative invention. Manchester County, where the principle happens is mythopoeic and akin to William Faulkner's Yoknapatawpha County, which this Mississippi writer famously called his "own little postage stamp of native soil":

> I discovered that my own little postage stamp of native soil was worth writing about and that I would never live long enough to exhaust it, and by sublimating the actual into the apocryphal I would have complete liberty to use whatever talent I might have to its absolute top.
>
> (Faulkner 1968, p. 255).

Faulkner's inventive, god-like freedom to defy conventional norms about time and space and especially the ability to "sublimate the actual into the apocryphal" perfectly express Edward P. Jones's unfettered imagination.

This act of sublimation and mythmaking as narrative practice in more literary historical terms is especially evident in Jones's radical departure from nineteenth and twentieth-century traditions of the African American Slave Narrative, the former of which is predicated on the "authority and authenticity" of the "lived experience," like *The Narrative of* the Life of Frederick Douglass, an American Slave* (1845), and Harriet Jacobs's *Incidents in the Life of a Slave Girl* (1861). These nineteenth-century memoirs of former slaves are characteristically written in the first-person voice rather than the ghost-written, or "as told to," narrative style that compromises both the authority and authenticity implicit in a work of nonfiction "written by himself," or "herself." This politically important phrase was affixed to both Douglass's and Jacobs's slave narratives, respectively, and rhetorically became the standard for veracity in the genre. Jones's *The Known World* is closer to, but still different from, the twentieth-century "neo-slave narratives" that are reconstructions of slavery through the literary imagination, whether narratively or poetically, rather than autobiographical, first-hand experience. A distinguished short list of titles in this modern slave narrative tradition includes Margaret Walker's *Jubilee* (1966), Gayl Jones's *Corregidora* (1975), Octavia E. Butler's *Kindred* (1979), Sherley Anne Williams's *Dessa Rose* (1986), Toni Morrison's *Beloved* (1987), and Colson Whitehead's *The Underground Railroad* (2016). In profoundly inventive ways each of these books creates its own "known world" about nineteenth-century American slavery.

The Known World is comprised of twelve chapters, and what may accurately be called an epilogue, each of which makes time a fluid mix, rather than a static, linear relation of present, past, and future through flashback, flash-forward, and lateral hold – basic filmic devices – that create small histories, or parables of individual lives and events from the 1830s to the early twentieth century. Jones's deployment of flash-forwards are too numerous to count, but rhetorically constitute one of the novel's most significant narrative strategies because more than the oppressive present of a slave's daily life, or a past that haunts the present, the razor-thin possibility of freedom lies in a future informed by everything – regret, love, hate, pain – that shapes the "lived experience." The ubiquitous use of flash-forwards in *The Known World* are a rhetorical sign that slavery is *not* an absolute condition that obviates the future – "not just fixed, paralyzing moment[s] of horror, but also a catalytic space where agency and progress, hope and being are possible" (Bryant 2005, p. 551). Flash-forwards emphasize life as an asynchronous, fluid progression that cannot be absolutely predetermined. Here is one brief example. A young slave girl named, Tessie, is holding a doll her father, Elias, has recently carved – partly out of love and partly to quell his restless urge to run for freedom (2003, p. 77) – when Fern Elston, a teacher and free Black woman who owns slaves, says to the child "That's such a pretty doll."

> "My daddy made it for me," Tessie said. "She would repeat those words just before she died, a little less than ninety years later. Her father had been on her mind all that dying morning, and she asked one of her great-grandchildren to go the attic and find the doll."
>
> (2003, p. 350)

This simple exchange in the present between a slave-holder and a slave establishes the reality of human bondage that links the daughter and father to what seems immutable. However, the flash-forward, "ninety years later," subverts the absoluteness of slavery as an institution. The doll carved by "restless hands" and the generations it passes to affirm a future that does not simply repeat the past but revises, transforms it. And by doing so, the novel consistently critiques and subverts the ideology, which Fern Elston, the Black slave owning schoolteacher, expresses that keeps the "peculiar" logic of the "known world" in place: "All of us do only what the law and God tell us we can do. No one of us [white or Black slaver-holders] who believes in the law and God does more than that" (2003, p. 109).

Beginning with its title and from the first chapter, *The Known World* is an extended metaphor for slavery's dominantly classist system of commodifying bodies, white and Black, free and enslaved, men, women, and children. In this morally minimalist, sometimes magically real, and systemically violent "cosmos" of generationally bound characters almost too numerous to remember, race matters, but is complicated by a competing and perverse belief in a power and privilege sanctioned by "law and God" (2003, p. 109). The tension between the known and the unknown is presented almost immediately, and throughout the novel, with Moses, the Black overseer on a Black-owned plantation, who eats dirt, lies naked on the ground under the stars in rain or fair weather, and masturbates to intimately *know* the circumference of his hierarchal place in the world. Moses knows everything within the boundaries of Henry Townsend's plantation and absolutely nothing beyond them. He is "world stupid," as Elias, the slave with "restless hands" and feet who is unafraid of boundaries, calls him. The trope here implies a duality of power – sensory domination over everything he can see, hear, touch, and taste, including animals, outbuildings, people, and the earth itself – and vulnerability to what lies beyond his knowledge that makes him cruel, untouchable, and afraid. In one singular instance, for example, Moses inadvertently ventures beyond the Townsend estate and suddenly realizes

> he did not know enough about the world to know he was going south. He could have found his way around Caldonia's [Henry Townsend's widow] plantation with no eyes and even no hands to touch familiar trees, but where he was walking now was not that place.
>
> (2003, p. 334)

Alice, "the woman without a mind" (2003, p. 12), whom Moses derisively calls "the night walker" (p. 60), and who, reportedly, has been kicked in the head by a mule on a previous owner's plantation, is the counterpoint to Moses and revises a paradigm of power and vulnerability in thematically central ways. First, as in nineteenth-century slave narratives, vulnerability means disability, whether physically – like the slave named Celeste whose leg is deformed; or, mutilated like Elias whose ear has been partially cut off (p. 94); or hobbled, as Moses ultimately is (p. 373) – or psychologically damaged, as wandering Alice is presumed to be. And disability, of any stripe, implies powerlessness. However, power and agency are precisely what Alice's feigned madness accords her because vulnerability engenders fear in some, like the "night patrollers" who think Alice bewitched, or too simple minded to be dangerous or a threat to run away and, in effect, give her a "pass" to roam the roads at night. In a revision of the paradigm, Alice's "vulnerability" is the source of power that allows her to secretly know the world – by the permission to roam madness grants her – well beyond the small circumference of Moses, or any other enslaved person, and ultimately enables Alice to escape to freedom.

Finally, there are at least two propositions that *The Known World* seems to urge. First is the unarguable fact that human nature is flawed, inherently good *and* fully capable of insensate evil – regardless of race, or gender, or moral, or logical biases. If the major premise that determines behavior is that "*all of us do only what the law and God tell us we can do,*" then any human arrangements are possible, no matter how malign, how cruel, or how justified. It is Alice, now "Alice Night" in the novel's final italicized section who has found her way – and the way for others from Manchester County and Henry Townsend's plantation, including Moses's wife Priscilla – to freedom in Washington, DC, where so much of Edward P. Jones's fiction happens. Here, Alice Night has put aside the ingenuity of madness for the creative genius of two "maps" on display in a hotel lobby: both are *"made with every kind of art man ever thought to represent himself. Yes, clay. Yes paint. Yes, cloth."* The second "Creation," *"may well be even more miraculous than the one of* [Manchester County]," perhaps because it is of a true known world that includes the people who make it a reality – miraculously *all* the people, the living and the dead. *"Not single person is missing"* (2003, p. 384). Alice Night's art may be a version of Revelations, the Last Judgment, "a great gettin up mornin." Perhaps. But the "Creations," taken together, represent the truest "known world" possible in which each life is present and counted without exception.

SEE ALSO: Butler, Octavia; Jones, Gayl; Morrison, Toni; Whitehead, Colson; Williams, Sherley Anne

REFERENCES

Bryant, Cedric Gael. (2005). *"The Soul has Bandaged Moments"*: reading the African American gothic in Wright's "Big Boy Leaves Home," Morrison's *Beloved*, and Gomez's *Gilda*. *African American Review* 39 (4): 541–553.

Faulkner, William. (1968). Interview with Jean Stein Vanden Heuvel. In: *Lion in the Garden: Interviews with William Faulkner: 1926–1962* (ed. James B. Meriwether and Michael Millgate), 237–256. Lincoln: University of Nebraska Press.

Hughes, Langston. (1995). "Harlem." In: *The Collected Poems of Langston Hughes* (ed. Arnold Rampersand). New York: Vintage.

Iser, Wolfgang. (1974). The reading process: a phenomenological approach. *The Implied Reader: Patterns of Communication in Prose Fiction from Bunyan to Beckett*. Baltimore: Johns Hopkins University Press.

Jones, Edward P. (2003). *The Known World*. New York: Amistad/HarperCollins.

Jones, Edward P. (2005). Foreword. In: *Black Boy* (by Richard Wright). New York: Harper Perennial.

Jones, Edward P. (2007). Introduction. *Being a Black Man: at the Corner of Progress and Peril* (ed. Kevin Merida). New York: Public Affairs.

Jones, Edward P. (2012). *Lost in the City*. New York: Amistad/HarperCollins; 1st ed. 1992.

Miller, E. Ethelbert. (2012). The writing life: poet/writer E. Ethelbert Miller talks with writer Edward P. Jones. Howard County Poetry and Literature Society of Columbia Maryland. https://youtu.be/W5sPWxFiVZI (accessed July 21, 2021).

Oates, Joyce Carol. (1996). Introduction. *American Gothic Tales*, 1–9. New York: Penguin Books.

FURTHER READING

Donica, Joseph L.V. (2011). Hierarchies of knowledge and the limits of law and theology in *The Known World*. *Edward P. Jones: New Essays* (ed. Daniel D. Wood), 135–157. Melbourne: Whetstone Press.

Jones, Edward P. (2019). Preface. In: *Hue and Cry* (by James A. McPherson). New York: Harper Collins.

Maucione, Jessica. (2011). Neighborhood as the new lost world. In: *Lost in the City. Edward P. Jones: New Essays* (ed. Daniel D. Wood), 75–91. Melbourne: Whetstone Press.

Wood, Daniel Davies. (2011). Reader, writer, mentor, man: a portrait of Edward P. Jones. In: *Edward P. Jones: New Essays* (ed. Daniel D. Wood), 11–60. Melbourne: Whetstone Press.

Jones, Gayl

SHARADA BALACHANDRAN ORIHUELA
University of Maryland, USA

Born in segregated Lexington, Kentucky, on November 23, 1949, African American writer Gayl Jones is best known for her novels *Corregidora* (1975), *Eva's Man* (1976), *The Healing* (1998), and *Mosquito* (1999). Having pursued an undergraduate degree at Connecticut College before pursuing master and doctor of arts degrees at Brown University, Jones demonstrated an early affinity for storytelling from a young age. She attended Connecticut College on a scholarship arranged by fellow Lexington writer Elizabeth Hardwick, and while attending

Connecticut College studied with US Poet Laureate Robert Hayden. While at Brown University, she studied under Michael S. Harper, who remains a close friend even now as Jones has receded from public social life. Jones is included in the canon of the great American writers of the twentieth century, and her first novel, *Corregidora*, was published by Random House during Toni Morrison's tenure as editor at the publishing house. Indeed, Morrison noted that after *Corregidora* "no novel about any black woman could ever be the same after this" (Ghansah 2015). Since then, Jones's work has been favorably compared to works by Morrison, especially given their shared concerns with Black life and sociality both in the United States and across the hemisphere.

Jones's distinctive style is characterized by polyvocality, plurality, and formal experimentation. She has described *Eva's Man* as a "dramatic story" that began as a "lyrical novel," and calls her style "improvisational" (Tate 1979, p. 143). Her intensely personal, first-person narrative voice and style in turn recalls the forms of storytelling in which Jones is invested. Indeed, her deep interest in the "oral traditions of storytelling," as well as in personal and intimate histories, has produced a unique style that has garnered critical acclaim (p. 143). It is never more clearly apparent than in her first published novel, *Corregidora*, which centers on a blues singer, the titular Ursa Corregidora, who uses storytelling and the blues to deliver her painful family history rooted in Brazilian chattel slavery. For Jones, her distinctive style results in a form of intimacy between the storyteller/novelist and the listener/reader, an intimacy which she is committed to strengthening and fostering between the two over the course of a novel. As she discusses in an interview, "history and personality are interests [in *Corregidora*] – the relationship between history and personality – personal and collective history – history as a motivating force in personality" (Rowell 1982, p. 45). Jones repeatedly acknowledges the Chaucerian origins of her work, noting that storytelling's origin in English literature dates to the fourteenth and fifteenth centuries. Even Jones's poetry, works that include *Song of Anninho* (1981), for example, are what she calls "little fictions" or "poetic narratives" and strive to break with the "aesthetic boundaries of literary forms and categories," as well as with conventions of linear time and temporality (Rowell 1982, p. 39). Even some of her works of literary criticism, the book-length essay titled "The Quest for Wholeness: Re-Imagining the African-American Novel," for example, take an unconventional form. The introduction, which appears in a 1994 issue of *Callaloo*, speaks for the novel in the first-person in order to make a case for the formal innovations that emerge in communities attempting to decolonize their own novelistic and linguistic forms. While Jones's style might playful and lighthearted, the content of her works certainly is not.

Pervasive themes in her work include the vast and interconnected network of Black persons not only across the Atlantic, but also along the American hemisphere. Influenced by the likes of Gabriel García Márquez and Carlos Fuentes, as well as a long lineage of Black writers influenced by Caribbean and/or Latin American revolutionary politics such as Martin Delany, Langston Hughes, Paule Marshall, Audre Lorde, and Alice Walker, Jones's novels and works of narrative poetry are simultaneously works of social realism, as well as fantastic (Tate 1979, p. 143). Jones's work points to the concurrent rise in popularity of African American and Latin American writing in the US literary marketplace. Indeed, critics such as Stelamaris Coser have pointed out that the rise of visibility of Black women writers coincided with the increased popularity of Latin American writers in the United States. It is in this light that Black women writers such as Gayl Jones, writing about the expansive reach of Black life across the United States, the Caribbean, and

Latin America, were able to bridge the two major shifts taking place in the post-1960s US literary marketplace. Jones's most well-read novel, *Corregidora*, is explicit in its interest in exposing the central place "of black women during and after slavery in Brazil as well as in the United States," as is her poetry collection, *Song for Anninho* (Coser 1995, p. 14). By casting the Black female protagonists in *Corregidora* and *Song for Anninho* as American descendants of chattel slavery in Brazil, Jones deftly links the Americas. And so, Jones's conception of race "foregrounds heterogeneity" and multiplicity, as well as transnationalism (Mills and Mitchell 2006, p. 3). In her later works, Gayl Jones also explores the place of Black persons living along the US–Mexico border alongside Latino and Native American persons, thereby irreversibly enriching the canon of Black writers engaging with this region in US contemporary literature. Certainly, Jones seems to be moved by Latin American revolutions and political change in Chile, Mexico, and Brazil (Harper 1977, p. 706). As she notes, "I'd like to be able to deal with the whole American continent in my fiction – the whole Americas – and to write imaginatively of blacks anywhere/everywhere" (Rowell 1982, p. 40).

Published most recently, *Mosquito* received largely negative reviews. In *The New York Times*, Henry Louis Gates (1999) wrote, "It is as if wanted to deliver a dissertation about orality in literature by transcribing hours of tapes from a loquacious storyteller" and called it a "sprawling, formless, maddening tale." The novel itself demonstrates Jones's commitment to exploring the unique racial and ethnic landscape of the US Southwest because of its proximity to the US–Mexico border. *Mosquito*'s namesake character, Sojourner Nadine Jane Johnson, is a Black woman truck driver who transports ecological detergents between the United States and Mexico. It is during one of these trips that Mosquito finds a pregnant undocumented woman, Maria Barriga, hiding in the cabin of her truck. There begins Mosquito's participation in the sanctuary movement in South Texas which transports and helps to protect Latin American refugees attempting to migrate to the United States. Part romance, part realist novel, and part stream-of-consciousness narrative, *Mosquito* defies generic categorization. The text even includes extended segments of quoted text from another character's literary magazine. Loosely organized around Mosquito's increased commitment to this "new" underground railroad, the novel is structured around a series of encounters between the titular character and a number of different figures, including Monkey Bread, Mosquito's best friend with whom she discusses Black politics; Delgadina, a Chicana bartender in South Texas with whom she pontificates on the transnational ebbs and flows of persons and capital; and Father Ray, her Pilipino lover responsible for her radicalization and increased participation in the sanctuary movement. Together they present a robust view and discussion of Latino immigration and refugees, pan-Africanism, neoliberal trade, and human geography. More significantly, *Mosquito* is insistent on drawing a close relationship between the United States and Mexico. As Mosquito notes, "I know they had that slavery in Mexico same as the US and a lot of them Africans that didn't escape to Canada escaped to Mexico. I even heard tales of Africans jumping off the slave ships headed for the United States and swimming to Mexico, 'cause they abolished that slavery in Mexico earlier than in the States" (Jones 1999, p. 190). *Mosquito*'s commitment to exploring the contours of the complex relationships between nations and persons is a reflection of Jones's long-standing interests in the Americas as a whole.

In addition to repeatedly acknowledging the influence of third-world liberation movements in the settings and characters she has created, Jones has also drawn a meaningful link between the African American and Latin American literature, noting that these two literary traditions also share their roots in the unique forms that emerge from the process of decolonization. As she writes in her work of imaginative literary criticism, "The Quest for Wholeness: Re-Imagining the African-American Novel. An Essay on Third World Aesthetics," "novels are patterns of stories and patterns of ideas that take place in time and space and that deal with perspective. In liberating themselves, colonized people also liberate their stories. Every group and nation want to be able to pattern its stories, pattern its ideas, and handle space, time, and perspective in its own unique way" (Jones 1994, p 511). Moreover, as she says in an interview with her mentor, Michael S. Harper, "Of course, black writers – it goes without saying why we've always had to hear. And Native American writers, and Latin American writers. It's all tied in with linguistic relationships, and with the whole socio-psychological-political-historical manifestations of these linguistic relationships" (Harper 1977, p. 694). Thus, for Jones, engaging with Latin America and its literature is not simply a way of understanding the multiplicity of race and the transnational origins of chattel slavery, but is also a necessary contact point with African American literary history through its emphasis on the linguistic relationships between persons and across generations. This dynamism and commitment to exploring the diverse implications of working in the tradition of storytelling is reflected both in her narrative poetry and in her fiction.

Jones's interest in Latin America and Latin American literature was enriched during her time in graduate school, where she studied Spanish language and literature (Coser 1995, p. 122). Jones notes her influences from Latin American writers are related to her knowledge of "image, myth, history, language, metaphor, movement between different kinds of language and levels of reality, different kinds of reality," and adds that "their influence has to do with the use of language, the kinds of imagery, the relationship between past and present with landscape" (Harper 1977, p. 705). These "different kinds of languages" are apparent in Jones's works, and the close relationship between written and oral language, and fluidity between the two, is part of Jones's distinctive style. Indeed, for Jones, oral and aural traditions are as much an aesthetic as a political choice. Thus, Latin American literature informs Jones's representation of different realities as coterminous. As she notes in a later interview: "I'm especially interested in Afro-American, African and other Third World folk narratives that contain magic and transformations/metamorphosis-myths that challenge or provide creative alternatives to European ones of that sort of imagination. Also (*sic*) I'm interested in studying how time and space are handled (and transformed) in them" (Rowell 1982, p. 34). And so, critics of Jones's work have seized upon the important contributions of her novels to linking the US South to the Global South. Indeed, it would seem that Jones anticipates later criticism linking these two souths through their rich oral traditions, as well as through their capacity to link the oral to the written.

Like *Mosquito*, *The Healing*, too, is a temporally and spatially decentered first-person narrative, and includes some of the same characters that appear in *Mosquito*, including Mosquito herself. Indeed, the form of intertextuality found in *The Healing* functions to draw connections not only between texts, but also between literary traditions. In this novel, Jones marries Latin American magical realism to critical fabulation – what Jones calls "confabulation" – a genre that Saidiya Hartman (2008) believes to be critical to conveying Black narrative and history, to tell the story of Harlan Jane Eagleton, a Black faith healer. The novel draws upon a long history of transatlantic religious and narrative syncretism to foreground Harlan's narrative of her first healing told in reverse chronological order, and only revealed in the final pages of the novel. As the reader is told, Harlan is stabbed by her longtime friend, Joan, who, after stabbing Harlan notes, "I thought you were a real person . . . But you're not even a human woman, you're not even a real human woman" (Jones 1998, p. 280). In response, Harlan simply puts her "hand to the wound and it healed" (p. 280), leading to her discovery that not only can she heal herself, but she can also heal others.

Jones's interests in the relationship between different narrative forms and genres extends to her first book of criticism, *Liberating Voices: Oral Tradition in African American Literature*, published by Harvard University Press in 1991, where Jones examines the works of African American poets and fiction writers ranging from Langston Hughes to her graduate mentor, Michael S. Harper, to Zora Neale Hurston, Amiri Baraka, Alice Walker, and Toni Morrison. Organized around forms of orality ranging from dialect to jazz modalities and blues ballads, Jones notes that interpenetration of "art" and "folk" forms in African American literature correspond to the "moral or social vision(s)" of their authors, and these forms have the capacity to reshape American literature across the nineteenth and twentieth centuries (1991, p. 1). Careful to mention the work of these authors' Latin American counterparts, Jones's expansive work of literary criticism is remarkable in its scope and the boldness of its argument: in Jones's estimation, American literature is characterized by its conscious employment of dialect and oral traditions (p. 8). Indeed, as she argues, this "American language," found in African American writing, is the cornerstone of twentieth-century American literary history, and demonstrates the twentieth-century writers' struggle to balance innovation with tradition.

While these are the most pervasive themes and topics present in Jones's works, violence and sexuality, too, appear throughout Jones's works. Indeed, her works have sometimes faced criticism due to her treatment of the relationships between Black men and women, as well as its use of the oft-trodden representations of these populations. To this, Jones has responded with a resistance to limiting her erotic imagination or the erotic imagination of her female protagonists for the sake of propriety or because of the heightened scrutiny that Black writers face when representing Black female sexuality lest it appear "as if you're supporting the sexual stereotypes about blacks" (Rowell 1982, p. 46). And yet, by her own admission, Jones remains attentive to these representations and admits to a certain "double-consciousness" when writing about sex and sexuality (p. 47). Critics have alternately said her work spreads "sinister misinformation about women – about women, in general, about black women in particular, and especially about young black girls forced to deal with the sexual, molesting violations of their minds and bodies by their fathers, their mothers' boyfriends, their cousins and uncles," as much as it represents a new frontier of Black women's writing (Jordan 1976). However, most critics find that Jones works within this dialectic in order to "situate the black female subject in a position of indeterminacy, and coextensively work to empower the subject" (Robinson 1991, p. 138). Either way, Jones's attention to the violent and traumatic transnational history of slavery makes works like *Corregidora* and its representation of the abuses under chattel slavery as powerful as the representations of the sexual abuse found in *Eva's Man*. Thus, the forms of grotesque sexualized violence found in Jones's works, the sexual violence and rape found in *Corregidora*, the castration found in *Eva's Man*, and even the excision of women's breasts in *Song for Anninho*, function to recall violence and victimization, as well as endurance and survival.

Jones's personal life has, by some accounts, overshadowed the critical and commercial success of her works. And yet, even amidst personal and familiar turmoil, Jones was prolific and published several works, including *The Hermit-Woman* (1983), the novel *Die Volgelfaengerin* (*The Birdwatcher*) and a collection of poetry, *Xarque and Other Poems*, both published in 1985, as well as a collection of short stories titled *Raveena* (1986). Since then, Jones has fallen into relative obscurity barring her publication of *The Healing* and *Mosquito* in 1998 and 1999, respectively. Even so, Jones's contribution to American literature cannot be understated. Jones repeatedly writes about the shifting and changing nature of her own work and her shifting consciousness. As she writes in the closing paragraph of "The Quest for Wholeness," "I should rephrase the question. This is a chapter not on 'How I Became Decolonized' but 'How I Am Becoming Decolonized,' for no matter how much I imagine or re-imagine my own decolonization, most all Third World novels are in the process of becoming decolonized, but decolonization like independence itself is a multiplex demanding physical, spiritual, and economic independence. All these elements of decolonization are necessary for complex artistic decolonization before we can achieve the full decolonization of any novel" (Jones 1994, p. 514). Jones's continuous desire to achieve the state of decolonization and literary and imaginative independence, and this continuous state of "becoming," speaks to the lasting value of both Jones and her work in American literary history. Jones's rich opus demonstrates the great gains and costs of Jones's *becomings*.

SEE ALSO: Black Atlantic; Border Fictions; Contemporary Regionalisms; Marshall, Paule; Morrison, Toni; Multiculturalism; Walker, Alice

REFERENCES

Coser, Stelamaris. (1995). *Bridging the Americas: The Literature of Paule Marshall, Toni Morrison, and Gayl Jones*. Philadelphia: Temple University Press.

Gates, Henry Louis. (1999). Sanctuary. Review of *Mosquito* by Gayl Jones. *The New York Times* (November 14, 1999). https://archive.nytimes.com/www.nytimes.com/books/99/11/14/reviews/991114.14gatest.html?scp=95&sq=black%2520women&st=cse (accessed July 7, 2021).

Ghansah, Rachel Kaadzi. (2015). The radical vision of Toni Morrison. *The New York Times* (April 8, 2015). https://www.nytimes.com/2015/04/12/magazine/the-radical-vision-of-toni-morrison.html (accessed July 7, 2021).

Harper, Michael S. (1977). Gayl Jones: an interview. *The Massachusetts Review* 18 (4): 692–715.

Hartman, Saidiya. (2008). Venus in two acts. *Small Axe* 12 (2): 1–14.

Jones, Gayl. (1991). *Liberating Voices: Oral Tradition in African American Literature*. Cambridge: Harvard University Press.

Jones, Gayl. (1994). From *The Quest for Wholeness*: re-imagining the African-American novel: an essay on third world aesthetics. *Callaloo* 17 (2) 507–518.

Jones, Gayl. (1998). *The Healing*. Boston: Beacon.

Jones, Gayl. (1999). *Mosquito*. Boston: Beacon.

Jordan, June. (1976). All about Eva. *The New York Times* (May 16, 1976). https://www.nytimes.com/1976/05/16/archives/all-about-eva-evas-man.html (accessed July 7, 2021).

Mills, Fiona and Mitchell, Keith B. (2006). *After the Pain: Critical Essays on Gayl Jones*. New York: Peter Lang.

Robinson, Sally. (1991). *Engendering the Subject: Gender and Self-Representation in Contemporary Women's Fiction*. Albany: State University of New York Press.

Rowell, Charles H. (1982). An interview with Gayl Jones. *Callaloo* 16 (16): 32–53.

Tate, Claudia C. (1979). An interview with Gayl Jones. *Black American Literature Forum* 13 (4): 142–148.

FURTHER READING

Clabough, Casey. (2005). Afrocentric recolonizations: Gayl Jones's 1990s fiction. *Contemporary Literature* 46 (2): 243–274.

Clabough, Casey. (2006). Speaking the grotesque: the short fiction of Gayl Jones. *The Southern Literary Journal* 38 (2): 74–96.

Clabough, Casey. (2006). "Toward an all-inclusive structure": the early fiction of Gayl Jones. *Callaloo* 29 (2): 634–657.

Edwards, Don, Webster, Sarah, and Bennett, Brian. (1998). Noted writer resurfaces in a tragedy. *The Baltimore Sun* (February 24, 1998).

Ward, Jerry W. (1982). Escape from Trublem: the fiction of Gayl Jones. *Callaloo* 16 (16): 95–104.

Jones, Stephen Graham

BILLY J. STRATTON
University of Denver, USA

Stephen Graham Jones currently holds the position of Ivena Baldwin Professor of English and Professor of Distinction at the University of Colorado at Boulder. Acclaimed for a prolific literary output that shows little sign of slowing, with the publication of *Night of the Mannequins* (2020) and *The Only Good Indians* (2020) Jones is author to twenty novels, four novellas, a co-written novel, five story collections, a graphic novel, and more than 300 individual stories, with translations into Spanish, French, Russian, German, and Turkish. Born in Midland, Texas and having grown up on the surrounding plains of West Texas, Jones traces his love for literature and writing to his childhood with the reading of *Where the Red Fern Grows* (1961) by Wilson Rawls. Beyond the story itself, the descriptive images from the novel's final scene of an old rusty ax head stuck in a tree with a lantern hanging from it resonated in his mind. For Jones this symbolic motif came to represent the capacity of the written word to inspire imagination and allow him to travel beyond the boundaries of space and time. He identifies Hal Borland's young adult classic, *When the Legends Die* (1963), as another important influence. This work tells the story of a young native man and his struggles to come to terms with the complexities of identity – an especially prevalent theme in late-twentieth-century native American literature, and one conspicuously absent from Jones' body of work. By high school, a portion of which was spent on a military base in Colorado, he'd become a voracious reader of fiction and developed a particular fondness for genre writing, especially Louis L'Amour's tales of Western adventure. During this time, Jones was also exploring other branches of the literary tree commencing what was to become an interstate love affair with horror after reading Whitley Strieber's *The Wolfen* (1978) and Stephen King's *Tommyknockers* (1987) – works that continue to have an indelible influence on his writing and life.

But like many who cultivate an appreciation for literature and the ineffable power of the written word, Jones is quick to admit he never imagined that these interests could lead to a career as a writer. Reflecting back on his college experience as one of his life's unexpected detours in a 2016 interview, he stated, "I always thought I'd just farm in the day and write at night," before going on to add, "I got lucky" (Jones and Stratton 2016, p. 16). Being a writer of native Blackfeet identity also holds a significant place in Jones's story, of course, but it is not necessarily an attribute that he considers as a defining feature of his life and work. He has made this clear in the biographical sketches and dedications that accompany many of his novels and story collections, but perhaps more significantly in what has been left unsaid. Jones has often shared such views on this subject in responses given for interviews found in numerous journals. When asked about his "heritage" by one interviewer, for instance, Jones's response – "I don't know, does MTV count?" – articulates a clear discomfort with the type of essentialist thinking that tends to divide the world into social constructs and oppositions (Hart 2007, quoted in Stratton 2016, p. 10). In a similar vein, Jones turns what is framed as a common, yet tiresome, observation about the length of his hair into an entry on the FAQ now found on his website, DemonTheory.net (Jones n.d.). The witty, yet biting response Jones gives as an answer – "Long hair because I used to want to look like George Lynch, back when he was part of Dokken. Indians, actually, can have any-length hair. It's a crazy world" – pushes us to think more deeply about one of the major focal points of essentialist expectation as being reducible to physical appearances.

The reflections he offers on his life and experience in a world which only seems to be getting more bizarre by the minute should not be taken as a disavowal of his native identity, either. Instead, such statements seem offered as an acknowledgment, one shared with James Baldwin and other writers from marginalized communities like Saul Bellow and Philip Roth, that particular elements of identity serve simply as discrete traits among many that combine to form the essence of a person's identity, while also, perhaps, acting to balance the forces of contingency, determinacy, and agency. Reflections such as these call out to remind us of something Jones has often expressed throughout his career, that whenever one includes "an adjective before 'writer' it's a way of dismissing the writer" (Kinsella 2012, p. 24). Jones's statement echoes the wisdom shared by Baldwin in his *New York Times* piece, "The Discovery of What it Means to Be an American" (Baldwin 1959). Writing about his emigration to Europe in his mid-twenties, Baldwin reveals that part of the reason he left the United States was "to prevent myself from becoming *merely* a Negro; or, even a Negro writer" (section BR, p. 4), while at the same time trying to reveal the sense of the shared human experience at the heart of the complexity of American culture. Further, the posture that both Baldwin and Jones maintain can also be seen as underscoring the value of writing and the creation of literature, which, at least in their ideal forms, are offered as a means of intersubjective communication and understanding across a diverse array of social, cultural, historical, and geographic boundaries.

At the same time, the ideas Jones expresses about identity formation and culture serve to challenge the impulse of both readers and critics alike who may be inclined to classify his writing through such an elemental, superficial means of engagement, which all too often serves as a substitute for engaged interpretation and critical analysis. Or worse yet, as a sort of one-way mirror that gives safe access into sites of alterity and exoticization for voyeurs to satisfy the puerile curiosities of colonial imagination that attach to native/ Indigenous others. In the face of such systems of cultural surveillance, Jones is driven by a compulsion to carve out a unique and deeply personal presence in the world through the magic of words inscribed on a page. Words that achieve their most immediate power and are transformed into a sort of substance when combined into stories that carry the inexhaustible capacity to create connections with and between readers, and to ignite the luminance of potential and emergent realities.

Turning to the significance of Stephen Graham Jones's literary production, his career as a novelist got off to an auspicious start with the publication of his groundbreaking novel, *The Fast Red Road: A Plainsong* (2000) – a work that evolved from his dissertation titled "Glory Dog: A Plainsong," completed as a doctoral student for Florida State University's doctoral program in creative writing. Serving itself as an indirect repudiation of the anxieties invoked by the Y2K hysteria, while reflecting a more pressing set of concerns about American colonialism, *The Fast Red Road* is animated by equal parts native American activism, historical critique, postmodern playfulness, and country music, all while drawing on the picaresque tradition and its antecedent, the mock-heroic epic. Further, and more specifically in terms of plot, structure, and narrative style, *The Fast Red Road* brings together an expansive network of intertextual and referential circuits that pay fitting homage to the works of writers who had an especially potent influence on his thinking and aspirations to become a writer. The diversity of literary voices represented in this group, which included such figures as Franz Kafka and Samuel Beckett to Thomas Pynchon, Gerald Vizenor, and Louise Erdrich, is instructive. The adoption, for instance, of the conspiracy-laden narrative frame of Pynchon's *The Crying of Lot 49* (1965) supplies the most obvious connection through Jones's integration of the themes of secrecy, paranoia, and indecidability. Moreover, the relentless critique of colonialism expressed throughout the narrative, and the fractured subjectivity through which the experiences of the crossblood protagonist, Pidgin Del Gato, are articulated, expose narrative traces that connect the efforts undertaken to come to terms with his father's life and death, to the journeys of the trickster characters of Vizenor's *Bearheart: The Heirship Chronicles* (1990; originally titled *Darkness in Saint Louis: Bearheart*). Jones reveals himself to be an intricate weaver of words through *The Fast Red Road*, over-, under-, and cross-stitching the seemingly disconnected story threads into a cohesive narrative whole with references to the iconic ballads of Marty Robbins found on his 1960 album *El Paso*, and fortified with literary allusions that combine the absurdity of Samuel Beckett's *Ill Seen Ill Said* (1982) with the intensity of description found in Franz Kafka's short fiction. The final product of these discursive literary features, which can present a challenge to even the most sophisticated readers, and are attributable to the wide variety and diversity of the references and source materials Jones deploys, allows him to push the limits of native/American fiction into previously unexplored territories. All the while producing a profoundly complex and inimitable artistic vision, one that can be simultaneously exhilarating, entertaining, and exasperating.

Given the distinctive qualities of *The Fast Red Road*, reinforced through its publication by Fiction Collective 2 – an independent press distinguished for its advancement of contemporary avant-garde and experimental writing – Jones was well on his way to establishing himself as a bold and innovative new voice in contemporary fiction. As the novel gained notoriety from its inclusion in literature courses, typically at universities with offerings in native literature, it acquired a cult following for its narrative distinctiveness, use of obscure and esoteric historical and philosophic references, and strong sense of humor, irony, and play in the face of traumatic experience. In the two decades since the publication of *The Fast Red Road*, which noted scholar Grace Dillon has since classified as one of the founding texts of "Native slipstream" (Dillon 2016, p. 347), the novel's influence has only continued to grow within the American literary establishment, reaching beyond the usual readership that would be expected given the novel's cultural and social groundings. Jones has attracted an increasingly enthusiastic following among readers, a group that extends well beyond the conventional boundaries of contemporary native/American literature, through elements that also appeal to readers with interests in popular forms of speculative and genre fiction such as horror, dark fantasy, and science fiction.

Jones was quick to solidify his reputation as a writer unconstrained by artificial literary, social, or cultural boundaries throughout the 2000s with the publication of several subsequent novels, while obtaining his initial academic position as a professor of English at Texas Tech University. His intensive labors were rewarded during this period with the publication of three additional novels, *All the Beautiful Sinners* (2003), *The Bird is Gone: A Monograph Manifesto* (2003), and *Demon Theory* (2006), along with his first short story collection, *Bleed Into Me* (2005). These novels are distinguished by the unconventional and unsettling nature of the narratives they contain, each of which is expressed in divergent literary forms. Among these readers find a detective novel fused with the fabled dreamscape of *The Wizard of Oz* (1939), a fragmented, yet cohesive, elaboration of the postcolonial intervention begun in *The Fast Red Road*, and a multilayered story of psychological horror deftly outfitted with an intertextual literary scaffolding with elements drawn from nineteenth-century gothic fiction, to which is added a collection of incisive and profound short stories that together provide a scintillating glimpse into the expansiveness of Jones's literary talent.

These novels and stories also serve to highlight the sheer inventiveness of Jones's writing as he continued to develop and hone experimental forms and techniques, while anticipating the subsequent crossover into story modes that would arise out of this wide-ranging literary foundation, and often in astonishing ways. In *Ledfeather* (2008), a veritable tour de force of historical fiction that concludes the narrative trajectory initiated in *The Fast Red Road*, Jones delicately addresses the legacy of Blackfeet history in the aftermath of the heart-wrenching cruelty of the Marias River massacre, placing it among only a handful of contemporary native novels set in the timeframe of initial colonial contact. Add to this *The Long Trial of Nolan Dugatti* (2008) – originally written for a 72-hour novel writing contest – a work that sensitively engages with the issue of suicide and mortality through the unsettling parallel digital reality of video games. Despite their widely divergent plotlines and exposition on distinctive philosophic concerns, these works highlight the impressive strides Jones has made in the development of his use of formal literary structure, narrative perspective, and linguistic complexity.

Jones continued his ascension as a major presence in native literary production through the 2010s and into the present with the release of another collection of stories, *The Ones That Got Away* (2010), and a volume of microfictions, *States of Grace* (2014), which is remarkable for its elegance and for the deeply personal resonance of faces and images frozen in time similar to those Ezra Pound once described at a station in the Paris Metro. These are qualities that are likewise articulated, yet even more intensely given the freedom allowed by long-form fiction, in his brilliantly rendered contribution to the genre of autofiction, *Growing Up Dead in Texas* (2012). Narrated by a character named Stephen Graham Jones who returns to rural Texas to solve a mystery surrounding a devastating cotton fire that occurred in his community's distant past, the narrative Jones weaves his readers into succeeds in conveying an uncanny sense of alternate lives and realities trapped in the midst of a haunted landscape, which stands in good stead alongside the complex examination of self and other so nimbly related by Bret Easton Ellis in *Lunar Park* (2005).

These texts, combined with others written during this period, display the ever broader range of Jones's fascinations whereby he has managed to establish himself as a significant voice in contemporary genre fiction through the publication of an ever-expanding body of speculative texts. These include a selection of wildly inventive novels: *It Came From Del Rio* (2010), *Zombie Bake-Off* (2010), *The Last Final Girl* (2012), *Flushboy* (2013), *The Least* of *My Scars* (2013), *The Gospel of Z* (2014), *Sterling City* (2014), *Not for Nothing* (2014), *Mongrels* (2016), *Mapping the Interior* (2017), *My Hero* (2017), *The Only Good Indians*, and *Night of the Mannequins*, along with the story collections *Three Miles Past* (2012), *Zombie Sharks With Metal Teeth* (2013), and *After the People Lights Have Gone Off* (2014). All of which contribute to Jones's growing reputation in the realms of horror, comics and graphic novels, crime fiction, science fiction, and dark fantasy.

It is on the reception Jones has garnered from these later works that he has gained much positive recognition as a multiple-nominated finalist for the Shirley Jackson and Bram Stoker awards for horror fiction – the latter of which he finally won in 2018 for *Mapping the Interior*. His fascination with the monstrous and monstrosity is on clear display in such works, exploring and reinforcing, perhaps, the role Donna J. Haraway has attributed to our world's "chthonic ones" as beings who "demonstrate and perform consequences" (Haraway 2016, p. 2). And it has been in precisely these texts, as the fellow horror writer Paul Tremblay observes, that readers are able to most clearly comprehend the mirror by which Jones reflects "a piece of himself, of his experience, of the fight, of the place he's forged" (Tremblay 2016, p. 358). What becomes apparent in these narratives, Tremblay goes on to say, is not only the story of the person and writer that this entry identifies as a significant literary figure, but also that "the ghosts of our past, present, and future are all represented. And we are all haunted by them" (p. 358).

In addition to a literary output that is impressive by any standard, Jones has continued to enlarge an ever-growing archive of short stories, consistently published in prominent literary journals and scores of edited collections in furtherance of the genres cited above. The accounting of just a few from among these examples highlights his inclusion in an impressive selection of online journals, to which he has also added the digital-only novelettes *The Elvis Room* (2014), *Chapter Six* (2014), and *The Night Cyclist* (2016), as well as the collaborative novel *Floating Boy and the Girl Who Couldn't Fly* (2014), written with the aforementioned Paul Tremblay. Given the breadth and range of these texts in light of the considerable number of works Jones has produced thus far, readers can only wonder as to where the future will carry him in the next decade and beyond. Yet, one thing seems assured – it will most likely be somewhere new and with an innovative edge, slipped onto a shelf where we may not expect to find him.

SEE ALSO: After Postmodernism; Contemporary Regionalisms; Danielewski, Mark Z.; Erdrich, Louise; Indigenous Narratives; King, Stephen; Momaday, N. Scott; Pynchon, Thomas; Silko, Leslie Marmon; Vizenor, Gerald

REFERENCES

Baldwin, James. (1959). The discovery of what it means to be an American. *The New York Times* (January 25, 1959): 4.

Dillon, Grace. (2016). Native slipstream: Blackfeet physics in *The Fast Red Road*. In: *The Fictions of Stephen Graham Jones: A Critical Companion* (ed. Billy J. Stratton), 343–355. Albuquerque: University of New Mexico Press.

Haraway, Donna J. (2016). *Staying with the Trouble: Making Kin in the Chthulucene*. Durham, NC: Duke University Press.

Hart, Rob. (2007). The dark professor: an interview with Stephen Graham Jones. The Cult: The Official Fan Site of Chuck Palahniuk (November 28, 2007). https://web.archive.org/web/20080526014158/ (accessed July 5, 2021).

Jones, Stephen Graham. (n.d.). FAQ. DemonTheory.net. https://www.demontheory.net/ (accessed July 5, 2021).

Jones, Stephen Graham and Stratton, Billy J. (2016). Observations on the shadow self: dialogues with Stephen Graham Jones. In: *The Fictions of Stephen Graham Jones: A Critical Companion* (ed.

Billy J. Stratton), 14–59. Albuquerque: University of New Mexico Press.

Kinsella, Bridget. (2012). Unfettered imagination: Stephen Graham Jones. *Publishers Weekly* (May 4, 2012). https://www.publishersweekly.com/pw/by-topic/authors/profiles/article/51817-unfettered-imagination-stephen-graham-jones.html (accessed July 5, 2021).

Stratton, Billy J. (ed.) (2016). *The Fictions of Stephen Graham Jones: A Critical Companion*. Albuquerque: University of New Mexico Press.

Tremblay, Paul. (2016). Afterword. In: *The Fictions of Stephen Graham Jones: A Critical Companion* (ed. Billy J. Stratton), 357–358. Albuquerque: University of New Mexico Press.

FURTHER READING

Dillon, Grace. (ed.) (2012). *Walking in the Clouds: An Anthology of Indigenous Science Fiction*. Tucson: University of Arizona Press.

Van Alst, Theodore, Jr. (2015). *The Faster Redder Road: The Best UnAmerican Stories of Stephen Graham Jones*. Albuquerque: University of New Mexico Press.

K

Kennedy, William

PATRICK O'DONNELL
Michigan State University, USA

Born in 1928, William Kennedy is the author of nine novels, three works of nonfiction, two plays, two screenplays, and two children's books (co-authored). The bulk of his fictional output – eight novels extending from *Legs* (1975) to *Changós Beads and Two-Tone Shoes* (2012) – comprises the Albany Cycle, a succession of novels about outlaws, writers, politicians, and working-class protagonists that include a mobster, a grifter, a vagrant, an orphaned novelist, a political hack, and a journalist recording tumultuous events of the late 1950s and 1960s. As this last descriptor suggests, Kennedy's novels are replete with local and national histories that occur within the time-frames of individual stories and coalesce across the loose framework of the Albany Cycle. Relatives and ancestors cross over in several of the novels, many of them of Irish Catholic descent as is Kennedy himself, born of working-class parents in Albany's northern end and educated at the Christian Brothers Academy in Albany and Siena College, a Franciscan liberal arts college in nearby Loudonville, New York. Like Kennedy, many of his protagonists struggle to achieve their callings in life, even as they are given unique, oftentimes eccentric voices in novels where history and character intersect at every moment. As an all-too-rare writer who characteristically focuses on the proletariat, Kennedy's importance to contemporary American fiction cannot be overstated.

Kennedy's difficulties in becoming a published author has been assessed both by scholars of his work and by Kennedy himself, whose *New York Times* essay, "Why It Took So Long," provides a record of struggle and perseverance. There, Kennedy writes that, having studied journalism at Siena, he became a local sports reporter and then was drafted into the army in 1950 during the Korean War, where he continued his journalistic career writing for military newspapers, and was "thrown in with the literate and subliterate malcontents who populated the public information section" (Kennedy 2021). Among this group were a number of aspiring writers who introduced Kennedy to the work of Faulkner, Dos Passos, Mailer, O'Connor, and others and kindled his desire to become an author of stories. Thus began a career that waited nearly two decades before the publication of his first novel, *The Ink Truck* (1969) as Kennedy labored to find his own voice: "in the year or two after I left the

---

The Encyclopedia of Contemporary American Fiction 1980–2020, First Edition. Edited by Patrick O'Donnell, Stephen J. Burn, and Lesley Larkin.
© 2022 John Wiley & Sons Ltd. Published 2022 by John Wiley & Sons Ltd.

Army I managed to write dialogue that sounded very like Hemingway and John O'Hara, I could describe the contents of a refrigerator just like Wolfe, I could use intelligent obscenity just like Mailer, I could keep a sentence running around the block, just like Faulkner. But where was Kennedy?" (Kennedy 2021). The stories that he was writing in the years after he left the army he "came to loathe, as did my family, my friends, and fiction editors coast to coast" (Kennedy 2021). In the decades that transpired between his departure from the military, Kennedy would take on various journalism jobs, quit in order to write a novel, then return to journalism in order to put food on the table, then quit again to work on a novel, and so on. It was a cycle that landed him in Puerto Rico as the managing editor of a newspaper where he fortuitously took a course from Saul Bellow who was teaching creative writing at the University of Puerto Rico for a term, and who became something of a mentor to Kennedy. It was also a cycle that eventually led through sheer determination to the publication of *The Ink Truck*, a novel set in Albany (though not generally considered to be part of the Albany cycle) that records the adventures of its protagonist during a newspaper strike. The novel was based on a real strike at the Albany *Times-Union*, the newspaper that Kennedy worked on part-time in the 1960s as a feature writer of local stories – much of this material becoming the basis for *O Albany!* (1983), subtitled *Improbable City of Political Wizards, Fearless Ethnics, Spectacular Aristocrats, Splendid Nobodies, and Underrated Scoundrels*. The stories garnered him a nomination for the Pulitzer Prize from the newspaper's editors.

With *Legs*, the story of the last days of a real American gangster, Jack "Legs" Diamond, the Albany Cycle proper begins, and the succession of the following novels, *Billy Phelan's Greatest Game* (1978) and *Ironweed* (1983) catapulted Kennedy to international recognition and the 1984 Pulitzer Prize for Fiction. This initial trilogy of novels captures the essence of the Albany Cycle with protagonists ranging from Diamond – the final, downward curve in the arc of his violent life told from the perspective of his lawyer, Marcus Gorman – to Billy Phelan, a pool hustler who has become involved in the kidnapping of the son of a corrupt political boss, to Francis Phelan (various members of the Phelan family are scattered throughout Kennedy's fiction), an alcoholic who has accidentally killed his infant son, become a vagrant in the aftermath, and returns twenty-two years later to the Albany neighborhood where he lived before a life spent on the road. Each novel is replete with notable, often eccentric characters met along the way, and stories related in distinctive narrational voices, grounded in Kennedy's realism which consistently compares personal experience with historical event, and pits legend, rumor, ghost story, and memory against stark actuality.

Legs, for example, begins with a conversation between Gorman and three old friends as they discuss rumors of Legs Diamond's death; this leads to Gorman's recollections of his friendship with the gangster that begin with a mythmaking eulogy: "I had come to see Jack as not merely the dude of all gangsters, the most active brain in the New York underworld, but as one of the truly new American Irishmen of his day; Horatio Alger out of Finn McCool and Jesse James, shaping the dream that you could grow up in America and shoot your way to glory and riches" (1983a, p. 13). Throughout the novel, the seeming glamor of Legs' existence is compared to the tawdriness of his final days and the brutality of his lifestyle: he, thus, joins a succession of real and fictional American outlaws – Billy the Kid, John Dillinger, Michael Corleone, Tony Soprano – in whom the American dream of riches and success cohabits with the ugliness, violence, and corruption that underlie that dream.

Billy Phelan's Greatest Game recounts the lives and troubles of two protagonists: Martin Daugherty, a journalist who hangs out with and (like Kennedy himself) tells the stories of the city's gamblers, small-time criminals, and hustlers, and Billy Phelan, a pool shark and Martin's friend. Early on, Martin describes Billy's swagger and vision:

> Billy's native arrogance might well have been a gift of miffed genes, then come to splendid definition through the tests to which a street like Broadway puts a young man on the make: tests designed to refine a breed, enforce a code, exclude all simps and gumps, and deliver into the city's life a man worthy of functioning in this age of nocturnal supremacy. Men like Billy Phelan, forged in the brass of Broadway, send, in the time of their splendor, telegraphic statements of mission: I, you bums, am a winner.
>
> (1983b, p. 8)

The novel is, in part, a fictionalization of the 1933 kidnapping of John O'Connell, the nephew of two important Democratic political bosses in Albany, one of them the city's mayor. The kidnappers demanded a $250,000 ransom (equivalent to over $20 million in today's currency); eventually the ransom was negotiated down to $40,000, O'Connell was released unharmed, and the gang of kidnappers caught, tried, and convicted, but the series of events surrounding the kidnappers garnered local and national attention for years, especially when three of the criminals staged a spectacular jailbreak during a transfer to Alcatraz.

In the novel, Billy Phelan, a close friend of the kidnap victim, the nephew of Albany political bosses the McCalls, is caught up between the Albany political machine and members of the local criminal underground with whom Billy has been involved in several minor schemes, the former seeking any information he might have about the kidnapping, the latter seeking to insure that Billy will not become a "snitch." It is Billy's popularity and mobility – his capacity to overhear and spread stories and rumors as a "young man on the make" – that implicates him in the kidnapping. (Notable among Billy's charismatic gifts is his occasional capacity for second sight, one of the early instances of the "departures from material reality... sometimes magical, sometimes mystical, sometimes quasi-scientific, and sometimes extra-sensory" that critic Kathryn Hume claims are interwoven with realism in much of Kennedy's fiction [Hume 2000, p. 523]). When it becomes known that Billy has supplied some incidental information about the kidnapping, the rumor mill spins it that Billy has turned informer, and he is unfairly shunned by the proprietors of the bars, poker parlors, and poolhalls where he had been a favored client. At the same time, because of the trust invested in him by both criminals and politicians, Martin Daugherty is chosen to help deliver the ransom and free the kidnap victim. Because of his newly-found celebrity and cache, Daugherty's defense of Billy Phelan in print leads to the charismatic figure's return to the neighborhoods in which he has sporadically thrived, and the novel concludes as a comic satire on the political/official and criminal/unofficial environments of Albany, especially as they mirror each other in the personalities of Martin Daugherty and Billy Phelan.

Francis Phelan, the father of Billy, is the central figure of Kennedy's most renowned novel – the third in the Albany trilogy – *Ironweed*. Winning the Pulitzer Prize in 1984, the novel was adapted for a highly-successful film released in 1987 with Kennedy himself credited as screenwriter, and starring Meryl Streep and Jack Nicholson who received

Oscar best actor nominations for their efforts (Kennedy had previously written the screenplay for *The Cotton Club* in 1984 with the film's director, Francis Ford Coppola). The novel relates a few days in the life of ex-baseball player Francis Phelan in the waning days of the Great Depression, soon after the events of *Billy Phelan's Greatest Game*. Having lived much of his life as a "hobo" on the road attempting to flee his past and the literal ghosts that haunt his present, Phelan decides to return to Albany twenty-two years after accidentally dropping and killing the infant son he was holding, presumably while drunk. His homecoming is marked by the resurgence of a traumatic past and a life spent drifting, as well as encounters with his surviving son, Billy, an old girlfriend, Helen, his fellow "bum," Rudy, and his wife, Annie. The return to the "scene of the crime" induces multiple parallels between Francis's violent life (he recollects the ghosts of those he has killed through the sheer need to survive in the vagrant undergrounds of America), and his need for redemption and return to home. The novel's events intertwine local politics and the circumstances of Francis's and his family's and friend's private lives, clearly suggesting the complex series of responsibilities and connections that exist between those who live "off the grid" and those who can survive with the parameters of legality and normality. In the end, Rudy and Francis are attacked in a homeless camp by local citizens; Francis kills a man while attempting, failingly, to save Rudy's life, and hops aboard an outbound freight, his future uncertain: he may continue as a social outcast, the brief interlude of an abortive homecoming behind him, or he may attempt to return more permanently to the home and family he has temporarily regained once things have settled down in Albany. This indecisiveness is characteristic of Kennedy's novels, protagonists, and narrators, as they are inevitably perched between public and private lives, the legal and the criminal, putative normalcy and marginalization.

In the remaining volumes in the Albany Cycle, Kennedy both broadens and deepens the narrative trajectories commenced in the initial three novels of the cycle. We meet more characters from the neighborhoods inhabited by the Phelans, the family history of the Phelans themselves is developed in more detail, and while twentieth-century Albany history, politics, and culture receive further elaboration, the action extends in several novels back to the nineteenth century and outwards, in the case of his last novel, to pre-Castro Cuba. In *Quinn's Book* (1988), the eponymous protagonist, Daniel Quinn (the ancestor of Danny Quinn, Billy Phelan's cousin who makes an appearance at the age of ten in *Billy Phelan's Greatest Game*), reminisces about his young adult life and his adventures as a journalist. The novel begins in 1849 with the disastrous scene of a boat capsizing on the Hudson River and 14-year-old Daniel participating in the rescue efforts, where he has the first glimpses of the woman he will pursue throughout his life. As he rises from riverboat apprentice to becoming a celebrated journalist of the Civil War, many of the critical events that would come to define the America in which his twentieth-century descendants struggle to survive are narrated through Daniel's eyes, including the war itself, the evolution of the Underground Railroad, the New York draft riots of 1864, and the burgeoning union movements of the 1860s in New York and Pennsylvania. Kennedy deploys a variety of literary styles as Daniel's story takes place not only within the parameters of the national history upon which he reports, but also within those of the cultural history of upstate New York and scenes of theatergoing, prize fighting, and sports racing. He also envisions a scene of a woman being raised from the dead that may be the most spectacular yet in the Albany novels where historical realism is interspersed with instances of magic, ghosts, and extrasensory perception. Like Legs Diamond, Billy Phelan and, in his way, Francis Phelan, Daniel Quinn is an adventurer whose remarkable inner life is refracted in the remarkable historical circumstances he lives through, and though set back in time from the other novels in the cycle, the novel is also a tale of the present in a sequence of work that, as Kennedy claims to an interviewer, "about my own time, whether I'm writing *Quinn's Book* in 1849 or the life of Legs Diamond . . . they always seem to me to be very modern books . . . products of my own contemporary consciousness, my own insights into how we live now" (Baruth 1998, p. 122).

The next three novels in the Albany Cycle, *Very Old Bones* (1992), *The Flaming Corsage* (1996), and *Roscoe* (2002), extend the character lines and historical circumstances of the previous works. *Very Old Bones* is a multigenerational novel that relates the history of the Phelan family and the curse it seems to suffer from, told through the eyes of Orson Purcell, the illegitimate son of Peter Phelan, younger brother of Francis; Purcell has returned to the family home in Albany in hopes of being acknowledged by his father. The time frame of the novel stretches from 1887 to 1958 as the disaster-ridden lives of the Phelan family, beset by madness, criminality, alcoholism, professional failure, and occasional transcendence are revealed. At the heart of this novel in which Francis Phelan returns in an important role as reflected through the lens of his erstwhile nephew, the difficult and thwarted quest for home, community, and family belonging is set within the circumstances of the local neighborhoods and evolving city that serve as the historical backdrops to all of Kennedy's novels.

The protagonists of the flamboyantly named *The Flaming Corsage* are Edward and Katrina Daugherty, the parents of Martin Daugherty who was last seen in *Billy Phelan's Greatest Game* as friend of the ambitious hustler and primary narrator of his adventures. Truly in love, Edward and Katrina marry against family wishes (his family is Catholic; hers is Protestant, the marriage taking place in the waning years of the nineteenth century when such "mixed" marriages were frowned upon). Though Edward begins to establish a career as a successful dramatist, their marriage is irretrievably damaged by the catastrophe of a hotel fire at a banquet in which Katrina is severely injured, her corsage set afire by falling debris, and by ensuing infidelities as Katrina has an affair with a young Francis Phelan and Edward with a young actress. The marriage declines into alienation and depression, the sporadic progress toward dissolution imagined through the celebrated play that Edward writes with the same title as that of the novel. The novel is widely considered to be the least successful of the Albany Cycle as it seems to depend more on melodrama, and less on the combination of historical circumstance with personal dreams, memories, and histories than previous novels.

In *Roscoe*, Kennedy returns to the political scene in mid-twentieth-century Albany. The protagonist is Roscoe Conway, a key figure in the Albany Democratic political machinery whose role is that of an intermediary between political factions, the police, and the corrupt underworld that has everywhere infiltrated the social order. In the attempt to extricate himself from Albany politics, Conway calls up ghosts of the past, interacts with various figures that appear in previous novels of the cycle, and attempts to mediate conflicts between the McCall brothers (who made a prominent appearance running City Hall in *Billy Phelan's Greatest Game*) and their political enemies. The final novel of the cycle thus far, the unusually-titled *Changós Beads and Two-Tone Shoes*, moves between Cuba just before Castro's accession to power in 1957 and Albany in 1968 in throes of racial strife following the assassination of Robert Kennedy. The protagonist is a journalist, Daniel Quinn, grandson of the Quinn of *Quinn's Book*, who depicts his career and troubled relationship with a woman mired in Cuban revolutionary politics charted against a historical backdrop that implicitly connects events in an island-nation just over a hundred miles from the Florida Keys to racial strife in the capital city of Albany. As everywhere in Kennedy's work, the personal and the political are inextricably intertwined as the primary elements of story and history.

Beyond the Albany Cycle, Kennedy's work includes three works of nonfiction (*O Albany!*, *The Making of Ironweed* [1988], and *Riding the Yellow Trolley Car* [1993]), the two screenplays of *The Cotton Club*, with Francis Ford Coppola (1986), and *Ironweed* (1987), two plays (*Grand View* [1996], and *In the System* [2003]), and two children's books (*Charlie Malarkey and the Belly Button Machine* [1986], and *Charley Malarkey and the Singing Moose* [1994], both co-authored with Brendan Kennedy). Like comparable contemporary writers such as E.L. Doctorow and Russell Banks, Kennedy writes novels that describe class struggle in America set against the larger backdrop of American history. Over his four decades of writing, Kennedy has established himself as a major voice in the annals of contemporary American fiction – one who exposes the ignored corners and unconventional, marginalized characters of American life upon whom history takes its inevitable toll.

SEE ALSO: Banks, Russell; Contemporary Regionalisms; Doctorow, E.L.; Fictions of Work and Labor; Urban Fiction

REFERENCES

Baruth, Philip. (1998). William Kennedy on the surreal and the unconscious, the religious, the sublime, and the gonzo. *New England Review* 19 (1): 116–126.

Hume, Kathryn. (2000). The semiotics of fantasy in William Kennedy's fiction. *Philological Quarterly* 79 (4): 523–548.

Kennedy, William. (1983a). *Legs*. New York: Penguin. 1st ed. 1975.

Kennedy, William. (1983b). *Billy Phelan's Greatest Game*. New York: Penguin. 1st ed. 1978.

Kennedy, William. (2021). Why it took so long. *The New York Times* (May 20, 1991). https://www.nytimes.com/1990/05/20/books/why-it-took-so-long.html (accessed August 15, 2021).

FURTHER READING

Gillespie, Michael. (2001). *Reading William Kennedy*. Syracuse, NY: Syracuse University Press.

Michener, Christian. (2005). *From Then Into Now: William Kennedy's Albany Novels*. Scranton, PA: University of Scranton Press.

Reilly, Edward C. (1991). *William Kennedy*. New York: Twayne.

Seshachari, Neila C. (ed.) (1997). *Conversations with William Kennedy*. Jackson: University of Mississippi Press.

Van Dover, J. Kenneth. (1991). *Understanding William Kennedy*. Columbia: University of South Carolina Press.

Kincaid, Jamaica

JANA EVANS BRAZIEL
Miami University (Ohio), USA

Jamaica Kincaid is one of the most important contemporary anglophone writers in the Americas. Writing across the transnational and diasporic terrain of the United States and the Caribbean, Kincaid alters diasporic and literary frames for understanding subjectivity, language, nationality, history, colonialism, and race. Kincaid's fictional texts, many published first in serial form in the *New Yorker*, where she was a staff writer, include the 1983 short story collection *At the Bottom of the River*, the novels *Annie John* (1985), *Lucy* (1990), and *The Autobiography of My Mother*

(1996). Kincaid has also published important works of nonfiction: *A Small Place* (1988), refused by the *New Yorker*, on the exploitation of her homeland Antigua, specifically, and the broader Caribbean region, more generally, by the structural violences of European colonialism and the neocolonialist abuses of the global tourism industry; a memoir of her brother, *My Brother* (1997), following his harrowing death from AIDS; a collection of essays about gardening, colonialism, race, and history in the Americas, *My Garden (Book)* (1999); and a collection of her early writings for the "The Talk of the Town" series in the *New Yorker*, published as *Talk Stories* by Farrar, Straus, Giroux in January 2001. Since 2000, Kincaid has published a fictionalized biographical novel entitled *Mr. Potter* (2002); a nonfiction reflection on botany through travel writing titled *Among Flowers: A Walk Through the Himalaya* (2005); an edited volume of essays entitled *My Favorite Tool* (2007); and the novel *See Then Now* (2013).

Born Elaine Potter Richardson in Antigua on May 25, 1949, in Holberton Hospital in St. John's, Antigua, Jamaica Kincaid, her literary *nom du guerre*, was the oldest child and the only daughter of Annie Victoria Richardson and presumably one of many children born to Frederick Potter (christened Roderick Nathaniel Potter in the novel *Mr. Potter*), the biological father who abandoned her mother before she was even born. Kincaid was raised by her mother Annie and her stepfather David Drew, a man whom she has written affectionately about and whom she believed to be her biological father throughout childhood. As the only child for nine years, Kincaid was doted on by her mother until 1958, as she recounts for her readers, when her brother Joseph was born; Dalma and Devon, her younger brothers, were born soon after Joseph. This perceived loss (or division) of her mother's affection was experienced as a tragic loss for Kincaid, one that she has written about extensively in her alterbiographical novels (*Annie John, Lucy, My Brother*); however, critics who would reduce Kincaid's writings to a mother-daughter drama neglect (at least partially) Kincaid's literary engagements with history, colonialism, slavery, violence and genocide in the Caribbean and in the Americas. Antigua remained under British colonial rule until 1981, when it won its independence; and after 1981, it remained part of the British Commonwealth, its government overseen for decades by the V.C. Bird family, a family "plagued by corruption" (Paravisini-Gebert 1999, p. 1).

In 1965, at the age of 16, Kincaid emigrated to New York to work as an *au pair*. Soon frustrated by the expected servility of working as an *au pair*, Kincaid left the family for New York City and began working as a freelance writer, first for *Ingénue* and *Ms.*, and later working as a fulltime writer for the prestigious literary magazine the *New Yorker*. In the early 1970s, the emergent writer experimented in self-creation, renaming herself "Jamaica Kincaid." As a young, rebellious, and iconoclastic Antiguan woman coming of age in New York City, Kincaid also experimented with self and identity, writing in 1995 of her early forays in self-creation that she was "making ... a type of person that did not exist in the place where I was born" (1995, p. 93). During this time, Kincaid also experimented as a creative writer, publishing short stories and essays in the *New Yorker* under the editorial guidance of William Shawn.

While writing for the *New Yorker*, then edited by William Shawn, Kincaid met her then future husband Allen Shawn, the senior Shawn's son and a musical composer, whom she married in 1979, but from whom she is now divorced. Kincaid wrote for the *New Yorker* from 1976 to 1995, leaving after a public dispute with Tina Brown, who took over the editorship of the magazine in the 1990s. In addition to writing, Kincaid has also taught literature and writing – first at Bennington College in Vermont and later (still) at Harvard University in Cambridge, Massachusetts.

Kincaid's first book, a collection of short stories entitled *At the Bottom of the River*, was published in 1983. Composed of ten interlocking short stories, seven first published in the *New Yorker*, the collection astounded critics with its breathtaking lyricism, fluid images, and innovative lines of poetic prose, even as it confounded critics and readers alike with its abstract language, its abstruse and ethereal narratives, and its recesses of metamorphic meaning. Opening with the terse, dialogic story "Girl," the collection explores the mother-daughter melodrama so often a central motif in Kincaid's literary texts, but it also creates alternate states of existences: *alter-narratives* in which a girl becomes a man who married "a red-skin woman with black bramblebrush hair and brown eyes" (2000, p. 11), in which "blue bells fall to the cool earth; dying and living in perpetuity" (p. 19); in which a girl throws stones at a monkey who throws the stones back (p. 44); in which a child "passing through a small beam of light . . . [becomes] transparent" (p. 49); in which the girl's mother grows "plates of metal-colored scales on her back" (p. 55), and "a world in which the sun and moon shone at the same time" (p. 77). It is the shapeshifting creatures and polyvocalic tones, the stunning metamorphoses, of the stories that fascinate and singe. And these cryptic stories seem shattered mirrors into the writer's own imaginary.

Kincaid's *Annie John*, the author's first novel, is a Bildungsroman or a coming-of-age narrative about the protaginst and title character in her homeland Antigua. The daughter Annie John intimately recounts her daily life, her at-times asphyxiating closeness, then her increasing alienation from her mother Annie Drew as she enters other intimate childhood and girlhood relations with best friend Gwen, with alluring yet forbidden red girl, with figures of death and illness and as she herself becomes ill and becomes nursed back to health by Ma Chess, her Dominican grandmother who travels to Antigua with herbal medicines and knowledge of Obeah. As a stunningly charming and lyrical first novel, or literary debut, *Annie John* marks an important contribution to postcolonial Caribbean literatures and ethnic American literatures in English.

Kincaid's *Lucy*, a fictionalized autobiographical novel, recounts the experiences of the young protagonist leaving her island home in Antigua, a hot tropical island in the Caribbean, to arrive in the urban northeastern United States in mid-January – if Manhattan, another island, but one that is bleak, windy, cold, icy and dreary. While we do not discover the name of the protagonist until the final chapter of the novel; nor does the author fully disclose the name of the northeastern US city where the young woman has arrived, the title itself reveals her name: Lucy. Having taken a position as an *au pair* in order, first, to save money to remit to her family back home and to pay tuition for nursing school (her mother's ambitions for her diasporic daughter), Lucy finds herself for the first time isolated, alone, lonely, and separate from her mother, a dominating, even suffocating force in her life. *Lucy* thus begins as *Annie John* ends with the island "girl" from a "small place" charting routes, departing mother and motherland to begin a new life in diaspora – for Lucy, in New York; for Annie John, in London.

The Autobiography of My Mother is a novel in autobiographical form about Xuela Claudette Richardson, the protagonist, who at the age of seventy retrospectively recounts the events of her life as they have unfolded in Dominica. She begins by telling the readers that her mother (a beautiful Carib woman named Xuela who was herself orphaned as an infant) died "at the moment that she was born," and this loss is the central preoccupation of the novel. We discover that Xuela's mother was abandoned as an infant by her own Carib mother who left her outside a convent where she was discovered by a nun named Claudette Desvarieux and from whom she acquired her full name: Xuela Claudette Desvarieux. After her mother's death, her father Alfred Richardson (himself the son of Mary, an African mother, and John Richardson, a "Scots-man") delivers her to the care of Ma Eunice Paul, a wet nurse who provides the infant shelter and nourishment but no love. Complex interwoven narrative lines in *The Autobiography of My Mother* swirl concentrically and even obsessively around a single problematic: that of autobiography.

Within Kincaid's literary oeuvre, *My Brother* offers the most extended literary imprinting of death as a "biographical autograph" that philosophically troubles the genre of biography, or "life writing." Biographical questions and generic problems recur in the memoir *My Brother*: the memoir destabilizes and metonymically displaces the writing self, or the autobiographical "I," and its presumed referentiality into the biographical brother Devon Drew, the author's youngest half-brother. Written following the death of her youngest half-brother from AIDS-related medical complications, the memoir poignantly reflects on Devon's life and his death, her relationship with her sibling, who was only a toddler when she left Antigua for New York, and the relationship of both children to their dominating, overpowering mother Annie Drew. In the memoir, the mother Annie Drew is configured as the guardian of death, the sister Jamaica Kincaid as biographer, life-writer, and thus, also life-giver, and the brother Devon Drew as a liminal body that is half-dead and half-alive. Mrs. Drew is also the divine-mother – not only creator of children, hearth, and home, but also the vengeful God of retribution and judgment – and her divinity imbues her with the destructive forces of nature and elemental power: Annie's offspring, her children, people the paradise she creates, but they are eventually cast out, punished, forsaken: they fall; they dwell in postlapsarian worlds. Like Lucy in the autobiographical of the same title, whose namesake is Lucifer, Annie Drew's children – her oldest child and only daughter Elaine Potter Richardson and her sons Dalma, Joe, and Devon Drew – are *fallen angels*.

Kincaid's *Mr. Potter* marks a significant foray into the complex and challenging terrain of autofiction (a hybrid genre intermingling fiction and autobiography); or more precisely, *alterbiography*, a textual rending of autobiography through the inscriptions of alterity and difference. The novel is subtle, nuanced, lyrical, passionate, and literary. *Mr. Potter* recounts the simple, sparse life of a chauffeur (who first works for an exiled Lebanese merchant and later for himself) on the island of Antigua, the place of Kincaid's own birth. The story reveals the daily events of Mr. Potter's life: his affairs and the numerous daughters (who all share his nose) that he birthed, but for whom he never provided and certainly never loved; his illiteracy and his humble attempts to make a life for himself, if not for his children. The novel is not just a biography of this man (who could not read or write), but also the autobiographical reflections of his daughter (the one who could read and write): Elaine Cynthia Potter. In the novel, Kincaid movingly tells of Mr. Potter's abandonment and rejection of the young girl (born on May 25, 1949), after her own mother, Annie Victoria Richardson (then Drew), seven months pregnant at the time, left with his money that had been saved and hidden under the mattress and with which he intended to buy a car. Through his story, we discover that he too has suffered loss and abandonment: his father, Nathaniel Potter, refused to acknowledge his paternity of the boy Roderick, and his mother, Elfrida Robinson, committed suicide by walking into the sea when he was just a small child. The book is a painful account of loss and desire, and it memorializes the pain itself, as much as the man who suffered it, and the man who in his own turn, passed on this line of disinheritance o his daughters, the legatees of his illegitimacy, anonymity, and illiteracy, save one: Jamaica Kincaid.

See Then Now, regarded by many critics as intensely autobiographical yet vehemently denied by the author as such, is set in small town New England – in Vermont, to be precise – and tells the tale of Mr. and Mrs. Sweet and their children Persephone and Heracles, recounts their daily humdrum lives, their eventual falling apart as a family. As Kincaid narrates from the perspective of Mrs. Sweet in the opening pages of the novel: "her husband, the dear Mr. Sweet, hated her very much" (2013, p. 6). Mr. Sweet is a composer, plays a Steinway piano, and who loved "ballet and Wittgenstein and opera" (p. 26); Mrs. Sweet, depressed and doting, a housewife, knits socks and watches her marriage unravel. As readers learn, Mr. Sweet, a musician, leaves Mrs. Sweet to be with a younger woman, also a musician. Kincaid, the writers, spares no one; and the story told is anything but sweet. Echoing the rhythmic and even hynoptic cadences of everyday life as captured in *Mr. Potter*, Kincaid's *See Then Now* similarly reveals the devastations of love, marriage, families, and the monotic passing of time. Evoking comparisons to Virginia Woolf, James Joyce, and Gertude Stein, particularly their modernist meditations on time and temporality, its flow and its disruptions, critics both celebrate and decry this most recent work of fiction by Jamaica Kincaid.

SEE ALSO: Black Atlantic; Danticat, Edwige; Díaz, Junot; James, Marlon; Literature of the Americas; Morrison, Toni; Multiculturalism; Paule, Marshall

REFERENCES

Kincaid, Jamaica. (1995). Putting myself together. *The New Yorker* (February 20–27, 1995): 93. https://www.newyorker.com/magazine/1995/02/20/putting-myself-together (accessed September 15, 2021).

Kincaid, Jamaica. (2000). *At the Bottom of the River.* New York: Farrar, Straus and Giroux; 1st ed. 1983.

Kincaid, Jamaica. (2013). *See Then Now.* New York: Farrar, Straus and Giroux.

Paravisini-Gebert, Lizabeth. (1999). *Jamaica Kincaid: A Critical Companion.* Westport, CT: Greenwood Press.

FURTHER READING

Bouson, J. Brooks. (2005). *Jamaica Kincaid: Writing Memory, Writing Back to The Mother.* Albany, NY: SUNY.

Braziel, Jana Evans. (2009). *Caribbean Genesis: Jamaica Kincaid and The Writing of New Worlds.* Albany, NY: SUNY.

Dance, Daryl Cumber. (2016). *In Search of Annie Drew: Jamaica Kincaid's Mother and Muse.* Charlottesville: University of Virginia Press.

Edwards, Justin D. (2007). *Understanding Jamaica Kincaid.* Columbia: University of South Carolina Press.

Ferguson, Moira. (1994). *Jamaica Kincaid: Where The Land Meets The Body.* Charlottesville: University of Virginia Press.

King, Stephen

ERIN MERCER
Massey University, New Zealand

Stephen King (b. September 21, 1947) is one of the most successful – and prolific – writers in the American literary tradition. To date, he has published over sixty novels in an array of genres, including horror, fantasy, science fiction, and crime, and has sold more than 350 million copies worldwide. He has published over 200 short stories, eighteen screenplays, and five nonfiction books. His popular success is matched by critical acclaim (although King has his share of detractors who tend to conflate popular success with poor literary value). He has received several prestigious awards, including the National Book Foundation Medal for Distinguished Contribution to American Letters in 2003, and in 2015, King was awarded a National Medal of Arts for his contributions to literature. King began publishing in 1974 and the novels of that decade – *Carrie* (1974), *'Salem's Lot* (1975), *The Shining* (1977), and *The Stand* (1978) – established his preoccupation with supernatural horror and psychological decay. Although King is certainly a master of horror, his work is also attuned to the realities of American social life, meaning that novels that focus on telekinetic teenagers, vampires, haunted hotels, and apocalyptic plagues are simultaneously concerned with "real life" horrors such as bullying, substance abuse, and domestic violence. This is evident in the major novels that King has published since the 1980s.

In *Pet Sematary* (1983), a middle-class nuclear family leaves the hustle of Chicago in favor of the rural idyll of Maine, where central protagonist Louis Creed takes up a job as a doctor at the local university. The house where the Creeds reside is seemingly perfect, as are the elderly neighbors who take the family under their wing, but there is something wrong in this seemingly ideal vision of the American Dream. Just beyond the Creed's house is a patch of land where local children bury their dead pets, and just beyond this is a darker place where evil resides. The novel's sinister pet cemetery and revenant cat are certainly the stuff of horror, but the most harrowing parts of *Pet Sematary* are the scenes depicting the debilitating grief that the Creeds experience when their youngest child, Gage, is killed on the busy road outside their house. In an effort to save his family from this grief, and to alleviate his own feelings of guilt at not being able to stop Gage from running into the road, Louis begins to contemplate the unthinkable: to disinter his son's corpse from the local cemetery and bury it in the woods. The novel's engagement with the figure of the zombie allows it to explore similar themes to those in Mary Shelley's *Frankenstein* (1818): hubris, the tension between religious and scientific perspectives, and what should remain taboo. As Heidi Strengell notes, both *Frankenstein* and *Pet Sematary* "analyze the concept of free will, hence apparently suggesting that although fate undeniably rules and the mechanistic world of the Gothic is in place, the characters still possess free will to make moral choices" (Strengell 2005, p. 55). Additionally, King introduces a political concern by identifying the environment that houses the power capable of resurrecting corpses with Native Americans. The Creeds are told that the land surrounding their house is the subject of claims by local tribes to have it returned to their ownership, which implicates a colonial past as at least part of the cause of a horrific present.

The sins of the past that refuse to remain buried is a key aspect of another important novel published in the 1980s: *IT* (1986). Again set in Maine (which is a recurring environment in King's fiction), this time the small town of Derry, *IT* is a sprawling novel that covers two time periods in the lives of its central protagonists: the 1950s when the protagonists are children; and the 1980s when they return to Derry as adults. As 11-year-olds, King's protagonists experience an array of traumas that are part of King's ongoing critique of American culture, including domestic abuse, incest, bullying, and racial hatred. The darkness that lies just beneath the pretty surface of Derry manifests as one of King's most recognizable monsters: Pennywise the Dancing Clown. Capable of taking on an array of guises according to what its victim most fears, the monstrous entity known as IT is an otherworldly being which haunts and feeds off the negativity that defines Derry. IT is cyclical, just like history, and returns to feed off the town's children every twenty-seven years. First as children, and then as adults, the protagonists who call themselves "the Losers' Club" come up against IT and attempt to vanquish it. As in so much of King's fiction, including *The Stand* and *Desperation* (1996), *IT* represents a soiled American reality defined by violence, hatred, and oppression. Nevertheless, there is goodness to be found – and in King's work it is often to be found in children – and the forces of good must engage in an apocalyptic battle against the forces of evil.

King's apocalyptic imaginary is particularly apparent in *The Stand*, which was republished in its complete and uncut form in 1990. Here King's concern with good and evil is expressed through a deadly plague that decimates the population, leaving just a tiny proportion of those who are mysteriously immune. Some of these people experience dreams that draw them toward Mother Abigail, an elderly African American woman who will eventually lead them to Boulder, Colorado, while others are drawn to Las Vegas and the seductive allure of the demonic Randall Flagg. In this novel, King contrasts the violence and greed that characterizes Las Vegas with the decency and sacrifice of those residing in Boulder. Flagg is a representative of Satan, just as Mother Abigail has been allowed to live for over a hundred years so that she can do God's bidding. *The Stand* is much more religious than *IT*, which makes little mention of God, but it similarly represents apocalyptic destruction as a necessary cleansing agent that will rid the world of evil.

King is certainly critical of many aspects of American society, repeatedly highlighting petty meanness, greed, misuse of power, and corruption, but his work also insists on the power of good. Thus, *The Stand* represents Randall Flagg as dangerously powerful, but not so powerful that he can thwart the power of decent people who are willing to sacrifice themselves for others. This optimism is also found in *Desperation*, which is similarly apocalyptic. Again, this novel takes as its central concern the battle between good and evil, and this conflict similarly plays out in the apocalyptic environment of the Western desert. Far beneath the earth of the Nevada town of Desperation lurks an evil entity referred to as Tak, which escapes the pit where it is confined by projecting itself into the bodies of others. In the body of the local policeman Entragian, Tak massacres the town's population, which King's disparate protagonists discover as they are variously drawn to the desert town. Like Mother Abigail in *The Stand*, who is chosen by God, 11-year-old David Carver is a special boy. Not particularly religious, David experiences a profound conversion when God grants his prayer to save his best friend's life after he is hit by a car. Following this, David is a believer, and he is tasked with destroying the evil entity that terrorizes Desperation. King's representations of God are not of the saccharine variety. Much of his work represents a divine power that demands significant sacrifice from his followers, which David discovers when his promise to owe God a favor in return for his friend's life involves him losing his entire family. The repeated refrain of *Desperation* is "God is cruel" but that cruelty is never malicious. Rather, God's will is enacted by free will rather than fate, and his cruelty is designed to refine the good as in a crucible.

Another concern that distinguishes King's writing is writing itself, and many of his novels have writers as characters. In *IT*, young Bill

Denborough becomes a successful writer of horrors, and David Carver's accomplice in the attack on Tak is a famous writer in the vein of Norman Mailer. In *Misery* (1987), King removes any supernatural element in order to focus primarily on the relationship between writer and reader. The central protagonist, Paul Sheldon, is a best-selling author of historical romances that feature a character named Misery Chastain. When the narrative begins, he has recently killed her off in a final novel in order to focus on the "serious" writing that he considers better than his popular series. When Paul is injured in a car accident, he emerges from unconsciousness to discover himself in the home of a former nurse, Annie Wilkes, who lives on a remote farm in Colorado. Although Paul is in severe pain from his serious injuries, which include two broken legs, Annie refuses to take him to a hospital, treating him herself and liberally providing pain killers that Paul is soon addicted to. Slowly it transpires that Annie is deranged; worse, she is a fan of the Misery series and is enraged to discover that Misery dies in the final instalment. Annie declares herself to be Paul's "number one fan" and demands that he write a new Misery novel, punishing him severely when he misbehaves – including chopping of a foot with an axe and cauterising his ankle with a blow torch. Finally, Annie reveals that she plans to kill Paul and herself when the manuscript is completed so that Misery's continued existence can be guaranteed. *Misery* is sensitive to the desire of writers to be creatively challenged and explore different modes of writing, but it is also sensitive to the desires of readers whose devotion to an author's work might involve a certain kind of responsibility. King has experienced this dilemma himself when his reputation as a writer of supernatural horror was challenged by his forays into fantasy with *The Eyes of the Dragon* (1984) and the Dark Tower series, the first of which appeared in 1982. Perhaps even more personal are King's own struggles with addiction. He wrote *Misery* in the throes of substance abuse and suggests that "I knew what I was writing about. There was never any question. Annie was my drug problem, and she was my number one fan. God, she never wanted to leave" (Wood 2017, p. 123).

The centrality of Annie Wilkes in *Misery* marks a significant turning point in King's writing, which came under fire during the 1980s for stereotypical representations of women. In *Pet Sematary*, for instance, Louis Creed's wife, Rachel, does little asides from cook eggs, bake apple pie, service her husband's sexual needs, and collapse into hysterics at moments of stress. Although Annie is monstrous, she is a fully rounded female character with layered psychology, idiosyncrasies, and a considerable amount of agency. This is a trend that King continued in two novels of the 1990s that focus on female experience, *Dolores Claibourne* (1993) and *Rose Madder* (1995). As in *Misery*, *Dolores Claibourne* eschews the supernatural, but King departs from his omniscient third-person narration, using instead a first-person monologue that represents Dolores's recorded confession to law enforcement, who suspect her of murdering her employer. Dolores is innocent of this crime, but confesses instead to the murder of her husband, who has physically abused his wife and molested his daughter. The concerns of *Dolores Claibourne* are domestic rather than supernatural, and the first-person monologue represents the narrator's experience in her own terms. *Rose Madder* is similarly concerned with the domestic abuse experienced by a woman, and like Dolores Claibourne, Rose is eventually able to escape the oppression of her husband in order to find a better life.

Between 1970 and 2012, King published the eight novels that constitute The Dark Tower series. Incorporating elements of fantasy, science fiction, and Western, the series focuses on the adventures of Roland Deschain and is a key tool in clarifying King's "multiverse." That is, while representing the quest of gunslinger Roland to find and protect the Dark Tower, the series also makes connections with King's standalone novels. For example, the nature of the ancient turtle that appears toward the end of *IT* is never clearly explained in that text; it is only in the Dark Tower series that the cosmology of King's fictional multiverse is revealed. The turtle spirit is known as Maturin, who originates in the Macroverse, a plane of reality outside that which contains Earth, and who essentially created Earth by vomiting it up. Similarly, the series references the rabid St Bernard dog that terrorizes the protagonists in *Cujo* (1981) and Paul Sheldon of *Misery*, even including a fictional version of Stephen King himself who appears in the sixth novel of the series, *Song of Susannah* (2004). In this novel, Roland and his companion Eddie Dean meet King, who fears that dark forces are conspiring in order to prevent him from completing the Dark Tower story. In a metafictional twist, King is a conduit for Gan the creator's will and by writing the series he is essentially enabling Roland's quest. If King dies, the quest for the Tower fails and the Crimson King, Gan's evil "other," will triumph. King's real-life accident that almost claimed his life in 1999 (when he was hit by a vehicle while out walking) is thus avoided in the novel so that he is able to keep writing the story.

King's fiction consistently engages with its cultural context, whether through references to brand names and popular culture, or through intertextual references and snippets of songs. In *Cell* (2006), King takes two aspects of twenty-first-century life – terrorism and cell phones – and lends new life to the zombie narrative. Once again, the protagonist of this novel is a writer, Clayton Riddell, whose life is disrupted when a mysterious pulse surges through the global cell phone network rendering all who hear it into murderous zombie-like figures soon referred to as "phoners." At once an indictment of the mindless swiping commonly associated with excessive use of mobile devices, *Cell* also engages with the threat of terrorism that has defined the Western world since the terrorist attacks of 9/11. The novel suggests that the Pulse is the work of a terrorist organization, while the double meaning of the novel's title – cell as in cellular phone and cell as in terrorist cell – works to reinforce this. Furthermore, the novel complicates just who might be defined as a terrorist as the group of unaffected survivors joined by Clayton undertakes to brutally destroy phoners. In one particularly vivid scene, a cluster of sleeping phoners are blown to pieces with dynamite by the survivors, which clearly casts Clayton and his friends as indiscriminate murderers, in contrast to the phoners, many of whom are peaceful. *Cell* ultimately suggests that terrorists might not just be an external threat, but a far more dangerous one from within, as civilians turn against those deemed to be "other."

In 2008, King published *Duma Key*, his first novel to be set in the state of Florida. The following year, *Under the Dome* (2009) appeared, which saw King return to the multiple character perspectives that define *The Stand*. In this novel, King is particularly attuned to character psychology, carefully tracing the effects on a town's inhabitants when they are sealed off by an invisible wall. In a slightly different return to roots, King wrote a sequel to *The Shining*, *Doctor Sleep* (2013), which finds Danny Torrance as a deeply troubled man in his forties. The novel reveals that despite surviving the violent events at the Overlook Hotel when he was a boy, Danny has not escaped unscathed. In fact, Danny is afflicted with the very alcoholism that helped ruin his father. *Doctor Sleep* traces the legacy of violence, while also continuing King's interest in supernatural horror, as Danny must protect a young girl with psychic powers from a group of vampire-like creatures whose power comes from imbibing the essence of children. In a quite different vein, King began writing crime thrillers during this decade, publishing *Mr Mercedes* (2014), *Finders Keepers* (2015) and *End of Watch* (2016), which constitute the Bill Hodges Trilogy about a retired police detective. Most recently, *The Institute* (2019) details the unethical and inhuman treatment of paranormally gifted children whose talents are exploited by a shadowy organization in order to manipulate global politics. Once again, King's work demonstrates a concern for the vulnerable who are terrorized by corrupt forces, whether supernatural or realistic.

The sheer amount of King's fiction – which also includes short stories, work published under the pseudonym Richard Bachman, novellas, and screenplays – is daunting, as is the imaginative power that generates a fictional output of such size and scope. What unites King's fiction is undoubtedly horror, but it is ultimately the horrors of what we recognize as real rather than supernatural that give his narratives such continuing resonance. Certainly, the demonic clown of *IT* that lures children to watery graves in the sewers of Derry is terrifying, as is the storeowner of *Needful Things* (1991) who has just what his customers want – in exchange for their souls – but underlying the tropes of horror fiction are small American towns riven by hatred, prejudice, and greed. King's characters consistently deal with violence, particularly domestic violence, and are repeatedly assaulted by the sins of a past that refuses to remain buried. Perhaps one possible answer as to why King's work is so enduringly popular might lie in the fact that his essentially good protagonists, more often than not, succeed in vanquishing the threats they face. King's work, while steeped in horror, also provides readers with the reassurance of a happy ending when that horror is ultimately contained.

SEE ALSO: Contemporary Regionalisms; Fiction and Terrorism; Mailer, Norman; Mixed-Genre Fiction; Post-9/11 Narratives; Religion and Contemporary Fiction

REFERENCES

Strengell, Heidi. (2005). *Dissecting Stephen King: From the Gothic to Literary Naturalism.* Madison: University of Wisconsin Press.

Wood, Rocky. (2017). *Stephen King: A Literary Companion.* Jefferson: McFarland.

FURTHER READING

Badley, Linda. (1996). *Writing Horror and the Body: The Fiction of Stephen King, Clive Barker, and Anne Rice.* Westport, CT: Greenwood Press.

Ingebretsen, Edward J. (2016). *Maps of Heaven, Maps of Hell: Religious Terror as Memory from the Puritans to Stephen King.* Abingdon, UK: Routledge.

Russell, Sharon. (1996). *Stephen King: A Critical Companion.* Westport, CT: Greenwood Press.

Sears, John. (2011). *Stephen King's Gothic.* Cardiff: University of Wales Press.

Simpson, Philip L. and McAleer, Patrick. (eds.) (2015). *Stephen King's Contemporary Classics: Reflections on the Modern Master of Horror.* Lanham, ML: Rowman & Littlefield.

Kingsolver, Barbara

DANA PHILLIPS
Towson University, USA

Since 1988, Barbara Kingsolver (b. 1955) has published eight novels, a volume of short stories, two collections of essays, a book on food and farming, two volumes of poetry, and a nonfiction account of a miners' strike in Arizona. Her Appalachian roots, long residence in Tucson, Arizona, education (undergraduate and graduate degrees in biology), wide-ranging travel, and political convictions have informed her writing from the start of her career.

Kingsolver's *The Bean Trees* (1988) and its sequel, *Pigs in Heaven* (1993), helped shape her reputation as a writer alert to the complexities of family, community, race, class, and environment. In the first novel, Taylor Greer leaves Kentucky in a derelict Volkswagen and heads west. In Oklahoma, she stops at a rundown bar and grill for a hamburger and as she leaves is given a toddler, a girl who seems traumatized. Because of the little girl's tenacious grip, Taylor names her Turtle. In Kentucky, it is proverbial that when mud turtles bite they won't let go until it thunders. The name also resonates with Turtle's identity: she is Cherokee.

Before leaving Kentucky, Taylor avoided an early pregnancy and a bad-luck marriage. Now, all at once, she has become a mother. The novel follows the story of her attempt to be a good parent as she adapts herself to the new community – human and nonhuman – that she discovers in Tucson. This community includes her employer, Mattie, the owner of a tire repair service and a key player in the Sanctuary movement. Taylor becomes the housemate of another displaced Kentuckian, Lou Ann, who like Taylor is a single mother. Other important characters include two refugees from Guatemala, Estevan and Esperanza, who have had to flee political turmoil.

Despite its solemn themes and dramatic plot, *The Bean Trees* is often a comic novel thanks to the rootedness of Taylor Greer's character in rural Kentucky. She does not try to shed her native Appalachian speech, and her grounded folk sensibility makes her role ironic and playful. This is a trademark of Kingsolver's fiction: she manages to treat very serious events in humorous but not flippant ways, avoiding the sentimentality and melodrama that otherwise would be generated by her plots. Taylor has native wit and intellectual curiosity. When she crosses the Arizona state line, she comments on the improbability of the desert Southwest: "The whole scene looked too goofy to be real. We whizzed by a roadside sign on which I could make out a dinosaur. I wondered if it told what kind of rocks they were, or if it was saying that they were actually petrified dinosaur turds. I was laughing my head off" (Kingsolver 1988, p. 47). She admits her idea of the desert was shaped by "old Westerns and Quickdraw McGraw cartoons" (p. 217). Yet Taylor is not naive; she knows better than to take herself and her first impressions too seriously, and is willing to change her mind. Later in the novel, Mattie, Taylor, Estevan, and Esperanza go to watch the first rain of the summer from a vantage point in the mountains outside Tucson. Typically, Kingsolver will allow a character like Taylor to experience a change of heart, and perhaps even an epiphany, only to undercut the character's elevation of spirit with a dose of fact. She does this when Taylor is moved by the desert rain:

> That was when we smelled the rain. It was so strong it seemed like more than just a smell. When we stretched out our hands we could practically feel it rising up from the ground. I don't know how a person could ever describe that scent. It certainly wasn't sour, but it wasn't sweet either, not like a flower. "Pungent" is the word Esteban used. To my mind it was like nothing so much as a wonderfully clean, scrubbed pine floor.
>
> Mattie explained that it was caused by the greasewood bushes, which she said produced a certain chemical when it rained.
>
> (1988, p. 219)

In her depiction of the natural world – for many readers, one of the chief attractions of her fiction – Kingsolver always takes care, as she does here, to temper the poetic with the astringency of fact.

Turtle is also at the center of the story told in *The Bean Trees*, as she will again be in *Pigs in Heaven*. She figures as a problem to be resolved in both novels. She is, at first, mute. When she does begin to speak, her talk focuses on plants and seeds, the names of which she employs as the vocabulary of a primitive and nearly private language. Her first word is "bean" (1988, p. 130), and when she is given dolls to play with she attempts to plant them. The title of the first novel echoes the name Turtle gives to wisteria vines, which after flowering produce long pods filled with bean-like seeds (p. 194). Yet Turtle does not assign names based solely on her childish grasp of taxonomy; she also studies seed catalogues. Plants provide her with a way back into the world. Turtle has been damaged physically and psychologically, but she proves to be resilient and even resourceful – and therefore is a good partner for Taylor. Together, the two invent a new life and a new home for themselves, which acquires some legitimacy when they travel to Oklahoma where, with the aid of Esteban and Esperanza, who pose as her birth parents, Taylor is able to formally adopt Turtle.

Pigs in Heaven takes up the story of Taylor Greer and her daughter a few years after the events described in the first novel. It complicates any notion her readers might have entertained of Kingsolver as a regionalist writer anchored in the South and Southwest: here the action moves from Tucson to the Grand Canyon and then to Chicago (where Turtle and Taylor appear on the Oprah show), with a sojourn in Seattle to follow, before the scene shifts once more back to Oklahoma and the Cherokee Nation. Taylor and Turtle are displaced several times, and spend long hours on the highway, before coming to a new understanding of home. Their new understanding depends on a plot filled with incident and movement, as well as with considerable coincidence. Taylor's mother also travels to the Cherokee Nation and learns that she and Taylor have enough native heritage to qualify for birth rights. Though a Cherokee lawyer is asserting the tribe's right to Turtle, its lost child, she also makes a match between Taylor's mother and Cash Stillwater, who has recently returned to Oklahoma after a few years in Jackson Hole. He proves to be Turtle's grandfather and sole next of kin, but allows Taylor to retain custody of her adoptive daughter when Taylor's mother agrees to marry him. Thus *Pigs in Heaven* achieves closure in the classic fashion of comedies: family is restored and a marriage celebrated. Crucially, the novel is saved from sentimentality by its many subtle ironies, as in Kingsolver's description of Cash's return to his native place:

> At a bend in the road outside Locust Grove, Cash is moved by the sight of a little field with a heartbreaking hedgerow of wild pink roses and one small, sweet hickory in the center, left standing because the Cherokee man or woman who plowed that field wouldn't cut down a hickory. He keeps an eye out, afraid to miss one single sight as he makes his way. Crowds of black-eyed susans stand up to be counted, and five beagles sit side by side in someone's yard, reverent as a choir, blessing his overdue return.
>
> (1993, p. 182)

The imperfectly plowed field and the five beagles are evidence of Kingsolver's awareness of the woebegone and mildly absurd features that home can acquire in the eyes of a returning native. The most succinct example of this in Kingsolver's fiction may be the moment in the title story of her collection *Homeland and Other Stories* (1989) when a "full-blood" Cherokee woman tells her excited granddaughter, during their visit to the tourist-trap town of Cherokee, North Carolina, "I've never been here before" (1990, p. 18).

Kingsolver also borrows from other native cultures in her second novel, *Animal Dreams* (1990). Its protagonist, Codi Noline, returns to her hometown of Grace, Arizona, a place where she never felt comfortable as an Anglo growing up among Hispanics. Now, after years away and a stalled medical career, she feels more alienated than ever. She has returned during troubled times. Her father Homer, the town doctor, is dying; Grace is experiencing a conflict between the mining company and its laborers; and the town is undergoing an environmental crisis, as the river that flows through the canyon where Grace is located has been poisoned with heavy metals from the mine. The toxic water is, in turn, killing the orchards that families have tended for generations. As is usually the case in Kingsolver's novels, lines of conflict and alliance in Grace are complex and entangled. Codi's father is actually a native of the place, Homero Nolino, and she is descended from one of the original Gracela sisters, immigrants from Spain, who gave the town its name. Her old neighbors do not see her as an outsider, recall her childhood with fondness, and invite her to join their fight against the mining company.

Again, despite the drama of her plot (which also includes the death of Codi's sister in Nicaragua, where she has gone to give agricultural advice to peasant farmers during the Sandinista revolution), Kingsolver infuses the novel with humor. This has to do with Codi's gradual realization of the deceptiveness of appearances and the heterogeneous nature of life in Grace. When she reunites with Loyd Peregrina (he impregnated her in high school, though she never told him), she begins to immerse herself in Grace and in the region in new ways. Loyd is White Mountain Apache. Codi knew about his native identity in high school, but now she learns that he also has ties to the Navajo Reservation and to Santa Rosalia, one of the pueblos near the Jemez Mountains of New Mexico. After an erotic interlude at the hot springs near Jemez pueblo (it is winter and the couple is alone), Kingsolver once again returns her character to reality: "After showing me his secret hot springs, Loyd had told me the Jemez Mountains were being mined savagely for pumice, the odd Styrofoam-like gravel I'd thrown into the air in handfuls. Pumice was required for the manufacture of so-called distressed denim jeans" (1991, p. 248). This habit of discounting the more romantic moments of her fiction by underscoring the bottom line of socioeconomic life reveals the critical intentions of Kingsolver's work.

To put the point another way, Kingsolver is and always has been a political novelist. This became fully apparent to her readers when she published *The Poisonwood Bible* in 1998. While the novel retains familiar features of her earlier work, it expands the scope of Kingsolver's fiction in terms of its length and complexity, and in terms of its geographical and historical reach. The plot concerns the failed mission of Nathan Price, his wife Orleanna, and their four daughters to a village in the Congo in the early 1960s, just as Belgian rule is coming to an end and Patrice Lumumba is about to become the newly independent country's first native president.

The Poisonwood Bible is more than a clever rewrite, from an American and a feminine perspective (Orleanna and her daughters serve as storytellers), of Conrad's *Heart of Darkness* (1899) and Achebe's *Things Fall Apart* (1958), texts to which Kingsolver's narrators sometimes allude. Multigenerational and multiply voiced, and tracing the history of decades of Congolese, European, and American interactions, the novel is at once a colonial, a postcolonial, and a neocolonial epic though it focuses on the life of a single family. Its storyline begins with tragedy, as Orleanna Price acknowledges when she reflects on the past from the vantage of her home on Sanderling Island along the Georgia coast: "What is the conqueror's wife, if not a conqueror herself? For that matter, what is *he*? When he rides in to vanquish the untouched tribes, don't you think they fall down with desire before those sky-colored eyes? And itch for a turn with those horses, and those guns? That's what we yell back at history, always, always. It wasn't just me; there were crimes strewn six ways to Sunday, and I had my own mouths to feed. I didn't know. I had no life of my own" (1999, p. 9). Orleanna couches this reflection in terms of a classic scenario of colonial encounter (blue eyes, horses, and guns versus tribesmen). But the terms of her own encounter are specific: she loses her husband to his religious mania, her youngest daughter to snakebite, and her oldest to the wiles of a South African mercenary, who works for the CIA and flies Rachel off to Johannesburg. Of her twin middle daughters, Leah remains in the Congo and marries the local schoolteacher, who is also a political activist. Only Adah, who has a physical disability (a lame leg) and a gnomic sensibility (she is obsessed with palindromes), returns to the United States with Orleanna.

From early on in the novel, Adah provides disenchanted and distanced commentary on events. Here is how she describes her father's failed attempt to feed his flock with fish from the nearby river by throwing sticks of dynamite into the water: "He performed a backward version of the loaves and fishes, trying to stuff ten thousand fish into fifty mouths, did the Reverend Price. [. . .] Our village was blessed for weeks with the smell of putrefaction. Instead of abundance it was a holiday of waste. No ice. Our Father forgot, for fishing in the style of modern redneck Georgia you need your ice" (1999, p. 70). Adah is always alert to the absurdity alloyed with the tragedy of Nathan Price's mission to the Congo. Her sister Leah, who is moved by the plight of the Congo and its politics, also comes to realize the folly of her father's actions. She describes his inability to cope with his congregation's desire to vote on whether to accept Christianity or continue to embrace their own spiritual traditions: "Tata Ndu turned to Father and spoke almost kindly:

'Jesus is a white man, so he will understand the law of *la majorité*, Tata Price. *Wenda mbote*.' Jesus Christ lost, eleven to fifty-six" (p. 334). The adoption of Western-style democracy by Congolese society produces a different, less whimsical result elsewhere in the novel.

Kingsolver returns to her own native ground in her next novel, *Prodigal Summer* (2000), which concerns two women and a lonely widower (all three with an interest in Appalachian biology and ecology) living in the mountains along the border between Tennessee and Virginia. However, her more recent novels have had the same concern with geopolitics and the same historical scale as *The Poisonwood Bible*. *The Lacuna* (2009), which won the Orange Prize for Fiction in 2010, represents an even more dramatic departure from Kingsolver's earlier subject matter. It depicts the radical politics of the 1930s, and the reaction they provoked in the 1940s and 1950s, by telling the story of Harrison Shepherd, the son of a Mexican mother and an American father, and his relationship with historical figures like Diego Rivera, Frida Kahlo, and Leon Trotsky.

Flight Behavior (2012) is also geopolitical, but in this case the politics are environmental. Its main character, Dellarobia Turnbow, is an unhappy housewife who discovers a population of monarch butterflies overwintering in the fir trees on her husband's family farm in the mountains of Tennessee. The butterflies are a spectacle she struggles to comprehend: "These things were all over, dangling like giant bunches of grapes from every tree she could see" (2013, p. 12). The monarchs' sudden shift from their usual wintering grounds in the mountains of northern Mexico to Tennessee is fantastic, since few species can adapt readily to the climate change that has altered their flight behavior. Soon, the farm is playing host to Dr. Ovid Byron, an entomologist and leading expert on the fate of the monarchs. The butterfly's story is entwined with Dellarobia's: her ambition was to leave home for college and a life elsewhere, but her own flight has been checked by an early marriage and motherhood.

Kingsolver's most recent novel, *Unsheltered* (2018), tells the story of the Donald Trump era from the perspective of a woman who has been forced to move from a college town in Virginia after her husband loses his job as a professor to the less idyllic Vineland, New Jersey. She begins to research the life of a nineteenth-century school teacher who, like her, moved to Vineland – and struck up a friendship with his neighbor, an eccentric woman and a brilliant naturalist who corresponded with Charles Darwin. Once more, Kingsolver anchors a story about politics and history in the life of a woman struggling to keep her family intact in a changing world.

SEE ALSO: Contemporary Regionalisms; Ecocriticism and Environmental Fiction

REFERENCES

Kingsolver, Barbara. (1988). *The Bean Trees*. New York: Harper.
Kingsolver, Barbara. (1990). *Homeland and Other Stories*. New York: Harper Perennial; 1st ed. 1989.
Kingsolver, Barbara. (1991). *Animal Dreams*. New York: Harper Perennial; 1st ed. 1990.
Kingsolver, Barbara. (1993). *Pigs in Heaven*. New York: HarperCollins.
Kingsolver, Barbara. (1999). *The Poisonwood Bible*. New York: Harper Perennial; 1st ed. 1998.
Kingsolver, Barbara. (2013). *Flight Behavior*. New York: Harper Perennial; 1st ed. 2012.

FURTHER READING

Houser, Heather. (2017). Knowledge work and the commons in Barbara Kingsolver's and Ann Pancake's Appalachia. *Modern Fiction Studies* 63 (1): 95–115.
Johns-Putra, Adeline. (2019). *Climate Change and the Contemporary Novel*. Cambridge: Cambridge University Press.
Jones, Suzanne W. (2006). The Southern family farm as endangered species: possibilities for survival in Barbara Kingsolver's *Prodigal Summer*. *Southern Literary Journal* 39 (1): 83–97.
Leder, Patricia. (ed.) (2010). *Seeds of Change: Critical Essays on Barbara Kingsolver*. Knoxville: University of Tennessee Press.
Strehle, Susan. (2008). Chosen people: American exceptionalism in Kingsolver's *The Poisonwood Bible*. *Critique: Studies in Contemporary Fiction* 49 (4): 413–429.

Kingston, Maxine Hong

LAUREN KURYLOSKI
SUNY, University at Buffalo, USA

Maxine Hong Kingston (b. 1940) is a writer known for her ability to transition between genres with ease, seamlessly moving between fiction, (auto)biography, essay, myth, and poetry, often all in one text. Across these many literary forms, there remains a constant: the belief in writing's ability to serve a valuable social function. Kingston explains, "We tell stories and we listen to stories in order to live. To stay conscious. To connect one with another. To understand consequences. To keep history. To rebuild civilization" (2006, p. 1). Over the course of a celebrated career, Kingston has used her writing to recover the forgotten and neglected histories of Chinese Americans, critique gender and racial injustice, and build communities of peace through artistic pacifist means. While her writing often has a kaleidoscopic effect, shifting in form and content, these are the foundational concepts to which she returns in each major work, continually revising and reframing her understanding of her own life and the communities she inhabits. Kingston's innovative writing, both highly personal and overtly political, has garnered critical accolades as well as popular appeal, and is recognized as having ushered in an Asian American literary renaissance in contemporary literature.

Maxine Ting Ting Hong was born in Stockton, California on October 27, 1940, to parents Tom and Ying Lan Hong, two figures who feature prominently in her work. She enrolled at the University of California, Berkeley, in 1958, eventually graduating with a degree in English. While at Berkeley, she met fellow student Earll Kingston, whom she married in 1962. The couple were politically active in protests against the Vietnam War, but eventually grew disillusioned with the state of the antiwar movement in the Berkeley area and relocated to Hawai'i in 1967, believing (mistakenly, as it would turn out) that they were moving as far from the war as possible. For the next seventeen years, Kingston worked as a teacher, while also writing her first major book. In 1976, *The Woman Warrior: Memoirs of a Girlhood Among Ghosts*, was published to immediate acclaim. *The Woman Warrior* established many of the themes that have remained central to Kingston's work in the ensuing decades, including the hybridization of genres, the incorporation of family lore and Chinese mythology, the critique of racial injustice in the United States, and what Shirley Geok-lin Lim has called Kingston's "translinguistic stylistics," or the creation of polyvocal texts that integrate multiple languages (Lim 2008, p. 162).

Much of Kingston's literary output recreates the act of "talk story," or the sharing of stories, myths, and legends between members of a community, or, as is often the case in her work, between members of a family. Her second major publication, *China Men* (1980), enacts "talk story" on the page, both chronicling and mythologizing the experiences of the Chinese men who came to the United States in the nineteenth and twentieth centuries. In an interview, Kingston explains "I saw *China Men* as a history book, and it would be a story that has been left out of history... the migrations to America from the east and not from Europe" (Lim 2008, p. 159). In order to piece together the missing history of the men in her family, and by extension, the larger Chinese immigrant population, Kingston calls upon a variety of sources: the existing yet incomplete historical record, stories passed down within her family, and her own imagination. Speaking directly to her father in one chapter, she asserts "I'll tell you what I suppose from your silences and few words, and you can tell me that I'm mistaken" (Kingston 1980, p. 15). Blending fact and fiction, in *China Men* Kingston deftly moves between different immigrant experiences, including a harrowing account of her grandfather building the Transcontinental Railroad, a factual listing of various laws, acts, and treaties that have impacted Chinese immigrants in the United States, and an imagined narrative of her own father's arrival in the country, creating a version of family history in which he crossed the sea hidden in a crate as a stowaway before arriving in New York City. The text relies on the power of talk story to tell a fuller, and in some ways more authentic and truthful, version of the Chinese American experience than that which exists in the standard historical record.

Kingston's interrogation of how immigrants and communities of color are treated within the United States is further developed in subsequent texts. In *Hawai'i One Summer* (1987), a slim collection of autobiographical essays originally published in *The New York Times*, Kingston articulates feelings of discomfort when writing about the island as a non-native Hawaiian. Although recognized as a Living Treasure of Hawai'i in 1980, she is hesitant to adopt the Hawaiian language and mythology for fear of appropriating stories that are not hers to share. This anxiety is compounded by the fact that during her time there the United States was using Hawai'i as the waypoint for soldiers and military equipment being sent to Vietnam. Although

Kingston believed Hawai'i would offer an escape from the war, she is instead confronted with the United States' militarization of the island and its history of colonization, both of which she writes about as manifestations of racialized violence.

The commitment to challenging racial injustice is a central feature of Kingston's only novel, *Tripmaster Monkey: His Fake Book* (1989). Set in the late 1960s and written in a stream of consciousness style, the novel follows the exploits of Wittman Ah Sing, a fifth-generation Chinese American, recent Berkeley graduate, beatnik, and aspiring playwright whose ultimate goal is to write a play that will end the Vietnam War. A clear allusion to the canonical American poet Walt Whitman, Wittman's name is both an honorific and a kind cultural critique. Although Wittman certainly longs to be a part of the American literary establishment, full recognition as an American citizen, as well as the avenues to artistic and literary success, are not readily available to Wittman due to his ethnicity. Fittingly, he is also modeled on Sun Wu Kong, the Monkey King and trickster figure of Chinese legend. Wittman's desire to disrupt the status quo finds him taking aim at the unjust treatment of minorities in the United States, as he vociferously asserts his own identity as both a significant American playwright and a champion of Chinese tradition by establishing a radical Chinese theater scene in San Francisco.

While *Tripmaster Monkey* won the PEN USA West Award in Fiction upon publication, critics and general readers alike have often described Wittman as a brash and unlikeable character. Nevertheless, he is the figure that Kingston has repeatedly returned to throughout her writing career. In Wittman, Kingston appears to find a kind of literary alter ego or companion, and in the rest of her published work she not only brings Wittman along, but also carries on his project of using art for pacifist means. As Julia Lee has noted, Kingston's later work is "less about the Chinese American community and more about creating communities of peace" through the act of writing (2018, p. 80). As both a writer and a teacher of writing for many years, it is perhaps unsurprising that her later works often have a pedagogical component, offering writing instruction and demonstrating the importance of continual revision. She enacts these values in her texts, often returning to narratives, themes, and characters established in her earlier work in order to revise and refine her approach.

Kingston gives readers intimate access to her writing process in *To Be the Poet* (2002), material originally given as part of the William E. Massey Sr. Lectures in American Studies at Harvard University in 2000. In the first of three chapters, Kingston states "I have almost finished my longbook. Let my life as Poet begin," thus announcing her intention to transition to poetry, a form that she believes will offer an "easiness" not to be found in prose (2002, p. 1). Characteristically, she troubles this initial assumption in subsequent chapters by revealing her personal struggles with the process of "becoming" a poet. In various interviews, essays, and lectures throughout her career, Kingston has described her approach as a writing teacher, including her method of encouraging students to write by telling them they will be graded on quantity instead of quality. Her belief that words on the page will eventually amount to something valuable is illustrated in *To Be the Poet*, as Kingston includes drafts of fledgling poems, mostly short pieces that discuss the day-to-day elements of her life. Just as Kingston calls upon students to become writers through the sustained labor of writing, she sets her intention to become "the poet" through the continued production and revision of her poetry. Her poems reflect the influence of William Carlos Williams, whose *In the*

American Grain (1925) Kingston repeatedly cites as a critical literary reference point. Well known for the line "no ideas but in things" (Williams 1951, p. 233), Williams modeled an approach to writing that foregrounds tangible objects, even the quotidian elements of everyday life, over abstract concepts. Kingston's faith in the written word's power to shape our lived reality in demonstrable ways becomes a focal point in her later work.

The "longbook" that Kingston references with a noticeable degree of frustration in *To Be the Poet*, is *The Fifth Book of Peace* (2003), a work of prose that explores the traumatic effects of violence and offers writing as a potential source of healing. *The Fifth Book of Peace* has its genesis in fire. Inspired by Chinese legends of three books of peace that were lost to fires throughout history, Kingston set to work on what was to be the fourth book of peace, a sequel to *Tripmaster Monkey*. However, the manuscript was lost when the Oakland Firestorm of 1991 destroyed Kingston's home and much of her community. From these ashes emerges *The Fifth Book of Peace*, Kingston's attempt to create something positive from personal and communal trauma.

A hybrid text that blends memoir, fiction, and essay, *The Fifth Book of Peace* begins by recounting Kingston's own experience with the Oakland fire and transitions into a recreation of the lost manuscript, an extended piece of fiction that reunites readers with Wittman Ah Sing as he moves to Hawai'i with his wife and son (their experiences closely mirroring Kingston's own). The final section of the book is an exploration of writing as a form of antiwar activism. Kingston recounts her work organizing a series of writing workshops for veterans with the goal of creating a community of writers working toward peace. She instructs the veterans to "Make a story. Tell the story until a happy ending" (Kingston 2003, p. 329). Her call for a happy ending is not intended to control the kinds of narratives they produce, but rather it is an appeal to use the writing process as a way to work through personal and collective trauma. In sharing their stories, they might write themselves to a place of peace. These workshops culminated in the anthology *Veterans of War, Veterans of Peace* (2006), for which Kingston penned the introduction. In her preface to the collection, she offers, "by writing the unspeakable . . . the writer shapes and forms experience, and thereby . . . changes the past and remakes the existing world" (Kingston 2006, pp. 1–2). Both *The Fifth Book of Peace* and *Veterans of War, Veterans of Peace* were published during the Iraq War, an event that further inspired Kingston's activism and her own drive to "remake" or transform the world.

Kingston's commitment to antiwar activism culminates in her arrest for protesting the Iraq War outside of the White House in 2003, an event featured in *I Love a Broad Margin to My Life* (2011), a memoir written entirely in verse. Her most recent published work, the text revisits familiar territory from her life and career, bringing Wittman Ah Sing along for the ride. When Kingston travels to China she extends an invitation to her fictional character to join her: "Wittman, son, brother, imaginary friend, I need you. Help me again" (2011, p. 211). Transitioning between her own experience of traveling to China as an aging woman and that of Wittman's journey to China as an older man, the twin travelers return to stories and concepts featured throughout her oeuvre. In so doing, Kingston performs a thoughtful act of "re-vision," looking at familiar concepts through the ever-evolving lens of her life's experience.

Kingston's return to familiar material is not the act of an accomplished writer resting on her laurels, but rather a generative process of attempting to revise her previous work in order to reflect her current understanding of the world. Kingston's willingness to reconceptualize even her most famous work is evident in her treatment of Fa Mook Lan, first introduced as Fa Mu Lan in *The Woman Warrior*. The famous swordswoman of Chinese legend is featured in one of the most memorable scenes in Kingston's first book, an extended take on the classic myth in which Kingston imagines Mu Lan's experience of training to become a warrior and eventually securing success in battle. Kingston returns to Mu Lan in *The Fifth Book of Peace*, chronicling the warrior woman's struggles to return to civilian life after leaving her military post. In the trip to China recounted in *Broad Margin*, Kingston learns a new detail of the legend that she has never heard before, that the swordswoman is said to have taken her own life. Reading Mu Lan's actions through a contemporary lens, one shaped by her work with war veterans, Kingston attributes her suicide to post-traumatic stress disorder (PTSD). She follows this revision of Mu Lan's story with the number of veteran suicides recorded by the year 2009. Kingston's alteration of the Mu Lan legend is her means of demonstrating the devastating effects of violence across space and time, as well as an appeal for peace.

During the course of a distinguished career, Kingston's work has not gone without critique. Frank Chin, among the most vocal of her critics, has accused Kingston of creating a "fake" Chinese mythology in order to cater to white readers, specifically white feminist readers (Chin 1991, p. 2). As Stella Bolaki notes, "Kingston has been praised for extricating Chinese myth from its patriarchal network of signification through her translations, but also has been condemned for twisting and distorting the meaning of the original in order to please her white sisters" (2009, p. 42). Some critics have also expressed frustration that Kingston's work, based as it is on her very personal experience, has often been taken as representative of *the* Chinese American experience. Rather than faulting Kingston for this phenomenon, critics might instead take to task the larger publishing industry and the hesitancy of publishers to take a perceived risk on ethnic writers in general, and specifically on those whose work diverges from what has previously been established as a successful model.

Ultimately, the impact of Maxine Hong Kingston's work on generations of writers cannot be understated. The publication of her first work sparked a renaissance in Asian American literature, and she has paved the way for innumerable writers, including Amy Tan, Gish Jen, and Viet Thanh Nguyen, among many others. She has been the recipient of numerous awards and honors, including the National Books Critics Circle Award for Nonfiction, the Anisfield-Wolf Race Relations Award, and the National Endowment for the Arts Award. She has received a Guggenheim Fellowship, been the runner-up for the Pulitzer Prize, and been awarded the National Medal of Arts by President Barack Obama in 2013.

In a 2020 interview published in *The New Yorker*, Kingston hints at a work in progress, a piece jokingly titled "Posthumously, Maxine" (Hsu 2020). In a career defined by adventurous storytelling, literary tricksterism, and politically conscious activism, any new material will undoubtedly work to expand the Kingston canon in meaningful and innovative ways.

SEE ALSO: Jen, Gish; Mixed-Genre Fiction; Nguyen, Viet Thanh; Tan, Amy; Trauma and Fiction

REFERENCES

Bolaki, Stella. (2009). It translated well: the promise and the perils of translation in Maxine Hong Kingston's *The Woman Warrior*. *MELUS* 34 (4): 39–60.

Chin, Frank. (1991). Come all ye Asian American writers of the real and the fake. In: *The Big Aiiieeee!: An Anthology of Chinese American and Japanese American Literature* (ed. Jeffery Paul Chan *et al.*), 1–92. New York: Meridian.

Hsu, Hua. (2020). Maxine Hong Kingston's genre-defying life and work. *The New Yorker* (June 1, 2020). https://www.newyorker.com/magazine/2020/06/08/maxine-hong-kingstons-genre-defying-life-and-work (accessed July 20, 2021).

Kingston, Maxine Hong. (1980). *China Men*. New York: Vintage International.

Kingston, Maxine Hong. (2002). *To Be the Poet*. Cambridge: Harvard University Press.

Kingston, Maxine Hong. (2003). *The Fifth Book of Peace*. New York: Vintage International.

Kingston, Maxine Hong. (ed.) (2006). *Veterans of War, Veterans of Peace*. Kihei, HI: Koa Books.

Kingston, Maxine Hong. (2011). *I Love a Broad Margin to My Life*. New York: Vintage International.

Lee, Julia. (2018). *Understanding Maxine Hong Kingston*. Columbia: University of South Carolina Press.

Lim, Shirley G. (2008). Reading back, looking forward: a retrospective interview with Maxine Hong Kingston. *MELUS* 33 (1): 157–170.

Williams, William Carlos. (1951). "Paterson" (1926). *The Collected Earlier Poems*. Cambridge, MA: New Directions.

FURTHER READING

Grice, Helena. (2006). *Maxine Hong Kingston*. Manchester: Manchester University Press.

Huntley, Edelma D. (2000). *Maxine Hong Kingston: A Critical Companion*. Westport, CT: Greenwood Press.

Skenazy, Paul and Martin, Tera. (ed.) (1998). *Conversations with Maxine Hong Kingston*. Jackson: University Press of Mississippi.

Krauss, Nicole

CORINNE BANCROFT
The University of Victoria, Canada

Nicole Krauss is perhaps as well known for the books she's yet to write as she is for her four current, internationally celebrated novels: *Forest Dark* (2017), *Great House* (2010), *The History of Love* (2005), and *Man Walks Into a Room* (2002). In 2010, *The New Yorker* chose Krauss as one of "20 under 40" authors who "are, or will be, key to their generation," and, three years earlier, *Granta* named her one of the "Best Young American Novelists." All of her novels have either won or been shortlisted for literary prizes. The forward-facing nature of Krauss's fame recognizes the innovative and influential nature of her work. Krauss writes not only with a sensitivity to loneliness and loss, but also with the conviction that if anything can bridge the seemingly unassailable distance between people or make life bearable after deep suffering, it is fiction. As the author asserts in an interview, "literature affords us this absolutely unique possibility – in no other moment in life . . . in no other art form can you step so directly, so vividly without any mediation into another's inner life" (PBS NewsHour 2010). In other words, for Krauss, literature is the medium of empathy: it is the only way we can come close to knowing "what it is to be another person" (PBS NewsHour 2010). Krauss's works help to shape an emerging novel form, the braided narrative, that is particularly fitted to engage these questions of recognition and connection. By twining together many, seemingly unrelated narrative threads (distinct in terms of teller and told), Krauss requires her readers to make sense of multiple narrators' experiences, even when they conflict. By placing incomparable griefs side by side, Krauss invites her readers to develop an empathy that resonates with each. The way Krauss renders these concerns both acknowledges and moves beyond traditional tenets of trauma studies. In addition to dealing with the way catastrophic violence such as the Holocaust forecloses cognitive registration (Laub 1992) and resists representation (Caruth 1996), Krauss focuses on how people might reinvent themselves and form meaningful attachments, even in the wake of catastrophic violence. For Krauss, the activities associated with literary fiction – imagining what it's like to be another person, constructing a narrative out of a series of experiences, finding truth in artifice – are the primary means through which people can make life worth living.

Krauss was born in New York on April 18, 1974, and, while this city serves as one important setting in all of her novels, the transnational trajectory of her parents and grandparents plays perhaps a larger role. In interviews, Krauss often explains that, because all of her grandparents were born in places to which they could not return either because the places no longer exist or because they were so stained with loss, she grew up with the sense that home is not a place, but a time in the past. As the grandchild of those who escaped the Holocaust when so many of their friends and family did not, Krauss writes with an awareness of irrevocable loss and a respect for the self-reinvention that surviving such violence requires. At the same time, Krauss finds, as she puts it in an interview, "an incredible bottomless sense of place" associated with her "Jewish intellectual legacy," a long tradition of thought that values "willful uncertainty, the importance of asking the questions rather than providing the answers" (Arts and Ideas at the JCCSF 2014). Krauss does not limit herself to the Jewish forefathers who critics often relate to her work; she refers just as easily to her admiration of Roberto Bolaño or Samuel Beckett as she does to her friendship with Joseph Brodsky or Philip Roth. Her cosmopolitan education also underscores her aesthetic openness: she studied English at Stanford University and traveled to Oxford for a master's in art history. Krauss has two children, Cy and Sasha, with Jonathan Safran Foer, her husband from 2004 to 2014. Critics have noted some resonance between Krauss and Foer's second and most recent novels: their earlier works feature meaningful relationships between millennial children and Holocaust survivors, and their later novels consider the ways marriages can come undone. Krauss now lives in Brooklyn and spends time in Israel, the predominant setting of *Forest Dark*.

Krauss's first novel, *Man Walks Into a Room* (shortlisted for the Los Angeles Times Book Prize in 2003) introduced her thematic interest in memory and its relationship to self-invention and the potential for empathy. A benign brain tumor causes protagonist Samson Greene to lose twenty-four years of memories; the 36-year-old can only remember the first twelve years of his life. The cherry-sized hole that the tumor leaves behind provides a space for Krauss to stage her well-researched inquiry into the way one's sense of self is a narrative composed of a series of memories. The dissolution of Samson's marriage to Anna, now a stranger, attests to the way attachments depend not only on this sense of self, but also on shared memories. When an eccentric scientist recruits Samson for an experiment in "*true* empathy" where he transfers another's memory into Samson's mind, the protagonist realizes that compassion might not be as much about internalizing the experience of another as it is about making sense of their experience in relationship to one's own (Krauss 2002, p. 105). While the majority of *A Man Walks Into The Room* details, in the third-person, Samson's post-surgery struggles to find the self he lost with his memories, the prologue and epilogue presage the narrative innovations that will come to characterize Krauss's work. The novel opens with the jarring four-page, first-person memory that will be inserted into Samson's mind 150 pages later and closes in Anna's nostalgic voice recalling a moment when Samson still remembered her.

Krauss's next two novels, *The History of Love* and *Great House* expand this shift in perspective by twining together multiple story lines, each narrated by a distinct narrator. In this way, these novels help to shape the emerging novel genre of the braided narrative. Krauss divides each novel among three or more different narrators who tell stories that sometimes take place on different continents in different decades. Like the disconcerting shift in *Man Walks Into a Room* between the opening memory and Samson's story, the transition between narrators in each of Krauss's subsequent novels can be jarring, and the relationship between the narrative threads often does not become clear until the end. The curious confusion that this narrative shifting elicits furthers Krauss's interest in the possibility of empathy. By placing potentially incommensurate stories alongside each other, Krauss requires her readers to countenance different ethical claims. Because Krauss does not always make the connections between these multiple characters explicit, she relies on readers' imaginations to fill in what she doesn't write, a strategy that might improve readers' impulse to imagine the experiences of nonfictional others as well.

Krauss's second novel, *The History of Love*, rotates among three narrative strands that are held together by an eponymous book-within-a-book. First, in what he believes to be the final years of his life, octogenarian Leo Gursky recounts his daily attempts to be seen in the sixty-odd years he's spent in New York and records memories from his youth before and during the Nazi occupation of Slonim. Second, in a series of numbered diary entries, Brooklyn teenager Alma Singer researches the book-within-a-book in an attempt to find another lover for her mother, seven years after her father's death. Next, a third-person narrator narrates "[w]hat is not known about Zvi Litvinoff," Leo's childhood friend who escaped to Chile, translated "The History of Love" into Spanish, and published it as his own (Krauss 2005, p. 68). Before the novel's end, Alma's younger brother Emmanuel Chaim, better known as Bird, begins reading her diary and adding his own entries, an intervention that makes the novel's culminating recognition scene possible. In this penultimate chapter, Alma *sees* Leo in an encounter that Krauss renders textually by alternating between Leo's perspective on the left-hand pages and Alma's on the right. By placing the experiences of two men who escaped the Holocaust alongside the story of a teenager who has lost her father, Krauss interrogates possibilities of recognition – even if these characters' sufferings are different and incomparable, can they forge meaningful attachments?

The History of Love's critical reception responds to Krauss's innovative approach to writing after the Holocaust. While some reviews found the novel too humorous or sentimental to deal adequately with atrocity, scholars lauded Krauss's work as simultaneously respecting the importance of history and looking toward the future. At the same time, *The History of Love* is Krauss's most celebrated novel: it won the Edward Lewis Wallant Award (2005), the Prix du Meilleur Livre Étranger (2006), and the William Saroyan Prize for Writing (2008), and was a finalist for the Orange Prize for Fiction (2006), Prix Médicis (2006), and Prix Femina (2006). Jessica Lang considers Krauss "a third-generation Holocaust writer" because her novel is removed from "the eye-witness testimony" central to survivors' texts and the "questions of theodicy and suicide" that she, like Alan Berger, associates with second-generation novels (Lang 2009, pp. 44, 45, 53). Instead, as Lang argues, Krauss not only acknowledges the particularity of suffering and importance of memory but also foregrounds the human potential for survival and love. As Krauss affirms, "I've written very little about the Holocaust in terms of the actual events. What interests me is the response to catastrophic loss" (Rothenberg Gritz 2010). Berger and Asher Milbauer, who also consider Krauss a "paradigmatic third-generation" writer, praise her novels as "markers of memory transmission as well as memory transformation" arguing that "Krauss provides her readers with a map of the future outlines of Holocaust memory" (Berger and Milbauer 2013, pp. 64, 83). Twining together multiple voices and experiences is a key stylistic strategy that attends to the past while imagining the future.

Like *The History of Love*, *Great House*, Krauss's third novel, moves among multiple narrative threads that are introduced in the first part of the book and repeat, in a different order, in the second. First, Nadia, a New York novelist, tells an unnamed judge the story of her failed relationships in an attempt to explain the accident that hospitalized him. Second, Aaron, an Israeli grandfather, addresses his missing adult son, in an effort to repair their damaged relationship, an apostrophe that expresses regrets he cannot bring himself to share in person. Third, Arthur, a retired British romanticist, describes his wife's deepest secret to convince himself of their intimacy. Fourth, Isabel, an American student, narrates her turn from the anxieties of reading modernist literature at Oxford to the pleasures of studying the enigma of a particular person. While the first three narrators each have another section in the second part of *Great House*, Krauss introduces a fifth narrator where Isabel's second section might have been. This final narrator, Weisz, appears as a character in Isabel, Nadia, and Arthur's stories and focuses here on his quest to rebuild his father's study, destroyed in 1944 by the Gestapo. An oversized, many-drawered writing desk and its one-time owner Daniel Varsky, a Chilean poet, connect most of the narrative threads. As characters, one of whom escaped the Holocaust, contend with Daniel's "disappearance" (a synonym for torture and murder under Pinochet's regime), Krauss expands the scope of her work to address, as one narrator describes it, "not one nightmare but many" (Krauss 2010, p. 104). While Krauss is careful not to conflate any individual's suffering with another's nor to equate any two historical catastrophes, placing them alongside each other shines light on the importance of human connection, however fragile. *Great House* was a finalist for the National Book Award (2010) and short-listed for The Orange Prize for Fiction (2011) and the Anisfield-Wolf Book Award (2011).

Krauss's most recent novel, *Forest Dark*, alternates between two distinct narratives. First, a third-person narrator recounts Jules Epstein's turn from the material world to the spiritual one and an ultimate disappearance into the desert. Second, an author-narrator named Nicole, feeling lost in her work and marriage, travels to the Tel Aviv Hilton and receives an invitation to finish Kafka's last work, a request that gets her stranded in the desert, but, unlike Epstein, she eventually returns home. While Krauss's previous two novels featured material objects and encounters that connect characters in the same story world, *Forest Dark*, as Krauss says, follows "two parallel stories that never really cross but are going over the same physical and metaphysical ground" (Dueben 2017). The parallel rather than braided structure of *Forest Dark* models Krauss's version of the multiverse theory, an interest of (and reality for) her self-named narrator. In place of some physicists' suggestion that an infinite number of universes exist, Nicole wonders whether people actually dream the multiple universes into existence: "what if we're the ones who have unwittingly been made subordinate to space, to its elegant design to propagate itself infinitely through the dreams of finite beings?" (Krauss 2017, p. 48).

While *Forest Dark*'s second narrator, Nicole, seems to represent Krauss's largest foray into autofiction, the author reimages reality in all her work. Many of Krauss's protagonists' biographies reference fragments of their author's life. *Forest Dark*'s second narrator not only shares Krauss's first name, but also her literary oeuvre, childhood memories, number of children, and centrifugal marriage. Nadia, *Great House*'s author-narrator, writes at an enormous, inherited writing desk inspired by the author's own. *The History of Love*'s "sixteen *different* pie charts" that explain Alma's ancestry could also describe the complexity of Krauss's (2005, p. 96, italics in original). Many characters, such as *Man Walks Into a Room*'s Uncle Max, *The History of Love*'s Alma Mereminski and Leo Gursky, and *Great House*'s Lotte Berg, reference Krauss's own grandparents, whose photographs appear in the dedication of *The History of Love*. Krauss's construction of these older characters shows that she's interested not only in referencing personal and political history, but also in imagining what might have been. For instance, like Krauss's grandmother, Lotte Berg escapes on the last Kindertransport, but rather than writing a fictional version of her grandmother's life, Krauss uses the history of her grandmother's escape as the premise for her character.

Krauss moves from the potentially autobiographical to the reimagining of history not only for her own family but also for literary figures. Nicole's narrative in *Forest Dark* unfolds in a world, perhaps one of many multiverses, where Franz Kafka did not die of tuberculosis in 1924, but instead survived by faking his death and moving to Palestine. While this plot strand refers to historical facts about Kafka's life and works, including the long legal battle over the ownership of his papers, it also imagines an alternative reality that raises questions about an author's relationship to the nation. In a less direct way, *The History of Love* alludes to Bruno Schulz and his lost masterpiece. Instead of dying at the hands of a Nazi in 1942 as Schulz did, Leo, Krauss's great Polish author-character, escapes to New York and continues to write, only to be published under another's name and in another's language. That Leo may have borrowed bits of his great novel from his friend Bruno, who may have been killed by Nazis, suggests that even when great writers die, their words and influence may live on through art and friendship.

All of Krauss's novels celebrate the way activities associated with literature make it possible not only to survive horrific violence but also to forge meaningful relationships. Krauss casts almost all of her protagonists as writers themselves or as serious readers. In addition to the author characters in *The History of Love*, *Great House*'s Nadia is prolific novelist, Lotte Berg an accomplished author of short stories, and even Dov (Nadia and Aaron's narratee) secretly writes short stories. *Forest Dark*'s author-narrator is named Nicole. Krauss marks the major characters who aren't writers as readers. Samson Greene of *Man Walks Into a Room* and *Great House*'s Arthur Bender taught English at Columbia and Oxford, respectively. *History of Love*'s Alma and Bird and *Great House*'s Aaron surreptitiously read other characters' writing. While writing and reading stand for the attempt to connect with another person, imagination, the medium of fiction, is the means through which that recognition is possible. As reading and writing connects characters and helps them to survive the traumas they face, the books that Krauss writes invite her readers to open ourselves both to the experiences of others and to the possibility that this act of imagination itself might make loss easier to bear.

SEE ALSO: The Brain and American Fiction Erdrich, Louise; Foer, Jonathan Safran; Globalization; Ozick, Cynthia; Roth, Philip; Trauma and Fiction

REFERENCES

Arts and Ideas at the JCCSF. (2014). Nicole Krauss in conversation with Elisabeth Rosner. https://www.youtube.com/watch?v=5JCcnvhRPQY (accessed July 7, 2021).

Berger, Alan and Milbauer, Asher. (2013). The burden of inheritance. *Shofar: An Interdisciplinary Journal of Jewish Studies* 31 (3): 64–85.

Caruth, Cathy. (1996). *Unclaimed Experience: Trauma, Narrative, and History*. Baltimore: Johns Hopkins University Press.

Dueben, Alex. (2017). What appears to be fiction: a conversation with Nicole Krauss. *The Rumpus* (September 25, 2017). https://therumpus.net/2017/09/the-rumpus-interview-with-nicole-krauss (accessed July 7, 2021).

Jack, Ian. (2007). Best of young American novelists 2: introduction. *Granta* (April 16, 2007). https://granta.com/introduction-boyan-2 (accessed July 7, 2021).

Krauss, Nicole. (2002). *Man Walks Into a Room*. New York: Random House.

Krauss, Nicole. (2005). *The History of Love*. New York: Norton.

Krauss, Nicole. (2010). *Great House*. New York: Norton.

Krauss, Nicole. (2017). *Forest Dark*. New York: HarperCollins.

Lang, Jessica. (2009). *The History of Love*, the contemporary reader, and the transmission of Holocaust memory. *Journal of Modern Literature* 33 (1): 43–56.

Laub, Dori. (1992). Bearing witness or the vicissitudes of listening. In: *Testimony: Crises of Witnessing in Literature, Psychoanalysis, and History* (with Shoshana Felman), 57–75. New York: Routledge.

PBS NewsHour. (2010). Conversation: Nicole Krauss' *Great House*. https://www.youtube.com/watch?v=ABV34eCgmEE (accessed July 7, 2021).

Rothenberg Gritz, Jennie. (2010). Nicole Krauss on fame, loss, and writing about Holocaust survivors. *The Atlantic* (October 21, 2010). https://www.theatlantic.com/entertainment/archive/2010/10/nicole-krauss-on-fame-loss-and-writing-about-holocaust-survivors/64869/ (accessed July 7, 2021).

The Editors. (2010). 20 under 40. *The New Yorker* (June 7, 2010). https://www.newyorker.com/magazine/2010/06/14/20-under-40 (accessed July 7, 2021).

FURTHER READING

Bancroft, Corinne. (2018). The braided narrative. *Narrative* 26 (3): 262–281.

Gwyer, Kirstin. (2018). "You think your writing belongs to you?": Intertextuality in contemporary Jewish post-Holocaust literature. *Humanities* 7 (1). https://doi.org/10.3390/h7010020

Hadar, David. (2018). Author-characters and authorial public image: the elderly protagonists in Philip Roth and Nicole Krauss. *Narrative* 26 (3): 282–301.

Krasuska, Karolina. (2016). Narratives of generationality in 21st-century North American Jewish literature: Krauss, Bezmozgis, Kalman. *East European Jewish Affairs* 46 (3): 285–310.

Krauss, Nicole. (2017). Do women get to write with authority? *The New York Times* (September 22, 2017) https://www.nytimes.com/2017/09/22/opinion/sunday/i-knew-i-had-to-fight-for-authority-so-i-wrote-like-a-man.html

Weisel-Barth, Joye. (2013). The fetish in Nicole Krauss' *Great House* and in clinical practice. *Psychoanalytic Dialogues* 23 (2): 180–196.

Kushner, Rachel

JUSTUS NIELAND
Michigan State University, USA

With three critically celebrated novels to date and one collection of stories, Rachel Kushner has emerged as one of contemporary fiction's most ambitious and original voices. The only writer to have been a finalist for the National Book Award for her first two novels – *Telex from Cuba* (2008) and *The Flamethrowers* (2013) – Kushner has received glossy profiles in venues like the *New Yorker*, a Guggenheim Fellowship (2013), and increasing academic interest in her writing. At a moment when the very category of "the contemporary," an "essentially empty category," is undergoing intense theoretical scrutiny (Martin 2018, p. 125), Kushner's fiercely intelligent prose fiction is boldly redefining what is possible in the contemporary novel. As Kushner herself explains: "All fiction is engagement. Contemporary doesn't mean that there's, like, an iPod in the book. It means the writer has something to say about the conditions of people's lives" (Hart and Rocca 2015, p. 210).

Kushner's contemporaneity is defined by a keen awareness of and material conditions of agency and action, even as the historical present of her prose is ripe with eventfulness, crackling with contingency and revolutionary possibility. Circumstances are understood intersectionally. The mutually ramifying categories of class, race, age, gender, and sexuality condition the perspectives of her characters and demarcate what is possible and thinkable in the way of freedom. The complex social and institutional matrices of her novels are inflected by macro-historical processes that she limns with brilliant detail: the legacies of colonialism and neocolonialism in *Telex from Cuba*; the global history of Fordist industrialization and the post-Fordist remaking of labor and life in *The Flamethrowers*; the dehumanizing impress of the prison-industrial complex in her most recent – and most despairing – novel, *The Mars Room* (2018), set in California's near present. To be contemporary, as Kushner understands it, is to "somehow understand large mechanisms, and to create characters who bear some human mark of those mechanisms" (Hart and Rocca 2015, p. 210).

Those characters also bear the mark of Kushner's own offbeat upbringing. Born in 1968, Kushner was raised by bohemian parents, then doctoral students in biology at the University of Oregon. Her mother was an avid skier, a sport Kushner took up early, and which features prominently in *The Flamethowers*. Her father came from a Jewish New York family involved the Communist Party. Her parents wanted their children to be creative artists and encouraged their independence, raising them in what Kushner has called "beatnik poverty" (Goodyear 2008). At sixteen, Kushner enrolled at UC-Berkeley, completing a degree in political economy and writing a thesis on US policy in Nicaragua. After returning to San Francisco, she eventually enrolled in Columbia University's MFA program. In New York, she became connected to a number of downtown artists, and after finishing her MFA in 2000, she began working as an editor for the literary magazine *Grand Street* and writing for venues like *BOMB* and *Artforum*.

While her work is not autofiction, Kushner's first three novels feature characters whose itineraries often echo her own, allowing her to scrutinize the operations of various forms of privilege and inequality within larger social mechanisms and institutions. In a recent interview, Kushner described her preoccupation with "the lucky and the unlucky" as a conceptual problem: "It's easier to say that I achieved the things I did by virtue of my intelligence, and my pluck, and my persistence, and my hard work, rather than by simply having been born into the circumstances that would give you the nurturing that would result in the successes that one has achieved in their life" (Kushner and Shawn 2020). In her novels to date, this basic political insight about class and historical contingency is pursued carefully, spread across varying contexts and geographies.

Kushner's debut, *Telex from Cuba*, is a lush and deeply researched historical novel loosely structured through the point of view of two American expatriate children whose fathers work in different levels of management for the United Fruit Company and a US owned-nickel mining firm in Cuba during the revolution. It is based in part on Kushner's excavation of the childhood stories of her mother and aunts, who lived in 1950s in Preston, Cuba – the regional headquarters of United Fruit. Kushner's maternal grandfather worked across the bay in Nicaro as a metallurgist in a nickel-processing plant. This family history, which Kushner explored archivally, and in research in Cuba, is appropriated in the service of a fictionalized corporate history of one of the most aggressive North American monopolies operating in Latin America.

The novel opens in January, 1958, as K.C. Stites – the 13-year-old son of the chief executive of United Fruit's Cuban

Division – narrates retrospectively his dawning awareness of revolutionary upheaval. Castro's rebels, including, it appears, K.C.'s radicalized older Anglo brother, have set fire to the firm's sugarcane fields near his family's plantation. The bravura opening chapter crystallizes the interlocking structures of class, race, and power that demarcate K.C.'s childhood, and the systems of colonial and neocolonial violence that secured his privilege, and now appear perilously fragile. It includes, for example, meditations on the family's Black maid and chauffeur, and memories of the living conditions of the cane cutters. The once-implacable vastness of this exploitive system of neocolonial exploitation set aflame in the novel's opening pages appears in K.C.'s recollection of a map of the region of Oriente, "Cuba's largest, poorest, blackest province," hanging in his father's office: "United Fruit's property was marked in green. Practically the whole map was green – 330,000 acres of arable land – with one small grey area that wasn't ours marked 'owned by others.' People have no idea, the scale of things" (Kushner 2008, p. 15).

Kushner's narrative structure explores the full complexity of the map's materialist lesson in a revolutionary context, while filtering intertwined corporate and political histories of this Cold War moment through the world-systems naivete of its child narrators, and in two temporalities. K.C.'s first-person narration looks back on his childhood from 2004, after the expulsion of his family, while the third-person narration of Everly Lederer transpires in the historical present of the 1950s. Telling the story of her family's expatriation from their arrival in Cuba in 1952, where her father has taken a job at Nicaro Nickel at the moment of Batista's coup, Everly's dawning social-political awareness serves as the reader's own introduction to the rituals and customs of this corporate enclave and its brilliantly drawn range of Anglo families.

Like K.C., Everly shares the class-based blindspots and often racist assumptions of her family, even as she struggles to observe and better understand the meaning of the revolution and her family's relationship to it. This plays out in Everly's friendship with Willy Bloussé, a young Black Haitian servant of the Lederer's, sold into manual servitude by his father, who schools Everly in the moral politics of class and the so-called "troublemakers": "But Willy made it sound like the troublemakers were the good guys. They just wanted to be paid fair wages and to live in decent conditions" (2008, p. 155). Eventually, we come to learn of Willy's own role in the underground; he narrowly escapes execution by Batista's Rural Guard when K.C. Stites identifies him as an old friend of his father's. K.C., like Every, is learning the *realpolitik* of race and power: "Did a white person know him? If so, he goes free. If not, they shoot him along with the other boys and string him up in a tree along the main highway" (p. 185).

Kushner's narrative architecture balances the privileged expat Anglo children's high-priced white innocence with two deeply knowing, even cynical characters, both based on historical personages: Rachel K, a burlesque dancer and high-class sex worker of European (and likely Jewish) descent, and Christian de La Mazière, "ex-Charlemagne Division Waffen SS, minor aristocrat, memoirist, and traitor to the state of France" (2008, p. 55). An amoral and charismatic fascist, La Mazière is an arms dealer working in the Caribbean to capitalize on geopolitical insecurity. Like Rachel K, his itinerary through the novel is an ingenious and playful historiographic device that allows Kushner to interleave various political figures, historical personages, and plot lines. Representing the labor of sex and the business of violent revolution, Rachel

K and La Mazière also allow Kushner to explore a series of conceptual questions about the relationship between reality and performance, fact and fantasy, often sexist male fantasy, and the aestheticization of politics – all themes that lie at the heart of her next novel, *The Flamethrowers*.

A carefully curated book steeped in Kushner's own taste and political sensibility, *The Flamethrowers* is largely set in the New York art world of the 1970s. Like *Telex*, though, its geography and settings are vast, shifting between deindustrializing New York and Italy, from the dawn of the Fordist century through the so-called Years of Lead of the 1970s. Also like *Telex*, *The Flamethrowers* introduces its reader to various scenes of incipient revolt through the perspective of an less-knowing outsider – here, a young, female Nevada art student new to the city's downtown scene.

Unnamed, but dubbed "Reno" by her artist friends in New York, the book's protagonist is an aspiring filmmaker and accomplished skier who, in an early scene, crashes her motorcycle at 148 mph at Utah's Bonneville Flats, and survives. She plans to photograph the traces of her tracks etched in the earth to capture "the experience of speed" (Kushner 2013, p. 30). Reno's ride is both real and a performance, an aesthetic stunt knowingly informed by Land Art and a range of post-Minimalist gestures she has begun to learn in New York. In Kushner's hands, though, the crash and its inhuman agent – a brand-new 1977 Moto Valera motorcycle – epitomize her strategy of scaling from manufactured object to larger processes and histories of industrialization, deindustrialization, and global political upheaval. This motorcycle is another small mechanism embedded, like the novels' characters, in the larger mechanisms that shape them.

Valera, a fictional Italian corporation modeled on Pirelli and Moto Guzzi, is the family firm of an older artist that will become Reno's boyfriend in New York, Sandro Valera, whose "artworks were large aluminum boxes, open on top, empty inside," and "stamped by the factory that produced them" (2013, pp. 92–93). Part of the book's achievement is its skillful threading of industrial and post-industrial histories through the generational wealth of Sandro Valera's family and the abiding global violences of industrial capitalism.

Sandro's factory aesthetic, for example, allows Reno to reckon with the post-Fordist status of the materiality of aesthetic production in the 1970s, as it shifted from Warholian mimicry of industrial production and the minimalist objecthood of Sandro's boxes to what art critic Lucy Lippard famously called the "disappearance of the object" at the dawn of the service economy. Artmaking, like other forms of production and labor, became curiously immaterial in the period, moving from object to image. Like the rest of the sharply drawn characters in the book's networked artworld, many of them near-satires of legendary artists (Donald Judd, Richard Serra, Richard Prince, Dan Flavin, Cindy Sherman, etc.), Sandro and his downtown crew offer Reno object lessons in aesthetic self-fashioning and the insurrectionist gesture.

But Kushner's hip *Künstlerroman* repeatedly shifts gears and directions, moving backwards in time, for example, from Reno's crash to tell the story of Sandro's father, and of Italy in the first half of the twentieth century. Like Reno, T.P. Valera fell in love with motorcycles early on. But he ran with the futurists, and served in a motorcycle battalion in World War I, before inheriting his own father's construction empire and expanding the firm during Italy's postwar economic miracle. Introduced in Reno's crash as a medium, the motorcycle is also an achievement of advanced industrial production, an object of erotic fascination and war, and a prized commodity. And the Valera firm – not unlike

Telex's United Fruit – is an emblem of the rapacious accumulation of twentieth-century capitalism writ large.

The novel carefully embeds the Valera family history in a longer sweep of colonial exploitation and in masculinist mythologies of speed and violence, later abetted by the rise of Italian fascism. The keen attention Kushner pays to various forms of labor and the materiality of production in *Telex* returns in *The Flamethrowers*, especially the chapters set in the Brazilian Amazon, and devoted to the Valera company's practices of rubber extraction, "conscripting nature into service," and doing violence to Indigenous workers (2013, p. 126). Kushner's materialism is also a green infrastructuralism, sourcing the industrial products of the world in the buried conditions of matter and labor.

This, Kushner demonstrates, is part of the prehistory of the revolutionary moment of the Autonomist movement 1970s in Italy that consumes much of novel's final movement, when Reno – visiting the Valera family villa, travels to a Valera factory to film some the workers during a general strike, and discovers Sandro's sexual betrayal. This abrupt awareness of her boyfriend's lies and dissimulation is doubled by her political awakening, when she finds herself holed up in Rome with a young man, Gianni, who appears a laborer at the Valera Villa, and turns out to be a leader of the Red Brigades.

Reno's movement in the novel between more experienced men like Sandro and Gianni might seem to suggest a certain failure of action on her part, a curious passivity. For Kushner, this first-person narration – observant, receptive, immediate – works as a kind of strategic neutrality that allows her narrative to be repeatedly taken over by other, more aggressive storytellers, generally male. Citing the narrative style of Roberto Bolaño's *The Savage Detectives* (1998), Kushner describes this as first person "that came across like thought, who could be drowned out and overrun by others" (Baron 2013) and she contrasts it with the agential mode of Sandro, a particular kind of "male actor" that "threads the century" (Hart and Rocca 2010, p. 202).

In *The Flamethrowers*, many of Kushner's models for conceptualizing alternate forms time and female agency are drawn from cinema, as in the book's sustained dialogue with Barbara Loden's feminist masterpiece *Wanda* (1970). The film's plot is detailed over several pages of the novel, and Kushner includes a still of its eponymous central character as she is framed in an early scene against the employee punch clock of her boss's office. While Sandro thinks Loden's film is about the "the human element of industry," and "the stark life in a coal-mining town," Reno knows it "was about being a woman, about caring and not caring about what happens to you" (2013, p. 199).

It is also a revisionist crime film, in which Wanda, a notoriously passive and blank Bonnie, sipping beer in a dive bar in her hair curlers, meets her Clyde, a schlub named Mr. Dennis, in the act of robbing the joint. Wanda is directionless, simply doing nothing, and so she becomes an accomplice to Mr. Dennis's ill-fated bank robbery. Reno calls this "curler time," and to her it "seemed almost religious, a waiting that was more important than what the waiting was for" (2013, p. 200). But for Reno, and Kushner, this empty time of waiting is also a site of possibility, of futurity. She ends the novel on the cusp of a similar temporality – empty and full – suspended in the "spell of waiting," yet realizing the need to tear from it, and "move on to the next question" (p. 383).

In other words, Kushner is exploring the dialectical conditions of a specific mode of passive agency that is at once specifically female and proto-political, even revolutionary. The possibility of freedom lies in that now-time, an "open absence" (2013, p. 383). The work of her bracing prison novel, *The Mars Room*, is in part to explore the structural conditions of human freedom and possibility, which her first two novels approach in revolutionary contexts, through their negation in systemic unfreedom – namely, mass incarceration in the United States. "We can all agree now," Kushner has written, that "American prisons are a malignant feature of contemporary life, broadening inequalities, destroying families, worsening racial disparities, and facilitating widespread state-sanctioned death" (Kushner and Fleetwood 2020). In *The Mars Room*, Kushner scrutinizes this malignancy, and the larger institutional culture that produces it, through the lens of Romy Hall, a stripper at a San Francisco club (the titular Mars Room) sentenced to life without parole for killing her stalker – an obsessive regular customer.

For Kushner, Romy's sentence – called "LWOP" within the institution – is the cruel limit condition of suspended agency, a brutal dead time that is the constant product of a dehumanizing penal system. Romy's backstory, told retrospectively in the first person during her imprisonment, is set largely in San Francisco's working-class Sunset district, where Kushner's own family moved when she was ten. These parts of the *Mars Room* – including descriptions of the kind of tough-luck kids she hung out with as an adolescent – may work as fictionalized memoir, but the book is best understood as an institutional analysis of prison life and carceral culture, and a devastating brief for prison abolition in novelistic form.

A committed abolitionist, and founding member of Justice Now, an Oakland-based legal organization devoted to helping inmates combat human-rights abuses in prison, Kushner began visiting prisons in 2014. She aimed to study "incarceration as a way to understand the contemporary," and life "rendered invisible" by the state (Goodyear, 2018). Stanville prison, where Romy lives LWOP, is modeled on the Central California Women's Facility Chowchilla, ensconced deep in the Central Valley, and many of Romy's fellow inmates are based on the actual experiences of women in Chowchilla that Kushner befriended during her research – relationships she has sustained over the years, by helping the women with their cases, and sending them books. As Kushner explains, this engagement is not about "usurping the lives of people for my own gain," but a kind of ethics: "It's about caring for people whose life trajectories are totally different from my own, and stepping out there so that our lives can intersect" (Goodyear 2018).

The Mars Room is a bleak book, cut by a very dark humor. How could it be otherwise? Kushner shifts her sustained focus on scions of privilege in her earlier novels to consider directly the lives and survival skills and modes of creativity of the socially marginalized, especially as their human capacities and talents are violently reshaped by the institution of prison. While Romy, the book's protagonist, is white, most of her fellow inmates are Black and Brown women, all of whose histories, like Romy's, are shaped indelibly by trauma and abuse. Deep histories of violence and cruelty also define the book's male characters, including Romy's stalker and a crooked police officer, whose warped psychologies and pathological sexual fantasies – fantasies that are the quotidian trade of Romy, like Rachel K before her – Kushner again parses with great skill.

Much like *Telex*'s expat community, or the New York art scene in *The Flamethrowers*, Stanville is both its own enclosed world with specific rituals and institutional protocols, and deeply, systemically connected to the violence of world outside. The institution of prison, Kushner knows, is also a capitalist industry. One of the strengths of the book is its emphasis on the ecological surround of Stanville – situated in the heart of industrial farming in the San Joaquin Valley. "We were surrounded by agriculture," Romy observes on the bus to Stanville. "I saw no human beings working in the fields. The fields were abandoned to machines" (Kushner 2018, p. 29). Embedded in a larger system of environmental devastation that its very presence abets, the prison is another dehumanizing mechanism – its violence echoes other crimes against nature.

The Mars Room is also an ugly book, strategically so. It is about the forms that human capacities take – including the capacity to experience beauty – under carceral conditions. At one point, a character named Gordon Hauser, a teacher in the prison who becomes attracted to Romy, and lends her novels, describes "his acquired taste for valley-beauty – to the untrained eye, not beautiful. It was a brutal, flat, machined landscape ... It was the size of industrial agriculture, scaled for that. It was difficult to imagine what it had looked like before it was farmed" (2018, p. 217). Romy and her fellow inmates at Stanville must make do with the vastness of a similar system of unnatural living-in-captivity that, tragically, can and does become second nature, and produces its own kind of contemporary beauty – a "carceral aesthetics" (Kushner and Fleetwood, 2020). Hauser, notably, lives alone in a cabin in the woods outside Stanville – a nod to Thoreauvian romanticism that Kushner undercuts by interspersing into the novel journal entries from another nature-lover living in radical isolation, Unabomber Ted Kaczinski.

During her unsuccessful prison escape at the novel's conclusion, Romy is captured in the woods, surrounded by gigantic sequoia that point to other scales of life and time than those through which the state has measured her sentence: LWOP. This natural idyll, cruel in its brevity, makes Romy think of her young son, Jackson: "I gave him life. It is quite a lot to give" (2018, p. 336). With this realization – that Romy has both given and lost *everything* – Kushner makes visible the obscene conditions of contemporary life, and perhaps, the conditions of our own luck, which we'd rather not see. Their ugliness is our great shame.

SEE ALSO: The Bolaño Effect; DeLillo, Don; Ecocriticism and Environmental Fiction; Fictions of Work and Labor; Franzen; Jonathan; Globalization; Intermedial Fiction; Lerner, Ben; Literary Magazines

REFERENCES

Baron, Jesse. (2013). Insurrection: an interview with Rachel Kushner. *The Paris Review* (April 3, 2013). https://www.theparisreview.org/blog/2013/04/03/insurrection-an-interview-with-rachel-kushner/ (accessed August 9, 2021).

Goodyear, Dana. (2018). Rachel Kushner's immersive fiction. *The New Yorker* (April 30, 2018). https://www.newyorker.com/magazine/2018/04/30/rachel-kushners-immersive-fiction (accessed August 9, 2021).

Hart, Matthew and Rocca, Alexander. (2015). An interview with Rachel Kushner. *Contemporary Literature* 56 (2): 193–215.

Kushner, Rachel. (2008). *Telex from Cuba*. New York: Scribner's.

Kushner, Rachel. (2013). *The Flamethrowers*. New York: Scribner's.

Kushner, Rachel. (2018). *The Mars Room*. New York: Scribner's.

Kushner, Rachel and Fleetwood, Nicole. (2020). Carceral aesthetics. *Artforum* 59 (1). www.artforum.com/print/202007/nicole-r-fleetwood-in-conversation-with-rachel-kushner-83681 (accessed August 9, 2021).

Kushner, Rachel and Shawn, Wallace. (2020). Wallace Shawn and Rachel Kushner: a conversation. (December 3, 2020). https://www.youtube.com/watch?v=el9An7aMhtA (accessed August 9, 2021).

Martin, Theodore. (2018). Contemporary, Inc. *Representations* 142 (1): 124–144.

FURTHER READING

Kushner, Rachel. (2012). Woman in revolt. *Artforum* 51 (3): 254–259.

Kushner, Rachel. (2015). *The Strange Case of Rachel K*. New York: New Directions.

Kushner, Rachel. (2021). The hard crowd. *The New Yorker* (January 18, 2021): 26–31. https://www.newyorker.com/magazine/2021/01/18/the-hard-crowd